Territorial Growth of the United States
Lake Superior
St. Lawrence R.
ME.
VT.
N.H.
WIS.
Lake Michigan
Lake Huron
Lake Ontario
N.Y.
MASS.
NN.
MICH.
CONN.
R.I.
Lake Erie
Mississippi R.
PA.
WA
N.J.
MASON-DIXON LINE
ATLANTIC OCEAN
ILL.
IND.
OHIO
MD.
DEL.
Ohio R.
W. VA.
VA.
KY.
MO.
THE ORIGINAL UNITED STATES
(BY TREATY WITH BRITAIN, 1783)
N. C.
36° 30'
TENN.
ARK.
S. C.
The Political Consolidation of Continental America, 1783-1853
GA.
MISS.
ALA.
LA.
(1810)
(1813)
FLA.
(SEIZED FROM SPAIN)
FLORIDA
(BY TREATY WITH SPAIN, 1819)
GULF OF MEXICO

THE AMERICAN PAGEANT

7th Edition

The American Pageant

A HISTORY OF THE REPUBLIC

Thomas A. Bailey
Stanford University
David M. Kennedy
Stanford University

D. C. HEATH AND COMPANY
Lexington, Massachusetts   Toronto

THOMAS A. BAILEY, a native of California, is Byrne Professor of American History, Emeritus, at Stanford University, his alma mater, where he has been a faculty member since 1930. While stationed at Stanford, he held temporary lectureships at Harvard, Cornell, Johns Hopkins, and other leading universities. He is past president of the Organization of American Historians and two other historical societies.

He is the author, co-author, or editor of about twenty books in the field of American history, most of them relating to American foreign policy. His *Diplomatic History of the American People*, first published in 1940, is now in its tenth edition. Since "retirement" in 1968, he has averaged about one new book or revision a year, including his autobiography, *The American Pageant Revisited* (1982).

With the present publisher, D.C. Heath and Company, Dr. Bailey has edited a companion volume to *The American Pageant*, namely, *The American Spirit* (4th edition, 1978), a compilation of provocative human-interest documents. He has also published with Heath an exposure of numerous historical myths entitled *Probing America's Past* (1973). This book complements *The American Pageant*, as does his *Voices of America: The Nation's Story in Slogans, Sayings, and Songs* (1976).

DAVID M. KENNEDY, a native of Seattle, received his undergraduate education at Stanford University. He earned his Ph.D. degree from Yale University in American Studies, combining the fields of history, economics, and literature. His first book, *Birth Control in America: The Career of Margaret Sanger* (Yale University Press, 1970), was honored with both the John Gilmary Shea Prize and the Bancroft Prize. His most recent book is *Over Here: The First World War and American Society* (Oxford University Press, 1980). Kennedy has received research fellowships from the American Council of Learned Societies and the John Simon Guggenheim Foundation. He has taught at the University of Florence, Italy, and lectured on American history in Bologna, Rome, Helsinki, Copenhagen, Istanbul, and Dublin. A member of the Stanford History Department since 1967, Kennedy chaired the university's Program in International Relations from 1977 to 1980, and is currently serving as Associate Dean of the School of Humanities and Sciences. He is now working on the volume covering the New Deal and World War II in the *Oxford History of the United States.*

COVER: "Centennial Progress," by Montgomery Tiers, 1875. From the American Stanhope Hotel Collection, New York City. Photograph courtesy of American Heritage Publishing Company.

Published simultaneously in Canada.

Printed in the United States of America.

International Standard Book Number: 0-669-05270-1

Library of Congress Catalog Card Number: 82-81619

Preface

This seventh edition of *The American Pageant* carries forward the collaboration we began on the sixth edition, which was the most thorough revision of the book since it first appeared in 1956. We have once again gone over the book carefully, enlivening the existing text in many places, and incorporating new material that reflects recent scholarship and the evolving concerns of our fellow historians. As before, we have enriched the *Pageant* by combining our diverse yet complementary areas of expertise—Thomas A. Bailey's in political, diplomatic, constitutional, and military history; David M. Kennedy's in social, economic, cultural, and intellectual history.

Readers will find substantially new treatment of several topics, including American Indian life in the pre-Columbian era, the Spanish impact on the New World, colonial social and economic history (particularly in the Chesapeake region), 19th-century immigration and social mobility, and the First World War. We have also added much material on changes in the structure of the family and the roles of women in the 19th Century, and on the implications of emancipation for masters and slaves alike. In addition, we have extensively recast the section on the Gilded Age, in order to highlight the important political changes of that period. We have similarly rewritten the chapters on the 1920s, to emphasize the extraordinary cultural and economic developments of that era. An entirely new chapter on the Carter administration and the beginning of the Reagan presidency brings the account fully up to date.

We have made other improvements as well. All bibliographies have been updated, as have charts and tables, where appropriate. We have added explanatory material to virtually every map, and to many of the illustrations. Parallel changes have been made in the accompanying *Guidebook* and *Quizbook*.

Readers often tell us that *The American Pageant* is one of the few textbooks with a personality, and we have preserved that personality in this edition. Believing that the way to hold the attention of students is to present the subject in an engaging way, we have worked to make this edition, like its predecessors, as lively as possible without distorting the often sobering reality of the past. As in previous editions, we have maintained a strong chronological narrative and a writing style that emphasizes clarity, concreteness, and a measure of wit. We hope that readers of this book will enjoy learning from it, and will come to share our enjoyment of the study of American history.

THOMAS A. BAILEY
Department of History
Stanford University
Stanford, California

DAVID M. KENNEDY
Department of History
Stanford University
Stanford, California

Contents

1
New World Beginnings
1

Europe in the 16th Century. The search for a water route to the East. Columbus and the early explorers. Native Americans. Spanish America and rivalry with England. The beginnings of English colonization. The Chesapeake region. The Southern colonies.

2
Completing the Thirteen Colonies
20

The Puritan faith. Plymouth, Massachusetts Bay, and Rhode Island Colonies. The New England Confederation, 1643–1684. The Dominion of New England, 1686–1689. The New England mind. The Middle Colonies.

3
The Duel for North America
41

New France. Anglo-French colonial rivalries. Europe, America, and the first "world wars." The French and Indian War, 1754–1763. The ouster of France from North America, 1763. The question of colonial union.

4
Colonial Society on the Eve of Revolution
59

Peopling the colonies. Immigrants and slaves. The colonial social structure. Regional differences. Earning a living. The Atlantic economy. The "Great Awakening" of the 1730s. Education and culture. Political patterns.

5
The Road to Revolution
81

The merits and menace of mercantilism. The Stamp Act crisis, 1765. The Townshend Acts, 1767. The Boston Tea Party, 1773. The "Intolerable Acts" and the Continental Congress, 1774. Lexington, Concord, and the gathering clouds of war, 1775.

6
America Secedes from the Empire
100

Early skirmishes, 1775. The Declaration of Independence, 1776. The Loyalists. The fighting fronts. The French Alliance, 1778. Yorktown, 1781. The Peace of Paris, 1783.

7
The Confederation and the Constitution
119

Political and economic changes. The Articles of Confederation, 1781–1788. The Northwest Ordinance, 1787. Shays's Rebellion, 1786. The Constitutional Convention, 1787. Ratifying the Constitution, 1787–1790.

8
Launching the New Ship of State
140

Problems of the young Republic. The first presidency, 1789–1793. Hamilton's economic policies. The Whiskey Rebellion, 1794. The emergence of political parties.

9
Federalists and Foreign Friction
152

Foreign policy conflicts. Jay's Treaty, 1794. President Adams keeps the peace. The Alien and Sedition Acts, 1798. The Virginia and Kentucky Resolutions, 1798–1799. Jefferson defeats the Federalists, 1800.

10
The Triumph of Jeffersonian Democracy
167

The Jefferson presidency. John Marshall and the Supreme Court. Barbary pirates. The Louisiana Purchase,1803. Anglo-French War. The Embargo, 1807–1809.

11
James Madison and the Second War for Independence
184

Napoleon manipulates Madison. War Hawks and the West. Invasion of Canada, 1812. The war at sea. Triumph at New Orleans, 1815. Treaty of Ghent, 1814. The Hartford Convention, 1814–1815. A new national identity.

12
The Post-War Upsurge of Nationalism, 1815-1824
202

The Tariff of 1816. James Monroe and the Era of Good Feelings. The Panic of 1819. The Missouri Compromise, 1820. The Supreme Court under John Marshall. Canada and Florida. The Monroe Doctrine, 1823.

13
The Rise of Jacksonian Democracy
221

The spread of the suffrage. The "corrupt bargain" of 1824. President John Quincy Adams. The "Tariff of Abominations," 1828. The "Jacksonian Revolution," 1828. The spoils system. The Maysville Road veto, 1830. The Webster-Hayne debate, 1830.

14
Jacksonian Democracy at Flood Tide
238

The South Carolina nullification crisis, 1832. Jackson's war on the Bank of the United States. The removal of the Southeast Indians. Revolution in Texas, 1835–1836. Martin Van Buren in the White House. The depression of 1837. The Independent Treasury. Harrison's "log cabin" campaign, 1840.

15
Manifest Destiny in the Forties
256

"Tyler Too" becomes President, 1841. Fixing the Maine boundary, 1842. The annexation of Texas, 1845. Oregon and California. James K. Polk, the "dark horse" of 1844. War with Mexico, 1846–1848.

16
Shaping the National Economy, 1790-1860
274

The coming of the factory system. Capitalists and workers. The ripening of commercial agriculture. The transportation revolution. The emergence of a continental economy. America and the Atlantic economy. Clipper ships and the Pony Express.

17
Creating an American Character 1790-1860
293

Pioneer democracy. European immigration. The Germans and the Irish. Religious revivals. The Mormons. Educational advances.

18
The Ferment of Reform and Culture, 1790-1860
313

Scientific achievements. Reform stirrings. Temperance. Women's roles and women's rights. Utopian experiments. Art and architecture. A national literature.

19
The South and the Slavery Controversy
329

The Cotton Kingdom. The white South. The black South. The "peculiar institution." Abolitionists. The Southern response.

20
Renewing the Sectional Struggle, 1848-1854
346

Popular sovereignty. Zachary Taylor and California statehood. The Compromise of 1850. The Fugitive Slave Law, 1850. President Pierce and expansion, 1853–1857. The Kansas-Nebraska Act, 1854.

21
Drifting Toward Disunion, 1854-1861
365

Abolitionist appeals to the North. The contest for Kansas. The election of James Buchanan, 1856. The Dred Scott case, 1857. The Panic of 1857. The Lincoln-Douglas debates, 1858. John Brown's raid on Harpers Ferry, 1859. Lincoln and Republican victory, 1860. Secession.

22
The War for Southern Independence
387

The attack on Sumter, April 1861. The crucial Border States. The threat of European intervention. Southern and Northern assets. The Emancipation Proclamation, 1863. Grant in the West. Sherman in Georgia. Hammering the Army of Virginia. Appomattox, 1865.

23
Behind the Lines: North and South
411

Friction with France and England. Men in uniform. Financing the Blue and the Gray. The economic impact of the war. Lincoln and civil liberties. Wartime politics. The assassination of Lincoln, 1865.

24
The Ordeal of Reconstruction
429

The defeated South. The freed slaves. Andrew Johnson versus the Radical Republicans. Military Reconstruction, 1867–1877. "Black Reconstruction." Impeachment. The legacy of Reconstruction.

25
Politics in the Gilded Age, 1869-1889
453

U. S. Grant, soldier-president. Corruption and reform in the post-Civil War era . The depression of the 1870s. Political parties and partisans. The compromise of 1877 and the end of Reconstruction, Civil Service reform. Grover Cleveland and the tariff.

26
Industry Comes of Age, 1865-1900
476

The railroad boom. Speculators and financiers. Early efforts at government regulation. Lords of industry. The New South. The laboring class.

27
New Social and Cultural Horizons, 1865-1900
498

Immigrants and nativists. The rise of the city. Changes in the churches. Educational gains. Black leaders: Washington and Du Bois. The "New Woman" and the new morality. Reformers and writers.

28
The Great West and the Agricultural Revolution, 1865–1890

522

The conquest of the Indians. The mining and cattle frontiers. Free lands and fraud. The industrialization of agriculture. The Populist protest.

29
The Revolt of the Debtor, 1889–1900

541

President Harrison and the "Billion-Dollar Congress." Cleveland regains the White House, 1892. The Panic of 1893. The Pullman strike, 1894. The Wilson-Gorman tariff, 1894. Bryan versus McKinley, 1896.

30
The Path of Empire

559

Blaine and American expansion. Cleveland and the Venezuelan boundary dispute, 1895–1896. The explosion of the *Maine*, February 15, 1898. The Spanish-American War, 1898. The liberation of Cuba. Acquiring Hawaii (1898) and the Philippines (1899).

31
America on the World Stage, 1899–1909

580

Crushing the Filipino insurrection. The Open Door Notes, 1899. TR becomes President, 1901. The Panama Canal. The "Roosevelt Corollary" to the Monroe Doctrine, 1905. Roosevelt and the Far East.

32
Progressivism and the Republican Roosevelt

598

Muckrakers. The politics of progressivism. Roosevelt, labor, and the trusts. Consumer protection. Conservation. The Roosevelt legacy.

33
William Howard Taft and the Progressive Revolt

617

The Payne-Aldrich Tariff, 1909. The Ballinger-Pinchot conservation controversy, 1909. Taft's "Dollar Diplomacy." TR breaks with Taft, 1912. The "Bull Moose" party, 1912. Wilson wins the White House, 1912.

34
Woodrow Wilson and the New Freedom

632

President Wilson. The Underwood Tariff, 1913. The Federal Reserve Act, 1913. The Clayton Anti-Trust Act, 1914. Wilson's diplomacy in Mexico.

35
The Road to World War I

649

War erupts in Europe, 1914. Germany, Britain, and American neutrality. Submarine warfare. The sinking of the *Lusitania*, May 1915. The campaign for preparedness, 1916. "He Kept Us Out of War," 1916. The U-boat forces Wilson's hand, 1917.

36
The War to End War, 1917-1918
667

Wilsonian idealism and the Fourteen Points. Mobilizing factories and farms. Aiding the Allies with dollars and "doughboys." Propaganda and civil liberties. The American Expeditionary Forces in France.

37
Making and Unmaking the Peace
686

The congressional elections of 1918. Wilson and the Big Four at Paris. The League of Nations. The Senate opposes the President's treaty. Wilson's collapse, 1919. The defeat of the Versailles Treaty.

38
American Life in the "Roaring Twenties"
701

The "Red Scare," 1919–1920. Immigration restriction, 1921–1924. Prohibition and gangsterism. The emergence of a mass-consumption economy. The automobile age. Radio and the movies. Music and literature in the "delirious decade." The economic boom.

39
The Politics of Boom and Bust, 1920-1932
723

The Republicans return to power, 1921. Disarmament and isolation. The Harding scandals. Calvin Coolidge's foreign policies. The international debt snarl. Herbert Hoover, cautious progressive. The Great Crash, 1929. Hoover and the Great Depression.

40
The Great Depression and the New Deal
749

The "Hundred Days," 1933. The National Recovery Administration, 1933–1935. The Agricultural Adjustment Administration, 1933–1936. The Social Security Act, 1935. Gains for organized labor. The election of 1936 and the "Roosevelt coalition." The Supreme Court fight, 1937.

41
Franklin D. Roosevelt and the Shadow of War
774

Roosevelt's early foreign policies. The Neutrality Acts, 1935–1939. The destroyer-bases deal with Britain, 1940. The Lend-Lease Act, 1941. The Atlantic Charter, 1941. Pearl Harbor, December 7, 1941.

42
America in World War II
794

The home front. The turning Japanese tide in the Pacific, 1942. North Africa (1942) and Italy (1943). D-Day in Normandy, June 6, 1944. Germany surrenders, May 1945. Atomizing Hiroshima and Nagasaki, August 1945.

43
Harry S Truman and the Cold War
816

Truman takes command, 1945. Yalta (February 1945) and the post-war world. Creating the United Nations. Origins of the Cold War. The Marshall Plan and the Truman doctrine, 1947. Truman's triumph in 1948.

44
Korea and the Eisenhower Era
836

The Korean War, 1950–1953. The menace of McCarthyism. Desegregating the South. John Foster Dulles and the "New Look" foreign policy. Eisenhower re-elected, 1956. Kennedy versus Nixon, 1960.

45
The Stormy Sixties
857

The Kennedy spirit. The Bay of Pigs invasion (1961) and the missile crisis (1962) in Cuba. Kennedy assassinated, November 22, 1963. Lyndon Baines Johnson and the "Great Society." The black revolution. The Vietnam disaster. The election of Nixon, 1968.

46
The Rise and Fall of Richard Nixon
879

Nixon and the Supreme Court. Ending the Asian war. Nixon trounces McGovern, 1972. Israelis, Arabs, and oil. The Watergate trauma. Nixon resigns, August 9, 1974.

47
The Carter Interlude and the Reagan Revolution
903

Jimmy Carter's diplomatic successes in Panama and the Middle East. The sagging economy in the seventies. Carter's energy program. The Iranian hostage crisis. The emergence of the "new right" and the election of Ronald Reagan. Budget battles and tax cuts. Reagan's foreign policy in Europe, the Middle East, and Central America. The "New Federalism."

48
The American People Since World War II
970

The post-war population boom. The rise of the "Sunbelt." Prosperity and its problems. Minorities on the march. Culture and "counter-culture." The American prospect.

APPENDIX
Declaration of Independence **i**
Constitution of the United States of America **iv**
Growth of U.S. Population and Area **xxi**
Admission of States **xxi**
Presidential Elections **xxii**
Presidents and Elected Vice-Presidents **xxv**

INDEX **xxvi**

COLOR PORTFOLIOS
American Life in Painting, 1750–1865
Between 266 and 267
American Life in Painting, 1865–Present
Between 682 and 683

Maps

Territorial Growth of the United States *Inside front cover*
The United States and Its Possessions *Inside back cover*
The United States Today **xx–xxi**
The World Known to Europe, 1492 **3**
Trade Routes with the East **4**
North American Indian Tribes at the time of European Colonization **5**
Principal Voyages of Discovery **6**
Principal Spanish Explorations and Conquests **7**
Early Maryland and Virginia **14**
Early Carolina and Georgia Settlements **17**
New England Settlements About 1650 **22**
The Great Puritan Migration **24**
Massachusetts Bay, the Hub of New England **27**
Andros's Dominion of New England **30**
Early Settlements in the Middle Colonies **34**
Early French Settlements **42**
France's American Empire at Greatest Extent, 1700 **44**
British Territory After Two Wars, 1713 **48**
Scenes of the French Wars **50**
The Ohio Country, 1753–1754 **50**
Braddock's March, 1755 **53**
Events of 1755–1760 **53**
North America Before 1754 and After 1763 **54**
Settled Areas at End of French and Indian War, 1763 **57**
Nationalities in 1775 **62**
Colonial Trade Patterns, c. 1770 **67**
Quebec Before and After 1774 **93**
Revolution in the North, 1775–1776 **103**
New York and New Jersey, 1776–1777 **107**
New York, Pennsylvania Theater, 1777–1778 **108**
War in the South, 1780–1781 **112**
George Rogers Clark's Campaign, 1778–1779 **113**
United States in 1783 **116**
Western Lands, 1783, 1802 **124**
Main Centers of Spanish and British Influence After 1783 **128**
Main Shaysite Centers in Massachusetts, 1786–1787 **129**
The Struggle over Ratification **136**
American Posts Held by British After 1783 **155**
Presidential Election of 1800 **165**
Four Barbary States of North Africa **172**
Louisiana Purchase, 1803 **174**
Exploring the Louisiana Purchase **176**
The Three U.S. Thrusts of 1812 **190**
Campaigns of 1813 **191**
British Invasion, 1814 **191**
The Southwest, 1814–1815 **193**
Presidential Election of 1812 **197**
The Missouri Compromise and Slavery, 1820–1821 **210**
U.S.–British Boundary Settlement, 1818 **214**
Acquiring the Floridas, 1810–1819 **214**
The West and Northwest, 1819–1824 **217**
Presidential Election of 1828 **230**
Southern Tribes Before Transplanting **245**
The Texas Revolution, 1835–1836 **249**
Maine Boundary Settlement, 1842 **260**
The Oregon Controversy **263**
Texas, 1845–1846 **268**
Major Campaigns of Mexican War **270**

Industrial Plants in the Early 1840s **275**
Cumberland (National) Road and Main Connections **283**
The Pattern of American Agricultural Production in 1860 **283**
Erie Canal and Main Branches **285**
Principal Canals in 1840 **286**
Railroads in Operation in 1850, 1860 **288**
Main Routes West Before the Civil War **291**
Westward Movement of Center of Population, 1790–1980 **294**
The Mormon Trek, 1846–1847 **305**
The Extent of Prohibition, 1855 **316**
Early Emancipation in the North **335**
Texas and the Compromise of 1850 **349**
Slavery After the Compromise of 1850 **354**
Central America, c. 1850, Showing British Possessions and Proposed Canal Routes **357**
Gadsden Purchase, 1853 **360**
Kansas and Nebraska, 1854 **363**
Bleeding Kansas, 1854–1860 **367**
Presidential Election of 1856 **372**
Presidential Election of 1860 **381**
Southern Opposition to Secession, 1860–1861 **383**
Proposed Crittenden Compromise, 1860 **384**
Seceding States **390**
Main Thrusts, 1861–1865 **399**
Peninsular Campaign, 1862 **402**
Emancipation in the South **404**
The Mississippi River and Tennessee, 1862–1863 **406**
Sherman's March, 1864–1865 **407**
Lee's Chief Battles, December 1862–July 1863 **408**
Grant's Virginia Campaign, 1864–1865 **410**
Presidential Election of 1864 **424**
Military Reconstruction, 1867 **442**
Alaska and the Lower Forty-Eight States **450**
Hayes-Tilden Disputed Election of 1876 **461**
Presidential Election of 1884 **469**
Federal Land Grants to Railroads **477**
Early Pacific Railway Lines **480**
States of the Great West **523**
Indian Reservations, 1883 **526**
Cattle Trails **529**
Average Annual Precipitation **532**
Presidential Election of 1892 **546**
Presidential Election of 1896 **555**
Protecting the Seals **561**
The Venezuela–British Guiana Boundary Dispute **562**
Samoa, 1899 **565**
The Hawaiian Islands **565**
Dewey's Route in the Philippines, 1898 **570**
The Cuban Campaign, 1898 **573**
Big Stick in the Caribbean **588**
The Alaskan Boundary Settlement, 1903 **592**
Far East, 1904–1905 **593**
The Extent of Erosion, 1934 **610**
Presidential Election of 1912 **629**
Possible Interflow of Twelve Federal Reserve Districts and Banks **638**
The United States in the Caribbean **643**
The United States and Mexico, 1914–1917 **647**
British Military Area **655**
German Submarine War Zone **656**
Presidential Election of 1916 **661**
Major U.S. Operations in France, 1918 **680**
Prohibition on the Eve of the 18th Amendment, 1919 **684**
Presidential Election of 1920 **698**
Presidential Election of 1924 **733**
Presidential Election of 1928 **738**
TVA Area **762**
Destroyer Deal Bases **785**
Presidential Election of 1940 **787**
Main Flow of Lend-Lease Aid **788**
Corregidor–Bataan **801**
United States Thrusts in the Pacific, 1942–1945 **802**
Allied Thrusts in North Africa and Italy, 1942–1945 **805**
Final Allied Thrusts in Europe, 1944–1945 **808**
Battle of the Bulge **811**
Post-War Partition of Germany **825**
United States Foreign Aid, Military and Economic, 1945–1954 **827**
The Shifting Front in Korea **838**
Presidential Election of 1952 **839**
The Far East, 1955–1956 **846**
Presidential Election of 1956 **848**
Presidential Election of 1960 **854**
Vietnam and Southeast Asia **860**
Presidential Election of 1968 **876**
Presidential Election of 1972 **888**
Presidential Election of 1980 **915**
The Middle East **920**
Central America and the Caribbean **921**
Population Increase in the Sunbelt States: 1950–1979 **927**

Charts and Tables

4,000 B.C. Recorded History Begins—World War II Ends **2**
Columbus's Discovery—World War II Ends **2**
The Tudor Rulers of England **10**
The Thirteen Original Colonies **15**
The Stuart Dynasty in England **28**
Later English Kings **46**
The Nine World Wars **48**
Estimated Population Elements, 1790 **62**
The Colonial Social Pyramid, 1775 **64**
Estimated Religious Census, 1775 **71**
Established (Tax-Supported) Churches in the Colonies, 1775 **71**
Colonial Colleges **73**
Britain Against the World **111**
Surveying the Old Northwest **126**
Evolution of Federal Union **133**
Strengthening the Central Government **135**
Ratification of the Constitution **137**
Evolution of the Cabinet **143**
Hamilton's Financial Structure Supported by Revenues **145**
Pennsylvania's Whiskey Rebellion, 1794 **147**
War Vote in House of Representatives, 1812 **187**
House Vote on Tariff of 1816 **204**
Election of 1824 **223**
House Vote on Tariff of 1828 **227**
House Vote on Tariff of 1832 **239**
House Vote on Compromise Tariff of 1833 **240**
Tariff Levies on Dutiable Imports, 1815–1880 **241**
House Vote on Tariff of 1846 **265**
Population Increase, Including Slaves and Indians, 1790–1860 **297**
Irish and German Immigration by Decade **298**
Cotton Exports Compared with Total Exports, 1800–1860 **331**
Slaveowning Families, 1850 **333**
Compromise of 1850 **353**
Election of 1860 **380**
Manufacturing by Sections, 1860 **393**
Immigration to U.S., 1860–1866 **395**
Enlistees North and South **416**
Civil War Financing in the North **417**
Union Party, 1864 **423**
Principal Reconstruction Proposals and Plans **440**
Southern Reconstruction by State **444**
Lynching: Aftermath of Reconstruction **447**
Composition of the Electoral Commission, 1877 **462**
Growth of Classified Civil Service **467**
Cotton Manufacturing Moves South **491**
Annual Immigration, 1860–1978 **499**
Old and New Immigration **501**
The Shift to the City **503**
The Decline of Illiteracy **506**
High-School and College Graduates, 1870–1970 **508**
Marriages and Divorces, 1890–1980 **516**
Homesteads from the Public Lands **533**
Average Percentage Rates on Dutiable Goods, 1890–1922 **544**
The Presidential Vote, 1912 **629**
Organization of Holding Companies **639**
Principal Foreign Elements in the United States **651**

U.S. Exports to Belligerents, 1914–1916 **653**
Merchant Tonnage Sunk by German U-Boats **670**
Approximate Comparative Losses in World War I **683**
Interlocking Treaty Structure **699**
Annual Immigration and the Quota Laws **704**
Limits Imposed by Washington Conference **728**
Aspects of the Financial Merry-Go-Round, 1921–1933 **735**
Tariff Trends, 1920–1979 **739**
Index of Common Stock Prices **740**
Selected Stock Prices, Sept.–Nov. 1929 **740**
Principal New Deal Acts During Hundred Days Congress, 1933 **753**
Bank Failures and the Banking Act of 1933 **755**
Farm Foreclosures and Defaults, 1929–1945 **756**
Later Major New Deal Measures, 1933–1939 **757**
The Rise of Organized Labor, 1900–1978 **765**
Unemployment, 1929–1942 **771**
National Debt, 1915–1955 **800**
Merchant Tonnage Sunk by German U-Boats **804**
Presidential Election of 1948 **832**
Presidential Election of 1964 **866**
The History of the Consumer Price Index, 1967–1981 **929**
Comparative Tax Burdens **930**
The Federal Budget Dollar and How It Is Spent, by Major Category **942**

Sail, sail thy best, ship of Democracy,
Of value is thy freight, 'tis not the Present only,
The Past is also stored in thee,
Thou holdest not the venture of thyself alone, not of the Western continent alone,
Earth's résumé entire floats on thy keel, O ship, is steadied by thy spars,
With thee Time voyages in trust, the antecedent nations sink or swim with thee,
With all their ancient struggles, martyrs, heroes, epics, wars, thou bear'st the other continents,
Theirs, theirs as much as thine, the destination-port triumphant. . . .

WALT WHITMAN
Thou Mother with Thy Equal Brood, 1872

The United States Today

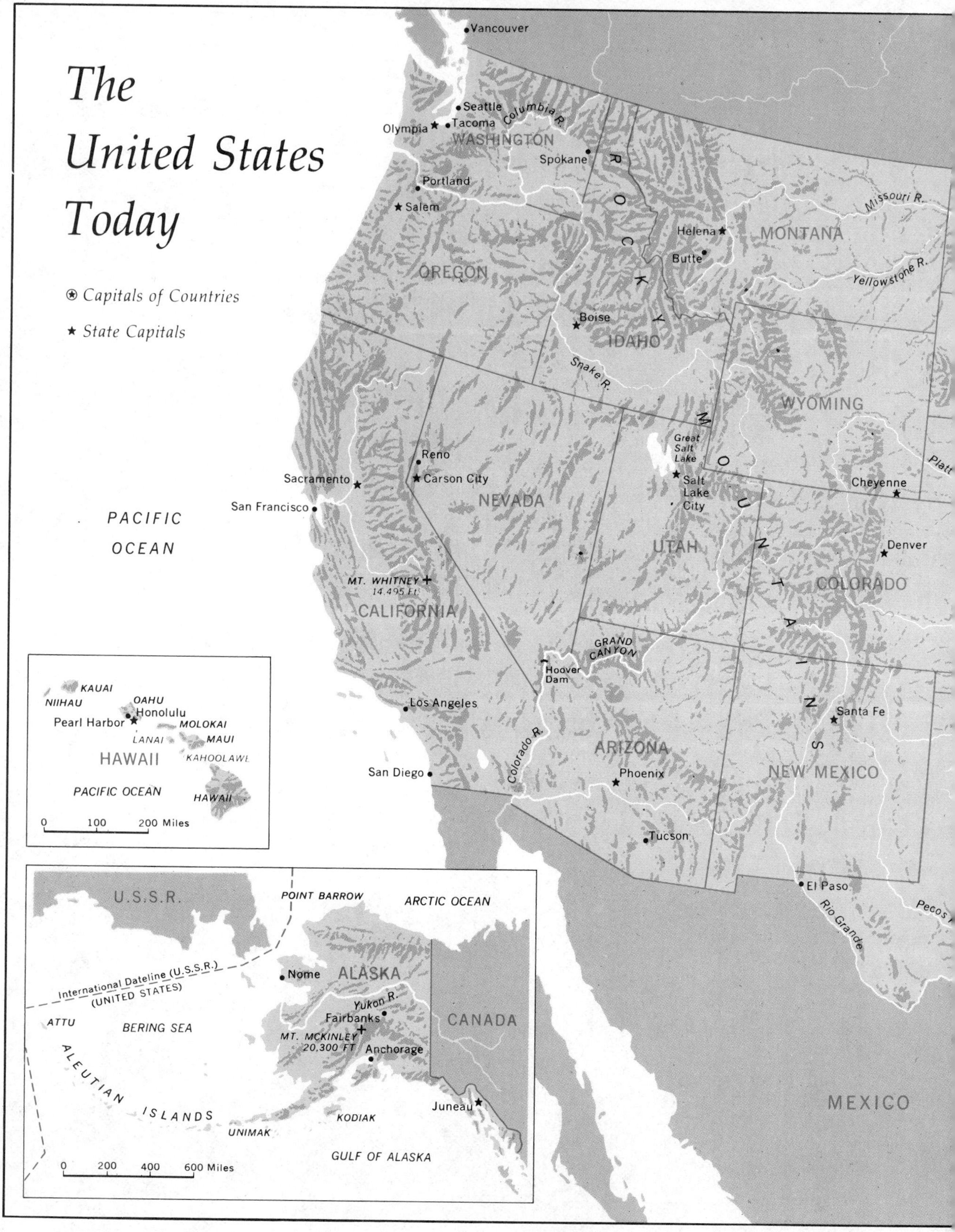

Capitals of Countries
State Capitals
Vancouver
Seattle
Olympia
Tacoma
Columbia R.
WASHINGTON
Spokane
Portland
Salem
ROCKY MOUNTAINS
Helena
MONTANA
Missouri R.
Butte
Yellowstone R.
OREGON
Boise
IDAHO
Snake R.
WYOMING
Great Salt Lake
Reno
Sacramento
Carson City
Salt Lake City
Cheyenne
Platt
San Francisco
NEVADA
PACIFIC OCEAN
UTAH
Denver
MT. WHITNEY
14,495 Ft.
COLORADO
CALIFORNIA
GRAND CANYON
Hoover Dam
Los Angeles
Santa Fe
Colorado R.
ARIZONA
San Diego
Phoenix
NEW MEXICO
Tucson
El Paso
Rio Grande
Pecos R.
MEXICO
KAUAI
NIIHAU
OAHU
Honolulu
Pearl Harbor
MOLOKAI
LANAI
MAUI
HAWAII
KAHOOLAWE
PACIFIC OCEAN
HAWAII
0
100
200 Miles
U.S.S.R.
POINT BARROW
ARCTIC OCEAN
International Dateline (U.S.S.R.)
(UNITED STATES)
Nome
ALASKA
Yukon R.
Fairbanks
MT. MCKINLEY
20,300 FT
Anchorage
CANADA
ATTU
BERING SEA
ALEUTIAN ISLANDS
Juneau
KODIAK
UNIMAK
GULF OF ALASKA
0
200
400
600 Miles

CANADA
Lake of the Woods
LAKE SUPERIOR
Ottawa R.
Ottawa
Quebec
St. Lawrence R.
Montreal
MAINE
Eastport
Augusta
Portland
Montpelier
VT.
N.H.
Concord
NEW YORK
MASS.
Boston
Albany
Hudson R.
Providence, R.I.
R.I.
Hartford
CONN.
Toronto
LAKE ONTARIO
Rochester
Buffalo
LAKE HURON
LAKE MICHIGAN
MICHIGAN
Lansing
Grand Rapids
Detroit
LAKE ERIE
Cleveland
Toledo
ORTH
AKOTA
smarck
Duluth
MINNESOTA
St. Paul
Minneapolis
WISCONSIN
OUTH
erre
AKOTA
Milwaukee
Madison
Mississippi R.
Missouri R.
IOWA
Des Moines
Chicago
South Bend
Ft. Wayne
OHIO
PENNSYLVANIA
Harrisburg
Pittsburgh
New York
Trenton
NEW JERSEY
Philadelphia
Dover
MD.
Baltimore
DELAWARE
Annapolis
Washington, D.C.
EBRASKA
Omaha
Lincoln
ILLINOIS
Indianapolis
Columbus
INDIANA
Springfield
Cincinnati
WEST VIRGINIA
Charleston
APPALACHIAN MOUNTAINS
Richmond
VIRGINIA
Norfolk
Kansas City
Topeka
Kansas City
St. Louis
Frankfort
Louisville
Ohio R.
KANSAS
Jefferson City
MISSOURI
KENTUCKY
ROANOKE ISLAND
CAPE HATTERAS
Arkansas R.
Wichita
Raleigh
Knoxville
Nashville
NORTH CAROLINA
Tennessee R.
Charlotte
TENNESSEE
Tulsa
Memphis
Columbia
Oklahoma City
ARKANSAS
SOUTH CAROLINA
OKLAHOMA
Little Rock
Atlanta
Savannah R.
Birmingham
Charleston
Red R.
Mississippi R.
ALABAMA
GEORGIA
MISSISSIPPI
Savannah
ATLANTIC OCEAN
Ft. Worth
Dallas
Montgomery
Jackson
EXAS
Sabine R.
Pearl R.
LOUISIANA
Jacksonville
Mobile
Tallahassee
Colorado R.
Austin
Baton Rouge
New Orleans
Houston
FLORIDA
San Antonio
Tampa
Miami
Rio Grande
0
100
200
300
400
500 Miles

1

New World Beginnings

. . . For I shall yet live to see it [*Virginia*] *an Inglishe nation.*

SIR WALTER RALEIGH, 1602

Planetary Perspectives

Several billion years ago that whirling speck of dust known as the earth, fifth in size among the planets, came into being.

About six thousand years ago—only the day before yesterday geologically—recorded history of the Western world began. Certain peoples of the Middle East, developing a primitive culture, gradually emerged from the haze of the past.

Nearly five hundred years ago—only yesterday—the American continents were stumbled on by Europeans. This epochal achievement, one of the most dramatic in the chronicles of mankind, opened breathtaking new vistas, and forever altered the future of both the Old World and the New.

The two new continents eventually brought forth a score of sovereign republics. By far the most influential of this brood—the United States—was born a pygmy and grew to be a giant. It was destined to leave a deep imprint upon the rest of the world as a result of its refreshingly liberal ideals, its revolutionary democratic experiment, and its boundless opportunities for the common folk of foreign lands. The enormous output of its robust economy ultimately made it a decisive weight in the world balance of power. Its achievements in science, technology, and culture shaped people's lives in every corner of this planet.

Fascinating though it is, the pageant of the American people does not loom large on the time chart of man's known past. But the roots of the United States reach down into the subsoil of the formative colonial years more deeply than is commonly supposed.

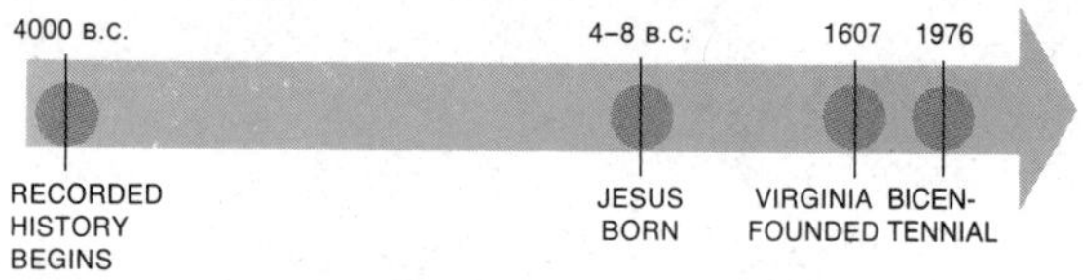

The American Republic, which is still relatively young when compared with the Old World, was from the outset richly favored. It started from scratch on a vast and virgin continent, which was so sparsely peopled by Indians that they could be eliminated or shouldered aside. Such a magnificent opportunity for a great democratic experiment may never come again, for no other huge, fertile, and relatively uninhabited areas are left in the temperate zones of this crowded planet.

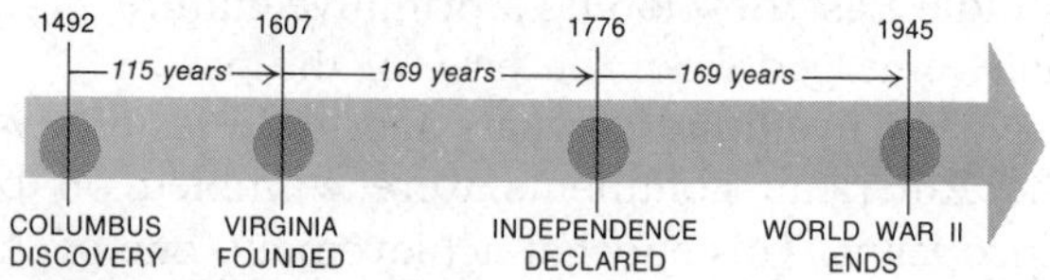

Despite its marvelous development, the United States will one day reach its peak, like Greece and Rome. It will ultimately fall upon evil days, as they did. But whatever uncertainties the future may hold, the past at least is secure and will richly repay examination.

Indirect Discoverers of the New World

The American continents were slow to yield their virginity. The all-conquering Romans, a half century after the birth of Christ, expanded their empire northwestward as far as Britain. But for nearly fifteen hundred years thereafter, the New World lay unknown and unsuspected to Europeans, awaiting its discoverers. It is true that about the year A.D. 1000, blond-bearded Norsemen from Scandinavia chanced upon the northeastern shoulder of North America, at a place abounding in wild grapes, which they named Vinland. But their settlements were soon abandoned, and the discovery was forgotten, except in Scandinavian saga and song.

America was to be a child of Europe, not of a specific country, such as England. One must seek in the Old World that momentous chain of events which led to a drive toward the Far East—and a completely accidental discovery of the New World.

Christian Crusaders must take high rank among the indirect discoverers of America. Tens of thousands of these European warriors, clad in shining armor, invaded Palestine from the 11th to the 14th Century. Whatever their true motives, they were avowedly attempting to wrest the Holy Land from the polluting hand of the Moslem infidel. Foiled in their repeated assaults, these Christian soldiers did manage to come into closer contact with the exotic delights of Asia—delights already introduced to Europe on a limited scale. European "barbarians" learned more fully the value of spices for spoiled and monotonous food; of silk for rough skins; of drugs for aching flesh; of perfumes for unbathed bodies; and of colorful draperies for gloomy castles.

But the luxuries of the Far East were almost too expensive in Europe. They had to be transported enormous distances from the Spice Islands (Indonesia), China, and India, in creaking ships and on swaying camel back, to the ports of the eastern Mediterranean. Moslem middlemen exacted a heavy toll en route. By the time the strange-smelling goods reached the Italian merchants at

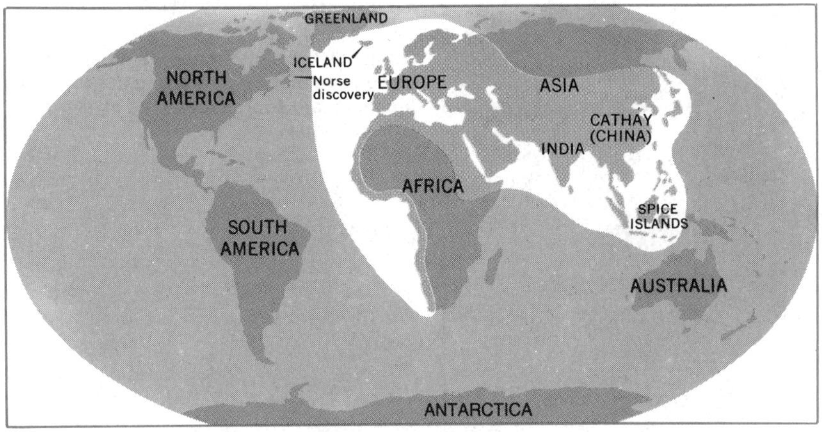

THE WORLD KNOWN TO EUROPE, 1492

Venice and Genoa, they were so costly that purchasers and profits alike were narrowly limited. Consumers and distributors of Western Europe were naturally eager to find a less costly route to the riches of Eastern Asia—one that would also break the monopoly of the Italian cities.

European appetites were further whetted when foot-loose Marco Polo, an Italian adventurer, returned to Europe in 1295, after a stay of nearly twenty years in China. Several years later, while a war prisoner, he dictated a classic account of his travels. He too must be regarded as an indirect discoverer of the New World, for his book, with its descriptions of rose-tinted pearls and golden pagodas, stimulated European desires for a cheaper route to the treasures of the Indies.

An urge to find a shortcut waterway to Eastern Asia was strong, but success awaited new horizons and new facilities. Fortunately the Renaissance, which dawned in the 14th Century, shot hopeful rays of light through the mists of the Middle Ages. Better maps reduced superstitious fears of the unknown. The mariner's compass, possibly borrowed from the Arabs, eliminated some of the uncertainties of navigation. Printing presses, introduced about 1450, facilitated the spread of scientific knowledge. An atmosphere of rebirth also accompanied the Renaissance and created a healthy spirit of optimism, self-reliance, and venturesomeness.

Portuguese Pathfinders

As the kings gradually subordinated the nobles, the modern national state emerged in Western Europe from the feudalism of the Middle Ages. This new type of government alone had the unity, power, and resources to shoulder the formidable tasks of discovery, conquest, and colonization.

The first nations to unite were the first to flourish as colonial empire builders—Portugal, Spain, England, France, and the Netherlands. Those countries that did not achieve unity until the 19th Century, notably Germany and Italy, were left with crumbs dropped by the early feasters.

Little Portugal took the lead in discovering what came to be the coveted water route to the Indies. A courageous band of Portuguese navigators, edging cautiously down the pistol-handle coast of Africa, pushed southeasterly in the general direction of Asia. In 1488, four years before Columbus chanced upon America, Bartholomeu Diaz rounded the southernmost tip of the Dark Continent. Complete success crowned Portuguese efforts in 1498 when Vasco da Gama finally reached India (hence the name "Indies," given to all the mysterious lands of the Orient). He coaxed few jewels and spices from the natives, but later voyagers reaped lush profits from this treasure trove.

Portuguese empire builders ultimately estab-

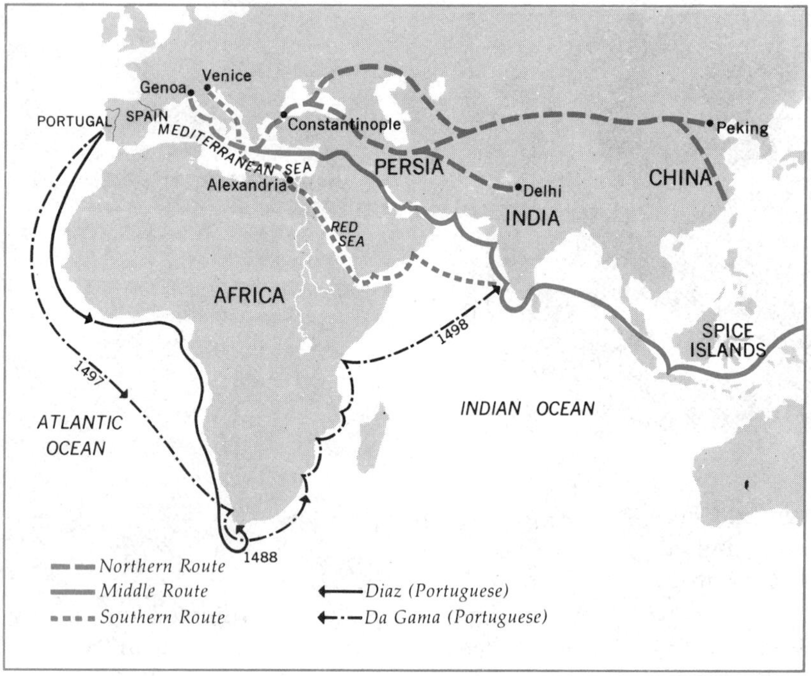

TRADE ROUTES WITH THE EAST
Goods on the early routes were passed through so many hands along the way that their ultimate source remained mysterious to Europeans.

lished flourishing trading stations in India, Africa, China, and the East Indies. Immense wealth flowed to European coffers from these varied ventures. In turn, the ballooning prices of Asian products collapsed, and the monopolistic grip of the Italian commercial cities was broken.

Brazil, by sheer accident, was unveiled in 1500. An India-bound Portuguese navigator, Pedro Cabral, touched upon the giant bulge of South America eight years after the first voyage of Columbus. Portugal subsequently erected a huge empire in the Brazilian wilderness. But the net return from this New World outpost was only a small fraction of the profits that the Portuguese garnered from exploiting their water route to the riches of the Indies.

Columbus Stumbles Upon a New World

The Kingdom of Spain became united—an event pregnant with destiny—late in the 15th Century. This new unity resulted primarily from the marriage of two sovereigns, Ferdinand and Isabella, and from the brutal expulsion of the "infidel" Moslem Moors. Glorying in their new strength, the Spaniards were eager to outstrip their Portuguese rivals in the race for the fabled Indies.

Christopher Columbus, a skilled Italian seaman, now stepped upon the stage of history. A man of vision, energy, resourcefulness, and courage, he finally managed, after heartbreaking delays, to gain the ear of the Spanish rulers. Like all of his informed contemporaries, he was convinced that the world was round. Then why not find the way to East Asia by sailing directly westward into the darkness of the Atlantic, instead of eastward for unnecessary miles around Africa?

The Spanish monarchs at last decided to gamble on the persistent mariner. They helped outfit him with three tiny but seaworthy ships, manned by a motley crew. Daringly, he spread the sails of his cockleshell craft. Winds were friendly and progress was rapid, but the superstitious sailors, fearful of sailing over the edge of the world, grew increasingly mutinous. Nearly six long weeks passed and failure loomed ahead when, on October 12, 1492, land was sighted—an island in the Bahamas. A new world thus swam within the vision of Europeans.

Columbus's sensational achievement has obscured the fact that he was one of the most successful failures of history. Seeking a new water route to the fabled Indies of the East, he had in fact bumped into an enormous land barrier blocking the ocean pathway. For decades thereafter explorers strove to get through it—or around it. The truth gradually dawned that sprawling new continents had been discovered. Yet Columbus stubbornly maintained until his death in 1506 that he had skirted the rim of the "Indies." So certain was he that he called the near-naked natives "Indians," a gross geographical misnomer that somehow stuck.

Ironically, the remote ancestors of these Native Americans were the true discoverers of America. Some 10,000 to 20,000 years earlier they had ventured across the narrow waters from Asia to what is now Alaska. From there they roamed slowly southward as far as South America. Over the centuries they had split into hundreds of tribes and language groups. Some of these aboriginal peoples had evolved stunning civilizations. Incas in Peru, Aztecs in Mexico, and Mayans in Central America developed advanced agricultural practices, based on the cultivation of corn (a gift from the Indians to the Old World), that supported populations of millions. They erected bustling, elaborately carved stone cities, rivaling in size those of contemporary medieval Europe. They carried on far-flung commerce, studied mathematics, and made strikingly accurate astronomical observations.

Indian life in North America was cruder, though high levels of cultural development were found among the Pueblos in the Southwest, the Creeks in the Southeast, and the Iroquois in the Northeast. Most native settlements were small, scattered, and often impermanent. So thinly spread across the land was the North American Indian population that large areas were virtually uninhabited, with whispering, primeval forests and sparkling, virgin waters. Perhaps one million Indians dwelled in all of the present-day United States at the time of Columbus's discovery. They ate corn, fish, wild game, nuts, and berries. Private property, especially private landholding, was a concept almost unknown to the Indians until the white Europeans moved in on them. Political organization was equally unfamiliar; loose, independent tribal structures served the Indians well until they clashed with the powerful governments

NORTH AMERICAN INDIAN TRIBES AT THE TIME OF EUROPEAN COLONIZATION

This map illustrates the great diversity of the Indian population—and suggests the inappropriateness of identifying all the Native American peoples with the single label "Indian." The more than 200 tribes were deeply divided by geography, language, and life-style.

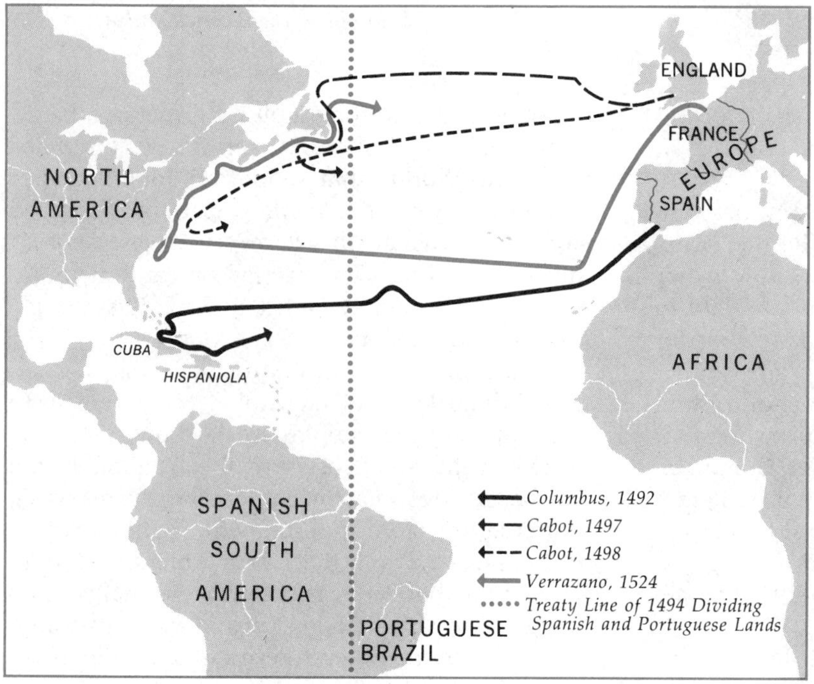

PRINCIPAL VOYAGES OF DISCOVERY

Spain, Portugal, France, and England reaped the greatest advantages from the New World, but much of the earliest exploration was done by Italians, notably Christopher Columbus of Genoa. John Cabot, another native of Genoa (his original name was Giovanni Caboto), sailed for England's King Henry VII. Giovanni da Verrazano was a Florentine employed by France.

of the whites. Europeans encountered only a handful of Indian institutions larger than the tribal unit, such as the Iroquois Confederacy in the region of present-day New York, and the Powhatan Confederacy in Virginia.

The Spanish Conquistadores

Gradually the realization sank in that the American continents held rich prizes of their own—especially the glittering gold of the advanced Indian civilizations in the southern continent. Spain secured its claim to Columbus's discoveries in the Treaty of Tordesillas (1494), dividing with Portugal the "heathen lands" of the New World. The lion's share went to Spain, but Portugal received compensating territory in Africa and Asia, and also title to lands that would one day be Brazil.

Spain now became the dominant exploring and colonizing power in the 1500s. Love of God joined with the lure of gold in spurring the Spaniards on, as zealous priests sought to convert the pagan natives to Catholic Christianity. On Spain's long roster of heroic deeds two spectacular exploits must be headlined. Vasco Nuñez Balboa, hailed as the discoverer of the Pacific Ocean, waded into the foaming waves off Panama in 1513 and claimed for his King all the lands washed by that sea! Ferdinand Magellan started from Spain in 1519 with five tiny ships. After discovering the storm-lashed strait off South America that bears his name, he was slain by the natives in the Philippines, but his one remaining vessel creakily completed the first circumnavigation of the globe in 1522.

Exploratory beginnings were launched by other adventuresome Spaniards in what was destined to be the United States. In 1513 Juan Ponce de León discovered Florida, which he thought an island. Debauched by high living, he was seeking the mythical Fountain of Youth. He found instead death—from an Indian arrow. Francisco Coronado, in quest of golden cities that turned out to be primitive pueblos, wandered in 1540–1542 with a clanking cavalcade through Arizona and New Mexico as far east as Kansas. His expedition discovered en route two impressive natural wonders: the Grand Canyon of the Colorado and enormous herds of buffalo (bison).

Hernando de Soto, with six hundred armor-

Typical Spanish *Conquistador.*
By Frederic Remington, artist of the West.

plated men, undertook a fantastic gold-seeking expedition during 1539–1542. Floundering through marshes and pine barrens, from Florida westward, he discovered and crossed the majestic Mississippi north of the Arkansas River. After cruelly misusing the Indians with iron collars and fierce dogs, he at length died of fever and wounds. His remains were secretly buried at night in the Mississippi, lest the Indians abuse the dead body of their abuser.

All these meanderings had little impact upon the events that gave birth to the United States, with two noteworthy exceptions. Hernando Cortés, with seven hundred men and eighteen horses (which awed the horseless natives), tore open the coffers of the Mexican Aztecs in 1519–1521. Francisco Pizarro, an iron-fisted conqueror, crushed the Peruvian Incas in 1532, and added another incredible hoard of gold and silver to the loot from Mexico. The Spanish invaders not only robbed the Indians, but subsequently enslaved them and put them to work digging up precious metals. By 1600, Spain was swimming in New World silver, mostly from the fabulously rich mines at Potosi, Peru.

The Spanish conquerors (*conquistadores*), curiously enough, were indirect founding fathers of the United States. Their phenomenal success excited the envy of Englishmen, and helped spur some of the early attempts at colonization. Moreover, the dumping of the enormous Indian treasure chests upon Europe inflated the currency and drove prices upward. The pinch further distressed underpaid English toilers, many of whom in turn were later driven to the New World. There,

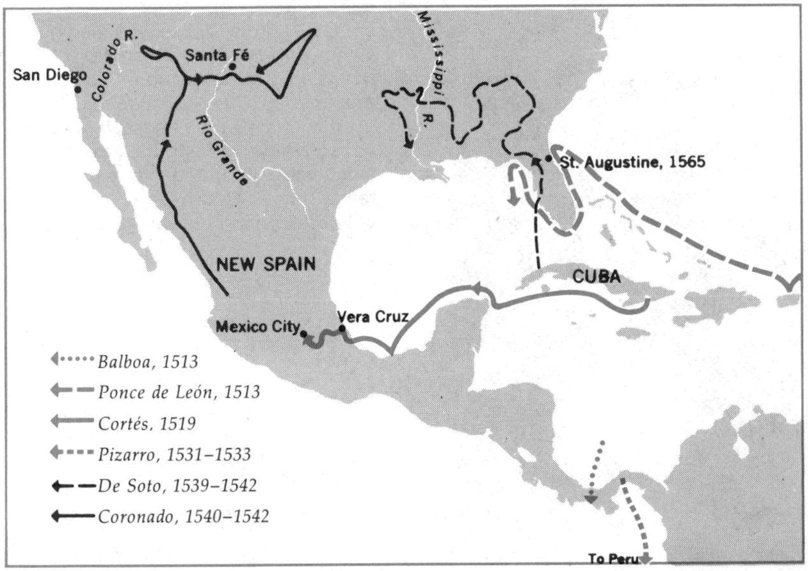

PRINCIPAL SPANISH EXPLORATIONS AND CONQUESTS

Note that Coronado traversed northern Texas and Oklahoma. In present-day eastern Kansas he found, instead of the great golden city he sought, a drab encampment, probably of Wichita Indians.

ironically, they challenged Spanish supremacy.

These plunderings by the Spaniards unfortunately obscured their substantial colonial achievements, and helped give birth to the "Black Legend." This false concept meant that the conquerors merely tortured and butchered the Indians ("killing for Christ"), stole their gold, infected them with smallpox, and left little but misery behind. The Spanish invader did kill thousands of natives and exploit the rest, but he intermarried with them as well, creating a distinctive South American culture of *mestizos*—people of mixed Indian and European heritage. He erected a colossal empire, sprawling from California and the Floridas to Tierra del Fuego. He transplanted and engrafted his culture, laws, religion, and language, and laid the foundations for a score of Spanish-speaking nations.

The bare statistics of Spain's colonial empire are alone impressive. By 1574, thirty-three years before the first primitive English shelters in Virginia, there were about two hundred Spanish cities and towns in North and South America. A total of 160,000 Spanish inhabitants, mostly men, had subjugated some 5 million Indians—all in the name of the gentle Jesus. Majestic cathedrals dotted the land, printing presses were turning out books, and literary prizes were being awarded. Two distinguished universities were chartered in 1551, one at Mexico City and the other at Lima, Peru. Both of them antedated Harvard, the first college established in the English colonies, by eighty-five years.

It is clear that the Spaniards, who had more than a century's head start over the English, were genuine empire builders in the New World. As compared with their Anglo-Saxon rivals, their colonial establishment was larger and richer, and it lasted more than a quarter of a century longer.

The Gilbert and Raleigh Fiascos

Feeble indeed were the efforts of England in the 1500s to compete with the sprawling Spanish empire. Sir Humphrey Gilbert tried to plant a colony

North Carolina Indians "Sitting at Meate." Painted by John White, a member of Sir Walter Raleigh's second expedition, 1585. Indians such as these may have absorbed the more than one hundred "lost colonists" from Sir Walter Raleigh's ill-starred venture on Roanoke Island. In one nearby county of present-day North Carolina, blue-eyed and fair-haired characteristics have persisted among the Indians, along with Elizabethan words and the family names of forty-one Roanoke colonists. (Library of Congress.)

Sir Walter Raleigh (c. 1552–1618). Here he is shown "drinking tobacco," as smoking was first called. He is credited with introducing both tobacco and the potato into England. A dashing courtier, he launched important colonizing failures in the New World. After seducing (and marrying) one of Queen Elizabeth's maids of honor, he fell out of favor and was ultimately beheaded for treason.

on the bleak coast of Newfoundland, but lost his gamble and his life in 1583, when his ship sank in a storm. Sir Walter Raleigh, Gilbert's gallant half-brother, attempted in the 1580s to establish a colony in warmer climes. The settlers chose North Carolina's Roanoke Island, which lay just off the coast of Virginia—a vague region named by the Virgin Queen Elizabeth in honor of herself. With Raleigh busy at home, the ill-starred Roanoke colony mysteriously vanished, swallowed up by the wilderness. Most probably disease and hostile Indians wiped out many of the colonists. Among them was Virginia Dare, the first of many millions of babies of English blood to be born in the New World. Her known life lasted nine days.

The Anglo-Saxons were plainly losing out. When the reign of "Good Queen Bess" ended in 1603, England did not have a single permanent habitation in all the Americas. Her backwardness contrasted strikingly with the imperial achievements of both Spain and Portugal.

Huge empires cannot be erected on shoestrings. The failures of lone wolves like Gilbert and Raleigh merely proved that the risky business of colony building was beyond the resources of a single private purse. But the child must creep before he can walk, and these discouraging setbacks taught badly needed lessons.

A Troubled England on the Eve of Empire

By the early 1600s the English were ready to enter the colonial scramble in dead earnest. Why?

Economic motivations were strong. A vigorous middle class had risen, challenging the social position of the nobles, and providing an active group of merchants who could furnish business leadership and wealth for colonial enterprises. Moreover, the joint-stock company—forerunner of the modern corporation—was now perfected. It had the virtue of enabling a considerable number of investors ("adventurers") to pool their capital—an advantage that the luckless Gilbert and Raleigh had not enjoyed.

England was also burdened with a surplus population. At least she thought she was, even though her 4 million inhabitants totaled only about half those of London in the mid-20th Century. The woolen industry was experiencing boom days, and farms were being turned into grazing lands, with the sheep displacing many soil tillers. Catholic monasteries and nunneries, which had formerly cared for the poor, had been seized by the anti-papal Crown. Penniless souls, in a period of increasingly hard times, were being turned loose on the country. In the late 1500s the land swarmed with "sturdy beggars and paupers," who engaged in "lewd and naughty practices" and who might well be dumped on America.

English colonization was also profoundly influenced by the Protestant Reformation. Martin Luther, a German who dramatically launched his reformist attack on the Church of Rome in 1517, was another indirect founding father of the United States. Much-married Henry VIII of England, using the Reformation for his own devices and divorces, broke with Rome and made himself head of the Church of England. Unhappy Protes-

The Tudor Rulers of England

(SEE P. 28 FOR CONTINUATION OF TABLE.)

Name, Reign	*Relation to America*
Henry VII, 1485–1509	Cabot voyages, 1497, 1498
Henry VIII, 1509–1547	English Reformation begun
Edward VI, 1547–1553	Strong Protestant tendencies
"Bloody" Mary, 1553–1558	Catholic reaction
Elizabeth, 1558–1603	Break with Rome final; Drake; Spanish Armada defeated

tants, especially those who felt that their king had not parted company completely with the Papacy, came to look upon America as a desirable haven for people of their faith. Many persecuted Catholics, who believed that their sovereign had gone too far, likewise began to regard America as a possible refuge.

International religious rivalry, in addition, spurred English colonization. The King of England ruled the leading Protestant nation; the King of Spain ruled the leading Catholic nation. A bitter contest between these two powers for the spoils of North America was, curiously, to take on some of the features of a religious crusade extended to the New World. English America was in some degree a child of Catholic-Protestant strife.

Elizabeth I (1533–1603). Although accused of being vain, fickle, prejudiced, and miserly, she proved to be an unusually successful ruler. She never married ("The Virgin Queen"), although various royal matches were projected. (National Portrait Gallery, London.)

Sir Francis Drake and the Spanish Armada

Hardy English freebooters swarmed out upon the shipping lanes in the mid-1500s. They sought to promote the twin goals of Protestantism and plunder by seizing Spanish treasure ships, even though England and Spain were technically at peace. The most famous of these semi-piratical "sea dogs" was the courtly Francis Drake. He plundered his way around the planet, and returned in 1580 with his ship heavily ballasted with Spanish silver and gold. The venture netted profits of about 4,600 percent to his financial backers, among whom, in secret, was Queen Elizabeth I. Defying the protests of Spain, she brazenly knighted Drake on the deck of his barnacled ship. Seldom has patriotic piracy been so handsomely rewarded. Elizabeth further outraged the Spanish Crown by sending English troops to the Netherlands, where they helped the partially Protestant Dutch to wrest their independence from Catholic Spain.

A showdown came in 1588 when Philip II of

Spain, self-anointed foe of the Protestant Reformation, amassed his "Invincible Armada" of some 130 ships bearing troops for an invasion of England. The English sea dogs fought back. They inflicted heavy damage in four running engagements, using craft that were swifter, more maneuverable, more numerous, and better armed. Then devastating storms took over, causing even greater damage. About half of the crippled Spanish fleet finally crept back into port. Spanish prestige, and with it the Catholic cause, had suffered a humiliating blow.

The defeat of the Spanish Armada was a red-letter event in American history. It dampened the fighting spirit of Spain, and gave further proof of the decline in her power, though by no means its end. The triumph also helped to insure England's naval dominance in the North Atlantic. It started her well on her way to becoming Mistress of the Seas—a fact of enormous importance to the American people. Control of the watery highways enabled England, with relative ease, not only to plant her colonies but to supply and protect them as well. Specifically, the victory helped clear the way for the English to settle on the Atlantic coast as far south as Virginia. This area was regarded by Spain as her own private preserve, for there she had already planted a Jesuit missionary outpost in 1570 which had soon been wiped out by Indians.

Ark Royal, the English Flagship Used in the Defeat of the Spanish Armada. (Reproduced by courtesy of the Trustees of the British Museum.)

England's rocky road to settlement in America was further smoothed in 1603, when Queen Elizabeth died. She carried her personal feud with Spain to her grave, and the next year the two rivals signed an uneasy peace.

A wondrous flowering of the English national spirit also followed the crippling of the Spanish Armada. A golden age of literature dawned in this exhilarating atmosphere, with Shakespeare, who was at the forefront, making occasional poetical reference to England's American colonies. Englishmen were seized with restlessness, with thirst for adventure, and with curiosity regarding the unknown. Everywhere there blossomed a new spirit of self-confidence, of vibrant patriotism, and of boundless faith in the future of the English nation.

England Plants the Jamestown Seedling

In 1606, two years after peace with Spain, the hand of destiny beckoned toward Virginia. A joint-stock company, known as The Virginia Company of London, received a charter from King James I of England for a settlement in the New World. The main attraction was the promise of gold, although there was also a strong desire to convert the Indians to Christianity and to find a passage through America to the Indies. Like most joint-stock companies of the day, The Virginia Company was intended to endure for only a few years, after which its stockholders hoped to liquidate it for a profit. This arrangement put severe pressure on the luckless colonists, who were threatened with abandonment in the wilderness if they did not quickly strike it rich on the company's behalf. Few of the investors thought in terms of long-term colonization. Apparently no one even faintly suspected that the seeds of a mighty nation were being planted.

The charter of the Virginia Company is a significant document in American history. It guaranteed to the overseas settlers the same rights of

King James I had scant enthusiasm for the Virginia experiment, partly because of his hatred of tobacco smoking, which had been introduced into the Old World by the Spanish discoverers. In 1604 he published the pamphlet *A Counterblast to Tobacco:* "A custom loathsome to the eye, hateful to the nose, harmful to the brain, dangerous to the lungs, and in the black stinking fume thereof, nearest resembling the horrible Stygian smoke of the pit [Hades] that is bottomless."

Englishmen that they would have enjoyed if they had stayed at home. This precious boon was gradually extended to the other English colonies, and became a foundation stone of American liberties.

Unluckily, the site selected in 1607 for the tiny colony was Jamestown, on the wooded and malarial banks of the James River, named in honor of King James I. Although mosquito-infested and unhealthful, the spot was easy to defend.

The early years at Jamestown proved to be a nightmare for all concerned—except the buzzards. Forty would-be colonists perished during the initial voyage in 1606–1607. Another expedition in 1609 lost its leaders and many of its precious supplies in a shipwreck in Bermuda. Of the 400 settlers who managed to make it to Virginia, only 60 survived the "starving time" winter of 1609–10. Ironically, the woods rustled with game and the rivers flopped with fish, but the greenhorn settlers wasted valuable time grubbing for nonexistent gold when they should have been gathering provisions. Diseased and despairing, the colonists dragged themselves aboard homeward-bound ships in the spring of 1610—only to be met at the mouth of the James River by a relief party, which ordered them back to Jamestown.

Disease continued to reap a gruesome harvest among the Virginians, and Indian raids added to the death toll. One Indian uprising in 1622 left 347 settlers dead. By 1625, Virginia contained only some 1200 hard-bitten survivors of the nearly 8000 adventurers who had tried to start life anew in the ill-fated colony.

Virginia was saved from collapse at the start largely by the leadership and resourcefulness of an incredible young adventurer, Captain John Smith. Taking over in 1608, he whipped the gold-hungry colonists into line with the rule, "He who will not work shall not eat." The brown-skinned Indian maiden Pocahontas may not have saved his life, as he dramatically related, by suddenly interposing her head between his and the war clubs of his Indian captors. But there can be little doubt that she contributed to the salvation of the colony by helping to preserve peace and provide foodstuffs. At times of scarcity the settlers were forced to eat "dogges, Catts, Ratts, and Myce." One hungry man killed, salted, and ate his wife, for which misbehavior he was executed.

Virginia: Child of Tobacco

John Rolfe, who married Pocahontas in 1613 and became father of the tobacco industry, was also an economic savior of the Virginia colony. By 1616 he perfected methods of raising and curing the pungent weed (another Indian gift to Europe) which eliminated much of the bitter tang. Tobacco-rush days began, as crops were planted even

Pochantas (c. 1595–1617). Taken to England by her husband, she was received as a princess. She died when preparing to return, and her infant son ultimately reached Virginia, where hundreds of his descendants have lived, including the second Mrs. Woodrow Wilson. (National Portrait Gallery, Smithsonian Institution, Washington, D.C.)

in the streets of Jamestown and between the numerous graves. So heavy was the concentration on the yellow leaf that some foodstuffs had to be imported.

Virginia's prosperity was finally built on tobacco smoke. This "bewitching weed" played a vital role in putting the colony on firm foundations, and in setting an example for other successful colonizing experiments. But tobacco—King Nicotine—was something of a tyrant. It was ruinous to the soil when greedily planted in successive years, and it enchained the prosperity of Virginia to the fluctuating price of a single crop. Finally, tobacco promoted the broad-acred plantation system, and with it a brisk demand for slave labor.

In 1619, the year before the Plymouth Pilgrims landed in New England, what was described as a Dutch warship appeared off Jamestown and sold some twenty black Africans. (The scanty record does not reveal whether they were purchased as lifelong slaves or as servants committed to limited years of servitude.) Yet black slaves were too costly for most of the hard-pinched white colonists to acquire, and for decades they were imported only in driblets. Virginia counted but 300 blacks in 1650, although by the end of the century blacks made up approximately 14 percent of the colony's population.

Representative self-government was also born in primitive Virginia, in the same cradle with slavery and in the same year—1619. The London Company authorized the settlers to summon an assembly, known as the House of Burgesses. A momentous precedent was thus feebly established, for this assemblage was the first of many miniature parliaments to mushroom from the soil of America.

The wife of a Virginia governor wrote to her sister in England in 1623 of her voyage: "For our Shippe was so pestered with people and goods that we were so full of infection that after a while we saw little but throwing folkes over board: It pleased god to send me my helth till I came to shoare and 3 dayes after I fell sick but I thank god I am well recovered. Few else are left alive that came in that Shippe. . . ."

"Cavalier" Virginia and Bacon's Rebellion

As time passed, James I grew increasingly hostile to Virginia. He detested tobacco and he distrusted the representative House of Burgesses, which he branded a "seminary of sedition." In 1624 he arbitrarily revoked the charter of the bankrupt Virginia Company, thus making Virginia a royal colony directly under his control. He next planned to abolish the House of Burgesses; but he died the next year, and in the subsequent change-over the newborn assembly was allowed to continue.

To add to the confusion, civil wars convulsed England in the 1640s. The personal rule of King Charles I, supported by his loyal "Cavaliers," was openly challenged by the Parliamentarians ("Roundheads"). They ultimately found their great leader in Oliver Cromwell. The Virginians showed surprising loyalty to the distant Crown, and when the Parliamentarians triumphed and Charles I was beheaded, a sprinkling of the vanquished Cavaliers fled to hospitable Virginia. Only a handful of them were of noble birth; most of them were Cavaliers only by sentiment or political attachment. But the tradition of aristocratic origins spread rapidly in Virginia—later "the Cavalier State"—and the belief that many of its founders were exiled noblemen came to have a profound impact on the Southern mind.

Cavalier or not, class and sectional tensions quickly jelled in colonial Virginia. Lace-bedecked gentry monopolized the rich tidewater lands of the coastal areas; the Byrd family alone eventually amassed 179,000 acres. Poorer folk were forced into the wild and dangerous back country. There, though unrepresented or underrepresented in the House of Burgesses, they were compelled to bear the full brunt of the Indian attacks.

Rebellion was clearly in the making. Autocratic old Governor Berkeley, who was allegedly involved in fur trade with the Indians, was unwilling to antagonize them by fighting back. About a thousand angry back-country men broke out of control in 1676, under the leadership of a twenty-nine-year-old planter, Nathaniel Bacon, whose overseer had been slain. They chastised the Indians, friendly and hostile alike, routed Governor Berkeley, and burned Jamestown. In the hour of victory Bacon suddenly died, amid rumors that he had been poisoned by the Berkeleyites. The governor thereupon crushed the uprising with needless cruelty, hanging in all more than twenty rebels. Back in England Charles II complained, "That old fool has put to death more people in that naked country than I did here for the murder of my father."

Bacon's ill-fated rebellion was symptomatic of much that was to be American. It highlighted the cleavage between the old order of aristocracy and special privilege, on the one hand, and the emerging new order of free enterprise and equal opportunity, on the other. The outburst arrayed the despised commoners against the lordly governing class, and the back-country frontier against the tidewater aristocracy. Bacon and his followers showed at this early date that aroused colonists would unite and die for what they regarded as their rights as free men.

Maryland: Catholic Haven

Maryland—the second plantation colony but the fourth English colony to be planted—was founded in 1634 by Lord Baltimore, of a prominent English Catholic family. He embarked upon the venture partly to reap financial profits and partly to create a refuge for his co-religionists. Protestant England was still persecuting Roman Catholics; among numerous discriminations, a couple seeking wedlock could not be legally married by a Catholic priest.

Absentee proprietor Lord Baltimore hoped that the 200 settlers who founded Maryland at St. Mary's, on Chesapeake Bay, would be the vanguard of a vast new feudal domain. Huge estates were to be awarded to his largely Catholic relatives, and gracious manor houses, modeled on those of England's aristocracy, were intended to sprout from the fertile forests. But colonists proved willing to come only if offered the right to acquire land of their own. Soon they were dispersed around the Chesapeake region on modest farms, and the haughty land barons, mostly Catholic, were surrounded by resentful back-country planters, mostly Protestant. Resentment flared into open rebellion near the end of the century, and the Baltimore family for a time lost its proprietary rights.

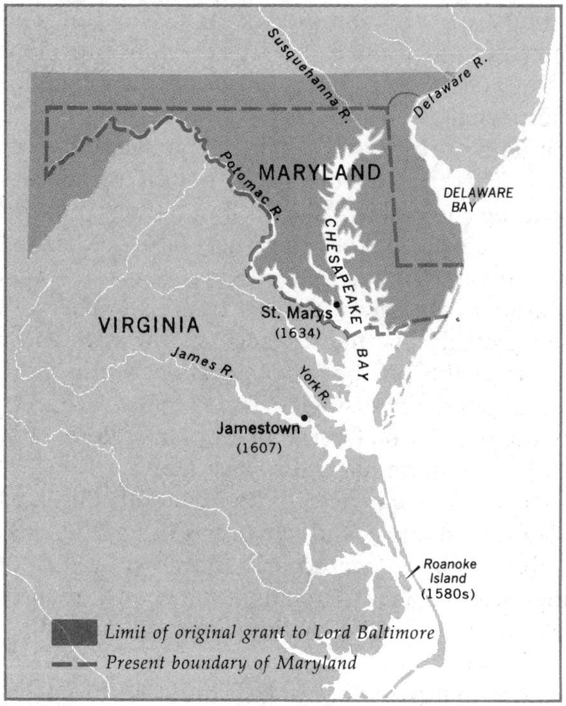

EARLY MARYLAND AND VIRGINIA

Despite these tensions, Maryland prospered. Like Virginia, it blossomed forth in acres of tobacco. Like Virginia, it depended for labor in its early years mainly on white indentured servants—penniless persons who bound themselves to work for a number of years to pay their passage. In both colonies it was only in the later years of the 17th Century that black slaves began to be imported in large numbers—a response to the rising price of white labor, and perhaps to fears of further troubles with rebellious white settlers like Nathaniel Bacon. At the same time, laws began to appear on the books that formally decreed the iron conditions of black slavery. These earliest "slave codes" made blacks and their children the property for life of their white masters. Not even conversion to Christianity could qualify a slave for freedom. Thus did the God-fearing whites put the fear of God into their hapless black laborers.

Lord Baltimore, a canny soul, permitted unusual freedom of worship at the outset. He hoped that he would thus purchase toleration for his own fellow worshipers. But the heavy tide of Protestants threatened to submerge the Catholics and place severe restrictions on them, as in England. Faced with disaster, the Catholics of Maryland threw their support behind the famed Act of Toleration, which was passed in 1649 by the local representative assembly.

Maryland's new religious statute guaranteed toleration to all Christians. But it decreed the death penalty for those, like Jews and atheists, who denied the divinity of Jesus. The law thus sanctioned less toleration than had previously existed in the settlement, but it did extend a temporary cloak of protection to the uneasy Catholic minority. One result was that when the colonial era ended, Maryland probably sheltered more Roman Catholics than any other English-speaking colony in the New World.

Cecelius Calvert (Lord Baltimore), c. 1605–1675. Inheriting the land grant from his father, he served as the first proprietor of Maryland, named after the English queen. He never saw his colony but governed through deputies. The present Anne Arundel county, embracing Annapolis and Baltimore, was named after his wife. (Enoch Pratt Free Library. Photograph from the Maryland Historical Society.)

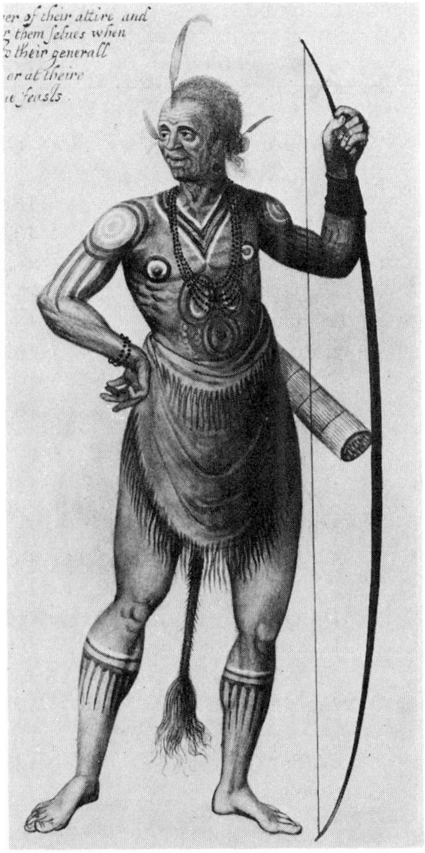

A North Carolina Indian. A painting by John White, who was a member of the Raleigh expedition of 1585. (Library of Congress.)

Colonizing the Carolinas

The Carolinas were formally created in 1670, after Charles II had granted to eight of his court favorites—Lords Proprietors—an expanse of wilderness ribboning across the continent to the Pacific. These aristocratic founders hoped to make their fortunes in this warm climate by producing non-English products, such as silk, wine, and olive oil.

South Carolina started auspiciously. There was no "starving time," as in Virginia, though the first fleet was on short rations when it arrived. Moss-festooned Charles Town—named after

The Thirteen Original Colonies

Name	Founded by	Year	Charter	Made Royal	1775 Status
1. Virginia	London Co.	1607	1606, 1609, 1612	1624	Royal (under the Crown)
Plymouth	Separatists	1620	None		(Merged with Mass., 1691)
Maine	F. Gorges	1623	1639		(Bought by Mass., 1677)
2. New Hampshire	John Mason and others	1623	1679	1679	Royal (absorbed by Mass., 1641–1679)
3. Massachusetts	Puritans	c.1628	1629	1691	Royal
4. Maryland	Lord Baltimore	1634	1632	—	Proprietary (controlled by proprietor)
5. Connecticut	Mass. emigrants	1635	1662	—	Self-governing (under local control)
6. Rhode Island	R. Williams	1636	1644, 1663	—	Self-governing
New Haven	Mass. emigrants	1638	None		(Merged with Conn., 1662)
7. N. Carolina	Virginians	1653	1663	1729	Royal (separated informally from S.C., 1691)
8. New York	Dutch	c.1613			
	Duke of York	1664	1664	1685	Royal
9. New Jersey	Berkeley and Carteret	1664	None	1702	Royal
10. S. Carolina	Eight nobles	1670	1663	1729	Royal (separated formally from N.C., 1712)
11. Pennsylvania	William Penn	1681	1681	—	Proprietary
12. Delaware	Swedes	1638	None	—	Proprietary (merged with Penn., 1682; same governor, but separate assembly, granted 1703)
13. Georgia	Oglethorpe and others	1733	1732	1752	Royal

King Charles II—rapidly became the most important seaport of the South. Many high-spirited younger sons of English noble families, deprived of an inheritance, came to the Charleston area and lent it a rich aristocratic flavor. The village also became a melting-pot community, to which French Protestant refugees and others were attracted by religious toleration.

South Carolina prospered and gradually developed close economic and cultural ties with the flourishing British West Indies. In a broad sense, the mainland colony was but the most northwesterly of these islands. Rice and the indigo plant, which then provided the most important blue dyestuff, were grown profitably on large plantations. The hot sun and swampy land combined to create a strong demand for African slaves; by 1776 South Carolina was the only colony in which blacks outnumbered whites, by nearly two to one.

Nearby, in Florida, the Catholic Spaniards bitterly resented the intrusion of these English heretics. South Carolina's frontier was often aflame. Spanish-incited Indians brandished their tomahawks, and armor-clad warriors of Spain attacked or were attacked during the successive Anglo-Spanish wars. But by 1700 South Carolina was too strong to be wiped out.

The wild northern expanse of the huge Carolina grant bordered on Virginia. From the older colony there drifted down a motley group of poverty-stricken outcasts and religious dissenters. Many of them had been repelled by the rarefied atmosphere of Virginia, dominated as it was by big-plantation aristocrats belonging to the Church of England. North Carolinians, as a result, have been called "the quintessence of Virginia's discontent." The newcomers, who frequently were "squatters" without legal right to the soil, raised their tobacco and other crops on small farms, with little need for slaves.

Distinctive traits developed rapidly in North Carolina. The poor but sturdy inhabitants, regarded as riffraff by their snobbish neighbors, earned a reputation for being irreligious and hospitable to pirates. Isolated from neighbors by raw wilderness and stormy Cape Hatteras, "graveyard of the Atlantic," the North Carolinians developed a strong spirit of resistance to authority. Their location between aristocratic Virginia and aristocratic South Carolina caused the area to be dubbed "a vale of humility between two mountains of conceit." Following much friction with governors, North Carolina was officially separated from South Carolina in 1712, and subsequently each segment became a royal colony.

North Carolina shares with tiny Rhode Island several distinctions. These two outposts were the most democratic, the most independent-minded, and the least aristocratic of the original thirteen English colonies.

EARLY CAROLINA AND GEORGIA SETTLEMENTS

Late-Coming Georgia: The Buffer Colony

Pine-forested Georgia, with the harbor of Savannah nourishing its chief settlement, was formally founded in 1733. It proved to be the last of the thirteen colonies to be planted—fifty-two years after Pennsylvania. Chronologically it belongs elsewhere, but geographically it may be grouped with its Southern neighbors.

Georgia was valued by the English Crown chiefly as a buffer. It would serve to protect the more valuable Carolinas from inroads by vengeful Spaniards from Florida, and by hostile Frenchmen from Louisiana. Georgia in truth suffered much buffeting, especially when wars broke out between Spain and England in the European cockpit. As a vital link in imperial defense, the exposed colony received monetary subsidies from the British government at the outset—the only one of the "original thirteen" to enjoy this boon in its founding stage.

Named in honor of George II of England, Georgia was launched by a high-minded group of philanthropists. Aside from producing silk and wine, and strengthening the empire, they were determined to create a haven for wretched souls imprisoned for debt. The ablest of the founders was the dynamic soldier-statesman James Oglethorpe, who became keenly interested in prison reform after one of his friends had died in a debtors' jail. As an able military leader, Oglethorpe repelled savage Spanish attacks. As an imperialist and a philanthropist, he saved "the Charity Colony" by his energetic leadership and by mortgaging heavily his own personal fortunes.

The hamlet of Savannah, like Charleston, was a melting-pot community. German Lutherans and kilted Scots Highlanders, among others, added color to the pattern. Religious toleration was extended to all Christian worshipers except

Catholics. The early days of the colony were vexed by the presence of too many religious prima donnas, some of whom came for missionary work among debtors and Indians. Prominent among them was young John Wesley, who, after various adventures and misadventures, returned to England and later founded the Methodist Church.

Georgia grew with painful slowness and at the end of the colonial era was perhaps the least populous of the colonies. Prosperity through a large-plantation economy was thwarted by an unhealthful climate, by early restrictions on black slavery, and by demoralizing Spanish attacks.

The Plantation Colonies

Certain distinctive features were shared by England's Southern mainland colonies: Maryland, Virginia, North Carolina, South Carolina, and Georgia.

Broad-acred, these outposts of empire were all in some degree dominated by a plantation economy. Profitable staple crops were the rule, notably tobacco, rice, and indigo, though to a lesser extent in small-farm North Carolina. Immense acreage in the hands of a favored few fostered a strong aristocratic atmosphere, except in North Carolina and to some extent in debtor-tinged Georgia. The wide scattering of plantations and farms, often along stately rivers, made the establishment of churches and schools both difficult and expensive. In 1671 testy Governor Berkeley, who had become something of a tyrant, thanked God that no free schools existed in Virginia, though there were then actually two.

All the plantation colonies were agitated by an underprivileged back-country element, which was seeking a larger voice in government. This was again less true of North Carolina, which from the beginning had attracted a poorer class of people.

All the plantation colonies were in some degree expansive. "Soil butchery" by excessive growing of tobacco drove men westward, and the long, lazy rivers invited penetration of the continent.

All the plantation colonies permitted some religious toleration. The tax-supported Church of England became the dominant faith, though weakest of all in non-conformist North Carolina. The Calvinistic Puritanism of New England, with its rather gloomy outlook on life, did not flourish in the sunny South. Many of the people, especially the wealthy landowners, were much more interested in racing horses and chasing foxes than in fighting the Devil and listening to lengthy hell-fire sermons.

VARYING VIEWPOINTS

The history of discovery and the earliest colonization raises perhaps the single most fundamental question about all American history. Should it be understood as the extension of European civilization into the New World, or as the gradual development of a uniquely "American" culture? An older school of thought tended to emphasize the Europeanization of America. Historians of that persuasion thus paid close attention to the situation in Europe, particularly in England and Spain, in the 15th and 16th Centuries. They also focused on the various means by which the values and institutions of the Mother Continent were exported to the new lands in the Western sea. Some European writers have varied this general question by asking what transforming effect the discovery of America had on Europe itself. But both of these approaches are Eurocentric. More recently, historians have concentrated on the distinctive aspects of America, especially the Americanization of Europeans and the interactions among various races that have been among the noteworthy characteristics of the American experience.

SELECT READINGS

Edward Cheyney ably describes *The European Background of American History, 1300–1600* (1904). The immediate English backdrop is colorfully presented in Peter Laslett, *The World We Have Lost* (1965), and in Carl Bridenbaugh, *Vexed and Troubled Englishmen, 1590–1642* (1968). A modern classic is Wallace Notestein, *The English People on the Eve of Colonization, 1603–1630* (1954). See also A. L. Rowse, *Elizabethans and America* (1959). Early English relations with the New World are treated in David B. Quinn, *England and the Discovery of America, 1481–1620* (1974). The ablest summation of the Spanish experience is Charles Gibson, *Spain in America* (1966); James Lang, *Conquest and Commerce: Spain and England in the Americas* (1975), is a comparative chronicle of colonial rivalries. A fascinating brief synthesis of early European contact with the Americas is J. H. Elliott, *The Old World and the New, 1492–1650* (1970). Samuel E. Morison has written several masterful accounts of the discoveries; among the best are *Admiral of the Ocean Sea* (2 vols., 1942; condensed as *Christopher Columbus, Mariner,* 1956), *The European Discovery of America: The Northern Voyages,* A.D. *500–1600* (1971), and *The European Discovery of America: The Southern Voyages,* A.D. *1492–1616* (1974). An excellent brief account of the process of discovery is J. H. Parry, *The Establishment of the European Hegemony, 1415–1715* (1961). The impact on Europe is given in Earl J. Hamilton, *American Treasure and the Price Revolution in Spain, 1501–1650* (1934), a seminal work that inspired much later scholarship. Recent studies that pursue the same theme are C. Cipolla, *European Culture and Overseas Expansion* (1970), and I. Wallerstein, *The Modern World-System: Capitalist Agriculture and the Origins of the European World-Economy in the Sixteenth Century* (1974). A marvelous volume, richly illustrated, portraying the impact of America on the European imagination is Hugh Honour, *The New Golden Land* (1975). A good introduction to early American conditions is C. L. Ver Steeg, *The Formative Years: 1607–1763* (1964). The best general discussion of the Southern colonies is W. F. Craven, *The Southern Colonies in the Seventeenth Century, 1607–1689* (1949). Virginia's story is found in P. L. Barbour, *The Three Worlds of Captain John Smith* (1964), and in Alden Vaughan, *American Genesis: Captain John Smith and the Founding of Virginia* (1975). The Chesapeake region has recently received much fresh attention, especially in Aubrey C. Land, et al., *Law, Society, and Politics in Early Maryland* (1977); T. W. Tate and D. L. Ammerman, eds., *The Chesapeake in the Seventeenth Century* (1979); and Paul G. E. Clemens, *The Atlantic Economy and Colonial Maryland's Eastern Shore* (1980). The role of slavery in early colonial society gets perceptive treatment in Edmund S. Morgan, *American Slavery, American Freedom* (1975). See also Winthrop Jordan's monumental *White Over Black* (1968), and Peter Wood's account of South Carolina, *Black Majority* (1974). Gary Nash analyzes relations among all three races in *Red, White, and Black: The Peoples of Early America* (1974). Native Americans get special attention in W. E. Washburn, *The Indian in America* (1975), and in Francis Jennings, *The Invasion of America* (1975). See also Karen Ordahl Kupperman, *Settling with the Indians: The Meeting of English and Indian Cultures in America, 1580–1640* (1980), and Bernard W. Sheehan, *Savagism and Civility: Indians and Englishmen in Colonial Virginia* (1980). Nathan Wachtel presents the Indians' view of the Spanish conquest in *The Vision of the Vanquished* (1977). Nathaniel Bacon is somewhat downgraded in W. E. Washburn, *The Governor and the Rebel* (1957).

2

Completing the Thirteen Colonies

God hath sifted a Nation that he might send Choice Grain into this Wilderness.

WILLIAM STOUGHTON [of Massachusetts Bay], 1669

Calvinism Conceives Puritanism

Little did the religious reformer John Calvin know, when he fled his native France in 1534, that he was to shape the destinies of a yet unheralded nation. Arriving in Switzerland, this radical young zealot gave the Protestant Reformation a twist that profoundly affected the thinking and character of generations of Americans yet unborn. Calvinism, ultimately somewhat watered down, became the basic theology of the dominant Puritan group in New England. It was also the creed of the Scottish Presbyterians, the French Huguenots, and communicants of the Dutch Reformed Church. The members of all these sects, as immigrants, played an influential role in American moral and spiritual life.

The awesome doctrine of predestination was a distinguishing feature of Calvinism. God in His infinite wisdom had predestined a mass of sinners, including babes in the womb, to be tortured in hell for an eternity. The Almighty had also chosen a selected few—the "elect"—to enjoy eternal bliss. Nothing that the damned could do would save them, whether faith, repentance, or good deeds. The complexities of Calvinism were later summed up by a rhymester:

> You can and you can't,
> You will and you won't.
> You'll be damned if you do,
> You'll be damned if you don't.

Calvinists were a peculiar lot, partly because no believers could be completely sure that they were of the "elect." A gnawing doubt led to much soul searching and Scripture reading. It also led to a denial of the pleasures of this earth in a preoccupation with the satisfactions of a future life. Even though a Calvinist might be convinced that he was of the "elect," he could not be certain that his neighbors were, and this curiosity led to much Puritanical prying into the lives of others. Nor was toleration tolerated by the extreme Calvinists; anyone who denied the truth of Calvinism was clearly a heretic.

The Puritans of Old England, even before 1620, were unhappy over the snail-like progress of the Protestant Reformation. They were especially eager to de-Catholicize further the Church of England. To them it was still "popish" and "idolatrous," with its Roman creed and ritual, and with its long black robes and other vestments.

Puritan reformers fell into two general groups. The first consisted of the Non-conformists, who sought to change the Church of England by boring from within. Devoted and sincere though they were, they constituted a difficult and militant minority. The second type of Puritans were Separatists. They wished to separate entirely from the Church of England and its "Romish" practices, in order that they might worship God and combat the Devil in their own way.

King James I, a shrewd Scotsman, was head of both the state and the church in England. He quickly perceived that if his subjects could defy him as their spiritual leader, they might one day defy him as their political leader, as in fact they later defied his son, Charles I. He therefore threatened to harass the more bothersome Separatists out of the land.

Pilgrims on *Mayflower* Leave England

The Pilgrims End Their Pilgrimage at Plymouth

The most famous congregation of Separatists, fleeing royal wrath, departed for Holland in 1608. During the ensuing twelve years of toil and poverty, they were increasingly distressed by the "Dutchification" of their children. They longed to find a haven where they could live and die as Englishmen. America was the logical refuge, despite the early ordeals of Jamestown, and despite tales of cannibals roasting steaks from their white victims before open fires.

A group of the Separatists in Holland, after negotiating with the Virginia Company, at length secured rights to settle under its jurisdiction. But their crowded *Mayflower,* sixty-five days at sea, missed its destination and arrived off the rocky coast of New England in 1620, with a total of 102 persons. One had died en route—an unusually short casualty list—and one had been born and appropriately named Oceanus. Fewer than half

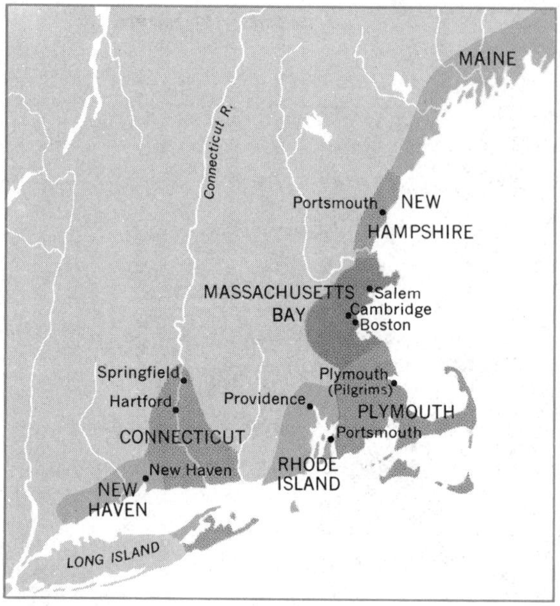

NEW ENGLAND SETTLEMENTS ABOUT 1650

of the entire party were Separatists. Prominent among the non-belongers was a peppery and stocky soldier of fortune, Captain Myles Standish, dubbed by one of his critics "Captain Shrimp." He later rendered indispensable service as an Indian fighter and negotiator.

The Pilgrims did not make their initial landing at Plymouth Rock, as commonly supposed, but undertook a number of preliminary surveys. They finally chose for their site the shore of inhospitable Plymouth Bay. This area was outside the domain of the Virginia Company, and consequently the settlers became squatters. They were without legal right to the land, and without specific authority to establish a government.

Before disembarking, the Pilgrim Fathers drew up and signed the brief Mayflower Compact. Though setting an invaluable precedent for later written constitutions, this document was not a constitution at all. It was a simple agreement to form a body politic, and to submit to the will of the majority under the regulations agreed upon. The Compact was signed by forty-one adult males, eleven of them with the exalted rank of "mister," though not by the servants and two seamen. The pact was a promising step toward genuine self-government, for soon the adult male settlers were assembling to make their own laws in open-discussion town meetings—a great laboratory of liberty.

The winter of 1620–1621 was a bone-chilling one, with cold and disease taking a grisly toll. Only 44 out of the 102 survived. At one time only seven were well enough to lay the dead in their frosty graves. Yet when the *Mayflower* sailed back to England in the spring, not a single one of the courageous band of Separatists left. As one of them wrote, "It is not with us as with other men, whom small things can discourage." The Pilgrim Mothers endured the same hardships as the Pilgrim Fathers, plus others, including childbearing.

God prospered His children, so the Pilgrims believed. The next autumn, that of 1621, brought bountiful harvests, and with them the first Thanksgiving Day in New England. In time the frail colony found sound economic legs in fur, fish, and lumber. But the beaver and the Bible were the early mainstays: the one for the sustenance of the body, the other for the sustenance of the soul. Plymouth proved that Englishmen could maintain themselves in this uninviting region.

The Pilgrims were extremely fortunate in their leaders. Prominent among them was the cultured

The Pilgrims Land, 1620. (Scribner's "History of the United States.")

William Bradford wrote in *Of Plymouth Plantation,* "Thus out of small beginnings greater things have been produced by His hand that made all things of nothing, and gives being to all things that are; and, as one small candle may light a thousand, so the light here kindled hath shone unto many, yea in some sort to our whole nation."

William Bradford, a self-taught scholar who read Hebrew, Greek, Latin, French, and Dutch. He was chosen governor thirty times in the annual elections. His descendants are now numbered by the thousands, and the descendants of Priscilla and John Alden, who were immortalized by Longfellow's "Courtship of Myles Standish," by the tens of thousands.

Quiet and quaint, the little colony of Plymouth was never important economically or numerically. It claimed only seven thousand souls by 1691, when, still charterless, it merged with its giant neighbor, the Massachusetts Bay Colony. But the tiny settlement of Pilgrims was big both morally and spiritually.

Aye, call it holy ground,
  The soil where first they trod!
They have left unstained what there they found—
  Freedom to worship God!*

The Bay Colony Bible Commonwealth

Bustling fishing villages and other settlements gradually sprouted to the north, on the storm-lashed shores of Massachusetts Bay, where many people were as much interested in cod as God. In 1629 an energetic group of non-Separatist Puritans in England, organizing the Massachusetts Bay Company, secured a charter from the Crown. Prompted by both economic and religious motives, they proposed to plant a settlement in the infertile Massachusetts area, with Boston soon becoming its hub. Stealing a march on both King and Church, the newcomers brought their charter with them. For many years they used it as a kind of constitution, out of immediate reach of royal authority. They steadfastly denied that they wanted to separate from the Church of England, only from its impurities. But back in the Mother Country the highly orthodox Archbishop Laud snorted that the Bay Colony Puritans were "swine which rooted in God's vineyard."

The Massachusetts Bay enterprise was singularly blessed. The massive expedition of 1630, with eleven vessels and hundreds of colonists, started the establishment off on a larger scale than any of the other English colonies. Another distinctive feature was the large proportion of fairly prosperous members of the middle class, including an unusual number of university graduates. "Dukes don't emigrate," the saying goes, for if men enjoy wealth and security they do not ordinarily expose their lives in the wilderness. The power of deep religious convictions is further attested by the presence in Massachusetts of well-to-do pillars of English society, notably Governor John Winthrop.

Puritan settlers on Massachusetts Bay, despite their preoccupation with things of the spirit, gave conscientious attention to earning a livelihood. Their settlements grew marvelously, as fur trading, fishing, and shipbuilding blossomed into important industries, especially fish and ships. The Massachusetts Bay Colony rapidly shot to the fore as not only the biggest but the most influential of the New England outposts.

Additional and enriching waves of Puritans were tossed upon the shores of Massachusetts in the 1630s. Persecution of Puritans at home by Archbishop Laud, arbitrary rule by Charles I, and economic insecurity in England resulted in the "Great Puritan Migration" of 1629–1640. Altogether, about 75,000 refugees left the Motherland. But not all of them were Puritans, and only about one-third came to the English mainland of North America. Many were attracted by the warm and fertile West Indies, especially by the sugar-rich island of

*Felicia D. Hemans, "The Landing of the Pilgrim Fathers."

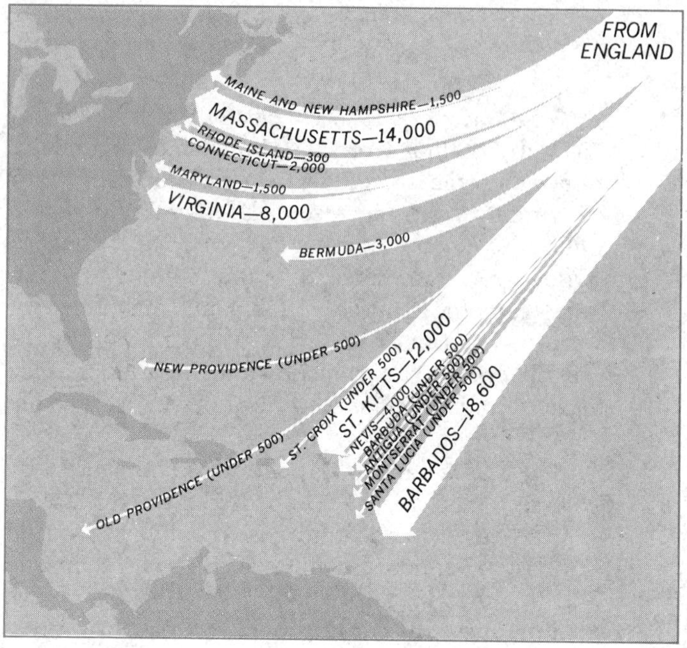

THE GREAT PURITAN MIGRATION

Much of the early history of the United States was written by New Englanders, who were not disposed to emphasize the larger exodus of Puritans to the southerly islands. When the mainland colonials declared independence in 1776, they hoped that these island outposts would join them, but the existence of the British navy had a chilling effect.

Barbados. More Puritans came to this Caribbean islet, rather surprisingly, than to all Massachusetts.

At first the Bay Colony was a "Bible Commonwealth." For more than fifty years no resident of the colony could vote in provincial elections unless he belonged to the Puritan Church, which in time was generally called the Congregational Church. On this basis, only about one-fifth of the adult white males enjoyed the ballot. The other males, as non-church members, were voteless, as were women. Yet they were taxed—an early instance of "taxation without representation." And the principal duty of the government was always to enforce "God's laws."

Religious leaders or "theocrats" also wielded much unofficial authority in the Bay Colony. Prominent among the "Saints" was fiery John Cotton, whose zeal sometimes prompted him to preach and pray as much as six hours in a single day. Such men exercised great influence through their spiritual leadership, as well as through their prestige as ministers of a church intimately associated with the government.

But the power of the preachers was not absolute; they were barred from holding formal political office. Puritans in England had suffered too much at the hands of a "political" Anglican clergy to permit in the New World another unholy union of religious and governmental power. In a limited way, the Bay Colonists thus endorsed the idea of the separation of church and state.

Religious Intolerance in Massachusetts

The age was not tolerant, whether in Europe or America, and the early religious leaders of Massachusetts Bay were not tolerant. Newcomers either conformed to the established Puritan Church, kept quiet, or departed—sometimes in haste. As custodians of the "true light," the Puritan emigrants from England, themselves the victims of intolerance, had little tolerance for other dissenters. Quakers, who flouted the authority of the Massachusetts rulers, were persecuted with fines, floggings, and banishment. Four Quakers who defied expulsion, one of them a woman, were hanged on the Boston Common. But this was an extreme case.

The age was not democratic—and the early Massachusetts leaders, often branded "blue-nosed bigots" by later generations, were not democrats. Holding unusual power in their own hands, they strove, like aristocrats in the other colonies, to

Colonel Robert E. Lee (later General) reflected a common Southern view when he wrote to his wife in 1856, "Is it not strange that the descendants of those Pilgrim Fathers who crossed the Atlantic to preserve their own freedom of opinion have always proved themselves intolerant of the spiritual liberty of others?"

keep it from falling into the hands of the rabble. "If the people be governors," queried the Reverend John Cotton, "who shall be governed?" The able John Winthrop feared and distrusted the "commons" as the "meaner sort," and thought that democracy was the "meanest and worst" of all forms of government.

Yet the religious and political leaders of the Bay Colony, try as they would, could not completely choke the rising voice of the masses. Beginnings of popular rule may be discerned in the charter of the colony; in the self-governing and hence democratic congregations of the Congregational Church; and above all in the "direct" or "pure" democracy of the town meeting. There the qualified voters enjoyed the priceless boon of publicly discussing local issues, often with much heat, and of voting on them by a majority-rule show of hands.

The arbitrary nature of Anne Hutchinson's trial is reflected in the record of the court:
GOVERNOR WINTHROP: Mrs. Hutchinson, you hear the sentence of the Court. It is that you are banished from out of our jurisdiction as being a woman not fit for our society. And you are to be imprisoned till the Court send you away.

MRS. HUTCHINSON: I desire to know wherefore I am banished.

GOVERNOR WINTHROP: Say no more. The Court knows wherefore, and is satisfied.

A sharp challenge to the authority of the clergymen of Massachusetts came from Mistress Anne Hutchinson. She was an intelligent, strong-willed, and talkative woman, ultimately the mother of fourteen children. Boasting a more intimate contact with God than even the Puritan clergy could claim, she committed the "sin" of interpreting their sermons to others. Banished as a "leper" after a farcical trial in 1638, she set out on foot for Rhode Island, though pregnant. She finally moved to New York, where she and all but one of her household were murdered by the Indians. Back in the Bay Colony, the pious John Winthrop saw "God's hand" in her fate.

The Trial of Anne Hutchinson. Mistress Hutchinson (1591–1643) was not only a religious leader but one of the earliest American feminists. A kindly soul, she not only held unorthodox religious discussions in her home but also committed the sin of invading the domain of the clergy, a calling hitherto reserved for the male sex.

More dangerous to the Puritan leaders was a fellow clergyman, Roger Williams, a young man with radical ideas and an unrestrained tongue. Among various alarming proposals, he defended Indian claims to the soil, and he agitated—horrifying thought to the ruling caste!—for a complete separation of church and state. He argued that religious groups should be supported by voluntary contributions of members, rather than by taxes imposed upon the population at large. He was accused of inciting others to cut the cross out of an English flag, and he branded the state-connected sects as "ulcered and gangrened."

Their patience exhausted by 1635, the Bay Colony authorities found Williams guilty of disseminating "newe & dangerous opinions," and ordered him banished. He was permitted to remain several months longer because of illness, but he kept up his criticisms. The outraged magistrates, fearing that he might organize a rival colony of malcontents, then planned to exile him to England.

The Rhode Island "Sewer"

Aided by friendly Indians, Roger Williams fled to the Rhode Island area in 1636, in the midst of a bitter winter. But he found, as he wrote, that

> God makes a path, provides a guide,
> And feeds in wilderness!

At Providence, the courageous and far-visioned Williams built a Baptist church, probably the first in America. He established complete freedom of religion, even for Jews and Catholics. In this respect he was not only far ahead of his age, but ahead of any of the other English settlements in the New World. He demanded no oaths regarding one's religious beliefs, no compulsory attendance at worship, no taxes to support a state church. He even sheltered the abused Quakers, although disagreeing sharply with their views.

Those outcasts who clustered about Roger Williams enjoyed additional blessings. They exercised simple manhood suffrage from the start, though this boon was later modified by a property qualification. Opposed to special privilege of any sort, the doughty Rhode Islanders managed to achieve remarkable freedom of opportunity.

Other scattered settlements soon dotted Rhode Island. They consisted largely of malcontents and exiles, some of whom could not bear the stifling theological atmosphere of the Bay Colony. Many of these restless souls in "Rogues' Island" were neither democratic nor tolerant, including Anne Hutchinson, who had little in common with Roger Williams—except banishment. The Puritan clergy back in Boston sneered at Rhode Island as "that sewer" in which the "Lord's debris" had collected and rotted.

Planted by dissenters and exiles, Rhode Island became strongly individualistic and stubbornly independent. With good reason "Little Rhody" was later known as "the traditional home of the otherwise minded." Begun as a squatter colony in 1636 without legal standing, it finally established rights to the soil when it secured a charter from Parliament in 1644. A huge bronze statue of the "Independent Man" appropriately stands today on the dome of the state house in Providence.

New England Spreads Out

The smiling valley of the Connecticut River, one of the few highly fertile expanses of any size in all New England, had meanwhile attracted a sprinkling of Dutch and English settlers. Hartford was founded in 1635. The next year witnessed a spectacular beginning of the centuries-long westward movement across the continent. An energetic group of Boston Puritans, led by the Reverend Thomas Hooker, swarmed as a body into the Hartford area, with Mrs. Hooker riding a horse litter.

Three years later, in 1639, the settlers of the new Connecticut River colony drafted in open meeting a trail-blazing document known as the Fundamental Orders. It was in effect a modern constitution, which established a regime democratically controlled by the "substantial" citizens. Essential features of the Fundamental Orders

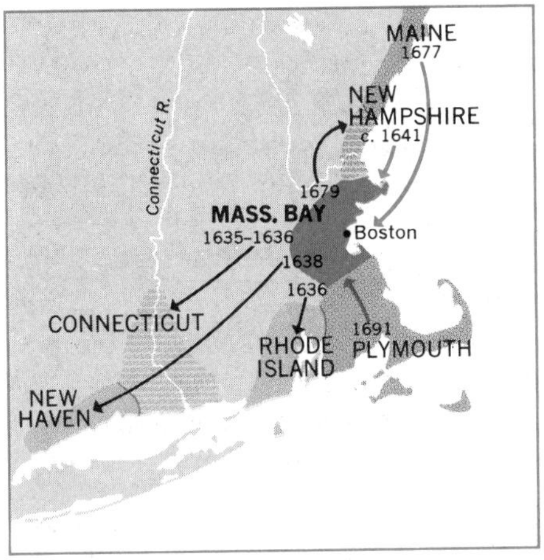

MASSACHUSETTS BAY,
THE HUB OF NEW ENGLAND
All earlier colonies grew into it; all later colonies grew out of it.

were later borrowed by Connecticut for her colonial charter, and ultimately for her state constitution.

Another flourishing Connecticut settlement began to spring up at New Haven in 1638. It was a prosperous group, containing many souls who could not endure the overbearing Puritan rulers of the Bay Colony. Themselves overbearing, they contrived to set up an ironclad regime which was even more autocratic than that of Boston. Although only squatters without a charter, the colonists dreamed of making New Haven a flourishing seaport. But they fell into disfavor with Charles II, as a result of having sheltered two of the judges who had condemned his father, Charles I, to death. In 1662, to the acute distress of the New Havenites, the Crown granted a charter to Connecticut which merged New Haven with the more democratic settlements in the Connecticut Valley.

Far to the north, enterprising fishermen and fur traders had been active on the coast of Maine for a dozen or so years before the founding of Plymouth. After disheartening attempts at colonization in 1623 by Sir Ferdinando Gorges, this land of lakes and forests was absorbed by Massachusetts Bay after a formal purchase in 1677 from the Gorges heirs. It remained a part of Massachusetts for nearly a century and a half, and then became a separate state.

Granite-ribbed New Hampshire also sprang from the fishing and trading activities along her narrow coast. She was absorbed in 1641 by the grasping Bay Colony, under a strained interpretation of the Massachusetts charter. The King, annoyed by this display of greed, arbitrarily separated New Hampshire from Massachusetts in 1679, and made her a royal colony.

Seeds of Colonial Unity and Independence

A path-breaking experiment in union was launched in 1643, when four colonies banded together to form the New England Confederation. Old England was then deeply involved in civil wars, and hence the colonials were thrown upon their own resources. The primary purpose of the Confederation was defense against foes or potential foes, notably the Indians, the French, and the Dutch. Purely intercolonial problems, such as runaway servants and criminals who had fled from one colony to another, also came within the jurisdiction of the Confederation. Each member, regardless of size, wielded two votes—an arrangement highly displeasing to the most populous one, Massachusetts Bay.

The Confederation was essentially an exclusive Puritan club. It consisted of the two Massachusetts colonies (the Bay Colony and bantam-sized Plymouth) and the two Connecticut colonies (New Haven and the scattered Valley settlements). The Puritan leaders blackballed Rhode Island, as well as the Maine outposts. These places, it was charged, harbored too many heretical or otherwise undesirable characters. Shockingly, one of the Maine towns had made a tailor its mayor, and had even sheltered an excommunicated minister of the gospel.

Weak though it was, the Confederation was

"Philip, King of Mount Hope." Philip was not only shot and killed but, as a "traitor" to the King, beheaded, drawn, and quartered. His head was exhibited at Plymouth for many years. (An engraving by Paul Revere, Courtesy of The American Antiquarian Society.)

the first notable milestone on the long and rocky road toward colonial unity. The delegates took tottering but urgently needed steps toward acting together on matters of intercolonial importance. Rank-and-file colonists, for their part, received valuable experience in delegating their votes to properly chosen representatives.

The New England Confederation functioned usefully during the bloody war in 1675–1676 with the Indian chieftain King Philip, whose followers struck back at encroachments by whites on their lands. Several hundred settlers were killed and dozens of towns were burned, but the whites finally emerged victorious. If the Confederation had been continued and strengthened, it almost certainly would have spared the colonials much grief in their subsequent conflicts with the French and Indians.

Back home in England, the King paid little attention to the American colonies during the early years of their planting. They were allowed, in effect, to become semi-independent republics. This era of "salutary neglect" was further prolonged when the Crown, struggling to retain its power, became involved during the 1640s in civil wars with the Parliamentarians. A climax came in 1649 when Charles I was beheaded. Meanwhile the American colonists, like children neglected by their parents, became increasingly impatient of overseas restraints.

Following the restoration of the English Crown in 1660, the royalists (including the Church of England element) were once more firmly in the saddle. Hopes of purifying the established faith fled. A renewed stream of embittered Puritans departed for America, where they added to the festering groups of malcontents already there and to the future sources of friction with the King.

The Stuart Dynasty in England
(SEE P. 10 FOR PREDECESSORS; P. 46 FOR SUCCESSORS.)

Name, Reign	*Relation to America*
James I, 1603–1625	Va., Plymouth founded; Separatists persecuted
Charles I, 1625–1649	Civil Wars, 1642–1649; Cavalier tradition; Mass., Md. founded
(Interregnum, 1649–1660)	Commonwealth; Protectorate (the Cromwells)
Charles II, 1660–1685	The Restoration; Carolinas, Penna., N.Y. founded; Conn. chartered
James II, 1685–1688	Catholic trend; Glorious Revolution, 1688
William & Mary, 1689–1702 (Mary died 1694)	King William's War, 1689–1697

Deepening colonial defiance was nowhere more glaringly revealed than in Massachusetts. One of the King's agents in Boston was mortified to find that royal orders had no more effect than old issues of the London *Gazette*. Punishment was soon forthcoming. As a slap at Massachusetts, Charles II granted to rival Connecticut in 1662 a sea-to-sea charter grant, which legalized the squatter settlements. The very next year the outcasts in Rhode Island received a new charter, which gave kingly sanction to the most democratic government yet devised in America. A final and crushing blow fell on the stiff-necked Bay Colony in 1684, when her precious charter was revoked by the London authorities.

Sir Edmund Andros (1637–1714). An able but iron-fisted administrator, Andros was three times recalled from North American colonial posts because of local resentment at his rule. He ended his career as governor of the tiny island of Guernsey, in the English Channel.

Andros Promotes the First American Revolution

Massachusetts suffered further humiliation in 1686, when the Dominion of New England was created by royal authority. Unlike the homegrown New England Confederation, it was imposed from London. Embracing at first all New England, it was expanded two years later to include New York and East and West Jersey. The Dominion also aimed at bolstering colonial defense in the event of war with the Indians, and hence from the imperial viewpoint of London was a statesmanlike move.

More importantly, the Dominion of New England was designed to promote urgently needed efficiency in the administration of the English Navigation Laws. Those laws, reflecting the intensifying colonial rivalries of the 17th Century, sought to stitch England's overseas possessions more tightly to the Motherland. Like colonial peoples everywhere, the Americans chafed at such confinements, and smuggling became an increasingly common and honorable occupation.

At the head of the new Dominion stood autocratic Sir Edmund Andros, an able English military man, conscientious but tactless. Establishing headquarters in Puritanical Boston, he generated much hostility by his open affiliation with the despised Church of England. The colonials were also outraged by his noisy and Sabbath-profaning soldiers, who were accused of teaching the people "to drink, blaspheme, curse, and damn."

Andros was prompt to use the mailed fist. He ruthlessly curbed the cherished town meetings, and laid heavy restrictions on the courts, the press, and the schools. Dispensing with the popular assemblies, he taxed the people without the consent of their duly elected representatives. He also strove to enforce the unpopular Navigation Laws and suppress smuggling. Liberty-loving colonials, accustomed to unusual privileges during long decades of neglect, were goaded to the verge of revolt.

The people of Old England, likewise resisting oppression, stole a march on the people of New England. In 1688–1689 they engineered the memorable Glorious (or Bloodless) Revolution. Dethroning the despotic and unpopular Catholic James II, they enthroned the Protestant rulers of the Netherlands, the Dutch-born William III and his English wife, Mary, daughter of James II.

When the news of the Glorious Revolution reached America, the ramshackle Dominion of New England collapsed like a house of cards. A Boston mob, catching the fever, rose against the existing regime. Sir Edmund Andros attempted to flee in woman's clothing, but was betrayed by

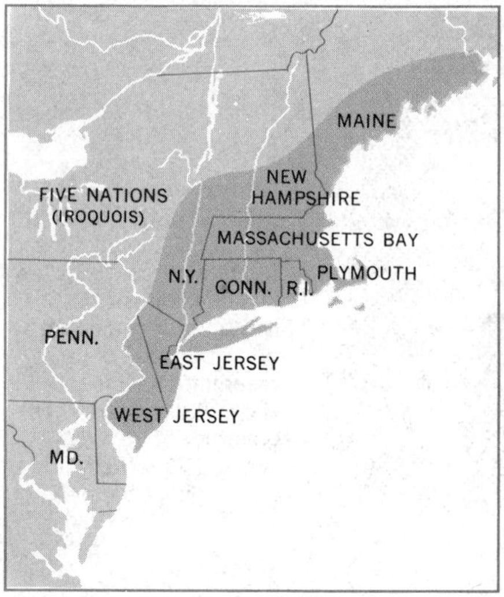

ANDROS'S DOMINION OF NEW ENGLAND

boots protruding beneath his dress. He was then shipped off to England.

Massachusetts, though rid of the despotic Andros, did not gain as much from the upheaval as she had hoped. In 1691 she was arbitrarily made a royal colony, with a new charter and a new royal governor. The permanent loss of the ancient charter was a staggering blow to the proud Puritans, who never fully recovered. Worst of all, the privilege of voting, once a monopoly of church members, was now to be enjoyed by all qualified male property holders.

England's Glorious Revolution had a far-flung impact, for unrest erupted from New England to the Carolinas. The upheaval resulted in a permanent abandonment of many of the objectionable features of the Andros system, as well as a temporary breakdown of the new imperial policy of enforcing the Navigation Laws.

Molding the New England Conscience

Oddly enough, the story of early New England was largely written by rocks. The heavily glaciated soil was strewn with countless stones, many of which were forced to the surface after the winter freeze. In a sense the Puritan fathers did not possess the soil; it possessed them by reshaping their character. Scratching a living from the protesting earth was an early American success story. Back-bending toil put a premium on industry and penny-pinching frugality, as in Scotland. Traditionally sharp Yankee traders, some of them palming off wooden nutmegs, made their mark. Connecticut in time came to be called good-humoredly "the Nutmeg State." Cynics exaggerated when they said that the three stages of progress in New England were "to get on, to get honor, to get honest."

The grudging land also left colonial New England less ethnically mixed than its southern neighbors. European immigrants were not attracted in great numbers to a site where the soil was so stony—and the religion so sulfurous.

Climate likewise molded character. New England summers were often uncomfortably hot, and the winters were cruelly cold. This combination of soil, climate, and Calvinism made for energy, purposefulness, sternness, stubbornness, self-reliance, and resourcefulness.

> New England says, "Make do, or go without,"
> So they make do.*

Connecticut, not surprisingly, was known as "the Land of Steady Habits." Yet there were a great many Puritans—legend to the contrary—who enjoyed simple pleasures: they ate plentifully, drank heartily, sang songs occasionally, and made love discreetly.

Yet life was serious business, and hell-fire was real—a hell where sinners shriveled and shrieked for divine mercy. An immensely popular poem in New England, selling one copy for every twenty persons, was clergyman Michael Wigglesworth's "Day of Doom" (1662). Especially horrifying were his descriptions of the fate of the damned:

> They cry, they roar for anguish sore,
> and gnaw their tongues for horrour.
> But get away without delay,
> Christ pitties not your cry:
> Depart to Hell, there may you yell,
> and roar Eternally.

---

*Bianca Bradbury, "Rule of Thumb."

Religious tolerance was generally slow to appear. The Puritan oligarchy tried to prod sinful people into saintliness by the famous "blue laws." These regulations, among other restraints, required rigid observance of the Sabbath and the repression of certain harmless human instincts. All other colonies passed similar laws, but those of New England were the most severe. In New Haven, for example, a young unmarried couple was fined twenty shillings for the crime of kissing, and in later years Connecticut came to be dubbed "the Blue Law State."

New England's tense and repressive atmosphere ultimately found a frightening outlet. In Salem, Massachusetts, a hysterical witchcraft delusion brought about the legal lynching in 1692 of twenty persons, nineteen of whom were hanged and one of whom was pressed to death. Two dogs were also hanged. Larger-scale witchcraft persecutions were common in Europe, and several outbreaks had already flared forth in the colonies. But the reign of horror in Salem reached an all-time peak in American experience, and seriously weakened the prestige of the Puritan clergy, some of whom had supported it.

On the positive side, the Puritan stress on unity of purpose also stimulated the growth of self-government. Democracy in Congregational Church government led logically to democracy in political government. The town meeting, in which the freemen met together and each man voted, exhibited democracy in its purest form. It was, observed Thomas Jefferson, "the best school of political liberty the world ever saw."

Witches Hanged in England as in America.

The Sacred Cod. As displayed in the Boston State House. (George M. Cushing.)

Righteous Puritans also prided themselves on being God's chosen people. They long boasted that Boston was "the Hub of the Universe"—at least spiritually. A famous jingle of later days ran:

> I come from the city of Boston,
> The home of the bean and the cod,
> Where the Cabots speak only to Lowells,
> And the Lowells speak only to God.

New England's impact on the rest of the nation has been incalculable. Countless tens of thousands of New Englanders, ousted by their sterile soil, were destined to pull up stakes and re-create New England towns all the way to Oregon and Hawaii. A people courageous, conscientious, and willing to sacrifice for their beliefs, they made the idealism represented by Plymouth Rock a national symbol. As flinty as their stones, as stiff as their cuffs and collars, they cross-fertilized innumerable other communities with their ideals and democratic practices. The New England conscience added something indispensable to the fiber and backbone of the American people.

The soil and climate of New England encouraged a diversified agriculture and industry. Staple products like tobacco did not flourish, as in the South. Black slavery, although tried, could not exist profitably on small farms, especially where the surest crop was stones. No broad, fertile hinterland, comparable to that of the South, beckoned men inland. The mountains ran fairly close to the shore, and the rivers were generally short and rapid.

Repelled by the rocks, the hardy New Englanders turned instinctively to their fine natural harbors. Hacking timber from their dense forests, they became proficient in shipbuilding and commerce. They were also ceaselessly active in exploiting the inexhaustible and self-perpetuating codfish lode off the coast of Newfoundland—the fishy "gold mines of New England," which have yielded more wealth than all the treasure chests of the Aztecs. During colonial days the wayfarer seldom got far from the sound of the ax and hammer, or the swift rush of the ship down the ways to the sea, or the smell of rotting fish. As a reminder of the importance of fishing, a handsome replica of the "sacred cod" is proudly displayed to this day in the Massachusetts State House in Boston.

Puritan Textbooks. A page from the *New England Primer;* and the hornbook for children, so called because the printing was protected by transparent horn.

The New England Way of Life

Sturdy New Englanders evolved a compact social structure, the basis of which was small farms and villages. This development was but natural in a people who were partially anchored by geography and hemmed in by Indians, Frenchmen, and Dutchmen. Calvinism, combined with a closely knit community life, likewise made for unity of purpose, and also for nosiness regarding the affairs of one's neighbors. It was no accident that the later crusade for abolishing black slavery—with Massachusetts agitators in the forefront—sprang in some degree from the New England conscience, with its Puritanical and Calvinistic coloration.

In the Chesapeake region the expansion of settlement was somewhat random and was usually undertaken by lone-wolf planters on their own initiative, but New England society grew in a more orderly fashion. New towns were legally chartered by the colonial authorities, and the distribution of land was entrusted to the steady hands of sober-minded town fathers. Towns of more than fifty families were required to provide elementary education, and as early as 1636 the Massachusetts Puritans established Harvard College, today the oldest corporation in America, to train local boys for the ministry.

Yet worries plagued the God-fearing pioneers of these tidy settlements. The pressure of population was gradually dispersing the Puritans onto outlying farms, away from the control of church and neighbors. The passage of time was depleting the first generation's religious zeal. About the middle of the 17th Century a new form of sermon began to be popular in Puritan pulpits—the "jeremiad." Taking their cue from the doom-saying Old Testament prophet Jeremiah, sober preachers scolded parishioners for their waning piety. Especially alarming was the apparent decline in "conversions"—testimonials by individuals that they had received God's grace and therefore deserved to be admitted to the church as members of the "elect." Troubled ministers in 1662 announced a new formula for church membership, the "Half-Way Covenant." It offered partial membership rights to persons not yet "converted."

The "Half-Way Covenant" dramatized the difficulty of maintaining at fever pitch the religious fervor of the founding generation. Jeremiads continued to thunder from the pulpits, but as time went on the doors of the Puritan churches swung fully open to all comers, whether converted or not. This widening of church membership gradually erased the distinction between the "elect" and other members of society, and it tended to water down the burning theology of the earliest days.

Old Netherlanders at New Netherland

Late in the 16th Century, the oppressed people of the Netherlands unfurled the standard of rebellion against Catholic Spain. After bloody and protracted fighting, they finally succeeded, with the aid of Protestant England, in winning their independence.

The 17th Century—the era of Rembrandt and other famous artists—was a golden age in Dutch history. This vigorous little lowland nation finally emerged as a major commercial and naval power, and then ungratefully challenged the supremacy of her former benefactor, England. Three great Anglo-Dutch naval wars were fought in the 17th Century, with as many as a hundred ships on each side. The sturdy Dutchmen dealt blows about as heavy as they received.

Holland also became a leading colonial power, with by far her greatest activity in the East Indies. There she maintained an enormous and profitable empire for over three hundred years. The Dutch East India Company was virtually a state within a state, and at one time supported an army of 10,000 men and a fleet of 190 ships, forty of them men-of-war.

Seeking greater riches, this enterprising company employed an English explorer, Henry Hudson. Disregarding orders to sail northeast, he ventured into Delaware Bay and New York Bay in 1609 and then ascended the Hudson River, hoping that at last he had chanced upon the coveted shortcut through the continent. But, as the event proved, he merely filed a Dutch claim to a magnificently wooded and watered area.

Henry Hudson (?–1611). An English explorer of little known antecedents, he made two famous voyages. The first, for the Dutch East India Company, resulted in the discovery of the Hudson River in 1609; the second, for some English merchants, in the discovery of Canada's Hudson Bay in 1610. His crew, suffering from extreme cold and other hardships, finally mutinied and set him adrift to die with his small son and seven others.

Much less powerful than the mighty Dutch East India Company was the Dutch West India Company, which maintained profitable enterprises in the Caribbean. At times it was less interested in trading than in raiding, and at one fell swoop in 1628 captured a fleet of Spanish treasure ships laden with loot worth $15 million. The company also established outposts in Africa and a flourishing sugar industry in Brazil, which for several decades was its principal center of activity in the New World.

New Netherland, in the beautiful Hudson River area, was planted in 1623–1624 on a permanent basis. Established by the Dutch West India Company for its quick-profit fur trade, it was never more than a secondary interest of the founders. The company's most brilliant stroke was to buy Manhattan Island from the Indians (who did not actually "own" it) for trinkets worth about $24—22,000 acres of what is now perhaps the most valuable real estate in the world for one-tenth of a cent an acre.

New Amsterdam—later New York City—was a company town. It was run by and for the Dutch company, in the interests of the stockholders. The investors had no enthusiasm for religious toleration, free speech, or democratic practices; and the governors appointed by the company as directors-general were usually harsh and despotic. In response to repeated protests by the colonists, a semi-representative body was at length reluctantly granted. Religious dissenters who opposed the official Dutch Reformed Church were looked upon with suspicion, and for a while Quakers were savagely abused.

This picturesque Dutch colony took on a strongly aristocratic tinge, and retained it for generations. Vast feudal estates fronting the Hudson

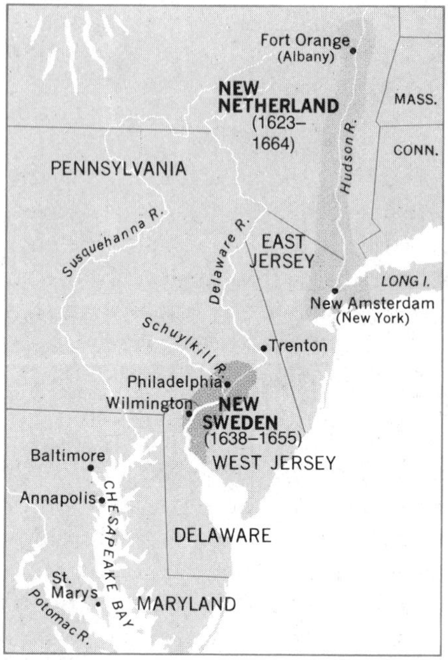

EARLY SETTLEMENTS IN THE MIDDLE COLONIES

River, known as patroonships, were granted to promoters who would settle fifty persons on them. One of the largest in the Albany area was slightly larger than the later state of Rhode Island.

Colorful little New Amsterdam attracted a cosmopolitan population, as is common in seaport towns. A French Jesuit missionary, visiting in the 1640s, noted that eighteen different languages were being spoken in the streets. The later babel of immigrant tongues was thus foreshadowed.

Friction with English and Swedish Neighbors

Vexations of various sorts beset the Dutch company-colony from the beginning. The directors-general were generally incompetent, though Washington Irving's later characterization of one of them as "a beer barrel on skids" is unfair. Company shareholders demanded their dividends, even at the expense of the colony's welfare. The Indians, infuriated by Dutch cruelties, retaliated with horrible massacres. As a defense measure, the hard-pressed settlers on Manhattan Island erected a stout wall, from which Wall Street derived its name.

New England was hostile to the growth of its Dutch neighbor, and the people of Connecticut finally ejected intruding Hollanders from their verdant valley. Three of the four member colonies of the New England Confederation were eager to wipe out New Netherland with military force. But Massachusetts, which would have had to provide most of the troops, vetoed the proposed foray.

The Swedes in turn trespassed on Dutch preserves, from 1638 to 1655, by planting the anemic colony of New Sweden on the Delaware River.

Peter Stuyvesant (1602–1682). Despotic in government and intolerant in religion, he lived in a constant state of friction with the prominent men of New Netherland. When protests arose, he replied that he derived his power from God and the Company, not the people. He opposed popular suffrage on the grounds that "the thief" would vote "for the thief" and "the rogue for the rogue."

This was the golden age of Sweden, during and following the Thirty Years' War of 1618–1648, in which her brilliant King Gustavus Adolphus had carried the torch for Protestantism. This outburst of energy in Sweden caused her to enter the costly colonial game in America, albeit on something of a shoestring.

Resenting the Swedish intrusion on the Delaware, the Dutch dispatched a small military expedition in 1655. It was led by the ablest of the directors-general, the energetic and hotheaded Peter Stuyvesant, who was dubbed "Father Wooden Leg" by the Indians. The main fort fell after a bloodless siege, whereupon Swedish rule came to an abrupt end. The colonists were absorbed by New Netherland.

New Sweden was never important. It faded away, leaving behind in later Delaware a sprinkling of Swedish place names and Swedish log cabins (the first in America), as well as an admixture of Swedish blood.

Dutch Residues in New York

The days of the Dutch on the Hudson were numbered, for the English regarded them as intruders. In 1664, after Charles II had granted the area to his brother, the Duke of York, a strong English squadron appeared off the decrepit defenses of New Amsterdam. A fuming Peter Stuyvesant, short of all munitions except courage, was forced to surrender without firing a shot. New Amsterdam was thereupon renamed New York, in honor of the Duke of York. England won a splendid harbor, strategically located in the middle of the mainland colonies, and a stately Hudson River penetrating the interior. The English banner now waved triumphantly, with the removal of this foreign wedge, over a solid stretch of territory from Maine to the Carolinas.

As the neglected stepchild of a trading company, New Netherland was destined from the beginning to be English. Lacking vitality, and representing only a secondary commercial interest of the Dutch, it lay under the shadow of the vigorous English colonies to the north. In addition, it was honeycombed with New England immigrants. Numbering about one-half of New Netherland's 10,000 souls in 1664, they might in time have seized control from within.

The conquered Dutch province tenaciously retained many of the illiberal features of earlier days. An autocratic spirit survived, and the aristocratic element gained strength when certain corrupt English governors granted immense acreage to their favorites. Influential landowning families —such as the Livingstons and the De Lanceys— wielded disproportionate power in the affairs of colonial New York. These monopolistic land policies, combined with the lordly atmosphere, discouraged many European immigrants from coming. The physical growth of New York was correspondingly retarded.

The short-lived Dutch colony contributed little of major significance, whether to democracy, government, education, toleration, or literature.

New Amsterdam (New York) in 1673. (The J. Clarence Davies Collection, Museum of the City of New York.)

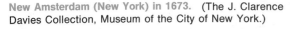

A possible exception would be the Knickerbocker themes that Washington Irving developed in the 19th Century with such charm. The Dutchmen peppered place names over the land, including Harlem (Haarlem), Brooklyn (Breuckelen), and Hell Gate (Hellegat). They likewise left their imprint on the gambrel-roofed architecture. As for social customs and folkways, no other foreign group of comparable size has made so colorful a contribution. Noteworthy were Easter eggs, Santa Claus, waffles, sauerkraut, bowling, sleighing, skating, and kolf (golf)—a dangerous game played with heavy clubs and forbidden in settled areas.

Diluted Dutch blood from New Netherland runs through the veins of many of America's "best families," including a host of "vans" and "velts." Three Presidents of the United States traced their ancestry back to the precarious colony: Martin Van Buren, Theodore Roosevelt, and Franklin D. Roosevelt. The last of the trio, when inclined to be stubborn, would speak of getting his "Dutch" up.

Penn's Holy Experiment in Pennsylvania

A remarkable group of dissenters, commonly known as Quakers, arose in England during the mid-1600s. Their name derived from the report that they "quaked" when under deep religious emotion. Officially they were known as the Religious Society of Friends.

Quakers were especially offensive to the authorities, both religious and civil. They refused to support the established Church of England with taxes. They built simple meetinghouses, without a paid clergy, and "spoke up" in meeting themselves when moved. Believing that they were all children in the sight of God, they kept their broad-brimmed hats on in the presence of their "betters," and addressed others with simple "thees" and "thous," rather than with conventional titles. They would take no oaths, because Jesus had said, "Swear not at all." This peculiarity often embroiled them with government officials, for "test oaths" were

Quakers Abused in England. New England persecutions were similarly harsh.

still required to establish the fact that a person was not a Roman Catholic.

The Quakers, beyond a doubt, were a people of deep conviction. They abhorred strife and warfare, and refused military service. As advocates of passive resistance, they would turn the other cheek and rebuild their meetinghouse on the site where their enemies had torn it down. Their courage and devotion to principle finally triumphed. Though at times they seemed stubborn and unreasonable, they were a simple, devoted, democratic people, contending in their own odd way for religious and civic freedom.

William Penn, a well-born and athletic young Englishman, was attracted to the Quaker faith in 1660, when only sixteen years old. His father, disapproving, administered a sound flogging. After various adventures in the army (the best portrait of the peaceful Quaker has him in armor), the youth firmly embraced the despised faith and suffered much persecution. The courts branded him a "saucy" and "impertinent" fellow. Several hundred of his less fortunate co-religionists died of cruel treatment, and thousands more were fined, flogged, or cast into "nasty stinking prisons."

Penn's thoughts naturally turned to the New World, where a sprinkling of Quakers had already fled, notably to Rhode Island, North Carolina, and New Jersey. Eager to establish an asylum for his people, he also hoped to experiment with liberal ideas in government, and at the same time make a profit. Finally, in 1681, he managed to secure from the King an immense grant of fertile land, in consideration of a monetary debt owed to his deceased father by the Crown. The King called the area Pennsylvania ("Penn's Woodland") in honor of the sire. But the modest son, fearing that critics would accuse him of naming it after himself, sought unsuccessfully to change the name.

Pennsylvania was by far the best advertised of all the colonies. Its founder—the "first American advertising man"—sent out paid agents and distributed countless pamphlets printed in English, Dutch, French, and German. Unlike the lures of many another American real estate promoter, then and later, Penn's inducements were generally truthful. He especially welcomed forward-looking spirits and substantial citizens, including industrious carpenters, masons, shoemakers, and other manual workers. His liberal land policy, which encouraged substantial holdings of land, was instrumental in attracting a heavy inflow of immigrants.

William Penn (1644–1718). He wrote in 1682, "Any government is free to the people under it where the laws rule and the people are a party to the laws." Penn was among the few English colonizers who learned to speak an Indian tongue.

Quaker Pennsylvania and Her Neighbors

Penn formally launched his colony in 1681. His task was simplified by the presence of several thousand "squatters"—Dutch, Swedes, English, Welsh—who were already scattered along the banks of the Delaware River. Philadelphia, meaning "brotherly love" in Greek, was more carefully planned than most colonial cities, and consequently enjoyed wide and attractive streets. Penn farsightedly bought land from the Indians, including Chief Tammany, later patron saint of New York's political Tammany Hall. His treatment of the red men was so fair that the Quaker "Broad Brims" went among them unarmed, and even employed them as baby tenders.

Penn's new proprietary regime was unusually liberal, and included a representative assembly elected by the landowners. There was no tax-supported state church. Freedom of worship was guaranteed to all residents, although Penn, under pressure from London, was forced to deny Catholics and Jews the privilege of voting or holding office. The death penalty was imposed only for treason and murder, as compared with some two hundred capital crimes in England.

Among other noteworthy features, no provision was made by the peace-loving Quakers of Pennsylvania for a military defense. No restrictions were placed on immigration, and naturalization was made easy. The humane Quakers early developed a strong dislike of black slavery, and in the genial glow of Pennsylvania some progress was made toward social reform.

With its many liberal attractions, Pennsylvania attracted a richly mixed racial group. The lot included numerous religious misfits who were repelled by the harsh practices of neighboring colonies. This Quaker haven boasted a surprisingly modern atmosphere in an unmodern age, and to an unusual degree afforded economic opportunity, civil liberty, and religious freedom. Even so, there were some "blue laws" aimed at "ungodly revelers," stage plays, playing cards, dice, May games, and excessive hilarity.

Under such generally happy auspices, Penn's brainchild grew lustily. The Quakers were shrewd businessmen, and in a short time the settlers were exporting grain and other foodstuffs. Within two years Philadelphia claimed 300 houses and 2,500 people. Within nineteen years—by 1700—the colony was surpassed in population and wealth only by long-established Virginia and Massachusetts.

William Penn, who altogether spent about four years in Pennsylvania, was never fully appreciated by his colonists. His governors, some of them incompetent and tactless, quarreled bitterly with the people, who were constantly demanding greater political control. Penn himself became too friendly with James II, the deposed Catholic King. Thrice arrested for treason, thrust for a time into a debtors' prison, and racked by apoplectic fits, he died full of sorrows. His enduring monument was not only a noble experiment in government but also a new commonwealth. Based on civil and religious liberty, and dedicated to freedom of conscience and worship, it held aloft a hopeful torch in a world of semi-darkness.

Smaller Quaker settlements flourished next door to Pennsylvania. New Jersey was started in 1664, when two noble proprietors received the area from the Duke of York. A substantial number of New Englanders, including many whose weary soil had petered out, flocked to the new colony. One of the proprietors sold West New Jersey in 1674 to a group of Quakers, who here set up a sanctuary even before Pennsylvania was launched. East New Jersey was also acquired in later years by the Quakers, whose wings were clipped in 1702 when the Crown combined the two Jerseys in a royal colony.

Swedish-tinged Delaware consisted of only three counties—two at high tide, the witticism goes—and was named after Lord de la Warr. Harboring some Quakers, and closely associated with Penn's flourishing colony, Delaware was granted its own assembly in 1703. But until the American Revolution it remained under the governor of Pennsylvania.

> In a Boston lecture (1869), Ralph Waldo Emerson declared, "The sect of the Quakers in their best representatives appear to me to have come nearer to the sublime history and genius of Christ than any other of the sects."

The Middle Way in the Middle Colonies

The Middle Colonies—New York, New Jersey, Delaware, and Pennsylvania—enjoyed certain features in common.

In general, the soil was fertile and the expanse of land was broad, unlike rock-bestrewn New England. Pennsylvania, New York, and New Jersey came to be known as the "Bread Colonies," by virtue of their heavy exports of grain.

Rivers also played a vital role. Broad, languid streams—notably the Susquehanna, the Delaware, and the Hudson—tapped the fur trade of the interior and beckoned adventuresome spirits into the back country. The rivers had few cascading waterfalls, unlike New England's, and hence presented little inducement to manufacturing with water-wheel power.

A surprising amount of industry, nonetheless, flourished in the Middle Colonies. Virginal forests abounded for lumbering and shipbuilding. The presence of deep river estuaries and landlocked harbors stimulated commerce and the growth of seaports, such as New York and Philadelphia. Even Albany, more than a hundred miles up the Hudson, was a port of some consequence in colonial days.

The Middle Colonies were in many respects midway between New England and the Southern plantation group. Except in aristocratic New York, the land holdings were generally intermediate in size—smaller than in the big-acreage South but larger than in small-farm New England. Local government lay somewhere between the personalized town meeting of New England and the diffused county government of the South. There were fewer industries in the Middle Colonies than in New England, more than in the South.

Yet the Middle Colonies, which in some ways were the most American part of America, could claim certain distinctions in their own right. Generally speaking, the population was more racially mixed than that of other settlements. The people were blessed with an unusual degree of religious toleration and democratic control. Earnest and devout Quakers, in particular, made a contribution to human freedom out of all proportion to their numbers. Desirable land was more easily acquired in the Middle Colonies than in New England or in the tidewater South. One result was that a considerable amount of economic and social democracy prevailed, though less so in aristocratic New York.

Modern-minded Benjamin Franklin, entering Philadelphia as a seventeen-year-old youth with a roll of bread under each arm, found a congenial home in the urbane atmosphere of the city. It is true that he was born a Yankee in Puritanical Boston, but, as one Pennsylvanian later boasted, "He came to life at seventeen, in Philadelphia."

First Church in Philadelphia

Long before 1760 the thirteen colonies as a group revealed striking similarities, even though they had developed wide differences. They were all basically English. They all exercised certain priceless Anglo-Saxon freedoms. They all possessed some measure of self-government, though by no means complete democracy. They all enjoyed some degree of religious toleration and educational opportunity. They all afforded unusual advantages for economic and social self-development. Finally—and perhaps most significantly—they were all separated from home authority by a billowing ocean moat 3,000 miles wide.

VARYING VIEWPOINTS

Not only New England, but New Englanders—from William Bradford in the 17th Century to Samuel Eliot Morison in the 20th Century—have dominated our understanding of the colonial era. Their traditional histories stressed the religious character of the "Puritan experiment," and usually emphasized the slow secularization of colonial life. More recent scholars have begun to move away from this exclusive focus on intellectual history. They have suggested that the decline in piety that so worried the Puritans and so preoccupied their patriotic chroniclers was but one aspect of a general disintegration of traditional social forms. Local histories, using sophisticated quantitative techniques and relying on modern demographic theories, illustrate the innumerable stresses that a rough wilderness existence put upon transplanted Europeans. These stresses strained religious faiths, family life, economic organization, and landholding patterns.

SELECT READINGS

New England has received more scholarly attention than any other colonial region. A rich contemporary account is William Bradford, *Of Plymouth Plantation,* available in an edition edited by S. E. Morison in 1952. See also Morison's sweeping survey, *Builders of the Bay Colony* (1930), and J. E. Pomfret, *Founding the American Colonies, 1583–1660* (1970). An incisive short account is Edmund S. Morgan, *The Puritan Dilemma: The Story of John Winthrop* (1958). A brilliant and complex intellectual history is Perry Miller, *The New England Mind* (2 vols., 1939, 1953), a work that has long been a landmark for other scholars. Robert Middlekauff focuses on *The Mathers: Three Generations of Puritan Intellectuals, 1596–1728* (1971), and Larzer Ziff, on *The Career of John Cotton* (1962). David Levin deals with his subject's youthful years in *Cotton Mather* (1978). See also Ziff's *Puritanism in America* (1973). Sacvan Bercovitch traces the heritage of the New England temperament in *The Puritan Origins of the American Self* (1975). Edmund S. Morgan describes the crisis that beset the original Puritans when their children displayed a lesser degree of religiosity in *Visible Saints* (1963). Social structure and politics are analyzed in R. E. Brown, *Middle-Class Democracy and the Revolution in Massachusetts, 1691–1780* (1955). Economic questions receive critical attention from Bernard Bailyn in *The New England Merchants in the Seventeenth Century* (1955). Some less attractive features of the New England experience are treated in Chadwick Hansen, *Witchcraft at Salem* (1969), and Paul Boyer and Stephen Nissenbaum, *Salem Possessed: The Social Origin of Witchcraft* (1974). Family life and local history are imaginatively scrutinized in Edmund S. Morgan, *Puritan Family* (1944), B. Bailyn, *Education in the Forming of American Society* (1960), S. C. Powell, *Puritan Village* (1963), D. Rutman, *Winthrop's Boston* (1965), J. Demos, *A Little Commonwealth: Family Life in Plymouth Colony* (1970), P. Greven, *Four Generations: Population, Land, and Family in Colonial Andover, Massachusetts* (1970), K. Lockridge, *New England Town: Dedham* (1970), Roger Thompson, *Women in Stuart England and America* (1974), Lyle Koehler, *A Search for Power: The "Weaker Sex" in Seventeenth-Century New England* (1980), and P. Greven, *The Protestant Temperament* (1977), which analyzes child-rearing practices. Religious issues are discussed in Sidney Mead, *The Lively Experiment* (1963), and in the early portions of Sidney Ahlstrom's monumental *Religious History of the American People* (1972). J. T. Ellis pays special attention to such issues in *Catholics in Colonial America* (1965), and O. E. Winslow, in *Master Roger Williams* (1957). Areas outside New England are dealt with in T. J. Wertenbaker, *The Founding of American Civilization: The Middle Colonies* (1938). Michael Kammen describes *Colonial New York* (1975). Pennsylvania is treated in E. B. Bronner, *William Penn's 'Holy Experiment'* (1962), Mary Maples Dunn, *William Penn: Politics and Conscience* (1967), and Gary Nash, *Quakers and Politics: Pennsylvania, 1681–1726* (1971). Comprehensive are David Grayson Allen, *In English Ways* (1981), a comparative study of England and Colonial America, and T. H. Breen, *Puritans and Adventurers* (1980), which discusses "localism" in both New England and Virginia.

3

The Duel for North America

A torch lighted in the forests of America set all Europe in conflagration.

François Voltaire, c. 1756

France Finds a Foothold in Canada

France was another latecomer in the scramble for New World real estate, like England and Holland, and for basically the same reasons. She was convulsed during the 1500s by foreign wars and domestic strife, including the frightful clashes between the Roman Catholics and the Protestant Huguenots. On St. Bartholomew's Day, 1572, over 10,000 Huguenots—men, women, and children—were butchered in cold blood.

A new era dawned in 1598 when the Edict of Nantes, issued by the Crown, granted limited toleration to the French Protestants. Religious wars ceased, and in the 1600s France blossomed into the mightiest and most-feared nation in Europe. Leadership of a high order was provided by a series of brilliant ministers, and by the vainglorious King Louis XIV. *Le Grand Monarque*

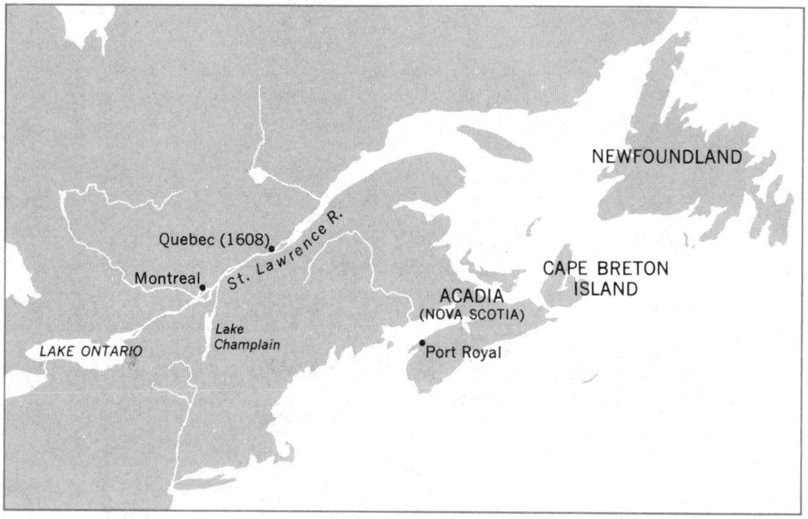

EARLY FRENCH SETTLEMENTS
By the 1980s French-speakers made up nearly 30 per cent of the total Canadian population of about 24 million, and a strong separatist movement had developed among them in Quebec—just one legacy of the Colonial-era duel for North America.

reigned majestically, beginning as a five-year-old boy, for an incredible seventy-two years (1643–1715). Though involved with a glittering court and numerous mistresses, he was deeply interested in overseas colonies, and bestirred himself to promote their welfare.

Even earlier, while the religious wars were still raging in the mid-1500s, the French had planted a few colonial seedlings. Noteworthy were the short-lived Catholic settlements on the St. Lawrence River, and the havens which the harassed Huguenots strove to create in Brazil, Florida, and South Carolina. But all these feeble experiments collapsed, either of their own weight or under the sword of Catholic enemies, whether Portuguese or Spaniards.

Success finally crowned the exertions of France in the New World. In 1608, the year after Jamestown, the permanent beginnings of a vast empire were established at Quebec, a rocky sentinel commanding the St. Lawrence River. The leading figure was Samuel de Champlain, an intrepid soldier

Champlain Fights the Iroquois, 1609. This illustration commemorates the battle on Lake Champlain. Champlain's explorations extended French claims as far inland as Wisconsin. He was fittingly buried in Quebec. (By permission of the Houghton Library, Harvard University.)

and explorer whose energy and leadership fairly earned for him the title "Father of New France."

Champlain entered into friendly relations—a fateful friendship—with the nearby Huron Indian tribes. Yielding to their entreaties, he joined them in battle against their feathered foes, the federated Iroquois tribes of the upper New York area. Two shots from the "lightning sticks" of the whites routed the terrified Indians, who left behind three dead and one wounded. France, to her sorrow, thus earned the lasting enmity of the Iroquois tribes. These painted warriors hampered French penetration of the Ohio Valley, ravaged French settlements, and served as allies of the British in the prolonged struggle for supremacy on the continent.

Old Feudalism in New France

The government of New France (Canada) finally fell under the direct control of the King, after various commercial companies had faltered or failed. This royal regime was almost completely autocratic. There were no popularly elected assemblies, as in the English colonies; there was no trial by jury—merely the decision of the magistrate.

Feudalism was dying out in Europe, but some of its most picturesque trappings were transplanted to New France. Noteworthy were the huge feudal estates, fronting the river highways, and the medieval customs, including the annual dues to the lord in chickens and other produce. The peasants (*habitants*) were little more than serfs. The autocracy thus established in the wilderness, unlike the regime in the English colonies, was ideal for military defense. It insured unity of purpose, speed of action, precision of movement, and a maximum concentration of meager resources.

Population in Catholic New France grew with painful slowness: as late as 1750 there were only 60,000 or so whites. Wintry blasts did not appeal to the peasants of sunny France, and the stubborn soil was uninviting. Protestant Huguenots were not allowed refuge in the raw colony, although some 400,000 were driven from their homeland by the termination of the Edict of Nantes in 1685. They would have added a thrifty and industrious element, but they no doubt would have caused internal friction.

Officials in New France, unable to recruit more than a dribble of immigrants, tried with some success to stimulate the birthrate. Bachelors were subjected to heavy restrictions. Fathers of unmarried daughters of sixteen were fined, and a small number of well-chaperoned "King's girls" were imported and married, following whirlwind courtships on the docks.

All things considered, the importance of New France was secondary to Old France. In the 1600s and 1700s the scattered French islands in the Caribbean, rich in sugar and rum, comprised a much more profitable enterprise than the snow-cloaked wilderness of the northern colony.

Red Men and Black Robes in Canada

Fur was the big "money crop" of New France. Lush pelts, especially beaver, were popular in Europe for their warmth, adornment, and proof of social position. More than 100,000 beaver skins were trapped in the best years, and the Indian fur flotilla which reached Montreal in 1693 numbered four hundred canoes.

But the fur-trapping business had fatal drawbacks. It was cannibalistic, for it ate up its own capital. Retreating animals had to be followed into the interior, and the lure of the sharp-toothed beaver dangerously diluted the already scanty vanguard of French inhabitants. English settlers, on the other hand, were dammed up east of the Allegheny barrier, and did not finally flow over the mountains in numbers until they had first been pressed together into a compact social structure.

Indians who trapped the furs were jerked from the stone age to the iron age almost overnight. Bows and arrows gave way to firearms. Red men became different creatures as they were debauched by the white man's diseases and alcohol—"bottled suicide"—sometimes adulterated with pepper. French Catholic missionaries tried desperately

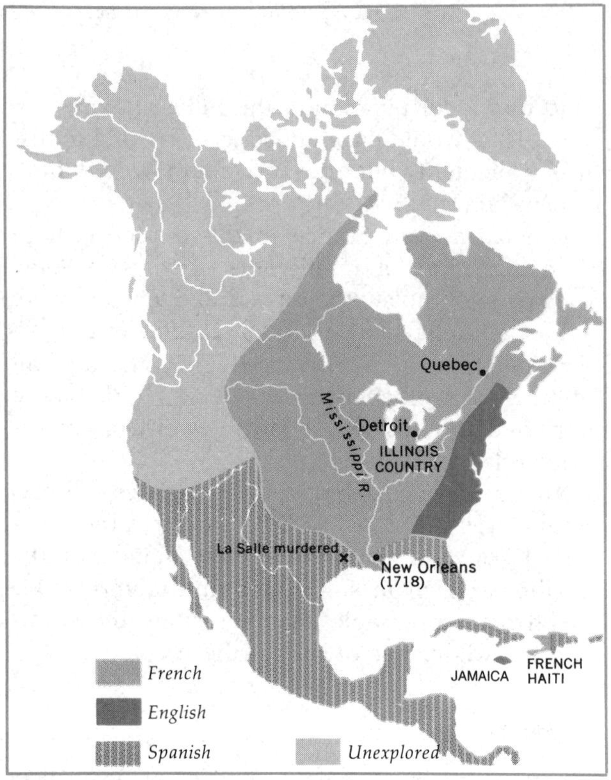

FRANCE'S AMERICAN EMPIRE AT GREATEST EXTENT, 1700

Father Jogues (1607–1646). With a hand mutilated by the Mohawks, he escaped and was granted special dispensation by the Pope to celebrate mass. He returned to the Mohawks, who tortured and then killed him. The Pope canonized him in 1930.

to block the sale of "firewater." But they were met with the crushing rebuttal that a denial of French brandy would force the Indian to exchange his furs for the rum of the English and Dutch traders, who were Protestant heretics.

French Catholic missionaries, notably the Jesuits, labored zealously to save both the bodies and souls of the heathen Indians. The Black Robes were at odds with the fur traders, whose chief purpose was to get the red man drunk and rob him of his peltries for a few strings of beads. Some of the Jesuit missionaries, their efforts unappreciated, suffered unspeakable tortures at the hands of the Indians. Conspicuous among the martyrs were Father Isaac Jogues and the giant Jean de Brébeuf, who is said to have kissed the stake at which he was burned, and whose skull is still preserved as a relic in Quebec.

The role of the Jesuits was vital to New France. It is true that they made few permanent converts, despite their heroic sacrifices in establishing missions. But in the capacity of explorers, geographers, and teachers they did much to publicize New France in Old France, and thus helped to save the colony.

New France Fans Out

Daring French explorers and traders were inevitably drawn deeper and deeper into the heart of the continent. They walked, rode, snowshoed, sailed, or paddled amazing distances. They were eager to find a shorter waterway to the Indies; to discover fabulous mines like those uncovered by the Spaniards in Mexico; to check Spanish penetration into the region of the Gulf of Mexico; and to thwart English traders pushing into the Ohio Valley. Partly for this last purpose Antoine Cadillac founded Detroit, "The City of Straits," in 1701.

Most famous of all the French explorers was the haughty but far-visioned La Salle. In 1682 he floated down the mighty Mississippi to the point where it mingles with the Gulf, and named the interior basin "Louisiana," in honor of his sovereign, Louis XIV. Dreaming of empire, La Salle proceeded to fit out a colonizing expedition of four ships in France. But he landed in Spanish Texas, after missing the delta of the Mississippi, and in 1687 was murdered by his own men.

Undismayed, French officials persisted in their efforts to forestall Spain on the Gulf of Mexico. They planted several fortified posts in present-day Mississippi and Louisiana, the most important of which was New Orleans (1718). Commanding the outlet of the Mississippi River, this strategic outpost also tapped the fur trade of the great interior basin. The fertile Illinois country, where missions and trading-post forts were firmly established, became the garden of France's North American empire. Surprising amounts of grain were floated down the Mississippi for transshipment to the West Indies and to Europe.

French explorers were lured still farther inland by the siren call of the unknown. They ranged in a gigantic arc from the border of Texas northward through the valleys of the Arkansas, Missouri, and Platte Rivers into Saskatchewan and Manitoba of present-day Canada. In 1743 a party of Frenchmen, though preceded some years earlier by Spaniards, glimpsed the Rocky Mountains.

Robert De La Salle (1643–1687). This Frenchman envisioned a North American empire for France.

But French influence was buttered too thin over a vast continent, and its lasting effect, except in Canada, was not great. French Canadians served as explorers and traders and, in the role of backwoods engineers, as trailblazers and city founders. Far-ranging *coureurs de bois* ("runners of the woods") were also runners of risks—two-fisted drinkers, free spenders, free livers, and free lovers ("squaw men"). Singing, paddle-swinging French *voyageurs* left behind a brood of half-breeds, and peppered the land with scores of place names, including Baton Rouge (red stick), Terre Haute (high land), and Des Moines (some monks).

Other French impacts were significant, if less direct. The character of the English colonists to the south and east was toughened by a series of bitter wars with the French, prolonged throughout three-fourths of a century. New France also diverted a considerable stream of Huguenots to English America by barring her own gates to them. Among these refugees were the ancestors of such distinguished Americans as the diplomat John Jay, the abolitionist poet John Greenleaf Whittier, and the silversmith-horseman Paul Revere, originally Revoire.

The Clash of Empires in Two Hemispheres

As the 17th Century neared its sunset, a titanic struggle was shaping up for mastery of the North American continent. It involved three civilizations: English, French, and Spanish.

Large-scale armed conflict was avoided until 1689. Why? At first there was enough elbowroom for all. Hundreds of miles of trackless forest separated the English from the French in the north and west, and from the Spaniards in the west and south. Rivalry for the furs taken by the Indians could be kept within bounds.

International politics and intrigue also promoted peace. The Stuart kings of England who reigned from 1660 to 1688—Charles II and James II—not only had strong Catholic leanings toward France but also were striving to build up a despotism at

English Caricature of Louis XIV. This French "Sun King," shown here with and without royal regalia, was feared and hated in England.

home. Finding Parliament stingy, they secured secret monetary subsidies from Louis XIV of France. And who bites the hand that feeds him? But the picture changed sharply in 1689, when the Catholic Louis XIV backed the exiled Catholic King of England, James II, against the two imported Protestants from Holland, William and Mary. War erupted in that year—the first of a series in a duel unto death.

In Europe, the two antagonists were fairly well matched. England boasted the stronger navy, France the stronger army, largely because of some 20 million inhabitants, as compared with only 5.5 million English people.

But in America, when the final showdown came in 1754, the English settlers enjoyed an overwhelming advantage in population of about 1.5 million to 60,000. Colonists under the British flag, though of mixed racial and national origins, were predominantly English. They were also relatively compact, confined to the Eastern seaboard by the ramparts of the Alleghenies and by unfriendly Frenchmen, Spaniards, and Indians.

Yet the population of New France, though sparse and diffuse, was far stronger than mere numbers would indicate. Being French Catholic, it was less racially mixed than its southern neighbor. New France also contained a higher proportion of arms-bearing men than the English colonies, especially Pennsylvania, where the Quakers condemned war.

Government in Canada was well designed for war making. It was tightly unified, highly centralized, heavily paternalistic, and sternly autocratic. The full might of the French Canadians could more easily be mobilized and manipulated by a few leaders.

In contrast, the numerical superiority of the English colonies was largely offset by loose governmental control, both at home and from London. As a result of the numerous religious sects and extensive popular rule, authority was widely decentralized and diluted. Andros's limited Dominion of New England, which would have provided some unity, had collapsed. Squabbling between the locally elected assemblies and the London-appointed governors was incessant. At times the colonials seemed more interested in fighting their royal governors than in fighting their French and Indian foes. There was also much intercolonial friction over boundaries and other local disputes. All these discords contributed to a high degree of disunity, and to a general unwillingness to assist neighbors in a common cause.

Yet elements of strength flowed from these apparent weaknesses in the English colonies. The existence of popular government and extensive democratic control encouraged individualism, self-reliance, and resourcefulness. These qualities were invaluable assets to the English settlers in the prolonged series of Anglo-French clashes.

England's colonies, moreover, possessed an overwhelming economic advantage. They enjoyed

Later English Kings
(SEE PP. 10, 28 FOR EARLIER ONES.)

Name, Reign	*Relation to America*
William III, 1689–1702	War of Spanish Succession begun
Anne, 1702–1714	Queen Anne's War, 1702–1713
George I, 1714–1727	Navigation Laws laxly enforced ("salutary neglect")
George II, 1727–1760	Ga. founded; King George's War; French and Indian War
George III, 1760–1820	American Revolution, 1775–1783

Canadiens en Raquette allant en guerre sur la nege

Canadian Dressed for Winter Warfare. (Boston Public Library.)

a wide diversification of industry, with all that this meant in self-sufficiency. But French Canada was weak economically. It rested uneasily on the back of the westward-retreating beaver and, except for furs, lacked a profitable overseas commerce. The frigid Canadian colony never produced enough grain for its own use, and was forced to import large quantities of foodstuffs for its military and civilian personnel.

Other military advantages were unevenly distributed. England's colonies enjoyed the direct shield of the potent British navy, and the indirect shield of the formidable Iroquois Confederacy. The French, who also enlisted painted allies, were blessed with front-rank military leaders. Towering among them were the Comte de Frontenac and the Marquis de Montcalm, who were able to work wonders with scanty tools. The English at first were cursed with inept generals, but finally secured able ones by costly methods of trial and error—chiefly error.

Colonial Pawns on the European Chessboard

The four Anglo-French intercolonial wars, from 1689 to 1763, were in a sense American backwashes of European conflicts. Each of the first three erupted in Europe and spread to America, where there was a reciprocal open season on Frenchmen and Englishmen. The bulk of the English settlers, especially in these early frays, were not eager to start butchering their neighbors when dynastic rivalry in Europe led to shooting. But the colonials, as vanguards of empire, were caught in a squeeze. To a large extent the New World settlements were regarded by Europeans as puppets whose strings could be pulled by overseas monarchs.

All four of these Anglo-French conflicts, which involved groupings of the powers, were world wars. They resulted in a death struggle for European mastery of the seas, and were fought in the waters and on the soil of two hemispheres. Counting these first four clashes, there have been nine world wars since 1688. The American people, whether as British subjects or American citizens, were unable to stay out of a single one of them. Isolation from the broils of Europe was all too often a hope rather than a reality.

The first of the Anglo-French collisions was known in America as King William's War, and it grew in part from the opposition of the French monarch to the expulsion of James II and the seating of William III. Fierce fighting was waged mainly in the various theaters of Europe, as well as in India, North and South America, and the Caribbean.

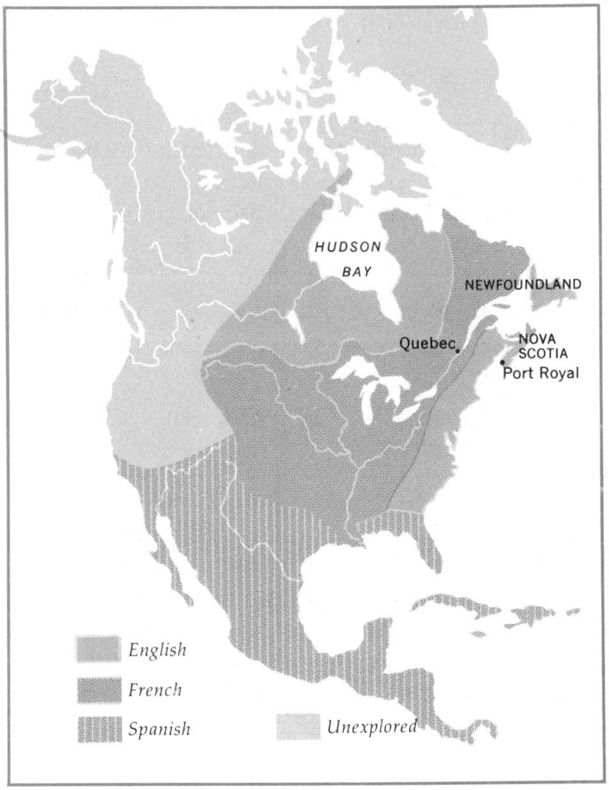

BRITISH TERRITORY AFTER TWO WARS, 1713

In America the fortunes of battle seesawed. War-whooping Indians, led by Frenchmen, ravaged with torch and tomahawk the frontiers of New England, and wiped out the village of Schenectady, New York. The English colonials, after failing miserably in attempts to capture Quebec and Montreal, temporarily seized the stronghold of Port Royal in Acadia. The war abroad ended in a virtual draw, and by the terms of the treaty of peace in 1697 all captured territory was returned.

An uneasy truce ending King William's War lasted a scant four years. In 1701 hostilities broke out anew, following the brazen attempt of Louis XIV to eliminate the traditional boundary of the Pyrenees Mountains by seating his grandson on the throne of Spain. England could not and would not tolerate this dangerous unbalancing of the balance of power.

The subsequent struggle, known as the War of Spanish Succession, was the most far-flung yet fought in Europe: England and her European allies were banded together against France, Spain, and their allies. Though extending to the Caribbean, the fighting occurred principally in Europe, where England captured and retained the defiant Rock of Gibraltar.

This roaring conflagration spread rapidly to America. Spain was now on the side of France, so the South Carolinians engaged in bloody but inconclusive skirmishes with the Spaniards in Florida. War cries of the French-led Indians, as before, split the night air along the northern frontier, notably at Deerfield, Massachusetts. The ill-trained colonials, happily combining pluck with luck, again captured the French fortress of Port Royal in Acadia.

Peace terms, signed in 1713, revealed how badly France and her Spanish ally had been beaten. England was rewarded with Acadia (renamed Nova Scotia or New Scotland), Newfoundland,

The Nine World Wars

Dates	*In Europe*	*In America*
1688–1697	War of the League of Augsburg	King William's War, 1689–1697
1701–1713	War of Spanish Succession	Queen Anne's War, 1702–1713
1740–1748	War of Austrian Succession	King George's War, 1744–1748
1756–1763	Seven Years' War	French and Indian War, 1754–1763
1778–1783	War of the American Revolution	American Revolution, 1775–1783
1793–1802	Wars of the French Revolution	Undeclared French War, 1798–1800
1803–1815	Napoleonic Wars	War of 1812, 1812–1814
1914–1918	World War I	World War I, 1917–1918
1939–1945	World War II	World War II, 1941–1945

> The Duke of Marlborough's triumph inspired Robert Southey's "The Battle of Blenheim" (1798):
> "And everybody praised the Duke,
> Who this great fight did win."
> "But what good came of it at last?"
> Quoth little Peterkin.
> "Why, that I cannot tell," said he;
> "But 'twas a famous victory."

and the bleak Hudson Bay region. These immense areas applied the pincers to the St. Lawrence settlements of France, and foreshadowed their ultimate doom. Except for Nova Scotia, the English colonials themselves had not captured any of these spoils. The final New World transfers were actually determined by the successes of British arms in the Old World. In Germany the Duke of Marlborough, for example, scored a notable victory against the French at Blenheim (1704). A generation of peace ensued, during which Britain provided her American colonies with decades of "salutary neglect"—fertile soil for the roots of independence.

European Wars Create American Sideshows

By the treaty of 1713 the British had won limited trading rights in Spanish America, but these later involved much friction over smuggling. Ill feeling flared up when an English Captain Jenkins, encountering Spanish revenue authorities, had one ear sliced off by a sword. The Spanish commander reportedly sneered, "Carry this home to the King, your master, whom, if he were present, I would serve in like fashion." The victim, with a tale of woe on his tongue and a shriveled ear in his hand, aroused furious resentment when he reached England.

The War of Jenkins' Ear, curiously named, broke out in 1739 between the English and the Spaniards. It was confined to the Caribbean Sea and to the much buffeted buffer colony of Georgia and its environs, where the philanthropist-soldier James Oglethorpe fought his Spanish foe to a standstill.

This small-scale scuffle with Spain in America soon merged with the large-scale War of Austrian Succession in Europe. It exploded with full fury in 1740, when Frederick the Great of Prussia treacherously seized the province of Silesia from his Austrian neighbor, the young and beautiful Maria Theresa. The talented empress fought back with all the fury of a woman scorned, and when Spain and France joined the Prussians, England entered the fray on the side of Austria.

As usual, the War of Austrian Succession was waged mainly in Europe, although sideshow skirmishes erupted in the Caribbean and along the thinly manned English colonial frontier in North America. The French had built a reputedly impregnable fortress, Louisbourg, on Cape Breton Island, commanding the Gulf of St. Lawrence and serving as a pistol pointed at the heart of New England. An expedition of rustic New Englanders was organized to seize it. With the support of a British fleet, and with incredibly good luck, the raw and sometimes drunken recruits blundered into victory and captured the prize in 1745.

But the peace terms of 1748 were determined by the global balance sheet. In Europe, the fighting had again proved inconclusive, except that Frederick of Prussia retained the rich province he had faithlessly wrested from his queenly neighbor. The British had lost Madras in India to France, and in regaining this valuable foothold in the general restoration, they handed back Louisbourg to their foe. The victorious New Englanders were outraged. Taking a narrowly provincial stand, they felt that their interests had been sacrificed to the imperial selfishness of Old Englanders. Although they were finally reimbursed in part for the expenses of their expedition, money did not completely salve their pride or quiet their fears. France was still powerful and unappeased.

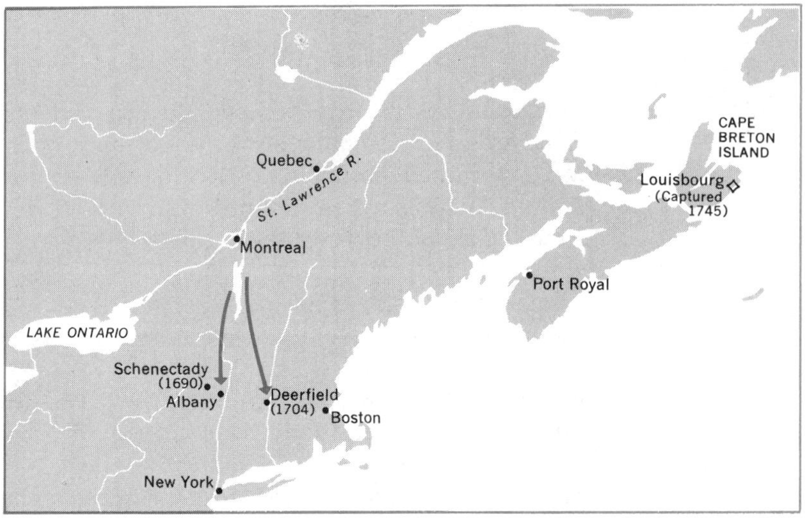

SCENES OF THE FRENCH WARS

The arrows indicate French-Indian attacks. The primitive settlement of Schenectady was burned to the ground in the raid of 1690. At Deerfield the attackers killed 50 inhabitants, took over 100 prisoners, and sent the rest of the village's 300 residents fleeing for their lives into the wintry February wilderness.

George Washington Inaugurates War with France

As the drama unfolded in the New World, the Ohio Valley became the chief bone of contention between the French and British. The Ohio country was the critical area into which the westward-pushing English would inevitably penetrate. It was the key to the continent which the French had to retain, particularly if they were going to link their Canadian holdings with those of the lower Mississippi Valley. By the mid-1700s the English colonials, painfully aware of these basic truths, were no longer so reluctant to bear the burdens of empire. Alarmed by French land-grabbing and cutthroat fur-trade competition in the Ohio Valley, they were determined to fight for their economic security and for the supremacy of their way of life in North America.

Rivalry for the lush lands of the upper Ohio Valley brought tensions to the snapping point. In 1749 a group of English colonial speculators, chiefly influential Virginians including the Washington family, had secured rights to some 500,000 acres in this region. In the same disputed wilderness the French were in the process of erecting a chain of forts commanding the strategic Ohio River.

In 1753 the governor of Virginia ushered George Washington, a twenty-one-year-old surveyor and fellow Virginian, onto the stage of history. The tall, athletic youth was commissioned to warn the French that they must leave the Ohio Valley; and while delivering the message he was to spy out their armed strength. Already marked out as an able and ambitious young man of promise, Washington completed this dangerous mission, after several brushes with death. But the French were not going to be ejected by mere words. They tightened their hold on the Ohio Valley by building a strong outpost, Fort Duquesne, at the strate-

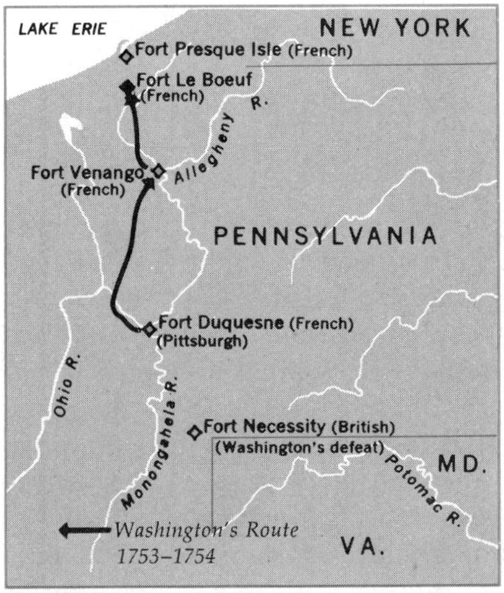

THE OHIO COUNTRY, 1753–1754

gic point where the Monongahela and Allegheny Rivers join to form the Ohio—the later site of Pittsburgh.

In 1754, shortly after his hazardous errand, Washington was sent to the Ohio country as a lieutenant-colonel in command of about 150 Virginia militiamen. Encountering a small detachment of French troops in the forest about forty miles from Fort Duquesne, the Virginians opened fire—the first shots of the globe-girdling new war. The French leader was killed and his men retreated. An exultant Washington wrote: "I heard the bullets whistle, and believe me, there is something charming in the sound." It soon lost its charm.

The French promptly returned with reinforcements, which surrounded Washington behind his hastily constructed breastworks, Fort Necessity. After a ten-hour siege he was forced to surrender his entire command in July 1754—ironically the Fourth of July. But he was permitted to march his men away with the full honors of war.

With the shooting already started and in danger of spreading, the British authorities in Nova Scotia took vigorous action. Understandably fearing a stab in the back from the French Acadians, whom England had acquired in 1713, the British brutally uprooted some 4,000 of them in 1755. These unhappy French deportees were scattered as far south as Louisiana, where the descendants of the French-speaking Acadians are now called "Cajuns" and number perhaps half a million.

Global War and Colonial Disunity

The first three Anglo-French colonial wars had all started in Europe, but the tables were now reversed. A fourth struggle, known as the French and Indian War, began in America. Touched off by George Washington in the wilds of the Ohio Valley in 1754, it rocked along on an undeclared basis for two years, and then widened into the most titanic conflict the world had yet seen—the Seven Years' War. It was fought not only in America but in Europe, in the West Indies, in the Philippines, in Africa, and on the ocean. The Seven Years' War was a seven seas war.

In Europe the principal adversaries were England and Prussia on one side, arrayed against France, Spain, Austria, and Russia on the other. The bloodiest theater was in Germany, where Frederick the Great deservedly won the title of "Great" by repelling French, Austrian, and Russian armies, often with the manpower odds three to one against him. The London government, unable to send him effective troop reinforcements, liberally subsidized him with gold. Luckily for the English colonials, the French wasted so much strength in this European bloodbath that they were unable to throw an adequate force into the New World. "America was conquered in Germany," declared Britain's great statesman William Pitt.

In previous intercolonial clashes, the Americans had revealed an astonishing lack of unity. Colonists who were nearest the shooting had responded much more generously with volunteers and money than those enjoying the safety of remoteness. Even the Indians had laughed at the inability of the colonials to pull together. With bullets already whining in the Ohio country, the crisis called for concerted action.

In 1754 the British government summoned an intercolonial Congress to Albany, New York, near the Iroquois Indian country. Travel-weary delegates from only seven of the thirteen colonies showed up. The immediate purpose was to keep the scalping knives of the Iroquois tribes loyal to the British in the spreading war. The chiefs were harangued at length and then presented with thirty wagon loads of gifts, including guns.

The longer-range purpose at Albany was to achieve greater colonial unity, and thus bolster the common defense against France. A month before the Congress assembled, ingenious Benjamin Franklin published in his *Pennsylvania Gazette* the most famous cartoon of the colonial era. Showing the separate colonies as parts of a disjointed snake, it broadcast the slogan, "Join, or Die."

Famous Cartoon by Benjamin Franklin. Delaware and Georgia were omitted.

Franklin himself, a wise and witty counselor, was the leading spirit of the Albany Congress. His outstanding contribution was a well-devised scheme for colonial home rule. It was unanimously adopted by the Albany delegates, but was spurned by the individual colonies and by the London regime. To the colonials, it did not seem to give enough independence; to the British officials, it seemed to give too much. The disappointing result confirmed one of Franklin's sage observations: all people agreed on the need for union, but their "weak noddles" were "perfectly distracted" when they attempted to agree on details.

Braddock's Blundering and Its Aftermath

The opening clashes of the French and Indian War went badly for the English colonials. Haughty and bull-headed General Braddock, a sixty-year-old officer experienced in European warfare, was sent to Virginia with a strong detachment of British regulars. After gathering scanty supplies from the reluctant colonists, he set out in 1755 with some 2,000 men to capture Fort Duquesne. A considerable part of his force consisted of ill-disciplined colonial militiamen ("buckskins"), whose behind-the-tree methods of fighting Indians won "Bulldog" Braddock's professional contempt.

General Edward Braddock (1695–1755). Braddock was buried in the road of retreat so that his grave could not be detected by the enemy. His last, futile words were reported to be, "We shall know better how to deal with them next time."

Braddock's expedition, dragging heavy artillery, moved slowly. Axmen laboriously hacked a path through the dense forest, thus opening a road that was later to be an important artery to the West. A few miles from Fort Duquesne, Braddock encountered a much smaller French and Indian army. At first the enemy force was repulsed, but it quickly melted into the thickets and poured a murderous fire into the ranks of the Redcoats. George Washington, an energetic and fearless aide to Braddock, had two horses shot from under him and four bullet holes in his coat, and Braddock himself was mortally wounded. The entire force was routed after appalling losses.

Inflamed by this easy victory, the Indians took to a wider warpath. The whole frontier from Pennsylvania to North Carolina, left virtually naked by Braddock's bloody defeat, felt their fury. Scalping forays occurred within eighty miles of Philadelphia, and in desperation the local authorities offered bounties for Indian scalps: $50 for a squaw and $130 for a brave. George Washington, with only 300 men, did heroic work in helping to defend the scorched frontier.

The British launched a full-scale invasion of Canada in 1756, now that the undeclared war in America had at last merged into a world conflict. But they unwisely tried to attack a number of exposed wilderness posts simultaneously, instead of throwing all their strength at Quebec and Montreal. If these strongholds had fallen, all the outposts to the west would have withered on the vine for lack of river-borne supplies. But the British ignored such sound strategy, and defeat after defeat tarnished their arms, both in America and in Europe.

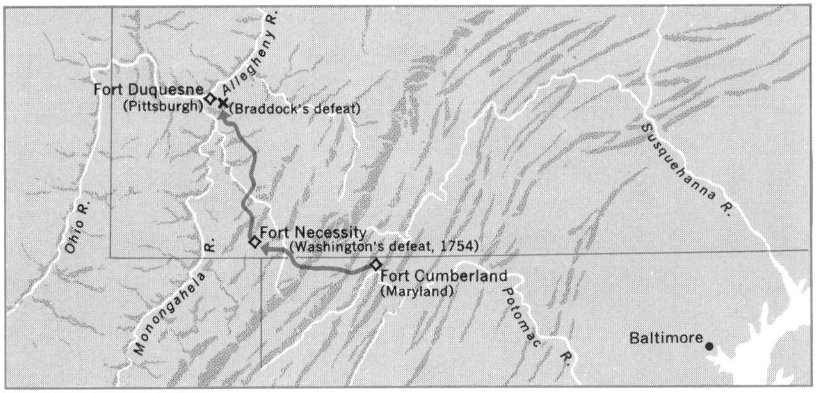

BRADDOCK'S MARCH, 1755

Pitt's Palms of Victory

In the hour of crisis Britain brought forth, as she repeatedly has, a superlative leader—William Pitt. A tall and imposing figure, whose flashing eyes were set in a hawk-like face, he was popularly known as the "Great Commoner." Pitt drew much of his strength from the common people, who admired him so greatly that on occasion they kissed his horses. A splendid orator endowed with a majestic voice, he believed passionately in his cause, in his country, and in himself.

In 1757 Pitt became a foremost leader in the London government. Throwing himself headlong into his task, he soon earned the title "Organizer of Victory." He wisely decided to soft-pedal assaults on the French West Indies, which had been bleeding away much British strength, and to concentrate on the vitals of Canada—the Quebec-Montreal area. He also picked young and ener-

EVENTS OF 1755–1760

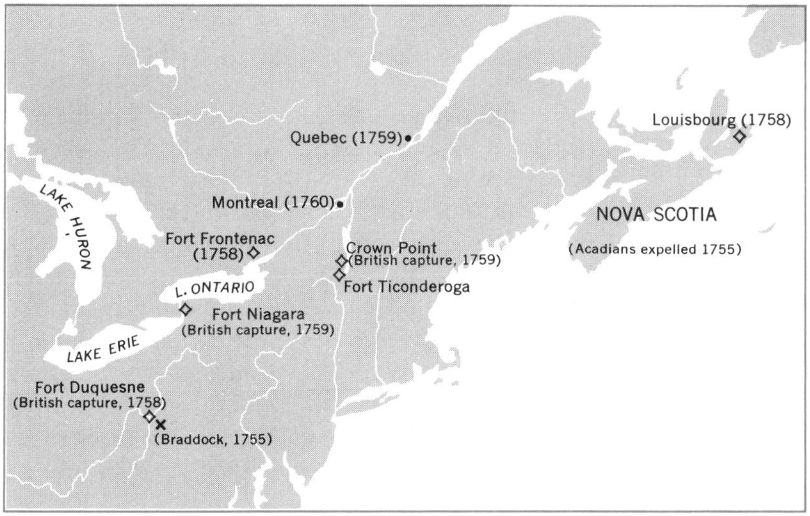

William Pitt (1708–1778). He opposed the King's stubborn policies against the colonies but never favored complete independence.

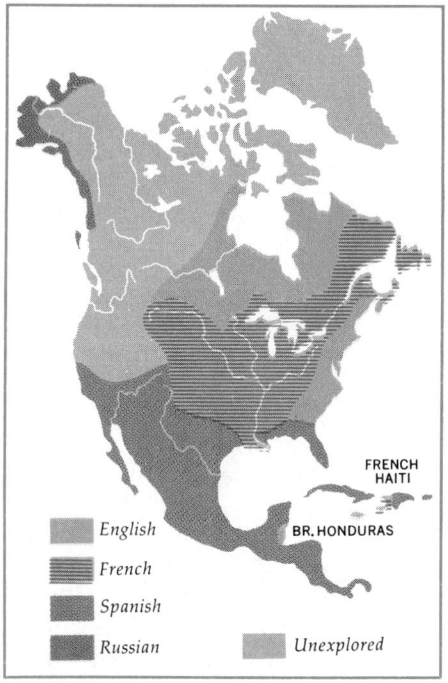

NORTH AMERICA BEFORE 1754

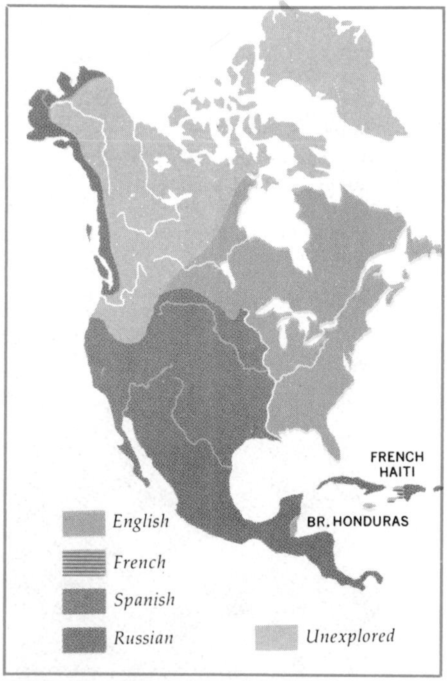

NORTH AMERICA AFTER 1763
(after French losses)

getic leaders, thus bypassing incompetent and cautious old generals.

Pitt first dispatched a powerful expedition in 1758 against Louisbourg. The frowning fortress, though it had been greatly strengthened, fell after a blistering siege. Wild rejoicing swept England, for this was the first significant British victory of the entire war.

Quebec was next on Pitt's list. For this crucial expedition he chose the thirty-two-year-old James Wolfe, who had been an officer since the age of fourteen. Though slight and sickly, Wolfe combined a mixture of dash with painstaking attention to detail. The British attackers were making scant progress when Wolfe, in a daring move, sent a detachment up a poorly guarded part of the rocky eminence protecting Quebec. This vanguard scaled the cliff, pulling itself upward by the bushes and showing the way for the others. In the morning the two armies faced each other on the Plains of Abraham on the outskirts of Quebec, one under Wolfe and the other under Montcalm. Both commanders fell fatally wounded, but the French were defeated and the city surrendered.

The battle of Quebec ranks as one of the most significant engagements in British and American history. Yet it was only one of the bumper crop of victories in 1759, known in British history as "the wonderful year." The English writer Horace Walpole noted, "We were forced to ask every morning what victory there is, for fear of missing one."

Yet the triumph at Quebec was not completely decisive. Winter descended, ice-locking the St. Lawrence River, and leaving the scurvy-ridden and outnumbered British army facing heavy attacks from Montreal. But with spring, the ice broke and reinforcements arrived. Montreal fell in 1760, and the French flag waved in Canada for the last time. Even so, the war continued globally for three more years. France and Spain were lucky to escape as well as they did, but the bad beating they received was reflected in severe peace terms.

By the peace settlement at Paris (1763), French

power was thrown completely off the continent of North America, leaving behind a fertile French population that is to this day a strong minority in Canada. This bitter pill was sweetened somewhat when the French were allowed to retain several small but valuable sugar islands in the West Indies, and two never-to-be-fortified islets in the Gulf of St. Lawrence for fishing stations. A final blow came when the French, to compensate their luckless Spanish ally for her losses, ceded to Spain all trans-Mississippi Louisiana, plus the outlet of New Orleans. Spain, for her part, turned Florida over to England in return for Cuba, where Havana had fallen to British arms.

Great Britain thus emerged as the dominant power in North America, while taking her place as the leading naval power of the world.

Mother-and-Daughter Friction

England's colonials, baptized by fire, emerged with increased confidence in their military strength. They had borne the brunt of battle at first; they had fought bravely beside the crack British regulars; and they had gained valuable experience, officers and men alike. In the closing days of the conflict some 20,000 American recruits were under arms.

Anti-Quaker Cartoon. Non-combatant Pennsylvania Quakers traded with the French, and in this cartoon (c. 1760) Franklin points out that the Quaker (with fox's head) will flourish, regardless of who wins. (The Historical Society of Pennsylvania.)

The French and Indian War, while bolstering colonial self-esteem, simultaneously shattered the myth of British invincibility. On Braddock's bloody field the "buckskin" militia had seen the demoralized regulars huddling helplessly together or fleeing their unseen enemy.

Ominously, friction had developed during the war between arrogant English officers and the raw colonial "boors." Displaying the contempt of the professional soldier for amateurs, the British refused to recognize any American militia commission above the rank of captain—a demotion humiliating to "Colonel" George Washington. They also showed the usual condescension of snobs from the civilized Old Country toward the "scum" who had confessed failure by fleeing to the "outhouses of civilization." General Wolfe referred to the colonial militia, with exaggeration, as "in general the dirtiest, most contemptible, cowardly dogs that you can conceive." Energetic and hardworking American settlers, on the other hand, sensed that they were the cutting edge of British civilization. They believed that they deserved credit rather than contempt for risking their lives to erect a New World empire.

British officials were further distressed by the reluctance of the colonials to support the common cause wholeheartedly. American shippers, using fraudulent papers, developed a golden traffic with the enemy ports of the Spanish and French West Indies. This treasonable trade in foodstuffs actually kept some of the hostile islands from starving at the very time when the British navy was trying to subdue them. In the last year of the war the British authorities, forced to resort to drastic measures, forbade the export of all supplies from New England and the Middle Colonies.

Nor had the conduct of other colonials been

> The Reverend Andrew Burnaby, an observant Church of England clergyman who visited the colonies in the closing months of the French and Indian War, scoffed at any possibility of unification (1760): ". . . for fire and water are not more heterogeneous than the different colonies in North America. Nothing can exceed the jealousy and emulation which they possess in regard to each other. . . . In short . . . were they left to themselves there would soon be a civil war from one end of the continent to the other, while the Indians and Negroes would . . . impatiently watch the opportunity of exterminating them all together."

praiseworthy. Self-centered and regarding the war as remote, large numbers of them had been loath to provide men and money for the conflict. They demanded the rights and privileges of Englishmen, without the duties and responsibilities of Englishmen. Not until Pitt had offered to reimburse the colonies for a substantial part of their expenditures—some £900,000—did they move with some enthusiasm. If the Americans had to be bribed to defend themselves against a relentless and savage foe, would they ever unite to strike the Mother Country?

The curse of intercolonial disunity, present from early days, had continued throughout the recent hostilities. It had been caused mainly by enormous distances; by geographical barriers like rivers; by conflicting religions, from Catholic to Quaker; by varied national backgrounds, from German to Irish; by differing types of colonial governments; by numerous boundary disputes; and by the resentment of the crude back-country democracy against the aristocratic bigwigs. Many of the colonials felt much more kindly toward Englishmen in England than they did toward Englishmen next door.

Yet unity received some encouragement during the French and Indian War. When soldiers and statesmen from widely separated colonies met around common campfires and council tables, they were often agreeably surprised by what they found. Despite deep-seated jealousy and suspicion, they discovered that they were all fellow Americans who generally spoke the same language and shared common ideals. Barriers of disunity began to melt, although a long and rugged road lay ahead before a nation could emerge.

American Men of Destiny

The removal of the French menace in Canada profoundly affected American attitudes. While the French hawk had been hovering in the North and West, the colonial chicks had been forced to cling close to the wings of the mother hen. Now that the hawk was killed, they could range far afield with a new spirit of independence.

Frenchmen, humiliated by the British and saddened by the fate of Canada, consoled themselves with one wishful thought. Perhaps the loss of their American empire would one day result in Britain's loss of her American empire. In a sense the history of the United States began with the fall of Quebec and Montreal; the infant republic was cradled on the Plains of Abraham.

The Spanish and Indian menaces, in like manner, were removed by the recent war. Spain was eliminated from Florida, although now entrenched in Louisiana and New Orleans. And the Indian allies of France were left in the lurch. A violent post-war flare-up against the white men occurred in the Ohio Valley and Great Lakes region in 1763, with the vengeful chieftain Pontiac as the principal leader. Catching the British napping, the red men wiped out a number of their posts. But the whites, rallying in superior numbers, crushed the uprising and pacified the frontier, temporarily.

Land-hungry American colonials were now free to burst over the dam of the Appalachian Moun-

SETTLED AREAS AT END OF FRENCH AND INDIAN WAR, 1763

This map, showing the colonies thirteen years before the Declaration of Independence, helps to explain why the British would be unable to conquer their offspring. The Colonials were spreading rapidly into the back-country, where the powerful British navy could not flush them out. During the Revolutionary War, the British at one time or another captured the leading colonial cities—Boston, New York, Philadelphia, and Charleston; but the more remote interior remained a sanctuary for rebels.

tains, and flood out over the grassy Western lands. A tiny rivulet of men like Daniel Boone had already trickled into Tennessee and Kentucky; other courageous pioneers were preparing for the long trek over the mountains.

Then, out of a clear sky, the London government issued its Proclamation of 1763. It flatly prohibited settlement in the area beyond the Appalachian Mountains, pending further adjustments. The truth is that this hastily drawn document was not designed to oppress the colonials at all, but to work out the Indian problem fairly in the interests of the fur traders and the other groups concerned.

But countless Americans, especially land speculators, were dismayed and angered. Was not the land beyond the mountains their birthright? Had they not, in addition, bought it with their blood in the recent war? In complete defiance of the paper Proclamation, they clogged the westward trails. In 1765 an estimated 1,000 wagons rolled through the town of Salisbury, North Carolina, on their way "up west." This wholesale flouting of royal authority boded ill for the longevity of British rule in America.

The French and Indian War also caused the colonials to develop a new vision of their ultimate destiny. With the path cleared for the conquest of a continent, with their birthrate high and their energy boundless, they sensed that they were a potent people on the march. And they were in no mood to be restrained.

Lordly Britons, whose suddenly swollen empire had tended to produce swollen heads, were in no mood for back talk. Puffed up over their recent victories, they were already annoyed with their unruly colonials. The stage was set for a violent family quarrel.

VARYING VIEWPOINTS

The duel for North America was but one episode in the epochal story of the worldwide expansion of European commerce and culture after 1500. Scholarly inquiry has revolved around four principal questions: How did New World developments fit into the overall pattern of rivalries among the great European powers? What were the relative strengths and weaknesses of the British and French imperial systems that spelled the final triumph of the British and the defeat of the French? How well or poorly did the British Empire function? Finally, were the Americans well or badly treated in the British imperial system? In short, how economically justifiable was the eventual American Revolution?

SELECT READINGS

The workings of the British mercantile system are detailed in G. L. Beer, *The Origins of the British Colonial System* (1908), and *The Old Colonial System* (2 vols., 1912). See also C. M. Andrews' vast *Colonial Period of American History* (4 vols., 1935–1938), and L. Gipson's still more ambitious *British Empire before the American Revolution* (15 vols., 1936–1970). Recent efforts to analyze the colonial empire are M. Hall, *Edward Randolph and the American Colonies, 1676–1703* (1960), J. Henretta, *"Salutary Neglect": Colonial Administration under the Duke of Newcastle* (1972), and Michael Kammen's especially interesting *Empire and Interest* (1970). The French colonial effort is described in G. M. Wrong, *The Rise and Fall of New France* (2 vols., 1928), and in S. Morison, *Samuel de Champlain: Father of New France* (1972). The Anglo-French struggle is recounted in H. H. Peckham, *The Colonial Wars, 1689–1762* (1964), and in Max Savelle, *The Origins of American Diplomacy: The International History of Angloamerica, 1492–1763* (1967). Classic accounts are Francis Parkman's several volumes, including *Count Frontenac and New France under Louis XIV* (1877), *Montcalm and Wolfe* (2 vols., 1884), and *A Half-Century of Conflict* (1892). Parkman's tomes are condensed, without serious loss of flavor, in *The Battle for North America* (ed. John Tebbel, 1948) and *The Parkman Reader* (ed. S. E. Morison, 1955). A recent military history is C. P. Stacey, *Quebec, 1759: The Siege and the Battle* (1959). An impressive biography is D. S. Freeman, *Young Washington* (2 vols., 1948), a subject treated in less detail in J. T. Flexner, *George Washington: The Forge of Experience* (1965). See also B. Knollenberg's revealing *George Washington: The Virginia Period* (1965).

4

Colonial Society on the Eve of Revolution

Driven from every other corner of the earth, freedom of thought and the right of private judgment in matters of conscience direct their course to this happy country as their last asylum.

SAMUEL ADAMS, 1776

Conquest by the Cradle

The common term "thirteen original colonies" is misleading. There were thirty-two colonies under British rule in North America by 1775, including Canada, the Floridas, and the various islands of the Caribbean. But only thirteen of them unfurled the standard of revolt. A few of the nonrebels, such as Canada and Jamaica, were larger, wealthier, or more populous than some of the thirteen. And even among the revolting thirteen, dramatic differences in economic organization, social structure, and ways of life were evident.

All the eventually rebellious colonies did have one outstanding feature in common: their population was growing by leaps and bounds. In 1700 they contained fewer than 300,000 souls, about 20,000 of whom were black. By 1775, 2.5 million

Early Advertising. Appeal in England for American colonists.

persons inhabited the thirteen colonies, of whom about half a million were black. White immigrants made up nearly 400,000 of the increased number, and black "forced immigrants" accounted for almost as many again. But most of the spurt stemmed from the remarkable natural fertility of all Americans, white and black. To the amazement and dismay of Europeans, the colonists were doubling their numbers every twenty-three years. Unfriendly Dr. Samuel Johnson, back in England, growled that the Americans were multiplying like their own rattlesnakes. This was especially true in New England, where the people were fertile even if the soil was not. Lower population densities slowed the spread of contagious microbes, making American death rates lower than those of the relatively crowded Old World. Simply put, America was a healthier place than Europe, though the southern colonies remained deathtraps until late in the 17th Century. Even the captive black population of the Chesapeake region reached the point of sustained natural increase sometime around 1720—about two generations later than the southern white settlers—making it one of the few slave societies in history to perpetuate itself by its own natural reproduction.

Early marriage encouraged the booming birthrate. Women were scarce and seldom stayed single for long. An unwed girl of twenty-one could be labeled "an antique virgin." In the courtship stages and in places where heating was a problem, "bundling" was occasionally permitted; that is, the young couple would cuddle together in bed fully clothed. Unwanted pregnancies sometimes re-

Graveyard Art. These New England colonists evidently died in the prime of life. Carving likenesses on grave markers was a common way of commemorating the dead. (American Antiquarian Society.)

sulted, although one New England rhymester defended the practice:

Since in a bed a man and maid
May bundle and be chaste,
It doth no good to burn up wood;
It is a needless waste.

Babies arrived with sometimes frightening frequency. Benjamin Franklin was one of seventeen by two mothers; William Phips, a Massachusetts governor was one of twenty-seven—all by the same mother. Ceaseless child-bearing drained the vitality of many pioneer women, as the weather-eroded colonial tombstones eloquently reveal, and a number of the largest families were borne by several mothers. Yet these maternal sacrifices had political consequences. In 1700 there were twenty Englishmen for each American colonist. By 1775 the English advantage in numbers had fallen to three-to-one—setting the stage for a momentous shift in the balance of power between colonies and the mother country.

The bulk of the population was cooped up east of the Alleghenies, although by 1775 a vanguard of pioneers had trickled into the stump-studded clearings of Tennessee and Kentucky. The most populous colonies in 1775 were Virginia, Massachusetts, Pennsylvania, North Carolina, and Maryland—in that order. There were only four communities that might properly be called cities: Philadelphia, including suburbs, was first with about 34,000, while New York, Boston, and Charleston were strung out behind. About 90 percent of the people lived in rural areas.

A Mingling of the Races

Colonial America was a melting pot, and had been from the outset. The population, although basically English in stock and language, was picturesquely mottled with sizable foreign groups.

Heavy-accented Germans constituted about 6 percent of the total population, or 150,000, by 1775. Fleeing religious persecution, economic oppression, and the ravages of war, they had flocked to America in the early 1700s, and had settled chiefly in Pennsylvania. Known popularly but erroneously as the Pennsylvania Dutch (a corruption of the German word *Deutsch*), they totaled about one-third of the colony's population. In Philadelphia the street signs were painted in both German and English.

These German newcomers moved into the back country of Pennsylvania, where their splendid stone barns gave—and still give—mute evidence of industry and prosperity. Not having been brought up as Englishmen, they had no deep-rooted loyalty to the British Crown, and they clung tenaciously to their German language and customs. But as permanent settlers they became the forebears of many distinguished Americans, including George Herman ("Babe") Ruth, the home-run king, and President Dwight D. Eisenhower.

The Scotch-Irish, who in 1775 numbered about 175,000, or 7 percent of the population, were an important non-English group, although English-speaking. They were not Irish at all, but turbulent Scots Lowlanders. Over a period of many decades, they had first been transplanted to Northern Ireland, where they had not prospered. The Irish Catholics already there, hating Scotch Presbyterianism, resented the intruders, and still do. The economic life of the Scotch-Irish was severely hampered, especially when the English government placed burdensome restrictions on their production of linens and woolens.

> A young Frenchman named Crèvecoeur wrote about 1770 of the mixed population. "They are a mixture of English, Scotch, Irish, French, Dutch, Germans, and Swedes. From this promiscuous breed, that race now called Americans have arisen. . . . I could point out to you a family whose grandfather was an Englishman, whose wife was Dutch, whose son married a French woman, and whose present four sons have now four wives of different nations."

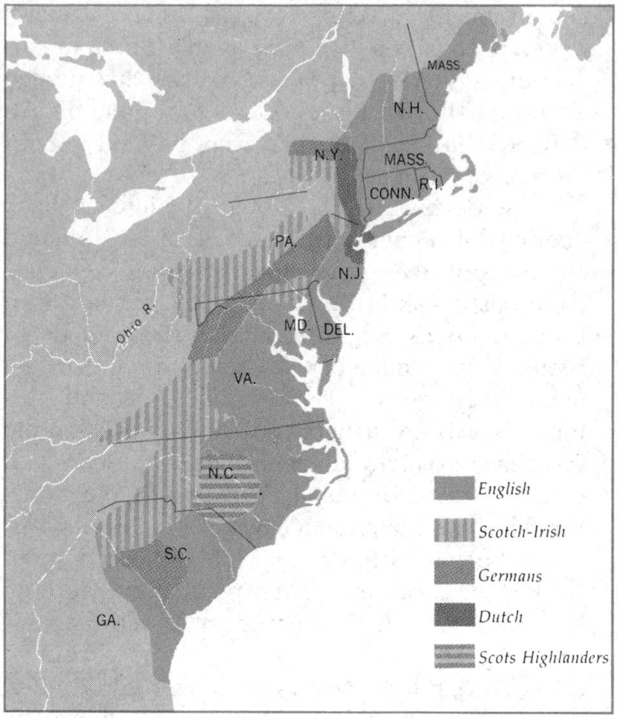

NATIONALITIES IN 1775

Early in the 1700s tens of thousands of embittered Scotch-Irish finally pulled up stakes and came to America, chiefly to tolerant and deep-soiled Pennsylvania. Finding the best acres already taken by Germans and Quakers, they pushed out onto the frontier. There many of them illegally but defiantly squatted on the unoccupied lands, and quarreled with both red and white owners. It was said, somewhat unfairly, that the Scotch-Irish kept the Sabbath—and all else they could lay their hands on. Pugnacious, lawless, and individualistic, they brought with them the Scottish secrets of whiskey distilling and proceeded to set up their own stills. Already experienced colonizers and agitators in Ireland, they proved to be superb frontiersmen and Indian fighters. They cherished no love for the British government which had uprooted them, and many of them—including the youthful Andrew Jackson—joined the embattled American Revolutionists. All told, about a dozen future Presidents were of Scotch-Irish descent.

Approximately 5 percent of the multi-colored colonial population consisted of other foreign groups. These embraced French Huguenots, Welsh, Dutch, Swedes, Jews, Irish, Swiss, and Scots Highlanders—as distinguished from the Scotch-Irish. Except for the Scots Highlanders, such hodgepodge elements felt little loyalty to the British Crown.

By far the largest single non-English group was African. Perhaps 400,000 blacks were carried in chains to colonial North America, yet they were only a tiny fraction of the millions brought to the New World as a whole in the centuries preceding the American Revolution. The small and struggling colonial economy did not at first provide an attractive market for slave traders. Most of the early human cargoes taken from West Africa's "slave coast" on the Gulf of Guinea went to South America or the West Indies. Throughout most of the 17th Century, nearly half the slaves brought to mainland America came by way of the West Indies, not directly from Africa. They had originally been captured in Africa by African coastal tribes, who traded them in crude markets on the shimmering tropical beaches to itinerant European flesh merchants. The captives were herded aboard sweltering ships for the gruesome "middle passage," on

Estimated Population Elements, 1790*
(BASED ON FAMILY NAMES)

Ethnic Groups	*Number*	*Percentage*
English and Welsh	2,605,699	66.3%
Scotch (including Scotch-Irish)	221,562	5.6
German	176,407	4.5
Dutch	78,959	2.0
Irish	61,534	1.6
French	17,619	0.4
All other whites	10,664	0.3
Black	757,181	19.3
GRAND TOTAL	3,929,625	

*Rossiter, *A Century of Population Growth* (1909). Later estimates by Barker and Hansen (1931) are not used here because they are confused by the inclusion of Spanish and French elements *later* a part of the United States.

TO BE SOLD,
On Saturday the 27th inſtant, at the London Coffee houſe;
Twelve or Fourteen
Valuable NEGROES,
Conſiſting of young men, women, boys and girls.
THEY have all had the ſmall pox, can talk E glish, and are ſeaſoned to the country. The ſale to begin at twelve o'clock.

A Pennsylvania Advertisement for Slaves in the 1760s. Note that the slaves are said to have had smallpox and to be able to speak English. (Rare Book Division, The New York Public Library, Astor, Lenox and Tilden Foundations.)

which death rates ran as high as 20 percent. Terrified survivors were eventually shoved onto auction blocks in New World ports.

Slave imports to the American colonies mounted rapidly after about 1690, as white labor became more expensive. In 1698 the Royal African Company lost its crown-granted monopoly on carrying slaves to the colonies. Enterprising Americans then rushed to cash in on the lucrative slave trade. "Guinea ships," mostly from New England, plied the grim course directly from Africa to America. Newport, Rhode Island, became a main port of entry, though it was dwarfed by the giant slave market at Charleston, South Carolina.

The population of the thirteen colonies, though mainly Anglo-Saxon, was perhaps the most mixed to be found anywhere in the world. The South, holding about 90 percent of the slaves, already displayed its historic black-and-white racial composition. New England, mostly staked out by the original Puritan migrants, showed the least ethnic diversity. The middle colonies, especially Pennsylvania, received the bulk of later white immigrants, and boasted an astonishing variety of peoples. Of the fifty-six signers of the Declaration of Independence in 1776, eighteen were non-English, and eight had been born outside the colonies.

Frontier Patricians

Crude frontier life did not permit the flagrant display of class distinctions, and 17th-Century colonial society had a certain simple sameness to it. Yet many settlers, who considered themselves of the "better sort," tried to re-create on a modified scale the social structure they had known at home. To some extent, they were successful, though yeasty democratic forces frustrated their full triumph. The most remarkable feature of the social ladder was the rags-to-riches ease with which an ambitious colonial, even a former indentured servant, might rise from a lower rung to a higher one, quite unlike in Old England.

Would-be American bluebloods resented the pretensions of the "meaner sort" and passed laws to keep them in their place. Massachusetts in 1651 prohibited poorer folk from "wearing gold or silver lace," and in 18th-Century Virginia a tailor was fined and jailed for arranging to race his horse—"a sport only for gentlemen."

Elites feathered their nests more finely in the 18th Century. People came to be seated in churches and schools according to their social rank. (Future President John Adams was placed fourteenth in a class of twenty-four at Harvard, where ability also affected one's standing.) At the top of the social ladder in the New England and Middle colonies roosted the merchant princes. Many of them laid the foundations of their fortunes with profits made as military suppliers during the wars of the 1690s and early 1700s. In the Southern colonies, land-holding was the passport to power, prestige, and wealth. The Virginia gentry proved remarkably able to keep its lands in a small circle of families over several generations—largely because they parceled out their huge holdings among several children, rather than just to the eldest son, as was the custom in England. A clutch of extended clans, such as the Fitzhughs, the Lees, and the Washingtons, owned amongst them vast tracts of Virginia real estate, and together they dominated Virginia politics. Just before the Revolutionary War, 70 percent of the leaders of the

House of Burgesses came from families established in Virginia before the 1690s—the famed "First Families of Virginia," or "FFV's."

The power of the great planters was also bolstered by their disproportionate ownership of slaves. The riches created by the swelling slave population in the 18th Century were not distributed evenly among the whites. Wealth tended to concentrate in the hands of the largest slave owners—thus widening the gap between the prosperous gentry and the "poor whites," with relatively few whites in between. In all the colonies, the ranks of the upper crust were further enhanced by the more successful professional men, the clergy of the established churches, and the well-dressed British officials, including the governors and other "ruffle-shirted Anglicans."*

The Lower Rungs of Society

Below the aristocracy was the middle class—the backbone of the colonies. Largest in New England, it consisted chiefly of the small farmers, often clad in buckskin breeches, who owned modest holdings and tilled them with their own hands and

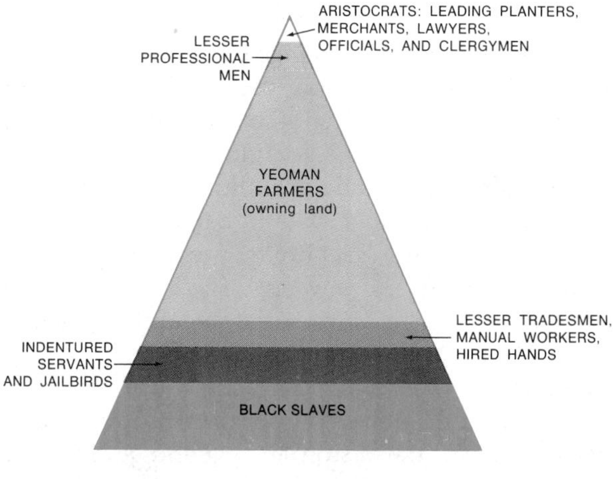

THE COLONIAL SOCIAL PYRAMID, 1775
(an approximation)

*See Gilbert Stuart's painting of "The Skater," color portfolio, for a rendition of an elegantly clad Revolutionary-era aristocrat.

Franklin's Press. Benjamin Franklin, a many-sided Philadelphian, was the best known and most prosperous colonial printer. He rose to hobnob with European royalty.

horses. Closely associated with this group were the skilled artisans, with their well-greased leather aprons, and the smaller tradesmen. America's most famous printer, Benjamin Franklin, was never fully accepted by the snobs of his adopted Philadelphia. The son of a Boston candlemaker, he was looked down upon as a social climber—a person in "trade."*

Below the prosperous middle class were "hired hands" and other landless poor whites. Happily, the ne'er-do-wells were not numerous; extreme poverty and extreme wealth were both rather rare.

Even lower on the social ladder were the indentured servants, of whom perhaps 250,000 had arrived by 1775. These "white slaves" were mainly persons who could not afford to pay their passage across the Atlantic. In return for transportation, they voluntarily mortgaged the sweat of their bodies for a period of years, usually four or more. Their lot was often harsh, and runaways were common.

Indentured servants, upon serving their time, frequently were given or otherwise secured land, and the more enterprising souls often became prosperous. Nor did any serious social stigma attach to them. Some even broke into the upper crust of aristocracy, and two became signers of the Declaration of Independence. The inden-

*For a portrait of another famous Colonial craftsman, Paul Revere, see John Singleton Copley's painting in the color portfolio.

tured-servant system admittedly inflicted much hardship, but it did give tens of thousands of impoverished people a chance to start anew in the Land of Opportunity.

Far less desirable than the voluntary indentured servants were the paupers and convicts who were involuntarily shipped over as indentured servants. Altogether, about 50,000 "jayle birds" were dumped on the American colonies by the London authorities. This riffraff crowd, including robbers, rapists, and murderers, was generally sullen and undesirable, and not bubbling over with goodwill for the King's government. But many convicts were the unfortunate victims of circumstances and of a viciously unfair penal code that included about 200 capital crimes. Some of the deportees, in fact, came to be highly respected citizens.

Slave-Catcher Advertisment. Runaway slaves were so numerous in colonial days that newspapers kept on hand stock woodcuts like those here reproduced. One Virginia owner offered five pounds reward for the return of Toby, a fourteen-year-old mulatto boy "with a scar on the right side of his throat", and with "an old brown jacket, tow shirt and check trousers, which are supposed to be worn out by this time."

Colonial Slavery

Luckless black slaves remained in society's basement. Enchained in all the colonies, the blacks were heavily concentrated in the South, where their numbers rose dramatically throughout the 18th Century. Blacks accounted for nearly half the population of Virginia by midcentury. In South Carolina they outnumbered whites two to one. There the climate was hostile to health and the labor was life draining. Isolated rice and indigo plantations were lonely hells-on-earth where gangs of mostly male blacks toiled and perished. Only fresh imports could sustain the slave population in the deep South. In 1739 more than fifty resentful blacks in South Carolina exploded in revolt and tried to march to Spanish Florida, but were stopped by the local militia.

Blacks in the tobacco-growing Chesapeake region had a somewhat easier lot. Farms were closer together, permitting more frequent contact with friends and relatives, and tobacco was a less physically demanding crop than those of the deeper South. By about 1740 the proportion of females in the slave population had begun to rise, making family life possible. The increasing presence of native-born Afro-Americans also contributed to the growth of a stable and distinctive slave culture, a mixture of African and American elements of speech, religion, and folkways.

Fears of black rebellion plagued the whites. Some of the colonial legislatures, notably South Carolina's in 1760, sensed the dangers present in a heavy concentration of rebellious slaves, and attempted to restrict or halt their importation. But the British authorities vetoed all such efforts. Many colonials looked upon this veto as a callous disregard of their welfare, although it was done primarily in the interests of imperial policy and of the British and New England slave trade. Thomas Jefferson, himself a slaveholder, assailed such vetoes in an early draft of the Declaration of Independence, but his proposed clause was finally dropped, largely out of regard for Southern sensibilities.

A few of the blacks had been freed, but the vast majority were condemned to a life under the lash. The universal passion for freedom vented itself during the colonial era in numerous cases of arson, murder, and insurrection or near-insurrection. A slave revolt erupted in New York City in 1712 which cost the lives of a dozen whites and caused the execution of twenty-one blacks, some of them burned at the stake over a slow fire. Yet the Africans made a significant contribution to America's early development through their labor, chiefly the sweaty toil of clearing swamps, grubbing out trees, and other menial tasks. A few of them were permitted to become artisans—carpenters, bricklayers, tanners—thus refuting the common prejudice that black people lacked the intelligence to perform skilled labor.

Clerics, Physicians, and Jurists

Most honored of the professions was the Christian ministry. In 1775 clergymen wielded less influence than in the early days of Massachusetts, when fanaticism had burned more fiercely. But they still occupied a position of high prestige.

Most physicians, on the other hand, were poorly trained and not highly esteemed. Not until 1765 was the first medical school established, although European centers attracted some students. Aspiring young doctors served for a while as apprentices to older practitioners, and were then turned loose on their "victims." Bleeding was a favorite and often fatal remedy; when the physician was not available, a barber was often summoned.

Plagues were a constant nightmare. Especially dreaded was smallpox (one of Europe's "gifts" to the New World), which afflicted one out of five persons, including the heavily pockmarked George Washington. A crude form of inoculation was introduced in 1721, despite the objections of many physicians and some of the clergy, who opposed tampering with the will of God. Powdered dried toad was a favorite prescription for smallpox. Diphtheria was also a deadly killer, especially of young people. One epidemic in the 1730s took the lives of thousands. This grim reminder of their mortality may have helped to prepare many colonists in their hearts and minds for the religious revival that was soon to sweep them up.

> On doctors and medicine Benjamin Franklin's *Poor Richard's Almanack* offered some homely advice:
>
> "God heals and the doctor takes the fee."
>
> "He's the best physician that knows the worthlessness of most medicines."
>
> "Don't go to the doctor with every distemper,
> nor to the lawyer with every quarrel,
> nor to the pot for every thirst."

At first the law profession was not favorably regarded. In this pioneering society, which required much honest manual labor, the parties to a dispute often presented their own cases in court. Lawyers were commonly regarded as noisy windbags or troublemaking rogues; an early Connecticut law classed them with drunkards and brothel keepers. When future President John Adams was a young law student, the father of the woman whom he eventually married frowned upon him as a suitor.

By about 1750, seaboard society had passed the pioneering stage, and trained attorneys were generally recognized as useful. Able to defend colonial rights against the Crown on legal grounds, lawyers like the eloquent James Otis and the flaming Patrick Henry took the lead in the agitation that led to revolt. Other lawyer-orators played hardly less important roles in forging new constitutions and in serving in representative bodies.

Workaday America

Agriculture was the leading industry, involving about 90 percent of the people. Cheap land continued to attract farmers. An acre of virgin soil cost about what an American carpenter could earn in one day as wages, which were roughly three times those of his European counterpart. Tobacco continued to be the staple crop in Maryland and Virginia. The fertile Middle ("Bread") Colonies produced large quantities of grain, and by 1759 New York alone was exporting 80,000 barrels of flour a year. Seemingly the farmer had only to tickle the soil with a hoe and it would laugh with a harvest.

COLONIAL TRADE PATTERNS, c. 1770

Future President John Adams noted about this time that "the commerce of the West Indies is a part of the American system of commerce. They can neither do without us, nor we without them. The Creator has placed us upon the globe in such a situation that we have occasion for each other."

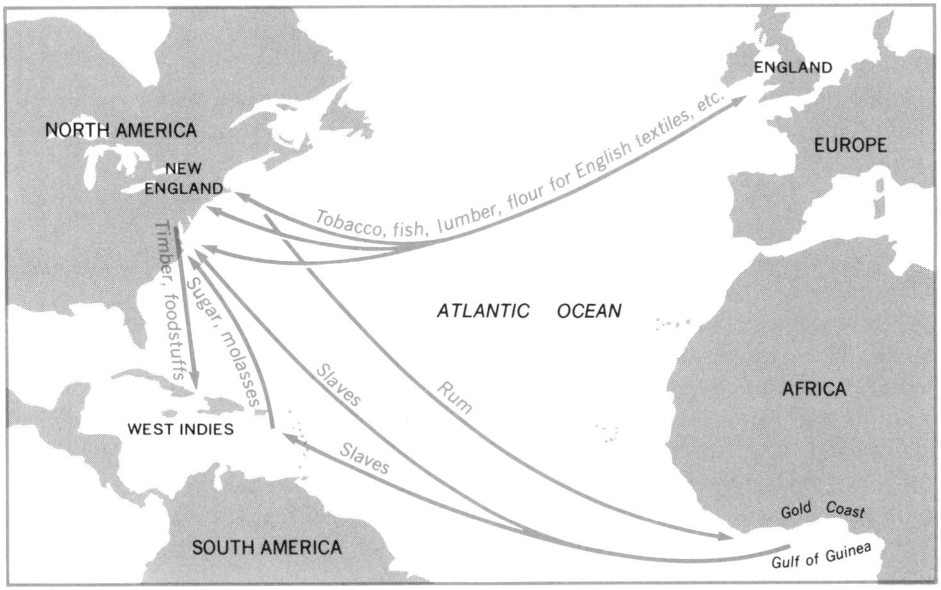

Fishing (including whaling), though ranking far below agriculture, was rewarding. Pursued in all the colonies, this harvesting of the sea was a major industry in New England, which exported smelly shiploads of dried cod to the Catholic countries of Europe. The fishing fleet also stimulated shipbuilding and served as a nursery for the seamen who manned the navy and merchant marine.

A bustling commerce, both coastwise and overseas, enriched all the colonies, especially the New England group, New York, and Pennsylvania. Commercial ventures and land speculation, in the absence of later get-rich-quick schemes, were the surest avenues to speedy wealth. Yankee seamen were famous in many climes not only as skilled mariners but as tight-fisted traders.* They provisioned the Caribbean sugar islands with food and forest products. They hauled Spanish and Portuguese gold, wine, and oranges to London, to be exchanged for industrial goods, which were then sold for a juicy profit in America.

The so-called triangular trade was infamously profitable, though small in relation to total colonial commerce. A skipper, for example, would leave a New England port with a cargo of rum and sail to the Gold Coast of Africa. Bartering the fiery liquor with African chiefs for captured African slaves, he would proceed to the West Indies with his screaming and suffocating cargo sardined below deck. There he would exchange the survivors for molasses, which he would then carry to New England, where it would be distilled into rum. He would then repeat the trip, making a handsome profit on each leg of the triangle.

Manufacturing in the colonies was of only secondary importance, although there was a surprising variety of small enterprises. As a rule, workmen could get ahead faster in soil-rich America by tilling the land. Huge quantities of "kill devil" rum were distilled in Rhode Island and Massachusetts; and even some of the "elect of the Lord" developed an overfondness for it. Handsome beaver hats were manufactured in quantity, despite British restrictions. Smoking iron forges, including Pennsylvania's Valley Forge, likewise dotted the land, and in fact were more numerous in 1775, though generally smaller, than those of England. In addition, household manufacturing, including spinning and weaving by womenfolk, added up to an impressive output. As in all pioneering countries, strong-backed laborers and

*Sea-going Yankees also found time for play, as shown in John Greenwood's painting of "Sea Captains Carousing in Surinam" in the color portfolio.

skilled craftsmen were scarce and highly prized. In early Virginia a carpenter who had committed a murder was freed because he was needed.

Lumbering was perhaps the most important single manufacturing activity. Countless cartloads of virgin timber were consumed by shipbuilders, at first chiefly in New England, and then elsewhere in the colonies. By 1770 about 400 vessels of assorted sizes were splashing down the ways each year, and about one-third of the British merchant marine was American-built.

Colonial naval stores—such as tar, pitch, rosin, and turpentine—were highly valued, for Britannia was anxious to gain and retain a mastery of the seas. London offered generous bounties to stimulate production of these items; otherwise Britain would have to turn to the uncertain and possibly hostile Baltic areas. Towering trees, ideal as masts for His Majesty's Navy, were marked with the King's broad arrow for future use. The luckless colonial who was caught cutting down this reserved timber was subject to a fine. Even though there were countless unreserved trees and the ones marked were being saved for the common defense, this shackle on free enterprise engendered considerable bitterness.

Americans held an important flank of a thriving, many-sided Atlantic economy by the dawn of the 18th Century. Yet strains appeared in this complex network as early as the 1730s. Fast-breeding Americans demanded more and more English products—yet the slow-growing English population early reached the saturation point for absorbing imports from America. How, then, could the colonists sell the goods to make the money to buy what they wanted in the mother country? The answer was obvious: by seeking foreign (non-English) markets.

By the eve of the revolution the bulk of Chesapeake tobacco was filling pipes in France and other continental countries, though it passed through the hands of English re-exporters, who took a slice of the profits. More important was the trade with the West Indies, especially the French islands. West Indian purchases of North American timber and foodstuffs provided the crucial cash for the colonists to continue to make their own purchases in England. In 1733, bowing to pressure from influential British West Indian planters, Parliament passed the Molasses Act, aimed at squelching North American trade with the *French* West Indies. If successful, this scheme would have struck a crippling blow to American international trade, and to the colonists' standard of living. American merchants responded by bribing and smuggling their way around the law. Thus was foreshadowed the impending imperial crisis, when headstrong Americans would revolt rather than submit to the dictates of a far-off Parliament, apparently bent on destroying their very livelihood.

Horsepower and Sailpower

All sprawling and sparsely populated pioneer communities are cursed with oppressive problems of transportation. America, with a scarcity of both money and manpower, was no exception.

Not until the 1700s were there roads connecting even the major cities, and these dirt thoroughfares were treacherously poor. A wayfarer could have rumbled along more rapidly over the Roman highways in the days of Julius Caesar, nearly 2,000 years earlier. It actually took twenty-nine days for the news of the Declaration of Independence—the story of the year—to reach Charleston from Philadelphia.

Roads were often clouds of dust in the summer and quagmires of mud in the winter. Stagecoach travelers braved such additional dangers as tree-strewn roads, rickety bridges, carriage overturns, and runaway horses. A man venturesome

Stagecoach Advertisement, 1781

Early Colonial Mail Carrier Trumpeting His Arrival

enough to journey from Philadelphia to New York, for example, would not think it amiss to make his will and assemble his family for prayers before departing.

Where man-made roads were wretched, heavy reliance was placed on God-grooved waterways. Population tended to cluster along the banks of navigable rivers. There was also much coastwise traffic, and although it was slow and undependable, it was relatively cheap and pleasant.

Taverns sprang up along the main routes of travel, as well as in the cities. Their attractions customarily included such items as bowling alleys, pool tables, bars, and gambling equipment. Before a cheerful, roaring log fire all social classes would mingle, including the village loafers and drunks. The tavern was yet another cradle of democracy.

Gossips also gathered at the taverns, which were clearinghouses of information, misinformation, and rumor—frequently stimulated by alcoholic refreshment and impassioned political talk. A successful politician, like the wire-pulling Samuel Adams, was often a man who had a large alehouse acquaintance in places like Boston's Green Dragon Tavern. Taverns were important in crystallizing public opinion, and proved to be hotbeds of agitation as the Revolutionary movement gathered momentum.

An intercolonial postal system was established by the mid-1700s, although private couriers remained. Some mail was handled on credit. Service was slow and infrequent, and secrecy was problematical. Mail carriers, serving long routes, would sometimes pass the time by reading the letters entrusted to their care.

Religious Ferment and the Great Awakening

Religion still had a fiery grip on the people. Sunday customs generally were observed with rigidity, church attendance was faithful (though often compulsory), and long-winded sermons were absorbed with rapt attention. The Bible was almost universally read as the infallible word of God, supplemented by such religious books as Bunyan's *Pilgrim's Progress* and Baxter's *Call to the Unconverted.* The famed *New England Primer* pounded home such precepts as:

> Christ crucify'd,
> For Sinners dy'd.

Yet the life of the spirit was not the all-absorbing concern in 1775 that it had been in the heyday of the Puritan fathers. Existence in the 1600s had been harsh, and religion had taken on the stern character of its pioneer surroundings. But as men attained more ease and luxury, the appeal of a fire and brimstone religion became less attractive, and fanaticism faded. Decidedly more liberal doctrines were sharply challenging Calvinism. They proclaimed that human beings were not necessarily predestined to damnation, but might save themselves by repentance and good works. Many of the unorthodox worshipers even argued that a spiritual conversion was not necessary for church

Franklin's *Poor Richard's Almanack* contained such thoughts on religion as:

"A good example is the best sermon."

"Many have quarreled about religion that never practiced it."

"Serving God is doing good to man, but praying is thought an easier service, and therefore more generally chosen."

"How many observe Christ's birthday; how few his precepts! O! 'tis easier to keep holidays than commandments."

membership, and some of the orthodox churches grudgingly made concessions to this new heresy.

In the 1730s and 1740s a reaction to this move away from hell-fire religion exploded into the Great Awakening—a rousing series of mass revivals that began in Europe and spread throughout America. Revivalist theologians (or "New Lights," as they were called) dwelt on man's evil and helpless nature. Revivalist ministers developed an electrifying new style of preaching, heaping abuse on sinners and scaring enormous audiences with emotional appeals. One preacher cackled hideously in the faces of hapless wrongdoers. Another, naked to the waist, leaped frantically about in the light of flickering torches.

The foremost Great Awakener in America was a tall, delicate, and intellectual Massachusetts theologian and preacher, Jonathan Edwards ("the Artist of Damnation"). He proclaimed with burning conviction the need for a complete conversion from sin to righteousness. Warming to his subject, he would paint in lurid detail the landscape of hell and the eternal torments of the damned. "Sinners in the Hands of an Angry God" was the title of one of his most famous sermons. He believed that hell was "paved with the skulls of unbaptized children."

George Whitefield, a former alehouse attendant, was a less intellectual but more emotional English pulpit-thumper. His magnificent voice could be heard by many thousands of enthralled listeners in an open field, and his eloquence caused the skeptical and thrifty Benjamin Franklin to empty his pockets into the collection plate. During these roaring revival meetings, countless sinners professed conversion, while hundreds of the "saved" groaned, shrieked, or rolled in the snow from religious excitation.

> Jonathan Edwards preached hell-fire, notably in one famous sermon: "The God that holds you over the pit of hell, much as one holds a spider or some loathsome insect over the fire, abhors you, and is dreadfully provoked. His wrath toward you burns like fire; he looks upon you as worthy of nothing else but to be cast into the fire."

George Whitefield (1714–1770). A great open-air revivalist, he was a leader in England of the Calvinistic Methodist Church. He made seven trips to America.

The Great Awakening touched off the first significant battle in America between fundamentalist evangelism and liberalism in religion. The more cautious "Old Light" clergy were deeply skeptical of the theatrical antics of the new revivalists. Congregationalists and Presbyterians split over this issue, and many of the believers in religious conversion went over to the Baptists and other more emotional sects. This denominational spin-off, which weakened the hold of the old-line clergy, also made for more democratic control.

Significantly, the Great Awakening was the first spontaneous mass movement of the American people. As such, it tended to break down sectional boundaries as well as denominational lines. It foreshadowed revolutionary new departures elsewhere, even in governmental control. The King would have done well to keep a more careful eye on his colonies.

Estimated Religious Census, 1775

Name	*Number*	*Chief Locale*
Congregationalists	575,000	New England
Anglicans	500,000	N.Y., South
Presbyterians	410,000	Frontier
German Churches (incl. Lutheran)	200,000	Penn.
Dutch Reformed	75,000	N.Y., N.J.
Quakers	40,000	Penn., N.J., Del.
Baptists	25,000	R.I., Penn., N.J., Del.
Roman Catholics	25,000	Md., Penn.
Methodists	5,000	Scattered
Jews	2,000	N.Y., R.I.
ESTIMATED TOTAL MEMBERSHIP	1,857,000	
ESTIMATED TOTAL POPULATION	2,493,000	
PERCENTAGE CHURCH MEMBERS	74%	

Dominant Denominations

Two "established" or tax-supported churches were conspicuous in 1775: the Anglican and the Congregational. A considerable segment of the population, surprisingly enough, did not worship in any church. And in those colonies where there was an "established" religion, only a minority of the people belonged to it.

The Church of England, whose members were commonly called Anglicans, became the official faith in Georgia, North and South Carolina, Virginia, Maryland, and a part of New York. Established also in England, it served in America as a major prop of kingly authority. British officials naturally made vigorous efforts to impose it on additional colonies, but they ran into a stone wall of opposition.

In America the Anglican Church fell distressingly short of its promise. Secure and self-satisfied, like the parent establishment in England, it clung to a faith that was less fierce and more worldly than the religion of Puritanical New England. Sermons were shorter; hell was less scorching; and amusements, like Virginia fox hunting, were less frowned upon. So dismal was the reputation of the Anglican clergy in 17th-Century Virginia that the College of William and Mary was founded in 1693 to train a better class of clerics.

The influential Congregational Church, which had grown out of the Puritan Church, was formally established in all the New England colonies, except independent-minded Rhode Island. At first Massachusetts taxed all residents to support Congregationalism, but later relented and exempted members of other well-known denominations. Presbyterianism, though closely associated with Congregationalism, was never made official in any of the colonies.

Ministers of the gospel, turning from the Bible to this sinful world, increasingly grappled with burning political issues. As the early rumblings of

Established (Tax-Supported) Churches in the Colonies, 1775

Colonies	*Churches*	*Year Disestablished*
Mass. (incl. Me.)	Congregational	1833
Connecticut	Congregational	1818
New Hampshire	Congregational	1819
New York	Anglican (in N.Y. City and three neighboring counties)	1777
Maryland	Anglican	1777
Virginia	Anglican	1786
North Carolina	Anglican	1776
South Carolina	Anglican	1778
Georgia	Anglican	1777
Rhode Island	None	
New Jersey	None	
Delaware	None	
Pennsylvania	None	

Note the persistence of the Congregational establishment in New England.

revolution against the British Crown could be heard, sedition flowed freely from pulpits. Presbyterianism, Congregationalism, and Rebellion were triplets. Many of the leading Anglican clergymen, aware of what side their tax-provided bread was buttered on, naturally supported their King.

Anglicans in the New World were seriously handicapped by not having a resident bishop, whose presence would be convenient for the ordination of young ministers. American students of Anglican theology had to travel to England to be ordained. On the eve of the Revolution there was serious talk of creating an American bishopric, but the scheme was violently opposed by many non-Anglicans, who feared a tightening of the royal reins. This controversy poured holy oil on the smoldering fires of rebellion.

Religious toleration had indeed made enormous strides in America, at least when compared with halting steps abroad. Roman Catholics were still generally discriminated against, as in England, even in office holding. But there were fewer Catholics in America, and hence the anti-papist laws were less severe and less strictly enforced. In general, a man could worship—or not worship—as he pleased.

Schools and Colleges

A time-honored English ideal regarded education as a boon reserved for the aristocratic few, not for the unwashed many. Education should be for leadership, not citizenship, and primarily for the male sex. Only slowly and painfully did the colonials break the chains of these ancient restrictions.

> John Adams, the future second President, once wrote to his wife:
>
> "The education of our children is never out of my mind. Train them to virtue. Habituate them to industry, activity, and spirit. . . . For God's sake make your children *hardy, active*, and *industrious*; for strength, activity, and industry will be their only resource and dependence."

Puritan New England, largely for religious reasons, was more zealously interested in education than any other section. Dominated by the Congregational Church, it stressed the need for Bible reading by the individual worshiper. The primary goal of the clergy was to make good Christians rather than good citizens. A more secular approach was evident late in the 18th Century, when some children were warned:

> He who ne'er learns his A.B.C.
> Forever will a blockhead be.
> But he who learns his letters fair
> Shall have a coach to take the air.

Education, principally for boys, flourished almost from the outset in New England. Population was compact and boasted an impressive number of graduates from the English universities, especially Cambridge, the intellectual center of England's Puritanism. New Englanders, at a relatively early date, established primary and secondary schools, which varied widely in the quality of instruction and in the length of time that their doors remained open each year. Back-straining farm labor drained much of the youth's time and energy.

Fairly adequate primary and secondary schools were also hammering knowledge into the heads of reluctant "scholars" in the Middle Colonies and in the South. Some of these institutions were tax-supported; others were privately operated. The South, with its white and black population diffused over wide areas, was severely handicapped in attempting to establish an effective school system. Wealthy families leaned heavily on private tutors.

The general atmosphere in the colonial schools and colleges continued grim and gloomy. Most of the emphasis was placed on religion and on the classical languages, Latin and Greek. The stress was not on experiment and reason, but on doctrine and dogma. The age was one of orthodoxy, and independence of thinking was discouraged. Disci-

Harvard College About 1770. Engraving by Paul Revere, Boston silversmith of "midnight ride" fame. (Harvard University.)

pline was severe, with many a mettlesome lad being sadistically "birched" with a switch cut from a birch tree. Sometimes punishment was inflicted by an indentured-servant teacher, who could himself be whipped for his failures as a worker, and who therefore was not inclined to spare the rod.

College education was regarded—at least at first in New England—as more important than instruction in the ABCs. Churches would wither if a new crop of ministers was not trained to lead the spiritual flocks. Many well-to-do families, especially in the South, sent their boys abroad to English institutions.

For purposes of convenience and economy, nine local colleges were planted during the colonial era. Student bodies were small, numbering about 200 boys at the most; and at one time a few lads as young as eleven were admitted to Harvard. Instruction was poor by present-day standards. The curriculum was still heavily loaded with theology and the "dead" languages, although by 1750 there was a distinct trend toward "live" languages and other modern subjects. A significant contribution was made by Benjamin Franklin, who had a large hand in launching what became the University of Pennsylvania, the first American college free from denominational control.

Culture in the Backwoods

The dawn-to-dusk toil of pioneer life left little vitality or aptitude for artistic effort. Americans were too busy chopping down trees to sit around painting landscapes, especially when a hostile Indian might burst from a nearby bush. There was no strong esthetic tradition; many clergymen, in fact, regarded art as an invention of the Devil.

As the colonists gradually acquired some wealth and leisure, their surplus energy went into religious and political leadership, not art. The materialistic atmosphere was not favorable to artistic endeavor. One famous painter, John

Colonial Colleges

Name	*Original Name (If Different)*	*Location*	*Opened or Founded*	*Denomination*
1. Harvard		Cambridge, Mass.	1636	Congregational
2. William and Mary		Williamsburg, Va.	1693	Anglican
3. Yale		New Haven, Conn.	1701	Congregational
4. Princeton	College of New Jersey	Princeton, N.J.	1746	Presbyterian
5. Pennsylvania	The Academy	Philadelphia	1751	Nonsectarian
6. Columbia	King's College	New York City	1754	Anglican
7. Brown	Rhode Island College	Providence, R.I.	1764	Baptist
8. Rutgers	Queen's College	New Brunswick, N.J.	1766	Dutch Reformed
9. Dartmouth (begun as an Indian missionary school.)		Hanover, N.H.	1769	Congregational

Trumbull of Connecticut (1756–1843), was discouraged in his youth by his father with the chilling remark, "Connecticut is not Athens." Charles W. Peale (1741–1827), best known for his portraits of George Washington, ran a museum, stuffed birds, and practiced dentistry. Gifted Benjamin West (1738–1820) and precocious John S. Copley* (1738–1815) succeeded in their ambition to become famous painters, but they had to go to England to complete their training. Only there could they find subjects who had the leisure to sit for their portraits, and the money to pay handsomely for them. Copley was regarded as a Loyalist during the Revolutionary War, while West, a close friend of George III and official court painter, was buried in London's St. Paul's Cathedral.

Architecture was largely imported from the Old World, and modified to meet the peculiar climatic and religious conditions of the New World. Even the lowly log cabin was apparently borrowed from Sweden. The red-bricked Georgian style, so common in the pre-Revolutionary decades, was introduced about 1720, and is best exemplified by the beauty of now-restored Williamsburg, Virginia.

Colonial literature, like art, was generally undistinguished, and for much the same reasons. Among numerous handicaps, it was dominated by theology, although many sermons had literary quality. What little writing emerged is known only to specialists, with several noteworthy exceptions.

Of unusual interest is the precocious black poetess Phillis Wheatley (c. 1753–1784), a slave girl brought to Boston at age eight and never formally educated. Taken to England when twenty years of age, she published a book of verse, and subsequently wrote other polished poems that revealed the influence of Alexander Pope. She died when about thirty. Her verse compares favorably with the best of the poetry-poor colonial period, but the remarkable fact is that, considering her grave handicaps, she could write any poetry at all.

Greatest of the "Great Awakeners" was Jonathan Edwards, who customarily arose at four o'clock to put in a fourteen-hour day. His religious writings were as numerous as they were hairsplitting, and established him as the finest theological mind ever produced in America. Some of his treatises, rivaling those of John Calvin in explaining Calvinism, were widely read in Presbyterian Scotland. His most famous work, *On the Freedom of the Will,* was perhaps the first American book of world importance. It was translated into many languages, including Arabic.

Many-sided Benjamin Franklin, often called "the first civilized American," also shone as a literary light. Although his autobiography is now a classic, he was best known to his contemporaries for *Poor Richard's Almanack*, which he edited from 1732 to 1758. This famous publication, containing many pithy sayings culled from the thinkers of the ages, emphasized such homespun virtues as thrift, industry, morality, and common sense. Examples are: "What maintains one vice would bring up two children"; "Plough deep while sluggards sleep"; "Honesty is the best policy"; and "Fish and visitors stink in three days." "Poor Richard" was well known in Europe and was more widely read in America than anything else, except the Bible. As a teacher of both old and young, Franklin's influence in shaping American character was incalculable. His down-to-earth approach to life did much to offset the influence of clergymen like Jonathan Edwards.

Science, rising above the shackles of theology and superstition, was making some progress, though lagging behind the Old World. A few botanists, mathematicians, and astronomers had won some repute, but Benjamin Franklin was perhaps the only first-rank scientist produced in the American colonies. His spectacular but dangerous experiments with electricity, includ-

*See color portfolio for painting by Copley.

ing the kite-flying episode, won him numerous honors in Europe. But his mind had a practical turn, and among his numerous inventions were bifocal spectacles and the highly efficient Franklin stove. His lightning rod, not surprisingly, was condemned by the less liberal clergy as "presuming on God" by attempting to control the "artillery of the heavens."

Pioneer Presses

Stump-grubbing Americans were too poor to buy quantities of books and too busy to read them. One South Carolina merchant in 1744 advertised the arrival of a shipment of "printed books, Pictures, Maps, and Pickles." A few private libraries of fair size could be found, especially among the clergy. The Byrd family of Virginia enjoyed perhaps the largest collection in the colonies, consisting of about 4,000 volumes. Bustling Benjamin Franklin established in Philadelphia the first privately supported circulating library in America; and by 1776 there were about fifty public libraries and collections supported by subscription.

Hand-operated printing presses were active in running off pamphlets, leaflets, and journals. On the eve of the Revolution there were about forty colonial newspapers, chiefly weeklies which consisted of a single large sheet folded once. Columns ran heavily to dull essays, frequently signed with such pseudonyms as Cicero, Philosophicus, and Pro Bono Publico (for the public good). The "news" often lagged many weeks behind the event, especially in the case of overseas happenings, in which the colonials were deeply interested. Newspapers proved to be a powerful agency for airing colonial grievances and building up opposition to British control.

> Andrew Hamilton concluded his eloquent plea in the Zenger case with these words: "The question before the court and you, gentlemen of the jury, is not of small nor private concern. It is not the cause of a poor printer, nor of New York alone, which you are now trying. No! It may, in its consequence, affect every freeman that lives under a British government on the main[land] of America. It is the best cause. It is the cause of liberty."

A celebrated legal case, in 1734–1735, involved John Peter Zenger, a newspaper printer. Significantly, the case arose in New York, reflecting the tumultuous give-and-take of politics in the middle colonies, where so many different ethnic groups jostled against one another. Zenger's newspaper had assailed the corrupt royal governor. Charged with seditious libel, the accused was haled into court, where he was defended by a distinguished Philadelphia lawyer, Andrew Hamilton, then nearly eighty. Zenger argued that he had printed the truth, while the bewigged royal chief justice ruled that the mere fact of printing, irrespective of the truth, was enough to convict. Yet the jury, swayed by the eloquence of Hamilton, defied the red-robed judges and daringly returned a verdict of "not guilty." Cheers burst from the spectators.

The Zenger decision was epochal. It pointed the way to the kind of freedom of expression required by the diverse society that was colonial New York, and that all America was to become. Though contrary to existing law and not accepted by other royal judges, in time it helped set a precedent against judicial tyranny in libel suits. Newspaper editors had something of a burden lifted from their backs, even though complete freedom of the press was unknown during the pre-Revolutionary era.

The Great Game of Politics

American colonials may have been backward in natural or physical science, but they were making noteworthy contributions to political science.

The thirteen colonial governments presented a varied structure. By 1775, eight of the colonies had royal governors, who were appointed by the King. Three were under proprietors who themselves chose the governors—Maryland, Pennsylvania, and Delaware. And two—Connecticut and Rhode Island—elected their own governors under self-governing charters.

Practically every colony utilized a two-house legislative body. The upper house, or council, was normally appointed by the Crown in the royal colonies, and by the proprietor in the proprietary colonies. It was chosen by the voters in the self-governing colonies. The lower house, as the popular branch, was elected by the people—or rather by those persons who owned enough property to qualify as voters. In several of the colonies, the back-country elements were seriously underrepresented, and they hated the ruling colonial clique perhaps more than they did kingly authority. Legislatures, in which the people enjoyed direct representation, voted such taxes as they chose for the necessary expenses of colonial government. Self-taxation through representation was a precious privilege which Americans had come to cherish above most others.

Governors appointed by the King were generally able men, sometimes outstanding figures, and their households were an important outcropping of Europe's cultural frontier. But the appointees were sometimes incompetent or corrupt, and included broken-down politicians badly in need of jobs. The worst of the group was impoverished Lord Cornbury, first cousin of Queen Anne, who was made governor of New York and New Jersey in 1702. He proved to be a drunkard, a spendthrift, a grafter, an embezzler, a religious bigot, and a vain fool, especially when he appeared in public dressed like a woman. Even the best of the King's appointees had trouble with the colonial legislatures, basically because the royal governor embodied a bothersome transatlantic authority some 3,000 miles away.

But the colonial assemblies were by no means defenseless. Some of them employed the trick of withholding the governor's salary unless he yielded to their wishes. He was normally in need of money—otherwise he would not have come to this God-forsaken country—so the power of the purse usually forced him to terms. But one governor of North Carolina died with his salary eleven years in arrears.

Junius, the pseudonym for a critic (or critics) of the British government from 1768 to 1772, published a pointed barb in criticizing one new appointee: "It was not Virginia that wanted a governor but a court favorite that wanted a salary."

The London government, in leaving the colonial governor to the tender mercies of the legislature, was guilty of poor administration. In the interests of simple efficiency the British authorities should have arranged to pay him from independent sources. As events turned out, control over the purse by the colonial legislatures led to prolonged bickering, which proved to be one of the persistent irritants that generated a spirit of revolt.*

Administration at the local level was also varied. County government remained the rule in the plantation South; town-meeting government predominated in New England; and a modification of the two developed in the Middle Colonies. In the town meeting, with its open discussion and open voting, direct democracy functioned at its best. In this unrivaled cradle of self-government, Americans learned to cherish their privileges and exercise their duties as citizens of the New World commonwealths.

Yet the ballot was by no means a birthright.

*Parliament finally arranged for separate payment of the governors through the Townshend taxes of 1767, but by then the colonials were in such an ugly mood over taxation that this innovation only added fresh fuel to the flames.

Heated Public Gathering. The spirit of the New England town meeting. (Library of Congress.)

Religious or property qualifications for voting, with even stiffer qualifications for office holding, existed in all the colonies in 1775. The privileged upper classes, fearful of democratic excesses, were unwilling to grant the ballot to every "biped of the forest." Perhaps half of the adult white males were thus disfranchised. But because of the ease of acquiring land and thus satisfying property requirements, the right to vote was not beyond the reach of most industrious and enterprising colonials.

By 1775 America was not yet a true democracy—socially, economically, or politically. But it was far more democratic than England and Europe. Colonial institutions were giving freer rein to the democratic ideals of tolerance, educational advantages, equality of economic opportunity, freedom of speech, freedom of the press, freedom of assembly, and representative government. And these democratic seeds, planted in rich soil, were to bring forth a lush harvest in later years.

Colonial Folkways

Everyday life in the colonies may now seem glamorous, especially as reflected in antique shops. But judged by modern standards, it was drab and tedious. For the mass of the people, the labor was heavy and constant—from daybreak to backbreak.

Food was plentiful, though the diet could be coarse and monotonous. Americans probably ate more bountifully, especially of meat, than any people in the Old World. Lazy or sickly was the man who could not manage to fill his stomach.

Basic comforts now taken for granted were lacking. Churches were not heated at all, except for charcoal foot-warmers which the womenfolk carried. During the frigid New England winters, the preaching of hell-fire may not have seemed altogether unattractive. Drafty homes were poorly heated, chiefly by inefficient fireplaces. There was no running water in the houses, no plumbing, and probably not a single bathtub in all colonial America. Flickering lights were inadequate, for illumination was provided by candles and whale-oil lamps. Garbage disposal was primitive. Long-snouted hogs customarily ranged the streets to consume refuse, while buzzards, protected by law, flapped greedily over tidbits of waste.

Amusement was eagerly pursued where time and custom permitted. The militia assembled periodically for "musters," which consisted of several days of drilling, liberally interspersed with merrymaking and eyeing the girls. On the frontier, pleasure was often combined with work at house-raisings, quilting bees, husking bees, and apple parings. Funerals and weddings everywhere afforded opportunities for social gatherings, which customarily involved the swilling of much strong liquor.

Winter sports were common in the North, while in the South card playing, horse racing, cockfighting, and fox hunting were favorite pastimes. George Washington, not surprisingly, was a superb rider. In the non-Puritanical South, dancing was the rage—jigs, square dances, the Virginia reel—and the agile Washington could swing his fair partner with the best of them.

Other diversions beckoned. Lotteries were universally approved, even by the clergy, and were used to raise money for churches and colleges, including Harvard. Stage plays became popular in the South, but were disapproved in the Quaker and Puritan colonies, and in some places were even forbidden by law. Many New England clergymen regarded play-acting as time-consuming and immoral; they preferred religious lectures, from which their flocks derived much spiritual satisfaction.

Holidays were everywhere celebrated, but Christmas was frowned upon in New England as an offensive reminder of "Popery." "Yuletide is fooltide" was a common Puritan sneer. Thanksgiving Day came to be a truly American festival, for it combined thanks to God with an opportunity for jollification, gorging, and guzzling.

Early lumbering. An 18th Century sawmill in colonial New York. (The William L. Clements Library.)

England's American colonists in 1775 were a remarkable people: restless, energetic, ambitious, resourceful, ingenious, and independent-minded. With every passing year they were less willing to bow their necks to the yoke of overseas authority. They were like a fast-growing and well-muscled farm boy who is coming of age, and who expects to be treated as an adult and not as a lackey. With a boundless continent before them, with impressive pioneer achievements behind them, and with an astonishing fertility within them, they had caught a vision of their destiny and were preparing to grasp it. Woe unto him who should try to thwart them!

VARYING VIEWPOINTS

It has always been difficult to view the history of the 18th Century in any way other than as a prelude to the Revolution of 1776. Historians of the "imperial school" used to emphasize the transatlantic economic motifs of the period as an overture to revolution. But as in so many other areas of American history, recent scholars have increasingly stressed social history. They now want to know the "preconditions" of American society in the mid-18th Century so as to answer the key question: Just how "revolutionary" was the Revolution? Thus issues like social structure, extent of the suffrage, and distribution of wealth have in recent years taken on increased significance.

SELECT READINGS

Social history is painted with broad strokes in J. Henretta, *The Evolution of American Society, 1700–1815* (1973), in D. Boorstin, *The Americans: The Colonial Experience* (1958), and in L. B. Wright, *The Cultural Life of the American Colonies, 1607–1763* (1957). Richard Hofstadter takes a suggestive snapshot view in *America at 1750* (1971). Indispensable as well as entertaining is Benjamin Franklin's classic *Autobiography;* "Poor Richard's" best biographer is still C. Van Doren, *Benjamin Franklin* (1938). Population trends are detailed in E. B. Greene and V. Harrington, *American Population before the Federal Census of 1790* (1932), and in R. V. Wells, *The Population of the British Colonies in America before 1776* (1975). Black "immigrants" are studied in P. Curtin, *The African Slave Trade: A Census* (1969), indentured servants, in A. E. Smith, *Colonists in Bondage* (1947), and colonial immigration in general, in the early portions of Maldwyn Jones, *American Immigration* (1960). J. T. Main astutely analyzes *The Social Structure of Revolutionary America, 1763–1788* (1965). Access to the ballot is scrutinized in C. Williamson, *American Suffrage: From Property to Democracy, 1760–1860* (1961). C. Bridenbaugh looks closely at social history in *Myths and Realities* (1952), *Cities in the Wilderness* (1938), and *Cities in Revolt* (1955). See the same author's *Fat Mutton and Liberty of Conscience* (1976). The toiling classes are probed in R. B. Morris, *Government and Labor in Early America* (1946), and in G. W. Mullin, *Flight and Rebellion: Slave Resistance in Eighteenth-Century Virginia* (1972). Large-scale economic patterns are traced in R. Davis, *Rise of the Atlantic Economies* (1973), and in Stuart Bruchey, *The Roots of American Economic Growth, 1607–1861* (1965). Transatlantic cultural relations are treated in Michael Kraus, *The Atlantic Civilization: Eighteenth-Century Origins* (1949). Religious revivalism is chronicled in E. S. Gaustad, *The Great Awakening in New England* (1957), and the broad social implications of the Awakening are analyzed in R. L. Bushman, *From Puritan to Yankee: Character and Social Order in Connecticut, 1690–1765* (1967). Consult also J. M. Bumsted and J. E. Van de Wetering, *What Must I Do To Be Saved?*

(1976). Cultural history is imaginatively presented in H. M. Jones, *O Strange New World: American Culture in the Formative Years* (1964). Comprehensive is Henry May, *The Enlightenment in America* (1976). The sometimes heroic dedication to education is portrayed by L. Cremin, *American Education: The Colonial Experience, 1607–1783* (1970), and the general social implications of the early educational system are studied in J. Axtell, *School upon a Hill* (1974). Colonial politics are interpreted in a most suggestive way in B. Bailyn, *The Origins of American Politics* (1965). More fine-grained local studies are R. E. and B. K. Brown, *Virginia 1705–1786: Democracy or Aristocracy?* (1964), P. Bonomi, *A Factious People: Politics and Society in Colonial New York* (1971), James T. Lemon, *The Best Poor Man's Country* (1972), which deals with Pennsylvania, and Daniel Blake Smith, *Inside the Great House: Planter Family Life in Eighteenth-Century Chesapeake Society* (1980). Broader is Richard B. Davis, *Intellectual Life in the Colonial South, 1585–1763* (3 vols., 1978).

5

The Road to Revolution

The Revolution was effected before the war commenced. The Revolution was in the minds and hearts of the people.

JOHN ADAMS, 1818

The Deep Roots of Revolution

In a broad sense, the American Revolution was not the same thing as the American War of Independence. The war itself lasted only eight years. But the revolution lasted over a century and a half, and began when the first permanent English settlers set foot on the new continent. Insurrection of thought usually precedes insurrection of deed. And over the years such a ferment occurred in the thinking of the colonists that the revolution was partially completed in their minds before the musket balls began to fly. America was a revolutionary force from the day of its discovery.

England's colonies were settled largely by emigrants who were discontented or rebellious in spirit—by people who had failed to adjust themselves to their harsh lot in the Old World. Most of

NOVA BRITANNIA.
OFFERING MOST
Excellent fruites by Planting in
VIRGINIA.
Exciting all ſuch as be well affected
to further the ſame.
LONDON
Printed for SAMVEL MACHAM, and are to be ſold at
his Shop in Pauls Church-yard, at the
Signe of the Bul-head.
1609.

Advertisement of a Voyage to America, 1609

them had not been able to get along, whether socially, politically, economically, or religiously. Some of them were tired of taking off their hats and standing bareheaded in the presence of their "betters." Others wanted a larger share in government, or a richer portion of this world's goods, or an opportunity to worship God in their own peculiar way.

The nightmare of crossing the Atlantic normally lasted about six to eight weeks, often much longer. Ships were frequently turned into "floating coffins" by food shortages or epidemics of disease; in one extreme case 350 of 400 passengers and crew perished. Cannibalism was not unknown, and starving men fought over the bodies of vermin. As a sailor's song ran:

> We ate the mice, we ate the rats,
> And through the hold we ran like cats.

Such a perilous crossing left many emotional scars. Survivors who staggered ashore on the Promised Land were, as a rule, isolated spiritually from the faraway Old World. They were more than ever aware that the long arm of the London government, enfeebled by 3,000 miles of ocean, could not reach them nearly so effectively as at home. Distance weakens authority; great distance weakens authority greatly.

America's lonely wilderness likewise stimulated ideas of independence. Back in England some villagers had lived near graveyards that contained the bones of their ancestors for a thousand years past. Born into such conservative surroundings, the poor plowman did not question the social rut in which he found himself. But in the New World he was not held down by the scowl of his overlords.

In America all was strange, crude, different. Dense forests and the rugged pioneering conditions changed patterns of living, and consequently habits of thought. Those wretched settlers perished who could not adapt themselves to their raw surroundings, and hundreds of the early Virginia colonists paid the supreme penalty. Before long, men were eating Indian corn, wearing Indian moccasins and buckskin, and in extreme instances on the frontier uttering the war whoop as they scalped their fallen red foe. Hacking a home out of the wildwood with an ax developed strength, self-confidence, individualism, and a spirit of independence.

As the Americans matured, they acquired privileges of self-government enjoyed by no other colonial peoples. They set up thirteen parliaments of their own, and aped the parliamentary methods of the Mother Country. Ultimately they came to regard their own legislative bodies as more or less on a footing with the great Mother of Parliaments in London. One governor of Rhode Island would wear no wig unless it had been made in England and was exactly like that worn by the Speaker of the British House of Commons.

The Mercantile Theory

Britain's empire was acquired in a "fit of absent-mindedness," as the old saying goes, and there is much truth in it. Not one of the original thirteen colonies, except Georgia, was formally planted by the British government. The actual founding was done haphazardly by trading companies, religious groups, land speculators, and others. Authorities in London did not even dream that a new nation was being born. And the colonials themselves, busy chopping down trees, were no less short-visioned.

Machinery in Britain for controlling the colonies was relatively simple. As it had evolved by 1696, the principal agency was the Board of Trade, joined in an advisory capacity by certain other prominent officials. With the passage of time, interest in the board flagged, and membership on it became something of a joke. Yet the recommendations of the board regarding the colonies were often made into law, either by act of Parliament or in regulations adopted by the Privy Council (the King's advisers).

The theory that shaped and justified English exploitation of the American colonies was mercantilism. According to this doctrine the colonies existed for the benefit of the Mother Country; they should add to its wealth, prosperity, and self-sufficiency. Otherwise why go to all the trouble and expense of governing and protecting them? The settlers were regarded more or less as tenants. They were expected to produce tobacco and other products needed in England, and not to bother their heads with dangerous experiments in agriculture or self-government.

Specifically, how were the American colonies to benefit the Mother Country? First of all, they were to insure Britain's naval supremacy by furnishing ships, ships' stores, seamen, and trade. In addition, they were to provide a profitable consumer's market for the English manufacturers at home. Finally, they were to keep gold and silver money within the empire by growing products, such as sugar, that otherwise would have to be bought from foreigners. The ideal of "Buy British" would thus be promoted in a manner that foreshadowed later protective tariffs.

> Adam Smith, the Scottish "Father of Modern Economics," frontally attacked mercantilism in 1776: "To prohibit a great people, however, from making all that they can of every part of their own produce, or from employing their stock and industry in the way that they judge most advantageous to themselves, is a manifest violation of the most sacred rights of mankind."

Mercantilist Trammels on Trade

Numerous measures were passed by Parliament to enforce the mercantile system. Most famous were the Navigation Laws. The first of these, enacted in 1650, was aimed at rival Dutch shippers who were elbowing their way into the American carrying trade. These Navigation Laws, as finally perfected, restricted commerce to and from the colonies to English vessels. Such regulation not only kept money within the empire but bolstered the British—and colonial—merchant marine, which in turn was an indispensable auxiliary to the Royal Navy.

An alert Parliament from time to time enacted additional laws favorable to the Motherland. European goods consigned to America had to be landed first in England, where customs duties could be collected and where the British middleman would get his cut of the profit. Still other curbs required certain "enumerated" products, notably tobacco, to be shipped to England and not to a foreign market, though prices in Europe might be higher.

> As the *Boston Gazette* declared in 1765, "A colonist cannot make a button, a horseshoe, nor a hobnail, but some snooty ironmonger or respectable buttonmaker of Britain shall bawl and squall that his honor's worship is most egregiously maltreated, injured, cheated, and robbed by the rascally American republicans."

In the interests of the empire, settlers were even restricted in what they might produce at home. They were forbidden to manufacture for export certain products, such as woolen cloth and beaver hats, because the colonies were supposed to complement and not compete with English industry.

Americans also felt the pinch in the area of currency. No banks existed in the colonies, and the money problem on the eve of the Revolution was acute. Industrious colonials were now busily buying more goods from England than they were selling to her, so the difference had to be made up in hard cash. Every year gold and silver money, much of it in quaint Spanish coins from the West Indies, was drained out of the colonies. The colonials simply did not have enough left for the convenience of everyday purchases. Barter became necessary, and even butter, nails, pitch, and feathers were used for purposes of exchange.

Currency problems came to a boil when dire need finally forced many of the colonies to issue paper money, which unfortunately depreciated. British merchants and creditors, understandably worried, squawked so loudly that Parliament was forced to act. It restrained the colonial legislatures from printing paper currency and from passing lax bankruptcy laws—practices that might result in defrauding British merchants. The Americans, who felt that their welfare was again being sacrificed, reacted angrily. Another burning grievance was thus heaped upon the pile of combustibles already smoldering.

London officialdom naturally kept a watchful eye on the legislation passed by the colonial assemblies. If such laws conflicted with British regulations or policy, they were declared null and void by the Privy Council—just as the Supreme Court of the United States today declares some laws unconstitutional.

The Female Combatants. Britain is symbolized as a lady of fashion, and her rebellious daughter as an Indian princess. (Lewis Walpole Library, Farmington.)

This "royal veto" was necessary for efficient government, but it was used rather sparingly—469 times in connection with 8,563 laws. The colonies naturally took a narrower view. Some of them were aggrieved when, in the interests of the Mother Country, they were forbidden to make reforms that they deemed desirable, such as curbing the degrading trade in African slaves.

The Merits of Mercantilism

Red-blooded Americans have long regarded the British mercantile system as thoroughly selfish

John Hancock (1736–1793). A merchant prince, he was the wealthiest New Englander on the Patriot side during the Revolution. Attaining popularity through the lavish expenditure of money, he served as president of the Continental Congress when independence was declared in 1776. His signature is the first, largest, and boldest on the famous Declaration, penned, it was said, so that George III could read Hancock's name without his glasses.

and deliberately oppressive, if not downright malicious. The truth is that until 1763 the Navigation Laws imposed no intolerable burden, partly because they were laxly enforced. Ingenious colonial merchants early learned to disregard or evade restrictions that they found vexatious. In fact, some of the early American fortunes were amassed by wholesale smuggling. Wealthy and vain John Hancock of Massachusetts came to be known as the "King of Smugglers," though his illicit activity was greatly exaggerated.

Americans, in addition, were fortunate enough to reap direct benefits from the mercantile system. London paid liberal bounties or price supports to those colonials who produced ships' parts and ships' stores, even though English competitors complained heatedly. When independence came, the bounties dried up and many of these American producers were forced to the wall.

Virginia tobacco planters, in particular, enjoyed valuable privileges. While forbidden to ship their pungent yellow leaf to any place other than England, they were guaranteed a monopoly of the British market. Tobacco growing was also outlawed in England and Ireland, although the plant had already been raised in England with some success.

American colonials additionally fared well in other fields. They enjoyed the undiluted rights of Englishmen, as well as unusual opportunities for self-government. They were not compelled to tax themselves to support a professional army and navy for protection against the French, Dutch, Spaniards, Indians, and pirates. Although the colonists went to some little expense in "training" militiamen, they enjoyed the shield of a strong army of British Redcoats and the mightiest navy in the world—without a penny of cost. After independence, the Americans would themselves be required to pay the costs of maintaining a tiny army and navy, both of which afforded inadequate protection.

In manufacturing and trade the New World settlers did not fare badly. They were denied the privilege of fabricating specified articles for export, notably fur hats, but this regulation worked no serious hardships, because it was laxly enforced and because other pursuits were usually more profitable. Americans were forced to deal with the British middleman, but they would have done so anyhow, owing to a common language, standard pounds and shillings, liberal credit arrangements, and familiar business methods.

"Prosperity trickles down" is a common saying; and in truth the Americans enjoyed a generous share of Britain's profits under the time-honored mercantile system. The average American was probably better off economically than the average Englishman at home. If the colonies existed for the benefit of the Mother Country, it was hardly less true that the Mother Country existed for the benefit of the colonies. The well-meaning officials in London were working for the welfare of the empire as a whole, and they gave overall unity to its policies. A wise man does not disembowel or starve the goose that lays the golden eggs. Mistakes were made by the British authorities, but they were not, until revolt was precipitated, the mistakes of malice.

Mercantilism had sufficient merit to be widely adopted and long perpetuated. All other colonial nations of that age, including Spain and France, embraced mercantilistic principles completely and enforced them ironhandedly. Mercantilism has endured to the present century, even in the United States. Interested groups of Americans seek to insure prosperity for manufacturers and wage earners by protective tariffs, and to bolster the national defense by subsidies to shipbuilders. American Navigation Laws—shades of the 17th Century!—are still designed to prevent foreign shippers from encroaching on coastwise trade, even that between Hawaii and the mainland.

The Menace of Mercantilism

Even when painted in its rosiest colors, the mercantile system burdened the colonials with annoying liabilities. Economic initiative was stifled because Americans were not at complete liberty to buy, sell, ship, or manufacture under conditions that they found most profitable. Southern colonies, as "pets," were generally favored over the Northern ones, chiefly because they grew non-English products like tobacco, sugar, and rice. Revolution was one seed that sprouted vigorously from the stony soil of New England, for the proud sons of the Puritans resented being treated like unwanted relatives.

One-crop Virginians, despite London's preference for Southern colonies, also nursed rankling grievances. Forced to sell their tobacco in England, they were at the mercy of British merchants, who often gouged them. Many of the fashionable Virginia planters were plunged into debt by the falling price of tobacco, and were forced to buy their necessities in England by mortgaging future crops. Some debts, becoming hereditary, were bequeathed by father to son.

Impoverished Virginia vied for leadership with restless Massachusetts in agitating for revolt against England; and unfriendly critics sneered that her cry, "Liberty or Death," might better have been "Liberty or Debt." While this charge was unfair in many cases, countless Virginians welcomed the opportunity to end their economic bondage to the Mother Country.

Finally—and of supreme importance—mercantilism was debasing to the Americans. The colonies, many of them felt, were being used or milked, as cows are milked. They were to be kept in a state of perpetual economic adolescence, and never allowed to come of age. As Benjamin Franklin wrote in 1775:

> We have an old mother that peevish is grown;
> She snubs us like children that scarce walk alone;
> She forgets we're grown up and have sense of our own.

Revolution broke out, as Theodore Roosevelt later remarked, because England failed to recognize an emerging nation when she saw one.

> English statesman Edmund Burke warned in 1775: "Young man, there is America—which at this day serves for little more than to amuse you with stories of savage men and uncouth manners; yet shall, before you taste of death, show itself equal to the whole of that commerce which now attracts the envy of the world."

The Stamp Tax Uproar

The costly Seven Years' War, which ended in 1763, marked a new relationship between Britain and her transatlantic colonies. A revolution in British colonial policy precipitated the American Revolution.

Victory-flushed Britain emerged from the conflict possessing one of the biggest empires in the world—and also, less happily, the biggest debt. It amounted to £140 million, about half of which had been incurred in defending the American colonies. British officials wisely had no intention of asking the colonials to help pay off this crushing burden. But London felt that the Americans should be asked to defray one-third the cost of maintaining a garrison of some 10,000 Redcoats, presumably for their own protection.

Prime Minister George Grenville, an honest and able financier not noted for tact, moved vigorously. Dedicated to efficiency, he aroused the resentment of the colonials in 1763 by ordering the British navy to enforce the Navigation Laws. He also secured from Parliament the so-called Sugar Act of 1764, the first law ever passed by that body for raising revenue in the colonies for the Crown. Among various provisions, it increased the duty on foreign sugar imported from the West Indies. After bitter protests from the colonials, the duties were lowered substantially, and the agitation died down. But resentment was kept burning by the Quartering Act of 1765. It required certain colonies to provide food and quarters for British troops.

Then in the same year, 1765, Grenville proposed the most ominous measure of all: a stamp tax, to raise revenues to support the new military force. The Stamp Act required the use of stamped paper or the affixing of stamps, certifying payment of tax. Involved were about fifty trade items and certain types of commercial and legal documents, including playing cards, pamphlets, newspapers, diplomas, bills of lading, and marriage licenses.

Grenville regarded all these measures as reasonable and just. He was simply asking the Americans to pay their fair share for colonial defense, through taxes that were already familiar in England. In fact, Englishmen for two generations had endured a stamp tax far heavier than that passed for the colonies.

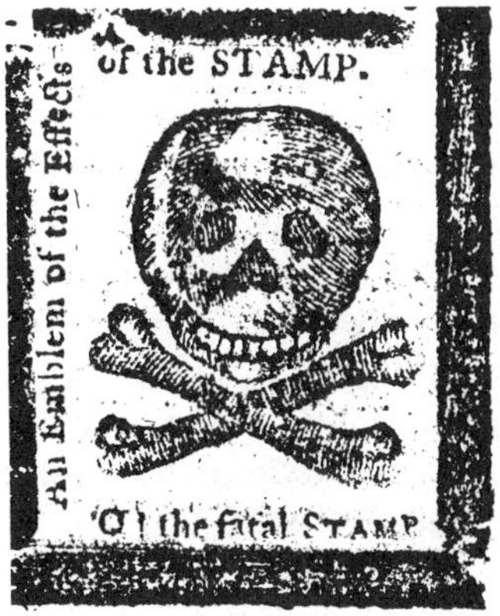

A Parody of the "Fatal Stamp"

A Royal Stamp. The motto in French is translated "Shame to him who evil thinks."

Yet the Americans were angrily aroused at what they regarded as Grenville's fiscal aggression. The new laws did pinch their pocketbooks. Earlier parliamentary imposts on the colonies had been mostly indirect taxes, designed primarily to regulate trade. They had been more or less painlessly levied at the customs house, then passed on to consumers in higher prices. But the stamp tax was a direct tax, offensively obvious to the consumer and clearly aimed to raise revenue.

The colonists sensed that more than their livelihood was threatened. Grenville's legal looting, they grumbled, menaced the local liberties they had come to assume as a matter of right. Thus some colonial assemblies defiantly refused to comply with the Quartering Act or voted only a fraction of the supplies that it called for. Angry throats raised the cry, "No taxation without representation." There was irony in the slogan, because the seaports and tidewater towns that were most wrathful against Grenville had long denied full representation to their own "backcountry" pioneers. But now the agitated colonials took the high ground of principle. They scoffed at Grenville's theory of "virtual representation," which claimed that every member of Parliament represented all British subjects, even those in Boston or in Charleston who had never voted for a member of the London Parliament.

Worse still, Grenville's noxious legislation seemed to menace the basic rights of the colonists as Englishmen. Both the Sugar Act and the Stamp Act provided for trying offenders in the hated admiralty courts, where juries were not allowed. The burden of proof was on the defendant, who was assumed to be guilty unless he could prove himself innocent. Trial by jury and the doctrine of "innocent until proved guilty" were ancient privileges that Englishmen everywhere, including Americans, held most dear. And why was a British army needed at all in the colonies, now that the French were vanquished and Pontiac's red men crushed? Could its real purpose be to whip rebellious colonials themselves into line? Many Americans began to sniff the strong scent of a conspiracy to strip them of all their historic liberties. They lashed back violently, and the Stamp Act soon became a magnet that drew their most ferocious fire.

Many colonials did not really want direct representation in Parliament. If they had obtained it, any gouty member of the House of Commons could have proposed an oppressive tax bill for the colonies, and the American representatives could have been heavily outvoted. In these circumstances the colonists preferred taxation without representation to taxation with representation.

What the colonials really wanted was a return to the "good old days" before the French and Indian War. Then the Navigation Laws had been only laxly enforced, and the Americans had suffered no taxation, except by their own elected assemblies. Betraying a quite human preference for benefits without burdens, the colonists were unwilling to shoulder the new responsibilities that went with being part of a great empire.

> Nicholas Cresswell, a Tory, observed in 1774: "The New Englanders by their canting, whining, insinuating tricks have persuaded the rest of the Colonies that the Government is going to make absolute slaves of them."

> The famous circular letter from the Massachusetts House of Representatives (1768) stated: ". . . considering the utter impracticability of their ever being fully and equally represented in Parliament, and the great expense that must unavoidably attend even a partial representation there, this House think that a taxation of their constituents, even without their consent, grievous as it is, would be preferable to any representation that could be admitted for them there."

Parliament Forced to Repeal the Stamp Act

Colonial outcries against the hated stamp tax took various forms. The most conspicuous assemblage was the Stamp Act Congress of 1765, which brought together in New York City twenty-seven distinguished delegates from nine colonies. After dignified debate, the members drew up a statement of their rights and grievances, and besought the King and Parliament to repeal the odious legislation.

The Stamp Act Congress, which was largely ignored in England, made little splash at the time in America. But it did do something to break down sectional suspicions, for it brought together around the same table leading men from the different and rival colonies. It was one more halting but significant step toward intercolonial unity.

More effective than the Congress was the widespread adoption of non-importation agreements against British goods. Woolen garments of homespun became fashionable, and the eating of lamb chops was discouraged lest wool-bearing sheep not be allowed to mature. Non-importation agreements were in fact a promising stride toward

Hanging John Huske in Effigy. A Paul Revere engraving showing the fate in America of an alleged supporter of the Stamp Act. (American Antiquarian Society.)

union; they spontaneously united the American people for the first time in common action.

Violence also attended colonial protests. Groups of ardent spirits, known as Sons of Liberty and backed by Daughters of Liberty, took the law into their own hands. Crying "Liberty, Property, and No Stamps," they enforced the non-importation agreements against violators, often with a generous coat of tar and feathers. Houses of unpopular officials were ransacked, their money was stolen, and stamp agents were hanged on Liberty Poles, albeit in effigy.

Shaken by violence, the machinery for collecting the tax broke down. On that dismal day in 1765 when the new act was to go into effect, the stamp agents had all been forced to resign, and there was no one to sell the stamps. While flags flapped at half-mast, the law was openly and flagrantly defied—or rather, nullified.

England was hard hit. Merchants and manufacturers suffered from the colonial non-importation agreements, and hundreds of laborers were thrown out of work. Loud demands converged on Parliament for repeal of the Stamp Act. But many of the members could not understand why 7.5 million Britons had to pay heavy taxes to protect the colonies, while some 2 million colonials refused to pay for only one-third of the cost of their own defense.

After a stormy debate, and as a matter of expediency and not of right, Parliament in 1766 reluctantly repealed the Stamp Act. At the same time, and by an overwhelming vote, it saved face by passing the Declaratory Act. This futile measure proclaimed that Parliament had the right "to bind" the colonies "in all cases whatsoever." A bare assertion of this right was but a feeble victory for parental authority, for the unruly colonials had proved that the London government could be forced to yield to boycotts and mob action.

America forthwith burst into an uproar of rejoicing. Grateful residents of New York erected a leaden statue to King George III—a tribute which was later melted into thousands of bullets to be fired at his own troops.

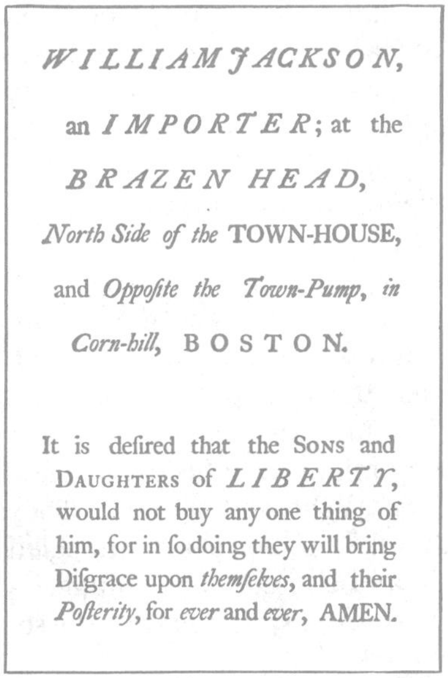

WILLIAM JACKSON,

an *IMPORTER*; at the

BRAZEN HEAD,

North Side of the TOWN-HOUSE,

and *Oppoſite the Town-Pump, in*

Corn-hill, BOSTON.

It is deſired that the SONS and DAUGHTERS of *LIBERTY*, would not buy any one thing of him, for in ſo doing they will bring Diſgrace upon *themſelves*, and their *Poſterity*, for *ever* and *ever*, AMEN.

Boycott Handbill

The Townshend Tea Tax and the Boston "Massacre"

Control of the British ministry was now seized by the gifted but erratic "Champagne Charley" Townshend, who could deliver brilliant speeches in Parliament while drunk. Rashly promising to pluck feathers from the colonial goose with a minimum of squawking, he persuaded Parliament in 1767 to pass the Townshend Acts. The most important of these new regulations was a light import duty on glass, white lead, paper, and tea. Townshend deferred to the sensitive colonials by making this tax, unlike the Stamp Act, an indirect customs duty payable at American ports.

Flushed with their recent victory over the stamp tax, the colonists were in a rebellious mood. The impost on tea was especially irksome, for an estimated 1 million persons drank "the cup that cheers" twice a day, and even tipplers used it when alcohol was not available.

The new Townshend revenues, worse yet, would be used to pay the salaries of the royal governors and judges in America. From the standpoint of efficient administration by London, this was a reform long overdue. But the ultra-suspicious Americans, who had beaten the royal governors into line by controlling the purse, regarded Townshend's tax as another attempt to enchain them. Their worst fears took on greater reality when the London government, after passing the Townshend taxes, suspended the legislature of New York for failure to comply with the Quartering Act in 1767.

Non-importation agreements, previously potent, were quickly revived against the Townshend Acts. But they proved less effective than those devised against the Stamp Act. The colonials, again enjoying prosperity, took the new tax less seriously than might have been expected, largely because it was light and indirect. They found, moreover, that they could secure smuggled tea at a cheap price, and consequently smugglers increased their activities, especially in Massachusetts.

Redcoats Landing in Boston

British officials, faced with a breakdown of law and order, landed two regiments of troops in Boston in 1768. Many of the soldiers, as might be expected, were drunken and profane characters. Liberty-loving colonials, resenting the presence of the red-coated "ruffians," taunted the "bloody backs" unmercifully.

A clash was inevitable. On the evening of March 5, 1770, a crowd of some sixty townspeople set upon a squad of about ten "bloody backs," one of whom was hit by a club and another of whom was knocked down. Acting apparently without orders but under extreme provocation, the troops opened fire and killed or wounded eleven "innocent" citizens. One of the first to die was Crispus Attucks, described by contemporaries as a powerfully built runaway "mulatto" and as a leader of the mob. Both sides were in some degree to blame, and in the subsequent trial only two of the soldiers could be found guilty of manslaughter. They were released after being branded on the hand.

The so-called Boston Massacre—"the Boston Brawl" rather than a "massacre"—further inflamed the colonials against the British, especially after the conviction spread that the Americans had been wholly unoffending. Paul Revere, the artist-horseman, wrote:

> Unhappy Boston! see thy sons deplore
> Thy hallowed walks besmear'd with guiltless gore.

Massacre Day was observed in Boston as a patriotic holiday until 1776, when the more glorious Fourth of July eclipsed it.

The Seditious Committees of Correspondence

By 1770 King George III, then only thirty-two years old, was strenuously attempting to restore the declining power of the British monarchy. He was a good man in his private morals, but he proved to be a bad ruler. Earnest, industrious, stubborn, lustful for power, and plagued with periodic fits of supposed madness, he surrounded himself with cooperative "yes men," notably his corpulent Prime Minister, Lord North.

The ill-timed Townshend Acts had failed to produce revenue, though producing near rebellion. Net proceeds from the tax in one year were £295, and during that time the annual military costs to Britain in the colonies had mounted to £170,000. Non-importation agreements, though feebly enforced, were pinching British manufacturers. The government of Lord North, bowing to various pressures, finally persuaded Parliament to repeal the Townshend revenue duties. But the three-pence tax on tea was retained to keep alive the principle of parliamentary taxation.

Flames of discontent in America continued to be fanned by numerous incidents, including the redoubled efforts of the British officials to enforce the Navigation Laws. Resistance was further whipped up by a master propagandist and engineer of rebellion, Samuel Adams of Boston, a cousin of John Adams. Unimpressive in appearance (his hands trembled), he had failed miserably in private life. His friends had to buy him a presentable suit of clothes when he left Massachusetts on intercolonial business. But zealous, tenacious, and courageous, he was ultrasensitive to infractions of colonial rights. Cherishing a deep faith in the common man, he appealed effectively to what was called his "trained mob." Skillful also as a pamphleteer, he soon became known as the "Penman of the Revolution."

Samuel Adams's signal contribution was to organize in Massachusetts the local committees of correspondence. After he had formed the first one in Boston during 1772, some eighty towns in the colony speedily set up similar organizations. Their chief function was to spread propaganda and information by interchanging letters, and thus keep alive opposition to British policy. One critic referred to the committees as "the foulest, subtlest, and most venomous serpent ever issued from the egg of sedition." No more effective device for stimulating resistance could have been contrived, and modern Communist revolutionists have adopted some of its underground techniques in establishing "cells."

Intercolonial committees of correspondence were the next logical step. Virginia led the way in 1773 by creating such a body as a standing committee of the House of Burgesses. Within a short time every colony had established a central committee through which it could exchange ideas and information with other colonies. These intercolonial groups, which were supremely significant in stimulating and disseminating sentiment in favor of united action, evolved directly into the first American Congresses.

Tea Parties at Boston and Elsewhere

Thus far—that is, by 1773—nothing had happened to make rebellion inevitable. Non-importation was weakening. Increasing numbers of colonials were reluctantly paying the tea tax, because the

Public Punishment. Boston customs official, John Malcolm, paraded after being tarred and feathered, January 25, 1774. (Detail from an English cartoon. Harvard College Library.)

legal tea was now cheaper than the smuggled tea, and cheaper than tea in England. Even John Adams on one occasion hoped that the tea he was drinking was smuggled Dutch tea, but he could not be sure and did not want to know.

A new ogre entered the picture in 1773. The powerful British East India Company, overburdened with 17 million pounds of unsold tea, was facing bankruptcy. If it collapsed, the London government would lose heavily in tax revenue. The ministry therefore decided to assist the company by awarding it a complete monopoly of the American tea business. The terms thus granted would enable the giant corporation to sell the coveted leaves more cheaply than ever before, even with the threepence tax added. But to many American consumers, principle was more important than price.

Violence was inevitable, for the new tea monopoly had many features that were hateful to the colonials. Above all, it seemed like a shabby attempt to trick the Americans, with the bait of cheaper tea, into acceptance of the detested tax. Once more the colonials rose in their wrath. Not a single one of the several thousand chests of tea shipped by the company reached the hands of the consignees. At Annapolis, the Marylanders burned both the cargo and the vessel, while proclaiming "Liberty and Independence or death in pursuit of it." At Boston, which was host to the most famous tea party of all, a band of white townsfolk, disguised as Indians, boarded the three tea ships on December 16, 1773. They smashed open 342 chests and dumped the "cursed weed" into the harbor, while a silent crowd watched approvingly from the wharves as salty tea was brewed for the fish.

Reactions varied. Extremists in America rejoiced; conservatives shuddered. This wanton destruction of private property was going too far. The British at home were outraged; even friends of America hung their heads. Punishment and coercion were the only possible responses of the London authorities, as long as the mercantilist philosophy prevailed and the colonials refused to accept responsibility. The granting of some kind of home rule to the Americans might have prevented rebellion, but the Britons of that age were not blessed with such vision. Edmund Burke, a friend of America in Parliament, declared, "To tax and to please, no more than to love and be wise, is not given to men."

Parliament Passes the "Intolerable Acts"

An outraged Parliament responded speedily to the Boston Tea Party with measures that brewed a revolution. By huge majorities in 1774 it passed a series of "Repressive Acts," which were designed to chastise Boston in particular, Massachusetts in general. They were branded in America as "the Massacre of American Liberty."

Most drastic of all was the Boston Port Act. It closed the tea-stained harbor until damages were paid and order could be assured. By other "Intolerable Acts"—as they were called in America—many of the chartered rights of colonial Massachusetts were swept away. Restrictions were likewise placed on the precious town meet-

QUEBEC BEFORE AND AFTER 1774

Young Alexander Hamilton voiced the fears of many colonists when he warned that the Quebec Act of 1774 would introduce "priestly tyranny" into Canada, making that country another Spain or Portugal. "Does not your blood run cold," he asked, "to think that an English Parliament should pass an act for the establishment of arbitrary power and Popery in such a country?"

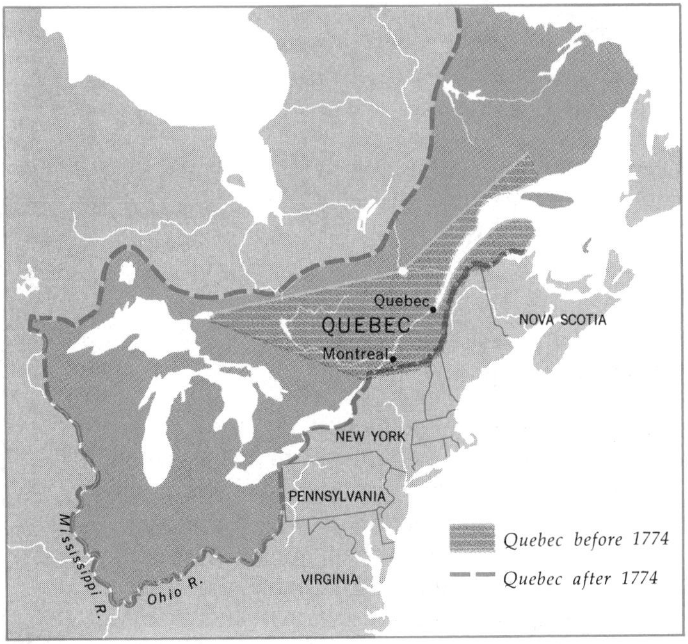

ings. Contrary to previous practice, enforcing officials who killed colonials in line of duty could now be sent to England for trial. There, suspicious Americans assumed, they would be likely to get off scot-free.

By a fateful coincidence, the "Intolerable Acts" were accompanied in 1774 by the Quebec Act. Passed at the same time, it was erroneously regarded in English-speaking America as one of the "repressive" measures. Actually, the Quebec Act was a good law in bad company. For many years the British government had debated how it should administer the 60,000 or so conquered French subjects in Canada, and it had finally framed this farsighted and statesmanlike measure. The French were guaranteed their Catholic religion. They were also permitted to retain many of their old customs and institutions, which did not include a representative assembly or trial by jury in civil cases. In addition, the old boundaries of the Province of Quebec were now extended southward all the way to the Ohio River.

> Josiah Quincy, a prominent Boston patriot and orator, lashed out against the Boston Port Act: "Blandishments will not fascinate us, nor will threats of a 'halter' [noose] intimidate. For, under God, we are determined that wheresoever, whensoever, or howsoever we shall be called to make our exit, we will die free men." He died at sea the next year while on a diplomatic mission to England.

The Quebec Act, from the viewpoint of the French Canadians, was a shrewd and conciliatory measure. If England had only shown as much foresight in dealing with her English-speaking colonies, she might not have lost them.

But from the viewpoint of the American colonials as a whole, the Quebec Act was the most intolerable of the "Intolerable Acts." All the other "repressive" laws slapped directly at Massachusetts, but this one had a much wider range. It seemed to set a dangerous precedent in America against jury trials and popular assemblies. It alarmed land speculators, who were distressed to see the huge trans-Allegheny area snatched from their grasp. It aroused the host of anti-Catholics, who were shocked by the extension of Roman Catholic jurisdiction southward into a huge region that had once been earmarked for Protestantism—a region about as large as the thirteen original colonies. One angry Protestant cried that there ought to be a "jubilee in hell" over this enormous gain for "popery."

The Continental Congress and Bloodshed

American dissenters, outraged by the Quebec Act, responded sympathetically to the plight of Massachusetts. She had put herself in the wrong by the wanton destruction of the tea cargoes; now the Mother Country had put herself in the wrong by brutal punishment that did not seem to fit the crime. Flags were flown at half-mast throughout the colonies on the day that the Boston Port Act went into effect, and sister colonies rallied to send food to the stricken city. Rice was shipped even from faraway South Carolina.

Most memorable of the responses to the "Intolerable Acts" was the summoning of a Continental Congress in 1774. It was to meet in Philadelphia to consider ways of redressing colonial grievances. Twelve of the thirteen colonies, with Georgia alone missing, sent fifty-five distinguished men, among them Samuel Adams, John Adams, George Washington, and Patrick Henry. Intercolonial frictions were partially melted away by social activity after working hours; in fifty-four days George Washington dined at his own lodgings only nine times.

The First Continental Congress deliberated for seven weeks, September 5 to October 26, 1774. It was not a legislative but a consultative body; it was a convention rather than a Congress. John Adams played a stellar role. Eloquently swaying his colleagues to a revolutionary course, he helped defeat by the narrowest of margins a proposal by the moderates for a species of American home rule under British direction. After prolonged argument, the Congress drew up several dignified papers. These included a ringing Declaration of Rights, as well as solemn appeals to other British American colonies, to the King, and to the British people.

Samuel Adams (1722–1803). A second cousin of John Adams, he contributed a potent pen and tongue to the American Revolution as a political agitator and organizer of rebellion. He was the leading spirit in hosting the Boston Tea Party. A failure in the brewing business, he was sent by Massachusetts to the First Continental Congress of 1774. He signed the Declaration of Independence and served in Congress until 1781. (Courtesy, Museum of Fine Arts, Boston. Deposited by the City of Boston.)

The most significant action of the Congress was the creation of The Association. Unlike previous non-importation agreements, this one called for a *complete* boycott of British goods: non-importation, non-exportation, and non-consumption. A document known as The Association, by providing for concerted action, was the closest approach to a written constitution that the colonies as a unit had yet devised. But still there was no genuine drive toward independence—merely an effort to bring about a repeal of the offensive legislation and a return to the happy days before parliamentary taxation. If colonial grievances were redressed, well and good; if not, the Congress was to meet again in May 1775.

But the deadly drift toward war continued. The petitions of the Continental Congress were rejected, after considerable debate, by strong majorities in Parliament. In America chickens squawked and tar kettles bubbled as violators of The Association were tarred and feathered.

Muskets were being collected, men were openly drilling, and a clash seemed imminent.

In April 1775, the British commander in Boston sent a detachment of troops to nearby Lexington and Concord. They were to seize stores of colonial gunpowder, and also to bag the "rebel" ringleaders, Samuel Adams and John Hancock. At Lexington, the colonial "Minute Men" refused to disperse rapidly enough, and shots were fired which killed eight Americans and wounded several more. The affair was more the "Lexington Massacre" than a battle. The Redcoats pushed on to Concord, whence they were forced to retreat by the homespun Americans, whom Emerson immortalized:

> By the rude bridge that arched the flood,
> Their flag to April's breeze unfurled,
> Here once the embattled farmers stood,
> And fired the shot heard round the world.*

The bewildered British, fighting off murderous fire from militiamen crouched behind thick stone walls, finally regained the sanctuary of Boston. Licking their wounds, they could count about 300 casualties, including some 70 killed. England now had a war on her hands.

Imperial Strength and Weakness

Aroused Americans had brashly rebelled against a mighty empire. The population odds were about three to one against the rebels—some 7.5 million Britons to 2.5 million colonials. The odds in monetary wealth and naval power were overwhelmingly in favor of the Mother Country.

Black people were only a partial asset to the American cause, for they could hardly be expected to fight for a society that had enslaved them. Still, about 5,000 saw military service, whether as freemen or as slaves promised freedom, and in a number of engagements fought bravely. Even larger numbers, often guaranteed freedom with no strings attached, fled to enemy lines and left the country when the British departed.

Britain then boasted a professional army of some 50,000 men, as compared with the numerous but wretchedly trained American militia. George III, in addition, had the money with which to hire foreign soldiers, and some 30,000 Germans—so-called Hessians—were ultimately employed. The British enrolled about 50,000 American Loyalists and enlisted the services of many Indians, who though unreliable fair-weather fighters, ravaged long stretches of the frontier. One British officer boasted that the war would offer no problems that could not be solved by an "experienced sheep herder."

Yet the Mother Country was weaker than she seemed at first glance. Oppressed Ireland was a latent volcano, and British troops had to be detached to watch her. France, bitter from her recent defeat, was awaiting an opportunity to stab Britain in the back. The London government was confused and inept. There was no William Pitt, "Organizer of Victory," only the stubborn George III and his pliant Lord North.

Many earnest and God-fearing Britons had no desire whatever to kill their American cousins. William Pitt withdrew a son from the army rather than see him thrust his sword into fellow Anglo-Saxons struggling for liberty. The English Whig factions, opposed to Lord North's Tory factions,

> Privately (1776) General Washington expressed his distrust of militia: "To place any dependence upon militia is assuredly resting on a broken staff. . . . The sudden change in their manner of living . . . brings on sickness in many, impatience in all, and such an unconquerable desire of returning to their respective homes that it not only produces shameful and scandalous desertions among themselves, but infuses the like spirit in others. . . . If I was called upon to declare upon oath whether the militia have been most serviceable or hurtful upon the whole, I should subscribe to the latter."

*Ralph Waldo Emerson, "Concord Hymn."

Lord North (1732–1792). A staunch Tory and a loyal supporter of George III, he served as Prime Minister from 1770 to 1782, when his plan to reconquer America had evidently failed. His overreaction to the Boston Tea Party (1773) did much to precipitate the American Revolution.

openly cheered American victories—at least at the outset. Aside from trying to embarrass the Tories politically, many Whigs believed that the battle for English freedom was being fought in America. If George III triumphed, his rule at home might become tyrannical. This outspoken sympathy in England, though plainly that of a minority, greatly encouraged the Americans. If they continued their resistance long enough, the Whigs might come into power and deal generously with them.

Britain's army in America had to operate under endless difficulties. The generals were second-rate; the soldiers, though generally capable, were brutally treated. There was one extreme case of 800 lashes on the bare back for striking an officer. Provisions were often scarce, rancid, and wormy. On one occasion a supply of biscuits, captured some fifteen years earlier from the French, was softened by dropping cannon balls on them.

Other handicaps loomed. The Redcoats had to conquer the Americans; a draw would be a victory for the colonials. Britain was operating some 3,000 miles (4,830 kilometers) from her home base, and distance added greatly to the delays and uncertainties arising from storms and other mishaps. Military orders were issued in London which, when received months later, would not fit the changing situation.

America's geographical expanse was enormous: roughly 1,000 by 600 miles (1,600 by 970 kilometers). The United Colonies had no urban nerve center, like France's Paris. British armies captured every city of any size, yet like a boxer punching a feather pillow, they made little more than a dent in the entire country. The Americans wisely traded space for time. Benjamin Franklin calculated that during the prolonged campaign in which the Redcoats captured Bunker Hill and killed some 150 Yankees, about 60,000 American babies were born.

American Pluses and Minuses

The Revolutionists were blessed with outstanding leadership. George Washington was a giant among men; Benjamin Franklin was a master among diplomats. Open foreign aid, theoretically possible from the start, eventually came from France. Numerous European officers, many of them unemployed and impoverished, volunteered their swords for pay. In a class by himself was a wealthy young French nobleman, the Marquis de Lafayette. Fleeing from boredom, loving glory and ultimately liberty, at age nineteen the "French gamecock" was made a major general in the colonial army. His commission was largely a recogni-

General Lafayette (1757–1834). He gave to America not only military services but some $200,000 of his private funds. He returned to France after the American Revolution to play a conspicuous but disappointing role in the French Revolution.

tion of his family influence and political connections, but the services of this teenage general in securing further aid from France were invaluable.

Other conditions aided the Americans. They were fighting defensively, with the odds, all things considered, favoring the defender. In agriculture, the colonies were mainly self-sustaining, like a kind of Robinson Crusoe's island. Colonial "buckskins," moreover, were a tough, self-reliant people. As marksmen, they far outshone the British, who often pointed rather than aimed their muskets. A competent American rifleman could hit a man's head at 200 yards (183 meters).

In addition, the Americans enjoyed the moral advantage that came from belief in a just cause. The historical odds were not impossible. Other peoples had triumphed in the face of greater obstacles: the Greeks against Persians, the Swiss against Austrians, the Dutch against Spaniards.

Yet the American rebels were badly organized for war. From earliest days they had been almost fatally lacking in unity, and the new nation lurched forward uncertainly like an uncoordinated centipede. Even the Continental Congress, which directed the conflict, was hardly more than a debating society, and it grew feebler as the struggle dragged on. "Their Congress now is quite disjoint'd," jibed an English satirist, "Since Gibbits (gallows) [are] for them appointed." Disorganized colonials fought almost the entire war before adopting a written constitution—the Articles of Confederation—in 1781.

Jealousy everywhere raised its hideous head. Individual states, proudly regarding themselves as sovereign, resented the attempts of Congress to exercise its weak powers. Sectional jealousy boiled up over the appointment of military leaders; some distrustful New Englanders almost preferred British officers to Americans from other sections.

Economic difficulties were well-nigh insuperable. Metallic money had already been heavily drained away. A cautious Continental Congress, unwilling to raise anew the explosive issue of taxation, was forced to print "Continental" paper money profusely. As this currency poured from the presses, it depreciated until the expression became current, "not worth a Continental." One barber contemptuously papered his shop with the almost worthless dollars. The confusion worsened when the individual states were compelled to issue depreciated paper money of their own.

Inflation of the currency inevitably skyrocketed prices. Families of the soldiers at the fighting front were hard hit, and hundreds of anxious husbands and fathers deserted. Debtors easily acquired handfuls of the semi-worthless money and gleefully paid their debts "without mercy"—sometimes with the bayonets of the authorities to back them up.

A Thin Line of Heroes

Basic military supplies in the colonies were dangerously scanty, especially firearms and powder. Benjamin Franklin seriously proposed going back to the bow and arrow. Even where food was accumulated, wagons were often not available to haul it. At Valley Forge, in the winter of 1777–1778, the shivering American soldiers were without bread for three successive days. In one Southern campaign some men fainted for lack of food.

Manufactured goods were generally in short supply in agricultural America, and clothing and shoes were appallingly scarce. The path of the patriot fighting men was often marked by bloody snow. At frigid Valley Forge, during one anxious period, 2,800 men were barefooted or nearly naked. Woolens were desperately needed against the wintry blasts; and in general the only real uniform of the colonial army was uniform raggedness. During a grand parade at Valley Forge some of the officers appeared wrapped in woolen bed covers. One Rhode Island unit was known as the "Ragged, Lousy, Naked Regiment."

American militiamen were numerous but highly unreliable. Able-bodied American males—perhaps several hundred thousand of them—had received rudimentary training, and many of these recruits served for short terms in the rebel armies. But poorly trained plowboys, though better shots, could not stand up in the open field against professional British troops advancing with bare bayonets. Many of these undisciplined warriors would, in the words of Washington, "fly from their own shadows."

A few thousand regulars—perhaps 7,000 or 8,000 at war's end—were finally whipped into shape by stern drillmasters. Notable among these officers was an organizational genius, the salty German Baron von Steuben. He spoke no English when he reached America, but he soon taught his men that bayonets were not for broiling beefsteaks over open fires. As they gained experience, these soldiers of the Continental Line could hold their own in open battle against crack British troops.

Morale in the Revolutionary army was badly undermined by American profiteers. These grasping gentry, putting profits before patriotism, sold to the British because the invader could pay in gold. Speculators forced prices sky-high; and some Bostonians made profits of 50 percent to 200 percent on army clothing while the American army was freezing at Valley Forge. Washington never had as many as 20,000 effective troops in one place at one time, despite bounties of land and other inducements. Yet if the rebels had thrown themselves into the struggle with Revolutionary zeal, they could easily have raised many times that number.

> General Washington's disgust is reflected in a diary entry for 1776: "Chimney corner patriots abound; venality, corruption, prostitution of office for selfish ends, abuse of trust, perversion of funds from a national to a private use, and speculations upon the necessities of the times pervade all interests."

The brutal truth is that only a select minority of the American colonials attached themselves to the cause of independence with a spirit of selfless devotion. These were the dedicated souls who bore the burden of battle and the risks of defeat; these were the freedom-loving patriots who deserved the gratitude and esteem of generations yet unborn. Seldom have so few done so much for so many.

VARYING VIEWPOINTS

Historians once assumed that the Revolution was just another chapter in the unfolding story of human liberty—a kind of divinely ordained progress toward perfection in human affairs. This approach is often called the Whig view of history. Around the beginning of this century, the concept was sharply challenged by the so-called progressive historians, who argued that not God but a sharp struggle among different social groups brought about change. "Progressives" thus saw the Revolution as stemming from class conflict and ending in a truly transformed social order. As one of them put it, the Revolution was not only about home rule, but about "who should rule at home." Since World War II, scholars have questioned this interpretation. They have uncovered evidence that the British imperial system really was not unduly burdensome to the colonists, and more important, that colonial society was *already* fairly democratic before 1776 (at least as regards white people).

Two questions naturally arise: What really caused the divorce of Mother Country and colonists, and precisely how "revolutionary" was the Revolution? Interestingly, recent scholarship has tended to emphasize not economic or political friction, but ideological and even psychological factors. The root causes of the Revolution may well have been the felt need to defend existing political liberties, combined with an exaggerated fear of conspiracy against them.

SELECT READINGS

Edmund S. Morgan, *The Birth of the Republic, 1763–1789* (1956), is among the best brief accounts of the Revolutionary era. It stresses the happy coincidence of the Revolutionaries' principles and their interests. L. Gipson, *The Coming of the Revolution, 1763–1775* (1954), summarizes his 15-volume masterwork (cited in Chapter 3). Merrill Jensen, *The Founding of a Nation* (1968), is a more recent effort at a general synthesis, as is Page Smith's massive *A New Age Now Begins: A People's History of the American Revolution* (1976). R. R. Palmer, *The Age of the Democratic Revolution: A Political History of Europe and America, 1760–1800* (2 vols., 1959, 1964), masterfully places American events in the larger context of Western history. Two enlightening collections of essays are J. P. Greene, ed., *The Reinterpretation of the American Revolution, 1763–1789* (1968), and A. F. Young, ed., *The American Revolution* (1976), which generally represents a "new left" revisionist view. An interesting effort to blend British and American perspectives is I. R. Christie and B. W. Labaree, *Empire or Independence, 1760–1776* (1976). The sources of American dissatisfaction with the British imperial system can be traced in C. Ubbelohde, *The American Colonies and the British Empire, 1607–1763* (1968), and T. C. Barrow, *Trade and Empire: The British Customs Service in Colonial America* (1967). O. M. Dickerson, *The Navigation Acts and the American Revolution* (1951), concludes that the navigation system did not put undue burdens on the colonies. B. Knollenberg examines the effects of the British tightening of the imperial system in the 1760s in *Origin of the American Revolution, 1759–1766* (1960), as does Michael Kammen in *Empire and Interest* (1970). John Shy imaginatively explores an important aspect of the imperial system's effect on America in *Toward Lexington: The Role of the British Army in the Coming of the American Revolution* (1965). A perceptive short account of the American reaction to British initiatives is E. S. and H. M. Morgan, *The Stamp Act Crisis* (1953). B. W. Labaree discusses another instance of American reaction in *The Boston Tea Party* (1964). P. Maier focuses on the crucial role of the "mob" in *From Resistance to Revolution: Colonial Radicals and the Development of American Opposition to Britain, 1756–1776* (1972). The British side is told in P. D. G. Thomas, *British Politics and the Stamp Act Crisis* (1975). Light is shed on the same subject and others in J. Brooke, *King George III* (1972). C. Bridenbaugh, *Mitre and Sceptre* (1962), explains the colonial fears of a British-imposed Anglican episcopate. A. Heimert, *Religion and the American Mind from the Great Awakening to the Revolution* (1966), seeks to find connections between the religious upheavals of the early 18th Century and the political uprising of 1776. C. Rossiter, *Seedtime of the Republic* (1953), stresses the importance of ideas in pushing the Revolution forward, as does B. Bailyn's seminal *Ideological Origins of the American Revolution* (1967), which also emphasizes the colonists' fears of a conspiracy against their liberties. Helpful biographies of key Revolutionary figures include J. C. Miller, *Sam Adams* (1936), R. D. Meade, *Patrick Henry* (1957), M. Peterson, *Thomas Jefferson and the New Nation* (1970), Dumas Malone, *Jefferson and His Time* (5 vols., 1948–1974), and P. Maier, *The Old Revolutionaries: Political Lives in the Age of Samuel Adams* (1980). Imaginative cultural history is found in Robert A. Gross, *The Minutemen and Their World* (1976). Gary B. Nash emphasizes class conflict in *The Urban Crucible: Social Change, Political Consciousness, and the Origins of the American Revolution* (1979). Two recent books take a psychological approach to the problem of the revolutionary generation's assault on established authority: Kenneth S. Lynn, *A Divided People* (1977), and Jay Fliegelman, *Prodigals and Pilgrims: The American Revolution against Patriarchal Authority, 1750–1800* (1982).

6

America Secedes from the Empire

These are the times that try men's souls. The summer soldier and the sunshine patriot will, in this crisis, shrink from the service of their country; but he that stands it now, *deserves the love and thanks of man and woman.*

THOMAS PAINE, December 1776

Congress Drafts George Washington

Bloodshed at Lexington and Concord, in April 1775, was a clarion call to arms. About 20,000 musket-bearing "Minute Men" swarmed around Boston, there to coop up the outnumbered British.

The Second Continental Congress met in Philadelphia the next month, on May 10, 1775; and this time the full slate of thirteen colonies was represented. The conservative element in Congress was still strong, despite the shooting in Massachusetts. There was no real sentiment for independence—merely a desire to continue fighting in the hope that King and Parliament would consent to a redress of grievances. Congress hopefully drafted new appeals to the British people and

King—appeals that were spurned. Anticipating a possible rebuff, the delegates also adopted measures to raise money and to create an army and navy.

Perhaps the most important single action of the Congress was to select George Washington, one of its members already in officer's uniform, to head the hastily improvised army besieging Boston. This choice was made with considerable misgivings. The tall, powerfully built, dignified, blue-eyed Virginia planter, then forty-three, had never risen above the rank of a colonel in the militia. His largest command had numbered only 1,200 men, and that had been some twenty years earlier. Falling short of true military genius, he was actually destined to lose more pitched battles than he won.

But the distinguished Virginian was gifted with outstanding powers of leadership and immense strength of character. He radiated patience, courage, self-discipline, and a sense of justice. He was a great moral force rather than a great military mind—a symbol and a rallying point. Men instinctively trusted him; they sensed that when he put himself at the head of a cause, he was prepared, if necessary, to go down with the ship. He insisted on serving without pay, though he kept a careful expense account amounting to more than $100,000. Later he sternly reprimanded his steward at Mount Vernon for providing the enemy, under duress, with supplies. He would have preferred to see the enemy put the torch to his mansion.

The Continental Congress, though dimly perceiving Washington's qualities of leadership, chose more wisely than it knew. His selection, in truth, was largely political. Americans in other sections, already jealous, were beginning to distrust the large New England army being collected around Boston. Prudence suggested a commander from Virginia, the largest and most populous of the colonies. As a man of wealth, both by inheritance and by marriage, Washington could not be accused of being a fortune seeker. As an aristocrat, he could be counted on to check the excesses of the masses.

Martha Washington (1732–1802). Destined to be the first First Lady, she was the daughter of a prominent Virginia planter. Her first husband died, leaving her a wealthy young widow with two children. Two years later she married George Washington. Known as "Lady Washington" for her charm and aristocratic graciousness, she brought considerable status to the Patriot cause. She bore Washington no children. It was said that fate had ordained that he was to be only the Father of his Country.

Bunker Hill and Hessian Hirelings

The clash of arms continued on a strangely contradictory basis. On the one hand, the Americans were emphatically affirming their loyalty to the King, and earnestly voicing their desire to patch up existing difficulties. On the other hand, they were raising armies and shooting down His Majesty's soldiers. This curious war of inconsistency was fought for fourteen long months—from April 1775 to July 1776—before the fateful plunge into independence was taken.

Gradually the tempo of warfare increased. In May 1775, a tiny American force, under Ethan Allen and Benedict Arnold, surprised and captured the British garrisons at Ticonderoga and Crown Point, on the scenic lakes of upper New York. A priceless store of powder and artillery for the siege of Boston was thus secured. In June

1775, the colonials seized a hill, now known as Bunker Hill (actually Breed's Hill), from which they menaced the enemy in Boston. The British, instead of cutting off the retreat of their foes by flanking them, blundered bloodily when they launched a frontal attack with 3,000 men. Sharpshooting Americans, numbering 1,500 and strongly entrenched, mowed down the advancing foe with frightful slaughter. But their scanty store of powder finally gave out, and they were forced to abandon the hill in disorder. With two more such victories, remarked the French foreign minister, the British would have no army left in America.

Following Bunker Hill, the King slammed the door on all hope of reconciliation. In August 1775, he formally proclaimed the colonies in rebellion, with all that this implied in the way of future hangings. The next month he further widened the chasm when he completed arrangements for hiring thousands of German troops (so-called Hessians) to help crush his rebellious subjects. Six German princes involved in the transaction needed the money (one reputedly had seventy-four children); George III needed the men.

News of the Hessian deal shocked the colonials. The quarrel, they felt, was within the family. Why bring in outside mercenaries, especially fiercely mustached foreigners, who had an exaggerated reputation for butchery and bestiality?

Hessian hirelings proved to be good soldiers in a mechanical sense, but many of them were more interested in booty than in duty. For good reason they were dubbed "Hessian flies." Seduced by American promises of land, hundreds of them finally deserted and remained in the United States to become respected citizens.

The Abortive Conquest of Canada

The unsheathed sword continued to take its toll. In October 1775, on the eve of a cruel winter, the British burned Falmouth (Portland), Maine. In that same autumn the rebels daringly undertook a two-pronged invasion of Canada. American leaders believed, erroneously, that the conquered French were explosively restive under the British yoke. A successful assault on Canada would add a fourteenth colony, while depriving Britain of a valuable base for striking at the colonies in revolt. But this large-scale attack, involving some 2,000 American troops, contradicted the claim of the colonials that they were merely fighting defensively for a redress of grievances. Invasion northward was undisguised offensive warfare.

This bold stroke for Canada narrowly missed success. One invading column under the Irish-born General Richard Montgomery, formerly of the British army, pushed up the Lake Champlain route and captured Montreal. He was joined at Quebec by the bedraggled army of General Benedict Arnold, whose men had been reduced to eating dogs and shoe leather during their grueling march through the Maine woods. An assault on Quebec, launched on the last day of 1775, was beaten off. The able Montgomery was killed; the dashing Arnold was wounded in one leg. Scattered remnants under his command retreated up the St. Lawrence River, reversing the way Montgomery had come. French-Canadian leaders, who had been generously treated by the British in the Quebec Act of 1774, showed no real desire to welcome the plundering anti-Catholic invaders.

General Benedict Arnold, Hero-Traitor (1741–1801). He died in England twenty years after fleeing the country. Legend has him repenting on his deathbed, "Let me die in my old uniform. God forgive me for ever putting on any other."

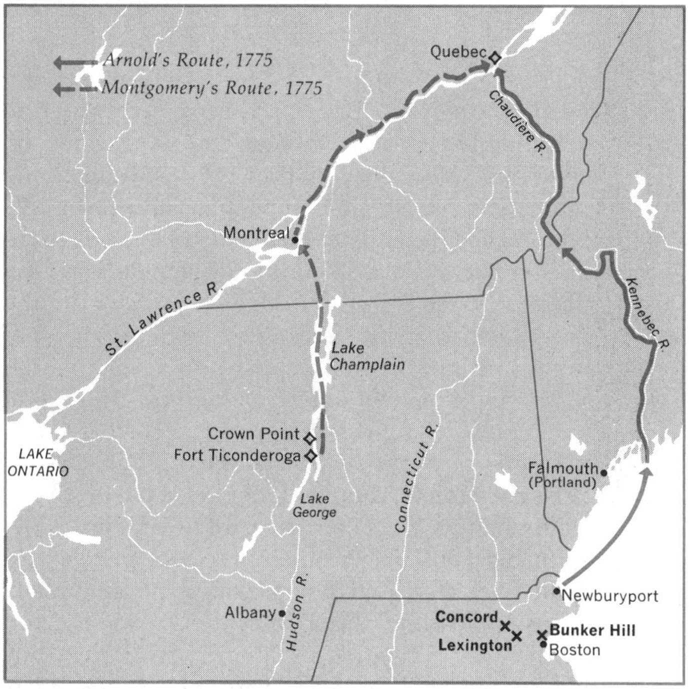

REVOLUTION IN THE NORTH, 1775–1776
Benedict Arnold's troops were described as "pretty young men" when they sailed from Massachusetts. They were considerably less pretty on their arrival in Quebec, after eight weeks of struggling through wet and frigid forests, often without food. "No one can imagine," one of them wrote, "the sweetness of a roasted shot-pouch [ammunition bag] to the famished appetite."

Bitter fighting continued in the colonies, though the Americans still disclaimed all desire for independence. In January 1776, the British set fire to the Virginia town of Norfolk. In March they were finally forced to evacuate Boston, taking with them the leading friends of the King. (Evacuation Day is still celebrated annually in Boston.) In the South the rebellious colonials won two victories in 1776; one in February against some 1,500 Loyalists at Moore's Creek Bridge, in North Carolina; and the other in June against an invading British fleet at Charleston harbor.

Thomas Paine Preaches Common Sense

Why did Americans continue to deny any intention of independence? Loyalty to the empire was deeply ingrained; colonial unity was poor; and open rebellion was dangerous, especially against a formidable Britain. Irish rebels of that day were customarily hanged, drawn, and quartered. American rebels might have fared no better. As late as January 1776—five months before independence was declared—the King's health was being toasted by the officers of Washington's mess near Boston. "God save the King" had not yet been replaced by "God save the Congress."

Gradually the Americans were shocked into an awareness of their inconsistency. Their eyes were opened by harsh British acts like the burning of Falmouth and Norfolk, and especially by the hiring of the Hessians. Early in 1776 came the publication of *Common Sense,* one of the most potent pamphlets ever written. Its author was the radical Thomas Paine, once an impoverished corset-maker's apprentice, who had come over from England a year earlier. His tract became a whirlwind best seller, and within a few months reached the astonishing total of 120,000 copies.

Paine flatly branded the shilly-shallying of the colonials as contrary to "common sense." Why not throw off the cloak of inconsistency? Nowhere in the physical universe did the smaller heavenly body control the larger one. Then why should the tiny island of England control the vast continent of America? As for the King, whom the Americans professed to revere, he was nothing but "the Royal Brute of Great Britain." America

> Paine rose to heights of eloquence in *Common Sense:* "O! ye that love mankind! Ye that dare oppose not only the tyranny but the tyrant, stand forth! Every spot of the Old World is overrun with oppression. Freedom hath been hunted round the globe. Asia and Africa have long expelled her. Europe regards her as a stranger and England hath given her warning to depart. O! receive the fugitive and prepare in time an asylum for mankind."

had a sacred mission—a moral obligation to the world—to set herself up as an independent, democratic republic, untainted by association with corrupt and monarchical Britain.

Paine's passionate protest was simple and somewhat shallow, but it was direct and persuasive. It was both high-class journalism and high-class propaganda. Thousands of American waverers, their eyes jolted open, were prodded into going the whole way. They not only perceived the folly of their position, but—perhaps most important—they realized that they could not hope for open aid from France as long as they swore allegiance to the King. The French Crown was interested in the destruction of the British Empire, not in its reconstruction under a plan of reconciliation.

Jefferson's "Explanation" of Independence

Members of the Philadelphia Congress, instructed by their respective colonies, gradually edged toward a clean break. On June 7, 1776, fiery Richard Henry Lee of Virginia moved that "These United Colonies are, and of right ought to be, free and independent states. . . ." After considerable debate, the motion was adopted nearly a month later, on July 2, 1776.

The passing of Lee's resolution was the formal "declaration" of independence by the American colonies, and technically this was all that was needed to cut the British tie. John Adams wrote confidently that ever thereafter July 2 would be celebrated annually with fireworks. But something more was required. An epochal rupture of this kind called for some formal explanation to "a candid world." An inspirational appeal was also needed to enlist other English colonies in the Americas, to invite assistance from foreign nations, and to rally resistance at home.

Shortly after Lee made his memorable motion on June 7, Congress appointed a committee to prepare an appropriate statement. The task of drafting it fell to Thomas Jefferson, a tall, freckled, sandy-haired Virginia lawyer of thirty-three. Despite his youth, he was already recognized as a brilliant writer, and he measured up splendidly to his opportunity. After some debate and amendment, the Declaration of Independence was formally approved by the Congress on July 4, 1776. It might better have been called "the Explanation of Independence" or, as one contemporary described it, "Mr. Jefferson's advertisement of Mr. Lee's resolution."

Jefferson's pronouncement, couched in a lofty style, was magnificent. He gave his appeal universality by invoking the "natural rights" of mankind —not just British rights. He argued persuasively that because the King had flouted these rights, the colonials were justified in cutting their connection. He then set forth a long list of the presumably tyrannous misdeeds of George III. The overdrawn bill of indictment included imposing taxes without consent, dispensing with trial by jury, abolishing valued laws, establishing a military dictatorship, maintaining standing armies in peacetime, cutting off trade, burning towns, hiring mercenaries, and inciting savage Indians.*

Jefferson's withering blast was admittedly one-sided. But he was in effect the prosecuting attorney, and he took certain liberties with historical truth. He was not writing history; he was making it through what has been called "the world's

*For an annotated text of the Declaration of Independence, see Appendix.

George III (1738–1820). America's last king, he was a good man, unlike some of his scandal-tainted brothers and sons, but a bad king. Doggedly determined to regain arbitrary power for the Crown, he antagonized and then lost the thirteen American colonies. During much of his sixty-year nominal reign, he seemed to be insane, but recently medical science has found that he was suffering from a rare metabolic and hereditary disease called porphyria. (Reproduced by courtesy of the Trustees of the British Museum)

greatest editorial." He owned many slaves, and his affirmation that "all men are created equal" was to haunt him and his countrymen for generations.

The formal declaration of independence cleared the air as a thundershower does on a muggy day. Foreign aid could be solicited with greater hope of success. Those patriots who defied the King were now rebels, not loving subjects shooting their way into reconciliation. They must all hang together, Franklin is said to have grimly remarked, or they would all hang separately. Or, in the eloquent language of the Great Declaration, "We mutually pledge to each other our lives, our fortunes and our sacred honor."

Jefferson's defiant Declaration of Independence had a universal impact unmatched by any other American document. This "shout heard round the world" has been a source of inspiration to countless revolutionary movements against arbitrary authority. Lafayette hung a copy on a wall in his home, leaving beside it room for a future French Declaration of the Rights of Man—a declaration that was officially born thirteen years later.

Patriots and Loyalists

The War of Independence, strictly speaking, was a war within a war. Colonials loyal to the King (Loyalists) fought the American rebels (Patriots), while the rebels also fought the British Redcoats. Loyalists were derisively called "Tories" after the dominant political factions in England, while Patriots were called Whigs after the opposition factions in England. A popular definition of a Tory among the Patriots betrayed bitterness: "A Tory is a thing whose head is in England, and its body in America, and its neck ought to be stretched."

Like many revolutions, the American Revolution was a minority movement. Roughly one-third of the people were apathetic or neutral, including those Byrds of Virginia who sat on the fence. Perhaps somewhat more than one-third were in varying degrees rebellious; probably somewhat fewer than one-third were Loyalists who remained true to their King. Families were often split over the issue of independence: Benjamin Franklin supported the Patriot side, while his handsome illegitimate son, William Franklin (the last royal governor of New Jersey), upheld the Loyalist cause.

The Loyalists were tragic figures. For generations Englishmen in the New World had been taught fidelity to their King. Loyalty is ordinarily

> The American signers had reason to fear for their necks. In 1802, twenty-six years later, George III approved this death sentence for seven Irish rebels: ". . . you are to be hanged by the neck, but not until you are dead; for while you are still living your bodies are to be taken down, your bowels torn out and burned before your faces, your heads then cut off, and your bodies divided each into four quarters, and your heads and quarters to be then at the King's disposal; and may the Almighty God have mercy on your souls."

regarded as a major virtue—loyalty to one's family, one's friends, one's country. If the King had triumphed, as he seemed likely to do, the Loyalists would have been acclaimed patriots, and defeated rebels like Washington would have been disgraced, severely punished, and probably forgotten.

Conservative Americans generally remained loyal—the people of education and wealth, of culture and caution. These moderate souls were satisfied with their lot, and believed that any violent change would only be for the worse. They feared that the "dirty rabble," inflamed by violence, might break out of control. "If I must be devoured," moaned one aristocrat, "let me be devoured by the jaws of a lion, and not gnawed to death by rats and vermin." Loyalists were also more numerous among the older generation. Young men make revolutions, and from the outset energetic, purposeful, and militant young men surged forward—figures like the sleeplessly scheming Samuel Adams and the impassioned Patrick Henry. His flaming outcry before the Virginia Assembly—"Give me liberty or give me death!"—still quickens patriotic pulses.

Loyalists also included the King's officers and other beneficiaries of the Crown—men who knew which side their daily bread came from. The same was generally true of the Anglican clergy and a large portion of their flocks, all of whom had long been taught obedience to the King.

Usually the Loyalists were most numerous where the Anglican Church was strongest. A notable exception was Virginia, where the debt-burdened Anglican aristocrats flocked into the rebel camp. The King's followers were well entrenched in aristocratic New York City and Charleston, and also in Quaker Pennsylvania and New Jersey, where General Washington felt that he was fighting in "the enemy's country." While his men were starving at Valley Forge, nearby Pennsylvania farmers were selling their produce to the British for the King's gold.

Loyalists were least numerous in New England, where self-government was especially strong and mercantilism especially weak. Rebels were the most numerous where Presbyterianism and Congregationalism flourished, notably in New England. Invading British armies vented their contempt and anger by using Yankee churches for pigsties.

The Loyalist Exodus

Before the Declaration of Independence in 1776, persecution of the Loyalists was relatively mild. Yet they were subjected to some brutality, including tarring and feathering and riding astride fence rails.

After the Declaration of Independence, which sharply separated Loyalists from Patriots, harsher methods prevailed. The rebels naturally desired a united front. Putting loyalty to the colonies first, they regarded their opponents, not themselves, as

Tory Suspended, While Goose is Plucked for Coat of Feathers. (The Bettmann Archive, Inc.)

traitors. Loyalists were roughly handled; hundreds were imprisoned; and a few noncombatants were hanged. But there was no wholesale reign of terror comparable to that which later bloodied both France and Russia. For one thing, the colonials reflected Anglo-Saxon regard for order; for another, the leading Loyalists were prudent enough to flee to the British lines.

About 80,000 loyal supporters of George III were driven out or fled, but several hundred thousand or so of the mild Loyalists were permitted to stay. The estates of many of the fugitives were confiscated and sold—a relatively painless way of helping to finance the war. Confiscation often worked great hardship, as, for example, when two aristocratic old ladies were forced to live in their former chicken house.

Some 50,000 Loyalist volunteers at one time or another bore arms for the British. They also helped the King's cause by serving as spies, by inciting the Indians, and by keeping Patriot soldiers at home to protect their families. Ardent Loyalists had their hearts in their cause, and a major blunder of the haughty British was not to make full use of them in the fighting.

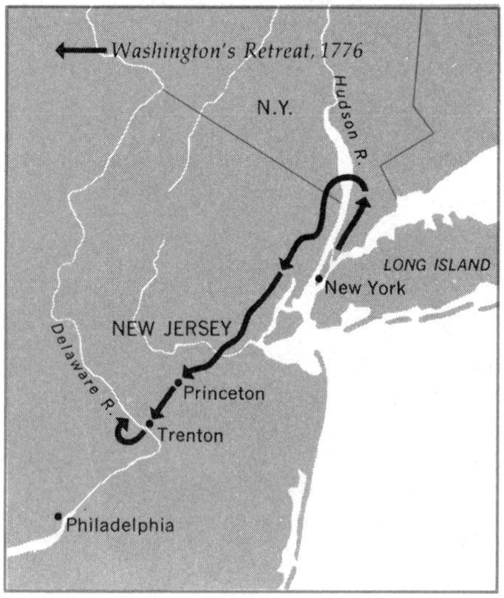

NEW YORK AND NEW JERSEY, 1776–1777

General Washington at Bay

With Boston evacuated in March 1776, the British concentrated on New York as a base of operations. Here was a splendid seaport, centrally located, where the King could count on cooperation from the numerous Loyalists. An awe-inspiring British fleet appeared off New York in July 1776. It consisted of some 500 ships and 35,000 men—the largest armed force to be seen in America until the Civil War. General Washington, dangerously outnumbered, could muster only 18,000 ill-trained troops with which to meet the crack army of the invader.

Disaster befell the Americans in the summer and fall of 1776. Outgeneraled and outmaneuvered, they were routed at the Battle of Long Island, where panic seized the raw recruits. By the narrowest of margins, and thanks to a favoring wind and fog, Washington escaped to Manhattan Island. Retreating northward, he crossed the Hudson River to New Jersey, and finally reached the Delaware River with the British close at his heels. Tauntingly, enemy buglers sounded the fox-hunting call, so familiar to Virginians of Washington's day. The Patriot cause was at low ebb when the rebel remnants fled across the river, after collecting all available boats to forestall pursuit.

The wonder is that Washington's adversary, General William Howe, did not speedily crush the demoralized American forces. But he was no military genius, and he well remembered the horrible slaughter at Bunker Hill, where he had commanded. The country was rough, supplies were slow in coming, and as a professional soldier Howe did not relish the rigors of winter campaigning. He evidently found more agreeable the bedtime company of his mistress, the wife of one of his subordinates—a scandal with which American satirists had a good deal of ribald fun.

Washington, now almost counted out, stealthily recrossed the ice-clogged Delaware River. At Trenton, on December 26, 1776, he surprised and captured a thousand Hessians who were sleeping off the effects of their Christmas celebration. A

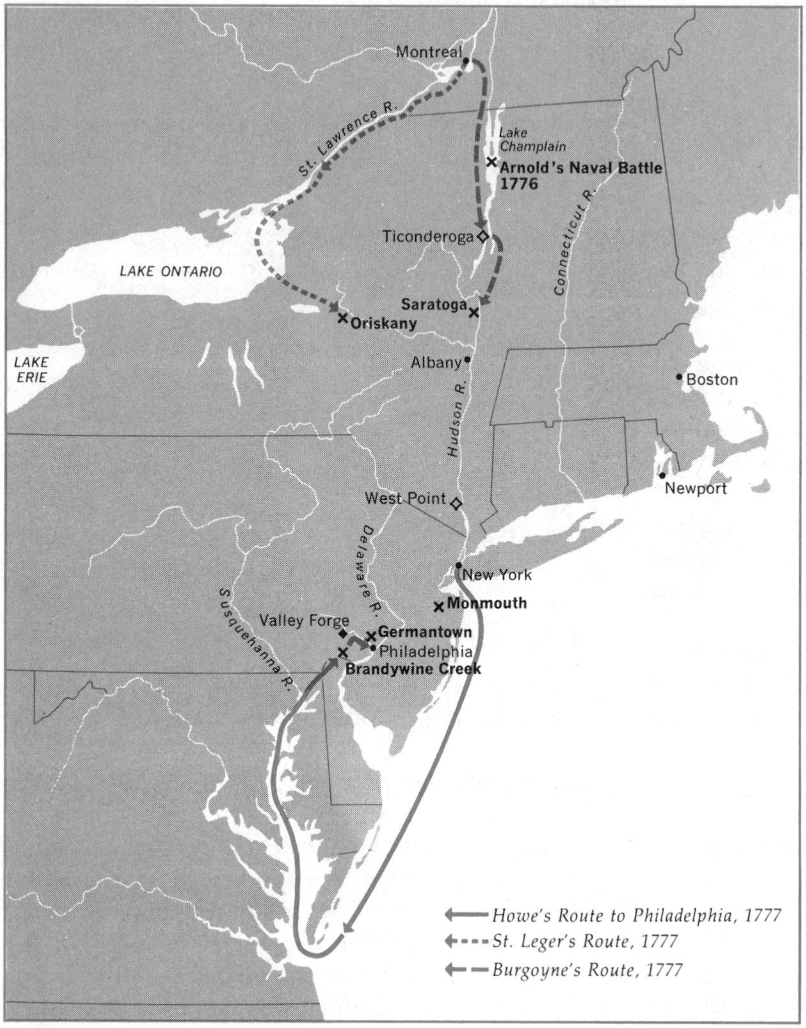

NEW YORK–PENNSYLVANIA THEATER, 1777–1778

Distinguished members of the Continental Congress fled from Philadelphia in near-panic as the British army approached. Thomas Paine reported that at three o'clock in the morning the streets were "as full of Men, Women, and Children as on a Market Day." John Adams had anticipated that "I shall run away, I suppose, with the rest," since "we are too brittle ware, you know, to stand the dashing of balls and bombs." Adams got his chance to decamp with the others into the interior of Pennsylvania, and tried to put the best face on things. "This tour," he commented, "has given me an opportunity of seeing many parts of this country which I never saw before."

week later, leaving his campfires burning as a ruse, he slipped away and inflicted a sharp defeat on a smaller British detachment at Princeton. This brilliant New Jersey campaign, crowned by these two lifesaving victories, revealed "Old Fox" Washington at his military best.

Burgoyne's Blundering Invasion

London officials adopted an intricate scheme for capturing the vital Hudson River Valley in 1777. If successful, the British would sever New England from the rest of the states and paralyze the American cause. The main invading force, under an actor-playwright-soldier, General ("Gentleman Johnny") Burgoyne, would push down the Lake Champlain route from Canada. General Howe's troops in New York, if needed, could advance up the Hudson River to meet Burgoyne near Albany. A third and much smaller British force, commanded by Colonel St. Leger, would come in from the west by way of Lake Ontario and the Mohawk Valley.

British planners did not reckon with General Benedict Arnold. After his repulse at Quebec in 1775, he had retreated slowly along the St. Lawrence River back to the Lake Champlain area, by heroic efforts keeping an army in the field. The

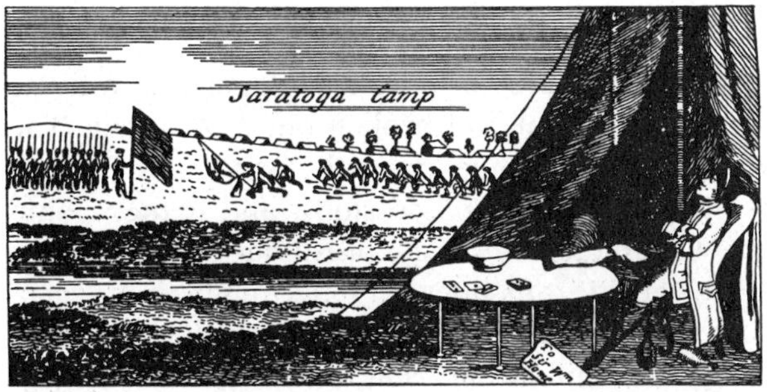

The Generals in America Doing Nothing, or Worse Than Nothing. British satire on the sloth and indifference of General Burgoyne. After playing solitaire and drinking heavily, he falls asleep as his plea to General Howe for help drops to the floor. Meanwhile Burgoyne's army is surrendering.

British had pursued his tattered force to Lake Champlain in 1776. But they could not move farther south until they had won control of the lake, which, in the absence of roads, was indispensable for carrying their supplies.

Tireless, Arnold assembled a small fleet, and the British had to stop to construct a larger one. His tiny flotilla was finally destroyed after desperate fighting, but winter was descending and the British were forced to retire to Canada. General Burgoyne had to start anew from this base the following year. If Arnold had not contributed his daring and skill, the British invaders of 1776 almost certainly would have penetrated as far south as Fort Ticonderoga. If Burgoyne had started from this springboard in 1777, instead of Canada, he almost certainly would have succeeded in his venture. (At long last the apparently futile American invasion of Canada in 1775 was beginning to pay rich dividends.)

General Burgoyne began his fateful invasion with 7,000 regular troops. He was encumbered by a heavy baggage train and a considerable number of women, many of whom were wives of his officers. Progress was painfully slow, for sweaty axmen had to chop a path through the forest, while American militiamen began to gather like hornets on Burgoyne's flanks.

General Howe, meanwhile, was causing astonished eyebrows to rise. At a time when it seemed obvious that he should be starting up the Hudson River from New York to join his slowly advancing colleague, he deliberately embarked with the main British army for an attack on Philadelphia, the rebel capital. As scholars now know, he wanted to force a general engagement with Washington's army, destroy it, and leave the path wide open for Burgoyne's thrust. Howe apparently assumed that he had ample time to assist Burgoyne directly, should he be needed.

General Washington, keeping a wary eye on the British in New York, hastily transferred his army to the vicinity of Philadelphia. There, late in 1777, he was defeated in two pitched battles, at Brandywine Creek and Germantown. Pleasure-loving General Howe then settled down comfortably in the lively capital, leaving Burgoyne to flounder through the wilds of upper New York. Benjamin Franklin, recently sent to Paris as an envoy, truthfully jested that Howe had not captured Philadelphia but that Philadelphia had captured Howe. Washington finally retired to winter quarters at Valley Forge, a strong hilly position some twenty miles northwest of Philadelphia, and there his frost-bitten and hungry men were short of about everything except misery. This rabble was nevertheless whipped into a professional army by the recently arrived Prussian drillmaster, the profane but patient Baron von Steuben.

Burgoyne meanwhile had begun to bog down north of Albany, while a host of American militiamen, scenting the kill, swarmed about him. In a series of sharp engagements, in which General Arnold was again shot in the leg wounded at Quebec, the British army was trapped. Meanwhile the Americans had driven back St. Leger's force at Oriskany. Unable to advance or retreat, Burgoyne was forced to surrender his entire command at Saratoga, on October 17, 1777, to the American General Gates.

Saratoga ranks high among the decisive battles of both American and world history. The victory immensely revived the faltering colonial cause. Even more important, it made possible the urgently needed foreign aid from France which in turn helped insure American independence.

Strange French Bedfellows

France, thirsting for revenge, was eager to inflame the quarrel that had broken out in America. The New World colonies were by far Britain's most valuable overseas possessions, and if they could be wrested from her, she presumably would cease to be a front-rank power. France might then regain her former position and prestige, the loss of which in the recent Seven Years' War rankled deeply.

America's cause rapidly became something of a fad in France. The bored aristocracy, which had developed some interest in the writings of liberal French thinkers like Rousseau, was rather intrigued by the ideal of American liberty. Hard-headed French officials, on the other hand, were not prompted by a love for America but by a realistic concern for the interests of France. Any marriage with the United States would be strictly one of convenience.

After the shooting at Lexington, in April 1775, the French agents undertook to blow on the embers. They secretly provided the Americans with lifesaving amounts of powder and other munitions, chiefly through a sham company rigged up for that purpose. About 90 percent of all the gunpowder used by the Americans in the first two and a half years of the war came from French arsenals.

The Horse *America* Throwing His Master. The rider is Lord North, British Prime Minister, represented with a whip of swords. Note the Frenchman in the background. (A British cartoon in the New York Public Library.)

Secrecy enshrouded all these French schemes. Open aid to the American rebels might provoke England into a declaration of war; and France, still weakened by her recent defeat, was not ready to fight. She feared that the American rebellion might fade out, for the colonies were proclaiming their desire to patch up differences. But the Declaration of Independence in 1776 showed that the Americans really meant business; and the smashing victory at Saratoga seemed to indicate that they had an excellent chance of winning their freedom.

After the humiliation at Saratoga in 1777, the British Parliament belatedly passed a measure which in effect offered the Americans home rule within the empire. This was essentially all that the colonials had ever asked for—except independence. If the French were going to break up the British Empire, they would have to bestir themselves. Wily and bespectacled old Benjamin Franklin, whose simple fur cap and witty sayings had captivated the French public, played skillfully on France's fears of reconciliation.

The French King, Louis XVI, was reluctant to intervene. Although somewhat stupid, he was alert enough to see grave dangers in aiding the Americans openly and incurring war with Britain. But his ministers at length won him over. They argued that hostilities were inevitable, sooner or later, to undo the victor's peace of 1763. If England should regain her colonies, she might join with them to seize the sugar-rich French West Indies, and thus secure compensation for the cost of the recent rebellion. The French had better fight while they could have an American ally, rather than wait and fight both Britain and her reunited colonials.

So France, in 1778, offered the Americans a treaty of alliance. It promised everything that Britain was offering—plus independence. Both allies bound themselves to wage war until the United States had won its freedom, and until both agreed on terms with the common foe.

This was the first entangling military alliance in the experience of the Republic, and one that later caused prolonged trouble. The American

> After concluding the alliance, France sent a minister to America, to the delight of one Patriot journalist: "Who would have thought that the American colonies, imperfectly known in Europe a few years ago and claimed by every pettifogging lawyer in the House of Commons, every cobbler in the beer-houses of London, as a part of their property, should to-day receive an ambassador from the most powerful monarchy in Europe."

people, with ingrained isolationist tendencies, accepted the French entanglement with distaste. They were painfully aware that it involved a hereditary foe which was also a Roman Catholic power. But when one's house is on fire, one does not inquire too closely into the background of those who carry the water buckets.

The Colonial War Becomes a World War

England and France thus came to blows in 1778, and the shot fired at Lexington rapidly widened into a global conflagration. Spain entered the fray against Britain in 1779, as did Holland. Combined Spanish and French fleets outnumbered those of England, and on two occasions the British Isles seemed to be at the mercy of hostile warships.

The weak maritime neutrals of Europe, who had suffered from Britain's dominance over the seas, now began to demand more respect for their rights. In 1780 the imperious Catherine the Great of Russia took the lead in organizing the Armed Neutrality, which she later sneeringly called the "Armed Nullity." It lined up almost all the remaining European neutrals in an attitude of passive hostility toward England. The war was now being fought not only in Europe and North America, but also in South America, the Caribbean, and Asia.

To say that America, with some French aid, defeated England is like saying, "Daddy and I killed the bear." To the Mother Country, struggling for her very life, the scuffle in the New World became secondary. The Americans deserve credit for having kept the war going until 1778, with secret French aid. But they did not achieve their independence until the conflict erupted into a multi-power world war that was too big for Britain to handle. From 1778 to 1783, France provided the rebels with large sums of money, immense amounts of equipment, about one-half of America's regular armed forces, and practically all of the new nation's naval strength.

Britain Against the World

Britain and Allies	*Enemy or Unfriendly Powers*	
Great Britain Some Loyalists and Indians 30,000 hired Hessians (*Total population on Britain's side: c. 8 million*)	Belligerents (*Total population: c. 39.5 million*)	United States, 1775–1783 France, 1778–1783 Spain, 1779–1783 Holland, 1779–1783
		Ireland (restive)
	Members of the Armed Neutrality (with dates of joining)	Russia, 1780 Denmark–Norway, 1780 Sweden, 1780 Holy Roman Empire, 1781 Prussia, 1782 Portugal, 1782 Two Sicilies, 1783 (after peace signed)

France's entrance into the conflict forced the British to change their basic strategy in America. Hitherto they could count on blockading the colonial coast and commanding the seas. Now the French had powerful fleets in American waters, chiefly to protect their own valuable West Indian islands, but in a position to jeopardize Britain's blockade and lines of supply. The British therefore decided to evacuate Philadelphia and concentrate their strength in New York City.

In June 1778, the withdrawing Redcoats were attacked by General Washington at Monmouth, New Jersey, on a blisteringly hot day. Scores of men collapsed or died from sunstroke. But the battle was indecisive, and the British escaped to New York, although about one-third of their Hessians deserted. Henceforth, except for the Yorktown interlude of 1781, Washington remained in the New York area hemming in the British.

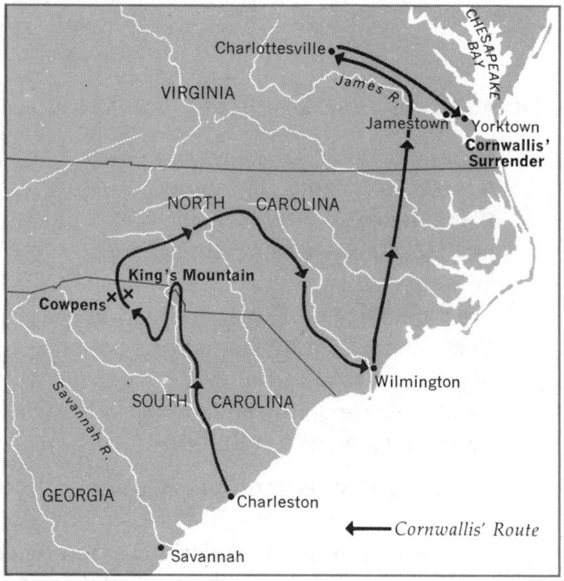

WAR IN THE SOUTH, 1780–1781

Blow and Counterblow

In the summer of 1780 a powerful French army of 6,000 regular troops, commanded by the Comte de Rochambeau, arrived in Newport, Rhode Island. The Americans were somewhat suspicious of their former enemies; in fact, several ugly flare-ups, involving minor bloodshed, had already occurred between the new allies. But French gold and goodwill melted restraints. Dancing parties were arranged with the prim Puritan maidens; and one French officer related, doubtless with exaggeration, "The simple innocence of the Garden of Eden prevailed." No real military advantage came immediately from this French reinforcement, although preparations were made for a Franco-American attack on New York.

Comte de Rochambeau (1735–1807). He got along so well with Washington that one observer said that the Comte was created to understand the American general. A statue of Rochambeau, a gift from France in 1902, was placed in Lafayette Square, across from the White House in Washington, D.C. (National Portrait Gallery, Smithsonian Institution, Washington, D.C.)

Improving American morale was staggered later in 1780, when General Benedict Arnold turned traitor. A leader of undoubted dash and brilliance, he was ambitious, greedy, unscrupulous, and suffering from a well-grounded but petulant feeling that his valuable services were not fully appreciated. He plotted with the British to sell out the key stronghold of West Point, which commanded the Hudson River, for £6,300 and an officer's commission. By the sheerest accident the plot was detected in the nick of time, and Arnold fled to the British. "Whom can we trust now?" cried General Washington in anguish.

The British meanwhile had devised a plan to roll up the colonies, beginning with the South, where the Loyalists were numerous. Georgia was ruthlessly overrun in 1778–1779; Charleston, South Carolina, fell in 1780. The surrender of the city to the British involved the capture of 5,000 men and 400 cannon, and was a heavier loss to the

Americans, in relation to existing strength, than that of Burgoyne was to the British.

Warfare now intensified in the Carolinas, where Patriots bitterly fought their Loyalist neighbors. It was not uncommon for prisoners on both sides to be butchered in cold blood after they had thrown down their arms. A turn of the tide came late in 1780 and early in 1781, when American riflemen wiped out a British detachment at King's Mountain, and then defeated a smaller force at Cowpens. In the Carolina campaign of 1781, General Nathanael Greene, a Quaker-reared tactician, distinguished himself by his strategy of delay. Standing and then retreating, he exhausted his foe, General Cornwallis, in vain pursuit. By losing battles but winning campaigns, the "Fighting Quaker" finally succeeded in clearing most of Georgia and South Carolina of British troops.

The Land Frontier and the Sea Frontier

The West was ablaze during much of the war. Indian allies of George III, hoping to protect their land, were busy with torch and tomahawk; they were egged on by British agents branded as "hair buyers" because they allegedly paid bounties for American scalps. Fateful 1777 was known as "the Bloody Year" on the frontier. Yet the human tide of westward-moving pioneers did not halt its flow. Eloquent testimony is provided by place names in Kentucky, such as Lexington (named after the battle) and Louisville (named after America's new ally, Louis XVI).

In the wild Illinois country the British were vulnerable to attack, for they held scattered posts which they had captured from the French. An audacious frontiersman, George Rogers Clark, conceived the idea of seizing these forts by surprise. With the blessing of Virginia and £1,200 in depreciated currency, he floated down the Ohio River with about 175 men and captured in quick succession Kaskaskia, Cahokia, and Vincennes. These daring forays no doubt helped quiet the Indians. But Clark's admirers have also assumed, without positive proof, that his occupation of

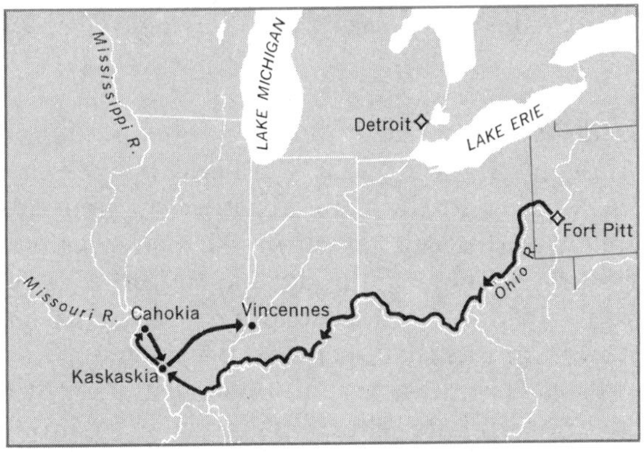

GEORGE ROGERS CLARK'S CAMPAIGN, 1778–1779

the southwest corner of the great area north of the Ohio River forced the British to cede the whole region to the United States at the peace table in Paris.

America's infant navy had meanwhile been laying the foundations of a brilliant tradition. The naval establishment consisted of only a handful of nondescript ships, commanded by daring officers, the most famous of whom was a hard-fighting young Scotsman, John Paul Jones. As events turned out, this tiny naval force never made a real dent in Britain's thunderous fleets. Its chief contribution was in destroying British merchant shipping, and thus carrying the war into the waters around the British Isles. An English song of the time, critical of the Royal Navy, began:

> The tradesmen stand still, and the merchant bemoans
> The losses he meets with from such as Paul Jones.

More numerous and damaging than ships of the regular American navy were swift privateers. These craft were privately owned armed ships—legalized pirates in a sense—specifically author-

Early American Naval Flag. The flag is shown with a yellow background and a rattler striking.

ized by Congress to prey on enemy shipping. Altogether over 1,000 American privateers, responding to the call of patriotism and profit, sallied forth with about 70,000 men ("sailors of fortune"). They captured some 600 British prizes, while British warships captured about as many American merchantmen and privateers.

Privateering was not an unalloyed asset. It had the unfortunate effect of diverting manpower from the main war effort and involving Americans, including Benedict Arnold, in speculation and graft. But the privateers brought in urgently needed gold, harassed the enemy, and raised American morale by providing victories at a time when victories were few. British shipping was so badly riddled by privateers and by the regular American navy that insurance rates skyrocketed. Merchant ships were compelled to sail in convoy, and British shippers and manufacturers brought increasing pressure on Parliament to end the war on honorable terms.

Yorktown and the Final Curtain

One of the darkest periods of the war was 1780–1781, before the last decisive victory. Inflation of the currency was continuing at full gallop. Not only was the government virtually bankrupt but Congress had been forced to repudiate its financial obligations, in part, on a forty-to-one basis. Despair was prevalent; disunion was increasing among the states; and mutiny over back pay was spreading in the army.

Meanwhile the British General Cornwallis was blundering into a trap. After futile operations in Virginia, he had fallen back to Chesapeake Bay at Yorktown, there to await seaborne supplies and reinforcements. He assumed that Britain would continue to control the sea. But these few fateful weeks just happened to be one of the brief periods during the war in America when British naval superiority slipped away.

The French were now prepared to cooperate energetically in a brilliant stroke. Admiral de Grasse, operating with a powerful fleet in the West Indies, advised the Americans that he was free to join with them in an assault on Cornwallis at Yorktown. Quick to seize this opportunity, General Washington made a swift march of more than 300 miles (483 kilometers) to the Chesapeake from the New York area. Accompanied by Rochambeau's French army, he beset the British by land, while De Grasse blockaded them by sea after beating off the British fleet. Completely cornered, Cornwallis surrendered his entire force of 7,000 men, on October 19, 1781, as his band appropriately played "The World Turn'd Upside Down." The triumph was no less French than American: the French provided essentially all the seapower and about half of the regular troops in the besieging army of some 16,000 men.

Stunned by news of the disaster, Prime Minister Lord North cried, "Oh God! It's all over! It's all over!" But it was not. George III stubbornly planned to continue the struggle, for England was far from being crushed. She still had 54,000 troops in North America, including 32,000 in the United States. Washington returned with his army to New York, there to continue keeping a vigilant eye on the British force of 10,000 men.

Fighting actually continued for more than a year after Yorktown, with Patriot-Loyalist warfare in the South especially savage. "No quarter for Tories" was the common battle cry. One of Washington's most valuable contributions was to keep the languishing cause alive, the army in the field, and the states together during these

Lord George Germain, secretary of state for the colonies and a chief architect of war plans, swelled with confidence after Yorktown: "So very contemptible is the Rebel Force now in all Parts, and so vast is Our Superiority everywhere, that no resistance on their [Americans'] Part is to be apprehended, that can materially obstruct the Progress of the King's Army in the Speedy Suppression of the Rebellion."

Benjamin Franklin (1706–1790). He left school at age ten, and became a wealthy businessman; a journalist; an inventor; a scientist; a legislator; and pre-eminently a statesman-diplomatist. He was sent to France in 1776 as the American envoy at age seventy, and he remained there until 1785, negotiating the alliance with the French and helping to negotiate the treaty of peace. His fame had preceded him, and when he discarded his wig for the fur cap of a simple "American agriculturist," he took French society by storm. The ladies, with whom he was a great favorite, honored him by adopting the high *coiffure à la Franklin* in imitation of his cap.

critical months. Otherwise a satisfactory peace treaty might never have been signed.

Peace at Paris

After Yorktown, the war-weary British were increasingly ready to come to terms. They had suffered heavy reverses in India and in the West Indies. The island of Minorca in the Mediterranean had fallen; the Rock of Gibraltar was tottering. Lord North's ministry collapsed in March 1782, temporarily ending the personal rule of George III. A Whig ministry, rather favorable to the Americans, replaced the Tory regime of Lord North.

Three American peace negotiators had meanwhile gathered at Paris: the aging but astute Benjamin Franklin; the flinty John Adams, vigilant for New England interests; and the impulsive John Jay of New York, deeply suspicious of Old World intrigue. The three envoys had explicit instructions from Congress to make no separate peace, and to consult with their French allies at all stages of the negotiations. But the American representatives chafed under this directive. They well knew that it had been written by a subservient Congress, with the French Foreign Office indirectly guiding the pen.

France was in a painful position. She had induced Spain to enter the war on her side, in part by promising to deliver British-held Gibraltar. Yet the towering rock was defying frantic joint assaults by Frenchmen and Spaniards. Spain also coveted the immense trans-Allegheny area, on which restless American pioneers were already settling.

France, ever eager to smash Britain's empire, desired an independent United States, but one feebly independent. She therefore schemed to keep the new republic cooped up east of the Allegheny Mountains. A weak America—like a horse gentle enough to plow but not vigorous enough to kick—would be easier to manage in promoting French interests and policy. France was paying a heavy price in men and treasure to win America's independence, and she wanted to get her money's worth.

But John Jay was unwilling to play France's game. Suspiciously alert, he perceived that the French could not satisfy the conflicting ambitions of both Americans and Spaniards. He saw signs—or thought he did—which indicated that the Paris Foreign Office was about to betray America's trans-Allegheny interests to satisfy those of Spain. He therefore secretly made separate overtures to London, contrary to his instructions from Congress. The hard-pressed British, eager to entice one of their enemies from the alliance, speedily came to terms with the Americans. A preliminary treaty of peace was signed in 1782; the final peace, the next year.

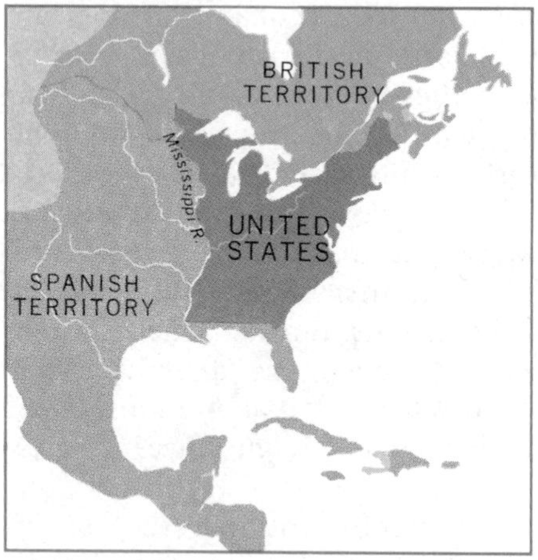

UNITED STATES IN 1783

By the Treaty of Paris of 1783, the British formally recognized the independence of the United States. In addition, they granted generous boundaries, stretching majestically to the Mississippi on the west, to the Great Lakes on the north, and to Spanish Florida on the south. (Spain had recently captured Florida from Britain.) The Yankees, though now divorced from the Empire, were to retain a share in the priceless fisheries of Newfoundland. The Canadians, of course, were profoundly displeased.

The Americans, on their part, had to yield important concessions. Loyalists were not to be further persecuted, and Congress was to *recommend* to the state legislatures that confiscated Loyalist property be restored. As for the debts long owed to British creditors, the American states were bound to put no lawful obstacles in the way of their collection. Unhappily for future harmony, the assurances regarding both debts and Loyalists were not carried out in the manner hoped for by London.

> Blundering George III, a poor loser, wrote this of America: "Knavery seems to be so much the striking feature of its inhabitants that it may not in the end be an evil that they become aliens to this Kingdom."

A New Nation Legitimized

Britain's terms were liberal almost beyond belief. The enormous trans-Allegheny area was thrown in as a virtual gift, for George Rogers Clark had captured only a small segment of it. Why the generosity? Had the United States beaten the Mother Country to her knees?

The key to the riddle may be found in the Old World. At the time the peace terms were drafted, England was trying to seduce America from her French alliance, so she made the terms as alluring as possible. The shaky Whig ministry, hanging on by its fingernails for only a few months, was more friendly to the Americans than were the

The Reconciliation Between Britannia and Her Daughter America. America (represented by an Indian) is invited to buss (kiss) her mother. (Detail from an English cartoon. New York Public Library.)

Tories. It was determined, by a policy of liberality, to salve recent wounds, reopen old trade channels, and prevent future wars over the coveted trans-Allegheny region. This far-visioned policy was regrettably not followed by the successors of the Whigs.

In spirit, the Americans made a separate peace—contrary to the French alliance. In fact, they did not. The Paris Foreign Office formally approved the terms of peace, though disturbed by the lone-wolf course of its American ally. France was immensely relieved by the prospect of bringing the costly conflict to an end, and of freeing herself from her embarrassing promises to the Spanish Crown.

America alone gained from the world-girdling war. The British, though soon to stage a comeback, were battered and beaten. The French gained sweet revenge, but plunged headlong down the slippery slope to bankruptcy and revolution. In truth, Dame Fortune smiled benignly on the Americans. Snatching their independence from the furnace of world conflict, they began their national career with a splendid territorial birthright and a priceless heritage of freedom. Seldom, if ever, has any people been so favored.

VARYING VIEWPOINTS

The consequences of the Revolution have recently been re-examined in much the same way as its causes. Scholars used to think that the conflict brought sweeping changes in social life and political institutions. Some historians now consider that view greatly exaggerated. They tend to agree with John Adams, who once said that history had already made radicals out of the Americans—and that the Revolution, therefore, was a conservative protest to maintain existing liberties. But this emphasis does not necessarily deny the real radicalism of the Revolution. There were sweeping changes, modern scholars conclude, but not so much in daily life as in people's minds. Democratic and egalitarian ideas had been current in the colonial period but always surrounded by a certain air of illegitimacy and impermanency. Now they could be seen as fully legitimate, correct, and successful. This sense of rightness began to spill over into many areas of life, creating pressures for social change in later movements of American history, such as Jacksonian democracy and the drive to abolish slavery. But problems remain with this persuasive view. What, for example, are historians to make of the Loyalists, supposedly arch-conservatives, if in fact we regard the Patriots themselves as conservative defenders of existing conditions?

SELECT READINGS

The war is sketched briefly in H. H. Peckham, *The War for Independence* (1958); more fully in J. R. Alden, *A History of the American Revolution* (1969). An excellent military history is D. Higginbotham, *The War of American Independence: Military Attitudes, Policies and Practice, 1763–1789* (1971). A highly original essay is John Shy, *A People Numerous and Armed: Reflections on the Military Struggle for American Independence on the Military Struggle for American Independence* (1976). Highly imaginative is Charles Royster, *A Revolutionary People at War: The Continental Army and the American Character* (1980). The conflict is considered in its European setting in Piers Mackesy, *The War for America, 1775–1783* (1964). Carl Becker's classic *The Declaration of Independence* (1922) is masterful; on the same subject, see also David Hawke, *A Transaction of*

Free Men (1964). Propaganda is analyzed in Carl Berger, *Broadsides and Bayonets* (1961). The role of the Loyalists is treated in W. H. Nelson, *The American Tory* (1961), W. Brown, *The Good Americans: The Loyalists in the American Revolution* (1969), R. Calhoon, *The Loyalists in Revolutionary America* (1973), and B. Bailyn's unusually sensitive biography of the governor of colonial Massachusetts, *The Ordeal of Thomas Hutchinson* (1974). A general treatment of an often neglected subject is B. Quarles, *The Negro in the American Revolution* (1961). See also D. MacLeod, *Slavery, Race and the American Revolution* (1974), and D. B. Davis, *The Problem of Slavery in the Age of Revolution, 1770–1823* (1975), an able, gracefully written book. International implications are developed in S. F. Bemis, *The Diplomacy of the American Revolution* (1935), W. C. Stinchcombe, *The American Revolution and the French Alliance* (1969), J. H. Hutson, *John Adams and the Diplomacy of the American Revolution* (1980), and in R. B. Morris, *The Peacemakers: The Great Powers and American Independence* (1965). See also the same author's *The American Revolution Reconsidered* (1967). Gary Wills has trenchantly reexamined the Declaration in *Inventing America: Jefferson's Declaration of Independence* (1980). Attention to the social history of the Revolution has been largely inspired by J. F. Jameson's seminal *The American Revolution Considered as a Social Movement* (1926). J. R. Main, *The Social Structure of Revolutionary America* (1969), takes the exploration further along the same lines, with conclusions somewhat at variance with Jameson's. See also James Hutson and S. Kurz, *Essays on the American Revolution* (1973). Interesting biographies are S. E. Morison's swashbuckling *John Paul Jones* (1959); E. Foner's *Tom Paine and Revolutionary America* (1976); O. Aldridge's study of the same subject, *Man of Reason* (1959); J. T. Flexner, *George Washington in the American Revolution, 1775–1783* (1968); and R. Burlingame, *Benjamin Franklin: Envoy Extraordinary* (1967). British troubles are laid bare in G. S. Brown, *The American Secretary: The Colonial Policy of Lord George Germain, 1775–1778* (1963), and in W. B. Willcox, *Portrait of a General: Sir Henry Clinton in the War of Independence* (1964). Women are the subject of Linda K. Kerber, *Women of the Republic: Intellect and Ideology in Revolutionary America* (1980), and Mary Beth Norton, *Liberty's Daughters: The Revolutionary Experience of American Women* (1980). Jack N. Rakove has provided a masterful history of the Continental Congress in *The Beginnings of National Politics* (1979). An excellent guide to the scholarly controversies about the period is Jack P. Greene, ed., *The Reinterpretation of the American Revolution* (1968). Michael Kammen brilliantly evokes the ways the Revolution has been enshrined in the national memory in *A Season of Youth: The American Revolution and the Historical Imagination* (1978).

7

The Confederation and the Constitution

This example of changing the constitution by assembling the wise men of the state, instead of assembling armies, will be worth as much to the world as the former examples we have given it.

THOMAS JEFFERSON, 1787

The Residue of Revolution

The American Revolution was not a revolution in the sense of a radical or total change. It was not a sudden and violent overturning of the political and social framework, such as later occurred in France and Russia, when both were already independent nations. Significant changes were ushered in, but they were not breathtaking. What happened was accelerated evolution rather than outright revolution. During the conflict itself people went on working and praying, marrying and playing. Most of them were not seriously disturbed by the actual fighting, and many of the more isolated communities scarcely knew that a war was on.

The impact of the American Revolution was worldwide. About 1783 a British ship stopped at some islands off the East African coast, where the natives were revolting against their Arab masters. When asked why they were fighting they replied, "America is free. Could not we be?"

America's War of Independence heralded the birth of three modern nations. One was Canada, which received its first large influx of English-speaking population from the thousands of Loyalists who fled there from the United States. Another was Australia, which became a convict dumping ground, now that America was no longer available for jailbirds. The third newcomer (by far the most important)—the United States—based itself squarely on republican principles.

Yet even the political overturn was not so revolutionary as one might suppose. In some states, notably Connecticut and Rhode Island, the war largely ratified a colonial self-rule already existing. Hated British officials, everywhere ousted, were replaced by a home-grown governing class, which promptly sought a local substitute for King and Parliament.

After the shooting started, the thirteen independent states were forced to devise new constitutions. For a time the manufacturing of governments was more pressing than the manufacturing of gunpowder. In the cases of Connecticut and Rhode Island, the yellowing charters were kept essentially intact but were retouched a bit to conform to new conditions. Significantly, none of the state constitutions was a radical departure from what the people had been accustomed to in the older colonial charters.

The newly forged state constitutions enjoyed many features in common. Their similarity, as it turned out, made easier the drafting of a workable federal charter when the time was ripe. Some of the state constitutions included bills of rights, specifically guaranteeing long-prized liberties. Most of them required the annual election of legislators, who were thus forced to toe the mark. All of them had weak executive and judicial branches, at least by present-day standards. The explanation is that the legislatures, now granted sweeping powers, were more directly representative of the people and hence more responsive to popular control. A generation of quarreling with His Majesty's officials had implanted a deep distrust of despotic governors and arbitrary judges.

At the end of the shooting, as before, none of the states enjoyed universal manhood suffrage, and only a few women were allowed to vote. In all of them a voter or officeholder was required to own property or pay taxes. During the war the restrictions on voting were eased in about half the states, but were increased in a few others.

Yet encouraging gains were registered for political democracy. More people—probably many more—could vote after the Revolution than before. This was especially true of the scorned backcountry folk, notably the Germans and Scotch-Irish of Pennsylvania. Tories, quite understandably, had sneered:

> Down at night a bricklayer or carpenter lies,
> Next sun a Lycurgus, a Solon doth rise.

New Social Fabrics

Social changes were striking but not bewildering. The expulsion of some 80,000 substantial Loyalists robbed the new ship of state of valuable leadership as well as of needed conservative ballast. This loss also weakened the aristocratic upper crust, with all its culture and elegance, and produced a gain for democratic "leveling."

War inevitably breeds a loosening of moral standards, often manifested in a spirit of "eat, drink, and be merry, for tomorrow we die." Sixty distilleries had operated in Massachusetts during the war. Alarmists pointed to the sharp increase of juvenile delinquency, of Sabbath breaking, of absenteeism from churches, and of the spread of

French radical ideas, notably those of the free-thinking Voltaire.

Church buildings had suffered severely from the conflict. Many of them were destroyed or damaged by invading armies, which thus vented their wrath against Whiggish preachers of sedition. Old South Church in Boston, for example, was made into a riding school for British cavalry.

The Anglican Church, tainted by association with the British Crown, was ruined. A new, de-Anglicized American church had to be built on the ashes of the old one. The Protestant Episcopal Church was therefore launched shortly after the guns fell silent. This blow to the Anglican Church, combined with the feverish democratic spirit aroused by the war, encouraged the spread of other faiths, especially on the frontier. Conspicuous among them were the more zestful Baptists and Methodists, whose popularity resulted in part from their more democratic organization.

Charleston Slave Advertisement. *State Gazette of South Carolina,* 1787.

A protracted fight for separation of church and state resulted in spectacular gains. Although the well-entrenched Congregational Church continued to be legally established in some New England states, the Anglican Church was everywhere disestablished. The struggle for a complete divorce between religion and government proved to be bitterest in Virginia. It was prolonged to 1786, when free-thinking Thomas Jefferson and his co-reformers, including the lowly Baptists, won a complete victory. (See table of established churches, p. 70.)

Social democracy was further stimulated by the widening of the franchise and the growth of trade organizations for artisans and laborers. Citizens in many states, flushed with republican fervor, also sawed off the remaining shackles of medieval inheritance laws, such as primogeniture, which awarded all a father's property to the eldest son.

The Revolutionary War likewise weakened the institution of slavery. Hostilities had hampered the noxious trade in "black ivory," and most of the new state constitutions forbade its renewal. Several Northern states either abolished slavery outright or provided for the gradual emancipation of black bondsmen. These laws codified the Declaration's concept that "all men are created equal," though laws against interracial marriage sprang up at the same time. Even in slave-burdened Virginia, a few idealistic masters freed their human chattels. In this revolution of sentiments, symbolized and inspired by the Declaration of Independence, were to be found the frail first sprouts of the later abolitionist movement.

Historians have searched with less success in the record of the Revolutionary era for the seeds of the feminist movement. Some women did serve (disguised as men) in the military, and New Jersey's new constitution in 1776 even temporarily gave women the vote. But though Abigail Adams teased her husband John Adams in 1777 that "the ladies" were determined "to foment a rebellion" of their own if they were not given political rights, most women were still doing traditional women's work.

Why in this dawning democratic age did abolition not go further and blot the evil of slavery from the fresh face of the new nation? The sad truth is that the fledgling idealism of the Founding Fathers was sacrificed to political expediency. A fight over the slavery issue would have fractured the fragile national unity that was so desperately needed. Nearly a century later, the same issue did wreck the Union—temporarily.

Education was temporarily blighted by the war, as schools were physically damaged, put on a part-time basis, or completely closed. Yet a refreshing spirit of liberalism began to suffuse the college curricula, partly as a result of the French alliance and the presence of French officers and troops in America. In 1782 Harvard College, one of the last holdouts, finally permitted the substitution of French for Hebrew.

Economic Crosscurrents

Economic changes begotten by the war were likewise noteworthy, but not overwhelming. States seized control of former Crown lands, and although rich speculators had their day, many of the large Loyalist holdings were confiscated and eventually cut up into small farms. Roger Morris' huge estate in New York, for example, was sliced into 250 parcels—thus accelerating the spread of economic democracy. The frightful excesses of the French Revolution were avoided, partly because cheap land was easily available. Men do not chop off heads so readily when they can chop down trees. It is highly significant that in the United States economic democracy, broadly speaking, preceded political democracy.

A sharp stimulus was given to manufacturing by the pre-war non-importation agreements, and later by the war itself. Goods that had formerly been imported from England were mostly cut off, and the ingenious Yankee was forced to make his own. Ten years after the Revolution the busy Brandywine Creek, south of Philadelphia, was turning the waterwheels of numerous mills along an 8-mile (13-kilometer) stretch. Yet America remained overwhelmingly a nation of soil-tillers.

Economically speaking, independence had drawbacks. Much of the coveted commerce of the Mother Country was still reserved for the loyal parts of the empire; and now that the Americans were aliens, they were forced to find new customers. Fisheries were disrupted, and bounties for ships' stores had abruptly ended. In some respects, the hated British Navigation Laws were more disagreeable after independence than before.

> Thomas Jefferson, then minister to France, was not overjoyed by the prospect of much manufacturing. As he wrote (1784), "While we have land to labor then, let us never wish to see our citizens occupied at a work-bench, or twirling a distaff. . . . For the general operations of manufacture, let our workshops remain in Europe. . . . The mobs of great cities add just so much to the support of pure government, as sores do to the strength of the human body."

New commercial outlets, fortunately, compensated partially for the loss of old ones. Americans could now trade freely with foreign nations, subject to local restrictions—a boon they had not enjoyed in the old days of mercantilism. Enterprising Yankee shippers ventured boldly—and profitably—into the Baltic and China seas. In 1784 the *Empress of China*, carrying a valuable weed (ginseng) that was highly prized by Chinese herb doctors as a cure for impotence, led the way into the East Asian markets.

Yet the general economic picture was far from being rosy. War had spawned demoralizing extravagance, speculation, and profiteering, with profits as indecently high as 300 percent. Runaway inflation had been ruinous to middle-class citizens on fixed incomes, and Congress had failed in its feeble attempts to curb economic laws by fixing prices. Probably the average citizen was worse off financially at the end of the shooting than he had been at the beginning.

The whole economic and social atmosphere was unhealthy. A newly rich class of profiteers was noisily conspicuous, while many once-wealthy people were left destitute. The controversy leading to the war had bred a keen distaste for taxes; and the wholesale seizure of Loyalist estates had encouraged disrespect for private property. John

Adams had been shocked when gleefully told by a horse-jockey neighbor that the courts of justice were all closed—a plight that proved to be only temporary.

A Shaky Start Toward Union

What would the Americans do with the independence they had so dearly won? London had dumped the responsibility of creating and operating a new central government squarely into their laps.

Prospects for erecting a lasting regime were far from bright. It is always difficult to set up a new government, doubly difficult to set up a new type of government. The picture was further confused in America by men preaching "natural rights" and looking suspiciously at all persons clothed with authority. America was more a name than a nation, and unity ran little deeper than the color on the map.

Disruptive forces stalked the land. The stabilizing Tory element had been tossed overboard. Patriots had fought the war with a high degree of disunity, but they had at least enjoyed the unifying cement of a common cause. Now even that was gone. It would have been almost a miracle if any government fashioned in all this confusion had long endured.

Hard times, the bane of all regimes, set in shortly after the war, and hit bottom in 1786. As if other troubles were not enough, British manufacturers, with dammed-up surpluses, began flooding the American market with cut-rate goods. War-baby American industries, in particular, suffered industrial colic from such ruthless competition. One Philadelphia newspaper in 1783 urged the use of ill-fitting homespun cloth:

> Of foreign gewgaws let's be free,
> And wear the webs of liberty.

Yet hopeful signs could be discerned. The thirteen sovereign states were basically alike in governmental structure, and functioned under similar constitutions. Americans enjoyed a rich political inheritance, derived partly from England and partly from their own homegrown devices for self-government. Finally, they were blessed with political leaders of a high order in men like George Washington, James Madison, John Adams, Thomas Jefferson, and Alexander Hamilton.

Creating a Confederation

The Second Continental Congress of Revolution days was little more than a conference of ambassadors from the thirteen states. It was totally without constitutional authority, and in general did only what it dared to do. In all respects the states were sovereign, for they coined money, raised armies and navies, and erected tariff barriers. The legislature of Virginia even ratified separately the treaty of alliance of 1778 with France.

Shortly before declaring independence in 1776, the Congress appointed a committee to draft a written constitution for the new nation. The finished product was the Articles of Confederation. Adopted by Congress in 1777, it was translated into French after the battle of Saratoga so as to convince France that America had a genuine government in the making. In due course this new constitution was sent out to the states for their

A View of the State-House in Philadelphia.

Independence Hall. Here the Declaration of Independence, Articles of Confederation, and U.S. Constitution were signed. (Free Library of Philadelphia.)

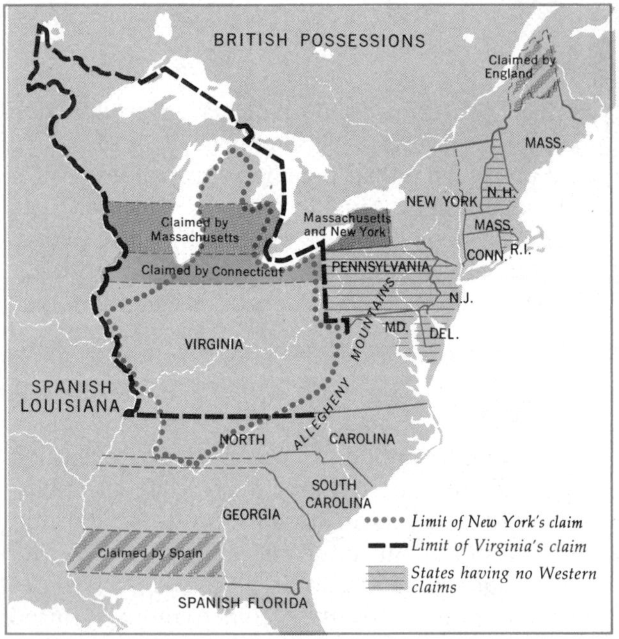

WESTERN LANDS, 1783

WESTERN LANDS, 1802

approval. But final action was delayed for four years, until 1781, less than eight months before the decisive victory at Yorktown.

The chief apple of discord was western lands. Six of the jealous states, including Pennsylvania and Maryland, had no holdings beyond the Allegheny Mountains. Seven, notably New York and Virginia, were favored with enormous acreage, on the basis of earlier sea-to-sea charter grants. The six landless states argued that their more fortunate sisters would not have retained possession of this splendid prize if all the other states had not fought for it also. A major complaint was that the land-blessed states could sell their trans-Allegheny tracts, and thus pay off pensions and other debts incurred in the common cause. States without such holdings would have to tax themselves heavily to defray these obligations. Why not turn the whole western area over to the central government?

Unanimous approval of the Articles of Confederation by the thirteen states was required, and landless Maryland stubbornly held out until March 1, 1781. She at length gave in when New York surrendered her western claims, and Virginia seemed about to do so. To sweeten the pill, Congress pledged itself to dispose of these vast areas for the "common benefit." It further agreed to carve from the new public domain not colonies but a number of "republican" states, which in time would be admitted to the Union on terms of complete equality with all the others. This extraordinary commitment faithfully reflected the anti-colonial spirit of the Revolution, and the pledge was later fully redeemed in the famed Northwest Ordinance of 1787.

Fertile public lands thus transferred to the central government proved to be an invaluable bond of union. The states that had thrown their heritage into the common pot had to remain in the Union if they were to reap their share of the advantages from the land sales. An army of westward-moving pioneers purchased their farms from the federal government, directly or indirectly, and they learned to look to the national capital, rather than to the state capitals—with a consequent weakening of local influence. Finally, a uniform national land policy was made possible.

The Articles of Confederation: America's First Constitution

The Articles of Confederation—some have said "Articles of Confusion"—provided for a loose confederation or "firm league of friendship." Thirteen independent states were thus linked together for joint action in dealing with common problems, such as foreign affairs. A clumsy Congress was to be the chief agency of government. There was no executive branch—George III had left a bad taste—and the vital judicial arm was left almost exclusively to the states, which remained sovereign.

Congress, though dominant, was closely hobbled. All bills dealing with specified subjects of importance required at least a two-thirds vote; any amendment of the Articles themselves required a unanimous vote. Unanimity was almost impossible, and this meant that the amending process, perhaps fortunately, was unworkable. If it had been workable, the Republic might have struggled along with a patched-up Articles of Confederation rather than adopting an effective new Constitution.

The shackled Congress was weak—and was purposely designed to be weak. Suspicious states, having just won control over taxation and commerce from Britain, had no desire to yield their newly acquired privileges to an American Parliament—even one of their own making.

Two handicaps of the Congress were crippling. It had no power to regulate commerce, and this weakness left the states free to establish conflictingly different laws regarding tariffs and navigation. Nor could the Congress enforce its tax-collection program. It established a tax quota for each of the states, and then asked them please to contribute their share on a voluntary basis. The central authority—a "government by supplication"—was lucky if in any year it received one-fourth of its requests.

The feeble national government in Philadelphia could advise and recommend and request. But in dealing with the independent states it could not command or coerce or enforce. It could not act directly upon the individual citizens of a sovereign state; it could not even protect itself against gross indignities. In 1783 a dangerous threat came from a group of mutinous Pennsylvania soldiers who demanded back pay. After Congress had appealed in vain to the state for protection, the members were forced to move in disgrace to Princeton College in New Jersey. The new Congress, with all its paper powers, was even less effective than the old Continental Congress, with no constitutional powers at all.

> Jefferson was never a friend of strong government (except when himself President), and he viewed with suspicion the substitute that was proposed for the Articles of Confederation: "Indeed, I think all the good of this new Constitution might have been couched in three or four new articles, to be added to the good, old, and venerable fabric."

Yet the Articles of Confederation, weak though they were, proved to be a landmark in government. They were for those days a model of what a loose *con*federation ought to be. Thomas Jefferson enthusiastically hailed the new structure as the best one "existing or that ever did exist." To compare it with the European governments, he thought, was like comparing "heaven and hell." But although the Confederation was praiseworthy as confederations went, the troubled times demanded not a loose *con*federation but a tightly knit federation. This involved the yielding by the states of their sovereignty to a completely new federal government, which in turn would leave them free to control their local affairs.

Despite their defects, the Articles of Confederation were a significant steppingstone toward the present Constitution. They clearly outlined the general powers that were to be exercised by the central government, such as making treaties and establishing a postal service. As the first written constitution of the Republic, the Articles kept alive the flickering ideal of union and held the

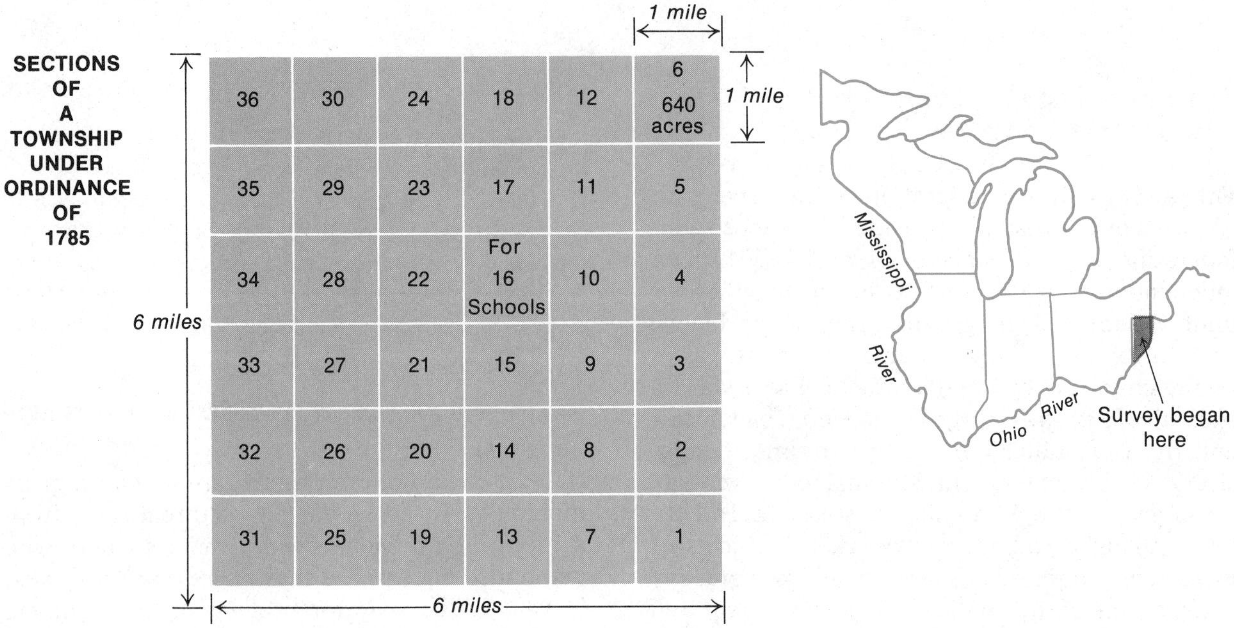

SURVEYING THE OLD NORTHWEST

states together—until such time as they were ripe for a strong constitution by peaceful, evolutionary methods. The anemic Articles represented what the states regarded as an alarming surrender of their power. Without this intermediary jump, they probably would never have consented to the breathtaking leap from the old boycott Association of 1774 to the Constitution of the United States.

Landmarks in Land Laws

Handcuffed though the Congress of the Confederation was, it managed to pass two supremely farsighted pieces of legislation. These related to an immense part of the public domain recently acquired from the states, and commonly known as the Old Northwest. This area lay northwest of the Ohio River, east of the Mississippi River, and south of the Great Lakes.

The first of these red-letter laws was the Land Ordinance of 1785. It provided that the acreage of the Old Northwest should be sold, and that the proceeds should be used to help pay off the national debt. The vast area was to be surveyed before sale and settlement, thus forestalling endless confusion and lawsuits. It was to be divided into townships six miles square, each of which in turn was to be split into thirty-six sections of one square mile each. The sixteenth section of each township was set aside to be sold for the benefit of the public schools—a priceless gift to education in the Northwest.

Even more noteworthy was the Northwest Ordinance of 1787, which related to governing of the Old Northwest. This law came to grips with the problem of how a nation should deal with its colonial peoples—the same problem that had bedeviled the King and Parliament in London. The solution provided by the Northwest Ordinance was a judicious compromise: temporary tutelage, then permanent equality. First, there would be two evolutionary territorial stages, during which the area would be subordinate to the federal government. Then, when a territory could boast 60,000 inhabitants, it might be admitted by Congress as a state, with all the privileges of the thirteen charter members. (This is precisely what the Continental Congress had promised the states when they surrendered their lands in 1781.) The Ordinance also forbade slavery in the Old Northwest—a path-breaking gain for freedom.

The wisdom of Congress in handling this explosive problem deserves warm praise. If it had attempted to chain the new territories in permanent subordination, a second American Revolution almost certainly would have erupted in later years, fought this time by the West against the East. Congress thus neatly solved the seemingly insoluble problem of empire. The scheme worked so well that its basic principles were ultimately carried over from the Old Northwest to other frontier areas.

The World's Ugly Duckling

Foreign relations, especially with London, continued troubled during these anxious years of the Confederation. The Mother Country resented the stab in the back from her rebellious offspring, and for eight years she refused to send a minister to America's "backwoods" capital. She suggested, with barbed irony, that if she sent one she would have to send thirteen.

Britain flatly declined to make a commercial treaty or to repeal her ancient Navigation Laws. Lord Sheffield, whose ungenerous views prevailed, argued persuasively in a widely sold pamphlet that England would win back America's trade anyhow. Commerce, he insisted, would naturally follow old channels. So why go to the Americans hat in hand? The British also officially shut off their profitable West Indian trade from the United States, though the Yankees, with their time-tested skill in smuggling, illegally shared some of it nonetheless.

Scheming British agents were also active along the far-flung northern frontier. They intrigued with the disgruntled Allen brothers of Vermont, and sought to annex that troubled area to Britain. Along the northern border the Redcoats continued to hold a chain of trading posts on United States soil, and there they maintained their profitable fur trade with the Indians. One plausible excuse for remaining was the failure of the American states to carry out the treaty of peace in regard to debts and Loyalists. But probably the main purpose of Britain in hanging on was to curry favor with the red men and keep their tomahawks lined up on the side of the King as a barrier against future American attacks on Canada.

All these grievances against England were maddening to patriotic Americans. Some citizens demanded, with more heat than wisdom, that the United States force the British into line by imposing restrictions on their imports to America. But Congress could not control commerce, and the states refused to adopt a uniform tariff policy. Some "easy states" deliberately lowered their tariffs in order to attract an unfair share of trade.

Ethan Allen (1738–1789). A Vermont leader, a Revolutionary hero, and a major-general in the local militia. On May 10, 1775, more than a year before independence was declared, Ethan Allen and his Green Mountain Boys captured the key British fort of Ticonderoga on Lake Champlain. Allen is reported to have demanded surrender "In the name of the Great Jehovah and the Continental Congress." Actually, he appears to have had no commission from either source.

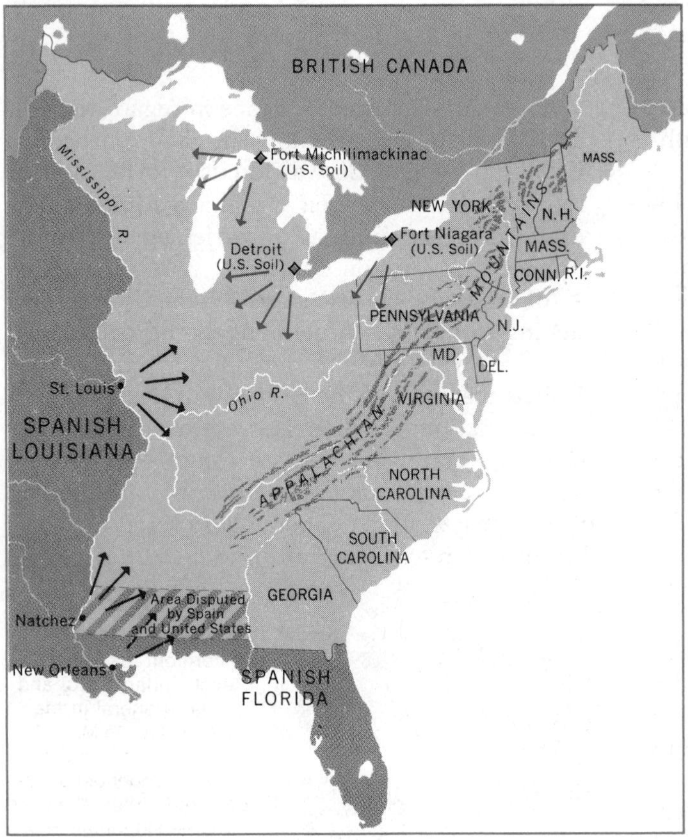

MAIN CENTERS OF SPANISH AND BRITISH INFLUENCE AFTER 1783

This map shows graphically that the United States in 1783 achieved complete independence in name only, particularly in the area west of the Appalachian Mountains. Not until twenty years had passed did the new republic, with the purchase of Louisiana from France in 1803, eliminate foreign influence from the area east of the Mississippi River.

Spain, though recently an enemy of England, was openly unfriendly to the new Republic. She controlled the mouth of the all-important Mississippi, down which the pioneers of Tennessee and Kentucky were forced to float their produce. The West was thus threatened with strangulation. Spain likewise claimed a large area north of the Gulf of Mexico, including Florida, granted to the United States by the British in 1783. At Natchez, on disputed soil, she held an important fort. She also intrigued with the neighboring red men to hem the Americans in east of the Alleghenies. Spain and England together, radiating their influence out among warlike Indian tribes, prevented America from exercising effective control over about half of its total territory.

Even America's French ally, now that she had humbled Britain, cooled off. She demanded the repayment of money loaned during the war; she restricted trade with her bustling West Indies and other ports.

Pirates of the North African states, including the arrogant Dey of Algiers, were ravaging America's Mediterranean commerce and enslaving Yankee seamen. The British purchased protection for their own subjects, and as colonials the Americans had enjoyed this shield. But as an independent nation the United States was too weak to fight and too poor to bribe. A few Yankee shippers engaged in the Mediterranean trade with forged British protection papers, but not all were so bold or so lucky.

John Jay, secretary for foreign affairs, derived some hollow satisfaction from these insults. He hoped they would at least humiliate the American people into framing a new government at home that would be strong enough to command respect abroad.

The Horrid Specter of Anarchy

Economic storm clouds continued to hang low in the mid-1780s. The requisition system of raising money was breaking down; some of the states refused to pay anything, while complaining bitterly about the tyranny of "King Congress." Interest on the public debt was piling up at home, while the nation's credit was evaporating abroad.

Individual states were getting out of hand. Several of them were quarreling over boundaries, which generated several minor pitched battles. Some of the states were levying duties on goods from their neighbors; New York, for example, taxed firewood from Connecticut and cabbages from New Jersey. A number of the states were again starting to grind out depreciated paper currency, and a few of them had passed laws sanctioning the semi-worthless "rag money." As a contemporary rhymester put it:

> Bankrupts their creditors with rage pursue;
> No stop, no mercy from the debtor crew.

An alarming uprising, known as Shays's Rebellion, flared up in western Massachusetts in 1786. Impoverished back-country farmers, many of them Revolutionary War veterans, were losing their farms through mortgage foreclosures and tax delinquencies. Led by Captain Daniel Shays, a veteran of the Revolution, these desperate debtors demanded cheap paper money, lighter taxes, and a suspension of mortgage foreclosures. Hundreds of angry men, again seizing their muskets, attempted to enforce their demands.

Massachusetts authorities responded with drastic action. Supported partly by contributions from wealthy citizens, they raised a small army under General Lincoln. Several skirmishes occurred—at Springfield three Shaysites were killed and one was wounded—and the movement collapsed. Daniel Shays, who believed that he was fighting anew against tyranny, was condemned to death but was later pardoned.

> Regarding popular disorders, Jefferson wrote privately in 1787: "A little rebellion, now and then, is a good thing, and as necessary in the political world as storms in the physical. . . . It is a medicine necessary for the sound health of government."

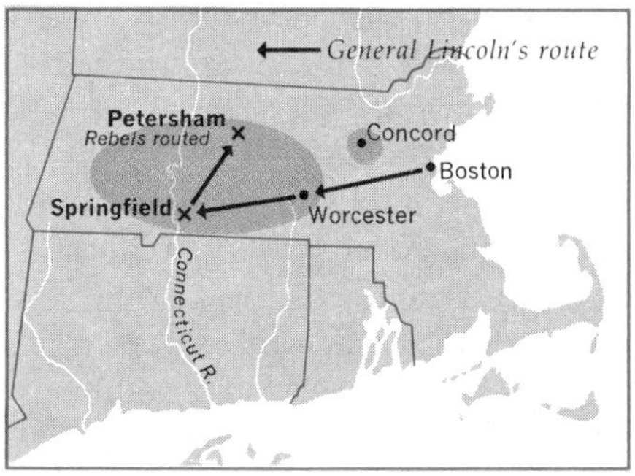

MAIN SHAYSITE CENTERS IN MASSACHUSETTS, 1786–1787
Disaffection existed in all parts of the state, but was concentrated in shaded areas.

Shays's followers were crushed—but the nightmarish memory lingered on. The outbursts of these and other distressed debtors struck fear in the hearts of the propertied men, who began to suspect that the Revolution had raised up a Frankenstein's monster of "mobocracy." "Good God!" burst out George Washington, who felt that only a Tory or a Briton could have predicted such disorders. There was obviously a crying need for a stronger central government. A few panicky citizens even talked of importing a European monarch to carry on where George III had failed.

How critical were conditions under the Confederation? Conservatives, anxious to safeguard their wealth and position, naturally exaggerated the seriousness of the nation's plight. They were eager to persuade their countrymen to scrap the Articles of Confederation, under which the states were sovereign, in favor of a muscular central government, in which the federal authority would be sovereign. But the poorer states'-rights people, who favored at most a simple amending of the

Articles, pooh-poohed the talk of anarchy. Many of them were debtors who feared that a powerful federal government would force them to pay their creditors.

Yet friends and critics of the Confederation generally agreed that it needed strengthening. Popular toasts were "Cement to the Union" and "A hoop to the barrel." The chief differences arose over how this goal should be attained, and how a maximum amount of states' rights could be reconciled with a strong central government. America probably could have muddled through somehow with amended Articles of Confederation. But the adoption of a completely new constitution certainly spared the Republic much costly indecision, uncertainty, and turmoil.

The nationwide picture was actually brightening before the Constitution was drafted. Nearly half the states had not issued semi-worthless paper currency; and some of the monetary black sheep showed signs of returning to the sound-money fold. Congressional control of commerce was in sight, specifically by means of an amendment to the Articles of Confederation. Prosperity was beginning to emerge from the fog of depression. By 1789 overseas shipping had largely regained its place in the commercial world. If conditions had been as grim in 1787 as painted by foes of the Articles, the move for a new constitution would hardly have encountered such heated opposition.

A Convention of "Demi-Gods"

Control of commerce, more than any other problem, touched off the chain reaction that led to a constitutional convention. Interstate squabbling over this issue had become so alarming by 1786 that Virginia, taking the lead, issued a call for a convention at Annapolis, Maryland. Nine states appointed delegates, but only five were finally represented. With so feeble a showing, nothing could be done about the ticklish question of commerce. A classic-featured New Yorker, thirty-one-year-old Alexander Hamilton, brilliantly saved the convention from complete failure by engineering the adoption of his report. It called upon Congress to summon a convention to meet in Philadelphia the next year, not to deal with commerce alone but to bolster the entire fabric of the Articles of Confederation.

Congress, though slowly dying in New York City, was reluctant to take a step that might be the signing of its own death warrant. But after six of the states had seized the bit in their teeth and appointed delegates anyhow, Congress belatedly issued the call for a convention *"for the sole and express purpose of revising"* the Articles of Confederation.

Every state chose representatives, except independent-minded Rhode Island (still "Rogues' Island"), a stronghold of paper-moneyites. These statesmen were all appointed by the state legislatures, whose members had been elected by voters who could qualify as property holders. This double distillation inevitably brought together a select group of propertied men.

A quorum of the fifty-five emissaries from twelve states finally convened at Philadelphia on May 25, 1787, in the imposing red-brick statehouse. The smallness of the assemblage facilitated intimate acquaintance and hence compromise. Sessions were held in complete secrecy, with armed sentinels posted at the doors. Delegates knew that they would generate heated differences, and they did not want to advertise their own dissensions, or put crippling arguments into the mouths of the opposition.

The caliber of the participants was extraordinarily high—"demi-gods," Jefferson called them. The crisis was such as to induce the ablest men to drop their personal pursuits and come to the aid of their country. Most of the members were lawyers, and most of them fortunately were old hands at constitution-making in their own states.

George Washington, towering austere and aloof among the "demi-gods" was unanimously elected chairman. His enormous prestige, as "the Sword of the Revolution," served to quiet overheated tempers. Benjamin Franklin, then eighty-one, added the urbanity of an elder statesman, though

Alexander Hamilton clearly revealed his class-interest views of an aristocratic government in his Philadelphia speech (1787): "All communities divide themselves into the few and the many. The first are the rich and wellborn, the other the mass of the people. . . . The people are turbulent and changing; they seldom judge or determine right. Give therefore to the first class a distinct, permanent share in the government. They will check the unsteadiness of the second, and as they cannot receive any advantage by change, they therefore will ever maintain good government."

Alexander Hamilton (1755–1804). He was one of the youngest and most brilliant of the Founding Fathers, who might have become President but for his ultraconservatism, an adulterous scandal, and a duelist's bullet. (Copyright Yale University Art Gallery)

he was inclined to be indiscreetly talkative in his declining years. James Madison, then thirty-six and a profound student of government, made contributions so notable that he has been dubbed "the Father of the Constitution." Alexander Hamilton, then only thirty-two, was present as an advocate of a super-powerful central government. His five-hour speech in behalf of his plan, though the most eloquent of the convention, netted only one favorable vote—his own.

Most of the flaming Revolutionary leaders of 1776 were absent. Thomas Jefferson and Thomas Paine were in Europe; Samuel Adams and John Hancock were not elected by Massachusetts. Patrick Henry, ardent champion of states' rights, was chosen as a delegate from Virginia but declined to serve, declaring that he "smelled a rat." It was perhaps well that these architects of revolution were absent. The time had come to yield the stage to statesmen interested in fashioning solid political systems.

Jefferson, despite his high regard for the statesmen at the Philadelphia convention, still was not unduly concerned about Shaysite rebellions. He wrote (November 1787): "What country before ever existed a century and a half without a rebellion? . . . The tree of liberty must be refreshed from time to time with the blood of patriots and tyrants. It is its natural manure."

Patriots in Philadelphia

The fifty-five delegates were a conservative, well-to-do body: lawyers, merchants, shippers, land speculators, and moneylenders. Not a single spokesman was present from the poorer, debtor groups.

Some forty of the fifty-five members owned depreciated securities of the existing regime. These men probably suspected that the value of their holdings would sharply increase if they succeeded in establishing a strong new government. Unfriendly critics of a later era have charged the Founding Fathers with having deliberately set out to feather their own nests. What is the truth about these so-called pocketbook patriots?

Many men in the Philadelphia assemblage, including the self-sacrificing Washington, were clearly prompted by patriotic motives, though some may not have been. The delegates realized that while they themselves might profit personally from a sounder government, so would the nation as a whole. If every man who stood to gain financially from a new constitution had bowed out, the country would have been robbed of its key leadership, and there probably would have been no Constitution.

What were the Founding Fathers after? They desired above all else a firm, dignified, and respected government. In a broad sense the piratical Dey of Algiers, who drove the delegates to their work, was a Founding Father. They aimed to clothe the central authority with genuine power, especially in controlling tariffs, so that the United States could wrest satisfactory commercial treaties from foreign nations. The shortsighted hostility of the British mercantilists spurred the constitution-framers to their task, and in this sense the illiberal Lord Sheffield was a Founding Father.

Other motives were present in the stately Philadelphia hall. Delegates were determined to preserve the Union, forestall anarchy, and insure security of life and property against dangerous uprisings by the "mobocracy." The specter of the recent outburst in Massachusetts held them to their labors, and in this sense Daniel Shays was a Founding Father. Grinding necessity extorted the Constitution from a reluctant nation. Fear occupied the fifty-sixth chair.

Hammering Out a Bundle of Compromises

Some of the travel-stained delegates, when they first reached Philadelphia, decided upon a daring step. They would completely *scrap* the old Articles of Confederation, despite explicit instructions from Congress to *revise*. Technically, these bolder spirits were determined to overthrow the existing government of the United States by peaceful means. The sovereign states were in danger of losing their sovereignty.

A scheme proposed by populous Virginia, and known as "the large-state plan," was first pushed forward as the framework of the Constitution. Its essence was that representation in Congress should be based on population—an arrangement that would naturally give the larger states an advantage.

Tiny New Jersey, suspicious of Virginia, countered with "the small-state plan." This provided for equal representation in Congress by states, regardless of size and population, as under the existing Articles of Confederation. The weaker states feared that under the Virginia scheme the stronger states would band together and lord it over the rest. Angry debate, heightened by a stifling heat wave, led to deadlock. The danger loomed that the convention would break up in complete failure. Even skeptical old Benjamin Franklin seriously proposed that the daily sessions be opened with prayer by a local clergyman.

After bitter and prolonged debate, the "Great Compromise" of the convention was hammered out and agreed upon. A cooling of tempers came coincidentally with a cooling of the temperature. The larger states were conceded representation by population in the House of Representatives (Art. I, Sec. II, para. 3; see Appendix at end of this book), and their smaller sisters were appeased by equal representation in the Senate (see Art. I, Sec. III, para. 1). Each state, no matter how poor or small, would have two senators. The big states, which would have to bear the major burden of taxation, obviously yielded more. As a sop to them, the delegates agreed that every tax bill or revenue measure must originate in the House, where population counted the more heavily (see Art. I, Sec. VII, para. 1). This critical compromise broke the logjam, and from then on success seemed within reach.

Gouverneur Morris (1752–1816). A delegate from Pennsylvania to the Constitutional Convention of 1787, he spoke more frequently than any other member and served as principal draftsman of that superbly written document. A wealthy and rock-ribbed conservative, he had joined the Revolutionary movement with reluctance and to the end feared the "riotous mob." (The New York Historical Society)

The Constitution as drafted was a bundle of compromises; they stand out in every section. A vital compromise was the method of electing the President indirectly by the Electoral College, rather than by direct means (see Art. II, Sec. I, para. 2). One Virginia delegate insisted that to leave the choice to the people was like asking a blind man to choose colors.

Sectional jealousy also intruded. Should the voteless slave of the Southern states count as a person in apportioning direct taxes and also representation in the House of Representatives? The South, not wishing to be deprived of influence, answered "yes." The North replied "no," arguing that the North might as logically have additional representation based on its horses. As a compromise between total representation and none at all, it was decided that a slave might count as three-fifths of a person. Hence the memorable, if somewhat illogical, "three-fifths compromise" (see Art. I, Sec. II, para. 3), an idea seriously discussed four years earlier.

Most of the states wanted to shut off the African slave trade. But South Carolina and Georgia, requiring slave labor in their rice paddies and malarial swamps, raised vehement protests. By way of compromise the convention stipulated that the slave trade might continue until the end of 1807, at which time Congress could turn off the spigot (see Art. I, Sec. IX, para 1). It did so as soon as the prescribed interval had elapsed. Meanwhile all the new state constitutions except Georgia's forbade overseas slave trade.

Evolution of Federal Union

Years	*Attempts at Union*	*Participants*
1643–1684	New England Confederation	4 colonies
1686–1689	Dominion of New England	7 colonies
1754	Albany Congress	7 colonies
1765	Stamp Act Congress	9 colonies
1772–1776	Committees of Correspondence	13 colonies
1774	First Continental Congress (adopts The Association)	12 colonies
1775–1781	Second Continental Congress	13 colonies
1781–1789	Articles of Confederation	13 states
1789–1790	Federal Constitution	13 states

Safeguards for Conservatism

Heated clashes among the delegates have been overplayed. The area of agreement was actually large; otherwise the convention would have speedily disbanded. Economically, the members generally saw eye to eye; they demanded sound money and the protection of private property. Politically, they were in basic agreement; they favored a stronger government, with three branches and with checks and balances among them—what critics called a "triple-headed monster." Finally, the convention was virtually unanimous in believing that manhood-suffrage democracy—government by "democratick babblers"—was something to be feared and fought.

Daniel Shays, the prime bogeyman, still frightened the conservative-minded delegates. They deliberately erected safeguards against the excesses of the "mob," and they made these barriers as strong as they dared. The awesome federal judges were to be appointed for life. The powerful President was to be elected *indirectly* by the Electoral College; the lordly senators were to be chosen *indirectly* by state legislatures (see Art. I, Sec. III, para. 1). Only in the case of one-half of one of the three great branches—the House of Representatives—were qualified (propertied) citizens permitted to choose their officials by *direct* vote (see Art. I, Sec. II, para. 1).

Yet the new charter also contained democratic elements. Above all, it stood foursquare on the great principle that the only legitimate government was one based on the consent of the governed. "We the people," the Preamble began, in a ringing affirmation of the doctrine of popular sovereignty.

At the end of seventeen muggy weeks—May 25 to September 17, 1787—only forty-two of the original fifty-five members remained to sign the Constitution. Three of the forty-two, refusing to do so, returned to their states to resist ratification. The remainder, adjourning to the City Tavern, appropriately celebrated the occasion. They little suspected that one day an 18th Amendment would be added forbidding the manufacture and sale of alcoholic beverages.

No members of the convention were completely happy about the result. They were too near their work—and too weary. Whatever their personal desires, they finally had to compromise and adopt what was acceptable to the entire body, and what presumably would be acceptable to the entire country.

The Clash of Federalists and Anti-Federalists

The Framing Fathers early foresaw that nationwide acceptance of the Constitution would not be easy to obtain. A formidable barrier was unanimous ratification by all thirteen states, as required for amendment by the still-existent Articles of Confederation. But since absent Rhode Island was certain to veto the Constitution, the delegates boldly adopted a different scheme. They stipulated that when *two-thirds* of the states—that is, nine—had registered their approval through specially elected conventions, the Constitution would become the supreme law of the land in those states ratifying (see Art. VII).

This was extraordinary, even revolutionary. It was in effect an appeal over the heads of the Congress that had called the convention, and over the heads of the legislatures that had chosen its members, to the people—or those of the people who could vote. In this way the framers could claim greater popular sanction for their handiwork.

> One of the Philadelphia delegates recorded in his journal a brief episode involving Benjamin Franklin, who was asked by a lady when the convention ended, "Well, Doctor, what have we got, a republic or a monarchy?" He answered, "A republic, if you can keep it."

Congress reluctantly submitted the document to the states on this basis, without recommendation of any kind.

People were somewhat shocked, so well had the secrets of the convention been kept. The public had expected the old Articles of Confederation to be patched up; now it was handed a frightening document in which, many thought, the precious jewel of state sovereignty was swallowed up. One of the hottest debates of American history forthwith erupted. The anti-federalists, who opposed the stronger federal government, were arrayed against the federalists, who naturally favored it.

A motley crowd gathered in the anti-federalist camp. It consisted primarily, though not exclusively, of the states'-rights devotees, the back-country men, the one-horse farmers, the work-soiled artisans, the ill-educated and illiterate—in general, the poorer classes. They were joined by paper-moneyites and debtors, many of whom feared that a potent central government would force them to pay off their debts—and at full value. Large numbers of anti-federalists suspected that something sinister was being put over on them by the aristocrats.

Silver-buckled federalists were more respectable; they generally embraced the cultured and propertied groups. Most of them lived in the settled areas along the seaboard, not in the raw back country. They were in outlook rather closely akin to the conservative Loyalist group of Revolutionary days. In fact, many of the remaining former Loyalists gave vigorous support to the Constitution; without them it might have failed of ratification.

Anti-federalists, their worst fears aroused, voiced vehement objections to the "gilded trap" known as the Constitution. They cried with much truth that it had been drawn up by the aristocratic elements, and hence was anti-democratic. They likewise charged that the sovereignty of the states was being swallowed up, and that the freedoms of the individual were jeopardized by the absence of a bill of rights. They decried the dropping of annual elections for congressmen; the setting up of a federal stronghold ten miles square (later the

Strengthening the Central Government

Under Articles of Confederation	*Under Federal Constitution*
A loose confederation of states	A firm union of people
1 vote in Congress for each state	2 votes in Senate for each state; representation by population in House (see Art. I, Secs. II, III)
⅔ vote (9 states) in Congress for all important measures	Simple majority vote in Congress, subject to presidential veto (see Art. I., Sec. VII, para. 2)
Laws executed by committees of Congress	Laws executed by powerful President (see Art. II, Secs. II, III)
No congressional power over commerce	Congress to regulate both foreign and interstate commerce (see Art. I, Sec. VIII, para. 3)
No congressional power to levy taxes	Extensive power in Congress to levy taxes (see Art. I, Sec. VIII, para. 1)
No federal courts	Federal courts, capped by Supreme Court (see Art. III)
Unanimity of states for amendment	Amendment less difficult (see Art. V)
No authority to act directly upon individuals, and no power to coerce states	Ample power to enforce laws by coercion of individuals and to some extent of states

District of Columbia); the creation of a standing army; the omission of any reference to God; and the highly questionable procedure of ratifying with only two-thirds of the states. A Philadelphia newspaper added that Franklin was "a fool from age," and Washington "a fool from nature."

The Great Debate in the States

Special elections, some apathetic but others hotly contested, were held in the various states for members of the ratifying conventions. Candidates—federalist or anti-federalist—were elected on the basis of their pledges for or against the Constitution.

The newly forged document was quickly accepted by four small states, for they had come off much better than they could have expected. Pennsylvania, number two on the list of ratifiers, was the first large state to act, but not until high-handed irregularities had been employed by the federalist legislature in calling a convention. These included the forcible seating of two anti-federalist members, their clothes torn and their faces red with rage, in order to complete a quorum.

Massachusetts, the second most populous state, provided an acid test. If the Constitution had failed there, the entire movement might easily have bogged down. The Boston ratifying convention at first contained an anti-federalist majority. It included weather-beaten Shaysites and the suspicious Samuel Adams, that aging "Engineer of Revolution" who now distrusted change. The assembly buzzed with dismaying talk of summoning another constitutional convention, as though the nation had not already shot its bolt. Clearly the choice was not between this Constitution and a better one, but between this Constitution and the creaking Articles of Confederation. The absence of a bill of rights was especially alarming to the anti-federalists. But the federalists gave solemn assurances that the first Congress would add such

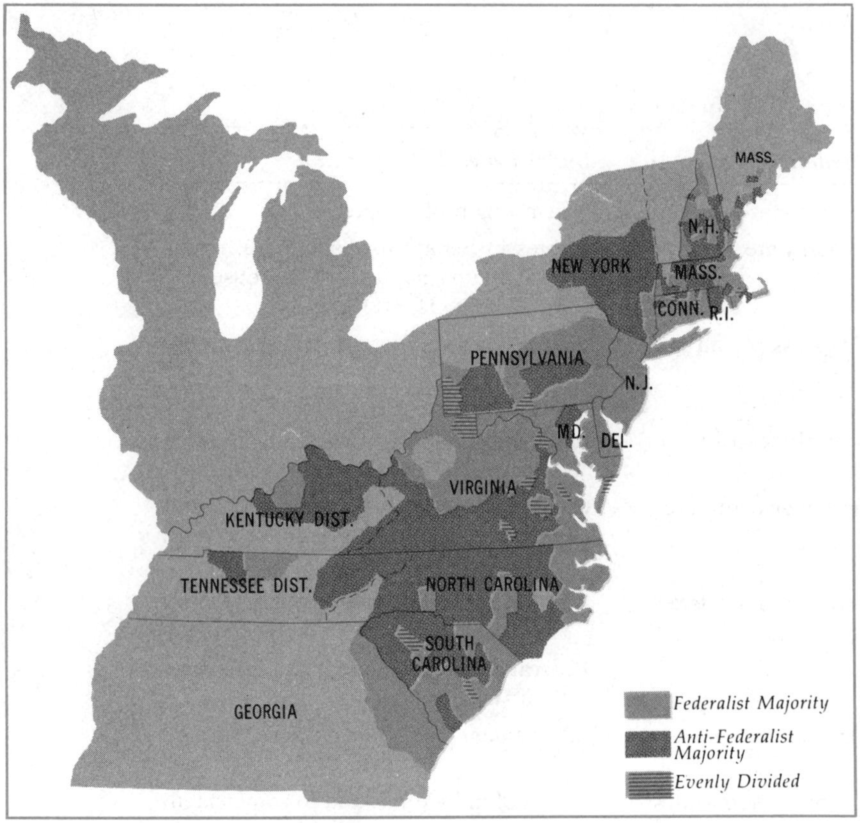

THE STRUGGLE OVER RATIFICATION
This mottled map shows that Federalist support tended to cluster around the coastal areas, which had enjoyed profitable commerce with the outside world, including the export of grain and tobacco. Impoverished frontiersmen, suspicious of a powerful new central government under the Constitution, were generally Anti-Federalists.

a safeguard by amendment, and ratification was then secured in Massachusetts by the rather narrow margin of 187 to 168.

Three more states fell into line. The last of these was New Hampshire, whose convention at first had contained a strong anti-federalist majority. The federalists cleverly engineered a prompt adjournment, and then won over enough waverers to secure ratification. Nine states—all but Virginia, New York, North Carolina, and Rhode Island—had now taken shelter under the "new federal roof," and the document was officially adopted on June 21, 1788. Francis Hopkinson exulted in his song "The New Roof":

> Huzza! my brave boys, our work is complete;
> The world shall admire Columbia's fair seat.

But such rejoicing was premature so long as the four dissenters, conspicuously New York and Virginia, remained outside the fold.

> In the Massachusetts ratifying convention, one member expressed distrust of the taxing power of the new government: "These lawyers, and men of learning, and moneyed men . . . expect to get into Congress themselves. . . . And then they will swallow up all us little folks . . . just as the whale swallowed up Jonah."

The Four Laggard States

Proud Virginia, the biggest and most populous state, provided fierce anti-federalist opposition. There the college-bred federalist orators, for once, encountered worthy antagonists, including the fiery Patrick Henry. He professed to see in the fearsome parchment the death warrant of liberty. George Washington, James Madison, and John

Ratification of the Constitution

State	Date	*Vote in Convention*	*Rank in Population*	*1790 Population*
1. Delaware	Dec. 7, 1787	Unanimous	13	59,096
2. Pennsylvania	Dec. 12, 1787	46 to 23	3	433,611
3. New Jersey	Dec. 18, 1787	Unanimous	9	184,139
4. Georgia	Jan. 2, 1788	Unanimous	11	82,548
5. Connecticut	Jan. 9, 1788	128 to 40	8	237,655
6. Massachusetts (incl. Maine)	Feb. 7, 1788	187 to 168	2	475,199
7. Maryland	Apr. 28, 1788	63 to 11	6	319,728
8. South Carolina	May 23, 1788	149 to 73	7	249,073
9. New Hampshire	June 21, 1788	57 to 46	10	141,899
10. Virginia	June 26, 1788	89 to 79	1	747,610
11. New York	July 26, 1788	30 to 27	5	340,241
12. North Carolina	Nov. 21, 1789	195 to 77	4	395,005
13. Rhode Island	May 29, 1790	34 to 32	12	69,112

Marshall, on the federalist side, lent influential support. With New Hampshire about to ratify, the new Union was going to be formed anyhow, and Virginia could not very well continue comfortably as an independent state. After a close and exciting debate in the state convention, ratification carried, 89 to 79.

New York, which also experienced an uphill struggle, was the only state that permitted a manhood-suffrage vote for the members of the ratifying convention. The result was a heavy anti-federalist majority. Alexander Hamilton at heart favored a much stronger central government than that under debate, but he contributed his sparkling personality and persuasive eloquence to whipping up support. He also joined John Jay and James Madison in penning a masterly series of articles for the New York newspapers. Though designed as propaganda, these essays remain the most penetrating commentary ever written on the Constitution, and are still widely sold in book form as *The Federalist.*

New York finally yielded. Realizing that the state could not prosper apart from the Union, the convention ratified the document by the close count of 30 to 27. At the same time, it approved thirty-two proposed amendments and—vain hope—issued a call for yet another convention to modify the Constitution.

Last-ditch dissent developed in only two states. A hostile convention met in North Carolina, then adjourned without taking a vote. Rhode Island

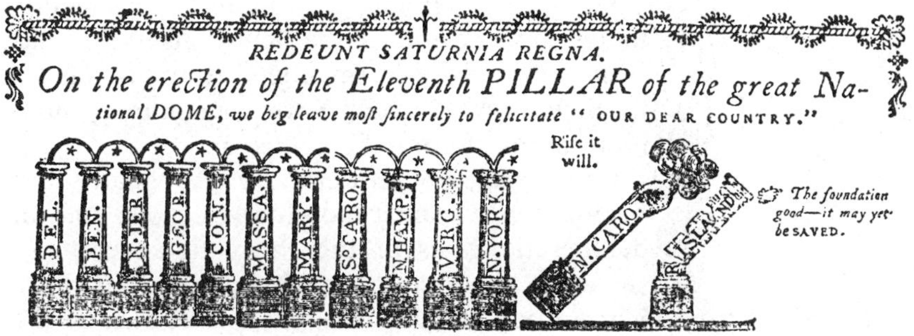
REDEUNT SATURNIA REGNA.
On the erection of the Eleventh PILLAR of the great National DOME, we beg leave most sincerely to felicitate "OUR DEAR COUNTRY."
Rise it will.
DEL.
PEN.
N.JER.
GEOR.
CON.
MASSA.
MARY.
S. CARO.
N.HAMP.
VIRG.
N.YORK.
N.CARO.
R.ISLAND.
The foundation good—it may yet be SAVED.

A Triumphant Cartoon. It appeared in the *Massachusetts Centinel* on August 2, 1788. Note the two laggards, especially the sorry condition of Rhode Island.

Hamiltonian Frigate. A victory parade in New York City honoring Hamilton and the ratification of the Constitution. At the key New York ratifying convention at Poughkeepsie, Hamilton, by sheer eloquence and cogent argument, turned a two-thirds majority against the Constitution into a majority of three in favor of it. (Brown Brothers)

did not even summon a ratifying convention. The two most ruggedly individualist centers of the colonial era—homes of the "otherwise minded"—thus ran true to form. They were to change their course, albeit unwillingly, only after the new government had been in operation for some months.

The battle for ratification, despite much apathy, was close and extremely bitter in some localities. No lives were lost, but riotous disturbances broke out in New York and Pennsylvania, involving bruises and bloodshed. There was much behind-the-scenes pressure on delegates who had solemnly promised their constituents to vote against the Constitution. The last four states ratified, not because they wanted to, but because they had to. They could not safely exist apart from the Union.

> Referring to the belief that self-government is better than good government, Fisher Ames of Massachusetts, a Federalist member of the new Congress, is quoted as having said: "A monarchy is like a merchantman [merchant ship]. You get on board and ride the wind and tide in safety and elation but, by and by, you strike a reef and go down. But democracy is like a raft. You never sink, but, damn it, your feet are always in the water."

A Conservative Triumph

The minority had triumphed—doubly. A militant minority of American radicals had engineered the military revolution which cast off the unwritten British constitution. A militant minority of conservatives—now embracing many of the earlier radicals—had engineered the peaceful revolution which overthrew the inadequate constitution known as the Articles of Confederation. Eleven states, in effect, had seceded from the Confederation, leaving two out in the cold.

A majority had not spoken. Only about one-fourth of the adult white males in the country, chiefly the propertied people, had voted for delegates to the ratifying conventions. Careful estimates indicate that if the new Constitution had been submitted to a manhood-suffrage vote, as in New York, it would have encountered much more opposition, probably defeat.

Conservatism was victorious. Safeguards had been erected against mob-rule excesses, and the democratic gains of the Revolution were conserved in the face of possible anarchy. Radicals like Patrick Henry, who had overthrown British rule, had in turn been overthrown by American conservatives. The result was a kind of peaceful counter-revolution. It restored the economic and political stability of colonial years, and set the drifting ship of state on a more promising course. Yet if the architects of the Constitution were conservative, it is worth emphasizing that what they conserved was the principle of popular, democratic government, made forever sacred in the fires of the Revolution. One of the distinctive—and enduring—paradoxes of American history was thus revealed: in the United States, conservatives and radicals alike have championed the heritage of democratic revolutionism.

VARYING VIEWPOINTS

Charles Beard's book, *An Economic Interpretation of the Constitution of the United States* (1913), has long defined the area around which debate on the constitutional period has revolved. Beard described the Constitution as the "reactionary" phase of the Revolutionary era—a shrewd maneuver by conservative men of property to curtail the democratic excesses let loose in 1776. Most modern scholars, if they accept Beard's argument at all, accept it only with severe qualifications. The most recent discussions of the Constitution have been cast in terms of reflections on the ancient riddle of republicanism: Does republican self-government rest on the virtue of the people or on the formal political institutions which channel and control human behavior? Seen in this light, the men who made the Constitution appear more "radical" than their opponents. They trusted human nature enough to go forward with the bold experiment of a strong national government based on republican principles. The anti-federalists, on the other hand, so feared man's weakness for corruption that they shuddered at the prospect of putting powerful political weapons in his hands. In this sense, the Constitution represents a vote of confidence in human rationality—the fulfillment, not the repudiation, of the most advanced ideas of the Revolutionary era. Thus it was "radical"; but whether it was "right" is an issue that will be endlessly debated.

SELECT READINGS

John Fiske, in *The Critical Period of American History* (1888), portrayed America under the Articles of Confederation as a crisis-ridden country. His view has been sharply qualified by the work of Merrill Jensen, summarized in *The Making of the American Constitution* (1964). On the Constitutional Convention, see Clinton Rossiter, *1787: The Grand Convention* (1966). Especially learned is G. S. Wood's massive and brilliant *The Creation of the American Republic, 1776–1787* (1969). See also Willi Paul Adams, *The First American Constitutions* (1980). Charles A. Beard shocked conservatives with *An Economic Interpretation of the Constitution of the United States* (1913). It is seriously weakened by two blistering attacks: R. E. Brown, *Charles Beard and the Constitution* (1956), and Forrest McDonald, *We the People: The Economic Origins of the Constitution* (1958). See also the latter author's *E Pluribus Unum: The Formation of the American Republic, 1776–1790* (1965). J. T. Main, *The Anti-Federalists* (1961), partially rehabilitates Beard. S. Lynd explores another aspect of the topic in *Class Conflict, Slavery, and the United States Constitution* (1967). More detailed is H. J. Henderson, *Party Politics in the Continental Congress* (1974). See also L. Levy, *Essays on the Making of the Constitution* (1969). Sectionalism is developed in J. R. Alden, *The First South* (1961), and W. N. Chambers, *Political Parties in a New Nation* (1963). Finance is treated fully in C. P. Nettels, *The Emergence of a National Economy, 1775–1815* (1962). David Szatmary is perceptive on *Shays's Rebellion* (1980). Relevant biographical studies of merit are J. C. Miller, *Alexander Hamilton: Portrait in Paradox* (1959); and Irving Brant, *James Madison* (6 vols., 1941–1961).

8

Launching the New Ship of State

I shall only say that I hold with Montesquieu, that a government must be fitted to a nation, as much as a coat to the individual; and, consequently, that what may be good at Philadelphia may be bad at Paris, and ridiculous at Petersburg [Russia].

ALEXANDER HAMILTON, 1799

A New Ship on an Uncertain Sea

When the Constitution was launched in 1789, the Republic was continuing to grow at an amazing rate. Population was still doubling about every twenty-three years, and the first official census of 1790 recorded almost 4 million souls. Cities had blossomed proportionately: Philadelphia numbered 42,000; New York, 33,000; Boston, 18,000; Charleston, 16,000; and Baltimore, 13,000.

America's population was still about 90 percent rural, despite the flourishing cities; all but 5 percent lived east of the mountains. The trans-Allegheny overflow was concentrated chiefly in Kentucky, Tennessee, and Ohio, all of which were welcomed as states within fourteen years. (Vermont had preceded them, becoming the fourteenth state in 1791.) Foreign travelers everywhere looked down their noses at the roughness and crudity resulting from ax-and-rifle pioneering life. Yet, critical though they might be, they were impressed by evidences of energy, self-confidence, and material well-being.

The new ship of state, despite these promising signs of fair weather, did not spread its sails to the most favorable breezes. Within twelve troubled years the American people had risen up and thrown overboard their first two constitutions: the British constitution and the Articles of Confederation. A decade of constitution-smashing and lawbreaking was not the best training for government-making. Americans had come to regard a central authority, replacing that of George III, as a necessary evil—something to be distrusted, watched, and curbed.

Men of the western waters, in the stump-studded clearings of Kentucky, Tennessee, and Ohio, were restive and dubiously loyal. The mouth of the Mississippi, their life-giving outlet, lay in the hands of unfriendly Spaniards. Smooth-tongued Spanish and British agents, jingling gold, moved freely among the settlers and held out seductive promises of independence.

Finances of the infant government were likewise precarious. The revenue had declined to a trickle, while the public debt, with interest heavily in arrears, was mountainous. Worthless paper money, both state and national, was as plentiful as metallic money was scarce.

> The French statesman Turgot had high expectations for a *united* America: "This people is the hope of the human race. . . . The Americans should be an example of political, religious, commercial and industrial liberty. . . . But to obtain these ends for us, America . . . must not become . . . a mass of divided powers, contending for territory and trade."

The Americans, moreover, were brashly attempting to erect a republic on an immense scale. They ignored the fact that hitherto a democratic form of government had succeeded only on a tiny scale, notably in Switzerland. The eyes of a skeptical world were on the upstart United States, and the bejeweled monarchs of Europe in particular feared that the new Republic would provide a dangerous example for their long-oppressed subjects.

Washington's Pro-Federalist Regime

General Washington, the esteemed war hero, was unanimously drafted as President by the Electoral College in 1789—the only presidential nominee ever to be honored by unanimity. He would not run for the office; he would not run from the office. His presence was imposing: 6 feet 2 inches, 175 pounds (1.88m, 79.5kg), broad and sloping shoulders, strongly pointed chin, and pockmarks (from smallpox) on nose and cheeks. Much preferring the quiet of Mount Vernon to the turmoil of politics, he was perhaps the only President who

Washington Being Sworn in at Federal Hall, New York. Being the first President under the Constitution, Washington could neither cite precedents nor blame a predecessor. (Stokes Collection, New York Public Library.)

President-Elect Washington Honored in New Jersey. Before leaving home he wrote, "My movements to the chair of government will be accompanied by feelings not unlike those of a culprit who is going to the place of his execution." (Lithograph, Library of Congress.)

did not in some way angle for this exalted office. But his name and fame, which had spread throughout two hemispheres, made him an "indispensable man." Balanced rather than brilliant, he commanded men by strength of character rather than by the arts of the politician.

Washington's long journey from Mount Vernon to New York City, the temporary capital, was a triumphal procession. He was greeted by roaring cannon, pealing bells, flower-carpeted roads, and singing and shouting citizens. With appropriate ceremony, he solemnly and somewhat nervously took the oath of office on April 30, 1789, on a crowded balcony overlooking Wall Street, which some have regarded as a bad omen. A cold but able New Englander, John Adams, was sworn in as Vice-President—an office which Benjamin Franklin thought should have carried the title "His Superfluous Excellency."

The Constitution does not mention a Cabinet; it merely provides that the President "may require" written opinions of the heads of his departments (see Art. II, Sec. II, para. 1). But this system proved so cumbersome, and involved so much homework, that Cabinet meetings gradually evolved in the Washington administration. The President thus secured an invaluable body of special advisers. Along with numerous other features not specifically authorized, the Cabinet has become an integral part of the "unwritten Constitution."

At first there were only three full-fledged department heads under the President: Secretary of State Thomas Jefferson, Secretary of the Treasury Alexander Hamilton, and Secretary of War Henry Knox. The last-named was a 300-pound (136-kg) Revolutionary general to whom were entrusted both the infant army and the newborn navy.

The shining star in this governmental galaxy was smooth-faced Alexander Hamilton, just thirty-four years old. He was once called the "bastard brat of a Scotch peddler," though the sneer was unfair. His parents could not legally marry because of a technicality connected with his mother's divorce from her first husband. Hamilton's genius was unquestioned, but doubts about his character and his loyalty to the democratic experiment always swirled about his head. He was said to have shocked Jefferson by exclaiming, "Your people, sir, are a Great Beast!"

Critics claimed that Hamilton loved his country more than he loved his countrymen. Born on a tiny island in the British West Indies, he never de-

Evolution of the Cabinet

Original Members	Added, 1798–1913	Added, 1947–1979
Secy. of State, 1789	Secy. of Navy, 1798 (Loses Cabinet status, 1947)	Secy. of Defense, 1947 (Subordinate to him, without Cabinet rank, are Secys. of Army, Navy, Air Force)
Secy. of Treasury, 1789	Postmaster General, 1829 (Loses Cabinet status, 1970)	Secy. of Health, Education, and Welfare, 1953 (divided in 1979)
Secy. of War, 1789 (Loses Cabinet status, 1947)	Secy. of Interior, 1849	Secy. of Housing and Urban Development, 1965
Attorney General, 1789 (Not head of Justice Dept. until 1870)	Secy. of Agriculture, 1889	Secy. of Transportation, 1966
	Secy. of Commerce and Labor, 1903 (Office divided in 1913)	Secy. of Energy, 1977
	Secy. of Commerce, 1913	Secy. of Health and Human Services, 1979
	Secy. of Labor, 1913	Secy. of Education, 1979

veloped that passionate state loyalty which dominated so many Americans. Hamilton regarded himself as a kind of prime minister in Washington's Cabinet, and on occasion thrust his hands into the affairs of other departments, including that of his arch-rival, Thomas Jefferson.

Other newly sawed governmental planks were nailed into place. Effective federal courts were created under the Judiciary Act passed by Congress in 1789. The first Congress likewise passed twelve amendments to the Constitution, of which ten were ratified by the states in 1791. Popularly known as the Bill of Rights, the new safeguards guaranteed the most precious of American principles. Among these are assurances against unreasonable search and the right to jury trial, as well as freedom of religion, freedom of speech, freedom of the press, freedom of assembly, and freedom of petition (see Amendments I–X).

Hamilton Revives the Corpse of Public Credit

Financial vexations, which had crippled the Articles of Confederation, were the most pressing. Alexander Hamilton, a financial wizard, sprang to the rescue. His plan was to shape the fiscal policies of the administration in such a way as to favor the wealthier groups. They, in turn, would gratefully lend the government monetary and moral support. The new federal regime would flourish, the propertied classes would grow fat, and prosperity would trickle down to the masses.

The youthful financier's first objective was to bolster the national credit. Without public confidence in the government, Hamilton could not secure the funds with which to float his risky schemes. He therefore boldly urged Congress to "fund" the entire national debt at par, and to assume completely the debts incurred by the states during the recent war.

"Funding at par" meant that the federal government would pay off its debts at face value, plus accumulated interest—a then enormous total of more than $54 million. So many people believed the infant Treasury incapable of meeting those obligations that government bonds had depreciated to ten or fifteen cents on the dollar. Yet speculators held fistfuls of them, and when Congress passed Hamilton's measure in 1790, they grabbed for more. Some of them galloped into rural areas ahead of the news, buying for a song the depreciated paper holdings of farmers, war veterans, and widows.

Hamilton was bitterly reproached for not having sought out the original holders of these securities. But such a course would have been impossible to carry out with complete fairness. Besides, Con-

> One of the most eloquent tributes to Hamilton came from Daniel Webster in the Senate (1831): "He smote the rock of the national resources, and abundant streams of revenue gushed forth. He touched the dead corpse of public credit, and it sprung upon its feet."

President Washington's "White House" in Philadelphia, 1794. The first national capital was New York (1789–1791) followed by Philadelphia (1791–1800), and then Washington.

gress, with some speculators in its ranks, flatly rejected such a proposal.

Some cynics have dubbed the first congressmen "Funding Fathers," with reference to their pocket-lining practices. Yet many of these legislators were convinced that the success of the new government depended on their approval of Hamilton's schemes. They could hardly have been expected to vote "nay" just because principle and personal profit happened to coincide.

Assuming the State Debts

Hamilton was willing, even eager, to have the new government shoulder additional obligations. While pushing the funding scheme, he urged Congress to assume the debts of the states, totaling some $21.5 million.

The secretary made a convincing case for "assumption." The state debts could be regarded as a proper national obligation, for they had been incurred in the war for independence. But foremost in Hamilton's thinking was the belief that assumption would chain the states more tightly to the "federal chariot." Thus, the secretary's maneuver would shift the attachment of wealthy creditors from the states to the federal government. The support of the rich for the national administration was a crucial link in Hamilton's political strategy of strengthening the central government.

States that were burdened by heavy debts, like Massachusetts, were delighted by Hamilton's proposal. States that had small debts, or had taken energetic steps to pay them off, were less happy. They saw no good reason why they should be taxed by the central government to pull their less thrifty sisters out of a fiscal hole. The fight against assumption was vigorously led by Virginia, and took on the semblance of another North-South sectional struggle. In some of the states there was even irresponsible talk of leaving the Union.

The stage was set for some old-fashioned horse trading. Virginia did not want the state debts assumed, but she did want the forthcoming federal district*—now the District of Columbia—to be located on the Potomac River. She would thus gain in commerce and prestige. Hamilton persuaded a reluctant Jefferson, who had recently come home from France, to line up enough votes in Congress for assumption. In return, Virginia would have the federal district on the Potomac. The bargain was carried through in 1790, though Jefferson later claimed that he had been outwitted. It proved to be one of the earliest instances of congressional logrolling.†

Customs Duties and Excise Taxes

The new ship of state thus set sail dangerously overloaded. The national debt had swelled to $75 million owing to Hamilton's insistence on honoring the outstanding federal and state obligations alike. A man less determined to establish a healthy

---

*Authorized by the Constitution, Art. I, Sec. VIII, para. 17.

†On the frontier, heavy logs in clearings were rolled into place by enlisting the assistance of neighbors. Mutual aid in legislative bodies to pass laws for special interests came to be called logrolling—"an aye for an aye."

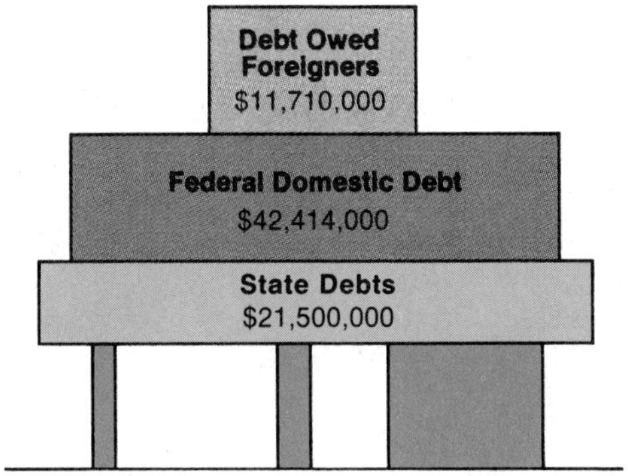

HAMILTON'S FINANCIAL STRUCTURE SUPPORTED BY REVENUES

public credit could have sidestepped $13 million in back interest, and could have avoided the state debts entirely.

But Hamilton, "Father of the National Debt," was not greatly worried. His objectives were as much political as economic. He believed that, within limits, a national debt was a "national blessing"—a kind of cement of union. The more creditors to whom the government owed money, the more people there would be with a personal stake in the success of his ambitious enterprise. His unique contribution was to make a debt—ordinarily a liability—an asset for vitalizing the financial system as well as the government itself.

Where was the money to come from to pay interest on this huge debt and to run the government? Hamilton's first answer was customs duties, derived from a tariff. Tariff revenues, in turn, depended on a vigorous foreign trade, another crucial link in Hamilton's overall economic strategy for the new Republic.

The first tariff law, a low one of about 8 percent on the value of dutiable imports, was speedily passed by the first Congress in 1789, even before Hamilton was sworn in. Revenue was by far the main goal, but the measure was also designed to erect a low protective wall around infant industries, which bawled noisily for more shelter than they received. Hamilton had the vision to see that the Industrial Revolution would soon reach America, and he argued strongly in favor of more protection for the well-to-do manufacturing groups—another vital element in his economic program. But Congress was still dominated by the agricultural and commercial interests, and it voted only two slight increases in the tariff during Washington's presidency.

Hamilton, with characteristic vigor, sought additional internal revenue, and in 1791 secured from Congress an excise tax on a few domestic items, notably whiskey. The new levy of seven cents a gallon was borne chiefly by the distillers who lived in the back country, where the wretched roads forced the farmer to reduce his bulky bushels of grain to horseback proportions. Whiskey flowed so freely on the frontier that it was used for money; a gallon of the fiery liquid passed for one shilling—or about twenty-five cents.

But Hamilton was not unduly bothered by the cries of outrage from the backwoods. The federal regime had to be bolstered, no matter how unpopular his measures. Besides, the excise would accustom the people, especially the reluctant states'-rights advocates, to a direct tax by the federal government. In any case, the secretary had little sympathy for the Western distillers, many of whom from the outset had opposed the powerful new Constitution and Hamilton's centralizing schemes.

Hamilton Battles Jefferson for a Bank

As the capstone of his financial system, Hamilton proposed a Bank of the United States. An enthusiastic admirer of most things English, he took as his model the Bank of England. Specifically, he proposed a powerful private institution, of which the government would be the major stockholder, and in which the Federal Treasury would deposit its surplus monies. The central government not only would have a convenient strongbox, but federal funds would stimulate business by remaining in circulation. The Bank would also print urgently needed paper money, and thus provide a sound and stable national currency, badly needed since the days when the Continental dollar was "not worth a Continental."

Ardent champions of states' rights, spearheaded by Secretary of State Jefferson, cried out against a giant Bank. They predicted that their cherished state banks could not survive competition from this monopolistic monster. More alarming, the states'-righters feared that their precious liberties would be jeopardized by a grasping banking colossus which, in fact, came to enjoy a virtual monopoly of the government's surplus funds.

Jefferson, whose written opinion Washington requested, argued vigorously against the Bank. There was, he insisted, no specific authorization in the Constitution for such a financial octopus. He was convinced that all powers not specifically granted to the central government were reserved to the states, as provided in the about-to-be-ratified Bill of Rights (see Art. X). He therefore concluded that the states, not Congress, had the power to charter banks. Believing that the Constitution should be interpreted "literally" or "strictly," Jefferson and his states'-rights disciples zealously embraced the theory of "strict construction."

Hamilton, also at Washington's request, prepared a brilliantly reasoned reply to Jefferson's arguments. He boldly invoked that clause of the Constitution which stipulates that Congress may pass any laws "necessary and proper" to carry out the powers vested in the various governmental agencies (see Art. I, Sec. VIII, para. 18). The government was explicitly empowered to collect taxes and regulate trade. In carrying out these basic functions, Hamilton argued, a national bank would be not only "proper" but "necessary." By inference or implication—that is, by virtue of "implied powers"—Congress would be fully justified in establishing the Bank of the United States. In short, Hamilton contended for a "loose" or "broad" interpretation of the Constitution. He and his federalist followers thus evolved the theory of "loose construction" by invoking the "elastic clause" of the Constitution—a precedent for enormous federal powers.

Hamilton's financial views prevailed. His eloquent and realistic arguments were accepted by Washington, who reluctantly signed the Bank

The First Bank of the United States. The first bank of the United States, established in Philadelphia, lasted from 1789 to 1811; the second, from 1816 to 1836. (Library of Congress.)

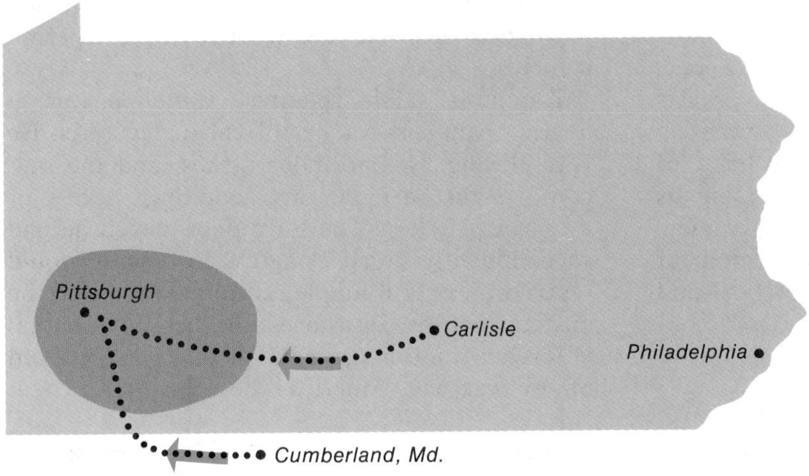

PENNSYLVANIA'S WHISKEY REBELLION, 1794
Hamilton regarded the "Whiskey Boys" not as mere tax resisters but as traitors scheming to detach the West from the newborn union. Yet after sharp interrogation of several captured rebels, the Treasury Secretary was forced to conclude that no secessionist plot existed. Even so, he wanted to leave an army of occupation in the whiskey country, to stop "the political putrefaction of Pennsylvania." Washington vetoed this heavy-handed measure.

measure into law. This explosive issue had been debated with much heat in Congress, where the old North-South cleavage again appeared ominously. The most enthusiastic support for the Bank naturally came from the commercial and financial centers of the North, while the strongest opposition arose from the agricultural South.

The Bank of the United States, as created by Congress in 1791, was chartered for twenty years. Located in Philadelphia, it was to have a capital of $10 million, one-fifth of it owned by the federal government. Stock was thrown open to public sale. To the agreeable surprise of Hamilton, a milling crowd oversubscribed in less than two hours, pushing aside many would-be purchasers.

Mutinous Moonshiners in Pennsylvania

The Whiskey Rebellion, which flared up in southwestern Pennsylvania in 1794, sharply challenged the new national government. Hamilton's excise bore harshly on these homespun pioneer folk. They regarded it not as a tax on a luxury but as a burden on an economic necessity and a medium of exchange. Even preachers of the gospel were paid in "Old Monongahela rye." Defiant distillers finally erected Whiskey Poles, similar to the Liberty Poles of anti–Stamp Tax days in 1765, and raised the cry "Liberty and No Excise." Boldly tarring and feathering revenue officers, they brought collections to a halt.

President Washington, once a Revolutionist, was alarmed by what he called these "self-created societies." With the warm encouragement of Hamilton, he summoned the militia of several states. Anxious moments followed the call, for there was much doubt as to whether men in other states would muster to crush a rebellion in a sister state. Despite some opposition, an army of about 13,000 rallied to the colors, and two widely separated columns marched briskly forth in a gorgeous, leaf-tinted Indian summer, until knee-deep mud slowed their progress. Washington accompanied the troops a part of the way; Hamilton all the way.

The federal force was overpoweringly strong—larger in fact than Washington's army during much of the Revolutionary War. When the troops reached the hills of western Pennsylvania, they found no insurrection. The "Whiskey Boys" were overawed, dispersed, or captured. Washington, with an eye to healing old sores, pardoned the two small-fry convicted culprits. Hamilton, disgusted by this turn of affairs, wanted to punish the real ringleaders. Ironically, the cost of crushing the rebels cost more than three years' net revenue from the excise.

The Whiskey Rebellion was small—some three

rebels were killed—but its consequences were large. George Washington's government, now substantially strengthened, commanded a new respect. Yet the numerous foes of the federalists condemned the administration for its brutal display of force—for having used a sledge hammer to crush a gnat. The ranks of the Jeffersonians were consequently enlarged. Back-country men, taught a harsh lesson, now saw the wisdom of forsaking the tar kettle for the ballot box—and voting for Jefferson.

The Hamiltonian Balance Sheet

Almost overnight Hamilton's fiscal feats had established the public credit. The Treasury was now able to secure needed funds in the Netherlands on terms more favorable than those being extended to any other borrowing nation.

The dynamic secretary, under the leadership of Washington, also strengthened the government politically while bolstering it financially. His major schemes—funding, assumption, the excise, the Bank—all encroached sharply upon states' rights. This trend, facilitated by "loose construction," was destined to continue its controversial course to the Civil War and beyond.

States'-rights people naturally condemned Hamilton in harsh terms. The Constitution had been ratified by a painfully narrow margin; and if the voters had foreseen how the states were going to be overshadowed by the federal colossus, they almost certainly would have voted it down. Hamilton in general believed that what the Constitution did not forbid it permitted; Jefferson in general believed that what it did not permit it forbade.

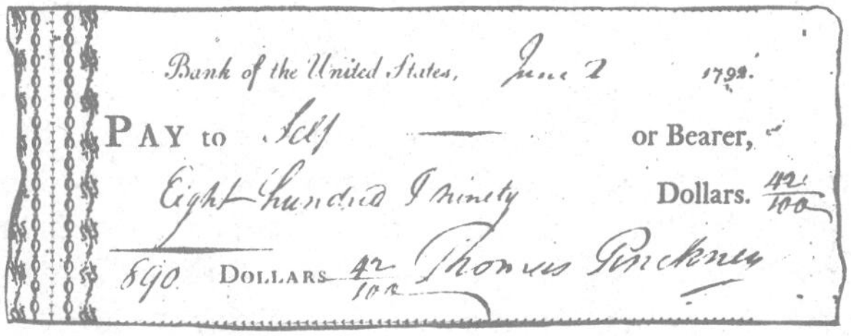

Check on the Bank of the U.S. By Thomas Pinckney, minister to England.

Though a skillful planner, Hamilton was at heart a gambler—a taker of calculated risks. He was playing for enormous stakes, and the outcome might be either a resounding success or a crashing failure. The huge debt, which he had so confidently urged Congress to assume, could be paid off only if ample receipts flowed into the customs-houses. Disaster would befall the nation if foreign trade languished, or if it were choked off by war with America's best customer, Great Britain.

Luck was with Hamilton. Returning prosperity preceded the Constitution, and floated it over the financial reefs. A full-blown foreign war was avoided for more than two decades, and by that time the experimental stage had passed. Even so, the race between mounting expenditures and increasing revenues was nip and tuck for about ten years.

Government by the Wellborn

Hamilton navigated skillfully on the sea of economic policy, but politically he encountered increasingly heavy weather. Out of the resentment against his revenue-raising and centralizing policies an organized opposition began to emerge.

National political parties, in the modern sense, were unknown to America when George Washington took the inaugural oath. There had been Whigs and Tories, federalists and anti-federalists, but these groups were factions rather than parties. They had sprung into existence over hotly contested special issues; they had faded away when their cause had triumphed or had become hopelessly lost.

American political parties date their birth from the bitter clashes between Hamilton and Jefferson, chiefly over fiscal policy and foreign affairs. By 1792–1793 two well-defined groupings had crystallized: the Hamiltonian Federalists and the Jeffersonian Republicans. The two-party system

> Jefferson, who became one of the ablest political organizers in American history, was distrustful of the evils spawned by parties. He wrote in 1789, "If I could not go to Heaven but with a party I would not go there at all."

has existed in the United States since that day, and has provided indispensable machinery for self-government. The party of the "outs" has traditionally played the invaluable role of both critic and brake—"the loyal opposition."

As might be expected, most federalists of the pre-Constitution period (1787–1789) became Federalists in the Washington era. By 1793 they were welded into an effective group, largely through the magnetic leadership and organizational genius of Alexander Hamilton.

Federalists openly advocated rule by the "best people." They believed in a government by the upper classes, with secondary attention to the masses. "Those who own the country," remarked Federalist John Jay, "ought to govern it." With their intellectual arrogance and Tory tastes, the Hamiltonians deplored democratic tendencies and distrusted the common man. They regarded democracy as the mother of all mischiefs, and feared the "swayability" of the crowd. Let the rich rule, insisted many Federalist leaders, for they had the leisure with which to study the problems of governing. They also enjoyed all the advantages of intelligence, education, and culture. The untutored masses would only throw monkey wrenches into the machinery; democracy was too important to be left to the people.

Hamiltonians likewise advocated a potent central government. It would maintain law and order, crush democratic excesses (like Shays's Rebellion), and protect the lives and estates of the wealthy. The foreign-born Hamilton, in pursuit of these goals, would subordinate the sovereignty-loving states.

Hamiltonian Federalists also believed that the national government should foster business, not interfere with it. This attitude was only natural in a group dominated by merchants, manufacturers, and shippers. The great majority of Federalists lived in the urban areas of the seaboard, where commerce and manufacturing flourished. If a gunner could have fired cannonballs 50 miles (80.5 kilometers) inland, he would have hit few Hamiltonians.

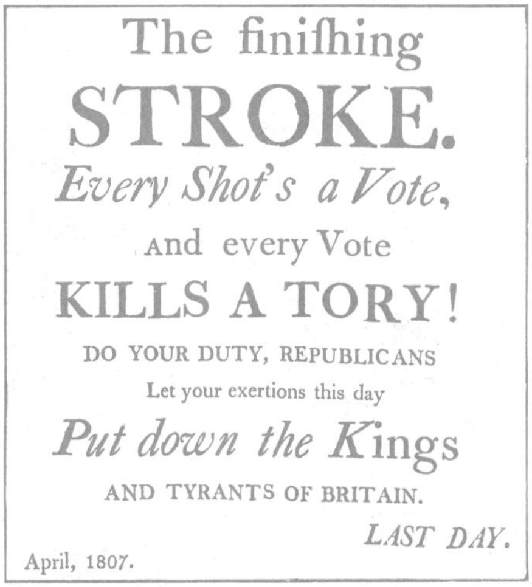
The finiſhing
STROKE.
Every Shot's a Vote,
And every Vote
KILLS A TORY!
DO YOUR DUTY, REPUBLICANS
Let your exertions this day
Put down the Kings
AND TYRANTS OF BRITAIN.
LAST DAY.
April, 1807.

Jeffersonian Republican Leaflet. It treats Federalists as Tories as late as 1807.

The Federalists, in addition, were at bottom pro-British. Though Americans first of all, they felt that the nation's foreign policy should be slanted toward friendship with England, above any other outside power. Foreign trade, especially with England, was a key element in Hamilton's entire fiscal machinery. Many Hamiltonians were mild Loyalists, leftovers from Revolutionary days. Basically conservative in their outlook, they welcomed the Federalist bias for the Mother Country, to which they retained much sentimental attachment.

Jeffersonian Idealism and Idealists

Leading the anti-Federalist forces was Thomas Jefferson. Lanky and relaxed in appearance, lacking personal aggressiveness, weak-voiced, and unable to deliver a rabble-rousing speech, he be-

Monticello, Jefferson's Self-Designed Architectural Marvel. A talented inventor, he installed a number of gadgets, including a device for pulling up chilled bottles of wine from the cellar to the dining table. (Virginia Chamber of Commerce, photo by D'Adamo.)

came a master political organizer through his ability to lead men rather than drive them. His strongest appeal was to the middle class and to the underprivileged—the "dirt" farmers, the laborers, the artisans, and the small shopkeepers.

Liberal-thinking Jefferson, with his aristocratic head set on a farmer's frame, was a bundle of inconsistencies. By one set of tests he should have been a Federalist, for he was a Virginia aristocrat and slaveowner who lived in an imposing hilltop mansion at Monticello. A so-called traitor to his upper class, Jefferson cherished uncommon sympathy for the common man, especially the downtrodden, the oppressed, and the persecuted. As he wrote in 1800, "I have sworn upon the altar of God eternal hostility against every form of tyranny over the mind of man."

Jeffersonian Republicans, or Democratic-Republicans, as they were called, demanded a weak central regime. They believed that the best government was the one that governed least. The bulk of the power, Jefferson argued, should be retained by the states. There the people, in intimate contact with local affairs, could keep a more vigilant eye on their public servants. Otherwise, a dictatorship might develop. Central authority—a kind of necessary evil—was to be kept at a minimum through a strict interpretation of the Constitution. The national debt, which Jefferson regarded as a curse illegitimately bequeathed to later generations, was to be paid off.

Jeffersonians, themselves primarily agrarians, insisted that there should be no special privileges for special classes, particularly manufacturers. Agriculture, to Jefferson, was the favored branch of the economy. He regarded farming as essentially ennobling; it kept men away from wicked cities, out in the sunshine and close to the sod—and God. Most of his followers naturally came from the agricultural South and Southwest.

Above all, Jefferson advocated the rule of the people. But he did not propose thrusting the ballot into the hands of *every* adult white male. He favored government *for* the people, but not by *all* the people—only by those men who were literate enough to inform themselves and wear the mantle of American citizenship worthily. Universal education would have to precede universal suffrage. The ignorant, he argued, were incapable of self-government. But he had profound faith in the reasonableness and teachableness of the masses, and in their collective wisdom when taught. His enduring appeal was to America's better self.

The open-minded Jefferson championed free speech, because without free speech the misdeeds of tyranny could not be exposed. He even went so far as to say that as between "a government without newspapers" and "newspapers without a government," he would choose the latter. No American statesman, except perhaps Lincoln, ever suffered more foul abuse from editorial pens; he might well have prayed for freedom *from* the Federalist press. Yet in 1801 he declared, "Error of opinion may be tolerated where reason is left free to combat it."

Jeffersonian Republicans, unlike the Federalist "British boot-lickers," were basically pro-French. They earnestly believed that it was to America's advantage to support the liberal ideals of the

French Revolution, rather than applaud the reaction of the English Tories. So it was that foreign policy and domestic politics became perilously intermingled, as the fledgling American Republic was caught up in the bloody international conflicts of the French Revolutionary era.

VARYING VIEWPOINTS

The Federalist era witnessed some of the sharpest political conflicts in American history. Certain critics see this period as virtually the *only* time in the nation's experience when major differences of ideology separated the main political leaders. In the clash between Hamiltonians and Jeffersonians, historians have generally sympathized with the liberal Virginian. Yet most scholars agree that it was fortunate for the Republic that the Federalists had the helm for a time. Their leaders put federal finances and foreign policy on a sound conservative foundation, thus permitting the later construction of a "liberal" Jeffersonian edifice.

SELECT READINGS

Perceptive introductions are provided by Marcus Cunliffe's succinct *The Nation Takes Shape, 1789–1837* (1959), and J. C. Miller's more detailed *The Federalist Era, 1789–1801* (1960). On administration, consult L. D. White, *The Federalists* (1948); on finance, D. F. Swanson, *The Origins of Hamilton's Fiscal Policies* (1963), and the book by Nettels cited in the previous chapter. See also those by Chambers on politics and the biographical studies by Brant, Miller, Mitchell, and Rossiter. Also illuminating is Gerald Stourzh, *Alexander Hamilton and the Idea of Republican Government* (1970). A comprehensive biography is James T. Flexner, *George Washington and the New Nation, 1783–1793* (1969). Consult also Forrest McDonald, *The Presidency of George Washington* (1974). Of special interest is R. H. Kohn, *Eagle and Sword: The Federalists and the Creation of the Military Establishment in America, 1783–1802* (1975).

9

Federalists and Foreign Friction

And ne'er shall the sons of Columbia be slaves,
While the earth bears a plant, or the sea rolls its waves.

POPULAR SONG BY ROBERT TREAT PAINE,
"Adams and Liberty," 1798

The Impact of the French Revolution

When Washington's first administration ended early in 1793, domestic controversies had already formed two political camps—Hamiltonian Federalists and Jeffersonian Republicans. As his second term began, issues of foreign policy brought differences to a fever pitch.

Only a few weeks after Washington's inauguration in 1789, the curtain had arisen on the first act of the French Revolution. Twenty-six years were to pass before the seething continent of Europe settled back into a peace of exhaustion. Few non-American events have left a deeper scar on American political and social life. In a sense, the French Revolution was misnamed: it was a *world* revolution that touched all civilized peoples.

In its early stages the upheaval was surprisingly

peaceful, involving as it did a successful attempt to impose constitutional shackles on Louis XVI. The American people, loving liberty and deploring despotism, were pleased. They were flattered to think that the outburst in France was but the second chapter of their own glorious revolution, as to some extent it was. Only a few ultra-conservative Federalists—fearing change, reform, and "leveling" principles—were from the outset dubious or outspokenly hostile to the "despicable mobocracy." The more ardent Jeffersonians were overjoyed.

The French Revolution entered upon a more ominous phase in 1792, when France declared war on hostile Austria. Powerful ideals and powerful armies alike were on the march. Late in that year the electrifying news reached America that French citizen armies had hurled back the invading foreigners, and that France had proclaimed herself a republic. American enthusiasm found expression in singing "The Marseillaise" and other French revolutionary songs, and in renaming thoroughfares. King Street in New York, for example, became Liberty Street, while in Boston Royal Exchange Alley became Equality Lane.

But centuries of pent-up poison could not be purged without baleful results. The guillotine was set up, the King was beheaded in 1793, Christianity was abolished, and the head-rolling Reign of Terror was begun. Back in America, God-fearing Federalist aristocrats nervously fingered their tender white necks and eyed the Jeffersonian masses apprehensively. Lukewarm Federalist approval of the early Revolution turned, almost overnight, to heated opposition to "blood-drinking cannibals."

Sober-minded Jeffersonians regretted the bloodshed. But they felt, with Jefferson, that one could not expect to be carried from "despotism to liberty in a feather bed," and that a few thousand aristocratic heads were a cheap price to pay for human freedom. When the news came of Louis XVI's beheading, the Pittsburgh *Gazette* brutally rejoiced, "Louis Capet has lost his caput."

Such gloating was shortsighted, for dire peril loomed ahead. The earlier battles of the French Revolution had not hurt America directly, but now

> William Cobbett wrote of the frenzied reaction in America to the death of Louis XVI: "Never was the memory of any man so cruelly insulted as that of this mild and humane monarch. He was guillotined in effigy, in the capital of the Union [Philadelphia], twenty or thirty times every day, during one whole winter and part of the summer. Men, women and children flocked to the tragical exhibition, and not a single paragraph appeared in the papers to shame them from it."

Britain was sucked into the titanic conflict. The conflagration speedily spread to the New World, where it vitally affected the expanding young Republic. Thus was repeated the familiar story of every major European war, beginning with 1689, that involved a death struggle for control of the Atlantic Ocean. (See table on p. 48.)

Washington's Neutrality Proclamation

Ominously, the Franco-American alliance of 1778 was still on the books. By its own terms it was to last "forever." It bound the United States to help the French defend their West Indies against future foes; and the booming British fleets were certain to attack these strategic islands.

Many Jeffersonian Republicans favored honoring the alliance, though dubious about defending the French island outposts at the risk of war. Aflame with the liberal ideals of the French Revolution, red-blooded Jeffersonians were eager to enter the conflict against Britain, the recent foe, at the side of France, the recent friend. America owed France her freedom, they argued, and now was the time to pay the debt of gratitude.

But President Washington, level-headed as usual, was not swayed by the clamor of the crowd. Backed by Hamilton, he perceived that war had to be avoided at all costs. The nation in 1793 was militarily weak, economically wobbly, and politi-

The Contrast. Adaptation of an English cartoon. C. C. Coffin, *Building a Nation,* 1882. (Boston Public Library.)

> A contemporary later wrote, "Can it ever be forgotten what a racket was made with the citizen Genêt? The most enthusiastic homage was too cold to welcome his arrival; and his being the first minister of the infant [French] republic . . . was dwelt upon. . . . What hugging and tugging! What addressing and caressing!"

cally disunited. But solid foundations were being laid, and American cradles were continuing to rock a bumper crop of babies. Washington sagaciously reasoned that if America could avoid the broils of Europe for a generation or so, she would then be populous enough and strong enough to assert her maritime rights with vigor and success. Otherwise, she might invite disaster. This strategy of delay—of playing for time while the birthrate fought America's battles—was a cardinal policy of the Founding Fathers. Hamilton and Jefferson, often poles apart on other issues, were in agreement here.

Accordingly, Washington boldly issued his Neutrality Proclamation in 1793, shortly after the outbreak of war between Britain and France. This epochal document not only proclaimed the government's official neutrality in the widening conflict, but sternly warned American citizens to be impartial toward both armed camps. It was America's first formal declaration of aloofness from Old World quarrels, and as such proved to be a major prop of the spreading isolationist tradition.

The pro-French Jeffersonians were enraged by the Neutrality Proclamation; the pro-British Federalists were enheartened. A few days earlier an impetuous, thirty-year-old representative of the French Republic, Citizen Genêt, had landed at Charleston, South Carolina. With unrestrained zeal, he undertook to fit out privateers and otherwise take advantage of the existing Franco-American alliance. The giddy-headed envoy—all sail and no anchor—was soon swept away by his enthusiastic reception by the Jeffersonian Republicans. He foolishly came to believe that the Neutrality Proclamation did not reflect the true wishes of the American people, and he consequently embarked upon unneutral activity not authorized by the French alliance. After he had threatened to appeal over the head of "Old Washington" to the sovereign voters, the President demanded Genêt's withdrawal and the Frenchman was replaced by a less impulsive spokesman.

Washington's Neutrality Proclamation clearly illustrates the truism that self-interest is the basic cement of alliances. In 1778, both France and America stood to gain; in 1793, only France. Technically, the Americans did not flout their obligation, because France never officially called upon them to honor it. Her homeland, and especially her blockaded West Indian Islands, were urgently in need of Yankee foodstuffs. If the Americans had entered the war, the British fleets would have blockaded their coasts and cut off those desperately needed supplies. America was much more useful to France as a prosperous provider than as a prostrate partner.

Embroilments with Britain

President Washington's far-visioned policy of neutrality was sorely tried by the British. For ten long years they had been retaining the chain of northern frontier posts on United States soil, all in defiance of the peace treaty of 1783. There they openly sold firearms and firewater to the Indians, who continued to attack pale-faced pioneers invading their lands. When General "Mad Anthony" Wayne crushed the Northwest Indians at the Battle of Fallen Timbers on August 20, 1794, the fleeing foe left on the field British-made arms, as well as the corpses of a few British-Canadians. In the Treaty of Greenville in 1795, the Indians, finally abandoned by their red-coated friends, ceded their claims to a vast virgin tract in the Ohio country.

On the sea frontier, the British were eager to starve out the French West Indies, and naturally expected the United States to defend them under the Franco-American alliance. Hard-boiled commanders of the Royal Navy, acting under instructions from London in 1793, struck savagely. They seized about 300 American merchant ships in the West Indies, impressed scores of seamen into service on English vessels, and threw hundreds of others into foul dungeons.

These outrages were intolerable. A mighty outcry arose, chiefly from Jeffersonians, that America should once again fight George III in defense of her liberties. At the very least, she should cut off all supplies to her oppressor through a nationwide embargo.

But the Federalists stoutly resisted all demands for drastic action. War with Britain would be a lethal blow at the heart of the Hamiltonian financial system. About 90 percent of the revenue supporting the nation's still-shaky financial structure flowed from customs duties, and some 75 percent of all customs duties came from British imports. An armed clash with England would dry up this life-giving revenue.

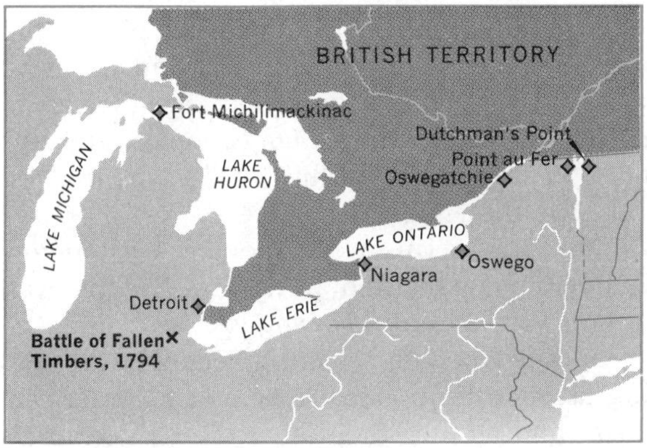

AMERICAN POSTS HELD BY BRITISH AFTER 1783

John Jay Negotiates a Treaty

President Washington, in a last desperate gamble to avert war, decided to send John Jay to London in 1794. The Jeffersonians were acutely unhappy over the choice, partly because they feared that so notorious a Federalist and Britain-lover would sell out his country. Arriving in London, Jay gave the Jeffersonians further cause for alarm when, at the presentation ceremony, he routinely kissed the Queen's hand.

Unhappily, Jay entered the negotiations with weak cards, which were further weakened by Hamilton. The latter, fearful of war with England, secretly supplied the British with the details of America's bargaining strategy. Not surprisingly, Jay won few concessions. The British did promise to evacuate the chain of posts on United States soil—a concession that inspired little confidence, since it had been made before in Paris (to the same John Jay!) in 1783. In addition, Britain consented to pay damages for the recent seizures of American ships. But the British stopped short of pledging anything about *future* maritime seizures and impressments, or about Indian butcheries. And they forced Jay to give ground by binding the United States to pay the debts still owed to British merchants on pre-Revolutionary accounts.

> Evidently satirizing Jay's obeisance to the British Queen, one American journal wrote, "Hear the voice of truth, hear and believe! John Jay, ah! the arch traitor—seize him, drown him, hang him, burn him, flay him alive! Men of America, he betrayed you with a kiss!"

John Jay Burned in Effigy. (After a drawing by F. O. C. Darley.)

When the Jeffersonians learned of Jay's concessions, their rage was fearful to behold. The treaty seemed like an abject surrender to Britain, as well as a betrayal of the Jeffersonian South. Southern planters would have to pay the major share of the pre-Revolutionary debts, while rich Federalist shippers were collecting damages for recent British seizures. Jeffersonian mobs hanged, burned, and guillotined in effigy that "damn'd archtraitor, Sir John Jay." His unpopular pact, more than any other issue, vitalized the newborn Democratic-Republican party of Thomas Jefferson.

President Washington was now confronted with an agonizing decision. He realized that the treaty was highly disappointing, but he also perceived, as did Hamilton, that the choice was either this treaty or none. If it was none, war would almost certainly ensue. And war might well be ruinous, given America's financially overstrained condition. So Washington, in one of the most courageous acts of a courageous life, threw his immense prestige behind the pact.

The President's course was both condemned and condoned. "Damn George Washington," reportedly cried John Randolph of Virginia in a public toast. Other violent Jeffersonians guillotined the President in effigy. But the Senate, after a stormy debate, approved the treaty by the narrowest of margins. Thus war with Great Britain was averted for seventeen years.

A memorable pact with Spain was one of the aftermaths of Jay's Treaty, which in some ways was more important for its by-products than for its provisions. Spain feared that the Anglo-American pact foreshadowed an Anglo-American alliance—to her detriment. She therefore made haste to conclude with the United States the Pinckney Treaty of 1795. Unlike Jay's Treaty, it conceded virtually everything the Americans demanded. At long last Spain granted free navigation of the Mississippi; she yielded the large area north of Florida that had been in dispute for over a decade. (See map on p. 128.) America's totally unexpected diplomatic successes in this quarter were again a direct result of Spain's European distresses.

George Washington's Farewell

A weary Washington had hoped to retire in 1793, at the end of his first term. But his friends and advisers, including the arch-rivals Jefferson and Hamilton, begged him to stay. This was no time to turn from a leader of international eminence to one of sectional stature, like the disagreeably stiff New Englander, John Adams. Washington was unanimously re-elected, simply because the nation could not do without him. Many people could still sing "God save great Washington," to the tune of "God Save the King."

But two full terms were enough. Washington was not only exhausted physically, but he was weary of verbal abuse. Having lost his non-partisan standing when he became a Federalist, he was being assailed by political foes as an "American Caesar" and as the "Stepfather of His Country." Although he had no serious constitutional scruples against a third election, his decision to retire con-

> Thomas Paine, then in France and resenting George Washington's anti-French policies, addressed the President in an open letter (1796) that reveals his bitterness: "And as to you, sir, treacherous in private friendship (for so you have been to me, and that in the day of danger) and a hypocrite in public life, the world will be puzzled to decide, whether you are an apostate or an imposter; whether you have abandoned good principles, or whether you ever had any."

tributed powerfully to establishing the two-term tradition.*

Washington's Farewell Address was not delivered orally, but was published in the newspapers of 1796. The bulk of the document, legend to the contrary, was not concerned with foreign affairs. About two-thirds of it was devoted to domestic problems, including a sage warning against partisan bitterness. Its admonition about alliances has been most misunderstood. Washington did not say that the nation should never make any alliances of any kind under any circumstances. As a military man, he favored "temporary alliances" for "extraordinary emergencies." But he strongly advised the avoidance of "permanent alliances," like the still-vexatious French Treaty of 1778.

Washington added still other words of paternal wisdom. With the pro-British Federalists and the pro-French Jeffersonians clearly in mind, he urged that the Republic avoid tying its political fortunes to the tail of a foreign kite. Subservience to overseas nations would cause America to become "in some degree a slave." With the plottings of Genêt and other French agents fresh in memory, Washington urged that the nation banish foreign intrigue from both domestic and diplomatic affairs.

The Farewell Address was not received with unanimous acclaim. Jeffersonians, on fire to help the French ally, assailed Washington's impartial words as though they were a declaration of war on France. The truth is that the President, in urging no "permanent" foreign entanglements, was giving admirable advice to a weak and divided nation in the year 1796. But what is sound counsel for a growing boy may not apply later to a muscular giant.

Washington's contributions as President were enormous, even though the sparkling Hamilton at times seemed to outshine him. The central government, its fiscal feet now under it, was solidly established. The West was expanding. The merchant marine was plowing the seas. Above all, Washington had kept the nation out of both overseas entanglements and foreign wars. The experimental stage had passed, and the presidential chair could now be turned over to a less impressive figure. But republics are notoriously ungrateful. When Washington left office in 1797, he was showered with the brickbats of partisan abuse, quite in contrast with the bouquets that had greeted his coming. Though the vast majority of his countrymen honored his name, the more venomous Jeffersonians hailed his departure as ending tyranny and graft. "This day," cried journalist Benjamin Franklin Bache, a grandson of "Old Ben," "ought to be a jubilee in the United States."

"Bonny Johnny" Adams Becomes President

Who should succeed the exalted "Father of His Country"? Alexander Hamilton was the best-known member of the Federalist party, now that Washington had bowed out. But his financial policies, some of which had fattened the speculators, had made him so unpopular that he could not hope to be elected President. The Federalists were forced to turn to the experienced but ungracious John Adams, a rugged chip off old Plymouth Rock. The Democratic-Republicans natur-

*Not broken until 1940 by Franklin D. Roosevelt, and made a part of the Constitution in 1951 by the 22nd Amendment.

John Adams, Flinty Second President. He was the first to move into the White House (1800), and his wife Abigail used the unfinished East Room for drying the family wash. An unusually intelligent woman, she was dubbed "Mrs. President" by critics who accused her of influencing her husband unduly.

ally rallied behind their master-organizer and leader, Thomas Jefferson.

Political passions ran feverishly high in the presidential canvass of 1796. The presence of Washington had hitherto imposed some restraints; now the lid was off. Cultured Federalists like Fisher Ames referred to the Jeffersonians as "fire-eating salamanders, poison-sucking toads." Federalists and Democratic-Republicans even drank their liquor in separate taverns. The issues of the campaign, as it turned out, focused heavily on personalities. But the Jeffersonians again assailed the too-forceful crushing of the Whiskey Rebellion and, above all, the negotiation of Jay's hated treaty.

John Adams, with most of his support in New England, squeezed through by the narrow margin of 71 votes to 68 in the Electoral College. The resulting taunt, "President by three votes," was galling to his pride, which was highly developed. Jefferson, as runner-up, became Vice-President.*

*The possibility of such an inharmonious two-party combination in the future was removed by the 12th Amendment to the Constitution in 1804. (See text in Appendix.)

> Jefferson wrote privately of John Adams in 1787, "He is vain, irritable, and a bad calculator of the force and probable effect of the motives which govern men. This is all the ill which can possibly be said of him. He is as disinterested as the Being who made him."

One of the ablest statesmen of his day, Adams at sixty-two was a stuffy figure. Sharp-featured, bald, short (5 feet 7 inches; 1.7 meters) and thickset ("His Rotundity"), he impressed observers as a man of stern principles who did his duty with stubborn devotion. Though learned and upright, he was a tactless and prickly intellectual aristocrat, with no appeal to the masses, and with no desire to cultivate any. Many citizens regarded him with "respectful irritation."

The crusty New Englander suffered from other handicaps. He had stepped into Washington's shoes, which no successor could hope to fill. In addition, Adams was hated by Hamilton, who had resigned from the Treasury in 1795, and who now headed the war faction of the Federalist party. The famed financier even secretly plotted with certain members of the Cabinet against the President, who had a conspiracy rather than a Cabinet on his hands. Most ominous of all, Adams inherited a violent quarrel with France—a quarrel which foreshadowed blazing gunpowder.

Unofficial Fighting with France

Frenchmen were infuriated by Jay's Treaty. They condemned it as the initial step toward an alliance with England, their relentless foe. They further assailed the pact as a flagrant violation of the Franco-American Treaty of 1778. French warships, in retaliation, began to seize defenseless American merchant vessels, altogether about 300 by mid-1797. Adding insult to outrage, the Paris regime haughtily refused to receive America's newly appointed envoy, and even threatened him with arrest.

President Adams kept his head, temporarily, even though the nation was mightily aroused. True to Washington's policy of steering clear of war at all costs, he tried again to reach an agreement with the French, and appointed a diplomatic commission of three men, including John Marshall, the future chief justice.

Adams' envoys, reaching Paris in 1797, hoped to meet Talleyrand, the crafty French foreign minister. They were secretly approached by three gobetweens, later referred to as X, Y, and Z in the published dispatches. The French spokesmen, among other concessions, demanded an unneutral loan of 32 million florins, plus what amounted to a bribe of $250,000 for the privilege of merely talking with Talleyrand.

These terms were intolerable. The American trio knew that bribes were standard diplomatic devices in Europe, but they gagged at paying a quarter of a million dollars for mere talk, without any assurances of a settlement. Negotiations quickly broke down, and John Marshall, on reaching New York in 1798, was hailed as a conquering hero for his steadfastness.

War hysteria swept the United States, catching up President Adams. The slogan of the hour became "Millions for defense, but not one cent for tribute." The song of the hour was "Hail Columbia," which was sung lustily in theaters and taverns:

> Immortal patriots, rise once more!
> Defend your rights, defend your shore.

The Federalists were delighted at this unexpected turn of affairs, while all except the most rabid Jeffersonians hung their heads over the misbehavior of their fine-feathered French friends.

War preparations in America were pushed feverishly, despite considerable Jeffersonian opposition in Congress. The Navy Department was created; the three-ship navy was expanded; the Marine Corps was established. A new army of 10,000 men was authorized (but never fully raised), to be headed by the redoubtable but aging General Washington. He reluctantly heeded the call of duty, but stipulated that the active command be

Preparation for War to Defend Commerce. The building of the frigate *Philadelphia*. In 1803 this frigate ran onto the rocks near Tripoli harbor, and about 300 officers and men were imprisoned by the Tripolitans. The ship was refloated for service against the Americans, but Stephen Decatur led a party of men that set her afire. (Prints Division, The New York Public Library, Astor, Lenox and Tilden Foundations.)

entrusted to the younger Alexander Hamilton, who became a major general. A frustrated military genius, Hamilton was intoxicated by dreams of conquest. He would lead a victorious American army, supported by the British navy, against the possessions of France's Spanish ally—specifically the Floridas, Louisiana, Mexico, and perhaps points south.

Bloodshed was confined to the sea, and principally to the West Indies. In two and one-half years of undeclared hostilities (1798–1800), American privateers and men-of-war of the new navy captured over eighty armed vessels flying the French colors, though several hundred Yankee merchantmen were lost to the enemy. Evidently only a slight push would plunge both nations into a full-dress war.

Adams Puts Patriotism Above Party

Embattled France, her hands full in Europe, wanted no war. An outwitted Talleyrand realized that to fight the United States would merely add one more foe to his enemies. The British, who were lending the Americans cannon and other war supplies, were actually driven closer to their wayward cousins than they were to be again for many years. Talleyrand therefore let it be known, through roundabout channels, that if the Americans would send a new minister, he would be received with proper respect.

This French furor brought to Adams a degree of personal acclaim that he had never known before—and was never to know again. The song "Adams and Liberty" was hardly less popular than "Hail Columbia." He doubtless perceived that a full-fledged war, crowned by the conquest of the Floridas and Louisiana, would bring new plaudits to the Federalist party—and perhaps a second term to himself. But the heady wine of popularity did not sway his final judgment. He realized full well, like other Founding Fathers, that war must be avoided while the country was relatively weak.

> Adams' firmness was revealed in his message to Congress (June 1798), "I will never send another minister to France without assurances that he will be received, respected, and honored as the representative of a great, free, powerful, and independent nation."

Adams unexpectedly exploded a bombshell when, early in 1799, he submitted to the Senate the name of a new minister to France. Hamilton and his war-hawk faction were enraged. But public opinion—Jeffersonian and reasonable Federalist alike—was favorable to one last try for peace.

America's envoys (now three) found the political skies brightening when they reached Paris early in 1800. The ambitious "Little Corporal," the Corsican Bonaparte, had recently seized dictatorial power. He was eager to free his hands of the American squabble so that he might continue to redraw the map of Europe, and perhaps create a New World empire in Louisiana. The distresses and ambitions of the Old World were again working to America's advantage.

After prolonged haggling, a memorable treaty known as the Convention of 1800 was signed in Paris. As finally amended, it brought about a mutually acceptable settlement. France agreed to grant a divorce from the twenty-two-year-old marriage of (in)convenience, but as a kind of alimony the United States itself agreed to pay the damage claims of American shippers. So ended the nation's only peacetime military alliance for a century and a half. Its troubled history does much to explain the traditional antipathy of the American people to foreign entanglements.

Adams, flinty to the end, deserves immense credit for his belated push for peace, even though moved in part by jealousy of Hamilton. He not only avoided the hazards of war, but unwittingly smoothed the path for the peaceful purchase of Louisiana three years later. He should indeed rank high among the forgotten purchasers of this vast domain. If America had drifted into a full-blown war with France in 1800, Napoleon would not have sold her Louisiana on any terms in 1803.

In 1815 Adams wrote privately, "I will defend my missions to France, as long as I have an eye to direct my hand, or a finger to hold my pen. They were the most disinterested and meritorious actions of my life. I reflect upon them with . . . satisfaction."

President Adams, the bubble of his popularity pricked by peace, was aware of his signal contribution to the nation. He later suggested as the epitaph for his tombstone (not used): "Here lies John Adams, who took upon himself the responsibility of peace with France in the year 1800."

The Federalist Witch Hunt

Exulting Federalists had meanwhile capitalized on the anti-French frenzy to drive through Congress in 1798 a sheaf of laws designed to reduce or gag their Jeffersonian foes.

The first of these oppressive laws was aimed at supposedly pro-Jeffersonian "aliens." Most European immigrants, lacking wealth, were scorned by the aristocratic Federalist party. But they were welcomed as voters by the less prosperous and more democratic Jeffersonians. The Federalist Congress, hoping to discourage the "dregs" of Europe, erected a disheartening barrier. They raised the residence requirements for aliens who desired to become citizens from a tolerable five years to an intolerable fourteen. This drastic new law violated the traditional American policy of open-door hospitality and speedy assimilation.

Two additional Alien Laws struck heavily at undesirable immigrants. The President was empowered to deport dangerous foreigners in time of peace, and to deport or imprison them in time of hostilities. Though defensible as a war measure —and an officially declared war with France seemed imminent—this was an arbitrary grant of power contrary to American tradition and to the spirit of the Constitution.

But the Alien Laws were not so senseless as they may seem. Hundreds of foreign firebrands, fleeing the wrath of the homeland authorities, were pouring into America from France, England, and Ireland. Most of these outcasts joined the ranks of the Jeffersonians, where they naturally clamored for an anti-British policy. A few of them were French spies who should have been expelled; many were what President Adams called "foreign liars."

The stringent Alien Laws were never enforced. But they frightened out of the country certain foreign agitators, including a reported two shiploads of Frenchmen. In addition, an undetermined number of other foreigners were discouraged from sailing to the now not-so-promising Promised Land.

The "lockjaw" Sedition Act, the last of the harsh Federalist measures, was a direct slap at two priceless freedoms guaranteed in the Constitution by the Bill of Rights—freedom of speech and freedom of the press (1st Amendment). This law provided that anyone who impeded the policies of the government or falsely defamed its officials, including the President, would be liable to a heavy fine and imprisonment. Severe though the measure was, the Federalists believed that it was justified. The verbal violence of the day was unrestrained, and foul-penned editors, some of them exiled aliens, assailed Adams' anti-French policy in vicious terms.

Many outspoken Jeffersonian editors were indicted under the Sedition Act, but only ten were brought to trial. All of them were convicted, often by packed juries swayed by prejudiced Federalist judges. A few of the victims were harmless partisans, who should have been spared the notoriety of martyrdom. Among them was Congressman Matthew Lyon (the "Spitting Lion"), who had earlier gained fame by spitting in the face of a Federalist. He was sentenced to four months in jail for writing of President Adams' "unbounded thirst for ridiculous pomp, foolish adulation, and selfish avarice." Another culprit was lucky to get off with a fine of $100 after he had expressed the wish that the wad of a cannon fired in honor of

Congressional Pugilists. Satirical representation of Matthew Lyon's fight in Congress with the Federalist Representative Roger Griswold. (Courtesy of The New York Public Library, Astor, Lenox and Tilden Foundations.)

Adams had landed in the seat of the President's breeches.

The Sedition Act, at least in spirit, was in direct conflict with the Constitution. But the Supreme Court, dominated by Federalists, was of no mind to declare this Federalist law unconstitutional. (The law expired, in March 1801, to much rejoicing from Jeffersonians.) This attempt by the Federalists to crush free speech and silence the opposition party, high-handed as it was, undoubtedly made many converts for the Jeffersonians.

> James Callender published in 1800 a pamphlet which assailed the President in this language: "The reign of Mr. Adams has, hitherto, been one continued tempest of *malignant* passions. As president, he has never opened his lips, or lifted his pen, without threatening and scolding. The grand object of his administration has been to exasperate the rage of contending parties, to caluminiate and destroy every man who differs from his opinions. . . . Every person holding an office must either quit it, or think and vote exactly with Mr. Adams." For such blasts Callender was prosecuted under the Sedition Act, fined $200, and sentenced to prison for nine months.

Yet the Alien and Sedition Laws, despite pained outcries from the Jeffersonians, commanded widespread popular support. Anti-French hysteria played directly into the hands of witch-hunting conservatives. In the congressional elections of 1798–1799 the Federalists, riding a wave of popularity, scored the most sweeping victory of their entire history.

The Virginia (Madison) and Kentucky (Jefferson) Resolutions

Resentful Jeffersonians naturally refused to take the Alien and Sedition Laws lying down. Jefferson himself feared that if the Federalists managed to choke free speech and free press, they would then wipe out other precious constitutional guarantees. His own political party might even be stamped out of existence. If this had happened, the country might have drifted into a dangerous one-party dictatorship.

As Vice-President under Adams, Jefferson was in an awkward position to protest openly against the Alien and Sedition Laws. Fearing prosecution for sedition, he secretly penned a series of resolutions, which the Kentucky legislature approved in 1798 and 1799. His friend and fellow Virginian, James Madison, drafted a similar but less extreme statement which was adopted by the legislature of Virginia in 1798.

Both Jefferson and Madison stressed the compact theory—a theory popular among English political philosophers in the 17th and 18th Centuries. As applied to America by the Jeffersonians, this concept meant that the thirteen sovereign states, in creating the federal government, had entered into a "compact" or contract regarding its jurisdiction. The national government was consequently the agent or creation of the states. Since water can rise no higher than its source, the individual states were the final judges of whether their agent had broken the "compact" by overstepping the authority originally granted. Invoking this logic, Jefferson's Kentucky resolutions concluded that the federal regime had exceeded its constitutional powers, and that with regard to the Alien and Sedition Acts "nullification" was the "rightful remedy."

If Federalists bent the bow too far in passing the Alien and Sedition Acts, Jefferson bent the bow too far in his reply. If the Federalist indiscretion had made many Jeffersonian voters, Jefferson's indiscretion made many Federalist voters. No other state legislatures, despite Jefferson's hopes, fell into line. Some of them flatly refused to endorse the Virginia and Kentucky resolutions. Others, chiefly in Federalist states, added ringing condemnations. Many Federalists argued that the people, not the states, had made the original compact, and that it was up to the Supreme Court–not the states–to nullify unconstitutional legislation passed by Congress. This practice, though not specifically authorized by the Constitution, was finally adopted by the Supreme Court in 1803.

The Providential Detection (Federalist Propaganda). The American Eagle snatches the Constitution from Jefferson, who is about to burn it (together with the works of Voltaire, Paine, and others) on the altar to French revolutionary despotism. (Massachusetts Historical Society.)

The Virginia and Kentucky resolutions were a brilliant formulation of the extreme states'-rights view regarding the Union. They were later used by Southerners to support nullification–and ultimately secession. Yet neither Jefferson nor Madison, as Founding Fathers of the Union, had any intention of breaking it up: they were groping for ways to preserve it. Their resolutions were basically campaign documents designed to crystallize opposition to the Federalist party, and to unseat it in the upcoming presidential election of 1800. The only real nullification that Jefferson had in view was the nullification of Federalist abuses.

Federalist and Republican Mudslingers

In the heated presidential contest of 1800, Adams and Jefferson were again the standard-bearers of their respective parties. The Federalists labored under heavy handicaps. Their Alien and Sedition Acts had aroused a host of enemies, although most of these critics were dyed-in-the-wool Jeffersonians anyhow. The Hamiltonian wing of the Federalist party, robbed of its glorious war with France, split openly with President Adams. Hamilton, a victim of arrogance, was so indiscreet as to attack the President in a privately printed pamphlet. Jeffersonians soon got hold of it and gleefully published it.

The most damaging blow to the Federalists was the refusal of Adams to give them a rousing fight with France. Their feverish war preparations had swelled the public debt and had required disagreeable new taxes, including a stamp tax. After all these unpopular measures, the war scare had petered out, and the country was left with an all-dressed-up-but-no-place-to-go feeling. The military preparations now seemed not only unnecessary but extravagant, as seamen for the "new navy" were called "John Adams' Jackasses."

I◻II◻II◻II◻II◻II◻II◻II◻II◻II◻II◻II◻II◻II◻II◻II◻II◻II◻II◻I

> The Reverend Timothy Dwight, president of Yale College, predicted that in the event of Jefferson's election "the Bible would be cast into a bonfire, our holy worship changed into a dance of [French] Jacobin phrensy, our wives and daughters dishonored, and our sons converted into the disciples of Voltaire and the dragoons of Marat."

I◻II◻II◻II◻II◻II◻II◻II◻II◻II◻II◻II◻II◻II◻II◻II◻II◻II◻II◻I

Adams himself was known as "The Father of the American Navy."

Thrown on the defensive, the Federalists concentrated their fire on Jefferson himself, who became the victim of one of the earliest "whispering campaigns." He was accused of having robbed a widow and her children of a trust fund, and of having fathered numerous mulatto children by his own slave women. As a liberal in religion, he had earlier incurred the wrath of the orthodox clergy, largely through his successful struggle to separate church and state in Virginia. From the New England stronghold of Federalism and Congregationalism, the preachers thundered against his atheism, although he did believe in God. Old ladies of Federalist families, fearing Jefferson's election, even buried their Bibles or hung them in wells.

The Jeffersonian "Revolution of 1800"

Jefferson won by a majority of 73 electoral votes to 65. But the colorless and presumably unpopular Adams polled more electoral strength than he had gained four years earlier—except for New York. The Empire State fell into the Jeffersonian basket, and with it the election, largely because Aaron Burr, a master wirepuller, turned New York to Jefferson by the narrowest of margins. The Virginian polled the bulk of his strength in the South and West, particularly in those states where manhood suffrage had been adopted.

Jeffersonians rejoiced wildly over the end of the "Federalist Reign of Terror." Some of them, with alcoholic enthusiasm, bawled the song "Jefferson and Liberty":

> Lord! how the Federalists will stare,
> At Jefferson, in Adams' chair!

But Jeffersonian joy was dampened by an unexpected deadlock. Through a technicality Jefferson, the presidential candidate, and Burr, his vice-presidential running mate, received the same number of electoral votes for the presidency. Under the Constitution the tie could be broken only by the House of Representatives (see Art. II, Sec. I, para. 2). This body was controlled for several more months by the lame-duck Federalists, who had been swept into office during the French war scare and who were eager to elect Burr.*

Voting in the House moved slowly to a climax. As ballots were taken in wearisome succession, congressmen snored in their seats; a sick member lay in an adjoining room. Historians used to think that Hamilton, bargaining secretly with Jefferson, played a decisive role. But the evidence indicates that the deadlock was broken when a few Federalists, despairing of electing Burr and hoping for moderation from Jefferson, refrained from voting. The election then went to the rightful candidate.

Jefferson later claimed that the election of 1800 was a "revolution" comparable in principle to that of 1776. In truth the outcome was not a mass upheaval or a popular mandate from anybody for anything. A switch of some 250 votes in New York would have defeated Jefferson. He did not—and could not—extend the suffrage. That was a privilege of the states. But he did persuade the apathetic and overawed marginal voter to go to the polls—the citizen who had just enough property to vote but who hesitated to speak up against his "betters." Above all, the electoral clash led to a peaceful transfer of power, remarkable in that

*A "lame duck" has been humorously defined as a politician whose political goose has been cooked at the recent elections. The possibility of another such tie was removed by the 12th Amendment in 1804 (for text, see Appendix). Before then, each elector had two votes, with the second-place finisher becoming Vice-President.

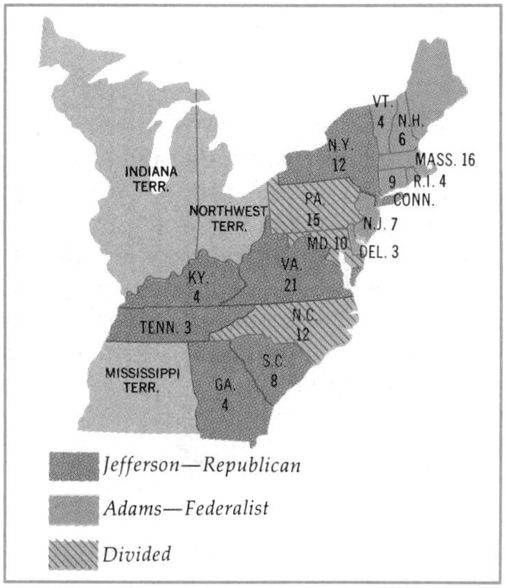

PRESIDENTIAL ELECTION OF 1800
(with electoral vote by state)
New York was the key state in this election, and Aaron Burr helped swing it away from the Federalists with tactics that anticipated the political "machines" of a later day. Federalists complained that Burr "travels every night from one meeting of Republicans to another, haranguing . . . them to the most zealous exertions. [He] can stoop so low as to visit every low tavern that may happen to be crowded with his dear fellow citizens." But Burr proved that the price was worth it. "We have beat you," Burr told kid-gloved Federalists after the election, "by superior *Management*."

age, especially after all the partisan bitterness.

Yet the election was also in part a class struggle. Budding democracy was arrayed against entrenched aristocracy more openly than in any previous presidential election. The battle of the ballots resulted in a gratifying victory for the "forgotten man"—and clipped the wings of fine-feathered Federalist aristocrats.

The Federalist Finale

John Adams, as fate would have it, was the last Federalist President of the United States. His party sank slowly into the mire of political oblivion, and ultimately disappeared completely in the days of Andrew Jackson.

Whatever their shortcomings, the Federalists were of the elite. They boasted a much higher concentration of brains, talent, and ability than any other major American political party, past or present. Their political and financial leaders had built enduring foundations for the new government. Their diplomats, with a strong helping hand from Europe's distresses, had signed advantageous treaties with England, Spain, and France. Their statesmen had kept the peace during a crucial period when peace had to be kept.

After all the turmoil of the American Revolution, a conservative party served a needed function in preserving democratic gains and fending off anarchy. The Federalists provided a welcome breathing spell, a chance for the nation to get its bearings. They served, in the words of historian Henry Adams, great-grandson of John Adams, as the "half-way house between the European past and the American future."

But by 1800 the Federalists, blessed with more talent than wisdom, were out of place. The bustling new Republic knew instinctively where it was going. It was eager to take the high road over the mountains that would one day lead to the fulfillment of America's democratic experiment. The Federalists lost out because they were content to mark time, and failed to get in step with the westward march of progress. They were unable or unwilling to unbend and appeal to the common man. They could not adapt—so they died, like the dinosaur. Distinguished though their past service had been, it was no substitute for a capacity to grapple democratically with future problems. The victorious Jeffersonians were prepared to keep the Federalist edifice while ousting the Federalist architects.

VARYING VIEWPOINTS

Historians have rightly regarded the Federalist era as the seedtime of the nation's foreign policy. As debate continues over America's role abroad, so does argument still swirl about the diplomacy of the Federalists. Was George Washington the father of unreasoning "isolationism," or did he set forth a realistic policy for the infant nation to follow? Was that policy equally applicable when the infant nation had matured? What was the historical basis of Washington's ideas? Some scholars regard his policies as opportune rationalizations of the country's weak position. Others see them as high expressions of all the best Enlightenment thought about an ideal international order. This question—concerning the degree to which American foreign policy reflects self-interest or idealism—has continued to be argued from Washington's day to the present.

SELECT READINGS

Brief introductions are Marcus Cunliffe, *The Nation Takes Shape, 1789–1837* (1959), and his *George Washington* (1958). More detailed is J. C. Miller, *The Federalist Era, 1789–1801* (1960). Biographical studies of Hamilton and Madison listed for Chapter 7 are relevant. See also Dumas Malone, *Jefferson and the Rights of Man* (1951), and *Jefferson and the Ordeal of Liberty* (1962); also J. A. Carroll and M. W. Ashworth, *George Washington: First in Peace* (1957), and J. T. Flexner, *George Washington: Anguish and Farewell, 1793–1799* (1972). On the rise of parties consult N. E. Cunningham, *The Jeffersonian Republicans* (1958). On aspects of foreign policy, see Alexander De Conde, *Entangling Alliance* (1958), and his *The Quasi-War: The Politics and Diplomacy of the Undeclared War with France, 1797–1801* (1966); Gilbert Lycan, *Alexander Hamilton and American Foreign Policy* (1970); Jerald Combs, *The Jay Treaty* (1970); Lawrence S. Kaplan, *Colonies into Nation: American Diplomacy, 1763–1801* (1972); L. M. Sears, *George Washington and the French Revolution* (1960); P. A. Varg, *Foreign Policies of the Founding Fathers* (1963); Felix Gilbert, *To the Farewell Address* (1961); and Julian Boyd, *Number 7* (1964), on Hamilton's devious dealings with the British. For the view from across the Atlantic, see Charles R. Ritcheson, *Aftermath of Revolution: British Policy Toward the United States, 1783–1795* (1969). On Adams, consult Page Smith, *John Adams* (2 vols., 1962), and S. G. Kurtz, *The Presidency of John Adams* (1957). J. C. Miller, *Crisis in Freedom* (1951), and J. M. Smith, *Freedom's Fetters* (1956), treat the Alien and Sedition Laws, as does Leonard Levy, *Legacy of Suppression* (1960).

10

The Triumph of Jeffersonian Democracy

Timid men . . . prefer the calm of despotism to the boisterous sea of liberty.

THOMAS JEFFERSON, 1796

Responsibility Breeds Moderation

"Long Tom" Jefferson was inaugurated President on March 4, 1801, in the swampy village of Washington, the crude new national capital. Tall (6 feet 2.5 inches; 1.89 meters), with large hands and feet, reddish hair ("The Red Fox"), and prominent cheekbones and chin, he was an arresting figure. Believing that the customary pomp did not befit his democratic ideals, he spurned a horse-drawn coach and simply walked over to the Capitol from his boarding house.

The inaugural address, beautifully phrased, was a classic statement of democratic principles. Seeking to allay Federalist fears of a bull-in-the-china-closet overturn, Jefferson blandly stated, "We are all Republicans, we are all Federalists." As for foreign affairs, he pledged "honest friendship with all nations, entangling alliances with none."

Washington and Jefferson Contrasted. Note the emphasis on Jefferson's fondness for free-thinkers like Paine and Voltaire. Jefferson liked the democratic way of thinking and the aristocratic way of living. His personal wine bill at the White House ran to over $10,000. Widowed at thirty-nine, he is alleged to have fathered a half-dozen slave children by his mulatto woman Sally, but the charge has never been conclusively proved. (New York Historical Society.)

With its rustic setting, Washington lent itself admirably to the simplicity and frugality of the Jeffersonian Republicans. In this respect, it contrasted sharply with the elegant atmosphere of Federalist Philadelphia, the former temporary capital. Extending democratic principles to etiquette, Jefferson established the rule of pell-mell at official dinners—that is, seating without regard to rank. The resplendent British minister, who had enjoyed precedence among the pro-British Federalists, was insulted.

As a widower, Jefferson was shockingly unconventional. Having no wife to police his apparel, he would receive callers in sloppy attire—on one occasion in a dressing gown and heelless slippers. He started the precedent, unbroken for 112 years, of sending messages to Congress to be read by a clerk. Personal appearances, in the Federalist manner, suggested too strongly a monarchical speech from the throne. Besides, Jefferson was painfully conscious of his weak voice and unimpressive platform presence.

As if plagued by an evil spirit, Jefferson was forced to reverse many of the political principles he had so vigorously championed. There were in fact two Thomas Jeffersons. One was the private citizen, who had philosophized in his study. The other was the public official, who made the disturbing discovery that bookish theories worked out differently in the noisy arena of practical politics. The open-minded Virginian was therefore consistently inconsistent; it is easy to quote one Jefferson to refute the other.

The triumph of Jefferson's Democratic-Republicans and the eviction of the Federalists marked the first party overturn in American history. The vanquished naturally feared that the victors would grab all the spoils of office for themselves. But Jefferson, in line with his conciliatory inaugural address, showed unexpected moderation. To the dismay of his office-seeking friends, the new Pres-

> Jefferson's toleration was reflected in his inaugural address: "If there be any among us who would wish to dissolve this Union or to change its republican form, let them stand undisturbed as monuments of the safety with which error of opinion may be tolerated where reason is left free to combat it."

> President John F. Kennedy later greeted a large group of Nobel prizewinners as "the most extraordinary collection of talent, of human knowledge, that has ever been gathered together at the White House, with the possible exception of when Thomas Jefferson dined alone."

ident dismissed few public servants for political reasons. Patronage-hungry Jeffersonians watched the Federalist appointees grow old in office, and grumbled that "few die, none resign."

Jefferson quickly proved an able politician. He was especially effective in the informal atmosphere of a dinner party. There he wooed Congressmen while personally pouring imported wines and serving the tasty dishes of his French cook.

In part, Jefferson had to rely on his personal charm because his party was so weak-jointed. Denied the power to dispense patronage, the Democratic-Republicans could not build a loyal political following. Opposition to the Federalists was the chief glue holding them together, and as the Federalists faded, so did Democratic-Republican unity. The era of well-developed, well-disciplined political parties still lay in the future.

Jeffersonian Reform Without Revolution

At the outset, Jefferson was determined to undo the Federalist abuses begotten by the anti-French hysteria. The hated Alien and Sedition Laws had already expired. The incoming President speedily pardoned the "martyrs" serving sentences under the Sedition Law, and the government returned many fines. Shortly after the Congress met, the Jeffersonians enacted the new naturalization law of 1802. It reduced the unreasonable requirement of fourteen years of residence to the former and more reasonable requirement of five years.

Jefferson actually kicked away only one substantial prop of the Hamiltonian system. He hated the excise tax, which bred bureaucrats and bore heavily on his farmer following, and he early persuaded Congress to repeal it. His devotion to principle thus cost the federal government about a million dollars a year in urgently needed revenue.

Swiss-born and French-accented Albert Gallatin, "Watchdog of the Treasury," proved to be as able a secretary of the treasury as Hamilton. Gallatin agreed with Jefferson that a national debt was a bane rather than a blessing, and by strict economy succeeded in reducing it substantially while balancing the budget.

Except for excising the excise tax, the Jeffersonians left the Hamiltonian framework essentially intact. They launched no attack on the Bank of the United States, and they did not repeal the mildly protective Federalist tariff. In later years they embraced Federalism to such a degree as to recharter a bigger Bank and to boost the protective tariff to higher levels.

The "Revolution of 1800," so far as it was a revolution, thus turned out to be largely one of men rather than of measures, especially in the national government. Generally speaking, the agrarian aristocrats of the Republican South and West—men like Jefferson—elbowed aside the commercial and manufacturing aristocrats of the Federalist northern seaboard.

The "Dead Clutch" of the Judiciary

The "death bed" Judiciary Act of 1801 was one of the last important laws passed by the expiring Federalist Congress. It created sixteen new federal judgeships and other judicial offices. President Adams remained at his desk until nine o'clock in the evening of his last day in office, allegedly signing the commissions of the Federalist "midnight judges." (Actually only three commissions were signed on his last day.)

This Federalist-sponsored Judiciary Act, though a long-overdue reform, aroused bitter resentment. "Packing" these lifetime posts with anti-Jeffersonian partisans was, in Republican eyes, a brazen attempt by the defeated party to entrench itself in one of the three powerful branches of government. Jeffersonians condemned the "midnight judges" in violent language. To them, the trickery of the Federalists was open defiance of the people's will, as recently expressed at the polls.

The newly elected Republican Congress bestirred itself to repeal the Judiciary Act of 1801 in the year after its passage. Jeffersonians thus swept sixteen benches from under the recently appointed "midnight judges." Frustrated Federalists, in turn, were acidly critical of this "assault" on the judicial arm.

Jeffersonians likewise had their knives sharpened for the scalp of Chief Justice John Marshall, whom Adams had appointed to the Supreme Court (as a fourth choice) in the dying days of his term. The lanky Marshall, with his rasping voice and steel-trap mind, was a cousin of Thomas Jefferson. As a Virginia Federalist, he was cordially disliked by the states'-rights Jeffersonians. He served for about thirty days under a Federalist administration, and thirty-four years under the administrations of the Jeffersonian Republicans and their successors. The Federalist party died out, but Marshall went on handing down Federalist decisions serenely for many more years. He probably did more than Hamilton to engraft the Hamiltonian concept of a powerful central government upon the American political and economic system.

One of the "midnight judges" of 1801 presented John Marshall with a historic opportunity. He was obscure William Marbury, whom President Adams had named a justice of the peace for the District of Columbia. When Marbury learned that his commission was being held up by the new secretary of state, James Madison, he sued for its delivery. Chief Justice John Marshall knew that his Jeffersonian rivals, entrenched in the executive branch, would hardly spring forward to enforce a writ to deliver the commission to his fellow Federalist Marbury. He therefore dismissed Marbury's suit, avoiding a direct political showdown. But the wily Marshall snatched a victory from the jaws of this judicial defeat. In explaining his ruling, Marshall said that the part of the Judiciary Act of 1789 on which Marbury tried to base his appeal was unconstitutional. The Act had attempted to assign to the Supreme Court powers that the Constitution had not foreseen.

> Jefferson referred privately to Marshall (1820) as "a crafty chief judge," and noted that "his twistifications in the case of Marbury, in that of Burr, and the Yazoo case show how dexterously he can reconcile law to his personal biases."

In this self-denying opinion, Marshall greatly magnified the authority of the Court—and slapped at the Jeffersonians. Until the case of *Marbury* v. *Madison* (1803), controversy had clouded the question of who had the final authority to determine the meaning of the Constitution. Jefferson in the Kentucky resolutions (1798) had tried to assign that right to the individual states. But now his cousin on the Court had cleverly promoted the contrary principle of "judicial review"—that the black-robed tribunal of the Supreme Court alone had the last word on the question of constitutionality. In this epochal case, Marshall thus neatly inserted the keystone into the arch that supports the tremendous power of the Supreme Court in American life.*

Jefferson Threatens the Supremacy of the Supreme Court

Marshall's decision regarding Marbury spurred the Jeffersonians in their desire to lay rough hands on the Supreme Court through impeachment. Certain Federalist judges had become highly offensive, especially in Sedition Law cases, by de-

*The next invalidation of a federal law by the Supreme Court came fifty-four years later with the explosive Dred Scott decision (see p. 371).

Mad Tom in a Rage. A Federalist cartoon shows "Mad Tom" Jefferson, assisted by brandy and the Devil, trying to pull down the Federal edifice erected by Washington and Adams. (Houghton Library, Harvard.)

livering harangues from the bench against the Republican "mobocracy." Jefferson favored free speech, but not this kind of free speech. Accordingly, he urged action against an arrogant Supreme Court justice, Samuel Chase, who was so unpopular that Republicans named vicious dogs after him.

Early in 1804 impeachment charges against Chase were voted by the House of Representatives, which then passed the question of guilt or innocence on to the Senate. The indictment by the House was based on "high crimes and misdemeanors," as specified in the Constitution.* Yet the evidence was plain that the intemperate judge had not been guilty of "high crimes" but of bad manners, injudicious statements, and unrestrained partisanship. The Senate, after a determined prosecution, failed to muster enough votes to convict and remove Chase. The precedent thus established was fortunate. From that day to this, no really serious attempt has been made to reshape the Supreme Court by the impeachment weapon.

John Marshall viewed the attack on Chase with deep misgivings. He suspected, not unreasonably, that if it succeeded he would be next—and then his other Federalist colleagues. These fears were now laid to rest. Jefferson's ill-advised attempt at "judge breaking" was a reassuring victory for the independence of the judiciary, and for the separation of powers among the three branches of the federal government.

The Pacifist Jefferson Turns Warrior

As a passionate champion of freedom, Jefferson distrusted large standing armies as a standing invitation to dictatorship. Navies, though also suspect, were less to be feared: they could not march inland and "endanger liberties." Pinning his faith to the frail reed of an ill-trained militia, Jefferson reduced the military establishment to a mere police force of 2,500 officers and men. The Republicans, primarily agrarians, saw little point in protecting a few Federalist shippers with a costly navy that all the taxpayers would have to support. Pledged to rigid economy, Jefferson gladly reduced the navy to a peacetime footing, in accordance with legislation already passed by the outgoing Federalist Congress.

But harsh realities forced a penny-pinching Jefferson to change his tune on navies and war. Pirates of the North African states had long made a national industry of blackmailing and plundering merchant ships that ventured into the Mediterranean. Preceding Federalist administrations, in fact, had been forced to buy protection. At the time of the French crisis of 1798, when Americans were shouting, "Millions for defense, but not one cent for tribute," twenty-six barrels of blackmail dollars were being shipped to piratical Algiers.

At this price, war seemed cheaper than peace, and the showdown came in 1801. The Pasha of Tripoli, dissatisfied with his share of protection money, informally declared war on the United States by cutting down the flagstaff of the American consulate. A challenge was thus thrown squarely into the face of Jefferson—the noninterventionist, the pacifist, the critic of a big-ship navy, and the political foe of Federalist shippers. He reluctantly rose to the occasion by dispatching

---

*For impeachment, see Art. I, Sec. II, para. 5; Art. I, Sec. III, paras. 6, 7; Art. II, Sec. IV, in Appendix.

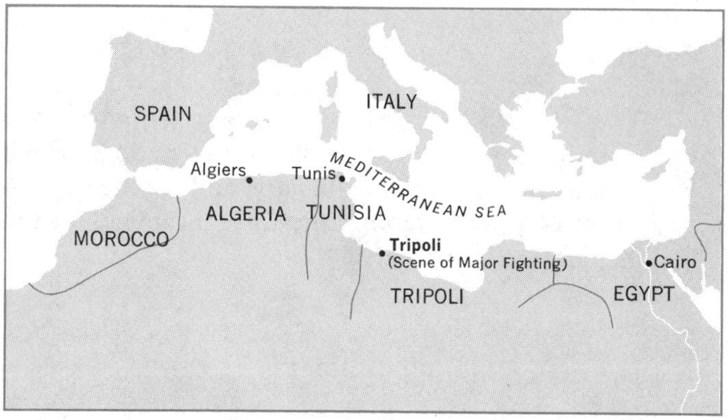

FOUR BARBARY STATES OF NORTH AFRICA

the infant navy to "the shores of Tripoli," as related in the song of the U.S. Marine Corps. After four years of intermittent fighting, marked by hair-raising exploits, Jefferson succeeded in extorting a treaty of peace from Tripoli in 1805. It was secured at the bargain price of only $60,000—a sum representing ransom payments for captured Americans.

With the pattern thus set, the punishment of other North African corsairs continued, off and on, until after the War of 1812. The navy reaped a rich harvest of experience, while strengthening its budding tradition. Foreign nations in general, and the Barbary cutthroats in particular, developed a wholesome respect for the United States—a nation willing and able to defend its rights with blazing guns.

Small gunboats, which the navy had used with some success in the Tripolitan War, fascinated Jefferson. Pledged to tax reduction, he advocated a large number of tiny coastal craft—"Jeffs" or the "mosquito fleet," as they were contemptuously called. He believed that these frail vessels would prove valuable in guarding American shores, although not in defending Federalist merchantmen on the high seas.

About two hundred tiny gunboats were constructed, democratically in small shipyards where votes could be made for Jefferson. Often mounting only one unwieldy gun, they were sometimes more of a menace to the crew than to the prospective enemy. During a hurricane and tidal wave at Savannah, Georgia, one of them was deposited eight miles (12.9 kilometers) inland in a cornfield, to the derisive glee of the Federalists. They drank toasts to American gunboats as the best in the world—on land. Jefferson's pinchpenny economizing backfired badly when the War of 1812 broke out and the whole swarm of gunboats proved virtually stingless. The money could have been much more wisely invested in a few frigates of the *Constitution* class.

Jefferson's One-Gun Gunboats, 1807
In June, 1813, fifteen of these gunboats, each with one heavy gun, attacked a becalmed British frigate near Norfolk, Va. Despite the superior numbers of American vessels, the frigate received only one or two shots in her hull. When the breeze arose, the British ship sailed away virtually unharmed—after killing one American and wounding two.

The Louisiana Godsend

A secret pact, fraught with peril for America, was signed in 1800. Napoleon Bonaparte induced the King of Spain to cede to France, for attractive considerations, the immense trans-Mississippi region of Louisiana, which included the New Orleans area.

Rumors of the transfer were partially confirmed in 1802, when the Spaniards at New Orleans withdrew the right of deposit guaranteed America by the treaty of 1795. Deposit privileges were vital to frontier farmers who floated their produce down the Mississippi to its mouth, there to await ocean-going vessels. A roar of anger rolled up the mighty river and into its tributary valleys. American pioneers talked wildly of descending upon New Orleans, rifles in hand. Had they done so, the nation probably would have been involved in war with both Spain and France.

Thomas Jefferson, both pacifistic and anti-entanglement, was again on the griddle. Louisiana in the senile grip of Spain posed no real threat; America could seize the territory when the time was ripe. But Louisiana in the iron fist of Napoleon, the pre-eminent military genius of his age, foreshadowed a dark and blood-drenched future. The United States would probably have to fight to dislodge him; and because it alone was not strong enough to defeat his armies, it would have to seek allies, contrary to the deepening anti-alliance policy.

Hoping to quiet the clamor of the West, Jefferson moved decisively. Early in 1803 he sent James Monroe to Paris to join forces with the regular minister there, Robert R. Livingston. The two envoys were instructed to buy New Orleans and as much land to the east as they could get for a maximum of $10 million. If these proposals should fail and the situation should become critical, negotiations were to be opened with England for an alliance.

Explaining the Western outburst over the closing of the river, James Madison wrote to Pinckney, "The Mississippi is to them every thing. It is the Hudson, the Delaware, the Potomac, and all the navigable rivers of the Atlantic States, formed into one stream."

Toussaint L'Ouverture (c. 1774–1803). A self-educated ex-slave and military genius, L'Ouverture was finally betrayed by the French, who imprisoned him in a chilly dungeon in France, where he coughed his life away. By indirection he did much to set up the sale of Louisiana to the United States. (Library of Congress.)

Nothing could better illustrate Jefferson's concern. Though a passionate hater of war and an enemy of entangling alliances, he was proposing to make an alliance with his old foe, England, against his old friend, France, with the object of waging a defensive war.

Napoleon now suddenly decided to sell all Louisiana and abandon his dream of a New World empire. He had failed in his efforts to reconquer the sugar-rich island of Santo Domingo, for which Louisiana was to serve as a granary. Infuriated ex-slaves, ably led by a gifted black, Toussaint L'Ouverture, had put up a stubborn resistance that was ultimately broken. Then the island's second line of defense—mosquitoes carrying yellow

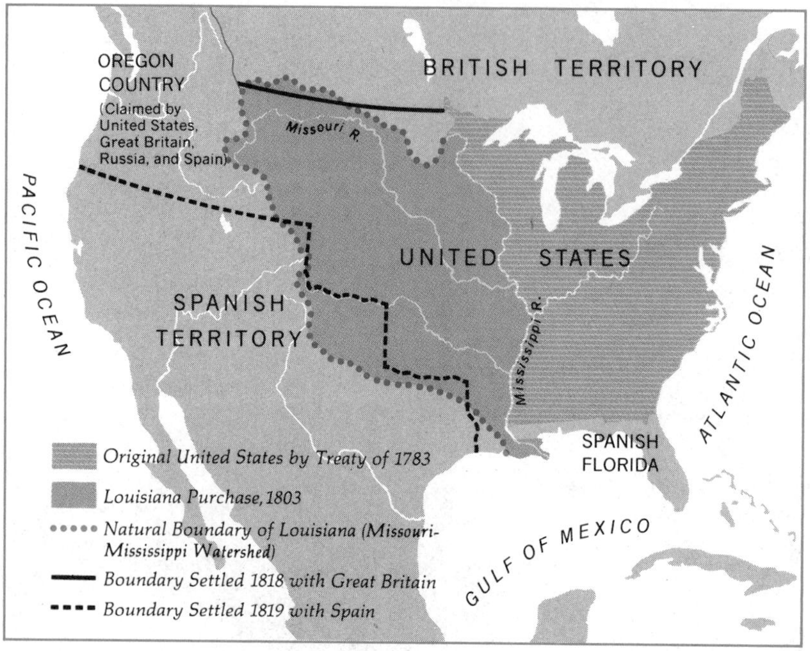

LOUISIANA PURCHASE, 1803
Seeking to avert friction with France by purchasing all of Louisiana, Jefferson bought trouble because of the vagueness of the boundaries. Among the disputants were Spain in the Floridas, Spain and Mexico in the Southwest, and Great Britain in Canada.

fever—had swept away thousands of crack French troops. Santo Domingo could not be reconquered, except perhaps at a staggering cost; hence there was no need for the granary. "Damn sugar, damn coffee, damn colonies!" burst out Napoleon.

Bonaparte was about to end the twenty-month lull in his deadly conflict with Britain. Because the British controlled the seas, he feared that he might be forced to make them a gift of Louisiana. Rather than drive America into the arms of England by attempting to hold the area, he decided to sell the huge wilderness to the Americans and pocket the money for his schemes nearer home. He hoped that the United States, strengthened by Louisiana, would one day grow up to be a military and naval power that would thwart the ambitions of the lordly British in the New World. The distresses of France in Europe were again paving the way for America's diplomatic successes.

Events now moved dizzily. The American Minister Livingston, pending the arrival of Monroe, was busily negotiating in Paris for a window on the Gulf of Mexico at New Orleans. Suddenly, out of a clear sky, the French foreign minister asked him how much he would give for all Louisiana. Scarcely able to believe his ears (he was partially deaf anyhow), Livingston nervously entered upon the negotiations. After about a week of haggling, while the fate of America trembled in the balance, treaties were signed, under the date April 30, 1803, ceding Louisiana to the United States for about $15 million.

The Devil and Napoleon. In England and among American Federalists, Napoleon came to be regarded as an anti-Christ, in league with the Devil. A contemporary French caricature.

Out-Federalizing the Federalists in Louisiana

When the news of the bargain reached America, Jefferson was startled. He had authorized his envoys to offer not more than $10 million for New Orleans, and as much to the *east* in the Floridas as they could get. Instead, they had signed three treaties which pledged $15 million for New Orleans, plus a vast wilderness entirely to the *west*—an area that would more than double the United States. They had bought a wilderness to get a city.

Once again the two Jeffersons wrestled with each other in private: the theorist and the former strict constructionist versus the realist and public official. Where in his beloved Constitution was the President authorized to negotiate treaties incorporating a huge new expanse into the union—an expanse containing some 50,000 red, white, and black inhabitants? There was no such clause.

Conscience-stricken, Jefferson secretly proposed that a constitutional amendment be passed. But his friends pointed out in alarm that in the interval Napoleon, for whom thought was action, might suddenly change his mind. So Jefferson shamefacedly submitted the treaties to the Senate, while privately admitting that the purchase was unconstitutional.

The senators were less finicky than Jefferson. Reflecting enthusiastic public support, they registered their prompt approval of the transaction. Land-hungry Americans were not disposed to split constitutional hairs when confronted with perhaps the most magnificent real estate bargain in history—828,000 square miles (2,144,520 square kilometers) at about three cents an acre.

If Louisiana made Jefferson a loose constructionist, it made many Federalists strict constructionists. (Hamilton, to his credit, was a partial exception.) Federalists argued vehemently that there was no constitutional warrant for the transfer. (Shades of the Federalists who had chartered the Bank of the United States!) Louisiana, so they claimed, was a worthless desert that would cost too much at a time when the Jeffersonians were pledged to rigid economy: $15 million in one pile of silver dollars would reach three miles into the air. (Shades of the Federalists who had cheerfully assumed Hamilton's debt of $75 million!)

What really worried the Federalists was that the signing of the Louisiana treaties was the signing of their own political death warrant. New states would be carved from the immense area—states that would outvote the thirteen charter members, including Federalist New England. The Jeffersonian agrarians would then become unassailable. At Williams College, in Massachusetts, a debating group voted fifteen to one that the purchase of Louisiana was undesirable. A few Federalist extremists even threatened to secede from the Union.

The purchase of Louisiana—the most glorious achievement of Jefferson as President—was a triumph for which neither he nor anyone else could claim much direct credit. Napoleon, for reasons purely selfish, dumped this rich prize into the laps of Livingston, Monroe, and Jefferson. Louisiana was so desirable that Jefferson found it less embarrassing to reverse himself on strict construction than to lose the magnificent windfall.

> In accepting the Louisiana Purchase, Jefferson thus compromised with conscience in a private letter: "It is the case of a guardian, investing the money of his ward in purchasing an important adjacent territory; and saying to him when of age, I did this for your good; I pretend to no right to bind you: you may disavow me, and I must get out of the scrape as I can: I thought it my duty to risk myself for you."

Louisiana in the Long View

Jefferson's bargain with France was epochal. By scooping up Louisiana, America secured at one bloodless stroke the western half of the richest river valley in the world, and further laid the foundations of a future major power. The ideal of a

EXPLORING THE LOUISIANA PURCHASE

An amazing Indian woman, Sacagawea, a Shoshone married to a Canadian interpreter, accompanied the Lewis and Clark expedition. She shared the hardships and privations with an infant strapped to her back. Without her assistance and the aid she obtained from the Shoshone Indians, Lewis and Clark might never have reached the Pacific Coast.

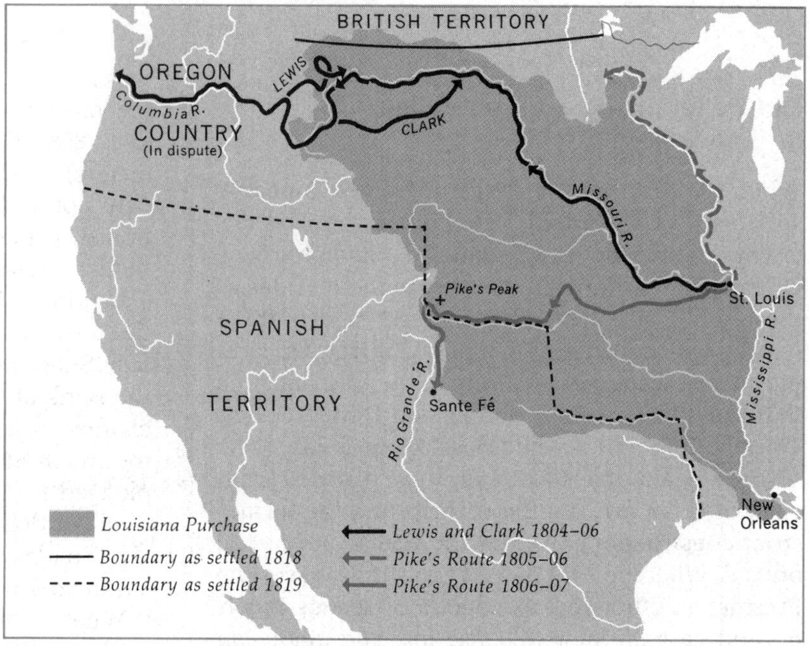

great agrarian democracy, as envisioned by Jefferson, would have elbowroom in the vast "Valley of Democracy." At the same time, the transfer established a precedent that was to be followed repeatedly: namely, the acquisition of foreign territory and peoples by purchase.

The extent of the huge new area was more fully unveiled by a series of explorations under the direction of Jefferson. He was keenly interested in the natural treasures of his purchase, including an enormous (and non-existent) mountain of salt. The expedition of Meriwether Lewis and William Clark ascended the "Great Muddy" Missouri River and struggled through the Rockies to the mouth of the Columbia River. This hazardous venture into the uncharted Western wilderness, from 1804 to 1806, bolstered America's claim to Oregon, while further opening the West to Indian trade and exploration. Zebulon M. Pike, in 1805–1806, explored the Louisiana territory near the headwaters of the Mississippi River, and in 1806–1807 ventured into Colorado and New Mexico, sighting the lofty peak that bears his name.

Lewis and Clark. A woodcut (1812) by Patrick Gass, a member of the expedition. (Rare Book Division, New York Public Library, Astor, Lenox and Tilden Foundations.)

Jefferson's reluctant purchase of Louisiana proved to be a landmark in American foreign policy. Overnight he avoided a possible rupture with France, and the consequent entangling alliance with England. The nation was thus able to continue the non-interventionist policies of the Founding Fathers, though it later quarreled with Spain and Britain over the vague boundaries of Louisiana, north, south, and west. Not needing the navy of the Mother Country, the United States drifted away from her, and eventually fought her in 1812. But by that time the Republic was bigger

> The French minister who negotiated the Louisiana Purchase treaties recalled that Minister Livingston had remarked at the signing, "We have lived long, but this is the noblest work of our whole lives. . . . From this day the United States take their place among the powers of the first rank. . . . The instruments which we have just signed will cause no tears to be shed: they prepare ages of happiness for innumerable generations of human creatures."

and stronger, and had Louisiana securely in its possession.

The Louisiana godsend likewise boosted national unity. Once-proud Federalists, now mere sectionalists, sank ever lower in public esteem as they were reduced to whining impotence. A few of their more extreme spokesmen attempted to plot with scheming Aaron Burr for the secession of New England and New York. But the intrigue failed, largely owing to the vigilance of Alexander Hamilton, who subsequently provoked Burr to a duel. The pistol that killed Hamilton in 1804 blew the brightest brain out of the Federalist party—and destroyed its one remaining hope of effective leadership.

A once-restive West, which now toasted the "immortal Jefferson," was more securely riveted to the Union by the purchase. Men of the western waters were grateful to the federal government for having safeguarded their interests, particularly in securing the mouth of the Mississippi. A new spirit of unity surged through the West.

Aaron Burr, turning his disunionist plottings to the trans-Mississippi West, was arrested in 1806 for treason. Tried the next year at Richmond, Virginia, he was freed after the presiding judge, Chief Justice Marshall, had infuriated the Jeffersonians by what seemed to be bias in favor of the accused. The government's case collapsed when two witnesses to the same overt act of treason could not be found, as required by the Constitution (see Art. III, Sec. III). Burr's schemes are still somewhat shrouded in mystery, but he apparently planned to separate the western part of the United States from the eastern and unite it with to-be-conquered Spanish territory west of the Louisiana Purchase. The very fact that so dashing a figure as Burr could muster only threescore followers was significant. It indicated, among other things, that the West was developing a deeper sense of loyalty to the Washington government.

America: A Nutcrackered Neutral

Jefferson was triumphantly re-elected in 1804, with 162 electoral votes to only 14 for his Federalist opponent. His success was not so much due to Republicanizing the Federalists, as he fondly supposed, as to Federalizing the Republicans. The iron hand of reality gradually forced him, quite unintentionally, to kill off the opposition party by stealing many of its principles and embracing them as his own. As was said, he caught the Federalists in bathing and made off with their clothes.

But the laurels of Jefferson's first administration soon withered under the blasts of the new storm that broke in Europe. After unloading Louisiana in 1803, Napoleon deliberately provoked a renewal of his war with Britain—a conflict that crashed to an awesome close eleven long years later.

For two years a maritime United States—the number one neutral carrier since 1793—enjoyed juicy commercial pickings. But a setback came in 1805. At the Battle of Trafalgar, one-eyed Lord Nelson achieved immortality by smashing the combined French and Spanish fleets off the coast

England (John Bull) Eats French Warships. Contemporary English caricature.

of Spain, thereby insuring Britain's supremacy on the seas. At the Battle of Austerlitz in Austria—the Battle of the Three Emperors—Napoleon crushed the combined Austrian and Russian armies, thereby insuring his mastery of the land. Like the tiger and the shark, France and Britain were supreme in their chosen elements. England ruled the waves and waived the rules.

Unable to hurt each other directly, the two antagonists were forced to strike indirect blows. The London government, beginning in 1806, issued a series of Orders in Council. As perfected, these edicts closed the ports under French continental control to foreign shipping, including American, unless the vessels first stopped at a British port. There they would pay the necessary fees and, if acceptable, secure clearance papers. Napoleon struck back savagely in a series of decrees. In effect, they ordered the seizure of all merchant ships, including American, that entered British ports.

Yankee skippers, like their predestined Calvinist ancestors, were seemingly damned if they did, damned if they did not. Even so, their trade prospered, because the greater the risk, the greater the profit. If only one vessel in three sailed over the reefs of French Decrees and past the shoals of British Orders in Council, the owner could make a comfortable gain.

Intercourse or Impartial Dealings. A cartoon by "Peter Pencil" (1809) shows Jefferson being victimized by both England (*left*) and France (*right*). (Houghton Library, Harvard.)

British Man-Stealing

Even more galling to American pride than the seizure of wooden ships was the seizure of flesh-and-blood American seamen. Impressment—the forcible enlistment of sailors—was a crude form of conscription which the British, among others, had employed for over four centuries. Clubs and stretchers (for men knocked unconscious) were standard equipment of press-gangs from His Majesty's man-hungry ships.

The London authorities themselves set limits to this ugly practice. They claimed the right to impress only British subjects on their own soil, in their own harbors, or on merchant ships on the high seas. But many fair-skinned Americans looked like Englishmen, and the benefit of the doubt was seldom given to an experienced seaman in those short-handed days. The result was that some 6,000 bona fide United States citizens, according to the best estimates, were impressed by the "piratical man-stealers" of England from 1808 to 1811 alone. A number of these luckless souls died or were killed in the service, leaving their kinfolk and friends bereaved and embittered.

On their side, the British had counter-complaints. America's navy and merchant marine openly encouraged the enlistment of deserters from the "floating hells" of the British navy, where discipline was taught to the tune of the cat-o'-nine-tails. An expanding American merchant marine, also short of sailors, paid seductively high wages—"dollars for shillings." British deserters, conniving with ingenious Americans, would often secure fraudulent naturalization papers. (One resourceful female conniver had an oversized cradle in her shop so she could swear she had known the sailor "from the cradle.") But His Majesty's press-gangs laughed aside such documents, whether genuine or not, holding to the principle "Once an Englishman, always an Englishman." The King expected every free-born Briton to do his duty in time of crisis.

Britain had her back to the wall, and her desperate plight colored her views. If the Yankee "dollar grubbers" had not encouraged so much desertion, the British impressers might have been willing to make fewer mistakes in acquiring sailors. But England would not abandon her brutal practice of sailor-snatching at the behest of an upstart United States. Britons were making war; Americans were making money. The British feared that they would lose the war if they gave up their hoary method of conscription—and they would fight before they did.

Britain's determination was spectacularly highlighted in 1807. A royal frigate overhauled a United States frigate, the *Chesapeake,* about ten miles off the coast of Virginia. The British captain bluntly demanded the surrender of four alleged deserters. London had never claimed the right to seize men from a foreign warship, and the American commander, though totally unprepared to fight, refused the request. The British warship thereupon fired three devastating broadsides at close range, killing three Americans and wounding eighteen. Four deserters were dragged away, and the bloody hulk called the *Chesapeake* limped back to port.

An infuriated America—Federalists and Republicans alike—joined in an outburst of national wrath. Nothing like it had been seen since the French XYZ insults of 1797. Jefferson, the peace lover, could easily have had war if he had wanted it. As the event proved, if America were going to fight at all, she should have fought when the country was united.

Britain was clearly in the wrong, as the London Foreign Office admitted. But Jefferson unwisely attempted to use the *Chesapeake* outrage as a lever to force the British to renounce impressment altogether. This they flatly refused to do. The affair rankled for five years; and when reparation was finally made, it came too late to salve old wounds.

> Regarding the *Chesapeake* affair, the Washington *Federalist* reported, "We have never, on any occasion, witnessed the spirit of the people excited to so great a degree of indignation, or such a thirst for revenge, as on hearing of the late unexampled outrage on the *Chesapeake.* All parties, ranks, and professions were unanimous in their detestation of the dastardly deed, and all cried aloud for vengeance."

Jefferson's Backfiring Embargo

National honor would not permit a slavish submission to British and French mistreatment. Yet a large-scale foreign war was contrary to the settled policy of the new Republic—and in addition it would be futile. The navy was weak, thanks largely to Jefferson's anti-navalism; and the army was even weaker. A disastrous defeat would not improve America's plight.

The warring nations in Europe were heavily dependent upon the United States for raw materials and foodstuffs. In his eager search for an alternative to war, Jefferson seized upon this essential fact. He reasoned that if America voluntarily cut off her exports, the offending powers would be forced to come, hat in hand, and agree to respect her rights.

Responding to the presidential lash, Congress hastily passed the Embargo Act late in 1807. This rigorous law forbade the export of all goods from the United States, whether in American or in foreign ships. It was a compromise between submission and shooting.

Jefferson, the onetime strict constructionist, had once more flip-flopped into the camp of the loose constructionists. In the interests of the Federalist shippers, whom he disliked, he was rereading the Constitution with strange bifocals. To him, it now meant that Congress, under its authority to "regulate" commerce, could go so far as to stop

The Embargo (Ograbme). As a snapping turtle, it halts overseas shipments. (Prints Division, New York Public Library, Astor, Lenox and Tilden Foundations.)

foreign trade altogether. Regulation thus became strangulation.

Federalist New England could well have prayed for relief from its newly found Virginia friend, "Mad Tom" Jefferson. Forests of dead masts gradually filled once-flourishing harbors; docks that had once rumbled were deserted (except for illegal trade); and soup kitchens cared for some of the hungry unemployed. Jeffersonian Republicans probably hurt the commerce of New England, which they avowedly were trying to protect, far more than Old England and France together were doing.

Farmers of the South and West, the strongholds of Jefferson, suffered no less disastrously than New England. They were alarmed by the mounting piles of exportable cotton, grain, and tobacco. Tart-tongued John Randolph of Virginia remarked that enacting the embargo was like cutting off one's toes to cure one's corns. Jefferson in truth seemed to be waging war on his fellow citizens, rather than on the offending belligerents.

The American people, from the days of the colonial Navigation Acts, have never submitted meekly to unpopular legislation. Though basically law-abiding, they habitually flout laws that are opposed by large numbers of the population. An enormous illicit trade mushroomed in 1808, especially along the Canadian border, where bands of armed Americans on loaded rafts overawed or overpowered federal agents. Irate citizens cynically transposed the letters of "Embargo" to read "O Grab Me," "Go Bar 'Em," and "Mobrage," while heartily denouncing the "Dambargo."

Jefferson nonetheless induced Congress to pass iron-toothed enforcing legislation. It was so inquisitorial and tyrannical as to cause some Americans to think more kindly of George III, whom Jefferson had berated in the Declaration of Independence. One indignant New Hampshire poet burst out in song:

> Our ships all in motion,
> Once whiten'd the ocean;
> They sail'd and return'd with a Cargo;
> Now doom'd to decay
> They are fallen a prey,
> To Jefferson, worms, and EMBARGO.

New England seethed with talk of secession; and Jefferson later admitted that he felt the foundations of government tremble under his feet.

An alarmed Congress, bowing to the storm of public anger, finally repealed the embargo, on March 1, 1809, three days before Jefferson's retirement. A half-loaf substitute was provided by the Non-Intercourse Act. This measure formally reopened trade with all the nations of the world, except the two most important, England and

A Federalist circular in Massachusetts against the embargo cried out, "Let every man who holds the name of America dear to him, stretch forth his hands and put this accursed thing, this *Embargo* from him. Be resolute, act like sons of liberty, of God, and your country; nerve your arm with vengeance against the Despot [Jefferson] who would wrest the inestimable germ of your independence from you—and you shall be *Conquerors!!!*"

France. Though thus watered down, economic coercion continued to be the policy of the Jeffersonians from 1809 to 1812, when the nation finally plunged into war.

The Wooden-Gun Embargo: A Successful Failure

Why did the embargo, Jefferson's most daring act of statesmanship, collapse after fifteen dismal months? First of all, he underestimated the bulldog determination of the British, as others have, and overestimated their dependence on America's trade. Bumper grain crops blessed the British Isles during these years, and the revolutionary Latin American republics unexpectedly threw open their ports for compensating commerce.

The hated embargo was not continued long enough or tightly enough to achieve the desired results. But a statesman must know the temper of his people, and Jefferson should have foreseen that such a self-crucifying weapon could not possibly command public support. The Americans, notoriously people of action, did not take kindly to the passive type of heroism. They much preferred commercial activity, with all its risks, to enforced inactivity, with no chance of profit.

A crestfallen Jefferson himself admitted that the embargo was three times more costly than war. The irony is that with only a fraction of its cost to the country, he could have built a fairly strong navy. Such a fighting force would have won more respect for American rights on the high seas, and might well have prevented the War of 1812.

The embargo further embroiled relations with both Britain and France. It embittered the British, partly because it hit them more forcibly than it did Napoleon. The French despot naturally applauded the embargo, for it was an indirect American blockade of his foe. He cynically helped enforce it by seizing scores of Yankee merchant ships in his ports; by the terms of the Embargo Act, he argued, these vessels should have been tied up at home. His "cooperation" merely rubbed salt into old sores.

A stoppage of exports hurt Federalist shipping, but revived the Federalist party. Gaining new converts, its leaders hurled their nullification of the embargo into the teeth of the "Virginia lordlings" in Washington. In 1804, the discredited Federalists had polled only 14 electoral votes out of 176; in 1808, the embargo year, the figure rose to 47 out of 175.

Curiously enough, New England plucked a new prosperity from the ugly jaws of the embargo. With shipping tied up and imported goods scarce, the resourceful Yankees reopened old factories and erected new ones. The real foundations of modern America's industrial might were laid behind the protective wall of the embargo, followed by non-intercourse and the War of 1812. Jefferson, the avowed critic of factories, may have unwittingly done more for American manufacturing than Alexander Hamilton, the outspoken friend of factories.

Jefferson's embargo, followed in modified form by non-intercourse, undeniably pinched England. Many British importers and manufacturers suffered severe losses, especially those dependent on American cotton. As thousands of factory workers were thrown out of jobs, agitation mounted for a repeal of the restrictions that had brought on the embargo. A petition to Parliament in 1812, from the city of Birmingham alone, bore 20,000 names on a sheet of parchment 150 feet long. So strong was public pressure that two days before Congress declared war in June 1812, the British foreign secretary announced that the offensive Orders in Council would be immediately suspended. The supreme irony is that Jefferson's policy of economic coercion did win in the end, but America was not patient enough to reap the reward of her sacrifices.

The Living Jefferson

Thomas Jefferson retained much of his popularity, even though it was severely tarnished by the embargo. One public toast ran: "May he receive from his fellow citizens the reward of his merit, a halter

> Early in 1805 Jefferson privately foresaw the two-term 22nd Amendment (1951): "General Washington set the example of voluntary retirement after eight years. I shall follow it, and a few more precedents will oppose the obstacle of habit to anyone after a while who shall endeavor to extend his term. Perhaps it may beget a disposition to establish it by an amendment of the Constitution."

[hangman's noose]." But his grip on his party was such that he could easily have won a third nomination and election. The international crisis was still acute; and although Jefferson was sixty-five years old, he was mentally alert and physically vigorous. He lived eighteen more years, glad to have escaped what he called the "splendid misery" of the presidential penitentiary.

Jefferson, rather than Washington, was the real father of the two-term tradition. Unlike the first President, who had no serious constitutional qualms, he feared that more than two terms might open the door to dictatorship. Yet Jefferson strongly favored the nomination and election of a kindred spirit, his friend and fellow Virginian, the quiet, intellectual, and unassuming James Madison.

Though bitterly assailed, Jefferson left office with the consolation that he had remained true to the guiding star of the other Founding Fathers. He had kept the country out of a serious foreign war. Despite numerous reversals of policy under the whiplash of practicality, he never lost his faith in democracy and in the common man. He brought a renovation rather than a revolution; the real revolution that did occur was in his own thinking. If the Federalists were the steppingstone between monarchical Europe and republican America, then the Jeffersonians were the steppingstone between aristocratic Federalism and democratic Jacksonianism.

Thomas Jefferson and John Adams died on the same day—appropriately the Fourth of July, 1826. The last words of Adams, then ninety-one, were: "Thomas Jefferson still survives." He was wrong, for three hours earlier Jefferson had breathed his last. But Thomas Jefferson still survives in the democratic ideals and liberal principles of the great nation which he risked his all to found, and which he served so long and faithfully.

VARYING VIEWPOINTS

The Jeffersonian era has long presented observers with a series of paradoxes: How did the pacifistic President lead the country so far down the path toward war? Why did America's most famous advocate of small government so greatly enlarge the federal domain and expand the power of the presidency? How did the man who proclaimed, "We are all Republicans, we are all Federalists," come to preside over one of the most bitterly partisan periods in American history? This last question has perhaps attracted the most attention from recent scholars. Many of them now view the Federalist and Jeffersonian decades as the seedbed of the modern system of political parties. How did the parties organize? How did the idea of *legitimate* opposition crystallize? On what basis were the people at large—the traditionally marginal masses—brought into the organized political system and infused with a sense of meaningful participation in national affairs?

SELECT READINGS

A monument of American historical writing is Henry Adams, *History of the United States during the Administrations of Jefferson and Madison* (9 vols., 1889–1891), available in a one-volume abridgment edited by Ernest Samuels. Especially fascinating are Adams' epilogue and prologue on the United States in 1800 and 1817. A brief introduction by a British scholar is Marcus Cunliffe, *The Nation Takes Shape, 1789–1837* (1959); greater detail is given in M. Smelser, *The Democratic Republic 1801–1815* (1968). Problems with the judiciary can be traced in A. J. Beveridge's still-respected *Life of John Marshall* (4 vols., 1919). A more recent and succinct analysis is R. E. Ellis, *The Jeffersonian Crisis: Courts and Politics in the New Republic* (1971). Politics are handled in N. E. Cunningham, *The Jeffersonian Republicans in Power* (1963), and treated in a broader, imaginative context in J. S. Young, *The Washington Community, 1800–1829* (1966), L. D. White brings administrative history to life in *The Jeffersonians* (rev. ed., 1959). Forrest McDonald is highly critical of his subject in *The Presidency of Thomas Jefferson* (1976). L. Levy debunks Jefferson's liberalism in *Jefferson and Civil Liberties* (1963), while B. W. Sheehan examines another important aspect of policy in *Seeds of Extinction: Jeffersonian Philanthropy and the American Indian* (1973). See also R. Horsman, *Expansion and American Indian Policy, 1783–1812* (1967). A first-class study of the negotiator of the Louisiana Purchase is G. Dangerfield, *Chancellor Robert R. Livingston of New York* (1960).

The development of political parties is dissected in W. N. Chambers, *Political Parties in a New Nation* (1963), and in Noble E. Cunningham, *The Jeffersonian Republicans: The Formation of Party Organization, 1789–1801* (1958). See also R. Buel, Jr., *Securing the Revolution* (1972), and Richard Hofstadter, *The Idea of a Party System* (1969), Lance Banning, *The Jeffersonian Persuasion* (1978), Drew McCoy, *The Elusive Republic: Political Economy in Jeffersonian America* (1980), and Robert E. Shalhope, *John Taylor of Caroline* (1980). Noble E. Cunningham, Jr., has carried his discussion forward in *The Process of Government under Jefferson* (1979). The standard scholarly biography is D. Malone, *Jefferson and His Time* (5 vols., 1948–1974). More compact is M. D. Peterson, *Thomas Jefferson and the New Nation: A Biography* (1970). Peterson has also scrutinized *The Jeffersonian Image in the American Mind* (1960). An expansionist thesis is fully developed in A. De Conde, *This Affair of Louisiana* (1976). The Embargo is treated in Burton Spivak, *Jefferson's English Crisis: Commerce, Embargo, and the Republican Revolution* (1979). D. Boorstin vividly evokes the intellectual climate of the age in *The Lost World of Thomas Jefferson* (1948). John C. Miller, *The Wolf by the Ears: Thomas Jefferson and Slavery* (1977), probes the third President's attitudes on an important question. I. Brant looks at *James Madison, Secretary of State* (1953), and F. E. Ewing examines Jefferson's powerful treasury secretary in *America's Forgotten Statesman: Albert Gallatin* (1959).

11

James Madison and the Second War for Independence

The Existing War—the Child of Prostitution. May no American Acknowledge it Legitimate.

A FEDERALIST TOAST DURING THE WAR OF 1812

Madison: Dupe of Napoleon

Scholarly James Madison took the presidential oath on March 4, 1809, as the awesome conflict in Europe was roaring to its climax. Small of stature (5 feet 4 inches; 1.62 meters), light of weight (about 100 pounds; 45 kilograms), bald of head, and weak of voice, he fell tragically short of providing vigorous executive leadership. Crippled also by factions within his Cabinet, he was unable to dominate his party, as Jefferson had once done.

The Non-Intercourse Act of 1809—the limited substitute for the embargo aimed solely at Britain and France—would expire in about a year. Congress, desperately attempting to uphold American rights, adopted in 1810 a bargaining measure known as Macon's Bill No. 2. While permitting American trade with all the world, it dangled an attractive lure. If either England or France repealed her commercial restrictions, America would restore non-importation against the non-repealing nation. In short, the United States would bribe the belligerents into respecting its rights.

This opportunity was made to order for Napoleon, a past master of deceit. He was eager to have non-importation clamped down once more on the British, because it would serve as a partial blockade which he would not have to raise a finger to enforce. He was hopeful that such a boycott would embroil the Americans in war with Britain, for then they would be serving as his indirect allies to weaken his arch-enemy. Accordingly, he blandly announced, in August 1810, that his objectionable decrees had been repealed. At the same time, he secretly ordered the sale of confiscated Yankee ships.

Responsible Americans, rising above self-delusion, should have examined the hollow-sounding French announcement with extreme caution. Napoleon, prince of liars, had no intention whatever of repealing his damaging decrees. But Madison, frantically seeking to wrest a recognition of American rights from England, accepted French bad faith as good faith. He formally announced, in November 1810, that France had complied with the terms of Macon's Bill No. 2, and that non-importation would consequently be re-established against Britain.

Madison's decision was fateful. Britons were angered by America's apparent willingness to be the dupe and partner of Napoleon. The wily Bonaparte, who continued to seize American merchantmen, was delighted by the success of his transparent scheme. Once Madison had aligned his nation against England commercially, he found himself gravitating toward France politically—and edging toward the whirlpool of war.

War Whoops Arouse the War Hawks

The complexion of the Twelfth Congress, which met late in 1811, differed markedly from that of its predecessor. Recent elections had swept away many of the older "submission men" and replaced

Henry Clay (1777–1852). A glamorous, eloquent, and ambitious member of the House and Senate for many years, Clay was thrice an unsuccessful candidate for the highest office in the land. "Sir," he declared in the Senate in 1850, "I would rather be right than be President." Right or wrong, he never made the grade but his devotion to the Union was inspirational. (Library of Congress)

them with young hotheads, chiefly from the South and West. The youthful newcomers—"the boys," John Randolph sneeringly called them—were on fire for a new war with the old enemy. Not having had a conflict in their own generation, these War Hawks were weary of hearing how their fathers had "whipped" the British single-handedly. They won control of the House of Representatives, and elevated to the speakership the tall (6 feet 2 inches; 1.88 meters), eloquent, and magnetic Henry Clay of Kentucky, the gallant "Harry of the West," then only thirty-four years old.

Western War Hawks, first of all, were eager to wipe out the renewed Indian resistance against the white settlers streaming steadily into the Western wilderness. As this white flood spread through the forests, more and more red men were pushed farther and farther toward the setting sun. Two

Tecumseh (1768?–1813). A Shawnee Indian born in the Ohio country, he was probably the most gifted organizer and leader of his people in U.S. history. A noted warrior, he fought the tribal custom of torturing prisoners and opposed the practice of permitting any one tribe to sell land that, he believed, belonged to all Indians.

remarkable Shawnee twin brothers, Tecumseh and the Prophet, knew that if this onrushing tide were ever to be stopped, that time had come. They began to weld together a far-flung confederacy of all the tribes east of the Mississippi. Their braves forswore firewater in order to be fit for the last-ditch battle with the "paleface" intruders. To make matters worse, the sturdy pioneers and their War Hawk representatives in Congress widely believed that the red men's firearms and scalping knives were being furnished by British "hair buyers" in Canada.

Only a few days after the War Hawk Congress convened in Washington, news of stirring events on the frontier further inflamed anti-Indian and anti-British feeling. General William H. Harrison, advancing with 1,000 men upon the Indian headquarters, repelled a surprise attack at Tippecanoe, in present Indiana, on November 7, 1811. He then put the torch to the settlement.

Harrison's onslaught broke the back of the red men's rebellion. It also made the blood course faster in the veins of the impetuous War Hawks. Men like Representative Felix Grundy of Tennessee, three of whose brothers had been murdered, cried that there was only one way to remove the menace of the Indians: wipe out their Canadian base.

Canada, in itself, was a lush prize. War Hawks made no bones about their desire to seize this enormous and richly wooded area, so near, so desirable, and apparently so defenseless. "On to Canada, on to Canada," was their ominous chant. Southern expansionists, less vocal, cast a covetous eye on Florida, then weakly held by Britain's ally, Spain.

A free sea, as well as free land, was a goal of the War Hawks. One of their most popular slogans ran, "Free Trade and Sailors' Rights." Yet why should men beyond the mountains, many of whom had never seen a body of salt water larger than a salt lick, want to fight for maritime rights?

Westerners, strange to relate, did have a vital interest in a free sea. They were proud, patriotic, and intensely nationalistic. The manhandling of an American sailor, though far away, struck these freedom-loving pioneers as outrageous. They might not have ships on the ocean, but they did have dammed-up agricultural products which, because of the odious British Orders in Council, could not be shipped to Europe. In short, Westerners, despite all their misleading clamor for Canada, did have a genuine emotional and financial stake in a free sea.

Militant War Hawks, with scattered but essential support from other sections, finally engineered a declaration of war in June 1812. The vote in the House was 79 to 49; in the Senate, 19 to 13. The close tally betrayed a dangerous degree of national disunity. Congressmen from the pro-British maritime and commercial centers of New England, as well as from the Middle Atlantic States, almost solidly opposed hostilities. Thus the West and Southwest, mostly landlocked, presented the sea-fronting East with a war for a free sea that the East vehemently resented.

Britain or Napoleon: A Choice of Foes

Why did the United States fight Britain and not France? Napoleonic seizures of Yankee ships since 1803 had numbered 558, as compared with 917 for Britain. Logically, the Americans should have fought both offenders, if the Republic were going to fight at all.

War Vote in House of Representatives, 1812
(SHOWING WESTERN AND SOUTHWESTERN WAR SENTIMENT)

States	*Regions*	*For War*	*Against War*
N.H.	Frontier New England	3	2
Vt.		3	1
Mass.	Maritime and Federalist New England; Mass. includes frontier Maine	6	8
R.I.		0	2
Conn.		0	7
N.Y.	Commercial and Federalist Middle States	3	11
N.J.		2	4
Del.		0	1
Penn.	Jeffersonian Middle States	16	2
Md.		6	3
Va.	Jeffersonian Southern States	14	5
N.C.		6	3
S.C.		8	0
Ga.		3	0
Ohio	The trans-Allegheny West—nest of the War Hawks	1	0
Ky.		5	0
Tenn.		3	0
		79	49

Why single out England? The Mother Country was the historic foe, and the Jeffersonian Republican party was traditionally anti-British and pro-French. This Gallic attachment partly explains why the Jeffersonians, disliking Federalist shippers, were ostensibly going to war to protect those shippers.

Nearness of offenses was also a vital factor. Napoleon had confiscated Yankee ships and imprisoned Yankee sailors, but his misdeeds were far away. British impressments and seizures, on the other hand, often took place within plain view. And on the frontier the Indian "hell hounds," bearing British arms, were smashing into the cabins of American pioneers.

> "The injuries received from *France,*" insisted the editor of Niles's *Weekly Register* (June 27, 1812), "do not lessen the enormity of those heaped upon us by *England*. . . . In this 'straight betwixt two' we had an unquestionable right to select our enemy. We have given the preference to *Great Britain* . . . on account of her more flagrant wrongs."

To declare war on France would avail nothing, for she was not vulnerable. America had no border in common with her, and hence (fortunately) could not come to grips with Napoleon's armies. But a victorious war with England, aside from avenging grievances, would be profitable as well as patriotic. Her merchant marine, the richest in the world, would fall easy prey to swarming Yankee privateers. And Canada, the choicest prize of all, looked like a sitting duck.

Costly illusions beckoned from the north. The invasion of Canada, Americans fondly believed, would be absurdly simple—a "frontiersmen's frolic"; a "mere matter of marching," said Jefferson. The trick could be turned, boasted Henry Clay, "the Cock of Kentucky," by the militiamen of his state alone.

Population odds justified such optimism. The United States numbered over 6 million whites, as compared with some 500,000 for Canada. A majority of the Canadians were Frenchmen, whose loyalty was dubious, and many of the rest were quite recent American emigrants, whose loyalty was even more dubious. England, bogged down in the Napoleonic War, could spare few troops for North America. Europe's distresses were again pointing the way to military successes.

The Northern mirage thus helped destroy America's last precious stores of patience. If Canada had not been so inviting and so helpless (seemingly), the administration probably would have endured British offenses a few more months. If it had done so, it would have learned of London's official announcement of the forthcoming repeal of her objectionable Orders in Council—an announcement made ironically two days *before* Congress voted war. If there had then been an Atlantic cable, the War Hawks probably could not have forced a formal declaration of hostilities through the Senate. A change of three votes would have brought a tie. But the tempting proximity of Canada turned American heads, and President Madison plunged into the conflict, contrary to the stall-for-time policy of the Founding Fathers.

American Allies of the Napoleonic Anti-Christ

New England, though fronting the sea, damned the declaration of war for a free sea. The news was greeted with muffled bells, flags at half-mast, and public fasting. One congressman, who had voted for war, was kicked through the streets of Plymouth, Massachusetts, by a frenzied mob.

Why the opposition? For one thing, violations of American rights were an old story; they had been continuing for about twenty years. The extent of impressment, though serious, had been exaggerated. Manufacturing in New England was mushrooming, and the luckier shippers, despite costly confiscations, were still raking in money. Profits dull patriotism. New England was also the traditional stronghold of pro-British Federalism, and it resented the pro-French favoritism of the "Virginia Dynasty" in Washington.

Federalist New England, moreover, had long been allied in sympathy with Old England. The Mother Country—"that fast-anchored isle"—was the last real bulwark of constitutional government left in the Old World. At a time when she was straining every nerve to defeat the despotism of Napoleon, the Federalists believed that Americans should be helping her. Instead the United States—the presumed friend of freedom and constitutionalism—was stabbing her in the back. Cold-bloodedly and calculatingly, Madison had concluded that Britain's war to the death with Napoleon, in indirect defense of American liberties, would enable America to seize some territory.

Nor did the sinfulness of the conflict, in Federalist eyes, end here. Not only had Madison treacherously pushed the Mother Country into the abyss of an unwanted war, but he had permitted himself to be tricked into it by her arch-enemy, Napoleon. More than that, Madison had become a virtual ally of the "Corsican butcher"—the "anti-Christ of the age."

The Present State of Our Country. Partisan disunity over the War of 1812 threatens the nation's very existence. The pro-war Jeffersonian at the left is attacking the pillar of federalism; the anti-war Federalist at the right is trying to pull down Democracy. The spirit of Washington warns that the country's welfare depends upon all three pillars, including Republicanism. (A cartoon by William Charles. New York Public Library.)

Pennsylvania State Militiaman, 1812. This fighting man appears deceptively well outfitted. In fact, colonial distrust of a standing army produced ill-prepared, poorly trained militiamen under the new post-Revolutionary governments.

Federalist charges of a quasi-alliance with France contained much distasteful truth. As the war in Europe ground on, Jeffersonian Republicans rejoiced over Napoleon's triumphs, while Federalists, no less loudly, acclaimed the victories of Britain and her allies over Bonaparte.

Federalists also condemned the War of 1812 because they opposed the acquisition of Canada. The seizure of this vast area, like the purchase of Louisiana, would merely add more agrarian states from the wild Northwest. These, in turn, would increase the voting strength of the Jeffersonians. Some New England Federalists feared the New West far more than they did Old England. They were determined, wrote one versifier,

> To rule the nation if they could,
> But see it damned if others should.

The bitterness of the New England Federalists against "Mr. Madison's War" led to treason or near treason. In a sense, America fought two enemies simultaneously: Old England and New England. Money holders of New England, possessing much of the nation's gold, probably lent more dollars to the British than to the Federal Treasury. Farmers of New England sent huge quantities of supplies north to Canada, including droves of cattle; and these foodstuffs enabled the British armies to invade New York. Governors of New England, thinking first of local defense, stubbornly refused to permit their militia to serve outside their states, though men were badly needed in the regular army.

Yet the disloyalty of New England has been overplayed. Jeffersonians in this section, comprising a substantial minority, vigorously opposed Federalist obstructionism. New England states actually contributed a surprising number of volunteers to the regular army; Massachusetts alone sent more than Virginia.

Unpreparedness and the Abortive Invasion of Canada

The War of 1812, largely because of widespread disunity, easily ranks as America's worst-fought major war. There was no burning national anger, as in 1807, following the *Chesapeake* outrage. War Hawks in Congress were no more than a zealous minority. President Madison, while supporting their aims, knew that there was serious disunity. But he made the near-fatal error of sponsoring a declaration of war in the hope that it would cause the nation to rally around the flag. New England and other Federalist centers were content to let the spangled banner fall into the mire.

America's manpower pool was deceptively large; there were at least a million males of arms-bearing age. But the government never mustered more than 7,000 men for any one battle. The supreme lesson of this conflict was the folly of leading a divided and apathetic people into war.

The Republic was dangerously unprepared, despite warnings going back nineteen years to the outbreak of the European war in 1793. The nation was still suffering from its own embargo and nonintercourse, which it had partially enforced for the better part of four years. Congress had shortsightedly permitted the Bank of the United States to expire in 1811, at a time when a powerful financial institution was needed. It was knifed largely by the jealousies of the competing state banks.

The regular army was scandalously inadequate, for it was ill-trained, ill-disciplined, and widely scattered. It had to be supplemented by the even more poorly trained militia, who were sometimes distinguished by speed of foot in leaving the battlefield. Some of the ranking generals were semisenile heirlooms from the Revolutionary War, rusting on their laurels and lacking in vigor and vision. By a process of trial and error—chiefly costly error—the mossbacks were gradually weeded out by 1814. But by that time the golden prize of Canada had slipped from America's grasp.

Offensive strategy adopted in Washington was poorly conceived. Roads in Canada were few and bad, so the bulk of the population was scattered along the St. Lawrence, its tributary rivers, and the Great Lakes. Over these waterways all essential supplies had to be transported. Once Montreal was captured, everything to the west was bound to die, just as the leaves of a tree wither when the trunk is girdled. If the United States had thrown everything it had against Montreal when the defenders were heavily outnumbered, all of Canada probably would have fallen.

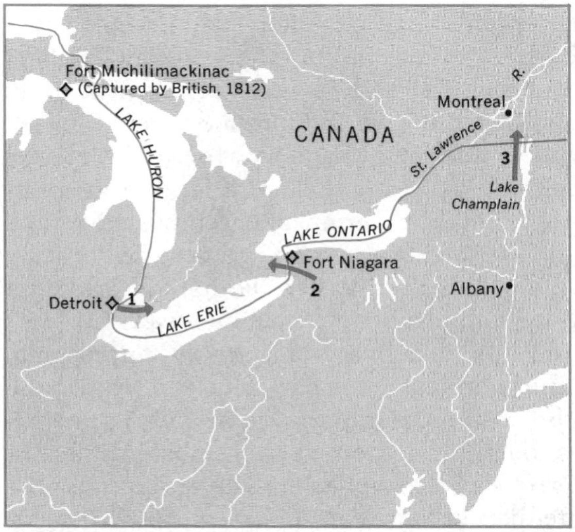

THE THREE U.S. THRUSTS OF 1812
Red line delineates the Canadian border.

But instead of laying ax to the trunk, the Americans frittered away their strength in the three-pronged invasion of 1812. One thrust started from the wilderness outpost of Detroit, under General Hull. He quickly retired to his base, and then surrendered his entire army to a numerically inferior enemy without firing a shot. The second American invasion, launched across the Niagara River, was beaten back. New York's militia balked at crossing the Canadian line, while their countrymen on the other side were being shot down or forced to surrender. A third force marched bravely for Montreal along the shores of Lake Champlain, but turned back when the state militia refused to cross the New York–Canada border.

By contrast, the British and Canadians from the outset displayed energy. Early in the war they captured the American fort of Michilimackinac, commanding the upper Great Lakes and a huge Indian-inhabited area to the south and west. In their brilliant defensive operations, the Canadians received vital help from a small but efficient force of professional British soldiers. Above all, they were blessed with an inspired British leader, General Isaac Brock, ably assisted (in the American camp) by "General Mud" and "General Confusion."

Invasion in Reverse and War on the Lakes

In 1813 the several American invasions of Canada were again hurled back in disarray. The Canadians, many of them descended from the evicted American Loyalists of 1776–1783, fought bravely for their new homes and firesides. They had not impressed Yankee sailors or seized Yankee ships, and they regarded the invasion as a wanton attack—"the War of Defense," they called their side of it.

Control of the Great Lakes was vital for transporting military supplies westward, and an energetic American naval officer, Oliver Hazard Perry, busied himself on the shores of Lake Erie. He managed to build a fleet of green-timbered ships, manned largely by even greener seamen, plus some Kentucky riflemen. In a furious engage-

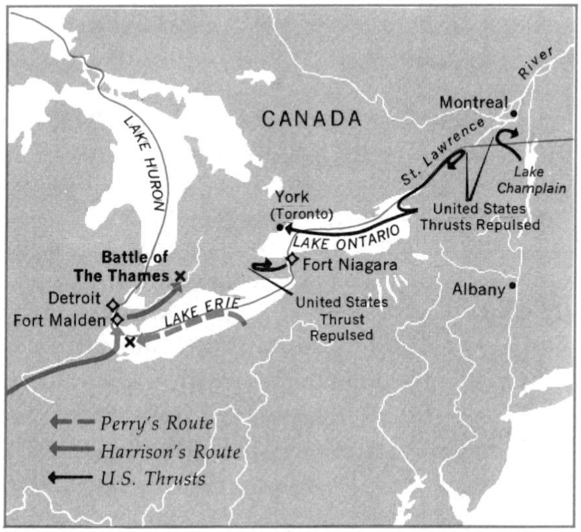

CAMPAIGNS OF 1813
Red line denotes Canadian boundary.

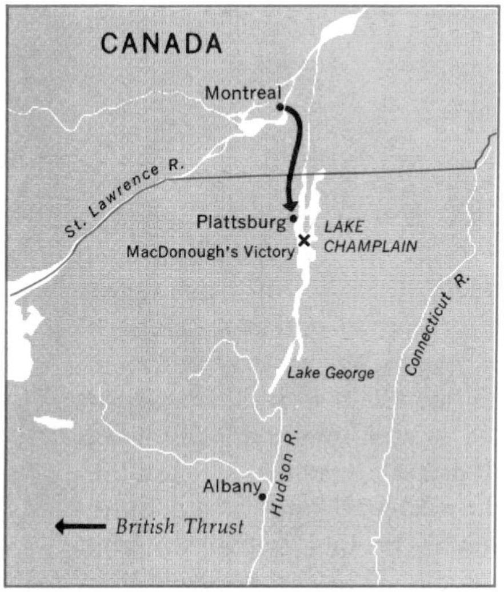

BRITISH INVASION, 1814
Red line denotes Canadian boundary.

ment on Lake Erie, he captured a less powerful British fleet. "We have met the enemy and they are ours," he reported to his superior, "two ships, two brigs, one schooner, and one sloop." His victory, combined with his slogan, infused new life into the drooping American cause.

With the control of Lake Erie firmly in American hands, the British holdings to the west, both at Malden and at captured Detroit, quickly withered. Forced to withdraw eastward into Canada, the retreating Redcoats were overtaken by General Harrison's army and beaten at the Battle of the Thames. There, in October 1813, the gifted Indian leader Tecumseh, now a brigadier general in the British army, lost his life.

Despite these successes, the Americans by late 1814, far from invading Canada, were grimly defending their own soil against the invading British. In Europe, the diversionary power of Napoleon was destroyed in mid-1814, and the dangerous despot was marooned on the Mediterranean isle of Elba. The United States, which had so brashly provoked war behind the protective skirts of Napoleon, was now left to face the music alone. As thousands of red-coated veterans began to pour into Canada, Europe's distresses, for once, failed the Americans.

Assembling some 10,000 crack troops, the British prepared in 1814 for a crushing blow into New York, along the familiar lake-river route. In the absence of roads, the invader was forced to bring his supplies over the Lake Champlain waterway. A weaker American fleet, commanded by the thirty-year-old Thomas Macdonough, challenged the British. The ensuing battle was desperately fought near Plattsburg, on September 11, 1814, on floating slaughterhouses. The American flagship at one point was in grave trouble. But Macdonough, unexpectedly turning his ship about with cables, confronted the enemy with a fresh broadside, and snatched victory from the fangs of defeat.

The results of this heroic naval battle were momentous. The invading British army, its supply line blocked, was forced to retreat, after having gained an initial minor success at Plattsburg over an outnumbered force of American recruits. Macdonough thus saved at least upper New York from conquest, New England from further disaffection, and the Union from possible dissolution. He also profoundly affected the concurrent negotiations of the Anglo-American peace treaty in Europe. The victories of Perry and Macdonough, though achieved on inland lakes, were by far the most decisive naval engagements of the war. The triumph of Macdonough, though the more important, is largely forgotten, partly because he devised no rousing slogan.

Washington Burned and New Orleans Defended

A second formidable British force, numbering about 4,000, landed in the Chesapeake Bay area in August 1814. Advancing rapidly on Washington, it easily dispersed some 6,000 panicky militia at Bladensburg ("the Bladensburg races"). The invaders then entered the capital and set fire to most of the public buildings, including the Capitol and the White House ("the Yankee Palace"). President Madison and his aides, chased into the surrounding hills like frightened rabbits, witnessed from afar the billowing smoke. The British fleet next appeared before Baltimore, a nest for privateers, but was beaten off by the doughty defenders at Fort McHenry, despite "bombs bursting in air." At the same time the American land defenders, though driven back at first, caused the attacking army to withdraw.

The wanton destruction of Washington reflected little credit on the British. They claimed that they had acted in retaliation for the unauthorized burning of certain public buildings by an American raiding party at York (Toronto) in 1813. But the deliberate application of the torch served only to inflame anti-British bitterness. The memory of the Chesapeake campaign was further kept alive when Francis Scott Key, a detained American anxiously watching the bombardment at Baltimore from a British ship, was inspired to write the words of "The Star-Spangled Banner." Set to the tune of a saucy old English tavern refrain, the song quickly attained popularity.

President James Madison (1751–1836). Though an eminent constitutionalist, legislator, and diplomatist, he was not a strong Chief Executive. Foolishly, he was the only President ever to go directly to the fighting front, but he quickly rode away as the British advanced on Washington in 1814.

A third British blow of 1814, aimed at New Orleans, menaced the entire Mississippi Valley. Gaunt and hawk-faced Andrew Jackson, fresh from crushing the Southwest Indians at the Battle of Horseshoe Bend in what is now Alabama, was placed in command. His hodgepodge force consisted of 7,000 sailors, regulars, pirates, and Frenchmen, as well as militiamen from Louisiana, Kentucky, and Tennessee. Among the defenders were two Louisiana regiments of free black volunteers, numbering about 400 men. The Americans threw up their entrenchment, and

> Behind it stood our little force—
> None wished it to be greater;
> For ev'ry man was half a horse,
> And half an alligator.*

The overconfident British, numbering some 8,000 battle-seasoned veterans, blundered badly. They made the mistake of launching a frontal assault, on January 8, 1815, on the entrenched American riflemen and cannoneers. The attackers suffered the most devastating defeat of the entire war, losing over 2,000, killed and wounded, in half an hour, as compared with some 70 for the Americans. This slaughter was as useless as it was horrible, for the treaty of peace had been signed at Ghent, in Europe, two weeks earlier. But Jackson became more than ever the hero of the West. Was he not greater than Napoleon, for had he not

*Popular song, "The Hunters of Kentucky." This song helped create the legend that the riflemen rather than the cannoneers inflicted the most damage.

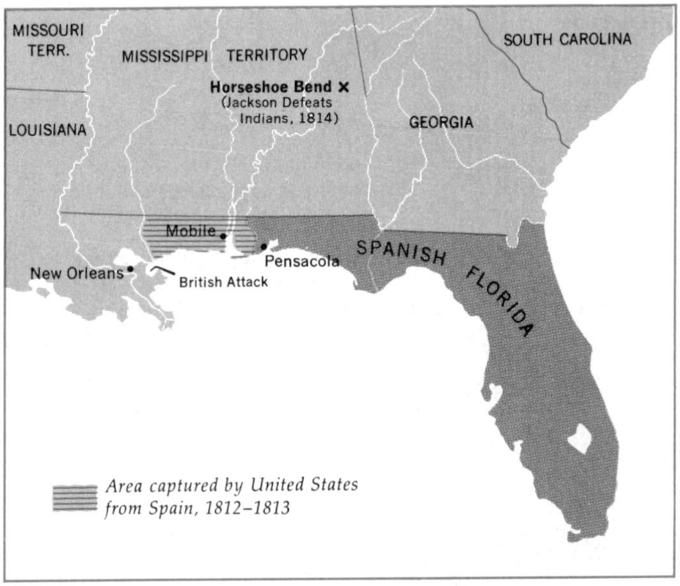

THE SOUTHWEST, 1814–1815

whipped the British veterans, who in turn had whipped Napoleon?

The smashing triumph at New Orleans was the only decisive American land victory that had not been set up by naval power. Yet if a nation is going to win only one such battle, a better aftertaste is left if it is the last one. The "glorious news" from New Orleans reached Washington early in February 1815, and about two weeks later came the tidings of the treaty of peace. Naive citizens promptly concluded that the British, beaten to their knees by Jackson, had hastened to make terms. More support was thus given to the legend that America soundly "thrashed" the British for a second time in the War of 1812—and with poorly trained militia at that.

Ship Duels and Privateer Prizes

Man for man and ship for ship the American navy did much better than the army. But the results of its heroism have been exaggerated.

Britain's navy in 1812 boasted more than 800 men-of-war. Of these oaken craft, 219 were ships-of-the-line of the 74-gun class, and 296 were frigates of roughly the 44-gun class. Little wonder that the motto of the British *Naval Register* was:

> The winds and seas are Britain's wide domain,
> And not a sail, but by permission, spreads.

America, by contrast, had only 16 ships in her entire navy, the largest of which were a few 44-gun frigates, unable to stand up to British ships-of-the-line. There could obviously be no saltwater fleet engagements in the slam-bang Trafalgar tradition; the only fleet battles were fought on the interior lakes.

American frigates and smaller sloops did clash with the enemy in a series of spectacular duels. In the frigate class, the Americans won four out of five of the single-ship contests, and in the sloop class, eight out of nine. American craft on the whole were more skillfully handled, had better gunners, and were manned by non–press-gang crews who were burning to avenge numerous indignities. The American frigates were specially designed super-frigates, notably the *Constitution* ("Old Ironsides"). They had thicker sides, heavier firepower, and larger crews, of which one sailor in six was a free black. These ships should have defeated their foes in the same category, and generally did, amid angry enemy charges that they were "disguised" ships-of-the-line.

The British were deeply humiliated by their naval defeats, all the more so because they had

***Constitution* and *Guerrière*, 1812.** The *Guerrière* was heavily outweighed and outgunned, yet her British captain eagerly—and foolishly—sought combat. His ship was totally destroyed. Historian Henry Adams later concluded that this duel "raised the United States in one half hour to the rank of a first-class Power in the world." (U.S. Naval Academy Museum.)

sneered at America's "few fir-built frigates, manned by a handful of bastards and outlaws." In a few months they lost more warships to the Yankees than the French and Spaniards together had captured in years of fighting.

After three straight losses in frigate duels, Englishmen rang the bells of London Tower in joy over one gratifying victory. The ill-starred American frigate *Chesapeake*, rashly taken into battle with an inexperienced crew, had been captured off Boston by the British frigate *Shannon* on June 1, 1813. From the dying lips of the American commander, Captain Lawrence, came the stirring slogan "Don't give up the ship. Blow her up." The British at length put an end to American single-ship frigate victories when they ordered their frigates to sail in pairs.

The loss of a dozen or so ships by the Royal Navy was negligible. But the victory-hungry Americans gathered from these triumphs a badly needed boost to their morale. When the conflict ended, there were only two or three ships of the American navy at large; Britain still had over 800. The United States obviously did not win the war on the sea. But the dramatic sloop and frigate duels gave further support to the legend that the navy had vanquished the British.

Swift and annoying American privateers—the "militia of the sea"—numbered about 500. They were in fact much more damaging than the regular navy, and had an important bearing on the coming of peace. Built to fly from stronger ships, rather than fight them, these speedy craft captured or destroyed some 1,350 British merchantmen, even pursuing them into the English Channel and the

> Smarting from wounded pride on the sea, the London *Times* urged chastisement for Americans: "The people—naturally vain, boastful, and insolent—have been filled with an absolute contempt of our maritime power, and a furious eagerness to beat down our maritime pretensions. Those passions, which have been inflamed by success, could only have been cooled by what in vulgar and emphatic language has been termed 'a sound flogging.'" (Dec. 30, 1814)

Irish Sea. Assisted by fast-sailing sloops of the navy, Yankee privateers were so destructive that Lloyd's of London refused to insure unconvoyed British merchantmen crossing the Irish Sea. (At the same time British warships and privateers were capturing hundreds of American merchant ships.)

Yet the American privateers were not an unmixed blessing. They lost scores of their own craft, and diverted valuable manpower from the navy and army. But they brought urgently needed wealth into the country, boosted sagging morale, and slowed up British operations in Canada and elsewhere by capturing arms and supplies. More than that, the privateers brought the war home to British manufacturers, merchants, and shippers, who in turn exerted strong pressure on Parliament to end this costly war.

Its wrath aroused, the Royal Navy finally retaliated by throwing a ruinous naval blockade along America's coast, and by landing raiding parties almost at will. American economic life, including fishing, was crippled. Customs revenues were choked off, and near the end of the war the bankrupt Treasury was unable to meet its maturing obligations.

British Peace Demands at Ghent

Czar Alexander I of Russia, late in 1812, unexpectedly proposed mediation between the clashing Anglo-Saxon cousins. He was then hard-pressed by Napoleon's invading Grand Army, and did not wish to see his British ally fritter away its strength in America. Nothing came of the Czar's feeler immediately, but it set the machinery in motion which, in 1814, brought five American peacemakers to the quaint city of Ghent, now in Belgium. This bickering group was headed by the early-rising and puritanical John Quincy Adams, son of John Adams, who deplored the late-hour card playing of his high-living colleague Henry Clay.

Britain's envoys were instructed to make sweeping demands. Their position was bolstered by the knowledge that His Majesty's forces occupied the eastern portion of Maine, and still held Fort Niagara. Britain, through her red allies, also loosely controlled a vast region between the Great Lakes and the Mississippi. The British negotiators therefore felt justified in demanding a neutralized Indian buffer state in this general area. Thrust between Canada and the United States, it would deprive the American pioneers of an immense field for future expansion.

The British diplomats further insisted upon control of the Great Lakes, so as to forestall a future invasion of Canada. With the defense of Canada also in mind, they demanded a substantial part of conquered Maine. They coveted this territory for a military road from Halifax to Quebec, to be employed during those months when the St. Lawrence River was ice-locked.

Such demands from London, harsh though they seemed, were not too far out of line with British military successes, past and prospective. But the American negotiators flatly rejected the proposed terms without even waiting to hear from the secretary of state.

Then, as if by magic, the atmosphere at Ghent changed. The British had presented their drastic proposals with complete confidence; they fully

"Bruin Becomes Mediator" or "Negotiation for Peace." The Russian Bear attempts to mediate between America and a chastened John Bull. America expresses concern over John Bull's horns, the Orders in Council. (A cartoon by William Charles. Courtesy of The New York Public Library, Astor, Lenox and Tilden Foundations.)

"A Wasp on a Frolic." U.S. sloops-of-war *Wasp* and *Hornet* sting John Bull's pride. The *Wasp* captured the *Frolic.* Contemporary American cartoon.

expected that news would soon arrive of crushing victories. But when instead tidings came of the repulses in upper New York and at Baltimore, London was more willing to compromise. The Madison administration, for its part, was now reluctantly prepared to keep silent on the issue of impressment, even though it had originally insisted on abandonment of this infuriating practice.

In England, the atmosphere likewise changed. Irate Britons were impatient to humiliate the "insolent" and "treacherous" Yankees. But the "Iron Duke" of Wellington, conqueror of Napoleon, warned that the United States could not be successfully invaded without British control of the Great Lakes. Such control could be achieved only at a heavy cost, if at all; and England was debt-burdened and war-weary from her twenty-year clash with France. American sloops and privateers were taking their deadly toll. The Congress of Vienna, designed to unscramble the map of Europe, was at a critical stage. France was restive, and Napoleon might forsake nearby Elba to meet his Waterloo (which he soon did).

Revenge was sweet—but expensive. Much as the British yearned to thrash their upstart offspring, they finally decided that this satisfaction would cost too much, while involving them too deeply at a time when they had to keep a vigilant eye on France. The British lion unhappily resigned himself to licking his wounds. Once again the distresses of Europe were bringing diplomatic success, for the War of 1812 was largely "won" in Europe, so far as it was won at all by the United States.

The Gains of Ghent

The Treaty of Ghent, signed on Christmas Eve in 1814, was essentially an armistice. Both sides simply agreed to stop fighting and to restore conquered territory. No mention was made of those grievances for which America had ostensibly fought: the Indian menace, search and seizure, Orders in Council, impressment, and confiscations. These maritime omissions have often been cited as further evidence of the insincerity of the War Hawks. Rather, they are proof that the Americans did not defeat the British decisively. With neither side able to impose its will, the treaty negotiations—like the war itself—ended as a virtual draw.

Time—the great healer—solved certain problems that the negotiators could not untangle. Impress-

> The War of 1812 won a new respect for America among many Britons. Michael Scott, a young lieutenant in the British navy, wrote: "I don't like Americans; I never did, and never shall like them. . . . I have no wish to eat with them, drink with them, deal with, or consort with them in any way; but let me tell the whole truth, *nor fight* with them, were it not for the laurels to be acquired, by overcoming an enemy so brave, determined, and alert, and in every way so worthy of one's steel, as they have always proved."

PRESIDENTIAL ELECTION OF 1812 (with electoral vote by state)
The Federalists showed impressive strength in the North, and their presidential candidate, DeWitt Clinton, the future "father of the Erie Canal," almost won. If the 25 electoral votes of Pennsylvania had gone to the New Yorker, he would have won, 114 to 103.

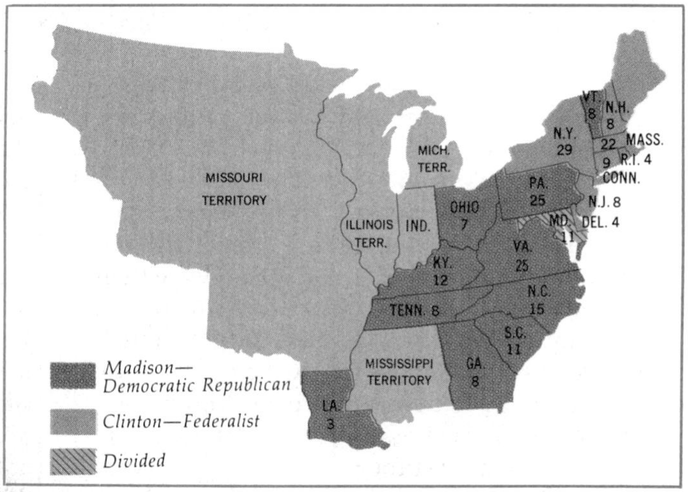

ment was never thereafter a burning issue. The British navy was reduced to a peace footing, and less brutal methods of enlistment were devised. The Peace of Ghent, like Jay's Treaty of 1794, was also a victory for arbitration: four boundary disputes were referred to arbitral commissions.

The "Truce of Ghent," which realistically swept problems under the rug, had one great merit. It was not a victor's peace; hence no territorial booty had to be won back. There were wounds—but not unhealable wounds. The treaty had done nothing, so nothing had to be undone. Therein lay the secret of its longevity.

The news from Ghent triggered an outburst of rejoicing in the United States. Many Americans had rather expected to lose some territory, so dark was the military outlook early in 1815. But when the treaty arrived, the public mood rocketed from gloom to glory. The popularity of the pact was so overwhelming that it was unanimously approved by the Senate. A slogan of the hour became "Not One Inch of Territory Ceded or Lost"—a watchword that contrasted strangely with "On to Canada" at the outset of the war.

Federalist Grievances and the Hartford Convention

Defiant New England remained a problem. She was by far the most prosperous section during the conflict, owing largely to illicit trade with the enemy in Canada and to the absence of a British blockade until 1814. But the embittered opposition of the Federalists to the war continued unabated. Late in 1812, when the first wartime presidential election was held, unhappy Federalists combined with disaffected Republicans and almost unseated President Madison. If the state of Pennsylvania alone had been transferred to their electoral column, they would have won.

As the war dragged on, New England extremists became more vocal. A small minority of them proposed secession from the Union, or at least a separate peace with England. Ugly rumors were afloat about "Blue Light" Federalists—treacherous New Englanders who supposedly flashed lanterns on the shore so that blockading British cruisers would be alerted to the attempted escape of American ships.

The most spectacular manifestation of Federalist discontent was the ill-omened Hartford Convention. Late in 1814, when the capture of New Orleans seemed imminent, Massachusetts issued a call for a convention at Hartford, Connecticut. The states of Massachusetts, Connecticut, and Rhode Island dispatched full delegations, while New Hampshire and Vermont sent partial representation. This group of prominent men, twenty-six in all, met in complete secrecy for about three weeks—December 15, 1814, to January 5, 1815—to discuss their grievances and to seek redress for their wrongs.

In truth, the Hartford Convention was less radical than alarmists supposed. Its immediate goal was to secure financial assistance from Washington, because the shores of New England were then being menaced by British blockading squadrons. A minority of the delegates gave vent to much wild talk of secession, but they were outvoted by the moderate Federalists. The report and resolutions adopted by the Convention, in fact, resemble a modern political platform.

The Hartfordites, resenting the war-bent policies of the administration, were eager to restore New England to her stellar role on the national stage. They recommended amendments to the Constitution aimed at hobbling Congress and restoring Federalist influence by a kind of minority veto. These proposals would require a two-thirds vote before an embargo could be imposed, before new Western states could be admitted, and before war could be declared—except in case of invasion.

Three special envoys from Massachusetts, bearing demands of the Hartford Convention for financial support to promote defense, journeyed to the burned-out capital of Washington. The trio arrived just in time to be overwhelmed by the glorious news from New Orleans, followed by that from Ghent. Pursued by the sneers and jeers of the press, they slunk away into obscurity and disgrace.

The Hartford resolutions, as it turned out, were the death song of the Federalist party. In 1816, the next year, the Federalists nominated their last presidential candidate. He was lopsidedly defeated by James Monroe, yet another Virginian.

Unhappily, the stench of treason has clung to the Hartford Convention. The taint was not justified by its formal resolutions, which were an attempt of moderates to iron out rankling vexations by constitutional methods—in the American way. Yet if the war had not ended when it did, the Convention might well have paved the way for treasonable courses.

Federalist doctrines of disunity, which long survived the party, blazed a fateful trail. Until 1815, there was far more talk of nullification and secession in New England than in any other section, including the South. The outright flouting of the Jeffersonian embargo and the later crippling of the war effort were the two most damaging acts of nullification in America prior to the events leading to the Civil War.

"Three Wise Men of Gotham Went to Sea in a Bowl.—" This satirical anti-Federalist cartoon shows three Massachusetts men sailing precariously for Washington in a large chamber pot bearing Hartfordite demands. They are quieting their fears of sinking by exchanging off-color remarks. (Massachusetts Historical Society.)

The Second War for American Independence

The War of 1812 was a small war, involving about 6,000 Americans killed or wounded. It was but a footnote to the mighty European conflagration. In 1812, when Napoleon invaded Russia with about 500,000 men, Madison tried to invade Canada with about 5,000 men. But if the American conflict was globally unimportant, its results were highly important to the United States.

Oliver H. Perry's Battle Flag, 1813. Bearing Captain Lawrence's slogan, it now hangs conspicuously on a wall at the U.S. Naval Academy at Annapolis.

Americans wrested no formal recognition of their rights on the high seas, but informally they did. No longer did British aristocrats jeer at the "striped bunting" over "American cockboats." The Republic had shown that it would resent, sword in hand, what it regarded as grievous wrongs. Other nations developed a new respect for American fighting men. Naval officers like Perry and Macdonough were the most effective type of negotiators; the hot breath of their broadsides spoke the most eloquent diplomatic language. America's diplomats abroad were henceforth treated with less scorn. In a diplomatic sense, if not in a military sense, the conflict could be called the Second War for American Independence.

A new nation, moreover, was welded in the fiery furnace of armed conflict. Sectionalism, now identified with discredited New England Federalists, was given a black eye. The painful events of the war glaringly revealed, as perhaps nothing else could have done, the folly of sectional disunity. In a sense, the most conspicuous casualty of the war was the Federalist party.

The nation thrilled to the victories of its warriors. A brilliant naval tradition, already well launched, was strengthened by the exploits of the gallant seamen. Ineptitudes of insubordinate or fleeing militia were forgotten. The battle-singed regular army, which in the closing months of the war had fought bravely and well, had won its spurs. New war heroes emerged, men like Andrew Jackson, William Henry Harrison, and Winfield Scott. All three were to become presidential candidates, two of them successful.

Hostile Indians of the South had been crushed by Jackson at Horseshoe Bend (1814), and those of the North by Harrison at the Battle of the Thames (1813). Left in the lurch by their British friends at Ghent, the Indians were forced to make such terms as they could. They reluctantly consented, in a series of treaties, to relinquish vast areas of forested land north of the Ohio River.

Manufacturing increased behind the fiery wooden wall of the British blockade. In an economic sense, as well as in a diplomatic sense, the War of 1812 may be regarded as the Second War for American Independence. The industries that were thus stimulated by the fighting rendered America less dependent on the workshops of Europe.

Lingering Hates and Canadian Misgivings

Regrettably, the war revived and intensified bitterness toward the Mother Country. The uglier incidents of the conflict, notably the burning of Washington, added fuel to a century of Britain-hating and Britain-baiting. A contemporary American war song, "Johnny Bull," proclaimed:

> But if again he should be vain
> Or dare to be uncivil,
> We'll let him know his rebel foe
> Can thrash him like the D——.

Mutual suspicion and hate were perhaps the most enduring heritages of this frustrating little war. Few Americans could have guessed in 1815 that it was to be the nation's last armed conflict with England.

Canadian patriotism and nationalism, no less

than American patriotism and nationalism, received a powerful stimulus from the clash. The outnumbered Canadians, fighting bravely in defense of their homeland against the Yankee invader, won their full share of the laurels. Their stirring song, "The Maple Leaf," ringingly recalls these battles, including Chippewa and Lundy's Lane, which Americans regard as their victories.

All hope of annexing Canada, at least by nonforcible means, was given a deadly blow. Peaceful Yankee penetration might have won this rich prize, but caveman aggression defeated its own ends. It strengthened the arm of those Canadians, led by the sons of the Loyalists, who would die in the last ditch before they would live under the Stars and Stripes. The irony is that the Loyalists, whom America had defeated in her first war with England, helped thwart her in her second war with England.

Many Canadians, including Western fur traders, cried that they had been betrayed by the Treaty of Ghent. They were especially aggrieved by Britain's failure to secure the defensive bulwark of an Indian buffer state, or even mastery of the Great Lakes. Fully expecting the frustrated Yankee to come again, they felt naked in the face of their former enemy.

The U.S. Frigate *Constitution*. It was the pride of the scant American fleet.

Naval armament on the lakes continued to be inflammatory. When the war ended, the Americans and the British were both engaged in building powerful and costly warships. But economy-minded London officials, who perceived that such vessels were useless to the saltwater Royal Navy, finally became receptive to American proposals for arms limitation.

In 1817 Great Britain went so far as to negotiate with the United States the Rush-Bagot disarmament agreement. This memorable pact severely limited naval armament on the Great Lakes, despite Canadian misgivings and protests. The immediate fruits have been greatly overpraised, but the principle of disarmament was gradually extended to border fortifications, which disappeared in the 1870s. One happy result was that the United States and Canada ultimately came to share the longest unfortified boundary in the world—5,527 miles (8,899 kilometers) long, including Alaska.

Larger Anglo-American Legacies

Painful military lessons of the war went largely unheeded by the public, owing in part to overemphasis on spectacular naval duels. Forgotten were the perils of unpreparedness, the dangers of disunity, the muddlings of the militia. Americans assumed, mistakenly, that they had won the war decisively—without preparing for it. Then why go to all the expense of building an adequate military establishment if they could defeat their enemies without one? Unpreparedness was sanctified by seeming success.

Europe's finish-fight at Waterloo, in 1815, proved to be one of the decisive battles of American history. With a defeated Napoleon safely exiled on the island-rock of St. Helena, some 5,000 miles away, Europe slumped back into a peace of exhaustion. Deposed monarchs returned to battered thrones, as the Mother Continent prepared to take the rutted road back to conservatism, illiberalism, and reaction.

American citizens now experienced the joys of emancipation. Freed from the humiliating side blows of the belligerents, they no longer had to scan the Atlantic horizon for approaching sails—sails that might bring news of impending calamities. Americans thrilled to a new sense of nationality. They were like subject peoples attaining their majority, and for the first time shaking off the shackles of colonialism. Turning their backs on the Old World, they faced resolutely toward the untamed West. Unlike monarchy-cursed Europe, they were ready to take the high road toward democracy, liberalism, and freedom. The steady tramp, tramp, of the westward-moving pioneers came to be the giant drumbeat of a new destiny.

VARYING VIEWPOINTS

The causes and consequences of the War of 1812 have long sparked spirited debate. Was war the result of Western War Hawk expansionism or of British provocations on the high seas? Most recent historians emphasize the naval issue. The young nation's pride and independence, they argue, could not tolerate John Bull's repeated affronts. Perhaps more interestingly, scholars also have seen the first vague outlines of an American identity emerging from the smoke of the War of 1812. Henry Adams' magisterial *History* made this theme a central motif; Adams found evidence of a distinctive American character even in the tactics and techniques of Yankee seamen. The war does appear to have dissolved many localisms and to have begun to forge a genuine national consciousness—thus paving the way for the so-called Era of Good Feelings.

SELECT READINGS

Marcus Cunliffe, *The Nation Takes Shape, 1789–1837* (1959), provides a convenient introduction. More detailed are H. L. Coles, *The War of 1812* (1965), P. C. T. White, *A Nation on Trial: America and the War of 1812* (1965), J. M. Hitsman, *The Incredible War of 1812: A Military History* (1965), and R. Horsman, *The War of 1812* (1969). On causation, J. W. Pratt, *Expansionists of 1812* (1925), stresses Western pressures; Bradford Perkins, *Prologue to War: England and the United States, 1805–1812* (1961), and R. Horsman, *The Causes of the War of 1812* (1962), discuss free seas; R. R. Brown, *The Republic in Peril: 1812* (1964), emphasizes the need for saving the Republican form of government. The relevant volumes of Henry Adams' nine-volume *History of the United States* (1889–1891) still contain magnificent reading, both on the war and on the peace. For the general context of Anglo-American diplomacy, see B. Perkins, *Castlereagh and Adams: England and the United States, 1812–1823* (1964). An overall view can be found in J. K. Mahon, *The War of 1812* (1972). A popularized account of the Peace of Ghent is F. L. Engelman, *The Peace of Christmas Eve* (1962). Federalist reaction to Republican foreign policy is vividly etched in D. H. Fisher, *The Revolution of American Conservatism* (1965), and J. Banner, *To the Hartford Convention: The Federalists and the Origins of Party Politics in Massachusetts* (1970). Consult also James H. Broussard, *The Southern Federalists, 1800–1816* (1979). Irving Brant continues his strong pro-Madison bias in the relevant volumes of his six-volume work: *James Madison: The President, 1809–1812* (1956), and *James Madison: Commander-in-Chief, 1812–1836* (1961). See also Ralph Ketcham, *James Madison: A Biography* (1971). Other useful biographical studies are Bernard Mayo, *Henry Clay: Spokesman of the New West* (1937), G. G. Van Deusen, *The Life of Henry Clay* (1937) and Marquis James's spirited *Andrew Jackson: The Border Captain* (1933).

12

The Post-War Upsurge of Nationalism, 1815–1824

The American continents . . . are henceforth not to be considered as subjects for future colonization by any European powers.

James Monroe, December 2, 1823

Nascent Nationalism

The most impressive by-product of the War of 1812 was a heightened nationalism—the spirit of nation-consciousness or national oneness. America may not have fought the war as one nation, but she emerged one nation. So exhilarating was the post-war era that President Madison, despite his blunders, enjoyed the unusual distinction of being more popular when he left the White House in 1817 than when he entered it in 1809.

A weak nationalism had existed since Revolutionary days, but the vibrant new nationalism was composed of many additional ingredients. It sprang partly from pride in recent victories, partly from the setback to Federalist sectionalism and states'-rightism, partly from a lessening of economic and political dependence on Europe, and partly from an exulting confidence in the future.

Swelling numbers of citizens—although probably not yet a majority—were coming to regard themselves as first of all Americans, and secondarily as citizens of their respective states.

The changed mood even manifested itself in the birth of a distinctively national literature. Washington Irving and James Fenimore Cooper attained international recognition in the 1820s, significantly as the nation's first writers of importance to use American scenes and themes. School textbooks, often British in an earlier era, were now being written by Americans for Americans. In the world of magazines, the highly intellectual *North American Review* saw the light of day in 1815—the year of the triumph at New Orleans. Even American painters increasingly celebrated the glories of American landscapes on their canvases.

A fresh nationalistic spirit could be recognized in many other areas. A more handsome national capital began to rise from the ashes of Washington —a capital fit to symbolize America's prospective greatness. The army was expanded to 10,000 men, though this number was inadequate for a serious emergency. Old fears that liberties might be crushed by a standing army largely melted away in the warm sun of emerging nationalism.

The navy, for a time at least, also received reasonably satisfactory financial support. It further covered itself with glory in 1815, when the naval heroes of the late war administered a thorough beating to the piratical plunderers of North Africa. These gratifying victories, inspired by the spirit of nationalism, further inflamed nationalism.

A rising tide of nation-consciousness also touched finance. The War of 1812 had demonstrated the folly of permitting the Bank of the United States to expire in 1811, on the very eve of hostilities. Weak state banks, responding to the vacuum, had seemingly sprung up beside every village tavern. The country was flooded with depreciated banknotes that, incidentally, had hampered the war effort.

A revived Bank of the United States, in response to these obvious needs, was voted by Congress in 1816. It was modeled on the first one but had a total capital of $35 million—three and one-half times that of the original. Jeffersonian Republicans, taught a bitter lesson during the war, supported the revived institution. In fact, they cleverly but inconsistently borrowed the same arguments for a bank that Hamilton had used against Jefferson in 1791. The Federalist minority in Congress, opposing Republican measures with its dying gasps, no less inconsistently denounced the Federalist-spawned Bank as unconstitutional.

Stephen Decatur (1779–1820). Decatur was a naval hero of the War of 1812 and the North African war. Reflecting and encouraging the post-war nationalism, he is best remembered for a famous toast: "Our country! In her intercourse with foreign nations may she always be in the right; but our country, right or wrong!"

The Second Bank of the United States, unlike the first, started off on the wrong foot. Badly managed in its early years, it finally settled down and contributed richly to the economic life of the country. The "moneyed monster," as it was branded by its enemies, further broadened nationalism as it thrust its numerous branches out across state boundaries.

Industrial Nationalism and the Tariff

Nationalism likewise manifested itself in manufacturing. Patriotic Americans took pride in the factories that had recently mushroomed forth, largely as a result of the self-imposed embargoes and the war.

When hostilities ended in 1815, British competitors undertook to recover lost ground. They began to dump the contents of their bulging warehouses on the United States, often cutting their prices below cost in an effort to strangle the American war-baby factories in the cradle. The infant industries bawled lustily for protection. To many red-blooded Americans it seemed as though the British, having failed on the battlefield to crush Yankee fighters, were now seeking to crush Yankee factories.

A nationalist Congress, out-Federalizing the old Federalists, responded by passing the pathbreaking Tariff of 1816. The legislators were impressed with the desirability of saving the new industries for the national defense, while at the same time promoting the general welfare. The Tariff of 1816, significantly, was the first in American history with aims that were primarily protective. Its rates—roughly 20 to 25 percent on the value of dutiable imports—were not high enough to provide completely adequate safeguards, but the law was a bold beginning. A strongly protective trend was started that stimulated the appetites of the protected for more protection.

The battle in Congress over the Tariff of 1816 reflected North-South sectional crosscurrents. Thirty-four-year-old Representative John C. Calhoun of South Carolina—slender, handsome, black-haired, intense, and intellectual—played a stellar role in the debates. A recent War Hawk and an ardent nationalist, he supported the tariff bill with all his eloquence and vigor. In 1816 there was some likelihood that the destiny of his native South lay in manufacturing, as well as in the intensive cultivation of cotton. But within a few years Calhoun became a relentless foe of a highly protective tariff. He sadly concluded that it was being used to enrich a few Yankee manufacturers, rather than to build up the economic self-sufficiency and well-being of the entire nation.

House Vote on Tariff of 1816

Regions	*For*	*Against*
New England	17	10
Middle States	44	10
West (Ohio)	4	0
South and Southwest	23	34
	88	54

NOTE: Even in South Carolina, Calhoun's state, the vote in favor of the bill was 4 to 3.

Calhoun encountered a worthy adversary in Daniel Webster of New Hampshire, also thirty-four. Stocky, bushy-browed, and dark-haired, "Black Dan" Webster eloquently opposed the highly protective duties of the Tariff of 1816. He took this stand even though he was later to be a zealous nationalist and an ardent champion of high protection. The explanation is simple. Manufacturing in New England had not yet pushed shipping into a back seat, and the shippers of Webster's New Hampshire district feared that a tariff would interfere with their carrying trade. New England, though favoring some protection, was not yet completely willing to exchange the mainsail for the loom—but that day was slowly dawning.

Nationalism was further highlighted by a grandiose plan of Henry Clay for developing a profitable home market. Still radiating the nationalism of War Hawk days, he threw himself behind an elaborate scheme known by 1824 as the American System. First, there would be the protective tariff, behind which Eastern manufacturing would flourish. Revenues gushing from the tariff would provide funds for roads and canals, especially in the fast-developing Ohio Valley. Through these new arteries of transportation would flow foodstuffs and raw materials from the South and West to the North and East. In exchange, a stream of manufactured goods would flow in the return direction.

A wedding of tariff revenues to internal improvements looked promising on paper. The entire country would prosper, while state boundaries would tend to become mere surveyors' lines. America would grow more self-sufficient, and under the

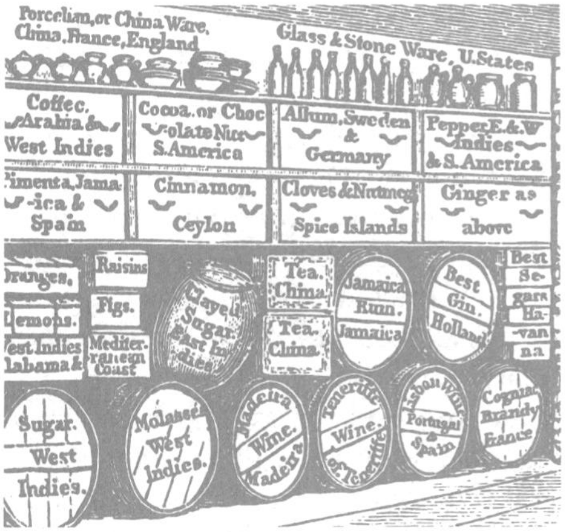

Pro-Tariff Woodcut Showing Foreign Goods on Shelves. Many Americans feared foreign goods more than foreign armies.

warm glow of prosperity the spirit of nationalism would deepen and broaden.

Roadblocks to Internal Improvements

Persistent and eloquent demands by Henry Clay and others for internal improvements struck a responsive chord with the public. The recent attempts to invade Canada had all failed partly because of oath-provoking roads—or no roads at all. Men who have dug wagons out of hub-deep mud do not quickly forget their blisters and backaches. An outcry for better transportation, rising most noisily in the road-poor West, was one of the most striking aspects of the nationalism inspired by the War of 1812.

Hope for more roads and canals came from an unexpected source. The Second Bank of the United States had been required to pay the federal government $1.5 million for its exclusive privileges. Calhoun, seeking to divert this sum to internal improvements, induced Congress in 1817 to pass the Bonus Bill, under which the Bank money would be parceled out to the states. But President Madison sternly vetoed this handout measure. In his view, the spending of federal funds for internal improvements within the individual states—but not across state lines—violated the Constitution, as interpreted strictly.

This anti-improvement veto threw a wet blanket over the upsurging nationalism. Madison's successor, President Monroe, generally followed the same line of negative reasoning—with the same disheartening results. The individual states, though lacking sufficient funds, were forced to venture ahead with building programs of their own. The most notable of these was the Erie Canal, triumphantly completed by New York in 1825.

On the transportation question, the Jeffersonian Republicans were not consistently inconsistent. On all other important problems, they were at last prepared to gulp down the Hamiltonian doctrine of loose construction. Madison and Monroe, political heirs of Jefferson, could easily have argued that roads and canals solely within the states contributed to the welfare of the country as a whole, while bolstering the common defense. But instead they timidly recommended an appropriate constitutional amendment to permit internal improvements at federal expense. It was never enacted.

The enfeebled Federalists, now turncoat strict constructionists, could grudgingly applaud the vetoes of the Jeffersonian Republican Presidents. New England, in particular, strongly opposed federally constructed roads and canals, because such outlets would further drain away population and create competing states beyond the mountains.

The So-Called Era of Good Feelings

James Monroe—6 feet (1.83 meters) tall, somewhat stooped, courtly, and mild-mannered—was nominated for the presidency in 1816 by the Republicans. They thus undertook to continue the so-called Virginia Dynasty of Washington, Jefferson, and Madison. The fading Federalists ran a candidate for the last time in their checkered history, and he was crushed by 183 electoral votes to 34.

The death of the once-proud Federalist party was due to various diseases, shortcomings, and misfortunes. A list would include its disgraceful

President James Monroe (1758–1831). Monroe fought in the Revolution (suffering a wound), served as minister to France, became co-purchaser of Louisiana, and rose to the presidency in 1817. An excellent administrator, he presided over the Era of Good Feelings. His inaugural address declared: "National honor is national property of the highest value." His name is imperishably attached to the Monroe Doctrine and Monrovia, the capital city of Liberia in Africa. He had strongly backed the colonization there of ex-slaves. His wife and two daughters had expensive tastes and, like plantation-owner Jefferson, he died deeply in debt. (The Metropolitan Museum of Art, Bequest of Seth Low, 1929.)

war record; its inability to choke down the new nationalistic program; and the theft of its tenets by the Jeffersonians. Many Federalists followed their stolen principles into the opposition camp; others gradually crawled away to the political graveyard. The irony is that the original Hamiltonians, while the party of the "ins," had been conspicuously nationalistic; now, as the party of the "outs," they scorned the nationalism of the Republicans.

In James Monroe, the man and the times auspiciously met. As the last President to wear an old-style cocked hat, he straddled two generations: the bygone age of the Founding Fathers and the emergent age of nationalism. Never brilliant, and perhaps not great, the serene Virginian with gray-blue eyes was in intellect and personal force among the least distinguished of the first eight Presidents. But the times called for sober administration, not heroics. And Monroe was an experienced, level-headed executive, with an ear-to-the-ground talent for interpreting popular rumblings.

Emerging nationalism was further cemented by a goodwill tour that Monroe undertook early in 1817, ostensibly to inspect military defenses. He pushed northward deep into New England, and then westward to Detroit, viewing en route the Niagara Falls. Even in Federalist New England, "the enemy's country," he received a heartwarming welcome; a Boston newspaper was so far carried away as to announce that an "Era of Good Feelings" had been ushered in. This happy phrase since then has been commonly used to describe the administrations of Monroe.

The Era of Good Feelings, unfortunately, was something of a misnomer. Considerable tranquillity and prosperity did in fact smile upon the early years of Monroe, but the period was a troubled one. The acute issues of the tariff, the Bank, internal improvements, and the sale of public lands were being hotly contested. Sectionalism was crystallizing, and the conflict over slavery was beginning to raise its hideous head.

> Boston's *Columbian Centinel* was not the only newspaper to regard President Monroe's early months as the Era of Good Feelings. The Washington *National Intelligencer* observed in July 1817, "Never before, perhaps, since the institution of civil government, did the same harmony, the same absence of party spirit, the same national feeling, pervade a community. The result is too consoling to dispute too nicely about the cause."

A vanquished Federalist party was breathing its dying gasps, leaving the field to the triumphant Republicans and one-party rule. But where there is only one party, or where one of the parties enjoys a lopsided majority, the tendency is for factions to develop and fight among themselves. By the early 1820s there was an Era of Inflamed Feelings. Political giants—men like Clay, Calhoun, Jackson, and John Quincy Adams— were elbowing for power and championing the clashing economic interests of their respective sections.

The Panic of 1819 and the Curse of Hard Times

Much of the goodness went out of the good feelings in 1819, when a paralyzing economic panic descended. It brought deflation, depression, bankruptcies, bank failures, unemployment, soup kitchens, and overcrowded pesthouses known as debtors' prisons.

This was the first of the national financial panics since President Washington took office. It was to be followed by a succession of others every twenty or so years, in what seemed an inevitable cycle. Many factors contributed to the catastrophe of 1819, but looming large was overspeculation in frontier lands. The Bank of the United States, through its Western branches, had become deeply involved in this popular type of outdoor gambling.

Financial paralysis from the panic, which lasted in some degree for several years, gave a rude setback to the nationalistic ardor. Various parts of the country tended to drift back toward the old sectionalism, as they concentrated on bailing themselves out. The West was especially hard hit. When the pinch came, the Bank of the United States forced the speculative ("wildcat") Western banks to the wall, and foreclosed mortgages on countless farms. All this was technically legal but politically unwise. In the eyes of the Western debtor, the Bank soon became a kind of financial devil.

A more welcome child of the panic was fresh legislation for the public domain. The plight of the Western farmer, combined with the evils of land speculation, laid bare the defects of the Land Act of 1800, as amended in 1804. By its terms, the pioneer could buy a minimum of 160 acres at $2 an acre over a period of four years, with a down payment of $80. When hard times came, whole communities would default on their installments. An improved Land Act of 1820 lightened the burden somewhat, for it permitted the buyer to secure 80 virgin acres at a minimum of $1.25 an acre in cash—for a total cost of $100. There was less acreage but less outlay.

The Panic of 1819 also created backwashes in the political and social world. It hit especially hard the poorer classes—the one-suspender men—and hence helped cultivate the seedbed of Jacksonian democracy. It also directed attention to the inhumanity of imprisoning debtors. In extreme cases, often overplayed, mothers were torn from their infants for owing a few dollars. Mounting agitation against imprisonment for debt bore fruit in remedial legislation in an increasing number of states.

Growing Pains of the West

Beyond doubt the West, out of which had swooped the War Hawks of 1812, was by far the most nationalistic of the sections. Being new, it had no long-established states'-rights tradition. Moreover, it had early learned to lean on the national government, from which it had secured most of its land, directly or indirectly. It was a mixing bowl within the huge American melting pot, for people from all the sections rubbed elbows on the frontier.

Marvelous indeed had been the onward march of the West; nine frontier states had joined the original thirteen between 1791 and 1819. With an eye to preserving the North-South sectional balance, most of these commonwealths had been admitted alternately, free or slave. (See Admission of States, in Appendix.)

Why this explosive expansion? Fundamentally, there was the generations-old westward movement, which had been going on since early colonial days. In addition, the siren call of cheap lands—"the Ohio fever"—had a special appeal to European immigrants. Quaintly garbed newcomers from abroad were beginning to shuffle down the gangplanks in impressive numbers, especially after the war of embargoes and bullets. Land exhaustion in the older tobacco states, where the soil was "mined" rather than cultivated, likewise drove people westward. Glib-tongued speculators, accepting small down payments, made easier the purchase of new holdings.

The western boom was stimulated by additional developments. Acute distress during the embargo years turned many saddened faces toward the setting sun. The crushing of the Indians in the Northwest and South, by Generals Harrison and Jackson, soothed the frontier and opened up vast virgin tracts. The building of highways improved the land routes to the Ohio Valley. Noteworthy was the Cumberland Road, begun in 1811, which ran ultimately from western Maryland to Illinois. The employment of the first steamboat on Western waters, also in 1811, heralded a new era of upstream navigation.

But the West, despite the inflow of settlers, was still weak in population and influence. Not potent enough politically to make its voice heard, it was forced to ally itself with sister sections. Thus strengthened, it demanded cheap acreage, and partially achieved its goal in the Land Act of 1820. It demanded cheap transportation, and slowly got it, despite the constitutional qualms of the Presidents and the hostility of Easterners. Finally, the West demanded cheap money, issued by its own "wildcat" banks, and fought the powerful Bank of the United States to attain its goal.

Hard Times in Ohio. A satire on Western migration, from a pamphlet of 1819. (American Antiquarian Society, Worcester, Massachusetts.)

Slavery and the Sectional Balance

Sectional tensions were nakedly revealed in 1819, when the territory of Missouri knocked on the doors of Congress for admission as a slave state. This fertile and well-watered area contained sufficient population to warrant statehood. But the House of Representatives threw a monkey wrench into the plans of the Missourians by passing the incendiary Tallmadge amendment. It stipulated that no more slaves should be brought into Missouri, and also provided for the gradual emancipation of children born to slave parents already there. A mounting roar of anger burst from slaveholding Southerners. They were joined by many depression-cursed pioneers who favored unhampered expansion of the West, and by many Northerners, especially diehard Federalists, who were eager to play politics.

Southerners saw in the Tallmadge amendment, which was defeated in the Senate, an ominous threat to the sectional balance. When the Constitution was adopted in 1788, the North and South were running neck and neck in wealth and population. But with every passing decade the North was becoming wealthier and more thickly settled—an advantage reflected in an increasing Northern majority in the House of Representatives. Yet in the Senate, with eleven states free and eleven slave, the Southerners had maintained equality. They were therefore in a good position to thwart any Northern effort to interfere with the expansion of slavery, and they did not want to lose this veto.

The future of the slave system caused Southerners profound concern. Missouri was the first state entirely west of the Mississippi River to be carved out of the Louisiana Purchase, and the Missouri emancipation amendment might set a damaging precedent for all the rest of the area. Even more disquieting was another possibility. If

Contemporary Anti-Slavery Propaganda. This also appeared as "Am I Not a Woman and a Sister?"

Congress could abolish the "peculiar institution" in Missouri, might it not attempt to do likewise in the older states of the South? The wounds of the Constitutional Convention of 1787 were once more ripped open.

Ugly moral questions also protruded, even though the main issue was political and economic balance. A small but growing group of anti-slavery agitators in the North seized the occasion to raise an outcry against the evils of slavery. They were determined that the plague of human bondage should not spread further into the virgin territories.

> While the debate over Missouri was raging, Jefferson wrote to a correspondent: "I thank you for your information on the progress and prospects of the Missouri question. It is the most portentous one which ever yet threatened our Union. In the gloomiest moment of the revolutionary war I never had any apprehensions equal to what I feel from this source." He also wrote that the "question, like a firebell in the night, awakened and filled me with terror." With slavery, the aging ex-President declared, "we have the wolf by the ears, and we can neither hold him nor safely let him go."

The Uneasy Missouri Compromise

Deadlock in Washington was at length broken in 1820 by the time-honored American solution of compromise—actually a bundle of three compromises. Courtly Henry Clay of Kentucky, gifted conciliator, played a leading role. Congress, despite abolitionist pleas, agreed to admit Missouri as a slave state. But at the same time free-soil

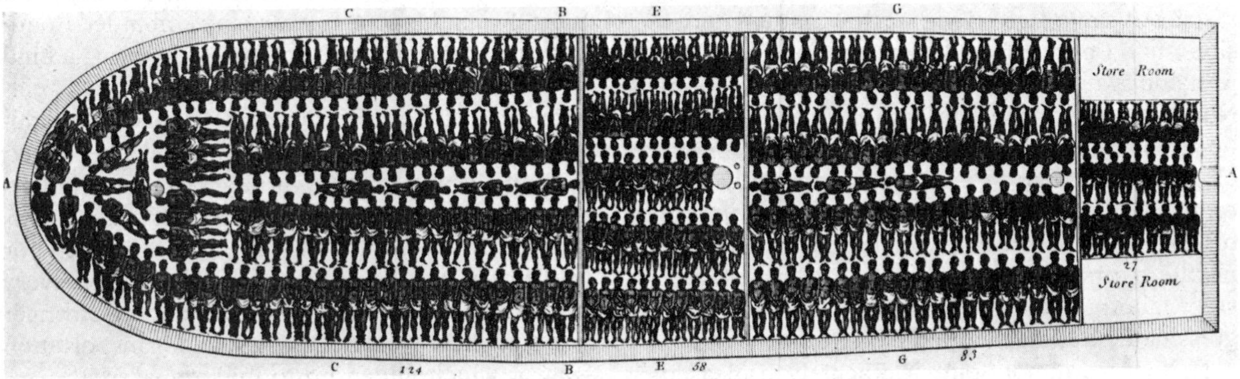

The "Middle Passage." Human Cargo in the hold of a slave ship. (The Mariners Museum.)

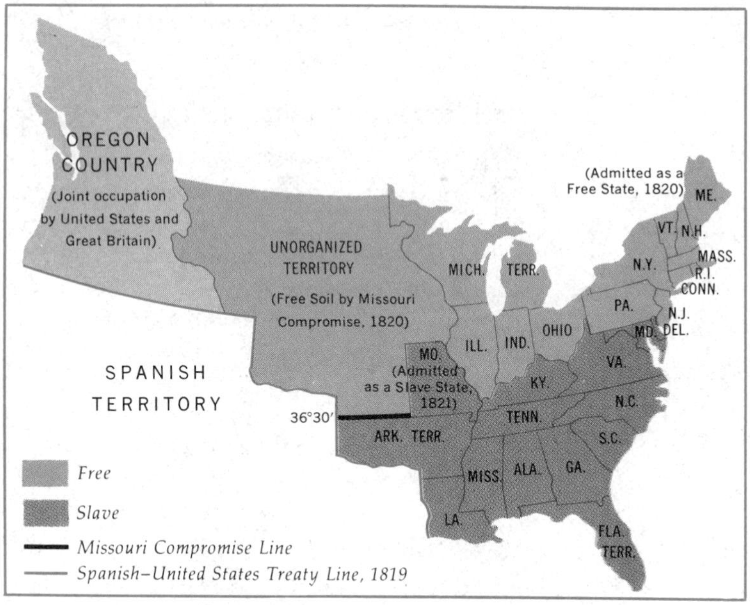

THE MISSOURI COMPROMISE AND SLAVERY, 1820–1821

In the 1780s Thomas Jefferson had written of slavery in America: "Indeed I tremble for my country when I reflect that God is just; that his justice cannot sleep forever; that . . . the Almighty has no attribute which can take side with us in such a contest." Now, at the time of the Missouri Compromise, Jefferson feared that his worst forebodings were coming to pass. "I considered it at once," he said of the Missouri question, "as the knell of the Union."

Maine, which until then had been a part of Massachusetts, was admitted as a separate state. The balance between North and South was thus kept at twelve states each, and remained there for fifteen years. Although Missouri was permitted to retain slaves, all future bondage was prohibited in the remainder of the Louisiana Purchase north of the line of 36° 30′—the southern boundary of Missouri.

This horse-trading adjustment was politically evenhanded, though denounced by extremists on each side as a "dirty bargain." Both North and South yielded something; both gained something. The South won the prize of Missouri as an unrestricted slave state. The North won the concession that Congress could forbid slavery in the remaining territories. More gratifying to many Northerners was the fact that the immense area north of 36° 30′, except Missouri, was forever closed to the blight of slavery. Yet the restriction on future slavery in the territories was not unduly offensive to the slaveowners, partly because the northern prairie land did not seem adapted to slave labor. Even so, a majority of Southern congressmen voted against the compromise.

Neither North nor South was acutely displeased, although neither was completely happy. Fortunately, the Missouri Compromise lasted thirty-four years—a vital formative period in the life of the young Republic—and during that time it preserved the shaky compact of the states. Yet the embittered dispute over slavery heralded the future breakup of the Union. Ever after, the morality of the South's "peculiar institution" was an issue that could not be swept under the rug. The Missouri Compromise only ducked the question—it did not resolve it. Sooner or later, Thomas Jefferson predicted, it will "burst on us as a tornado."

The Missouri dispute proved to be another serious setback to nationalism, and a tremendous stimulus to sectionalism—in the North, South, and West. From this time forward the embattled South began to develop a nationalism of its own—a kind of sectional nationalism. Needing sectional reinforcements, it cast flirtatious eyes upon the adolescent West, which in turn was seeking allies.

Hotheads in both the North and South, numbering only a tiny minority, clamored for secession or a shooting showdown in 1820. But fortunately for the Union, hostilities were postponed. With every passing decade the North was becoming stronger in population, wealth, industry, and transportation—all of which added up to military strength.

Admittedly, the Missouri solution was a compromise—a partial surrender on both sides. Subsequent generations have tended to sneer at Henry Clay and the other architects of the settlement as weak men—"appeasers." Yet the fact should not be overlooked that compromise and statesmanship are often Siamese twins. In a free and peaceful association of once-sovereign states, no group of them could lord it over the others—that is, if they were all going to live together under the same roof. Without compromise there could have been no Constitution in 1787. Compromise made the Union in 1789; compromise saved the Union until 1860. When compromise broke down, the Union broke up.

The Missouri Compromise and the concurrent Panic of 1819 should have dimmed the political star of President Monroe. Certainly both unhappy events had a dampening effect on the Era of Good Feelings. But smooth-spoken James Monroe was so popular, and the Federalist opposition so weak, that in the presidential election of 1820 he received every electoral vote except one. Unanimity was an honor reserved for George Washington. Monroe, as it turned out, was the only President in American history to be re-elected after a term in which a major financial panic began.

John Marshall and Judicial Nationalism

Upsurging nationalism of the post-Ghent years, despite setbacks, was further reflected and strengthened by the Supreme Court.

The august tribunal was dominated by the tall, thin, and aggressive Chief Justice John Marshall, a "deathbed" Federalist appointee of John Adams' expiring administration. He had served at Valley Forge during the Revolution, and while suffering from cold and hunger had been painfully impressed with the drawbacks of feeble central authority. Before Marshall mounted the Supreme Bench in 1801, the judiciary had been the weakest and most timid of the three arms of the federal government. But he boldly asserted the doctrine of judicial review of congressional legislation in the case of *Marbury* v. *Madison* (1803).* And long before the end of his thirty-four years of service, he had made the judiciary, in some respects, the strongest branch of the national government.

Marshall, whose formal legal schooling had lasted only six weeks, was a judicial statesman rather than a strictly impartial judge. He examined a case through the colored lenses of his Federalist philosophy, and undertook to find legal precedents to support his Hamiltonian preconceptions. Sure of his ground, he wrote some of his most important decisions even before the lawyers had concluded their arguments.

In the vain hope of offsetting Marshall's Federalism, President Jefferson and his successors appointed Republicans to the Supreme Court. But

*See p. 170.

John Marshall (1755–1835). Born in a log cabin on the Virginia frontier, he attended law lectures for only a few months at the college of William and Mary—his only formal education. (National Portrait Gallery, Smithsonian Institution, Washington, D.C.)

by this time many Republicans had come to accept the Federalist ideal of a strong central government, and the masterful Marshall found it easy to lead his colleagues the rest of the way. The Jeffersonians raged, while Jefferson himself privately condemned the "twistifications" of his cousin, "the crafty chief judge." But Marshall pushed ahead inflexibly on his Federalist course, though bending slightly in his final years before the rising popular demands for a more democratic control of government.

For over three decades, the ghost of Alexander Hamilton spoke through the lanky, black-robed judge. As a shaper of the Constitution in the direction of a more potent central government, Marshall ranks as the foremost of the Molding Fathers. As a wealthy businessman and land speculator, he instinctively shared Hamilton's preference for the propertied class. As a Virginia aristocrat, he deplored democratic excesses, and opposed manhood suffrage and the rule of the unwashed masses.

The Supreme Court Curbs States' Rights

One group of Marshall's decisions—perhaps the most famous—resulted in bolstering the power of the federal government at the expense of the states. A notable case in this category was *McCulloch* v. *Maryland* (1819). The suit involved an attempt by the state of Maryland to destroy a branch of the Bank of the United States by imposing a tax on its notes. John Marshall, speaking for the Court, declared the Bank constitutional by invoking the Hamiltonian doctrine of implied powers (see p. 146). At the same time, he strengthened federal authority and slapped at state infringements when he denied the right of Maryland to tax the Bank. With ringing emphasis, he affirmed "that the power to tax involves the power to destroy," and "that a power to create implies a power to preserve."

In 1819, he gave the doctrine of "loose construction" its most famous formulation. The Constitution, he said, derived from the consent of the people and thus permitted the government to act for their benefit. He further argued that the Constitution was "intended to endure for ages to come and, consequently, to be adapted to the various crises of human affairs." Finally, he declared: "Let the end be legitimate, let it be within the scope of the Constitution, and all means which are appropriate, which are plainly adapted to that end, which are not prohibited, but consist with the letter and spirit of the Constitution, are constitutional."

Two years later (1821) the case of *Cohens* v. *Virginia* gave Marshall one of his greatest opportunities. The Cohens, found guilty by the Virginia courts of illegally selling lottery tickets, appealed to the highest tribunal. Virginia won, in that the conviction of the Cohens was upheld. But she lost, in that Marshall resoundingly asserted the right of the Supreme Court to review the decisions of the state supreme courts in all questions involving powers of the federal government. The states'-rights people were aghast.

Hardly less significant in Marshall's career was the celebrated "steamboat case," *Gibbons* v. *Ogden* (1824). The suit grew out of an attempt by the state of New York to grant to a private concern a monopoly of waterborne commerce between New York and New Jersey. Marshall sternly reminded the upstart state that the Constitution conferred on Congress alone the control of interstate commerce (see Art. I, Sec. VIII, para. 3). He thus struck another blow at states' rights, while upholding the sovereign powers of the federal government. Interstate streams were thus cleared of this judicial snag, while the departed spirit of Hamilton may have applauded.

Judicial Dikes Against Democratic Excesses

Another sheaf of Marshall's decisions bolstered judicial barriers against democratic or demagogic attacks on property rights.

The notorious case of *Fletcher* v. *Peck* (1810) arose when a Georgia legislature, swayed by bribery, granted 35 million acres in the Yazoo River country (Mississippi) to private speculators. The next legislature, yielding to an angry public outcry,

Daniel Webster (1782–1852). Premier orator and statesman, he served many years in both Houses of Congress, and also as secretary of state. Often regarded as presidential timber, he was somewhat handicapped by an overfondness for good food and drink, and was often in financial difficulties. His devotion to the Union was inflexible. "One country, one constitution, and one destiny," he declaimed in 1837. (The Metropolitan Museum of Art, Gift of I. N. Phelps Stokes, Edward S. Hawes, Alice Mary Hawes, Marion Augusta Hawes, 1937)

canceled the crooked transaction. But the Supreme Court, with Marshall presiding, decreed that the legislative grant was a contract (even though fraudulently secured), and that the Constitution forbids state laws "impairing" contracts (Art. I, Sec. X, para. 1). The decision is perhaps most noteworthy as further protecting property rights against popular pressures. It is also one of the earliest clear assertions of the right of the Court to invalidate state laws conflicting with the federal Constitution.

A similar principle was upheld in the case of *Dartmouth College* v. *Woodward* (1819), perhaps the best-remembered of Marshall's decisions. The college had been granted a charter by King George III in 1769, but the democratic New Hampshire state legislature had seen fit to change it. Dartmouth appealed the case, employing as counsel its most distinguished alumnus, Daniel Webster ('01). The "Godlike Daniel" reportedly pulled out all the stops of his tear-inducing eloquence when he declaimed, "It is, sir, as I have said, a small college. And yet there are those who love it."

Marshall needed no dramatics in the Dartmouth case. He put the states firmly in their place when he ruled that the original charter must stand. It was a contract—and the Constitution protected contracts against state encroachments. The Dartmouth decision had the fortunate effect of safeguarding business enterprise from domination by the states. But it had the unfortunate effect of creating a precedent which enabled chartered corporations, in later years, to escape the handcuffs of needed public control.

If John Marshall was a Molding Father of the Constitution, Daniel Webster was an Expounding Father. Time and again he left his seat in the Senate, stepped downstairs, and there expounded his federalistic and nationalistic philosophy before the Supreme Bench. The eminent chief justice, so Webster reported, approvingly drank in the familiar arguments as a baby sucks in its mother's milk. The two men dovetailed with each other. Webster's classic speeches in the Senate, challenging states' rights and nullification, were largely repetitions of the arguments that he had earlier presented before a sympathetic Supreme Court.

During Marshall's judicial reign, manhood suffrage was flowering and America was veering toward stronger popular control. The chief justice stoutly held the judicial dike against these upwashing democratic waves. Almost singlehandedly, he shaped the Constitution along conservative, centralizing lines that ran somewhat counter to the new spirit of the century.

Marshall's decisions are felt even today. In this sense his nationalism was the most tenaciously enduring of the era. Even after the masses had won control under President Andrew Jackson, they could not successfully assault the highest towers of the judicial fortress. While buttressing the federal union and nascent nationalism, Marshall checked the excesses of popularly elected state legislatures, and thus stabilized business.

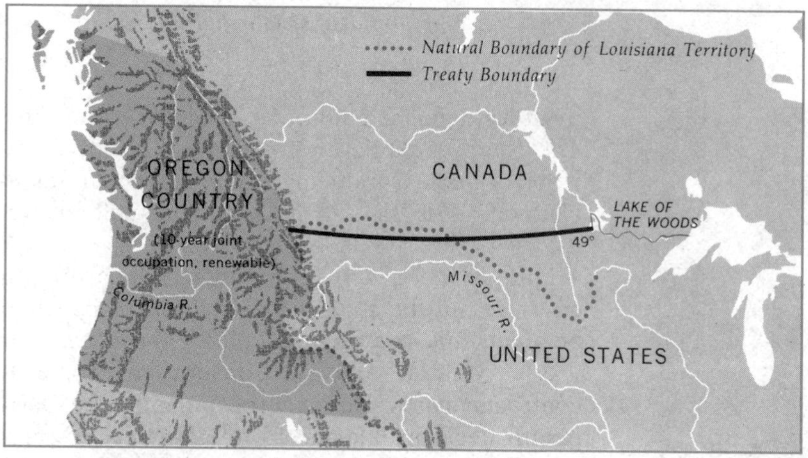

U.S.–BRITISH BOUNDARY SETTLEMENT, 1818
Note that the United States gained considerable territory by securing a treaty boundary rather than the natural boundary of the Missouri River watershed. The line of 49° was extended westward to the Pacific Ocean under the Treaty of 1846 with Britain (see p. 266).

Through him the conservative Hamiltonians triumphed from the tomb.

British Agreements and Spanish Friction

The yeasty nationalism of the years after the War of 1812 was likewise reflected in the shaping of foreign policy. To this end, the nationalistic President Monroe teamed with his nationalistic secretary of state, John Quincy Adams, the cold and scholarly son of the frosty and bookish ex-President. The younger Adams, a statesman of the first rank, happily rose above the ingrown Federalist sectionalism of his native New England and proved to be one of the great secretaries of state.

To its credit, the Monroe administration succeeded in negotiating with England the much underrated Treaty of 1818. This multi-sided agreement disposed of some of the unfinished business swept under the peace table at Ghent. For one thing, the Newfoundland fisheries quarrel had continued to bob up, and the new pact achieved a temporary settlement. The Americans were permitted to share again coveted fishing privileges with their Canadian cousins—privileges granted in 1783, and presumably ended by the War of 1812. In addition, the treaty makers agreed to define the vague northern limits of Louisiana, which henceforth would run along the 49th parallel to the Rocky ("Stony") Mountains.

The British-American negotiators of 1818 also discussed the possibility of running the same dividing line on to the Pacific. But agreement proved impossible. The Treaty of 1818 consequently provided for a ten-year joint occupation of the untamed Oregon Country, without surrender of the rights or claims of either America or Britain. With time on the side of an awesomely growing United States, the postponement of a decision foreshadowed a final settlement favorable to American demands.

To the south lay semi-tropical Spanish Florida, thrust like a giant thumb into the Gulf of Mexico. This coveted peninsula, many believed, occupied a part of the map which geography and Providence had destined for the United States. Already

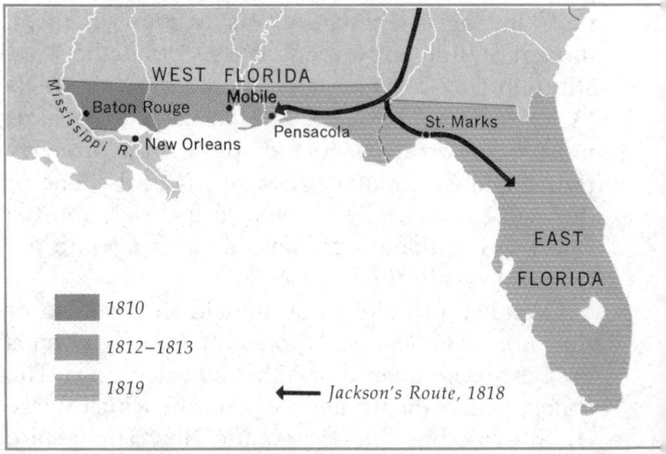

ACQUIRING THE FLORIDAS, 1810–1819

Americans had nibbled at West Florida, a region claimed by the federal government, rather flimsily, under the blanket of the Louisiana Purchase. Uninvited American settlers had moved into the area, and in 1810 rose to overthrow the hated Spanish flag. Congress formally ratified this grab in 1812 and added an even larger chunk to the east. During the War of 1812 with Britain (Spain's ally), a small American army seized the Mobile region, which the United States had already embraced (on paper). But the bulk of Florida remained, tauntingly, under Spain's flag.

When an epidemic of revolutions broke out in South America, Spain was forced to denude Florida of troops to fight the rebels. A chaotic situation rapidly developed in the swampy peninsula. Bands of Indians, runaway slaves, and white outcasts poured across the border into American territory, burning and scalping, and then fled to safety behind the surveyor's line.

General Andrew Jackson, idol of the West and scourge of the Indians, reappeared in 1817. The Monroe administration formally commissioned him to punish the Indians and, if necessary, to pursue them into Florida. But he was to respect all posts under the Spanish flag.

Early in 1818 Jackson swept across the Florida border with all the fury of an avenging angel. He hanged two Indian chiefs without ceremony and, after hasty military trials, executed two British subjects for assisting the Indians. He also seized the two most important Spanish posts in the area, St. Marks and then Pensacola, where he deposed the Spanish governor, who was lucky enough to escape Jackson's jerking noose.

Warrior Andrew Jackson, 1814. A self-taught and popularly elected major-general of the militia, Andrew Jackson became a major-general of the U.S. army in 1814. He was noted for his stern discipline, iron will ("Old Hickory"), and good luck.

Acquiring Florida from Spain

Jackson had clearly exceeded his instructions from Washington, unclear though they may have been. By dishonoring the Spanish flag, he had been guilty of a hostile act. By putting to death two British subjects who had a better right than he to be in Florida, he had caused a vengeful outcry for war to rise from British hotheads. With difficulty a sane London government quieted the jingoes.

President Monroe in alarm consulted his Cabinet. Its members were for disavowing or disciplining the overzealous Jackson—all except the lone wolf John Quincy Adams, who refused to howl with the pack. An ardent patriot and nationalist, the flinty New Englander finally won the others over to his point of view. Far from apologizing, he took the offensive and emphatically informed Spain that she had violated the Spanish-American Treaty of 1795 by not suppressing the outlaws of Florida. He then insisted that the alternatives were for the Spaniards to control the area (a task which they admitted was impossible) or cede it to the

United States (a course which was galling to their pride).

Again Spain's distresses, both at home and in her rebellious Latin American colonies, operated to America's advantage. The Spaniards perceived that they were going to lose Florida anyhow. They wisely decided to dispose of the alligator-infested area while they could get something for it, rather than lose it after a humiliating and costly war.

The Florida Purchase Treaty of 1819, so called, was mislabeled. It involved much more than Florida. The western boundary of the Louisiana territory, hitherto vague, was made to zigzag along the Rockies to the 42nd parallel. The line then turned due west to the Pacific, to divide Oregon from Spanish holdings. Texas, although claimed by the United States under the elastic blanket of the Louisiana Purchase, was excluded from American jurisdiction. The vast plains of Texas were more important to Spain than was fast-slipping Florida; Florida was more immediately important to the United States. Texas could come later—and did.

In 1819 Spain, in effect, ceded Florida and her shadowy rights to Oregon in exchange for America's dubious pretensions to Texas. The United States also agreed to assume claims for damages to the extent of $5 million—seemingly uncollectible claims which American citizens had filed against the Spanish government. Spain lost Florida, but saved face.

When the Spanish-American pact of 1819 was signed, it seemed like a fair bargain, even though Western-minded American patriots decried the so-called surrender of Texas. By one stroke of the pen, the United States ended protracted friction with Spain, rounded out its continental domain, and gave another boost to swelling national pride.

The Menace of Monarchy in America

After the Napoleonic nightmare, the rethroned autocrats of Europe banded together in a kind of monarchical protective association. Determined to restore the good old days, they undertook to stamp out the democratic tendencies that had sprouted from soil richly manured by the ideals of the French Revolution. The world must be made safe *from* democracy.

The crowned despots acted promptly. With complete ruthlessness, they smothered the embers of rebellion in Italy (1821) and in Spain (1823). According to the European rumor-factory, they were also gazing across the Atlantic. Russia, Austria, Prussia, and France, acting in partnership, would presumably send powerful fleets and armies to the revolted colonies of Spanish America, and there restore the autocratic Spanish King to his ancestral domains.

> The successful invasion of Spain, so Secretary of State Adams recorded in his diary, caused panic in official Washington: "I find him [President Monroe] . . . alarmed, far beyond anything that I could have conceived possible, with the fear that the Holy Alliance [of European powers] are about to restore immediately all South America to Spain."

Many Americans were alarmed. Sympathetic to democratic revolutions everywhere, they had cheered when the Latin American republics rose from the ruins of monarchy. Americans feared that if the European powers intervened in the New World, the cause of republicanism would suffer irreparable harm. The physical security of the United States—the Mother Lode of democracy—would be endangered by the proximity of powerful and unfriendly forces.

The southward push of the Russian Bear, from the chill region now known as Alaska, had already publicized the menace of monarchy to North America. In 1821 the Czar of Russia issued a decree extending Russian jurisdiction over 100 miles (161 kilometers) of the open sea down to the line of 51°, an area which embraced most of the

THE WEST AND NORTHWEST, 1819–1824

The British Hudson's Bay Company moved to secure its claim to the Oregon country in 1824, when it sent a heavily armed expedition led by Peter Skene Ogden into the Snake River country. In May, 1825, Ogden's party descended the Bear River, "and found it discharged into a large Lake of 100 miles in length"—the first documented sighting by white men of Great Salt Lake.

coast of present-day British Columbia. The energetic Russians had already established trading posts almost as far south as the entrance to San Francisco Bay, and the fear prevailed in the United States that they were planning to cut the Republic off from California, its prospective window on the Pacific.

Great Britain, still Mistress of the Seas, was now beginning to play a lone-hand role on the complicated international stage. In particular, she recoiled from joining hands with the Continental European powers in crushing the newly won liberties of the Spanish-Americans. These revolutionists had thrown open their monopoly-bound ports to outside trade, and British shippers, as well as Americans, had found the profits sweet.

Accordingly, in August 1823, George Canning, the haughty British foreign secretary, approached the American minister in London with a startling proposition. Would not the United States join with Britain in a joint declaration, specifically warning the European despots to keep their harsh hands off the Latin American republics? The American minister, lacking instructions, referred this fateful scheme to his superiors in Washington.

Mr. Monroe and His Doctrine

Reactions in America to the Canning proposal varied. The intimate advisers of President Monroe, including the aged Jefferson and Madison, recommended that the Republic lock arms with the hitherto distrusted Mother Country. The one notable exception was again the lone-wolf nationalist, Secretary Adams, who was hardheaded enough to beware of Britons bearing gifts. Why should the lordly British, with the mightiest navy afloat, need America as an ally—an America which had neither naval nor military strength? Such a union, argued Adams, was undignified—like a tiny American "cockboat" sailing "in the wake of the British man-of-war."

Adams, ever alert, thought that he detected the joker in the Canning proposal. The British feared that the aggressive Yankee would one day seize Spanish territory in the Americas—perhaps Cuba—

which would jeopardize England's possessions in the Caribbean. If Canning could seduce the United States into joining with him in support of the territorial integrity of the New World, America's own hands would be morally tied.

A self-denying alliance with Britain would not only hamper American expansion, concluded Adams, but it was unnecessary. He had good reason to suspect that the European powers had not agreed upon any definite plans for invading the Americas. In any event, the British navy would not permit hostile fleets to come, because the South American markets had to be kept open at all costs for English merchants. It was presumably safe for Uncle Sam, behind the protective wooden petticoats of the British navy, to blow a defiant, nationalistic blast at all Europe. The distresses of the Old World again set the stage for another American diplomatic coup.

The Monroe Doctrine was born late in 1823, when the nationalistic Adams won the nationalistic Monroe over to his way of thinking. The President, in his regular annual message to Congress of December 2, 1823, incorporated a stern warning to the European powers. Its two basic features were (1) non-colonization and (2) non-intervention.

Monroe first directed his verbal blast primarily at the lumbering Russian Bear in the Northwest. With emphatic tones he proclaimed, in effect, that the era of colonization in the Americas had ended, and that henceforth there would be a permanently closed season. What the great powers had they might keep, but neither they nor any other Old World powers could seize or otherwise acquire more. This lofty declaration was later resented by those nations, notably Germany and Italy, that were not unified and hence unable to take out colonial hunting licenses until late in the century.

At the same time Monroe sounded a trumpet blast against foreign intervention. He was clearly concerned with regions to the south, where fears were felt for the newly fledged Spanish-American republics. He bluntly warned the crowned heads of Europe to keep their hated monarchical systems out of this hemisphere. For its part, the United States would not intervene in the war that the Greeks were then fighting against the Turks for their independence.

Czar Alexander I. The Russian leader of European monarchs, he was an inspirer of the Monroe Doctrine.

Monroe's Dictum Abroad

Monroe's ringing declaration quickened the patriotic pulse of nationalistic young America. The American people were thrilled, even though they had no effective army or navy, to shake their collective fists at all the European despots and loudly warn them to stay away. While gratifying national pride and striking a blow for democratic rule, Monroe was also striking a blow for the "Almighty Dollar," as represented by the freshly opened Latin American markets.

Reactions in England were mixed. The British press, likewise savoring the juicy Latin American markets, was generally favorable to Monroe's forceful warning. But Canning was irked, for he perceived that the Monroe Doctrine was aimed at possible land-grabbing by Britain, as well as by Europe. "Hands off" applied to all outside powers, including proud Britain.

The ermined monarchs of Europe were angered. Having resented the incendiary American experiment from the beginning, they were now deeply offended by Monroe's high-flown pronouncement—all the more so because of the gulf between America's loud pretensions and her weak military strength. But though offended by the upstart

> Prince Metternich, the Austrian chancellor, wrote bitterly of the "dangerous" new manifesto with its "unprovoked attacks . . . indecent declarations . . . evil doctrines and pernicious examples."

Yankee, the European powers found their hands tied, and their frustration increased their annoyance. Even if they had worked out plans for invading the Americas, they would have been helpless before the booming broadsides of the British navy.

Monroe's solemn warning, when issued, made little splash in the newly hatched republics to the south. Anyone could see that Uncle Sam was only secondarily concerned about his neighbors, because he was primarily concerned about defending himself against future invasion. Only a relatively few upper-class Latin Americans knew of the message, and they generally recognized that the British navy—not the paper pronouncement of James Monroe—stood between them and a hostile Europe.

In truth, Monroe's message actually did not have much contemporary significance. Americans applauded it, and then forgot it as they turned back to such activities as felling trees and Indians. Not until 1845 did President Polk revive it, and not until mid-century did it become an important national dogma.

Ruins of One of the Bastions at Russia's Fort Ross (c. 1890). Established just north of San Francisco Bay in 1811 without Spain's permission, this trading post seemed to be evidence of Russia's imperialistic ambitions on America's future Pacific Coast.

The new doctrine was not even necessary, in a narrow sense, when given to the world. Secretary Adams, in firm diplomatic notes, had already warned Russia against trespassing on the Northwest Coast. Even before Monroe's stiff message, the Czar had decided to retreat. This he formally did in the Russo-American Treaty of 1824, which fixed his southernmost limits at the line of 54° 40′—the present southern tip of the Alaska panhandle.

Danger of an invasion of Latin America by the European powers was not imminent in 1823. But this does not mean that the monarchs, if unhampered, could not have drawn up a blueprint for conquest. Aside from the British navy, they were dissuaded from making incursions in later years by other attractions and deterrents. Among attractions were the richer and easier pickings of Asia and Africa; among deterrents was the growing strength of the United States and its neighbors.

Monroe's Self-Defense Doctrine in Retrospect

The Monroe Doctrine might more accurately have been called the Self-Defense Doctrine. President Monroe was concerned basically with the security of his own country—not of Latin America. The United States has never willingly permitted a powerful foreign nation to secure a foothold near its strategic Caribbean vitals. Yet in the absence of the British navy or other allies, the strength of the Monroe Doctrine has never been greater than America's power to eject the trespasser. The doctrine, as often noted, was just as big as the nation's armed forces—and no bigger. But attaching Monroe's name to the Self-Defense Doctrine has given it the prestige that comes from a distinguished personage.

Monroe and Adams must share about equally the credit for the authorship of the so-called Monroe Doctrine. But its basic principles, in one form or another, had been set forth earlier by Washington, Jefferson, Hamilton, and others. Monroe and Adams merely collected and codified existing ideas, giving them a new emphasis and slant.

The Monroe Doctrine has had a long career of ups and downs. It was never law—domestic or international. It was not, technically speaking, a pledge or an agreement. It was merely a simple, personalized statement of the policy of President Monroe. What one President says, another may unsay. And Monroe's successors have ignored, revived, distorted, or expanded the original version, chiefly by adding interpretations. Like ivy on a tree, it has grown with America's growth.

But the Monroe Doctrine in 1823 was largely an expression of the post-1812 nationalism energizing the United States. Although directed at a specific menace in 1823, and hence a kind of period piece, the doctrine proved to be the most famous of all the long-lived offspring of that nationalism. While giving vent to a spirit of patriotism, it simultaneously deepened the illusion of isolationism. Many Americans falsely concluded, then and later, that the Republic was in fact isolated from European dangers simply because it wanted to be, and because, in a nationalistic outburst, Monroe had publicly warned the Old World powers to stay away.

VARYING VIEWPOINTS

The Era of Good Feelings, not surprisingly, has generated little ill feeling among historians. They generally agree in seeing the period not in terms of conflict, but of consolidation. There were then few irreconcilable controversies, but rather a remarkable consensus on laying the new nation's institutional base. In effect, the era set up a political program for the future; defined the power of the Supreme Court and its relation to the other branches of government; stabilized national boundaries; established basic elements of foreign policy in the Monroe Doctrine; and drew up the battle lines on the explosive issues of the tariff and, especially, slavery.

SELECT READINGS

An excellent introduction is George Dangerfield, *The Awakening of American Nationalism, 1815–1828* (1965), which supplements his *The Era of Good Feelings* (1952). Consult also M. N. Rothbard, *The Panic of 1819* (1962); Glover Moore, *The Missouri Controversy, 1819–1821* (1953); E. S. Corwin, *John Marshall and the Constitution* (1919); and A. J. Beveridge, *The Life of John Marshall* (4 vols., 1916–1919). P. Miller, *The Life of the Mind in America* (1965), contains suggestive insights on legal thought and the role of the legal profession in the Marshall era. This and other topics are astutely placed in context by Lawrence Friedman, *A History of American Law* (1973). On the Monroe Doctrine the best single volume is Dexter Perkins, *A History of the Monroe Doctrine* (new ed., 1955). More recently, E. R. May has somewhat unconvincingly tied the doctrine to domestic politics, especially the impending election of 1824, in *The Making of the Monroe Doctrine* (1975). Related to the doctrine is J. A. Logan, Jr., *No Transfer: An American Security Principle* (1961). See also Harry Ammon, *James Monroe: The Quest for National Identity* (1971). On Calhoun consult M. L. Coit, *John C. Calhoun* (1950), and C. M. Wiltse's more detailed *John C. Calhoun, Nationalist, 1782–1828* (1944). See also G. M. Capers, *John C. Calhoun, Opportunist* (1960); R. N. Current, *John C. Calhoun* (1963); and S. F. Bemis, *John Quincy Adams and the Foundations of American Foreign Policy* (1949).

13

The Rise of Jacksonian Democracy

The most disagreeable duty I have to perform is the removals, and appointments to office. . . . You will see from the public journals we have begun reform, and that we are trying to cleans[e] *the Augean stables, and expose to view the corruption of some of the agents of the late administration.*

ANDREW JACKSON, 1829

The Spread of Manhood Suffrage

Democracy was something of a taint in the days of the Federalist aristocrats. Martha Washington (Mrs. George Washington), after a presidential reception, was shocked to find a greasy smear on the wallpaper, left there, she was sure, by an uninvited "filthy democrat."

But by the 1820s and 1830s, if not before, aristocracy was becoming a taint, and democracy was becoming respectable. Lucky indeed was the aspiring politician who could boast of birth in a log cabin. In 1840 Daniel Webster publicly apologized for not being able to claim so lowly a birthplace, though quickly adding that his brothers could.

The New Democracy, so called, was based on manhood suffrage rather than on the old property qualifications. Snobbish bigwigs, unhappy over the change, referred sneeringly to "coonskin congressmen" and to the enfranchised "bipeds of the forest." To them, the tyranny of King Numbers was no less offensive than that of King George.

The frontier state of Vermont, admitted in 1791, was the first to place the ballot in the hands of all adult white males. This trend continued, notably in the West, where land was so easily obtained as to render almost meaningless the old property qualifications. Property tests for office holding were also widely abolished, and even judges were now being popularly elected. The South trailed other regions in giving up property requirements.

Government *by* the masses—instead of government *of* the masses *by* the upper classes—was finally introduced at the national level in the days of Andrew Jackson. The common man was at last coming into his own: the sturdy American who donned plain trousers rather than silver-buckled knee breeches, who besported a plain haircut and a coonskin cap rather than an ornate wig, and who wore no man's collar, often not even one of his own. Instead of the old divine right of kings, America was now witnessing the divine right of the people.

David Crockett (1786–1836). A semi-literate Tennesseean, he failed at farming but won distinction as a rifleman, soldier, scout, humorist, and three-time congressman. Rejected in politics, he left Tennessee to fight for Texas against the Mexicans and fell, bullet riddled, in the final assault on the Alamo.

The Reign of King Numbers

Debasement of the political tone was one nasty by-product of the New Democracy, commonly called Jacksonian democracy. A statesman was unable to elevate the unlettered masses to his own intellectual level. Rather, the masses dragged the politician down to the level of their own emotions and prejudices. Mudslinging frequently proved more effective than a sober discussion of issues. Candidates for office also made increasing use of banners, badges, parades, barbecues, free drinks, and baby-kissing. Yet competition for public favor did have the virtue of "bringing out the vote."

Successful politicians were now forced to unbend and curry favor with the voting masses. Fatally handicapped was the candidate who appeared to be too clean, too well-dressed, too grammatical, too high-browishly intellectual, too conspicuously fit. The Western belief was spreading that a man was well qualified for high office if he was a superior militia commander or a victorious Indian fighter, like Andrew Jackson, or even an outstanding hunter. The semi-literate Davy Crockett was elected to the legislature of Tennessee, mainly on the basis of his prowess with the rifle. Later he killed 105 bears in a single season, and his constituents began to talk of running him for the presidency.

With the emergence of "nose-counting" democracy, the masses were demanding and securing a fuller measure of popular control. Jeffersonian democracy had proclaimed that the people should be governed as little as possible; Jacksonian democracy argued that the people might govern as much as they liked. Members of the Electoral College, to an increasing degree, were being chosen directly by the people, rather than by state legislatures. Presidential nominations by a congressional caucus, meeting secretly, were no longer in good odor. This procedure was now regarded as furtive, aristocratic, and subversive of good government. The delicate checks and balances among the three federal branches were weakened when the President was indirectly indebted to Congress for his exalted office.

New and more democratic methods of nominating presidential candidates would have to be found. In 1824 the voters, crying "The People Must Be Heard" and "Down with King Caucus," turned against the candidate (Crawford) who had been selected by the congressional clique. For a brief period nominations were made by some of the state legislatures. But these did not seem democratic either, and in 1831 the first of the circuslike national nominating conventions was held. Here the people appeared to exercise a higher degree of direct control, though their will was often thwarted by paunchy bosses in smoke-filled rooms.

Yet manhood suffrage, on balance, conferred incalculable benefits. It enhanced the dignity of the common man; and his greater personal responsibility led to a greater flowering of his talents. The national spirit was further unshackled for marvelous achievements. If the masses made mistakes, they made them themselves and were not the victims of aristocratic domination. If at times they stumbled, they stumbled forward.

The Adams-Clay "Corrupt" Bargaining

The woods were full of presidential timber in 1824. Four candidates towered above the others: Andrew Jackson of Tennessee, the tall, silver-maned, and hollow-cheeked "Old Hero" of New Orleans; Henry Clay of Kentucky, the gamey and gallant "Harry of the West"; William H. Crawford of Georgia, a giant of a man, able though ailing; and John Quincy Adams of Massachusetts, highly intelligent, experienced, and aloof.

All four rivals had much in common. They were all outstanding figures; they were all regarded as strong nationalists; and they were all presumed to have similar views on such active issues as the tariff and internal improvements. A colorful note was injected when "Hickory Boys" whooped it up for "Old Hickory" Jackson.

Election of 1824

Candidates	*Electoral Vote*	*Popular Vote*	*Popular Percentage*
Jackson	99	153,544	42.16%
Adams	84	108,740	31.89
Crawford	41	46,618	12.95
Clay	37	47,136	12.99

The results of the noisy campaign were interesting but confusing. Jackson, the war hero, clearly had the strongest personal appeal, especially in the West. He polled almost as many popular votes as his next two rivals combined, but he failed to win a majority of the electoral vote. In such a deadlock the House of Representatives, as directed by the 12th Amendment (see Appendix), must choose among the top three candidates. Clay was thus eliminated, yet he still presided over the very chamber that had to pick the winner. Since he enjoyed all the influence of a popular speaker of the House, he was in a position to throw the election to the candidate of his choice.

Clay reached his fateful decision by a process of elimination. Crawford, recently felled by a paralytic stroke, was out of the picture. Clay hated the "military chieftain" Jackson, who in turn bitterly resented Clay's public denunciation of his Florida foray in 1818. The only candidate left was the puritanical Adams, with whom Clay—a free-living gambler and duelist—had never established cordial personal relations. But the two men had much in common politically: both were fervid nationalists and advocates of the American System. Shortly before the final balloting in the House, Clay met privately with Adams and assured him of his support.

Decision day came early in 1825. The House of Representatives met amid tense excitement, with sick members being carried in on stretchers. On the first ballot, thanks largely to Clay's behind-the-scenes influence, Adams was elected President. A few days later, the victor announced that Henry Clay would be the new secretary of state.

The secretaryship of state was then the prize plum, even more so than today. Three of the four preceding secretaries had reached the presidency, and the high Cabinet office was regarded as an almost certain runway to the White House. By allegedly dangling the secretaryship as a bribe before Clay, Adams, the second choice of the people, apparently defeated the first choice of the people, Andrew Jackson.

Masses of angered Jacksonians, most of them common folk, raised a roar of protest against the "Corrupt Bargain." The clamor continued for nearly four years. Jackson condemned Clay as the "Judas of the West," and John Randolph of Virginia publicly assailed the alliance between "the Puritan [Adams] and the black-leg [Clay]." Randolph also said of Clay, "He shines and stinks like rotten mackerel by moonlight." Clay, outraged, challenged Randolph to a duel, the bloodless outcome of which proved nothing, except perhaps shaky nerves and poor marksmanship.

No positive evidence has yet been unearthed to prove that Adams and Clay entered into a formal bargain, corrupt or otherwise. But appearances were so damning as to render denials unconvincing. Even if a bargain had been struck, it was not necessarily corrupt, for "deals" of a similar nature are the stock-in-trade of politicians. But this "bargain" differed from others in its apparent flouting of the popular will by both Adams and Clay. Both men erred, the one by offering the post in circumstances sure to arouse suspicion, the other by accepting it. The best that can be said of them is that neither avoided the appearance of evil.

Suspicions of a "Corrupt Bargain" have been strengthened by entries in Adams' diary. On January 1, 1825, after a public dinner, we find: "He [Clay] told me [in a whisper] that he should be glad to have with me soon some confidential conversation upon public affairs. I said I should be happy to have it whenever it might suit his convenience." The diary entry for January 9 reads in part: "Mr. Clay came at six, and spent the evening with me in a long conversation explanatory of the past and prospective of the future." Exactly a month later, with Clay's backing, Adams was elected.

A Puritan Misfit in the Presidential Chair

John Quincy Adams was a chip off the old family glacier. Short (5 feet 7 inches; 1.7 meters), thickset, and billiard-bald, he was even more frigidly austere than his presidential father, John Adams. Shunning people, he often went for early morning swims, sometimes stark naked, in the then pure Potomac River. Essentially a closeted thinker rather than a politician, he was irritable, sarcastic, and tactless. Yet few men have ever come to the presidency with a more brilliant record in statecraft, especially in foreign affairs. He ranks as one of the most successful secretaries of state, yet one of the least successful Presidents.

A man of puritanical honor, Adams entered upon his four-year "sentence" in the White House smarting under charges of "bargain," "corruption," and "usurpation." Fewer than one-third of the voters had voted for him. As the first "minority President," he would have found it difficult to win popular support even under the most favorable conditions. Possessing almost none of the arts of the politician, he had achieved high office by commanding respect rather than by courting popularity. In an earlier era, an aloof John Adams could win the votes of propertied men by sheer ability. But with the raw New Democracy in the driver's seat, his cold-fish son could hardly hope for success at the polls.

Political spoilsmen annoyed Adams. Whether through high-mindedness or ineptitude, he re-

President John Quincy Adams (1767–1848). Adams wrote in his dairy, in June 1819, nearly six years before becoming President, "I am a man of reserved, cold, austere, and forbidding manners: my political adversaries say, a gloomy misanthropist, and my personal enemies, an unsocial savage."

solutely declined to oust efficient officeholders in order to create vacancies for political supporters. During his entire administration he removed only twelve public servants from the federal payroll. Such stubbornness caused countless Adams men to throw up their hands in despair. If the President would not reward party workers with political plums, why should they labor to keep him in office?

Adams' nationalistic views involved him in further woes. The old Jeffersonian Republican party was breaking into fragments, most of which tended to coalesce around a common hatred of the Adams-Clay partnership. The flinty President refused to recognize that the popular tide was turning away from the post-Ghent nationalism toward states' rights and sectionalism. Confirmed nationalist that he was, Adams urged upon Congress in his first annual message the construction of roads and canals. He renewed George Washington's proposal for a national university, and went so far as to advocate federal support for an astronomical observatory, similar to Europe's more than 130 "lighthouses of the skies."

The public reaction to some of these proposals was prompt and unfavorable. To many workaday Americans grubbing out stumps, astronomical observatories seemed like a scandalous waste of public funds. The South in particular bristled up. If the federal government should take on such heavy financial burdens, it would have to continue the hated tariff duties. If it could meddle in local concerns like education and roads, it might even try to lay its hand on the "peculiar institution" of black slavery.

Adams' land policy likewise antagonized the Westerners. They clamored for wide-open expansion, and were angered by the President's well-meaning attempts to curb feverish speculation in the public domain. The fate of the Cherokee Indians, who were about to be evicted from their holdings in Georgia, generated additional bitterness. Ruggedly honest Adams, in attempting to deal fairly with the friendless Indians, further offended the West in general and the state of Georgia in particular. The governor, who threatened a resort to arms, successfully resisted the efforts of the Washington government to interpose federal authority on behalf of the Indians. Another fateful chapter was thus written in the nullification of the national will.

Adams Fumbles Foreign Affairs

If Adams was inept politically, he was deft diplomatically, and in foreign affairs he was expected to shine. But he quickly ran afoul of his old British adversary, George Canning. The clever foreign secretary, still smarting from Secretary Adams' rebuff at the time of the Monroe Doctrine, apparently took delight in thwarting his antagonist at every turn.

Trade with the British West Indies continued to be a thorny issue. Ever since the United States had broken away from the empire in 1776, this rich traffic had been officially closed, or subjected

> The year after Secretary of State Adams stole a march on Foreign Secretary Canning by helping to frame the Monroe Doctrine, aimed in part at British influence in Latin America, the British government recognized the Spanish-American republics. Canning privately gloated, "The deed is done, the nail is driven, Spanish America is free; and if we do not mismanage our affairs badly, *she is English*." He was speaking, of course, of commercial ascendancy.

to annoying restrictions. When President Adams made a somewhat tactless attempt to induce the London government to reopen trade in 1826, Canning administered a stinging rebuff.

Another bitter cup was the Panama Congress of 1826. This assemblage of the American republics was summoned by Simón Bolívar, leading hero of the South American wars for independence. Its major purpose was to discuss common problems of defense and peaceful intercourse. Secretary Clay, a passionate pioneer of Pan-Americanism, eagerly accepted the invitation on behalf of the United States. President Adams thereupon appointed two delegates. But at the same time he unnecessarily and unwisely sought confirmation by the Senate, as well as expense money from Congress.

The ensuing debate in Congress was both windy and ill-tempered. Foes of Adams and Clay united to denounce the Panama scheme, while isolationists decried the dangers of foreign entrapments. The South, with an eye to its slave problem, was sensitive about sending delegates to a conference in which black South American representatives would be "putting on airs."

Adams finally won congressional approval, but his victory was little better than a defeat. One of the delegates died en route. The other reached Panama after the Congress, which had almost drowned in a sea of words, had adjourned without agreeing on anything of consequence. Hoots of derision were showered upon Adams' head. The tragedy is that the foes of the administration sacrificed a splendid opportunity to assume leadership of the Pan-American movement at the very outset.

The Tricky Tariff of Abominations

The tariff issue provided yet another headache for Adams. Congress had come to grips with the problem in 1824, under President Monroe, when it increased the protective tariff of 1816. Formerly the general level had been 20 to 25 percent on the value of dutiable goods; the change boosted the charge to new heights of about 37 percent. But the woolen manufacturers, dissatisfied with their share of protection, bleated for higher barriers still.

Rabid Jacksonites, seeking to unhorse Adams, seized this opportunity to play politics with the Tariff of 1828. They rigged up a bill that was seemingly more concerned with manufacturing a President than with protecting manufacturers. A part of their scheme was to push the duties as high as about 45 percent on the value of certain manufactured items. At the same time, they would impose a heavy tariff on certain raw materials, notably wool. These materials were so urgently needed for manufacturing, especially in New England, that even this industrial section would presumably vote against the entire measure. Adams, whose stronghold was New England, would thus be given another political black eye, and Jackson would receive a boost, especially in the Middle States. There many voters were politically uncertain but protection-prone.

But the New Englanders spoiled this clever little game. Though disliking the proposed duties, they were anxious to continue the principle of protection. As a consequence, enough of them choked down the dishonest Tariff of 1828, as amended, to force its passage. Daniel Webster, who had earlier fought the mild Tariff of 1816, and John C. Calhoun, who had sponsored it, had by this time completely reversed their positions. The future of New England clearly lay in the

House Vote on Tariff of 1828 ("Tariff of Abominations")
(COMPARE 1816 TARIFF, P. 204.)

Regions	*For*	*Against*
New England	16	23
Middle States	57	11
West (Ohio, Ind., Ill., Mo.)	17	1
South (incl. La.)	3	50
Southwest (Tenn., Ky.)	12	9
TOTAL	105	94

factory, rather than on the waves, while the destiny of the South lay in the cotton fields.

Southerners, as heavy consumers of manufactured goods, were shocked by what they regarded as the outrageous rates of the Tariff of 1828. Hotheads promptly branded it the "Black Tariff" or the "Tariff of Abominations." Several Southern states adopted formal protests; in South Carolina flags were lowered to half-mast. "Let the *New* England beware how she imitates the *Old*," cried one eloquent Carolinian who remembered 1776.

John C. Calhoun (1782–1850). Calhoun was a South Carolinian, partially educated at Yale. Beginning as a strong nationalist and Unionist, he reversed himself and became the ablest of the sectionalists and disunionists in defense of the South and slavery. As a foremost nullifier and secessionist, he died trying to reconcile strong states' rights with a strong Union. In his last years he advocated a Siamese-twin presidency, probably unworkable, with one President for the North and one for the South. His former plantation home is now the site of Clemson University. (National Archives.)

Why did the South, especially South Carolina, react so angrily against the tariff? The Old South—the seaboard area first settled—was the least flourishing of all the sections. The bustling Northeast was experiencing a boom in manufacturing; the developing West was prospering from rising property values and a multiplying population; and the energetic Southwest was expanding into virgin cotton lands. Overcropped acres of the Old South were petering out, and the price of cotton was falling sharply. John Randolph of Virginia grimly quipped that masters would soon cease to advertise for their fugitive slaves, and slaves would advertise for their fugitive masters. So the Old South was seeking a scapegoat, and the tariff proved to be a convenient and plausible one.

The Tariff Yoke in the South

Southerners believed, not illogically, that the "Yankee tariff" discriminated against them. They sold their cotton and other farm produce in a world market completely unprotected by tariffs, and were forced to buy their manufactured goods in an American market heavily protected by tariffs.

The plight of the South may be illustrated by a hypothetical case. Let us suppose that in 1828 an English manufacturer could sell his shoes in South Carolina at $1.25 a pair, whereas a Massachusetts factory would have to charge $1.50 for a pair of equal quality. South Carolinians would naturally buy the British footwear. But if a tariff of fifty cents a pair were levied on foreign shoes at the Charleston customs house, the British shoes would cost $1.75 a pair. Southerners, if economy-minded, would be forced to buy the Yankee product at $1.50. They would thus be taxed twenty-five cents

Tariff Inequalities, North and South. The protective tariff under which the North grows fat and prosperous brings economic hardship to the South. (*United States Weekly Telegram*, 1832.)

on each purchase to support Northern factories.

Towering tariff walls discourage imports. If a system of completely free trade had existed in 1828, the British would probably have bought more raw materials from those nations that consumed English manufactured goods. Rather than sail their ships away from American ports empty, they would have purchased more cotton, tobacco, and other products from the South. Little wonder that Southern leaders regarded the protective tariff as a foe of their economic development. On the other hand, many failed to appreciate that a prosperous manufacturing Northeast contributed to their prosperity by consuming their cotton and other farm produce.

South Carolinians took the lead in protesting against the "Tariff of Abominations." Their legislature went so far as to publish in 1828, though without formal endorsement, a pamphlet known as "The South Carolina Exposition." It had been secretly written by John C. Calhoun, one of the few top-flight political theorists ever produced by America. (As Vice-President, he was forced to conceal his authorship.) "The Exposition" boldly denounced the recent tariff as unjust and unconstitutional. Going a stride beyond the Kentucky and Virginia resolutions of 1798, it bluntly and explicitly proposed that the states should nullify the tariff—that is, they should declare it null and void within their borders.

Calhoun found himself caught in an awkward straddle. Still a Unionist and a nationalist, he was also a Southern sectionalist. He therefore desperately sought a formula that would protect the minority in the South from the "tyranny of the majority" in the North and West. Seizing upon nullification, he undertook by this explosive device to preserve the Union and prevent secession. His aim was not to destroy the Union, but to salvage it by quieting the fears of those forces that might one day destroy it.

Calhoun's "Exposition," at least immediately, was a false alarm. No other state joined South Carolina in her heated anti-tariff protest. But the disruptive theory of nullification was further publicized, while the even more dangerous doctrine of secession was foreshadowed. South Carolina was not then prepared to force the controversy to a showdown. The election of Carolina-born Andrew Jackson to the presidency had occurred two weeks earlier, and the "Old Hero"—a fellow cotton planter and slaveowner—was expected to sympathize with the plight of the South.

Going "Whole Hog" for Jackson in 1828

The presidential campaign for Andrew Jackson had started early. It began on February 9, 1825, the day of John Quincy Adams' controversial election by the House, and continued noisily for nearly four years.

Even before the election of 1828, the temporarily united Republicans of the Era of Good Feelings had split into two camps. One was the National Republicans, with the ultra-nationalistic Adams as their standard-bearer. The other was the Democratic-Republicans, with the fiery Jackson heading their ticket. Rallying cries of the Jackson zealots were "Bargain and Corruption," "Huzza for Jackson," and "All Hail Old Hickory." Jacksonites planted hickory poles for their hickory-tough hero; "Adamites" adopted the oak as the symbol of their oakenly independent candidate.

"Shall the people rule?" was the chief issue of 1828, at least to Jacksonians. They argued that the will of the voters had been thwarted in 1825 by the backstairs "bargain" of Adams and Clay. The only way to right the wrong was to seat Jackson, who would then bring about "reform" by sweeping out the "dishonest" Adams gang. "Jackson and Reform" was a widely mouthed slogan, while hickory brooms were brandished as tokens of a forthcoming "clean sweep." Seldom has the public mind been so successfully poisoned against an honest and high-minded President.

Mudslinging reached a disgraceful level, partly as a result of the taste of the new mass electorate for bare-knuckle politics. Adams would not stoop to gutter tactics, but many of his backers were less squeamish. They described Jackson's mother as a prostitute; they printed black-bordered handbills, shaped like coffins, recounting his numerous duels and brawls and trumpeting his hanging of six mutinous militiamen. The "Old Hero" was also branded an adulterer. He had married an estimable woman, Rachel Robards, confident that her divorce had been granted. To the consternation of both, they discovered two years later that it had not been, and they made haste to correct the marital miscue.

Anti-Jackson Cartoon of 1828. The cartoon recalls his hanging of mutinous militiamen.

Mrs. Andrew Jackson. A devoted wife who did not live to become First Lady, she had unwittingly and hence innocently involved herself and her husband in scandal. (National Archives.)

Rachel Jackson was crushed by the vicious charges of bigamy and adultery. She lived to see her husband win the presidency, but she died—supposedly of a broken heart—before she could become First Lady. Jackson, devotedly attached to his wife, was convinced that his enemies had killed her. He never forgave them.

Jackson men also hit below the belt. President Adams had purchased, with his own money and for his own use, a billiard table and a set of chessmen. In the mouths of rabid Jacksonites, these items became "gaming tables" and "gambling furniture" for the "presidential palace." Criticism

> One anti-Jackson newspaper declared, "General Jackson's mother was a Common Prostitute, brought to this country by the British soldiers! She afterwards married a MULATTO MAN with whom she had several children, of which number GENERAL JACKSON is one."

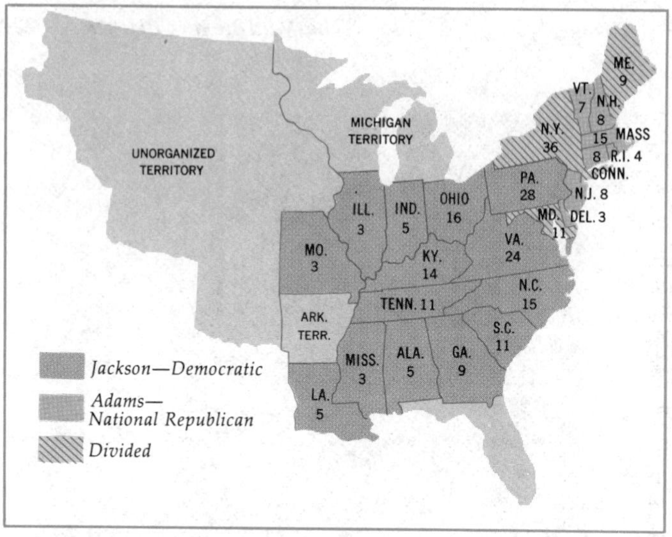

PRESIDENTIAL ELECTION OF 1828 (with electoral vote by state)

Note that Jackson swept the South and West, while Adams retained the old Federalist stronghold of the Northeast. Yet Jackson's inroads in the Northeast were decisive. He won 20 of New York's electoral votes, and all 28 of Pennsylvania's. If those votes had gone the other way, Adams would have been victorious—by a margin of one vote.

was also unfairly directed at the large sums that Adams had received over the years in federal salaries, well earned though they had been. He was even accused of having procured a servant girl for the lust of a Russian nobleman while minister to Russia—in short, of having served as a pimp.

The Jacksonian "Revolution" of 1828

General Jackson, victorious on the battlefields, was no less victorious at the ballot boxes. The popular tally was 647,286 votes for him to 508,064 for Adams, with an electoral count of 178 to 83. Support for Jackson came mainly from the West and South, and to a considerable extent from the sweat-stained laborers of the Eastern seaboard. Generally speaking, the common people—though by no means all of them—voted for the Hero of New Orleans. Adams won the backing of his own New England, as well as the propertied "better elements" of the Northeast.

The election of 1828 has often been called the "Revolution of 1828." Actually, as in 1800, there was no upheaval or landslide that swept out the incumbent. Adams, in fact, polled a respectable 44 percent of the popular vote. A considerable part of Jackson's support, moreover, was lined up by machine politicians, especially in New York and Pennsylvania, and not entirely among the leather-aproned artisans and other manual workers.

But the concept of a *political* revolution in 1828 is not completely farfetched. The increased turnout of voters proved that the common people, especially in the manhood-suffrage states, now had the vote and the will to use it for their ends. A discontented West, with its numerous rustics and debtors, generally voted for Jackson. The results show that the political center of gravity was continuing to shift away from the conservative seaboard East toward the emerging states across the mountains.

So in a broader sense the election was a "revolution," more than in 1800. It was a peaceful revolution, achieved by ballots instead of bullets, by counting heads instead of crushing them. "Shall the people rule?" cried the Jacksonians. The answering roar seemed to say, "The people shall rule!" In the struggle between the poorer masses and the entrenched classes, the homespun folk scored a resounding triumph. Rejecting the candidate who lacked the common touch, they rejoiced as though they had been delivered from some impending danger. Even so, there had been no mass turnout of voters; only about one-half the eligible persons balloted for a presidential candidate in 1828. But that proportion was already double the figure for 1824, and as the New Democracy infected the body politic, voter turnout rose dramatically. In the presidential election of

1840 ("Tippecanoe and Tyler too"), it reached 78 percent.

America hitherto had been ruled by an elite of brains and wealth, whether aristocratic Federalist shippers or aristocratic Jeffersonian planters. Jackson's victory accelerated the transfer of national power from the countinghouse to the farmhouse, from the East to the West, and from the snobs to the mobs. If Jefferson had been the hero of the gentleman farmer, Jackson was the hero of the dirt farmer. The plowholder was now ready to take over the government—*his* government.

Adams, though President-reject, was still destined for an enviable public career. Ever high-minded, he did not deem it beneath his dignity to accept election to the House of Representatives from Massachusetts. There he served with conspicuous success for seventeen fruitful years. Affectionately known as "Old Man Eloquent," he fought stalwartly for free government, free speech, free soil, and free men. A rough and savage debater, he finally was stricken on the job in 1848, at age eighty. His funeral was the greatest pageant of its kind that Washington had yet seen. Ironically, the popularity that had escaped him in life came to him in death.

The Advent of "Old Hickory" Jackson

Andrew Jackson cut a striking figure—tall (6 feet 1 inch; 1.86 meters), gaunt, and with bushy iron-gray hair brushed high above a prominent forehead, craggy eyebrows, and blue eyes. His irritability and emaciated condition (140 pounds; 64 kilograms) probably had resulted in part from long-term bouts with dysentery, malaria, tuberculosis, and lead poisoning from two bullets that he carried in his body from near-fatal duels. His autobiography was largely written in his lined face.

To a considerable degree, Jackson personified the New West. He reflected its individualism, its Jack-of-all-trades versatility, its opportunism, its energy, its directness, and its prejudices. He was a genuine folk hero—an uncommon common man. The backwoods preacher who cried that Jesus was "just another Andrew Jackson" reflected a sentiment that did not seem out of place to some.

Jackson's upbringing was not of the best. Born in the Carolinas and early orphaned, "Mischievous Andy" grew up without parental restraints. As a youth, he displayed much more interest in brawling and cockfighting than in his scanty opportunities for reading and spelling. Although he ultimately learned to express himself in writing with vigor and clarity, his grammar was always rough-hewn and his spelling was often original, like that of many contemporaries. He sometimes misspelled a word two different ways in the same letter.

The youthful Carolinian had the foresight to emigrate "up West" to Tennessee, where a fighting man was more highly regarded than a writing man. There—through native intelligence, force of personality, and powers of leadership—he became a judge and a member of Congress. His passions were so terrible that on occasion he would choke into silence when he tried to speak. He won his greatest fame as a commander of militia troops, who dubbed him "Old Hickory" in honor of his toughness. Afflicted with a violent temper, he early became involved in numerous duels, stabbings, and other bloody frays. But, rough and forthright as democracy itself, he made things move.

The Hermitage. Jackson's palatial Tennessee home. From an old print.

In 1824, Jefferson said of Jackson: "When I was President of the Senate he was a Senator; and he could never speak on account of the rashness of his feelings. I have seen him attempt it repeatedly, and as often choke with rage. His passions are no doubt cooler now . . . but he is a dangerous man."

The first President from the West, and the first without a college education, except Washington, Jackson was unique. His university was adversity. He had risen from the masses, but he was not one of them, except insofar as he shared many of their prejudices. Essentially a frontier aristocrat, he owned many slaves, cultivated broad acres, and lived in one of the finest mansions in America—the Hermitage, near Nashville, Tennessee. More Westerner than Easterner, more country gentleman than common clay, more courtly than crude, he was hard to fit into a neat category:

> He's none of your old New England stock,
> Or your gentry-proud Virginians,
> But a regular Western fighting-cock
> With Tennessee opinions.*

Contrary to legend, Jackson did not create the New Democracy. Before 1828, he had not contributed a single significant idea to it. As a clever and extremely lucky opportunist, he was the beneficiary of the New Democracy, and was tossed into office on the crest of its wave. He was the hero of the one-suspender man.

While President, Jackson proved to be a storm center. As a former military man, he demanded prompt and loyal support from his subordinates. If one was not for him, one was against him. Cherishing strong ideas as to his constitutional prerogatives, he ignored the Supreme Court on several conspicuous occasions. He likewise defied or dominated Congress as few Presidents have done. His six predecessors had wielded the veto ten times; during his two terms he employed it twelve times, sometimes on grounds of personal distaste rather than constitutional principle. Jackson's modest use of the veto axe was perfectly legitimate, but his numerous enemies condemned him as "King Andrew the First."

Jackson's inauguration symbolized the newly won ascendancy of the masses. "Hickoryites" poured into Washington from far places, sleeping on hotel floors or in hallways. They were curious to see their hero take office, and perhaps to pick up a well-paying office for themselves. Nobodies mingled with notables as the White House, for the first time, was thrown open to the multitude. A milling crowd of clerks, shopkeepers, hobnailed artisans, and grimy laborers surged in, wrecking the china and furniture, and threatening the "people's champion" with cracked ribs. Jackson was hastily spirited through a side door, and the White House miraculously emptied itself when the word was passed that huge bowls of well-spiked punch had been placed on the lawns. Such was "the inaugural brawl."

To conservatives, this orgy seemed like the end of the world. "King Mob" reigned triumphant as

"King Andrew the First." Jackson is here assailed as a tyrant who tramples underfoot the Constitution, the courts, and domestic welfare. (Houghton Library, Harvard.)

*"Andrew Jackson" from *A Book of Americans* by Rosemary & Stephen Vincent Benét. Copyright, 1933, by Rosemary & Stephen Vincent Benét. Copyright renewed ©, 1961, by Rosemary Carr Benét. Reprinted by permission of Brandt & Brandt Literary Agency, Inc.

Jacksonian vulgarity replaced Jeffersonian simplicity. Old ladies of both sexes shuddered, drew their blinds, and recalled the opening scenes of the French Revolution.

Jackson Nationalizes the Spoils System

Under Jackson the spoils system—that is, rewarding political supporters with public office—was introduced into the federal government on a large numerical scale. On a percentage basis, Jefferson, with reluctance and discrimination, had already made about as large a beginning. Jackson, with more ruthlessness, extended it to more people, while complaining about those "clamoring for a public tit from which to suck the treasury."

The basic idea was as old as politics. Its name came later from Senator Marcy's classic remark in 1832, "To the victor belong the spoils of the enemy." The system had already secured a firm hold in New York and Pennsylvania, where well-greased machines were operating. Professional politicians, by ladling out the "gravy" of office, had been able to make politics a full-time business, rather than a sideline. The emphasis was more on spoils than on responsibilities.

A house-cleaning of some sort in Washington was clearly needed. No party overturn had occurred since the defeat of the Federalists in 1800, and even that had not produced wholesale evictions. During the ensuing twenty-eight years, festering evils had developed in the civil service. The old colonial-system ideal of holding office during good behavior had bred some incompetence and corruption, as well as considerable indifference and insolence ("uncivil servants"). A few officeholders, their commissions signed by President Washington, were lingering on into their eighties, drawing breath and salary but doing little else.

Jackson fully shared the view of the New Democracy that "every man is as good as his neighbor"—perhaps "equally better." As this was believed to be so, and as the routine of office was also thought to be simple enough for any upstanding American to learn quickly, why encourage the development of an aristocratic, bureaucratic, officeholding class? Experience, of course, had some value. But alertness and new blood had more—at least in the eyes of Jacksonians.

The New Democracy also trumpeted the ideal of "rotation in office"—or "a turn about is fair play." Since experience was discounted, and since officeholding provided valuable training for citizenship, let as many citizens as possible feed at the public trough for at least a short time. This was a polite way of saying "Throw the rascals out and put our rascals in."

More Victors than Spoils

Elected as a reformer, Jackson believed that the swiftest road to reform was to sweep out the Adams-Clay gang and bring in his own trusted henchmen. Furiously aroused against his foes, he agreed that the old Adams "barnacles" must "be scraped clean from the Ship of State."

The spoilsmen now had their inning. Office seekers hounded Jackson at every turn and even invaded his privacy: for every appointee there were seemingly ten disappointees. In view of such pressures, one may marvel that he removed so few incumbents rather than so many. During his eight years, only about one-fifth of the old civil servants were dismissed, leaving more than 9,000 out of the original 11,000. The "clean sweeps" were to come in later administrations.

Even so, a demoralizing practice was begun on a national scale. Insecurity replaced security and discouraged many able citizens from entering the

> One elderly postmaster, a Revolutionary war veteran, while personally appealing to Jackson not to evict him from office, removed his coat to display his war wounds. Jackson later exclaimed: "By the eternal! I will not remove the old man. Do you know that he carries a pound of British lead in his body?"

public service. Terrible hardships were worked on poor men with large families. One discharged employee cut his throat from ear to ear; another went raving mad. Fitness, merit, and the ideal of public service were subordinated, while offices were prostituted to political ends. The questions were not "What can he do for the country?" but "What has he done for the party?" or "Is he loyal to Jackson?"

Scandal inevitably accompanied the new system. Men were appointed to high office who had openly bought their posts by campaign contributions. Illiterates, incompetents, and plain crooks were given positions of public trust; they lusted for the spoils of office rather than the toils of office. Samuel Swartwout, despite ample warnings of his untrustworthiness, was awarded the high-salaried post of collector of the customs of the port of New York. Nearly nine years later he "Swartwouted out" for England, leaving his accounts more than a million dollars short—the first man to steal a million dollars from the Washington government.

Finally, the spoils system built up a potent, personalized political machine. Its delicate gears were lubricated by gifts from expectant party members, and by percentage levies on the salaries of officeholders—a kind of political job insurance. The system at length secured such a tenacious hold that more than half a century passed before its grip could be partially loosened.

Cabinet Crises and Nationalistic Setbacks

Jackson's Cabinet was mediocre; its members were used primarily as executive clerks. The only person of conspicuous ability was the smooth-tongued and keen-witted secretary of state, Dutch-descended Martin Van Buren of New York, who shone as a gifted conciliator and wire-puller. A balding, sharp-featured little man, he was affectionately addressed by Jackson as "Matty." But he was known to his enemies as the "Little Magician."

The official Cabinet of six was privately supplemented by an extra-official cabinet of about thirteen ever-shifting members. It grew out of Jackson's informal meetings with his advisers, some of whom were newspapermen who kept him in touch with the fickle winds of public opinion. The enemies of the President branded these shirt-sleeved cronies "the Kitchen Cabinet." Subsequent generations have retained the picture of an uncouth clique gathering in the kitchen and spitting tobacco juice in the general direction of grimy spittoons. Actually, the group did not gather in the kitchen; it never met officially; its overall influence has been grossly exaggerated; and it was not unconstitutional. The President is free to consult with such unofficial advisers as he desires.

The regular Cabinet was wrecked in 1831, as a result of the "Eaton malaria." Secretary of War Eaton had married the daughter of a Washington boardinghouse keeper, pretty Peggy O'Neal, whom the tongue of scandal had perhaps unfairly linked with the male boarders. She was consequently snubbed by the ladies of Jackson's official family, conspicuously by the blue-blooded wife of Vice-President Calhoun. The President, whose own spouse had been victimized by scandalmongers, was chivalrously aroused in behalf of Mrs. Eaton's chastity. With a zeal worthy of a better cause, he tried to force the social acceptance of the black-haired beauty. But the all-conquering general finally had to acknowledge defeat in the "Petticoat War" at the hands of the female phalanx.

Peggy Eaton (1796–1879). Though scandal raised her to notoriety, she retained Jackson's favor. After her husband left the Cabinet, the President appointed him minister to Spain. For four years she basked in a brilliant Madrid society that had no prejudice against a woman with a past. (Library of Congress)

The Eaton scandal played directly into the hands of Secretary Van Buren. As a fancy-free widower, he further curried favor with Jackson by paying marked attention to Mrs. Eaton, whose physical charms lightened this self-imposed task. Jackson turned increasingly against Calhoun, and finally broke with him completely. Followers of the South Carolinian were purged from the Cabinet in 1831. Calhoun himself, resigning the vice-presidency the next year, entered the Senate as a champion of South Carolina.

It would be absurd to say that Peggy Eaton caused the Civil War. But up to this time Calhoun had publicly been a strong nationalist, despite his secret espousal of nullification in "The South Carolina Exposition" of 1828. As Vice-President, he thought himself in line for the presidency after Jackson had served one term. The open break with the incumbent, though foreshadowed earlier, blighted his hopes. He gradually abandoned his weakening nationalism and became an inflexible defender of Southern sectionalism. Seeking extreme medicines for protecting the states and preserving the Union, the "Great Nullifier" contributed to the almost fatal illness of the Union.

Jackson himself dealt nationalism a body blow by his hostility to localized roads and canals. It is true that he signed a number of measures which appropriated federal funds for ambitious internal improvements. But his states'-rights principles rebelled against spending money from the pinched Washington Treasury for roads built entirely within individual states and unrelated to an interstate network. He headlined his antagonism in 1830, when he vigorously vetoed a bill for improving the Maysville Road, which lay completely within Henry Clay's Kentucky (but which was connected with an interstate artery). This setback was incidentally a slap at the internal improvements aspect of the American System, so ardently championed by Clay, the "corrupt bargainer" whom Jackson never forgave. "Old Hickory's" veto was also a signal victory for Eastern and Southern states'-rightism in its struggle with Jackson's own West.

The Webster-Hayne Forensic Duel

Sectional jealousies found a spectacular outlet in the Senate during 1829–1830. Hidebound New England, resenting the marvelous expansion of the West, was determined to call a halt. The lavish distribution of Western acreage was draining off Eastern population, while further upsetting the political balance. Late in 1829, therefore, a New England senator introduced a resolution designed to curb the sale of public lands.

Sectional passions flared forth angrily in the Senate, as the Western senators sprang furiously to the defense of their interests. The South, seeking sectional allies in its controversies with the Northeast, promptly sided with the West. Its most persuasive spokesman was Robert Y. Hayne, of South Carolina, one of the silver-tongued orators of his generation.

Hayne's oratorical effort in the Senate was impressive. He roundly condemned the obvious disloyalty of New England during the War of 1812, as well as her selfish inconsistency on the protective tariff. Airing in detail the grievances of the South, he reserved his heavy fire for the "Tariff of Abominations" (1828). He then acclaimed Calhoun's dangerous doctrine of nullification as the only means of safeguarding the minority interests of his section. Hayne, like Calhoun, did not advocate a breakup of the Union; rather, he was seeking to protect Southern rights within the Union and under the Constitution. But his arguments were carefully stored up by nullifiers and secessionists for future use.

In 1839 Daniel Webster visited England, where his distinguished bearing and intellectual power made a great impression. The Reverend Sydney Smith, a merciless critic of America, reportedly remarked, "Daniel Webster struck me much like a steam-engine in trousers." He was also a "living lie, because no man on earth could be so great as he looked."

Webster challenged Hayne in these words: "The proposition that, in case of a supposed violation of the Constitution by Congress, the states have a constitutional right to interfere and annul the law of Congress is the proposition of the gentleman. I do not admit it. If the gentleman had intended no more than to assert the right of revolution for justifiable cause, he would have said only what all agree to. But I cannot conceive that there can be a middle course, between submission to the laws, when regularly pronounced constitutional, on the one hand, and open resistance, which is revolution or rebellion, on the other" (Jan. 26, 1830). Webster and Hayne thus clashed over the same question that had vexed Jefferson in the Kentucky resolutions and Marshall in *Marbury* v. *Madison*. Where did final authority to interpret the Constitution lie?

The "Godlike Daniel" Webster, spokesman for New England, now took the floor. Matchless orator and leader of the American bar, he awed audiences by his majestic presence, including craglike brows, flashing eyes, a sonorous voice, a noble head, and a well-chested frame. His life up to this point, including his frequent appearances before Chief Justice Marshall, had been a preparation for this nine-day running debate with Hayne in January of 1830.

After defending New England with vigor, if not complete candor, Webster, the ex-Federalist, passed on to the larger issue of Union. Insisting that the *people* and not the *states* had framed the Constitution (here he was on shaky historical ground*), he decried the insidious doctrine of nullification. Either the Supreme Court would judge the constitutionality of laws, or the Republic would be torn by revolution. If each of the twenty-four states was free to go its separate way in obeying or rejecting federal statutes, there would be no union but only a "rope of sand." Webster's concluding outburst, which brought tears to men's eyes, was a magnificent tribute to the Union, ending with those imperishable words: "Liberty and Union, now and forever, one and inseparable."

Websterian Cement for the Union

Webster did not overpower Hayne with his thunderous oratory; Hayne did not defeat Webster with his seductive eloquence. There were no official judges. The polished Southerner was sounder on historical and economic grounds; the impassioned New Englander was sounder on constitutional practicalities and common sense—on things as they were rather than as they had been. Each section was satisfied with its champion.

The impact of Webster's reply was spectacular. About 40,000 copies were printed in three months, and arguments for the Union were seared into the minds of countless Northerners. Among them was young Abraham Lincoln, just turning twenty-one and moving from Indiana to the Illinois frontier. Webster's inspirational peroration was printed in the school readers, and was memorized by tens of thousands of impressionable lads—the Boys in Blue who in 1861–1865 were willing to lay down their lives for the Union.

Webster, beyond a doubt, had a large hand in winning the Civil War. He probably did more than any other person to arouse the oncoming generation of Northerners to fight for the ideal of Union. His admirers have claimed that the nation was saved hardly less by the thunder of Webster's replies to Hayne than by the thunder of General Grant's replies to the cannonading of General Lee.

Hot-tempered "Old Hickory" had meanwhile been keeping strangely silent on Southern grievances. States'-rights leaders, at a Jefferson Day banquet in 1830, schemed to smoke him out. Their

*The original preamble of the Constitution of 1787 had read: "We the people of the states of"—and then they were listed by name. But when it was objected that all the states might not ratify, the formula "We the people of the United States" was adopted. (For the text of the Preamble, see Appendix.)

strategy was to devise a series of toasts in honor of Jefferson, onetime foe of centralization, that would lean toward states' rights and nullification. The plotters assumed that the "Old Hero"—a fellow Southerner—would be swept along by the tenor of the toasts and speak up in favor of states' rights.

Jackson, forewarned and inwardly fuming, had carefully prepared his response. At the proper moment he rose to his full height, fixed his eyes on Calhoun, and with dramatic intensity proclaimed:

"Our Union: It must be preserved!"

The Southerners were dumbfounded, and Calhoun haltingly replied, in part:

"The union, next to our liberty, most dear!"

Some seventy other anti-climactic toasts followed, but in effect the party was over.

Jackson's military ire was aroused. As commander-in-chief, he would stand for no back talk from the states, and particularly from the hated Calhoun. But, as fate decreed, the showdown with defiant South Carolina was postponed for over two years.

VARYING VIEWPOINTS

Aristocratic 19th-Century historians damned Jackson as a backwoods barbarian. They criticized Jacksonianism as democracy run riot—an irresponsible backcountry outburst that overturned the electoral system and raised hob with the national financial structure. Early-20th-Century "progressive" historians followed the lead of Frederick Jackson Turner in his famous 1893 essay, "The Significance of the Frontier in American History." They saw the frontier as the fount of democratic virtue, and they hailed Jackson as a popular hero sprung from the forests of the West. But with the publication of Arthur M. Schlesinger, Jr.'s *The Age of Jackson* in 1945, the focus of the debate on Jacksonianism shifted. Schlesinger argued that Jacksonians were strong in the urban East as well as in the Western woods. Ever since, the debate on Jacksonian democracy has tended to revolve around the question of social class rather than geographical section.

SELECT READINGS

The best general introductions are George Dangerfield, *The Awakening of American Nationalism, 1815–1828* (1965), and G. G. Van Deusen, *The Jacksonian Era, 1828–1848* (1959). A still-living classic treatise on the Jacksonian period is Alexis De Tocqueville, *Democracy in America* (1835, 1840). A. M. Schlesinger, Jr., in his pro-Jackson *The Age of Jackson* (1945), stresses the support of Eastern labor for Jackson, a view that has come under heavy attack in Lee Benson, *The Concept of Jacksonian Democracy: New York as a Test Case* (1961). See also Walter Hugins, *Jacksonian Democracy and the Working Class: A Study of the New York Workingmen's Movement, 1829–1837* (1960), and Marvin Meyers, *The Jacksonian Persuasion* (1957). More broadly conceived is J. W. Ward, *Andrew Jackson: Symbol for an Age* (1955). R. V. Remini has three revealing books: *Martin Van Buren and the Making of the Democratic Party* (1959); *The Election of Andrew Jackson* (1963); and *The Revolutionary Age of Andrew Jackson* (1976). On administrative aspects and the functioning of the spoils system consult L. D. White, *The Jacksonians* (1954), and S. H. Aronson, *Status and Kinship in the Higher Civil Service* (1964). See also Chilton Williamson, *American Suffrage from Property to Democracy, 1760–1860* (1960). S. F. Bemis, *John Quincy Adams and the Union* (1956), is the second and concluding volume of a distinguished biography. Robert Dalzell examines *Daniel Webster and the Trial of American Nationalism, 1843–1852* (1973). The standard work on the subject is Frank W. Taussig, *The Tariff History of the United States* (1931).

14

Jacksonian Democracy at Flood Tide

The vain threats of resistance by those who [in South Carolina] have raised the standard of rebellion shew their madness and folly. . . . In forty days, I can have within the limits of So. Carolina fifty thousand men. . . . The Union will be preserved.

ANDREW JACKSON, 1832

"Nullies" in South Carolina

The "abominable" Tariff of 1828 continued to rankle with hot-blooded South Carolinians. Some of them took to wearing ill-fitting homespun garments, untaxed by the hated Yankee tariff, while their slaves strutted about in discarded broadcloth. The nullifiers–"nullies," they were called–tried valiantly to muster the necessary two-thirds vote in the South Carolina legislature for nullification. But they were blocked by a determined minority of Unionists or "submission men."

Back in Washington, Congress touched off the fuse by passing the new Tariff of 1832, which fell far short of meeting all Southern demands. The measure did pare away the worst of the "abominations" of 1828, and it did lower the imposts to about the level of the moderate Tariff of 1824—roughly 35 percent, or a reduction of 10 percent. Yet the new law was frankly protective and to many Southerners it had a disquieting air of permanence.

South Carolina was now nerved for drastic action. Nullifiers and Unionists clashed head-on in the state election of 1832. "Nullies," defiantly wearing palmetto ribbons on their hats, emerged with more than a two-thirds majority. The state legislature then called for a special convention. Several weeks later the delegates, meeting in Columbia, solemnly declared the existing federal tariff to be null and void within South Carolina. The hotheaded assemblage also called upon the state legislature to undertake any necessary military preparations. As a final act of defiance, the convention threatened to take South Carolina out of the Union if the Washington regime attempted to collect the customs duties by force.

Calhoun Criticized. This contemporary cartoon shows Calhoun reaching for power over the dead bodies of the Constitution and the Union. Jackson, at the far right, threatens to hang the nullifiers. (The New York Public Library, Astor, Lenox and Tilden Foundations)

President-General Jackson, his military instincts rasped, reacted violently. Hating Calhoun and pledged to uphold the Union, he privately threatened to hang the nullifiers. But fortunately for compromise, he was much less pugnacious in public. He dispatched modest naval and military reinforcements to the Palmetto State, while quietly preparing a sizable army. He also issued a ringing proclamation against nullification, to which the governor of South Carolina, ex-Senator Hayne, responded with a counter-proclamation. If civil war was to be avoided, one side would have to surrender, or both would have to compromise.

Conciliatory Henry Clay of Kentucky, now in the Senate, stepped forward. An unforgiving foe of Jackson, he had no desire to see his old enemy win new laurels by crushing the Carolinians and returning with the scalp of Calhoun dangling from his belt. The gallant Kentuckian therefore threw his influence behind a compromise bill which would gradually reduce the Tariff of 1832 by about 10 percent over a period of eight years. By 1842 the rates would be at approximately the mildly protective level of 1816—that is, 20 percent to 25 percent on the value of dutiable goods.

House Vote on Tariff of 1832

Regions	*For*	*Against*	*Explanations*
New England	17	17	Divided on moderate tariff
Middle States	52	18	Pa., N.Y., protectionist strongholds
West (Ohio, Ind., Ill., Mo.)	18	0	Undeveloped West for tariff to support improvements
South (incl. La.)	27	27	Note division on moderate tariff
Southwest (Tenn., Ky.)	18	3	West favorable to tariff
TOTAL	132	65	

The vote was badly divided because the bill was really a compromise between extreme protection and free trade. Compare vote on 1828 tariff, p. 227.

House Vote on Compromise Tariff of 1833

Regions	*For*	*Against*	*Explanations*
New England	10	28	Opposition in manufacturing centers to lowered tariff
Middle States	24	47	
West	10	8	Divided on moderate tariff
South and Southwest	75	2	Strong Southern support for compromise
TOTAL	119	85	

The compromise Tariff of 1833 finally squeezed through Congress. Debate was bitter, with most of the opposition naturally coming from protectionist New England and the Middle States. Calhoun and the South favored the compromise, so it was evident that Jackson would not have to use firearms and rope. But at the same time, and partly as a face-saving device, Congress passed the Force Bill, known among Carolinians as the "Bloody Bill." It authorized the President to use the army and navy, if necessary, to collect federal tariff duties.

Militant South Carolinians welcomed this opportunity to extricate themselves without loss of face from a dangerously tight corner. To the consternation of the Calhounites, no other Southern states had sprung to their support, though Georgia and Virginia toyed with the idea. Moreover, an appreciable Unionist minority within South Carolina was gathering guns, organizing militia, and nailing the Stars and Stripes to flagpoles. Faced with civil war within and invasion from without, the Columbia convention met again and repealed the ordinance of nullification. As a final but futile gesture of fist-shaking, it nullified the unnecessary Force Act and adjourned.

Flag of South Carolina, with Palmetto Tree

A Victory for Both Union and Nullification

Neither Jackson nor the "nullies" won a clear-cut triumph. Admirers of "Old Hickory" insisted that he had avoided an armed clash, induced the South Carolinians to repeal their ordinance of nullification, and preserved the Union. On the other hand, the danger of disunion seems to have been exaggerated.

South Carolina actually emerged with colors flying. Although confronted with overwhelming odds, she had forced a reduction of the tariff to as reasonable a level as she could have expected. She had not only saved face but she had surrendered no principle. Unrepentant and defiant, she felt that she had won; and the people of Charleston—the "Cradle of Secession"—gave a gala "victory ball" for the volunteer troops. But ominously the South Carolinians gradually abandoned nullification in favor of the more extreme remedy of secession.

Later generations, gazing back through the smoke of the Civil War, have condemned the "appeasement" of South Carolina in 1833 as sheer folly. Unbloody and unbowed, she could have been voted the state most likely to secede. (In 1860 she was the first to go.) If Jackson had only strangled the serpent of secession in the cradle, so the argument runs, there might have been no costly Civil War. During the crisis of 1832 medals were struck off in honor of Calhoun bearing the words, "First President of the Southern Confederacy."

Yet force was the risky solution. The flare-up in South Carolina was no mere Whiskey Rebellion,

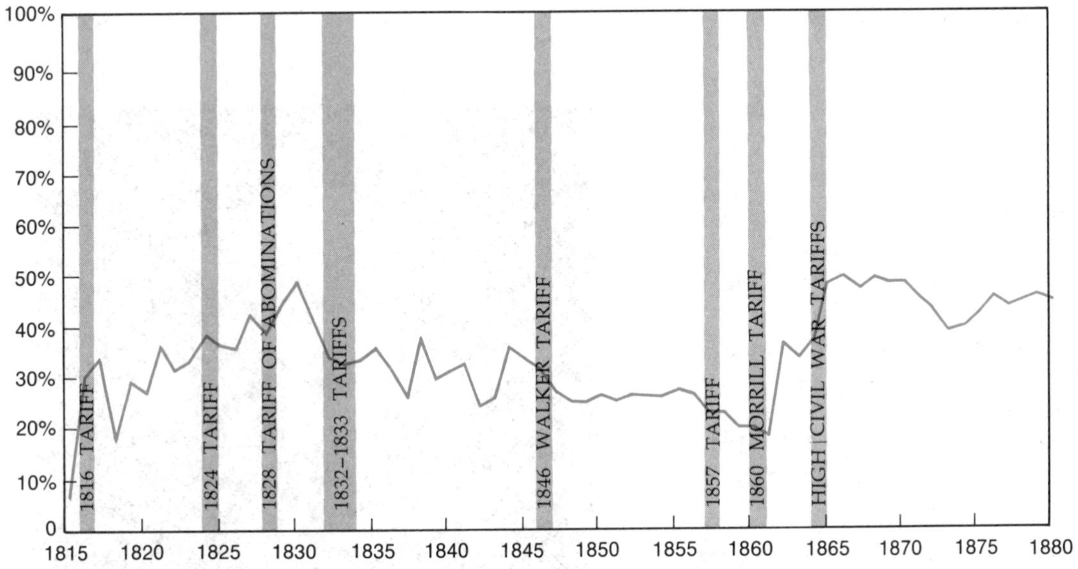

(The data before 1820 are approximations. Note that the effects of a tariff are often not immediately felt in the year of its passage.)

TARIFF LEVIES ON DUTIABLE IMPORTS, 1815–1880

and the nation was not yet ready to drink the cup of blood. Violence tends to beget violence. Armed invasion might have aroused other Southern states and touched off a civil war, at a time when the Unionists were even worse prepared for fighting than in 1861. Force is a confession that statesmanship has failed. Reasonable compromise was in the American tradition, and in 1833 any other course seemed unwise.

The Bank as a Political Football

President Jackson did not hate all banks and all businesses, but he distrusted monopolistic banking and over-big business, as did his followers. A man of violent dislikes, he came to share the prejudices of his own West against the "moneyed monster" known as the Bank of the United States (B.U.S.). He might have tolerated a renewal of its charter in 1836, with adequate safeguards. But hated Henry Clay aroused his ire by throwing himself behind a premature move in the Senate to recharter the Bank in 1832—four years early. "Gallant Harry" was the leading candidate of the National Republicans for the presidency, and with a fateful blindness he looked upon the Bank issue as a surefire winner.

Clay's scheme was to ram a recharter bill through Congress, and then send it on to the White House. If Jackson signed it, he would alienate his worshipful Western followers. If he vetoed it, as seemed certain, he would presumably lose the presidency in the forthcoming election by alienating the wealthy and influential groups in the East. Clay seems not to have fully realized that the "best people" were now only a minority, and that they generally feared Jackson anyhow. The President growled privately, "The Bank . . . is trying to kill me, but I will kill it."

The recharter bill slid through Congress on greased skids, as planned, but was killed by a scorching veto from Jackson. The "Old Hero" assailed the plutocratic and monopolistic Bank as unconstitutional. Of course the Supreme Court had earlier declared it constitutional in the case of *McCulloch* v. *Maryland* (1819), but Jackson acted as though he regarded the executive branch as superior to the judicial branch. He had taken an oath to uphold the Constitution as he understood it, not as his foe, John Marshall, understood it.

Banker Biddle wrote to Henry Clay (August 1, 1832) expressing his satisfaction: "I have always deplored making the Bank a party question, but since the President will have it so, he must pay the penalty of his own rashness. As to the veto message, I am delighted with it. It has all the fury of a chained panther biting the bars of his cage. It is really a manifesto of anarchy . . . and my hope is that it will contribute to relieve the country of the domination of these miserable [Jackson] people."

Jackson's veto message went on to condemn the Bank as not only anti-Western but anti-American. A substantial minority of its stockholders were foreigners, chiefly Britons, for whom Americans still harbored a war-born hate. Thus, at one bold stroke, Jackson succeeded in mobilizing the prejudices of the West against the East. He was setting the log cabin against the business office, the apprehensive debtor against the steely-eyed creditor. More than that, he was arousing the "native" American against the foreigner, the states'-righter against the centralizer.

The gods continued to misguide Henry Clay. Delighted with the financial fallacies of Jackson's message, but blind to its political appeal, he arranged to have thousands of copies printed as a campaign document. The President's sweeping accusations may indeed have seemed demagogic to the moneyed men of the country, but they made good sense to the common men. The Bank issue was now thrown into the noisy arena of the Clay-Jackson presidential canvass of 1832.

Brickbats and Bouquets for the Bank

What of Jackson's vigorous charges? The Bank was undeniably anti-Western in its strong hostility to the wobbly "wildcat banks" that provided financial fuel—often volatile paper—for Western expansion. It had foreclosed on many Western farms, and had thus drained "tribute" into its Eastern coffers. For that era, it was a mammoth super-bank—a "monster monopoly"—and hence out of touch with the sweaty New Democracy. It was undeniably plutocratic, run by an elite moneyed aristocracy, headed by the able but high-handed Nicholas Biddle (dubbed "Czar Nicholas I"). The Bank was also in some degree autocratic and tyrannical, especially when it turned the screws on the weak "rag money" banks.

Nicholas Biddle (1786–1844). A precociously brilliant linguist, writer, magazine editor, diplomat, legislator, and financier, he entered the University of Pennsylvania at age ten and completed the requirements for graduation at age thirteen. Drawn into high finance, he mastered the business and became president of the Bank of the United States. (Frick Art Reference Library)

The charge that the Bank was a "hydra of corruption" contained much truth. Biddle cleverly lent funds where they would make influential friends. In 1831 alone, a total of fifty-nine members of Congress borrowed sums from "Biddle's Bank" totaling about a third of a million dollars. Even a dog does not ordinarily bite the hand that feeds him. During one period Daniel Webster was a director of the Bank, its chief paid counsel, its debtor in the sum of thousands of dollars, and a member of the United States Senate, where he eloquently battled for his employer's interests. Judicious loans by Biddle to newspaper editors likewise insured a "good press," and led to the sneer, "Emperor Nick of the Bribery Bank." Whomever he could not corrupt, it was believed, he crushed.

Yet the Bank had much to commend it. An eminently sound organization, it was the only national financial institution of its kind in American history. It kept the fly-by-night Western banks under some restraint—banks that often consisted of little more than a few chairs and a suitcase full of printed notes. It reduced bank failures and, at a time when the country was flooded with depreciated paper money, issued sound banknotes ("Old Nick's Money"). It helped the West expand by making credit and sound currency reasonably abundant. It was a safe depository for the funds of the Washington government, which it also served by transferring and disbursing money. Admittedly it had a monopoly of surplus federal funds, but that monopoly had been specifically authorized by the people's representatives in Congress.

The Bank, in short, was a highly important and useful institution which had fallen into the hands of a wealthy clique. Its officers were not only arrogant, but they were not fully aware of their responsibilities to society in the management of what amounted to a public utility.

"Old Hickory" Crushes Clay in 1832

Clay, as a National Republican, and Jackson, as a Democrat, were the chief gladiators in the presidential contest of 1832. The gaunt old general, who had earlier favored one term for a President and rotation in office, was easily persuaded by his cronies not to rotate himself out of office. Presidential power is a heady brew—and habit-forming.

The ensuing campaign was colorful and noisy. The "Old Hero's" adherents again raised the hickory pole and bellowed, "Jackson Forever: Go the Whole Hog." Admirers of Clay shouted, "Freedom and Clay," while his foes harped on his dueling, gambling, cockfighting, and fast living.

Novel features made the campaign of 1832 especially memorable. Americans witnessed for the first time nominations by national nominating conventions (three of them), which now took over from the state legislatures the function of naming candidates. The first national party platform was

"Race Over Uncle Sam's Course." Clay, with his American System, is supposed to gain the White House as Jackson, with his veto club and Van Buren as running mate, falls on the Bank issue in 1832. A falsely optimistic Whig cartoon. (Boston Public Library.)

also published. And for the first time a third-party ticket entered the field—the short-lived anti-Masonic group, which opposed the fearsome secrecy of the Masonic order. But on the whole the "hurrah" froth of the preceding campaign was subordinated to the solid issue of the Bank.

Henry Clay and his overconfident National Republicans enjoyed impressive advantages. Ample funds flowed into their campaign chest, including $50,000 in "life insurance" from the B.U.S. Most of the newspaper editors, some of them "bought" with Biddle's Bank loans, dipped their pens in acid when they wrote of Jackson. Oratorical big guns, including the incomparable Webster, were lined up on the side of Clay, as was true of the middle- and upper-income groups.

Yet Jackson won easily over the sparkling Kentuckian. The popular count stood at 687,502 to 530,189; the electoral count at 219 to 49. A Jacksonian wave swept over the West and South, washed into Pennsylvania and New York, and even broke into rock-ribbed New England.

Henry Clay, long bitten by the presidential bug, was crushed. Himself magnetically appealing, he had enlisted on his side the big money, the brilliant oratory, the "solid" citizenry, and the sound financial reasoning. But the peppery President, the idol of the masses, won because he had the votes. The poor always outnumber the rich—and in 1832, as in 1824 and 1828, the poor voted for "Old Andy" Jackson.

Badgering Biddle's Bank

A vindictive Jackson was not one to let the financial octopus die in peace. He was convinced that he now had a "mandate" from the voters, and he had good reason to fear that the slippery Biddle might try to manipulate the Bank (as he did) so as to force its recharter. Jackson therefore decided to "remove" the federal deposits gradually, thus cushioning the final shock when the Bank expired in four years. He would accomplish his objective by depositing no more funds with Biddle, and by using existing deposits to defray the day-to-day expenses of the government.

> "The times are dreadfully hard," wrote a New York diarist, Philip Hone, Dec. 30, 1833. "The . . . act of tyranny which the President exercised in removing the deposits has produced a state of alarm and panic unprecedented in our city. . . . The truth is, we are smarting under the lash which the vindictive ruler of our destinies [Jackson] has inflicted upon us as a penalty for the sin which Nicholas Biddle committed in opposing his election. My share of the punishment amounts to $20,000, which I have lost by the fall of stocks in the last sixty days."

"Removing" the deposits involved nasty complications. Jackson, his dander up, was forced to reshuffle his Cabinet before he could find a secretary of the treasury who would bend to his iron will. Surplus federal funds henceforth were placed in several dozen state institutions—the so-called pet banks or Jackson's pets. These new depositories were selected partly because of their pro-Jackson sympathies, but in general they were not nearly so weak as pictured by the President's enemies.

Biddle, for his part, was compelled to retrench after losing the federal deposits. But he called in loans with unnecessary severity, and evidently for the purpose of forcing a reconsideration of the charter by Congress. A number of the wobblier banks were driven to the wall by "Biddle's Panic," and the vengeful conduct of the dying "monster" seemed to justify the earlier accusations of its foes.

The teetering financial structure of the country received an additional shock in 1836, the year the Bank breathed its last. "Wildcat" currency had become so unreliable in the West that Jackson authorized the Treasury to issue a Specie Circular —a decree that required all public lands to be purchased with "hard" or metallic money. This drastic step was overdue, but coming at that time it gave the speculative bubble another sharp prick. Hard money brought hard feelings and hard times to the West.

Inflationary pressures nevertheless continued. By 1835 the national debt was finally liquidated for the first time, but additional funds still poured into the federal Treasury. This revenue flowed principally from the customs houses, which were benefiting from the high tariff duties and the heavy imports resulting from flush times. In 1836 a scheme passed Congress for distributing the surplus above $5 million to the states. When this transfer began, early in 1837, the risky speculative spiral was given another boost. Later that year the panic broke, and the bothersome problem of the surplus became the even more bothersome problem of a deficit.

Transplanting the Tribes

Wondrous indeed was the continued expansion of the American population. The unflagging fertility of the people, reinforced by immigration, brought the total figure to nearly 13 million by 1830—or more than three times that of 1790.* Most of the states east of the Mississippi had been admitted, leaving islands of red men marooned on lands coveted by their white neighbors.

President Jackson, the veteran Indian fighter known as "Big Knife," was convinced of the folly of continuing to regard the tribes as separate nations within the individual states. When Georgia attempted to exercise control over the Cherokees, and the Supreme Court thrice upheld the rights of the Indians, Jackson viewed continued defiance by the state with unaccustomed composure. A state might flout federal law if white men thereby profited at the Indians' expense. In a callous sneer at the red men's defender, Jackson reportedly snapped, "John Marshall has made his decision; now let him enforce it."

Yet Jackson also harbored protective feelings toward the Indians. Their present condition, he told Congress in 1829, "contrasted with what they once were, makes a most powerful appeal to our sympathies." Could not something be done, he implored, to preserve "this much injured race"? Jackson proposed a bodily removal of the remaining Eastern tribes—chiefly Cherokee, Creek, Choctaw, and Chickasaw—beyond the Mississippi. Individual Indians might remain if they adopted white men's ways. Emigration should be voluntary, since it would be "cruel and unjust to compel the aborigines to abandon the graves of their fathers."

Jackson's policy was high-sounding, but it led to the more or less forcible uprooting of more than 100,000 Indians in the 1830s. Many died on the "Trail of Tears" to the newly established Indian Territory (present Oklahoma), where they were to be "permanently" free of white encroachments. The Bureau of Indian Affairs was established in 1836 to administer relations with America's original inhabitants. But as the landhungry "palefaces" pushed west faster than anticipated, the government's guarantees went up in smoke. The "permanent" frontier lasted about fifteen years.

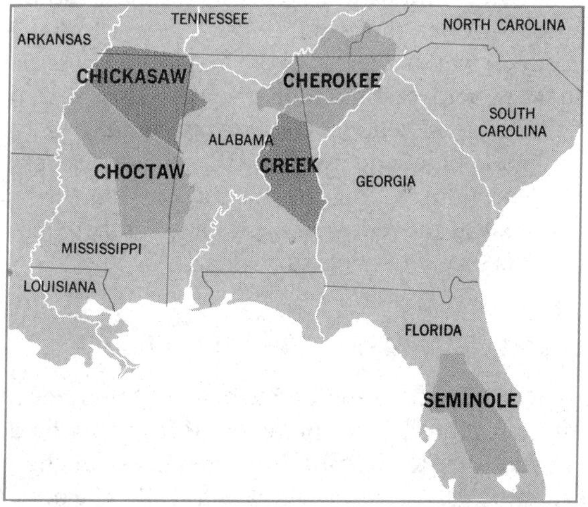

SOUTHERN TRIBES BEFORE TRANSPLANTING

*For population figures since 1790, see Appendix.

Black Hawk War, c. 1832. Resisting Indians in the Illinois country are dispatched by the white men's "fire sticks." (Rare Book Division, New York Public Library, Astor, Lenox and Tilden Foundations.)

Suspicious of white intentions from the start, braves from Illinois and Wisconsin, ably led by Black Hawk, resisted eviction. They were bloodily crushed in 1832 by regular troops, including Lieutenant Jefferson Davis of Mississippi, and by volunteers, including Captain Abraham Lincoln of Illinois.

In Florida the Seminole Indians, joined by runaway black slaves, retreated to the swampy Everglades. For seven years (1835–1842) they waged a bitter guerrilla war that took the lives of some 1,500 soldiers and proved to be the costliest Indian conflict in American experience. The spirit of the Seminoles was at last broken in 1837, when the American field commander treacherously seized their half-breed leader, Osceola, under a flag of truce. Some fled deeper into the Everglades, where their descendants now live, but about four-fifths of them were moved to present Oklahoma, where about 3,000 of the tribe survive.

Jackson's Brass-Knuckle Diplomacy

Trigger-tempered General Jackson was temperamentally unfitted for diplomacy. But in this field he turned out to be much more successful than President J. Q. Adams, his diplomatically seasoned predecessor.

How would Jackson get along with the British? Sober citizens had misgivings, for the fiery general had fought them in two wars. He had also borne on his head, since age fourteen, a sword scar brutally inflicted by an English officer. The problem of reopening trade with the British West Indies provided an acid test of Jackson's views. John Quincy Adams, the astute diplomat, had demanded reopening as a right. Jackson, with surprising moderation, requested it as a privilege. London, no doubt expecting a saber-rattling approach, was thrown off guard. Death had removed the imperious Foreign Secretary Canning from Downing Street, and the British were veering toward free trade, away from their ancient mercantilism. They therefore agreed to reopen this once-lucrative West Indian commerce, subject to the payment of normal customs duties.

As an international bill collector, Jackson proved equally successful, though much less velvet-gloved. In 1831 the Paris government belatedly agreed to pay the United States several million dollars, as compensation for American ships illegally seized during the Napoleonic upheaval. But partly because of political tensions in France, the initial payments were held back. Jackson, short on patience as usual, recommended in his annual message of 1834 that, if necessary, the federal government should seize French property in the United States and pay off the debt with the proceeds.

Gallic pride, traditionally thin-skinned, was hurt. The French closed their legation in Washington and ordered Chargé Alphonse Pageot home. He sailed with his American wife (whose father was a friend of Jackson) and his infant son, Andrew Jackson Pageot (whose godfather was the President). The American legation in Paris was likewise closed, as the buzz of war preparations increased on both sides. Jackson was urged by well-wishers to apologize, but he refused. "Apologize?" he reportedly burst out; "I'll see the whole race roasting in hell first!"

War with France seemed imminent. But the British, not wishing to see their French ally squander its strength in America, successfully mediated. Europe's distresses were still coming to America's aid. French officials, carefully rereading Jackson's messages to Congress, insisted that they now found in them a satisfactory apology—though Jackson loudly insisted that he had not apologized. At all events, arrangements were finally made to pay the debt; and Monsieur Pageot, Madame Pageot, and little Andrew Jackson Pageot sailed back to America.

Jackson had raised international blood pressures dangerously high over this relatively trifling affair. But he did get the money. He also ended a dispute that had explosive possibilities, and he created a new respect in European capitals for the robust young Republic. The Henry Clayites condemned the verbal violence employed, while the President's admirers elatedly retorted, "Hurrah for Jackson!" "No Explanations! No Apologies!"

> Jackson defiantly declared in his annual message to Congress (Dec. 7, 1835), in relation to French claims, "The honor of my country shall never be stained by an apology from me for the statement of truth and the performance of duty; nor can I give any explanation of my official acts except such as is due to integrity and justice and consistent with the principles on which our institutions have been framed."

The Lone Star of Texas Flickers

Land-hungry Americans continued to covet the vast expanse of Texas, which the United States had abandoned to Spain when acquiring Florida in 1819. The Spanish authorities were desirous of populating this virtually unpeopled area, but before they could carry through their contemplated plans, the Mexicans won their independence. A new regime in Mexico City thereupon concluded arrangements in 1823 for granting a huge tract of land to Stephen Austin, with the understanding that he would bring in 300 American families. Immigrants were to be of the established Roman Catholic faith, and in addition were to become properly Mexicanized.

These two restrictions were largely ignored. Hardy Texan pioneers remained Americans at heart, resenting the trammels imposed by a "foreign" government. They were especially annoyed by the presence of Mexican soldiers, many of whom were ragged ex-convicts.

Virile and prolific, Texas-Americans numbered about 30,000 by 1835. Most of them were law-abiding, God-fearing men, but some of them had left the "states" only one or two jumps ahead of the sheriff. "G. T. T." (Gone to Texas) became current descriptive slang. Among the adventurers were Davy Crockett, the fabulous rifleman, and James Bowie, the presumed inventor of the murderous knife that bears his name. It was widely known in the Southwest as the "genuwine Arkansas toothpick." A distinguished latecomer and leader was an ex-governor of Tennessee, Sam Houston. His life had been temporarily shattered in 1829 when his bride of a few weeks left him and he took up transient residence with the Arkansas Indians, who dubbed him "Big Drink." He subsequently took the pledge of temperance.

The pioneer individualists who came to Texas were not easy to push around. Friction rapidly increased between Mexicans and Texans over such issues as slavery, immigration, and local rights. The explosion finally came in 1835, when dictator Santa Anna wiped out cherished rights guaranteed by the Mexican constitution of 1824.

Early in 1836 the liberty-loving Texans declared their independence and unfurled their Lone Star flag—with Sam Houston as commander-in-chief. Santa Anna, at the head of about 6,000 men, swept ferociously into Texas. Trapping a band of nearly 200 defiant Texans at the Alamo in San Antonio, he wiped them out to a man after a thirteen-day siege. Their commander, Colonel W. B. Travis, had heroically declared, "I shall never surrender nor retreat. . . . Victory or Death." The victims included Jim Bowie, who was shot as he lay sick and crippled on his cot, and Davy Crockett, whose body was found riddled with bullets and surrounded by enemy corpses. But the Mexican losses were extremely heavy. A short time later a band of about 400 surrounded and defeated American volunteers, having thrown down their arms at Goliad, were butchered as "pirates." All these operations further delayed the Mexican advance.

Texan war cries—"Remember the Alamo!" "Remember Goliad!" and "Death to Santa Anna!" —swept up into the United States. Scores of vengeful Americans seized their rifles and rushed to the aid of relatives, friends, and compatriots. But despite their efforts, the Lone Star was in grave danger of being dimmed forever as General Sam Houston's small army continued its thirty-seven-day eastward retreat.

But Houston proved equal to the occasion. A commanding figure of a man and a natural leader of the Texans, he lured the pursuers onward to San Jacinto, near the site of the city that now bears his name. The invaders numbered about 1,300 men; the Texans about 900. Suddenly, on April 21, 1836, Houston turned. Taking full advantage of the Mexican siesta hour, he wiped out the invading force and captured Santa Anna, who was

The Alamo. An abandoned mission at San Antonio, the Alamo occupies a glorious spot in Texas history. Known as "The Cradle of Texas Liberty," the Alamo was constructed as a Franciscan chapel in the days of Spanish colonization in the eighteenth century. It had been abandoned for some time prior to its famous use as a fort in 1836. Badly destroyed in the Mexican attack, the Alamo was purchased by the state of Texas in 1883 and subsequently restored. (Courtesy, Texas State Library.)

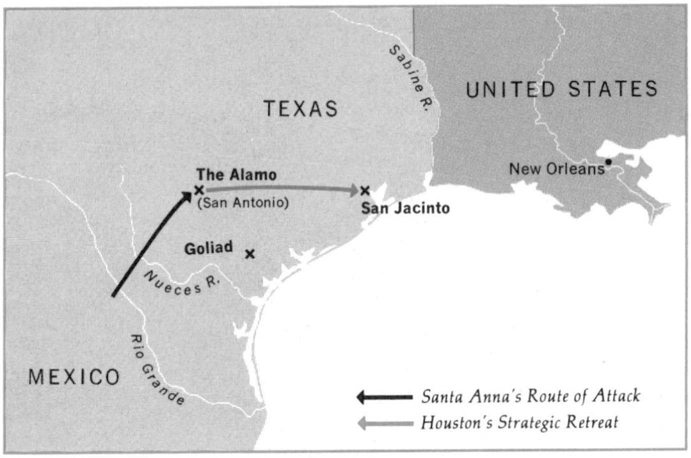

THE TEXAS REVOLUTION, 1835–1836
General Houston's strategy was to retreat and use defense in depth. His line of supply from the United States was shortened as Santa Anna's lengthened. The Mexicans were forced to bring up supplies by land because the Texas navy controlled the sea. This force consisted of only four small ships, but it was big enough to do the job.

found cowering in the tall grass near the battlefield. Confronted with thirsty Bowie knives, the quaking dictator was speedily induced to sign two treaties. By their terms he agreed to withdraw Mexican troops and to recognize the Rio Grande as the extreme southwestern boundary of Texas. When released, he repudiated the whole agreement as illegal and as extorted under duress.

Samuel Houston (1793–1863). After a promising career in Tennessee as a soldier, lawyer, congressman, and governor, Houston became the chief leader and hero of the Texas rebels. Elected to the U.S. Senate and the governorship of Texas, he was forced into retirement when his love for the Union caused him to spurn the Confederacy in the Civil War.

Texas: An International Derelict

Mexico no doubt had a genuine grievance against the United States. The Texans, though courageous, could hardly have won their independence without unneutral help in men and supplies from their American cousins. The Washington government, as the Mexicans bitterly complained, had a solemn obligation under international law to enforce its leaky neutrality statutes. But American public opinion, overwhelmingly favorable to the Texans, openly nullified the existing legislation. The federal authorities were powerless to act.

Jackson's heart was torn by the Texas issue. He disliked the Mexican overlords and admired the heroism of Sam Houston, his old comrade-in-arms against the Indians. But he was in no haste to recognize Texas formally as an independent republic. To do so would touch off the whole explosive issue of slavery, at a time when he was trying to engineer the election of his handpicked successor, Martin Van Buren. But after Van Buren had come safely under the wire, Jackson extended the right hand of recognition, the day before he left office in 1837.

Texas had every reason to expect a union with the United States, for what nation in its right mind would refuse so princely a dowry? The radiant Texan bride, officially petitioning for annexation in 1837, presented herself for marriage. But the expectant groom, Uncle Sam, was jerked back by the black hand of the slavery issue. Anti-slavery zealots in the North were opposing annexation with increasing vehemence; they contended that the whole scheme was merely a conspiracy cooked up by the Southern "slavocracy" to bring new slave pens into the Union.

At first glance, a "slavery plot" charge seemed plausible. Most of the early settlers in Texas, as well as American volunteers during the revolution, had come from the states of the South and Southwest. But scholars have concluded that the settlement of Texas was merely the normal and inexorable march of the westward movement. Most of the immigrants came from the South and Southwest simply because these states were closer. The explanation was proximity rather than conspiracy.

The jilted Texas bride was left in a dangerous predicament. Fearing the return of the "villain," Santa Anna, she understandably went so far as to flirt openly with Britain and France for support. An ugly situation, involving balance-of-power politics, began to develop below the underbelly of the United States. It could not be allowed to go on indefinitely.

The End of "King Andrew's" Reign

New parties were jelling as the 1830s lengthened. By 1834, the Democratic-Republicans of Andrew Jackson had unashamedly adopted the once-tainted name of "Democrats." National Republicans, glamorously led by Henry Clay, chose the time-honored name of Whig—a magic name closely associated with patriotism during the Revolutionary War. (See chart, p. 149.)

The Whig party was a hodgepodge of malcontents—"an organized incompatibility." Their guiding star at this time was opportunism; their chief cement was hatred of Jackson and hunger for the spoils of office. In the same political bed were gathered all kinds of Whigs: protectionists and free-traders, Southern nullifiers and Northern nationalists, rich Southern planters and poor Northern farmers.

As the presidential election of 1836 neared, the Whigs did not feel strong enough to beat the Jacksonian Democrats in a straight-out fight. Their strategy was to nominate several prominent "favorite sons," who would so scatter the vote that no candidate would get a majority. The deadlock would then have to be broken by the House of Representatives, where the Whigs had a chance. With Henry Clay bowing out of a near-hopeless race, the leading "favorite son" was heavy-jawed General William Henry Harrison of Ohio, so-called hero of the Battle of Tippecanoe.

Contemporary Election Parade. (Library of Congress.)

Martin Van Buren of New York, a smooth-as-silk politician, was Jackson's choice for "appointment" as his successor. The hollow-cheeked Jackson, now nearing seventy, was too old and ailing to consider a third term. But he was not loath to try to serve a third term through Van Buren, something of a "yes man," who was unconvincingly called "Young Hickory." Leaving nothing to chance, the general carefully rigged the nominating convention and rammed his favorite down the throats of the delegates. Van Buren was supported by the Jacksonites without wild enthusiasm, even though he had promised "to tread generally" in the military-booted footsteps of his predecessor.

The finespun schemes of the Whigs availed nothing. Van Buren, the dapper "Little Van," squirmed into office by the close popular vote of 762,678 to 735,651, but by the comfortable margin of 170 votes to 73 in the Electoral College. Jackson could now step down.

In retrospect, the Jackson years were yeasty ones. It is true that they were marred by noise and bluster, as well as by bull-in-the-china-closet finance and diplomacy. Yet the rough-hewn general —through forthrightness, energy, and strength of character—did far better than might have been expected. He demonstrated anew the value of strong executive leadership; he led the common people into national politics; he united them into the powerful and long-lived Democratic party; and he proved that they could be trusted with both the vote and high office. Reasserting the prestige of the presidency, he amazed weak-kneed politicians by showing that the courageous course often wins the most votes.

The other side of the ledger is less satisfying. Jackson cannot escape blame for his encouragement of the spoils system and of unsound finance, with its heartbreaking legacy of a century of thousands of bank failures. No one can deny that the B.U.S. was a powerful and ultimately a corrupting monopoly, which needed to have its wings clipped. But chopping off its head instead of its wings was of dubious benefit to the entire nation.

Dandified Martin Van Buren (1782–1862). He has been generally underrated as a President because of his skill as a politician. It was said of him that he rowed toward his objectives "with muffled oars." Yet he was a politician with principles, as evidenced by his strong stand against slavery expansion and by his hopeless run for the presidency in his later years (1848) as candidate of the Free Soil party.

Big Woes for the "Little Magician"

Martin Van Buren, eighth President, was the first to be born under the American flag. Bland of face, bald of head, slender of figure, the adroit little New Yorker has been described as "a first-class second-rate man." An accomplished wire-puller and spoilsman—"the wizard of Albany"—he was also a statesman of wide experience in both legislative and administrative life. In intelligence, education, and training, he was above the average of the Presidents since Jackson. The myth of his complete mediocrity sprouted from a series of misfortunes over which he had no control.

From the outset, the new politician-President labored under severe handicaps. As a machine-made candidate, he incurred the resentment of many Democrats—the men who objected to having a "bastard politician" smuggled into office beneath the tails of the old general's military coat. Jackson, the master showman, had been the dynamic type of executive whose administration had resounded with furious quarrels and cracked heads. Easygoing Martin Van Buren seemed to rattle about in the military boots of his testy predecessor. The people felt let down. Inheriting Jackson's mantle without his popularity, the polished New Yorker also inherited the ex-President's numerous and vengeful enemies.

Van Buren's four years overflowed with toil and trouble. A rebellion in Canada in 1837 stirred up ugly incidents along the northern frontier and threatened to trigger war with Britain. The President's attempt to play a neutral game led to the cry, "Woe to Martin Van Buren!" The anti-slavery agitators in the North were in full cry, and among other grievances were condemning the prospective annexation of Texas.

Worst of all, Van Buren inherited a searing depression from Jackson. Much of his energy had to be devoted to the purely negative task of battling the panic, and there were not enough rabbits in the "Little Magician's" tall silk hat. Hard times ordinarily blight the reputation of a President—and Van Buren was no exception.

Depression Doldrums and the Independent Treasury

The Panic of 1837 was a symptom of the financial sickness of the times. Its basic cause was evidently overspeculation, prompted by a mania of get-rich-quickism. Gamblers in Western lands were doing a "land-office business" on borrowed capital, much of it in the shaky currency of "wildcat banks." The speculative craze spread to canals, roads, railroads, and slaves.

But speculation alone did not cause the crash. Jacksonian finance, including the Bank War and the Specie Circular, gave an additional jolt to an already teetering structure. Failures of wheat crops, ravaged by the Hessian fly, deepened the distress. Grain prices were forced so high that mobs in New York City, three weeks before Van Buren took the oath, stormed warehouses and broke open flour barrels. The panic really began before Jackson left, but its full fury burst about Van Buren's bewildered head.

Financial stringency abroad likewise left its imprint on America. Late in 1836, while Jackson was still President, the failure of two prominent British banks created tremors and these in turn caused English investors to call in foreign loans. The resulting pinch in the United States, combined with other setbacks, heralded the beginning of the panic. Europe's economic distresses have often been America's distresses, for every major American financial panic has been affected by conditions overseas.

Hardship was acute and widespread. American banks collapsed by the hundreds, including some "pet banks," which carried down with them several millions in government funds. Commodity prices drooped, sales of public lands fell off, and customs revenues dried to a rivulet. Factories closed their doors; unemployed workers darkened the streets.

> Philip Hone, a New York businessman, described in his diary (May 10, 1837) a phase of the financial crisis: "The savings-bank also sustained a most grievous run yesterday. They paid 375 depositors $81,000. The press was awful; the hour for closing the bank is six o'clock, but they did not get through the paying of those who were in at that time till nine o'clock. I was there with the other trustees and witnessed the madness of the people—women nearly pressed to death, and the stoutest men could scarcely sustain themselves; but they held on as with a death's grip upon the evidences of their claims, and, exhausted as they were with the pressure, they had strength to cry 'Pay! Pay!'"

Unhappily, the masses simply had to wait for the economic blizzard to blow itself out. The view prevailed, substantially unchanged until the 1930s, that the less governmental interference there was the better. Luckless Van Buren, shackled by this hands-off philosophy, could cope with the crisis only indirectly.

A perplexed President sought to bring some relief through his much-debated "Divorce Bill." Convinced that some of the financial fever had come from injecting government funds into politics, he championed the principle of "divorcing" the public revenue from private banks. The so-called Independent Treasury Bill is his chief claim to constructive statesmanship. The scheme was to lock the surplus federal money in government vaults, which would be located in the larger cities. Funds could be disbursed as needed, and they would not only be safe but completely divorced from politics. Yet they would also be denied to the banking system as reserves, thus shriveling available credit resources. The need for political purity triumphed over enlightened economics.

Van Buren's "divorce" scheme was never highly popular. It was supported only lukewarmly by his fellow Democrats, many of whom longed for the risky but lush days of the "pet banks." The new policy was condemned by the Whigs, primarily because it would dampen their hopes for a revived Bank of the United States. After a prolonged struggle, the Independent Treasury Bill passed Congress in 1840. Repealed the next year by the victorious Whigs, the sub-treasury scheme was re-enacted by the triumphant Democrats in 1846, and then continued until merged with the Federal Reserve System in the next century.

"Tippecanoe" Versus "Little Van"

Van Buren, though panic-tainted, was renominated by the Democrats in 1840, albeit without great enthusiasm. They had no acceptable alternative to what the Whigs called "Martin Van Ruin." Not to have run him again would have been a damaging admission that the party had foisted an unsound choice upon the country in 1836.

The Whigs, hungering for the spoils of office, scented victory in the breeze. Pangs of the panic

President William Henry Harrison (1773–1841). Harrison can claim several distinctions. At sixty-eight, he was the oldest man ever to be sworn in; he delivered the longest inaugural address (two hours); dying of pneumonia, he served the shortest term (thirty-one days); he obviously accomplished the least of any President; and he was responsible for the most progeny: 10 children; 48 grandchildren; 106 great-grandchildren. One of his grandchildren, Benjamin Harrison, became the 23rd President.

were still being felt; and voters blindly blamed their woes on the party in power. The Whigs turned again not to their ablest statesman—Clay or Webster—but to their presumably ablest vote-getter: General Harrison, a coarse-featured military chieftain, with a long, thin face and medium build (5 feet 8 inches; 1.72 meters).

The aging hero, nearly sixty-eight when the campaign ended, was a small-bore candidate. Despite an inflated reputation, he had been only moderately successful in civilian and military life, notably at the Battles of Tippecanoe (1811) and the Thames (1813). "Old Tippecanoe" was then living quietly in a sixteen-room mansion, located on a 3,000-acre farm near North Bend, Ohio. His views on current issues were only vaguely known. He was nominated primarily because he was issueless and enemyless—and a most unfortunate precedent was thus set. John Tyler of Virginia, an afterthought, was selected as his vice-presidential running mate.

The Whigs played this political game with the cards close to their vests. They published no platform, fearing to make bothersome commitments and unwilling to reveal the deep divisions within their own patchwork party. They hoped to sweep their hero in by a frothy huzza-for-Harrison campaign.

A dull-witted Democratic editor played directly into Whig hands. Stupidly insulting the West, he sneered at Harrison as an impoverished old farmer who would be content with a pension, a log cabin, and a barrel of hard cider—the poor Westerner's champagne. Whigs gleefully took up the challenge and, stressing the hard cider and log cabin theme, turned the campaign into a huge political revival meeting. Harrisonites portrayed their hero as the poor "Farmer of North Bend," who had been called from his plow and his log cabin to drive corrupt Jackson spoilsmen from the "presidential palace."

A non-existent candidate rapidly began to take shape in the hands of Whig mythmakers. The real Harrison was not lowborn, but from one of the F.F.V.'s (First Families of Virginia). He was not poverty-stricken; he did not live in a one-room log

Hard Cider Triumphant. A contemporary sketch.

cabin; he did not swill down gallons of hard cider (he evidently prefered whiskey); and he did not plow his fields with his own "huge paws."

Whig propagandists made merry with little "Matty" Van Buren, the "Flying Dutchman." Although reared in poverty, he was denounced as a supercilious aristocrat, who wore corsets and ate French food with golden teaspoons from golden plates. Jackson's rough-timbered Democratic party, deeply rooted in the West, was thus saddled with a simpering dandy from the aristocratic East. The aristocratic Whig party of Webster and Biddle, no less inconsistently, had come up with a backwoods nominee from the Democratic West—a reasonably good facsimile of wrinkled old General Jackson. As a jeering Whig campaign song proclaimed:

> Old Tip, he wears a homespun shirt,
> He has no ruffled shirt, wirt, wirt.
> But Matt, he has the golden plate,
> And he's a little squirt, wirt, wirt.

The Log Cabins and Hard Cider of 1840

Eager Democrats, who had hurrahed Jackson into the White House, now discovered to their chagrin that this was a game two could play. Acres of Whig audiences and miles of Whig marchers shouted such slogans as: "Harrison, Two Dollars a Day and Roast Beef" and "With Tip and Tyler We'll Bust Van's Biler." Log cabins were dished up in every conceivable form. Bawling Whigs, stimulated by fortified cider, rolled huge inflated balls from village to village and state to state—balls that represented the snowballing majority for "Tip and Ty." As they pushed, they sang:

> Tippecanoe, and Tyler too.
> And with them we'll beat little Van, Van, Van,
> Oh! Van is a used-up man.

Claptrap was king, as the electoral debauch reached an all-time intellectual low. There was little sober discussion of solid issues. Democrats inquired earnestly about the Bank, internal improvements, and the tariff. The replies were "log cabin," "hard cider," "Harrison is a poor man." Van Burenites, protesting futilely, were drowned in a tidal wave of apple juice as America experienced its first mass-turnout election.

Harrison won by the surprisingly close margin of 1,275,016 popular votes to 1,129,102, but by the overwhelming electoral count of 234 to 60. The hard-ciderites had seemingly received a mandate to go to Washington, tear down the White House, and erect a log cabin.

A Hard Road to Hoe! Jackson urges Van Buren toward the White House over a road littered with log cabins and hard cider. Van Buren, handicapped also by his unpopular sub-treasury policy, would evidently prefer the smoother road back to his Kinderhook home. A campaign cartoon of 1840. (Library of Congress.)

Basically, the vote was a protest against hard times—a thunderous shout of "Out with the old and in with the new." But the blatant buncombe and silly slogans set an unfortunate example for future campaigns. Democracy calls for hard thinking, not hard cider; for dignity, not delirium. Yet an able, well-organized, and well-entrenched political party, committed to solid principles, was hooted out of office by an inane hoopla campaign.

The Democrats were baffled. They complained with much bitterness and no little truth that they had been shouted down, sung down, lied down, and drunk down. Yet, though out-sloganed, they had kept their ranks intact. Even in defeat they were a stronger party than the Whigs. Though temporarily overdosed with hard cider, they would be heard from again.

VARYING VIEWPOINTS

The debate over Jacksonianism has shifted from a concern with geography to a concern with social class. Simultaneously, the question of Jackson's precise class position—and the class interests he represented—has moved to center stage. Arthur Schlesinger, Jr., had identified him with the working class and thus preserved Jackson's "popular" image. But other historians see "Old Hickory" as an aspiring frontier aristocrat, and they appraise Jacksonianism as a movement to liberate emerging capitalism from the restraints of an older "establishment." Jackson's war on the Bank, in this view, was less a popular crusade against the moneyed interests and more a blow by one segment of the business class against another segment of the business class. Indian policy, which has recently come in for renewed scrutiny, seems to reinforce the image of the Jacksonians as ambitious capitalists, motivated less by regard for human rights than by their own acquisitiveness.

SELECT READINGS

G. G. Van Deusen, *The Jacksonian Era, 1828–1848* (1959), is an excellent introduction. Colorful detail abounds in Marquis James, *Andrew Jackson: Portrait of a President* (1937). Incisive analysis can be found in Richard Hofstadter's essay on Jackson in *The American Political Tradition* (1948). Edward Pessen finds little to praise in *Jacksonian America: Society, Personality, and Politics* (1969). The opposing sides in the nullification crisis may be studied in C. M. Wiltse, *John C. Calhoun, Nullifier* (1951), and C. G. Sellers, *Andrew Jackson and the States-Rights Tradition* (1963). A superior monograph is W. W. Freehling, *Prelude to Civil War: The Nullification Controversy in South Carolina* (1966). Jacksonians are charged with ignorance and hypocrisy in Bray Hammond, *Banks and Politics in America, from the Revolution to the Civil War* (1957), and T. P. Govan defends *Nicholas Biddle: Nationalist and Public Banker* (1959). John McFaul looks at the broader picture in *The Politics of Jacksonian Finance* (1972). Jackson's Indian policies are scrutinized in four recent books: Arthur DeRosier, *The Removal of the Choctaw Indians* (1970), Thurman Wilkins, *Cherokee Tragedy* (1970), R. N. Satz, *American Indian Policy in the Jacksonian Era* (1975), and M. P. Rogin's heavily psychoanalytic *Fathers and Children: Andrew Jackson and the Subjugation of the American Indians* (1975). For an intriguing intellectual history of the same subject, see R. N. Pearce, *The Savages of America* (1965). Important political transformations are handled in R. P. McCormick, *The Second American Party System: Party Formation in the Jacksonian Era* (1966), and in R. Formisano, *The Birth of Mass Political Parties: Michigan, 1827–1861* (1971). Peter Temin interprets *The Jacksonian Economy* (1969). The color of the frothy presidential campaign of 1840 comes through in R. G. Gunderson, *The Log-Cabin Campaign* (1957). Daniel W. Howe provides a stimulating analysis of ideology in *The Political Culture of the American Whigs* (1980).

15

Manifest Destiny in the Forties

Our manifest destiny [is] to overspread the continent allotted by Providence for the free development of our yearly multiplying millions.

JOHN L. O'SULLIVAN, 1845*

The Accession of "Tyler Too"

A horde of hard-ciderites descended upon Washington early in 1841, clamoring for the spoils of office. Newly elected President Harrison, bewildered by the uproar, was almost hounded to death by Whig spoilsmen.

The real leaders of the Whig party regarded "Old Tippecanoe" as little more than an impressive figurehead. Daniel Webster, as secretary of state, and Henry Clay, the uncrowned king of the Whigs and their ablest spokesman in the Senate, would grasp the helm. The aging general was finally forced to rebuke the over-zealous Clay and

*Earliest known use of the term "manifest destiny," sometimes called "manifest desire."

pointedly remind him that William Henry Harrison was President of the United States.

Unluckily for Clay and Webster, their schemes soon hit a fatal snag. Before the new term had fairly started, Harrison came down with pneumonia. Wearied by official functions and plagued by office seekers, the enfeebled old warrior died after only four weeks in the White House—the shortest administration by far in American history, following by far the longest inaugural address.

The "Tyler too" part of the Whig ticket, hitherto only a rhyme, now claimed the spotlight. What manner of man did the nation now find in the presidential chair? Six feet (1.83 meters) tall, slender, blue-eyed, and fair-haired, with classical features and a high forehead, Tyler was a Virginia gentleman of the old school—gracious and kindly, yet stubbornly attached to principle. He had earlier resigned from the United States Senate, quite unnecessarily, rather than accept distasteful instructions from the Virginia legislature. Still a lone wolf, he had forsaken the Jacksonian Democratic fold for that of the Whigs, largely because he could not stomach the dictatorial tactics of Jackson.

Tyler's enemies accused him of being a Democrat in Whig clothing, but this charge was only partially true. The Whig party was something of a catchall, and the accidental President belonged to the minority wing, which embraced a number of Jeffersonian states'-righters. Tyler had in fact been put on the ticket partly to attract the vote of this influential group, many of whom were Southern gentry.

Yet Tyler, high-minded as he was, should never have consented to run on the ticket. Though the dominant Clay-Webster group had published no platform, every alert politician knew what the unpublished platform contained. And on virtually every major issue the obstinate Virginian was at odds with the majority of his Whig party, which was pro-Bank, pro-protective tariff, and pro-internal improvements. "Tyler too" rhymed with "Tippecanoe," but there the harmony ended. As events turned out, President Harrison, the Whig, served for only four weeks, while Tyler, the ex-Democrat who was still largely a Democrat at heart, served for 204 weeks.

President John Tyler (1790–1862). The first "accidental President," he was faithful to his states'-rights convictions until death. A member of the Virginia secession convention in 1861, he served in the provisional congress of the Confederacy and was elected to a seat in the Confederate house of representatives. Invading Northern troops vengefully despoiled his beautiful Virginia estate, Sherwood Forest.

John Tyler: A President Without a Party

After their hard-won, hard-cider victory, the Whigs brought their secret platform out of Clay's waistcoat pocket. To the surprise of no one, it outlined a strongly nationalistic program.

Financial reform came first. The Whig Congress hastened to pass a law ending the Independent Treasury system, and President Tyler, disarmingly agreeable, signed it. Clay next drove through Congress a bill for a "Fiscal Bank," which would establish a new Bank of the United States.

Tyler's hostility to a centralized bank was notorious, and Clay—the "Great Compromiser"—would have done well to conciliate him. But the Kentuckian, robbed repeatedly of the presidency by lesser men, was in an imperious mood and riding for a fall. When the bank bill reached the presidential desk, Tyler flatly vetoed it on both practical and constitutional grounds. A drunken mob gathered late at night near the White House and shouted insultingly, "Huzza for Clay!" "A Bank! A Bank!" "Down with the Veto!"

The stunned Whig leaders tried once again.

Striving to meet Tyler's objections to a "Fiscal Bank," they passed another bill providing for a "Fiscal Corporation." But the President, still unbending, vetoed the offensive substitute. Democrats were jubilant: they had been saved from another financial "monster" only by the pneumonia that had felled Harrison.

Whig extremists, boiling with indignation, condemned Tyler as "His Accidency" and as an "Executive Ass." Widely burned in effigy, he received numerous letters threatening him with death. A wave of influenza then sweeping the country was called the "Tyler grippe." To the delight of Democrats, the stiff-necked Virginian was formally expelled from his party by a caucus of Whig congressmen, and a serious attempt to impeach him was made in the House of Representatives. His entire Cabinet resigned in a body, except Secretary of State Webster, who was then in the midst of delicate negotiations with England.

The proposed Whig tariff also felt the prick of the President's well-inked pen. Surprisingly enough, Tyler did sign a law passed in 1841 for bringing additional revenue to the depression-drained Treasury. But he looked with frosty eye on the major tariff scheme of the Whigs. It provided, among other features, for a distribution among the states of revenue from the sale of public lands in the West. Tyler could see no point in squandering federal money when the federal Treasury was not overflowing, and he again wielded an emphatic veto.

Chastened Clayites redrafted their tariff bill. They chopped out the offensive dollar-distribution scheme, and pushed down the rates to about the moderately protective level of 1832, roughly 32 percent on dutiable goods. Tyler had no fondness for a protective tariff, but realizing the need for additional revenue, he reluctantly signed the law of 1842. In subsequent months, the pressure for higher customs duties slackened as the country gradually edged its way out of the depression. The Whig slogan, "Harrison, Two Dollars a Day and Roast Beef," was rewritten by unhappy Democrats to read, "Ten Cents a Day and Bean Soup."

A War of Words with England

Hatred of England during the 19th Century came to a head periodically, and had to be lanced by treaty settlement or by war. The poison had festered ominously by 1842.

Anti-British passions were compounded of many ingredients. At bottom lay the bitter, redcoated memories of the two Anglo-American wars. In addition, the genteel pro-British Federalists had died out, eventually yielding to the boisterous Jacksonian Democrats. British travelers, sniffing with aristocratic noses at the crude scene, wrote acidly of American tobacco spitting, slave auctioneering, lynching, eye gouging, and other unsavory features of the rustic civilization. Travel books penned by these critics, whose views were avidly read on both sides of the Atlantic, stirred up angry outbursts in America.

But the literary fireworks did not end here. British magazines added fuel to the flames when, enlarging on the travel books, they launched sneering attacks on Yankee shortcomings. American journals struck back with "you're another" arguments, thus touching off the "Third War with

"Life In An American Hotel." An English caricature of American rudeness and readiness with the pistol. (*Punch*, 1856.)

England." Fortunately, it was fought with paper broadsides, and only ink was spilled. British authors, including Charles Dickens, entered the fray with gall-dipped pens, for they were being denied rich royalties by the absence of an American copyright law.*

Sprawling America, with expensive canals to dig and railroads to build, was a borrowing nation in the 19th Century. Imperial Britain, with her overflowing coffers, was a lending nation. The tight-fisted creditor is never popular with the debtor, and the phrase "bloated British bondholder" rolled bitterly from many an American tongue. When the Panic of 1837 broke, and several states defaulted on their bonds or repudiated them openly, honest Englishmen assailed Yankee trickery. One of them offered a new stanza for an old song:

> Yankee Doodle borrows cash,
> Yankee Doodle spends it,
> And then he snaps his fingers at
> The jolly flat [simpleton] who lends it.

Troubles of a more dangerous sort came closer to home in 1837, when a short-lived insurrection erupted in Canada. It was supported by such a small minority of Canadians that it never had a real chance of success. Yet hundreds of hot-blooded Americans, hoping to strike a blow for freedom against the hereditary enemy, furnished military supplies or volunteered for armed service. The Washington regime tried arduously, though futilely, to uphold its weak neutrality regulations. But again, as in the case of Texas, it simply could not enforce unpopular laws in the face of popular opposition.

A provocative incident on the Canadian frontier brought passions to a boil in 1837. An American steamer, the *Caroline,* was engaged in carrying supplies to the insurgents across the swift Niagara River. It was finally attacked on the New York shore by a determined British force, which set the vessel on fire. Lurid American illustrators showed the flaming ship, laden with shrieking souls, plunging over the Niagara Falls. The craft evidently sank short of the falls, and only one American was killed.

This unlawful invasion of American soil—a counter-violation of neutrality—had alarming aftermaths. The Washington officials lodged vigorous but ineffective protests. Three years later, in 1840, the incident was dramatically revived in the state of New York. A Canadian named McLeod, after allegedly boasting in a tavern of his part in the *Caroline* raid, was arrested and indicted for murder. The London Foreign Office, which regarded the *Caroline* raiders as members of an armed force and not as criminals, made clear that his execution would mean war. Fortunately, McLeod was freed after establishing an alibi. It must have been airtight, for it was good enough to convince a New York jury. The tension forthwith eased, but it snapped taut again in 1841, when British officials in the Bahamas offered asylum to 130 Virginia slaves who had rebelled and captured the American ship *Creole.*

Manipulating the Maine Maps

An explosive controversy of the early 1840s involved the Maine boundary dispute. The St. Lawrence River is icebound several months of the year, as the British, remembering the War of 1812, well knew. They were determined, as a defensive precaution against the Yankees, to build a road westward from the seaport of Halifax to Quebec. But the proposed route ran through disputed territory—claimed also by Maine under the misleading peace treaty of 1783. Tough-knuckled lumberjacks from both Maine and Canada entered the disputed no-man's-land of the tall-timbered Aroostook River Valley. Ugly fights flared up; both sides summoned the local militia. The small-scale lumberjack clash, dubbed the "Aroostook War," threatened to widen into a full-dress shooting war.

As the crisis deepened in 1842, the London Foreign Office took an unusual step. It sent to

*Not until 1891 did Congress extend copyright privileges to foreign authors.

Washington a non-professional diplomat, the conciliatory financier Lord Ashburton, who had married a wealthy American woman. He speedily established cordial relations with Secretary Webster, who had recently been lionized during a visit to England.

The two statesmen, their nerves frayed by protracted negotiations in the heat of a Washington summer, finally agreed to compromise on the Maine boundary. On the basis of a rough, split-the-difference arrangement, the Americans were to retain some 7,000 square miles (18,130 square kilometers) of the 12,000 square miles (31,080 square kilometers) of wilderness in dispute. The British got less land, but won the desired Halifax-Quebec route. During the negotiations the *Caroline* affair, dragged out since 1837, was patched up by an exchange of diplomatic notes.

The surrender of 5,000 square miles (12,950 square kilometers) of allegedly American soil to the British proved highly unpopular, especially among loyal Maine men. One irate United States senator branded the treaty a "solemn bamboozlement." But Webster had obtained an ancient map which indicated, ironically, that the British were entitled to the entire area in dispute. When he secretly displayed his find in Washington, the treaty quickly slipped through the Senate on greased skids.

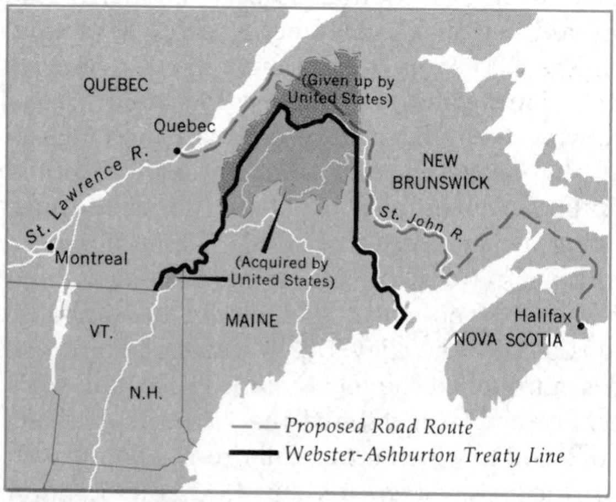

MAINE BOUNDARY SETTLEMENT, 1842

The London *Morning Chronicle* greeted the Webster-Ashburton treaty: "See the feeling with which the treaty has been received in America; mark the enthusiasm it has excited. What does this mean? Why, either that the Americans have gained a great diplomatic victory over us, or that they have escaped a great danger, as they have felt it, in having to maintain their claim by war."

British imperialists likewise condemned Lord Ashburton for his "capitulation." But their opposition also evaporated when the London officials turned up with another yellowing map: it proved that the *Americans* were entitled to the entire area in contention. Thus each party to the negotiation secretly held the other's trump card in the historic "Battle of the Maps."

Historians have since proved that the United States had a valid claim to the entire territory. This fact was not known at the time, perhaps fortunately, for the British were in no mood to give up the Halifax route. The yielding of 5,000 square miles (12,950 square kilometers) of pine-forested land, at least in 1842, seemed like a cheap price to pay for avoiding a senseless war.

An overlooked bonus was won in the same treaty when the British, in adjusting the boundary to the west, surrendered 6,500 square miles (16,835 square kilometers). The area was later found to contain the priceless Mesabi iron ore of Minnesota.

The Lone Star of Texas Shines Alone

The jilted Texan bride, during the uncertain eight years since 1836, had led a precarious existence. Mexico, refusing to recognize her independence, regarded the Lone Star Republic as a province in revolt, to be reconquered in the future. Mexican officials loudly threatened war if the American eagle should gather the fledgling republic under its protective wings.

General Santa Anna (1795–1876). Four-time president of Mexico, he lost California and the rest of the Mexican cession to the U.S. in 1848.

The Texans were forced to maintain a costly military establishment. Vastly outnumbered by their Mexican foe, they could not tell when he would strike again. Mexico actually did make two halfhearted raids which, though ineffectual, foreshadowed more fearsome efforts. Confronted with such perils, Texas was driven to open negotiations with England and France, in the hope of securing the defensive shield of a protectorate. In 1839 and 1840, the Texans concluded treaties with France, Holland, and Belgium.

Britain was intensely interested in an independent Texas. Such a republic would check the southward surge of the American colossus, whose bulging biceps posed a constant threat to nearby British possessions in the New World. A puppet Texas, dancing to strings pulled by Britain, could be turned upon the Yankees. Subsequent clashes would create a smoke-screen diversion, behind which foreign powers could move into the Americas and challenge the insolent Monroe Doctrine. French schemers were likewise attracted by the hoary game of divide and conquer. It would result, they hoped, in the fragmentation and militarization of America.

Dangers threatened from other foreign quarters. British abolitionists were busily intriguing for a foothold in Texas. If successful in freeing the few blacks there, they presumably would inflame the nearby slaves of the South. In addition, British merchants regarded Texas as a potentially important free-trade area—an offset to the tariff-walled United States. British manufacturers likewise perceived that those vast Texan plains constituted one of the great cotton-producing areas of the future. An independent Texas would relieve British looms of their fatal dependence on American fiber—a supply which might be cut off in time of crisis by embargo or war.

The Belated Texas Nuptials

Partly because of the fears aroused by British schemers, Texas became a leading issue in the presidential campaign of 1844. The foes of expansion assailed annexation, while Southern hotheads cried, "Texas or Disunion." The pro-expansion Democrats under James K. Polk finally triumphed over the Whigs under Henry Clay, the hardy perennial candidate. Lame-duck President Tyler thereupon interpreted the narrow Democratic victory, with dubious accuracy, as a "mandate" to acquire Texas.

Eager to crown his troubled administration with this splendid prize, Tyler deserves much of the credit for shepherding Texas into the fold. Many "conscience Whigs" feared that Texas in the Union would be red meat to nourish the lusty "slave power." Tyler despaired of securing the needed two-thirds vote for a treaty in the Senate, and he made haste to arrange for annexation by a joint resolution. This solution required only a simple majority in both houses of Congress. After a spirited debate, the resolution passed early in 1845, and Texas was formally invited to become the twenty-eighth star on the American flag. After some coyness, the waiting bride unpacked her mildewing wedding dress and was formally embraced as a full-fledged state.

Mexico angrily charged that the Americans had

Early Texas State House

despoiled her of Texas. This was to some extent true in 1836, but hardly true in 1845, for the area was no longer Mexico's to be despoiled of. As the years stretched out, realistic observers could see that the Mexicans would not be able to reconquer their lost province. Yet Mexico left the Texans dangling by denying their right to dispose of themselves as they chose.

By 1845, the Lone Star Republic had become a danger spot, inviting foreign intrigue that menaced the American people. Her continued existence as an independent nation threatened to involve the United States in a series of ruinous wars, both in America and in Europe. Americans were in a "lick all creation" mood when they sang "Uncle Sam's Song to Miss Texas":

> If Mexy back'd by secret foes,
> Still talks of getting you, gal;
> Why we can lick 'em all you know
> And then annex 'em too, gal.

What other power would have spurned the imperial domain of Texas? The bride was so near, so rich, so fair, so willing. Whatever the peculiar circumstances of the Texas revolution, the United States can hardly be accused of unseemly haste in achieving annexation. Nine long years were surely a decent wait between the beginning of the courtship and the consummation of the marriage.

Oregon Fever Populates Oregon

The so-called Oregon Country was an enormous wilderness. It sprawled magnificently west of the Rockies to the Pacific Ocean, and north of California to the line of 54° 40′—the present southern tip of the Alaska panhandle. All or substantial parts of this immense area were claimed at one time or another by four nations: Spain, Russia, Britain, and the United States.

Two claimants dropped out of the scramble. Spain, though the first to raise her banner in Oregon, bartered away her claims to the United States in the so-called Florida Treaty of 1819. The Russian Bear retreated to the line of 54° 40′ by the treaties of 1824 and 1825 with America and Britain. These two remaining rivals now had the field to themselves.

British claims to Oregon were strong—at least to that portion north of the Columbia River. They were based squarely on prior discovery and exploration, on treaty rights, and on actual occupation. The most important colonizing agency was the far-flung Hudson's Bay Company, which was trading profitably with the Indians of the Pacific Northwest for their furs.

Americans, for their part, could also point pridefully to exploration and occupation. Captain Robert Gray in 1792 had stumbled upon the majestic Columbia River, which he named after his ship; and the famed Lewis and Clark expedition of 1804–1806 had ranged overland through the Oregon Country to the Pacific. This shaky American toehold was ultimately strengthened by the presence of missionaries and other settlers, a sprinkling of whom reached the grassy Willamette River Valley, south of the Columbia, in the 1830s. These men of God, in saving the soul of the Indian, were instrumental in saving the soil of Oregon for the United States. They stimulated interest in a faraway domain which countless Americans had earlier assumed would not be settled for centuries.

Scattered American and British pioneers in Oregon continued to live peacefully side by side. At the time of negotiating the Treaty of 1818, the

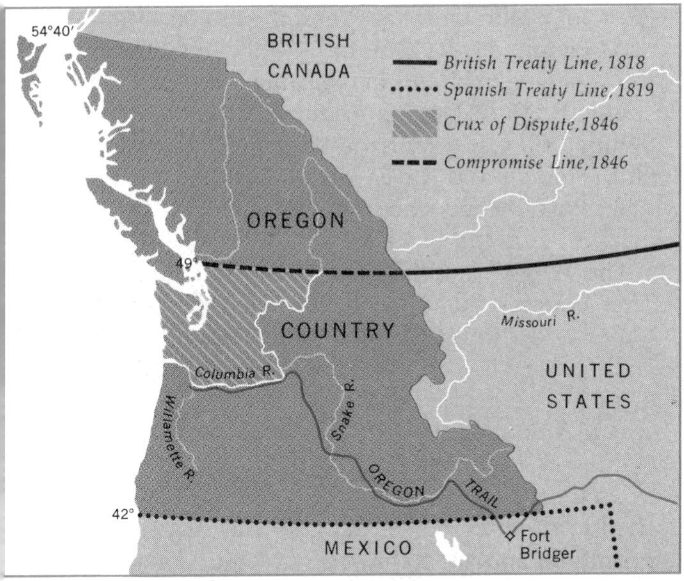

THE OREGON CONTROVERSY

United States had sought to divide the vast domain by the 49th parallel. But the British, who regarded the Columbia River as the St. Lawrence of the West, were unwilling to yield this vital artery. A scheme for peaceful "joint occupation" was thereupon adopted, pending a future settlement.

The handful of Americans in the Willamette Valley was suddenly multiplied in the early 1840s, when "Oregon fever" seized hundreds of restless pioneers. In increasing numbers their creaking covered wagons jolted over the 2,000-mile (3,200-kilometer) Oregon Trail as the human rivulet widened into a stream.* By 1846 there were about 5,000 American settlers south of the Columbia River, some of them tough "border ruffians," expert with Bowie knife and "revolving pistol."

The British, in the face of this rising torrent of humanity, could muster only 700 or so subjects

> In winning Oregon the Americans had great faith in their procreative powers. "Our people are spreading out," boasted one congressman in 1846, "with the aid of the American multiplication table. Go to the West and see a young man with his mate of eighteen; after the lapse of thirty years, visit him again, and instead of two, you will find twenty-two. That is what I call the American multiplication table."

north of the Columbia. Losing out lopsidedly in the population race, they were beginning to see the wisdom of arriving at a peaceful settlement before being engulfed by their neighbors.

A curious fact is that only a relatively small segment of the Oregon Country was in actual controversy by 1845. The area in dispute consisted of the rough triangle between the Columbia River on the south and the 49th parallel on the north. Britain had repeatedly offered the line of the Columbia; America had repeatedly offered the 49th parallel. The whole fateful issue was now tossed into the presidential election of 1844.

A Mandate(?) for Manifest Destiny

The two major parties nominated their presidential standard-bearers in May 1844. Ambitious but often frustrated Henry Clay, easily the most popular man in the country, was enthusiastically chosen by the Whigs at Baltimore. The Democrats, meeting later in the same city, seemed hopelessly deadlocked. Finally the expansionists, dominated by the pro-Texas Southerners, trotted out and nominated James K. Polk of Tennessee, the nation's first "dark horse" or "surprise" presidential candidate.

Polk may have been a dark horse, but he was not an unknown or decrepit horse. Speaker of the House of Representatives for four years and governor of Tennessee for two terms, he was a determined, industrious, ruthless, and intelligent

*The average rate of progress in covered wagons was one to two miles an hour. This amounted to about 100 miles (161 kilometers) a week or about five months for the entire journey. Thousands of humans, in addition to horses and oxen, died en route. One estimate is seventeen deaths a mile for men, women, and children.

James K. Polk (1795–1849). Distinguished for both determination and deviousness, Polk added more territory to the U.S. (by questionable means) than any other President. In tenaciously pursuing his goals, he broke himself down with overwork and died 103 days after his single term ended. His childless wife (and secretary) had banned all drinking and dancing in the White House. (National Archives.)

public servant. Sponsored by Andrew Jackson, his friend and neighbor, he was rather implausibly built up by Democrats as yet another "Young Hickory." Whigs attempted to jeer him into oblivion with the taunt, "Who is James K. Polk?" They soon found out.

The campaign of 1844 was in part an expression of the mighty emotional upsurge known as Manifest Destiny. Countless citizens in the 1840s and 1850s, feeling a sense of mission, believed that Almighty God had "manifestly" destined the American people for a hemispheric career. They would irresistibly spread their uplifting and ennobling democratic institutions over at least the entire continent, and possibly over South America as well. Land greed and ideals were thus conveniently conjoined.

Expansionist Democrats were strongly swayed by the intoxicating spell of Manifest Destiny. They came out flat-footedly in their platform for the "Reannexation of Texas"* and the "Reoccupation of Oregon," all the way to 54° 40′. Outbellowing the Whig log-cabinites in the game of slogans, they shouted "All of Oregon or None." They also condemned Clay as a "corrupt bargainer," a dissolute character, and a slaveowner. (Their own candidate, Polk, owned slaves—a classic case of the pot calling the kettle black.)

The Whigs, as noisemakers, took no back seat. They countered with such slogans as "Hooray for Clay" and "Polk, Slavery, and Texas, or Clay, Union, and Liberty." They also spread the lie that a gang of Tennessee slaves had been seen on their way to a Southern market with the initials J. K. P. (James K. Polk) branded on them.

On the crucial issue of Texas, the acrobatic Clay tried to ride two horses at once. The "Great Compromiser" appears to have compromised away the presidency when he wrote a series of confusing letters. They seemed to say that while he personally favored annexing slaveholding Texas (an appeal to the South), he also favored postponement (an appeal to the North). He might have lost more ground if he had not "straddled," but he certainly alienated the more ardent anti-slaveryites.

In the stretch drive, "Dark Horse" Polk nipped Henry Clay at the wire, 170 to 105 in the Electoral College and 1,337,243 to 1,299,062 in the popular column. Clay would have won if he had not lost New York State by a scant 5,000 votes. There the tiny anti-slavery Liberty party absorbed nearly 16,000 votes, many of which would otherwise have gone to the unlucky Kentuckian. Ironically, the anti-Texas Liberty party, by helping to insure the election of pro-Texas Polk, hastened the annexation of Texas.

Land-hungry Democrats, flushed with victory, proclaimed that they had received a mandate from the voters to take Texas. But a presidential election is seldom, if ever, a clear-cut mandate on anything.

---

*The United States had given up its claims to Texas in the so-called Florida Purchase Treaty with Spain in 1819 (see p. 214). The slogan "Fifty-four forty or fight" was evidently not coined until two years later, in 1846.

The only way to secure a true reflection of the voters' will is to hold a special election on a given issue. The picture that emerged in 1844 is not one of mandate but of muddle. What else could there have been when the results were so close, the personalities so colorful, and the issues so numerous—including Oregon, Texas, the tariff, slavery, the Bank, and internal improvements? Yet this unclear "mandate" was interpreted by President Tyler as a clear mandate to annex Texas—and he signed the joint resolution three days before leaving the White House.

Polk the Purposeful

"Young Hickory" Polk, unlike "Old Hickory" Jackson, was not an impressive figure. Of middle height (5 feet 8 inches; 1.72 meters), lean, white-haired (worn long), gray-eyed, and stern-faced, he took life seriously and drove himself mercilessly into a premature grave. His burdens were increased by an unwillingness to delegate authority. Methodical and hardworking but not brilliant, he was shrewd, narrow, conscientious, and persistent. "What he went for he fetched," wrote a contemporary. Purposeful in the highest degree, he developed a positive four-point program, and with remarkable success achieved it completely in less than four years.

President Polk's Flimsy House of Cards. He appears to be hatching troublesome eggs relating to vexatious issues. (*Yankee Doodle.*)

House Vote on Tariff of 1846

Regions	*For*	*Against*
New England	9	19
Middle States	18	44
West and Northwest	29	10
South and Southwest	58	20
TOTAL	114	93

Compare vote on 1832 tariff, p. 239.

One of Polk's goals was a lowered tariff. His secretary of the treasury, wispy Robert J. Walker, devised a tariff-for-revenue bill which reduced the average rates of the Tariff of 1842 from about 32 percent to 25 percent. With the strong support of low-tariff Southerners, Walker lobbied the measure through Congress, though not without loud complaints from the Clayites, especially in New England and the Middle States, that American manufacturing would be ruined. But these prophets of doom missed the mark. The Walker Tariff of 1846 proved to be an excellent revenue producer, largely because it was followed by boom times and heavy imports.

A second objective of Polk was the restoration of the Independent Treasury, unceremoniously dropped by the Whigs in 1841. Pro-Bank Whigs in Congress raised a storm of opposition, but victory at last rewarded the President's efforts in 1846.

The third and fourth points on Polk's "must list" were the acquisition of California and the settlement of the Oregon dispute.

"Reoccupation" of the "whole" of Oregon had been promised Northern Democrats in the campaign of 1844. But Southern Democrats, once they had "reannexed" Texas, rapidly cooled off. Polk, himself a Southerner, had no intention of insisting on the 54° 40′ pledge of his own platform. But feeling bound by the three offers of his predecessors to London, he again proposed the compromise line of 49°. The British minister in Washington, on

Ridiculous Exhibition. "Yankee noodle" putting his head into the British Lion's mouth. British view of American bluster on the Oregon issue. (*Punch,* 1846.)

his own initiative, brusquely spurned this olive branch.

The next move on the Oregon chessboard was up to Britain. Fortunately for peace, the ministry began to experience a change of heart. British anti-expansionists ("Little Englanders") were now persuaded that the Columbia River after all was not the St. Lawrence of the West, and that the turbulent American hordes might one day seize the Oregon Country. Why fight a hazardous war over this wilderness on behalf of an unpopular monopoly, the Hudson's Bay Company, which had already "furred out" much of the area anyhow?

Early in 1846 the British, hat in hand, came around and themselves proposed the line of 49°. Polk, irked by the previous rebuff, threw the decision squarely into the lap of the Senate. The senators speedily accepted the offer and approved the subsequent treaty, despite a few diehard shouts of "Fifty-four forty forever!" and "Every foot or not an inch!" The fact that the United States was then a month deep in the Mexican War doubtless influenced the final vote.

Satisfaction with the Oregon settlement among Americans was not unanimous. The Northwestern states, hotbed of Manifest Destiny and "fifty-four fortyism," joined the anti-slavery men in condemning what they regarded as a base betrayal by the South. Why *all* of Texas and not *all* of Oregon? Because, sneered the expansionist Senator Benton of Missouri, "Great Britain is powerful and Mexico is weak."

So Polk, despite all the campaign bluster, got neither "fifty-four forty" nor a fight. But he did get something that in the long run was better: a reasonable compromise without shedding a drop of blood.

Misunderstandings with Mexico

Faraway California was another worry of Polk's. He and other disciples of Manifest Destiny had long coveted its verdant valleys, and especially the spacious bay of San Francisco. This splendid har-

Senator Benton Speaking at His Desk. Thomas Hart Benton (1782–1858), four-time Missouri senator, had grown up in Tennessee, where he had engaged in a tavern brawl with Andrew Jackson. The two became reconciled, and "Old Bullion" Benton loyally supported Jackson's hard-money ("Benton's Mint Drops") and anti-Bank policies.

AMERICAN LIFE IN PAINTING 1750-1865

Paul Revere, c. 1768
by John Singleton Copley
(1738–1815)

Copley, a Bostonian who pursued the major portion of his career in London, left an eloquent artistic record of colonial life. This painting of the Massachusetts silversmith-horseman, Paul Revere, challenged convention by portraying an artisan in working clothes admiring a teapot he had just finished. Note how Copley has depicted the serene confidence of the master craftsman and Revere's quiet pride in his work. *Courtesy Museum of Fine Arts, Boston* (Gift of Joseph W., William B., and Edward H. R. Revere).

Sea Captains Carousing in Surinam, 1757–1758, by John Greenwood (1727–1792)

This playful portrayal of Yankee sea captains far from home is often regarded as America's first "genre painting," or a painting realistically showing a scene from everyday life. The South American setting in Dutch Guiana is a reminder of the distant trade connections established by American shippers in the colonial era. The lively ale-house merriment suggests that not all seamen were sober-sided Puritans. *The St. Louis Art Museum.*

The Skater (Portrait of William Grant), 1782
by Gilbert Stuart (1755–1828)

Stuart, a Rhode Islander, is most famous for his numerous portraits of the "American aristocracy." (The current dollar bill bears one of Stuart's several portraits of George Washington.) The skater's easy equilibrium suggests the poise and self-assurance of a well-to-do American gentleman of the era. Like Copley's *Paul Revere,* Stuart's skater is a model of self-confidence and individual dignity. Compare these renditions of 18th-Century people with George Tooker's portrayal of 20th-Century life in *The Subway* (second color section). *National Gallery of Art, Washington* (Andrew W. Mellon Collection).

Fur Traders Descending the Missouri, 1844
by George Caleb Bingham (1811–1879)

Bingham, a son of the Missouri frontier, achieved widespread popularity in his day with his paintings of scenes from the Western wilderness. Here he has portrayed a moment of calm in an obviously strenuous life. The fragile dugout canoe on the ominously placid water, the tethered animal in the bow, and the recently shot duck (contrasted with the flock in the distant sky) evoke the pioneer's constant battle with nature. *The Metropolitan Museum of Art, Morris K. Jesup Fund, 1933.*

Winter Scene in Brooklyn, c. 1817–1820, by Francis Guy (1760–1820)

Life in the cities of the early Republic was devoid of many of the amenities that made urban living attractive to later generations of Americans. This painting of Brooklyn, near the site of the later Brooklyn Bridge, shows that city-dwellers, like their country counterparts, still had to split their own firewood, draw their own water, and brave the icy elements as they went about their daily business. *The Brooklyn Museum, Gift of the Brooklyn Institute of Arts and Sciences.*

The Old Plantation, Late 18th Century, artist unknown

This painting by an unknown artist reveals a frolicsome moment in the lives of slaves on a Southern plantation. The fancy clothing worn by the dancing blacks suggests that this scene may have been idealized. The painting also suggests that African art forms survived in America. The small drum on the right closely resembles the "gudu-gudu" drum used by the Yoruba peoples of West Africa. It is identifiable primarily by the small drumsticks the slave is using, made of rolled strips of stiff leather. *Abby Aldrich Rockefeller Folk Art Center, Williamsburg, Virginia.*

The Residence of David Twining, 1787, 1845–1848, by Edward Hicks (1780–1849)

A Quaker sign-painter from Bucks County, Pennsylvania, Hicks reproduced many scenes of farm life and of a tranquil nature where all manner of animals and children mingled peaceably with one another. Elements of that eloquent Quaker vision can be seen in this vivid painting of David Twining's well-maintained eastern Pennsylvania farm, where different breeds of animals, different generations, and different races live in fertile harmony.
Abby Aldrich Rockefeller Folk Art Center, Williamsburg, Virginia.

The Quilting Party, Third quarter 19th Century, artist unknown

Pioneer families would often turn tiresome tasks into social events. Here several families gather while the women, young and old, piece together a patchwork quilt. The men serve the food and help mind the baby. The couple in the right-hand corner has taken advantage of the occasion to engage in a little discreet hand-holding. *Abby Aldrich Rockefeller Folk Art Center, Williamsburg, Virginia.*

Joseph Moore and His Family, 1839
by Erastus Salisbury Field (1805–1900)

New England small-town life had a certain austere elegance and sober dignity in the age of Jackson. Here Joseph Moore of Ware, Massachusetts, proudly poses with his family in their simple but properly appointed parlor. Note the formal attire on the children, who are portrayed as "little adults." *Courtesy Museum of Fine Arts, Boston* (M & M Karolik Collection).

Blacksmith Shop, Last third 19th Century, attributed to Francis A. Beckett.

This blacksmith shop in gold-rush California was exceptionally well outfitted. The leather-aproned owner sports a stovepipe hat, while his assistants wear mere derbies. Note the massive bellows suspended from the high ceiling. It could heat the fire to blast-furnace temperatures. *National Gallery of Art, Washington* (Gift of Edgar William and Bernice Chrysler Garbisch).

A Ride for Liberty, c. 1862 by Eastman Johnson (1824–1906)

Johnson was a New Englander who traveled widely in the South so as to understand better and properly interpret the hardships of black people under slavery. In this painting before emancipation, he brilliantly evoked the anxiety of fleeing slaves. *The Brooklyn Museum* (Gift of Miss Gwendolyn O. L. Conkling).

bor was widely regarded as America's future gateway to the Pacific Ocean.

The population of California in 1845 was curiously mixed. It consisted of some 7,000 sun-blessed Spanish-Mexicans, plus more than ten times as many dispirited Indians. There were fewer than a thousand foreigners, mostly Americans, some of whom had "left their consciences" behind them as they rounded Cape Horn. Given time, these transplanted Yankees might yet bring California into the Union by "playing the Texas game."

Polk was eager to buy California from Mexico, but relations with Mexico City were dangerously embittered. Among other friction points, the United States had claims against the Mexicans for some $3 million in damages to American citizens and their property. The revolution-riddled regime in Mexico had formally agreed to assume most of this debt, but had been forced to default on its payments.

A more serious bone of contention was Texas. The Mexican government, after threatening war if the United States should acquire the Lone Star Republic, had recalled its minister from Washington following annexation. Diplomatic relations were completely severed.

Deadlock with Mexico over Texas was further tightened by a question of boundaries. During the long era of Spanish-Mexican occupation, the southwestern boundary of Texas had been the Nueces River. But the expansive Texans, on rather farfetched grounds, were claiming the more southerly Rio Grande instead. Polk, for his part, felt a strong moral obligation to defend Texas in her claim, once she was annexed.

The Mexicans were far less concerned about this boundary quibble than the United States. In their eyes all of Texas was still theirs, although temporarily in revolt, and a dispute over the two rivers seemed pointless. Yet Polk was careful to keep American troops out of virtually all of the explosive no-man's-land between the Nueces and the Rio Grande, as long as there was any real prospect of peaceful adjustment.

The golden prize of California continued to cause Polk much anxiety. Disquieting rumors (now known to have been ill-founded) were circulating that the British Lion was about to buy or seize California—a grab that Americans could not tolerate under the Monroe Doctrine. In a last desperate throw of the dice, Polk dispatched John Slidell to Mexico City as minister late in 1845. The new envoy, among other alternatives, was instructed to offer a maximum of $25 million for California and territory to the east. But the proud Mexicans would not even permit Slidell to present his "insulting" proposition.

American Blood on American(?) Soil

A frustrated Polk was now prepared to force a showdown. On January 13, 1846, he ordered 4,000 men, under General Zachary Taylor, to march from the Nueces River to the Rio Grande, provocatively near Mexican forces. Polk's presidential diary reveals that he expected at any moment to hear of a clash. When none occurred after an anxious wait, he informed his Cabinet on May 9, 1846, that he proposed to ask Congress to declare war on the basis of (1) unpaid claims and (2) Slidell's rejection. These, at best, were rather flimsy pretexts. Two Cabinet members spoke up and said that they would feel better satisfied if Mexican troops should fire first.

That very evening, as fate would have it, news of bloodshed arrived. On April 25, 1846, Mexican troops had crossed the Rio Grande and attacked General Taylor's command, with a loss of sixteen Americans killed or wounded.

Polk, further aroused, sent a vigorous war message to Congress. He declared that despite "all our efforts" to avoid a clash, hostilities had been forced upon the country by the shedding of "American blood on the American soil." A patriotic Congress overwhelmingly voted for war, and enthusiastic volunteers cried, "Ho for the Halls of the Montezumas!" and "Mexico or Death!" Inflamed by the war fever, even anti-slavery Whig centers joined with the rest of the nation, though they later condemned "Jimmy Polk's war." As

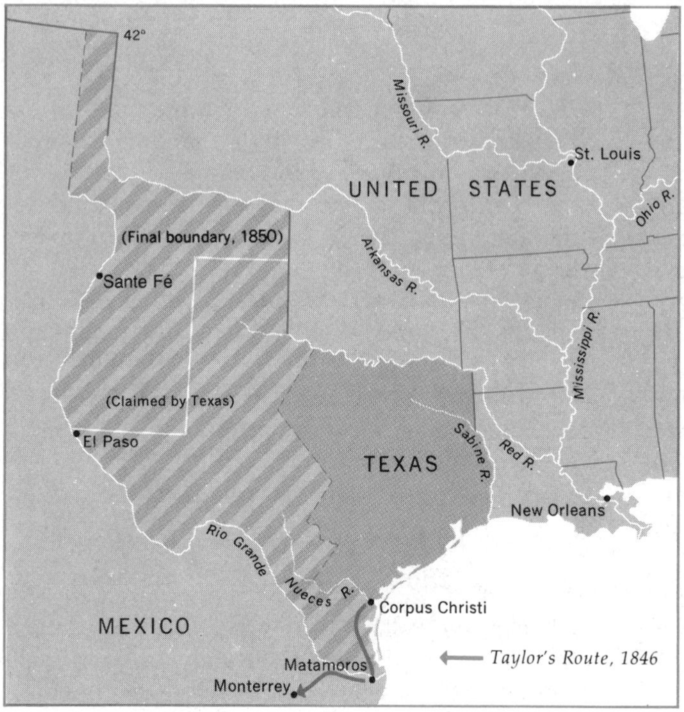

TEXAS, 1845–1846

Texas President Mirabeau Buonaparte Lamar, flushed with imperial dreams, tried to secure the Texas claim to the large striped area on this map by leading a military expedition in 1841 against the Mexicans at Santa Fe. But the weak and outgunned "army" of the Lone Star Republic, made up mostly of American drifters and adventurers, was speedily smashed. The Texans drew in their horns thereafter, and with renewed vigor sought annexation to the United States, rather than further expansion to the West of their precariously independent nation.

James Russell Lowell of Massachusetts lamented,

> Massachusetts, God forgive her,
> She's akneelin' with the rest.

In his message to Congress Polk was making history—not writing it. If he had been a historian, he would have explained that American blood had been shed on soil which the Mexicans had good reason to regard as their own. A gangling, rough-featured Whig congressman from Illinois, one Abraham Lincoln, introduced certain resolutions that requested information as to the precise "spot" on American soil where American blood had been shed. He pushed his "spot" resolutions with such persistence that he came to be known as the "spotty Lincoln," who could die of "spotted fever." The more extreme anti-slavery agitators of the North, many of them Whigs, branded the President a liar—"Polk the Mendacious."

Did Polk provoke war? California was an imperative point in his program, and Mexico would not sell it at any price. The only way to get it was to use force, or wait for an internal American revolt. Yet delay seemed dangerous, for the claws of the British Lion might snatch the ripening California fruit from the talons of the American Eagle. Grievances against Mexico were annoying yet tolerable; in later years America endured even worse ones. But in 1846 patience had ceased to be a virtue, as far as Polk was concerned. So he pushed the quarrel to a bloody showdown.

Both sides, in fact, were spoiling for a fight. Hotheaded Americans, especially Southwestern expansionists, were eager to teach the Mexicans a lesson. The Mexicans, in turn, were burning to humiliate the "Bullies of the North." Possessing a

> Less than a year before he became President, Lincoln wrote that "the act of sending an armed force among the Mexicans was unnecessary, inasmuch as Mexico was in no way molesting or menacing the United States or the people thereof; and that it was unconstitutional, because the power of levying war is vested in Congress, and not in the President" (June 1, 1860).

considerable standing army, heavily overstaffed with generals, they boasted of invading the United States, freeing the black slaves, and lassoing whole regiments of Americans. They were hoping that the quarrel with Britain over Oregon would blossom into a full-dress war, as it came near doing, and further pin down the hated *Yanquis*. A conquest of Mexico's vast and arid expanses seemed fantastic, especially in view of the bungling American invasion of Canada in 1812.

Both sides were fired by moral indignation. The Mexicans could fight with the flaming sword of righteousness, for had not the "insolent" Yankee picked a fight by polluting their soil? Many earnest Americans, on the other hand, sincerely believed that Mexico was the aggressor.

The Bear Flag of California. (California Historical Society Library.)

The Mastering of Mexico

Polk wanted California—not war. But when war came he hoped to fight it on a limited scale, and then pull out when he had won the prize. The dethroned Mexican dictator Santa Anna, then exiled with his teenage bride in Cuba, let it be known that if the American blockading squadron would permit him to slip into Mexico, he would sell out his country. This discreditable intrigue was finally carried through. But the double-crossing Santa Anna, self-styled "Napoleon of the West," rallied the Mexicans to a desperate defense of their soil.

American operations in the Southwest and in California were completely successful. In 1846 General Stephen W. Kearny led a detachment of about 1,700 troops over the famous Santa Fe trail, from Fort Leavenworth to Santa Fe. This sun-baked outpost, with its drowsy plazas, was easily captured. But before Kearny could reach California, the fertile province was won. When war broke out, Captain John C. Frémont, the dashing explorer, just "happened" to be there with several dozen well-armed men. In helping to overthrow Mexican rule in 1846, he collaborated with American naval officers and with the local Americans, who had hoisted the banner of the short-lived California Bear Flag Republic.

General Zachary Taylor meanwhile had been spearheading the main thrust. Known as "Old Rough and Ready" because of his iron constitution and incredibly unsoldierly appearance—he sometimes wore a Mexican straw hat—he fought his way across the Rio Grande into Mexico. After several gratifying victories, he reached Buena Vista. There, on February 22–23, 1847, his weakened force of 5,000 men was attacked by some 20,000 march-weary troops under Santa Anna. The Mexicans were finally repulsed with extreme difficulty, and overnight Zachary Taylor became the "Hero of Buena Vista." One Kentuckian was heard to say that "Old Zack" would be elected President in 1848 by "spontaneous combustion."

Sound American strategy now called for a crushing blow at the enemy's vitals—Mexico City. General Taylor, though a good leader of modest-sized forces, could not win decisively in the semi-deserts of northern Mexico. The command of the main expedition, which pushed inland from the coastal city of Vera Cruz early in 1847, was entrusted to General Winfield Scott. A handsome giant of a man, Scott had emerged as a hero from the War of 1812 and had later earned the nickname of "Old Fuss and Feathers" because of his resplendent uniforms and strict discipline. He was severely handicapped in the Mexican campaign by inadequate numbers of troops, by expiring enlistments, by a more numerous enemy, by mountainous terrain, by disease, and by political backbiting at home. Yet he succeeded in battling his way up to Mexico City by September 1847 in one of the most brilliant campaigns in American mili-

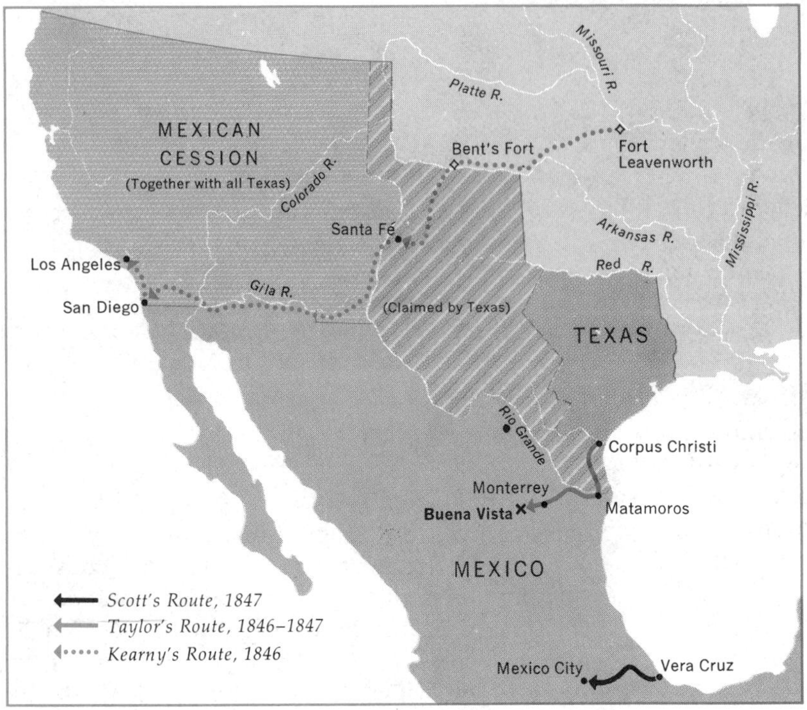

MAJOR CAMPAIGNS OF MEXICAN WAR

tary annals. He proved to be the most distinguished general produced by his country between 1783 and 1861.

Fighting Mexico for Peace

Polk was anxious to end the shooting as soon as he could secure his territorial goals. Accordingly, he sent along with Scott's invading army the chief clerk of the State Department, Nicholas P. Trist, who among other weaknesses was afflicted with an overfluid pen. Trist and Scott arranged for an armistice with Santa Anna, at a cost of $10,000. The wily dictator pocketed the bribe, and then used the time to bolster his defenses.

Negotiating a treaty with a sword in one hand and a pen in the other was ticklish business. Polk, disgusted with his blundering envoy, abruptly recalled Trist. The wordy diplomat then dashed off a sixty-five-page letter explaining why he was not coming home. The President was furious. But Trist, grasping a fleeting opportunity to negotiate, signed the Treaty of Guadalupe-Hidalgo on February 2, 1848, and forwarded it to Washington.

The terms of the treaty were breathtaking. They confirmed the American title to Texas, and yielded the enormous area stretching westward to Oregon and the ocean and embracing coveted California. This total expanse, including Texas, was about one-half of Mexico. The United States agreed to pay $15 million for the land, and to assume the claims of its citizens against Mexico in the amount of $3,250,000.

Polk submitted the treaty to the Senate. Although Trist had proved highly annoying, he had generally followed his original instructions. And speed was imperative. The anti-slavery Whigs in Congress—dubbed "Mexican Whigs"—were condemning this "damnable war" with increasing heat. Having secured control of the House in 1847, they were even threatening to vote down supplies for the armies in the field. If they had done so, Scott probably would have been forced to retreat, and the fruits of victory might have been tossed away.

Another peril impended. A swelling group of expansionists, intoxicated by Manifest Destiny, was clamoring for all of Mexico. If America had

Early in 1848 the New York *Evening Post* demanded: "Now we ask, whether any man can coolly contemplate the idea of recalling our troops from the [Mexican] territory we at present occupy . . . and . . . resign this beautiful country to the custody of the ignorant cowards and profligate ruffians who have ruled it for the last twenty-five years? Why, humanity cries out against it. Civilization and Christianity protest against this reflux of the tide of barbarism and anarchy." Such was one phase of Manifest Destiny.

seized it, the nation would have been saddled with an expensive and vexatious policing problem. Far-seeing Southerners like Calhoun, alarmed by the mounting anger of anti-slavery agitators, realized that the South would do well not to be too greedy. The treaty was finally approved by the Senate, 38 to 14. Oddly enough, it was condemned both by opponents who wanted all of Mexico and by opponents who wanted none of it.

Victors rarely pay an indemnity, especially after a costly conflict has been "forced" on them. Yet Polk, who had planned to offer $25 million before the war, arranged to pay $18,250,000 after winning the war. Cynics have charged that the Americans were pricked by guilty consciences; apologists have pointed proudly to the "Anglo-Saxon spirit of fair play." A decisive factor was the need for haste, while there was still a responsible Mexican government to carry out the treaty, and before political foes in the United States, notably the anti-slavery zealots, sabotaged Polk's expansionist program.

Profit and Loss in Mexico

As wars go, the Mexican War was a small one. It cost some 13,000 American lives, most of them taken by disease. But the fruits of the fighting were enormous.

America's total expanse, already vast, was increased by about one-third (counting Texas)—an addition even greater than that of the Louisiana Purchase. A sharp stimulus was given to the spirit of Manifest Destiny for, as the proverb has it, the appetite comes with eating.

As fate ordained, the Mexican War was the blood-spattered schoolroom of the Civil War. The campaigns provided priceless field experience for most of the officers destined to become leading generals in the forthcoming conflict, including Captain Robert E. Lee and Lieutenant U. S. Grant. The Military Academy at West Point, founded in 1802, fully justified its existence through the well-trained officers. Useful also was the navy, which did valuable work in throwing a crippling blockade around Mexican ports. The Marine Corps, in existence since 1798, won new laurels, and to this day sings in its stirring hymn about the Halls of Montezuma.

The army waged war without defeat and without a major blunder, despite formidable obstacles and a half dozen or so incredibly long marches. Chagrined British critics, as well as other foreign skeptics, reluctantly revised upward their estimate of Yankee military prowess. Opposing armies,

PLUCKED:
THE MEXICAN EAGLE BEFORE THE WAR!
THE MEXICAN EAGLE AFTER THE WAR!

A Cartoon from *Yankee Doodle*, 1847. This satiric drawing was symbolic of the "lick all creation" spirit of the times.

moreover, emerged with increased respect for each other. The Mexicans, though poorly led, fought heroically. At Chapultepec, near Mexico City, the teenage lads of the military academy there (*los niños*) perished to a boy.

Long-memoried Mexicans have never forgotten that their northern enemy tore away about half of their country. The argument that they were lucky not to lose all of it, and that they had been paid something for their land, did not lessen their bitterness. The war also marked an ugly turning point in the relations between the United States and Latin America as a whole. Hitherto, Uncle Sam had been regarded with some complacency, even friendliness. Henceforth, he was increasingly feared as the "Colossus of the North." Suspicious neighbors to the south condemned him as a greedy and untrustworthy bully, who might next despoil them of their soil.

Most ominous of all, the war rearoused the snarling dog of the slavery issue, and the beast did not stop yelping until drowned in the blood of the Civil War. Abolitionists assailed the Mexican conflict as one provoked by the Southern "slavocracy" for its own evil purposes. As James Russell Lowell had Hosea Biglow drawl in his Yankee dialect:

> They jest want this Californy
> So's to lug new slave-states in
> To abuse ye, an' to scorn ye,
> An' to plunder ye like sin.

In line with Lowell's charge, the bulk of the American volunteers were admittedly from the South and Southwest. But, as in the case of the Texan revolution, the basic explanation was proximity rather than conspiracy.

Quarreling over slavery extension also erupted on the floors of Congress. In 1846, shortly after the shooting started, Polk requested an appropriation of $2 million with which to buy a peace. Representative David Wilmot of Pennsylvania, fearful of the Southern "slavocracy," introduced a fateful amendment. It stipulated that slavery should never exist in any of the territory to be wrested from Mexico.

The disruptive Wilmot amendment twice passed the House, but not the Senate. Southern members, unwilling to be robbed of prospective slave states, fought the restriction tooth and nail. Anti-slavery men, in Congress and out, battled no less bitterly for the exclusion of slaves. The "Wilmot Proviso" soon came to symbolize the burning issue of slavery in the territories.

In a broad sense, the opening shots of the Mexican War were the opening shots of the Civil War. President Polk left the nation the splendid physical heritage of California and the Southwest, but also the ugly moral heritage of an embittered slavery dispute. Mexicans could later take some satisfaction in knowing that the territory wrenched from them had proved to be a frightful apple of discord that could well be called Santa Anna's revenge.

VARYING VIEWPOINTS

Historians have long probed for the real meaning behind the pulse-stirring phrase "Manifest Destiny." Some have emphasized the idealistic impulses behind continental expansion. Others have stressed the supposed "superiority" of Anglo-Saxon culture over Indian and Spanish civilizations. Still other writers have seen American expansion as simply another chapter in the familiar story of territorial conquest. In recent years many historians, no doubt influenced by the general reappraisal of America's relations with the rest of the world, have stressed the "hard"—even "imperialistic"—forces behind America's territorial growth. Scholars have also begun to show more interest in, and sympathy for, the peoples displaced or absorbed in America's sweep to the Western sea.

SELECT READINGS

A good introduction is G. G. Van Deusen, *The Jacksonian Era* (1959). R. A. Billington, *Westward Expansion* (rev. ed., 1974), is comprehensive. On Tyler, see R. Seager II, *And Tyler Too* (1963). Still useful is A. Weinberg, *Manifest Destiny* (1935), though it should be supplemented by Edward M. Burns, *The American Idea of Mission: Concepts of National Purpose and Destiny* (1957), and F. Merk, *Manifest Destiny and Mission in American History* (1963). See also F. Merk, *Monroe Doctrine and American Expansionism, 1843–1849* (1966). Paul Horgan, *Great River* (1954), is a magnificent history of the Southwest and the Rio Grande. *The Texas Revolution* is the subject of W. C. Binkley's 1952 study. It should be supplemented by F. Merk, *Slavery and the Annexation of Texas* (1972). For the Pacific region, see Francis Parkman's classic *The California and Oregon Trail* (1849), and N. A. Graebner's general account, *Empire on the Pacific* (1955). F. Merk is definitive on *The Oregon Question* (1967), and J. Caughey provides an excellent introduction to *California* (1970). C. G. Sellers analyzes *James K. Polk, Continentalist: 1843–1846* (1966). Recent studies of the conflict with Mexico are O. A. Singletary, *The Mexican War* (1960), and K. J. Bauer, *The Mexican-American War, 1846–1848* (1974). The other side's perspective is given in Gene M. Brack, *Mexico Views Manifest Destiny, 1821–1846* (1976). J. H. Schroeder analyzes an important aspect of the conflict in *Mr. Polk's War: American Opposition and Dissent, 1846–1848* (1973). D. Pletcher gives an overall view in *The Diplomacy of the Annexation of Texas, Oregon, and the Mexican War* (1973). See also B. DeVoto's popular *Year of Decision, 1846* (1943). W. H. Goetzmann brings to life *Army Exploration in the American West, 1803–1863* (1959). Unusually colorful social history of the Westward movement is provided in John Mark Faragher, *Women and Men on the Overland Trail* (1979), and John D. Unruh, Jr., *The Plains Across: The Overland Emigrants and the Trans-Mississippi West, 1840–1860* (1979).

16

Shaping the National Economy, 1790-1860

The progress of invention is really a threat [to monarchy]. Whenever I see a railroad I look for a republic.

RALPH WALDO EMERSON, 1866

The March of Mechanization

A gifted group of British inventors, beginning about 1750, perfected a series of machines for the mass production of textiles. This enslavement of steam multiplied the power of man's muscles some ten thousandfold, and ushered in the modern factory system.

The so-called Industrial Revolution has been misnamed. It was not a revolution in the sense of an overnight change or upheaval. The machines developed in England were gradually improved over several decades, and the people there were scarcely aware that a significant shift was taking place. Nor was the Industrial Revolution solely industrial. It was accompanied by a no less spectacular transformation in the methods of transportation and communication.

The factory system gradually spread from England—"the world's workshop"—to other lands. It took a generation or so to reach western Europe, and then the United States. Why was the youthful American Republic, destined to be an industrial giant, so slow to embrace the machine?

For one thing, virgin soil in America was cheap. Land-starved descendants of land-starved peasants were not going to coop themselves up in smelly factories when they might till their own acres in God's fresh air and sunlight. Labor was therefore generally scarce, and enough nimble hands to operate the machines were hard to find. Money for capital investment, moreover, was not plentiful in pioneering America. Raw materials lay undeveloped, undiscovered, or unsuspected. The Republic was one day to become the world's leading coal producer, but much of the coal burned in colonial times was imported all the way from England.

Just as labor was scarce, so were consumers. The young country at first lacked a domestic market large enough to make factory-scale manufacturing profitable.

Long-established British factories, which provided cutthroat competition, posed another problem. Their superiority was attested by the fact that a few unscrupulous Yankee manufacturers, out to make a dishonest dollar, learned to stamp their own products with faked English trademarks.

Early Waterwheel Powers New England Factory

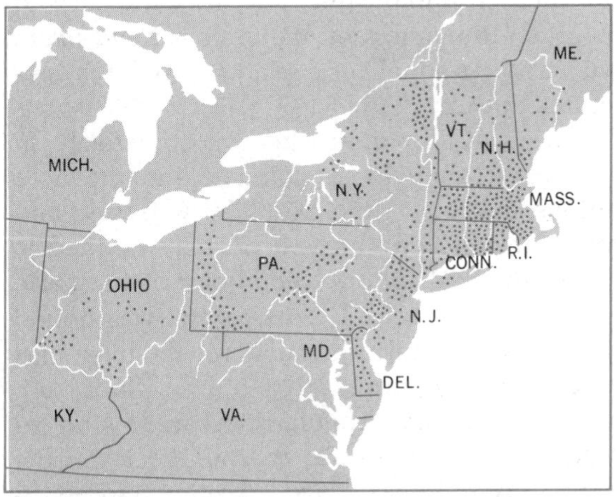

INDUSTRIAL PLANTS IN THE EARLY 1840s

The British also enjoyed a monopoly of the textile machinery, whose secrets they were anxious to hide from foreign competitors. Parliament enacted laws, in harmony with the mercantilistic system, forbidding the export of the machines, or the emigration of mechanics able to reproduce them.

Despite all these drawbacks, a surprising amount of small-scale manufacturing existed when the Republic was launched. As early as 1791, Alexander Hamilton reported that the wheels of seventeen different kinds of enterprises were humming. Yet the future industrial colossus was still snoring. Not until well past the middle of the next century did the value of the output of the factories exceed that of the farms.

Whitney Ends the Fiber Famine

Samuel Slater has been acclaimed the "Father of the Factory System" in America, and seldom can the paternity of a movement more properly be ascribed to one person. A skilled British mechanic of twenty-one, he was attracted by bounties being offered to English workmen familiar with the textile machines. After memorizing the plans for the machinery, he escaped in disguise to America, where he won the backing of Moses Brown, a Quaker capitalist in Rhode Island. Laboriously reconstructing the essential apparatus with the aid of a blacksmith and a carpenter, he put into operation in 1791 the first efficient American machinery for the spinning of cotton thread.

The ravenous mechanism was now ready, but where was the cotton fiber? Handpicking 1 pound

(0.45 kilogram) of lint from 3 pounds (1.36 kilograms) of seed was a full day's work for one slave, and this process was so expensive that cotton cloth was relatively rare. In 1785 eight bales of cotton were seized for fraudulent entry at Liverpool, England. The officials charged that so much cotton could not have been produced in America.

Another mechanical genius, Massachusetts-born Eli Whitney, now made his mark. After graduating from Yale College, he journeyed to Georgia to serve as a private tutor while preparing for the law. There he was told that the poverty of the South would be relieved if someone could only invent a workable device for separating the seed from the short-staple cotton fiber. Within ten days, in 1793, he constructed a crude machine which was fifty times more effective than the handpicking process. The cotton gin (short for en*gin*e) was so simple that rivals infringed on his patent, and he was to net only relatively small profits from this particular brainchild.

McCormick Reaper Works, 1850s. Contrast this scene of "Mass Production" with the workplace depicted in "Blacksmith Shop," in the color portfolio. (McCormick Collection, State Historical Society of Wisconsin.)

Few machines have ever wrought so wondrous a change. The gin affected not only the history of America but that of the world. Almost overnight the raising of cotton became highly profitable, and the South was tied hand and foot to the throne of King Cotton. Human bondage had been dying out, but the insatiable demand for cotton reriveted the chains on the limbs of the luckless Southern blacks.

South and North both prospered. Slave-driving planters cleared more acres for cotton, pushing the Cotton Kingdom westward off the depleted tidewater plains, over the Piedmont, and onto the black loam bottomlands of Alabama and Mississippi. Humming gins poured out avalanches of snowy fiber for the spindles of the Yankee machines. The American phase of the Industrial Revolution, which first blossomed in cotton textiles, was well on its way. Yet many decades were to pass before the old-fashioned spinning wheel was driven into the attic, and from there into the antique shops.

Early textile factories merely spun the fiber into cotton thread. The actual weaving into cloth was done laboriously by hand in the home or by contract weavers. Not until 1814, at Waltham, Massachusetts, was the first dual-purpose plant established: it spun the fiber and wove the finished cloth under the same roof. Water power and steam power were gradually supplanting mother-and-daughter power.

Factories at first flourished most actively in New England, though branching out into the more populous areas of New York, New Jersey, and Pennsylvania. The South, increasingly wedded to the production of cotton, could boast of comparatively little manufacturing. Its capital was bound up in slaves; its local consumers for the most part were desperately poor.

New England was singularly favored as an industrial center for several reasons. Her narrow belt of stony soil discouraged farming and hence made manufacturing more attractive than else-

> One observer in 1836 published a newspaper account of conditions in some of the New England factories: "The operatives work thirteen hours a day in the summer time, and from daylight to dark in the winter. At half past four in the morning the factory bell rings, and at five the girls must be in the mills. . . . So fatigued . . . are numbers of girls that they go to bed soon after their evening meal, and endeavor by a comparatively long sleep to resuscitate their weakened frames for the toil of the coming day."

where. A relatively dense population provided labor; shipping brought in capital; and snug seaports made easy the import of raw materials and the export of the finished products. Finally, the rapid rivers—notably the Merrimack in Massachusetts—provided abundant water power to turn the cogs of the machines. By 1860, more than 400 million pounds (182,000 metric tons) of Southern cotton poured annually into the gaping maws of over 1,000 mills, mostly in New England.

Marvels in Manufacturing

America's factories spread slowly until about 1807, when there began the fateful sequence of the embargo, non-intercourse, and the War of 1812. Stern necessity dictated the manufacture of substitutes for normal imports, while the stoppage of European commerce was temporarily ruinous to Yankee shipping. Both capital and labor were driven from the waves onto the factory floor, as New England, in the striking phrase of John Randolph, exchanged the trident for the distaff. Generous bounties were offered by local authorities for homegrown goods; "Buy American" and "Wear American" became popular slogans; and patriotism prompted the wearing of baggy homespun garments. President Madison donned some at his inauguration, where he was said to have been a walking argument for the better processing of native wool.

But the manufacturing boomlet broke abruptly with the Peace of Ghent in 1815. British competitors unloaded their dammed-up surpluses at ruinously low prices, and American newspapers were so full of British advertisements for goods on credit that little space was left for news. In one Rhode Island district, all 150 mills were forced to close their doors, except the original Slater plant. Responding to pained outcries, Congress provided some relief when it passed the mildly protective Tariff of 1816.

As the factory system flourished, it embraced numerous other industries in addition to textiles. Prominent among them was the manufacturing of firearms, and here the wizardly Eli Whitney again appeared with an epochal contribution. Frustrated in his earlier efforts to monopolize the cotton gin, he turned to the mass production of muskets for the United States army. Up to this time each part of a firearm had been hand-tooled, and if the trigger of one broke, the trigger of another might or might not fit. About 1798 Whitney seized upon the idea of having machines make each part, so that all the triggers, for example, would be as much alike as the successive imprints of a copperplate engraving. Journeying to Washington, he reportedly dismantled ten of his new muskets in the presence of skeptical officials, scrambled the parts together, and then quickly reassembled ten different muskets.

The principle of interchangeable parts was widely adopted by 1850, and it ultimately became the basis of modern mass-production, assembly-line methods. It gave to the North the vast industrial plant which insured military preponderance over the South. The Yankee Eli Whitney, by perfecting the cotton gin, gave slavery a renewed lease on life, and perhaps made inevitable the Civil War. The same Whitney, by popularizing the principle of interchangeable parts, caused factories to flourish in the North, and contributed heavily to the winning of that war by the Union.

Industrialization in the North received another

"The patent system," said Abraham Lincoln in a lecture in 1859, ". . . secured to the inventor for a limited time exclusive use of his invention, and thereby added the fuel of interest to the fire of genius in the discovery and production of new and useful things." Ten years earlier Lincoln had received patent No. 6469 for a scheme to buoy steamboats over shoals. It was never practically applied, but he remains the only President ever to have secured a patent.

strong boost about 1850, with the perfection of the sewing machine for making clothing, both in the home and in the factory. Here emerged the figure of Elias Howe, who suffered such extreme poverty that when his wife died he had to wear borrowed "Sunday" clothes to her funeral. He finally succeeded commercially where others had failed; and the royalties from his invention, patented in 1846, rapidly mounted to $4,000 a week. Even more successful in improving and promoting the machine was the versatile inventor Isaac Singer, whose name is still a household word. A new stitching device was also adapted before the Civil War for the mass production of boots and shoes.

The sewing machine was of incalculable significance. It was the foundation of the ready-made clothing industry, which took root about the time of the Civil War. It drove many a seamstress from the shelter of the private home to the factory where, like a human robot, she tended the clattering mechanisms.

Elias Howe's First Sewing Machine. The young republic often lacked the money to match the genius of its inventors, and Howe had to travel to England to secure the financial backing necessary to turn his revolutionary invention to practical use. (National Museum of History and Technology, Smithsonian Institution, Washington, D.C.)

Momentous inventions seem to unchain the human imagination and stimulate other inventions. American ingenuity before the Civil War is best revealed by the number of patents registered in Washington. The decade ending in 1800 saw only 306; the decade ending in 1860 saw the amazing total of 28,000. America was truly the land of the fertile-minded and the home of the ingenious. Yet in 1838 the clerk of the Patent Office had resigned in despair, complaining that all worthwhile inventions had been discovered.

Building the Business World

All these advances spurred changes in the form and legal status of business organizations. To take proper advantage of the new machine gadgetry, men needed to command great concentrations of capital and to find means to organize efficiently their far-flung affairs. Capital began to accumulate more rapidly as the principle of limited liability gained acceptance—permitting the individual investor, in cases of legal claims or bankruptcy, to risk no more than his own share of the corporation's stock. Fifteen Boston families formed one of the earliest and most powerful joint-capital ventures, the Boston Associates. They came to dominate not only the textile industry, but also the railroad, insurance, and banking business in all of Massachusetts.

The state of New York gave a powerful boost to budding capitalism in 1848, when it passed a General Incorporation Law. Businessmen no longer needed to apply for charters from the legislature; they could simply create a corporation if they complied with the terms of the law. "Free incorporation" statutes reflected the Jacksonian climate and were widely adopted in other states. They poured economic adrenalin into the veins of enterprising capitalists.

Other inventions tightened the sinews of an

Samuel Morse (1791–1872). Morse was the perfecter if not inventor of the electric telegraph and the Morse code.

increasingly complex business world. Prominent among them was the telegraph, developed by patriarch-bearded Samuel F. B. Morse, whose name is immortalized by the Morse code. A distinguished portrait painter, he was compelled by poverty to forsake his brush for the telegraph key. After prolonged disappointments and hunger, he finally secured from Congress, to the accompaniment of the usual jeers, an appropriation of $30,000 to support his experiment with "talking wires."

In 1844 Morse strung a wire 40 miles (64 kilometers) from Washington to Baltimore, and clicked out the historic message, "What hath God wrought?" The government might have controlled the telegraph, as it did the post office, but declined on the ground that the new device would not pay. But the invention brought fame and fortune to Morse, as he put distantly separated men of affairs in almost instant communication with one another.

Northern "Wage Slaves"

One ugly offspring of the factory system was an increasingly acute labor problem. Hitherto manufacturing had been done in the home, or in the small shop, where the master craftsman and his apprentice, rubbing elbows at the same bench, could maintain an intimate and friendly relationship. The Industrial Revolution submerged this personal association in the impersonal ownership of stuffy factories in "spindle cities." Around these,

Textile Workers of Lawrence (Mass.). Engraving by Winslow Homer, a famous painter. (*Harper's Weekly*, 1868.)

like tumors, the slum-like hovels of the "wage slaves" tended to cluster.

Clearly the early factory system did not shower its benefits evenly on all. While many owners waxed fat, workingpeople often wasted away at their workbenches. Hours were long, wages were low, and meals were skimpy and hastily gulped. Workers were forced to toil in unsanitary buildings that were poorly ventilated, lighted, and heated. They were forbidden by law to form labor unions to raise wages, for such cooperative activity was regarded as a criminal conspiracy. Not surprisingly, only twenty-four recorded strikes occurred before 1835.

Women and children were also sucked into the clanging mechanism of factory production. They typically toiled six days a week, earning a pittance for dreary stints of twelve or thirteen hours—"from dark to dark." The Boston Associates pridefully pointed to their textile mill at Lowell, Massachusetts, as a showplace factory. The workers were virtually all New England farm girls, carefully supervised on and off the job by watchful matrons. Escorted regularly to church from their company boardinghouses, forbidden to form unions, they were as disciplined and docile a labor force as any employer could wish. To the surprise of visitors, including Charles Dickens, they published their own newspaper. But the "Song of the Manchester Factory Girl" was no doubt overdrawn:

> She tends her loom, she watches the spindle,
> And cheerfully talketh away;
> Mid the din of wheels, how her bright eyes kindle!
> And her bosom is ever gay.

Few observers harbored such happy illusions about child workers. In 1820, half the nation's industrial toilers were children under ten years of age. Victims of factory labor, many children were mentally blighted, emotionally starved, physically stunted, and even brutally whipped in special "whipping rooms." In Samuel Slater's mill of 1791, the first machine tenders were seven boys and two girls, all under twelve.

Triumphs for American Toilers

The lot of the wage worker improved markedly in the 1820s and 1830s. In the full flush of Jacksonian democracy, many of the states granted the laboring man the vote. Brandishing the ballot, he first strove to lighten his burden through workingmen's parties. Aside from such goals as the ten-hour day, higher wages, and tolerable working conditions, he demanded public education for his children and an end to the inhuman practice of imprisonment for debt.

Employers, abhorring the rise of the "rabble" in politics, fought the ten-hour day to the last ditch. They argued that reduced hours would lessen production, increase costs, and demoralize the worker. He would have so much leisure time that the Devil would lead him into mischief. A red-letter gain was at length registered for labor in 1840, when President Van Buren established the ten-hour day for federal employees on public works. In ensuing years, a number of states gradually fell into line by reducing the hours of workingpeople.

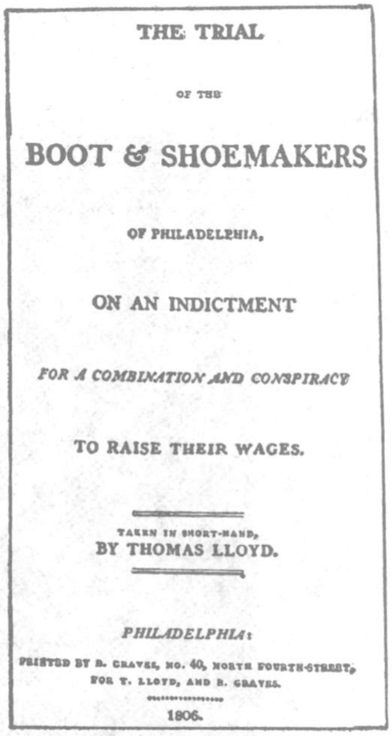
THE TRIAL
OF THE
BOOT & SHOEMAKERS
OF PHILADELPHIA,
ON AN INDICTMENT
FOR A COMBINATION AND CONSPIRACY
TO RAISE THEIR WAGES.
TAKEN IN SHORT-HAND,
BY THOMAS LLOYD.
PHILADELPHIA:
PRINTED BY B. GRAVES, NO. 40, NORTH FOURTH-STREET, FOR T. LLOYD, AND B. GRAVES.
1806.

Early Pamphlet on the Trial of Strikers for Striking

Day laborers at last learned that their strongest weapon was to lay down their tools, even at the risk of prosecution under the law. Dozens of strikes erupted in the 1830s and 1840s, most of them for higher wages, some for the ten-hour day, and a few for such unusual goals as the right to smoke on the job. The workers usually lost more strikes than they won, for the employer could resort to such tactics as the importing of strike-breakers—often derisively called "scabs" or "rats," and often fresh off the boat from the Old World. Labor long raised its voice against the unrestricted inpouring of wage-depressing and union-busting immigrant workers.

Labor's early and painful efforts at organization had netted some 300,000 trade unionists by 1830. But such encouraging gains were dashed on the rocks of hard times following the severe depression of 1837. As unemployment spread, union membership shriveled. Yet toilers won a hope-giving legal victory in 1842. The supreme court of Massachusetts ruled in the case of *Commonwealth* v. *Hunt* that labor unions were not illegal conspiracies, provided that their methods were "honorable and peaceful." This enlightened decision did not legalize the strike overnight throughout the country, but it was a significant signpost of the times. Trade unions still had a rocky row to hoe, stretching ahead for about a century, before they could meet management on relatively even terms.

> Violence broke out along the New York waterfront in 1836 when laborers striking for higher wages attacked "scabs." "The Mayor," Philip Hone's diary records, "who acts with vigour and firmness, ordered out the troops, who are now on duty with loaded arms. . . . These measures have restored order for the present, but I fear the elements of disorder are at work; the bands of Irish and other foreigners, instigated by the mischievous councils of the trades-union and other combinations of discontented men, are acquiring strength and importance which will ere long be difficult to quell."

Western Farmers Reap a Revolution in the Fields

As smoke-belching factories altered the Eastern skyline, flourishing farms were changing the face of the West. The trans-Allegheny region—especially the Ohio-Indiana-Illinois tier—was fast becoming the nation's breadbasket. Before long, it would become a granary to the world.

Pioneer farmers first hacked a clearing out of the forest, and then planted their painfully furrowed fields to corn. The yellow grain was amazingly versatile. It could be fed to hogs ("corn on the hoof") or distilled into liquor ("corn in the bottle"). Both these products could be more easily transported than the bulky grain itself, and they became the early Western farmer's staple market items. So many hogs were butchered, traded, or shipped at Cincinnati that the city was known as the "Porkopolis" of the West.

Most Western produce was at first floated down the Ohio-Mississippi River system, to feed the lusty appetite of the booming Cotton Kingdom. But Western farmers were as hungry for profits as Southern slaves and planters were for food. These soil tillers, spurred on by the easy availability of seemingly boundless acres, sought ways to bring more and more land into cultivation.

Ingenious inventors came to their aid. One of the first obstacles that frustrated the farmers was the thickly matted soil of the West, which snagged and snapped fragile wooden plows. John Deere of Illinois in 1837 finally produced a steel plow that broke the virgin soil. Sharp and effective, it was also light enough to be pulled by horses, rather than oxen.

Virginia-born Cyrus McCormick contributed the most wondrous contraption of all: a mechanical mower-reaper. The clattering cogs of McCormick's

Harvesting Grain by Hand and by McCormick Reaper. (*Above*, Prints Division, New York Public Library; *below*, from a company advertisement.)

horse-drawn machine were to the Western farmers what the cotton gin was to the Southern planters. Seated on his red-chariot reaper, a single husbandman could do the work of five men with sickles and scythes.

No other American invention cut so wide a swath. It made ambitious capitalists out of humble plowmen, who now scrambled for more acres on which to plant more fields of billowing wheat. Large-scale ("extensive"), specialized, cash-crop agriculture came to dominate the trans-Allegheny West. With it followed mounting indebtedness, as farmers bought more land and more machinery to work it. Soon hustling farmer-businessmen were annually harvesting a larger crop than even the South could devour. They began to dream of markets elsewhere—in the mushrooming factory towns of the East, or across the faraway Atlantic. But they were still largely landlocked. Commerce moved north and south on the river systems. Before it could begin to move east-west in bulk, a transportation revolution would have to occur.

Highways and Byways

In 1789, when the Constitution was launched, primitive methods of travel were still in use. Waterborne commerce, whether along the coast or on the rivers, was slow, uncertain, and often dangerous. Stagecoaches and wagons lurched over bone-shaking roads. Passengers would be routed out to lay nearby fence rails across muddy stretches, and occasionally horses would drown in muddy pits while wagons sank slowly out of sight.

Cheap and efficient carriers were imperative if raw materials were to be transported to the factories, and if the finished product was to be delivered to the consumer. On December 3, 1803, a firm in Providence, Rhode Island, sent a shipment of yarn to a point 60 miles (97 kilometers) away, notifying the purchaser that the consignment could be expected to arrive in "the course of the winter."

A promising change for the better came in the 1790s, when a private company completed the Lancaster turnpike in Pennsylvania. It was a broad, hard-surfaced highway that thrust 62 miles (100 kilometers) westward, from Philadelphia to Lancaster. As the driver approached the toll gate, he was confronted with a barrier of sharp pikes, which were turned aside when he paid his toll. Hence the term "turnpike."

The Lancaster Pike proved to be a highly successful venture, returning as high as 15 percent annual dividends to its stockholders. It attracted a rich trade to Philadelphia, and touched off a turnpike-building boom that lasted about twenty years. It also stimulated Western development. The turnpikes beckoned to the canvas-covered Conestoga wagons, whose creakings heralded an advance that would know no real retreat.

CUMBERLAND (NATIONAL) ROAD AND MAIN CONNECTIONS

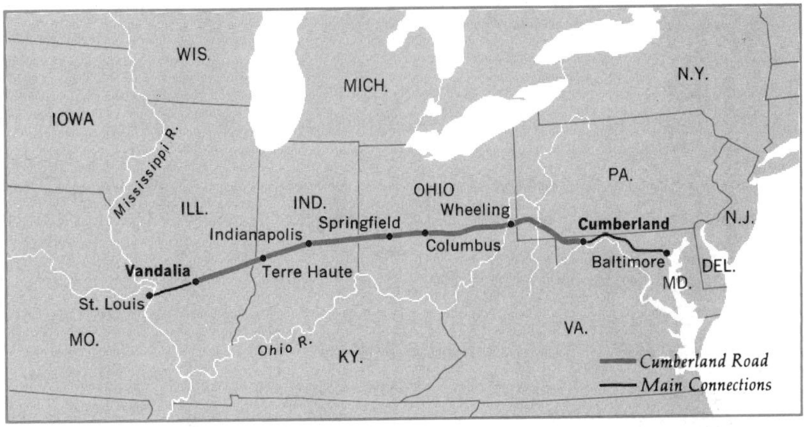

Western road building, always expensive, encountered many obstacles. Looming large among them were the noisy states'-righters, who opposed federal aid to local projects. Eastern states also protested against being bled of their populations by the westward-reaching arteries.

Westerners scored a notable triumph in 1811 when the federal government began to construct the elongated National Road, or Cumberland Road. This highway ultimately stretched from Cumberland, in western Maryland, to Vandalia, in Illinois, a distance of 591 miles (952 kilometers). The War of 1812 interrupted construction, and states'-rights shackles on internal improvements hampered federal grants. But the thoroughfare was belatedly brought to its destination, in 1852, by a combination of aid from the states and the federal government.

The famed Cumberland Road, with numerous branches, was a marvelous stimulant to American prosperity. As the vital highway to the West, it made freight carrying cheaper and faster. It hastened the flow of European immigrants over the mountains; it swelled population centers; it enhanced land values. It also wrote a colorful chapter in the history of transportation. Brightly painted stagecoaches, named after prominent statesmen and pulled by four to six foam-flecked horses, careened down the dusty highroad at breakneck speed, often better than 20 miles (32 kilometers) an hour. The age of rapid land transportation was dawning.

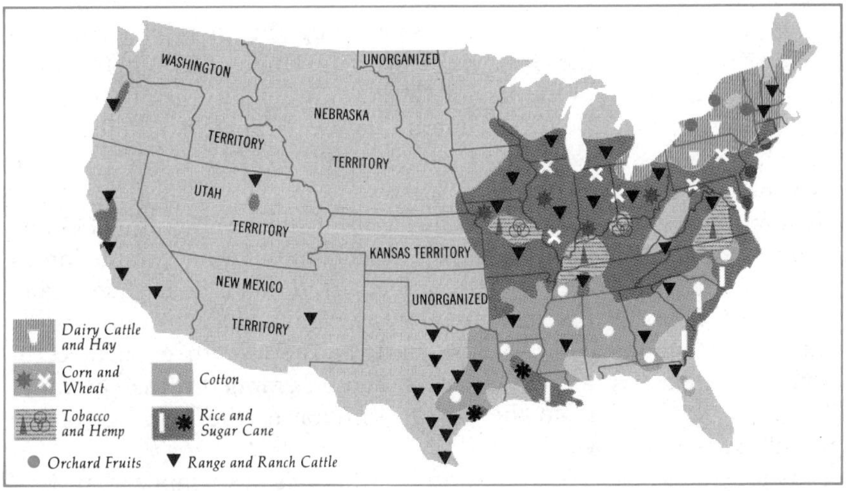

THE PATTERN OF AMERICAN AGRICULTURAL PRODUCTION IN 1860

Fulton's First Steamboat. The presence of the two sails indicates that the inventor anticipated engine trouble.

Fulton Reverses the Rivers

The steamboat craze, which overlapped the turnpike craze, was touched off by an ambitious painter-engineer named Robert Fulton. Several other men had earlier built steamboats, but these craft had all proved unprofitable, largely because of weak engines and even weaker financing.

Fulton, shrewder and luckier than the others, won financial backing from a wealthy New Yorker. He installed a powerful steam engine in a vessel which posterity came to know as the *Clermont* but which a dubious public dubbed "Fulton's Folly." On a historic day in 1807, the quaint little ship, belching sparks from its single smokestack, churned steadily from New York City up the Hudson River toward Albany. It made the run of 150 miles (242 kilometers) in 32 hours.

The success of the steamboat was sensational. Man could now in large degree defy wind, wave, tide, and downstream current. Within a few years Fulton had changed all of America's navigable streams into two-way arteries, thereby doubling their carrying capacity. Hitherto keelboats had been pushed up the Mississippi, with quivering poles and raucous profanity, at less than one mile an hour—a process that was prohibitively costly. Now the steamboats could churn rapidly against the current, ultimately attaining speeds in excess of 10 miles (16 kilometers) an hour. The mighty Mississippi had now met her master.

By 1820 there were some sixty steamboats on the Mississippi and its tributaries; by 1860, about one thousand, some of them luxurious river palaces. Keen rivalry among the swift and gaudy steamers led to memorable races. Excited passengers would urge the captain to pile on wood at the risk of bursting the boilers, which all too often exploded with tragic results for the floating firetraps.

Chugging steamboats played a vital role in the opening of the West and South, both of which were richly endowed with navigable rivers. Like bunches of grapes on a vine, population clustered along the banks of the broad-flowing streams. Cotton growers and other farmers made haste to take up the now-profitable virgin soil. Not only could they float their produce out to market but, hardly less important, they could ship in at low cost their shoes, hardware, and other manufactured necessities.

"Clinton's Big Ditch" in New York

A canal-cutting craze paralleled the boom in turnpikes and steamboats. A few canals had been built around falls and elsewhere in colonial days, but ambitious projects lay in the future. Resourceful New Yorkers, cut off from federal aid by states'-righters, themselves dug the Erie Canal, linking the Great Lakes with the Hudson River. They were blessed with the driving leadership of Governor DeWitt Clinton, whose grandiose project was scoffingly called "Clinton's Big Ditch" or "the Governor's Gutter."

Begun in 1817, the canal eventually ribboned 363 miles (585 kilometers). On its completion in 1825, a garland-bedecked canal boat glided from Buffalo, on Lake Erie, to the Hudson River and on to New York harbor. There, with colorful ceremony, Governor Clinton emptied a cask of water from the lake to symbolize "the marriage of the waters."

The water from Clinton's cask baptized an Em-

ERIE CANAL AND MAIN BRANCHES

The Erie Canal system, and others like it, tapped the fabulous agricultural potential of the Midwest, while canal construction and maintenance provided employment for displaced Eastern farmers squeezed off the land by competition from their more productive Midwestern cousins. The transportation revolution thus simultaneously expanded the nation's acreage under cultivation and speeded the shift of the work force from agricultural to manufacturing and "service" occupations. In 1820 more than three-quarters of American workers labored on farms; by 1850 only a little more than half of them were so employed.

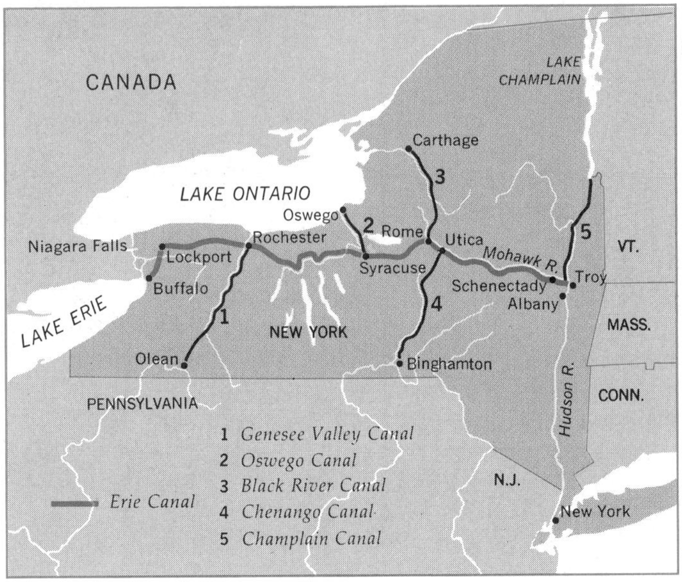

pire State. Mule-drawn passengers and bulky freight could now be handled with cheapness and dispatch, at the dizzy speed of 5 miles (8 kilometers) an hour. The cost of shipping a ton of grain from Buffalo to New York City fell from $100 to $5, and the time of transit from about twenty days to six.

Ever-widening economic ripples followed the completion of the Erie Canal. The value of land along the route skyrocketed, and new cities—like Rochester and Syracuse—sprouted up. Industry in the state boomed. The new profitableness of farming in the Old Northwest—notably in Ohio, Michigan, Indiana, Illinois—attracted thousands of European immigrants to the unaxed and untaxed lands now available. Flotillas of steamships soon plied the Great Lakes, connecting with waiting canal barges at Buffalo. Interior waterside villages like Cleveland, Detroit, and Chicago exploded into mighty cities.

Other profound economic and political changes followed the completion of the canal. The price of potatoes in New York City was cut in half, and many dispirited New England farmers, no longer able to face this ruinous competition, abandoned their rocky holdings and went elsewhere. Some

A Set of Locks on the Erie Canal. An engineering marvel, it had to raise boats 571 feet (174 meters) from the Hudson to Lake Erie. Thousands of laborers died of afflictions ranging from malaria to snake bite—conspicuously Irish immigrant laborers, some of whom worked for 37½ cents an hour plus whiskey. (Courtesy of The New-York Historical Society, New York City.)

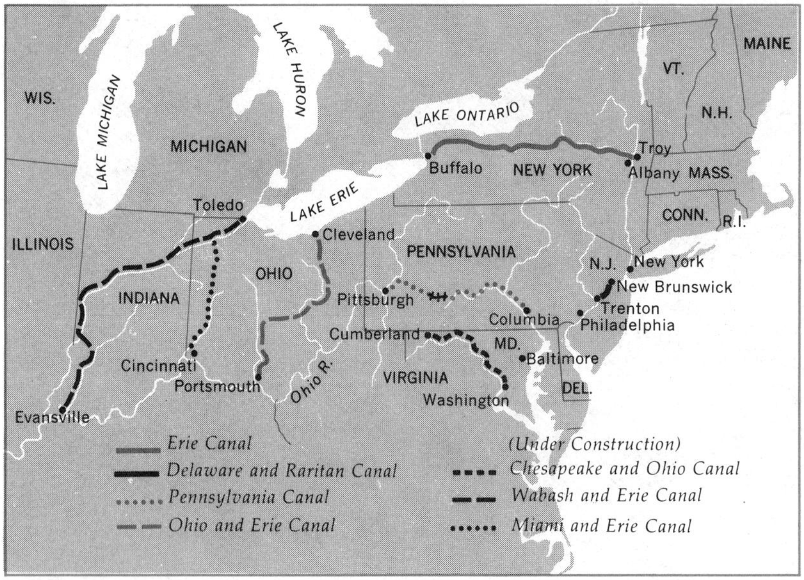

PRINCIPAL CANALS IN 1840

Note that the canals mainly facilitated east-west traffic, especially along the great Lake Erie artery. No comparable network of canals existed in the South—a disparity that helps to explain Northern superiority in the Civil War that came two decades later.

became mill hands, thus speeding the industrialization of America. Others, finding it easy to go west over the Erie Canal, took up new farmlands south of the Great Lakes, where they were joined by countless thousands of New Yorkers and other Northerners. Still others shifted to fruit, vegetable, and dairy farming. These transformations in the Northeast showed how long-established local market structures could be swamped by the emerging behemoth of a continental economy.

The astonishing success of the Erie Canal stimulated competition, especially from the urban rivals of New York City. Ingenious Philadelphians, defying both geography and gravity, constructed a temporarily profitable canal over the Allegheny Mountains. At a unique portage, a special railroad lifted barges to an elevation of nearly 2,300 feet (700 meters), from which they were lowered on the other side.

A web of canals was likewise dug in the Old Northwest to connect with the Great Lakes and the Mississippi River. On one of the Ohio waterways, the youthful James A. Garfield, later to become President, drove balky mules down the towpath.

When the Iron Horse Was a Colt

The railroad proved to be the most significant contribution to a solution of the great American problem of distance. It was fast, reliable, cheaper than canals to construct, and not frozen over in winter. Able to go almost anywhere, even through the Allegheny barrier, it defied terrain and weather.

Early experiments with railroads involved the use of various kinds of power, including wind, dogs, horses, and finally steam. The first important line was begun by the Baltimore and Ohio Company, significantly on Independence Day, 1828. At the colorful dedication ceremony, the first stone was laid at Baltimore by Charles Carroll, then aged ninety, the only surviving signer of the Declaration of Independence. But the steam locomotive for railroads—truly a declaration of independence from primitive transportation—was not, as commonly supposed, a Yankee invention. It had already been used to a limited extent in England.

American locomotives, though soon to make the grade, encountered initial setbacks. A famous nine-mile race was staged in 1830 between a horse-drawn car and the "Tom Thumb," the crack locomotive of the Baltimore and Ohio. The noisy iron horse was winning when it broke down. The gray quadruped then clattered on to victory, amid wild cheers from the foes of mechanical progress. But dumb animals rapidly lost out, as numerous railroads began to radiate from the main cities like spokes from the hub of a wheel. By 1860, only thirty-two years after the Baltimore and Ohio ceremony, the United States boasted 30,000 miles (48,000 kilometers) of railroad track, three-fourths of it in the rapidly industrializing North.

Pioneer Railroad Promoters

Inevitably the hoarse screech of the locomotive sounded the doom of various vested interests. They railed against progress and in defense of their pocketbooks, as people so often do. Turnpike investors and tavern keepers did not relish the loss of business, and farmers feared for their hay-and-horse market. The canal backers were especially violent. Mass meetings were held along the Erie Canal, and in 1833 the legislature of New York, anxious to protect its canal investment, prohibited the railroads from carrying freight—at least temporarily.

Objections to the Iron Monster did not end there. It was branded as undemocratic, for no ordinary citizen could own one. It was sacrilegious, for God had given men and animals legs. Finally, it was a public menace. Sparks set fire to haystacks and houses, and supposedly frightened chickens into not laying eggs. Good old four-legged Dobbin was preferred. He sent out no sparks, carried his own fuel, made little noise, and would not explode.

Early railway coaches were torture chambers on wheels, and no places for weaklings or cowards. Live cinders burned holes in clothes—one woman found thirteen in her gown. The brakes were so feeble that the engineer might miss the station twice, both coming and backing up. The rails were flimsy iron strips fastened on wood; and appalling accidents turned the wooden "miniature hells" into flaming funeral pyres.

Railroad pioneers ran into additional obstacles. Arrivals and departures were conjectural; timetables were little better than ill-kept promissory notes. Further complications were caused by the variance in gauge (or space between the rails). When a passenger came to a different line, he would often have to change cars, after wiping cinders from his eyes. In 1840 there were seven transfers between Philadelphia and Charleston. Violence flared up in Erie, Pennsylvania, in 1853, when the hotel and trucking men rebelled. Fearing that the trains would go through without stopping,

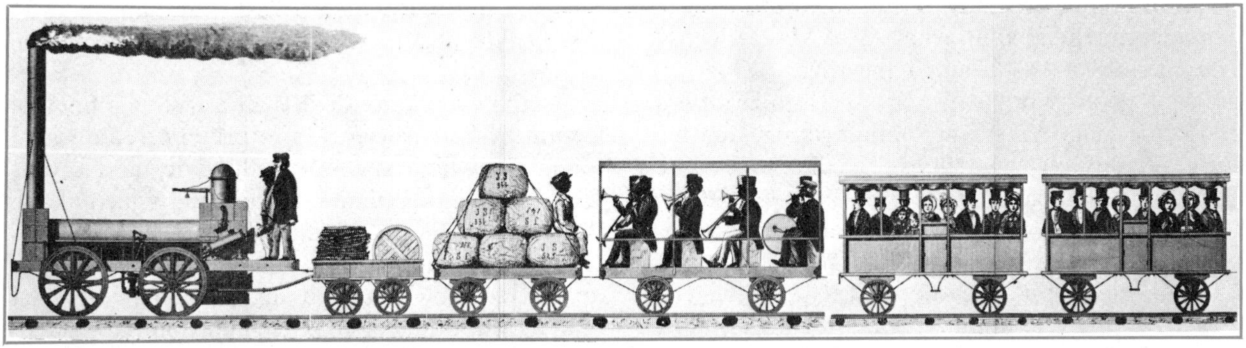

The "West Point." Second locomotive built for a railroad. (Library of Congress.)

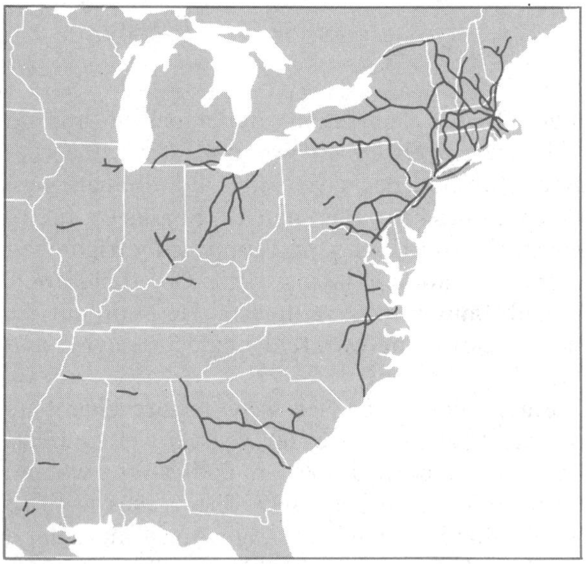

RAILROADS IN OPERATION IN 1850

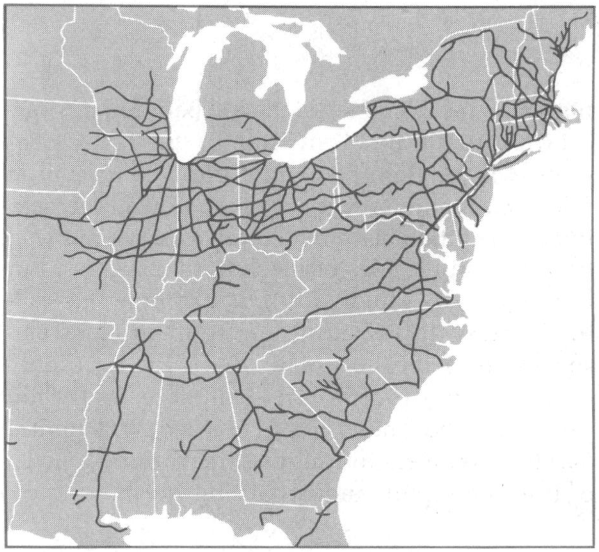

RAILROADS IN OPERATION IN 1860. Note concentration in North.

they unsuccessfully attempted to prevent standardization of the gauge.

But needed railway improvements were gradually installed. Gauges became standardized, safety devices were adopted, solid iron rails were laid, and the Pullman sleeping "palace" was introduced in 1859. America at long last was being bound together with ribs of iron—later steel.

The Transport Web Binds the Union

More than anything else, the desire of the East to tap the West stimulated the "transportation revolution." Until about 1830, the produce of the Western region drained southward to the cotton belt or to the heaped-up wharves of New Orleans. The steamboat vastly aided the reverse flow of finished goods up the watery Western arteries, and helped bind West and South together. But the truly revolutionary changes in commerce and communication came in the three decades before the Civil War, as canals and railroad tracks radiated out from the East, across the Alleghenies and into the blossoming heartland. The ditchdiggers and tie-layers were attempting nothing less than a conquest of nature itself. They would offset the "natural" flow of trade on the interior rivers by laying down an impressive grid of "internal improvements."

The builders succeeded beyond their wildest dreams. The Mississippi was increasingly robbed of its traffic, as goods moved eastward on chugging trains, puffing lake boats, and mule-tugged canal barges. Governor Clinton had in effect picked up the mighty Father of Waters and flung it over the Alleghenies, forcing it to empty into the sea at New York City. By the 1840s Buffalo handled more Western produce than New Orleans. Between 1836 and 1860, grain shipments through Buffalo increased a staggering sixtyfold. New York City became the seaboard queen of the nation, a gigantic port through which a vast hinterland poured its wealth, and to which it daily paid economic tribute.

By the eve of the Civil War, a truly continental economy had emerged. The principle of division of labor, which spelled productivity and profits in the factory, applied on a national scale as well. Each region now specialized in a particular type of economic activity. The South raised cotton for export to New England and Europe; the West grew grain and livestock to feed Southern slaves and Eastern factory workers; the East made machines and textiles for the other two regions.

The economic pattern thus woven had fateful political and military implications. Many Southerners regarded the Mississippi as a silver chain that naturally linked together the upper valley states and the Cotton Kingdom. They were convinced, as secession approached, that some or all of these states would have to secede with them or be strangled. But they overlooked the man-made links that now bound the upper Mississippi Valley to the East in intimate commercial union. Southern rebels would have to fight not only Northern armies, but the tight bonds of an interdependent continental economy. Economically, the two northerly sections were Siamese twins.

Wealth and Poverty

Revolutionary advances in manufacturing and transportation brought increased prosperity to all Americans, but they also widened the gulf between the rich and the poor. Millionaires had been rare in the early days of the Republic, but by the eve of the Civil War several specimens of colossal financial success were strutting across the national stage. Spectacular was the case of fur trader and real-estate speculator John Jacob Astor, who left an estate of $30 million on his death in 1848.

Cities bred the greatest extremes of economic inequality. Unskilled workers, then as always, fared worst. Many of them came to make up a floating mass of "drifters," buffeted from town to town by the shifting prospects for menial jobs. These wandering workers accounted at various times for up to half the population of the brawling industrial centers. Though their numbers were large, they left little behind them but the homely fruits of their transient labor. Largely unstoried and unsung, they are among the forgotten men and women of American history.

Many myths about "social mobility" grew up over the buried memories of these luckless day laborers. Mobility did exist in industrializing America—but not in the proportions that legend often portrays. Rags-to-riches success stories were relatively few.

Yet America, with its dynamic society and wide open spaces, undoubtedly provided more "opportunity" than did the contemporary countries of the Old World—which is why millions of immigrants packed their bags and headed for New World shores. Moreover, a rising tide lifts all boats, and the improvement in overall standards of living was real. Wages for unskilled workers in labor-hungry America rose about 1 percent a year from 1820 to 1860. This general prosperity helped to defuse the potential class conflict that might otherwise have exploded—and that did explode in several European countries.

Commerce and Cables

A new pattern of American foreign trade also emerged in the antebellum years, though businessmen concentrated on developing the wondrously rewarding domestic market. (Foreign commerce seldom added up to more than 7 percent of the national product.) Abroad as at home, cotton was king and regularly accounted for more than half the value of all American exports. After the repeal of the British exclusionary Corn Laws in 1846, the wheat gathered by McCormick's reapers began to play an increasingly important role in trade with Great Britain. Americans generally exported agricultural products and imported manufactured goods—and they generally imported more than they exported.

Most American foreign trade involved Great Britain. As time went on, a bustling Anglo-American transatlantic economy took shape. In 1818 New York's Black Ball Line inaugurated a regularly scheduled passenger and shipping service to England.

In 1858 Cyrus Field, a wealthy New York paper manufacturer, finally succeeded in stretching a cable between Newfoundland and Ireland. As "the greatest wire-puller of modern times," he had tried and failed in four previous attempts, amid much ridicule, to lay the cable through the 2 miles (3.2 kilometers) deep North Atlantic waters. When he achieved his goal, wild rejoicing rocked the nation. New York City reveled in a two-day cable carnival, and Queen Victoria exchanged congratulatory messages with President Buchanan. After three weeks and several hundred cablegrams, the cable went dead and remained useless for eight years. Heroes became villains overnight, and skeptics falsely accused the promoter of having sent faked messages so as to sell his stock at a high figure. But Field did not despair. In 1866, after the Civil War and another aborted try, he laid a heavier cable with gratifying success. The derided dreamer once more became an honored hero.

Clipper Captains and Pony Riders

The United States merchant marine encountered rough sailing during much of the early 19th Century. American vessels had been repeatedly laid up by the embargo, the War of 1812, and the panics of 1819 and 1837. American naval designers made few contributions to maritime progress. A pioneer American steamer, the *Savannah*, had crept across the Atlantic in 1819, but she used sail most of the time and was pursued for a day by a British captain who thought her afire.

In the 1840s and 1850s a golden age dawned for American shipping. Yankee naval yards, notably Donald McKay's at Boston, began to send down the ways sleek new craft called clipper ships. Long, narrow, and majestic, they glided across the sea under towering masts and clouds of canvas. In a fair breeze they could outrun any steamer.

> Stately as churches, swift as gulls,
> They trod the oceans, then—
> No man had seen such ships before
> And none will see again.*

The stately clippers sacrificed cargo space for speed, and their captains made killings by hauling high-value cargoes in record times. They wrested much of the tea-carrying trade between the Far East and England from their slower-moving British competitors, and they sped thousands of impatient adventurers to the gold fields of California and Australia.

But the hour of glory for the clipper was relatively brief. On the eve of the Civil War the British

---

*"Clipper Ships and Captains" from *A Book of Americans* by Rosemary & Stephen Vincent Benét. Copyright, 1933, by Rosemary & Stephen Vincent Benét. Copyright renewed ©, 1961, by Rosemary Carr Benét. Reprinted by permission of Brandt & Brandt Literary Agency, Inc.

A Clipper Ship. (The Peabody Museum of Salem, Massachusetts.)

MAIN ROUTES WEST BEFORE THE CIVIL WAR

Mark Twain described his stagecoach trip to California in the 1860s:

We began to get into country, now, threaded here and there with little streams. These had high, steep banks on each side, and every time we flew down one bank and scrambled up the other, our party inside got mixed somewhat. First we would all be down in a pile at the forward end of the stage, . . . and in a second we would shoot to the other end, and stand on our heads. And . . . as the dust rose from the tumult, we would all sneeze in chorus, and the majority of us would grumble, and probably say some hasty thing, like: "Take your elbow out of my ribs!—can't you quit crowding?"

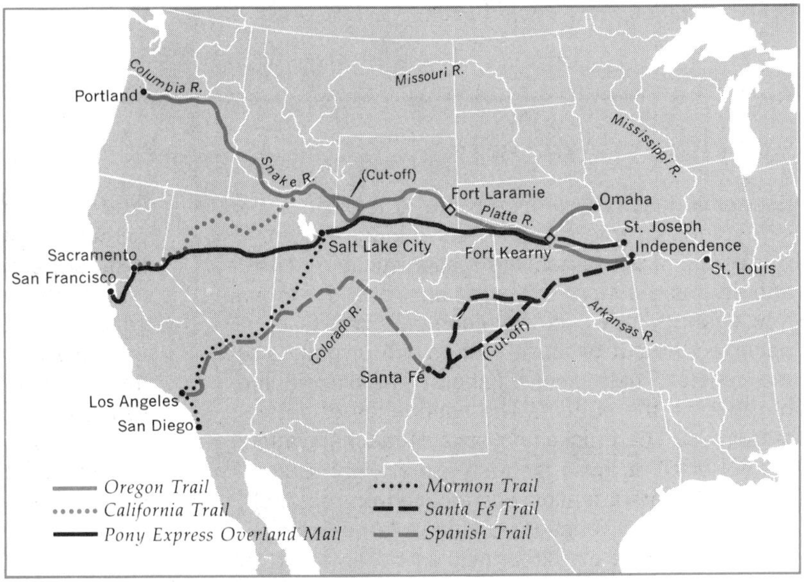

had clearly won the world race for maritime ascendancy with their iron tramp steamers ("teakettles"). Though slower and less romantic than the clipper, these vessels were steadier, more capacious, more reliable, and hence more profitable.

No story of rapid American communication would be complete without including the Far West. By 1858 horse-drawn overland stages, immortalized by Mark Twain's *Roughing It*, were a familiar sight. Their dusty tracks stretched into California from the right bank of the muddy Missouri River.

Even more dramatic was the Pony Express, established in 1860 to carry mail speedily the 2,000 lonely miles (3,220 kilometers) from St. Joseph, Missouri, to Sacramento, California. Daring, lightweight riders, leaping onto wiry ponies saddled at stations approximately 10 miles (16 kilometers) apart, could make the trip in an amazing ten days. These unarmed horsemen galloped on, summer or winter, day or night, through dust or snow, past red Indians and white bandits. The speeding postmen missed only one trip, though the whole enterprise lost money heavily and folded after only eighteen legend-leaving months.

Just as the clippers had succumbed to steam, so were the express riders unhorsed by Morse's clacking keys, which began tapping messages to California in 1861. The swift ships and the fleet ponies ushered out a dying technology of wind and muscle. In the future, machines would be in the saddle.

> As late as 1877 stagecoach passengers were advised in print: "Never shoot on the road as the noise might frighten the horses. . . . Don't point out where murders have been committed, especially if there are women passengers. . . . Expect annoyances, discomfort, and some hardships."

Pony Express. A short-lived epoch of speed. (Ernst Lehner, *American Symbols*, New York: Amiel Book Distributors.)

VARYING VIEWPOINTS

Economic history was once simply a tale of industrious inventors and inventive industrialists. But economics has become a sophisticated science, and so has the story of the material past. Historians now seek to know just *why* economic growth occurred. Was it because of the spirit or genius of the people? Their sheer numbers? The exploitation of those on the bottom? The abundance of natural resources? The quickening pace of mechanization? No doubt all of these factors were at work. But in recent years attention has focused on regional specialization of function—a kind of large-scale equivalent of the classic principle of division of labor. Thus a key to growth is seen in the national parceling-out of economic tasks: agriculture in the Midwest, cotton exports in the South, and manufacturing and services in the Northeast. This shaping of the national economic pattern, in turn, depended on the development of an efficient transportation system—hence the crucial importance of the canal and railroad network. Historians are also increasingly interested in the question: What people benefited most from economic growth? This is known as the "welfare" question, as distinct from the fact of growth alone.

SELECT READINGS

Solid introductions are P. W. Gates, *The Farmer's Age: Agriculture, 1815–1860* (1960), G. R. Taylor, *The Transportation Revolution, 1815–1860* (1951), and T. C. Cochran and W. Miller, *The Age of Enterprise* (1942). The events of the period are placed in a larger context of economic history in S. Bruchey, *The Roots of American Economic Growth, 1607–1861* (1965), and in W. W. Rostow, *The Stages of Economic Growth* (rev. ed., 1971). See also Lance Davis, *American Economic Growth: An Economist's History of the United States* (1972), and P. d'A. Jones, *The Consumer Society: A History of American Capitalism* (1969). C. M. Green treats the father of the factory system in *Eli Whitney and the Birth of American Technology* (1956). T. C. Cochran gives an overall view in *Business in American Life: A History* (1972). The laboring classes are chronicled in Norman Ware, *The Industrial Worker, 1840–1860* (1924), and in J. Rayback, *History of American Labor* (1966). Consult also Herbert Gutman's path-breaking *Work, Culture and Society in Industrializing America* (1976). Two fascinating case studies of the coming of industrialism are Alan Dawley, *Class and Community: The Industrial Revolution in Lynn* (1977), and Anthony F. C. Wallace, *Rockdale: The Growth of an American Village in the Early Industrial Revolution* (1978). Ideological aspects of this process are described in John F. Kasson, *Civilizing the Machine: Technology and Republican Values in America, 1776–1900* (1976). Highly informative is C. H. Danhof, *Change in Agriculture: The Northern United States, 1820–1870* (1969). The canal era is comprehensively described in C. Goodrich, *Government Promotion of American Canals and Railroads, 1800–1890* (1960). See also R. E. Shaw, *Erie Water West, A History of the Erie Canal, 1792–1854* (1966), and H. N. Scheiber, *The Ohio Canal Era* (1968). On railroads, consult Robert Fogel, *Railroads and American Economic Growth* (1964), which presents the startling thesis that the iron horse in fact did little to promote growth. For a different view, see A. Fishlow, *American Railroads and the Transformation of the Ante-Bellum Economy* (1965). An important aspect of the subject is studied in A. M. Johnston and B. E. Supple, *Boston Capitalists and Western Railroads* (1967). Douglas C. North has contributed a fascinating study of *Economic Growth in the United States, 1790–1860* (1961), which should be supplemented by his equally stimulating *Growth and Welfare in the American Past* (rev. ed., 1974). The clipper ships are lovingly described in C. C. Cutler, *Greyhounds of the Sea* (1930), and S. E. Morison, *By Land and By Sea* (1953). An excellent introduction to the romance of the tall ships is R. H. Dana's personal narrative, *Two Years before the Mast* (1840).

17

Creating an American Character, 1790-1860

America was bred in a cabin.

MORRIS BIRKBECK, 1817

American Children of Environment

"In the United States," wrote Gertrude Stein, "there is more space where nobody is than where anybody is. This is what makes America what it is." Even today, as a highly industrialized and technologically sophisticated people, Americans have not fully shaken off the effects of their centuries-long battle with the wilderness.

The West, with its raw frontier, was the most typically American part of America. George Washington, a product of tidewater Virginia, was outwardly an English aristocrat, who lived most of his life under the British flag; Andrew Jackson, a product of frontier Tennessee, was clearly an American. As Ralph Waldo Emerson wrote in 1844, "Europe stretches to the Alleghenies; America lies beyond."

The "go-aheaditive" Americans sprang from a restless breed of people. Thanks to an invigorating climate and the challenge of tremendous tasks,

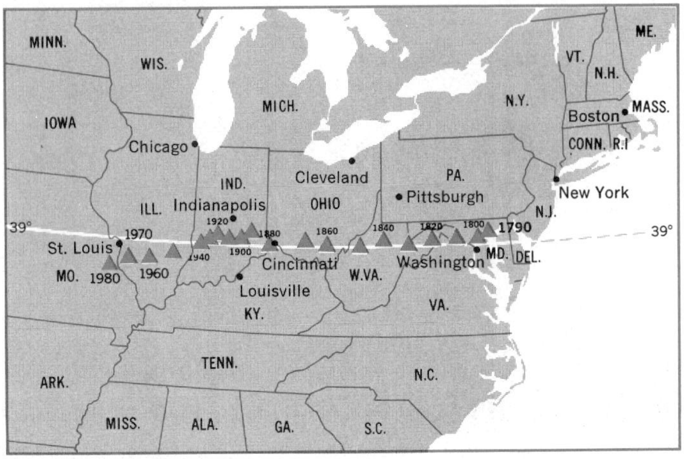

WESTWARD MOVEMENT OF CENTER OF POPULATION, 1790–1980
Note the remarkable equilibrium of the north-south pull from 1790 onward, and the strong spurt west and south after 1940. The 1980 census revealed that the nation's center of population had at last moved west of the Mississippi River.

they were nervous and energetic. Born hustlers—always "a-doin'"—they were footloose and frequently on the move. One "tall tale" of the frontier described chickens that voluntarily crossed their legs every spring, waiting to be tied for the annual move west. Even in repose, Americans were often whittling, sewing, chewing, jiggling, or rocking. The rocking chair—"the chair that travels but stays at home"—was a typically American device. At the dinner table, the rule seemed to be "gobble, gulp, and go." Americans had no time for four o'clock tea, as the English did. There was too much cream to be skimmed off the continent—furs, timber, wildlife—with a consequent wasting of soil and natural resources in some areas. All this restlessness came partly from youth; as late as 1850 the majority of Americans were under thirty.

The West attracted these nervous particles of human energy like a magnet. By 1840 the "demographic center" of the American population map had crossed the Alleghenies. On the eve of the Civil War, it had marched beyond the Ohio River. Legend portrays an army of muscular axmen triumphantly carving civilization out of the Western woods. But in reality life was downright grim for most pioneer families. Poorly fed, ill-clad, housed in hastily erected shanties, they were perpetual victims of disease, depression, and premature death. Above all, there was the awful loneliness, especially for women, who sometimes cracked under the strain. They were often cut off from human contact, especially neighbors, for whole days or even weeks, while confined to the cramped orbit of a dark cabin erected in a crude and secluded clearing. Breakdowns and even madness were all too frequently the "opportunities" that the frontier offered to pioneer women.

Rugged Pioneers

A mad scramble for riches led not only to waste but to superficiality. Wooden bridges were flung across streams, until time permitted the hurry-up American to build stone spans. The breathless pursuit of treasure inevitably led to accusations of money-chasing and crass materialism. John Stuart Mill, the noted English writer, remarked in the 1840s that in America the life of one sex was "devoted to dollar hunting, and of the other to the breeding of dollar hunters." Dollar grabbing was undeniably important, but the thrill of the chase was hardly less so. Wealth was everywhere recognized as the badge of success and the symbol of power.

The rough-and-tough American—especially the Westerner—was often crude, ruthless, brutal. Tobacco chewing and indelicate spitting—"the salivary propensity"—became a national scandal in the decades before the Civil War. One visiting Briton suggested that the spittoon, not the eagle, should be America's national emblem; and a group of Japanese visitors in 1860 noted that the white man had brown saliva. Frontier wrestling, often of the no-holds-barred type, sanctioned such niceties as the biting off of noses or the gouging out of eyes. "Look out, or I'll measure the length of your eyestrings [eye muscles]" was an expressive frontier warning. Nor was brutality directed solely at fellow white men. The Indians stood in the way of expansion, and when they fought back they were brushed aside or killed off, like the wild animals.

Americans were ingenious, inventive, adaptable, self-sufficient—jacks-of-all-trades. They had to be, especially on the frontier, where there was no place for specialists. "Root, hog, or die"—the Western saying directed at hogs left to root up their own food—might well have been the national motto.

Average Americans were strenuous, courageous, aggressive—overendowed with the "lick all creation" spirit. They had unshakeable faith in their military prowess, untrained though they might be. They were tough and tenacious. Learning to laugh at adversity, they fought the elements, the wild animals ("varmints"), their Canadian and Mexican neighbors, and, above all, the Indians. The Englishman Rudyard Kipling later wrote in grudging admiration:

He greets the embarrassed Gods, nor fears
To shake the iron hand of Fate
Or match with Destiny for beers.

"The Spitter." The famed English author, Charles Dickens, laid out his clothes one night on an American canal boat. The next morning he found them liberally bedewed with tobacco juice, the result of "a perfect storm and tempest of spitting." (*Vanity Fair.*)

Gamblers All

Marooned by geography, Americans were self-centered, provincial, and isolationist, whether in their hometowns or in the world community. First and foremost they were individualists. The men depended on their own trusty axes and especially their rifles, which, in the Western phrase, made them all "equally tall." Their political and social beliefs might not bear a radical stamp, for many observers noted the remarkable conformity of American opinion. But they were convinced that their way in the world was for them alone to make. Emerson's popular lecture-essay, "Self-Reliance," struck a deeply responsive chord. Popular literature of the period abounded in portraits of heroically unique, even isolated, figures like Cooper's Natty Bumppo and Melville's Captain Ahab—just as Jacksonian politics aimed to emancipate the lone-wolf, enterprising businessman. Vast space and fabulous economic abundance fostered this fond self-image, and gave it a certain reality. Yet even in this heyday of "rugged individualism" there were exceptions. Pioneers, in tasks clearly beyond their own individual resources, would call upon their neighbors for logrolling and barn-raising, and upon their federal government for help in building internal improvements.

Americans in general were confident, buoyant, optimistic—born boosters, tellers of "tall tales," admirers of the giant lumberjack, the fabled Paul Bunyan. Pessimism was a kind of treason; "knockers" were not wanted. The ancestors of the Americans, as well as the immigrants themselves, had to be courageously optimistic to undertake the stormy Atlantic crossing. "The cowards never started; the weak died on the way," ran the saying.

A British magazine thus satirized American boastfulness in 1870: "If an Arkansaw man cannot boast of the education of a Boston man, at any rate he can chew more tobacco and spit more, farther and straighter than any other man. If the Mississippi steamers are not so magnificent as some on the Hudson River, they sail faster and blow up oftener and shoot men higher than any other steamers in the country."

Those who reached the New World were all gamblers. They gambled their lives against disease and Indians, and their crops and fortunes against the elements. The American people are distilled not only from a select group of brave men and women but also from a long line of risk-takers. Even those who failed had at least one satisfaction: someone had to take the first steps if the Republic was to achieve its ultimate destiny. "It's better to be a has-been," one heard, "than a never-was."

Americans were boastful—a trait growing out of their easy optimism. The game of poker ("brag"), with its premium on successful bluffing, attained great popularity in the West, especially with Henry Clay. Americans were painfully aware of their nation's many physical and cultural shortcomings and, while smarting under the sneers of monocled foreigners, they would brag loudly and defensively about the splendid cities that would one day spring from their malarial swamps. Significantly, they boasted of the future, while Europeans boasted of their past. They also learned to worship bigness, partly because America excelled in size. Above all, they had unbounded faith in the future, in progress, in the "American dream."

The Torch of Democracy

The American people were essentially democratic except, conspicuously, for the blight of slavery. In their social democracy, especially beyond the mountains, they set little store by caste, tradition, or family trees. The first question was not "Who are you?" but "What can you do?" On the frontier, where all people were "equally better," a common expression was "I'm as good as you be." Or as a Hungarian immigrant later remarked, "The President is Mister and I am Mister too." The very first sentence of Alexis de Tocqueville's great treatise on *Democracy in America* (1835) proclaimed: "Nothing struck me more forcibly than the general equality of conditions among the people." One rousing song sung at religious camp meetings ran:

Come hungry, come thirsty, come ragged, come bare,
Come filthy, come lousy, come just as you are.

Political democracy was one of the nation's proudest boasts. White manhood suffrage came to be the rule. The people realized that the world was skeptically watching their vast experiment in political democracy, and this awareness contributed further to self-conscious boastfulness. Emerson once observed that the American eagle was something of a peacock.

Americans, moreover, were lovers of freedom. Not to be pushed about, they had forcibly overthrown George III and set up a republic. They cherished states' rights and localism, largely because these ideals enabled them to keep a more watchful eye on their public servants. They hailed freedom abroad, as well as in America. Responding to the flattery of imitation, they applauded democratic revolutions whenever they occurred, and often assisted them with money and volunteers. They cheered as thrones crashed, and they openly pitied people who did not have the "gumption" to rise up and break their autocratic chains. Mark Twain caught the spirit of anti-monarchical America when he had Huck Finn remark, "Sometimes I wish we could hear of a country that's out of kings."

Americans were intensely patriotic and nationalistic—America lovers, who annually cheered flag-flapping Fourth of July oratory. Instead of inheriting the land, they had subdued it them-

YEAR	WHITE	NON-WHITE	TOTAL POPULATION
1790	3,172,000	757,000	3,929,000
1800	4,306,000	1,002,000	5,308,000
1810	5,862,000	1,378,000	7,240,000
1820	7,867,000	1,772,000	9,639,000
1830	10,537,000	2,329,000	12,866,000
1840	14,196,000	2,874,000	17,070,000
1850	19,553,000	3,639,000	23,192,000
1860	26,922,000	4,521,000	31,443,000

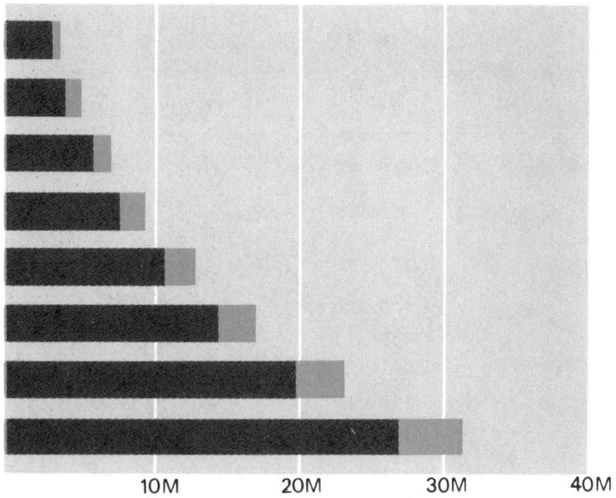

POPULATION INCREASE, INCLUDING SLAVES AND INDIANS, 1790–1860

selves, battling both the elements and the Indians. And one especially cherishes the possessions one has to fight for.

The March of the Millions

An amazing multiplication of people continued decade after decade, without serious slackening. By mid-century the population was still doubling approximately every twenty-three years, as in fertile colonial days.

By 1860 the original thirteen states had more than doubled in number: thirty-three stars graced the American flag. The United States was the fourth most populous nation in the Western world, exceeded by only three European countries—Russia, France, and Austria.

Urban growth continued explosively. In 1790 there had been only two cities that could boast 20,000 or more souls: Philadelphia and New York. By 1860 there were forty-three; and about 300 other places claimed over 5,000 inhabitants apiece. New York was the metropolis; New Orleans, the "Queen of the South;" and Chicago, the swaggering lord of the Midwest, destined to be "Hog Butcher for the World."

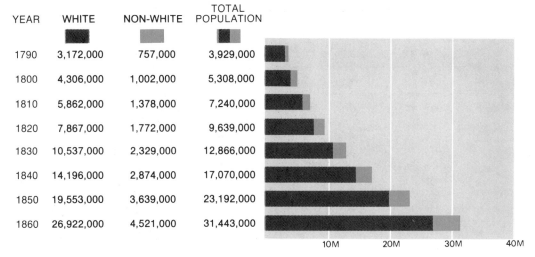

Cincinnati in 1843. Famous as a processor of hogs, this "Queen City of the West" was a town of 2,540 people in 1800, and 161,044 in 1860, 45 percent of them foreign born. Though tied to the South by down-river commerce on the Ohio and Mississippi rivers, it remained loyal to the North during the Civil War. (Cincinnati Public Library.)

Irish and German Immigration by Decade

Years	*Irish*	*German*	*All Others*	*Grand Total*
1820–1830	Unknown	Unknown	Unknown	151,824
1831–1840	207,381	152,454	239,290	599,125
1841–1850	780,719	434,626	497,906	1,713,251
1851–1860	914,119	951,667	732,428	2,598,214
1861–1870	435,778	787,468	1,091,578	2,314,824
1871–1880	436,871	718,182	1,657,138	2,812,191
1881–1890	655,482	1,452,970	3,138,161	5,246,613
1891–1900	388,416	505,152	2,793,996	3,687,564

Such overrapid urbanization unfortunately brought undesirable by-products. It intensified the problems of smelly slums, feeble street lighting, inadequate policing, impure water, foul sewage, ravenous rats, and improper garbage disposal. Hogs poked their scavenging snouts about many city streets as late as the 1840s. Boston in 1823 pioneered with a sewage system; and New York in 1842 abandoned wells and cisterns for a piped-in water supply. The city thus unknowingly eliminated the breeding places of many disease-carrying mosquitoes.

A continuing high birthrate accounted for most of the increase in population, but by the 1840s the tides of immigration were adding hundreds of thousands more. Before this decade, immigrants had been flowing in at the rate of about 60,000 a year, but suddenly the influx was tripled in the 1840s, and then quadrupled in the 1850s. During these two feverish decades, over a million and a half Irish, and nearly as many Germans, swarmed down the gangplanks. Why did they come?

The immigrants came partly because Europe seemed to be running out of room. The population of the Old World more than doubled in the 19th Century, and Europe began to generate a great seething pool of apparently "surplus" people. They were displaced and footloose in their homelands before they felt the tug of the American magnet. Indeed, at least as many people moved about *within* Europe as crossed the Atlantic. America benefited from these people-churning changes but did not set them all in motion. Nor was the United States the sole beneficiary of the process: of the nearly 60 million persons who abandoned Europe in the century after 1840, about 25 million went somewhere other than the United States.

Yet America still beckoned most strongly to the struggling masses of Europe, and the majority of migrants headed for the "land of freedom and opportunity." There was freedom from aristocratic caste and state church; there was abundant opportunity to secure broad acres and better one's condition. Much-read letters sent home by immigrants—"America letters"—often described in glowing terms the richer life: low taxes, no compulsory military service, and "three meat meals a day." The introduction of transoceanic steamships also meant that the immigrants could come speedily, in a matter of ten or twelve days instead of ten or twelve weeks. They were still jammed into unsanitary quarters, thus suffering an appalling death rate, but the nightmare was more endurable because it was shorter.

The Emerald Isle Moves West

Ireland, already groaning under the heavy hand of British overlords, was prostrated in the mid-1840s. A terrible rot attacked the potato crop, on which the people had become dangerously de-

Ragged Irish Immigrant Arriving in America. Bewildered newcomers were often whisked to "boardinghouses"—filthy hovels above a "grog shop" where whiskey flowed and a saucer of free tobacco sat on the bar. The hard-drinking Irish scandalized old-stock Americans, but Boston's Orestes Brownson predicted in 1852: "Out from these . . . dirty streets will come forth some of the noblest sons of our country, whom she will delight to own and honor."

pendent, and about one-fourth of them were swept away by disease and hunger. Starved bodies were found dead by the roadsides with grass in their mouths. All told, about 2 million perished.

Tens of thousands of destitute souls, fleeing the Land of Famine for the Land of Plenty, flocked to America in the "Black Forties." Ireland's great export has been population; and the Irish take their place beside the Jews as a dispersed people.

These uprooted newcomers, too poor to move west and buy the necessary land, livestock, and equipment, swarmed into the larger seaboard cities. Noteworthy were Boston and particularly New York, which rapidly became the largest Irish city in the world. Before many decades had passed, more people of Hibernian blood lived in America than on the "ould sod" of Erin's Isle.

The luckless Irish received no red-carpet treatment. Forced to live in squalor, they worsened already vile slum conditions. They were scorned by the older American stock, especially "proper" Protestant Bostonians, who regarded the scruffy Catholic newcomers as a social menace. Barely literate "Biddies" (Bridgets) took jobs as kitchen maids. Broad-shouldered "Paddies" (Patricks), were pushed into pick-and-shovel drudgery on canals and railroads, where thousands left their bones as victims of disease and accidental explosions. It was said that an Irishman lay buried under every railroad tie. Even so, the Irish were hated by native workers. "No Irish Need Apply" was a sign commonly posted at factory gates, and was often abbreviated to NINA. The Irish, in turn, fiercely resented the blacks, with whom they shared society's basement. Race riots between black and Irish dockworkers flared up in several port cities, and the Irish were always cool to the abolitionist cause.

The friendless Irish were forced to fend for themselves. The Ancient Order of Hibernians, a semisecret society founded in Ireland to fight rapacious landlords, served in America as a benevolent society, aiding the downtrodden. It also helped to spawn the "Molly Maguires," a shadowy Irish miners' union that rocked the Pennsylvania coal districts in the 1860s and 1870s.

The Irish tended to remain in low-skill occupations, but gradually improved their lot, usually by acquiring modest amounts of property. The education of children was cut short as families struggled to save money to purchase a home. But for humble Irish peasants, cruelly cast out of their homeland, property ownership counted as a grand "success."

Politics quickly attracted these gregarious Gaelic newcomers. A poet urged them in 1852:

> Fellow exiles! claim your station
> In the councils of the nation;
> Be not aliens in the soil
> Which exacts your sweat and toil.

They soon began to gain control of powerful city machines, notably New York's Tammany Hall, and reaped the patronage rewards. Before long, beguilingly brogued Irishmen dominated police departments in many big cities, where they now drove the "Paddy wagons" that had once carted their brawling forebears to jail.

American politicians made haste to cultivate the

Irish vote, especially in the politically potent state of New York. Irish hatred of the British lost nothing in the transatlantic transplanting. As the Irish-Americans increased in number—nearly 2 million arrived between 1830 and 1860—officials in Washington glimpsed political gold in those Hibernian hills. Politicians often found it politically profitable to fire verbal volleys at London—a process vulgarly known as "twisting the British Lion's tail."

The German Forty-Eighters

The influx of refugees from Germany between 1830 and 1860 was hardly less spectacular than that from Ireland. During these troubled years, over a million and a half thrifty Germans stepped onto American soil. The bulk of them were poor people, displaced by crop failures and by other hardships. But a strong sprinkling were liberal political refugees. Saddened by the collapse of the democratic revolutions of 1848, they had decided to leave the autocratic Fatherland and flee to America—the one brightest hope of democracy.

The liberal German "Forty-Eighters," who came to America for free government, are not to be confused with the "Forty-Niners," who came to California for free gold. The future history of Germany—and indeed of the world—might well have been less war-torn if these rare spirits had remained at home as a seedbed for genuine democracy. But Germany's loss was America's gain. Zealous German liberals like the lanky and public-spirited Carl Schurz, a relentless foe of slavery and public corruption, contributed richly to the elevation of American political life.

Many of the Germanic newcomers, unlike the Irish, possessed a modest amount of this world's goods. Most of them pushed out to the lush lands of the Middle West, notably Wisconsin, where they settled and established model farms. Like the Irish, they formed an influential body of voters whom American politicians shamelessly wooed. But the Germans were less potent politically because their strength was more widely scattered.

The hand of Germans in shaping American life was widely felt in still other ways. They had fled from the militarism and wars of Europe, and consequently came to be a bulwark of isolationist sentiment in the upper Mississippi Valley. Better educated on the whole than the stump-grubbing Americans, they warmly supported public schools, including their *Kindergarten* (children's garden). They likewise did much to stimulate art and music. As outspoken champions of freedom, they became relentless enemies of slavery during the fevered years before the Civil War.

Yet the Germans—often dubbed "damned Dutchmen"—were occasionally regarded with suspicion by their old-stock American neighbors. Seeking to preserve their language and culture, they sometimes settled in compact "colonies" and kept aloof from the surrounding community. Accustomed to the "Continental Sunday" and uncurbed by Puritan tradition, they made merry on the Sabbath and drank huge quantities of an amber beverage called *Bier* (beer), which dates its real popularity in America to their coming.* Their Old World drinking habits, like those of the Irish newcomers, gave a severe setback to the movement for greater temperance in the use of alcohol.

Flare-Ups of Anti-Foreignism

The invasion by this so-called immigrant "rabble" in the 1840s and 1850s inflamed the hates of American "nativists." They feared that these foreign hordes would outbreed, outvote, and overwhelm the old "native" stock. Not only did the newcomers take jobs from "native" Americans, but the bulk of displaced Irishmen were Roman Catholics, as were a substantial minority of the Germans. The Church of Rome was still widely regarded by many old-line Americans as a "foreign" church; convents were commonly referred to as "Popish brothels."

Roman Catholics were now on the move. They had formed a negligible minority during colonial

*Frederick Pabst and Joseph Schlitz were among the German immigrant brewers who "made Milwaukee famous."

> Strong anti-foreignism was reflected in the platform of the American (Know-Nothing) party in 1856: "*Americans must rule America;* and to this end, *native*-born citizens should be selected for all state, federal, or municipal offices of government employment, in preference to naturalized citizens."

days, and their numbers had increased gradually. But with the enormous influx of the Irish and Germans in the 1840s and 1850s, the Catholics became a powerful religious group. In 1840 they had ranked fifth, behind the Baptists, Methodists, Presbyterians, and Congregationalists. By 1850, with some 1.8 million communicants, they had bounded into first place—a position they have never lost.

"Native" Americans were alarmed by these mounting figures. They professed to believe that in due time the "alien riffraff" would "establish" the Catholic Church at the expense of Protestantism and would introduce "Popish idols." The noisier American "nativists" rallied for political action. In 1849 they formed the Order of the Star-Spangled Banner, which soon developed into the formidable American or "Know-Nothing" party—a name derived from its secretiveness. "Nativists" agitated for rigid restrictions on immigration and naturalization, and for laws authorizing the deportation of alien paupers. They also promoted a lurid literature of exposure, much of it pure fiction. The authors, sometimes posing as escaped nuns, described sin as they imagined it behind brick convent walls, including the secret burial of babies. One of these books—Maria Monk's *Awful Disclosures* (1836)—sold over 300,000 copies.

Even uglier was occasional mass violence. As early as 1834 a Catholic convent near Boston was burned by a howling mob, and in ensuing years there were a few scattered attacks on Catholic schools and churches. The most frightful flare-up occurred during 1844 in Philadelphia, where the Irish Catholics fought back against the threats of the "nativists." The City of Brotherly Love did not quiet down until two Catholic churches had been burned and some thirteen citizens had been killed and fifty wounded in several days of fighting. These outbursts of intolerance, though infrequent and generally localized in the larger cities, remain an unfortunate blot on the record of America's treatment of minority groups.

Crooked Voting. A bitter "nativist" cartoon charging Irish and German immigrants with "stealing" elections. (New York Public Library.)

Reviving Religion

Church attendance was still a fairly regular ritual for about three-fourths of the 23 million Americans in 1850. Yet the old Calvinist rigor was seeping out of American religion. The rationalist ideas of the French Revolutionary era had done much to undermine the older orthodoxy. Thomas Paine's widely circulated book, *The Age of Reason* (1794), had shockingly declared that all churches were "set up to terrify and enslave mankind, and monopolize power and profit." Free-thinking Paine penned his own religious declaration of independence: "My own mind is my own church."

Sheer distance also broke the grip of formal doctrine and centralized church control on American religious life. Scattered frontier communities

A Camp Meeting at Sing Sing, New York. Note the preacher with uplifted hands under the canopy at the left. A British visitor wrote in 1839 of a revival meeting: "In front of the pulpit there was a space railed off and strewn with straw, which I was told was the anxious seat, and on which sat those who were touched by their consciences." (Library of Congress.)

bred maverick congregations, unresponsive to the voice of "higher" authority in the East.

As doctrines softened, sects multiplied. One of the most important spin-offs from the dour Puritanism of the past was the Unitarian faith, which began to gather momentum about 1800, particularly in New England. It held that God existed only in *one* person (hence *uni*tarian), and not in the orthodox Trinity—the Father, the Son, and the Holy Spirit. This disturbing new sect found its inspiration in the liberal ideas set in motion by the American Revolution and other vitalizing forces. It was primarily a protest against the hell-fire doctrines of Calvinism, especially predestined damnation and total depravity. Although denying that Jesus was divine, the Unitarians stressed the essential goodness of human nature rather than its vileness; they proclaimed salvation through integrity and good works. Embraced by many leading thinkers (including Ralph Waldo Emerson), the Unitarian movement continued to be highly intellectual—and, thought some, *too* rational and optimistic.

A sharp reaction against the growing liberalism in religion set in about 1800. A fresh wave of roaring revivals sent a Second Great Awakening surging across the land. Huge "camp meetings" were held along the frontier, with as many as 25,000 persons gathering for an encampment of several days to drink the hell-fire gospel. As one of their hymns recounted:

> My thoughts on awful subjects roll,
> Damnation and the dead;
> What horrors seize a guilty soul
> Upon a dying bed!

Thousands of emotionally starved souls "got religion," and in their ecstasy engaged in orgies of rolling, dancing, barking, and jerking. Many of the "saved" soon backslid into their former sinful ways, but the revivals stimulated church membership and humanitarian reform. Easterners were moved to engage in missionary work in the Indian backwoods, in Hawaii, and in faraway Asia.

Methodists and Baptists reaped the biggest harvests of souls from the fields fertilized by revivalism. Both sects stressed personal conversion (contrary to predestination), a relatively democratic control of church affairs, and a rousing emotionalism. As a frontier jingle ran:

> The Devil hates the Methodist
> Because they sing and shout the best.

Bishop Francis Asbury (1745–1816), English-born and somewhat domineering, was the outstanding figure in early American Methodism. A tall, frail bachelor, he traveled an estimated 300,000 miles (483,000 kilometers) over wretched roads, praying, preaching, and organizing. He rode one horse about 25,000 miles (40,250 kilometers) in five years.

Powerful Peter Cartwright (1785–1872) was the best known of the later Methodist "circuit riders" or traveling frontier preachers. This ill-educated but sinewy servant of the Lord ranged for a half-century from Tennessee to Illinois, calling upon sinners to repent. With bellowing voice and flailing arms, he converted thousands of souls to the Lord. Not only did he lash the Devil with his tongue, but with his fists he knocked out rowdies who attempted to break up his meetings. His Christianity was definitely muscular.

The Circuit Preacher. (From the drawing by A. R. Waud in *Harper's Weekly,* Oct. 12, 1867.)

Denominational Diversity

Revivals also furthered the fragmentation of religious faiths. Western New York, where many descendants of New England Puritans had settled, was so blistered by sermonizers preaching "hell-fire and damnation" that it came to be known as the "Burned-Over District."

Millerites or Adventists, who mustered several hundred thousand adherents, rose from the super-heated soil of the Burned-Over region in the 1830s. Named after the eloquent and commanding William Miller, they interpreted the Bible to mean that Christ would return to earth on October 22, 1844. Donning their go-to-meeting clothes, they gathered in prayerful assemblies to greet their Redeemer. The failure of Jesus to descend on schedule dampened but did not destroy the movement.

Like the First Great Awakening, the Second Great Awakening tended to widen the lines between classes and regions. The more prosperous and conservative denominations in the East were little touched by revivalism, while Episcopalians, Presbyterians, Congregationalists, and Unitarians continued to rise mostly from the wealthier, better-educated levels of society. Methodists, Baptists, and the members of the other new sects spawned by the swelling evangelistic fervor tended to come from less prosperous, less "learned" communities in the rural South and West.

Religious diversity further reflected social cleavages when the churches faced up to the slavery issue. By 1844–1845 both the Southern Baptists and the Southern Methodists had split with their Northern brethren over human bondage. The Methodists came to grief over the case of a slave-owning bishop in Georgia, whose second wife added several household slaves to his estate. In 1857 the Presbyterians, North and South, parted company. The secession of the Southern churches foreshadowed the secession of the Southern states. First the churches split, then the political parties split, and then the Union split.

A Desert Zion in Utah

The smoldering spiritual embers of the Burned-Over District kindled one especially ardent flame in 1830. In that year Joseph Smith—a tall, blue-eyed, and visionary spirit—reported that he had received some golden plates from an angel. When deciphered, they constituted the Book of Mormon, and the Church of Jesus Christ of Latter-Day Saints (Mormons) was launched. It was a native American product, one of the few American-born denominations to spread its influence worldwide.

After establishing a religious oligarchy, Smith ran into serious opposition from his non-Mormon neighbors, first in Missouri and then in Illinois. His cooperative sect rasped rank-and-file Americans, who were individualistic and dedicated to free enterprise. The Mormons aroused further antagonism by voting as a unit and by openly but understandably drilling their militia for defensive purposes. Accusations of polygamy likewise arose and increased in intensity, for Joseph Smith was reputed to have several wives.

Continuing hostility finally drove the Mormons to desperate measures. In 1844 Joseph Smith and his brother were murdered and mangled by a mob in Carthage, Illinois, and the movement seemed near collapse. But the falling torch was seized by a remarkable Mormon Moses named Brigham Young, an aggressive leader, an eloquent preacher, and a gifted administrator. Determined to escape further persecution, Young in 1847–1848 led his oppressed and despoiled Latter-Day Saints over vast rolling plains to Utah as they sang "Come, Come, Ye Saints."

Overcoming pioneer hardships, the Mormons soon made the desert bloom like a new Eden by means of ingenious and cooperative methods of irrigation. The crops of 1848, threatened by hordes of crickets, were saved when flocks of gulls appeared, as if by a miracle, to gulp down the invaders. (A monument to the sea gulls stands in Salt Lake City today.)

Semi-arid Utah grew remarkably. By the end of 1848 some 5,000 settlers had arrived, and other

The Mormon Trail. Utah-bound Mormons with hand carts. (The Church of Jesus Christ of Latter-Day Saints.)

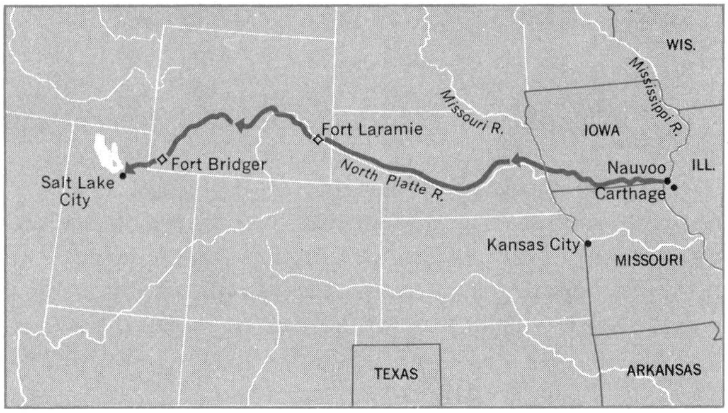

THE MORMON TREK, 1846–1847.
Accompanied by livestock, the first pioneer band, led by Brigham Young, set out for Utah in 1846. The party consisted of 146 young men and women driving 73 wagons.

large bands were to follow. Many dedicated Mormons in the 1850s actually made the 1,300-mile (2,090-kilometer) trek across the plains pulling two-wheeled carts.

Under the rigidly disciplined management of Brigham Young, the community became a prosperous frontier theocracy and a cooperative commonwealth. Young married as many as twenty-seven women—some of them wives in name only—and begot fifty-six children. The population was further swelled by thousands of immigrants from Europe, where the Mormons had established a flourishing missionary movement.

A crisis developed when the Washington government was unable to control the hierarchy of Brigham Young, who had been made territorial governor in 1850. A federal army marched in 1857 against the Mormons, who harassed its lines of supply and rallied to die in their last dusty ditch. Fortunately, the quarrel was finally adjusted without serious bloodshed. The Mormons later ran afoul of the anti-polygamy laws passed by Congress in 1862 and 1882, and their peculiar practice delayed statehood for Utah until 1896.

Polygamy was an issue of such consequence that it was bracketed with slavery in the Republican national platform of 1856: "It is both the right and the imperative duty of Congress to prohibit in the Territories those twin relics of barbarism—Polygamy and Slavery."

Daily Diversions

As the log-clearing phase passed, the masses were left with more leisure to enjoy the good things of life. The simple amusements of colonial days were continued, such as country dances, and the people still derived much satisfaction from religious and political meetings, which were primly attended in "Sunday best" clothes. But a wider range of diversions gradually beckoned.

The stage took on greater respectability as the 19th Century unfolded, even in Boston, where the Puritans had frowned upon the theater as "the Devil's chapel." Resourceful promoters attempted to quiet prejudices by stressing the moral value of their productions: one of Shakespeare's famous plays was advertised as: "Hamlet: Filial Piety." Classical English dramas continued their popularity, while in the 1850s *Uncle Tom's Cabin* and *Ten Nights in a Barroom* were also playing to packed houses.

Early in the century many of the leading actors were visitors from England, but eventually local stars began to flash across the American stage. Handsome and arrogant Edwin Forrest (1806–1872) was the first top-flight American performer, and his rivalry with a visiting English artist inflamed his New York devotees to riot in 1849. This frightful affair ended with twenty-two persons killed and thirty-six wounded.

Other headliners had their day. English-born Junius Brutus Booth (1796–1852), a marvelously gifted though alcoholic tragedian, often broke engagements and even upbraided audiences. Two of his sons trod the boards as tragedians: Edwin T. Booth (1833–1893), who gained fame as an actor; John Wilkes Booth (1838–1865), who gained infamy as the assassin of Lincoln. The most talented American actress of the century was contralto-voiced Charlotte Cushman (1816–1876), who proved to be a smash hit in male and female roles, including both Romeo and Juliet.

Sports continued to relieve the monotony of everyday drudgery. Horse racing still attracted an enthusiastic and open-pursed following. Embryonic baseball had attained so much popularity by 1845 that a uniform set of rules was adopted. Flashy and flammable showboats were churning the main rivers, bringing their variety shows to a gaping public. The traveling circus was drawing appreciative crowds, although the huge three-ring spectacles were not introduced until after the Civil War.

The most famous showman of the era was Phineas T. Barnum (1810–1891), a shrewd and cynical Connecticut Yankee, "the Prince of Humbug." He got his start during the 1830s and 1840s in New York City, where he displayed bearded ladies and other freaks. Realizing that the American public loved to be "humbugged," he operated on the golden assumption that a "sucker" was born every minute. One of his prize hoaxes was the wizened black "nurse" of George Washington, alleged to be 161 years old. (An autopsy indicated that she was about 80.)

Other activities were less amusing. Light-fingered gamblers were ever present to fleece the greedy and unwary, especially on the palatial river steamers. Dueling died hard in the honor-conscious South, its last stronghold. Crimes of violence still persisted in alarming numbers, partly as a result of the brutalizing influence of the frontier. Rough Western justice—often hempen injustice—still manifested itself to an alarming degree in lynching bees, popularly known as "necktie parties."

For the upper crust, fashionable "watering places" were established at Saratoga Springs (New York) and Newport (Rhode Island). These resorts were frequented by the gaudily dressed elite, including many cotton-rich Southerners. Growing numbers of wealthier Americans were also making the "Grand Tour" of Europe.

Culturally, by 1860 America had traveled a long and uphill road since crude pioneering days. But a high degree of polish and sophistication, at least by European standards, lay in the lap of the future.

Free Schools for a Free People

Tax-supported primary schools were scarce in the early years of the Republic. They had the odor of pauperism about them, since they existed chiefly to educate the children of the poor—the so-called ragged schools. Advocates of "free" public education met stiff opposition. A middlewestern legislator cried that he wanted only this simple epitaph when he died: "Here lies an enemy of public education."

Well-do-do, conservative Americans gradually saw the light. If they did not pay to educate "other folkses brats," the brats might grow up into a dangerous, ignorant rabble—armed with the vote. Taxation for education was an insurance premium that the wealthy paid for stability and democracy.

Tax-supported public education, though lagging in the slavery-cursed South, triumphed between 1825 and 1850. Grimy-handed laborers wielded in-

> Lincoln wrote of his education (1859): "There were some schools so-called [in Indiana], but no qualification was ever required of a teacher beyond 'readin', writin' and cipherin' ' to the rule of three. . . . There was absolutely nothing to excite ambition for education. Of course, when I came of age I did not know much. Still, somehow, I could read, write and cipher to the rule of three, but that was all. I have not been to school since. The little advance I now have upon this store of education, I have picked up from time to time under the pressure of necessity. I was raised to work, which I continued till I was twenty-two."

The Dunce. Idle, stupid, or misbehaving school children were forced to wear the dunce cap. (McGuffey's *First Eclectic Reader.*)

creased influence and demanded instruction for their children. Most important was the gaining of manhood suffrage for whites in Jackson's day. A free vote cried aloud for free education. A civilized nation that was both ignorant and free, declared Thomas Jefferson, "never was and never will be."

The famed little red schoolhouse—with one room, one stove, one teacher, and often eight grades—became the shrine of American democracy. Regrettably, it was an imperfect shrine. Early free schools stayed open only a few months of the year. Schoolmasters were too often ill trained, ill tempered, and ill paid. They frequently put more stress on "lickin'" (with a hickory stick) than on "larnin'." These knights of the blackboard often "boarded around" in the community, and some knew scarcely more than their older pupils. They usually taught only the "Three Rs"—"readin', 'ritin', and 'rithmetic." To many rugged Americans, suspicious of "book larnin'," this was enough.

Reform was urgently needed. Into the breach stepped Horace Mann (1796–1859), a brilliant and idealistic graduate of Brown University. As secretary of the Massachusetts Board of Education, he campaigned effectively for more and better schoolhouses, longer school terms, higher pay for teachers, and an expanded curriculum. His influence radiated out to other states, and impressive improvements were chalked up. Yet education remained an expensive luxury for many communities. As late as 1860 the nation counted only a few hundred public secondary schools—and nearly a million white adult illiterates.

> Horace Mann deplored indolence when he said, "Lost, yesterday, somewhere between sunrise and sunset, two golden hours, each set with sixty diamond minutes. No reward is offered, for they are gone forever."

Educational advances were aided by improved textbooks, notably those of Noah Webster (1758–1843), a Yale-educated Connecticut Yankee who was known as the "Schoolmaster of the Republic." His "reading lessons," used by millions of children in the 19th Century, were partly designed to promote patriotism. He devoted twenty years to his famous dictionary, published in 1828, which helped to standardize the American language.

Equally influential was Ohioan William H. McGuffey (1800–1873), a teacher-preacher of rare

The Wages of Sin. The sad fate of a boy who stopped to play in a pond on his way to school and was drowned. (McGuffey's *First Eclectic Reader.*)

power. His grade-school readers, first published in the 1830s, sold 122 million copies in the following decades. *McGuffey's Readers* hammered home lasting lessons in morality, patriotism, and idealism. One copy-exercise ran:

> Beautiful hands are they that do
> Deeds that are noble good and true;
> Beautiful feet are they that go
> Swiftly to lighten another's woe.

Higher Goals for Higher Learning

Higher education was likewise stirring. The religious zeal of the Second Great Awakening, beginning about 1800, led to the planting of many small, denominational, liberal arts colleges, chiefly in the South and West. Too often they were educationally anemic, established more to satisfy local pride than genuinely to advance the cause of learning. Like their more venerable, ivy-draped brethren, the new colleges offered a narrow, tradition-bound curriculum of Latin, Greek, mathematics, and moral philosophy. On new and old campuses alike there was little intellectual vitality and much boredom.

The first state-supported universities sprang up in the South, beginning with North Carolina in 1795. Federal land grants nourished the growth of state institutions of higher learning. Conspicuous among the early group was the University of Virginia, founded in 1819. It was largely the brain child of Thomas Jefferson, who designed its beautiful architecture, and who at times watched its construction through a telescope from his hilltop home. He dedicated the university to freedom from religious or political shackles, and modern languages and the sciences received unusual emphasis.

Women's higher education was frowned upon in the early decades of the 19th Century. A woman's place was in the home, and training in needlecraft seemed more important than training in algebra. In an era when the clinging-vine bride was the ideal, co-education was regarded as frivolous. Prejudices also prevailed that too much learning injured the feminine brain, undermined health, and rendered a young lady unfit for marriage. The teachers of Susan B. Anthony, the future feminist, refused to instruct her in long division.

Mary Lyon (1797–1849). An intrepid pioneer in the field of higher education for women, Mary Lyon was a gifted teacher who achieved an important breakthrough when, in the face of much antagonism, she managed to raise enough money to launch her "Female Seminary," now Mount Holyoke College. The year after it opened in 1837, she had to turn away some 400 applicants. She served as principal for twelve years.

Women's schools at the secondary level began to attain some respectability in the 1820s, thanks in part to the dedicated work of Emma Willard (1787–1870). In 1821 she established the Troy (New York) Female Seminary. Oberlin College, in Ohio, shocked traditionalists in 1833 when it opened its doors to women as well as men. In 1837, Mary Lyon established an outstanding women's school, Mount Holyoke Seminary (later College), in South Hadley, Massachusetts. Mossback critics scoffed that "they'll be educatin' cows next."

Adults who craved more learning satisfied their thirst for knowledge at private subscription libraries, or, increasingly, at tax-supported libraries. House-to-house peddlers also did a lush business in feeding the public appetite for culture. Traveling lecturers helped to carry learning to the masses through the lyceum lecture associations, which numbered about 3,000 by 1835. The lyceums provided platforms for speakers on science, literature, and moral philosophy. Talented talkers like Ralph Waldo Emerson journeyed thousands of miles on the lyceum circuits, casting their pearls of civilization before appreciative audiences.

Magazines flourished in the pre-Civil War years, but most of them withered after a short life. The *North American Review*, founded in 1815, was the long-lived leader of the intellectuals. *Godey's Lady's Book*, founded in 1830, survived until 1898, and attained the enormous circulation (for those days) of 150,000. It was devoured devotedly by countless millions of women.

The Changing American Family

The rustling pages of publications like *Godey's Lady's Book*, perused in parlors all over America, quietly heralded a subtle, slow-moving, but eventually sweeping revolution in American society. Women were growing more conscious of themselves as individuals, and as one another's "sisters" in a world where male and female sexual roles were becoming more sharply divided. Prompted in part by the wide circulation of women's magazines like *Godey's*, this dawning self-consciousness was beginning to change women's lives—and to transform society's most fundamental institution, the family.

It was still a man's world, in America and Europe, when the 19th Century opened. A wife was supposed to immerse herself in her home, and subordinate herself to her lord and master. Like black slaves, she could not vote; like black slaves, she could be legally beaten by her overlord "with a reasonable instrument." When she married, she could not retain title to her property; it passed to her husband.

Yet American women, though legally regarded as perpetual minors, fared better than their European cousins, partly because of their scarcity in frontier communities. A western woman could warn her spouse to be respectful, for "if you don't there's plenty will." Few American husbands were brutes; and women always had quiet ways of protecting themselves, regardless of law.

Despite these relative advantages, women were still "the submerged sex" in America in the early part of the century. But as the decades unfolded, women increasingly emerged to breathe the air of freedom and self-determination. In contrast to colonial times, many women avoided marriage altogether—about 10 percent of adult women remained "spinsters" at the time of the Civil War.

Opportunities for women to be economically self-supporting were still scarce, and consisted mainly of low-paying factory jobs, teaching, and domestic service. Perhaps one white family in ten employed servants at midcentury, most of whom

Godey's Lady's Book. The most popular women's magazine of the era. (Schlesinger Library, Radcliffe College; photo by Barry Donahue.)

were poor white, immigrant, or black women. About 10 percent of white women were working for pay outside their own homes in 1850, and estimates are that about 20 percent of all women had worked at some time prior to marriage.

The vast majority of working women were single. Upon marriage, they left their paying jobs and took up their new work (without wages) as wives and mothers. In the home they were enshrined in a "cult of domesticity," a widespread cultural creed that glorified the traditional functions of the homemaker. From their pedestal, married women commanded immense moral power, and they increasingly made decisions that altered the character of the family itself.

Families are like air—they surround most people so completely and so constantly that they have tended to be invisible, historically speaking.* But though they long went unrecorded, important changes were overtaking the life of the 19th-Century home—the traditional "women's sphere." Love, not parental "arrangement," more and more frequently determined the choice of a spouse—yet parents often retained the power of veto. Families thus became more closely knit and affectionate, providing the emotional refuge that made the threatening impersonality of big-city industrialism tolerable to many people.

Most striking, families grew smaller. The average household had nearly six members at the end of the 18th Century, but fewer than five members a century later. The "fertility rate," or number of births among women aged 14 to 45, dropped sharply among white women after the Revolution, and in the course of the 19th Century as a whole, fell by half. Birth control was still a taboo topic for polite conversation, and contraceptive technology was primitive, but clearly some form of family limitation was being practiced quietly and effectively in countless families, rural and urban alike. Women undoubtedly played a large part—perhaps the leading part—in decisions to have fewer children. This newly assertive role for women has been called "domestic feminism," because it signified the growing power and independence of women, even while they remained trapped in the "cult of domesticity."

Smaller families, in turn, meant child-centered families, since where children are fewer parents can lavish more care on them individually. European visitors to the United States in the 19th Century often complained about the unruly behavior of American "brats." But though American parents may have increasingly spared the rod, they did not spoil their children. Lessons were enforced by punishments other than the hickory stick. When the daughter of novelist Harriet Beecher Stowe neglected to do her homework, her mother sent her from the dinner table, and gave her "only bread and water in her own apartment." What Europeans saw as permissiveness was in reality the consequence of an emerging new idea of child rearing, in which the child's will was not to be simply broken, but shaped. In the little republic of the family, as in the Republic at large, good citizens were raised not to be meekly obedient to authority, but to be independent individuals who could make their own decisions on the basis of internalized moral standards. Thus the outlines of the "modern" family were clear by midcentury: it was small, affectionate, child-centered, and provided a special arena for the talents of women. Feminists of a later day might decry the stifling atmosphere of the Victorian home, but to many women of the time it seemed a big step upward from the conditions in which their mothers had lived.

Journalistic Giants

The newspaper—"the university of the public"—was further popularized by free, compulsory education and a consequent increase of literacy. Before 1830 a daily journal cost about six cents, a sum which the dollar-a-day manual laborer could ill afford to pay. The New York *Sun*, seeking the economies of mass production, reduced its price in 1833 to one cent. It thus inaugurated the era of the "penny dreadful"—dreadful because it

*See "The Quilting Party" and "Joseph Moore and His Family," color portfolio, for two artistic views of 19th-Century family life.

featured murders, scandals, and other human-interest stories in the manner of the modern tabloid.

A leader in the new "gutter journalism" was erratic James Gordon Bennett, who in 1835 founded the New York *Herald*. His office desk consisted of two flour barrels with a plank laid across them; and he was editor, reporter, proofreader, folder, and cashier. He believed that the function of newspapers was not only to instruct but to startle, and he and other editors lowered the public taste while lowering the price of their sheets. At all events, more Americans were now reading than ever before.

The influence of journalism was vastly increased by the march of mechanization. Telegraphy instantly updated the news, and "scoops" became the newspaperman's driving demon. Quick contact with events only hours old whetted the public's appetite for more newsprint, and publishers sought to multiply the output of their clanking presses. In 1846 Richard Hoe came to their aid with a cylindrical press that could spew forth 8,000 papers in an hour.

The decades just before the Civil War marked the dawn of the golden age of personal journalism. Newspaper publishing had not yet become a big business, and editors like Horace Greeley of the New York *Tribune* owned and published their own newspapers. His weekly edition enjoyed a wide circulation outside New York State, and

Horace Greeley, Outspoken Editor. He ran for the presidency in 1872 and was badly defeated.

since the idealistic Greeley was a merciless foe of slavery, his word was law among a host of followers. "Wait until the *Weekly Tribune* arrives," remarked a New York farmer when asked his opinion, "and then I can tell you what I think about it."

Passions ran incredibly high during this era of personalized, hit-below-the-belt journalism. The writing-fighting editors were frequently caned, stabbed, or shot by those whom they verbally abused. "You lie, you villain," wrote Greeley of a rival editor, "you sinfully, wickedly, basely lie."

Despite this violence and vulgarity, America was making praiseworthy progress in lifting the mental horizons of the masses. More people than ever were now able to inform themselves on current issues; and with increased knowledge went an increased ability to make democracy work.

VARYING VIEWPOINTS

Ever since the publication of Alexis de Tocqueville's *Democracy in America* (1835, 1840), the period from the Revolution to the Civil War has been regarded as a crucially formative phase in the shaping of American society. This was the time when new institutions were being tested, new peoples absorbed, and new values sorted out. All of these processes have traditionally been seen as adding up to a tremendous success story, in which Americans energetically forged a distinctive national culture. But recently some historians have questioned this rather upbeat view and have asked what elements were *lost* as the American people plunged so breathlessly toward the future. Did the rise of individualism corrode the cohesion of the community? What cultural baggage did the immigrants leave behind them? Were there severe social costs in the sudden flowering of numerous religious sects? Did the spread of formal education preserve or undermine traditional cultural forms?

SELECT READINGS

Satisfying detail may be found in R. B. Nye, *The Cultural Life of the New Nation, 1776–1830* (1960), and the same author's *Society and Culture in America, 1830–1860* (1974). Alexis de Tocqueville's classic account of life in the young republic is brilliantly analyzed by James R. Schlieffer in *The Making of Tocqueville's "Democracy in America"* (1980). R. A. Easterlin analyzes *Population, Labor Force, and Long Swings in Economic Growth: The American Experience* (1968). Brinley Thomas has written a landmark study of *Migration and Economic Growth: A Study of Great Britain and the Atlantic Economy* (1954). Also concentrating on the European side is Philip Taylor, *The Distant Magnet* (1971). Maldwyn Jones, *American Immigration* (1960), is a standard work. Consult also Marcus Hansen, *Atlantic Migration* (1940), and C. F. Wittke's pro-immigrant *We Who Built America* (rev. ed., 1964). Wittke has also examined *The Irish in America* (1956). Anti-Catholic bigotry is analyzed in R. A. Billington, *The Protestant Crusade* (1938), and in Carleton Beals's lurid *Brass-Knuckle Crusade: The Know-Nothing Conspiracy, 1820–1860* (1960). S. Ahlstrom, *Religious History of the American People* (1972), is sweeping. W. Sweet, *Religion in the Development of American Culture, 1765–1840* (1952), concentrates on the early national period. On revivalism, see W. G. McLoughlin, *Modern Revivalism: Charles Grandison Finney to Billy Graham* (1959), and Whitney Cross's absorbing *The Burned-Over District* (1950). Consult also B. Weisberger, *They Gathered at the River* (1958), C. A. Johnson, *The Frontier Camp Meeting* (1955), and Paul E. Johnson, *A Shopkeeper's Millenium: Society and Revivals in Rochester, New York, 1815–1837* (1978). On the Latter-Day Saints, consult T. F. O'Dea, *The Mormons* (1957), and Fawn Brodie's fascinating biography of Joseph Smith, *No Man Knows My History* (1945). Wallace Stegner writes interestingly about the Mormon Trail in *The Gathering of Zion* (1964). On education see Merle Curti, *Social Ideas of American Educators* (rev. ed., 1959), and R. M. Elson, *Guardians of Tradition: American Schoolbooks of the Nineteenth Century* (1964). Michael Katz is most provocative in *The Irony of Early School Reform* (1968), as is S. K. Schultz, *The Culture Factory: Boston Public Schools, 1789–1860* (1973). See also J. Messerli, *Horace Mann* (1972). Lawrence A. Cremin, *American Education: the National Experience, 1783–1876* (1980), is masterful, and can be usefully supplemented by David Nasaw, *Schooled to Order: A Social History of Public Schooling in the United States* (1979), and especially by Carl F. Kaestle and Maris A. Vinovskis, *Education and Social Change in Nineteenth-Century Massachusetts* (1980). Higher education is handled in F. Rudolph, *The American College and University* (1962), and in R. Hofstadter and W. P. Metzger, *The Development of Academic Freedom in the United States* (1955). A pathbreaking study is B. Wishy, *The Child and the Republic: The Dawn of Modern American Nurture* (1968). Indispensable on the same subject is R. H. Bremner, ed., *Children and Youth in America: A Documentary History* (1970–1971). Recent work of note on children and the family includes Joseph F. Kett, *Rites of Passage: Adolescence in America, 1790 to the Present* (1977), Lewis Perry, *Childhood, Marriage, and Reform: Henry Clarke Wright, 1797–1870* (1980), Carl N. Degler, *At Odds: Women and The Family in America from the Revolution to the Present* (1980), and Nancy's Cott's particularly sensitive *The Bonds of Womanhood: "Woman's Sphere" in New England, 1780–1835* (1977). Special topics are treated in Lewis O. Saum, *The Popular Mood of Pre-Civil War America* (1980), W. J. Rorabaugh, *The Alcoholic Republic* (1979), Morton J. Horowitz, *The Transformation of American Law, 1780–1860* (1977), James W. Hurst, *Law and Social Order in the United States* (1977), and James H. Kettner, *The Development of American Citizenship, 1608–1870* (1978). Also valuable are Ian R. Tyrrell, *Sobering Up: From Temperance to Prohibition in Antebellum America* (1979), and Ruth Bordin, *Woman and Temperance* (1981).

18

The Ferment of Reform and Culture, 1790–1860

We [Americans] will walk on our own feet; we will work with our own hands; we will speak our own minds.

RALPH WALDO EMERSON, "The American Scholar," 1837

The Dawn of Scientific Achievement

Early Americans, confronted with pioneering problems, were more interested in practical gadgets than in pure science. Thomas Jefferson, for example, was a gifted amateur who won a gold medal for a new type of plow. Noteworthy were the writings of the mathematician Nathaniel Bowditch (1773–1838) on practical navigation, and of the oceanographer Matthew F. Maury (1806–1873) on ocean winds and currents. All these writers promoted safety, speed, and economy. But as far as basic science was concerned, Americans were best known for borrowing and adapting the findings of Europeans.

Yet the Republic was not without scientific talent. The most influential American scientist of the first half of the 19th Century was Professor

Benjamin Silliman (1779–1864), a pioneer chemist and geologist who taught and wrote brilliantly at Yale College for more than fifty years. Professor Louis Agassiz (1807–1873), a distinguished French-Swiss immigrant, served for a quarter of a century at Harvard College. As a pathbreaking student of biology who sometimes carried snakes in his pockets, he insisted on original research and deplored the overemphasis on memory work. Professor Asa Gray (1810–1888) of Harvard College, the Columbus of American botany, published over 350 books, monographs, and papers. His textbooks set new standards for clarity and interest.

Lovers of American bird lore owed much to the French-descended John J. Audubon (1785–1851), who painted wild fowl in their natural habitat. His magnificently illustrated *Birds of America* attained considerable popularity. The Audubon Society for the protection of birds was named after him, although as a young man he shot much feathered game for sport.

Medicine in America, despite a steady growth of medical schools, was still primitive by modern standards. Bleeding remained a common remedy. Plagues of smallpox were still dreaded, and the terrible yellow fever epidemic of 1793 in Philadelphia took several thousand lives. "Bring out your dead!" was the daily cry of the drivers of the death wagons.

People everywhere complained of ill health—malaria, the "rheumatics," the "miseries," and the chills. Illness often resulted from improper diet, hurried eating, perspiring and cooling off too rapidly, and ignorance of germs and sanitation. "We was sick every fall, regular," wrote the mother of the future President Garfield. Life expectancy was still dismayingly short—about forty years for a white person born in 1850, and less for blacks. The suffering from decayed or ulcerated teeth was enormous; tooth extraction was often practiced by the muscular village blacksmith.

> An outbreak of cholera occurred in New York City in 1832, and a wealthy businessman, Philip Hone, wrote in his diary for the Fourth of July: "The alarm about the cholera has prevented all the usual jollification under the public authority. . . . The Board of Health reports to-day twenty new cases and eleven deaths since noon yesterday. The disease is here in all its violence and will increase. God grant that its ravages may be confined, and its visit short."

Self-prescribed patent medicines were common (one for man, two for horse), and included Robertson's Infallible Worm Destroying Lozenges. Among home remedies was the rubbing of tumors with dead toads. The use of medicine by the regular doctors was often harmful, and Dr. Oliver Wendell Holmes declared in 1860 that if the medicines, as then employed, were thrown into the sea, humans would be better off and the fish worse off.

Victims of surgical operations were ordinarily tied down, often after a stiff drink of whiskey. The surgeon then sawed or cut with breakneck speed, undeterred by the shrieks of the patient. A priceless boon came in the early 1840s when several American doctors and dentists, working independently, successfully used laughing gas and ether as anesthetics.

Humanitarian Stirrings

As the 19th Century slowly advanced, a strong reaction began to develop against the brutalities of earlier days. The crusade against slavery came to overshadow all other reforms; to some extent it hampered them by attracting so much energy to itself.

Reform campaigns of all types flourished in bewildering abundance. Zealots hawked "health" diets, fashion fads, and folk medicine. Many faddists were simply crackbrained cranks. But most reformers were intelligent, level-headed idealists. They tended to come from the old Puritan stronghold of New England, or from those Western regions to which the sons and daughters of the

Puritans had migrated. The religious reawakening of the age had stirred their Calvinist consciences from slumber.

Idealists dreamed anew the old Puritan vision of a perfected society: free from cruelty, war, intoxicating drink, discrimination, and—ultimately—slavery. Mainly middle-class descendants of pioneer farmers, most reformers were blissfully unaware that they were witnessing the dawn of the industrial era, which posed unprecedented problems and called for novel ideas. They either ignored the factory workers, for example, or blamed their problems on bad habits. With naive single-mindedness reformers applied conventional virtue to refurbishing an older order—while events hurtled them headlong into the new.

Imprisonment for debt continued to be a nightmare, though its extent has been exaggerated. As late as 1830 hundreds of penniless persons were languishing in filthy holes, sometimes for owing less than one dollar. The poorer working classes were especially hard hit by this merciless practice. But as the embattled laborer won the ballot and asserted himself, state legislatures gradually abolished debtors' prisons.

Criminal codes in the states were likewise being softened, in accord with more enlightened European practices. The number of capital offenses was being reduced, and brutal punishments, such as whipping and branding, were being slowly eliminated. A refreshing idea was taking hold that prisons should reform as well as punish—hence "reformatories," "houses of correction," and "penitentiaries" (for penance).

Sufferers from so-called insanity were still being treated with incredible cruelty. The medieval concept had been that the mentally deranged were cursed with unclean spirits; the 19th-Century idea was that they were willfully perverse and depraved—to be treated only as beasts. Many crazed persons were chained in jails or poorhouses with sane people.

Into this dismal picture stepped a quiet New England teacher-authoress, Dorothea Dix (1802–1887). A frail spinster afflicted with persistent lung

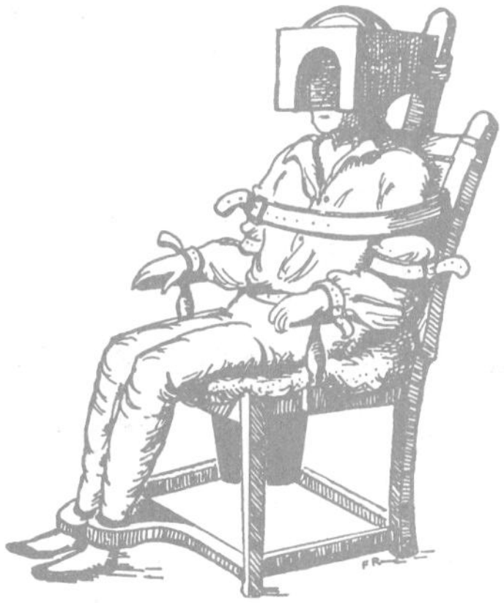

An Early Restraining Chair for the Insane

trouble, she possessed infinite compassion and will power. Never raising her voice to a screech, she traveled some 60,000 miles (97,000 kilometers) in eight years and assembled her damning reports on insanity from firsthand observations. Her classic petition of 1843 to the Massachusetts legislature, describing cells so foul that visitors were driven back by the stench, turned legislative stomachs and hearts. Her persistent prodding resulted in improved conditions and in a gain for the concept that the demented were not willfully perverse but mentally ill.

Agitation for peace also gained some momentum in the pre–Civil War years. In 1828 the American Peace Society was formed, with a ringing declaration of war on war. A leading spirit was William Ladd, who orated when his legs were so badly ulcerated that he had to sit on a stool. His ideas were finally to bear some fruit in the international organizations for collective security of the 20th Century. The American peace crusade, linked with the European crusade, was making promising progress by mid-century, when it was set back by the bloodshed of the Crimean War in Europe and the Civil War in America.

Demon Rum—The "Old Deluder"

The ever-present drink problem attracted dedicated reformers. Custom, combined with a hard and monotonous life, led to the excessive drinking

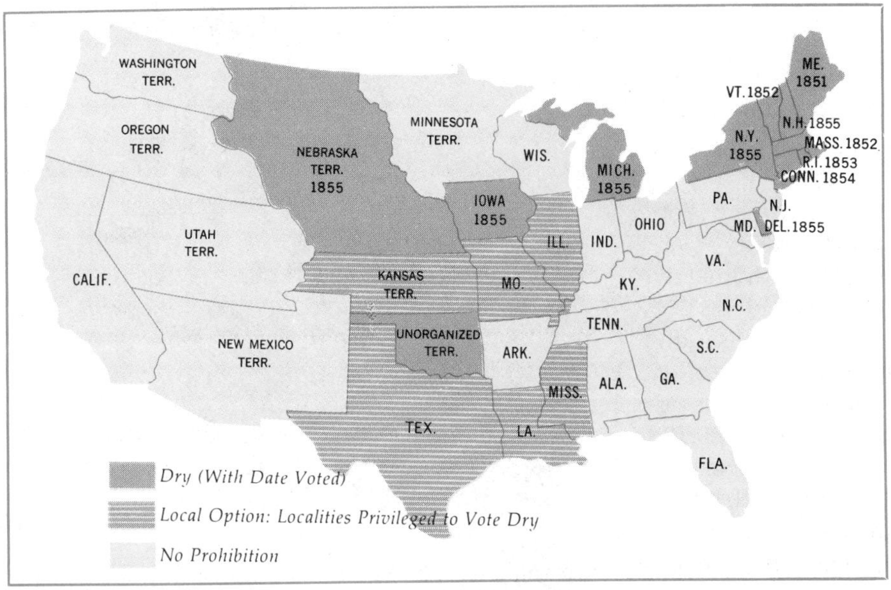

THE EXTENT OF PROHIBITION, 1855. Lax enforcement led a legendary tippler to comment that prohibition was far better than no liquor at all.

of hard liquor, even among women, clergymen, and members of Congress. Weddings and funerals all too often became disgraceful brawls, and occasionally a drunken man would fall into the open grave with the corpse. Heavy drinking decreased the efficiency of labor, while the introduction of poorly safeguarded machinery increased the danger of accident.

After earlier and feebler efforts, the American Temperance Society was formed at Boston in 1826. Within a few years about a thousand local groups sprang into existence. They implored drinkers to sign the temperance pledge and organized children's clubs, known as the "Cold Water Army." Temperance crusaders also made effective use of pictures, pamphlets, and lurid lecturers, some of whom were reformed drunkards. A popular temperance song ran:

> We've done with our days of carousing,
> Our nights, too, of frolicsome glee;
> For now with our sober minds choosing,
> We've pledged ourselves never to spree.

Demon Rum Plagues His Victim. One popular lecturer told of a tipsy man who fell into a pig sty. As the animals grunted in alarm, he muttered, "Hold your tongues; I'm as good as any of you." A contemporary cartoon.

The most popular anti-alcohol tract of the era was T. S. Arthur's melodramatic novel, *Ten Nights in a Barroom and What I Saw There* (1854). It described in shocking detail how a once-happy village was ruined by Sam Slade's tavern. The book was second only to Mrs. Stowe's *Uncle Tom's Cabin* as a best seller in the 1850s, and it enjoyed a highly successful run on the stage. Its touching theme song began with the words of a little girl:

> Father, dear father, come home with me now,
> The clock in the belfry strikes one.

Early foes of Demon Drink adopted two major lines of attack. One was to stiffen the individual's will to resist the wiles of the little brown jug. Moderate reformers thus stressed "temperance" rather than "teetotalism," or the total elimination of intoxicants. But less patient zealots gradually came to believe that temptation should be removed by legislation. Prominent among this group was Neal S. Dow of Maine, a blue-nosed reformer who, as a mayor of Portland and an employer of labor, had often witnessed the debauching effect of alcohol.

Dow—the "Father of Prohibition"—sponsored the so-called Maine Law of 1851, which supplanted an earlier effort in 1846. This drastic new statute, hailed as "the law of Heaven Americanized," prohibited the manufacture and sale of intoxicating liquor. Other states in the North followed Maine's example, and by 1857 about a dozen had passed various prohibitory laws. But these figures are deceptive, for within a decade some of the statutes were repealed or declared unconstitutional, if not openly flouted.

It was clearly impossible to legislate thirst out of existence, especially in localities where public sentiment was hostile. Yet on the eve of the Civil War the prohibitionists had registered inspiriting gains. There was much less drinking among women than earlier in the century, and probably much less per capita consumption of hard liquor.

Women in Revolt

Sexual differences were strongly emphasized in 19th-Century America. Women were thought to be physically and emotionally weak, but also artistic, refined, and endowed with finely tuned consciences. Men were considered strong but crude, always in danger of slipping into some savage or beastly way of life if not guided by the gentle hands of their loving ladies. But if sexual roles were sharply separated, men and women could still be regarded as equals. As a sign of the prestigious position of American women, French visitor Alexis de Tocqueville noted that in his native France rape was punished only lightly, while in America it was one of the few crimes punishable by death.

The home was woman's special sphere. But some women increasingly felt that the glorified sanctuary of the home was in fact a gilded cage. They yearned to tear down the bars that separated the woman's world from the man's.

A covey of clamorous female agitators emerged as the century neared its halfway point. Most of them were broad-gauge battlers; while demanding rights for women, they were simultaneously fighting for temperance and anti-slavery reform. Homegrown feminists received much encouragement from their sisters in Europe, where a parallel movement was gaining ground. Neither foul eggs nor foul words, when hurled by disapproving males, could halt America's fiery females.

The woman's rights movement was mothered by some arresting characters. Prominent among them was Lucretia Mott, a sprightly Quaker whose ire had been aroused when she and her fellow female delegates to the London anti-slavery convention of 1840 were not recognized. Elizabeth Cady Stanton, a mother of seven who had insisted on leaving "obey" out of her marriage ceremony, shocked fellow feminists by going so far as to advocate suffrage for women. Quaker-reared Susan B. Anthony, a militant lecturer for woman's rights, exposed herself to rotten garbage and vulgar epithets. She became such a conspicuous ad-

Susan B. Anthony (1820–1906). A woman of great militancy and singleness of purpose, she was a foremost fighter in the woman's rights movement, as well as in that for temperance and abolition. Arrested in 1872 in Rochester, New York, for having voted, she was found guilty and fined $100. She vowed that she would never pay and she never did. She lived to see four states grant equal suffrage to women.

What It Would Be If Some Ladies Had Their Own Way. The men are sewing, tending the baby, and washing clothes. This scene seemed absurd then but not a century later. (Historical Pictures Service, Chicago.)

vocate of female rights that progressive women everywhere were called "Suzy Bs."

Other feminists challenged the man's world. Dr. Elizabeth Blackwell, a pioneer in a previously forbidden profession for women, was the first female graduate of a medical college. Precocious Margaret Fuller edited a Transcendentalist journal, *The Dial,* and is remembered for having said, "I accept the universe." The talented Grimké sisters, Sarah and Angelina, spoke at anti-slavery gatherings and aroused the ire of conservatives. Lucy Stone retained her maiden name after marriage—hence the latter-day "Lucy Stoners," who follow her example. Amelia Bloomer revolted against the current "street sweeping" female attire by donning a semi-masculine short skirt with Turkish trousers—"bloomers," they were called—amid much bawdy ridicule about "Bloomerism" and "loose habits." A jeering male rhyme of the times jabbed:

Gibbey, gibbey gab
The women had a confab
And demanded the rights
To wear the tights
Gibbey, gibbey gab.

Fighting feminists met at Seneca Falls, New York, in a memorable Woman's Rights Convention (1848). The defiant Mrs. Stanton read a "Declaration of Sentiments," which in the spirit of the Declaration of Independence declared that "all men *and women* are created equal." One resolution formally demanded the ballot for females. The Seneca Falls meeting, which launched the modern woman's rights movement, not surprisingly became the object of scorn and denunciation from press and pulpit.

The crusade for woman's rights was eclipsed by that against slavery in the decade before the Civil War. Male idiots could still vote; women could not. Yet women were being gradually admitted to colleges, and some states, beginning with Mississippi in 1839, were even permitting wives to own property after marriage.

Wilderness Utopias

Leaders of the woman's rights movement often marched arm in arm with other reformers. Professional "do-gooders" popped up at every hand, giving the 1840s the distinction of being the "hot air period" of American history. About everything was tried, from communism to socialism, through polygamy and celibacy, to rule by a prophet and guidance by spirits. Societies were formed against tobacco, profanity, and the transit of mail on the Sabbath. Various faddist diets were promoted, including the whole-wheat graham bread and crackers of Sylvester Graham.

There was not "a reading man," observed Ralph Waldo Emerson, who was without some scheme for a new utopia in his "waistcoat pocket." Various reformers, ranging from the high-minded to the "lunatic fringe," set up more than forty communities of a cooperative, communistic, or "communitarian" nature. Seeking human betterment, a wealthy and idealistic Scottish textile manufacturer, Robert Owen, established in 1825 a communal society of about a thousand persons at New Harmony, Indiana. Little harmony prevailed in the colony, which, in addition to hardworking visionaries, attracted a sprinkling of radicals, lazy theorists, and outright scoundrels. The enterprise sank in a morass of contradiction and confusion.

Brook Farm in Massachusetts, comprising 200 acres of grudging soil, was started in 1841 with the brotherly cooperation of about twenty intellectuals. They prospered reasonably well until 1846, when they lost by fire a large new communal building shortly before its completion. The whole experiment in "plain living and high thinking" then collapsed in debt. Although a financial failure, Brook Farm was in some ways a social and educational success.

A more radical experiment was the Oneida Colony, founded in New York in 1848. It practiced free love ("complex marriage"), birth control, and the eugenic selection of parents to produce superior offspring. The leader finally fled to Canada to escape prosecution for adultery. This curious enterprise flourished for more than thirty years, largely because its craftsmen made superior steel traps and Oneida Community (silver) Plate. In 1879–1880 the group embraced monogamy and abandoned communism.

Various communistic experiments, mostly small-scale, have been attempted since Jamestown. But in competition with democratic free enterprise and free land, virtually all of them sooner or later failed or changed their methods. Perhaps the longest-lived sect has been the Shakers who, beginning in 1776, set up the first of a score or so of religious communities. They attained a membership of about 6,000 in 1840, but since they opposed both marriage and free love, they were virtually extinct by 1940.

Shakers in Dancing Ceremony

Artistic Endeavors and Achievements

Architecturally, America contributed little of note in the first half of the century. The rustic Republic, still under pressure to erect shelters in haste, was continuing to imitate European models. Public buildings and other important structures followed Greek and Roman lines, which seemed curiously out of place in a wilderness setting. A remarkable Greek revival came between 1820 and 1850, partly stimulated by the heroic efforts of the Greeks in the 1820s to wrest independence from the "terrible Turk." About mid-century strong interest developed in a revival of Gothic forms, with their emphasis on pointed arches and large windows.

Talented Thomas Jefferson, architect of revolution, was probably the ablest American architect of his generation. He brought a classical design to his Virginia hilltop home, Monticello—perhaps the most stately mansion in the nation (see p. 150). The quadrangle of the University of Virginia at Charlottesville, another creation of Jefferson, remains one of the finest examples of classical architecture in America.

The art of painting continued to be handicapped. It suffered from the dollar grabbing of a raw civilization; from the hustle, bustle, and absence of leisure; from the lack of a wealthy class to sit for portraits—and then pay for them. Some of the earliest painters were forced to go to England, where they found both training and patrons. America exported artists and imported art.

Painting, like the theater, also suffered from the Puritan prejudice that art was a sinful waste of time—and often obscene. John Adams boasted that "he would not give a sixpence for a bust of Phidias or a painting by Raphael." When Edward Everett, the eminent Boston scholar and orator, placed a statue of Apollo in his home, he had its naked limbs draped.

Competent painters nevertheless emerged. Gilbert Stuart (1755–1828), a spendthrift Rhode Islander and one of the most gifted of the early group, wielded his brush in England in competition with the best artists. He produced several portraits of Washington, all of them somewhat idealized and dehumanized. Truth to tell, the famous general had by then lost his natural teeth and some of the original shape of his face. Charles Willson Peale (1741–1827), a Marylander, painted some sixty portraits of Washington, who patiently sat for about fourteen of them. John Trumbull (1756–1843), who had fought in the Revolutionary War, recaptured its scenes and spirit on scores of striking canvases.

During the nationalistic upsurge after the War of 1812, American painters of portraits turned increasingly from human landscapes to romantic mirrorings of local landscapes. The Hudson River School excelled in this type of art. At the same time, portrait painters gradually encountered some unwelcome competition from the invention of a crude photograph known as the daguerreotype, perfected about 1839 by a Frenchman, Louis Daguerre.

America Bursts into Song

Music was slowly shaking off the restraints of colonial days, when the prim Puritans had frowned upon non-religious singing. Melody-minded Americans received much inspiration from the emergence of European musicians—Schubert, Mendelssohn, Chopin, Wagner. Growing numbers of citizens were studying music, and the song-loving German immigrants of the 1840s and 1850s added richly to American culture. A mid-century boom in the manufacture of pianos reflected improving tastes.

An appreciation of good music was increased by some noteworthy public performances. The New York Philharmonic Orchestra, one of the first, was organized in 1842. Ole Bull, the famous Norwegian violin virtuoso, held audiences spellbound during his five tours of the country, from 1843 to 1880. Golden-voiced Jenny Lind, the "Swedish Nightingale," who was also a talented actress and a rare Christian spirit, created a sensation in 1850–

A Satirical By-Product of Jenny Lind's Tour. (*Yankee Notions*, 1852.)

1852 ("Lindomania"). She received an unprecedented $1,000 for each of 150 concerts managed by showman Phineas T. Barnum, who for once did not "humbug" the public.

These visiting artists helped to elevate the nation's musical taste, but Americans themselves were making solid contributions. Gifted writers of hymns were adding to American hymnology. Notable in this group was Lowell Mason (1792–1872), who is perhaps best known for "Nearer, My God, to Thee" and "From Greenland's Icy Mountains."

Rhythmic and nostalgic "darky" tunes, popularized by white men, were becoming immensely popular by mid-century. Special favorites were the uniquely American minstrel shows, featuring white actors with blackened faces. "Dixie," later adopted by the Confederates as their battle hymn, was written in 1859, ironically in New York City by an Ohioan. The most famous black songs, also ironically, came from a white Pennsylvanian, Stephen C. Foster (1826–1864). His one excursion into the South occurred in 1852, after he had published "Old Folks at Home." Foster made a valuable contribution to American folk music by capturing the plaintive spirit of the slaves. An odd and pathetic figure, he finally lost both his art and his popularity, and died in a charity ward after drowning his sorrows in drink.

Sturdy yeomen were still too busy felling trees to write symphonies about their crashing. An eccentric Bohemian musician, A. P. Heinrich, undertook to play one of his own compositions about America at the White House. He was deeply affronted when President Tyler interrupted his piano-pounding to say, "That may all be very fine, sir, but can't you play us a good old Virginia reel?"

The Blossoming of a National Literature

"Who reads an American book?" sneered the British critic Sydney Smith in 1820. The painful truth was that the nation's rough-hewn, pioneering civilization gave little encouragement to "polite" literature. Much of the reading matter was imported or plagiarized from England.

Busy conquering a continent, the Americans poured most of their creative efforts into practical outlets. Praiseworthy were political essays, like *The Federalist* of Hamilton, Jay, and Madison; pamphlets, like Tom Paine's *Common Sense;* and political orations, like the masterpieces of Daniel Webster. In the category of non-religious books published before 1820, Benjamin Franklin's *Autobiography* (1818) is one of the few that achieved genuine distinction. His narrative is a classic in its simplicity, clarity, and inspirational quality. Even so, it records only a fragment of "Old Ben's" long, fruitful, and amorous life.

A genuinely American literature received a strong boost from the wave of nationalism that followed the War of Independence and especially the War of 1812. By 1820 the older seaboard areas were sufficiently removed from tree-chopping so that literature could be supported as a profession. The Knickerbocker Group in New York blazed brilliantly across the literary heavens, thus enabling America for the first time to boast of a literature to match her magnificent landscapes.

Washington Irving (1783–1859), born in New York City, was the first American to win international recognition as a literary figure. Steeped in the traditions of New Netherland, he published in 1809 his *Knickerbocker's History of New York,* with its amusing caricatures of the Dutch. When the family business failed, Irving was forced to turn to the goose-feather pen. In 1819–1820 he published *The Sketch Book*, which brought him immediate fame at home and abroad. Combining a pleasing style with delicate charm and quiet humor, he used English as well as American themes, and included such immortal Dutch-American tales as "Rip Van Winkle" and "The Legend of Sleepy Hollow." Europe was amazed to find at last an American with a feather in his hand, not in his hair. Later turning to Spanish locales and biography, Irving did much to interpret America to Europe and Europe to America. He was, said the Englishman William Thackeray,

Washington Irving's Character, Father Knickerbocker. (*The Knickerbocker,* 1834.)

"the first ambassador whom the New World of letters sent to the Old."

James Fenimore Cooper (1789–1851) was the first American novelist, as Irving was the first general writer, to gain world fame and make New World themes respectable. Marrying into a wealthy family, he settled down on the frontier of New York. Reading one day to his wife from an insipid English novel, he remarked in disgust that he could write a better one himself. She challenged him to do so—and he did.

After an initial failure, Cooper launched out upon an illustrious career in 1821 with his second novel, *The Spy*—an absorbing tale of the American Revolution. His stories of the sea were meritorious and popular, but his fame rests most enduringly on the *Leather Stocking Tales*. A deadeye rifleman named Natty Bumppo, one of nature's noblemen, meets with Indians in stirring adventures like *The Last of the Mohicans*. Cooper's novels had a wide sale among Europeans, some of whom came to think of all Americans as born with tomahawk in hand. Actually the author was seeking the good society somewhere between the anarchy of wilderness and the artificiality of modern civilization.

A third member of the Knickerbocker group in New York was the belated Puritan William Cullen Bryant (1794–1878), transplanted from Massachusetts. At age sixteen he wrote the meditative and melancholy "Thanatopsis" (published in 1817), which was one of the first high-quality poems produced in the United States. Critics could hardly believe that it had been written on "this side of the water." Although Bryant continued with poetry, he was forced to make his living by editing the influential New York *Evening Post*. For over fifty years he set a model for journalism that was dignified, liberal, and high-minded.

Trumpeters of Transcendentalism

A golden age in American literature dawned in the second quarter of the 19th Century, when an amazing outburst shook New England. One of the mainsprings of this literary flowering was Transcendentalism, especially in the Boston area, which preened itself as "the Athens of America."

The Transcendentalist movement of the 1830s resulted in part from a liberalizing of the strait-jacket Puritan theology. It also owed much to foreign thinkers, including the German romantic philosophers. The Transcendentalists rejected the prevailing theory, derived from John Locke, that all knowledge comes to the mind through the senses. Truth, rather, "transcends" the senses: it cannot be found by observation alone. Every man possesses an inner light that can illuminate the highest truth and put him in direct touch with God, or the "Oversoul."

These mystical doctrines of Transcendentalism defied precise definition, but they underlay concrete beliefs. Foremost was a stiff-backed individualism in matters religious as well as social. Closely associated was a commitment to self-reliance, self-culture, and self-discipline. These traits naturally bred hostility to authority and to formal institutions of any kind, as well as to all conventional wisdom. Finally came exaltation of the dignity of the individual, whether black or white—the mainspring of a whole array of humanitarian reforms.

Best known of the Transcendentalists was Boston-born Ralph Waldo Emerson (1803–1882).

Tall, slender, and intensely blue-eyed, he mirrored serenity in his noble features. Trained as a Unitarian minister, he early forsook his pulpit and ultimately reached a wider audience by pen and platform. He was a never-failing favorite as a lyceum lecturer, and for twenty years took a Western tour every winter. Perhaps his most thrilling public effort was a Phi Beta Kappa address, "The American Scholar," delivered at Harvard College in 1837. This brilliant appeal was an intellectual Declaration of Independence, for it urged American writers to throw off European traditions and delve into the riches of their own backyards.

Hailed as both a poet and a philosopher, Emerson was not of the highest rank as either. He was more influential as a practical philosopher, and through his fresh and vibrant essays enriched countless thousands of humdrum lives. Catching the individualistic mood of the Republic, he stressed self-reliance, self-improvement, self-confidence, optimism, and freedom. The secret of Emerson's popularity lay largely in the fact that his ideals reflected those of an expanding America. Among his most-quoted observations are: "Whoso would be a man, must be a non-conformist"; "A foolish consistency is the hobgoblin of little minds"; "God offers to every mind its choice between truth and repose."

Ralph Waldo Emerson (1803–1882). Emerson's philosophical observations include such statements as: "The less government we have, the better—the fewer laws, and the less confided power"; "To be great is to be misunderstood"; "Every hero becomes a bore at last"; "Shallow men believe in luck"; "When you strike a king, you must kill him." (Courtesy, Concord Free Public Library, Gift of Mrs. Arthur Holland)

In 1849 Thoreau published *On the Duty of Civil Disobedience,* asserting, "I heartily accept the motto, 'That government is best which governs least'; and I should like to see it acted up to more rapidly and systematically. Carried out, it finally amounts to this, which also I believe—'That government is best which governs not at all'; and when men are prepared for it, that will be the kind of government which they will have. Government is at best an expedient; but most governments are sometimes, inexpedient."

Henry David Thoreau (1817–1862) was Emerson's close associate—a poet, a mystic, a Transcendentalist, and a non-conformist. Condemning a government that supported slavery, he refused to pay his Massachusetts poll tax, and was jailed for a night.* A gifted prose writer, he is well known for *Walden: Or Life in the Woods* (1854). The book is a record of Thoreau's two years of simple existence in a hut which he built on the edge of Walden Pond, near Concord, Massachusetts. A stiff-necked individualist, he believed that he should reduce his bodily wants so as to gain time for a pursuit of truth through study and meditation. Thoreau's *Walden* and his essay on *Civil Disobedience* exercised a strong influence in furthering idealistic thought, both in America and abroad. His writings later encouraged Mahatma Gandhi to resist British rule in India.

*The story (probably apocryphal) is that Emerson visited Thoreau at the jail and asked, "Why are you here?" The reply came, "Why are you not here?"

Bold, brassy, and swaggering was the open-collared figure of Brooklyn's Walt Whitman (1819–1892). In his famous collection of poems, *Leaves of Grass* (1855), he gave free rein to his gushing genius with what he called a "barbaric yawp." Highly romantic, emotional, and unconventional, he dispensed with titles, stanzas, rhymes, and at times even regular meter. He handled sex with shocking frankness, although he laundered his verses in later editions, and his book was banned in Boston.

Whitman's *Leaves of Grass* was at first a financial failure. The only three enthusiastic reviews that it received were written by the author himself—anonymously. But in time the once-withered *Leaves of Grass,* revived and honored, won for Whitman an enormous following in both America and Europe. His fame increased immensely among "Whitmaniacs" after his death.

Leaves of Grass gained for Whitman the informal title "Poet Laureate of Democracy." Singing with Transcendental abandon of his love for the masses, he caught the exuberant enthusiasm of an expanding America that had turned her back on the Old World:

All the Past we leave behind;
We debouch upon a newer, mightier world, varied
world;
Fresh and strong the world we seize—world of
labor and the march—
Pioneers! O Pioneers!

Here at last was the native art for which critics had been crying.

Walt Whitman. This portrait of the young poet appeared in the first edition of *Leaves of Grass* (1855). (Rare Book Division, New York Public Library, Astor, Lenox and Tilden Foundations.)

In 1876 the London *Saturday Review* referred to Whitman as the author of a volume of "so-called poems which were chiefly remarkable for their absurd extravagances and shameless obscenity, and who has since, we are glad to say, been little heard of among decent people." In 1888 Whitman wrote, "I had my choice when I commenced. I bid neither for soft eulogies, big money returns, nor the approbation of existing schools and conventions. . . . I have had my say entirely my own way, and put it unerringly on record— the value thereof to be decided by time."

Glowing Literary Lights

Certain other literary giants were not actively associated with the Transcendentalist movement, though not completely immune to its influences. Professor Henry Wadsworth Longfellow (1807–1882), who for many years taught modern languages at Harvard College, was one of the most popular poets ever produced in America. Handsome and urbane, he lived a generally serene life, except for the tragic deaths of two wives, the second of whom perished before his eyes when her dress caught fire. Writing for the genteel classes, he was adopted by the less cultured masses. His wide knowledge of European literature supplied him with many themes, but some of his most admired poems were based on American traditions—*Evangeline, Hiawatha,* and *The Courtship of Miles Standish.* Immensely popular in Europe, Longfellow was the only American ever to be honored with a bust in the Poets' Corner of Westminster Abbey.

A fighting Quaker, John Greenleaf Whittier (1807–1892), with piercing dark eyes and swarthy complexion, was the uncrowned poet laureate of the anti-slavery crusade. Less talented as a craftsman than Longfellow, he was vastly more important in influencing social action. His poems cried aloud against inhumanity, injustice, and intolerance, against

> The outworn rite, the old abuse,
> The pious fraud transparent grown.

Undeterred by insults and the stonings of mobs, Whittier helped arouse a calloused America on the slavery issue. A great conscience rather than a great poet or intellect, Whittier was one of the moving forces of his generation, whether moral, humanitarian, or spiritual. Gentle and lovable, he was pre-eminently the poet of human freedom.

Many-sided James Russell Lowell (1819–1891), who succeeded Professor Longfellow at Harvard, ranks as one of America's better poets. He was also a distinguished essayist, literary critic, editor, and diplomat—a diffusion of talents that hampered his poetical output. He is remembered as a political satirist in his *Biglow Papers,* especially those of 1846 dealing with the Mexican War. Written partly as poetry in the Yankee dialect, the *Papers* condemned in blistering terms the alleged slavery-expansion designs of the Polk administration.

Slender Dr. Oliver Wendell Holmes (1809–1894), who taught anatomy with a sparkle at Harvard Medical School, was a prominent poet, essayist, novelist, lecturer, and wit. A non-conformist and a fascinating conversationalist, he shone among a group of literary lights who regarded Boston as "the hub of the universe." His poem "The Last Leaf," in honor of the last "white Indian" of the Boston Tea Party, came to apply to himself. Dying at age eighty-five, he was the "last leaf" among his distinguished contemporaries.*

The most noteworthy literary figure produced by the South before the Civil War, unless Edgar Allan Poe is regarded as a Southerner, was novelist William Gilmore Simms (1806–1870). Quantitatively, at least, he was great: eighty-two books flowed from his ever-moist pen, winning for him the title "the Cooper of the South." His themes dealt with the Southern frontier in colonial days and with the South during the Revolutionary War. But he was neglected by his own section, even though he married into the socially elite and became a slaveowner. The high-toned planter aristocracy would never accept the son of a poor Charleston storekeeper.

Literary Individualists and Dissenters

Not all writers in these years believed so keenly in human goodness and social progress. Edgar Allan Poe (1809–1849), who spent much of his youth in Virginia, was an eccentric genius. Orphaned at an early age, cursed with ill health, and married to a child-wife of fourteen who fell fatally ill of tuberculosis, he suffered hunger, cold, poverty, and debt. Failing at suicide, he took refuge in the bottle and dissipated his talent early. Poe was a gifted lyric poet, as "The Raven" attests. A master stylist, he also excelled in the short story, especially of the horror type, in which he shared his alcoholic nightmares with fascinated readers. If he did not invent the modern detective novel, he at least set new high standards in tales like "The Gold Bug."

Poe was fascinated by the ghostly and ghastly, as in "The Fall of the House of Usher" and other stories. He reflected a morbid sensibility distinctly at odds with the usually optimistic tone of American culture. Partly for this reason, Poe has per-

*Oliver Wendell Holmes had a son with the same name who became a distinguished justice of the Supreme Court (1902–1932) and who lived to be ninety-four, less two days.

haps been even more prized by Europeans than by his own countrymen. His brilliant career was cut short when he was found drunk in a Baltimore gutter and shortly thereafter died.

Two other writers reflected the continuing Calvinist obsession with original sin and with the never-ending struggle between good and evil. In somber Salem, Massachusetts, Nathaniel Hawthorne grew up in an atmosphere heavy with the memories of his Puritan forebears and the tragedy of his father's premature death on an ocean voyage. His masterpiece was *The Scarlet Letter* (1850), which described the Puritan practice of forcing an adultress to wear a scarlet A on her clothing.* The tragic tale chronicles the psychological effects of sin on the guilty heroine and her secret lover (the father of her baby), a minister of the gospel in Puritan Boston. In *The Marble Faun* (1860), Hawthorne dealt with a group of young American artists who witness a mysterious murder in Rome. He thus explored the concepts of the omnipresence of evil and the dead hand of the past weighing upon the present.

Herman Melville (1819–1891), an orphaned and ill-educated New Yorker, went to sea as a youth and served eighteen adventuresome months on a whaler. "A whale ship was my Yale College and my Harvard," he wrote. Jumping ship in the South Seas, he lived among cannibals, from whom he providentially escaped uneaten. His fresh and charming tales of the South Seas were immediately popular, but his masterpiece, *Moby Dick* (1851), was not. This epic novel was a complex allegory of good and evil, told in terms of the conflict between a whaling captain, Ahab, and a giant white whale, Moby Dick. Captain Ahab, who lost a leg to the marine monster, swore revenge. His pursuit finally ended when Moby Dick rammed and sank Ahab's ship, leaving only one survivor. The whale's exact identity and Ahab's motives remained obscure. In the end the sea, like the terrifyingly impersonal and unknowable universe of Melville's imagination, simply rolled on.

Moby Dick was widely ignored at the time of its publication; people were accustomed to more straightforward and upbeat prose. A disheartened Melville continued to write unprofitably for some years, part of the time eking out a living as a customs inspector, and then died in relative obscurity and poverty. Ironically, his brooding masterpiece about the mysterious white whale had to wait until the more jaded 20th Century for readers and proper recognition.

*This was how Hester Prynne got her A in *The Scarlet Letter.* An H stood for heresy and an I for incest.

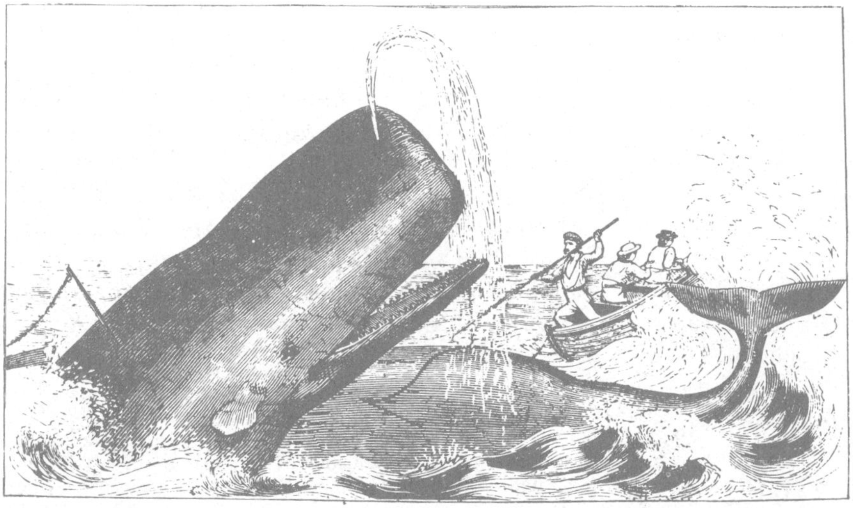

Hazardous Whaling. *Moby Dick* gives a vivid first-hand picture of whaling, which proved to be an important industry from colonial times to the end of the 19th Century. (From *Etchings of a Whaling Cruise* by John Ross Browne, 1846. Stanford University Libraries.)

Portrayers of the Past

A distinguished group of American historians was emerging at the same time that other writers were winning distinction. Energetic George Bancroft (1800–1891), who as secretary of the navy helped found the Naval Academy at Annapolis in 1845, has deservedly received the title "Father of American History." He published a spirited, superpatriotic history of the United States to 1789 in six (originally ten) volumes (1834–1876), a work that grew out of his vast researches in dusty archives in Europe and America.

Two other historians are read with greater pleasure and profit today. William H. Prescott (1796–1859), who accidently lost the sight of an eye while in college, conserved his remaining weak vision, and published classic accounts of the conquest of Mexico (1843) and Peru (1847). Francis Parkman (1823–1893), whose eyes were so defective that he wrote in darkness with the aid of a guiding machine, penned a brilliant series of volumes, beginning in 1851. In epic style he chronicled the struggle between France and England in colonial times for the mastery of North America.

George Bancroft, Historian. With unscholarly exaggeration, he wrote of the outbreak of the American Revolution: "With one impulse, the colonies sprung to arms; with one spirit, they pledged themselves to each other 'to be ready for the supreme event.' With one heart, the continent cried: 'Liberty or Death!'"

Early American historians of prominence were almost without exception New Englanders, largely because the Boston area provided well-stocked libraries and a stimulating literary tradition. These writers numbered abolitionists among their relatives and friends, and hence were disposed to view unsympathetically the slave-cursed South. The writing of American history for generations to come was to suffer from an anti-Southern bias perpetuated by this early "made in New England" interpretation.

VARYING VIEWPOINTS

The reformist and intellectual ferment of the antebellum era was extraordinary, and historians are still seeking a satisfying explanation of this many-sided activity. Was there some single origin of the multiple impulses that animated the movements for temperance, woman's rights, communalism, and eventually abolition? Some writers have suggested the Puritan spirit, as it was transformed and rejuvenated by the religious revivals of the early 19th Century. Others have pointed to a pervasive utopianism, seen both in social movements and in the unprecedented literary outpouring of the age. Utopianism is common in revolutionary societies (which the United States in many ways still was), and it was strengthened in America by the stimulating presence of a vast, near-virgin wilderness.

SELECT READINGS

General intellectual histories are M. Curti, *The Growth of American Thought* (3rd ed., 1964), and R. H. Gabriel, *The Course of American Democratic Thought* (2nd ed., 1956). See also Perry Miller's *Life of the Mind in America: From the Revolution to the Civil War* (1965). Also of general interest are Daniel Boorstin, *The Americans: The National Experience* (1965), and Rowland Berthoff, *An Unsettled People* (1971). Y. Arieli has an intriguing essay on *Individualism and Nationalism in American Ideology* (1964), and Carl Bode dissects *The Anatomy of American Popular Culture, 1840–1861* (1959). See also G. Daniels, *American Science in the Age of Jackson* (1968), to be supplemented by R. H. Shryock, *Medicine and Science in America* (1960). A solid biography is E. Lurie's study of *Louis Agassiz* (1960). An older but still standard discussion of reform is Alice F. Tyler, *Freedom's Ferment* (1944). For particular subjects, consult David Rothman, *The Discovery of the Asylum* (1971), and G. Grob, *Mental Institutions in America: Social Policy to 1875* (1973); on juvenile delinquency, Joseph Hawes, *Children in Urban Society* (1971); and on prohibition, J. Gusfield, *Symbolic Crusade* (1963). Large-scale histories of the woman's movement are Andrew Sinclair, *The Better Half* (1965), W. O'Neill, *Everyone Was Brave* (1970), and Page Smith, *Daughters of the Promised Land* (1970). Consult also E. Flexner, *Century of Struggle* (1959), and R. Riegel, *American Feminists* (1963). Women's history for this period has recently blossomed in a number of fine studies, including Ellen Carol Dubois, *Feminism and Suffrage* (1978), Barbara J. Berg, *The Remembered Gate: Origins of American Feminism—the Woman and the City, 1800–1860* (1977), Estelle B. Freedman, *Their Sisters' Keepers: Women's Prison Reform in America, 1830–1930* (1981), Keith E. Melder, *The Beginnings of Sisterhood* (1977), and, emphasizing intellectual and literary history, Ann Douglas, *The Feminization of American Culture* (1977). Communal experiments are treated in A. Bestor, *Backwoods Utopias* (1950), M. Holloway, *Heavens on Earth* (1951), and J. F. C. Harrison's analysis of the Owenites, *Quest for the New Moral World* (1969). K. Silverman provides an excellent *Cultural History of the American Revolution* (1976). F. O. Mathiessen's masterful *American Renaissance* (1941) is indispensable on the writers of the 1840s and 1850s. D. H. Lawrence, *Studies in Classic American Literature* (1923), is a classic in its own right. For provocative overviews of the literature of the period, consult A. N. Kaul, *American Vision: Actual and Ideal Society in Nineteenth-Century Fiction* (1963), F. Somkin, *Unquiet Eagle: Memory and Desire in the Idea of American Freedom, 1815–1860* (1967), and Joel Porte, *Representative Man: Ralph Waldo Emerson in His Time* (1979). See also O. W. Larkin, *Art and Life in America* (1949), to be supplemented by J. T. Flexner, *That Wilder Image* (1962), and by Neil Harris's imaginative *Artist in American Society: The Formative Years, 1790–1860* (1968), and especially by Barbara Novak's stimulating *Nature and Culture: American Landscape and Painting, 1825–1875* (1980). On history, see John Higham et al., *History* (1965), and David Levin, *History as Romantic Art* (1959). Particularly intriguing is Anne C. Rose, *Transcendentalism as a Social Movement* (1981).

19

The South and the Slavery Controversy

If you put a chain around the neck of a slave,
the other end fastens itself around your own.

RALPH WALDO EMERSON, 1841

"Cotton Is King!"

When George Washington first took the presidential oath, the economic wheels of the South were creaking badly. They were burdened with depressed prices, unmarketable products, overcropped lands, and the dead weight of an unprofitable slave system. Some Southern statesmen, including Thomas Jefferson, were talking openly of freeing their slaves, and confidently predicting that slavery would gradually die of economic anemia.

But the introduction of Whitney's cotton gin in 1793 changed the scene. The newly popularized short-staple cotton, which brought a premium price, gradually became the dominant Southern crop, eclipsing tobacco, rice, and sugar. Slavery was reinvigorated, with the slave being chained to the gin, and the planter to the slave.

Cotton as King. In this Northern Civil War cartoon, the Confederacy appears as a lighted bomb.

As time passed, the Cotton Kingdom developed into a huge agricultural factory, pouring out avalanches of the fluffy fiber. Quick profits drew planters to the virgin bottom lands of the Gulf states. As long as the soil was still vigorous, the yield was bountiful and the rewards were high. Caught up in an economic spiral, the planters bought more slaves and land to grow more cotton, so as to buy still more slaves and land.

Northern shippers reaped a large part of the profits from the cotton trade. They would load bulging bales of cotton at Southern ports, transport them to England, sell them for pounds sterling, and buy needed manufactured goods for sale in the United States. To a large degree the prosperity of both North and South rested on the bent backs of Southern slaves.

Cotton thus came to be by far the largest and most important American export. Not only was it valuable in establishing a balance between imports and exports, but it held foreign nations in partial bondage. Britain was then the leading industrial power. Her most important single manufacture in the 1850s was cotton cloth, from which about one-fifth of her population, directly or indirectly, drew its livelihood. About 80 percent of this precious supply of fiber came from the white-carpeted acres of the South.

Southern statesmen were fully aware that England was tied to them by cotton threads, and this dependence gave them a heady sense of power. In their eyes "Cotton was King," the gin was his throne, and the black bondsmen were his henchmen. If war should ever break out between North and South, Northern warships would presumably cut off the outflow of cotton. Fiber-famished British factories would then close their gates, starving mobs would force the London government to break the blockade, and the South would triumph. Cotton was a powerful monarch indeed.

Cavaliers All

Before the Civil War the South was in some respects not so much a democracy as an oligarchy—or a government by the few, in this case heavily influenced by a planter aristocracy. In 1850 only 1,733 families owned more than 100 slaves each, and this select group provided the cream of the political and social leadership of the section and nation. Here was the mint-julep South of the tall-columned and white-painted plantation mansion—the "big house," where dwelt the "cottonocracy."

Thomas Jefferson wrote in 1782: "The whole commerce between master and slave is a perpetual exercise of the . . . most unremitting despotism on the one part, and degrading submissions on the other. . . . Indeed I tremble for my country when I reflect that God is just; that his justice cannot sleep forever." Unlike Washington, Jefferson did not free his slaves in his will; he had fallen upon distressful times.

Cotton Exports Compared with Total Exports, 1800–1860*

Year	*Pounds of Cotton Exported*	*Value of Cotton Exported*	*Value of Total U.S. Exports*	*Percentage of Cotton in Relation to Total Exports*
1800	17,789,803	$ 5,000,000	$ 70,971,780	7%
1810	93,261,462	15,108,000	66,757,970	22
1820	127,860,152	22,308,667	69,691,669	32
1830	298,459,102	29,674,883	71,670,735	41
1840	743,941,061	63,870,307	123,668,932	51
1850	635,381,604	71,984,616	144,375,726	49
1860	1,767,686,338	191,806,555	333,576,057	57

*Note that the above figures show exports alone. Hinton R. Helper pointed out that in 1850 the value of the Northern hay crop, consumed locally, exceeded that of all leading Southern agricultural products combined.

The planter aristocrat, with his blooded horses and Chippendale chairs, enjoyed a lion's share of Southern wealth. He could educate his children in the finest schools, often in the North or abroad. His money provided the leisure for study, reflection, and statecraft, as was notably true of men like John C. Calhoun (a Yale graduate) and Jefferson Davis (a West Point graduate). He felt a keen sense of obligation to serve the public. It was no accident that Virginia and her Southern sisters produced a higher proportion of front-rank statesmen before 1860 than the "dollar-grubbing" North.

But even in its best light, dominance by a favored aristocracy was basically undemocratic. It widened the gap between rich and poor. It hampered tax-supported public education, because the rich planter could and did send his children to private institutions. Yet although inequities existed, schools of the South, especially at the secondary level, were more numerous and efficient than is commonly supposed.

Southern gentry were high-strung, though generally soft-spoken, courteous, hospitable, and chivalrous. Jealous of their honor, they clung to dueling long after it had died out in the North. They carried on the somewhat spurious "Cavalier" tradition of early Virginia, and developed a martial spirit that is still reflected in high-quality Southern military academies like The Citadel (Charleston) and the Virginia Military Institute (Lexington).

A favorite author of Southerners was Sir Walter Scott, whose manors and castles, graced by brave Ivanhoes and fair Rowenas, roughly mirrored their own semi-feudal society. Southern aristocrats, who would sometimes stage jousting tournaments, strove to perpetuate a type of medievalism that had died out in Europe—or was rapidly dying out.* Mark Twain later accused Sir Walter Scott of having had a hand in starting the Civil War. The British novelist, Twain said, aroused the Southerners to fight for a decaying social structure—"a sham civilization."

Slaves of the Slave System

Unhappily the moonlight-and-magnolia tradition concealed much that was worrisome, distasteful, and sordid. Plantation agriculture was wasteful, largely because King Cotton and his money-hungry subjects despoiled the good earth. Quick profits led to excessive cultivation or "land butchery," which in turn caused a heavy leakage of population to the West and Northwest. Soil exhaustion also forced attention to scientific agriculture, and the pre-war South excelled in farm journals and agricultural societies. Edmund Ruffin of Virginia, who later fired one of the first shots of the Civil

*Oddly enough, by legislative enactment jousting became the official state sport of Maryland in 1962.

Harvesting Cotton. Slaves of both sexes picked cotton on the great plantations. (Boston Public Library.)

War at Fort Sumter, did notable pioneering work in soil restoration. Yet his best efforts were inadequate to cope with the problem.

The economic structure of the South became increasingly monopolistic. As the land wore thin, many small farmers sold their holdings to more prosperous neighbors, and went north or west. The big got bigger and the small smaller. When the Civil War finally broke, a large percentage of Southern farms had passed from the hands of the families that had originally cleared them.

Another cancer in the bosom of the South was the financial instability of the plantation system. The temptation to overspeculate in land and slaves caused many a planter, including Andrew Jackson in his later years, to plunge in beyond his depth. Although the black bondsmen might in extreme cases be fed for as little as ten cents a day, there were other expenses. The slaves represented a heavy investment of capital, perhaps $1,200 each in the case of prime field hands; and they might deliberately injure themselves or run away. An entire slave quarter might be wiped out by disease or even by lightning, as happened in one instance to twenty luckless blacks.

Dominance by King Cotton likewise led to a dangerous dependence on a one-crop economy, whose price level was at the mercy of world conditions. The whole system discouraged a healthy diversification of agriculture and particularly of manufacturing, for which the South was almost ideally fitted. While concentrating on cotton, the plantations had to import huge quantities of pork and grain from the upper Mississippi Valley.

Southern planters resented watching the North grow fat at their expense. They were pained by the heavy outward flow of commissions and interest to Northern middlemen, bankers, agents, and shippers. True sons of the South, especially by the 1850s, deplored the fact that when born they were wrapped in Yankee-made swaddling clothes, and that they spent the rest of their lives in servitude to Yankee manufacturing. When they died, they were laid in coffins held together with Yankee nails, and were buried in graves dug with Yankee shovels. The South furnished the corpse and the hole in the ground.

The Cotton Kingdom also repelled large-scale European immigration, which added so richly to the manpower and wealth of the North. In 1860

> Basil Hall, an Englishman, visited part of the cotton belt on a river steamer (1827–1828). Noting the preoccupation with cotton, he wrote: "All day and almost all night long, the captain, pilot, crew, and passengers were talking of nothing else; and sometimes our ears were so wearied with the sound of cotton! cotton! cotton! that we gladly hailed a fresh inundation of company in hopes of some change—but alas! . . . 'What's cotton at?' was the first eager inquiry. 'Ten cents [a pound].' 'Oh, that will never do!' From the cotton in the market they went to the crops in the fields—the frost which had nipped their shoots—the hard times—the overtrading—and so round to the prices and prospects again and again."

only 4.4 percent of the Southern population was foreign-born, as compared with 18.7 percent for the North. German and Irish immigration to the South was generally discouraged by the competition of slave labor, by the high cost of fertile land, and by European ignorance of cotton growing. The diverting of non-English immigration to the North caused the white South to become the most Anglo-Saxon section of the nation.

Rich Whites and Poor Whites

Only a handful of Southern aristocrats lived in Grecian-pillared mansions. Below the 1,733 families in 1850 who owned 100 or more slaves were the less wealthy slaveowners. They totaled in 1850 some 345,000 families, representing about 1,725,000 white persons. Over two-thirds of these families—255,268 in all—owned fewer than ten slaves each.

Beneath the slaveowners was the great body of non-slaveowning whites who, by 1860, had swelled their numbers to 6,120,825. These rank-and-file citizens, comprising about three-fourths of the free population of the South, had no direct stake in slavery. They fell roughly into three groups: (1) the lowland whites, who were by far the most numerous; (2) the poor whites, who were generally disease-ridden; and (3) the semi-isolated mountain whites, who were the most independent-minded.

The hundreds of thousands of energetic lowland whites included such folks as mechanics, lesser tradesmen, and above all, small cotton farmers. Though owning no slaves themselves, they were among the stoutest defenders of the slave system. The carrot-on-the-stick ever dangling before their noses was the hope of buying a slave or two, and of parlaying their holdings into riches—all in accord with the "American dream." They also took fierce pride in their presumed racial superiority, which would be watered down if the slaves were freed. Many of the poorer lowland whites were hardly better off economically than the Afro-American; some, indeed, were not so well off. But they clung desperately to their one visible badge of presumed superiority.

Conspicuous among the millions of non-slaveholders was a considerable sprinkling of poor whites, whom even the slaves despised as the "poor white trash." Known also as "hillbillies," "crackers," or "clay eaters," they were often listless, pallid, shiftless, and misshapen. Later investigations have revealed that many of them were not so much lazy as sickly, suffering from malnutrition and disease, including hookworm.

Mountain whites of the South are not to be confused with the poor whites of the lowland cotton belt. They were more or less marooned in the valleys of the Appalachian range, stretching from western Virginia to northern Georgia and Alabama. Civilization had largely passed them by. They were a kind of living ancestry, for some of them retained Elizabethan speech forms and habits that had long since died out in England.

As independent small farmers, the mountain

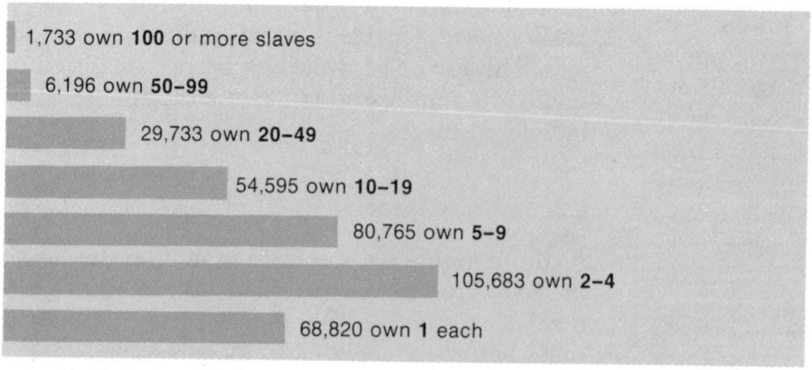

SLAVEOWNING FAMILIES, 1850
The philosopher Ralph Waldo Emerson, a New Englander, declared in 1856: "I do not see how a barbarous community and a civilized community can constitute a state. I think we must get rid of slavery or we must get rid of freedom."

whites had little in common with the aristocracy of the broad cotton lands. Many of them, including the future President Andrew Johnson of Tennessee, hated both the lordly planter and his gangs of blacks. They looked upon the impending strife between North and South as "a rich man's war but a poor man's fight."

The tough-fibered mountain whites constituted a vitally important peninsula of unionism jutting down into the secessionist Southern sea. They ultimately played a significant role in crippling the Confederacy. Their attachment to the Union party of Abraham Lincoln was such that, for generations after the Civil War, the only concentrated Republican strength in the Solid South was to be found in the Southern highlands.

Ex-Slave Douglass Resists Indiana Mob. At times he preached extremism. In 1852, he shocked a Pennsylvania audience by declaring: "My motto is extermination. The slaveholders not only forfeit their right to liberty but to life itself."

The Unfree Freedmen

Below the most wretched whites in the social scale of 1860 were about 250,000 free blacks, several thousand of whom owned a slave or two themselves.* They usually had been freed by kind masters, or had purchased their freedom with earnings from labor after hours. They were a kind of "third race." Their lot was unpleasant and their "fettered freedom" was precarious, because they might be highjacked back into slavery by unscrupulous white dealers. Yet as free men and women they were walking examples of what might be achieved by emancipation, and hence were frowned upon by defenders of the slave system.

Free blacks were also unpopular in the North, where several states forbade their entrance. In 1835 New Hampshire farmers, using oxen, dragged into a swamp a small schoolhouse that had enrolled fourteen black children. Northern ex-slaves were especially hated by the pick-and-shovel Irish immigrants, who feared wage-lowering competition. Much of the agitation in the North against the spread of slavery into the new territories in the 1840s and 1850s grew out of race prejudice, not humanitarianism.

Feeling against the blacks was in fact frequently stronger in the North than in the South. The gifted and eloquent ex-slave Frederick Douglass, an abolitionist and self-educated orator of rare power, was subjected to numerous mobbings and beatings by Northern rowdies. It was frequently observed that white Southerners, who were sometimes suckled and reared by black nurses, liked the black as an individual but despised his race. The white Northerner, on the other hand, often professed to like the race but disliked individual blacks.

Black Bondsmen

At the bottom of the social pyramid in the South of 1860 were nearly 4 million black human chattels. Black slaves had existed in all of the thirteen colonies before independence. Even preachers of the

*William T. Johnson, a free black and "the barber of Natchez," owned fifteen slaves. His diary records that in June 1848 he flogged two slaves and a mule.

gospel in the North owned them, including the godly Jonathan Edwards, who kept two. American slaves had been originally captured in Africa during raids or wars by fellow blacks, who sold them to white slave traders. The unfortunate victims were then crammed into slavers sailing to the New World. Many coffins had more room. As a contemporary ballad ran:

> We crowded them upon the deck
> and stored them all below
> With eighteen inches to the man,
> was all they had to go.

Some of the slave ships became so filthy that, with the wind in the right direction, they could be smelled before they were sighted. Death rates on the horrible "middle passage" were incredibly high, but so were the profits, which sometimes ran to 500 percent.

The transplanting of African slaves to English America was mostly done by Englishmen and New Englanders. Some Yankee traders were descendants of early Puritans and, ironically, ancestors of later abolitionists.

Black slavery gradually died out in the North during and after the Revolutionary War. Human bondage clashed with the philosophy of the Declaration of Independence, which proclaimed that "all men are created equal." But perhaps as important, slavery in the North had become unprofitable. Black babies, when weaned, were sometimes given away by their owners. Financial loss helps to create a tender conscience.

Slave Deck of the Slaver *Wildfire.* Captured by the U.S. navy, this slave ship was brought into Key West, Florida, in April 1860. The blacks were freed. (From a daguerreotype [photograph] published in *Harper's Weekly,* June 2, 1860.)

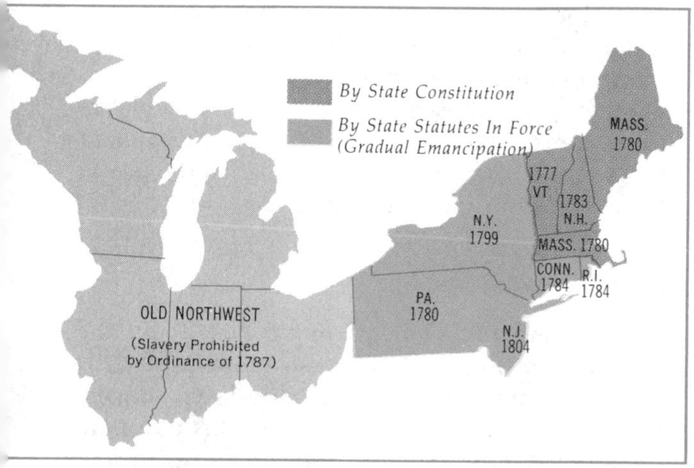

EARLY EMANCIPATION IN THE NORTH

Legal importations of African slaves into America ended in 1808, when Congress nailed up the bars. This action was taken precisely at the end of the twenty-year period of grace prescribed in the Constitution (see Art. I, Sec. IX, para. 1). But the price of "Black Ivory" was so high before the Civil War that uncounted thousands of blacks were smuggled into the South, despite the death penalty for slavers. Though several were captured, only one slave trader was ever executed, N. P. Gordon, and that was in New York in 1862, the second year of the Civil War.

After the cotton gin had made slavery profitable, the planters had the wolf by the ears. It was dangerous to hold on, death to let go. To ask slavemasters to free their blacks was to invite them to

The Slave Quarters. This Civil War—era photograph shows the stark simplicity of black family life in the South. South Carolina Senator Hammond declared in 1858: "In all social systems there must be a class to do the mean duties. . . . It constitutes the very mudsills of society. . . . Fortunately for the South, she found a race adapted to that purpose. . . . We use them for that purpose and call them slaves." (Library of Congress.)

throw away about $2 billion in human livestock and plunge into financial ruin. Even if the planters were paid for their slaves, they still feared that they would go bankrupt because they could not raise cotton profitably without a dependable labor supply. The masters believed that the blacks, unless threatened with the lash, would not toil in the blazing sun. Slaveowners also clung to the convenient fiction that white men could not labor in the fields without ruining their health. Actually, hundreds of thousands of red-necked whites hoed cotton and picked the bursting bolls without suffering ill effects.

It is true that after emancipation the ex-slaves adjusted themselves with much jarring to the wage-incentive system. But the masters doubted that this could be done—and they were unwilling to take the chance. Above all, the issue was not simply an economic one. Slavery was as much a system of racial dominance and subordination as it was a labor system. Even if the freed slaves should prove to be docile and efficient wage laborers, their freedom would weaken the notion of "white supremacy" and complicate the task of "keeping the Negroes in their place."

In theory, the race problem could have been solved—though not the labor problem—by transporting the blacks bodily back to Africa. But most of them did not want to return to a strange civilization after becoming partially Americanized. By 1860 the great majority of Southern slaves were native-born Afro-Americans, not Africans. The Republic of Liberia, on the fever-stricken West African coast, was established for ex-slaves in 1822, with its capital, Monrovia, named after President Monroe. (Ironically, Liberia itself continued to be a flourishing center for slave trade.) After much expense and effort on the part of both Southerners and Northerners, some 15,000 blacks were transplanted during the next thirty-eight years. About that many black babies were born in the South during a single month.

Human Livestock

White Southerners might romanticize about the singing, dancing, and banjo-strumming of their joyful "darkies," but how did the slaves actually live? There is no simple answer to this question. Conditions varied greatly from region to region, from large plantation to small farm, and from master to master. By the eve of the Civil War, more than half the slaves were concentrated in the "black belt" of the Deep South that stretched from South Carolina and Georgia through the new Southwest states of Mississippi, Alabama, and Louisiana. This was the region of the Southern frontier, into which the Cotton Kingdom had burst in a few short decades. As on all frontiers, life was often rough and raw, and in general the lot of the slave was harder here than in the more settled areas of the Old South.

A majority of the blacks lived on larger plantations that harbored communities of twenty or more slaves. In some counties of the Deep South, especially those along the lower Mississippi River, blacks accounted for more than 75 percent of the population. There the family life of the slaves tended to be relatively stable. Forced separations of husbands from wives and children from parents were evidently more common on smaller plantations. Marriage vows sometimes read, "Until death or *distance* do you part."

Slave auctions were brutal sights. The open selling of human flesh under the hammer, sometimes with cattle and horses, was a revolting practice. Families were separated with distressing frequency, usually for economic reasons, such as the division of "property" among heirs. Brokenhearted slaves were poor workers and potential runaways. As one black spiritual lamented:

> Nobody knows de trouble I've had,
> Nobody knows but Jesus.

Breeding slaves, as cattle are bred, was not openly encouraged. But thousands of blacks from the soil-exhausted slave states of the Old South, notably Virginia, were "sold down the river" to toil as field-gang laborers in the lower Mississippi Valley, where the lunch "hour" was often fifteen minutes and work sometimes continued in the moonlight. Women who bore thirteen or fourteen babies were regarded as "rattlin' good breeders," and some of these fecund females were promised their freedom when they had produced ten. All too frequently white males would force their attentions on female blacks, whether their own slaves or not.

Floggings were common, for the whip was the substitute for the wage-incentive system. As an abolitionist song of the 1850s lamented:

> To-night the bond man, Lord,
> Is bleeding in his chains;
> And loud the falling lash is heard
> On Carolina's plains!

A Slave Auction. A family being sold. In an address given in 1865, President Lincoln said: "Whenever I hear anyone arguing for slavery, I feel a strong impulse to see it tried on him personally."

> Frederick Douglass, the remarkable ex-slave, told of Mr. Covey, a white owner who bought a single female slave "as a breeder." She gave birth to twins at the end of the year. "At this addition to the human stock Covey and his wife were ecstatic with joy. No one dreamed of reproaching the woman or finding fault with the hired man, Bill Smith, the father of the children, for Mr. Covey himself had locked the two up together every night, thus inviting the result."

But savage beatings were normally not administered without some reason or provocation, because whipping made sullen laborers, and lash marks hurt resale values. There are, to be sure, always some sadistic monsters in any population. But for financial as well as humane reasons, the planter did not customarily go out and beat to death a valuable field hand before breakfast.

Slavery was undeniably degrading to the victims. They were deprived of the dignity and sense of responsibility that come from owning a home, caring for oneself, and finding labor of one's choice. They were normally denied an education, partly because reading brought ideas, and ideas brought discontent. Many states passed laws forbidding their instruction. Perhaps nine-tenths of the adult slaves at the beginning of the Civil War were totally illiterate.

Flogging Slaves. An example of anti-slavery propaganda, 1838. (Courtesy, American Antiquarian Society.)

The Burdens of Bondage

Victims of the "peculiar institution" universally pined for freedom. Many took to their heels as runaways. A black girl, asked if her mother was dead, replied, "Yassah, massah, she is daid, but she's free." Others rebelled, never successfully. In 1800 an armed insurrection led by a slave named Gabriel in Richmond, Virginia, was foiled by informers, and its leaders were hanged. Denmark Vesey, a free black, led another ill-fated rebellion in Charleston in 1822. Also betrayed by informers, Vesey and more than thirty followers were publicly strung from the gallows. In 1831 the semiliterate Nat Turner, a visionary black preacher, led an uprising that butchered about sixty white Virginians, mostly women and children. Reprisals were swift and bloody.

The dark taint of slavery also left its mark on the whites. It fostered the brutality of the whip, the bloodhound, and the branding iron. White Southerners increasingly lived in a state of imagined siege, surrounded by potentially rebellious blacks inflamed by abolitionist propaganda from the North. Their fears bolstered an intoxicating theory of biological racial superiority and turned the South into a reactionary backwater in an era of progress. The defenders of slavery were forced to degrade themselves, along with their victims. As Booker T. Washington, a distinguished black leader and ex-slave, later observed, a white man cannot hold a black man in a ditch without getting down there with him.

Reasonable Abolitionism

The inhumanity of the "peculiar institution" gradually caused anti-slavery societies to sprout forth. In the 1820s, in fact, they were far more numerous in the South than in the North, as many white Southerners felt shame and guilt about slavery. But in the 1830s and 1840s Northern crusaders intensified their efforts, partly caught up by the general reform movement sweeping the country. Additional support was given their cause by the unchaining of slaves in the British Empire in the 1830s, including the nearby British West Indies.

A leading abolitionist in these early decades was Theodore Dwight Weld, a passionate soul whose conscience had been deeply aroused by the revivalism of the Second Great Awakening. After studying for the ministry at Lane Theological Seminary in Cincinnati, Weld devoted himself to organizing and preaching against slavery. His potent propaganda pamphlet, *American Slavery As It Is* (1839), was among the most effective abolitionist tracts, and greatly influenced Harriet Beecher Stowe's *Uncle Tom's Cabin* (1852).

Weld was unflinching in his hatred of the "sin" of slavery, but he and his followers were "gradualists." They favored a gradual erasure of the black blot of slavery by action of the Southern legislatures. Serious economic and social maladjustments, they believed, would thus be avoided. Some moderate abolitionists even suggested at least partial financial compensation to the owners.

Garrisonian Militants

The atmosphere of moderation was shattered in 1831, when a new and ominous blast came from the trumpet of William Lloyd Garrison, a mild-looking reformer of twenty-six. As James Russell Lowell put it:

> There's Garrison, his features very
> Benign for an incendiary;
> Beaming forth sunshine through his glasses
> On the surrounding lads and lasses.

The emotionally high-strung son of a drunken father, Garrison published in Boston the first issue of his militant abolitionist newspaper, *The Liberator*. This was perhaps the first paper broadside of a thirty years' verbal war, and in a sense one of the opening guns of the Civil War.

At the outset, Garrison nailed his colors to the masthead of his weekly. He proclaimed in violent tones that he would never compromise with the poisonous growth of slavery, but would stamp it

William Lloyd Garrison (1805–1879). The most conspicuous and most hated of the abolitionists, Garrison was a nonresistant pacifist and a poor organizer. He favored Northern secession from the South, and antagonized both sections with his intemperate language.

out at once, root and branch. "I am in earnest—I will not equivocate—I will not excuse—I will not retreat a single inch—and I WILL BE HEARD!" A close associate of Garrison was Wendell Phillips, a Boston patrician and renowned orator who came to be known as "abolition's golden trumpet." He would eat no cane sugar and wear no cotton cloth: both were produced by Southern slaves.

Many free blacks rallied to Garrison's standard. Their ranks included David Walker, whose incendiary *Appeal to the Colored Citizens of the World* (1829) advocated a bloody end to white supremacy. Also noteworthy was Sojourner Truth, a freed black woman in New York, who reported hearing heavenly voices. Eloquent, though illiterate, she fought tirelessly for black emancipation and woman's rights.

The extreme Garrison wing of the abolition movement did not understand the complex problems of the South—and evidently had no real desire to do so. Few, if any, of the abolitionist leaders had ever been near a Southern plantation. Yet, "angry for the right," they demanded immediate abolition—without compensation. Why compensate the "sinful" slaveowners who, themselves, should compensate their own exploited slaves? As for "gradualism," should a mother, as Garrison proclaimed, "gradually extricate her babe from the fire into which it has fallen?"

The Garrisonians adopted an extreme approach to a dilemma that plagued all the abolitionists. The

Constitution upheld slavery, and the federal government had no legal authority to interfere with the "peculiar institution" in the existing states. Just what *political* means could be taken to topple the slave power?

The moderate abolitionists hoped to prod the conscience of the white South and meanwhile take what piecemeal political steps they could. These might include legislation prohibiting the interstate slave trade, ending slavery in the federal District of Columbia, and banning slavery from new territories brought into the Union.

But the Garrisonians appeared to be more interested in their own righteousness than in the substance of the slavery evil itself. They flayed the "slavocrats" as brothel keepers and criminals. Garrison himself repeatedly demanded that the "virtuous" North secede from the "wicked" South. Yet he did not explain how the creation of an independent slave republic would bring a speedy end to the "damning crime" of slavery. "All Hail Disunion" and "No Union with Slaveholders" became his slogans. As a deep-dyed "non-resistant" pacifist, he publicly burned a copy of the Constitution as "a covenant with death and an agreement with hell." He refused to commit the sin of voting under such a government. Renouncing politics, Garrison cruelly probed the moral wound in America's underbelly, but offered no acceptable balm to ease the pain.

"Am I Not a Woman and a Sister?" A popular appeal. (Garrison's *Liberator*.)

The error persists that Garrison was the "voice" of the abolitionists. Actually he and his colleagues were only a small minority—the "lunatic fringe"—of the whole abolitionist movement. But his voice was so shrill, and his antics were so spectacular, that he overshadowed and obstructed the efforts of the more sober anti-slave majority. His weekly *Liberator* was never self-supporting, and though widely known, attained a circulation of only 5,000 or so. This figure contrasts with the 28,000 in 1853 for the *National Era,* a weekly newspaper of the moderate abolitionists, and only one of the many anti-slavery papers. Most moderates, who favored the Union and the ballot box, disliked Garrison—the "Massachusetts Madman." Some of them came to hate the Garrisonians even more than they hated slavery itself.

Violence Begets Violence

Abolitionists—especially the extreme Garrisonians—were unpopular in many parts of the North. Northerners had been brought up to revere the Constitution, and to regard the clauses on slavery as a lasting bargain. The ideal of Union, hammered home by the thundering eloquence of Daniel Webster and others, had taken deep root; and Garrison's wild talk of secession grated harshly on Northern ears.

The North also had a heavy economic stake in Dixieland. By the late 1850s the Southern planters owed Northern bankers and other creditors about $300 million and much of this immense sum would be lost—as, in fact, it later was—should the Union dissolve. New England textile mills were fed with cotton raised by the slaves, and a disrupted labor system might cut off this vital supply and bring unemployment. The Union during these critical years was partly bound together with cotton threads, tied by Lords of the Loom in collaboration with the so-called Lords of the Lash. Not surprisingly, strong hostility developed in the

Lovejoy's Press Destroyed

North against the boat-rocking tactics of the radical anti-slaveryites.

Repeated tongue-lashings by the extreme abolitionists ultimately provoked scores of mob outbursts in the North, some of them led by respectable gentlemen. In 1835 Garrison, with a rope tied around him, was dragged through the streets of Boston by the so-called Broadcloth Mob, but escaped almost miraculously. The Reverend Elijah P. Lovejoy, of Alton, Illinois, not content to assail slavery, impugned the chastity of Catholic women. His printing press was destroyed four times, and in 1837 he was killed by a mob, thus becoming "the martyr abolitionist." So unpopular were the anti-slavery zealots that ambitious politicians, like Lincoln, usually avoided the taint of Garrisonian abolition like the plague.

Yet by the 1850s the abolitionist outcry had made a deep dent in the Northern mind. Many citizens had come to see the South as the land of the unfree and the home of a hateful institution. Few Northerners were prepared to abolish slavery outright, but a growing number, including Abraham Lincoln, opposed extending it to the territories in the West. Men of this stamp, commonly called "free-soilers," swelled their ranks as the Civil War approached.

The South Lashes Back

Anti-slavery sentiment was not unknown in the South, but after about 1830 the voice of white Southern abolitionism was silenced. Nat Turner's rebellion sent a wave of hysteria sweeping over the white cotton fields, and planters in increasing numbers slept with pistols by their pillows. Although Garrison had no demonstrable connection with the Turner conspiracy, his *Liberator* appeared at about the same time, and he was bitterly condemned as a terrorist and an inciter of murder. The state of Georgia offered $5,000 for his arrest and conviction.

The Nullification Crisis in 1832 further implanted haunting fears in Southern minds, which conjured up nightmares of black incendiaries and abolitionist devils. Jailings, whippings, and lynchings now greeted rational efforts to discuss the slavery problem in the South.

Pro-slavery whites responded by launching a massive defense of slavery as a positive good. In doing so, they forgot their own section's previous doubts about the morality of the "peculiar institution." Slavery, they claimed, was supported by the authority of the Bible and the wisdom of Aristotle. It was good for the Africans, who were lifted from the barbarism of the jungle and clothed with the blessings of Christian civilization. Slavemasters did indeed encourage religion in the slave quarters. A catechism for blacks contained such passages as:

> Q. Who gave you a master and a mistress?
> A. God gave them to me.
> Q. Who says that you must obey them?
> A. God says that I must.

White apologists also pointed out that master-slave relationships really resembled those of a family. On many plantations, especially those in the Old South of Virginia and Maryland, this argument had a certain plausibility. A slave's tombstone bore this touching inscription:

> JOHN:
> A faithful servant
> and true friend:
> Kindly, and considerate:
> Loyal, and affectionate:
> The family he served
> Honours him in death:
> But, in life they gave him love:
> For he was one of them

A Two-Way Pro-Slavery Cartoon. Published in New York, the cartoon shows a chilled and rejected free black in the North (left) disconsolately passing a grogshop, while (*right*) a happy Southern slave enjoys life with a fishing rod in the company of a white youth.

Southern whites were quick to contrast the "happy" lot of their "servants" with that of the overworked Northern wage slaves, including sweated women and stunted children. The blacks mostly toiled in the fresh air and sunlight, not in dark and stuffy factories. They did not have to worry about slack times or unemployment, as did the "hired hands" of the North. Provided with a jail-like form of Social Security, they were cared for in sickness and old age, unlike the Northern workers, who were turned adrift. And they were sometimes, though by no means always, spared dangerous work, like putting a roof on a house. If a neck was going to be broken, the master preferred it to be that of a wage-earning Irishman, rather than that of a field hand worth $1,200.

These curious pro-slavery arguments only widened the chasm between a backward-looking South and a forward-looking North—and indeed much of the rest of the Western world. The Southerners reacted to the pressure of their own fears and the merciless nagging of the Northern abolitionists. Increasingly the white South turned in upon itself and grew hotly intolerant of any embarrassing questions about the status of slavery.

Regrettably, also, the controversy over free men endangered free speech in the entire country. Piles of petitions poured in upon Congress from the anti-slavery reformers; and in 1836 sensitive Southerners drove through the House the so-called gag resolution. It required all such anti-slavery appeals to be tabled without debate. This attack on the right of petition aroused the sleeping lion in an aged ex-President, Representative John Quincy Adams, and he waged a successful eight-year fight for its repeal.

Southern whites likewise resented the flooding of their mails with incendiary abolitionist literature. Even if the blacks could not read, they could interpret the inflammatory drawings, such as those that showed masters knocking the teeth out of their slaves with clubs. In 1835 a mob in Charleston, South Carolina, looted the local post office and burned a pile of abolitionist propaganda. The authorities in Washington were unable to force the local postmasters to deliver such mail. Such was "freedom of the press" as guaranteed by the Constitution.

The Fruits of Extremism

The South no doubt took extremists like the Garrisonians much too seriously, and made the mistake of regarding them as the mouthpiece of the entire North. Southerners would have been well advised to hit the abolitionists with "a chunk of silence." But this was asking too much of human nature. The more violently the winds of abolitionism blew down from the North, the more tightly the South wrapped the black cloak of slavery about itself, and the more savagely it struck back at its tormentors. After thirty years of abolitionist agitation, the "peculiar institution" was more firmly rooted than ever before.

All this uproar produced a bitter harvest. For over a generation, it partially eclipsed other worthy reforms, including woman's rights. It blasted hope for gradual emancipation in the northernmost slave states, where the movement had been making encouraging progress. It contributed to a splitting of parties and churches into sectional groupings. It resulted in jeopardy to fundamental American rights, of both North and South, including the right to petition, freedom of speech, freedom of the press, freedom of inquiry, freedom of travel, and freedom of teaching—almost everything "free." These priceless freedoms were most severely restricted in the South, but occasionally there were disagreeable incidents in the North, as, for example, when a professor at Harvard College was dismissed for his anti-slavery views. Finally, mobbings and lynchings shook the foundations of law and order, while making more abolitionists by making more martyrs.

Radical abolitionists also helped destroy mutual respect between the sections—the goodwill that was the cement of union. Delicate social problems cannot be solved by name-calling, and the Garrisonians injected emotion into a situation that called for light—not heat. Shouting led inexorably to shooting.

The South, angered by the holier-than-thou abuse of the extreme abolitionists, responded in kind. Fiery South Carolina orators like Senator Rhett and Congressman Keitt could fully hold their own. This exchange of epithets, in an ever-widening circle, elicited even more violent epithets. Men spoke the same language, but no longer understood one another. Bonfires of hatred were lighted that in the end were only partially extinguished by buckets of blood. When secession finally came, many Southerners felt a sense of relief in getting away from "abolitionist nagging."

> Abraham Lincoln, in a speech at Springfield, Illinois (July 16, 1852), expressed little sympathy for the more fanatical abolitionists: "Those who would shiver into fragments the Union of these states, tear to tatters its now venerated Constitution, and even burn the last copy of the Bible, rather than slavery continue a single hour, together with all their more halting sympathizers, have received, and are receiving their just execration."

Was Bloodshed Necessary?

The heat generated by the extremists on both sides helped destroy all hope of compromise. The South finally worked itself into a state of mind that would not accept compensated emancipation, and the North into a state of mind that would not offer it.

"Like Meets Like." Garrison (*right*) is here pilloried as a foe of the Union no less dangerous than the South Carolina secessionist Keitt. (*Vanity Fair*, 1861.)

If the South had been approached more diplomatically, it might ultimately have accepted such a reasonable arrangement. Yet even this assumption is questionable because of the issue of presumed racial superiority.

Abolitionists, so their defenders say, helped prick the moral conscience of the North, at a time when there was widespread apathy and callousness. When someone assured the Massachusetts clergyman Theodore Parker that God in his own good time would end slavery, Parker shot back, "The trouble is God isn't in any hurry and I am." The abolitionists were generally men and women of goodwill and various colors who faced the cruel choice that people in many ages have had thrust upon them. When is evil so enormous that it must be denounced, even at the cost of bloodshed and butchery?

Abolitionist extremists no doubt hastened the freeing of the slave by a number of years. But emancipation came at the price of a civil conflict that tore apart the social and economic fabric of the South. About a million whites were to be killed or disabled before some 4 million slaves could be freed, under conditions that took the lives of tens of thousands of black soldiers and ex-slaves. The war itself cost some $20 billion, including interest and long-term pensions—for Union veterans only. Compensated emancipation at full value—about $2 billion—would have been far cheaper in dollars and cents.

The bewildered blacks were caught in the middle. Sudden, overnight liberation, though a giant step in the right direction, was in many ways a disillusionment. And freedom by no means solved the race problem or brought complete liberty.

Emotionalism on both sides thus slammed the door on any fair adjustment. Statesmen like Daniel Webster and Abraham Lincoln came to believe, not unreasonably, that the extreme abolitionists were doing more harm than good. All other Western nations, including Brazil, ultimately rid themselves of the tumor of slavery without the surgery of the sword, although admittedly their problems were different. Solution by civil war, even though it called forth much self-sacrifice and devotion to ideals, tragically scarred the body and soul of America. Its effects are visible even today.

VARYING VIEWPOINTS

Ulrich B. Phillips made two key points in his memorable study, *American Negro Slavery* (1918). One was that slavery was a relatively benign social system; the other was that slavery was a dying economic institution, unprofitable to the slaveowner and an obstacle to the economic development of the South as a whole. From these conclusions there followed two disturbing implications. First, the abolitionists had fundamentally misconstrued the nature of the "peculiar institution." Second, the Civil War was probably unnecessary, because slavery might eventually have expired from "natural" economic causes.

For more than half a century, historians have debated these issues, sometimes heatedly. Despite increasing sophistication of economic analysis, there is still no consensus on the degree of slavery's profitability. With regard to the social character of the system, a large number of modern scholars refuse to concede that slavery was a benign institution. On the other hand, much evidence confirms the health and vitality of black culture in slavery—the strength of family ties, religious institutions, and cultural forms of all kinds.

The reputation of the abolitionists, both moderate and extreme, has greatly improved, reflecting the changed pro-black atmosphere generated by the civil rights struggles of the 1960s and 1970s. Once vilified as irresponsible provokers of a needless war, they are now commonly hailed as champions of human rights.

SELECT READINGS

A good introduction to Southern history is Clement Eaton, *A History of the Old South: The Emergence of a Reluctant Nation* (1975). W. J. Cash, *The Mind of the South* (1941), is an engagingly written classic. Always incisive is C. Vann Woodward, *The Burden of Southern History* (1960) and *American Counterpoint* (1971). F. Owsley, *Plain Folk of the Old South* (1949), illuminates the lives of non-slaveholding whites. Eugene Genovese analyzes *The Political Economy of Slavery* (1965) and *The World the Slaveholders Made* (1970). J. H. Franklin, *The Militant South* (1956), stresses the tradition of violence. H. D. Woodman reviews an important controversy in *Slavery and the Southern Economy* (1966), which should be supplemented by Gavin Wright, *The Political Economy of the Cotton South* (1978). The literature on slavery and Afro-Americans is enormous; the best place to start is J. H. Franklin, *From Slavery to Freedom* (1974), and consult also Nathan Irving Huggins' sometimes lyrical *Black Odyssey* (1977). The modern debate on slavery began with Ulrich B. Phillips' classic *American Negro Slavery* (1918); a darker view of the same subject is found in K. M. Stampp, *The Peculiar Institution* (1956). Consult also Stanley Elkins' stimulating essay, *Slavery* (2nd ed., 1968). More recently, considerable furor has surrounded the publication of R. Fogel and S. Engerman, *Time on the Cross: The Economics of American Slavery* (2 vols., 1974). For contrasting views and rebuttals, see J. W. Blassingame, *The Slave Community* (rev. ed., 1979), H. Gutman, *Slavery and the Numbers Game* (1975), the same author's *The Black Family in Slavery and Freedom, 1750–1925* (1976), Paul David, *Reckoning with Slavery* (1976), E. Genovese, *Roll, Jordan, Roll* (1974), and Carl N. Degler's comparison of slavery and race relations in Brazil and the United States, *Neither Black nor White* (1971). Albert J. Raboteau describes *Slave Religion* (1978), and Lawrence W. Levine imaginatively recreates Afro-American folk-life in *Black Culture and Black Consciousness* (1977). R. Starobin examines *Industrial Slavery in the Old South* (1970), and Ira Berlin tells the story of free blacks in *Slaves without Masters* (1975). See also L. Litwack, *North of Slavery* (1961), for the situation of blacks outside the South. D. B. Davis provides indispensable background to the history of abolitionism in *The Problem of Slavery in Western Culture* (1966) and *The Problem of Slavery in the Age of Revolution* (1975). The best brief history of the abolitionists is James B. Stewart, *Holy Warriors* (1976). Lively and pro-abolitionist are G. H. Barnes, *The Anti-Slavery Impulse* (1933), and Louis Filler, *The Crusade against Slavery* (1960). Markedly unsympathetic to the white South is D. L. Dumond, *Antislavery* (1961). J. L. Thomas is critical of William Lloyd Garrison in *The Liberator* (1963), while Aileen Kraditor is much more favorably disposed in *Means and Ends in American Abolitionism: Garrison and His Critics* (1967). Consult also Lewis Perry, *Radical Abolitionists* (1973). Stanley Elkins' *Slavery* has interesting observations on abolitionist intellectuals. Benjamin Quarles examines *Black Abolitionists* (1969), as do J. H. and W. H. Pease in *They Who Would Be Free: Blacks Search for Freedom, 1830–1861* (1974). Arna Bontemps presents the life of Frederick Douglass, the most prominent black abolitionist, in *Free at Last* (1971). White attitudes can be studied in Winthrop Jordan's masterful *White over Black* (1968) and George Frederickson's incisive *The Black Image in the White Mind* (1971), as well as in Leonard Richard's illuminating *"Gentlemen of Property and Standing": Anti-Abolitionist Mobs in Jacksonian America* (1970). R. B. Nye looks at the effects of the slavery controversy on civil liberties in *Fettered Freedom* (1963). Carl Degler portrays the dilemma of some Southern abolitionists in *The Other South* (1974). William J. Cooper, Jr., probes his subject with keen intelligence in *The South and the Politics of Slavery, 1828–1856* (1978). J. Mills Thornton III, *Politics and Power in a Slave Society: Alabama, 1800–1860* (1981), is an intriguing, inventive study with implications that reach well beyond Alabama. The semi-mythical Underground Railway is treated in W. Breyfogle, *Make Free* (1958), Larry Gara, *The Liberty Line* (1961), and Henrietta Buckmaster, *Let My People Go* (1959). Willie Lee Rose offers her customarily sensitive insights on several aspects of the subject in *Slavery and Freedom* (1982).

20

Renewing the Sectional Struggle, 1848–1854

Secession! Peaceable secession! Sir, your eyes and mine are never destined to see that miracle.

Daniel Webster, Seventh of March speech, 1850

The Popular Sovereignty Panacea

The year 1848, highlighted by a rash of revolutions in Europe, was filled with unrest in America. Land recently wrested from Mexico proved to be a bone of contention, for it raised anew the issue of extending slavery into the territories. The danger was ever present that the explosive question might disrupt the ranks of both Whigs and Democrats.

Each of the two great political parties was a vital bond of national unity, for each enjoyed powerful support in both North and South. If they should be replaced by two purely sectional groupings, the Union would be in peril. To politicians, the wisest strategy seemed to be to sit on the lid of the slavery issue and ignore the boiling beneath. Even so, the cover bobbed up and down ominously in response to the agitation of zealous Northern abolitionists and hotheaded Southern "fire-eaters."

Anxious Democrats were forced to seek a new

standard-bearer in 1848. President Polk, broken in health by overwork and chronic diarrhea, had pledged himself to a single term. The Democratic national convention at Baltimore turned to an aging leader, General Lewis Cass, a veteran of the War of 1812. Though a senator and diplomat of wide experience and considerable ability, he was sour-visaged and somewhat pompous. His enemies dubbed him General "Gass," and quickly noted that Cass rhymed with jackass. The Democratic platform, in line with the lid-sitting strategy, was silent on the burning issue of slavery in the territories.

But Cass himself had not been silent. His views on the extension of slavery were well known, because he was the reputed father of "popular sovereignty." This was the doctrine that the sovereign people of a territory, under the general principles of the Constitution, should themselves determine the status of slavery.

Popular sovereignty had a persuasive appeal. The public liked it because it accorded with the democratic tradition of self-determination. Politicians liked it because it seemed a comfortable compromise between a ban on slavery in the territories and Southern demands that Congress protect slavery in the territories. Popular sovereignty tossed the slavery problem into the laps of the people in the various territories. Advocates of the doctrine thus hoped to dissolve the most stubborn national issue of the day into a series of local issues. Yet popular sovereignty had one fatal defect: it might serve to spread the blight of slavery.

Political Triumphs for General Taylor

The Whigs, meeting in Philadelphia, cashed in on the "Taylor fever." They nominated frank and honest Zachary Taylor, the "Hero of Buena Vista," who had never held civil office or even voted for President. Henry Clay, the living embodiment of Whiggism, should logically have been nominated. But he had made too many speeches—and too many enemies.

As usual, the Whigs pussyfooted in their platform. Eager to win at any cost, they dodged all troublesome issues and merely extolled the homespun virtues of their candidate. The self-reliant old frontier fighter, actually a babe in the woods politically, had not committed himself on the issue of slavery extension. But as a wealthy resident of Louisiana, living on a sugar plantation, he owned scores of slaves.

Ardent anti-slavery men in the North, distrusting both Cass and Taylor, organized the Free-Soil party. Aroused by the conspiracy of silence in the Democratic and Whig platforms, they made no bones about their own stand. They came out foursquare for the Wilmot Proviso and against slavery in the territories. Going beyond other anti-slavery groups, they broadened their appeal by advocating federal aid for internal improvements and by urging free government homesteads for settlers.

General Zachary Taylor. This Democratic campaign cartoon of 1848 charges that Taylor's reputation rested on Mexican skulls. (Courtesy of The New-York Historical Society, New York City.)

The new party trotted out wizened ex-President Van Buren, and marched into the fray shouting, "Free soil, free speech, free labor, and free men."

With the slavery issue officially shoved under the rug by the two major parties, the politicians on both sides opened fire on personalities. The amateurish Taylor had to be carefully watched, lest his indiscreet pen puncture the reputation won by his sword. His admirers puffed him up as a gallant knight and a Napoleon, and sloganized his remark, allegedly uttered during the Battle of Buena Vista, "General Taylor never surrenders."

Taylor's wartime popularity pulled him through. He harvested 1,360,099 popular and 163 electoral votes, as compared with Cass's 1,220,544 popular and 127 electoral votes. Free-Soiler Van Buren, although winning no state, polled 291,263 ballots, and apparently diverted enough Democratic strength from Cass in the crucial state of New York to throw the election to Taylor.

"Californy Gold"

Tobacco-chewing President Taylor—with his stumpy legs, rough features, heavy jaw, black hair, ruddy complexion, and squinty gray eyes—was a military square peg in a political round hole. He would have been spared much turmoil if he could have continued to sit on the slavery lid. But the discovery of gold in California, early in 1848, blew the cover off.

A horde of adventurers poured into the valleys of California. Singing "O Susannah!" and shouting "Gold! Gold! Gold!" they began tearing frantically at the yellow-graveled streams and hills. A fortunate few of the bearded miners "struck it rich" at the "diggings." But the luckless many, who netted blisters instead of nuggets, probably would have been money well ahead if they had stayed at home unaffected by the "gold fever," which was often followed by more deadly fevers. The most reliable profits were made by those who mined the miners, notably by charging outrageous rates for laundry and other personal services. Some soiled clothing was even sent as far away as the Hawaiian Islands for washing.

The overnight inpouring of tens of thousands of people into the future Golden State completely overwhelmed the one-horse government of California. A distressingly high proportion of the newcomers were lawless men, accompanied or followed by virtueless women. A contemporary song ran:

> Oh what was your name in the States?
> Was it Thompson or Johnson or Bates?
> Did you murder your wife,
> And fly for your life?
> Say, what was your name in the States?

An outburst of crime inevitably resulted from the presence of so many outcasts. Robbery, claim

The Washing-Bowl. One method of panning for gold. (*Harper's New Monthly Magazine.*)

> The idea that many ne'er-do-wells went west is found in Ralph Waldo Emerson's *Journals* (January 1849): "If a man is going to California, he announces it with some hesitation; because it is a confession that he has failed at home."

jumping, and murder were commonplace; and such violence was only partly discouraged by rough vigilante justice. In San Francisco, from 1848 to 1856, there were scores of lawless killings but only three semilegal hangings.

A majority of the Californians, as decent and law-abiding citizens needing protection, grappled earnestly with the problem of erecting an adequate state government. Privately encouraged by President Taylor, they drafted a constitution in 1849 which excluded slavery, and then boldly applied to Congress for admission. California would thus bypass the usual territorial stage, thwarting Southern congressmen seeking to block free soil. Southern politicians, alarmed by this "impertinent" stroke for freedom, arose in violent opposition. Would California prove to be the golden straw that broke the back of the Union?

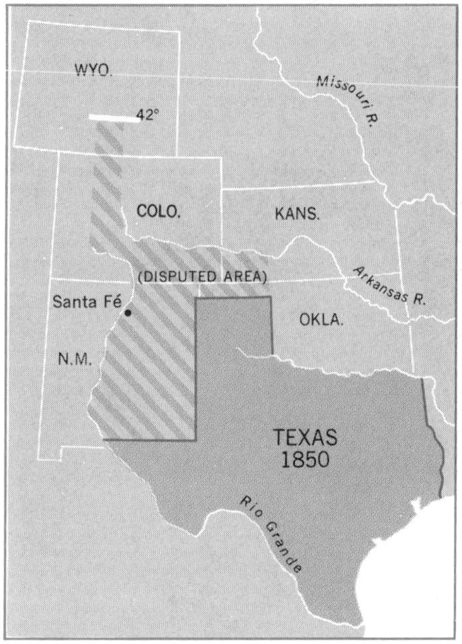

TEXAS AND THE COMPROMISE OF 1850

Sectional Balance and the Underground Railroad

The South of 1850 was relatively well off. It then enjoyed, as it had from the beginning, more than its share of the nation's leadership. It had seated in the White House the war hero Zachary Taylor, a Virginia-born, slave-owning planter from Louisiana. It had a majority in the Cabinet and on the Supreme Bench. If outnumbered in the House, the South had equality in the Senate, where it could hope to exercise a veto voice. Its cotton fields were expanding, and the price of the snowy fiber was profitably high. Few sane people, North or South, believed that slavery was seriously threatened where it already existed below the Mason-Dixon line.* The fifteen slave states could easily veto any proposed constitutional amendment.

Yet the South was deeply worried, as it had been for several decades, by the ever-tipping political balance. There were then fifteen slave states and fifteen free states. The admission of California would destroy the delicate equilibrium in the Senate, perhaps forever. Potential slave territory under the American flag was running short, if it had not already disappeared. Agitation had already developed in the territories of New Mexico and Utah for admission as nonslave states. The fate of California might well establish a precedent for the rest of the Mexican Cession territory—an area purchased largely with Southern blood.

Texas nursed an additional grievance of her own. She claimed a huge area east of the Rio Grande and north to the 42nd parallel, embracing in part about half the territory of present New Mexico. The federal government was proposing to detach this prize, while hot-blooded Texans were threatening to descend upon Santa Fe and seize what they regarded as rightfully theirs. The explosive quarrel foreshadowed shooting.

Many Southerners were also angered by the nagging agitation in the North for the abolition of slavery in the District of Columbia. They looked with alarm on the prospect of a ten-mile-square

*Originally the southern boundary of colonial Pennsylvania.

Resurrection of Henry Box Brown. Brown, a slave, was shipped to Philadelphia abolitionists from Virginia in a box. (Library of Congress.)

oasis of free soil, thrust between slaveholding Maryland and slaveholding Virginia.

Even more disagreeable to the South was the loss of runaway slaves, many of whom were assisted north by the Underground Railroad. It consisted of an informal chain of "stations" (antislavery homes), through which scores of "passengers" (runaway slaves) were spirited by "conductors" (usually white and black abolitionists) from the slave states to the free-soil sanctuary of Canada.

The most amazing of these "conductors" was an illiterate runaway slave from Maryland, fearless Harriet Tubman. During nineteen forays into the South, she rescued more than 300 slaves, including her aged parents, and deservedly earned the title "Moses." Lively imaginations later exaggerated the role of the Underground Railroad and its "station masters," but its existence was a fact. Another significant fact is that the most difficult part of the escape was to get to the Ohio River, for up to that point runaway slaves were generally on their own.

By 1850 Southerners were demanding a new and more stringent fugitive slave law. The old one, passed by Congress in 1793, had proved inadequate to cope with runaways, especially since unfriendly state authorities failed to provide needed cooperation. Unlike cattle thieves, the abolitionists who ran the Underground Railroad did not gain personally from their lawlessness. But to the slaveowners the loss was infuriating, whatever the motives. The moral judgments of the abolitionists seemed, in some ways, more galling than outright

Harriet Tubman, Premier Assistant of Runaway Slaves. John Brown called her "General Tubman" for her effective work in helping slaves escape to Canada. During the Civil War she served as a Union spy behind Confederate lines. Herself illiterate, she worked after the war to bring education to the freed slaves in North Carolina. (The New York Public Library, Astor, Lenox, and Tilden Foundations.) (Library of Congress)

theft. They reflected not only a holier-than-thou attitude but a refusal to obey the laws solemnly passed by Congress.

Estimates indicate that the South in 1850 was losing perhaps 1,000 runaways a year, out of its total of some 4 million slaves. In fact, the owners probably freed more blacks voluntarily than ever escaped. But the principle weighed heavily with the slavemasters. They rested their argument on the Constitution, which protected slavery, and on the laws of Congress, which provided for slavecatching.

Twilight of the Senatorial Giants

Southern fears were such that Congress was confronted with catastrophe in 1850. Free-soil California was banging on the door for admission, and "fire-eaters" in the South were voicing ominous threats of secession. The crisis brought into the congressional forum the most distinguished assemblage of statesmen since the Constitutional Convention of 1787—the Old Guard of the dying generation and the young gladiators of the new. That "immortal trio"—Clay, Calhoun, and Webster—appeared together for the last time on the public stage.

Henry Clay, now seventy-three years of age, played a crucial role. The "Great Pacificator" had come to the Senate from Kentucky to engineer his third great compromise. The once-glamorous statesman—though disillusioned, enfeebled, and racked by a cruel cough—was still eloquent, conciliatory, captivating. He proposed and skillfully defended a series of compromises. He was ably seconded by thirty-seven-year-old Senator Stephen A. Douglas of Illinois, the "Little Giant" (5 feet 4 inches; 1.62 meters), whose role was less spectacular but even more important. Clay urged with all his persuasiveness that the North and South both make concessions, and that the North partially yield by enacting a more effective fugitive slave law.

Senator John C. Calhoun, then sixty-eight and dying of tuberculosis, championed the South in his last formal speech. Too weak to deliver it himself, he sat bundled up in the Senate chamber, his eyes glowing within a stern face, while a younger colleague read his fateful words. Although approving the purpose of Clay's proposed concessions, Calhoun rejected them as not providing adequate safeguards. His impassioned plea was to leave slavery alone, return runaway slaves, give the South its rights as a minority, and restore the political balance. He had in view, as was later revealed, an utterly unworkable scheme of electing two Presidents, one from the North and one from the South, each wielding a veto.

Calhoun died in 1850, before the debate was over, uttering the sad words, "The South! The South! God knows what will become of her!" Appreciative fellow citizens in Charleston erected to his memory an imposing monument, which bore the inscription "Truth, Justice, and the Constitution." Calhoun had labored to preserve the Union, and had taken his stand on the Constitution, but his proposals in their behalf almost undid both.

Daniel Webster next took the Senate spotlight to uphold Clay's compromise measures in his last great speech, a three-hour effort. Now sixty-eight years old, and suffering from a liver complaint aggravated by high living, he had lost some of the fire in his magnificent voice. Speaking deliberately and before overflowing galleries, he urged all reasonable concessions to the South, including a new fugitive slave law with teeth.

As for slavery in the territories, asked Webster, why legislate on the subject? To do so was an act of sacrilege, for Almighty God had already passed the Wilmot Proviso. The good Lord had decreed—through climate, topography, and geography—that a plantation economy, and hence a slave economy, could not profitably exist in the Mexican Cession territory.* Webster sanely concluded that compromise, concession, and sweet reasonableness would provide the only solutions. "Let

*Webster was wrong here; within 100 years California had become one of the great cotton-producing states of the Union.

us not be pygmies," he pleaded, "in a case that calls for men."

Webster's famed Seventh of March speech, 1850, was his finest, if measured by its immediate effects. It helped turn the tide in the North toward compromise. The clamor for printed copies became so great that Webster mailed out more than 100,000, remarking that 200,000 would not satisfy the demand. His tremendous effort visibly strengthened Union sentiment. It was especially pleasing to the banking and commercial centers of the North, which stood to lose millions of dollars by secession. One prominent Washington banker canceled two notes of Webster's, totaling $5,000, and sent him a personal check for $1,000 and a message of congratulations.

But the abolitionists, who had regarded Webster as one of themselves, upbraided him as a traitor, worthy of bracketing with Benedict Arnold. The poet Whittier lamented:

> So fallen! so lost! the light withdrawn
> Which once he wore!
> The glory from his gray hairs gone
> For evermore!

These reproaches were most unfair. Webster, who had long regarded slavery as evil but disunion as worse, despised the abolitionists and never joined their ranks.

> Ralph Waldo Emerson, the philosopher and moderate abolitionist, was outraged by Webster's support of concessions to the South in the Fugitive Slave Act. In February 1851 he wrote in his *Journal:* "I opened a paper to-day in which he [Webster] pounds on the old strings [of liberty] in a letter to the Washington Birthday feasters at New York. 'Liberty! liberty!' Pho! Let Mr. Webster, for decency's sake, shut his lips once and forever on this word. The word *liberty* in the mouth of Mr. Webster sounds like the word *love* in the mouth of a courtesan."

Deadlock and Danger on Capitol Hill

The stormy congressional debate of 1850 was not finished, for the Young Guard from the North were yet to have their say. This was the group of newer statesmen who, unlike the aging Old Guard, had not grown up with the Union. They were more interested in purging and purifying it than in patching and preserving it.

William H. Seward, the wiry and husky-throated freshman senator from New York, was the able spokesman for many of the younger Northern radicals. A strong anti-slaveryite, he came out flat-footedly against concession. He seemed not to realize that compromise had brought the Union together, and that when the sections could no longer compromise, they would have to part company.

Seward argued earnestly that Christian legisla-

A Seward Caricature. He later became Lincoln's foremost rival for the presidency, and still later his secretary of state.

Compromise of 1850

Concessions to the North	*Concessions to the South*
California admitted as a free state	The remainder of the Mexican Cession area to be formed into the territories of New Mexico and Utah, without restriction on slavery, hence open to popular sovereignty
Territory disputed by Texas and New Mexico to be surrendered to New Mexico	Texas to receive $10 million from the federal government as compensation
Abolition of the slave trade (but not slavery) in the District of Columbia	A more stringent Fugitive Slave Law, going beyond that of 1793

tors must obey God's moral law as well as man's mundane law. He therefore appealed, with reference to excluding slavery in the territories, to an even "higher law" than the Constitution. This alarming phrase, wrenched from its context, may have cost him the presidential nomination and the presidency in 1860.

As the great debate in Congress ran its heated course, deadlock seemed certain. Blunt old President Taylor, who had allegedly fallen under the influence of men like "Higher Law" Seward, seemed bent on vetoing any compromise passed by Congress. His military ire was aroused by the threats of Texas to seize Santa Fe. He appeared to be doggedly determined to "Jacksonize" the dissenters, if need be, by leading an army against the Texans in person and hanging all "damned traitors." If troops had begun to march, the South probably would have rallied to the defense of her sister state, and the Civil War might have erupted in 1850.

Breaking the Congressional Logjam

At the height of the controversy in 1850, President Taylor unknowingly helped the cause of concession by dying suddenly, probably of an acute intestinal disorder. Portly, round-faced Vice-President Millard Fillmore, a colorless and conciliatory New York lawyer-politician, took over the reins. As presiding officer of the Senate, he had been impressed with the arguments for conciliation, and he gladly signed the series of compromise measures that passed Congress after seven long months of stormy debate. The balancing of interests in the Compromise of 1850 was delicate in the extreme.

The struggle to get these measures accepted by the country was hardly less heated than in Congress. In the Northern states, "Union savers" like Senators Clay, Webster, and Douglas orated on behalf of the compromise. The ailing Clay himself delivered more than seventy speeches, as a powerful sentiment for acceptance gradually crystallized in the North. It was strengthened by a growing spirit of goodwill, which sprang partly from a feeling of relief, and partly from an upsurge of prosperity enriched by California gold.

But the "fire-eaters" of the South were still violently opposed to concessions. One extreme South Carolina newspaper avowed that it loathed the Union and hated the North as much as it did Hell itself. A movement in the South to boycott Northern goods gained some headway, but in the end the Southern Unionists, assisted by the warm glow of prosperity, prevailed.

In mid-1850, an assemblage of Southern extremists had met in Nashville, Tennessee, ironically near the burial place of Andrew Jackson. The delegates not only took a strong position in favor of slavery, but condemned the compromise measures then being hammered out in Congress. Meeting again later in the year after the bills had passed, the convention proved to be a dud. By that

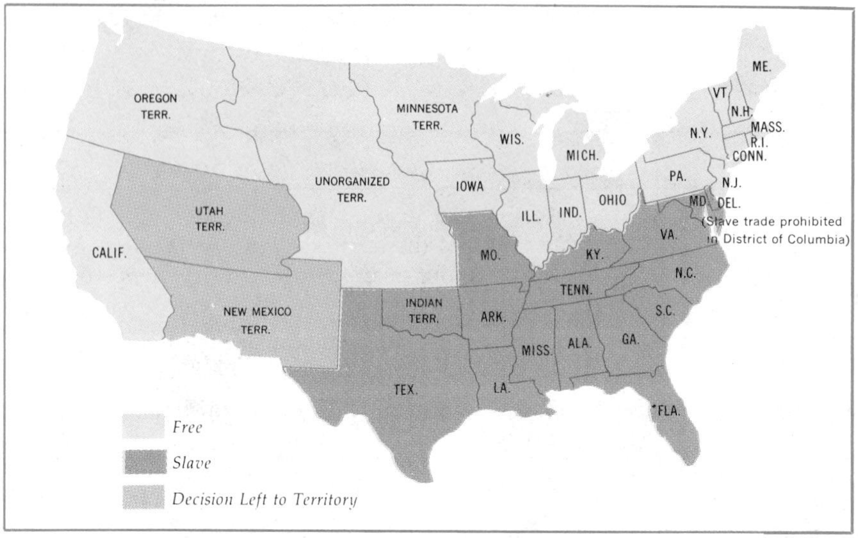

SLAVERY AFTER THE COMPROMISE OF 1850

time Southern opinion had reluctantly accepted the verdict of Congress.

Like the calm after a storm, a second Era of Good Feelings dawned. Disquieting talk of secession subsided. Reasonable men, both North and South, were determined that the compromises should be a "finality," and that the explosive issue of slavery should be buried. But this reign of reason proved all too brief.

Balancing the Compromise Scales

Who got the better of the Compromise of 1850?

The answer is clearly the North. California, as a free state, tipped the Senate balance permanently against the South. The territories of New Mexico and Utah were open to slavery on the basis of popular sovereignty. But the iron law of nature—the "highest law" of all—had loaded the dice in favor of free soil. The Southerners urgently needed more slave territory to restore the "sacred balance." If they could not carve new states out of the recent conquests from Mexico, where else would they get them?

Even the apparent gains of the South rang hollow. Disgruntled Texas was to be paid $10 million toward discharging her indebtedness, but in the long run this was a modest sum. The immense area in dispute had been torn from the side of slaveholding Texas, and was almost certain to be free. The South had halted the drive toward abolition in the District of Columbia, at least temporarily, by permitting the outlawing of the slave traffic. But even this move was an entering wedge toward complete emancipation in the nation's capital.

Most alarming of all, the drastic new Fugitive Slave Law—"the Bloodhound Bill"—stirred up a storm of opposition in the North. The fleeing slave could not testify in his own behalf, and he was denied a jury trial. These harsh practices threatened to create dangerous precedents for the whites. The federal commissioner who handled

> Regarding the Fugitive Slave Act of 1850, Ralph Waldo Emerson, the abolitionist, declared (May 1851) at Concord, Massachusetts: "The act of Congress . . . is a law which every one of you will break on the earliest occasion—a law which no man can obey, or abet the obeying, without loss of self-respect and forfeiture of the name of gentleman." Privately he wrote in his *Journal:* "This filthy enactment was made in the nineteenth century, by people who could read and write. I will not obey it, by God" (July 1851).

the case would receive five dollars if the runaway was freed, and ten dollars if not—an arrangement that strongly resembled a bribe. Freedom-loving Northerners who aided the slave to escape were liable to heavy fines and jail sentences. They might even be ordered to join the slavecatchers, and this possibility rubbed salt into old sores.

So savage was this "Man-Stealing Law" that it touched off an explosive chain reaction in the North. Many shocked moderates, hitherto passive, were driven into the swelling ranks of the abolitionists. Cried John Pierpont:

> Lashed with her hounds, must we
> Run down the poor who flee
> From Slavery's hell?

The Underground Railroad stepped up its timetable, while infuriated Northern mobs rescued slaves from their pursuers. Massachusetts, in a move toward nullification suggestive of South Carolina in 1832, made it a penal offense for any state official to enforce the new federal statute. Other states passed "personal liberty laws," which denied local jails to federal officials and otherwise hampered enforcement. The abolitionists rent the heavens with their protests against the man-stealing statute. A meeting presided over by Garrison in 1851 declared, "We execrate it, we spit upon it, we trample it under our feet."

Runaway Slaves Rout Slave Catchers. Christiana, Pa., 1851.

Beyond question, the Fugitive Slave Law was an appalling blunder on the part of the South. No single irritant of the 1850s was more persistently galling to both sides, and none did more to awaken in the North a spirit of antagonism against the South. The Southerners in turn were embittered because the Northerners would not in good faith execute the law—the one real and immediate "gain" from the Great Compromise. Slavecatchers, with some success, redoubled their efforts.

Should the shooting showdown have come in 1850? From the standpoint of the secessionists, yes; from the standpoint of the Unionists, no. Time was fighting for the North. With every passing decade this huge section was forging farther ahead in population and wealth—in crops, factories, foundries, ships, and railroads.

Delay also added immensely to the moral strength of the North— to its will to fight for the Union. In 1850 countless thousands of Northern moderates were unwilling to pin the South to the rest of the nation with bayonets. But the inflammatory events of the 1850s did much to bolster the Yankee will to resist secession, whatever the cost. This one feverish decade gave the North time to accumulate the physical and moral strength that provided the margin of victory. Thus the Compromise of 1850, from one point of view, won the Civil War for the Union.

Defeat and Doom for the Whigs

Meeting in Baltimore, the Democratic nominating convention of 1852 startled the nation. Hopelessly deadlocked, it finally stampeded to the second "dark horse" candidate in American history, an unrenowned lawyer-politician, Franklin Pierce, from the hills of New Hampshire. The Whigs tried to jeer him back into obscurity with the cry, "Who is Frank Pierce?" Democrats replied, "The Young Hickory of the Granite Hills."

Pierce, though handsome, was a weak and indecisive figure. Youngish, militarily erect, smiling, and convivial, he had served without real distinction in the Mexican War. As a result of a painful

President Franklin Pierce (1804–1869). Pierce was never a strong President. On the eve of his inauguration, he and his wife saw their one surviving son being mangled to death in a railroad wreck. In the White House the distraught First Lady wore only black and spent much time writing letters to one of her three dead sons.

groin injury that caused him to fall off a horse, he was known as the "Fainting General," though scandalmongers pointed to a fondness for alcohol. But he was enemyless because he had been inconspicuous, and as a pro-Southern Northerner he was acceptable to the slavery wing of the Democratic party. His platform came out emphatically for the finality of the Compromise of 1850, Fugitive Slave Law and all.

The Whigs, also convening in Baltimore, missed a splendid opportunity to capitalize on their record in statecraft. Able to boast of a praiseworthy achievement in the Compromise of 1850, they might logically have nominated President Fillmore or Senator Webster, both of whom were associated with it. But having won in the past only with military heroes, they turned to another, "Old Fuss and Feathers" Winfield Scott, perhaps the ablest American general of his generation. Although he was a huge and impressive figure, his manner bordered on haughtiness. His personality not only repelled the masses but eclipsed his genuinely statesmanlike achievements. The Whig platform praised the Compromise of 1850 as a lasting arrangement, though less enthusiastically than the Democrats.

With slavery and sectionalism to some extent soft-pedaled, the campaign again degenerated into a dull and childish attack on personalities. Democrats ridiculed Scott's pomposity; Whigs charged that Pierce was the hero of "many a well-fought *bottle.*" Democrats cried exultantly, "We Polked 'em in '44; we'll Pierce 'em in '52."

Luckily for the Democrats, the Whig party was hopelessly split. Anti-slavery Whigs of the North swallowed Scott as their standard-bearer but deplored his platform, which endorsed the hated Fugitive Slave Law. The current phrase ran, "We accept the candidate but spit on the platform." Southern Whigs, who doubted Scott's loyalty to the Compromise of 1850 and especially to the Fugitive Slave Law, accepted the platform but spat on the candidate. More than 5,000 Georgia Whigs—"finality men"—futilely voted for Webster, although he had died nearly two weeks before the election.

General Scott, victorious on the battlefield, met defeat at the ballot box. His friends remarked whimsically that he was not used to "running." Actually, he was stabbed in the back by his fellow Whigs, notably in the South. The pliant Pierce won in a landslide, 254 electoral votes to 42, though the

> In assailing the candidacy of "Fuss and Feathers" Scott, James Buchanan, himself elected President some four years later, declared that to elevate generals would cause "aspiring officers" to favor "foreign wars, as the best means of acquiring military glory. . . . Napoleon was endeared to his army by his designation of 'the little Corporal'; General Jackson, by that of 'Old Hickory'; and General Taylor was 'Rough and Ready'; but what shall we say to 'Fuss and Feathers'?"

CENTRAL AMERICA, c. 1850, SHOWING BRITISH POSSESSIONS AND PROPOSED CANAL ROUTES
Until President Theodore Roosevelt swung into action with his Big Stick in 1903, a Nicaraguan canal, closer to the United States, was generally judged more desirable than a canal across Panama.

popular count was closer, 1,601,274 to 1,386,580.

The election of 1852 was fraught with frightening significance, though it may have seemed tame at the time. It marked the effective end of the disorganized Whig party, and within a few years its complete death. The Whigs were governed at times by the crassest opportunism, and they won only two presidential elections (1840, 1848) in their colorful career, both with war heroes. They finally choked to death trying to gag down the Fugitive Slave Law. But their great contribution—and a noteworthy one indeed—was to help implant and uphold the ideal of Union through leaders like Clay and Webster. Both of these statesmen, by unhappy coincidence, died during the campaign. But the good that they had done lived after them, and contributed powerfully to the preservation of a united United States.

President Pierce the Expansionist

At the outset the Pierce administration displayed vigor. The new President, standing confidently before some 15,000 people on inauguration day, delivered from memory a clear-voiced inaugural address. His Cabinet contained aggressive Southerners, including as secretary of war one Jefferson Davis, future president of the Confederacy. The men of Dixie were determined to acquire more slave territory, and the compliant Pierce was prepared to be their willing tool.

The intoxicating victories of the Mexican War stimulated the spirit of Manifest Destiny, especially among "slaveocrats" lusting for new slave territory. The conquest of a Pacific frontage, and the discovery of gold on it, aroused lively interest in the trans-Isthmian land routes of Central America, chiefly in Panama and Nicaragua. Many Americans were looking even farther ahead to potential canal routes, and to the islands flanking them, notably Spain's Cuba.

Nicaragua was of vital concern to Great Britain, the world's leading maritime and commercial power. Fearing that the grasping Yankees would monopolize the trade arteries there, the British made haste to secure a solid foothold at Greytown, the eastern end of the proposed Nicaraguan canal route. This challenge to the Monroe Doctrine forthwith raised the ugly possibility of an armed clash. The crisis was surmounted in 1850 by the Clayton-Bulwer Treaty, which stipulated that neither America nor Britain would fortify or secure exclusive control over any future Isthmian waterway. This agreement, at the time, seemed necessary to halt the British, but to American canal promoters in later years it proved to be a ball and chain.

America had become a Pacific power with the acquisition of California and Oregon, both of which faced the Orient. The prospects of a rich trade with the Far East now seemed rosier. Americans had already established contacts with China, and shippers were urging Washington to push for commercial intercourse with Japan. The Mikado's empire, after some disagreeable experiences with the European world, had withdrawn into a cocoon of isolationism and had remained there for over 200 years. But by 1853, as events proved, Nippon was ready to emerge, partly because of the Russian menace.

The Washington government was now eager to pry open the bamboo gates of Japan. It dispatched a fleet of awesome, smoke-belching warships, commanded by Commodore Matthew C. Perry, brother of the hero of the Battle of Lake Erie in 1813. By a judicious display of force and tact, he persuaded the Japanese in 1854 to sign a memorable treaty. It provided for only a commercial foot in the door, but it was the beginning of an epochal relationship between the Land of the Rising Sun and the Western world. Ironically, this achievement attracted little notice at the time, partly because Perry devised no memorable slogan.

A Japanese Portrait of Commodore Perry. A blunt officer, known as "Old Bruin" by his men, he was held in high regard by the Japanese until World War II. Early in 1944, in the wake of American bombings, a monument to him in Yokohama was torn down.

Coveted Cuba: Pearl of the Antilles

Sugar-rich Cuba, lying off the nation's southern doorstep, was the prime objective of Manifest Destiny in the 1850s. Supporting a large population of enslaved blacks, it was coveted by the South as the most desirable slave territory available. Carved into several states, it would once more restore the political balance in the Senate.

Cuba was a kind of heirloom—the most important remnant of Spain's once-mighty New World empire. Polk, the expansionist, had taken steps to offer $100 million for it, but the sensitive Spaniards had replied that they would see it sunk into the ocean before they would sell it to the Americans at any price. With purchase completely out of the question, seizure was apparently the only way to pluck the ripening fruit.

Private adventurers from the South now undertook to shake the tree of Manifest Destiny. During 1850–1851 two filibustering expeditions, each numbering several hundred armed men, descended upon Cuba. Both feeble efforts were repelled, and the last one ended in tragedy when the leader and fifty followers—some of them from the "best families" of the South—were summarily shot or strangled. So outraged were the Southerners that an angry mob sacked Spain's consulate in New Orleans.

Spanish officials in Cuba rashly forced a showdown in 1854, when they seized an American

Cuban Discomfort. "Master Jonathan tries to smoke a Cuba, but it doesn't agree with him!" English chortle over America's Cuban blunder. (Punch, 1850.)

steamer, *Black Warrior,* on a technicality. Now was the time for President Pierce, dominated as he was by the South, to provoke a war with Spain and seize Cuba. The major powers of Europe—England, France, and Russia—were about to become bogged down in the Crimean War, and hence were unable to aid Spain.

An incredible cloak-and-dagger episode followed. The secretary of state instructed the American ministers in Spain, England, and France to prepare confidential recommendations for the acquisition of Cuba. Meeting initially at Ostend, Belgium, the three envoys drew up a top-secret dispatch, soon known as the Ostend Manifesto. This startling document urged that the administration offer $120 million for Cuba. If Spain refused, and if her continued ownership endangered American interests, the United States would "be justified in wresting" the island from her.

The secret Ostend Manifesto quickly leaked out. Northern free-soilers, already angered by the Fugitive Slave Law and other gains for slavery, rose in an outburst of wrath against the "manifesto of brigands." Confronted with disruption at home, the red-faced Pierce administration was forced to drop its brazen schemes for Cuba.

Clearly the slavery issue, like a two-headed snake with the heads at cross purposes, deadlocked territorial expansion in the 1850s. The North, flushed with Manifest Destiny, was developing a renewed appetite for Canada. The South coveted Cuba. Neither section would permit the other to get the apple of its eye, so neither got either. The shackled black hands of Harriet Beecher Stowe's Uncle Tom, who had already aroused the North, held the South back from Cuba. The internal distresses of the United States were such that, for once, it could not take advantage of Europe's distresses—in this case the Crimean War.

The first platform of the newly born (antislavery) Republican party in 1856 lashed out at the Ostend Manifesto, with its transparent suggestion that Cuba be seized. The plank read: "*Resolved,* That the highwayman's plea, that 'might makes right,' embodied in the Ostend Circular, was in every respect unworthy of American diplomacy, and would bring shame and dishonor upon any Government or people that gave it their sanction."

Pacific Railroad Promoters and the Gadsden Purchase

Acute transportation problems were another legacy of the Mexican War. The newly acquired prizes of California and Oregon might just as well have been islands some 8,000 miles (13,000 kilometers) west of the nation's capital. The sea routes to and from the Isthmus, to say nothing of those around South America, were too long. Covered-wagon travel past bleaching animal bones was possible, but it was slow and dangerous. A popular song recalled:

They swam the wide rivers and crossed the tall peaks,
And camped on the prairie for weeks upon weeks.
Starvation and cholera and hard work and slaughter,
They reached California spite of hell and high water.

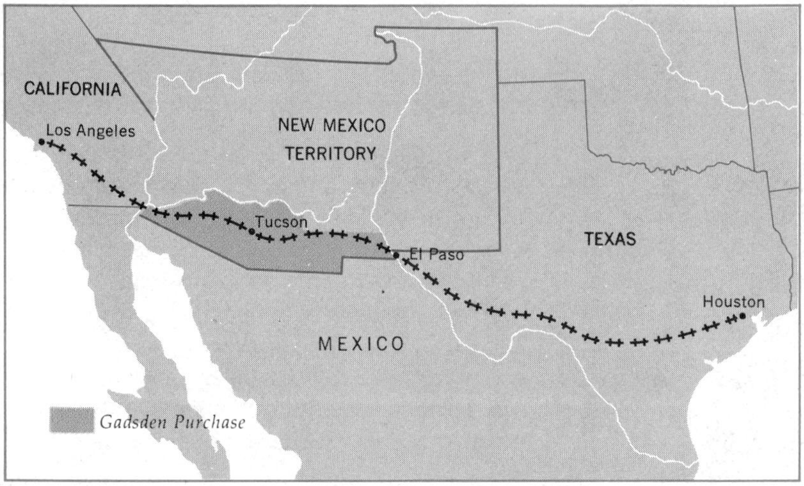

GADSDEN PURCHASE, 1853
Future Southern Pacific Railroad (completed 1882) is shown.

Feasible land transportation was imperative—or the newly won possessions on the Pacific Coast might break away. Camels were even proposed as the answer. Several score of these temperamental beasts—"ships of the desert"—were imported from the Near East, but mule-driving Americans did not adjust to them. A transcontinental railroad was clearly the only real solution to the problem.

Railway promoters, both North and South, had projected many drawing-board routes to the Pacific Coast. But the estimated cost in all cases was so great that for many years there could obviously be only one line. Should its terminus be in the North or in the South? The favored section would reap rich rewards in wealth, population, and influence. The South, losing the economic race with the North, was eager to extend a railroad through adjacent Southwestern territory all the way to California.

Another chunk of Mexico now seemed desirable, because the campaigns of the recent war had shown that the best railway route ran slightly south of the Mexican border. Secretary of War Jefferson Davis, a Mississippian, arranged to have James Gadsden, a prominent South Carolina railroad man, appointed minister to Mexico. Finding Santa Anna in power for the sixth and last time, and as usual in need of money, Gadsden made gratifying headway. He negotiated a treaty in 1853, which ceded to the United States the Gadsden Purchase area for $10 million. The transaction aroused much criticism among Northerners, who objected to paying a huge sum for a cactus-strewn desert nearly the size of Gadsden's South Carolina. Undeterred, the Senate approved the pact after shortsightedly eliminating a window on the Gulf of California.

No doubt the Gadsden Purchase enabled the South to claim the coveted railroad with even greater insistence. A southern track would be easier to build, because the mountains were less high and because the route, unlike the proposed northern lines, would not pass through unorganized territory. Texas was already a state, and New Mexico (with the Gadsden Purchase added) was a formally organized territory, with federal troops available to provide protection against marauding red men. Any northern or central line would have to be thrust through the unorganized territory of Nebraska, where the buffalo and Indians roamed.

Northern railroad boosters quickly replied that if organized territory was the test, then Nebraska should be organized. Such a move was not premature, because thousands of land-hungry pioneers were already poised on the Nebraska border. But all schemes proposed in Congress for organizing the territory were greeted with apathy or hostility by many Southerners. Why should the South help create new free-soil states, and thus cut its own throat by facilitating a northern railroad?

Douglas's Kansas-Nebraska Scheme

At this point in 1854 Senator Stephen A. Douglas of Illinois delivered a counterstroke to offset the Gadsden thrust for Southern expansion westward. A squat, bull-necked, and heavy-chested figure, the "Little Giant" radiated the energy and breezy optimism of the self-made man. An ardent booster for the West, he longed to break the North-South deadlock over westward expansion and stretch a line of settlements across the continent. He had also invested heavily in Chicago real estate and in railway stock, and was eager to have the Windy City become the eastern terminus of the proposed Pacific railroad. He would thus endear himself to the voters of Illinois, benefit his own section, and enrich his own purse.

Stephen A. Douglas (1813–1861). Despite having stirred up sectional bitterness, Douglas was so devoted to the Union that he warmly supported his rival, Lincoln, when war broke out. He attended the inauguration and reportedly held Lincoln's stovepipe hat while the President spoke. (National Portrait Gallery, Smithsonian Institution, Washington, D.C.)

A veritable "steam engine in breeches," Douglas threw himself behind a legislative scheme that would enlist the support of a reluctant South. The proposed Territory of Nebraska would be carved into two territories, Kansas and Nebraska. Their status regarding slavery would be settled by popular sovereignty—a democratic concept to which Douglas and his Western constituents were deeply attached. Kansas, which lay due west of slaveholding Missouri, would presumably choose to become a slave state. But Nebraska, lying west of free-soil Iowa, would presumably become a free state.

Douglas's Kansas-Nebraska scheme ran headlong into a formidable political obstacle. The Missouri Compromise of 1820 had forbidden slavery in the Nebraska Territory, which lay north of the sacred 36°30′ line; and the only way to open the region to popular sovereignty was to repeal the ancient compact outright. This bold step Douglas was prepared to take, even at the risk of shattering the uneasy truce patched up by the Great Compromise of 1850.

Many Southerners, who had not conceived of Kansas as slave soil, rose to the bait. Here was a chance to gain one more slave state. The pliable President Pierce, under the thumb of Southern advisers, threw his full weight behind the Kansas-Nebraska Bill.

But the Missouri Compromise, now thirty-four years old, could not be brushed aside lightly. Whatever Congress passes it can repeal, but by this time the North had come to regard the sectional pact as almost as sacred as the Constitution itself. Free-soil members of Congress struck back furiously. They met their match in the violently gesticulating Douglas, who was the ablest rough-and-tumble debater of his generation. Employing twisted logic and oratorical fireworks, he rammed the bill through Congress, with strong support from many Southerners. So heated were political passions that bloodshed was barely averted. Some members carried a concealed revolver or a bowie knife—or both.

Douglas's motives in prodding anew the snarling dog of slavery have long puzzled historians. His

Douglas Hatches a Slavery Problem. Note the already hatched Missouri Compromise, Squatter Sovereignty, and Filibustering (in Cuba), and the about-to-hatch Free Kansas and Dred Scott decision. So bitter was the outcry against Douglas at the time of the Kansas-Nebraska controversy that he claimed with exaggeration that he could have traveled from Boston to Chicago at night by the light from his burning effigies. Republican cartoon.

personal interests have already been mentioned. In addition, his foes accused him of angling for the presidency in 1856. Yet his admirers have argued plausibly in his defense that if he had not championed the ill-omened bill, someone else would have.

The truth seems to be that Douglas acted somewhat impulsively and recklessly. His heart did not bleed over the issue of slavery, and he declared repeatedly that he did not care whether it was voted up or down in the territories. What he failed to perceive was that hundreds of thousands of his fellow countrymen in the North *did* feel deeply on this moral issue. They regarded the repeal of the Missouri Compromise as an intolerable breach of faith, and they would henceforth resist to the last trench all future demands of the South for slave territory.

A genuine statesman, like a skillful chess player, must foresee the possible effects of his moves. Douglas predicted a "hell of a storm," but he grossly underestimated its proportions. His critics in the North, branding him a "Judas" and a "traitor," greeted his name with frenzied boos, hisses, and "three groans for Doug." But he still enjoyed a high degree of popularity among his own loyal following in the Democratic party, especially in Illinois, a stronghold of popular sovereignty.

Congress Legislates a Civil War

The Kansas-Nebraska Act—a curtain raiser to a terrible drama—was one of the most momentous measures ever to pass Congress. By one way of reckoning, it led directly down the slippery slope to Civil War.

Anti-slavery Northerners were angered by what they condemned as an act of bad faith by the "Neb-rascals" and their "Nebrascality." All future compromise with the South would be immeasurably more difficult, and without compromise there was bound to be conflict.

Henceforth the Fugitive Slave Law of 1850, previously enforced in the North only halfheartedly, was a dead letter. The Kansas-Nebraska Act wrecked two compromises: that of 1820, which it repealed specifically, and that of 1850, which Northern opinion repealed indirectly. Emerson wrote, "The Fugitive [Slave] Law did much to unglue the eyes of men, and now the Nebraska Bill leaves us staring."

Northern abolitionists and Southern "fire-eaters" alike were stirred to new outbursts. The growing legion of anti-slaveryites gained numerous recruits, who resented the grasping move by the "slavocracy" for Kansas. The Southerners, in turn, became inflamed when the free-soilers attempted to control Kansas, contrary to the presumed "deal."

The proud Democrats—a party now over half a century old—were shattered by the Kansas-Nebraska Act. They managed to elect a President two years later, but he was the last one they were

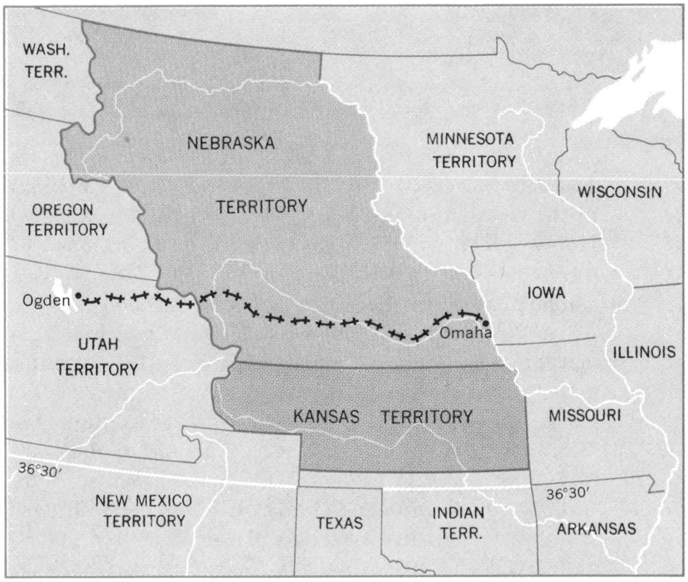

KANSAS AND NEBRASKA, 1854
Future Union Pacific Railroad (completed 1869) is shown. Note the Missouri Compromise line of 36°30′ (1820).

to boost into the White House for twenty-eight long years.

Undoubtedly the most durable offspring of the Kansas-Nebraska blunder was the new Republican party. It sprang up spontaneously in the Middle West, notably in Wisconsin and Michigan, as a mighty moral protest against the gains of slavery. Gathering together dissatisfied elements, it soon included disgruntled Whigs (including Abraham Lincoln), Democrats, Free-Soilers, Know-Nothings, and other foes of the Kansas-Nebraska Act. The hodgepodge party spread eastward with the rapidity of a prairie fire and with the zeal of a religious crusade. Unheard of and unheralded at the beginning of 1854, it elected a Republican speaker of the House of Representatives within two years. Never really a third-party movement, it erupted with such force as to become almost overnight the second major political party—and a purely sectional one at that.

At long last the dreaded sectional rift had appeared. The new Republican party would not be allowed south of the Mason-Dixon line. Countless Southerners subscribed wholeheartedly to the sentiment that it was "a nigger stealing, stinking, putrid, abolition party." The Union was in dire peril.

VARYING VIEWPOINTS

Historical treatments of the 1850s have long reflected the major controversy of that decade: whether the principal issue was slavery itself or simply the *expansion* of slavery into the Western territories. In short, did slavery need to be abolished or merely contained? Historians have generally emphasized the geographical factor, describing a contest for control of the territories, and for control of the central government that disposed of those territories. But recently some analysts, probably reflecting the pro–civil rights agitation of the times, have stressed broader issues, including morality. In this view the territorial question was real enough, but it also symbolized a pervasive threat by the slave-power to the "free" Northern way of life. In the end, the problems of Southern slavery and Western "free soil" proved inseparable and insoluble, except by war.

SELECT READINGS

The best account of the events of the 1850s is David Potter's masterful *The Impending Crisis, 1848–1861* (1976). Sketchy but penetrating is Roy F. Nichols, *The Stakes of Power, 1845–1877* (1961); see also his more detailed *The Disruption of American Democracy* (1948). Comprehensive treatments may be found in J. G. Randall and David Donald, *The Civil War and Reconstruction* (rev. ed., 1969), and Allan Nevins, *Ordeal of the Union* (2 vols., 1947). See also A. O. Craven, *The Coming of the Civil War* (2nd ed., 1957), his *Civil War in the Making* (1959), and his *Growth of Southern Nationalism* (1953). David Potter also offers illuminating insights in *The South and the Sectional Conflict* (1968). The standard work is Holman Hamilton, *Prologue to Conflict: The Crisis and Compromise of 1850* (1964). The emergence of the Republican party can be studied in Eric Foner's brilliant discussion of ideology, *Free Soil, Free Labor, Free Men* (1970), in J. G. Rayback's analysis of the election of 1848, *Free Soil* (1970), and in Michael Holt's perceptive *Forging a Majority: The Formation of the Republican Party in Pittsburgh* (1969). Foner's ideas can be pursued further in his *Politics and Ideology in the Age of the Civil War* (1980), while Holt has developed his views in *The Political Crisis of the 1850s* (1978), an unusually provocative book. Robert W. Johannsen, *Stephen Douglas* (1973), analyzes with perception the "Little Giant's" motives. Other useful biographies are M. L. Coit, *John C. Calhoun* (1950), C. M. Wiltse, *John C. Calhoun: Sectionalist* (1951), R. J. Rayback, *Millard Fillmore* (1959), R. F. Nichols, *Franklin Pierce* (1958), and G. G. Van Deusen, *William Henry Seward* (1967).

21

Drifting Toward Disunion, 1854–1861

A house divided against itself cannot stand. I believe this government cannot endure permanently half slave and half free.

ABRAHAM LINCOLN, 1858

Stowe and Helper: Literary Incendiaries

Sectional tensions were further strained in 1852, and later, by an inky phenomenon. Harriet Beecher Stowe, a wisp of a woman and the mother of a half-dozen children, published her heart-rending novel, *Uncle Tom's Cabin.* Dismayed by the passage of the Fugitive Slave Law, she was determined to awaken the North to the wickedness of slavery by laying bare its terrible inhumanity. Her book, though lacking high literary quality, was distinguished by powerful imagery and touching pathos. "God wrote it," she explained in later years.

The success of the novel at home and abroad was sensational. Several hundred thousand copies were published in the first year, and the totals soon ran into the millions as the tale was translated into more than a score of languages. It was also put on the stage in "Tom shows" for lengthy runs. No other novel in American history—perhaps in all history—can be compared with it as a political force. To millions of people it made slavery appear almost as evil as it really was.

When Mrs. Stowe was introduced to President Lincoln in 1862, he reportedly remarked with twinkling eyes, "So you're the little woman who wrote the book that made this great war." The truth is that *Uncle Tom's Cabin* helped start the Civil War—and win it. The South condemned that "vile wretch in petticoats" when it learned that hundreds of thousands of fellow Americans were reading and believing her "unfair" indictment. Mrs. Stowe had never witnessed slavery at first hand in the Deep South, but she had seen it briefly during a visit to Kentucky, and she had lived for many years in Ohio, a center of Underground Railway activity.

Harriet Beecher Stowe (1811–1896). She was a remarkable woman whose pen helped to change the course of history. (The Metropolitan Museum of Art, Gift of I. N. Phelps Stokes, Edward S. Hawes, Alice Mary Hawes, and Marion Augusta Hawes, 1937)

In the closing scenes of Mrs. Stowe's novel, Uncle Tom's brutal master, Simon Legree, orders the $1,200 slave savagely beaten (to death) by two fellow slaves. Through tears and blood Tom exclaims, "No! no! no! my soul an't yours, Mas'r! You haven't bought it—ye can't buy it! It's been bought and paid for by One that is able to keep it. No matter, no matter, you can't harm me!" "I can't!" said Legree, with a sneer; "we'll see—we'll see! Here, Sambo, Quimbo, give this dog such a breakin' in as he won't get over this month!"

Uncle Tom, endearing and enduring, left a profound impression on the North. Uncounted thousands of readers swore that henceforth they would have nothing to do with the enforcement of the Fugitive Slave Law. The tale was devoured by millions of impressionable youths in the 1850s—the later Boys in Blue who volunteered to fight the Civil War through to its grim finale. The memory of a beaten and dying Uncle Tom helped sustain them in their determination to wipe out the plague of slavery.

The novel was immensely popular abroad, especially in England and France. Countless readers wept over the kindly Tom and the angelic Eva, while deploring the brutal Simon Legree. When the guns in America finally began to boom, the common people of England sensed that the triumph of the North would spell the end of the black curse. The governments in London and Paris seriously considered intervening in behalf of the South, but they were sobered by the realization that many of their own people, aroused by the "Tom-mania," might not support them.

Another trouble-brewing book appeared in 1857, five years after the debut of Uncle Tom. Entitled *The Impending Crisis of the South,* it was written by Hinton R. Helper, a non-aristocratic white from North Carolina. Hating both slavery and blacks, he attempted to prove by an array of statistics that indirectly the non-slaveholding

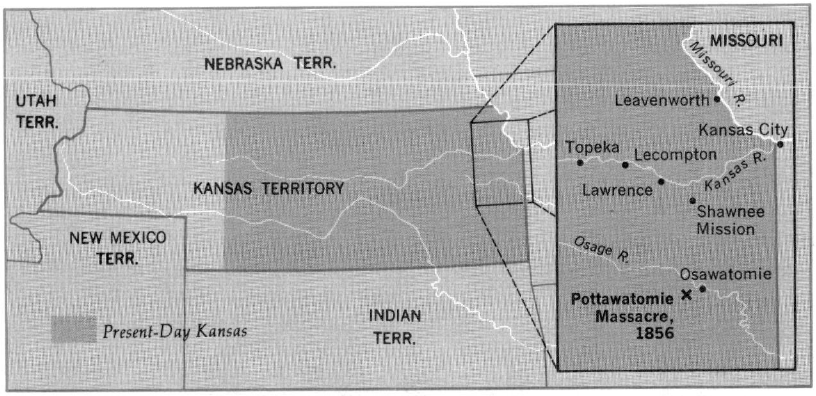

BLEEDING KANSAS, 1854–1860
Abolitionist newspapers had a field day reporting Kansas "atrocities" hatched by the proslavery party. Where facts were lacking, imaginations took over. Victims were portrayed as law-abiding, antislavery citizens, while aggressors were invariably "border ruffians," or "hired henchmen," maddened by whiskey. One notorious murder was later proved to have resulted from a purely personal quarrel between two men, *both* of whom were free-soilers.

whites were the ones who suffered most from the millstone of slavery. Unable to secure a publisher in the South, he finally managed to find one in the North.

Helper's influence was negligible among the poorer whites to whom he addressed his message. His book, with its "dirty allusions," was banned in the South, where book-burning parties were held. But in the North countless thousands of copies, many in condensed form, were distributed as campaign literature by the Republicans. Southerners were further embittered when they learned that their Northern brethren were spreading these wicked "lies." Thus the sons of the South, reacting much as they did to *Uncle Tom's Cabin,* became increasingly unwilling to sleep under the same federal roof with their hostile Yankee bedfellows.

The North-South Contest for Kansas

The rolling plains of Kansas had meanwhile been providing a horrible example of the workings of popular sovereignty, although admittedly under abnormal conditions.

Newcomers who ventured into Kansas were a motley lot. Most of the Northerners were just ordinary westward-moving pioneers in search of richer lands beyond the sunset. But a small part of the inflow was financed by groups of Northern abolitionists or free-soilers. The most famous of these anti-slavery organizations was the New England Emigrant Aid Company, which sent about 2,000 persons to the troubled area to forestall the South—and also to make a profit. Shouting "Ho for Kansas," many of them carried the deadly new breech-loading Sharps rifles, nicknamed "Beecher's Bibles" after the prominent clergyman who had helped raise money for their purchase. Many of the Kansas-bound pioneers sang Whittier's marching song (1854):

> We cross the prairie as of old
> The pilgrims crossed the sea,
> To make the West, as they the East,
> The homestead of the free!

Southern spokesmen, now more than ordinarily touchy, raised furious cries of betrayal. They had supported the Kansas-Nebraska scheme of Douglas with the informal understanding that Kansas would become slave and Nebraska free. The Northern "Nebrascals," allegedly by foul means, were now apparently out to "abolitionize" *both* Kansas and Nebraska.

A few Southern hotheads, quick to respond in kind, attempted to "assist" small groups of well-armed slaveowners to Kansas. Some carried banners proclaiming:

> Let Yankees tremble, abolitionists fall,
> Our motto is, "Give Southern Rights to All."

But planting blacks on Kansas soil was a losing game. The slave was valuable and volatile property, and foolish indeed were owners who would take him where bullets were flying, and where the soil might be voted free under popular sovereignty. The census of 1860 found only two slaves among 107,000 souls in all the territory, and only fifteen in Nebraska. There was much force in the charge that the whole quarrel over slavery in the territories revolved around "an imaginary Negro in an impossible place."

Crisis conditions in Kansas rapidly worsened. When the day came in 1855 to elect members of the first territorial legislature, pro-slavery "border ruffians" poured in from Missouri to vote early and often. The slavery men triumphed, and then set up their own puppet government at Shawnee Mission. The free-soilers, unable to stomach this fraudulent conspiracy, established an extra-legal regime of their own in Topeka. The confused Kansan thus had his choice between two governments —one based on fraud, the other on illegality.

Tension mounted as men also feuded over conflicting land claims. The breaking point came in 1856 when a gang of pro-slavery raiders, alleging provocation, shot up and burned a part of the free-soil town of Lawrence. This outrage was but the prelude to a bloodier tragedy.

John Brown (1800–1859). A militant abolitionist, Brown became perhaps the most sung-about man up to that time, except Jesus. From a primitive photograph (daguerreotype) taken in 1856. (Courtesy Kansas Historical Society.)

Kansas in Convulsion

The fanatical figure of John Brown now stalked upon the Kansas battlefield. Spare, gray-bearded, iron-willed, and narrowly ignorant, he was dedicated to the abolitionist cause. The power of his glittering gray eyes was such, so he claimed, that his stare could force a dog or cat to slink out of a room. Becoming involved in dubious dealings, including horse stealing, he moved to Kansas from Ohio with a part of his large family. Brooding over the recent attack on Lawrence, "Old Brown" of Osawatomie led a band of his followers to Pottawatomie Creek, in May 1856. There they literally hacked to pieces five surprised men, allegedly pro-slaveryites. This fiendish butchery, clearly the product of a deranged mind, besmirched the free-soil cause and brought vicious retaliation from the pro-slavery men.

Civil war in Kansas, which thus flared forth in 1856, continued intermittently until it merged with the large-scale Civil War of 1861–1865. Altogether, the Kansas conflict destroyed millions of dollars' worth of property, paralyzed agriculture in certain areas, and cost scores of lives.

Yet by 1857 Kansas had enough people, chiefly

> John Brown, an avid reader of the Old Testament, evidently believed in the principle of an eye for an eye, and a hand for a hand. A surviving son of one of his victims later testified under oath that "I found my father and one brother, William, lying dead in the road . . . I saw my other brother lying dead on the ground . . . in the grass, near a ravine; his fingers were cut off and his arms were cut off; his head was cut open; there was a hole in his breast. William's head was cut open, and a hole was in his jaw . . . and a hole was also in his side. My father was shot in the forehead and stabbed in the breast."

free-soilers, to apply for statehood on a popular-sovereignty basis. The pro-slavery men, then in the saddle, devised a tricky document known as the Lecompton Constitution. The people were not allowed to vote for or against the constitution as a whole, but for the constitution either "with slavery" or "with no slavery." If they voted against slavery, one of the remaining provisions of the constitution would protect the owners of slaves already in Kansas. So whatever the outcome, there would still be black bondage in Kansas. Many free-soilers, infuriated by this trick, boycotted the polls. Left to themselves, the slaveryites approved the constitution with slavery late in 1857.

The scene next shifted to Washington. President Pierce had been succeeded by the no-less-pliable James Buchanan, who was also strongly under Southern influence. Blind to sharp divisions within his own Democratic party, Buchanan threw the weight of his administration behind the notorious Lecompton Constitution. But Senator Douglas, who had championed true popular sovereignty, would have none of this semi-popular fraudulency. Deliberately tossing away his strong support in the South for the presidency, he fought courageously for fair play and democratic principles. The outcome was a compromise which, in effect, submitted the *entire* Lecompton Constitution to a popular vote. The free-soil men thereupon thronged to the polls and snowed it under. But Kansas was denied statehood until 1861, when the Southern secessionists left Congress.

President Buchanan, by antagonizing the numerous Douglas Democrats in the North, hopelessly divided the once-powerful Democratic party. Until then, it had been the only remaining *national* party, for the Whigs were dead and the Republicans were sectional. With the disruption of the Democrats came the snapping of one of the last important strands in the rope that was barely binding the Union together.

"Bully" Brooks and His Bludgeon

"Bleeding Kansas" also splattered blood on the floor of the United States Senate in 1856. Senator Charles Sumner of Massachusetts, a tall and imposing figure, was a leading abolitionist—one of the few prominent in political life. Highly edu-

SOUTHERN CHIVALRY — ARGUMENT VERSUS CLUB'S.
KANSAS

Sumner Beaten by Brooks. Note that the cartoonist has two of the senators smiling or laughing, and one of them preventing interference with his cane. Note also that Sumner is defending himself with a quill pen while Brooks is wielding a club. (Courtesy the New York Public Library, Astor, Lenox, and Tilden Foundations.)

cated but cold, humorless, intolerant, and egotistical, he had made himself one of the most disliked men in the Senate. Brooding over the turbulent miscarriage of popular sovereignty, he delivered a blistering speech entitled "The Crime against Kansas." Sparing few epithets, he condemned the pro-slavery men as "hirelings picked from the drunken spew and vomit of an uneasy civilization." He also referred insultingly to South Carolina, and to her white-haired Senator Butler, one of the best-liked members of the Senate.

Hot-tempered Congressman Brooks, of South Carolina, now took vengeance into his own hands. Ordinarily gracious and gallant, he resented the insults to his state and to her senator, a distant cousin. His code of honor called for a duel, but in the South one fought only with one's social equals. And had not the coarse language of the Yankee, who probably would reject a challenge, dropped him to a lower order? To Brooks, the only alternative was to chastise the senator as one would beat an unruly dog. On May 22, 1856, he approached Sumner, then sitting at his Senate desk, and pounded the orator with a heavy cane until it broke. The victim fell bleeding and unconscious to the floor, while several nearby senators refrained from interfering.

Sumner had been provocatively insulting, but this counter-outrage put Brooks in the wrong. The House of Representatives could not muster enough votes to expel the Carolinian, but he resigned and was triumphantly re-elected. Southern admirers deluged Brooks with canes, some of them gold-headed, to replace the one that had been broken. The injuries to Sumner's head and nervous system were serious. He was forced to leave his seat for three and a half years and go to Europe for treatment that was both painful and costly. Meanwhile Massachusetts defiantly re-elected him, leaving his seat eloquently empty. Bleeding Sumner was thus joined with Bleeding Kansas as a political issue.

The free-soil North was mightily aroused against the "uncouth" and "cowardly" "Bully" Brooks. Copies of Sumner's abusive speech, otherwise doomed to obscurity, were sold by the tens of thousands. Every blow that struck the senator doubtless made thousands of Republican votes. The South, although not unanimous in approving Brooks, was angered not only because Sumner had made such an intemperate speech but because it had been so extravagantly applauded in the North.

Regarding the Brooks assault on Sumner, one of the more moderate anti-slavery journals (*Illinois State Journal*) declared, "Brooks and his Southern allies have deliberately adopted the monstrous creed than any man who dares to utter sentiments which they deem wrong or unjust, shall be brutally assailed. . . . " One of the milder Southern responses came from the *Petersburg* (Virginia) *Intelligencer*: "Although Mr. Brooks ought to have selected some other spot for the altercation than the Senate chamber, if he had broken every bone in Sumner's carcass it would have been a just retribution upon this slanderer of the South and her individual citizens."

The Sumner-Brooks clash and the ensuing reactions revealed how dangerously inflamed passions were becoming, North and South. It was ominous that the cultured Sumner should have used the language of a barroom bully, and that the gentlemanly Brooks should have employed the tactics and tools of a thug. Emotion was displacing thought. The blows rained on Sumner's head were, broadly speaking, among the first blows of the Civil War.

"Old Buck" versus "The Pathfinder"

With bullets whining in Kansas, the Democrats met in Cincinnati to nominate their presidential standard-bearer of 1856. They shied away from both the weak-kneed President Pierce and the dynamic Douglas. Each was too heavily blackened

Frémont, the Explorer, in Heroic Pose. It was said with exaggeration that from the ashes of his campfires have sprung cities. Actually he was a pathmarker as much as a pathfinder; a great deal of the land he explored had already been traversed by fur-seeking "mountain men." (Library of Congress.)

by the Kansas-Nebraska Act. The delegates finally chose James Buchanan (pronounced by many *Buck*-anan), who was muscular, white-haired, and tall (6 feet; 1.83 meters), with a short neck and a protruding chin. Because of an eye defect, he carried his head cocked to one side. As a well-to-do Pennsylvania lawyer, he had been serving as minister to London during the recent Kansas-Nebraska uproar. He was therefore "Kansasless," and hence relatively enemyless. But in a crisis that called for giants, "Old Buck" Buchanan was mediocre, irresolute, confused.

Delegates of the fast-growing Republican party met in Philadelphia with bubbling enthusiasm. "Higher Law" Seward was their most conspicuous leader, and he probably would have arranged to win the nomination had he been confident that this was a "Republican year." The final choice was Captain John C. Frémont, the so-called Pathfinder of the West—a dashing but erratic explorer-soldier-surveyor who was supposed to find the path to the White House. The black-bearded and flashy young adventurer was virtually without political experience, but like Buchanan he was not tarred with the Kansas brush. The Republican platform came out vigorously against the extension of slavery into the territories, while the Democrats declared no less emphatically for popular sovereignty.

An ugly dose of anti-foreignism was injected into the campaign, even though slavery extension loomed largest. The recent horde of immigrants from Ireland and Germany had alarmed "nativists," as many old-stock Protestants were called. They organized the American party, known also as the Know-Nothing party because of its secretiveness, and in 1856 nominated the lackluster ex-President Fillmore. Anti-foreign and anti-Catholic, these superpatriots adopted the slogan "Americans Must Rule America." Remnants of the dying Whig party likewise endorsed Fillmore, and they and the Know-Nothings threatened to cut into Republican strength.

Republicans fell in behind Frémont with the zeal of crusaders. Shouting "We Follow the Pathfinder" and "We Are Buck Hunting," they organized glee clubs which sang (to the tune of the "Marseillaise"):

> Arise, arise ye brave!
> And let our war-cry be,
> Free speech, free press, free soil, free men,
> Fre-mont and victory!

"And free love," sneered the Buchanan men ("Buchaneers").

Mudslinging bespattered both candidates. "Old Fogy" Buchanan was assailed because he was a bachelor: the fiancée of his youth had died after a lovers' quarrel. Frémont was reviled because of his illegitimate birth, for his young mother had left her elderly husband, a Virginia planter, to run away with a French adventurer. In due season she gave birth to John in Savannah, Georgia—

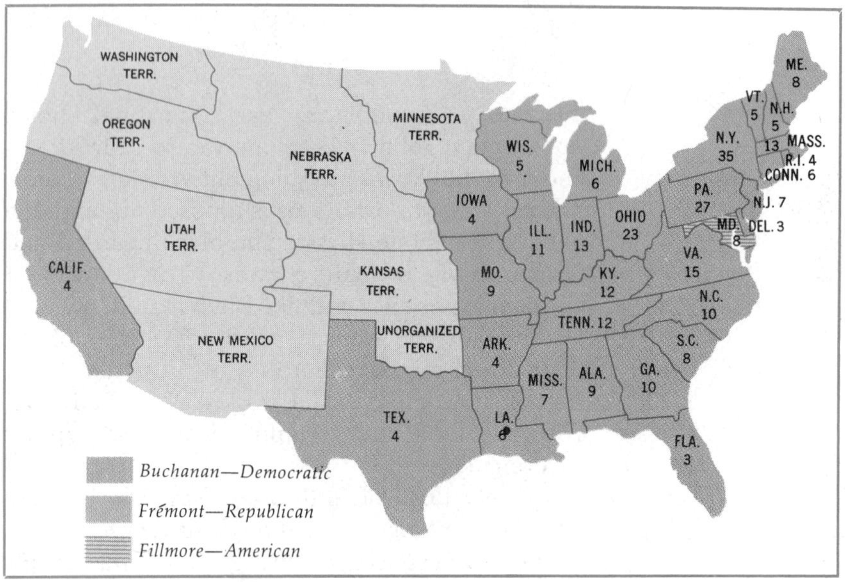

PRESIDENTIAL ELECTION OF 1856 (with electoral vote by state)
The fateful split of 1860 was here foreshadowed. The regional polarization in 1856, shown here, was to be even sharper four years later, as illustrated by the maps on p. 381.

further to shame the South. More harmful to Frémont was the allegation, which alienated many bigoted Know-Nothings and other "nativists," that he was a Roman Catholic.

The Electoral Fruits of 1856

A bland Buchanan, although polling less than a majority of the popular vote, won handily. His tally in the Electoral College was 174 to 114 for Frémont, with Fillmore garnering 8. The popular vote was 1,838,169 for Buchanan to 1,341,264 for Frémont, with 874,534 for Fillmore.

Why did the aroused Republicans go down to defeat? Frémont lost much ground because of grave doubts as to his honesty, capacity, and sound judgment. Perhaps more damaging were the violent threats of the Southern "fire-eaters" that the election of a sectional "Black Republican" would be a declaration of war on them, forcing them to secede. Many Northerners, anxious to save both the Union and their profitable business connections with the South, were thus intimidated into voting for Buchanan. Innate conservatism triumphed, assisted by so-called Southern bullyism.

It was probably fortunate for the Union that secession and civil war did not come in 1856, following a Republican victory. Frémont, an ill-balanced and second-rate figure, was no Abraham Lincoln. And in 1856 the North was more willing to let the South depart in peace than in 1860. Dramatic events from 1856 to 1860 were to arouse hundreds of thousands of still-apathetic Northerners to a fighting pitch.

Yet the Republicans in 1856 could rightfully claim a "victorious defeat." The new party—a mere two-year-old infant—had made an astonishing showing against the well-oiled Democratic machine. Whittier exulted:

Then sound again the bugles,
Call the muster-roll anew;
If months have well-nigh won the field,
What may not four years do?

> Spiritual overtones developed in the Frémont campaign, especially over slavery. The *Independent,* a foremost religious journal, saw in Frémont's nomination "the good hand of God." As election day neared it declared, "Fellow-Christians! Remember it is for Christ, for the nation, and for the world that you vote at this election! Vote as you pray! Pray as you vote!"

The election of 1856 cast a long shadow forward, and politicians, North and South, peered anxiously toward 1860.

The Dred Scott Bombshell

The Dred Scott decision, handed down by the Supreme Court on March 6, 1857, abruptly ended the two-day presidential honeymoon of the unlucky bachelor, James Buchanan. This pronouncement was one of the opening paper-gun blasts of the Civil War.

Basically, the case was simple. Dred Scott, a black slave, had lived with his master for five years in Illinois and Wisconsin Territory. Backed by interested abolitionists, he sued for freedom on the basis of his long residence on free soil.

The Supreme Court proceeded to turn a simple legal case into a complex political issue. It ruled, not surprisingly, that Dred Scott was a black slave and not a citizen, and hence could not sue in federal courts.* The tribunal could then have thrown out the case on these technical grounds alone. But a majority decided to go further, under the leadership of emaciated Chief Justice Taney from the slave state of Maryland. A sweeping judgment on the larger issue of slavery in the territories seemed desirable, particularly to forestall arguments by two free-soil members who were preparing dissenting opinions. The pro-Southern majority evidently hoped in this way to lay the vexed question to rest.

Taney's thunderclap rocked the free-soilers back on their heels. A majority of the Court had decreed that because a slave was private property, he could be taken into *any* territory and held there. The reasoning was that the 5th Amendment clearly forbade Congress to deprive persons of their property without due process of law. The Court, to be consistent, went further. The Missouri Compromise, banning slavery north of 36°30′, had been repealed three years earlier by the Kansas-Nebraska Act. But its spirit was still venerated in the North. Now the Court had ruled that the Compromise of 1820 had been unconstitutional all along: Congress had no power to ban slavery from the territories, regardless even of what the territorial legislatures themselves might want.

*This part of the ruling, denying blacks their citizenship, seriously menaced the precarious position of the South's quarter-million "free" blacks.

> Taney's decision, in the case of Dred Scott, referred to the status of slaves when the Constitution was adopted: "They had for more than a century before been regarded as beings of an inferior order; and altogether unfit to associate with the white race, either in social or political relations; and so far inferior that they had no rights which the white man was bound to respect. . . . This opinion was at that time fixed and universal in the civilized portion of the white race." Taney's statement was historically sound as it related to the United States, but highly offensive to anti-slaveryites when applied to conditions in 1857.

A cry of delight broke from Southern throats over this unexpected victory. Champions of popular sovereignty were aghast, including Senator Douglas and a host of Northern Democrats. Another lethal wedge was thus driven between the Northern and Southern wings of the once-united Democratic party.

Foes of slavery extension, especially the Republicans, were infuriated by the Dred Scott setback. Their chief rallying cry had been the banishing of bondage from the territories. They now insisted that the ruling of the Court was merely an opinion, not a decision, and just as binding as the views of a "Southern debating society." Republican defiance of the exalted tribunal was intensified by an awareness that a majority of its members were Southerners, and by the conviction that it had debased itself—"sullied the ermine"—by wallowing in the gutter of politics.

Southerners in turn were inflamed by all this defiance. They began to wonder anew how much longer they could remain married to a section that refused to honor the Supreme Court, to say nothing of the constitutional compact which had established it.

The Financial Crash of 1857

Bitterness caused by the Dred Scott decision was deepened by hard times, which dampened a period of feverish prosperity. Late in 1857 a panic burst about Buchanan's harassed head. The storm was not so bad economically as the Panic of 1837, but psychologically it was probably the worst of the 19th Century.

What caused the crash? Inpouring California gold played its part by helping to inflate the currency. The demands of the Crimean War had overstimulated the growing of grain, while frenzied speculation in land and railroads had further ripped the economic fabric. When the collapse came, over 5,000 businesses failed within a year. Unemployment, accompanied by hunger meetings in urban areas, was widespread. "Bread or Death" was one desperate slogan.

The North, including the grain growers, was hardest hit. The South, enjoying favorable cotton prices abroad, rode out the storm with flying colors. Panic conditions seemed further proof that cotton *was* king, and that his economic kingdom was stronger than that of the North. This fatal delusion helped drive the overconfident Southerners closer to a shooting showdown.

A New York Panic Scene, 1857

Financial distress in the North, especially in agriculture, gave a new vigor to the demand for free farms of 160 acres from the public domain. For several decades interested groups had been urging the federal government to abandon its ancient policy of selling the land for revenue. Instead, the argument ran, acreage should be given outright to the sturdy pioneers as a reward for risking health and life to develop it.

A scheme to make outright gifts of homesteads encountered two-pronged opposition. Eastern industrialists had long been unfriendly to free land; some of them feared that their underpaid workmen would be drained off to the West. The South was even more bitterly opposed, partly because gang-labor slavery could not flourish on a mere 160 acres. Free farms would merely fill up the territories more rapidly with free-soilers, and further tip the political balance against the South. In 1860, after years of debate, Congress finally passed a homestead act—one that made public lands available at a nominal sum of twenty-five cents an acre. But it was stabbed to death by the veto pen of Buchanan, near whose elbow sat leading Southern sympathizers.

The Panic of 1857 also created a clamor for higher tariff rates. Several months before the crash, Congress, embarrassed by a large Treasury surplus, had enacted the Tariff of 1857. The new law, responding to pressures from the South, reduced duties to about 20 percent on dutiable goods—the lowest point since the War of 1812. Hardly had the revised rates been placed on the books when financial distress descended like a black pall. Northern manufacturers, many of them Republicans, noisily blamed their misfortunes on the low tariff. As the surplus melted away in the Treasury, industrialists in the North pointed to the need for higher duties. But what really concerned them was their desire for increased protection. Thus the Panic of 1857 gave the Republicans two sure-fire issues for the election of 1860: protection for the unprotected and farms for the farmless.

An Illinois Rail Splitter Emerges

The Illinois senatorial election of 1858 now claimed the national spotlight. Senator Douglas's term was about to expire, and the Republicans decided to run against him a rustic Springfield lawyer, one Abraham Lincoln. The candidate–6 feet 4 inches (1.93 meters) in height and 180 pounds (81.7 kilograms) in weight–presented an awkward but arresting figure. His legs, arms, and neck were grotesquely long; his head was crowned by coarse, black, and unruly hair; and his face was sad, sunken, and weather-beaten.

Lincoln was no silver-spoon child of destiny. Born in a Kentucky log cabin to impoverished parents, he attended a frontier school for not more than a year; being an avid reader, he was mainly self-educated. All his life he said "git," "thar," "heered." Though narrow-chested and somewhat stoop-shouldered, he shone in his frontier community as a wrestler and weight-lifter, and spent some time, among other pioneering pursuits, as a splitter of logs for fence rails. A superb teller of earthy and amusing stories, he would oddly enough plunge into protracted periods of melancholy.

Lincoln's private and professional life was not especially noteworthy. He married "above himself" socially, into the influential Todd family of Kentucky; and the temperamental outbursts of his high-strung wife, known by her enemies as the "she wolf," helped to school him in patience and forbearance. After reading a little law, he gradually emerged as one of the dozen or so better-known trial lawyers in Illinois, although still accustomed to carrying important papers in his stovepipe hat. He was widely referred to as "Honest Abe," partly because he would refuse cases that he could not conscientiously defend.

The rise of Lincoln as a political figure was less than rocket-like. After making his mark in the Illinois legislature as a Whig politician of the log-rolling variety, he served one undistinguished term in Congress, 1847–1849. Until 1854, when he was forty-five years of age, he had done nothing to establish a claim to statesmanship. But the passage of the Kansas-Nebraska Act in that year lighted within him unexpected fires. After mounting the Republican bandwagon, he emerged as one of the foremost politicians and orators of the Northwest. At the Philadelphia convention of 1856, where Frémont was nominated, Lincoln actually received 110 votes for the vice-presidential nomination.

> In 1832, when Lincoln became a candidate for the Illinois legislature, he delivered a speech at a political gathering: "I presume you all know who I am. I am humble Abraham Lincoln. I have been solicited by many friends to become a candidate for the Legislature. My [Whiggish] politics are short and sweet, like the old woman's dance. I am in favor of a national bank. I am in favor of the internal-improvement system, and a high protective tariff. These are my sentiments and political principles. If elected, I shall be thankful; if not, it will be all the same." He was elected two years later.

The Great Debate: Lincoln versus Douglas

Lincoln, as Republican nominee for the Senate seat, boldly challenged Douglas to a series of joint debates. This was a rash act, because the stumpy senator was probably the nation's most devastating debater. Douglas promptly accepted the challenge, and seven meetings were arranged from August to October 1858.

At first glance, the two contestants seemed ill-matched. The well-groomed and polished Douglas, with stocky figure and bullish voice, presented a striking contrast to the lanky Lincoln, with his

A Lincoln-Douglas Debate. On one occasion, Lincoln charged that Douglas's logic would prove that a horse chestnut was a chestnut horse.

Abraham Lincoln, A Most Uncommon Common Man. Early photograph (daguerreotype) by Mathew B. Brady, distinguished photographer of the era.

baggy clothes and unshined shoes. Moreover, "Old Abe," as he was called in both affection and derision, had a piercing, high-pitched voice, and was often ill at ease when he began to speak. But as he threw himself into an argument, he seemed to grow in height, while his glowing eyes lighted up a rugged face. He relied on logic rather than on table-thumping.

The most famous of the forensic clashes came at Freeport, Illinois, where Lincoln neatly impaled his opponent on the horns of a dilemma. Suppose, he queried, the people of a territory should vote slavery down? The Supreme Court in the Dred Scott decision had decreed that they could not. Who would prevail, the Court or the people?

Legend to the contrary, Douglas and some Southerners had already publicly answered the Freeport question. The "Little Giant" therefore did not hesitate to meet the issue head on, honestly and consistently. He replied that no matter how the Supreme Court ruled, slavery would stay down if the people voted it down. Laws to protect slavery would have to be passed by the territorial legislatures. These would not be forthcoming in the absence of popular approval, and black bondage would soon disappear. Douglas, in truth, had American history on his side. Where public opinion does not support the federal government, as in the case of Jefferson's embargo, the law is almost impossible to enforce.

The upshot was that Douglas defeated Lincoln for the Senate seat. The "Little Giant's" loyalty to popular sovereignty, which still had a powerful appeal in Illinois, probably was decisive. Senators were then chosen by state legislatures; and in the general election that followed the debates, more pro-Douglas members were elected than pro-Lincoln members. Yet thanks to inequitable apportionment, the districts carried by Douglas men represented a smaller population than those carried by the Lincoln men. "Honest Abe" thus won a clear moral victory.

Lincoln possibly was playing for larger stakes than just the senatorship. Although defeated, he had shambled into the national limelight in company with the most prominent Northern politicians. Newspapers in the East published detailed accounts of the debates, and Lincoln began to emerge as a potential Republican nominee for President. But Douglas, in winning Illinois, hurt his chances of winning the presidency, while further splitting his splintering party. After his opposition to the Lecompton Constitution for Kansas and his further defiance of the Supreme Court at Freeport, Southern Democrats were determined to break up the party (and the Union) rather than accept him. The Lincoln-Douglas debate platform thus proved to be one of the preliminary battlefields of the Civil War.

The efforts of the Douglasites to represent Lincoln as a lover of the blacks were sharply rebutted by "Old Abe" in the opening of his debate at Charleston, Illinois: "While I was at the hotel to-day an elderly gentleman called upon me to know whether I was really in favor of producing a perfect equality between the negroes and white people. [Great laughter.] . . . I will say, then, that I am not, nor ever have been, in favor of bringing about in any way the social and political equality of the white and black races; [applause] that I am not, nor ever have been, in favor of making voters or jurors of negroes, nor of qualifying them to hold office, nor to intermarry with white people. . . . I as much as any other man am in favor of having the superior position assigned to the white race."

John Brown: Murderer or Martyr?

The gaunt, grim figure of John Brown of Kansas fame now appeared again in a more terrible way. His crackbrained scheme was to invade the South secretly with a handful of followers, call upon the slaves to rise, furnish them with arms, and establish a kind of black free state as a sanctuary. Brown secured several thousand dollars for firearms from Northern abolitionists, and finally arrived in hilly western Virginia with some twenty men. At scenic Harpers Ferry he seized the federal arsenal in October 1859, incidentally killing seven innocent people, including a free black, and injuring ten or so more. But the slaves refused to rise, and the wounded Brown and the remnants of his tiny band were quickly captured.

"Old Brown" was convicted of murder and treason, after a hasty but legal trial. His presumed insanity was supported by affidavits from seventeen friends and relatives, who were trying to save his neck. Actually thirteen of his near relations were regarded as insane, including his mother and grandmother. Governor Wise of

"A Premature Movement." John Brown hands the pike to the slave and says "Follow me!" but the startled black protests that they have not finished seeding "at our house." Brown had made the fatal error of not earlier asking the slaves in question if they were willing to rise. (*Harper's Weekly,* 1859.)

Virginia would have been most wise, so his critics say, if he had only clapped the culprit into a lunatic asylum.

But Brown—"God's angry man"—was given every opportunity to pose and to enjoy martyrdom. Though probably of unsound mind, he was clever enough to see that he was worth much more to the abolitionist cause dangling from a rope than in any other way. His demeanor during the trial was dignified and courageous, his last words were to become a classic, and he marched up the scaffold steps without flinching. His conduct was so exemplary, his devotion to freedom so inflexible, that he took on an exalted character, however deplorable his previous record may have been. So the hangman's trap was sprung, and Brown plunged not into oblivion but into world fame. A memorable marching song of the impending Civil War ran:

> John Brown's body lies a-mould'ring in the grave,
> His soul is marching on.

The effects of Harpers Ferry were calamitous. In the eyes of the South, already embittered, "Osawatomie Brown" was a wholesale murderer and an apostle of treason. Many Southerners asked how they could possibly remain in the Union while a "murderous gang of abolitionists" were financing armed bands to "Brown" them. Moderate Northerners, including Republican leaders, openly deplored this mad exploit. But the South naturally concluded that the violent abolitionist view was shared by the entire North, dominated by "Brown-loving" Republicans.

Abolitionists and other ardent free-soilers were infuriated by Brown's execution. Many of them were ignorant of his bloody past and his even more bloody purposes, and they were outraged because the Virginians had hanged so earnest a reformer who was working for so righteous a cause. On the day of his execution, free-soil centers in the North tolled bells, fired guns, half-masted flags, and held mass meetings. Some spoke of "Saint John" Brown, while the serene Ralph Waldo Emerson compared the new martyr-hero with Jesus. The gallows became a cross. E. C. Stedman wrote:

> And Old Brown,
> Osawatomie Brown,
> May trouble you more than ever,
> when you've nailed his coffin down!

The ghost of the martyred Brown would not be laid to rest.

> Sentenced to be hanged, John Brown wrote to his brother, "I am quite cheerful in view of my approaching end, being fully persuaded that I am worth inconceivably more to hang than for any other purpose. . . . I count it all joy. 'I have fought the good fight,' and have, as I trust, 'finished my course.' "

The Disruption of the Democrats

Beyond question the presidential election of 1860 was the most fateful in American history. On it hung the issue of peace or civil war.

Deeply divided, the Democrats met in Charleston, South Carolina, with Douglas the leading candidate of the Northern wing of the party. But the Southern "fire-eaters" regarded him as a traitor, as a result of his unpopular stand on the Lecompton Constitution and the Freeport Doctrine. After a bitter wrangle over the platform, the delegates from most of the cotton states walked out. When the remainder could not scrape together the necessary two-thirds vote for Douglas, the entire body dissolved in confusion. The first tragic secession was the secession of Southerners from the Democratic national convention. It became habit-forming.

The Democrats tried again in Baltimore. This time the Douglas Democrats, chiefly from the

I◻II◻II◻II◻II◻II◻II◻II◻II◻II◻II◻II◻II◻II◻II◻II◻I

> Alexander H. Stephens, destined the next year to become vice-president of the new Confederacy, wrote privately in 1860 of the anti-Douglas Democrats who seceded from the Charleston convention: "The seceders intended from the beginning to rule or ruin; and when they find they cannot rule, they will then ruin. They have about enough power for this purpose; not much more; and I doubt not but they will use it. Envy, hate, jealousy, spite . . . will make devils of men. The secession movement was instigated by nothing but bad passions."

I◻II◻II◻II◻II◻II◻II◻II◻II◻II◻II◻II◻II◻II◻II◻II◻I

North, were firmly in the saddle. Many of the cotton-state delegates again took a walk, and the rest of the convention enthusiastically nominated their hero. The platform came out squarely for popular sovereignty and, as a sop to the South, against obstruction of the Fugitive Slave Law by the states.

Angered Southern Democrats promptly organized a rival convention in Baltimore, in which many of the Northern states were unrepresented. They selected as their leader the stern-jawed Vice-President, John C. Breckinridge, a man of moderate views from the border state of Kentucky. The platform favored the extension of slavery into the territories and the annexation of slave-populated Cuba.

A middle-of-the-road group, fearing for the Union, hastily organized the Constitutional Union party, sneered at as the "Do Nothing" or "Old Gentleman's" party. It consisted mainly of former Whigs and Know-Nothings, a veritable "Gathering of Graybeards." Desperately anxious to elect a compromise candidate, they met in Baltimore and nominated for the presidency John Bell of Tennessee. They went into battle ringing hand bells for Bell, and voicing the slogan, "The Union, the Constitution, and the Enforcement of the Laws."

A Rail Splitter Splits the Union

Elated Republicans were presented with a heaven-sent opportunity. Scenting victory in the breeze as their opponents split hopelessly, they gathered in Chicago in a huge, boxlike wooden structure called the Wigwam. William H. Seward was by far the best known of the contenders. But his radical utterances, including his "irrepressible conflict" speech at Rochester in 1858, had fatally injured his prospects.* His numerous enemies coined the slogan "Success Rather than Seward." Lincoln, the favorite son of Illinois, was definitely a "Mr. Second Best," but he was a stronger candidate because he had made fewer enemies. Overtaking Seward on the third ballot, he was nominated amid scenes of the wildest excitement.

The Republican platform had a seductive appeal for just about every important non-Southern group. For the free-soilers, non-extension of slavery; for the Northern manufacturers, a protective tariff; for the immigrants, no abridgment of rights; for the Northwest, a Pacific railroad; for the West, internal improvements at federal expense; and for the farmers, free homesteads from the public domain. Seductive slogans were "Vote Yourselves a Farm" and "Land for the Landless."

Southern secessionists promptly served notice that the election of the "baboon" Lincoln—the "abolitionist" rail splitter—would split the Union. "Honest Abe," though hating slavery, was no abolitionist. But he saw fit, perhaps mistakenly, to issue no statements to quiet Southern fears. He had already put himself on record; and fresh statements might stir up fresh antagonisms.

As the election campaign ground noisily forward, Lincoln enthusiasts staged roaring rallies and parades, complete with pitch-dripping torches and oilskin capes. They extolled "High Old Abe," the "Woodchopper of the West," and the "Little Giant Killer," while groaning dismally for "Poor Little Doug." Enthusiastic "Little Giants" and

*Seward had referred to an "irrepressible conflict" between slavery and freedom, though not necessarily a bloody one.

A Republican Campaign Caricature. Douglas is represented as a pious character prepared to bury Lincoln politically. (*Vanity Fair,* 1860.)

"Little Dougs" retorted with "We want a statesman, not a rail splitter, as President." Douglas himself waged a vigorous speaking campaign, even in the South, and threatened to put the hemp with his own hands around the neck of the first secessionist.

The returns, breathlessly awaited, proclaimed a sweeping victory for Lincoln (see table below).

The Electoral Upheaval of 1860

Awkward "Abe" Lincoln had run a curious race. To a greater degree than any other President (except J. Q. Adams), he was a minority President. Sixty percent of the voters preferred some other candidate. He was also a sectional President, for in ten Southern states, where he was not allowed on the ballot, he polled no popular votes. The election of 1860 was virtually two elections: one in the North, the other in the South. South Carolinians rejoiced over Lincoln's victory; they now had their excuse to secede. In winning the North the "Rail Splitter" had split off the South.

Douglas, though scraping together only 12 electoral votes, made an impressive showing. He drew important strength from all sections, and ranked a fairly close second in the popular-vote column. In fact, the Douglas Democrats and the Breckinridge Democrats together amassed 366,484 more votes than Lincoln.

A myth persists that if the Democrats had only united behind Douglas, they would have triumphed. Yet the cold figures tell a different story. Even if the "Little Giant" had received all the electoral votes cast for all three of Lincoln's opponents, the "Rail Splitter" would have won, 169 to 134, instead of 180 to 123. Lincoln still would have carried the populous states of the North and the Northwest. On the other hand, if the Democrats had not broken up, they could have entered the campaign with higher enthusiasm and better organization, and might have won.

Significantly, the verdict of the ballot box did not indicate a strong sentiment for secession. Breckinridge, while favoring the extension of slavery, was no disunionist. Although the candidate of the "fire-eaters," in the slave states he polled fewer votes than the combined strength of his opponents, Douglas and Bell. He even failed to carry his own Kentucky.

Yet the South, despite its electoral defeat, was not badly off. It still had a five-to-four majority on

Election of 1860

Candidate	*Popular Vote*	*Percentage of Popular Vote*	*Electoral Vote*
Lincoln	1,867,198	39.79%	180 (every vote of the free states except for 3 of New Jersey's 7 votes)
Douglas	1,379,434	29.40	12 (only Missouri and 3 of New Jersey's 7 votes)
Breckinridge	854,248	18.20	72 (all the cotton states)
Bell	591,658	12.61	39 (Virginia, Kentucky, Tennessee)

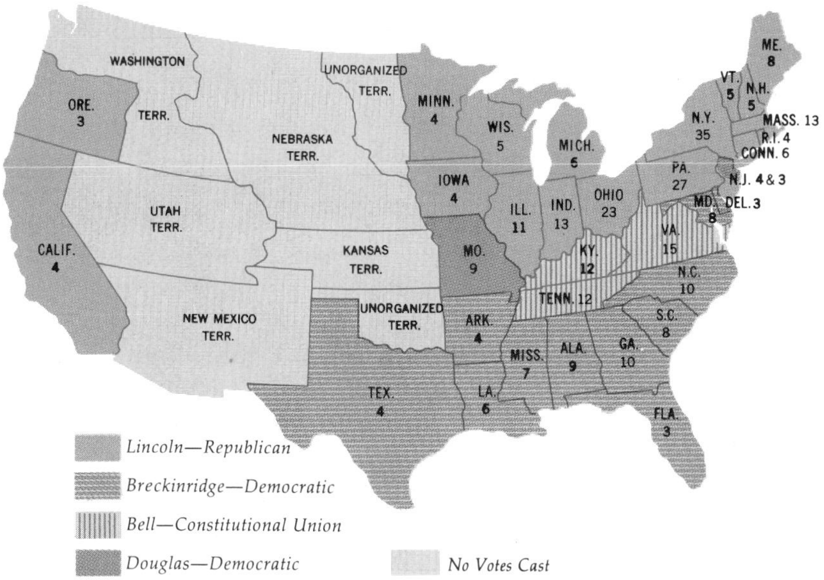

PRESIDENTIAL ELECTION OF 1860
(with electoral vote by state)
A surprising fact is that Lincoln, often rated among the greatest Presidents, ranks near the bottom in percentage of popular votes. In all the eleven states that seceded, he received only a scattering of one state's votes—about 1.5 percent in Virginia.

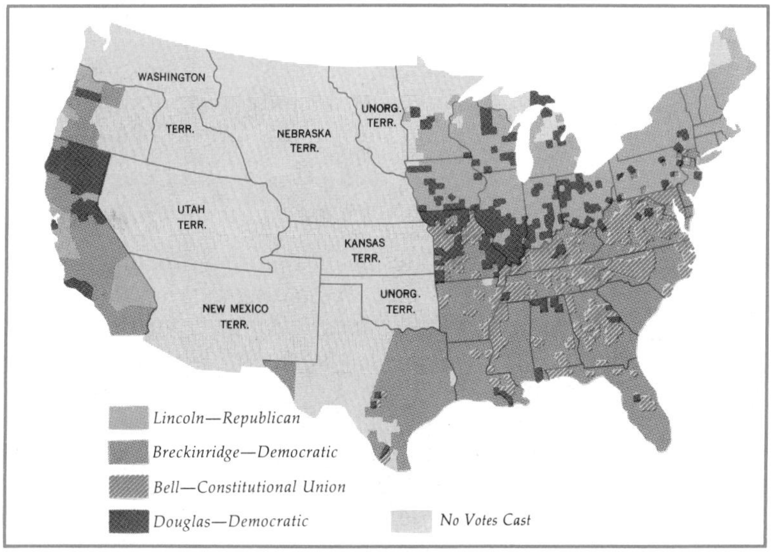

PRESIDENTIAL ELECTION OF 1860
(showing popular vote by county)
Note that the vote by counties for Lincoln was virtually all cast in the North. The Northern Democrat, Douglas, was also nearly shut out in the South, which divided its votes between Breckinridge and Bell. (Note that only citizens of states could vote; inhabitants of territories could not.)

the Supreme Bench. Although the Republicans had elected Lincoln, they controlled neither the Senate nor the House of Representatives. The federal government could not touch slavery in those states where it existed except by a constitutional amendment, and such an amendment could be defeated by one-fourth of the states. The fifteen slave states numbered nearly one-half of the total—a fact not fully appreciated by Southern hotheads.

The Secessionist Exodus

A tragic chain reaction of secession now began to explode. South Carolina, which had threatened to go out if the "sectional" Lincoln came in, was as good as her word. Four days after the election of the "Illinois Baboon" by "insulting" majorities, her legislature voted unanimously to call a special convention. Meeting at Charleston in December 1860, it unanimously voted to secede. During

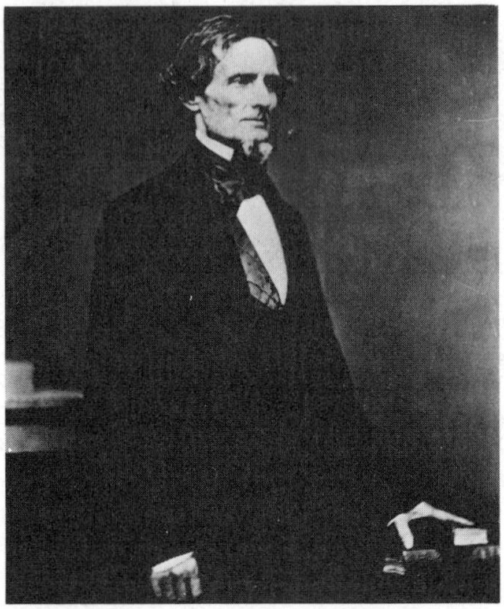

President Jefferson Davis (1808–1889). Faced with grave difficulties, he was probably as able a man for the position as the Confederacy could have chosen. The Davis family had moved south from Kentucky; the Lincoln family, north. If the migrations had been reversed, the presidential roles might have been reversed, as some have speculated. (Library of Congress.)

the next six weeks, six other states of the lower South, though somewhat less united, followed South Carolina over the precipice. Four more were to join them later, bringing the total to eleven.

With the eyes of destiny upon them, the seven seceders, formally meeting at Montgomery, Alabama, created a government known as the Confederate States of America. As their president they chose Jefferson Davis, a dignified and austere recent member of the United States Senate from Mississippi. He was a West Pointer and a former Cabinet member with wide military and administrative experience; but he suffered from chronic ill-health, as well as from a frustrated ambition to be a Napoleonic strategist.

The crisis, already critical enough, was deepened by the "lame duck"* interlude. Lincoln,

Three days after Lincoln's election, Horace Greeley's influential New York *Tribune* (November 9, 1860) had declared: "If the cotton States shall decide that they can do better out of the Union than in it, we insist on letting them go in peace. The right to secede may be a revolutionary one, but it exists nevertheless. . . . Whenever a considerable section of our Union shall deliberately resolve to go out, we shall resist all coercive measures designed to keep it in. We hope never to live in a republic, whereof one section is pinned to the residue by bayonets." After the secession movement got well under way, Greeley's *Tribune* changed its tune.

although elected President in November 1860, could not take office until four months later, March 4, 1861. During this period of protracted uncertainty, when he was still a private citizen in Illinois, seven of the eleven deserting states pulled out of the Union.

President Buchanan, the aging incumbent, has been blamed for not holding the seceders in the Union by sheer force—for wringing his hands instead of secessionist necks. Never a vigorous man and habitually conservative, he was now nearly seventy, and although devoted to the Union, he was surrounded by pro-Southern advisers. As an able bachelor-lawyer wedded to the Constitution, he did not believe that the Southern states could legally secede. Yet he could find no authority in the Constitution for stopping them with guns.

"Oh for one hour of Jackson!" cried the advocates of strong-arm tactics. But "Old Buck" Buchanan was not "Old Hickory," and he was faced with a far more complex and serious problem. One important reason why he did not resort to force was that the tiny standing army of some 15,000 men, then widely scattered, was urgently needed to control the Indians in the West. Public

*The "lame duck" period was shortened to ten weeks in 1933 by the 20th Amendment (See Appendix).

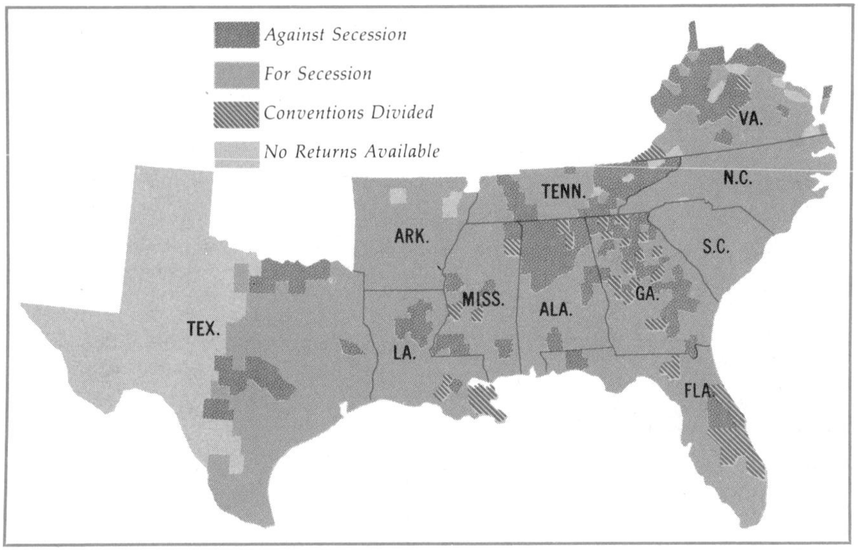

SOUTHERN OPPOSITION TO SECESSION, 1860–1861
(showing vote by county)
This county vote shows the opposition of the anti-planter, anti-slavery mountain whites in the Appalachian region. There was also considerable resistance to secession in Texas, where Governor Sam Houston, who led the Unionists, was deposed by secessionist hotheads.

opinion in the North, at that time, was far from willing to unsheathe the sword. Fighting would merely shatter all prospects of adjustment, and until the guns began to boom there was still a flickering hope of reconciliation rather than a contested divorce. The weakness lay not so much in Buchanan as in the Constitution and in the Union itself. Ironically, when Lincoln became President, he continued essentially Buchanan's wait-and-see policy.

The Collapse of Compromise

Impending bloodshed spurred final and frantic attempts at compromise—in the American tradition. The most promising of these efforts was sponsored by Senator Crittenden of Kentucky, on whose shoulders had fallen the mantle of a fellow Kentuckian, Henry Clay.

The proposed Crittenden amendments to the Constitution were designed to appease the South. Slavery in the territories was to be prohibited north of 36°30′, but south of that line it was to be given federal protection in all territories existing or "hereafter to be acquired" (such as Cuba). Future states, north or south of 36°30′, could come into the Union with or without slavery, as they should choose. In short, the slavery men were to be guaranteed full rights in the southern territories, as long as they were territories, regardless of the wishes of the majority under popular sovereignty. Federal protection in a territory south of 36°30′ might conceivably, though improbably, turn the entire area permanently to slavery.

Lincoln flatly rejected the Crittenden scheme, which offered some slight prospect of success, and all hope of compromise fled. For this refusal he must bear a heavy responsibility. Yet he had been elected on a platform that opposed the extension

One reason why the Crittenden Compromise failed in December 1860 was the prevalence of an attitude reflected in a private letter of Senator Hammond of South Carolina on April 19: "I firmly believe that the slave-holding South is now the controlling *power* of the world—that no other power would face us in hostility. Cotton, rice, tobacco, and naval stores command the world; and we have sense to know it, and are sufficiently Teutonic to carry it out successfully. The North without us would be a motherless calf, bleating about, and die of mange and starvation."

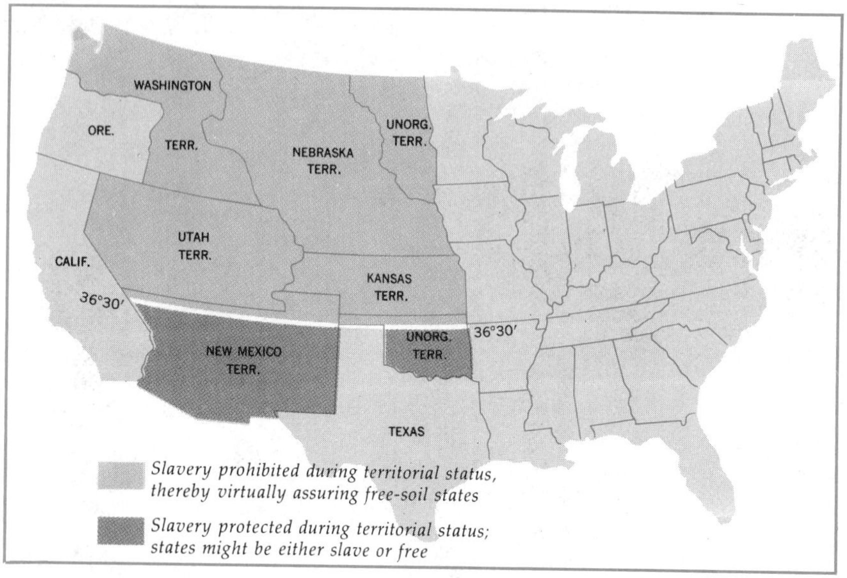

PROPOSED CRITTENDEN COMPROMISE, 1860
Stephen A. Douglas claimed that "if the Crittenden proposition could have been passed early in the session [of Congress], it would have saved all the States, except South Carolina." But Crittenden's proposal was doomed—Lincoln opposed it, and Republicans cast not a single vote in its favor.

of slavery, and he felt that as a matter of principle he could not afford to yield, even though gains for slavery in the territories might be only temporary. Larger gains might come later in Cuba and Mexico.

As for the supposedly spineless "Old Fogy" Buchanan, how could he have prevented the Civil War by starting a civil war? No one has yet come up with a satisfactory answer. If he had used force on South Carolina in December 1860, the fighting almost certainly would have erupted three months sooner than it did, and under less favorable circumstances for the Union. The North would have appeared as the heavy-handed aggressor. And the crucial Border States, so vital to the Union, probably would have been driven into the arms of their "wayward sisters."

"Wretched Condition of the Old Party at the White House." Buchanan is hard pressed between Southern threats of violence and Northern reminders of his obligation to uphold the Constitution. (*Harper's Weekly,* 1861.)

Farewell to Union

Secessionists who parted company with their sister states left for a number of avowed reasons, mostly relating in some way to slavery. They were alarmed by the inexorable tipping of the political balance against them—"the despotic majority of numbers." The "crime" of the North, observed James Russell Lowell, was the census returns. Southerners were also dismayed by the triumph of the new sectional Republican party, which seemed to threaten their rights as a slaveholding minority. They were weary of free-soil criticism, abolitionist nagging, and Northern interference, ranging from the Underground Railroad to John Brown's raid. "All we ask is to be let alone," declared president Jefferson Davis in an early message to his congress.

Many Southerners supported secession because they felt sure that their departure would be unopposed, despite "Yankee yawp" to the contrary. They were confident that the clodhopping and codfishing Yankee would not or could not fight. They believed that Northern manufacturers and bankers, so heavily dependent on Southern cotton and markets, would not dare to cut their own economic throats with their own swords. But should war come, the immense debt owed to Northern creditors by the South—happy thought—could be promptly repudiated, as it later was.

> James Russell Lowell, the Northern poet and essayist, wrote in the *Atlantic Monthly* shortly after the secessionist movement began: "The fault of the free States in the eyes of the South is not one that can be atoned for by any yielding of special points here and there. Their offence is that they are free, and that their habits and prepossessions are those of freedom. Their crime is the census of 1860. Their increase in numbers, wealth, and power is a standing aggression. It would not be enough to please the Southern States that we should stop asking them to abolish slavery: what they demand of us is nothing less than that we should abolish the spirit of the age. Our very thoughts are a menace."

Southern leaders regarded secession as a golden opportunity to cast aside their generations of "vassalage" to the North. An independent Dixieland could develop its own banking and shipping, and trade directly with Europe. The low Tariff of 1857, which had been passed largely by Southern votes, was not in itself menacing. But who could tell when the "greedy" Republicans would win control of Congress and drive through an oppressive protective tariff of their own? For decades there had been this fundamental friction between the North, with its manufacturing plants, and the South, with its agrarian economy.

Worldwide impulses of nationalism—then stirring in Italy, Germany, Poland, and elsewhere—were fermenting in the South. This huge area, with its distinctive culture, was not so much a section as a sub-nation. It could not view with complacency the possibility of being lorded over, then or later, by what it regarded as a hostile nation of Northerners.

The principles of self-determination—of the Declaration of Independence—seemed to many Southerners to apply perfectly to them. Few, if any, of the seceders felt that they were doing anything wrong or immoral. The thirteen original states had voluntarily entered the Union and now seven—ultimately eleven—Southern states were voluntarily withdrawing from it.

Historical parallels ran even deeper. In 1776, thirteen American colonies, led by the rebel George Washington, had seceded from the British Empire by throwing off the yoke of King George. In 1860–1861, eleven American states, led by the rebel Jefferson Davis, were seceding from the Union by throwing off the yoke of "King" Abraham Lincoln. With that burden gone, the South was confident that it could work out its own peculiar destiny more quietly, happily, and prosperously.

VARYING VIEWPOINTS

Few issues have generated as much heat among American historians as the causes of the War for Southern Independence. The very names chosen to describe the conflict—notably "Civil War" or "War Between the States"—reveal much about various authors' points of view. Opinions have naturally differed according to section, but in general the appraisals of the war have gone through four phases.

The so-called nationalist school in the late 19th Century found slavery and Union to be the fundamental causes of the bloodletting, and approved the war because it ended slavery and preserved the Union. In the early 20th Century, some writers, notably Charles Beard, argued that the war was not about slavery per se, but about the basic economic conflict between an industrial North and an agricultural South. Yet if there had been no slavery there would have been no Civil War, at least not in 1861.

After the disappointing results of World War I, some historians argued that the Civil War itself had been a great mistake, traceable not to any fundamentally "irreconcilable conflict," whether racial or economic, but to the breakdown of political institutions and the ineptitude of a blundering generation of leaders. But since World War II, a "neonationalist" view has generally prevailed. It pictures the Civil War as an all-but-inevitable clash between two cultures and two sets of social values, ending in victory for the forces of virtue and progress.

SELECT READINGS

Refer to the previous chapter for the titles by Nichols, Randall and Donald, and Craven. Richly detailed is Allan Nevins, *The Emergence of Lincoln* (2 vols., 1950). David Donald, *Charles Sumner and the Coming of the Civil War* (1960), is an outstanding biography. See also his able *Charles Sumner and the Rights of Man* (1970). Lincoln's rise is developed in Don E. Fehrenbacker's *Prelude to Greatness* (1962), and in Carl Sandburg's *Abraham Lincoln: The Prairie Years* (2 vols., 1926). Consult also Benjamin Quarles, *Lincoln and the Negro* (1962). Stanley W. Campbell describes *The Slave Catchers: Enforcement of the Fugitive Slave Law, 1840–1860* (1968). The explosive Kansas issue is dealt with in James A. Rawley, *Race and Politics: "Bleeding Kansas" and the Coming of the Civil War* (1969), and in Paul W. Gates, *Fifty Million Acres: Conflicts over Kansas Land Policy, 1854–1890* (1954). On the Lincoln-Douglas debates see H. V. Jaffa, *Crisis of the House Divided* (1959). Don E. Fehrenbacher brilliantly and thoroughly dissects *The Dred Scott Case* (1978). P. S. Klein, in *President James Buchanan* (1962), does his subject belated justice. The final moments before the fighting began are scrutinized in David Potter, *Lincoln and His Party in the Secession Crisis* (1942), and in K. M. Stampp, *And the War Came* (1950). The Southern side of the question appears in Steven A. Channing, *Crisis of Fear: Secession of South Carolina* (1970), W. L. Barney, *The Secessionist Impulse: Alabama and Mississippi* (1974), W. J. Evitts, *A Matter of Allegiances: Maryland from 1850 to 1861* (1974), and R. A. Wooster, *The Secessionist Conventions of the South* (1962). See also Michael P. Johnson, *Toward a Patriarchal Republic: The Secession of Georgia* (1977). Stephen B. Oates paints a vivid portrait of John Brown in *To Purge This Land with Blood* (1970). Thomas J. Pressley reviews the copious literature about the war in *Americans Interpret their Civil War* (1954). George Forgie offers a psychoanalytical explanation of the coming of the war in *Patricide in the House Divided: A Psychological Interpretation of Lincoln and His Age* (1979).

22

The War for Southern Independence

My paramount object in this struggle is to save the Union, and is not either to save or to destroy slavery.

ABRAHAM LINCOLN, 1862

President of the Disunited States of America

Abraham Lincoln solemnly took the oath of office on March 4, 1861, after having slipped into Washington at night, partially disguised to thwart assassins. He thus became President, not of the *United* States of America, but of the disunited states of America. Seven had departed; eight more were teetering on the edge. The girders of the unfinished Capitol dome loomed nakedly in the background, as if to symbolize the imperfect state of the Union.

Lincoln's inaugural address was firm yet conciliatory: there would be no conflict unless the South provoked it. Secession, the President declared, was wholly impracticable, because "Physically speaking, we cannot separate."

Here Lincoln put his finger on a profound geographical truth. The North and South were Siamese twins, bound inseparably together. If they had been divided by the Pyrenees Mountains or the Danube River, a sectional divorce would have been more feasible. But the Appalachian Mountains and the mighty Mississippi River both ran the wrong way.

Uncontested secession would only create new controversies. What share of the national debt should the South be forced to take with it? What portion of the jointly held federal territories, if any, should the Confederate states be allotted—areas so largely purchased with Southern blood? How would the fugitive-slave issue be dealt with? The Underground Railroad would certainly redouble its activity, and it would have to transport its passengers only across the Ohio River, not all the way to Canada. Was it conceivable that all such problems could have been solved without ugly armed clashes?

A united United States had hitherto been the top-dog republic in the Western Hemisphere. If this powerful democracy should break into two hostile parts, the European nations would be delighted. They could gleefully transplant to America their hoary concept of the balance of power. Playing the no less hoary game of divide and conquer, they could incite one snarling fragment of the dis-United States against the other. The colonies of the European powers in the New World, notably those of Britain, would thus be made safer against the rapacious Yankees. And European imperialists, with no unified republic to stand across their path, could the more easily defy the Monroe Doctrine and seize territory in the Americas.

Lincoln's Contentious Cabinet

A greedy horde of hungry office seekers, elbowing for the patronage gravy trough, overwhelmed Lincoln at the very outset. At a time when he needed a clear mind for pressing affairs of state, he was forced to worry about the "postmastership at Podunk." There were, in his earthy phrase, "too many hogs for the tits."

Secretary William H. Seward (1801–1872). Seward was a senator, a secretary of state, and the purchaser of Alaska ("Seward's Folly"), where both a peninsula and a city were named after him. (National Archives.)

The Cabinet was dominated by Lincoln's former rivals for the presidential nomination. Headstrong and egotistical William H. Seward, the front-running contender at Chicago in 1860, was of necessity made secretary of state. He regarded himself as a kind of prime minister, but after some difficulty Lincoln tactfully put him in his place. Happily, Seward turned out to be one of the abler secretaries of state.

Other Cabinet members were likewise problem children. The secretary of the treasury was a leading abolitionist, Salmon P. Chase of Ohio. A massive, handsome man, he was self-righteous, opinionated, and constantly stung by the presidential bee buzzing in his bonnet. The original secretary of war, Simon Cameron, became involved in graft, and was succeeded by bulldog-like Edwin M. Stanton, stocky, black-haired, and asthmatic. Though tireless and decisive, he was arrogant, irascible, vindictive, and double-dealing. A Democrat and a more distinguished lawyer than Lincoln, he had savagely criticized the "imbecility" of his future chief, whom he dubbed the "original gorilla."

Unhappily the Cabinet was never completely harmonious or loyal to the President. A minor civil war within his official family was but one of

Secretary of State Seward entertained the dangerous idea that if the North picked a fight with one or more European nations, the South would once more rally around the flag. On April Fool's Day, 1861, he submitted to Lincoln a memorandum recommending:

> "I would demand explanations from Spain and France, categorically, at once. I would seek explanations from Great Britain and Russia. . . . And, if satisfactory explanations are not received from Spain and France . . . would convene Congress and declare war against them."

Lincoln quietly but firmly quashed Seward's scheme.

the many crosses that Lincoln had to bear while prosecuting the larger Civil War.

The South Assails Fort Sumter

The plight of the federal forts had meanwhile partially overshadowed political squabbles. As the seceding states left, they had seized the United States arsenals, mints, and other public property within their borders. When Lincoln took office, only two significant forts in the South still flew the Stars and Stripes. The more important of the pair was square-walled Fort Sumter, in Charleston Harbor, with fewer than 100 men.

Ominously the choices presented to Lincoln by Fort Sumter were all bad. This stronghold had provisions that would last only a few weeks—until the middle of April 1861. If no supplies were forthcoming, its commander would have to surrender without firing a shot. Lincoln, quite understandably, did not feel that such a weak-kneed course squared with his obligation to protect federal property. But if he sent reinforcements, the South Carolinians would undoubtedly fight back; they could not tolerate a federal fort blocking the mouth of their most important Atlantic seaport.

After agonizing indecision, Lincoln adopted a middle-of-the-road solution. He notified the South Carolinians that an expedition would be sent to *provision* the garrison, though not to *reinforce* it. But in Southern eyes "provision" spelled "reinforcement."

A Union naval force was next started on its way to Fort Sumter—a move that the South regarded as an act of aggression. On April 12, 1861, the cannon of the Carolinians opened fire on the fort, while crowds in Charleston applauded and waved handkerchiefs. After a thirty-four-hour bombardment, which took no life, the dazed garrison surrendered.

The firing on the fort electrified the North, which at once responded with cries of "Remember Fort Sumter" and "Save the Union." Hitherto countless Northerners had been saying that if the Southern states wanted to go, they should not be pinned to the rest of the nation with bayonets.

"A House Divided Against Itself Cannot Stand." Contemporary cartoon of Lincoln.

"Wayward sisters, depart in peace" was a common sentiment, expressed even by the commander of the army, war hero General Winfield Scott, now so old at seventy-five that he had to be boosted onto his horse.

But the assault on Fort Sumter provoked the North to a fighting pitch: the fort was lost but the Union was saved. Lincoln had contrived to win a great strategic victory. Southerners had wantonly fired upon the glorious Stars and Stripes, and honor demanded an armed response. Lincoln promptly (April 15) issued a call to the states for 75,000 militiamen; and volunteers sprang to the colors in such enthusiastic numbers that many were turned away—a mistake not often repeated. On April 19 and 27 the President proclaimed a leaky blockade of Southern seaports.

The call for troops, in turn, aroused the South much as the attack on Fort Sumter had aroused the North. Lincoln was now waging war—from the Southern view an aggressive war—on the Confederacy. Virginia, Arkansas, and Tennessee, all of which had earlier voted down secession, reluctantly joined their embattled sister states, as did North Carolina. Thus the seven became eleven as the "submissionists" and "Union shriekers" were overcome. Yet Richmond in Virginia, replacing Montgomery in Alabama as the Confederate capital, was too near Washington for strategic comfort on either side.

James L. Petigru, a South Carolinian, was one of the few prominent citizens of the state to oppose secession. When asked by a stranger in December 1860 where the insane asylum could be found, he pointed out the Baptist church, in which the secession convention had gathered. "It looks like a church," he said, "but it is now a lunatic asylum; go right there and you will find one hundred and sixty-four maniacs within." They voted unanimously for secession.

Brothers' Blood and Border Blood

The only slave states left were the crucial Border States. This group consisted of Missouri, Kentucky, Maryland, Delaware, and later West Virginia—the "mountain white" area which somewhat

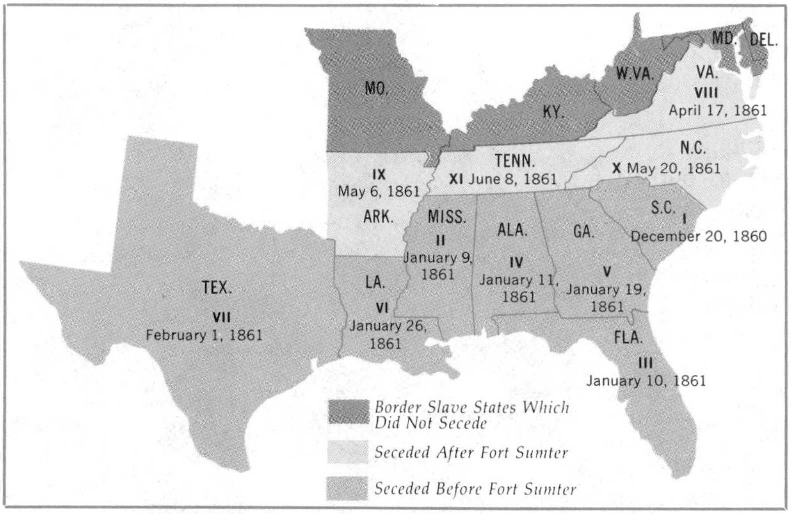

SECEDING STATES
(with dates and order of secession)
Note the long period of time between the secession of South Carolina, the first state to go, and that of Tennessee, the last state to leave the Union. These six months were a time of terrible trial for moderate Southerners. When a Georgia statesman pleaded for restraint and negotiations with Washington, he was rebuffed with the cry: "Throw the bloody spear into this den of incendiaries!"

illegally tore itself from the side of Virginia in mid-1861. If the North had fired the first shot, some or all of these doubtful states probably would have seceded, and the South might well have succeeded. The Border group actually boasted a white population more than half that of the entire Confederacy. Lincoln reportedly said that he hoped to have God on his side, but he had to have Kentucky.

In dealing with the Border States, the President did not rely solely on moral suasion but successfully used methods of dubious legality. In Maryland he declared martial law where needed and sent in troops, because this state threatened to cut off Washington from the North. He also deployed Union soldiers in western Virginia and notably in Missouri, where they fought beside Unionists in a local civil war within the larger Civil War.

Any official statement of the North's war aims was profoundly influenced by the teetering Border States. At the very outset, Lincoln was obliged to declare publicly that he was not fighting to free the blacks. An anti-slavery declaration would no doubt have driven the Border States into the welcoming arms of the South. Lincoln had to insist repeatedly—even though weakening his moral cause—that his primary purpose was to preserve the Union at all costs. Thus the war began not as one between slave soil and free soil, but one for the Union with slaveholders on both sides.

Unhappily, the conflict between "Billy Yank" and "Johnny Reb" was a brothers' war. There were many Northern volunteers from the Southern states, and many Southern volunteers from the Northern states. The "mountain whites" of the South sent north some 50,000 men, and the loyal slave states contributed some 300,000 soldiers to the Union. In many a family of the Border states, one brother rode north to fight with the Blue, another south to fight with the Gray. Senator Crittenden of Kentucky, who fathered the abortive Crittenden Compromise, fathered two sons: one became a general in the Union army, the other a general in the Confederate army.

Europe's Aristocracy Sticks Together

Confederates were inspired by the open sympathy of Europe's ruling classes, with the conspicuous exception of Russia. The South could reasonably hope for mediation or armed intervention, which almost came. At the very least, it could expect the sale of weapons, warships, and supplies, all of which did come.

Why were the upper classes of Western Europe so favorably disposed to the Confederacy? They had from the beginning abhorred the incendiary example of the American democratic experiment, and were overjoyed to see the long-smoking chimney at last "take fire." Moreover, the semi-feudal, aristocratic elements, especially in England, had long cherished something of a fellow feeling for the semi-feudal, aristocratic society of the South. The Foreign Offices of both Britain and France, reflecting these pro-Southern sentiments, naturally welcomed the breakup of the fast-growing and ever-threatening United States.

Leaders of British industrial and commercial life likewise hailed the newly born Confederacy. For one thing, it would provide the long-coveted independent cotton supply. For another, it would increase the opportunities of British shippers and

"Oh, Ain't We Sorry!" The cartoon shows what the tyrants of the Old World think of secession. Note that the royal group is doubled up with laughter. (*Harper's Weekly,* 1860.)

> Regarding the Civil War, the London *Times* (Nov. 7, 1861) editorialized: "The contest is really for empire on the side of the North, and for independence on that of the South, and in this respect we recognize an exact analogy between the North and the Government of George III, and the South and the Thirteen Revolted Provinces."

manufacturers to make profits from the South, without the hurdle of a Yankee protective tariff.

On the other hand, countless workingmen in England, and to some extent in France, were pulling or praying for the North. Many of them had read *Uncle Tom's Cabin*, and they sensed that a victory for the Union would result in freeing the slaves. The ending of human bondage anywhere would further dignify free labor everywhere.

The common folk in Britain could not yet cast the ballot, but they could cast the brick. Their certain hostility to any official intervention on behalf of the South evidently had a sobering effect on the British Cabinet. Thus the dead hands of Uncle Tom helped Uncle Sam by restraining the British and French ironclads from breaking the Union blockade.

Southern Assets

Both North and South were unready for war, as Americans are inclined to be. Each gained valuable experience from the other, and this fact partly explains why they battled so long on relatively even terms.

The South had only to fight defensively, behind interior lines, and hence needed fewer troops. The North had to invade the Confederacy, conquer it, and drag it back bodily into the Union—a prodigious task involving an area about as large as all Western Europe south of Scandinavia. Indeed the South did not have to win the war to win its independence; it had merely to repulse or discourage the invader. A draw would be a victory. The Confederate states would then be left independent—and this was all they really wanted.

Until the emancipation proclamations of 1862–1863, many observers conceded to the South the superior moral cause, despite the dark stain of slavery. It was fighting for self-determination, for self-government, for its peculiar social structure, for hearth and home, for fundamental freedoms (for whites, not slaves). Favorite slogans were "Death before Dishonor" and "For Our Altars and Our Firesides."

The South not only had talented officers but had them from the beginning. Conspicuous among the dozen or so first-rate leaders was General Robert E. Lee, with his florid face, graying hair, and knightly bearing. In poise, magnanimity, and sense of honor he embodied the Southern ideal. President Lincoln had unofficially offered him the command of the armies of the North, but when Virginia seceded Lee felt honor-bound to go along with his native state. His chief lieutenant was black-bearded and unpretentious young Thomas J. ("Stonewall") Jackson, a somewhat eccentric teacher of tactics and philosophy at the Virginia Military Institute. With his "foot cavalry," he was a master of speed and deception.

The North was much less fortunate. It was forced to use costly trial-and-error methods until it uncovered a general, in the person of Ulysses Simpson Grant, who would crunch his way to victory. The Union was further handicapped by numerous political officers, including the pompously incompetent General Benjamin F. ("Beast Ben") Butler, who aroused a storm by threatening harsh measures against the defiant women of New Orleans. His famous "woman order" decreed that females insulting his soldiers were to be jailed as common prostitutes. Their misbehavior stopped quickly.

Southern men were of a fighting breed. Accustomed to manage horses and bear arms from boyhood, they made excellent cavalrymen and foot soldiers. They were supremely self-confident, and their high-pitched "rebel yell" ("Yeeeahhhh") was designed to strike terror into the hearts of fuzz-chinned Yankee recruits known as "fresh fish." Yet the Northern "shopkeepers" and "clodhoppers" adjusted themselves surprisingly well to the rugged demands of military life. They may have been short on dash but they were long on discipline and determination.

Confederate Chances

The South, as primarily an immense farm, was severely hampered by the fewness of its factories. Yet it seized the weapons stored in federal arsenals when it seceded, and managed to sneak through the Union blockade an impressive mass of munitions. Displaying remarkable resourcefulness, the Southerners developed ironworks which, though limited, turned out much artillery. "Yankee ingenuity" was not confined to Yankees.

As the war dragged on, grave shortages developed among the Southerners in such necessities as shoes, uniforms, and blankets. There were immense stores of food in the South but the civilians and soldiers often went hungry. "Forward, men! They have cheese in their haversacks," was the reported cry of one Southern officer as he attacked the Yankees. Much of the hunger was caused by a breakdown of transportation, especially where the railroads were cut or destroyed by the Northern invader.

Formidable though all these handicaps were, the chances for Southern independence were unusually favorable. This was true even though the Confederates had to start from scratch in building a government, an army, and a navy. As one Southern general remarked, never was a major revolution undertaken with better prospects of success. Certainly the thirteen colonies in 1776 had faced more hazardous odds.

The might-have-beens are fascinating. *If* the Border States had seceded, *if* the uncertain states of the upper Mississippi Valley had turned against the Union, *if* a wave of Northern defeatism had demanded an armistice, and *if* England and/or France had broken the blockade, the South probably would have won. All of these possibilities came close to realities, but none of them happened. Successful revolutions, including the American Revolution of 1776, have generally succeeded because of foreign intervention. The South counted on it, did not get it, and lost.

Yankee Advantages

The North was not only a huge farm but a sprawling factory as well—and wars were already being fought with both smokestacks and guns. Yankees boasted about three-fourths of the nation's wealth, including overwhelming superiority in manufacturing, shipping, and banking. The Union also possessed nearly three-fourths of the 30,000 miles (48,000 kilometers) of railroads. Not only did it have longer and better trackage, but it had abundant facilities for repair and replacement, all of which the South sorely lacked.

Additionally the North controlled the sea. With

Manufacturing by Sections, 1860

Section	*Number of Establishments*	*Capital Invested*	*Average Number of Laborers*	*Annual Value of Products*	*Percentage of Total Value*
New England	20,671	$ 257,477,783	391,836	$ 468,599,287	24%
Middle States	53,387	435,061,964	546,243	802,338,392	42
Western States	36,785	194,212,543	209,909	384,606,530	20
Southern States	20,631	95,975,185	110,721	155,531,281	8
Pacific States	8,777	23,380,334	50,204	71,229,989	3
Territories	282	3,747,906	2,333	3,556,197	1
	140,533	$1,009,855,715	1,311,246	$1,885,861,676	

Tredegar Iron Works, Richmond, Virginia. This was by far the most important of the Confederate iron works. Using skilled slave labor, this plant equipped the army with nearly 1,200 scarce cannons. Without these works, the Confederacy probably would have collapsed. Their presence in Richmond helps to explain why the South fought so hard to keep the city.

its vastly superior navy, it established a blockade that choked off the bulk of Southern exports and imports. This stoppage not only hampered the South economically and militarily, but finally shattered its morale. While strangling the Confederacy with one hand, the North could simultaneously keep open the sea lanes to Europe. It was thus able to exchange huge quantities of grain for munitions, and in this way it used the factories of Europe to supplement its own. During the early months of the war, the North imported many more firearms from abroad than it was able to manufacture at home.

Union forces likewise enjoyed a much larger reservoir of manpower. The loyal states had a population of some 22 million; the seceding states, 9 million. This latter figure included about 3.5 million slaves. The population advantage of the North was somewhat greater than 2 to 1, and the estimated enlistments ran 1,556,000 to 1,082,000. Manpower odds against General Lee were ordinarily about 3 to 2, sometimes 3 to 1. Such superior numbers usually gave the North the advantage of choosing the point of attack.

A broad stream of European immigrants con-

Lieutenant Porter and Soldiers. Union soldiers of the 4th Michigan Infantry. (Library of Congress.)

Immigration to U.S., 1860–1866

Year	*Total*	*Britain*	*Ireland*	*Germany*	*All Others*
1860	153,640	29,737	48,637	54,491	20,775
1861	91,918	19,675	23,797	31,661	16,785
1862	91,985	24,639	23,351	27,529	16,466
1863	176,282	66,882	55,916	33,162	20,322
1864	193,418	53,428	63,523	57,276	19,191
1865*	248,120	82,465	29,772	83,424	52,459
1866	318,568	94,924	36,690	115,892	71,062

*Only the first three months of 1865 were war months.

tinued to pour into the North, thanks to Northern control of the seas. Though slowed down a bit by the war, especially during the first two years, the inflow totaled over 800,000 newcomers of both sexes from 1861 through 1865—or more than the total casualties in the armed services of the North. The bulk of the new arrivals were British, Irish, and German; and large numbers of them were induced to enlist in the Union armies. Tens of thousands of earlier immigrants, inspired by a love of freedom and gratitude to their adopted land, likewise joined the colors. Altogether, about one-fifth of the Union forces were foreign-born. In one division, commands were given in four different languages; and some German units even had guttural-accented officers of their own nationality. Southerners branded foreign enlistees as "Hessians" or "Yankee Hessians."

The two most prominent German-American generals, Franz Sigel and Carl Schurz, were both refugees from the German revolutions of 1848. Sigel did yeoman work in saving Missouri, with its large German population, for the Union. Both generals suffered reverses, but Schurz, through no fault of his own, was routed. German-speaking soldiers, when asked whom they were serving with, would reply, "I fights mit Sigel and I runs mit Schurz."

Black Men Battle Bondage

Altogether about 180,000 blacks served in the Union armies, most of them from the slave states but many from the free-soil North. Blacks accounted for about 10 percent of the total enlistments in Union forces, on land or sea, and included two Massachusetts regiments raised largely through the efforts of the ex-slave Frederick Douglass.

Black volunteers were at first rejected. Race prejudice, fear of arming blacks, and a feeling that white men should fight their own war raised a forbidding hand. But as manpower ran low and emancipation was proclaimed, black enlistees

Frederick Douglass (c. 1817–1895). Born a slave in Maryland, Douglass escaped to the North and became the most prominent black abolitionist. Gifted as an orator, writer, and editor, he continued to battle for the civil rights of his people after emancipation. Near the end of a distinguished career he served as U.S. Minister to Haiti. (Library of Congress.)

Proud Black Soldiers of the Union Army. (Library of Congress.)

were welcomed, although at first they were not paid as well as the whites. Strangely enough, the blacks had to fight for the privilege of fighting for freedom.

Black fighting men unquestionably had their hearts in a war against slavery. They participated in about 500 engagements, major and minor, and received 22 Congressional Medals of Honor—the highest military award. Their casualties were extremely heavy; over 38,000 died, whether from battle, sickness, or reprisals by vengeful masters. A few were put to death as slaves in revolt, for not until 1864 did the South recognize them as prisoners of war. In later years many Southerners blamed their defeat on the "unfair" use of blacks and foreigners.

> In August 1863, Lincoln wrote to Grant that enlisting black soldiers "works doubly, weakening the enemy and strengthening us." In December 1863, he announced that "it is difficult to say they are not as good soldiers as any." In August 1864, he said, "Abandon all the posts now garrisoned by black men, take 150,000 [black] men from our side and put them in the battle-field or cornfield against us, and we would be compelled to abandon the war in three weeks."

For reasons of pride, prejudice, and principle, the Confederacy could not bring itself to enlist slaves until a month before the war ended and then it was too late. Meanwhile tens of thousands were impressed into labor battalions, the building of fortifications, the supplying of armies, and other war-connected activities. Slaves moreover were "the stomach of the Confederacy," for they kept the farms going while the white men fought.

Ironically, the great mass of Southern slaves did little to help their Northern liberators, white or black. A thousand scattered torches in the hands of a thousand slaves would have brought the Southern soldiers home, and the war would have ended. Through the "grapevine," the blacks learned of Lincoln's Emancipation Proclamation. Yet the bulk of them, whether because of lethargy, loyalty, lack of leadership, or strict policing, did not cast off their chains. But tens of thousands revolted "with their feet," when they abandoned their plantations upon the arrival or imminent arrival of Union armies, with or without emancipation proclamations. About 25,000 joined Sherman's march through Georgia in 1864, and their presence in such numbers created problems of supply and discipline.

Rallying to the Flag of the Union

The ideal of Union was a tremendous asset to the North. This ideal was compounded largely of pride in the flag, in the past, and in the future. America could not hope to shame its monarchical critics and achieve its Manifest Destiny if it divided. The teachings of Webster and Clay had been driven home, as indicated by such popular Northern watchwords as "Union Forever" and "What God Hath Joined Let No Man Put Asunder." A rousing Northern song, widely sung since the 1850s, proudly proclaimed:

The union of lakes, the union of lands,
The union of States none can sever,
The union of hearts, the union of hands,
And the flag of our union forever.*

Devotion to the Union aroused the North with unexpected fury against the "flag of disunion," and helped to hold the Border States in line. The concept infused in the North the will to fight, and retained the Southerner-infiltrated states of the upper Mississippi Valley. Finally, the ideal provided the Northerners with the inspiring war cry of Union, until such time as the moral issue of slavery could be brought out into the open, as it was late in 1862.

Dethroning King Cotton

Textile mills in Britain were fatally dependent on Southern cotton, and the Confederates were supremely confident that the British fleet would be forced to break the blockade. Why did King Cotton fail them?

English manufacturers had on hand, when the shooting started in 1861, a heavy oversupply of fiber. The real pinch did not come until about a year and a half later, when thousands of hungry operatives were thrown out of work. But by this time Lincoln had announced his slave-emancipation policy, and the "wage slaves" of England were not going to demand a war for the slaveowners of the South.

The direst effects of the "cotton famine" in England were relieved in several ways. Hunger among unemployed workers was partially eased when certain kindhearted Americans sent over several cargoes of foodstuffs. As Union armies penetrated the South, they captured or bought considerable supplies of cotton and shipped them to England; and the Confederates also ran a limited quantity through the blockade. In addition, the cotton growers of Egypt and India, responding to high prices, increased their output. Finally, booming war industries in England, which supplied both North and South, relieved unemployment.

As the Civil War neared the end of its third year, the London *Times* (Jan. 7, 1864) could boast: "We are as busy, as rich, and as fortunate in our trade as if the American war had never broken out, and our trade with the States had never been disturbed. Cotton was no King, notwithstanding the prerogatives which had been loudly claimed for him."

King Wheat and King Corn—of the Northern agricultural royalty—proved to be more potent potentates than King Cotton. During these war years the North, blessed with ideal weather, produced bountiful crops of grain and harvested them with McCormick's mechanical reaper. In the same period the British suffered a series of bad harvests. They were forced to import huge quantities of grain from America, which happened to have the cheapest and most abundant supply. If the British had broken the blockade to get cotton, they would have provoked the North to war and would have cut off this precious granary. Unemployment for some seemed better than hunger for all. Hence one Yankee journal could exult:

Wave the stars and stripes high o'er us,
Let every freeman sing . . .
Old King Cotton's dead and buried:
brave young Corn is King.

President Davis versus President Lincoln

The Confederate government, like King Cotton, betrayed fatal weaknesses. Its constitution, borrowing liberally from that of the Union, had one deadly defect. Created by secession, it could not

*George P. Morris, "The Flag of Our Union."

logically deny future secession to its states. Jefferson Davis, while making his bow to states' rights, had in view a well-knit central government. But determined states'-rights men fought him bitterly to the end. The Richmond regime even encountered difficulty in persuading certain state troops to serve outside their own borders. Governor Brown of Georgia, a belligerent states'-righter, at times seemed ready to secede from the secession and fight both sides. States' rights were actually more damaging to the Confederacy than Yankee sabers.

Sharp-featured President Davis—tense, humorless, legalistic, stubborn—was repeatedly in hot water. Though an eloquent orator and an able administrator, he at no time enjoyed real personal popularity, and was often at loggerheads with his congress. At times there was serious talk of impeachment. Unlike Lincoln, Davis was somewhat imperious and inclined to defy rather than lead public opinion. Suffering acutely from neuralgia and other nervous disorders (including a tic) he overworked himself with the details of both civil government and military operations. No one could doubt his courage, sincerity, integrity, and devotion to the South, but the task proved beyond his powers. It was probably beyond the powers of any mortal man.

President Davis, the Acrobat, on Rope of Cotton. The "Confederacy" is a fuse bomb, the flag reads, "Let Us Alone," a Davis theme. The cotton rope is unraveling.

Lincoln also had his troubles, but on the whole they were less prostrating. The North enjoyed the prestige of a long-established government, financially stable and fully recognized both at home and abroad. Lincoln, the inexperienced prairie politician, proved superior to the more experienced but less flexible Jefferson Davis. Able to relax with droll stories at critical times, "Old Abe" grew as the war dragged on. Tactful, quiet, patient, yet firm, he developed a genius for interpreting and leading a fickle public opinion. Holding aloft the banner of Union with inspiring utterances, he revealed charitableness toward the South and forbearance toward backbiting colleagues. "Did [Secretary] Stanton say I was a damned fool?" he reportedly replied to a talebearer. "Then I dare say I must be one, for Stanton is generally right and he always says what he means."

Strangulation of the South by Sea

As finally developed, the general plan of Northern attack had four phases. First, slowly suffocate the South by blockading its coasts. Second, cut it in half by seizing control of the Mississippi River backbone. Third, chop it to pieces (a later idea) by sending troops through Georgia, and then north into the Carolinas. Fourth, strangle it by capturing its capital (Richmond), and by pounding its remaining armies into submission. The overall strategy called for slowly beating down the enemy rather than delivering a knockout punch.

The blockade started leakily: it was not clamped

MAIN THRUSTS, 1861–1865
Northern strategists at first believed that the rebellion could be snuffed out quickly by a swift, crushing blow. But the stiffness of Southern resistance to the Union's early probes revealed that the conflict would be a war of attrition, long and bloody.

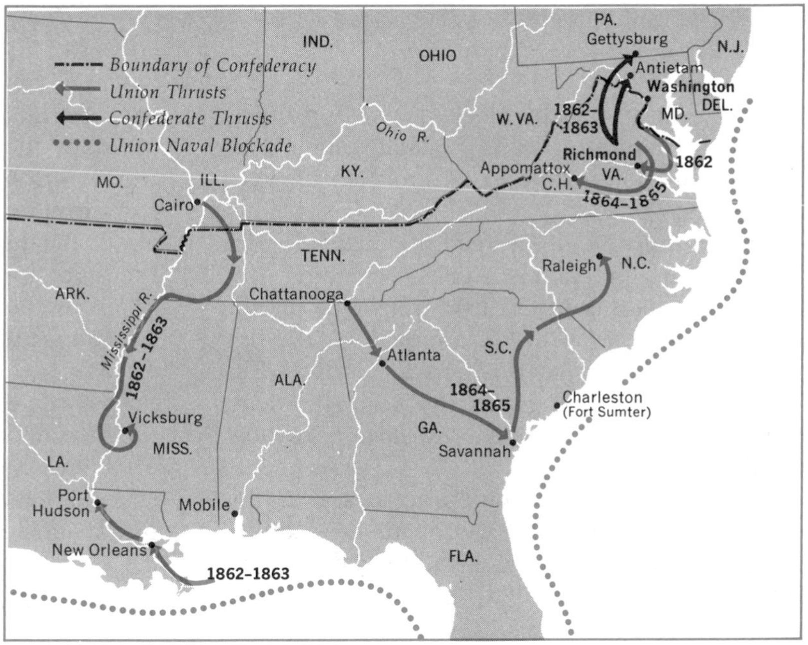

down all at once, but was extended by degrees. An airtight patrol of some 3,500 miles (5,635 kilometers) of coast was impossible for the hastily improvised Northern navy, which consisted partly of converted yachts and ferryboats. But blockading was simplified by concentrating on the principal ports and inlets. Only at such places were dock facilities available for loading bulky bales of cotton.

How was the blockade regarded by the naval powers of the world? Ordinarily, they probably would have defied it, for it was never completely effective, and was especially sievelike at the outset. But England, the greatest maritime nation, recognized it as binding, and warned her shippers that they ignored it at their peril. An explanation is easy. Blockade happened to be the chief offensive weapon of Britain, which was still Mistress of the Seas. She plainly did not want to tie her hands in a future war by insisting that Lincoln maintain impossibly high blockading standards.

Blockade-running soon became riskily profitable, as the growing scarcity of Southern goods drove prices skyward. The most successful runners were swift, gray-painted steamers, scores of which were specially built in Scotland. A leading rendezvous was the West Indian port of Nassau, in the British Bahamas, where at one time thirty-five of the speedy ships were counted. The low-lying craft would take on cargoes of arms brought in by tramp steamers from England, leave with fraudulent papers for "Halifax" (Canada), and return a few days later with a cargo of cotton. The risks were great, but the profits would mount to 700 percent and more for lucky gamblers. Two successful voyages might well pay for capture on a

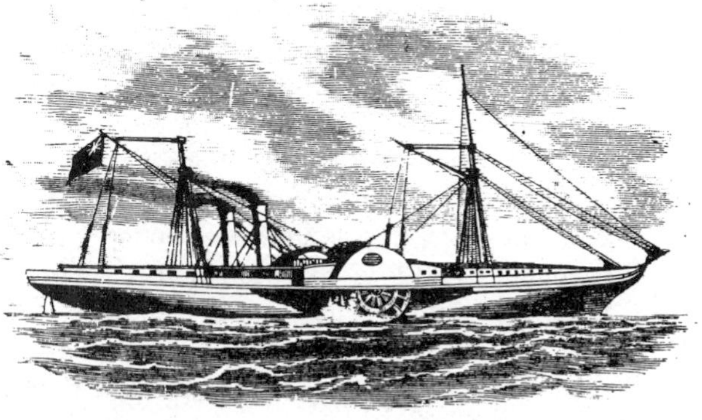

Confederate Blockade Runner. (Courtesy of The New York Public Library, Astor, Lenox and Tilden Foundations.)

third. The lush days of blockade-running finally passed as Union squadrons gradually pinched off the leading Southern ports, from New Orleans to Charleston.

The Northern navy enforced the blockade with high-handed practices. Yankee captains, for example, would seize British freighters on the high seas, if laden with war supplies for the tiny port of Nassau and other halfway stations. The justification was that obviously these shipments were "ultimately" destined, by devious routes, for the Confederacy.

London, although not happy, acquiesced in this disagreeable doctrine of "ultimate destination" or "continuous voyage." British blockaders might find such a farfetched interpretation highly useful in a future war—as in fact they did in the World War of 1914–1918.

The most alarming Confederate threat to the blockade came in 1862. Resourceful Southerners raised and reconditioned a former wooden United States warship, the *Merrimack*, and plated its sides with old iron railroad rails. Renamed the *Virginia*, this clumsy but powerful monster easily destroyed two wooden ships of the Union navy in the Virginia waters of Chesapeake Bay; it also threatened catastrophe to the entire Yankee blockading fleet. (Actually the homemade ironclad was not a seaworthy craft.)

> When news reached Washington that the *Merrimack* had sunk two wooden Yankee warships with ridiculous ease, President Lincoln, much "excited," summoned his advisers. Secretary of the Navy Welles records: "The most frightened man on that gloomy day . . . was the Secretary of War [Stanton]. He was at times almost frantic. . . . The *Merrimack*, he said, would destroy every vessel in the service, could lay every city on the coast under contribution, could take Fortress Monroe. . . . Likely the first movement of the *Merrimack* would be to come up the Potomac and disperse Congress, destroy the Capitol and public buildings."

A tiny Union ironclad, the *Monitor*, built in about 100 days, arrived on the scene in the nick of time. For four hours, on March 9, 1862, the little "Yankee cheesebox on a raft" fought the wheezy *Merrimack* to a standstill. Britain and France had already built several powerful ironclads, but the first battle-testing of these new craft heralded the doom of wooden warships. A few months after the historic battle, the Confederates destroyed the *Merrimack* to keep her from the grasp of advancing Union troops.

The Runners of Bull Run

By the summer of 1861, a Union army of some 30,000 men was being drilled near Washington. It was ill-prepared for battle, but Northern newspaper editors, eager to end the war in a hurry, raised the cry, "On to Richmond!" Proddings by the press and public finally forced action, contrary to the better judgment of some of the generals. This was a classic example of the dangerous pressure that can be exerted by an ill-informed public.

Preliminaries of the clash at Bull Run, on July 21, 1861, seemed like those of a sporting event. The raw Yankee recruits marched or straggled from the capital, accompanied by congressmen, ladies, and others riding out with lunch baskets to see the fun. The ill-trained Union force encountered a smaller Confederate army at Bull Run (Manassas Junction), some 30 miles (48 kilometers) southwest of Washington. At first the battle went well for the Yankees. But "Stonewall" Jackson's gray-clad warriors stood like a stone wall (here he won his nickname), and Confederate reinforcements arrived unexpectedly. Panic suddenly seized the weary Union soldiers, many of whom fled in disgraceful confusion. The Confederates, too exhausted or too disorganized to pursue effectively, feasted on captured lunches.

The "military picnic" at Bull Run, though not decisive militarily, was significant psychologically.

Defeat was better than victory for the Union, because it dispelled all illusions of a one-punch war and caused the Northerners to buckle down to the staggering task at hand. Conversely, the victory was worse than a defeat for the South, because it inflated an already dangerous overconfidence. Many soldiers deserted, some boastfully to display their trophies, others sure that the war was over. Southern enlistments fell off sharply, and preparations for a protracted war slackened.

"Tardy George" McClellan

Northern hopes brightened later in 1861, when General George B. McClellan was given command of the Army of the Potomac, as the major Union force near Washington was now called. Red-haired and red-mustached, strong and stocky, McClellan was a brilliant, thirty-four-year-old West Pointer. As a serious student of warfare who was dubbed "Young Napoleon," he had seen plenty of fighting, first in the Mexican War and then as an observer of the Crimean War in Russia.

Cocky George McClellan embodied a curious mixture of virtues and defects. He was a superb organizer and drillmaster, and he injected splendid morale into the Army of the Potomac. Hating to sacrifice his troops, he was idolized by his men, who affectionately called him "Little Mac." But he was a perfectionist who seems not to have realized that an army is never ready to the last button, and that wars cannot be won without running some risks. He consistently but erroneously believed that the enemy outnumbered him, partly because his intelligence reports from the head of Pinkerton's Detective Agency were unreliable. He was overcautious—Lincoln once accused him of having "the slows"—and he addressed the President in an arrogant tone which a less forgiving person would never have tolerated. Privately the general referred to his Chief as a "baboon."

As McClellan discreetly continued to drill his army without moving it toward Richmond, the derisive Northern watchword became "All Quiet along the Potomac." The song of the hour was "Tardy George" [McClellan]. After threatening to "borrow" the army if it was not going to be used, Lincoln finally issued firm orders to move.

> Lincoln treated McClellan's demands for reinforcements and his excuses for inaction with infinite patience. One exception came when the general complained that his horses were tired. Lincoln wrote, "I have just read your dispatch about sore-tongued and fatigued horses. Will you pardon me for asking what the horses of your army have done since the battle of Antietam that fatigues anything?" (October 24, 1862)

A reluctant McClellan decided upon a waterborne flanking approach to Richmond. Choosing the route up the peninsula formed by the James and York Rivers, he warily advanced toward the city in the spring of 1862 with about 100,000 men. After taking a month to capture historic Yorktown, which bristled with imitation wooden can-

"Masterly Inactivity, or Six Months on the Potomac." McClellan and his Confederate foe view each other cautiously, while their troops engage in visiting, marrying, and sports. (*Frank Leslie's Illustrated Newspaper,* 1862.)

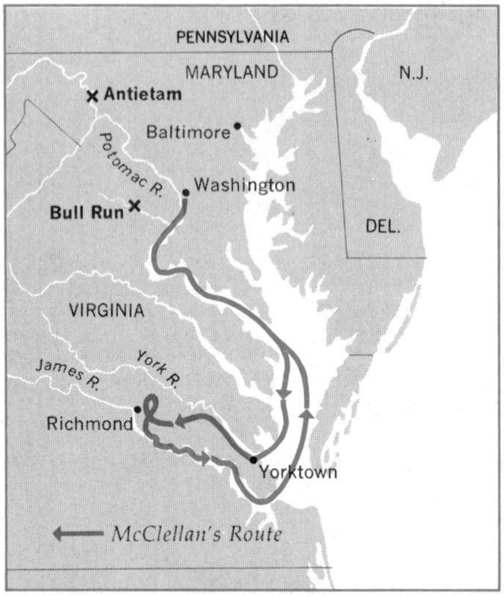

PENINSULAR CAMPAIGN, 1862

non, he finally came within sight of the spires of Richmond. Then General Lee suddenly struck with about 70,000 troops. Brilliantly assisted by "Stonewall" Jackson, he slowly drove McClellan back to his base on Chesapeake Bay. Although the Union army was still in fighting shape, the whole Peninsular Campaign was abandoned as a costly failure.

McClellan was now given a less active command, amid a storm of controversy. His enemies accused "Mac the Unready" of having moved too timorously. His defenders claimed that he would have captured Richmond if Lincoln had not withdrawn troops for the defense of Washington, which had been jeopardized by the lightning feints of General Jackson in the Shenandoah Valley. It is worth noting that McClellan was never decisively defeated, and that after the war Lee rated him the ablest of his many opponents.

A Union army near Washington, strengthened by units from McClellan's command, was now entrusted to overconfident General Pope. A handsome, dashing, soldierly figure, he boasted that in the Western theater, from which he had come, he had seen only the backs of the enemy. He quickly got a front view, for General Lee, at the Second Battle of Bull Run (August 29–30, 1862), furiously attacked him and inflicted a crushing defeat. Gloom once more enshrouded the North.

The Antietam Pivotal Point

Lee now undertook a daring thrust into Maryland. He hoped to win a victory that would not only encourage foreign intervention, but also seduce this wavering Border State and her sisters from the Union. The Confederate troops sang lustily:

> Thou wilt not cower in the dust,
> Maryland! my Maryland!
> Thy gleaming sword shall never rust,
> Maryland! my Maryland!

But the Marylanders did not respond to the siren song. The presence among the invaders of so many blanketless, hatless, and shoeless soldiers dampened the state's ardor.

Events finally shaped up for a critical battle at Antietam Creek, Maryland. Lincoln, responding to popular pressures, hastily restored "Little Mac" to active command of the main Northern army. The soldiers tossed their caps into the air and hugged his horse as they hailed his return. At Antietam, on September 17, 1862, McClellan succeeded in halting Lee in one of the bitterest and bloodiest days of the war.

Antietam was more or less a draw militarily. But Lee, finding his thrust parried, retired across the Potomac. McClellan, from whom much more had been hoped, was removed from his field command for the second and final time. His numerous critics, condemning him for not having boldly pursued the ever-dangerous Lee, finally got his scalp.

The landmark Battle of Antietam was one of the decisive battles of world history—probably the most decisive of the Civil War. Jefferson Davis was perhaps never again so near victory as on that fateful summer day. The British and French governments were on the verge of diplomatic mediation, a species of interference sure to be

Confederate Corpses at Antietam. Unknown to Lee, who had dangerously divided his army, McClellan had somehow obtained a copy of the Confederate battle plan. The Union forces thus had a great tactical advantage, and the result was appalling slaughter. The twelve-hour fight at Antietam Creek ranks as the bloodiest day of the war, with more than ten thousand Confederate casualties, and even more on the Union side. "At last the sun went down and the battle ended," one historian wrote, "smoke heavy in the air, the twilight quivering with the anguished cries of thousands of wounded men." (Library of Congress.)

angrily resented by the North. An almost certain rebuff by Washington might well have spurred Paris and London into armed intervention. But both capitals cooled off when the Union displayed unexpected power at Antietam, and their chill deepened with the passing months.

Bloody Antietam was also the long-awaited "victory" which Lincoln needed for launching his Emancipation Proclamation. The abolitionists had long been clamoring for action: Wendell Phillips was denouncing the President as a "first-rate second-rate man." By midsummer of 1862, with the Border States safely in the fold, Lincoln was ready to move. But he believed that to issue such an edict on the heels of a series of military disasters would be folly. It would seem like a confession that the North, unable to conquer the South, was forced to call upon the slaves to murder their masters. Lincoln therefore decided to await the outcome of Lee's invasion.

Antietam served as the needed emancipation springboard. The halting of Lee's offensive was just enough of a victory to justify Lincoln's issuing, on September 23, 1862, the preliminary Emancipation Proclamation. This hope-giving document announced that on January 1, 1863, the President would issue a final proclamation. On the scheduled date he fully redeemed his promise, and the Civil War became more of a moral crusade.

A Proclamation Without Emancipation

Lincoln's Emancipation Proclamation of 1863 declared "forever free" the slaves in those Confederate states still in rebellion. The blacks in the loyal Border States were not affected, nor were those in specific conquered areas in the South—all told, about 800,000. The tone of the document was dull and legalistic: there was no clarion call for a holy war to achieve freedom. Lincoln in fact is on record as favoring cash compensation to the owners of all slaves as late as February of 1865.

The presidential pen did not formally strike the shackles from a single slave. Where Lincoln could presumably free the slaves—that is, in the loyal Border States—he refused to do so, lest he spur disunion. Where he could not—that is, in the Confederate states—he tried to. In short, where he *could* he would not, and where he *would* he could not. Thus the Emancipation Proclamation was stronger on proclamation than emancipation.

Yet much unofficial do-it-yourself liberation did

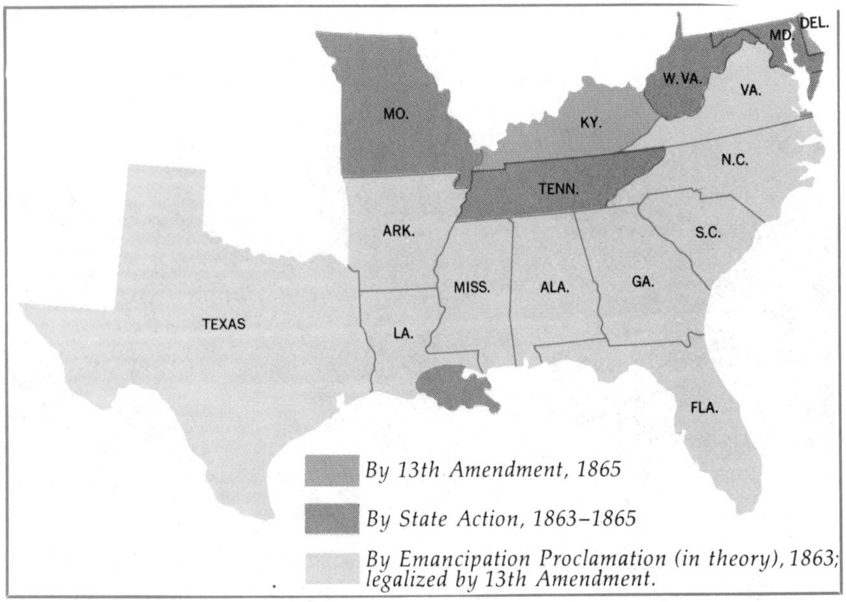

EMANCIPATION IN THE SOUTH
President Lincoln believed that compensated emancipation of the slaves would be fairest to the South. He formally proposed such an amendment to the Constitution in December, 1862. What finally emerged was the Thirteenth Amendment of 1865, which freed all slaves *without* compensation.

take place. Thousands of jubilant slaves, learning of the proclamation, flocked to the invading Union armies, sometimes hindering military operations. In this sense the Emancipation Proclamation was heralded by the patter of running feet. But many fugitives would have come anyhow, as they had from the war's outset. Actually, Lincoln did not go so far as legislation already passed by Congress for freeing enemy-owned blacks. His immediate goal was not so much to liberate the slaves as to strengthen the moral cause of the Union at home and abroad. This he succeeded in doing.

Many of the British aristocrats were unfriendly to the North, and the London *Spectator* sneered at Lincoln's so-called Emancipation Proclamation: "The Government liberates the enemy's slaves as it would the enemy's cattle, simply to weaken them in the coming conflict. . . . The principle asserted is not that a human being cannot justly own another, but that he cannot own him unless he is loyal to the United States."

At the same time his proclamation, though of dubious constitutionality, clearly foreshadowed the ultimate doom of slavery. This was legally achieved by action of the individual states and by their ratification of the 13th Amendment in 1865, eight months after the war had ended. (For text, see Appendix.)

Public reactions to the long-awaited proclamation of 1863 were varied. "God bless Abraham Lincoln," exulted the anti-slavery editor Horace Greeley in his New York *Tribune*. But many ardent abolitionists complained that Lincoln had not gone far enough. On the other hand, formidable numbers of Northerners, especially in the Old Northwest and the Border States, felt that he had gone too far. A Democratic rhymester sneered:

Honest old Abe, when the war first began,
Denied abolition was part of his plan;
Honest old Abe has since made a decree,
The war must go on till the slaves are all free.
As both can't be honest, will some one tell how,
If honest Abe then, he is honest Abe now?

Opposition mounted in the North against supporting an "abolition war"; ex-President Pierce and others felt that emancipation should not be "inflicted" on the slaves. Many Boys in Blue, especially from the Border States, had volunteered to fight for the Union, not against slavery. Desertions increased sharply. The crucial congressional elections in the autumn of 1862 went heavily against the administration, particularly in New York, Pennsylvania, and Ohio. Democrats even carried Lincoln's Illinois, although they failed to secure control of Congress.

The Emancipation Proclamation caused an outcry to rise from the South that "Lincoln the fiend" was trying to stir up the "hellish passions" of a slave insurrection. Aristocrats of Europe, noting that the proclamation applied only to rebel slaveholders, were inclined to sympathize with Southern protests. But the Old World working classes, especially in England, reacted otherwise. They sensed that the proclamation spelled the ultimate doom of slavery, and many laborers were more determined than ever to oppose intervention. Gradually the diplomatic position of the Union improved.

The North now had much the stronger moral cause. In addition to preserving the Union, it had committed itself to freeing the slaves. The moral position of the South was correspondingly weakened.

Lincoln "the Fiend." Unflattering English cartoon. Critics of Lincoln, North and South, called him "Caesar," "Buffoon," "Illinois Baboon," and "Simple Susan Tyrant." (London *Fun*.)

Lincoln Plays His Last Card. Lincoln's last card was the Emancipation Proclamation, shown as a black spade. (London *Punch*, 1862.)

Bisecting the South

Luckily the spectacular rise of Ulysses S. Grant provided Lincoln at last with an able general—and one who did not have to be shelved after every reverse. As a mediocre student at West Point, Grant had distinguished himself only in horsemanship, although he did fairly well in mathematics. After participating with credit in the Mexican War, he was stationed at lonely frontier posts, where boredom and loneliness drove him to drink. Resigning from the army to avoid a court martial for drunkenness, he failed at various business ventures, and when war came he was working in his father's leather store in Illinois at $50 a month.

Grant did not cut much of a figure. The shy and silent shopkeeper was short, stooped, awkward, stubble-bearded, and sloppy in dress. He managed with some difficulty to secure a colonelcy in the volunteers. From then on his military experience—combined with boldness, resourcefulness, and doggedness—brought a meteoric rise.

Grant's first signal success came in the northern Tennessee theater. After heavy fighting, he succeeded in capturing Fort Henry and Fort Donelson on the Tennessee and Cumberland Rivers in

February 1862. When the Confederate commander at Fort Donelson asked for terms, Grant bluntly demanded "an unconditional and immediate surrender."

This triumph in Tennessee was of major significance. Kentucky was riveted more securely to the Union, and the gateway was opened to the rest of Tennessee as well as to Georgia and the heart of the South. Grant's exploit also captured the imagination of the victory-starved North, and infused badly needed life into the Union cause.

"Unconditional Surrender" Grant was caught napping several weeks later at Shiloh, in southern Tennessee, April 6–7, 1862. But he finally managed to beat off the enemy on one of the goriest fields of the war. Lincoln resisted all demands for his removal by saying, "I can't spare this man, he fights." When talebearers later told Lincoln that Grant drank too much, the President allegedly replied, "Find me the brand, and I'll send a barrel to each of my other generals." There is no evidence that Grant's drinking habits had a seriously adverse effect on his performance.

Other Union thrusts were in the making. In the spring of 1862, a flotilla commanded by David G. Farragut joined with a Northern army to strike the South a staggering blow by seizing New Orleans. With Union gunboats both ascending and descending the Mississippi, the Eastern part of the Confederacy was left with a precarious back door. Through this narrowing entrance, between Vicksburg and Port Hudson, flowed herds of vitally needed cattle and quantities of other provisions from Louisiana and Texas. The fortress of Vicksburg, located on a hairpin turn of the Mississippi, was the South's sentinel protecting the lifeline to the Western sources of supply.

General Grant was now given command of the Union forces attacking Vicksburg, and in the teeth of grave difficulties displayed rare skill and daring. This was his best-fought campaign of the war. Vicksburg at length surrendered, on July 4, 1863, with the garrison reduced to eating mules and rats. Five days later came the fall of Port Hudson, the last Southern bastion on the Mississippi. The

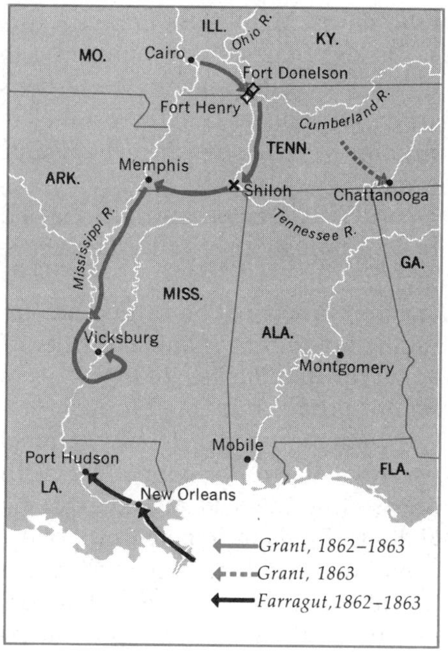

THE MISSISSIPPI RIVER AND TENNESSEE, 1862–1863

spinal cord of the Confederacy was now severed and, in Lincoln's quaint phrase, the Father of Waters at last flowed "unvexed to the sea."

Sherman Scorches Georgia

General Grant, the victor of Vicksburg, was now transferred to the east Tennessee theater. There, in November 1863, he won a series of desperate engagements in the vicinity of Chattanooga, including Missionary Ridge and Lookout Mountain ("the Battle above the Clouds"). The state was thus cleared of Confederates, and the way was opened for an invasion of Georgia. Grant was rewarded by being made general-in-chief.

The conquest of Georgia was entrusted to General William Tecumseh Sherman. Red-haired and red-bearded, grim-faced and ruthless, he captured and burned Atlanta in September 1864. He then daringly undertook to cut loose from his base of supplies, live off the country for some 250 miles

(402 kilometers), and emerge at Savannah on the sea. As a rousing Northern song ("Marching through Georgia") put it:

> "Sherman's dashing Yankee boys will never reach
> the coast!"
> So the saucy rebels said—and 't was a handsome
> boast.

But Sherman's hated "Blue Bellies," 60,000 strong, cut a 60-mile (97-kilometer) swath of destruction through Georgia. They burned buildings, leaving only the blackened chimneys ("Sherman's Sentinels"). They tore up railroad rails, heated them red-hot, and twisted them into "iron doughnuts" and "Sherman's hairpins." They bayoneted family portraits and ran off with valuable "souvenirs." "War . . . is all hell," admitted Sherman later, and he proved it by his efforts to "make Georgia howl." One of his major purposes was to destroy supplies destined for the Confederate army, and to weaken the morale of the men at the front by waging war on their homes.

Sherman was a pioneer practitioner of "total war." His success in "Shermanizing" the South was attested by increasing numbers of Confederate desertions. Although his methods were brutal, he probably shortened the struggle and hence saved lives. But there can be no doubt that the discipline of his army at times broke down, as roving riffraff (Sherman's "bummers") engaged in an orgy of pillaging. "Sherman the Brute" was universally damned in the South.

> A letter picked up on a dead Confederate in North Carolina and addressed to his "deer sister" concluded that it was "dam fulishness" trying to "lick shurmin." He had been getting "nuthin but hell & lots uv it" ever since he saw the "dam yanks" and he was "tirde uv it." He would head for home now, but his old horse was "plaid out." If the "dam yankees" had not got there yet it would be a "dam wunder." They were thicker than "lise on a hen and a dam site ornerier."

After seizing Savannah as a Christmas present for Lincoln, Sherman's army veered north into South Carolina, where the destruction was even more vicious. Many Union soldiers believed that this state, the "hell-hole of secession," had wantonly provoked the war. The capital city, Columbia, burst into flames, in all probability the handiwork of the Yankee invader. Crunching northward, Sherman's conquering army had rolled deep into North Carolina by the time the war ended.

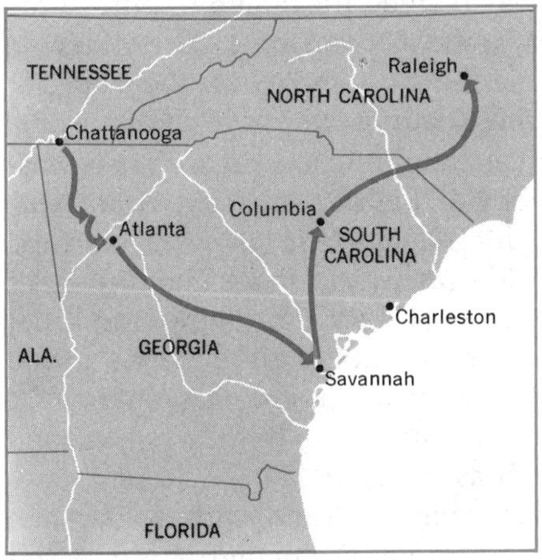

SHERMAN'S MARCH, 1864–1865

Lee's Last Lunge

After Antietam, Lincoln replaced McClellan as commander of the Army of the Potomac with General A. E. Burnside, whose ornate side-whiskers came to be known as "burnsides" or "sideburns." Protesting his unfitness for this responsibility, Burnside proved it when he launched a rash frontal attack on Lee's strong position at Fredericksburg, Virginia, on December 13, 1862. A chicken could not have lived in the line of fire, remarked one Confederate officer. More than 10,000 Northern soldiers were killed or wounded in "Burnside's Slaughter Pen."

A new slaughter pen was prepared when General Burnside yielded his command to "Fighting

Joe" Hooker, an aggressive officer but a headstrong subordinate. At Chancellorsville, Virginia, May 2–4, 1863, Lee daringly divided his numerically inferior force, and sent "Stonewall" Jackson to attack the Union flank. The strategy worked. Hooker, temporarily dazed by a near hit from a cannon ball, was badly beaten but not crushed. This victory was probably Lee's most brilliant, but it was dearly bought. Jackson was mistakenly shot by his own men in the gathering dusk, and died a few days later. "I have lost my right arm," lamented Lee. Southern folklore relates how Jackson outflanked the angels while getting into Heaven.

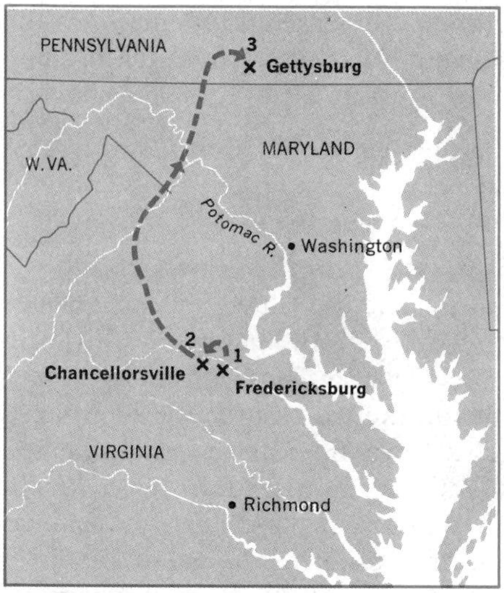

LEE'S CHIEF BATTLES, DECEMBER 1862–JULY 1863

Lee now prepared to follow up his brilliant victory by invading the North again, this time through Pennsylvania. A decisive blow would add strength to the peace movement in the North, while encouraging foreign intervention. Three days before the battle was joined, General George G. Meade—scholarly, unspectacular, abrupt—was aroused from his sleep at 2 A.M. with the unwelcome news that he would replace Hooker. The high tide of the Confederacy was at hand.

Quite by accident Meade took his stand on the green rolling hills near quiet little Gettysburg, Pennsylvania. There his 92,000 men in blue locked in furious combat with Lee's 76,000 gray-clad warriors. The battle seesawed throughout three days, July 1–3, 1863, and the outcome was in doubt until almost the very end. The failure of General Pickett's magnificent but bloodily futile charge finally broke the back of the Confederates.

Lee's defeat was his worst to date, but he took full responsibility for it, even though some of his subordinates had failed him. From now on the Southern cause was doomed, for Vicksburg had surrendered on the day after the reverse at Gettysburg. Yet the men of Dixie fought on, through sweat, blood, and weariness of spirit. The Confederacy was like a cut flower—outwardly blooming but slowly dying.

Later in that dreary autumn of 1863, with the graves still fresh, Lincoln journeyed to Gettysburg to dedicate the cemetery. He read a two-minute address, following a two-hour speech by the orator of the day. Lincoln's noble remarks were branded by the London *Times* as "ludicrous" and by Democratic editors as "dishwatery" and "silly." The address attracted relatively little attention at the time, but the President was speaking for the ages.

Grant Outlasts Lee

Grant was now brought in from the West over Meade, who was blamed for failing to pursue the defeated but always dangerous Lee. Lincoln needed a general who, employing the superior resources of the North, would have the intestinal stamina to drive straight ahead, regardless of casualties. A soldier of bulldog tenacity, Grant was the man for this meat-grinder type of warfare. His overall basic strategy was to assail the enemy's armies simultaneously, so that they could not assist one another, and hence could be destroyed piecemeal. His personal motto was "When in doubt, fight." Lincoln urged him "to chew and choke, as much as possible."

A grimly determined Grant, with more than 100,000 men, struck for Richmond. He engaged Lee in a series of furious battles in the Wilderness of Virginia, during May and June of 1864, notably

in the leaden hurricane of the "Bloody Angle" and "Hell's Half Acre." In this Wilderness Campaign Grant suffered about 50,000 casualties, or nearly as many men as Lee had at the start. But Lee lost about as heavily in proportion.

In a ghastly gamble, on June 3, 1864, Grant ordered a frontal assault on the impregnable position of Cold Harbor. The Union soldiers advanced to almost certain death with papers pinned on their backs bearing their names and addresses. In a few minutes, about 7,000 men were killed or wounded.

Public opinion in the North was appalled by this "blood and guts" type of fighting. Critics cried that "Grant the Butcher" had gone insane. But his basic strategy of hammering ahead seemed brutally necessary; he could trade two men for one and still beat the enemy to its knees. "I propose to fight it out on this line," he wrote, "if it takes all summer." It did—and all autumn, all winter, and a part of the spring.

Early in 1865 the Confederates, tasting the bitter dregs of defeat, tried desperately to negotiate for peace between the "two countries." But Lincoln could accept nothing short of Union, and the Southerners could accept nothing short of independence. So the war had to grind on—amid smoke and agony—to its terrible climax.

The end came with dramatic suddenness. Rapidly advancing Northern troops captured Richmond and cornered Lee at Appomattox Court House in Virginia, in April 1865. Grant—stubble-bearded and informally dressed—met with Lee on Palm Sunday and granted generous terms of surrender. Among other concessions, the hungry Confederates were allowed to keep their own horses for spring plowing.

General Ulysses S. Grant and General Robert E. Lee. Trained at West Point, Grant (*above*) proved to be a better general than a President. Oddly, he hated the sight of blood and recoiled from rare beef. Lee (*below*), a gentlemanly general in an ungentlemanly business, remarked when the Union troops were bloodily repulsed at Fredericksburg, "It is well that war is so terrible, or we should get too fond of it." (*Above and below,* National Archives.)

GRANT'S VIRGINIA CAMPAIGN, 1864–1865

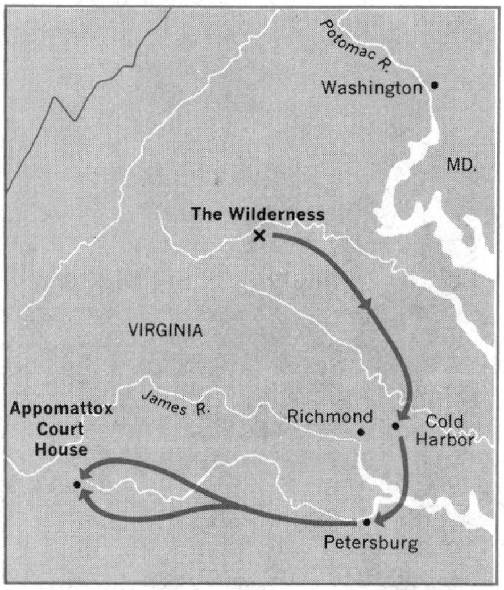

Tattered Southern veterans—"Lee's Ragamuffins"—wept as they took leave of their beloved commander. The elated Union soldiers cheered, but they were silenced by Grant's stern admonition, "The war is over; the rebels are our countrymen again." Unfortunately, as the tragic sequel proved, this soldierly forgiveness was not shared by all Northern hearts.

VARYING VIEWPOINTS

Why did the North win the Civil War? The usual answer is that superior industry and transportation tipped the scales in the Union's favor. This line of reasoning leads to the conclusion that the Civil War was the first "modern" war, in which victory turned at least as much on home-front economic mobilization as on battlefield prowess. And yet the war contained many traditional, "pre-industrial" features as well—for how else could the smaller, agrarian South have held out for four bloody years? Debate continues over the relative importance of battlefront and behind-the-lines factors in accounting for the North's crushing triumph.

SELECT READINGS

An able survey is J. G. Randall and David Donald, *The Civil War and Reconstruction* (rev. ed., 1969); greater detail appears in J. G. Randall, *Lincoln the President* (4 vols.; 1945–1955). A good one-volume history is Peter J. Parish, *The American Civil War* (1975). Full-scale accounts are Shelby Foote, *The Civil War* (3 vols., 1958–1974), and Allan Nevins' monumental *Ordeal of the Union* (8 vols., 1947–1971). Russell T. Weigley, *The American Way of War* (1973), puts military history in a broader context. R. N. Current, *Lincoln and the First Shot* (1963), partially exculpates Lincoln. See also T. H. Williams, *Lincoln and His Generals* (1952). J. H. Franklin, *The Emancipation Proclamation* (1963), is informative; consult also Robert Durden, *The Gray and the Black: The Confederate Debate on Emancipation* (1973). Bruce Catton has a series of a dozen or so books on aspects of the Civil War, all readable and knowledgeable, including *A Stillness at Appomattox* (1953) and *This Hallowed Ground* (1956). D. S. Freeman, *R. E. Lee* (4 vols., 1934–1935) and *Lee's Lieutenants* (3 vols., 1942–1944), are detailed but absorbing. See also Jay Luvaas, *The Military Legacy of the Civil War* (1959). D. T. Cornish, *The Sable Arm: Negro Troops in the Union Army* (1956), is an illuminating study. See also B. Quarles, *The Negro in the Civil War* (1953), and J. M. McPherson's collection of documents, *The Negro's Civil War* (1965). On the Confederacy see Clement Eaton, *A History of the Southern Confederacy* (1956), and Clifford Dowdey, *The Land They Fought For* (1955). Important too are B. I. Wiley, *Southern Negroes, 1861–1865* (1938), and the same author's descriptions of common soldiers, *The Life of Johnny Reb* (1943) and *The Life of Billy Yank* (1952). See also his *Plain People of the Confederacy* (1943). Hudson Strode has completed his detailed three-volume biography with *Jefferson Davis, Tragic Hero* (1964). Recent biographies are by W. W. Hassler on McClellan (1957); Freeman Cleaves on Meade (1960); Lenoir Chambers on Jackson (2 vols., 1959); Clifford Dowdey on Lee (1965); and William McFeeley on Grant (1981).

23

Behind the Lines: North and South

Long experience has shown that armies can not be maintained unless desertion shall be punished by the severe penalty of death. . . . [But] must I shoot a simple-minded soldier boy who deserts, while I must not touch a hair of a wily agitator who induces him to desert?

ABRAHAM LINCOLN, 1863

Diplomatic Warriors Abroad

America's diplomatic front, ordinarily second fiddle in wartime, has seldom been so critical as during the Civil War. The attitude of the major European countries, particularly France and Britain, was crucial. Both nations had formidable ironclads in their navies, and if either power had decided to intervene, it probably could have smashed the wooden blockading fleet of the Union with terrifying ease—at least in the early years of the war. If this had happened, the South almost certainly would have won its independence. An infuriated North no doubt would have turned its bayonets against British Canada, there to seek vengeance and compensation.

Napoleon III, the slippery dictator of France, was openly unfriendly to the North. Behind the smoke screen of the Civil War he was attempting to prop up his puppet, the Austrian nobleman Maximilian, on the throne of Mexico. The success of this hazardous venture depended on the collapse of the Union. Napoleon had the naval strength to break the Northern blockade, but because he did not have the nerve to go it alone, he sought the support of Britain. The London government saw fit to restrain him, so intervention never came.

British officialdom, heavily tinged with aristocracy, was personally more friendly to the aristocratic South than to the "shopkeeping" North. But London proclaimed an official neutrality, and observed it rather well—at least as well as it could with its leaky neutrality laws. The North had expected the British, who were anti-slavery, to sympathize with its cause, which initially was officially concerned only with preserving the Union, not freeing the slaves. In these circumstances the cold neutrality of Britain should not have been surprising, but it seemed like veiled hostility. James Russell Lowell sorrowfully addressed John Bull:

> We know we've gut a cause, John,
> Thet's honest, just, an' true;
> We thought 't would win applause, John,
> Ef nowheres else, from you.

The first real crisis with Britain came over the *Trent* affair, late in 1861. A Union warship cruising on the high seas north of Cuba stopped a British mail steamer, the *Trent*, and forcibly removed from it two Confederate diplomats who were on their way to England. The American captain was guilty of a serious error: he should have brought the entire ship to port for proper judicial judgment.

An outburst of rejoicing arose from the Northerners. They had as yet won no important military victory, and they regarded the seizure of these two eminent envoys as a brilliant stroke. Many a loyal Union man feared that if they had continued on their journey, they might have persuaded Britain and France to break the blockade. Besides, patriotic citizens, remembering the impressment days of 1812, thought it great sport to give John Bull a dose of his own medicine. Americans were now dragging men from the decks of British ships for a change.

Britons were outraged: upstart Yankees could not do this sort of thing to the Mistress of the Seas. War preparations buzzed, and red-coated troops embarked for Canada, with bands blaring, "I Wish I Was in Dixie." The London Foreign Office forthwith prepared an ultimatum, demanding a surrender of the prisoners and a proper apology.

Luckily the *Trent* crisis was surmounted, but only with grave difficulty. The recently laid Atlantic cable had gone dead, and the delays caused by slow steamship communication gave passions on both sides a chance to cool. Lincoln gradually perceived that the North had on its hands two "white elephants," and despite the popularity of their seizure, he reluctantly decided to release them. Secretary of State Seward was at pains to sweeten the pill for the American public. In a clever note he in effect congratulated the British on having accepted, at long last, the views for which the Republic had futilely fought them in the War of 1812.

Outraged by the outcome of the *Trent* affair, Representative Lovejoy of Illinois, who "literally wept tears of vexation," proclaimed on the floor of Congress: "I hate the British government. . . . I now here publicly avow and record my inextinguishable hatred. . . . I mean to cherish it while I live, and to bequeath it as a legacy to my children when I die. And if I am alive when war with England comes, as sooner or later it must, for we shall never forget this humiliation, and if I can carry a musket in that war I will carry it."

Destructive Confederate "Pirates"

A dangerous development for the United States came in the autumn of 1862. The British Cabinet, yielding to the urgings of Napoleon III, seemed about to join France in mediating between North and South, with consequent dangers of shooting. The Union "victory" at Antietam came as a bucket of cold water to such schemes, for Canada was vulnerable to Union bayonets and British shipping was exposed to Yankee privateers. Prime Minister Palmerston was reminded of the ancient couplet:

> Those who in quarrels interpose,
> Must often wipe a bloody nose.

A new major crisis in Anglo-American relations arose over the unneutral building in England of Confederate commerce-raiders, notably the *Alabama*. These vessels were not warships within the meaning of loopholed British law, because they left their shipyards unarmed and picked up their guns elsewhere. The *Alabama* escaped in 1862 to the Portuguese Azores, and there took on weapons and a crew from two English ships that followed her. Although flying the Confederate flag and officered by Confederates, she was manned by Britons and never entered a Confederate port. England was thus the chief naval base of the Confederacy.

The *Alabama* Sunk, 1864

The *Alabama* lighted the skies from Europe to the Far East with the burning hulks of Yankee merchantmen. All told, this "British pirate" captured over sixty vessels. Competing British shippers were delighted, while an angered North had to divert naval strength from its blockade for wild-goose chases. The barnacled *Alabama* finally accepted a challenge from a stronger Union cruiser off the coast of France in 1864, and was quickly destroyed. A picture of the battle, widely sold in the North, bore the words: "Built of English oak in an English yard, armed with English guns, manned by an English crew, and sunk in the English Channel."

As time passed, the shortsighted officials in London began to develop twinges of conscience. They were given no peace by the American minister, Charles Francis Adams, who persistently presented lists of sinkings and bills for damages by the British-built raider. The Foreign Office gradually perceived that it was sanctioning a dangerous precedent that might one day be used against Britain by a future foe—perhaps one without a navy (Ireland?) or even one without a seacoast. Fearing that provocation might push the Americans too far, London took drastic action in 1863. It openly violated its own leaky laws when it seized another raider being built for the South. In the subsequent trial the British government was assessed costs and damages, but its action was clear evidence of a determination to be truly neutral.

Confederate commerce-destroyers, chiefly British-built, captured in all more than 250 Yankee ships, including many whalers. The owners of several hundred others, fearing destruction, transferred them to foreign flags. Under existing federal laws, these could not be transferred back to American registry. Fortunately for the North,

Charles Francis Adams (1807–1886). Son of President John Quincy Adams, grandson of President John Adams, and father of author Henry Adams, he was himself widely regarded as of presidential timber, especially in 1872. His chief claim to distinction was his bold and dignified diplomacy in London during the Civil War. (Courtesy of the Harvard University Portrait collection)

the *Alabama*s did not cripple the war effort, because British and other neutral shipping was available. But the American merchant marine, only recently the proud challenger of England, was riddled. Earnest citizens, deeply angered, talked openly of securing both revenge and recompense by seizing Canada when the war was over.

Foreign Flare-Ups

A final Anglo-American crisis was touched off in 1863 by the Laird rams—two Confederate warships being constructed in Great Britain. Designed to destroy the wooden ships of the Union navy with their iron rams and large-caliber guns, they were far more dangerous than the swift and lightly armed *Alabama.* If delivered to the South, they probably would have sunk the blockading squadrons, and then brought Northern cities under their fire. In angry retaliation, the North doubtless would have invaded Canada, and a full-dress war with Britain would have erupted.

There were no legal grounds for detaining the rams, for their fraudulent papers indicated a non-Confederate purchaser. But Minister Adams took a hard line, warning that "this is war" if the rams were released. At the last minute the London government relented, and bought the two ships for the Royal Navy. Everyone seemed satisfied—except the disappointed Confederates. Britain also eventually repented her sorry role in the *Alabama* business. She agreed in 1871 to submit the *Alabama* dispute to arbitration, and in 1872 paid American claimants $15.5 million for damages caused by wartime commerce raiders. On the London Foreign Office wall was hung the cancelled draft for $15.5 million, as a warning to future ministries to be more careful.

American anger was also directed at Canada, where despite the vigilance of British authorities, Southern agents plotted to burn Northern cities. One Confederate raid into Vermont left three banks plundered and one American citizen dead. Hatred of England burned especially fiercely among Irish-Americans, and they unleashed their fury on Canada. They raised several tiny "armies" of a few hundred green-shirted men, and launched invasions of Canada, notably in 1866 and 1870. The Canadians condemned the Washington government for permitting such violations of neutrality, but the administration was hampered by the presence of so many Irish-American voters.

As fate would have it, two great nations emerged from the fiery furnace of the American Civil War. One was a reunited United States, the other was a united Canada. The British Parliament established the Dominion of Canada in 1867. It was partly designed to bolster the Canadians, both politically and spiritually, against the possible vengeance of the United States.

The Czar of Russia watched with interest as Anglo-American tensions mounted. He was himself on the verge of war with both Britain and France over Poland. In that event, he needed to make sure that his navy was not icebound or bottled up in the Baltic or Black Seas. Accordingly, he sent two fleets in the war-weary autumn of 1863 to visit New York and San Francisco. From those ports they might roam as *Alabama*s to ravage vulnerable British and French shipping. The Czar thus acted in his own self-interest—though many Americans leaped to the conclusion that his fleets were meant to forestall British and French intervention in the American Civil War. Several years later Oliver Wendell Holmes declared:

> Bleak are our shores with the blasts of December,
> Fettered and chill is the rivulet's flow;
> Throbbing and warm are the hearts that remember
> Who was our friend when the world was our foe.

The outpouring of friendship for Russia was based on mistaken assumptions, but in any case helped pave the way for the later purchase of Alaska.

The haughty Emperor Napoleon III of France dispatched a French army to occupy Mexico City in 1863. On the ruins of a crushed republic the following year he enthroned an Austrian tool, the Archduke Maximilian, as Emperor of Mexico. Both sending the army and installing Maximilian were done in flagrant violation of the Monroe Doctrine.

The North, as long as it was convulsed by war, pursued a walk-on-eggs policy toward France. But when the shooting stopped, Secretary of State Seward, speaking with the authority of nearly a million bayonets, prepared to march south. Napoleon realized that his costly gamble was doomed. He reluctantly took "French leave" of his ill-starred puppet in 1867, and Maximilian soon crumpled ingloriously before a Mexican firing squad. With his death the Monroe Doctrine took on new life.

Volunteers and Draftees: North and South

Ravenous, the gods of war demanded men—lots of men. Northern armies were at first manned solely by volunteers, with each state assigned a quota based on population. But in 1863, after volunteering had slackened off, Congress passed a federal conscription law for the first time on a nationwide scale in the United States. The provisions were grossly unfair to the poor. Rich boys, including young John D. Rockefeller, could hire substitutes to go in their places, or purchase exemption outright by paying $300. "Three-hundred-dollar men" was the scornful epithet applied to these slackers. Draftees who did not have the necessary cash complained that their bandit-like government demanded "three hundred dollars or your life."

The draft was especially damned in the Democratic strongholds of the North, notably in New York City. A frightful riot broke out in 1863, touched off largely by underprivileged and anti-black Irish-Americans who shouted, "Down with Lincoln!" and "Down with the Draft!" For several

The New York Draft Riot, 1863. Irish workmen resented competition for jobs by "nagurs." The free blacks in turn called the Irish "white niggers." (Museum of the City of New York.)

days the city was at the mercy of a burning, drunken, pillaging mob, and scores of lives were lost, including many lynched blacks. Elsewhere in the North conscription met with resentment and an occasional minor riot.

More than 90 percent of the Union armies were volunteers, since social and patriotic pressures to enlist were strong. As ablebodied men became scarcer, generous bounties for enlistment were offered by federal, state, and local authorities. An enterprising and money-wise volunteer might legitimately pocket more than $1,000.

With money flowing so freely, an unsavory crew of "bounty brokers" and "substitute brokers" sprang up, at home and abroad. They combed the poorhouses of the British Isles and Western Europe; and many an Irishman or German was befuddled with whiskey and induced to enlist. A number of the slippery "bounty boys" deserted, volunteered elsewhere, and netted another handsome haul. The records reveal that one "bounty jumper" repeated his profitable operation thirty-two times. But desertion was by no means confined to "bounty jumpers." The rolls of the Union army recorded about 200,000 deserters of all classes, and the Confederate authorities were plagued with a problem of similar dimensions.

Like the North, the South relied mainly on volunteers. But since the Confederacy was much less populous, it scraped the bottom of its manpower barrel much more quickly. The Richmond regime, robbing both "cradle and grave" (ages 17 to 50) was forced to resort to conscription as early as April 1862, nearly a year earlier than the Union.

A Northern Draft Drawing

Enlistees North and South
(NUMBER OF MEN IN UNIFORM AT DATE GIVEN)

Date	*Union*	*Confederate*
July 1861	186,751	112,040
January 1862	575,917	351,418
March 1862	637,126	401,395
January 1863	918,121	446,622
January 1864	860,737	481,180
January 1865	959,460	445,203

Confederate draft regulations also worked serious injustices. As in the North, a rich man could hire a substitute or purchase exemption. Slaveowners or overseers with twenty slaves might also claim exemption. These special privileges, later modified, made for bad feeling among the less prosperous, many of whom complained that this was "a rich man's war but a poor man's fight." Why sacrifice one's life to save slavery? No large-scale draft riots broke out in the South, as in New York City. But the Confederate conscription agents often found it prudent to avoid those areas inhabited by sharp-shooting mountain whites, who were branded "Tories," "traitors," and "Yankee-lovers."

The Dollar Goes to War

Blessed with a lion's share of the wealth, the North rode through the financial breakers much more smoothly than the South. Excise taxes on tobacco and alcohol were substantially increased by Congress. An income tax was levied for the first time in the nation's experience; and although the rates were painlessly low by later standards, they netted millions of dollars.

Customs receipts likewise proved to be important revenue-raisers. Early in 1861, after enough anti-protection Southern members had seceded, Congress passed the Morrill Tariff Act, superseding the low Tariff of 1857. It increased the existing duties some 5 to 10 percent, boosting them to about the moderate level of the Walker Tariff of 1846. But these modest rates were soon pushed sharply upward by the war. The increases were designed partly to raise additional revenue, and partly to provide more protection for the prosperous manufacturers who were being plucked by the new internal taxes. A protective tariff thus became identified with the Republican party, as American industrialists, predominantly Republicans, waxed fat on these welcome benefits.

The Washington Treasury also issued greenbacked paper money, totaling nearly $450 million at face value. This printing-press currency was inadequately supported by gold, and hence its value was determined by the nation's credit. Greenbacks thus fluctuated with the fortunes of Union arms, and at one low point were worth only 39 cents on the gold dollar. The holders of the notes, victims of creeping inflation, were indirectly taxed as the value of the currency slowly withered in their hands.

Yet borrowing far outstripped both greenbacks and taxes as a money-raiser. The Federal Treasury netted $2,621,916,786 through the sale of bonds, which bore interest and which were payable at a later date. The modern technique of selling these issues to the people directly through "drives" and payroll deductions had not yet been devised. Accordingly, the Treasury was forced to market its bonds through the private banking house of Jay Cooke and Company, which received a commission of three-eighths of 1 percent on all sales. With both profits and patriotism at stake, the bankers succeeded in making effective appeals to citizen purchasers.

A financial landmark of the war was the National Banking System, authorized by Congress in 1863. Launched partly as a stimulant to the sale of government bonds, it was also designed to establish a standard banknote currency. (The country was then flooded with depreciated "rag money" issued by unreliable bankers.) Banks that joined the National Banking System could buy government bonds and issue sound paper money backed by them. The war-born National Banking Act thus turned out to be the first significant step taken toward a unified banking network since 1836, when the "monster" Bank of the United States was killed by Andrew Jackson. Spawned by the war, this new system continued to function for fifty years.

Taxation by Inflation

An impoverished South was beset by different financial problems. Customs duties were choked off as the coils of the Union blockade tightened. Large issues of Confederate bonds were sold at home and abroad, amounting to nearly $400 million. The Richmond regime also increased taxes sharply, and imposed a 10 percent levy on farm produce. But in general the states'-rights Southerners were vigorously opposed to heavy direct taxation by the central authority: only about 1 percent of the total income was raised in this way.

As revenue began to dry up, the Confederate government was forced to print blue-backed paper money with complete abandon. "Runaway inflation" occurred as Southern presses continued to grind out the poorly backed treasury notes, total-

Civil War Financing in the North

Fiscal Year	*Customs*	*Internal Revenue and Income Tax*	*Total Taxes*	*Loans, Including Treasury Notes*
1861–1862	$ 49,056,397		$ 50,851,729	$ 433,663,538
1862–1863	69,059,642	$ 37,640,787	108,185,534	596,203,071
1863–1864	102,316,152	109,741,134	212,532,936	719,476,032
1864–1865	84,928,260	209,464,215	295,593,048	872,574,145
TOTAL	$305,360,451	$356,846,136	$667,163,247	$2,621,916,786

A contemporary (Oct. 22, 1863) Richmond diary portrays the ruinous effects of inflation: "A poor woman yesterday applied to a merchant in Carey Street to purchase a barrel of flour. The price he demanded was $70.

'My God!' exclaimed she, 'how can I pay such prices? I have seven children; what shall I do?'

'I don't know, madam,' said he coolly, 'unless you eat your children.'"

ing in all more than $1 billion. One breakfast for three in Richmond in 1864 cost $141. The Confederate paper dollar finally sank to the point where it was worth only 1.6 cents when Lee surrendered. The extent to which the Southern currency melted away in the pockets of its holder was the extent to which that citizen was taxed in a roundabout way by his government. Tens of millions of dollars were thus quietly filched from Confederate wallets. Yet inflation did not ruin the South, as was commonly believed. Rather, an inflation of the currency, together with the levy on farm produce, kept the Confederacy going to the end.

"Shoddy" Millionaires in the North

Wartime prosperity in the North was little short of miraculous. The marvel is that a divided nation could fight a costly conflict for four long years and then emerge seemingly more prosperous than ever before. It is true that the early months after secession, with the stoppage of cotton imports and other dislocations, brought temporary depression. But the clouds soon gave way to the sunshine of military orders and war-born civilian prosperity.

New factories, sheltered by the friendly umbrella of the new protective tariffs, mushroomed forth. Soaring prices, resulting from inflation, unfortunately pinched the day laborer and the white-collar worker to some extent. But the manufacturers and businessmen raked in "the fortunes of war."

The Civil War spawned a millionaire class for the first time in American history, though a few men of extreme wealth could have been found earlier. Many of these newly rich were noisy, gaudy, brassy, and given to extravagant living. Their emergence merely illustrates the truth that some gluttony and greed always mar the devotion and self-sacrifice called forth by war. The story of speculators and peculators was roughly the same in both camps. But graft was more flagrant in the North than in the South, partly because there was more to steal.

Yankee "sharpness" appeared at its worst. Dishonest agents, putting profits above patriotism, palmed off aged and blind horses on government purchasers. Unscrupulous Northern manufacturers supplied shoes with cardboard soles, and fast-disintegrating uniforms of reprocessed or "shoddy" wool, rather than virgin wool. Hence the reproachful term "shoddy millionaires." One

"Nightmare of a War Profiteer." A dead soldier forces on him the same poisonous food and drink with which he supplied the army. (*Vanity Fair,* 1861.)

profiteer reluctantly admitted that his profits were "painfully large."

Newly invented labor-saving machinery enabled the North to expand economically, even though the cream of its manpower was being drained off by the fighting front. The sewing machine wrought wonders in fabricating uniforms and military footwear. Clattering mechanical reapers, which numbered about 250,000 by 1865, proved hardly less potent than thundering guns. It not only released tens of thousands of farm boys for the army but fed them while there. It produced vast surpluses of grain which, when sent abroad, helped dethrone King Cotton. It provided profits with which the North was able to buy munitions and supplies from abroad. It contributed to the feverish prosperity of the North—a prosperity that enabled the Union to weather the war with flying colors.

Other industries were humming. The discovery of petroleum gushers in 1859 had led to a rush of "Fifty-Niners" to Pennsylvania. The result was the birth of a new industry, with its "petroleum plutocracy" and "coal oil Johnnies." Pioneers continued to push westward during the war, altogether an estimated 300,000 souls. Major magnets were free gold nuggets and free lands under the Homestead Act of 1862. Strong propellants were the federal draft agents. The only major Northern industry to suffer a crippling setback was the ocean-carrying trade, which fell prey to the *Alabama* and her sister raiders.

A Crushed Cotton Kingdom

Dismally different was the plight of the South, which had fought to exhaustion. The suffocation caused by the blockade, together with the destruction by invaders, took a terrible toll. Transportation collapsed. The South was even driven to the economic cannibalism of pulling up rails from the less-used lines to repair the main ones. Window weights were melted down into bullets; gourds replaced dishes; pins became so scarce that they were loaned with reluctance.

> The blockade produced acute shortages, including morphine for the wounded. One North Carolinian recalled his boyhood: "There was a poppy bed in every garden planted for this purpose, and when I was seven years old I worked daily for the soldiers, scraping the inspissated juice of the poppy from the bulbar ovaries which had been punctured a few days before, and, like everyone else, I worked under the eternal mandate, 'Don't taste it!' On some fifty poppy heads it was a morning's work to get a mass about as big as a small peanut."

To the brutal end, the South revealed magnificent resourcefulness and spirit. Women buoyed up their menfolk, many of whom had seen enough of war at first hand to be heartily sick of it. A proposal was made by a number of women that they cut off their long hair and sell it abroad. But the project was not adopted, partly because of the blockade. The self-sacrificing women took pride in denying themselves the silks and satins of their Northern sisters. The chorus of a song, "The Southern Girl," touched a cheerful note:

> So hurrah! hurrah! For Southern Rights, hurrah!
> Hurrah! for the homespun dress the Southern
> ladies wear.

The Northern Captains of Industry had conquered the Southern Lords of the Manor. A crippled South left the capitalistic North free to work its own way, with high tariffs and other benefits. The industrial giants of the North, ushering in the full-fledged Industrial Revolution, were destined for increased dominance over American economic and political life. Hitherto the agrarian "slavocracy" of the South, by using sectional alliances, had partially checked the rising plutocracy of the North. Now cotton capitalism had lost out to industrial capitalism. The South of 1865 was rich in little but amputees, war heroes, ruins, and memories.

Limitations on Wartime Liberties

"Honest Abe" Lincoln, when inaugurated, laid his hand on the Bible and swore a solemn oath to uphold the Constitution. Then, driven by sheer necessity, he proceeded to tear a few holes in that hallowed document. He sagely concluded that if he did not do so, and patch the parchment later, there might not be a Constitution of a *united* United States to mend. The "Rail Splitter" was no hairsplitter.

But such infractions were not, in general, sweeping. Congress, as is often true in time of crisis, generally accepted or confirmed the President's questionable acts. Lincoln, though accused of being a "Simple Susan Tyrant," did not believe that his ironhanded authority would continue, once the Union was preserved. As he pointedly remarked in 1863, a man suffering from "temporary illness" would not persist in feeding on bitter medicines for "the remainder of his healthful life."

The Yankee Guy Fawkes. Lincoln is represented as destroying American liberties by the draft, the suspension of habeas corpus, and the Emancipation Proclamation. (London *Fun*, 1863.)

Congress was not in session when war erupted, so Lincoln gathered the reins into his own hands. Brushing aside legal objections, he boldly proclaimed a blockade. (His action was later upheld by the Supreme Court.) He arbitrarily increased the size of the Federal army—something that only Congress can do under the Constitution (see Art. I, Sec. VIII, para. 12). (Congress later approved.) He directed the secretary of the treasury to advance $2 million without appropriation or security to three private citizens for military purposes—a grave irregularity contrary to the Constitution (see Art. I, Sec. IX, par. 7). He suspended the precious privilege of the writ of habeas corpus, so that anti-Unionists might be summarily arrested. In taking this step, he defied a ruling by the chief justice that the safeguards of habeas corpus could be set aside only by authorization of Congress, as provided in the Constitution (see Art. I, Sec. IX, para. 2). Nearly two years later, in 1863, Congress acquiesced in the suspension.

Lincoln's regime was also guilty of many other high-handed acts. For example, it arranged for "supervised" voting in the Border States. There the intimidated citizen, holding a colored ballot indicating his party preference, had to march between two lines of armed troops. The federal officials also ordered the suspension of certain

> Lincoln, Kentucky-born like Jefferson Davis, was aware of Kentucky's crucial importance. In September 1861 he remarked, "I think to lose Kentucky is nearly the same as to lose the whole game. Kentucky gone, we cannot hold Missouri, nor, I think, Maryland. These all against us, and the job on our hands is too large for us. We would as well consent to separation at once, including the surrender of this capital [Washington].

newspapers and the arrest of their editors on grounds of obstructing the war.

Jefferson Davis was less able than Lincoln to exercise arbitrary power, mainly because of confirmed states'-righters who revealed an intense spirit of localism. To the very end of the conflict the owners of horse-drawn vans in Petersburg, Virginia, prevented the joining of the incoming and outgoing tracks of a militarily vital railroad. The South seemed willing to lose the war before it would surrender local rights—and it did.

The Copperhead Party. The cartoon shows the party in favor of a vigorous prosecution of peace. (*Harper's Weekly,* 1863.)

The Curse of Copperheadism

Hundreds of Northern citizens were arrested by the military authorities, chiefly on charges of hindering the Union cause by preaching defeatism or peace-at-any-price-ism. Many were seized without a warrant and were held for prolonged periods without trial, as in Czarist Russia. A large percentage of the persons thus abused were so-called Copperhead Democrats. The Copperheads were partisans who obstructed the war effort by disloyal talk—or worse—and they were named after the poisonous snake, which strikes without warning rattle. Dubbed members of the "White Feather Party," the Copperheads accused the Lincolnites of urging "War to the knife, and the knife to the hilt" in this uncivil Civil War.

Notorious among the victims of autocratic arrest was a prominent Copperhead, Clement L. Vallandigham. This tempestuous character was an Ohio ex-congressman who possessed brilliant oratorical gifts and unusual talents for stirring up trouble. A Southern partisan, he publicly demanded an end to the "wicked and cruel" war. The civil courts in Ohio were open, and he should have been tried in them. But he was convicted by a military tribunal in 1863 for treasonable utterances, and was then sentenced to prison. Lincoln decided that if Vallandigham liked the Confederates so much, he ought to be banished to their lines. This was done.

Vallandigham was not so easily silenced. Working his way to Canada, he ran for the governorship of Ohio on foreign soil, and polled a substantial but insufficient vote. He returned to his own state before the war ended, and although he defied "King Lincoln" and spat upon a military decree, he was not further prosecuted. The strange case of Vallandigham inspired Edward Everett Hale to write his moving but fictional story of Philip Nolan, *The Man without a Country* (1863), which was immensely popular in the North and which helped stimulate devotion to the Union. Nolan was a young army officer found guilty of participation in the Aaron Burr plot of 1806. He had cried out in court, "Damn the United States! I wish I may never hear of the United States again!" For this outburst he was condemned to a life of complete exile on American warships.

Considering the hatreds aroused, civil liberties and constitutional rights fared rather well. Some of the power usurped by the Chief Executive was retained, but most of it was gradually restored to the courts and Congress after the shooting stopped. Wartime penalties on the whole were mild and pardons speedy. Thousands of unterrified and unmolested Copperhead Democrats openly denounced Lincoln as "the Illinois Ape," demanded an end to the "Nigger War," discouraged enlistments, and encouraged desertions.

Politics as Usual in 1864

Political infighting in the North added greatly to Lincoln's cup of woe. Factions within his own party, distrusting his ability, sought to tie his hands. Conspicuous among these critics was the group led by the overambitious Secretary of the Treasury Chase. The master stroke of the anti-Lincoln Republicans was the creation of the meddlesome Congressional Committee on the Conduct of the War, which may have stirred up about as much trouble as it smoothed over. The extreme abolitionists, in addition, clamored for an immediate freeing of the slaves, regardless of the political and military consequences.

Salmon P. Chase (1808–1873). Chase was so conspicuously identified with anti-slavery in Ohio that he was known as "The Attorney General for Fugitive Slaves." He served conspicuously during the Civil War as secretary of the treasury, in which capacity he inaugurated the National Banking System. (Frick Art Reference Library)

Most dangerous of all were the Northern Democrats. Deprived of the brains that had departed with the Southern wing, they were left with the taint of association with the seceders. A tragedy befell the Democrats—and the Union—when their gifted leader, Stephen A. Douglas, died of typhoid fever seven weeks after war began. Inflexibly devoted to the Union, he probably could have kept much of his following on the straight and narrow path of loyalty.

Lacking a leader, the Democrats became badly divided. A large group of so-called War Democrats patriotically supported the Lincoln administration, but tens of thousands of Peace Democrats and regular Democrats did not. Many of the dissenters were outright Copperheads. They ranged all the way from those who wished the enemy Godspeed to those who favored a restored Union—but one restored by negotiation, not war.

Lincoln's precarious authority depended on his retaining Republican control of Congress. His majority was menaced by the Copperheads, who were especially strong in Ohio, Indiana, and Illinois, all of which contained many Southerners. Only with difficulty did the war governors of these states manage to keep them cooperating with Washington.

Lincoln Defeats McClellan at the Polls

Presidential elections come by the calendar and not by the crisis. As fate would have it, the election of 1864 fell most inopportunely in the midst of war.

The Republican party, fearing defeat, executed a clever maneuver. Joining with the War Democrats, it proclaimed itself to be the Union party. Thus the Republican party passed temporarily out of existence.

Lincoln's renomination at first encountered surprisingly strong opposition. Hostile factions whipped up considerable agitation to shelve

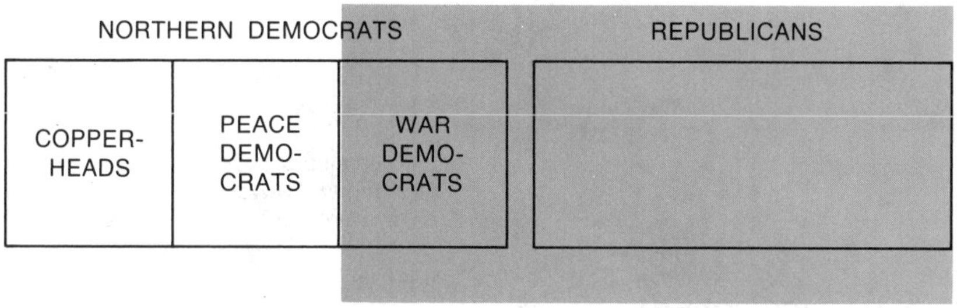

UNION PARTY, 1864

homely "Old Abe" in favor of handsome Secretary of the Treasury Chase. Lincoln was accused of lacking force; of being overready to compromise; of not having won the war; and of having shocked many sensitive souls by his ill-timed and earthy jokes. ("Prince of Jesters," one journal called him.) But the "ditch Lincoln" move collapsed, and the President was nominated by the Union party without serious dissent.

Lincoln's running mate was ex-tailor Andrew Johnson, a loyal War Democrat from Tennessee who had been a small slaveowner when the conflict began. He was placed on the Union party ticket to "sew up" the election by attracting War Democrats and the voters in the Border States, and not with proper regard for the possibility that Lincoln might die in office. Southerners and Copperheads alike condemned both candidates as birds of a feather: two ignorant, third-rate, boorish, backwoods politicians born in log cabins.

Embattled Democrats—regular and Copperhead—nominated the deposed and overcautious war hero, General McClellan. The Copperheads managed to force into the Democratic platform a plank denouncing the prosecution of the war as a failure. But McClellan, who could not otherwise have faced his old comrades-in-arms, repudiated this defeatist declaration.

The ensuing campaign was noisy and heated. The Democrats cried, "Old Abe removed McClellan. We'll now remove Old Abe." They also sang, "Mac Will Win the Union Back." The Union party men shouted for "Uncle Abe and Andy," and urged, "Vote as you shot." Their most effective slogan, growing out of a remark by Lincoln, was: "Don't swap horses in the middle of the river."

Lincoln's re-election was at first gravely in doubt. The war was going badly, as "Butcher" Grant continued to be bogged down in the Wilderness of Virginia. Lincoln himself gave way to despondency, fearing that political defeat was imminent. The anti-Lincoln Republicans, taking heart, started a new movement to "dump" Lincoln in favor of someone else.

But the atmosphere of gloom was changed electrically, as balloting day neared, by a succession of Northern victories. Admiral Farragut captured Mobile, Alabama, after defiantly shouting,

An Anti-Lincoln Cartoon. *Columbia:* "Where are my 15,000 sons—murdered at Fredericksburg?" *Lincoln:* "This reminds me of a little joke—" *Columbia:* "Go tell your joke at Springfield!" (*Harper's Weekly*, 1863.)

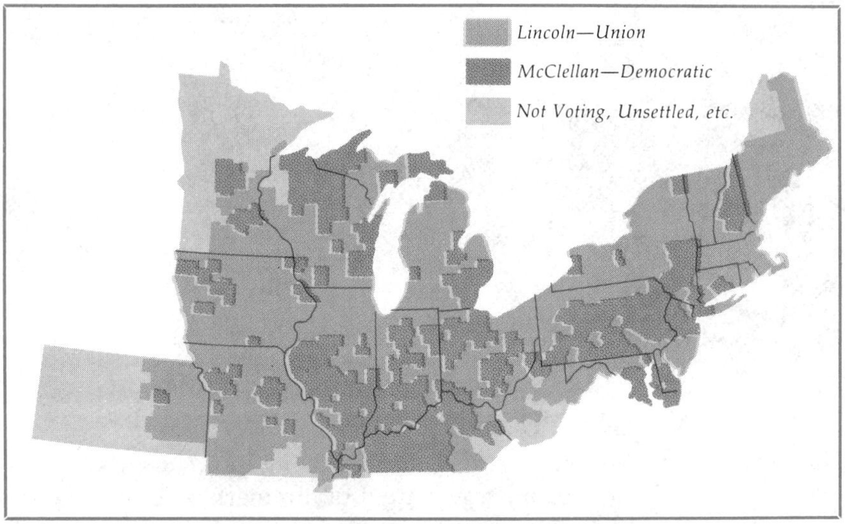

PRESIDENTIAL ELECTION OF 1864 (showing popular vote by county)
Lincoln also carried California, Oregon, and Nevada, but there was a considerable McClellan vote in each.

"Damn the torpedoes! Go ahead." General Sherman seized Atlanta. General ("Little Phil") Sheridan laid waste the verdant Shenandoah Valley of Virginia so thoroughly that in his words "a crow could not fly over it without carrying his rations with him."

The President pulled through, but nothing more than necessary was left to chance. At election time many Northern soldiers were furloughed home to support Lincoln. One Pennsylvania veteran voted forty-nine times—once for himself and once for each absent member of his company. Other soldiers were permitted to cast their ballots at the front.

Lincoln, who could have won anyhow without the "bayonet vote," vanquished McClellan by 212 electoral votes to 21, with the loss of only Kentucky, Delaware, and New Jersey. But "Little Mac" ran a much closer race than the electoral count indicates. He netted a surprising 45 percent of the popular vote, 1,805,237 to Lincoln's 2,213,665, piling up much support in the Southerner-infiltrated states of the Old Northwest, in New York, and in his native state of Pennsylvania.

One of the most crushing defeats suffered by the South was the defeat of the Northern Democrats in 1864. The removal of Lincoln was the last real hope for a Confederate victory, and the Southern soldiers would wishfully shout, "Hurrah for McClellan!" When Lincoln triumphed, desertions from the sinking Southern ship increased sharply.

The Martyrdom of Lincoln

On the night of April 14, 1865 (Good Friday), only five days after Lee's surrender, Ford's Theater in Washington witnessed its most sensational drama. A half-crazed, fanatically pro-Southern actor, John Wilkes Booth, slipped behind Lincoln as he sat in his box and shot him in the head. After lying unconscious all night, the Great Emancipator died the following morning. "Now he belongs to the ages," remarked the once-critical Secretary Stanton—probably the finest thing he ever said.

Lincoln expired in the arms of victory, at the very pinnacle of his fame. From the standpoint of his reputation, his death could not have been better timed if he had hired the assassin. A large number of his countrymen had not suspected his greatness, and many others had even doubted his ability. But his dramatic death helped to erase the memory of his shortcomings, and caused his nobler qualities to stand out in clearer relief. A contemporary, J. T. Trowbridge, lamented:

Heroic soul, in homely garb half-hid,
  Sincere, sagacious, melancholy, quaint;
What he endured, no less than what he did,
  Has reared his monument, and crowned him saint.

The full impact of Lincoln's death was not at once apparent to the South. Hundreds of bedraggled ex-Confederate soldiers cheered, as did some Southern civilians and Northern Copperheads, when they learned of the assassination. This reaction was only natural, because Lincoln had kept the war grinding on to the bitter end. If he had only been willing to stop the shooting, the South would have won.

As time wore on, increasing numbers of Southerners perceived that Lincoln's death was a calamity for them. Belatedly they recognized that his kindliness and moderation would have been the most effective shields between them and vindictive treatment by the victors. The assassination unfortunately increased the bitterness in the North, partly because of the fantastic rumor that Jefferson Davis had plotted it.

A few historians have argued that Andrew Johnson, now President-by-bullet, was crucified for Lincoln. The implication is that if the "Rail Splitter" had lived he would have run into serious trouble, perhaps impeachment, at the hands of the embittered members of his own party who demanded harsh treatment of the South.

The crucifixion thesis does not stand up under scrutiny. Lincoln no doubt would have clashed with Congress; in fact, he had already found himself in some hot water. The legislative branch normally struggles to win back the power that has been wrested from it by the executive in time of crisis. But the surefooted and experienced Lincoln could hardly have blundered into the same quicksands that engulfed Johnson. Lincoln was a victorious President; and there is no arguing with victory. Enjoying battle-tested powers of leadership, he possessed in full measure tact, sweet reasonableness, and an uncommon amount of common sense. Andrew Johnson, hot-tempered and impetuous, lacked all of these priceless qualities.

Ford's Theater, with its tragic murder of Lincoln, set the stage for the terrible ordeal of Reconstruction.

The powerful London *Times*, spokesman of the upper classes, had generally criticized Lincoln during the war, especially after the Emancipation Proclamation of 1862. He was then condemned as "a sort of moral American Pope" destined to be "Lincoln the Last." When the President was shot, the *Times* reversed itself (April 29, 1865): "Abraham Lincoln was as little of a tyrant as any man who ever lived. He could have been a tyrant had he pleased, but he never uttered so much as an ill-natured speech. . . . In all America there was, perhaps, not one man who less deserved to be the victim of this revolution than he who has just fallen."

The Aftermath of the Nightmare

The Civil War took a grisly toll in gore, about as much as all of America's subsequent wars combined. Over 600,000 men died in action or of disease, and in all over a million were killed or seriously wounded. To its lasting hurt, the white South lost the cream of its young manhood and potential leadership. In addition, tens of thousands of babies went unborn because potential fathers were at the front.

Direct monetary costs of the conflict totaled about $15 billion. But this colossal figure does not include continuing expenses, such as pensions and interest on the national debt. The intangible costs—dislocations, disunities, wasted energies, lowered ethics, blasted lives, bitter memories, and burning hates—cannot be calculated.

The greatest constitutional decision of the century, in a sense, was written in blood and handed down at Appomattox Court House, near which Lee surrendered. The extreme states'-righters were crushed. The national government, rewelded in the fiery furnace of war, emerged unbroken. Nullification and secession, those twin nightmares of previous decades, were laid to rest.

Union Troops Enter Richmond. Note the cheering blacks. (Valentine Museum, Richmond, Virginia.)

Beyond doubt the Civil War—the nightmare of the Republic—was the supreme test of American democracy. It finally answered the question, in the words of Lincoln at Gettysburg, whether a nation dedicated to such principles "can long endure." The preservation of democratic ideals, though not an officially announced war aim, was subconsciously one of the major objectives of the North.

Victory for Union arms also provided inspiration to the champions of democracy and liberalism the world over. The great English Reform Bill of 1867, under which Britain became a true political democracy, was passed two years after the Civil War ended. American democracy had proved itself, and its success was an additional argument used by the disfranchised British masses in securing similar blessings for themselves.

The "Lost Cause" of the South was lost, but few Americans today would argue that the end result was not for the best. America was again united physically, though for many years still divided spiritually by the passions of war. With the shameful cancer of slavery sliced away, free labor was further dignified by the removal of servile competition. Grave dangers were averted, including constant friction and conflict between North and South, each bristling with guns. The Monroe Doctrine, as foreigners could readily observe, took on more muscle. A strong and united nation was thus left free to fulfill its destiny as the overshadowingly powerful republic of the hemisphere—and ultimately of the world.

VARYING VIEWPOINTS

When the Civil War ended, slavery was officially defunct, secession was a dead issue, and industrial growth was surging forward. Charles Beard later hailed the war as the "Second American Revolution" because it had transformed the legal and institutional structure of government, and placed the levers of power firmly in the hands of a new business class. But did the bloody conflict neatly bisect the nation's history? In recent years many scholars have questioned the concept that the war constituted a dramatic turning point. Slavery may have formally disappeared, but blacks remained a scandalously subordinated social group. Regional differences persisted, even down to the present day. Thomas Cochran has even argued that the Civil War may have *retarded* overall industrialization. As for the rising commercial class of the post-war "Gilded Age," many historians now point to its antecedents in both the Whig and Jacksonian movements. History, it seems, is a mighty stream, which in time partially submerges even momentous events like the Civil War beneath the surface of its relentless flow.

SELECT READINGS

See the references for the previous chapter, especially those by Randall and Nevins. The best one-volume biography is B. P. Thomas, *Abraham Lincoln* (1952); see also R. H. Luthin, *The Real Abraham Lincoln* (1960). A multivolume, anecdotal work by a famed poet is Carl Sandburg, *Abraham Lincoln* (6 vols., 1926–1939). For social conditions see A. C. Cole, *The Irrepressible Conflict, 1850–1865* (1934); and E. D. Fite, *Social and Industrial Conditions in the North* (1910). A masterly synthesis is P. W. Gates, *Agriculture and the Civil War* (1965). Home-front politics are treated in J. A. Rawley, *The Politics of Union* (1974), and in Joel Silbey, *A Respectable Minority: The Democratic Party in The Civil War Era* (1977). Lincoln's problems are analyzed in W. B. Hesseltine, *Lincoln and the War Governors* (1948), J. G. Randall, *Constitutional Problems under Lincoln* (rev. ed., 1951), and T. H. Williams, *Lincoln and the Radicals* (1941). For a different view of the same subject, see H. L. Trefousse, *The Radical Republicans: Lincoln's Vanguard for Racial Justice* (1969). R. N. Current, *The Lincoln Nobody Knows* (1958), and David Donald, *Lincoln Reconsidered* (1956), offer interesting insights. On "disloyalty" see Wood Gray, *The Hidden Civil War* (1942), and especially F. L. Klement, *The Copperheads in the Middle West* (1960). Another aspect of Midwestern affairs is discussed in V. J. Voegeli, *Free but Not Equal: The Midwest and the Negro during the Civil War* (1967). Benjamin Quarles looks at *Lincoln and the Negro* (1962), and J. M. McPherson examines *The Struggle for Equality: Abolitionists and the Negro in the Civil War and Reconstruction* (1964). E. C. Murdoch analyzes the military draft in the North in *One Million Men* (1971), while Adrian Cook treats an important by-product of the draft, the New York City riots, in *Armies of the Street* (1974). Mary E. Massey presents the interesting story of women in the Civil War in *Bonnet Brigades* (1966); that topic also figures in Anne Firor Scott's *The Southern Lady* (1970). On the Confederacy, see E. M. Coulter, *The Confederate States of America* (1950), C. P. Roland, *The Confederacy* (1960), Emory M. Thomas, *The Confederate Nation, 1861–1865* (1979), and, for a fascinating first-person account, C. Vann Woodward, ed., *Mary Chestnut's Civil War* (1981). Diplomatic history is presented in F. L. Owsley's revised *King Cotton Diplomacy* (1959), and Martin Duberman's *Charles Francis Adams* (1961). See also Lynn M. Case and Warren F. Spencer, *The United States and France: Civil War Diplomacy* (1970). Economic matters are handled in R. T. Andreano, ed., *The Economic Impact of the American Civil War* (1962), and D. T. Gilchrist and W. D. Lewis, eds., *Economic Change in the Civil War Era* (1965). See David Donald, ed., *Why the North Won the Civil War* (1960). The war's literary legacy is keenly analyzed in Edmund Wilson's classic *Patriotic Gore* (1962) and in Daniel Aaron's *The Unwritten War: American Writers and the Civil War* (1973). For a fascinating discussion of Northern intellectuals and the conflict, consult George M. Frederickson, *The Inner Civil War* (1965).

24

The Ordeal of Reconstruction

With malice toward none, with charity for all, with firmness in the right as God gives us to see the right, let us strive on to finish the work we are in, to bind up the nation's wounds, to care for him who shall have borne the battle and for his widow and orphan, to do all which may achieve and cherish a just and lasting peace among ourselves and with all nations.

ABRAHAM LINCOLN, Second Inaugural, March 4, 1865

The Problems of Peace

Staggering tasks confronted the American people, North and South, when the guns grew cold. About a million and a half warriors in blue and gray had to be demobilized, readjusted to civilian life, and reabsorbed by the war-blasted economy. Civil government likewise had to be put back on a peacetime basis, and purged of encroachments by the military men.

The desperate plight of the South has eclipsed the fact that reconstruction had to be undertaken also in the North, though less spectacularly. War-inflated industries had to be deflated to a peace footing; factories had to be retooled for civilian needs.

Financial problems also loomed large in the North, now that the piper was to be paid. The national debt had shot up from a modest $65 million in 1860 to nearly $3 billion in 1865—a colossal sum for those days but one that a prudent government could pay. At the same time, war taxes had to be reduced to less burdensome levels.

Physical devastation inflicted by invading armies, chiefly in the South and Border States, had to be repaired. This herculean task was ultimately completed, but with discouraging slowness. Moral devastation in the North, most evident in greed and loose living, took longer to mend because it was deeper-rooted and harder to see.

Other weighty questions clamored for answers. What was to be done with approximately 4 million black slaves suddenly being plunged into the cold bath of freedom? Were the seceded states to be brought back into the Union on the old basis, and if so, with or without punishment?

What of the captured Confederate ringleaders, all of whom were liable to charges of treason? During the war a popular song had been "Hang Jeff Davis to a Sour Apple Tree," and even innocent children had lisped it. Davis was temporarily clapped into irons during the early days of his two-year imprisonment. But he and his fellow "conspirators" were finally released, partly

Richmond Devastated. Charleston, Atlanta, and other Southern cities looked much the same, resembling bombed-out Berlin and Munich in 1945. (Library of Congress.)

President Andrew Johnson (1808–1875). An "accidental President," Johnson was the only Chief Executive to be impeached by the House, though narrowly acquitted by the Senate. A former U.S. senator from Tennessee, he was re-elected in 1875 to the Senate that had formally tried him seven years earlier. As he said in a public speech in 1866: "I love my country. Every public act of my life testifies that is so. Where is the man who can put his finger upon one act of mine . . . to prove the contrary." (Library of Congress.)

because the odds were that no Virginia jury would convict them. All "rebel" leaders were finally pardoned by President Johnson as a Christmas present in 1868. But Congress did not remove all remaining civil disabilities until thirty years later.

The Prostrate South

Dismal indeed was the picture presented by the war-racked South when the rattle of musketry died. Not only had an age perished but a civilization had collapsed, in both its economic and its social structure. The moonlight-and-magnolia Old South of antebellum days, largely imaginary, had gone with the wind.

Handsome cities of yesteryear, like Charleston and Richmond, were gutted and weed-choked. An Atlantan returned to his once-fair home town and remarked, "Hell has laid her egg, and right here it hatched."

War had everywhere left its searing mark on social institutions. Churches were battered and dilapidated. The educational system was in chaos, with countless schools destroyed, many teachers killed in battle, and endowments wiped out. Sherman's Yankee invaders had reputedly stabled their horses in the dormitories of the University of South Carolina.

Economic life had creaked to a halt. Banks and business houses had locked their doors, ruined by runaway inflation. Factories were smokeless, silent, dismantled. The transportation system had broken down almost completely. Before the war, five different railroad lines had converged on Columbia, South Carolina; now the nearest connected track was twenty-nine miles (46.7 km) away. Efforts to untwist the rails corkscrewed by Sherman's soldiers were bumpily unsatisfactory.

Agriculture—the economic lifeblood of the South—was almost hopelessly crippled. Once-white cotton fields now yielded a lush harvest of green weeds. Seed was scarce, livestock had

A "Jeff Davis Necktie." A twisted iron rail after having been heated in a Yankee bonfire.

been driven off by plundering Yankees, and much of the black labor supply had taken off to enjoy the new freedom. Pathetic instances were reported of men hitching themselves to plows, while women and children gripped the handles. Not until 1870 did the seceded states produce as large a cotton crop as that of the fateful year 1860, and much of that came from new acreage in the Southwest.

Unfettered Freedmen

Confusion abounded in the still-smoldering South about the precise meaning of "freedom" for blacks. Emancipation took effect haltingly and unevenly in different parts of the conquered Confederacy, and in some regions planters stubbornly protested that slavery was legal until state legislatures or the Supreme Court might act. Newspapers in Mississippi earnestly discussed *gradual* emancipation. For many bondsmen, the shackles of slavery were not struck off in a single mighty blow; long-suffering blacks often had to struggle out of their chains link by link.

The variety of responses to emancipation, by whites as well as blacks, illustrated the sometimes startling complexity of the master-slave relationship. Unbending loyalty to "ole Massa" prompted many slaves to help their owners resist the liberating Union armies. Blacks blocked the door of the "big house" with their bodies, or stashed the plantation silverware under mattresses in their own humble huts, where it would be safe from the plundering "bluebellies." On other plantations, pent-up bitterness burst violently forth on the day of liberation. A group of Virginia slaves laid twenty lashes on the back of their former master—a painful dose of his own favorite medicine. Newly emancipated slaves sometimes eagerly accepted the invitation of Union troops to join in the pillaging of their master's possessions. One freedman said that he felt entitled to steal a chicken or two, since the whites had robbed him of his labor and his children.

> Carl Schurz described a Fourth of July affair in Savannah, Georgia, in 1865: "The colored firemen of this city desired to parade their engine on the anniversary of our independence. . . . In the principal street of the city the procession was attacked with clubs and stones by a mob . . . and by a crowd of boys swearing at the d——d niggers. The colored firemen were knocked down, some of them severely injured, their engine was taken away from them, and the peaceable procession dispersed."

Emancipation followed by re-enslavement, or worse, was the bewildering lot of many blacks, as Union armies marched in and out of various localities. A North Carolina slave estimated that he had celebrated emancipation about twelve times. As blacks in one Texas county flocked to the free soil of the liberated county next door, their owners bushwacked them with rifle fire as they swam for freedom across the river that marked the county line. The next day, trees along the riverbank were bent with swinging corpses—a grisly warning to others dreaming of liberty.

Prodded by the bayonets of Yankee armies of occupation, all masters were eventually forced to recognize their slaves' permanent freedom. The once-commanding planter would assemble his former human chattels in front of the porch of the "big house," and announce their liberty. This "Day of Jubilo" was the occasion of wild rejoicing. Tens of thousands of blacks naturally took to the roads. They sought long-separated loved ones, as formalizing a "slave marriage" was the first goal of many newly free men and women. Others travelled in search of economic opportunity in the towns or in the still-wild West. Many moved simply to test their new freedom.

Inexperienced ex-slaves unfortunately fell victims to the schemes of greedy whites. A "grapevine" rumor spread among blacks that on a given day the Washington government would present each family with "forty acres and a mule." White

Free at Last. A black family in South Carolina photographed just after Emancipation. Three generations are apparently present here, suggesting the cohesiveness and endurance of the Afro-American family, despite the harshness of slavery. (Library of Congress.)

swindlers sometimes sold for five dollars a set of red, white, and blue pegs, with which the trusting black had only to stake out his acreage. Quickly disillusioned, he was left with neither acres nor mule—nor his five dollars!

Uncertain about just how "free" they were, the former slaves were not instantly relieved of the yoke of centuries of oppression. Blacks had suffered many cruelties during slavery, but one of the cruelest strokes of all was being jerked from chains to freedom without adequate preparation or safeguards. In many ways, the war changed little. Poor, powerless, and illiterate, the majority of blacks carried on much as they had before. They worked at the same jobs for the same "massa," receiving pittance wages.

Desperately trying to bootstrap themselves up from slavery, blacks assembled in "Conventions of Freedmen" to fight for their newly gained rights. Led by ministers of God and free-born blacks from the North, these conventions expressed surprisingly moderate views. But moderation could not guarantee a warm reception by embittered white Southerners. The freed blacks were going to need all the friends—and the power—they could find in Washington.

A Dethroned but Defiant Aristocracy

The planter aristocrats were virtually ruined by the war. Reduced to proud poverty, they were confronted with damaged or burned mansions, lost investments, and semi-worthless land. In addition, their slaves, once worth about $2 billion, had been freed in one of the costliest confiscations of history. Some whites were assisted by the pitiful savings of their former slaves; a few peddled pies or took in washing. Women and children, some reared in luxury, were found begging from door to door.

Several thousand of the former "cotton lords" were unable to face up to their overpowering

"The Re-United States." This English cartoon reflects sympathy for the South. (*Punch,* 1865.)

burdens. They departed for the Far West, or for Mexico and Brazil, where their children gradually became Mexicanized or Brazilianized. A few desperate Southerners sought escape in suicide, including the distinguished Virginia soil expert, Edmund Ruffin, who ironically had fired one of the first shots at Fort Sumter.

But most of the impoverished planters labored courageously to restore the glory that had once been the South. General Robert E. Lee, for example, accepted the presidency of Washington College in Virginia—later Washington and Lee—and became a respected educator.

In teeter-totter fashion, the loss of the aristocrats was in some degree the gain of the common folk. The poor whites, not possessing much to begin with, stood to gain from change—and some of them did. As the once-rich abandoned their broad ancestral estates, a number of small farms became available. A kind of curious economic leveling took place, with the rich leveled down and the poor partially leveled up. But many dreary years were to pass before the economic health of the South equaled that of 1860.

The high-spirited Southerners, including many women, were unwilling to acknowledge defeat Having fought gallantly, they felt that they had not been beaten but had worn themselves out beating the North, like an arm-weary pugilist. Many of them, mourning the triumph of brute strength over righteousness, believed that they had won a moral victory. To them the struggle, though a "Lost Cause," was still a just war. They were conscious of no crime, and still believed that their view of secession was correct. A song sung in the South during the post-war years revealed no love for the Union:

I'm glad I fought agin her, I only wish we'd won,
And I ain't axed any pardon for anything I've done.

Continued defiance by Southerners was disquieting. It revealed itself in references to "damyankees" and to "your government" instead of "our government." A bishop in one Southern diocese even refused to pray for President Andrew Johnson, though the latter was in sore need of divine guidance. The Southerners would have avoided much misery if they had only realized that no great rebellion has ever ended with the victors sitting down to a love feast with the vanquished.

Black Codes in the Black South

Abolitionists had long preached that slavery was a degrading institution. Now the emancipators had to face the fact that the ex-slaves were in many ways actually degraded. The freedmen were largely unskilled, unlettered, without property or capital, and without even the knowledge of how to survive in free society. To cope with this problem throughout the conquered South, Congress created the Freedmen's Bureau in 1865. On paper at least, the bureau was to be a kind of primitive welfare

Primary School for Freedmen in Vicksburg, Mississippi. Note wide ranges of ages. (*Harper's Weekly*, 1866.)

agency. It was to provide food, clothing, and education both to white refugees and to freedmen. It was also authorized to distribute up to forty acres of abandoned or confiscated land to every adult male.*

In practice, the bureau met with scant success. But it did teach an estimated 200,000 black folk the elements of reading. Many ex-slaves had a passion for learning, partly because they wanted to close the gap between themselves and the whites, and partly because they longed to read the Word of God. In one elementary class in North Carolina sat four generations of the same family, ranging from a six-year-old tot to the seventy-five-year-old grandmother. But the bureau redistributed virtually no land, and its local administrators often yielded to white sentiment. Yet the white South resented the bureau as a meddlesome federal interloper that threatened to upset white racial dominance.

White Southern legislatures had their own ideas about how to handle the freedmen, and in 1865 and 1866 they enacted the iron-toothed Black Codes. These laws were designed to regulate the affairs of the emancipated blacks, much as the slave statutes had done in pre–Civil War days. The Black Codes aimed, first of all, to insure a stable labor supply. The crushed Cotton Kingdom could not rise from its weeds until the fields were once again put under the plow and hoe—and many whites feared that black plowmen and field hands would not work unless forced to do so.

Severe penalties were thus imposed by the codes on blacks who "jumped" their labor contracts. The ex-slaves could be made to forfeit their

---

*A Union general, Oliver O. Howard, was the first head of the Freedmen's Bureau. Sympathetic toward blacks, he founded and later served as president of Howard University, in Washington, D. C.

Black Huts at the Trent River Settlement, North Carolina. (*Harper's Weekly,* June 9, 1866.)

> Early in 1866 one congressman quoted a Georgian: "The blacks eat, sleep, move, live, only by the tolerance of the whites, who hate them. The blacks own absolutely nothing but their bodies; their former masters own everything, and will sell them nothing. If a black man draws even a bucket of water from a well, he must first get the permission of a white man, his enemy. . . . If he asks for work to earn his living, he must ask it of a white man; and the whites are determined to give him no work, except on such terms as will make him a serf and impair his liberty."

back wages, or could be forcibly dragged back to work by a paid "Negro-catcher." In Mississippi the captured freedman could be fined and then hired out to pay off his fine—an arrangement that closely resembled slavery itself.

The codes also aimed to restore as nearly as possible the pre-emancipation system of race relations. Freedom itself was legally recognized, as were some lesser privileges, such as the right to marry. But all the codes forbade a black to serve on a jury; some even barred blacks from renting or leasing land. A black could be punished for "idleness" by being sentenced to work on the chain gang.

These oppressive laws were a terrible burden to the unfettered blacks, struggling against ignorance and poverty to make their way as free persons. Thousands of impoverished ex-slaves slipped into the status of share crop farmers, as did many of the former landowning whites. The luckless sharecroppers gradually sank into a debtor's morass of virtual peonage, and remained there for generations. Formerly slaves to masters, countless blacks became slaves to the soil and their creditors.

The Black Codes naturally left a painful impression in the North. This was notably true of former anti-slavery centers, where the Southern restrictions were painted in especially lurid hues. If the ex-slaves were being re-enslaved, people asked one another, had not the Boys in Blue spilled their blood in vain? Had the North really won the war?

Johnson: The Tailor President

Few Presidents have ever been faced with a more perplexing sea of troubles than that confronting Andrew Johnson. What manner of man was this medium-built, dark-eyed, black-haired Tennessean, now Chief Executive by virtue of the bullet that killed Lincoln?

No citizen, not even Lincoln, has ever reached the White House from humbler beginnings. Born to impoverished parents in North Carolina and

Johnson's Tailor Shop. (Library of Congress.)

early orphaned, Johnson never attended school but was apprenticed to a tailor at age ten. Ambitious to get ahead, he taught himself to read, and later his wife taught him to write and do simple arithmetic. Like many another self-made man, he was inclined to overpraise his maker.

Johnson early became identified with politics in Tennessee, to which he had moved when seventeen years old. He shone as an impassioned champion of the poor whites against the planter aristocrats, although he himself ultimately owned a few slaves. He excelled as a two-fisted stump speaker before angry and heckling crowds, among whom on occasion he could hear a pistol being cocked. Elected to Congress, he attracted much favorable attention in the North (but not the South) when he refused to secede with his own state. After Tennessee was partially "redeemed" by Union armies, he was appointed war governor, and served courageously in an atmosphere of danger.

Destiny next thrust Johnson into the vice-presidency. Lincoln's Union party in 1864 needed to attract support from the War Democrats and other pro-Southern elements, and Johnson, a Democrat, seemed to be the ideal man. Unfortunately, he appeared at the vice-presidential inaugural ceremonies the following March in a scandalous condition. He had recently been afflicted with typhoid fever, and although not known as a heavy drinker, he was urged by his friends to take a stiff bracer of whiskey. This he did—with disgraceful results.

"Old Andy" Johnson was no doubt a man of parts—unpolished parts. He was intelligent, able, forceful, and gifted with homespun honesty. Steadfastly devoted to duty and to the people, he was a dogmatic champion of states' rights and the Constitution. He would often present a copy of the document to visitors, and he was buried with one as a pillow.

Yet the man who had raised himself from the tailor's bench to the President's chair was a misfit. A Southerner who did not understand the North, a Tennessean who had earned the distrust of the South, a Democrat who had never been accepted by the Republicans, a President who had never been elected President, he was not at home in a Republican White House. Hotheaded, contentious, and stubborn, he was the wrong man in the wrong place at the wrong time. A Reconstruction policy devised by the angels might well have failed in his tactless hands.

Johnson as a Parrot. He was constantly invoking the Constitution. (*Harper's Weekly.*)

Lenient Johnsonian Justice

Johnson got off on the right foot as far as vengeful Northerners were concerned. Upon Lincoln's death, his hatred of the "stuck-up" planter aristocrats again flared forth, and he threatened to reconstruct the South with fire and hemp.

Applause burst from Republicans, especially the Radical or dominant wing of the party. These were the extremists who had condemned Lincoln's go-slow abolition policy, and they were determined to reconstruct the South radically—that is, with a rod of iron. Many Radicals wanted to safeguard the rights of the blacks; others were also driven by an urge for power and punishment. Some of them were secretly pleased when the assassin's bullet removed Lincoln, for the martyred President had shown tenderness toward the South. Spiteful "Andy" Johnson would presumably be a pliant tool in their hands.

But time and responsibility sobered Johnson, and within a few weeks he veered toward Lincoln's "rosewater" 10-percent plan. Lincoln had decreed in 1863 that, as a first step, a group of voters equal to one-tenth of the voting population of any Southern state in 1860 must take the oath of allegiance to the United States. The next step would be the erection of a new state government under a constitution which accepted the abolition of slavery. Lincoln would then recognize the purified new regime.

Several conquered Southern states, taking advantage of Lincoln's lenient 10-percent proposal, had reorganized their governments by 1864. But Congress flatly refused to seat their duly elected representatives. The Radical Republicans, though by no means all Republicans, were determined that the South should suffer more severely for its sins.

The plan adopted by Johnson in 1865 rather resembled Lincoln's 10-percent scheme; in some respects it was even more generous. It disfranchised certain leading Confederates, including those with taxable property worth more than $20,000, but it permitted the other whites to reorganize their own state governments. Special state conventions were to be summoned. These would be required to repeal the ordinances of secession, repudiate all Confederate debts, and ratify the slave-freeing 13th Amendment.

> Before President Johnson softened his Southern policy, his views were Radical. Speaking on April 21, 1865, he declared: "It is not promulgating anything that I have not heretofore said to say that traitors must be made odious, that treason must be made odious, that traitors must be punished and impoverished. They must not only be punished, but their social power must be destroyed. If not, they will still maintain an ascendancy, and may again become numerous and powerful; for, in the words of a former Senator of the United States, 'When traitors become numerous enough, treason becomes respectable.'"

Republican Radicals in the Saddle

In the second half of 1865, the new Southern state governments were rapidly organized under the "soft" Lincoln-Johnson plan. Among the first acts of these regimes was the passage of the Black Codes, so offensive to the North. Elections were duly held for senators and representatives in Congress. When that body convened in December 1865, scores of distinguished Southerners were on hand to claim their seats.

The appearance of these ex-rebels was a natural but costly blunder. Voters of the South, seeking able representatives, had turned instinctively to their experienced statesmen. But most of the Southern leaders were "tainted" by active association with the "Lost Cause." Among the delegations elected to Congress were four former Confederate generals, five colonels, and various members of the Richmond cabinet and Congress. Worst of all, there was the 90-pound (40.8-kilogram) but brainy Alexander Stephens, former vice-president of the Confederacy, still under indictment for treason.

Inevitably, the presence of those "whitewashed rebels" infuriated the Radical Republicans in Congress. The war had been fought to restore the Union, but the Radicals wanted it restored on their own terms. They were in no hurry to embrace their former enemies, virtually all of them Democrats, in the chambers of the Capitol. While the South had been "out" from 1861 to 1865, the Republicans in Congress had enjoyed a relatively free hand. They had passed much legislation that favored the North, such as the Homestead Act and the Pacific Railroad Act. Now many Republicans balked at giving up this political advantage. On December 4, 1865, the first day of the session, they banged shut the door in the faces of the newly elected Southern delegations.

Looking to the future, the Radical Republicans were alarmed to note that a restored South would be stronger than ever in Congress. Before the war a black slave had counted as three-fifths of a person in apportioning congressional representation. Now he was five-fifths of a person. Eleven Southern states had seceded and had lost the war. But now, owing to full counting of free blacks, the rebel states were entitled to twelve more votes in Congress than they had previously enjoyed. Again the question was being raised in the North: Who won the war?

Radicals had good reason to fear that ultimately they would be elbowed aside. Southerners might join hands with ex-Copperheads and discontented farmers of the North and West, and then win control of Congress. If this happened, they could destroy the industrial and financial foundations of the Republican party, which had entrenched itself deeply behind the smoke screen of the Civil War. Specifically, the Southerners might lower the high war tariffs, restrict the new industrial monopolies, repeal the free-farm Homestead Act, and curtail the lavish grants of land to the railroads. The ex-Confederates might even go so far as to repudiate the national debt and re-enslave the blacks. These last two possibilities, though remote, alarmed Republican bondholders and ex-abolitionists alike.

Fearing such disasters, the Radical Republicans found a potent trump card—the black vote. If they could give the ballot to the ex-slave and induce him to vote Republican, they would hold a powerful hand. They probably could offset the efforts of the Southerners to unite with the numerous Northern agrarians to destroy Republican dominance in Washington.

Republican agitation for black suffrage—that is, more democracy—was prompted by both idealistic and selfish motives. Idealists like Senator Charles Sumner were striving not only for black freedom but for racial equality. They believed that the ex-bondsman should have the ballot for protection against the whites, and for the development of civic responsibility as well. But less idealistic Radical Republicans—how numerous one cannot say—were plainly more interested in the welfare of the party than in that of the black. They would "Republicanize" the South by making the freedman their tool; they would rule or ruin. For a time they did both.

Johnson Clashes with Congress

On what terms should the seceded states now be readmitted? Lincoln had argued—and Johnson agreed—that the Southern states had never legally withdrawn from the Union. Their formal restoration would therefore be relatively simple. But the Radical Republicans insisted that the seceders had forfeited all their rights—had committed "suicide"—and could be readmitted only as "conquered provinces" on such conditions as Congress should decree.

Most powerful of the Radical Republicans was crusty Congressman Thaddeus Stevens of Pennsylvania, then seventy-four years old. He was a curious figure, with a protruding lower lip, a heavy black wig on a bald head, and a deformed foot. A devoted friend of the blacks, he had defended runaway slaves without fee and, before dying, insisted on burial in a black cemetery. His hatred of the South, already violent, was intensified when Confederate cavalry raiders pillaged and burned his Pennsylvania ironworks. He even talked wildly at times of exterminating the ex-Confederates, and of handing their estates over to the ex-slaves as compensation for unpaid sweat.

When Congress convened for its fateful session

Thaddeus Stevens (1792–1868). Stevens, who regarded the seceded states as "conquered provinces," promoted much of the major Reconstruction legislation, including the 14th (civil rights) Amendment. He was among the foremost in the impeachment of President Johnson. (Library of Congress.)

An Inflexible President. This Republican cartoon shows Johnson knocking blacks out of the Freedmen's Bureau by his veto. (Thomas Nast, (*Harper's Weekly*, 1866.)

in December 1865, the Radical Republicans were prepared to call the tune. Led by the zealous Stevens, a masterly parliamentarian with a razor-sharp mind and withering sarcasm, they not only denied the Southern members seats, but promptly set up the Joint (House-Senate) Committee on Reconstruction. The domineering Stevens, as chairman of the House contingent, was the most influential member of this committee of fifteen. Cracking the whip relentlessly from his driver's seat, he became, as much as any one man, virtual ruler of the nation for more than a year.

A clash between the high-riding Radicals and the strong-willed Johnson was inevitable. It came in February 1866, when the President vetoed a bill (later repassed) to extend the life of the controversial Freedmen's Bureau. He stubbornly regarded the measure as an unconstitutional invasion of the rights of the Southern states.

Aroused, the Radicals quickly struck back. In March 1866, they passed the Civil Rights Bill, which conferred on the blacks the privilege of American citizenship and also struck at the Black Codes. Johnson resolutely vetoed this forward-looking measure on constitutional grounds, but in April the Radicals in Congress steam-rollered it over his veto—something they repeatedly did henceforth. The helpless President, dubbed "Sir Veto" and "Andy Veto," was reduced to a partial figurehead as Congress assumed the dominant role in running the government. One critic called Johnson "the dead dog of the White House."

The Radicals now undertook to rivet the principles of the Civil Rights Bill into the Constitution as the 14th Amendment. They feared that the Southerners might one day win control of Congress and repeal the hated law. The proposed amendment, as approved by Congress and sent to the states in June 1866, was sweeping. It (1) conferred civil rights (but not the vote) on the blacks; (2) reduced proportionately the representation of a state in Congress and in the Electoral College if it denied the blacks the ballot; (3) disqualified from federal and state office ex-Confederates who as federal officeholders had once taken an oath "to support the Constitution of the United States"; and (4) guaranteed the federal debt, while repudiating all Confederate debts. (See text of 14th Amendment in Appendix.)

Thus the scheme of the Radicals was roughly the broad 14th Amendment superimposed upon the lenient Lincoln-Johnson plan. These terms were not intolerably severe, though highly ob-

Principal Reconstruction Proposals and Plans

1864–1865	*1865–1866*	*1866–1867*	*1867–1877*
Lincoln's 10-percent proposal	Johnson's version of Lincoln's proposal	Congressional plan: 10-percent plan with 14th Amendment	Congressional plan of military Reconstruction: 14th Amendment plus black suffrage, later established nationwide by 15th Amendment

jectionable to the still-defiant white Southerners. Black suffrage was not yet forced on them, but they would be shorn of considerable political power if they did not adopt it voluntarily.

Swinging 'Round the Circle with Johnson

As 1866 lengthened, the battle intensified between the Radical Congress and the President. The root of the controversy went back to Johnson's "10-percent" governments that had passed the most severe Black Codes. Congress tried to temper the worst features of the codes by extending the life of the embattled Freedmen's Bureau and passing the Civil Rights Bill. Both measures Johnson had vetoed. Now the burning issue was whether Reconstruction was to be carried on with or without the drastic 14th Amendment. The Radicals would settle for nothing less; they insisted that the Southern states ratify the amendment as a condition for readmitting their representatives to Congress.

"The Reconstruction Dose." This Republican cartoon shows Johnson as a bad boy urging the South to reject the medicine with which Dr. Congress, backed up by Mrs. Columbia, is trying to restore her health. (*Frank Leslie's Illustrated Newspaper*, 1867.)

Collision Course. President Andrew Johnson and Radical Republican leader Thaddeus Stevens square off during Reconstruction. (Library of Congress)

The crucial congressional elections of 1866—more crucial than some presidential elections—were fast approaching. President Johnson was naturally eager to escape from the clutch of the Radical Congress by securing a majority favorable to his soft-on-the-South policy. Invited to dedicate a Chicago monument to Stephen A. Douglas, he undertook to speak at various cities en route in support of his views.

Johnson's famous "Swing around the Circle," beginning in the late summer of 1866, was a serio-comedy of errors. The President delivered a series of "give 'em hell" speeches, in which he accused the Radicals in Congress of having planned large-scale anti-black riots and murder in the South. As he spoke, hecklers hurled insults at him. Reverting to his stump-speaking days in Tennessee, he shouted back angry retorts, amid cries of "You be damned" and "Don't get mad, Andy." The dignity of his high office sank to a new low, as the old charges of drunkenness were revived.

As a vote-getter, Johnson was highly successful—for the opposition. His inept speechmaking heightened the cry "Stand by Congress" against the "Tailor of the Potomac." When the ballots were counted, the Radicals had rolled up more than a two-thirds majority in both Houses of Congress. Yet the outcome did not necessarily mean that

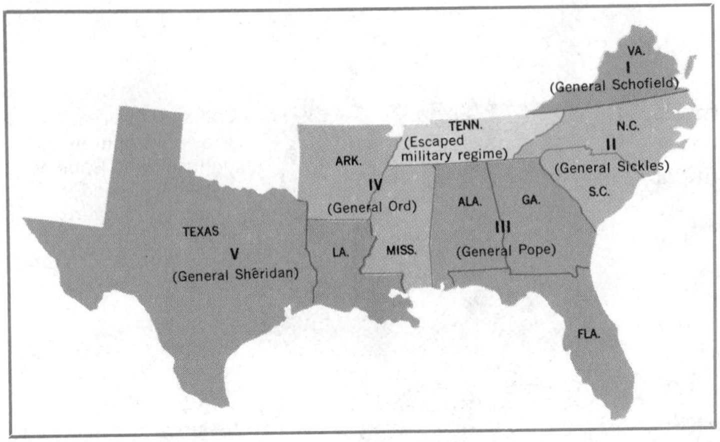

MILITARY RECONSTRUCTION, 1867
(five districts and commanding generals)
For many white Southerners, military reconstruction amounted to turning the knife in the wound of defeat. An often-repeated story of later years had a Southerner remark, "I was sixteen years old before I discovered that damnyankee was two words."

the country favored Radical Reconstruction. In many congressional districts the voters had a devil's choice between an ex-Copperhead and a Radical; they held their noses and chose the latter.

The setback at the polls merely widened the gap between the determined Radicals and the stiff-necked Southerners. If Johnson had been far-sighted, he would have urged the Southern states to accept the 14th Amendment as the best possible terms they could get. But he encouraged them to resist. They probably needed no prompting, for all of the "sinful eleven," except Tennessee, defiantly spurned the 14th Amendment. Their spirit was reflected in a Southern song:

> And I don't want no pardon for what I was or am,
> I won't be reconstructed and I don't give a damn.

Reconstruction by the Sword

Radicals in Congress now felt fully justified in imposing on the South the drastic Military Reconstruction Act of March 2, 1867, supplemented by three other measures. The controversial legislation swept away the lily-white Southern state governments, which had been reorganized under Johnson's auspices. It set up five military districts, each commanded by a Union general and policed by blue-clad soldiers, about 20,000 all told. More than that, the Radical restrictions, reinforced by requirements forced into the new state constitutions, disfranchised additional tens of thousands of Southern white leaders.

Congress additionally laid down stringent conditions for the readmission of the seceded states. The wayward sisters were required to ratify the 14th Amendment, thus giving the ex-slaves their rights as citizens. But the bitterest pill of all to white Southerners was the stipulation that they guarantee in their state constitutions full suffrage for their former slaves. One result was the election of more than a dozen black congressmen, including two senators, who as a group did creditable work.

The Radical Republicans were still worried. The danger loomed that once the unrepentant states were readmitted, they would amend their constitutions so as to withdraw the ballot from the blacks. The only ironclad safeguard was to incorporate black suffrage in the federal Constitution. This goal was finally achieved, three years after the Military Reconstruction Act of 1867, by the 15th Amendment. Passed by Congress in 1869, it was ratified by the required number of states in 1870. (For text, see Appendix.)

Military Reconstruction of the South was thus launched in 1867. Congress not only usurped certain functions of the President as commander-in-chief, but it set up a questionable martial regime. The Supreme Court had already ruled, in the case of *Ex parte Milligan* (1866), that military tribunals could not properly try civilians, even during wartime, in areas where the civil courts were open. Peacetime military rule, which involved an arbitrary suppression of newspapers, was obviously contrary to the spirit of the Constitution.

After shackling "Old Veto" Johnson, the Radicals even succeeded in subduing the Supreme Court. The learned justices, no doubt fearing that their own powers were in jeopardy, avoided giving serious offense to the Radical Congress. They even refused, on technicalities, to assert themselves when they might have intervened. But public sentiment in the North gradually turned against the Radicals. The Supreme Court took heart from this changing atmosphere, and beginning in 1876 it stamped the brand of unconstitutionality on a number of the congressional Reconstruction laws. But by this time—nine years after the first Military Reconstruction Act—the eggs had been scrambled.

Beginning in 1867, and under the stern eye of Union soldiers, new state governments had been set up in the South. They promptly fell under the control of the much-maligned "scalawags" and "carpetbaggers," who in turn used the blacks as political henchmen. The "scalawags" were Southerners, sometimes able Southern Unionists and ex-Whigs. They collaborated in creating the new regimes and hence were regarded as traitors by the ex-Confederates. The "carpetbaggers" were mainly Northern adventurers and fortune seekers ("vultures"), who supposedly packed all their worldly goods into a single carpetbag. Though many of these "damn Yankees" were offensive to the South, a kinder feeling was shown toward carpetbaggers who came down with some capital, a willingness to work, and a capacity to "mind their own business"—that is, not "meddle" with the blacks.

Senator Hiram R. Revels (1822–1901). The first black U.S. senator, Revels was elected in 1870 to the seat that had been occupied by Jefferson Davis when the South seceded. (Library of Congress.)

Prodded into line by federal officials, the Southern states got on with the distasteful task of constitution making. By 1870 all of them had reorganized their governments and had been accorded full rights. The hated "Blue Bellies" were withdrawn from police work only when the new Radical regimes seemed to be firmly entrenched. Finally, in 1877, ten years after the long ordeal of military Reconstruction had begun, the last federal bayonets were removed from state politics.

Enfranchised Freedmen

The ex-slaves were now free. But should they have the full rights of citizenship, including the most important of all, the right to vote? The question was a thorny one. In justice, if blacks were to be equal, they would have to wield the ballot. But many Radical Republicans at first hesitated to bestow suffrage on the freedmen. The 14th Amendment had conferred citizenship but had stopped short of guaranteeing the right to vote. It merely imposed relatively mild penalties on those states that refused to enfranchise blacks. But the Radicals soon grew steely in their determination to gain the power of the ballot box for the emancipated slaves.

White Southerners bitterly resented the efforts of the Republican Radicals from 1867 to 1870 to elevate the uneducated blacks to full political equality. The ex-slaves themselves were often

Southern Reconstruction by State

State	*Readmitted to Representation in Congress*	*Home Rule (Democratic Regime) Re-established*	*Comments*
Tennessee	July 24, 1866		Ratified 14th Amendment in 1866, and hence avoided Military Reconstruction.*
Arkansas	June 22, 1868	1874	
North Carolina	June 25, 1868	1870	
Alabama	June 25, 1868	1874	
Florida	June 25, 1868	1877	
Louisiana	June 25, 1868	1877	Federal troops restationed in 1877, as result of Hayes-Tilden electoral bargain.
South Carolina	June 25, 1868	1877	Same as above.
Virginia	January 26, 1870	1869	
Mississippi	February 23, 1870	1876	
Texas	March 30, 1870	1874	
Georgia	[June 25, 1868] July 15, 1870	1872	Readmitted June 25, 1868, but returned to military control after expulsion of blacks from legislature.

*For many years Tennessee was the only state of the secession to observe Lincoln's birthday as a legal holiday. Many Southern states still observe the birthdays of Jefferson Davis and Robert E. Lee.

bewildered by such unaccustomed responsibilities. When they registered to vote many of them did not know their ages; even boys of sixteen signed the rolls. Some of these future voters could not even give their last names, if indeed they had any, and many took any surname that popped into their heads, often that of old "Massa."

Representative Thaddeus Stevens, in a congressional speech on January 3, 1867, urged the ballot for blacks out of concern for them and out of bitterness against the whites: "I am for Negro suffrage in every rebel state. If it be just, it should not be denied; if it be necessary, it should be adopted; if it be a punishment to traitors, they deserve it."

Thousands of Southern whites were meanwhile being denied the vote, either by act of Congress or by the new state constitutions. At one dinner in South Carolina, the company consisted of a distinguished group of ex-governors, ex-congressmen, and ex-judges. The only voter in the room was the black waiter who served the meal. In some localities, about half the eligible white voters were temporarily disfranchised, and at one time the black voters in five Southern states outnumbered the white voters, many of whom were also illiterate.

By glaring contrast most of the Northern states, before the ratification of the 15th Amendment in

1870, withheld the ballot from their tiny black minorities. Southerners naturally concluded that the Radicals were hypocritical in insisting that blacks in the South be allowed to vote. One prominent North Carolinian jibed:

> To every Southern river shall Negro suffrage come,
> But not to fair New England, for that's too close
> to hum.

Both Presidents Lincoln and Johnson had proposed to give the ballot gradually to blacks who qualified for it through education, property ownership, or soldier-service. Such a moderate program might have proved more acceptable to the ex-Confederates. But in the stormy aftermath of the war, the voices of moderation were lost in the gale. Gradualism gave way to the hard insistence by Stevens and other Radicals that the ex-slaves be enfranchised wholesale and immediately. In the end, Radical policy backfired in many ways. It conferred only fleeting benefits on the blacks, envenomed the whites, and eventually crippled the Republican party for nearly 100 years in the ex-Confederate states.

"The First Vote." (Alfred R. Waud, *Harper's Weekly,* November 16, 1867.)

Black-and-White Legislatures in the South

In five states—Alabama, Florida, Louisiana, Mississippi, and South Carolina—the black voters enfranchised by the new state constitutions made up a majority. But only in South Carolina did they manage to dominate the lower house of the legislature. There were no state senates with a black majority, and no black governors during "black Reconstruction." Many of the newly elected black legislators were literate and able; more than a few came from the ranks of the pre-war free blacks, who had often acquired considerable education.

Yet in many Southern capitols, the ex-slaves, to the bitter resentment of their ex-masters, held offices ranging from doorkeeper to speaker. Blacks who had once raised cotton under the lash of an overseer were now raising points of order under the gavel of a parliamentarian. In many Southern states—as in many Northern states at the same time—graft and theft ran rampant. This was especially true of South Carolina and Louisiana, where promoters and other pocket-padders used politically inexperienced blacks as catspaws. The worst black-and-white legislatures purchased, under "legislative supplies," such "stationery" as hams, perfumes, suspenders, bonnets, corsets, champagne, and a coffin. One "thrifty" carpetbag governor in a single year "saved" $100,000 from a salary of $8,000.

To their credit, the black-and-white legislatures also passed much desirable legislation and introduced many overdue reforms. In some states the tax system was streamlined; charities were established; public works were launched; property rights were guaranteed to women; and free public schools were encouraged for blacks as well as whites. Many of these reforms were so welcome that they were retained even by the all-white "Redeemer" governments that later returned to power.

A white Virginian wrote from his deathbed: "Now with what will be my lastest breath, I here repeat and would willingly proclaim my unmitigated hatred to Yankee rule . . . and all connections with Yankees, and the perfidious, malignant and vile Yankee race." A Virginia woman noted at about the same time: "I have this morning witnessed a procession of nearly a thousand children belonging to colored schools. . . . When I thought that the fetters of ignorance were broken, and that they might not be forced from their parents and sold at auction to the highest bidder, my heart went up in adoring gratitude to the great God; not only on their account, but that we white people were no longer permitted to go on in such wickedness, heaping up more and more wrath of God upon our devoted heads."

Public debt in the Southern states doubled and tripled. Sometimes the expenditures were for legitimate purposes, such as rebuilding war-torn bridges or providing new educational services for the suddenly liberated blacks. Southern debts were further bloated by the unwillingness of Northern financiers to invest their capital in ravaged Dixieland. This reluctance proved so great that issues of Southern state bonds sold at deeply depressed discounts in the money markets of the North. And much of the new debt slipped down the sinkhole of fraud and corruption.

Tax rates meanwhile shot up ten- and fifteen-fold, and many propertied but disfranchised whites raised the ancient cry, "No taxation without representation." When these whites (the "Redeemers") finally regained control of their state governments, they openly repudiated over $100 million of the indebtedness they regarded as improperly incurred.

Knights of the White Sheet

Deeply embittered, some Southern whites resorted to savage measures against "Radical" rule. Many whites resented the success and ability of black legislators as much as they resented alleged "corruption." A number of secret organizations mushroomed forth, the most notorious of which was the "Invisible Empire of the South," or Ku Klux Klan, founded in Tennessee in 1866. Besheeted night riders, their horses' hoofs muffled, would approach the cabin of an "upstart" black and hammer on the door. In ghoulish tones one thirsty horseman would demand a bucket of water. Then, under pretense of drinking, he would pour it into a rubber attachment concealed beneath his mask and gown, smack his lips, and declare that this was the first water he had tasted since he was killed at the Battle of Shiloh. If fright did not produce the desired effect, force was employed.

Such tomfoolery and terror proved partially effective. Many ex-bondsmen and white "carpetbaggers," quick to take a hint, shunned the polls. But those stubborn souls who persisted in their "upstart" ways were flogged, mutilated, or even murdered. In one Louisiana parish in 1868, the whites in two days killed or wounded 200 victims; a pile of 25 bodies was found half-buried in the woods. By such atrocious practices was the black "kept in his place"—that is, down. The Klan be-

In a 1900 speech Senator Tillman of South Carolina brutally boasted: "We preferred to have a United States army officer rather than a government of carpetbaggers and thieves and scallywags and scoundrels who had stolen everything in sight and mortgaged posterity . . . by issuing bonds. When that happened we took the government away. We stuffed the ballot boxes. We shot them. We are not ashamed of it."

Lynching: Aftermath of Reconstruction
(PERSONS IN U.S. LYNCHED [BY RACE], 1882–1970*)

Year	*Whites*	*Blacks*	*Total*
1882	64	49	113
1885	110	74	184
1890	11	85	96
1895	66	113	179
1900	9	106	115
1905	5	57	62
1910	9	67	76
1915	13	56	69
1920	8	53	61
1925	0	17	17
1930	1	20	21
1935	2	18	20
1940	1	4	5
1945	0	1	1
1950	1	1	2
1965	0	0	0

*There were no lynchings in 1965–1970. In every year from 1882 (when records were first kept) to 1964 the number of lynchings corresponded roughly to the figures here given. The worst year was 1892, when 161 blacks and 69 whites were lynched (total 230); the next worst was 1884, when 160 whites and 51 blacks were lynched (total 211).

The Ku Klux Klan. Two contemporary views of the Klan—masked and unmasked. (*Left,* from an anonymous pamphlet of 1872; *right,* Archives of Rutherford B. Hayes Library.)

came a refuge for numerous bandits and cutthroats. Any scoundrel could don a sheet.

Radicals in Congress, outraged by this night-riding lawlessness, passed the harsh Force Acts of 1870 and 1871. Federal troops were able to stamp out much of the "lash law," but by this time the "Invisible Empire" had already done its work of intimidation. Many of the outlawed groups continued their tactics in the guise of "dancing clubs," "missionary societies," and "rifle clubs," though the net effect of all the hooded terrorists has probably been exaggerated. Economic reprisals were often more effective, especially when causing the black to lose his job.

The following excerpt is part of a pathetic appeal to Congress in 1871 by a group of Kentucky blacks:

"We believe you are not familiar with the description of the Ku Klux Klans riding nightly over the country, going from county to county, and in the county towns, spreading terror wherever they go by robbing, whipping, ravishing, and killing our people without provocation, compelling colored people to break the ice and bathe in the chilly waters of the Kentucky River.

"The [state] legislature has adjourned. They refused to enact any laws to suppress Ku-Klux disorder. We regard them [the Ku-Kluxers] as now being licensed to continue their dark and bloody deeds under cover of the dark night. They refuse to allow us to testify in the state courts where a white man is concerned. We find their deeds are perpetrated only upon colored men and white Republicans. We also find that for our services to the government and our race we have become the special object of hatred and persecution at the hands of the Democratic Party. Our people are driven from their homes in great numbers, having no redress only [except] the United States court, which is in many cases unable to reach them."

Shortsighted attempts by the Radicals to exploit the ex-slave as a voter failed miserably. The white South, for many decades, openly flouted the 14th and 15th Amendments. Wholesale disfranchisement of the black, starting conspicuously about 1890, was achieved by intimidation, fraud, and trickery. Among various underhanded schemes were the literacy tests, unfairly administered by whites to the advantage of illiterate whites. In the eyes of otherwise honorable Southerners, the goal of White Supremacy fully justified dishonorable devices.

A black leader protested to whites in 1868: "It is extraordinary that a race such as yours, professing gallantry, chivalry, education, and superiority, living in a land where ringing chimes call child and sire to the Gospel of God—that with all these advantages on your side, you can make war upon the poor defenseless black man."

Johnson Walks the Impeachment Plank

Radicals meanwhile had been sharpening their hatchets for President Johnson. Annoyed by the obstruction of the "drunken tailor" in the White House, they falsely accused him of maintaining there a harem of "dissolute women." Not content with curbing his authority, they decided to remove him altogether by constitutional processes.* Under existing law the president pro tempore of the Senate, the unscrupulous and rabidly Radical "Bluff Ben" Wade of Ohio, would then become President.

As an initial step, the Radicals in 1867 passed the Tenure of Office Act—as usual over Johnson's veto. Contrary to precedent, the new law required the President to secure the consent of the Senate before he could remove his appointees, once they had been approved by that body. One purpose of the Radicals was to freeze into the Cabinet the secretary of war, Edwin M. Stanton, a holdover from the Lincoln administration. Though outwardly loyal to Johnson, he was secretly serving as a spy and informer for the Radicals. Another purpose was to goad Johnson into breaking the law, and thus establish grounds for his impeachment.

An aroused Johnson was eager to get a test case before the Supreme Court, for he believed the Tenure of Office Act to be unconstitutional. (That slow-moving tribunal finally ruled indirectly in his favor fifty-eight years later.) Expecting reason-

*For impeachment, see Art. I, Sec. II, para. 5; Art. I, Sec. III, paras. 6, 7; Art. II, Sec. IV, in Appendix.

able judicial speed, Johnson abruptly dismissed the two-faced Stanton early in 1868. The President did not believe that the law applied to Lincoln's holdovers, even though the Radicals insisted otherwise.

A Radical-influenced House of Representatives struck back swiftly. By a count of 126 to 47, it voted to impeach Johnson for "high crimes and misdemeanors," as called for by the Constitution. Most of the specific accusations grew out of the President's so-called violation of the ("unconstitutional") Tenure of Office Act. Two added articles related to Johnson's verbal assaults on Congress, involving "disgrace, ridicule, hatred, contempt, and reproach."

A Not-Guilty Verdict for Johnson

With evident zeal, the Radical-led Senate now sat as a court to try Johnson on the dubious impeachment charges. The House conducted the prosecution. The trial aroused intense public interest and, with 1,000 tickets printed, proved to be the biggest show of 1868. Johnson kept his dignity and sobriety, and maintained a discreet silence. His battery of attorneys was extremely able, while the House prosecutors, including oily-tongued Benjamin F. Butler and embittered Thaddeus Stevens, bungled their flimsy case.

A Crippled Stevens Carried to the Trial. Stevens, too weak to walk, is borne into the Senate chamber for Johnson's impeachment trial. (Rare Book Division, The New York Public Library, Astor, Lenox and Tilden Foundations.)

On May 16, 1868, the day for the first voting in the Senate, the tension was electric, and heavy breathing could be heard in the galleries. By a margin of only one vote, the Radicals failed to muster the two-thirds majority for Johnson's removal. Seven independent-minded Republican senators, courageously putting country above party, voted "not guilty."

The Radicals were infuriated. "The country is going to the Devil!" cried the crippled Stevens as he was carried from the hall. President-to-be-Wade had even chosen his Cabinet, with the unscrupulous Benjamin F. Butler as secretary of state. But the nation, though violently aroused, accepted the verdict with a good temper that did credit to its political maturity. In a less stable Republic, an armed uprising might have erupted against the President.

A bad precedent was thus narrowly avoided that would have gravely weakened one of the three branches of the federal government. Johnson was clearly guilty of bad speeches, bad judgment, and bad temper, but not of "high crimes and misdemeanors." From the standpoint of the Radicals, his greatest crime had been to stand inflexibly in their path.

The Purchase of Alaska

Johnson's administration, though largely reduced to a figurehead, achieved its most enduring success in the field of foreign relations.

The Russians by 1867 were in a mood to sell the vast and chilly expanse now known as Alaska. They had already overextended themselves in North America, and they saw that in the likely event of another war with England they probably would lose their defenseless province to the sea-dominant British. Alaska, moreover, had been ruthlessly "furred out" and was a growing economic liability. The Russians were therefore eager

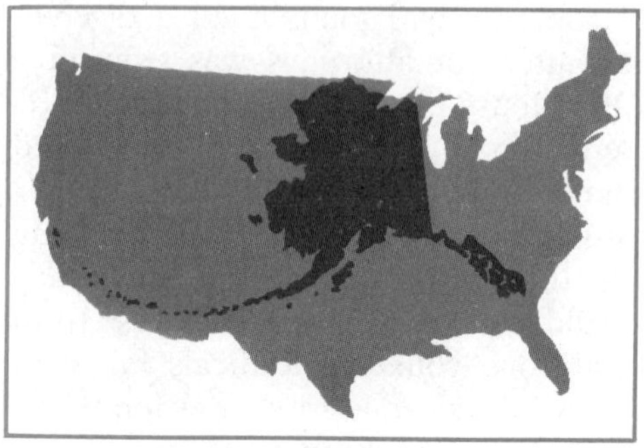

ALASKA AND THE LOWER FORTY-EIGHT STATES
(a size comparison)

to unload their "frozen asset" on the Americans, and they put out seductive feelers in Washington. They preferred the United States to any other purchaser, primarily because they wanted to strengthen further the Republic as a barrier against their ancient enemy, Britain.

In 1867 Secretary of State Seward, an ardent expansionist, signed a treaty with Russia which transferred Alaska to the United States for the bargain price of $7.2 million. But Seward's enthusiasm for these frigid wastes was not shared by his ignorant or uninformed countrymen, who jeered at "Seward's Folly," "Seward's Icebox," "Frigidia," and "Walrussia." The American people, still preoccupied with Reconstruction and other internal vexations, were economy-minded and anti-expansionist.

The Alaska Purchase Satirized. It is pilloried as a scheme to get votes for the Johnson administration. Ursus, a polar bear, is hailed as the bears' candidate. (American Antiquarian Society.)

Then why did Congress and the American public sanction the purchase? For one thing Russia, alone among the powers, had been conspicuously friendly to the North during the recent Civil War. Americans did not feel that they could offend their great and good friend, the Czar, by hurling his walrus-covered icebergs back into his face. Besides, the territory was rumored to be teeming with furs, fish, and gold, and it might yet "pan out" profitably—as it later did with natural resources, including oil and gas. So Congress and the country accepted "Seward's Polar Bear Garden," somewhat wry-facedly and derisively but nevertheless hopefully. The speculative nature of the transaction not only appealed to Yankee love of a bargain, but did something to dispel the gloom of the Reconstruction era.

Heritage of Reconstruction

Many historians have ranked Reconstruction as one of America's tragic failures. The Republic fumbled away the opportunity to close the bloody chasm between North and South. Yet such were the war-born hatreds that much of this unreason was perhaps inevitable.

The Civil War was fought openly—and on the whole honorably. When it was over, there were no wholesale blood purges. No one was executed for a purely political offense, though the foreign-born commander of a Confederate prison (Andersonville) was hanged for murder, as were surviving conspirators in the Lincoln assassination. Probably no large-scale and unsuccessful revolt has ever ended with so little head-rolling.

But if the Yankee victor chopped off no heads, the ex-Confederates regarded themselves as ground into the dust over the race issue. The Northern ideals of national unity and human freedom, they cried, were submerged in an orgy of

> The remarkable ex-slave Frederick Douglass, wrote in 1882: "Though slavery was abolished, the wrongs of my people were not ended. Though they were not slaves, they were not yet quite free. No man can be truly free whose liberty is dependent upon the thought, feeling, and action of others, and who has himself no means in his own hands for guarding, protecting, defending, and maintaining that liberty. Yet the Negro after his emancipation was precisely in this state of destitution. . . . He was free from the individual master, but the slave of society. He had neither money, property, nor friends. He was free from the old plantation, but he had nothing but the dusty road under his feet. He was free from the old quarter that once gave him shelter, but a slave to the rains of summer and the frosts of winter. He was, in a word, literally turned loose, naked, hungry, and destitute, to the open sky."

hate and corruption. To many white Southerners, reconstructing was a more grievous wound than the fighting; it left the "Angry Scar."

The Republican party, with its luckless black recruits, was indelibly tarred by the brush of Reconstruction. Southern devotees of White Supremacy were driven into the ranks of the Democratic party, and the Solid South solidified for decades as the Democratic South. The blacks were freed but only partially free.

In the light of hindsight, the Radical Reconstruction program seems for too narrowly conceived. It might well have embraced the social and economic rehabilitation of the South, including the blacks. At a time when weed-choked Southern lands were lying idle, hundreds of thousands of acres could have been made available to the ex-slaves at low cost, or no cost, as Thaddeus Stevens and others had urged. But indifference and ingrained American resistance to drastic change, especially regarding property rights, proved too strong.

VARYING VIEWPOINTS

Few topics have triggered as much intellectual warfare as the "dark and bloody ground" of Reconstruction. The period provoked questions—sectional, racial, and constitutional—about which people felt deeply and remain deeply divided even today. Scholarly argument goes back conspicuously to a Columbia University historian, William A. Dunning, and his *Reconstruction, Political and Economic* (1907). Dunning was influenced by the turn-of-the-century spirit of sectional reconciliation and by then current theories about black racial inferiority. Sympathizing with the white South, he wrote of Reconstruction as a kind of national disgrace, foisted upon a prostrate region by vindictive, self-seeking Radical Republican politicians. If the South had wronged the North by seceding, the North had wronged the South by reconstructing. For a long time this persuasive view held sway, reinforced by a widespread suspicion in the 1920s and 1930s that the Civil War itself had been a tragic and unnecessary blunder. Black historian W. E. B. Du Bois' *Black Reconstruction* in 1935 represented virtually the only serious attack on the "Dunning School" until World War II.

Following the Second World War, two developments in American culture encouraged a new examination of the Dunning approach. One was the spread of a more egalitarian attitude toward racial questions, especially following the black agitation of the 1960s. The other factor was the growing conviction that ideals counted for a great deal in this controversy. Consequently, many historians now showed much more interest in the real problems of the black freedmen, more admiration for the "helpful" Radical Republicans as genuine idealists rather than as self-seeking politicians, and less sympathy for the beaten and defiant white South. Kenneth Stampp's *Era of Reconstruction* (1965) probably best summarizes these newer views, which continue to spark debate.

SELECT READINGS

Overall accounts may be found in J. G. Randall and David Donald, *The Civil War and Reconstruction* (rev. ed., 1969), R. W. Patrick, *The Reconstruction of the Nation* (1967), Avery Craven, *Reconstruction* (1969), J. H. Franklin, *Reconstruction After the Civil War* (1961), and Kenneth Stampp, *The Era of Reconstruction* (1965), perhaps the best brief introduction. Howard K. Beale, *The Critical Year* (1930), is sympathetic to Johnson. More critical of the accidental President are E. L. McKitrick, *Andrew Johnson and Reconstruction* (1960), W. R. Brock, *An American Crisis* (1960), and LaWanda and J. H. Cox, *Politics, Principle, and Prejudice, 1865–1866* (1963). Sympathetic to the Radical Republicans are J. M. McPherson, *The Struggle for Equality* (1964), and H. L. Trefousse, *The Radical Republicans* (1969). See also David Montgomery, *Beyond Equality: Labor and the Radical Republicans, 1862–1872* (1967). Radiating pro-Southern indignation is E. M. Coulter, *The South during Reconstruction* (1947). Siding with the Radicals in the impeachment fight are M. L. Benedict, *The Impeachment and Trial of Andrew Johnson* (1973), and H. L. Trefousse, *Impeachment of a President* (1975).

Conditions in the South are analyzed in W. E. B. Du Bois's controversial classic, *Black Reconstruction* (1935), in Peter Kolchin, *First Freedom* (1973), and in Leon F. Litwack's brilliantly evocative *Been in the Storm So Long* (1979), a revealing study of the initial responses, by both blacks and whites, to emancipation. It can be usefully supplemented by Roger Ransom and Richard L. Sutch, *One Kind of Freedom: The Economic Consequences of Emancipation* (1977). See also James Roark, *Masters Without Slaves: Southern Planters in the Civil War and Reconstruction* (1977). Willie Lee Rose engagingly describes a *Rehearsal for Reconstruction: The Port Royal Experiment* (1964). O. A. Singletary discusses *The Negro Militia and Reconstruction* (1957). Local studies of merit are Joel Williamson, *After Slavery: The Negro in South Carolina during Reconstruction* (1965), J. W. Blassingame, *Black New Orleans, 1860–1880* (1973), and Thomas Holt, *Black Over White: Negro Political Leadership in South Carolina during Reconstruction* (1977). W. P. Vaughan examines the movement to educate the freedmen in *Schools for All* (1974). C. Vann Woodward looks for the roots of segregation in *The Strange Career of Jim Crow* (rev. ed., 1974). See also Robert Cruden, *The Negro in Reconstruction* (1969). A unique collection of documents is George P. Rawick, ed., *The American Slave: A Composite Autobiography* (19 vols., 1972), a collection of oral history interviews conducted with ex-slaves and their families by the Federal Writers Project during the Depression of the 1930s. For Southern white responses to Reconstruction, see Michael Perman, *Reunion without Compromise* (1973), and Allen W. Trelease, *White Terror* (1971).

Special studies of value are W. B. Hesseltine, *Lincoln's Plan of Reconstruction* (1960). W. S. McFeely, *Yankee Stepfather: General O. O. Howard and the Freedmen* (1968), J. B. James, *The Framing of the Fourteenth Amendment* (1956), W. Gillette, *The Right to Vote: Politics and the Passage of the 15th Amendment* (1965), S. I. Kutler, *Judicial Power and Reconstruction Politics* (1968), H. M. Hyman, *A More Perfect Union: The Impact of the Civil War and Reconstruction on the Constitution* (1973), R. P. Sharkey, *Money, Class, and Party: An Economic Study of Civil War and Reconstruction* (1959), and W. T. K. Nugent, *The Money Question during Reconstruction* (1967). Useful biographies are David Donald, *Charles Sumner and the Rights of Man* (1970), Fawn M. Brodie, *Thaddeus Stevens* (1959), and B. P. Thomas and H. M. Hyman, *Stanton* (1962). A comprehensive study of the climax of this troubled period is William Gillette, *Retreat from Reconstruction, 1869–1879* (1979).

25

Politics in the Gilded Age, 1869-1889

"Grant . . . had no right to exist. He should have been extinct for ages. . . . That, two thousand years after Alexander the Great and Julius Caesar, a man like Grant should be called—and should actually and truly be—the highest product of the most advanced evolution, made evolution ludicrous. . . . The progress of evolution, from President Washington to President Grant, was alone evidence enough to upset Darwin. . . . Grant . . . should have lived in a cave and worn skins."

HENRY ADAMS, *The Education of Henry Adams*, 1907

The "Bloody Shirt" Elects Grant

Disillusionment ran deep among idealistic Americans in the era after the Civil War. They had spilled their blood for Union, Emancipation, and Abraham Lincoln, who had promised "a new birth of freedom." Instead, they got a bitter dose of corruption, petty politics, and Ulysses S. Grant, a great soldier but a baby politician.

Wrangling between Congress and Andrew Johnson soured the people on professional politicians, and the notion still prevailed that a good general was bound to make a good President. Stubbily bearded General Grant, with his slightly stooped body measuring a shade over 5 feet 8 inches (1.72 meters), was by far the most popular Northern hero to emerge from the war. Grateful citizens of Philadelphia, Washington, and his home town of Galena, Illinois, passed the hat around and in each place presented him with a house. New Yorkers tendered him a check for $105,000. The general, silently puffing his cigar, accepted these gifts with open arms, as if the Republic owed them to him for having rescued the Union.

Unfortunately, this hard-riding soldier was a toddler in the political woods. He had almost no political experience, and his one presidential vote had been cast for the Democratic ticket in 1856. A better judge of horseflesh than of human beings, his cultural background was breathtakingly narrow. He once reportedly remarked that Venice (Italy) would be a fine city if only it were drained.

The Republicans, now freed from the Union party coalition of war days, enthusiastically nominated Grant for the Presidency in 1868. The party's platform sounded a clarion call for continued Reconstruction of the South under the glinting steel of federal bayonets. Yet Grant, always a man of few words, struck a highly popular note in his letter of acceptance when he said "Let us have peace." This noble sentiment became a leading campaign slogan, and was later engraved on his tomb beside the Hudson River.

Expectant Democrats, meeting in their own nominating convention, denounced military Reconstruction but could agree on little else. Wealthy Eastern delegates demanded a plank promising that federal bonds, issued during the war, be redeemed in gold—even though many of the bonds had been purchased with badly depreciated paper greenbacks. Poorer Middle Western delegates answered with the "Ohio Idea," forcing a "repudiation" plank into the platform. It called for redemption in greenbacks to the maximum extent possible. Down-on-their-luck agrarian Democrats thus hoped to keep more money in circulation, which would make loans less costly and easier to find.

The midwestern delegates got the platform but not the candidate, who turned out to be the conservative former governor of New York, Horatio Seymour. He promptly repudiated the "repudiation" plank, thereby sinking the Democrats' scant hopes for success at the polls. Republicans whipped up enthusiasm for Grant by energetically "waving the bloody shirt"—that is, reviving gory memories of the Civil War—which became for the first time a prominent feature of a presidential campaign.* "Vote As You Shot" was a powerful Republican slogan aimed at Union army veterans.

Grant won, with 214 electoral votes to 80 for Seymour. But despite his great popularity, the former general scored a majority of only 300,000 in the popular vote (3,013,421 to 2,706,829). Most white voters apparently supported Seymour, and the ballots of three still-unreconstructed Southern states were not counted. An estimated 500,000 former slaves gave Grant his margin of victory. To remain in power, the Republican party had somehow to continue to control the South—and to keep the ballot in the hands of the grateful freedmen. Republicans could not take future victories "for Granted."

The Era of Good Stealings

The population of the Republic continued to vault upward by vigorous leaps, despite the awful bloodletting of the Civil War. Census takers reported over 38 million souls in 1870, a gain of 22.6 percent over the previous decade, as the immigrant tide surged again. The United States was now the third largest nation of the Western world, ranking behind Russia and France.

But the moral stature of the Republic fell regrettably short of its physical stature. The war and

*The expression is said to have derived from a speech by Representative Benjamin F. Butler, who allegedly waved before the House the bloodstained nightshirt of a Klan-flogged carpetbagger.

its aftermath bred waste, extravagance, speculation, and graft. When so much money is thrown about with wild abandon, a great deal sticks to the wrong fingers.

A few skunks can pollute a large area. Although the great majority of businessmen and government officials conducted their affairs with decency and honor, the whole atmosphere was fetid. The Man in the Moon, it was said, had to hold his nose when passing over America. Railroad promoters sometimes left gullible bond buyers with only "two streaks of rust and a right of way." Unscrupulous stock-market manipulators were a cinder in the public eye. Too many judges and legislators put their power up for hire. Cynics defined an honest politician as one who, when bought, would stay bought.

Notorious in the financial world were two millionaires, "Jubilee Jim" Fisk and Jay Gould. The corpulent Fisk—bold, impudent, unprincipled—often paraded in public with "cuddlesome women" behind a span of fast horses. He provided the "brass," and the undersized and cunning Gould provided the brains of the combination. The crafty pair concocted a plot in 1869 to "corner" the gold market. Their slippery game would work only if the federal Treasury refrained from selling gold. The conspirators worked on President Grant directly, and also through his brother-in-law, who received $25,000 for his complicity. On "Black Friday" (September 24, 1869), Fisk and Gould madly bid the price of gold skyward, while scores of honest businessmen were driven to the wall. The bubble finally broke when the Treasury, contrary to Grant's supposed assurances, was compelled to release gold. A congressional probe concluded that Grant had done nothing crooked, though he had acted stupidly and indiscreetly.

The infamous Tweed Ring in New York City viv-

Jay Gould (1836–1892). A cold, calculating, unscrupulous, and tight-fisted financial buccaneer, Gould was widely disliked for his ruthlessly acquisitive financial practices, especially in combining railroads. He once said, "Anybody can make a fortune. It takes a genius to hold on to one."

James Fisk (1834–1872). A flashy speculator-capitalist, Fisk was one of the most notorious figures of the Grant era. Although married for seventeen years, he kept numerous mistresses, including a famous actress. He was fatally shot by a jealous male rival in New York's Grand Central Hotel.

Boss Tweed Manipulates Ballots. Another Nast cartoon had Tweed ask, "As long as I count the votes, what are you going to do about it?" (Thomas Nast in *Harper's Weekly*, 1871.)

idly displayed the ethics (or lack of ethics) typical of the age. Burly "Boss" Tweed—240 pounds (109 kilograms) of rascality—employed bribery, graft, and fraudulent elections to milk the metropolis of as much as $200 million. He adopted the cynical rule: "Addition, division, and silence." The books recorded, for example, a payment of $138,000 to a plasterer for two days of labor. Honest citizens were cowed into silence. Protestors found their tax assessments raised.

Tweed's luck finally ran out. The *New York Times* secured damning evidence in 1871 and courageously published it, though offered $5 million not to do so. A gifted cartoonist, Thomas Nast, pilloried Tweed mercilessly, after spurning a heavy bribe to desist. The portly thief reportedly complained that his illiterate followers could not help seeing "them damn pictures." A New York attorney, Samuel J. Tilden, headed the prosecution and gained fame that later paved the path to his presidential nomination. Unbailed and unwept, Tweed died behind bars.

A Carnival of Corruption

With the atmosphere so badly contaminated, it was small wonder that the easy-going Grant apparently failed to scent some of the worst evildoing in public life. His Cabinet was a nest of grafters and incompetents, with one notable exception, Secretary of State Hamilton Fish. Favor seekers haunted the White House, often plying Grant with cigars, wines, and horses. His election was a Godsend to his in-laws of the Dent family, several dozen of whom attached themselves to the public payroll.

Grant was tarred by the Crédit Mobilier scandal, though the dirtiest work had been done in 1867–68, before he took office. The Crédit Mobilier was a railroad construction company, formed by the insiders of the transcontinental Union Pacific Railway. They cleverly hired themselves to build the line, and sometimes paid themselves as much as $50,000 a mile for construction that cost $30,000 a mile. In one year, the Crédit Mobilier paid dividends of 348 percent. Fearing that Congress might blow the whistle, the company furtively distributed shares of its valuable stock to key congressmen.

A New York newspaper finally exposed the scandal in 1872, and a congressional investigation confirmed some of the worst charges. Two members of Congress were formally censured, and the Vice-President of the United States was shown to have accepted twenty shares of stock and some dividends.

The breath of scandal in Washington also reeked of alcohol. In 1875 the public learned that a sprawling Whiskey Ring had robbed the Treasury of millions in excise tax revenues. "Let no guilty man escape," insisted President Grant. But when his own private secretary turned up among the culprits, the President speedily changed his views. He volunteered a written statement to the jury, with all the weight of his exalted office behind it, and the thief escaped. News of further rottenness in the Grant administration broke in 1876, when Secretary of War Belknap was shown to have

"All Smoke." Cartoonist Thomas Nast makes light of the Grant scandals. Grant was a heavy cigar smoker who reportedly smoked twenty cigars a day; he died of cancer of the throat. (*Harper's Weekly*, 1872.)

pocketed some $24,000 by selling the privilege of disbursing supplies—often junk—to the Indians. The House voted unanimously to impeach him. Belknap resigned the same day, thus avoiding conviction by the Senate. Grant, ever loyal to his crooked cronies, accepted his resignation "with great regret."

The Liberal Republican Revolt of 1872

By 1872 a powerful wave of disgust with Grantism was beginning to build up throughout the nation, even before some of the worst scandals had been exposed. Reform-minded citizens banded together in the Liberal Republican party. Voicing the slogan, "Turn the Rascals Out," they urged purification of the Washington administration and an end to military Reconstruction.

The Liberal Republicans muffed their chance when their Cincinnati nominating convention, heavily studded with starry-eyed reformers, fell into the hands of amateurish newspapermen and scheming politicians. This "conclave of cranks" astounded the country by nominating the brilliant but erratic Horace Greeley for the Presidency. Greeley was a mind-boggling choice. Though he was a fearless editor of the *New York Tribune*, he was dogmatic, emotional, petulant, and notoriously unsound in his political judgments.

More astonishing still was the action of the office-hungry Democrats, who endorsed Greeley's candidacy. In swallowing Greeley, the Democrats "ate crow" in large gulps, for the eccentric editor had long blasted them as traitors, slave whippers, saloon keepers, horse thieves, and idiots. Yet Greeley pleased the Democrats, North and South, when he pleaded for a clasping of hands across "the bloody chasm." The Republicans dutifully renominated Grant, and the voters were thus presented with a choice between two candidates who had made their careers in fields other than politics, and who were both eminently unqualified, by temperament and lifelong training, for high political office.

Much mud was spattered along the campaign trail in 1872. Greeley was denounced as an atheist, a Communist, a free-lover, a vegetarian, a brown-bread eater, and a cosigner of Jefferson Davis's bail bond, which in fact he had signed. "Grant beat Davis—Greeley bailed him," ran the slogan. The much-defamed Greeley was heard to wonder if he were running for the Presidency or the penitentiary. Grant in turn was derided as an ignoramus, a drunkard, and a swindler. But the regular Republicans, chanting "Grant us another term," pulled the President through. The count in the electoral column was 286 to 66, in the popular column 3,596,745 to 2,843,446.

Greeley and the Democrats "Swallow" Each Other. A Republican jibe at the forced alliance between these former foes. General W. T. Sherman wrote from Paris to his brother: "I feel amazed to see the turn things have taken. Grant who never was a Republican is your candidate; and Greeley who never was a Democrat, but quite the reverse, is the Democratic candidate." (Thomas Nast in *Harper's Weekly*, 1872).

For Greeley, the outcome was tragic. Within a month he lost his wife, the election, his job, his mind, and his life. Liberal Republican agitation frightened the regular Republicans into cleaning their own house before they were thrown out of it. The Republican Congress in 1872 passed a general amnesty act, removing political disabilities from all but some 500 former Confederate leaders. Congress also moved to reduce high Civil War tariffs, and to fumigate the Grant administration with mild civil service reform. Like many American third parties, the Liberal Republicans left some enduring footprints, even in defeat.

Depression Doldrums in the Seventies

The evil repute of the scandal-scarred Grant years was worsened by the paralyzing panic that broke in 1873. Bursting with startling rapidity, the crash was one of those periodic plummets that roller-coastered the economy in this age of unbridled capitalist expansion. Overreaching promoters had laid more railroad track, sunk more mines, erected more factories, and cleared more grain fields than existing markets could bear. Bankers, in turn, had made too many imprudent loans to finance those enterprises. When profits failed to materialize, loans went unpaid, and the whole credit-based house of cards fluttered down.

The first severe shock came with the failure of the New York banking firm of Jay Cooke & Company, headed by the fabulously rich Jay Cooke, financier of the Civil War. Boom times became gloom times as more than 15,000 businesses went bankrupt; and in New York City an army of unemployed riotously battled the police.

Hard times breathed new life into the issue of greenbacks. During the war $450 million of the "folding money" had been issued, but it had depreciated under a cloud of popular mistrust and dubious legality.* By 1868 the Treasury had already withdrawn $100 million of the "battle-born currency" from circulation, and "hard money" men everywhere looked forward to its complete disappearance. But now afflicted agrarian and debtor groups—"cheap money" men—clamored for a re-issuance of the greenbacks. With a crude but essentially accurate grasp of monetary theory, they reasoned that more money meant cheaper money, and hence rising prices and easier-to-pay debts. Creditors, of course, reasoning from the same premises, advocated precisely the opposite policy.

"Substance and Shadow." The metallic (specie) dollar is the substance; the depreciated paper greenback is the shadow. (*Harper's Weekly,* 1875.)

The "hard money" men carried the day in 1874 when they persuaded the confused Grant to veto a bill to print more paper money. They scored another victory in the Resumption Act of 1875, which pledged the government to the further withdrawal of greenbacks from circulation, and to the redemption of all paper currency in gold at face value, beginning in 1879.

Down but not out, debtors now looked for relief to another precious metal, silver. The "sacred white metal," they claimed, had received a raw deal. In the early 1870s, the Treasury stubbornly and unrealistically maintained that an ounce of silver was worth only 1/16 as much as an ounce of gold, though open-market prices for silver were higher. Silver miners thus stopped offering their shiny product for sale to the federal mints. With no

*The Supreme Court in 1870 declared the Civil War Legal Tender Act unconstitutional. With the concurrence of the Senate, Grant thereupon added to the bench two Justices who could be counted on to help reverse that decision, which happened in 1871. This is how the Court grew to its current size of nine Justices.

silver flowing into the federal coffers, Congress formally dropped the coinage of silver dollars in 1873. Fate then played a sly joke when new silver discoveries later in the 1870s shot production up and forced silver prices down. Westerners from silver-mining states joined with debtors in assailing the "Crime of '73," demanding a return to the "Dollar of Our Daddies." This demand, like the demand for more greenbacks, was essentially a call for inflation.

Grant's name continued to be associated with sound money, though not with sound government. The Treasury began to accumulate gold stocks against the appointed day for resumption of metallic-money payments. Coupled with the reduction of greenbacks, this policy was called "contraction." It had a noticeable deflationary effect—the amount of money per capita in circulation actually *decreased* between 1870 and 1880, from $19.42 to $19.37. Contraction probably worsened the impact of the depression. But the new policy did restore the government's credit rating, and it brought the embattled greenbacks up to their full face value. When Redemption Day came in 1879, few greenback-holders bothered to exchange the lighter and more convenient bills for gold.

The fate of silver also disappointed the friends of easy money. "Soft money" advocates clamored for the unlimited coinage of all silver mined at the old value-ratio of 16 to 1. "Sound money" champions scornfully rejected the coinage of any silver at all. A compromise was struck with the Bland-Allison Act of 1878, masterminded by Representative Richard P. ("Silver Dick") Bland of Missouri. The law instructed the Treasury to buy and coin between 2 and 4 million dollars' worth of silver bullion each month. But the government dampened the hopes of inflationists when it stuck steadfastly to a policy of buying only the legal minimum.

Republican "hard money" policy had a political backlash. It helped elect a Democratic House of Representatives in 1874, and in 1878 it spawned a Greenback Labor Party that polled over a million votes and elected fourteen members of Congress.

Pallid Politics in the Gilded Age

The political see-saw was delicately balanced throughout most of the Gilded Age (a sarcastic name given to the post–Civil War era by Mark Twain in 1873). Even a slight nudge could tip the teeter-totter to the advantage of the opposition party. Every presidential election was a squeaker, and the majority party in the House of Representatives switched six times in the eleven sessions between 1869 and 1891. Wobbling in such shaky equilibrium, politicians were not inclined to take bold, firm stands. They tended, instead, to tiptoe timidly, producing a political record that was often trivial and petty.

Yet paradoxically, voter turnouts and party loyalty reached heights unmatched before or since. Nearly 80 percent of eligible voters cast their ballots in presidential elections in the three decades after the Civil War. On election days, droves of the party faithful tramped behind marching bands to the polling places, and "ticket splitting," or failing to vote the straight party line, was as rare as an honest alderman.

Democrats, still somewhat cursed with the charge of wartime Copperheadism, had a solid electoral base in the South. They also ran well in the Northern industrial cities, which were packed with immigrants and controlled by well-oiled political machines. Republicans could usually count on winning the midwest and the rural and small-town northeast, still populous enough to swing the northeastern states regularly into the Republican column. Grateful freedmen in the South contributed significant numbers of votes to the Republicans. Another important bloc of Republican ballots came from the members of the Grand Army of the Republic (G.A.R.)—a politically potent fraternal organization of several hundred thousand Union veterans of the Civil War. The initials G.A.R. were humorously interpreted to mean "Generally All Republicans." The lifeblood of both parties was patronage—disbursing jobs by the bucketful in return for votes, kickbacks, and party service. In this postwar era of vastly expanded government employment—especially in the postal service—the old practice of awarding the spoils to the victors had mushroomed into a big business.

Boisterous infighting beset the Republican party in the 1870s and 1880s. A "Stalwart" faction, led by the handsome and imperious Roscoe ("Lord Roscoe") Conkling, United States senator from New York, unblushingly embraced the time-honored system of swapping civil service jobs for votes. Once needled by a rival as having a "turkey gobbler strut," Conkling was forever after portrayed by cartoonists as a gobbling turkey, with the curl that he affected in the middle of his forehead. Opposed to the Conklingites were the "Half-Breeds," who flirted coyly with civil service reform, but whose real quarrel with the Stalwarts was over who should hold the ladle that dished out the spoils. The champion of the Half-Breeds was James G. Blaine, a radiantly personable congressman from Maine. Gifted with a photographic memory for names and faces, he was a politician's politician. He had a fine physical presence, flashing eyes, a thrilling speaking voice, and an elastic conscience. A perennial contender for the presidency, Blaine was inclined to demagoguery in his pursuit of the office. He would twist the British Lion's tail for Irish votes, and wave the Bloody Shirt for veterans' votes. The fact that he himself had not heard the whine of Confederate bullets led to the jibe, "Invisible in war, invincible in peace." But despite all the color of their personalities, Conkling and Blaine succeeded for the most part only in stalemating one another and deadlocking their party.

The Hayes-Tilden Stand-off, 1876

Hangers-on around Grant, like fleas urging their ailing dog to live, begged the "Old Man" to try for a third term in 1876. The general, blind to his own ineptitudes, showed a disquieting willingness. But the House of Representatives, by a lopsided bipartisan vote of 233 to 18, spiked the third-term boom. It passed a resolution that sternly reminded the country—and Grant—of the anti-dictator implications of the two-term tradition.

With Grant out of the running, and with the Conklingites and Blaineites checkmating each other, the Republicans turned to a compromise candidate, Rutherford B. Hayes, who was obscure enough to be dubbed "The Great Unknown." Of medium build, he displayed a high-domed forehead above a heavy reddish beard. Wounded several times as an officer in the Civil War, he appealed to veterans. His foremost qualification was the fact that he hailed from the electorally doubtful but potent state of Ohio, where he had served three terms as governor. So crucial were the "swing" votes of Ohio in the cliff-hanging presidential contests of the day that the state produced more than its share of presidential candidates. A political saying of the 1870s went:

> Some are born great,
> Some achieve greatness,
> And some are born in Ohio.

Pitted against the humdrum Hayes was the Democratic nominee, Samuel J. Tilden, who had

President Rutherford B. Hayes (1822–1893). Henry Adams wrote that Hayes "is a third-rate nonentity, whose only recommendation is that he is obnoxious to no one." (Library of Congress.)

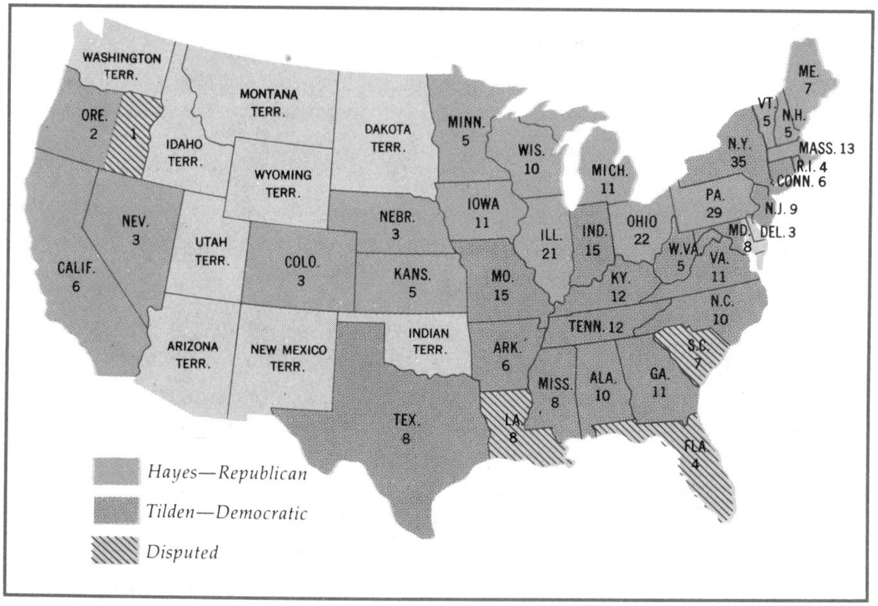

HAYES-TILDEN DISPUTED ELECTION OF 1876 (with electoral vote by state)
Nineteen of the twenty disputed votes comprised the total electoral count of Louisiana, South Carolina, and Florida. The twentieth was one of Oregon's three votes, cast by an elector who turned out to be ineligible because he was a federal office-holder (a postmaster), contrary to the Constitution (see Art. II, Sec. I, para. 2).

risen to fame as the man who bagged Boss Tweed in New York. Boyish-faced and smooth-shaven (unusual in that bewhiskered age), he was slightly built, nervous, droopy eyed, and weak voiced ("Whispering Sammy"). Campaigning against Republican scandal and for sweeping civil service reform, Tilden racked up 184 electoral votes of the needed 185, with 20 votes in four states doubtful because of irregular returns (see map). Surely Tilden could pick up at least one of these, especially in view of the fact that he had polled 247,448 more popular votes than Hayes, 4,284,020 to 4,036,572.

Both parties scurried to send "visiting statesmen" to the contested Southern states of Louisiana, South Carolina, and Florida. All three disputed states submitted two sets of returns, one Democratic and one Republican. As the weeks drifted by, the paralysis tightened. Here were the makings of an epochal Constitutional crisis. The Constitution merely states that the electoral returns from the states shall be sent to Congress, and in the presence of the House and Senate they shall be *opened* by the President of the Senate (see Art. XII). But who should *count* them? On this point the Constitution was silent. If counted by the President of the Senate (a Republican), the Republican returns would be selected. If counted by the Speaker of the House (a Democrat), the Democratic returns would be chosen.

The Compromise of 1877

Clash or compromise was the stark choice. The danger loomed that there would be no President on Inauguration Day, March 4, 1877. "Tilden or Blood!" cried Democratic hotheads, and some of their "Minute Men" began to drill with arms. But behind the scenes frantically laboring statesmen gradually hammered out an agreement in the Henry Clay tradition—the Compromise of 1877.

The election deadlock itself was to be broken by the Electoral Count Act, which passed Congress early in 1877. It set up an electoral commission consisting of fifteen men selected from the Senate, the House, and the Supreme Court. The fifteenth member of the commission, according to Democratic schemes, was to have been the giant-sized Justice David Davis, an independent—with Democratic leanings. But at the last moment he resigned from the Bench to go to the Senate, and the only remaining members of the Supreme Court were Republicans. A Republican rhymester chortled at the Democrats:

> They digged a pit, they digged it deep,
> They digged it for their brother;
> But through their sin they did fall in
> The pit they digged for t'other.

In February 1877, about a month before inaug-

Thomas Nast Favors a Truce. (*Harper's Weekly,* 1877.)

uration day, the Senate and House met together in an electric atmosphere to settle the dispute. The roll of the states was tolled off alphabetically. When Florida was reached—the first of the three Southern states with two sets of returns—the disputed documents were referred to the electoral commission, which sat in a nearby chamber. After prolonged discussion the members agreed, by the partisan vote of eight Republicans to seven Democrats, to accept the Republican returns. Outraged Democrats in Congress, smelling defeat, undertook to launch a filibuster "until hell froze over."

Renewed deadlock was avoided by the rest of the complex Compromise of 1877, already partially concluded behind closed doors. The Democrats reluctantly agreed that Hayes might take office in return for his withdrawing intimidating federal troops from the two states in which they remained, Louisiana and South Carolina. Among various concessions, the Republicans assured the Democrats a place at the presidential patronage trough, and support for a bill subsidizing the Texas and Pacific Railroad's construction of a Southern transcontinental line. Not all of these promises were kept in later years, including the Texas and Pacific subsidy. But the deal held together long enough to break the dangerous electoral stand-off. The Democrats permitted Hayes to receive the remainder of the disputed returns—all by the partisan vote of 8 to 7. So close was the margin of

Composition of the Electoral Commission, 1877

Members	*Republicans*	*Democrats*
Senate (Republican majority)	3	2
House (Democratic majority)	2	3
Supreme Court	3	2
TOTAL	8	7

safety that the explosive issue was settled only three days before the new President was officially sworn in.

The compromise bought peace at a price. Violence was averted by sacrificing the black freedmen in the South. With the Hayes-Tilden deal, the Republican party quietly abandoned its commitment to black equality. That commitment had been weakening, in any case. The Civil Rights Act of 1875 was in a sense the last feeble gasp of the congressional Radical Republicans. The Act supposedly guaranteed equal accommodations in public places and prohibited racial discrimination in jury selection, but the law was born toothless and stayed that way for nearly a century. Hayes clinched the bargain soon after his inauguration, when he appointed former Confederate General D. M. Key as postmaster general. Hayes also withdrew the last federal troops that were propping up

Troop Removal in South Extracts Aching Bayonet Tooth. Contemporary cartoon.

carpetbag governments, and the bayonet-backed Republican regimes collapsed as the blue-clad soldiers departed. The Solid Democratic South speedily solidified, and speedily suppressed the now friendless blacks. Reconstruction, for better or worse, was officially ended.

Cold-water Integrity on the Potomac

Rutherford ("Rutherfraud") B. Hayes was the only President, except possibly J. Q. Adams, to take office with a cloud on his title. Newspapers pilloried him as "Old 8-to-7" and "His Fraudulency," and cartoonists sketched him with "Fraud" on his honest brow. All this cut him deeply. A man of unsullied honor and high ideals—a "Queen Victoria in breeches"—he believed himself rightfully elected. Lucy Webb Hayes, his wife and childhood sweetheart, was a kindred spirit. Family prayers were offered daily; and because both the President and Mrs. Hayes were temperance advocates, "Lemonade Lucy" served no alcohol. The "cold-water administration" swept the fetid, smoke-laden atmosphere out of the wineless White House.

Hayes's years in office were turbulent. The President displayed his stiff integrity when he removed the federal troops from the South, calling down on his head the outraged cries of Republican carpetbaggers who craved "four more years of good stealing." He further enraged Republican regulars when he undertook to clean out the New York Customs House. This key agency was a vital cog in Senator Conkling's political machine, and was overseen by one of Conkling's chief henchmen, Chester A. Arthur. Arthur supervised a payroll of some 1,300 persons, who, together with their families, wielded a sizeable bloc of votes. Hayes, determined to curb the spoils system in New York, fired Arthur, touching off prolonged political warfare with the powerful New York senator.

Labor disturbances rumbled throughout the country during Hayes's term. The explosive atmosphere was largely a by-product of the long years of depression and deflation following the Panic of 1873. Mass disorders convulsed a number of major Eastern cities in 1877. The paralyzing railroad strikes of that year, which verged on civil war in places like Baltimore and Pittsburgh, forced Hayes to call out the federal troops. Order was restored only after scores of rioters had been killed or injured.

Economic unrest swept to California and included hard-working Chinese laborers among its victims. By 1880 the Golden State counted 75,000 of these Oriental newcomers, about 9 percent of its entire population. In San Francisco, Irish-born demagogue Denis Kearney incited his followers to violent abuse of the hapless Chinese. The Kearneyites, many of whom were recently arrived immigrants from Europe, fiercely resented the competition of cheap labor from the still more recently arrived Chinese. The beef eater, they claimed, had no chance against the rice eater in a life-and-death struggle for jobs and wages. The present tens of thousands of Chinese "coolies" were regarded as a menace; the prospective millions as a calamity. Taking to the streets, gangs of Kearneyites terrorized the Orientals by shearing off precious pigtails. Some Chinese victims were murdered outright.

Congress finally responded to all this uproar in 1879, when it passed a bill severely restricting the influx of Chinese immigrants. But Hayes, ever the man of honor, vetoed this discriminatory measure on the grounds that it violated the existing treaty

"Pacific Chivalry." A California Kearneyite abuses a Chinese immigrant. (Thomas Nast, *Harper's Weekly*, 1869.)

with China. Angry Californians burned the President in effigy. Once the scrupulous Hayes was out of the way, in 1882, Congress slammed the door on Chinese laborers, and it stayed slammed until 1943.

Hayes accomplished little that was lasting—except writing "finished" to Reconstruction. His legislative record was negligible, and his political record was a disaster. As the presidential campaign of 1880 approached, Hayes was a man without a party. Denounced as "Granny" Hayes and a "Goody Two-Shoes" reformer, he was openly repudiated by the old-line politicians. He had earlier declared himself to be a single-termer, and this decision proved to be a face-saver because he probably could not have won renomination in any event.

The Garfield Interlude

Deadlocked for thirty-five ballots by the usual Stalwart-Half Breed standoff, Republicans finally broke the impasse when they nominated for the presidency in 1880 a "dark horse" candidate, James A. Garfield of Ohio. Broad-shouldered and tall (6 feet; 1.83 meters), Garfield enjoyed many political assets. Born in a log cabin in the electorally powerful state of Ohio, "Boatman Jim" had struggled up from poverty by driving mules along the towpaths of the Ohio Canal. He had served honorably as a Civil War officer, rising to the rank of major general.

Crestfallen spoilsmen received some slight consolation. The delegates chose for the vice-presidency a notorious Stalwart, Senator Conkling's henchman, Chester A. Arthur of New York. The platform declared emphatically for the protective tariff, and somewhat feebly for reform of the civil service, sneeringly labelled the "snivel service" by those who plundered it for their own political gain. One Republican delegate from Texas blurted out, "What are we here for except the offices?"

Wrathful Democrats, still seething over having been robbed of the presidency in 1876, nominated another former Civil War general, Winfield S. Hancock. He appealed to veterans as a hero wounded at Gettysburg, and he was popular in the

Campaign Banner, Election of 1880. (Smithsonian Institution, Division of Political History)

South, where he had fair-mindedly headed one of the military Reconstruction districts. The Democratic platform called for civil service reform and a "tariff for revenue only."

The campaigners shunned real controversy like leprosy, as happened in so many electoral contests during this politically cautious era. Republicans turned their backs on deepening economic and social injustices, and strove desperately to wring another President from the Bloody Shirt by verbally refighting the Civil War. They drenched Indiana with Republican money ("soap"), helping to grease it into the Republican column. Energetic Democrats, harping on Garfield's alleged receipt of $329 in stock dividends in the Crédit Mobilier scandal, chalked those telltale figures on buildings, walls, and fences.

Garfield, "the Canal Boy," barely scraped across the electoral reefs. He polled only 39,213 more votes than Hancock—4,453,295 to 4,414,082—but his margin in the electoral column was a comfortable 214 to 155. The new President was an able and generous man, and a devoted son who turned and kissed his mother after taking the inaugural oath. But he had one serious weakness. He hated to hurt people's feelings by saying "no."

Office-hungry Republicans besieged the White House. "My God!" exclaimed an exasperated Garfield, "What is there in this place that a man should ever want to get into it?" He rewarded his chief political benefactor, James G. Blaine, with the prize plum of the secretaryship of state. The "Half-Breed" Blaine immediately set out to persuade the President to clip the wings of his perennial "Stalwart" nemesis, the "turkey-gobbler" Senator Roscoe Conkling of New York. Conkling, a colossus of conceit, fought back bitterly, especially when the President appointed a staunch anti-Conklingite to the coveted office of collector of the port of New York.

Then, as the political battle was raging, tragedy struck. A disappointed and mentally deranged office-seeker, Charles J. Guiteau, shot President Garfield in the back in a Washington railroad station. The victim lingered in agony for eleven weeks, and died on September 19, 1881. Guiteau, when

President James A. Garfield (1831–1881). He was the second President to be killed by an assassin's bullet. He may have had a premonition; two days before the shooting he called in Lincoln's son for an hour of recollection of the 1865 assassination.

seized, reportedly cried, "I am a Stalwart. Arthur is now President of the United States." The implication was that now the Conklingites would all get good jobs. At his trial, Guiteau went so far as to ask all those who had benefited politically by the assassination to contribute to his defense fund. The appeal availed little, as he was found guilty of murder and hanged.

Statesmen are dead politicians, the saying goes, and Garfield's "martyrdom" undoubtedly enhanced his reputation. Brutal though the thought is, Garfield's greatest single service to his country probably was to die when he did and as he did. An unwitting martyr to the evils of spoils seeking, he departed this life in such a way as to shock public servants into taking action to correct flagrant abuses. The nation might well bow its head in shame when it was a case of "an office—or your life."

Chester Arthur Takes Command

Garfield's death was rendered all the more shocking by the low repute of his successor. Arthur had no apparent qualifications for the presidency, though he was well endowed in other ways. The new President was a wealthy, handsome widower who enjoyed a richly-stocked wine cellar and a wardrobe that included eighty pairs of trousers. He could wear his clothes to advantage, for he was tall (6 feet 2 inches; 1.88 meters), well proportioned, and sported a mustache with billowing sideburns. His previous political experience consisted almost entirely of faithful service as a spoilsman in Conkling's sprawling political machine.

The Office Makes the Man. Besieged by his former New York cronies, Arthur tries to assert the dignity of his new presidential office. ("The Proper Thing," James A. Wales, as printed in *Judge*, November 19, 1881. Courtesy, Harvard College Library)

But observers at first underestimated Arthur. He proved to have unsuspected reserves of intelligence, idealism, and integrity. A Phi Beta Kappa graduate of Union College, he had served as a lawyer for the abolitionist cause while a young man in New York. Now the responsibilities of the highest office in the land lifted "Prince" Arthur to new, unexpected heights. He prosecuted with vigor certain post-office frauds, and gave his former Conklingite cronies a frosty reception when they came seeking favors.

Disgust with the circumstances of Garfield's murder churned the public's clamor for civil service reform into an irresistible wave, and Arthur commendably threw his influence behind the movement. The Republican party itself began to reveal a previously undetected enthusiasm for reform. Republicans lost control of the House in the midterm elections of 1882, and they rightly feared further political hemorrhaging if they failed to find a cure for the ravages that the spoils system was inflicting on the body politic.

The Pendleton Act of 1883—the so-called Magna Carta of civil service reform—was the medicine finally applied to the long-suffering organs of the federal government. It prohibited, at least on paper, financial assessments on jobholders, including lowly scrubwomen. It established a merit system of making appointments to office on the basis of aptitude rather than "pull." It set up a Civil Service Commission, charged with administering open competitive examinations to applicants for posts in the classified service. Offices not "classified" by the President remained the fought-over footballs of politics.

Ironically, the success of the new anti-spoilsmen law depended largely on the cooperation of a seasoned former spoilsman, President Arthur. Fortunately, he cooperated with vigor. By 1884 he had classified nearly 14,000 federal offices, or about 10 percent of the total. A century later, about 90 percent of federal offices were classified.

Civil service reform was a necessary idea whose time had come. Yet like many well-intentioned reforms it bred unintended problems of its own.

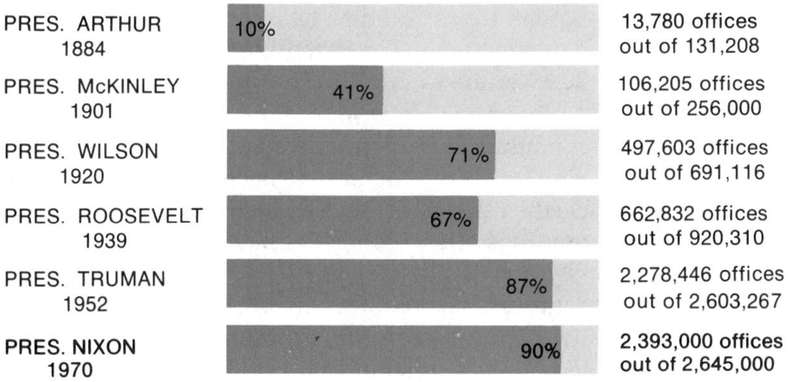

GROWTH OF CLASSIFIED CIVIL SERVICE (subject to competitive requirements)

The law skimmed off much of the cream of federal patronage, and put it safely beyond the reach of grasping politicians. They were now forced to look elsewhere for money, "the mother's milk of politics." Increasingly, they turned to the bulging coffers of the big corporations. A new breed of "boss" emerged—less skilled at mobilizing small armies of immigrants and other voters on election day, but more adept at milking dollars from manufacturers and lobbyists. The Pendleton Act partially divorced politics from patronage, but it helped drive politicians into "marriages of convenience" with big businessmen.

Reform was also needed in America's worm-eaten navy, which still carried on its rolls the pre-1812, wooden frigate *Constitution*. The Civil War fleet, a collection of "floating washtubs," had been allowed to rust and rot away as the nation concentrated on internal expansion. With only two iron ships, the navy was no match for modern European fleets, and in some respects was inferior to the navy of Chile. Prodded by President Arthur, who wanted to make productive use of a growing Treasury surplus, Congress appropriated money for four new ships—the nucleus of a modern steel navy. (By the time the Spanish-American War broke out in 1898, the U.S. Navy ranked about fifth among world fleets, and was able to give an impressive account of itself.)

U.S. Salutes Foreign Ships with Peashooters. A satire. (*Harper's Weekly,* 1881.)

One good term deserves another, and President Arthur's surprising display of integrity deserved to be rewarded with a presidential nomination "in his own right." But his reforms had offended too many powerful Republicans. His ungrateful party turned him out to pasture, and in 1886 he died of a cerebral hemorrhage.

The Blaine-Cleveland Mudslingers of 1884

James G. Blaine's persistence in pursuit of the presidential nomination finally paid off in 1884. The dashing Down-Easter, blessed with almost every political asset except a reputation for honesty, was the clear choice of the Republican convention in Chicago. But many reform-minded Republicans gagged on Blaine's candidacy. They

Congressman James G. Blaine. His very political adroitness during a long public career ironically cast doubts on his moral integrity, and helped to deny him the Presidency. (Courtesy of the National Archives)

referred contemptuously to Blaine as the "tattooed man"—tattooed with countless political villainies. Blaine's enemies publicized the fishy-smelling "Mulligan letters," written by Blaine to a Boston businessman, and linking the powerful politician to a corrupt deal involving federal favors to a Southern railroad. At least one of the damning documents ended with the furtive warning "Burn this letter." Some reformers, unable to swallow Blaine, bolted to the Democrats. They were sneeringly dubbed "Mugwumps," a word of Indian derivation apparently meaning "great man" or "holier than thou."*

Victory-starved Democrats, scenting their own success in the nomination of a tainted Republican, turned enthusiastically to a noted reformer, Grover Cleveland. A burly bachelor with a soup-straining mustache and a taste for chewing tobacco, Cleveland was a solid but not brilliant lawyer of forty-seven. He had rocketed from the mayoralty of Buffalo to the governorship of New York and the presidential nomination in three short years. He enjoyed a well-deserved reputation for probity in office, gained especially by his veto, while governor, of a popular bill reducing fares on New York City's elevated railroads. Moralistic Americans, hungry for a candidate whose character they could applaud, seemed to have found their man at last in "Grover the Good."

Unfortunately, Cleveland's admirers soon got something of a shock. Resolute Republicans, digging for dirt in the past of bachelor Cleveland, unearthed the report that he had been involved in an amorous affair with a Buffalo widow, to whom an illegitimate son had been born, now eight years old. Although several other men had been attentive to her at the same time, Cleveland had forthrightly assumed full responsibility and had made financial provision for the unwelcome offspring. Democratic elders, who had launched the campaign on a high moral plane, were demoralized. They hurried to Cleveland and urged him to lie like a gentleman, but their ruggedly honest candidate insisted, "Tell the truth."

The campaign of 1884 sank to perhaps the lowest level in American experience, as the two parties grunted and shoved for the hog trough of office. Few fundamental differences separated them.

A Banner from Cleveland's First Presidential Campaign. This elaborate, fringed banner was typical of the ornate style of the Gilded Age. (Smithsonian Institution)

*Latter-day punsters jibed that the Mugwumps were priggish politicians who sat on the fence with their "mugs" on one side and their "wumps" on the other.

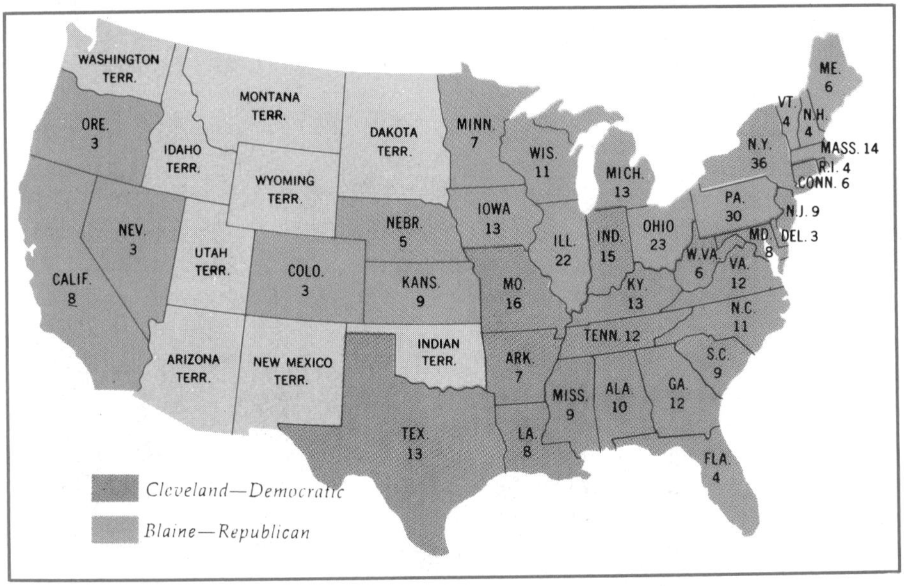

PRESIDENTIAL ELECTION OF 1884 (with electoral vote by state)

Even the Bloody Shirt had faded to a pale pink.* Personalities, not principles, claimed the headlines. Enormous crowds of Democrats surged through city streets, chanting—to the rhythm of left, left, left, right, left—"Burn, burn, burn this letter!" Republicans taunted in return: "Ma, ma, where's my pa?" Defiant Democrats shouted back, "Gone to the White House, ha, ha, ha!"

The contest hinged on the state of New York, where Blaine blundered badly in the closing days of the campaign. A witless Republican clergyman damned the Democrats before an Irish-American audience as the party of "Rum, Romanism, and Rebellion"—insulting at one stroke the race, the faith, and the patriotism of his listeners. Blaine was present but lacked the presence of mind to repudiate the statement at once. The pungent phrase, shortened to "RRR," stung and stuck. Blaine's silence seemed to give consent, and the wavering Irishmen who deserted his camp helped to account for Cleveland's paper-thin plurality of about 1,000 votes in New York state.

*Neither Blaine nor Cleveland had served in the Civil War. Cleveland had hired a substitute to go in his stead while he supported his widowed mother and two sisters. Blaine was the only candidate nominated by the Republicans from Grant through McKinley (1868 to 1900) who had not been a Civil War officer.

Cleveland swept the Solid South and squeaked into office with 219 to 182 electoral votes, and 4,879,507 to 4,850,293 popular votes. Basically, the issue narrowed down to a choice between public dishonesty and private immorality. The desertion of the Mugwumps, and Blaine's mishaps in New York, were the deciding factors.

"I Want My Pa!" Malicious anti-Cleveland cartoon. (*Puck.*)

"Old Grover" Takes Over

Bull-necked Cleveland in 1885 was the first Democrat to take the oath of presidential office since Buchanan, twenty-eight years earlier. Huge question marks hung over his portly frame (5 feet 11 inches, 250 pounds; 1.8 meters, 113 kilograms). Could the "party of disunion" be trusted to govern the Union? Would desperate Democrats, ravenously hungry after twenty-four years of exile, trample the frail sprouts of civil service reform in a stampede to the patronage trough? Could Cleveland restore a measure of respect and power to the maligned and enfeebled presidency?

Cleveland was not a suave or skillful political leader. Inclined to put his foot down rather than slide it down, he could not work well in party harness. His fame had been built on his vetoes, and he at first showed little stomach for taking bold political initiatives. A staunch apostle of the hands-off creed of *laissez-faire*, the new President caused the hearts of businessmen and bankers to beat with contentment. He summed up his political philosophy in 1887 when he vetoed a bill to provide seeds for drought-ravaged Texas farmers. "Though the people support the government," he declared, "the government should not support the people." As tactless as a mirror and as direct as a bulldozer, he was outspoken, unbending, and profanely hot-tempered.

Democratic Office-Seekers Haunt Cleveland's White House. By promoting civil service reform, Grover Cleveland hoped to eliminate scenes like this one. (*Frank Leslie's Illustrated Newspaper,* March 9, 1889)

Grover Cleveland (1837–1908). Cleveland, President for two nonconsecutive terms, was a strong supporter of civil service reform and tariff reduction. When Pullman strikers in Chicago obstructed movement of mail, he sent U.S. troops to intervene. (By permission of the Houghton Library, Harvard University.)

At the outset, Cleveland calmed the disquiet of some of his critics. He narrowed the North-South chasm by naming to his Cabinet two former Confederates, but he stopped far short of handing over the government to former rebels. As for the civil service, Cleveland was whipsawed between the demands of the Democratic faithful for jobs and the demands of the Mugwumps, who had helped elect him, for reform. Believing in the merit system, Cleveland at first favored the cause of the reformers; but he eventually caved in to the carpings of Democratic bosses and fired almost two-thirds of the 120,000 federal employees, including 40,000 incumbent (Republican) postmasters.

Military pensions gave Cleveland some of his most painful political headaches. The Union had tried to treat its veterans generously, but by the 1880s the pension legislation contained gaping loopholes and was aggressively abused. The prospect of easy access to Treasury dollars attracted grafters as honey attracts flies. Slippery pension attorneys ferreted out able-bodied veterans and induced them to file fraudulent claims. If the Pension Bureau proved uncompliant, the claimant might appeal to his congressman, who, mindful of the politically powerful G.A.R., would often introduce a special bill.

Hundreds of private pension bills were thus logrolled through Congress and then sent to the White House. Handouts were granted to deserters, to bounty jumpers, to men who had never served, and to former soldiers who in later years had incurred disabilities in no way connected with war service. Cleveland, a slave to his conscience, read these bills carefully, vetoed several hundred of them, and then laboriously penned individual veto messages for Congress. Sometimes he waxed sarcastic, as when referring to one man's "terrific encounter with the measles." A Democrat and a nonveteran, Cleveland was in a vulnerable position when it came to fighting the pension-grabbers. Yet he showed real courage in taking them on. His fortitude was exceptionally displayed in 1887 when he risked the retribution of the G.A.R. and vetoed a bill adding several hundred thousand new pensioners to the rolls.

Cleveland Battles for a Lower Tariff

During the Civil War, tariff schedules had been jacked up to new high levels, partly to raise revenues for the insatiable military machine. American industry, which was preponderantly in Republican hands, had profited from this protection and hated to see the sheltering benefits reduced in peacetime. But the high duties continued to pile up revenue at the customhouses, and by 1881 the Treasury was running an annual surplus amounting to an embarrassing $145 million. Most of the government's income, in those pre-income tax days, came from the tariff.

Congress could reduce the vexatious surplus in two ways. One was to squander it on pensions and "pork-barrel" bills, and thus curry favor with veterans and other self-seeking groups. The other was to lower the tariff—something that the big industrialists vehemently opposed. Grover Cleveland, the rustic Buffalo attorney, had known little and cared less about the tariff before entering the White House. But as he studied the subject, he was much impressed by the arguments for downward revision of the tariff schedules. Lower barriers would mean lower prices for consumers. Most important, they would mean an end to the Treasury surplus, a standing mockery of Cleveland's professed belief in fiscal orthodoxy and small-government frugality. After much hesitation, Cleveland saw his duty and overdid it.

Rejecting the advice of Democratic politicians, Cleveland decided to prod the hornet's nest of the tariff issue. "What's the use," he insisted, "of being elected or reelected unless you stand for some-

Cleveland Files Rough Edges from Tariff. (*Harper's Weekly,* 1888.)

thing?" With characteristic bluntness, Cleveland tossed his appeal for lower tariffs like a bombshell into the lap of Congress in late 1887. The annual message of the President had always been devoted to a review of the year's events, but Cleveland concentrated his fire solely on the tariff.

The response was electric. Cleveland succeeded admirably in smoking the issue out into the open. Democrats were deeply depressed at the obstinacy of their chief. Republicans rejoiced at his apparent recklessness. The old warrior Blaine gloated that "There's one more President for us in [tariff] protection." For the first time in years, a real issue divided the two parties and would dominate the upcoming presidential election of 1888.

Harrison Ousts Cleveland in 1888

Dismayed Democrats, seeing no alternative, somewhat dejectedly nominated Cleveland in their St. Louis convention. Eager Republicans turned to

Benjamin Harrison (1833–1901). A staunch charter member of the Republican party, Harrison was a distinguished but colorless corporation lawyer, who hailed from his President-grandfather's town of North Bend, Ohio. He was described as so aloof and cool in his dealings with other people that he "could carry a piece of ice in each pants pocket on a July afternoon and never lose a drop." (By permission of the Houghton Library, Harvard University.)

A "Campaign Ball" Used in Harrison's Campaign, 1888. Ball-rolling, torchlight parades and rallies, and similar sorts of hoopla were common features of political campaigns in the late 19th Century. (Library of Congress)

Benjamin Harrison, whose grandfather was former President William Henry ("Tippecanoe") Harrison. The grandson, "Little Ben," was joyously hailed as "Young Tippecanoe," and was pictured wearing his grandfather's military hat. Democrats maliciously cartooned the pint-sized Indianan as rattling around ridiculously in the oversize martial headgear.

The campaign proceeded on a fairly high level, despite some feeble flapping of the Bloody Shirt, and some further probing of Cleveland's private life. The "Beast of Buffalo," who had married his beautiful twenty-one-year-old ward (twenty-seven years his junior) during his second year in the White House, was absurdly accused of beating his wife during drunken fits. But the tariff was the prime issue. The two parties flooded the country with some 10 million pamphlets on the subject.

The British Lion's tail came in for some energetic twisting, especially when a California man claiming English birth wrote to the British Minister in Washington, Sir Lionel Sackville-West, for advice on how to vote. The foolish diplomat replied, in effect, that a vote for Cleveland, with his low-tariff policies, was a vote for England, the champion of "free trade." Republicans jubilantly trumpeted the indiscreet letter and made it a front-page sensation. The crucial Irish vote in New York, normally Democratic, began to slip away. Cleveland was forced to send the "damned Englishman" packing off to England. Crowds of gleeful Republicans tramped through New York chanting:

> West, West, Sackville-West
> He didn't want to go home
> But Cleveland thought it best.

The specter of a lowered tariff spurred the Republicans to frantic action. In an impressive demonstration of the post–Pendleton Act politics of alliances with big business, they raised a war chest of some $3 million—the lushest yet—largely by "frying the fat" out of nervous industrialists. The money was widely used to line up corrupt "voting cattle" known as "repeaters" and "floaters." In Indiana, always a crucial "swing" state, votes were shamelessly purchased for as much as $20 each.

On election day, Harrison nosed out Cleveland, 233 to 168 electoral votes. A change of 6,502 ballots in New York would have reversed the outcome. Cleveland actually polled more popular votes, 4,879,507 to 4,850,293. Such are the curiosities of the Electoral College.

Grover Cleveland, the first sitting President to be voted out of his chair since Martin Van Buren in 1840, could count some noteworthy achievements of his four-year term. Two legislative landmarks in 1887 were the Dawes Act, designed to control the Indians (see p. 527), and the Interstate Commerce Act (see p. 483), designed to curb the railroads. Cleveland's administration also retrieved for the government some 81 million acres of the public domain in the West—land that in many cases had been improperly acquired by the "cattle barons" or the railroad "octopus" (see p. 477).

But for the most part, Cleveland, despite his gruff integrity and occasional courage, was tied down in office by the same threads that held all the Presidents of the day to Lilliputian levels. Grant, Hayes, Garfield, Arthur, and Harrison are often referred to as the "forgettable Presidents." They were all bearded and bland in person, and they left mostly blanks—or blots—on the nation's political record. In this dull galaxy even such a dim light as Cleveland shone like a bright star. What little political vitality existed was to be found in local settings, or in Congress, which overshadowed the White House during most of the Gilded Age.

As the 19th Century drew to a close, observers were asking "Why are the 'best men' not in politics?" One answer was that they had been lured away from public life by the lusty attractions of the booming industrial economy. Talented men ached for profits, not the presidency; they dreamed of controlling corporations, not Congress. What the nation lost in political leadership, it gained in an astounding surge of economic growth. Though still in many ways a political dwarf, the United States was about to stand up before the world as an industrial colossus.

On the night before the inauguration of Harrison, a crowd of jubilant Republicans tauntingly serenaded the darkened White House with a popular campaign ditty directed at Grover Cleveland:

> Down in the cornfield
> Hear that mournful sound;
> All the Democrats are weeping—
> Grover's in the cold, cold ground!

But Grover was to rise again and serve as President for four more years.

VARYING VIEWPOINTS

Few significant economic issues separated the major parties in the Gilded Age. Democrats and Republicans saw very nearly eye to eye on questions like the tariff, currency, and even civil service reform. Yet despite their rough agreement on these national matters, the two parties were fiercely competitive with one another. Probably at no time in American history have political parties been so tightly organized, or partisan loyalties so intense, as they were in the late 19th Century. How can this apparent paradox of political consensus and partisan fervor be explained?

Recent scholarship has suggested that the answer lies in ethnic and cultural differences between the two parties—in distinctions of style and tone and even religious sentiment. Republican voters tended to adhere to those creeds that traced their lineage to Puritanism. They stressed strict codes of personal morality and believed in the possibility of establishing Christian perfectionism on earth—by government fiat, if necessary. Democrats, among whom immigrant Catholics and Lutherans figured heavily, were more likely to belong to faiths that took a less stern view of human weakness, that professed toleration of differences in an imperfect world, and that were decidedly uninterested in a government that tried to impose a single moral standard on the entire society.

These differences in temperament and religious values often produced ferocious political contests at the local level, where issues like prohibition and education loomed large. It is there, rather than in the national arena, that the explanation of the era's passionate political behavior is to be found.

SELECT READINGS

The scandal-rocked Grant era is treated with brevity in J. G. Randall and David Donald, *The Civil War and Reconstruction* (rev. ed., 1969), and at greater length in William Gillette, *Retreat from Reconstruction* (1979), and James M. McPherson, *Ordeal by Fire* (1981). Consult also W. B. Hesseltine, *Ulysses S. Grant* (1935), and W. McFeeley, *Grant* (1981). On politics, see Paul Kleppner, *The Third Electoral System, 1835–1892* (1979), Morton Keller, *Affairs of State: Public Life in Nineteenth-Century America* (1977), and John A. Garraty, *The New Commonwealth, 1877–1890* (1968). Also valuable are Mathew Josephson, *The Politicos* (1938), Ari A. Hoogenboom, *Outlawing the Spoils* (1961), David J. Rothman, *Politics and Power: The U.S. Senate, 1869–1901* (1966), and H. W. Morgan, *From Hayes to McKinley* (1969). Robert D. Marcus focuses on the *Grand Old Party: Political Structure in the Gilded Age* (1971). Administrative history is handled in L. D. White, *The Republican Era, 1869–1901* (1958). Money questions are treated in Irwin Unger, *The Greenback Era* (1964), W. T. K. Nugent, *Money and American Society, 1865–1880* (1968), and Allen Weinstein's account of the "Crime of '73", *Prelude to Populism* (1970). C. Vann Woodward sharply analyzes the Compromise of 1877 in *Reunion and Reaction* (rev. ed., 1956). Some of the consequences of the compromise are scrutinized in Vincent P. DeSantis, *Republicans Face the Southern Question: The New Departure Years, 1877–1897* (1959), J. Morgan Kousser, *The Shaping of Southern Politics* (1974), and R. W. Logan, *The Negro in American Life and Thought: The Nadir, 1877–1901* (1954). Sectional reconciliation is stressed in S. P. Hirshon, *Farewell to the Bloody Shirt* (1962), and Paul H. Buck's classic, *The Road to Reunion, 1865–1900* (1937). Consult also Harry Barnard, *Rutherford B. Hayes and His America* (1954). The great strikes are described in R. V. Bruce, *1877: Year of Violence* (1959). California receives special attention in Alexander Saxton, *The Indispensable Enemy: Labor and the Anti-Chinese Movement in California* (1975).

Useful biographies include Allan Peskin, *Garfield* (1978), G. F. Howe, *Chester A. Arthur* (1934), D. S. Muzzey, *James G. Blaine* (1934), and Allan Nevins, *Grover Cleveland* (1932). J. G. Sproat looks at liberal reformers in *"The Best Men"* (1968). Foreign policy is treated in D. M. Pletcher, *The Awkward Years: American Foreign Relations under Garfield and Arthur* (1962). The fullest treatment is H. J. Clancy, *The Presidential Election of 1880* (1958). Henry Adams penned some perceptive and sour observations on the era in his autobiographical *Education of Henry Adams* (1907) and in his novel, *Democracy* (1880). See also the classic satire by Mark Twain and Charles Dudley Warner, *The Gilded Age* (1873).

26

Industry Comes of Age, 1865-1900

The railroads are not run for the benefit of the dear public. That cry is all nonsense. They are built for men who invest their money and expect to get a fair percentage on the same.

William H. Vanderbilt, 1882

The Iron Colt Becomes an Iron Horse

The feverish years after the Civil War witnessed an unparalleled outburst of railroad construction. When Lincoln was shot in 1865, there were only 35,000 miles (56,350 kilometers) of steam railways in the United States, mostly east of the Mississippi. By 1900 the figure had spurted up to 192,556 miles (310,115 kilometers), or more than that for all Europe combined.

Transcontinental railroad building was so costly and risky as to require governmental subsidies. The extension of rails into thinly peopled regions was unprofitable until the areas could be built up; and private promoters were unwilling to suffer heavy initial losses. Congress, impressed by arguments supporting military and postal needs, began to advance liberal money loans to two favored

FEDERAL LAND GRANTS TO RAILROADS
The color portions indicate areas within which the railroads *might* have been given some land. The heavy black lines are in proportion to the land finally granted to the railroads.

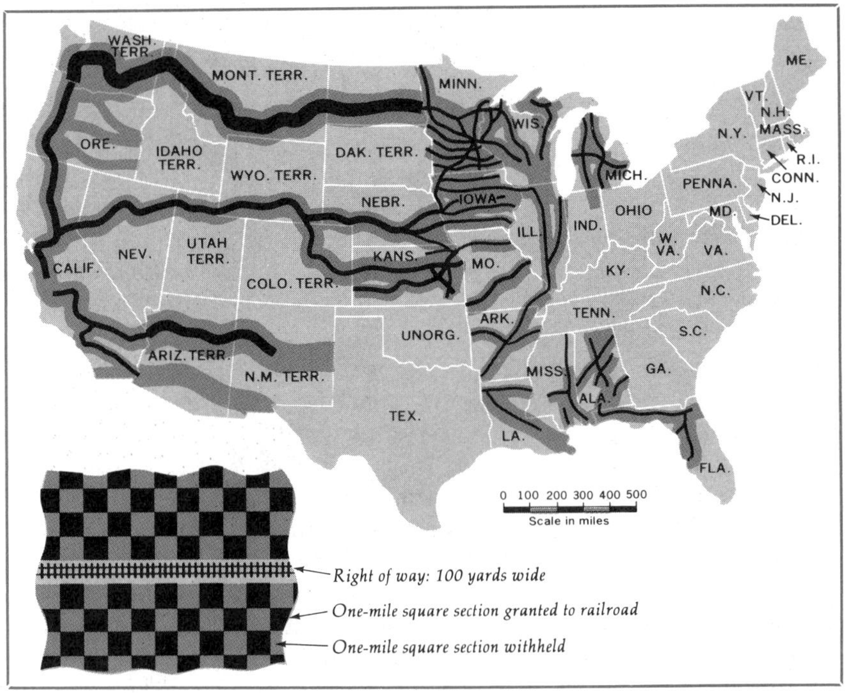

cross-continent companies in 1862, and added enormous donations of acreage paralleling the tracks. All told, Washington rewarded the railroads with 155,504,994 acres, while the Western states contributed 49 million more—a total area larger than Texas.

Grasping railroads tied up even more land than this for a number of years. Land grants were made in broad belts along the proposed route. Within these belts, the railroads were allowed to choose *alternate* mile-square sections in checkerboard fashion (see map). But until they determined the precise location of their tracks and decided which sections were the choicest selections, the railroads withheld *all* the land from other users. President Cleveland put an end to this foot-dragging practice in 1887 and threw open to settlement the still-unclaimed public portions of the land-grant areas.

Noisy criticism, especially in later years, was leveled at the "giveaway" of so valuable a birthright to greedy corporations. But the government did receive beneficial returns, including long-term preferential rates for postal service and military traffic. Granting land was also a "cheap" way to subsidize a much-desired transportation system, because it avoided new taxes for direct cash grants. The railroads could turn the land into gold by using it as collateral for loans or, later, by selling it. This they often did, at an average price of $3 an acre. Critics were also prone to overlook the fact that the land did not have even that relatively modest value until the railroads had ribboned it with steel.

Frontier villages touched by the magic wand of the iron rail became flourishing cities; those that were bypassed often withered away as "ghost towns." Little wonder that communities fought one another for the privilege of playing host to the railroads. Ambitious towns customarily held out monetary and other attractions to the builders, who sometimes blackmailed them into contributing more generously.

Spanning the Continent with Rails

Deadlock in the 1850s over the proposed transcontinental railroad was broken when the South seceded, leaving the field to the North. In 1862, the year after the guns first spoke at Fort Sumter, Congress made provision for starting the much-talked-about line. One weighty argument for action was the urgency of bolstering the Union, already disrupted, by binding the Pacific Coast more securely to the rest of the Republic.

The *Union* Pacific Railroad—note the word "Union"—was thus commissioned by Congress to thrust westward from Omaha, Nebraska. For each mile (1.6 kilometers) of track constructed, the company was granted 20 square miles (51.8 square kilometers) of land, alternating in 640-acre sections on either side of the track. For each mile the builders were also to receive a generous federal loan, ranging from $16,000 on the flat prairie land to $48,000 for mountainous country. The laying of rails began in earnest after the Civil War ended in 1865; and with juicy loans and land grants available, the "groundhog" promoters made all possible haste.

Sweaty construction gangs, containing many Irish "Paddies" (Patricks) who had fought in the Union armies, worked at a frantic pace. On one record-breaking day, a sledge-and-shovel army of some 5,000 men laid 10 miles (16 kilometers) of track. A favorite song was:

Then drill, my Paddies, drill;
  Drill, my heroes, drill;
Drill all day,
  No sugar in your tay,
Workin' on the U. P. Railway.

When hostile Indians attacked, the laborers would drop their picks and seize their rifles. Scores of men lost their lives as they built the line with one hand and fended off the attacking red men with the other. Relaxation and conviviality were provided by the tented towns, known as "hells on wheels," which sprang up at rail's end, sometimes numbering as many as 10,000 men and a sprinkling of painted prostitutes. The fabulous profits of the huge enterprise were reaped by the insiders of the Crédit Mobilier construction company. They slyly pocketed $73 million for some $50 million worth of breakneck construction, while bribing congressmen to look the other way.

Rail laying at the California end was undertaken by the Central Pacific Railroad. This line pushed boldly eastward from boom-town Sacramento, over and through the towering, snow-clogged Sierra Nevada. Four farseeing men—the so-called Big Four—were the chief financial backers of the enterprise. The quartet included the heavyset, enterprising ex-Governor Leland Stanford of California, who had useful political connections, and the burly, energetic Collis P. Huntington, an adept lobbyist. The Big Four cleverly operated through two construction companies, and although they pocketed tens of millions in profits, they kept their hands relatively clean by not becoming involved in the bribery of congressmen.

The Central Pacific, which was granted the same princely subsidies as the Union Pacific, had the same incentive to haste. Some 10,000 pig-tailed Chinese "coolies," with picturesque basket hats and flapping pantaloons, proved to be cheap, efficient, docile, and expendable (hundreds lost their lives in premature explosions and other mishaps). The rocky Sierra Nevada presented a formidable barrier; and the nerves of the Big Four were strained when the "coolies" could chip only a few inches a day through rocky tunnels, while

Leland Stanford (1824–1893). Multimillionaire railroad builder, California governor, and U.S. senator, he founded Stanford University as a memorial to his only son, who died as a youth. (Stanford University.)

Cheyenne Indians Interrupt Work on the Union Pacific Railroad. (*Harper's Weekly,* 1867.)

the Union Pacific was sledgehammering westward across the plains.

A "wedding of the rails" was finally consummated near Ogden, Utah, in 1869, as two locomotives gently kissed cowcatchers. The colorful ceremony included the breaking of champagne bottles and the driving of a last ceremonial (golden) spike, with Governor Stanford clumsily wielding a silver sledgehammer.* In all, the Union Pacific built 1,086 miles (1,739 kilometers); the Central Pacific, 689 miles (1,110 kilometers).

Completion of the transcontinental line—a magnificent engineering feat for that day—was one of America's most impressive peacetime undertakings. It spiked the West Coast more firmly to the Union, and facilitated a flourishing trade with the Orient. It penetrated the arid barrier of the deserts, while paving the way for the phenomenal growth of the Great West. Men compared this electrifying achievement with the Declaration of Independence and the emancipation of the slaves; jubilant Philadelphians again rang the cracked bell of Independence Hall.

* The spike was promptly removed and is now exhibited at the Stanford University Museum. There were two other gold ceremonial spikes.

Binding the Country with Railroad Ties

With the westward trail now blazed, four other transcontinental lines were completed before the century's end. None of them secured monetary loans from the federal government, as did the Union Pacific and the Central Pacific. But all of them except the Great Northern received generous grants of land.

The Northern Pacific Railroad, stretching from Lake Superior to Puget Sound, reached its terminus in 1883. On this gala occasion, builder Henry Villard, the German-born journalist–railroad man, dispatched his "Gold Spike Special," loaded with notables.

Two other lines ran parallel to some extent in New Mexico, Arizona, and California. One—the Atchison, Topeka, and Santa Fe—stretching through the Southwestern deserts to California, was completed in 1884. The other, the Southern Pacific, ribboned from New Orleans to San Francisco, and was consolidated in the same year. Two of the Big Four of Central Pacific fame—Huntington and Stanford—had a large hand in the construction and exploitation of the Southern Pacific (with which the Central Pacific later merged). The South had finally won its direct route to the West Coast.

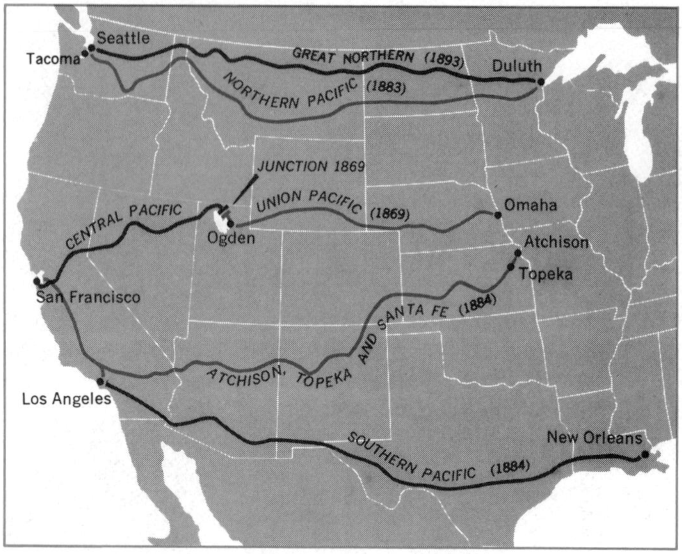

EARLY PACIFIC RAILWAY LINES
(with completion dates)
The Great Northern line claimed several distinctions: it was the last-built of the major transcontinental roads, the only one constructed without lavish federal subsidies, and the most northerly. Its larger-than-life promoter, James J. Hill, once declared: "You can't interest me in any proposition in any place where it doesn't snow. . . . No man on whom the snow does not fall ever amounts to a tinker's dam."

The last spike of the last of the five transcontinental railroads of the 19th Century was hammered home in 1893. The Great Northern, which ran from Duluth to Seattle north of the Northern Pacific, was the creation of a far-visioned Canadian-American, James J. Hill, a bearlike man who was probably the greatest railroad builder of all. Endowed with a high sense of public duty, he perceived that the prosperity of his railroad depended on the prosperity of the area that it served. He ran agricultural demonstration trains through the "Hill Country," and imported from England blooded bulls, which he distributed to the farmers.

In 1892, General Weaver, nominee of the Poplists, wrote regarding the railroad magnates: "In their delirium of greed the managers of our transportation systems disregard both private right and the public welfare. Today they will combine and bankrupt their weak rivals, and by the expenditure of a triflling sum possess themselves of properties which cost the outlay of millions. Tomorrow they will capitalize their booty for five times the cost, issue their bonds, and proceed to levy tariffs upon the people to pay dividends upon the fraud."

His enterprise was so soundly organized that it rode through later financial storms with flying colors.

Yet the romance of the rails was not without its sordid side. Much of the early construction was dangerously hasty and flimsy. A main object of subsidy chasers seemed to be to throw down any kind of line so as to get the lavish federal bounties, and then go back and repair later.

Pioneer builders were often guilty of gross overoptimism. Avidly seeking land bounties and pushing into areas that lacked enough potential population to support a railroad, they sometimes laid down rails that led "from nowhere to nothing." When prosperity failed to smile upon their coming, they went into bankruptcy, carrying down with them the savings of trusting investors. Many of the large railroads in the post–Civil War decades passed through seemingly endless bankruptcies, mergers, or reorganizations.

Railroad Consolidation and Mechanization

The success of the Western lines was facilitated by welding together and expanding the older Eastern networks, notably the New York Central. The moving genius in this enterprise was "Commodore" Cornelius Vanderbilt—burly, boisterous, white-whiskered. Having made his millions in steamboating, he daringly turned, in his late sixties, to a new career in railroading. Though ill-educated, ungrammatical, coarse, and ruthless, he was clear-visioned. Offering superior service at lower rates, he amassed a fortune of $100 million. His name is perhaps best remembered through his contribution of $1 million to the founding of Vanderbilt University in Tennessee.

Two significant new improvements proved a boon to the railroads. One was the steel rail, which Vanderbilt helped popularize when he replaced the old iron tracks of the New York Central with the tougher metal. Steel was safer and more economical because it could bear a heavier load. A standard gauge of track width likewise came into wide use during the post-war years, thus eliminating the expense and inconvenience of numerous changes from one line to another.

Cornelius Vanderbilt (1794–1877). Vanderbilt established a shipping-land transit line across Nicaragua, in response to the California gold rush. In 1873 he was the first to connect New York and Chicago by rail.

Other refinements played a vital role in railroading. The Westinghouse air brake, generally adopted in the 1870s, was a marvelous contribution to efficiency and safety. The Pullman Palace Cars, advertised as "gorgeous traveling hotels," were introduced on a considerable scale in the 1860s. Alarmists condemned them as "wheeled torture chambers" and potential funeral pyres, for the wooden cars were equipped with swaying kerosene lamps. Appalling accidents continued to be almost daily tragedies, despite safety devices like the telegraph ("talking wires"), double-tracking, and (later) the block signal.

Revolution by Railways

Metallic fingers of the railroads touched intimately countless phases of American life. For the first time a sprawling nation became united in a physical sense, bound together with ribs of iron and steel.

More than any other single factor, the railroad network spurred the amazing industrialization of the post–Civil War years. Puffing locomotives opened fresh markets for manufactured goods and sped raw materials to the factory. The forging of the rails themselves provided the largest single backlog for the adolescent steel industry.

The screeching iron horse likewise stimulated mining and agriculture, especially in the West. It took the farmer out to his land, carried the fruits of his toil to market, and brought him his manufactured necessities. Clusters of farm settlements paralleled the railroads, just as earlier they had followed the rivers.

Railways boomed the cities and played a leading role in the great cityward movement of the last decades of the century. The iron monsters could feed enormous concentrations of people, and at the same time insure them a livelihood by providing raw materials and markets.

Railroad companies also stimulated the mighty stream of immigration. Seeking settlers to whom their land grants might be sold at a profit, they advertised seductively in Europe, and sometimes offered to transport the newcomers free to their farms.

Finally, the railroad, more than any other single factor, was the maker of millionaires. A raw new aristocracy, consisting of "lords of the rail," replaced the old Southern "lords of the lash." The multiwebbed lines became the playthings of Wall Street; and colossal wealth was amassed by stock speculators and railroad wreckers like "Jubilee Jim" Fisk and the pious rascal "Uncle Daniel" Drew. As the Benéts have said,

> He toiled not, neither did he spin,
> But how he raked the dollars in!*

Wrongdoing in Railroading

Corruption lurks nearby when fabulous fortunes can be amassed overnight. The fleecings administered by the railroad construction companies, such as the Crédit Mobilier, were but the first of the bunco games that the railroad promoters learned to play. Methods soon became more refined, as fast-fingered financiers executed multimillion-dollar maneuvers beneath the noses of a bedazzled public. Jay Gould was the most adept of these ringmasters of rapacity. For nearly thirty years he boomed and busted the stocks of the Erie, the Kansas Pacific, the Union Pacific, and the Texas and Pacific in an incredible circus of speculative skullduggery.

One of the favorite devices of the moguls of manipulation was "stock watering." The term originally referred to the practice of making cattle thirsty by feeding them salt, and then having them bloat themselves with water before they were weighed in for sale. Thus railroad stock promoters grossly inflated their claims about a given line's assets and profitability, and sold stocks and bonds far in excess of the railroad's actual value. "Promoters' profits" often were the tail that wagged the iron horse itself. Railroad managers were forced to charge extortionate rates and wage ruthless competitive battles in order to pay off the exaggerated financial obligations with which they were saddled.

The Public Be Damned! Wealthy William H. Vanderbilt traveling in one of his palace cars. (New York *Daily Graphic.*)

The public interest was frequently trampled underfoot as the railroad titans waged their brutal wars. Crusty old Cornelius Vanderbilt, when told that the law stood in his way, reportedly exclaimed: "Law! What do I care about the law? Hain't I got the power?" On another occasion he supposedly threatened some associates: "I won't sue you, for the law is too slow. I'll ruin you." His son, William H. Vanderbilt, when asked in 1883 about the discontinuance of a fast mail train, reportedly snorted, "The public be damned!"

While abusing the public, the railroaders blandly bought and sold men in public life. They bribed judges and legislatures, employed arm-twisting lobbyists, and elected their own "creatures" to high office. They showered free passes on journalists and politicians in profusion. One railroad man noted in 1885 that in the West "no man who has money, or official position, or influence thinks he ought to pay anything for riding on a railroad."

Railroad kings were, for a time, virtual indus-

*"Daniel Drew" from *A Book of Americans* by Rosemary & Stephen Vincent Benét. Copyright, 1933, by Rosemary & Stephen Vincent Benét. Copyright renewed ©, 1961, by Rosemary Carr Benét. Reprinted by permission of Brandt & Brandt Literary Agency, Inc.

trial monarchs. As manipulators of a huge natural monopoly, they exercised more direct control over the lives of more people than did the President of the United States—and their terms were not limited to four years. They increasingly shunned the crude bloodletting of cutthroat competition and began to cooperate with one another to rule the railroad dominion. Sorely pressed to show at least some returns on their bloated investments, they entered into defensive alliances to protect precious profits.

The earliest form of combination was the "pool"—an agreement to divide the business in a given area and share the profits. Other rail barons granted secret rebates or kickbacks to powerful shippers in return for steady and assured traffic. Often they slashed their rates on competing lines, but they more than made up the difference on non-competing ones, where they might actually charge more for a short haul than for a long one.

Government Bridles the Iron Horse

It was not healthy that so many should be at the mercy of so few. Impoverished farmers, especially in the Middle West, began to wonder if the nation had not escaped from the slavery power only to fall into the hands of the money power, as represented by the railroad plutocracy.

But the American people, though quick to respond to political injustice, were slow to combat economic injustice. Dedicated to free enterprise and to the principle that competition is the soul of trade, they cherished a traditionally keen pride in progress. They remembered that Jefferson's ideals were hostile to governmental interference with business. Above all, there shimmered the "American dream": the hope that in a catch-as-catch-can economic system anyone might become a millionaire.

The depression of the 1870s finally goaded the embattled farmers into protesting against being "railroaded" into bankruptcy. Under pressure from organized agrarian groups like the Grange (Patrons of Husbandry), several Midwestern legislatures attempted to regulate the railroad monopoly.

These scattered state efforts came to a screeching halt in 1886. The Supreme Court, in the famed *Wabash* case, decreed that individual states had no power to regulate *inter*state commerce. If the mechanical monster were to be corralled, the Washington government would have to do the job.

Easygoing President Cleveland did not look kindly on effective regulation. But Congress ignored his grumbling opposition and passed the epochal Interstate Commerce Act in 1887. It prohibited rebates and pools, and required the railroads openly to publish their rates. It also forbade unfair discrimination against shippers, and outlawed charging more for a short haul than a long one over the same line. Most important, it set up the Interstate Commerce Commission (I.C.C.) to enforce and administer the new legislation.

Despite acclaim, the Interstate Commerce Act emphatically did not represent a popular victory over corporate wealth. One of the leading corporation lawyers of the day, Richard Olney, shrewdly noted that the new Commission "can be made of great use to the railroads. It satisfies the popular clamor for a government supervision of railroads, at the same time that such supervision is

"Uncle Sam's Wild West Show." The new Interstate Commerce Commission cautiously sets about lassoing refractory railroads under Uncle Sam's watchful eye. (*Harper's Weekly,* 1887.)

almost entirely nominal. . . . The part of wisdom is not to destroy the Commission, but to utilize it."

What the new legislation did do was to provide an orderly forum where competing business interests could resolve their conflicts in peaceable ways. The country could now avoid ruinous rate wars among the railroads, and outraged, "confiscatory" attacks on the lines by pitchfork-prodded state legislatures. This was a modest accomplishment but by no means an unimportant one. The Interstate Commerce Act tended to stabilize, not revolutionize, the existing business system.

Yet the act still ranks as a red-letter law. It was the first large-scale attempt by Washington to regulate business in the interest of society at large. It foreshadowed the doom of free-wheeling, buccaneering business practices, and served full notice that there was a public interest in private enterprise that the government was bound to protect.

Miracles of Mechanization

Post-war industrial expansion, partly a child of the railroad network, rapidly began to assume gigantic proportions. When Lincoln was elected in 1860, the Republic ranked only fourth among the manufacturing nations of the world. By 1894 it had spurted into first place; and it has never relinquished that leadership. Why the sudden upsurge?

Liquid capital, previously scarce, was now becoming abundant. The word "millionaire" had not been coined until the 1840s, and in 1861 only a handful of men were in this class. But the Civil War, partly through profiteering, created immense fortunes; and these accumulations could now be combined with the customary borrowings from foreign capitalists.

The amazing natural resources of the nation were now about to be fully exploited, including coal, oil, and iron. For example, the Minnesota–Lake Superior region, which had yielded some iron ore by the 1850s, contributed the rich deposits of the Mesabi range by the 1890s. This priceless bonanza, where mountains of red-rusted ore could be scooped up by steam shovels, ultimately became a cornerstone of a vast steel empire.

> Regarding the exploitation of immigrant labor, Ralph Waldo Emerson wrote in 1860: "The German and Irish millions, like the Negro, have a great deal of guano in their destiny. They are ferried over the Atlantic, and carted over America, to ditch and to drudge, to make corn cheap, and then to lie down prematurely to make a spot of green grass on the prairie."

Unskilled labor, both homegrown and imported, was now cheap and plentiful. Steel, the keystone industry, came to be based largely on the sweat of low-priced immigrant labor, working in two twelve-hour shifts, seven days a week.

American ingenuity at the same time played a vital role in the Second American Industrial Revolution. Techniques of mass production, pioneered by Eli Whitney, were being perfected by the Captains of Industry. American inventiveness flowered luxuriantly in the post-war years: between 1860 and 1890 some 440,000 patents were issued. Business operations were facilitated by the cash register, the stock ticker, and Christopher Sholes's typewriter ("literary piano"), which attracted home-confined women to industry. Urbanization was speeded by the refrigerator car, the electric dynamo, and F. J. Sprague's electric railway, which displaced animal-drawn cars. A New Orleans mass meeting proclaimed:

> Lincoln Set the Negroes Free!
> Sprague Has Set the Mule Free!
> The Long-Eared Mule No More Shall Adorn Our Streets.

One of the most ingenious inventions was the telephone, introduced by Alexander Graham Bell in 1876. A teacher of the deaf who was given a dead man's ear to experiment with, he remarked that if he could make the dumb talk, he could make iron speak. America was speedily turned into

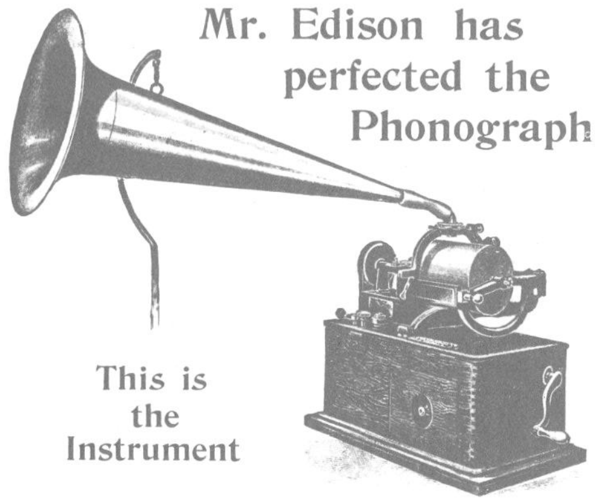
Mr. Edison has
perfected the
Phonograph
This is
the
Instrument

Advertisement for the New Edison Phonograph. *(Harper's Weekly.)*

a nation of "telephoniacs," as a gigantic system was erected on his invention. The social impact of this instrument was further revealed when an additional army of "number please" women was attracted from the home into industry. Telephone boys were at first employed at switchboards but their profanity shocked patrons.

The most versatile inventor of all was Thomas A. Edison, who as a boy had been considered so dull-witted that he was taken out of school. This "Wizard of the Wires" ran a veritable invention factory in New Jersey. He is perhaps best known for his perfection in 1879 of the electric light, which he unveiled after trying some 6,000 filaments. So deaf that he was not easily distracted, he displayed sleepless energy and a flair for practical money-making schemes rather than pure science. He invented, perfected, or did useful exploratory work on the phonograph, the mimeograph, the dictaphone, and the moving picture. "Genius," he said, "is one percent inspiration and ninety-nine percent perspiration."

The Trust Titan Emerges

Despite pious protests to the contrary, competition was the bogeyman of most business leaders of the day. Tycoons like Andrew Carnegie, the steel king, John D. Rockefeller, the oil baron, and J. Pierpont Morgan, the bankers' banker, exercised their genius in devising ways to ruin rivals and monopolize markets. Carnegie integrated every phase of his steel-making operation. His miners scratched the ore from the earth in the Mesabi range; Carnegie ships floated it across the Great Lakes; Carnegie railroads delivered it to the blast furnaces at Pittsburgh. When the molten metal finally poured from the glowing crucibles into the waiting ingot molds, no other hands but those in Carnegie's employ had touched the product.

Rockefeller likewise pursued a policy of "vertical integration," and he perfected another device for controlling competitors—the "trust." Stockholders in various smaller oil companies assigned their stock to the board of directors of Rockefeller's Standard Oil Company. It then consolidated and concerted the operations of the previously competing enterprises. "Let us prey" was said to be Rockefeller's unwritten motto. Wielding vast power with ruthless efficiency, Standard Oil soon cornered virtually the entire world petroleum market. Weaker competitors, left out of the trust agreement, went to the wall. Rockefeller's

J. P. Morgan (1837–1913). As the most influential banker of his day, he symbolized to many people the power and arrogance of "finance capitalism." (Library of Congress.)

stunning success inspired many imitators, and the word "trust" came to be generally used to describe any large-scale business combination.

The imperial Morgan devised still other schemes for eliminating wasteful competition. The depression of the 1890s drove into his welcoming arms many bleeding businessmen, wounded by cutthroat competition. His prescribed remedy was to consolidate rival enterprises, and to insure future harmony by placing officers of his own banking syndicate on their various boards of directors. These came to be known as "interlocking directorates."

The Supremacy of Steel

"Steel is king!" might well have been the exultant war cry of the new industrialized generation. The mighty metal ultimately held together the new steel civilization, from skyscrapers to coal scuttles, while providing it with food, shelter, and transportation. Steel making, notably rails for railroads, typified the dominance of "heavy industry," with its "capital goods," as distinct from the production of "consumer goods" such as clothes and shoes.

Now taken for granted, steel was a scarce commodity in the wood-and-brick America of Abraham Lincoln. Considerable iron went into railroad rails and bridges, but steel was expensive and was used largely for products like cutlery. The early iron horse snorted exclusively (and dangerously) over iron rails; and when in the 1870s "Commodore" Vanderbilt of the New York Central began to use steel rails, he was forced to import them from England.

Yet within an amazing twenty years the United States had outdistanced all foreign competitors, and was pouring out more than one-third of the world's supply of steel. By 1900 the Americans were producing as much as England and Germany combined.

What wrought the transformation? Chiefly the invention in the 1850s of a method of making cheap steel—the Bessemer process. It was named after a derided British inventor, although an American had stumbled on it a few years earlier. William Kelly, a Kentucky manufacturer of iron kettles, discovered that cold air blown on red-hot iron caused the metal to become white-hot by igniting the carbon and thus eliminating impurities. He tried to apply the new "air boiling" technique to his own product, but his customers decried "Kelly's fool steel" and his business declined. Gradually the Bessemer-Kelly process won acceptance, and these two "crazy men" ultimately made possible the present steel civilization.

A revolutionary steel-fabricating process was not the whole story. America was one of the few places in the world where one could find relatively close together abundant coal for fuel, rich iron ore for smelting, and other essential ingredients for making steel. The nation also boasted an abundant labor supply, guided by industrial know-how of a high order. The stage was set for miracles of production.

Carnegie and Other Men of Steel

Kingpin among steelmasters was Andrew Carnegie, an undersized, charming Scotsman. As a towheaded lad, he was brought to America by his impoverished parents in 1848, and got a job as a bobbin boy at $1.20 a week. Mounting the ladder of success so fast that he was said to have scorched the rungs, he forged ahead by working hard, doing the extra chore, cheerfully assuming responsibility, and smoothly cultivating influential people.

After accumulating some capital, Carnegie entered the steel business in the Pittsburgh area. A gifted organizer and administrator, he achieved success by picking high-class associates and by eliminating many of the middlemen. Although inclined to be tough-fisted in business, he was not a monopolist and disliked monopolistic trusts. His remarkable organization was a partnership which involved, at its maximum, about forty "Pittsburgh millionaires." By 1900 Carnegie was producing one-fourth of the nation's Bessemer steel, and the partners were dividing profits of $40 million a year, with the "Napoleon of the Smoke-

Carnegie Presents the Trust as a Trustworthy Beast. Steel, oil, coal, lumber, sugar, and salt are all represented. (*Harper's Weekly.*)

stacks" himself receiving a cool $25 million. These were the pre-income tax days, when millionaires were really rich and profits represented take-home pay.

Into the picture now stepped the financial giant of the age, J. Pierpont Morgan. "Jupiter" Morgan had made a legendary reputation for himself and his Wall Street banking house by financing the reorganization of railroads, insurance companies, and banks. An impressive figure of a man, with massive shoulders, shaggy brows, piercing eyes, and a bulbous, acne-cursed red nose, he had established an enviable reputation for integrity. He did not believe that "money power" was dangerous, except when in dangerous hands—and he did not regard his hands as dangerous.

The force of circumstances brought Morgan and Carnegie into collision. By 1900 the canny little Scotsman, weary of turning steel into gold, was eager to sell his holdings. Morgan had meanwhile plunged heavily into the manufacture of steel pipe tubing. Carnegie, cleverly threatening to invade the same business, was ready to ruin his rival

> Carnegie wrote in 1889: "The man who dies leaving behind him millions of available wealth, which was his to administer during life, will pass away 'unwept, unhonored, and unsung,' no matter to what uses he leaves the dross which he cannot take with him. Of such as these the public verdict will then be: 'The man who dies thus rich dies disgraced.' "

if he did not receive his price. The steelmaster's agents haggled with the imperious Morgan for eight agonizing hours, and the financier finally agreed to buy out Carnegie for over $400 million. Fearing that he would die "disgraced" with so much money, Carnegie dedicated the remaining years of his life to giving it away for public libraries, pensions for professors, and other philanthropic purposes—in all disposing of about $350 million.

Morgan moved rapidly to expand his new industrial empire. He took the Carnegie holdings, added others, "watered" the stock liberally, and in 1901 launched the enlarged United States Steel Corporation. Capitalized at $1.4 billion, it was America's first billion-dollar corporation—a larger sum than the total estimated wealth of the nation in 1800. The Industrial Revolution, with its hot Bessemer breath, had at last come into its own.

Rockefeller Grows an American Beauty Rose

A sudden emergence of the oil industry was one of the most striking developments of the years during and after the Civil War. Traces of oil found on streams had earlier been bottled for back-rub and other patent medicines, but not until 1859 did the first well in Pennsylvania—"Drake's Folly"—pour out its liquid "black gold." Almost overnight an industry was born which was to take more wealth from the earth—and more useful wealth at that—than all of the gold extracted by the Forty-Niners and their Western successors. The soaring popularity of kerosene as an illuminant for lamps struck a crippling blow at the old whale-oil business.

John D. Rockefeller—lanky, shrewd, ambitious, abstemious (he neither drank, smoked, nor swore)—came to dominate the oil industry. Born to a family of precarious income, he became a successful businessman at age nineteen. One upward stride led to another, and in 1870 he organized the Standard Oil Company of Ohio, nucleus of the great trust formed in 1882. Locating his refineries in Cleveland, he sought to eliminate the middleman and squeeze out competitors.

Pious and parsimonious, Rockefeller flourished in an era of completely free enterprise. So-called piratical practices were employed by "corsairs of finance," and business ethics were distressingly low. Rockefeller, operating "just to the windward of the law," pursued a policy of rule or ruin. "Sell all the oil that is sold in your district" was the hard-boiled order that went out to his local agents. By 1877 Rockefeller controlled 95 percent of all the oil refineries in the country.

Rockefeller—"Reckafellow," as Carnegie once called him—showed little mercy. A kind of primitive savagery prevailed in the jungle world of big business, where only the fittest survived. Or so Rockefeller believed. His son later explained that the giant American Beauty rose could be produced "only by sacrificing the early buds that grew up around it." His father pinched off the small buds with complete ruthlessness. Employing spies and extorting secret rebates from the railroads, he even forced the lines to pay him rebates on the freight bills of his competitors!

Rockefeller Nips Competing Buds. His grandson, Nelson A. Rockefeller, later remarked that the original "John D." broke no laws but "a lot of laws were passed because of him." His sharp practices finally alerted legislatures. (*Literary Digest*, 1905.)

Rockefeller himself thought he was simply obeying a law of nature. "The time was ripe" for aggressive consolidation, he later reflected. "It had to come, though all we saw at the moment was the need to save ourselves from wasteful conditions . . . . The day of combination is here to stay. Individualism has gone, never to return."

On the other side of the ledger, Rockefeller's oil monopoly did turn out a superior product at a relatively cheap price. It achieved important economies, both at home and abroad, by its large-scale methods of production and distribution. This, in truth, was the tale of the other trusts as well. The efficient use of expensive machinery called for bigness, and consolidation proved more profitable than ruinous price wars.

Other trusts blossomed along with the American Beauty of oil. These included the Sugar Trust, the Tobacco Trust, the Leather Trust, and the Harvester Trust, which amalgamated some 200 competitors. The meat industry arose on the backs of bawling Western herds, and Meat Kings like Gustavus F. Swift and Philip Armour took their place among the new royalty. Wealth was coming to dominate the commonwealth.

These untrustworthy trusts, and the "pirates" who captained them, were disturbingly new. They eclipsed an older American aristocracy of modestly successful merchants and professional men. An arrogant class of "new rich" now was elbowing aside the patrician families in the mad scramble for power and prestige. Not surprisingly, the ranks of the reformers were frequently spearheaded by the "best men"—genteel old-family do-gooders who were not radicals but conservative defenders of their own vanishing influence.

The Gospel of Wealth

Monarchs of yore invoked the divine right of kings, and America's industrial plutocrats took a somewhat similar stance. Some candidly cred-

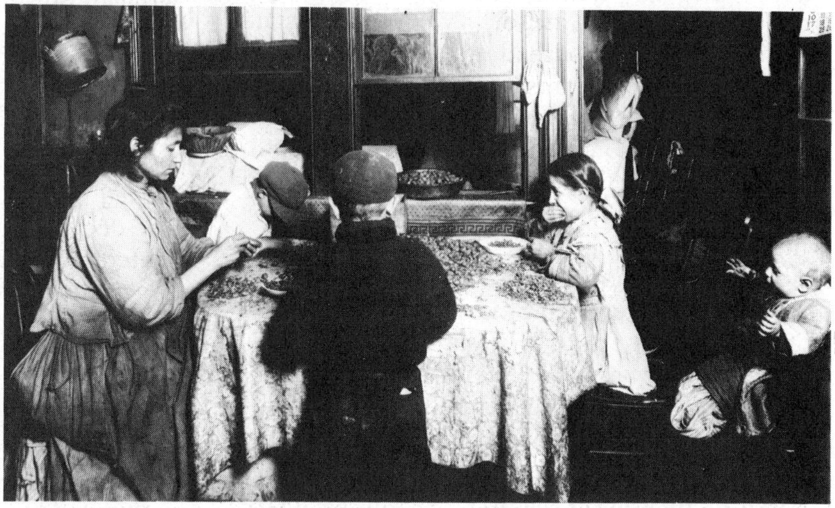

The New Rich and the New Immigrants. A well-to-do family out for a jaunt (*above*) and a tenement family doing "piece-work" at home—shelling nuts for commercial use (*below*). The young girl at the table seems to be "snitching" some nuts for herself. The apparently growing gulf between the super-rich and the squalid poor deeply worried reformers in the late 19th Century. They feared that democracy could not survive in the face of such gross inequality. (*Above*, Brown Brothers; *below,* International Museum of Photography at George Eastman House.)

ited heavenly help. "Godliness is in league with riches," preached the Episcopal bishop of Massachusetts, and hard-fisted John D. Rockefeller piously acknowledged that "the good Lord gave me my money." But most defenders of wide-open capitalism relied more heavily on the survival-of-the-fittest theories of Charles Darwin. "The millionaires are a product of natural selection," concluded Yale Professor William Graham Sumner. "They get high wages and live in luxury, but the bargain is a good one for society." Despite plutocracy and deepening class divisions, the Captains of Industry provided material progress.

Self-justification by the wealthy inevitably involved contempt for the poor. Many of the rich, especially the newly rich, had pulled themselves up by their own bootstraps; hence they concluded that those who stayed poor must be lazy and lacking in enterprise. The Reverend Russell Conwell of Philadelphia became rich by delivering his lecture "Acres of Diamonds" thousands of times. In it he said, "There is not a poor person in the

> Industrial millionaires were condemned in the Populist platform of 1892: "The fruits of the toil of millions are boldly stolen to build up colossal fortunes for a few . . . and the possessors of these, in turn despise the Republic and endanger liberty. From the same prolific womb of governmental injustice we breed the two great classes—tramps and millionaires."

United States who was not made poor by his own shortcomings." Such attitudes were a formidable roadblock to social reform.

Plutocracy, like the earlier slavocracy, took its stand firmly on the Constitution. The clause which gave Congress sole jurisdiction over interstate commerce was a godsend to the monopolists; their high-priced lawyers used it time and again to thwart controls by the state legislatures. Giant trusts likewise sought refuge behind the 14th Amendment, which had been originally designed to protect the rights of the ex-slaves as persons. The courts ingeniously interpreted a corporation to be a legal "person," and decreed that as such it could not be deprived of its property by a state without "due process of law" (see Art. XIV, para.1). There is some questionable evidence that slippery corporation lawyers deliberately inserted this loophole when the 14th Amendment was being fashioned in 1866.

Great industrialists likewise sought to incorporate in "easy states," like New Jersey, where the restrictions on Big Business were mild or nonexistent. For example, the Southern Pacific Railroad, with much of its trackage in California, was incorporated in Kentucky.

The growing concentration of capital, through trusts and other combines, was astounding. By 1890 the value of all property in the United States was estimated at $65 billion, of which $25 billion represented the assets of corporations. Cynics sneered that U.S.A. meant United Syndicates of America.

Government Tackles the Trust Evil

At long last, the masses of the people began to mobilize against monopoly. They first tried to control the trusts through state legislation, as they had earlier attempted to curb the railroads. Failing here, as before, they were forced to appeal to Congress. After prolonged pulling and hauling, the Sherman Anti-Trust Law of 1890 was finally signed into law.

The Sherman Act flatly forbade combinations in restraint of trade, without any distinction between "good" trusts and "bad" trusts. Bigness, not badness, was the sin. The law proved ineffective, largely because it had only baby teeth or no teeth at all, and because it contained legal loopholes through which clever corporation lawyers could wriggle. But the new act was unexpectedly effective in one respect. Contrary to its original intent, it was used to curb labor unions or labor combinations which were deemed to be restraining trade.

Early prosecutions of the trusts by the Justice Department under the Sherman Act of 1890, as it turned out, were neither vigorous nor successful. The decisions in seven of the first eight cases presented by the attorney general were adverse to the government. More new trusts were formed in the 1890s under President McKinley than during any other like period. Not until 1914 were the paper jaws of the Sherman Act fitted with reasonably sharp teeth. Until then, there was some question whether the government would control the trusts or the trusts the government.

But the iron grip of monopolistic corporations was being threatened. A revolutionary new principle had been written into the law books by the Sherman Anti-Trust Act of 1890, as well as by the Interstate Commerce Act of 1887. Private greed must henceforth be subordinated to public need.

The South in the Age of Industry

The industrial tidal wave that washed over the North after the Civil War caused only feeble ripples in the backwater of the South. The plantation

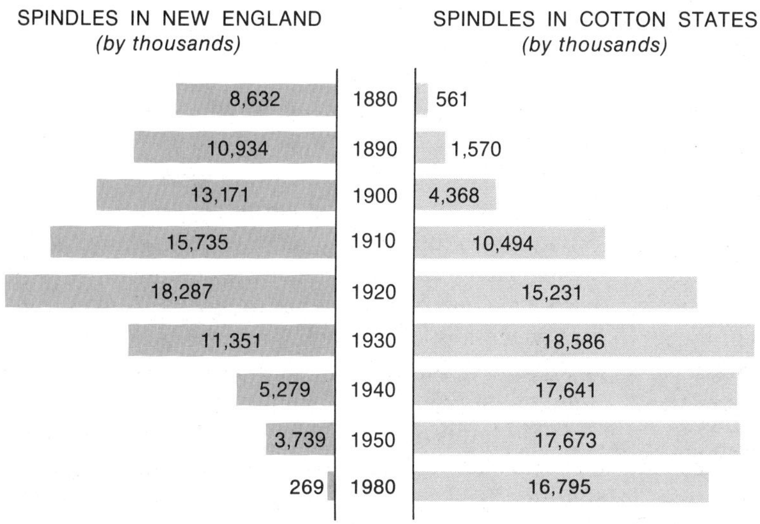

COTTON MANUFACTURING MOVES SOUTH

Textile manufacturing usually looms large in the early stages of industrial development. In later stages, it gives way to higher-technology businesses. This trend can be seen here, both in the migration of textile manufacturing to the Southern United States, and in the decline in the number of spindles in the United States as a whole since the 1930s, as developing Third World countries became major textile producers.

system had degenerated into a pattern of absentee land ownership. White and black sharecroppers now tilled the soil for a share of the crop, or they became tenants, in bondage to landlords who controlled needed credit and supplies.

Southern agriculture received a welcome boost in the 1880s, when machine-made cigarettes replaced the roll-your-own variety and tobacco consumption shot up. James Buchanan Duke took full advantage of the new technology to mass-produce the dainty "coffin nails." In 1890, in what was becoming a familiar pattern, he absorbed his main competitors into the American Tobacco Company. The cigarette czar later showed such generosity to Trinity College, near his birthplace in Durham, North Carolina, that the trustees gratefully changed its name to Duke University.

> Henry Grady, the Atlanta editor, urged the New South to industrialize. In a Boston speech in 1889 he described the burial in Georgia of a Confederate veteran: "The South didn't furnish a thing on earth for that funeral but the corpse and the hole in the ground. . . . They buried him in a New York coat and a Boston pair of shoes and a pair of breeches from Chicago and a shirt from Cincinnati, leaving him nothing to carry into the next world with him to remind him of the country in which he lived, and for which he fought for four years, but the chill of blood in his veins and the marrow in his bones."

Industrialists tried to coax the agricultural South out of the fields and into the factories, but with only modest success. The region remained overwhelmingly rural. Prominent among the boosters of a "New South" was silver-tongued Henry W. Grady, editor of the Atlanta *Constitution.* He tirelessly exhorted the ex-Confederates to become "Georgia Yankees" and outplay the North at the commercial and industrial game.

Yet formidable obstacles lay in the path of Southern industrialization. One was the paper barrier of regional rate-setting systems imposed by the Northern-dominated railroad interests. Railroads gave preferential rates to manufactured goods moving southward from the north, but in the opposite direction they discriminated in favor of Southern raw materials. The net effect was to keep the South in a kind of "third world" servitude to the Northeast—as a supplier of raw materials to the manufacturing metropolis, unable to develop a substantial industrial base of its own.

A bitter example of this economic discrimination against the South was the "Pittsburgh plus" pricing system in the steel industry. Rich deposits of coal and iron ore near Birmingham, Alabama, worked by cheap Southern labor, should have given steel manufacturers there a competitive edge, especially in Southern markets. But the steel lords of Pittsburgh brought pressure to bear on the compliant railroads. As a result, Birmingham steel, no matter where it was delivered, was charged a fictional fee, as if it had been shipped from Pittsburgh. This stunting of the South's natural economic advantages throttled the growth of the Birmingham steel industry.

In manufacturing cotton textiles the South fared considerably better. Southerners had long resented shipping their fiber to New England, and now their cry was "Bring the mills to the cotton." Beginning about 1880, Northern capital began to erect cotton mills in the South, largely in response to tax benefits and the prospect of cheap and nonunionized labor. Many smokestacks now pricked the Southern skyline, but as late as 1900 the South still produced a smaller percentage of the nation's manufactured goods than it had before the Civil War. (See chart on preceding page.)

The Impact of the New Industrial Revolution on America

Economic miracles wrought during the decades after the Civil War enormously increased the wealth of the Republic. The standard of living rose sharply, and the well-fed American worker enjoyed more physical comforts than his coworkers in any other powerful nation. Urban centers mushroomed as the insatiable factories demanded more American labor, and as immigrants poured into the vacuums created by new jobs.

Early Jeffersonian ideals were withering before the smudgy blasts from the smokestacks. As agriculture declined in relation to manufacturing, America could no longer aspire to be a nation of small freehold farms. Jefferson's concepts of free enterprise, with neither help nor hindrance from Washington, were being thrown out the factory window. Tariffs had already provided assistance, but the long arm of federal authority was now committed to decades of corporation curbing and "trust busting."

Probably no single group was more profoundly affected by the new Industrial Age than women. Sucked into industry by recent inventions, chiefly the typewriter and the telephone switchboard, millions of stenographers and "hello girls" achieved a new economic and social independence. Careers for women also meant delayed marriages and smaller families.

The clattering Machine Age likewise accentuated class division. "Industrial buccaneers" flaunted bloated fortunes, while their rags-to-riches spouses displayed glittering diamonds. Such extravagances evoked bitter criticism. Some of it was envious but much of it rose from the small and increasingly vocal group of socialists and other radicals, many of whom were recent European immigrants. The existence of an oligarchy of money was amply demonstrated by the fact that by 1900 about one-tenth of the people owned and controlled nine-tenths of the nation's wealth.

Finally, strong pressures for foreign trade developed as the tireless machine threatened to flood the domestic market. American products radiated out all over the world—notably the five-gallon kerosene can of the Standard Oil Company. The flag follows trade, and empire tends to follow the flag—a harsh lesson that America was soon to learn.

In Unions There Is Strength

Sweat of the laborer lubricated the vast new industrial machine. Yet the wageworker did not share proportionately with his employers the benefits of the Age of Big Business.

The workingman, suggestive of the Roman galley slave, was becoming a lever-puller in a giant mechanism. His originality and creativeness were being stifled, and less value than ever before was being placed on manual skills. Before the Civil War he might have toiled in a small plant, whose owner hailed him in the morning by his first name and inquired after his wife's gallstones. But now

> The Reverend Henry Ward Beecher of Brooklyn (1813–1887), the most distinguished (and notorious) clergyman of the era after the Civil War, said, "The trade union, which originated under the European system, destroys liberty. I do not say a dollar a day is enough to support a working man, but it is enough to support a man. Not enough to support a man and five children if a man insists on smoking and drinking beer."

the factory hand was employed by a corporation—depersonalized, bodiless, soulless, and often conscienceless. The directors knew him not; and in fairness to their stockholders they did not feel that they could engage in large-scale private philanthropy.

As new machines were invented, many of the regular employees were thrown out of work. In the long run more jobs were created than destroyed, but in the short run the manual worker was often hard hit. Labor is the most perishable of all commodities. A pair of shoes unsold may be sold tomorrow, but a day's labor not sold today is lost forever.

A glutted labor market, moreover, severely handicapped the wage earners. The vast new railroad network could shuttle unemployed workers, including blacks and immigrants, into areas where wages were high, and thus beat standards down. Inpouring Europeans further worsened conditions. During the 1880s and 1890s and later, the labor market had to absorb several hundred thousand unskilled workers a year.

Individual workers were powerless to battle singlehandedly against giant industry. Forced to organize and fight for basic rights, they found the dice heavily loaded against them. The corporation could dispense with the individual worker much more easily than the worker could dispense with the corporation. The employer could pool vast wealth through thousands of stockholders, retain high-priced lawyers, buy up the local press, and put pressure on the politicians. He could import strikebreakers ("scabs") and employ thugs to beat up labor organizers. In 1886 Jay Gould reputedly boasted, "I can hire one-half of the working class to kill the other half."

Corporations had still other weapons in their arsenals. They could call upon the federal courts—presided over by well-fed and conservative judges—to issue injunctions ordering the strikers to cease striking. If defiance and disorders ensued, the company could request the state and federal authorities to bring in troops. An employer could lock his doors against rebellious workers—a process called the "lockout"—and then starve them into submission. He could compel them to sign "ironclad oaths" or "yellow dog contracts," both of which were solemn agreements not to join a labor union. He could put the names of agitators on a "black list" and circulate it among fellow

"The Root of the Matter." Foreign-appearing labor agitator urges a work stoppage on a reluctant artisan. Smearing the labor movement as a "foreign" import was a common tactic of employers. (Thomas Nast in *Harper's Weekly*, May 8, 1886.)

employers. A corporation might even own the "company town," with its high-priced grocery stores and "easy" credit. Oftentimes the worker sank into perpetual debt—a status that strongly resembled serfdom. Countless thousands of blackened coal miners were born in a company house, nurtured by a (high-priced) company store, and buried in a company graveyard—prematurely dead.

The public, annoyed by recurrent strikes, grew deaf to the outcry of the worker. American wages were perhaps the highest in the world, although a dollar a day for pick-and-shovel labor does not now seem excessive. Carnegie and Rockefeller had battled their way to the top, and the view was common that the laborer could do likewise. Somehow the strike seemed like a foreign importation—socialistic and hence unpatriotic. Big Business might combine into trusts to raise prices, but the worker must not combine into unions to raise wages. Unemployment seemed to be an act of God, who somehow would take care of the laborer.

Labor Limps Along

Labor unions, which had been few and disorganized in 1861, were given a strong boost by the Civil War. This bloody conflict, with its drain on manpower, put more of a premium on labor; and the mounting cost of living provided an urgent incentive to unionization. By 1872 there were several hundred thousand organized workers and thirty-two national unions, including such crafts as bricklayers, typesetters, and shoemakers. They were not concerned with the sweet by-and-by but with the bitter here and now.

The National Labor Union, organized in 1866, represented a giant-boot stride by the workingmen. It lasted six years and attracted the impressive total of some 600,000 members, including the skilled, unskilled, and farmers. Its keynote was social reform, although it agitated for such specific goals as the eight-hour day and the arbitration of industrial disputes. It finally succeeded in winning an eight-hour day for government workers, but the devastating depression of the 1870s dealt it a knockout blow. Labor was generally rocked back on its heels during these hectic years. Wage reductions in 1877 touched off a series of strikes on the railroads which were so violent as to verge on civil war.

> Henry George, the tax reformer, observed in 1879, "The methods by which a trade union can alone act are necessarily destructive; its organization is necessarily tyrannical."

A new organization—the Knights of Labor—seized the torch dropped by the defunct National Labor Union. Officially known as The Noble and Holy Order of the Knights of Labor, it began inauspiciously in 1869 as a secret society, with a private ritual, passwords, and a grip. Secrecy, which continued until 1881, would forestall possible reprisals by employers.

The Knights of Labor, like the National Labor Union, sought to include all workers in "one big union." Their slogan was: "An injury to one is the concern of all." A welcome mat was rolled out for the skilled and unskilled, for men and women, for whites and underprivileged blacks, some 90,000 of whom joined. The Knights excluded only liquor dealers, professional gamblers, lawyers, bankers, and stockbrokers.

Setting up broad goals, the embattled Knights refused to thrust their lance into politics. Instead, they campaigned for economic and social reform, including producers' cooperatives and codes for safety and health. Voicing the war cry, "Labor is the only creator of values and capital," they frowned upon industrial warfare while fostering industrial arbitration. The ordinary workday was then ten hours or more, and the Knights waged a determined campaign for the eight-hour stint. A favorite song of these years ran:

> Hurrah, hurrah, for labor,
>   it is mustering all its powers,
> And shall march along to victory
>   with the banner of eight hours.

Under the eloquent leadership of Terence V. Powderly, an Irish-American of nimble wit and fluent tongue, the Knights won a number of strikes for the eight-hour day. By 1886, though their claim of a million members was evidently exaggerated, they were clearly a force to be reckoned with.

Unhorsing the Knights of Labor

Despite their outward success, the Knights were riding for a fall. They became involved in a number of May Day strikes in 1886, about half of which failed. A focal point was Chicago, which contained about 80,000 Knights. The city was also honeycombed with a few hundred anarchists, many of them foreign-born, who were advocating a violent overthrow of the American government.

Tensions rapidly built up to the bloody Haymarket Square episode. Labor disorders had broken out, and on May 4, 1886, the Chicago police advanced on a meeting called to protest alleged brutalities by the authorities. Suddenly a dynamite bomb was thrown which killed or injured several dozen persons, including policemen.

Hysteria swept the Windy City. Eight anarchists were rounded up, although nobody proved that they had anything to do directly with the bomb. But the judge and jury held that since they had preached incendiary doctrines, they could be charged with conspiracy. Five were sentenced to death, one of whom committed suicide, and the other three were given stiff prison terms.

Agitation for clemency mounted. In 1892, some six years later, John P. Altgeld, a German-born Democrat of strong liberal tendencies, was elected governor of Illinois. After studying the Haymarket case exhaustively, he pardoned the three survivors. Violent abuse was showered on him by conservatives, unstinted praise by those who thought the men innocent. He was defeated for re-election, and died a few years later in relative obscurity, "The Eagle Forgotten." Whatever the merits of the case, Altgeld displayed courage in opposing what he regarded as a gross injustice.

The Haymarket Square bomb helped blow the props from under the Knights of Labor. They were associated in the public mind, though mistakenly, with the anarchists. The eight-hour movement suffered correspondingly, and subsequent strikes by the Knights met with scant success. The right to choose to strike carried with it the right to lose the strike.

Knights of Labor at Odds with Skilled Craft Unions. Capital looks on happily. (Thomas Nast, *Harper's Weekly*, 1886.)

Another fatal handicap of the Knights was their inclusion of both skilled and unskilled workers. Unskilled labor could be easily replaced by strikebreaking "scabs." High-class craft unionists, who enjoyed a semi-monopoly of skills, could not readily be supplanted, and hence enjoyed a superior bargaining position. They finally wearied of sacrificing this advantage in order to pull the chestnuts of the unskilled out of the fire. By 1890 the Knights had melted away to 100,000 members, and these gradually fused with other protest groups of the 1890s.

The AF of L to the Fore

The powerful American Federation of Labor, which next stole the spotlight, was largely a creation of squat, square-jawed Samuel Gompers. This colorful Jewish cigar maker, born in a London tenement and removed from school at age ten, was brought to America when thirteen. Taking his turn at reading informative literature to fellow cigar makers in New York, he was pressed into overtime service because of his strong voice. Rising spectacularly in labor ranks, he was elected president of the American Federation of Labor every year except one from 1886 to 1924.

Samuel Gompers (1850–1924). Samuel Gompers declared, "Show me the country in which there are no strikes and I'll show you that country in which there is no liberty." In later years this was notably true of authoritarian countries. (National Archives.)

Significantly, the American *Federation* of Labor was just what it called itself—a federation. It consisted of an association of self-governing national unions, each of which kept its independence, with the AF of L unifying overall strategy. No individual laborer as such could join the central body.

Gompers adopted a down-to-earth approach, soft-pedaling attempts to engineer sweeping social reform. A bitter foe of socialism, he kept the Federation squarely on the cautious path of conservatism. He had no quarrel with capitalism as such, but he wanted labor to win its fair share. All he wanted, he said simply, was "more." His objectives were better wages and hours, as well as other improved conditions for the worker. Another major goal of Gompers was the "trade agreement" authorizing the "closed shop"—or all-union labor. His chief weapons were the walkout and the boycott, enforced by "We don't patronize" signs. The stronger craft unions of the Federation, by pooling funds, were able to amass a war chest that would enable them to ride out prolonged strikes.

The AF of L thus established itself on solid foundations. Although attempting to speak for all workers, it fell far short of being representative of them. Composed of skilled crafts, like the carpenters and the bricklayers, it was willing to let unskilled laborers, especially blacks, shift for themselves. Though hard-pressed by big industry, the Federation was basically non-political. But it did attempt to persuade members to reward friends and punish foes at the polls. The AF of L weathered the Panic of 1893 reasonably well, and by 1900 it could boast a membership of 500,000. Critics referred to it, with questionable accuracy, as "the Labor Trust."

Labor disorders continued throughout the years from 1881 to 1900, during which there was an alarming total of over 23,000 strikes. These disturbances involved 6,610,000 workers, with a total loss to both employers and employees of $450 million. The strikers lost about half their strikes, and won or compromised the remainder.* Perhaps the gravest weakness of organized labor was that it still embraced only a small minority of all working people—about 3 percent in 1900.

But attitudes toward labor had begun to change perceptibly by 1900. The public was beginning to concede the right of workingmen to organize, to bargain collectively, and to strike. As a sign of the times, Labor Day was made a legal holiday by act of Congress in 1894. A few enlightened industrialists had come to perceive the wisdom of avoiding costly economic warfare by bargaining with the unions and signing agreements. But the vast majority of employers continued to fight organized labor, which achieved its grudging gains only after recurrent strikes and frequent reverses. Nothing was handed to it on a silver platter. Management still held the whip hand, and several trouble-fraught decades were to pass before labor was to gain a position of relative equality with capital. If the Age of Big Business had dawned, the Age of Big Labor was still some distance from the horizon.

---

*For an artist's view of a late 19th Century strike, see the painting by Robert Koehler, color portfolio

VARYING VIEWPOINTS

The capitalists who forged an industrial America in the late 19th Century were once called Captains of Industry—a respectful title that bespoke the awe due their wondrous material accomplishments. But these economic innovators have never been universally admired. During the Great Depression of the 1930s, when the entire industrial order they had created seemed to have collapsed utterly, it was fashionable to speak of them as "Robber Barons"—a term implying scorn for their high-handed methods. This sneer came often to the lips and pens of left-wing critics like Matthew Josephson, who sympathized with the working classes that were allegedly brutalized by the factory system. Criticism has also come from writers nostalgic for a pre-industrial past. These critics see farmers, not factory workers, as the chief victims of America's great economic transformation. But in recent years, as attention has focused on problems of economic development in the "Third World," American industrialization in the 19th Century has come to be regarded as relatively painless and commendably successful. The reputation of the leading capitalists responsible for that process has risen accordingly.

SELECT READINGS

A penetrating survey is Samuel P. Hays, *The Response to Industrialism, 1885–1914* (1957). Other useful general accounts include Ray Ginger, *Age of Excess* (1965), John A. Garraty, *The New Commonwealth* (1968), Matthew Josephson, *The Robber Barons* (1934), and three studies by E. C. Kirkland: *The Coming of the Industrial Age* (1960), *Industry Comes of Age* (1961), and *Dream and Thought in the Business Community, 1860–1900* (1956). Rendigs Fels provides valuable detail in *American Business Cycles* (1959), and Stuart Bruchey puts the period in context in *The Growth of the Modern Economy* (1975). Consult also Robert Higgs, *The Transformation of the American Economy, 1865–1914* (1971), and C. H. Hession and Hyman Sardy, *Ascent to Affluence: A History of American Economic Development* (1969). The thought and attitudes characteristic of the new industrial age are examined by Richard Hofstadter, *Social Darwinism in American Thought* (rev. ed., 1955), Sidney Daniel T. Rodgers, *The Work Ethic in Industrial America, 1850–1920* (1978), and J. G. Cawelti, *Apostles of the Self-Made Man: Changing Concepts of Success in America* (1965). On the railroads see G. R. Taylor and I. D. Neu, *The American Railroad Network, 1861–1890* (1956), Robert Fogel, *The Union Pacific Railroad* (1960), and the same author's provocative *Railroads and American Economic Growth* (1964). Consult also James McCague, *Moguls and Iron Men* (1964), for the story of the first transcontinental railroad. On regulation, see Gabriel Kolko, *Railroads and Regulation, 1877–1916* (1965), and Lee Benson, *Merchants, Farmers, and Railroads* (1955). Hans B. Thorelli, *Federal Antitrust Policy* (1955), is comprehensive. Joseph F. Wall is insightful on *Andrew Carnegie* (1970). Allan Nevins is favorably disposed toward *John D. Rockefeller* (2 vols., 1953); on the same subject see H. F. Williamson and A. R. Daum, *The American Petroleum Industry: The Age of Illumination, 1859–1899* (1959). On steel, consult Peter Temin, *Iron and Steel in Nineteenth-Century America* (1964). C. Vann Woodward has provided a masterful analysis of *Origins of the New South, 1877–1913* (1951), which can be profitably supplemented by Jonathan M. Wiener, *Social Origins of the New South* (1978). Joseph G. Rayback, *History of American Labor* (1959), gives an overall picture. More specialized studies include Philip Taft, *The A.F. of L. in the Time of Gompers* (1957), Bernard Mandel, *Samuel Gompers* (1963), Robert Smuts, *Women and Work in America* (1959), David M. Katzman, *Seven Days A Week: Woman and Domestic Service in Industrializing America* (1978), Gerald N. Grob, *Workers and Utopia, A Study of Ideological Conflict in the American Labor Movement, 1865–1900* (1961), and Herbert Gutman's stimulating *Work, Culture, and Society in Industrializing America* (1976).

27

New Social and Cultural Horizons, 1865-1900

We heartily approve all legitimate efforts to prevent the United States from being used as the dumping ground for the known criminals and professional paupers of Europe.

Democratic National Platform, 1892

Aliens Within the Gates

The nation's upsurging population foreshadowed momentous social and cultural changes—changes hardly less spectacular than those occurring in industry. The census of 1870 enumerated 39,818,449 souls; in 1900 it recorded nearly twice as many. Booming urban centers stretched city limits everywhere, owing largely to expanding industry and multiplying railroads. By 1890, three out of ten Americans were city dwellers, in striking contrast to the rustic population of stagecoach days.

Despite the jostling of movement and change, a sturdy and honest middle class continued to provide stability. Proud possessors of homes and farms, these solid, industrious folk formed the nation's backbone. But increasingly the middle

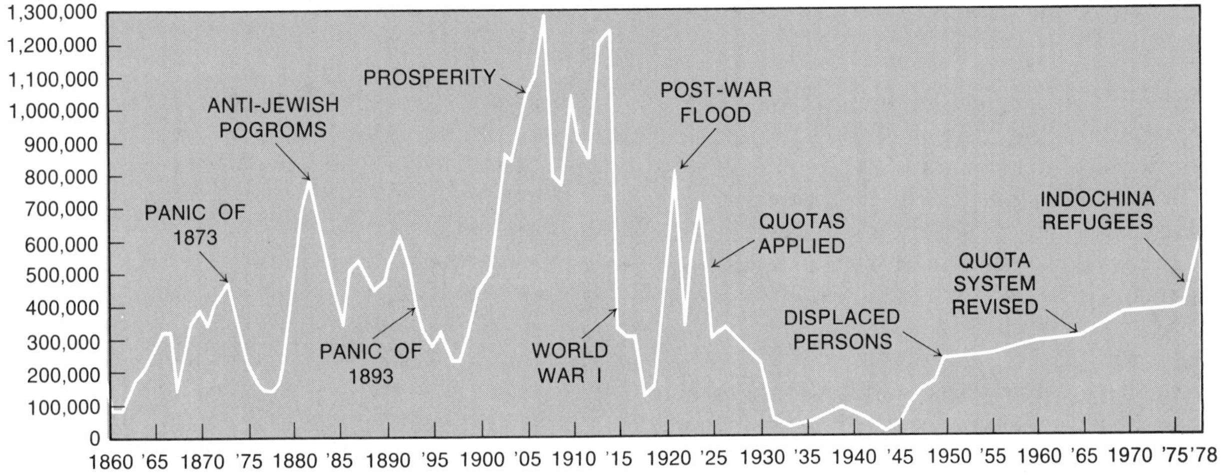

ANNUAL IMMIGRATION, 1860–1978

class found itself squeezed between the sweaty laborers and the gaudy new millionaires of the Gilded Age. These get-rich-quick gentry were striving desperately to rise from the cash register to the social register.

A brightly colored stream of immigrants continued to pour in from Europe. In every decade from the 1850s through the 1870s, more than 2 million aliens had stepped upon America's shores. By the 1880s the stream had become a rushing torrent, for in that decade a record-breaking total of more than 5 million flooded in. A new high for a single year was reached in 1882, when 788,992 arrived—or over 2,100 a day. This figure was not exceeded until 1903.

Until the 1880s, the bulk of these immigrants were easy to assimilate. Most of them had come from the British Isles and Western Europe, chiefly Germany and Scandinavia. They were generally fair-skinned Anglo-Saxon and Teutonic types; and they were usually Protestants, except for the Catholic Irish and many Catholic Germans. They boasted a comparatively high degree of literacy and were accustomed to some kind of constitutional government. Their native institutions were such that their Americanization was usually speedy, especially when they took up farms.

But in the 1880s a new element appeared, commonly known as the New Immigration. For the first time in American experience, a substantial proportion of the new arrivals came from Southern and Eastern Europe. Among them could be found swarthy and black-bearded Italians, Croats, Slovaks, Greeks, and Poles. In the 1880s these picturesque new peoples totaled 19 percent of the inpouring immigrants; by the first decade of the next century they constituted an astonishing 66 percent of the total inflow. "Old-line" Americans asked if the nation had become a melting pot, a stew kettle, or a dumping ground.

South Europe Uprooted

Why were these bright-shawled and quaint-jacketed strangers hammering on the gates? An unfortunate few were paupers, feeble-minded, or criminals, whose home governments were eager to assist them out of the fatherland. Some were fleeing compulsory military service. But the vast majority emigrated because America was painted as the Land of Opportunity; and they sought to escape the poverty and squalor of their native soil. Unfortunately, many of them merely exchanged one slum for another; their children, rather than they, profited from the transplanting.

"America fever" proved highly contagious in Europe. The New World "paradise" was often described in glowing colors by the "America letters" of those already here—letters that were soiled by the hands of many readers. "We eat here every day," wrote one jubilant Pole, "what we get only for Easter in our [native] country." The Land of the Free was also blessed with high wages, free homesteads for the settler, religious freedom, unusual civil liberties, and the absence of a ruling caste.

Profit-seeking Americans trumpeted throughout Europe the attractions of the new Promised Land. Industrialists wanted cheap labor, railroads wanted buyers for their land grants, states wanted more population, and steamship lines wanted more human cargo for their holds. In fact, the ease and cheapness of emigrating greatly accelerated the transoceanic flood. Travel in steerage was an ordeal; but it was not the nightmare of colonial days, and it was soon over.

> Mary Antin, who came to America from Russian Poland in 1894, when thirteen years of age, later wrote in *The Promised Land* (1912): "So at last I was going to America! Really, really going, at last! The boundaries burst. The arch of heaven soared. A million suns shone out for every star. The winds rushed in from outer space, roaring in my ears, 'America! America!'"

As the century lengthened, savage persecution of minorities in Europe drove many shattered souls to American shores. In the 1880s the Russians turned violently upon their own Jews, chiefly in the Polish areas. Tens of thousands of these

The Steerage. A group of immigrants aboard a ship bound for the American "promised land" in 1901. Crowding like this was common. Though several women are pictured here, many immigrants were men who left their families behind. An Italian song of the 19th Century went:

"Christopher Columbus, what have you done?
You've left Italy with hardly a son.
The men seek America, gold to own.
The women weep tears, at home all alone."

(Museum of the City of New York.)

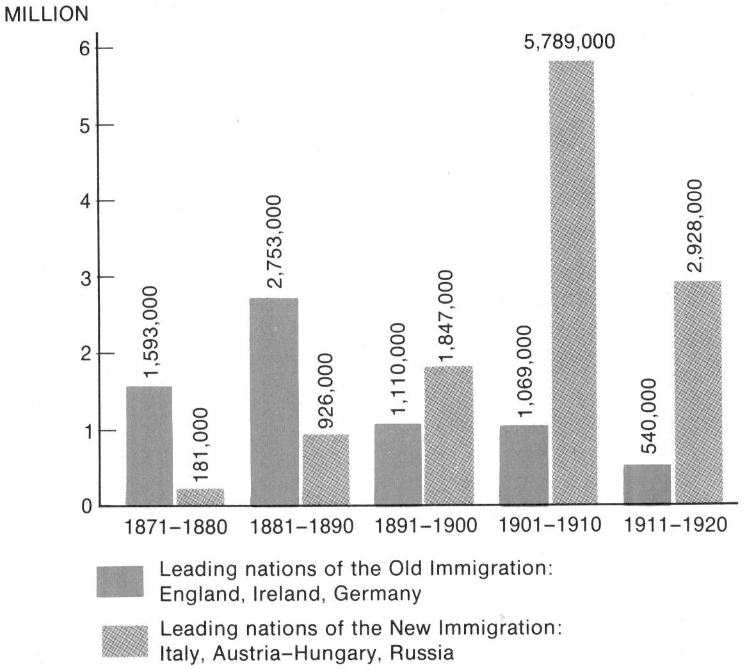

OLD AND NEW IMMIGRATION (by decade)
By the 1970s, the sources of immigration to the United States had shifted yet again. The largest number of immigrants came from Latin America (especially Mexico), the next largest from Asia. The old "mother continent" of Europe accounted for only 19 percent of the immigrants to America in the 1970s.

nerve-racked refugees, fleeing their burning homes, arrived in the seaboard cities of the Atlantic Coast, notably New York. Too poor to move farther, they huddled together in the already stinking slums, and there they found Americanization unusually difficult.

Anti-foreignism, or "nativism," earlier touched off by the Irish and Germans in the 1840s and 1850s, once more flared forth. The hordes from Eastern and Southern Europe seemed especially hard to digest, even though the percentage of foreign-born in America remained relatively constant. They were non-Teutonic and preponderantly Roman Catholic; they had been accustomed to cringe before despotism; they were generally illiterate; they were poverty-stricken; and they tended to hive together in the jam-packed cities rather than move out to farms. The "Little Italys" and "Little Polands" of New York and Chicago were soon to claim more inhabitants than many of the largest cities of the same nationality in the Old World.

These newcomers, who threatened to drown the earlier comers in a foreign sea, aroused widespread alarm. They were not only numerous but they had a high birthrate, as is common among people with a low standard of living and enough youth and vigor to pull up stakes. Old-stock Americans protested that the original Anglo-Saxon Puritan stock would soon be outbred and outvoted. Still more horrifying was the prospect that it would be mongrelized by a mixture of "inferior" South European blood, and that the Anglo-Saxon types would disappear in a darker blend. T.B. Aldrich, a son of New England, cried out in anguish:

> O Liberty, white Goddess! is it well
> To leave the gates unguarded?

"Native" Americans voiced additional complaints. They objected to the creation of new rabbit-hutch slums in the seething cities; they condemned what they branded as the pauperism and bad morals of "smelly" Europeans. The alien arrivals were also assailed for a willingness to work for "starvation" wages, and for importing in their intellectual baggage such dangerous "isms" as socialism, communism, and anarchism. Many Big Business leaders, who welcomed the flood of cheap manual labor, began to fear that they had embraced a Frankenstein's monster.

> Sociologist E. A. Ross wrote in 1914: "Observe immigrants . . . in their gatherings. You are struck by the fact that from ten to twenty per cent are hirsute, low-browed, big-faced persons of obviously low mentality. . . . They . . . clearly belong in skins, in wattled huts at the close of the Great Ice Age. These oxlike men are descendants of those who always stayed behind."

Narrowing the Welcome Mat

Anti-foreign organizations, common in the 1840s and 1850s, were now revived in a different guise. Notorious among them was the American Protective Association (A.P.A.), which was created in 1887 and which soon claimed a million militant members. In seeking its "nativist" goals, the A.P.A. urged voting against Roman Catholic candidates for office, and sponsored the publication of lustful fantasies about runaway nuns.

Organized labor was quick to throw its weight behind the move to choke off the rising tide of foreigners. The newly arrived Europeans, frequently used as strikebreakers, were hard to unionize because of the language barrier, the strangeness of their new surroundings, and their willingness to work for low wages that seemed to them like princely sums. Labor leaders argued, not illogically, that if American industry was entitled to protection from foreign goods, the American workingman was entitled to protection from foreign laborers.

Congress finally erected partial bars against the inpouring immigrants. The first restrictive law —that of 1882—banged the gate in the faces of paupers, criminals, and convicts, all of whom had to be returned at the expense of the careless or greedy shipper. Congress further responded to pained outcries from organized labor when, in 1885, it prohibited the importation of workmen under contract—usually for sub-standard wages. In later years, other federal laws lengthened the list of undesirables by adding such categories as the insane, polygamists, prostitutes, alcoholics, anarchists, and persons afflicted with contagious diseases. A proposed literacy test, long a goal of the "nativists" because it would favor the Old Immigration over the New, met vigorous opposition. It was not enacted until 1917, after three Presidents had vetoed it on the grounds that literacy was more a test of opportunity than of intelligence.

The year 1882, in addition to the first federal restrictions against certain undesirables, brought forth a law to bar completely one racial group—the Chinese (see p. 463). Hitherto America had gathered to her mighty breast the oppressed and underprivileged of all races and climes. Hereafter the gates would be padlocked against defective undesirables—plus the Chinese. Four years later, in 1886, the Statue of Liberty was erected in New York harbor as a gift from the people of France. On its base were inscribed the words of Emma Lazarus:

> Give me your tired, your poor,
> Your huddled masses yearning to breathe free,
> The wretched refuse of your teeming shore.

To many "nativists," those noble words described only too accurately the "scum" washed up by the New Immigrant tides.

The advocates of more rigid restriction specifically accused the New Immigrants of exploiting America. This charge was partially true of those who came with the intention of going back to

> President Cleveland declared in 1897: "It is said . . . that the quality of recent immigration is undesirable. The time is quite within recent memory when the same thing was said of immigrants who, with their descendants, are now numbered among our best citizens."

the Old Country when they had "made their pile." Of the approximately 20 million newcomers who arrived from 1820 to 1900, about 5 million "birds of passage" returned. But most of the aliens who came were exploited to some extent by dollar-conscious Americans, whether in rat-infested city slums or sooty mining slums. These displaced Europeans, unlike "nativists" born in America, became American citizens the hard way. They stepped off the ship, many of them full-grown and well muscled, ready to put their shoulders to the nation's industrial wheels. The Republic owes much to these later comers—to their brawn, their brains, their courage, and their reforming zeal.

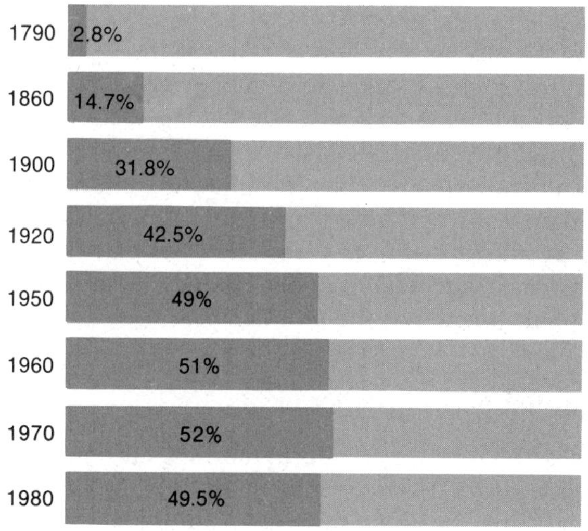

THE SHIFT TO THE CITY
Percent of total population living in cities of 10,000 or more. Note the reversal of the cityward trend in the 1970s.

New Frontiers in the Cities

A vast cityward movement was gathering momentum in the 1880s and 1890s, not only in the United States but elsewhere in the world. In 1860 no American city could boast a million inhabitants; by 1890, New York, Chicago, and Philadelphia had spurted past the million mark. By 1900 New York, with some 3.5 million, was the second largest city in the world, outranked only by London. It was dubbed "a nightmare in stone."

This spectacular drift to the city is not hard to explain. It was speeded by machine-made jobs, by seductively high wages, and by the growing monotony of the farm, where there were too many cows to milk and hogs to feed. Urban centers were becoming more attractive, with their network of telephones and their bright lights, especially after the flickering gaslight era gave way to electricity. Noteworthy also were improvements in central heating, public water systems, indoor plumbing, sewage disposal, asphalt pavements, and transportation. The giant Brooklyn Bridge, dedicated in 1883, blazed the way for bigger and better spans. Electric-powered elevated cars and subways were introduced near the end of the century, inspiring the quip "The public be jammed." Congestion in the cities was markedly relieved by the cloud-brushing skyscraper in 1885; the Americans were apparently becoming modern cliff dwellers.

But the jagged skyline of America's perpendicular civilization could not conceal the ugliness of a feverish growth. Some of the showier cities, like skyscrapered New York, resembled beautiful women with dirty necks and out-at-the-toes shoes. Human pigsties, known as slums, became more crowded, more dirty, more rat-infested, more unhealthful. Thousands of families were trapped in ill-ventilated and foul-smelling shacks and cellars, without plumbing. In these wretched tenements, conspicuously in New York's infamous "Lung Block," hundreds of immigrants coughed away their lives. "Flophouses" abounded where the half-starved and unemployed might sleep for a few cents on verminous mattresses. Democracy found difficult rootage in the garbage-strewn alleyways. Yet, marvelous to relate, the vast majority of these underprivileged souls grew up to be decent and law-abiding citizens.

Crime and corruption, like lice, flourished in the teeming cities. Criminals ranged from burly thugs with blackjacks to "city slickers" palming off "gold bricks" on "hayseeds" from the country. Crookedness in city government was most luridly exemplified by New York's notorious Tweed Ring. The boss and the machine made willing tools of the befuddled and purchasable immigrants, whose loyalty was paid for in jobs, social welfare, and progress toward Americanization. America's governmental system, nurtured in wide-open spaces, was least successful in the cement forests and asphalt jungles of the great cities.

Challenges to the Church

Bells tolling every Sunday morning in countless belfries sounded deceptive tones. Worshipers had vastly increased in numbers, but they had decreased in the intensity of their religious convictions. In the age-old struggle between God and the Devil, the Wicked One had registered dismaying gains. The mounting emphasis was on materialism; distressing numbers of devotees worshiped "the bitch goddess success." Money was the accepted measure of achievement, and the new Gospel of Wealth proclaimed that God prospered the righteous.

The traditional faith of the Fathers received additional blows from new trends, including a booming sale of books on comparative religion and on historical criticism as applied to the Bible. Most unsettling of all was *On the Origin of Species,* a highly controversial volume published in 1859, on the eve of the Civil War, by the English naturalist Charles Darwin. He set forth in lucid form the sensational theory that man had slowly evolved from lower forms of life—a theory that was soon summarized to mean "the survival of the fittest." In American minds the struggle for the survival of the Union eclipsed for a time that for the survival of the fittest, and the real impact of Darwinism was delayed until the post-war years.

Evolution cast serious doubt on a literal interpretation of the Bible, which relates how God created the heaven and the earth in six days. Conservatives, or "Fundamentalists," stood firmly on the Scripture as the inspired and infallible Word of God, and they condemned the "bestial hypothesis" of the Darwinians. "Modernists" parted company with the "Fundamentalists," and flatly refused to accept the Bible in its entirety as either history or science.

> Darwin wrote in 1871: "Man is descended from a hairy, tailed quadruped, probably arboreal in its habits. . . . For my part I would as soon be descended from a baboon . . . as from a savage who delights to torture his enemies, . . . treats his wives like slaves, . . . and is haunted by the grossest superstitions."

This furious battle over Darwinism created rifts in the churches and colleges of the post–Civil War era. "Modernist" clergymen were removed from their pulpits; teachers of biology who embraced evolution were dismissed from their chairs. But as time wore on, an increasing number of liberal thinkers were able to reconcile Darwinism with Christianity. They heralded the revolutionary theory as a newer and grander revelation of the ways of the Almighty. As W. H. Carruth observed:

> Some call it Evolution,
> And others call it God.

But Darwinism undoubtedly did much to loosen religious moorings and to promote unbelief among the gospel-glutted. The most bitterly denounced skeptic of the era was a golden-tongued orator, Colonel Robert G. Ingersoll, who lectured widely

> A famous and vehement evangelist, Billy Sunday, declared in 1908, "I have studied the Bible from Genesis to Revelation, I have read everything that Bob Ingersoll ever spouted. . . . And if Bob Ingersoll isn't in hell, God is a liar and the Bible isn't worth the paper it is printed on."

on "Some Mistakes of Moses" and "Why I Am an Agnostic." He might have gone far in public life if he had stuck to politics and refrained from attacking orthodox religion by "giving hell hell," as he put it.

Denominational Gains and Losses

Protestant churches, in particular, suffered heavily from the weakening of religious ties. The larger houses of worship, with their stained-glass windows and thundering pipe organs, were tending to become a kind of sacred diversion or amusement. Growing complacent with wealth, the churches were distressingly slow to raise their voices against social and economic vices. John D. Rockefeller was a pillar of the Baptist Church; J. Pierpont Morgan, of the Episcopal Church. Trinity Episcopal Church in New York actually owned some of the city's worst slum property. Critics charged that theology was drowning out true religion, and the more cynical remarked that the Episcopal Church had become "the Republican party at prayer."

Some Protestant clergymen were seeking to apply the Christian religion to the slums and factories. Noteworthy among them was Walter Rauschenbusch, who in 1886 became pastor of a German Baptist church in New York City. Also conspicuous was Washington Gladden, who took over a Congregational church in Columbus, Ohio, in 1882. Preaching the "Social Gospel," they both insisted that the churches tackle the burning social and economic injustices of the day. The Sermon on the Mount, they declared, was the science of society, and many Social Gospelers predicted that socialism would be the logical outcome of Christian doctrine. These "Christian Socialists" did much to prick calloused consciences, thus preparing the path for the progressive reform movements after the turn of the century.

Simultaneously, the Roman Catholic and Jewish faiths were gaining enormous strength from the New Immigration. By 1900 the Roman Catholics had increased their lead as the largest single denomination, numbering nearly 9 million communicants. Roman Catholic and Jewish groups kept the common touch better than many of the leading Protestant churches. Cardinal Gibbons (1834–1921), an urbane Catholic leader devoted to American unity, was immensely popular with Roman Catholics and Protestants alike. Acquainted with every President from Johnson to Harding, he employed his liberal sympathies to assist the American labor movement.

By 1890 the variety-loving American could choose from 150 religious denominations, two of them newcomers. One was the band-playing Salvation Army, whose soldiers without swords invaded America from England in 1879 and established a beachhead on the street corners. Appealing frankly to the down-and-outers, the so-called Starvation Army did much practical good, especially with free soup.

The other important new faith was the Church of Christ, Scientist (Christian Science), founded by Mary Baker Eddy in 1879, after she had suffered much ill health. Preaching that the true practice of Christianity heals sickness, she set forth her views in a book entitled *Science and Health with Key to the Scriptures* (1875), which sold an amazing 400,000 copies before her death.

Mary Baker Eddy (1821–1910). Her *Science and Health* declared: "We classify disease as error, which nothing but Truth or Mind can heal, and this Mind must be divine, not human." (Used with permission © 1929, renewed 1957 The Christian Science Publishing Society. All Rights Reserved.)

A fertile field for converts was found in America's hurried, nerve-racked, and urbanized civilization, to which Mrs. Eddy held out the hope of relief from discords and diseases through prayer as taught by Christian Science. By the time she passed on in 1910, she had founded an influential church which embraced several hundred thousand devoted worshipers.

The Lust for Learning

Public education continued its upward climb. The ideal of tax-supported elementary schools, adopted on a nationwide basis before the Civil War, was still gathering strength. Americans were accepting the truism that a free government cannot function successfully if the people are shackled by ignorance. Beginning about 1870, more and more states were making at least a grade-school education compulsory, and this gain, incidentally, helped check the frightful abuses of child labor.

Spectacular indeed was the spread of the high schools, especially by the 1880s and 1890s. Before the Civil War, private academies at the secondary level were common, and tax-supported high schools were rare, numbering only several hundred. But the concept was now gaining impressive support that a high-school education, as well as a grade-school education, was the birthright of every citizen. By 1900 there were some 6,000 high schools. In addition, free textbooks were being provided in increasing quantities by the taxpayers of the states during the last two decades of the century.

Other trends were noteworthy. Teacher-training schools, then called "normal schools," experienced a striking expansion after the Civil War. In 1860 there were only 12 of them; in 1910, over 300. Kindergartens, earlier borrowed from Germany, also began to gain strong support. The New Immigration in the 1880s and 1890s brought vast new strength to the private Catholic parochial schools, which were fast becoming a major pillar of the nation's educational structure.

Public schools, though showering benefits on children, excluded millions of adults. This deficiency was partially remedied by the Chautauqua movement, a successor to the lyceums, which was launched in 1874 on the shores of Lake Chautauqua, in New York. The organizers achieved gratifying success through nationwide public lectures, often held in tents and featuring well-known speakers, including the witty Mark Twain. In addition, there were extensive

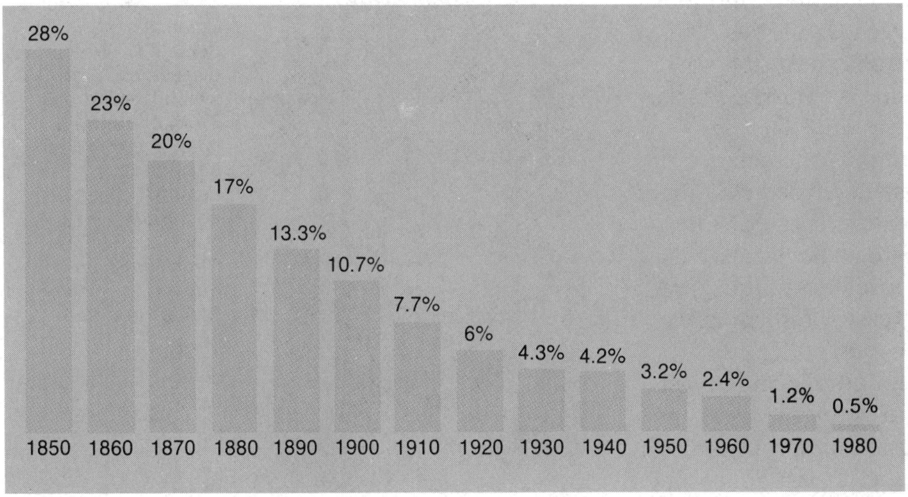

THE DECLINE OF ILLITERACY (in persons over 10 years old; the 1980 figure is for persons 15 years of age and older). This graph shows the percentage of the population that was illiterate. Such figures do not include the "functionally illiterate" graduates of grade schools and high schools.

Chautauqua courses of home study, for which 100,000 persons enrolled in 1892 alone.

Crowded cities, despite their cancers, generally provided better educational facilities than the old one-room, one-teacher red schoolhouse. The success of the public schools is confirmed by the falling of the illiteracy rate from 20 percent in 1870 to 10.7 percent in 1900. Americans were developing a profound faith in education, often misplaced, as the sovereign remedy for their ills.

Booker Washington and Education for Black People

War-torn and impoverished, the South lagged far behind its sister states in public education, and the blacks suffered most severely. A staggering 44 percent of non-whites were illiterate in 1900. Some help came from Northern philanthropists, but the foremost champion of black education was an ex-slave, Booker T. Washington, who had slept under a board sidewalk to save pennies for his schooling. Called in 1881 to head the black normal and industrial school at Tuskegee, Alabama, he began with forty students in a tumble-down shanty. Undaunted by adversity, he succeeded in teaching his people useful trades so that they could gain self-respect and merit a position of economic equality with the whites. But he stopped short of advocating *social* equality.

Booker T. Washington (1856–1915). In a famous speech in Atlanta, Washington accepted social separateness for blacks: "In all things that are purely social, we can be as separate as the fingers, yet one as the hand in all things essential to mutual progress." (Tuskegee Institute.)

A stellar member of the Tuskegee faculty, beginning in 1896, was slave-born George Washington Carver, who as an infant in Missouri was kidnapped and ransomed for a horse worth $300. He became an internationally famous agricultural chemist who helped the economy of the South by discovering hundreds of new uses for the lowly peanut (shampoo, axle grease), sweet potato (vinegar), and soy bean (paints).

Other black leaders, notably Dr. W. E. B. Du Bois, assailed Booker T. Washington as an "Uncle Tom," who was condemning their race to manual labor and perpetual inferiority. Born in Massachusetts, Du Bois was a mixture of African, French, Dutch, and Indian blood ("Thank God, no Anglo-Saxon," he would add). After a determined struggle, he earned a Ph.D. at Harvard, the first of his race to achieve this goal. He demanded full equality for the blacks, social as well as economic, and helped to found the National Association for the Advancement of Colored People in 1910. He was especially determined that the "talented tenth" of the black community be given the opportunity to develop their capacities so as to be able to help their race on its difficult upward climb. An exceptionally talented historian, sociologist, and poet, he died as a self-exile in Africa in 1963, at the age of ninety-five.

The Hallowed Halls of Ivy

Colleges and universities also shot up like lusty young saplings in the decades after the Civil War. Parents in multiplying numbers were eager to make sacrifices so that their children might secure a college education—something that now seemed indispensable in the scramble for the golden apple of success. The educational battle for women,

High-School and College Graduates, 1870–1970

Year	Number Graduating from High School	Number Graduating from College	Interim Population Increase
1870	16,000	9,371	
1880	23,634	10,353	26.0%
1890	43,731	15,539	25.5
1900	94,883	27,410	20.7
1910	156,429	37,199	21.0
1920	311,266	48,622	14.9
1930	666,904	122,484	16.1
1940	1,221,475	186,500	7.2
1950	1,199,700	432,058	14.5
1960	1,864,000	392,440	18.4
1970	2,906,000	792,000	13.3

only partially won before the war, now turned into a rout of the masculine diehards. Women's colleges, like Vassar, were gaining ground; and universities open to both sexes were blossoming forth, notably in the Middle West.

The almost phenomenal growth of higher education owed much to the Morrill Act of 1862. This enlightened law, passed after the South had seceded, provided a generous grant of the public lands to the states for support of education. "Land-grant colleges," most of which became state universities, in turn bound themselves to provide certain services, such as military training. The Hatch Act of 1887, supplementing the Morrill Act, provided federal funds for the establishment of agricultural experiment stations in connection with the land-grant colleges.

Private philanthropy richly supplemented federal grants to higher education. Many of the new industrial millionaires, developing tender social consciences, donated immense fortunes to educational enterprises. A "philanthropist" was cynically described as "one who steals privately and gives publicly." In the twenty years from 1878 to 1898 these money barons gave away about $150 million. Noteworthy among the new private universities of high quality to open their doors were Cornell (1865) and Leland Stanford Junior (1891), the latter founded in memory of the deceased fifteen-year-old only child of a builder of the Central Pacific Railroad. The University of Chicago, opened in 1892, speedily forged into a front-rank position, owing largely to the lubricant of Rockefeller's oil millions. A Chicago newspaper was prompted to proclaim:

> Let us then be up and doing,
> All becoming money kings;
> Some day we may be endowing
> Universities and things.

Rockefeller died at 97, after having given some $550 million for philanthropic purposes.

Significant also was the sharp increase in professional and technical schools, where modern laboratories were replacing the solo experiment performed by the instructor in front of his class. Towering among the specialized institutions was the Johns Hopkins University, opened in 1876, which maintained the nation's first high-grade graduate school. Several generations of American scholars, repelled by snobbish English cousins and attracted by painstaking Continental methods, had attended German universities. Johns Hopkins ably carried on the Germanic tradition of profusely footnoted tomes. Reputable scholars no longer had to go abroad for a gilt-edged graduate degree; and Dr. Woodrow Wilson, among others, received his Ph.D. at Johns Hopkins.

The March of the Mind

Cut-and-dried, the old classical curriculum in the colleges was on the way out, as the new industrialization brought insistent demands for "practical" courses and specialized training in the sciences. The elective system, which permitted students to choose more courses in cafeteria fashion, was gaining popularity. It received a powerful boost in the 1870s, when Dr. Charles W. Eliot, a vigorous young chemist, became president of Harvard College and embarked upon a lengthy career of educational statesmanship. During the closing decades of the century, summer school courses and university extension work were securing a promising foothold.

Winds of "dangerous doctrines" threatened to shipwreck freedom of teaching in the colleges. Disagreeable incidents involved the dismissal of professors who taught evolution or expressed hostility to high tariffs. For many years, some of the Big Business alumni of Yale vainly sought the bald scalp of the low-tariff economist and sociologist William Graham Sumner.

Medical schools and medical science after the Civil War were prospering. Despite the enormous sale of patent medicines and Indian remedies—"good for man or beast"—the new scientific gains were reflected in improved public health. Revolutionary discoveries abroad, such as those of the French scientist Louis Pasteur and the English physician Joseph Lister, left their imprint on America.* The popularity of heavy whiskers waned as the century ended; such hairy adornments were now coming to be regarded as germ traps. As a result of new health-giving precautions, including campaigns against public spitting, life expectancy at birth was measurably increased.

Many capable scientists and thinkers adorned university faculties, but few enjoyed international reputations. American genius shone best in applying scientific knowledge to practical problems, as was notably true of the wizardly Thomas A. Edison. One of the most brilliant philosophers thus far produced in America, the slight and sickly William James (1842–1910), served for thirty-five years on the Harvard faculty. Through his numerous writings he gave wide currency to the philosophical concept known as pragmatism, which emphasized the practical side of thinking. Truth was to be tested, above all, by the practical consequences of belief, by action rather than theories. This kind of reasoning chimed in with the mood of a materialistic, cash-value America, which was already hotly in pursuit of the dollar.

*From Pasteur came the word "pasteurize"; from Lister came "Listerine."

Edison in His Laboratory. In 1878 he declared: "I speak without exaggeration when I say that I have constructed three thousand different theories in connection with the electric light. . . . Yet in only two cases did my experiments prove the truth of my theory."

The Appeal of the Press

Books continued to be a major source of edification and enjoyment, for both juveniles and adults. Best sellers of the 1880s were generally old favorites like *David Copperfield* and *Ivanhoe.*

American authors, many with unpublished manuscripts on their hands, were greatly encouraged by new copyright arrangements. In 1891, after a half-century or so of debate, Congress enacted a law making possible an international copyright. Foreign writers could henceforth secure royalties from America, and American writers could hope to reap rewards from abroad. (Longfellow had been "honored" by some twenty unauthorized publishers in England.) Aspiring young American authors no longer had to fear the competition of cheap, royaltyless foreign reprints.

Well-stocked public libraries—the poor man's university—were making encouraging progress, especially in Boston and New York. The magnificent Library of Congress building, which opened its doors in 1897, provided 13 acres of floor space in the largest and costliest edifice of its kind in the world. A new era was inaugurated by the generous gifts of Andrew Carnegie. This open-handed Scotsman, book-starved in his youth, contributed $60 million for the construction of public libraries all over the country. By 1900 there were about 9,000 free circulating libraries in America, each with at least 300 books.

Roaring newspaper presses, spurred by the invention of the linotype in 1885, more than kept pace with the demands of a word-hungry public. But the heavy investment in machinery and plant was accompanied by a growing fear of offending advertisers and subscribers. Bare-knuckle editorials were, to an increasing degree, being supplanted by feature articles and non-controversial syndicated material. The day of slashing journalistic giants like Horace Greeley was passing.

Sensationalism, at the same time, was beginning to debase the public taste. The semi-literate immigrants, combined with strap-hanging urban commuters, created a profitable market for news that was simply and punchily written. Sex, scandal, and other human-interest stories burst into the headlines, as a vulgarization of the press accompanied the growth of circulation. Critics complained in vain of "presstitutes."

Two new journalistic tycoons emerged. Joseph Pulitzer, Hungarian-born and near-blind, was a leader in the techniques of sensationalism in St. Louis and especially with the New York *World.* His use of the colored comic supplements, featuring the "Yellow Kid," gave the name of yellow journalism to his lurid sheets. A close and ruthless competitor was youthful William Randolph Hearst, who had been expelled from Harvard College for a crude prank. Able to draw on his California father's mining millions, he ultimately built up a powerful chain of newspapers, beginning with the San Francisco *Examiner* in 1887.

Scotsman Carnegie Besieged by Money Seekers. (Minneapolis *Tribune,* 1899.)

Unfortunately, the overall influence of Pulitzer and Hearst was not altogether wholesome. Although both championed many worthy causes, both prostituted the press in their struggle for increased circulation; both "stooped, snooped, and scooped to conquer." Their flair for scandal and sensational rumor was happily somewhat offset by the introduction of syndicated material and by the strengthening of the news-gathering Associated Press, which had been founded in the 1840s.

Apostles of Reform

Magazines partially satisfied the public appetite for good reading, notably old standbys like *Harper's,* the *Atlantic Monthly,* and *Scribner's Monthly.* Possibly the most influential journal of all was the liberal and highly intellectual New York *Nation,* which was read largely by professors, preachers, and publicists as "the weekly Day of Judgment." Launched in 1865 by the Irish-born Edwin L. Godkin, a merciless critic, it crusaded militantly for civil service reform, honesty in government, and a moderate tariff. The *Nation* attained only a modest circulation—about 10,000 in the 19th Century—but Godkin believed that if he could reach the right 10,000 leaders, his ideas through them might reach the 10 millions.

Another journalist-author, Henry George, was an original thinker who left an enduring mark. Poor in formal schooling, he was rich in idealism and in the milk of human kindness. After seeing poverty at its worst in India, and land grabbing at its greediest in California, he took pen in hand. His classic treatise, *Progress and Poverty,* undertook to solve "the great enigma of our times"—"the association of progress with poverty." Arguing that poverty was attributable to rent, he concluded that a single tax on land was the remedy for many social and economic ills.

George soon became one of the most controversial figures of his age. His single-tax ideas were so horrifying to propertied men that his manuscript was rejected by numerous publishers. Finally brought out in 1879, the book gradually broke into the best-seller lists and ultimately sold some 3 million copies. George also lectured widely in America, where he influenced thinking about the maldistribution of wealth, and in Britain, where he left an indelible mark on English Fabian socialism.

Henry George, in *Progress and Poverty* (1879), wrote: "Our boasted freedom necessarily involves slavery, so long as we recognize private property in land. Until that is abolished, Declarations of Independence and Acts of Emancipation are in vain. So long as one man can claim the exclusive ownership of the land from which other men must live, slavery will exist, and as material progresses on, must grow and deepen!"

Edward Bellamy, a quiet Massachusetts Yankee, was another journalist-reformer of remarkable power. In 1888 he published a socialistic novel, *Looking Backward,* in which the hero, falling into a hypnotic sleep, awakens in the year 2000. He "looks backward" and finds that the social and economic injustices of 1887 have melted away under an idyllic government. To a nation already alarmed by the trust evil, the book had a magnetic appeal and sold over a million copies. Scores of Bellamy Clubs sprang up to discuss this mild Utopian socialism, and they definitely influenced American reform movements near the end of the century.

Post-War Writing

As literacy increased, so did book reading. Post–Civil War Americans devoured millions of "dime novels," usually depicting the wilds of the woolly West. Paint-bedaubed Indians and quick-triggered gunmen like "Deadwood Dick" shot off vast quantities of powder, and virtue invariably triumphed. These lurid "paperbacks" were frowned upon by parents, but goggle-eyed youths read them in haylofts or in schools behind the broad covers of geography books. The king of dime novelists was Harlan F. Halsey, who made a fortune by dashing off about 650 novels, often one in a day.

General Lewis Wallace—lawyer-soldier-author—was a colorful figure. Having fought with distinction in the Civil War, he sought to combat the prevailing wave of Darwinian skepticism with his novel *Ben Hur: A Tale of the Christ* (1880). A phenomenal success, the book sold an estimated 2 million copies in many languages, including Arabic and Chinese, and later appeared on stage and screen. It was the *Uncle Tom's Cabin* of the anti-Darwinists, who found in it support for the Holy Scriptures.

An even more popular writer was Horatio ("Holy Horatio") Alger, a Puritan-reared New Englander, who in 1866 forsook the pulpit for the pen. Deeply interested in New York newsboys, he wrote more than a hundred volumes of juvenile fiction that sold over 100 million copies. His stock formula was that virtue, honesty, and industry are rewarded by success, wealth, and honor—a kind of survival of the purest, especially non-smokers, non-drinkers, non-swearers, and non-liars. Although Alger's own bachelor life was criticized, he implanted morality and the conviction that there is always room at the top (especially if one is lucky enough to save the life of the boss's daughter and marry her).

In poetry, Walt Whitman was one of the few luminaries of yesteryear who remained active. Although shattered in health by service as a Civil War nurse, he brought out successive—and purified—revisions of his hardy perennial, *Leaves of Grass.* The assassination of Lincoln inspired him to write two of the most moving poems in American literature, "O Captain! My Captain!" and "When Lilacs Last in the Dooryard Bloom'd."

The curious figure of Emily Dickinson, one of America's most gifted lyric poets, did not emerge until 1886, when she died and her poems were discovered. A Massachusetts spinster and recluse, disappointed in love, she wrote over a thousand short lyrics on odd scraps of paper. Only two were published during her lifetime, and those without her consent. As she wrote:

> How dreary to be somebody!
> How public, like a frog
> To tell your name the livelong day
> To an admiring bog!

Among the lesser poetical lights was a tragic Southerner, Sidney Lanier (1842–1881). Oppressed by poverty and ill health, he was torn between flute playing and poetry. Dying young of tuberculosis, he wrote some of his finest poems while afflicted with a temperature of 104° F (40° C). He is perhaps best known for his "The Marshes of Glynn," a poem of faith inspired by the current clash between Darwinism and orthodox religion.

No other Southern poet came as close as Lanier

Emily Dickinson (1830–1886). A great American poet, she never married but pursued intense intellectual relationships with several men, including the abolitionist Thomas Wentworth Higginson. (Amherst College Library.)

to the first rank in the post-war years of the 19th Century. Undistinguished for literature before the Civil War, Dixieland had even less reason for distinction after it. An obscure poet, J. G. Coogler, wrote in 1879:

> Alas for the South: her books have grown fewer—
> She never was much given to literature.

Literary Landmarks

In novel writing, the romantic sentimentality of a youthful era was giving way to a rugged realism that reflected more faithfully the materialism of an industrial society. American authors now turned increasingly to the coarse human comedy of the world around them to find their subjects.

Mustachioed Mark Twain (1835–1910) had leapt to fame with *The Celebrated Jumping Frog of Calaveras County* (1867) and *The Innocents Abroad* (1869). He teamed up with Charles Dudley Warner in 1873 to write *The Gilded Age.* An acid satire on post–Civil War politicians and speculators, the book gave a name to an era. With his scanty formal schooling in frontier Missouri, Twain typified a new breed of American authors in revolt against the elegant refinements of the old New England school of writing. Christened Samuel L. Clemens, he served for a time as a Mississippi river boat pilot and later took his pen name, Mark Twain, from the boatman's cry that meant two fathoms. After a brief stint in the armed forces, Twain journeyed westward to California, a trip he described, with a mixture of truth and tall tales, in *Roughing It* (1872).

Many other books flowed from Twain's busy pen. His *The Adventures of Tom Sawyer* (1876) and *The Adventures of Huckleberry Finn* (1884) rank among American masterpieces, though initially regarded as "trash" by snobbish Boston critics. His later years were soured by bankruptcy growing out of unwise investments, and he was forced to take to the lecture platform and amuse what he called "the damned human race." A great tribute was paid to his self-tutored genius—and to American letters—when England's Oxford University awarded him an honorary degree in 1907. Journalist, humorist, satirist, and foe of social injustice, he made his most enduring contribution in recapturing frontier realism and humor in the authentic American dialect.

Another author who wrote out of the West and achieved at least temporary fame and fortune was Bret Harte (1836–1902). A foppishly dressed New Yorker, Harte struck it rich in California with

> In 1935 Ernest Hemingway wrote: "All modern American literature comes from one book by Mark Twain called *Huckleberry Finn*. . . . All American writing comes from that. There was nothing before. There has been nothing as good since."

Mark Twain on his Celebrated Jumping Frog. From a poster advertising one of his public lectures.

gold-rush stories, especially "The Luck of Roaring Camp" and "The Outcasts of Poker Flat." Catapulted suddenly into notoriety by those stories, he never again matched their excellence or their popularity. He lived out his final years in London as little more than a hack writer.

William Dean Howells (1837–1920), a printer's son from Ohio, could boast of little school-house education, but his busy pen carried him high into the literary circles of the East. In 1871 he became the editor-in-chief of the prestigious Boston-based *Atlantic Monthly,* and was subsequently presented with honorary degrees from six universities, including Oxford. He wrote about ordinary people and about contemporary and sometimes controversial social themes. *A Modern Instance* (1882) deals with the once-taboo subject of divorce; *The Rise of Silas Lapham* (1885) describes the trials of a newly rich paint manufacturer caught up in the caste system of Brahmin Boston. *A Hazard of New Fortunes* (1890) portrays the reformers, strikers, and Socialists in gilded-age New York.

Stephen Crane (1871–1900), the fourteenth son of a Methodist minister, also wrote about the seamy underside of life in urban, industrial America. His *Maggie: A Girl of the Streets* (1893), a brutal tale about a poor prostitute driven to suicide, was too grim to find a publisher. Crane had to

> Crane wrote in *The Red Badge of Courage:* "At times he regarded the wounded soldiers in an envious way. He conceived persons with torn bodies to be peculiarly happy. He wished that he, too, had a wound, a red badge of courage."

> Dreiser's pessimism was reflected in *Sister Carrie:* "Our civilization is still in a middle stage, scarcely beast, in that it is no longer wholly guided by instinct; scarcely human, in that it is not yet wholly guided by reason."

have it printed privately. He rose quickly to prominence with *The Red Badge of Courage* (1895), the stirring story of a bloodied young Civil War recruit ("fresh fish") under fire. Crane himself had never seen a battle and wrote entirely from the printed Civil War records. He died of tuberculosis in 1900, when only twenty-nine.

Henry James (1843–1916), brother of Harvard philosopher William James, was a New Yorker who turned from law to literature. Taking as his dominant theme the confrontation of innocent Americans with subtle Europeans, James penned a remarkable number of brilliant novels, including *Daisy Miller* (1879), *The Portrait of a Lady* (1881), and *The Wings of the Dove* (1902). In *The Bostonians* (1886) he wrote one of the first novels about the rising feminist movement. James frequently made women his central characters, exploring their inner reactions to complex situations with a deftness that marked him as a master of "psychological realism." Long resident in England, he became a British subject shortly before his death.

Candid portrayals of contemporary life and social problems were the literary order of the day by the turn of the century. Jack London (1876–1916), famous as a nature writer in such books as *The Call of the Wild* (1903), turned to depicting a possible fascistic revolution in *The Iron Heel* (1907). Frank Norris (1870–1902), like London a Californian, wrote *The Octopus* (1901), an earthy saga of the stranglehold of the railroad and corrupt politicians on California wheat-ranchers. A sequel, *The Pit* (1903), dealt with the making and breaking of speculators on the Chicago wheat exchange.

Conspicuous among the new "social novelists" rising in the literary firmament was Theodore Dreiser (1871–1945), a homely, gangling writer from Indiana. He burst upon the literary scene in 1900 with *Sister Carrie,* a graphically realistic narrative of a poor working girl in Chicago and New York. She becomes one man's mistress, then elopes with another, and finally strikes out on her own to make a career on the stage. The fictional Carrie's disregard for prevailing moral standards so offended Dreiser's publisher that the book was soon withdrawn from circulation.

> Jack London, the socialist who hated strikebreakers known as "scabs," said: "No man has a right to scab so long as there is a pool of water to drown his carcass in, or a rope long enough to hang his body with. Judas Iscariot was a gentleman compared with a scab. For betraying his master, he had character enough to hang himself. A scab has not."

Women in Arms

Victoria Woodhull, who was real flesh and blood, also shook the pillars of conventional morality when she publicly proclaimed her belief in free love in 1871. Woodhull was a beautiful and eloquent divorcée, sometime stockbroker, and tireless feminist propagandist. Together with her sister she published a far-out weekly periodical, *Woodhull and Claflin's Weekly.* The sisters again shocked respectable society in 1872 when their journal struck a blow for the new morality by charging that Henry Ward Beecher, the most famous preacher of his day, had for years been carrying on an adulterous affair.

Pure-minded Americans sternly resisted these affronts to their moral principles. Their foremost champion was a portly crusader, Anthony Comstock, who made lifelong war on the "immoral." Armed after 1873 with a federal statute—the notorious "Comstock Law"—this self-appointed defender of sexual purity boasted that he had confiscated no fewer than 202,679 "obscene pictures and photos," 4,185 "boxes of pills, powders, etc., used by abortionists," and twenty-six "obscene pictures, framed on walls of saloons." His proud claim was that he had driven at least fifteen people to suicide.

The antics of the Woodhull sisters and Anthony Comstock exposed to daylight the battle going on in late 19th-Century America over sexual attitudes and the place of women. Switchboards and typewriters in the booming cities became increasingly the tools of women's liberation. In the 1890s, more than a million females entered the work force for the first time, many of them as telephone operators and secretaries. Economic freedom encouraged sexual freedom, and the "new morality" began to be reflected in soaring divorce rates, the spreading practice of birth control, and increasingly frank discussion of sexual topics. By 1913, said one popular magazine, the chimes had struck "sex o'clock in America."

Prosecution of Victoria Woodhull and Tennessee Claflin, 1872. The government banned their sending "obscene" literature through the mails, namely, *Woodhull and Claflin's Weekly.* (By permission of the Houghton Library, Harvard University.)

Women's Rights and Wrongs

Fiery feminists continued to insist on the ballot. They had been demanding the vote since before the Civil War, but many female reformers had temporarily shelved the cause of women to fight for the rights of blacks. In 1890, militant suffragists formed the National American Women's Suffrage Association. Its leaders included Elizabeth Cady Stanton, an aging pioneer who had helped organize the first woman's rights convention in 1848. Prominent also was Susan B. Anthony, the radical Quaker spitfire who had courted jail by trying to cast a ballot in the 1872 presidential election. By the end of the century the suffragists had registered encouraging gains, despite showers of rotten eggs and the jeers of critics who insisted that women were made for loving, not voting.

Growing numbers of women were being permitted to vote in local elections, particularly on issues relating to the schools. Wyoming Territory—later called "the Equality State"—reflected the high regard of the West for the scarcer sex when it granted unrestricted suffrage to women in 1869. This important breach in the dike once made, many states followed Wyoming's example. Paralleling these triumphs, most of the states by 1890 had passed laws to permit wives to own or control their property after marriage.

Women were becoming more independent, though American females had long enjoyed a degree of freedom unknown in Europe. Industrialization and urbanization were luring tens of thousands of women into business. A career was now an attractive alternative to early matrimony; hence marriages were being delayed and parents were having fewer children. Smaller families were also a result of crowded conditions in the cities, higher living standards, and the spread of birth control.

Marriages and Divorces, 1890–1980

Year	*Marriages*	*Divorces*	*Ratio of Divorces to Marriages*
1890	570,000	33,461	1:17
1900	709,000	55,751	1:12
1910	948,166	83,045	1:11
1920	1,274,476	170,505	1:7
1930	1,126,856	195,961	1:5
1940	1,595,879	264,000	1:6
1950	1,667,231	385,144	1:4.3
1960	1,523,381	393,000	1:3.8
1970	2,159,000	708,000	1:3
1980	2,393,000	1,184,000	1:2

A gradual emancipation of females was reflected in a disquieting increase in the divorce rate. A partial explanation was that many women no longer would tolerate abuse at the hands of their lords and masters. Uniformity in divorce laws, owing to the chaotic states'-rights tradition, was lamentably lacking, and "easy states," like Nevada and Wyoming, did a bustling business in divorce.

Putting the Burden Where It Belongs. The cartoonist argues that the costs of crime and pauperism, the offspring of alcohol, should be borne by the dealers in alcohol. (*Harper's Weekly,* 1883.)

Prohibition of Alcohol and Social Progress

Alarming gains by Demon Rum spurred the temperance reformers to redoubled zeal. Especially obnoxious to them was the shutter-doored corner saloon, appropriately called "the poor man's club." It helped keep both him and his family poor. Liquor consumption had increased during the nerve-racking days of the Civil War; and immigrant groups, accustomed to alcohol in the Old Country, were hostile to restraints. Whiskey-loving foreigners in Boston would rudely hiss temperance lecturers.

The National Prohibition party, organized in 1869, polled a sprinkling of votes in some of the ensuing presidential elections. Among the favorite songs of these sober souls were "I'll Marry No Man If He Drinks," "Vote Down the Vile Traffic," and "The Drunkard's Doom." Typical was:

Now, all young men, a warning take,
And shun the poisoned bowl;
'Twill lead you down to hell's dark gate,
And ruin your own soul.

Militant ladies entered the alcoholic arena, notably when the Woman's Christian Temperance Union (W.C.T.U.) was organized in 1874. The white ribbon was its symbol of purity; the saintly Frances E. Willard—also a champion of planned parenthood—was its leading spirit. Less saintly was a muscular and mentally deranged "Kansas Cyclone," Carrie A. Nation, whose first husband had died of alcoholism. With her hatchet she boldly smashed saloon bottles and bars, and her "hatchetations" brought considerable disrepute to the prohibition movement by the violence of her one-woman crusade.

But rum was now on the run. The potent Anti-Saloon League was formed in 1893, with its members singing "The Saloon Must Go" and "Vote for Cold Water, Boys." Female supporters sang "The Lips That Touch Liquor Must Never Touch Mine." Statewide prohibition, which had registered surprising gains in Maine and elsewhere before the Civil War, was sweeping new states into the "dry" column. The great triumph—but only a temporary one—came in 1919, when the national prohibition amendment (18th) was attached to the Constitution.

Banners of other social crusaders were aloft. The American Society for the Prevention of Cruelty to Animals was created by Henry Bergh in 1866, after he had witnessed brutality to horses in Russia. The American Red Cross was launched in 1881, with the dynamic 5-foot (1.52 meters) Clara Barton, an "angel" of Civil War battlefields, as a leading spirit. Organized philanthropy, a forerunner of annual charity drives, was becoming popular, beginning with Buffalo in the 1870s, and was replacing the old haphazard methods of giving. More money went into salaries and other collection costs, but the recipients of charity also got more, despite a poet's protest against

> The organized charity, scrimped and iced,
> In the name of a cautious, statistical Christ.

Clara Barton (1821–1912). A shy Massachusetts school teacher, she was afflicted with attacks of nervous prostration during the first half of her life. She established the American National Red Cross, which she headed from 1881 to 1904. (Brown Brothers)

Carrie Nation Advertised as a Lecturer. She holds her famous hatchet. Carrie Nation took her antidrink crusade to several universities, including Harvard and Yale, which she denounced as "hellholes." Predictably, the students greeted her with wild burlesque. (Courtesy Kansas Historical Society.)

Artistic Triumphs

America still lacked artists to match her magnificent mountains. Art had been of sickly growth in the rustic years of the Republic, largely because of an absence of leisure and wealth. The nation now had both, but the results were unspectacular. Perhaps the roar of the industrialized civilization repelled the delicate muses; perhaps art itself was becoming mechanized. Roll-film cameras, popularized by George Eastman in the 1880s, enabled every man to be his own artist.

Yet several portrait painters of distinction emerged, notably James Whistler (1834–1903). This eccentric and quarrelsome Massachusetts Yankee had earlier been dropped from West Point after failing in chemistry. "Had silicon been a gas," he later jested, "I would have been a major general." Moving to Europe, he did much of his work in England, including the celebrated portrait of his mother. Another gifted portrait painter, likewise self-exiled in England, was John Singer Sargent (1856–1925). His flattering but somewhat superficial likenesses of the British nobility were highly prized.

Other brush wielders, no less talented, brightened the artistic horizon. Self-taught George Inness (1825–1894) looked like a fanatic with his long hair and piercing gaze, but he became America's leading landscapist. Thomas Eakins (1844–1916) attained a high degree of realism in his paintings, a quality not appreciated by portrait sitters who wanted their moles overlooked. Boston-born Winslow Homer (1836–1910), who as a youth had secretly drawn sketches in school, was perhaps the greatest painter of the group. Earthily American and largely resistant to foreign influences, he revealed rugged realism and boldness of conception. His canvases of the sea and of fisherfolk were masterly, and probably no American artist has excelled him in portraying the awesome power of the ocean.

Probably the most gifted sculptor yet produced by America was Augustus Saint-Gaudens (1848–1907). Born in Ireland of an Irish mother and a French father, he became an adopted American. Although he sculptured many noble statues, his most striking work is the "Adams Monument," a shrouded and enigmatic female figure representing grief or a kindred emotion. It was erected in a Washington cemetery by the historian Henry Adams in memory of his beloved wife, who had committed suicide.

Music too was gaining popularity. America of the 1880s and 1890s was assembling high-quality symphony orchestras, notably in Boston and Chicago. The famed Metropolitan Opera House of New York was erected in 1883. In its fabled "Diamond Horseshoe" the newly rich, often under the pretense of enjoying the imported singers, would flaunt their jewels, gowns, and furs. A marvelous discovery was the reproduction of music by mechanical means. The phonograph, though a squeakily imperfect instrument when invented by the deaf Edison, had by 1900 reached over 150,000 homes. Americans were rapidly being dosed with "canned music," as the "sitting room" piano increasingly gathered dust.

The most original architects of the era sought to escape the hodgepodge borrowings from Europe by stressing usefulness of design—realism in building. The most noteworthy contribution of this sort was the steel-skeleton skyscraper. Coming first as a ten-story building in Chicago in 1884, it was made practicable by the perfecting of the elevator. An opinionated Chicagoan, Louis H. Sullivan (1856–1924), added much to the skyscraper by his guiding principle, "Form follows function."

"New York a Few Years from Now." A curiously prophetic cartoon by Thomas Nast in 1881, three years before the first skyscraper was completed (in Chicago). (*Harper's Weekly*, August 27, 1881.)

Hamlin Garland, the well-known novelist and writer of short stories, was immensely impressed by the cultural value of the Chicago Columbian Exposition. He wrote to his aged parents on their Dakota farm, "Sell the cook stove if necessary and come. You *must* see this fair."

A revival of classical architectural forms—and a setback for realism—came with the great Columbian Exposition. Held in Chicago in 1893, it honored the four hundredth anniversary of Columbus's first voyage. This so-called dream of loveliness, which was visited by 27 million people, did much to raise American artistic standards and promote city planning, although many of the spectators were attracted primarily by the torsal contortions of a hootchy-kootchy dancer, "Little Egypt."

MISS ANNIE OAKLEY,
THE PEERLESS LADY WING-SHOT.

Annie Oakley (1860–1926). Raised in backwoods Ohio, she began to shoot rabbits and quail when she was nine years old. In Cincinnati she beat a crack marksman in a vaudeville contest; they fell in love and were married. She ultimately received top billing in his show. (Historical Pictures Service, Chicago.)

The Business of Amusement

Fun and frolic were not neglected by the workaday American. The pursuit of happiness, heralded in the Declaration of Independence, had by century's end become a frenzied scramble. People sought their pleasures fiercely, as they had overrun their continent fiercely. And now they had more time to play.

Varied diversions beckoned. As a nation of "joiners" contemptuous of royalty, Americans inconsistently sought to escape from democratic equality in the aristocratic hierarchies of lodges. The legitimate stage still flourished, as appreciative audiences responded to the lure of the footlights. Vaudeville, with its coarse jokes and graceful acrobats, continued to be immensely popular during the 1880s and 1890s.

The circus—high-tented and multi-ringed—finally emerged full-blown. Phineas T. Barnum, the master showman who had early discovered that "the public likes to be humbugged," joined hands with James A. Bailey in 1881 to stage the "Greatest Show on Earth."*

Colorful "Wild West" shows, first performed in 1883, were even more distinctively American. Headed by the knightly, goateed and free-drinking William F. ("Buffalo Bill") Cody, the troupe included war-whooping Indians, live buffalo, and deadeye marksmen. Among them was the girlish Annie Oakley. Rifle in hand, at thirty paces she could perforate a tossed-up card half a dozen times before it fluttered to the ground. (Hence the

*Now Ringling Bros. and Barnum and Bailey Combined Shows, Inc.

term "Annie Oakley" for a punched ticket, later for a free pass.)

Baseball, already widely played before the Civil War, was clearly emerging as the national pastime, if not a national mania. A league of professional players was formed in the 1870s, and in 1888 an all-star baseball team toured the world, using the pyramids as a backstop while in Egypt.

A gladiatorial trend toward spectators' sports, rather than participants' sports, was well exemplified by football. This rugged game, with its dangerous flying wedge, had become popular well before 1889, when Yaleman Walter C. Camp chose his first "All American" team. The Yale-Princeton game of 1893 drew 50,000 excited spectators, while foreigners complained that the nation was getting sports "on the brain."

Even pugilism, with its long background of bare-knuckle brutality, gained a new and gloved respectability in 1892. Agile "Gentleman Jim" Corbett, a scientific boxer, wrested the world championship from the aging and alcoholic John L. Sullivan, the fabulous "Boston Strong Boy."

Two crazes swept the country in the closing decades of the century. Croquet became enormously popular, though condemned by moralists of the "naughty nineties" because it exposed feminine ankles and promoted flirtation. The low-framed "safety" bicycle came to replace the high-seated model. By 1893 a million bicycles were in use, and thousands of young ladies, jokesters remarked, were turning to this new "spinning wheel."

Basketball was invented in 1891 by James Naismith, a Y.M.C.A. instructor in Springfield, Massachusetts. Designed as an active indoor sport that could be played during the winter months, it spread rapidly and enjoyed enormous popularity in the next century.

The land of the skyscraper was plainly becoming more standardized, owing largely to the new industrialization. To an increasing degree, Americans were falling into the ways of lock-step living—playing, reading, thinking, and talking alike. They were eating the same canned food and wearing the same ready-made clothes. But what they had lost in variety, they were gaining in efficiency. They were still inseparably wedded to the ideal of unlimited human progress, and they still glimpsed, with invincible optimism, the unexplored vistas that stretched into the future.

VARYING VIEWPOINTS

In addition to industrialization, three major developments seemed to alter the fabric of American life in the late 19th Century: massive immigration, urbanization, and the further advance of the woman's movement. Historians have long concentrated on the innovative and transforming features of these processes. They have asked, for example, how America was changed by the great immigrant influx—or, alternatively, how migration changed the immigrants themselves. How did city life alter life-styles and political institutions? How did the "new woman" change the basis of family organization and sexual behavior? Increasingly, scholars have been answering "not so much as expected" to all these questions. Recent investigations have tended to emphasize the persistence of ethnic identities among immigrants, the preservation of small-town or village values in the booming metropolitan centers, and even the modest dimensions of the 19th-Century "sexual revolution." True revolutions are rare in history. Even the massive social upheavals of this fermenting era did not fully displace older customs and attitudes.

SELECT READINGS

See previous chapter for titles by Hays, Ginger, and Garraty for useful surveys. Maldwyn Jones, *American Immigration* (1960), is a well-written introduction. Oscar Handlin, *The Uprooted* (1951), is an imaginative account of the immigrant experience. John Higham examines the "nativist" reaction in *Strangers in the Land* (1955). Ronald T. Takaki finds nativism and racism rampant in *Iron Cages: Race and Culture in Nineteenth-Century America* (1979). For a more detached perspective, see Milton Gordon, *Assimilation in American Life* (1964). Specific "new immigrant" groups are studied in John W. Briggs, *An Italian Passage: Immigrants to Three American Cities, 1890–1930* (1978), Dino Cinel, *From Italy to San Francisco: The Immigrant Experience* (1982), Humbert Nelli, *Italians in Chicago, 1880–1930* (1970), Thomas Kessner, *The Golden Door: Italian and Jewish Immigrant Mobility in New York City, 1880–1915* (1977), Moses Rischin, *The Promised City: New York's Jews, 1870–1914* (1962), and Irving Howe's monumental and moving account of Jewish immigration, *World of Our Fathers* (1976). Consult also Stephan Thernstrom, *Poverty and Progress* (1964), and his *The Other Bostonians* (1973). *The Rise of the City, 1878–1898* (1933) is a classic study by Arthur M. Schlesinger. More recent are Gunther Barth, *City People: The Rise of Modern City Culture in Nineteenth-Century America* (1980), Blake McKelvey, *The Urbanization of America, 1860–1915* (1963), Howard Chudacoff, *The Evolution of American Urban Society* (1975), and Sam Bass Warner, Jr., *The Urban Wilderness* (1972). Specific cities are discussed in Warner's *The Private City: Philadelphia in Three Periods of Its Growth* (1968), and in his study of Boston, *Streetcar Suburbs* (1962). Richard Sennet looks at Chicago in *Families against the City* (1970). Morton and Lucia White examine attitudes toward urbanism in *The Intellectual versus the City* (1962). Religious changes are scrutinized in Henry May, *Protestant Churches and Industrial America* (1949). On medicine, consult Morris J. Vogel, *The Invention of the Modern Hospital: Boston, 1870–1930* (1980). On education, see Lawrence Cremin, *The Transformation of the School* (1961), and Lawrence Veysey, *The Emergence of the American University* (1965). Black history for this period is illuminated by three studies: August Meier, *Negro Thought in America, 1880–1915* (1963), L. R. Harlan, *Booker T. Washington: The Making of a Black Leader, 1865–1901* (1972), and E. M. Rudwick, *W. E. B. Du Bois: A Study in Minority Group Leadership* (1960). On the "new woman" and the new morality, see William L. O'Neill, *Everyone was Brave* (1969), Lois Banner, *Elizabeth Cady Stanton* (1980), William Leach, *True Love and Perfect Union: The Feminist Reform of Sex and Society* (1980), Eleanor Flexner, *Century of Struggle* (1959), Aileen Kraditor, *Ideas of the Woman Suffrage Movement* (1965), Hal D. Sears, *The Sex Radicals* (1977), and Ann Douglas, *The Feminization of American Culture* (1977). On working women, consult Susan Estabrook Kennedy, *If All We Did Was to Weep at Home: A History of White Working-Class Women in America* (1979). Interesting also is Elaine Tyler May, *Great Expectations: Marriage and Divorce in Post-Victorian America* (1980). On reformers and writers, see the titles cited in the previous chapter by Hofstadter and Fine, as well as H. S. Commager, *The American Mind* (1950), Daniel Aaron, *Men of Good Hope* (1951), Jay Martin, *Harvests of Change: American Literature, 1865–1914* (1967), and Larzer Ziff, *The American 1890s* (1966). For architecture, see Sherman Paul, *Louis Sullivan* (1962), on sport, F. R. Dulles, *America Learns to Play* (1940). Of special interest is Neil Harris, *Humbug: The Art of P. T. Barnum* (1973). Bruce Kuklick examines Harvard's star-studded philosophy department in *The Rise of American Philosophy* (1977). Two fascinating studies document the rise of a "new" middle-class mentality: B. J. Bledstein, *The Culture of Professionalism* (1976), and T. Haskell, *The Emergence of Professional Social Science* (1977).

28

The Great West and the Agricultural Revolution, 1865–1890

Up to our own day American history has been in a large degree the history of the colonization of the Great West. The existence of an area of free land, its continuous recession, and the advance of American settlement westward, explain American development.

FREDERICK JACKSON TURNER, 1893

The Indian Barrier to the West

When the Civil War crashed to a close, the frontier line was still wavering westward. A long fringe of settlement, bulging outward here and there, ran roughly north through central Texas and onward to the Canadian border. Between this jagged line and the settled areas on the Pacific slope, there were virtually no white people. The only exceptions worth mentioning were the islands of Mormons in Utah, occasional trading posts and gold camps, and a few scattered Spanish-Mexican settlements in the Southwest.

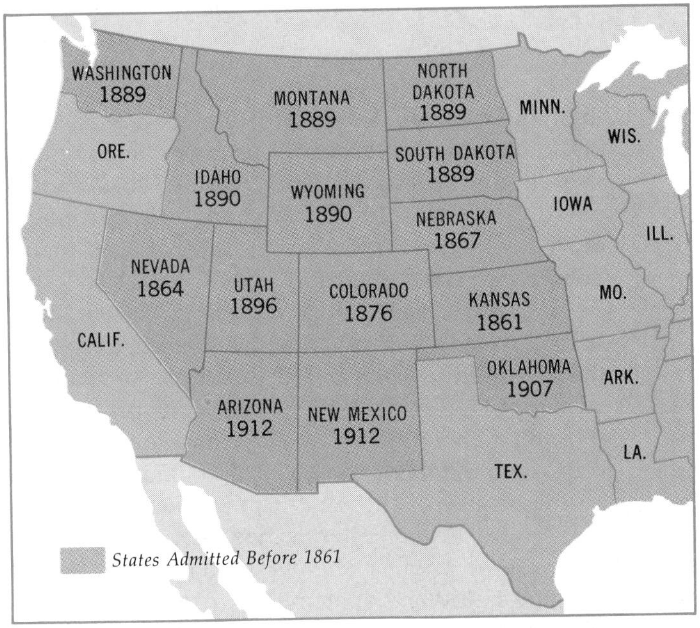

STATES OF THE GREAT WEST
(with dates of admission)
For exact order of admission, see table in Appendix. This map reflects the way that settlement leapfrogged to the Pacific Coast over the Great Plains and the Great Basin. Utah was settled by Mormons in the 1840s, but its admission to statehood was long delayed because of controversy over the Mormon belief in polygamy. The Mormon church prohibited the practice in 1890, paving the way to statehood six years later.

Sprawling in expanse, the Great West was a rough square which measured about 1,000 miles (1,600 kilometers) on each side. Embracing mountains, plateaus, deserts, and plains, it was the habitat of the Indian, the buffalo, the wild horse, the prairie dog, and the coyote. Twenty-five years later—that is, by 1890—the entire domain had been carved into states, except for four territories. Men flung themselves greedily on this enormous prize, as if to ravish it. Never before in human experience, probably, had so huge an area been reduced so rapidly to a semblance of civilization.

The Indians, to their misfortune, stood in the path of the white settlers. Like the blades of mighty scissors, two lines of onward-moving pioneers were closing in simultaneously—one from the Pacific Coast, the other from the trans-Mississippi East. A clash was inevitable between an acquisitive civilization and a traditional culture, as the march of modernity crushed under its feet the hunting grounds and hence the food supply of the red inhabitants.

Tens of thousands of buffalo-hunting Indians roamed the spacious Western plains in 1860. In three centuries the Spanish-introduced horse had transformed the culture of the Plains Indians, causing the tribes to become more nomadic and more warlike. The red warriors had become superbly skilled riders and fighters.

In 1851, the Washington government, yielding to expansionist pressures, determined to crack the great Indian barrier in the West and induce the tribes to "concentrate" in certain "inviolable" areas to the north and south of intended white settlement. In the 1860s Washington intensified this policy and herded the Indians into still smaller confines. The Sioux were to be "guaranteed" the sanctuary of the Black Hills in Dakota Territory. Certain southern tribes were to be relocated in the "Indian Territory" of present Oklahoma.

The Indians surrendered their ancestral lands only when they had received solemn promises from the Great White Father in Washington that

> One disheartened Indian complained to the white Sioux Commission created by Congress, "Tell your people that since the Great Father promised that we should never be removed we have been moved five times. . . . I think you had better put the Indians on wheels and you can run them about wherever you wish."

they would be left alone and provided with food, clothing, and other supplies. Regrettably, the federal Indian agents were often corrupt. They palmed off moth-eaten blankets, spoiled beef, and other defective provisions on the friendless Indians. One of these cheating officials, on an annual salary of $1,500, returned home after four years with an estimated "savings" of $50,000.

Grasping white men were guilty of many additional provocations. They flagrantly disregarded treaty promises, openly seized the land of the Indians, wantonly slaughtered their game, and occasionally debauched their women. During the Civil War the Sioux of Minnesota, facing starvation and taking advantage of the sectional quarrel, went on the warpath and murdered several hundred settlers. The uprising was finally crushed by federal troops, and nearly forty of the Indians, after a summary trial, were hanged at a well-attended mass execution.

From 1868 to about 1890, almost incessant warfare raged in various parts of the West between Indians and whites. A printed list of the names of the engagements alone covers over 100 pages. The fighting was fierce and harrowing, especially the winter campaigning in sub-zero weather. Many of the regular troops were veterans of the Civil War, and their ranks embraced four crack black units, including the famous 10th Cavalry. All told, about one-fifth of all soldiers assigned to the frontier during these years were black. Generals Sherman, Sheridan ("the only good Indian is a dead Indian"), and Custer, all of whom had won their spurs in the Civil War, gathered further laurels in the West. They were matched against formidable adversaries, for the Indians of the Plains, unlike those first encountered by the American colonists, rode swift ponies and enjoyed baffling mobility. To the disgust of the American soldiers, "the hostiles" were often better armed than the federal troops sent against them with clumsy muzzle-loaders. The War Department was perhaps not so much to blame as conscienceless white fur traders, who provided the Indians with the most modern repeating rifles.

Cavalrymen in the West. Drawing by Frederic Remington.

Receding Red Population

Savagery was not all on the side of the Indians. Where fighting is protracted and uncivilized, the ethics of combat are ordinarily pulled down to a primitive level. Whites were often the immediate aggressors, and they sometimes shot peaceful red men on sight, just to make sure they would give no trouble. At Sand Creek, Colorado, in 1864, Colonel J. M. Chivington's militia massacred in cold blood some 400 Indians who apparently thought they had been promised immunity. Squaws were shot praying for mercy, children had their brains dashed out, and braves were tortured, scalped, and unspeakably mutilated. On several notorious occasions, innocent Indians were killed for outrages committed by their fellow tribesmen; sometimes they were shot just for "sport."

Unquestionably, the most spectacular of these clashes was the Sioux War of 1876–1877, touched off when a horde of gold-greedy white men rushed into the Black Hills of South Dakota during the stampede of 1875. The proud and warlike Sioux, their lands invaded despite treaty guarantees, took to the warpath. Conspicuous among their leaders

> A young lieutenant told Colonel Chivington that to attack the Indians would be a violation of pledges. "His reply was, bringing his fist down close to my face, 'Damn any man who sympathizes with Indians.' I told him what pledges were given the Indians. He replied that he 'had come to kill Indians, and believed it to be honorable to kill Indians under any and all circumstances.' "

was heavyset Sitting Bull, a medicine man as wily as he was influential.

Sioux braves were hotly pursued by impetuous George A. Custer, the buckskin-clad "boy general," now demoted to lieutenant-colonel. Attacking what turned out to be a superior force of some 2,500 well-armed warriors near the Little Big Horn River in present Montana, the "White Chief with Yellow Hair" and his 264 officers and men were completely wiped out in 1876 when two supporting columns failed to come to their rescue.* (Sitting Bull sat out this battle, safely "making medicine" in his tent, while Crazy Horse played a stellar role.) But white reinforcements later arrived, and Sitting Bull and the remnants of his band were finally driven to Canada, whence hunger forced them to return and surrender.

The Nez Percé Indians of Idaho were likewise goaded into warfare in 1877, when gold-crazed white miners trespassed upon their beaver streams. Chief Joseph, a noble and unusually humane leader, established himself as a remarkable strategist when he undertook a roundabout retreat of 1,500 miles (2,400 kilometers) to Canada, only to be cornered 30 miles (48 kilometers) from safety.

Fierce Apache tribes of Arizona and New

Geronimo (c. 1829–1909). He was the most famous Apache leader. (National Archives.)

Mexico were the most difficult to subdue. Led by Geronimo, whose eyes blazed hatred of the whites, they were pursued into Mexico by federal troops using the sun-flashing heliograph, a communication device, which impressed the Indians as "big medicine." Scattered remnants of the braves were finally persuaded to surrender after their squaws had been exiled to Florida. The Apaches ultimately became successful farmers in Oklahoma, where they raised stock instead of raiding settlements.

This relentless fire-and-sword policy of the

*When the whites wiped out red men, the engagement (in white history books) was usually a "battle"; when the Indians wiped out whites, it was a "massacre." Strategy, when practiced by red men, was "treachery."

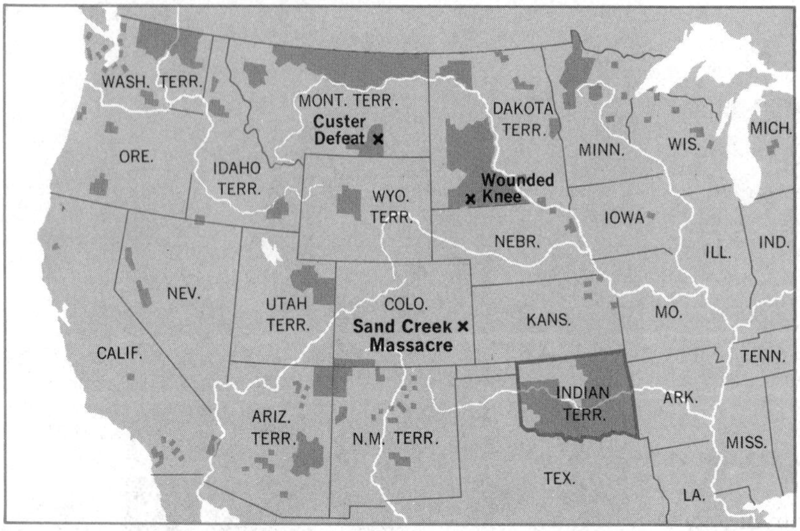

INDIAN RESERVATIONS, 1883
Surrendering in 1877, Chief Joseph of the Nez Percé declared: "Our chiefs are killed. . . . The old men are all dead. . . . The little children are freezing to death. . . . I want to have time to look for my children. . . . Hear me, my chiefs. My heart is sick and sad. From where the sun now stands I will fight no more forever."

whites at last shattered the spirit of the Indians. The vanquished red people were finally ghettoized in "human zoos," known as reservations, there to eke out a sullen existence as wards of the government. Their white masters had at last discovered that the Indians were much cheaper to feed than to fight. Even so, for many decades they were almost ignored to death.

The taming of the Indians was engineered by a number of factors. Of cardinal importance was the railroad, which shot an iron arrow through the heart of the West. Locomotives ("bad medicine wagons") could bring out unlimited numbers of troops, farmers, cattlemen, sheepherders, and settlers. The luckless Indians were also ravaged by the white people's diseases, to which they showed little resistance, and by their firewater, to which they showed almost no resistance. Finally, the virtual extermination of the buffalo resulted in the near-extermination of the Plains Indians.

Bellowing Herds of Bison

Tens of millions of buffalo—described by early Spaniards as "hunchback cows"—blackened the Western prairies when the white Americans first arrived. These shaggy, lumbering animals were the staff of life for the Indian. Their flesh provided food; their dried dung provided fuel ("buffalo chips"); their hides provided clothing, lariats, bowstrings, and harness.

When the Civil War closed, there were still some 15 million of these meaty beasts grazing on the Western plains. In 1868 one of the Kansas Pacific locomotives had to wait eight hours for a herd to amble across the tracks; experience had shown that trying to smash through would produce only mangled flesh and derailment. Much of the food supply of the railroad construction gangs came from juicy buffalo steaks. "Buffalo Bill" Cody—sinewy, telescopic-eyed, and a crack shot—killed over 4,000 animals in eighteen months while employed by the Kansas Pacific.

Buffalo Crossing. Trains in the West were halted, sometimes for hours, while enormous bison herds crossed the tracks. (Smithsonian Institution; painting by Newbold H. Trotter.)

With the building of the railroad, the massacre of the herds began in deadly earnest. Most of the stupid creatures were slain for their hides and in response to the insatiable demand for buffalo robes, then highly fashionable. Others were felled merely for their tongues or a few other choice cuts, while the rest of the carcass was left to be picked by the vultures. Countless buffalo were shot with repeating rifles for sheer amusement. "Sportsmen" on lurching railroad trains would lean out the windows and blaze away at the brutes to satisfy their lust for slaughter or excitement.

Such wholesale butchery could have only one end. By 1885 fewer than 1,000 buffalo were left, and the once-numerous quadrupeds were in danger of complete extermination. Somewhat like the Indians, a few thousand of the beefy animals have been kept alive, largely as living museum pieces. The whole story is a shocking example of the greed and waste that accompanied the conquest of the continent.

The Indian's Portion. (*Puck*, 1880.)

The End of the Trail

By the 1880s the national conscience began to stir uneasily against the policy of corralling and then exterminating the Indians. Helen Hunt Jackson, a Massachusetts writer of children's literature, pricked the moral sense of whites in 1881, when she published *A Century of Dishonor*. The book chronicled the sorry record of governmental ruthlessness and chicanery in dealing with the Indians. Her later novel *Ramona* (1884), a love story of injustice to the California aborigines, sold some 600,000 copies and further inspired sympathy for the red people.

Debate seesawed. Humanitarians wanted to treat the Indians kindly and persuade them thereby to "walk the white man's road." Yet hardliners insisted on the current policy of forced containment and brutal punishment. Neither side showed much respect for traditional Indian culture. Christian reformers, who often administered educational facilities on the reservations, sometimes withheld precious food to force the Indians to give up their tribal religion. In 1884 these zealous white souls joined with military men in successfully persuading the federal government to outlaw the sacred Sun Dance. When the "Ghost Dance" cult later spread to the Dakota Sioux, the army bloodily stamped it out in 1890 at the so-called Battle of Wounded Knee. In the fighting thus provoked, an estimated 200 braves, squaws, and children were killed, as well as 29 invading soldiers.

The misbegotten offspring of the movement to reform Indian policy was the Dawes Severalty Act of 1887. Reflecting the forced-civilization views of the reformers, the act dissolved many tribes as legal entities, wiped out tribal ownership of land, and set up individual Indian family heads with 160 free acres. If the Indians behaved themselves like "good white settlers," they would get full title to their holdings, as well as citizenship, in twenty-five years. The probationary period was later extended, but full citizenship was granted to all Indians in 1924.

The Dawes Act struck directly at the organization of the tribe and tried to make rugged individualists out of the Indians. Whatever its good intentions, this legislation did much to accelerate the already advanced decay of traditional Indian culture. The Dawes Act remained the government's official Indian policy until 1934, when the Indian Reorganization Act ("The Indian New

Deal") reversed the individualistic approach and belatedly tried to restore the tribal basis of Indian life.

Under these new federal policies, defective though they were, the Indian population started to mount slowly. The total number had been reduced by 1887 to about 243,000—the result of bullets, bottles, and bacteria—but the census of 1970 counted nearly 800,000, urban and rural. Possibly more Indians dwell in the United States today than were here when Columbus came, even though their blood is much diluted with that of their conquerors.

Mining: From Dishpan to Ore-Breaker

Beyond doubt the conquest of the Indians and the coming of the railroad were life-giving boons to the mining frontier. The golden gravel of California continued to yield "pay dirt," and in 1858 an electrifying discovery convulsed Colorado. Avid "Fifty-Niners" or "Pike's Peakers" rushed west to rip at the ramparts of the Rockies. But there were more miners than minerals; and many a gold-grubber, with "Pike's Peak or Bust" inscribed on the canvas of his covered wagon, creaked wearily back with the added inscription, "Busted, by Gosh." Yet countless bearded fortune seekers stayed on, some to strip away the silver deposits, others to extract non-metallic wealth from the earth in the form of golden grain.

"Fifty-Niners" also poured feverishly into Nevada in 1859, after the fabulous Comstock Lode had been uncovered. A fantastic amount of gold and silver, worth more than $340 million, was mined by the "Kings of the Comstock" from 1860 to 1890. The scantily populated state of Nevada, "child of the Comstock Lode," was prematurely railroaded into the Union in 1864, partly to provide three electoral votes for President Lincoln.

Smaller "lucky strikes" drew frantic gold- and silver-seekers into Montana, Idaho, and other Western states. Boom towns, known as "Helldorados," sprouted from the desert sands like magic. Every third cabin was a saloon, where sweat-stained miners drank bad liquor ("rotgut") in the company of bad women. Lynch law and hempen vigilante justice, as in early California, preserved a crude semblance of order. And when the "diggings" petered out, the gold-seekers de-

Helena, Montana, 1865. Mining towns such as this one sprang up wherever gold- and silver-diggers thought they would strike it rich. They would abandon such towns as soon as the "diggings" were depleted, leaving "ghost towns" behind. (Montana Historical Society.)

camped, leaving picturesque "ghost towns" silhouetted in the desert, such as Virginia City, Nevada. Begun with a boom, these towns ended with a whimper.

Once the loose surface gold was gobbled up, ore-breaking machinery was imported to smash the gold-bearing quartz. This operation was so expensive that it could ordinarily be undertaken only by corporations pooling the wealth of stockholders. Gradually the Age of Big Business came to the mining industry. Dusty, bewhiskered miners, dishpans in hand, were replaced by the impersonal and beardless corporations, with their costly machinery and trained engineers. The once-picturesque gold-washer became just another day laborer, for it took gold to get gold.

Yet the mining frontier had played a vital role in subduing the continent. Magnetlike, it attracted population and wealth, while advertising the wonders of the Wild West. The amassing of precious metals helped finance the Civil War, facilitated the building of railroads, and forced a partial solution to the Indian problem. The outpouring of silver and gold enabled the Treasury to resume specie payments in 1879, and injected the silver issue into American politics. "Silver Senators," representing the thinly peopled "acreage states" of the West, used their disproportionate influence to promote the interests of the silver men. Finally, the mining frontier added to American folklore and literature, as the writings of Bret Harte and Mark Twain so colorfully attest.

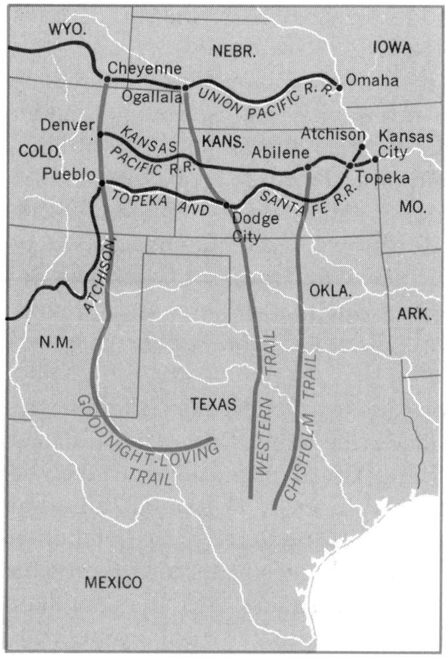

CATTLE TRAILS

Beef Bonanzas and the Long Drive

When the Civil War ended, the grassy plains of Texas supported several million tough, long-horned cattle. These scrawny beasts, whose horn spread sometimes reached 8 feet (2.4 meters), were killed primarily for their hides. There was no way of getting their meat profitably to market.

The problem of marketing was neatly solved when the transcontinental railroads thrust their iron fingers into the West. Cattle could now be shipped bodily to the stockyards and, under "beef barons" like the Swifts and Armours, the highly industrialized meat-packing business sprang into existence as a main pillar of the economy. Drawing upon the gigantic stockyards at Kansas City and Chicago, the packers could ship their fresh products to the East Coast in the newly perfected refrigerator cars.

A spectacular feeder of the new slaughterhouses was the "Long Drive." Texas cattle raisers, with herds numbering from 1,000 to 10,000 head, would drive their animals slowly over the unfenced and unpeopled plains until they reached a railroad terminal. The bawling beasts grazed en route on the free government grass. Favorite terminal points were fly-specked "cow towns" like Dodge City— "the Bibulous Babylon of the Frontier"— and Abilene (Kansas), Ogallala (Nebraska), and Cheyenne (Wyoming). At Abilene, order was maintained by "Judge Colt" in the person of Marshal James B. ("Wild Bill") Hickok, a fabulous gunman who reputedly killed only in self-defense or in line of duty, and who was finally shot in the back while playing poker.*

As long as lush grass was available, the Long Drive proved profitable—that is, to the luckier cattlemen who escaped the Indians, stampedes, cattle fever, and other hazards. From 1866 to 1888 bellowing herds, totaling over 4 million steers, were driven northward from the beef bowl of Texas. In peak years the profits to some cattlemen would soar as high as 40 percent. The steer was king in a Cattle Kingdom richly carpeted with grass.

What the Lord giveth, the Lord also taketh away. The railroad made the Long Drive; the railroad unmade the Long Drive, primarily because the locomotives ran both ways. The same rails that bore the cattle from the open range to the kitchen range brought out the homesteader and the sheepherder. Both of these intruders, amid flying bullets, built barbed-wire fences that were too numerous to be cut down by the cowboys. Furthermore the terrible winter of 1886–1887, with blinding blizzards reaching 68° below zero (−56°C), left thousands of dazed cattle starving and freezing. Overexpansion and overgrazing likewise took their toll, as the cowboys slowly gave way to ploughboys.

The only escape for the stockman was to make cattle raising a big business and avoid the perils of overproduction. Breeders learned to fence their ranches, lay in winter feed, import blooded bulls, and produce fewer and meatier animals. They also learned to organize. The Wyoming Stock-Growers' Association, especially in the 1880s, virtually controlled the state and its legislature. Many high-handed and illegal practices went on, but such was the overrapid taming of the Wild West.

These were the days when cowboyhood was in flower. The equipment of the lone cowhand—from "shooting irons" and ten-gallon hat to chaps and high-heeled boots—served a useful, not an ornamental, function. A "genuwine" gun-toting cowpuncher, riding where men were men and smelled like horses, could justifiably boast of his toughness.

The Long Drive. *(Harper's Weekly, 1874.)*

These bowlegged Knights of the Saddle, with colorful trappings and cattle-lulling songs, became an authentic part of American folklore. A substantial number of them were blacks, perhaps 5,000, who especially enjoyed the new-found freedom of the open range.

Free Land for Free Families

A new day dawned for Western farmers with the Homestead Act of 1862—an epochal measure vigorously opposed by the South before secession. The law provided that a settler could acquire as much as 160 acres of land (a quarter section) by living on it five years, improving it, and paying a nominal fee of ten dollars. Pre-emption, or first choice, was still possible for certain squatters at $1.25 an acre.

The Homestead Act marked a drastic departure from previous policy. Hitherto public land had

*Frontier marshals like Hickok, Wyatt Earp, and "Bat" Masterson have been highly romanticized; some were little better than criminals who shot men from behind curtains: hooligans, not heroes. They were less "fast on the draw" and less accurate with their "six-guns" than commonly portrayed. A Western saying was that God did not make all men equal; Colonel Colt did.

been sold primarily for revenue; now it was to be given away to encourage a rapid filling of empty spaces and to provide a stimulus to the family farm—"the backbone of democracy." The new law was a godsend to a host of farmers who could not afford to buy large holdings; and during the forty years after its passage about half a million families carved out new homes in the vast open stretches. Five times that many families *purchased* their land from the railroads, land companies, or the states.

But the Homestead Act often turned out to be a cruel hoax. The standard 160 acres, quite adequate in the well-watered Mississippi basin, frequently proved quite inadequate on the rain-scarce Great Plains. Thousands of homesteaders, perhaps two out of three, were forced to give up the one-sided struggle against drought. Uncle Sam, it was said, bet 160 acres against ten dollars that the settler could not live on his homestead for five years. One of these unsuccessful gambles in Greer County, western Oklahoma, inspired a folk song:

> Hurrah for Greer County! The land of the free,
> The land of the bedbug, grasshopper, and flea;
> I'll sing of its praises, I'll tell of its fame,
> While starving to death on my government claim.

Naked fraud was spawned by the Homestead Act and sister laws. Perhaps ten times more of the public domain wound up in the clutches of land-grabbing promoters than in the hands of bona fide farmers. Unscrupulous corporations would use "dummy" homesteaders—often aliens bribed with cash or a bottle of beer—to grab the best properties containing timber, minerals, and oil. Settlers would later swear that they had "improved" the property by erecting a "twelve by fourteen" dwelling, which turned out to measure twelve by fourteen *inches.* In later years the Washington officials were only partially successful in unraveling the tangled skein of deceit. So functioned the government's first big "giveaway" program.

A Bona Fide Residence. A removable house for fraudulent purposes. (Illustration in A. B. Richardson's *Beyond the Mississippi,* 1866.)

Taming Western Deserts

The life-giving railways also played a major role in developing the agricultural West, largely through the profitable marketing of crops. In addition, some railroad companies induced Americans and European immigrants to buy the cheap lands earlier granted by the government. A leader in such "induced colonization" was the Northern Pacific Railroad, which at one time had nearly 1,000 paid agents in Europe distributing roseate leaflets in various languages.

A shattering of the myth of the Great American Desert further opened the gateways to the agricultural West. The windswept prairies were for the most part treeless, and the tough sod had been pounded solid by millions of buffalo hoofs. Pioneer explorers and trappers had assumed that the soil must be sterile, simply because it was not heavily watered and did not support immense forests. But once the prairie sod was broken—and this was done in Kansas with special plows pulled by four powerful yoke of oxen—the earth proved to be astonishingly fruitful.

This boom in Western farming was aided by additional stimulants. Improved irrigation techniques—"the miracle of water"—caused deserts to bloom, notably in Mormon Utah. Tough strains of wheat that were resistant to cold and drought were imported from Russia, and they blossomed into billowing yellow carpets. New flour-milling

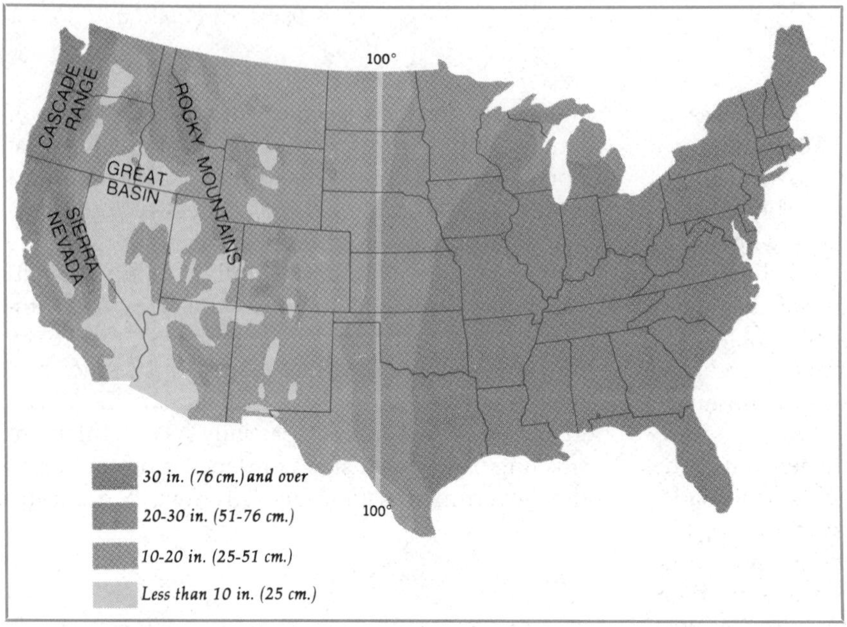

AVERAGE ANNUAL PRECIPITATION
In the northern hemisphere, storms usually circle the globe in a west-to-east direction. Much of the life-nourishing water in these storms is dumped as rainfall on the western slopes of the cloud-high Pacific Coastal ranges and the Rocky Mountains. This weather pattern creates deep, dry "rain-shadows" in the Great Basin and in the plains area immediately east of the Rockies.

processes, which brought John S. Pillsbury of Minneapolis both fame and fortune, increased the demand for grain.

Wheat growers were lured out onto the poorer marginal lands, owing to the high prices in the 1870s resulting from crop failures in other parts of the world. Farmers rashly pushed beyond the 100th meridian as far west as the semi-arid regions of eastern Colorado and Montana, where they developed the special techniques of "dry" farming, including frequent shallow cultivation. To their dismay, they were to discover in the next decade that dry farming succeeds best in wet years, and that dusty farms produce dust bowls. "Pioneering does not pay," observed steelman Andrew Carnegie.

Barbed wire, hardly less than the railroad, bound together the Great West. Fences were necessary to contain livestock, as well as to enclose water holes. Wood was too scarce on the treeless prairies to be used for fencing, and ordinary wire would not hold a rampaging steer. In 1874 Joseph F. Glidden invented a superior type of barbed wire, and in 1883 the company using his patent was turning out 600 miles (966 kilometers) of the new product each day. Among other contributions, barbed wire gave the farmer greater protection against trespassing cattle, although further spelling the doom of the Long Drive.

The Far West Comes of Age

The Great West experienced a fantastic growth of population from the 1870s to the 1890s. A current quip was that one could not tell the truth about the West without lying. Confederate and Union veterans alike moved into the sunset with their families, as did tens of thousands of inpouring immigrants.

A parade of new Western states proudly joined their Eastern sisters. Boom-town Colorado, offspring of the Pike's Peak gold rush, was greeted in 1876 as "the Centennial State." In 1889–1890 a Republican Congress, eagerly seeking more Republican electoral and congressional votes, admitted in a wholesale lot six new states: North Dakota, South Dakota, Montana, Washington, Idaho, and Wyoming. The Mormon Church formally and belatedly banned polygamy in 1890, but not until 1896 was Utah deemed worthy of admission. Only Oklahoma, New Mexico, and Arizona remained to be erected into states from contiguous territory on the mainland of North America.

In a last gaudy fling, the Washington government made available to settlers vast stretches of fertile plains formerly occupied by the Indians in the district of Oklahoma ("the Beautiful Land"). Scores of overeager and well-armed "sooners," illegally jumping the gun, had entered Oklahoma Territory. They had to be evicted repeatedly by federal troops, who on occasion would shoot the horses of intruders. On April 22, 1889, all was in readiness for the legal opening, and some 50,000 "boomers" were poised expectantly on the boundary line. At high noon the bugle shrilled, and a horde of "Eighty-Niners" poured in on lathered horses or careening vehicles. That night a lonely spot on the prairie had mushroomed into the tented city of Guthrie, with over 10,000 souls. By the end of the year Oklahoma boasted 60,000 inhabitants, and Congress made it a territory. In 1907 it became "The Sooner State."

"Boomers" in Oklahoma

The mad haste of the "boomers" underscored the fact that fertile free land was no longer abundant. In 1890—a watershed date—the superintendent of the census announced that for the first time in America's experience a frontier line was no longer discernible. All the unsettled areas were now broken into by isolated bodies of settlement.

Actually, few Americans in 1890 realized that the fading frontier line had disappeared. The Homestead Act remained on the books—and still does—and more millions of acres were taken up after 1890 than between 1862 and 1890. But in general the new lands were less desirable, and many sterile or parched farms, though well watered with sweat, had to be abandoned. To this

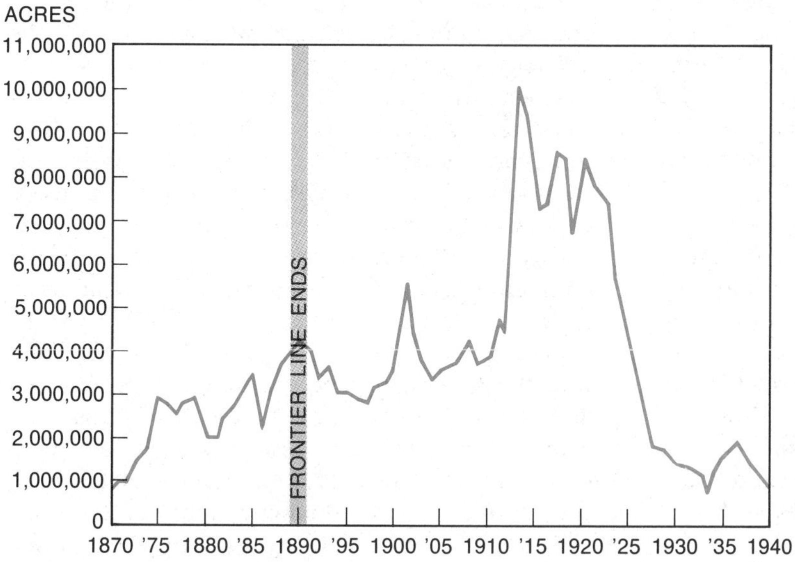

HOMESTEADS FROM THE PUBLIC LANDS (acreage covered by perfected entries)

day the federal government, which owns nearly one-fourth of all American soil, has many millions of acres which may be homesteaded. But they are mostly grazing lands and other marginal areas incapable of sustaining a decent standard of living. From time to time, considerable acreage was rendered attractive for homesteading by the completion of irrigation or reclamation projects. In these ways the frontier survived its "death" by several decades.

As the 19th Century neared its sunset, the westward-tramping American people were disturbed to find that their fabled free land was going or had gone. The secretary of war had prophesied in 1827 that 500 years would be needed to fill the West. But when the nation learned that its land was not inexhaustible, the seeds were planted in the public mind for the belated conservation movement of later decades.

The Folding Frontier

The frontier was more than a place: it was also a state of mind and a symbol of opportunity. Its passing ended a romantic phase of the nation's internal development, and created new economic and psychological problems.

Traditionally footloose, Americans have been notorious for their mobility; the automobile trailer is a typically American vehicle. The nation's farmers, unlike the peasants of Europe, have seldom remained rooted to their soil. The sale of land for a profit, as settlement closed in, was often the settler's most profitable crop.

Much has been said about the frontier as a "safety valve." The theory is that when hard times came, the unemployed who cluttered the city pavements merely moved west, took up farming, and prospered.

In truth relatively few city dwellers, at least in the populous Eastern centers, migrated to the frontier during depressions. Most of them did not know how to farm; few of them could raise enough money to transport themselves west and then pay for livestock and expensive machinery. The initial outlay for equipment had become so heavy by the 1880s and 1890s that the West was decreasingly a land of opportunity for farmers, though it might be for ranchers, miners, and day laborers. A large proportion of the settlers who moved west came from farms on the older frontier, which was within striking distance of the new frontier.

But the "safety-valve" theory does have some validity. For one thing, free acreage lured westward a host of immigrant farmers. Many of these newcomers would have stayed in the Eastern cities to worsen problems of unemployment and slum-festering. The frontier also drew off some restless spirits, and no doubt exercised a powerful psychological influence. Even though Easterners seldom pulled up stakes and moved west, in theory they could always flee to the frontier. This prospect often gave a lift to these drooping spirits—and perhaps also a lift to the wages paid by their employers.

Once the fertile and well-watered free lands were gone, farmers could no longer move west in significant numbers. They had to stand and fight, and consequently they voiced their grievances more and fled from them less. Some farmers actually turned their backs upon the West and moved east. In fact, the vast cityward movement near the end of the century partially replaced the old Westward Movement.

American history cannot be properly understood unless it is viewed in the light of this westward-moving experience—an experience that was centuries-long and soul-searing. Though raucous and raw, the frontier was the cradle of youthful and robust Americanism, and it left an enduring imprint on the older settlements. The Wild West, with its pistol-popping days, was about to disappear. But much of its distinctive flavor remained with the American people, among whom lingered its incurable optimism, its resilient toughness, its handyman resourcefulness, its zestful eagerness for social and economic reform. Its spirit still endures in the cowboy-worship of the ever-popular Western fiction and movies, which recapture the flavor of the sagebrush saga, when men were men and women were scarce and highly prized.

The Farm Becomes a Factory

The role of the American farmers, who had once been jacks-of-all-trades, was rapidly changing. In colonial days they had lived on a kind of Robinson Crusoe's island; they had raised their own food, and the women had woven the clothing. But diversification of crops declined with the passing decades; and after the Civil War, if not earlier, the immense grain-producing areas of the Mississippi Valley found themselves in the throes of an agricultural revolution. Prices were so favorable that the farmers were concentrating on a single money-crop, such as wheat or corn. They could use their profits to buy their foodstuffs at the country store, instead of raising them themselves. They could secure their manufactured goods in town or by mail order, perhaps from the Chicago firm of Aaron Montgomery Ward, established in 1872, with its first catalog a single sheet.

Large-scale farmers were now both specialists and businessmen. As cogs in the vast industrial machine, they were intimately tied in with banking, railroading, and manufacturing. They had to buy expensive machinery to plant and to harvest their crops. A powerful steam engine could drag behind it simultaneously the plow, seeder, and harrow. The speed of harvesting wheat was immensely increased in the 1870s by John F. Appleby's twine binder, and then in the 1880s by the "combine"—the combined reaper-thresher, which was drawn by twenty to forty horses, and which both reaped and bagged the grain. Widespread use of such costly equipment naturally called for first-class management. But the farmers, often unskilled as businessmen, were inclined to blame the banks and railroads, rather than their own shortcomings, for their losses.

This amazing mechanization of agriculture in the post-war years was almost as striking as the mechanization of industry. America was rapidly becoming the world's breadbasket and butcher shop. The farm was attaining the status of a factory—an outdoor grain factory. Bonanza wheat farms of the Minnesota–North Dakota area, for example, were enormous. By 1890 there were at least a half-dozen of them larger than 15,000 acres, with communication by telephone from one part to another. King Wheat was achieving an increasingly prominent position in the galaxy of agriculture potentates.

Harvesting the Wheat. Equipment like this enormous reaper was both efficient and expensive. The "skinner," or driver, had his hands full. (The Bettmann Archive Inc.)

Deflation Dooms the Debtor

Once the farmers became chained to a one-crop economy—wheat or corn—they were in the same leaky boat with the cotton growers of the South. As long as prices stayed high, all went well. But when they skidded in the 1880s, bankruptcy fell like a blight upon the farm belts.

The grain farmers were no longer the masters of their own destinies. They were engaged in one of the most fiercely competitive of businesses, for the price of their product was determined in a world market by the world output. If the wheat fields of Argentina, Russia, and other foreign countries smiled, the price of the farmers' grain would fall and American sod-busters would face ruin, as they did in the 1880s and 1890s.

Low prices and a deflated currency were the chief worries of the frustrated farmers—North, South, and West. If a family had borrowed $1,000 in 1855, when wheat was worth about a dollar a bushel, they expected to pay back the equivalent of 1,000 bushels, plus interest, when the mortgage fell due. But if they let their debt run to 1890, when wheat had fallen to about fifty cents a bushel, they would have to pay back the price of 2,000 bushels for the $1,000 they had borrowed, plus interest. This unexpected burden struck them as unjust, though their steely-eyed creditors often branded the complaining farmers slippery and dishonest rascals.

The deflationary pinch on the debtor flowed partly from the static money supply. There were simply not enough dollars to go around, and as a result prices were forced down. In 1870, the currency in circulation for each person was $19.42; in 1890 it was only $22.67. Yet during these twenty years business and industrial activity, increasing manyfold, had intensified the scramble for available currency.

The forgotten farmers were caught on a treadmill. Despite unremitting toil, they operated year after year at a loss and lived off their fat as best they could. In a vicious circle, their farm machinery increased their output of grain, lowered the price, and drove them even deeper into debt. Mortgages engulfed homesteads at an alarming rate; by 1890 Nebraska alone reported more than 100,000 farms blanketed with mortgages. The repeated crash of the sheriff-auctioneer's hammer kept announcing to the world that another sturdy American husbandman had become landless in a landed nation.

Ruinous rates of interest, running from 8 to 40 percent, were charged on mortgages, largely by agents of Eastern loan companies. The windburned sons of the sod, who felt that they deserved praise for developing the country, cried out in despair against the loan sharks and the Wall Street octopus. Laws against excessive interest charges brought little relief.

Farm tenancy rather than farm ownership was spreading like stinkweed. The trend was especially marked in the sharecropping South, where cotton prices also sank dismayingly. By 1880 one-fourth of all American farms were operated by tenants. The United States was ready to feed the world, but under the new industrial feudalism the farmers were about to sink into a status suggesting Old World serfdom.

> A contemporary farm protest song, "The Kansas Fool," ran:
>
> The bankers followed us out west;
> And did in mortgages invest;
> They looked ahead and shrewdly planned,
> And soon they'll have our Kansas land.

Unhappy Husbandmen

Even Dame Nature ceased smiling, as her powerful forces conspired against agriculture. Mile-wide clouds of grasshoppers, leaving "nothing but the mortgage," periodically ravaged prairie farms. The terrible cotton-boll weevil was also wreaking havoc by the early 1890s.

The good earth was going sour. Floods added to the waste of erosion, which had already washed the topsoil off millions of once-lush Southern acres. Expensive fertilizers were urgently needed. A long succession of droughts seared the trans-Mississippi West, beginning in the summer of 1887. Whole towns were abandoned. "Going home to the wife's folks" and "In God we trusted, in Kansas we busted" were typical laments of many impoverished farmers, as they fled their weather-beaten shacks and sun-baked sod houses. One irate "poet" proclaimed:

> Fifty miles to water,
> A hundred miles to wood,
> To hell with this damned country,
> I'm going home for good.

To add to their miseries, the soil-tillers were gouged by their government—local, state, and national. Their land was overassessed and they paid painful local taxes, while wealthy Easterners concealed their stocks and bonds in safe-deposit boxes. Protective tariffs of these years, while pouring profits into the pockets of the manufacturer, imposed heavy burdens on agriculture, especially in the South. Cotton producers or grain growers had to sell their low-priced, unprotected product in a fiercely competitive world market, while buying high-priced, manufactured goods in a protected home market.

The farmers were also "farmed" by the corporations and processors. They were at the mercy of the Harvester Trust, the Barbed Wire Trust, and the Fertilizer Trust, all of which could control output and raise prices to extortionate levels. Middlemen took a juicy "cut" from the selling price of the goods that the farmers bought, while storage rates for their grain at warehouses and elevators were pushed up by the operators.

In addition, the railroad octopus had the grain growers in its grip. Freight rates could be so high that the farmers sometimes lost less if they burned their corn for fuel than if they shipped it. If they raised their voices in protest, the ruthless railroad operators might let their grain spoil in damp places, or refuse to provide them with cars when needed.

By 1890 the farmers comprised nearly one-half of the population, but they were hopelessly disorganized. The manufacturers and railroads, which were well organized, employed persuasive lobbyists. But the farmers were by nature independent and individualistic—dead set against consolidation or regimentation. They never did organize successfully to restrict production until forced to do so by Washington nearly half a century later, in Roosevelt's New Deal days. Meanwhile they were slowly being goaded into a large-scale political uprising.

Pioneer Sod House in Nebraska, 1888. Lumber was scarce. Note deer antlers on well top and mule-drawn grain mower on left. (S. D. Butcher Collection, Nebraska State Historical Society.)

The Farmers Take Their Stand

Agrarian unrest had flared forth earlier in the Greenback movement shortly after the Civil War. Prices sagged in 1868, and a host of farmers unsuccessfully sought relief from low prices and high indebtedness by demanding an inflation of the currency with paper money.

The National Grange of the Patrons of Husbandry—better known as the Grange—was organized in 1867. Its leading spirit was Oliver H. Kelley, a shrewd and energetic Minnesota farmer then working as a clerk in Washington. A primary objective at first was to stimulate the minds of the farm folk by social, educational, and fraternal activities.

With picnics, music, and lecturers, the Grange had much colorful appeal. Kelley, a Mason, introduced a mumbo-jumbo of passwords and secrecy, as well as a four-ply hierarchy, ranging (for men) from Laborer to Husbandman, and (for women) from Maid to Matron. The movement was a godsend to the sun-bonneted and bony-handed womenfolk, who were cursed with loneliness in widely separated farmhouses. The Grange spread like an old-time prairie fire, and by 1875 claimed 800,000 members, chiefly in the Middle West and South. Buzzing with gossip, these ginghamed and calloused folk often met in red schoolhouses around pot-bellied stoves.

The Grangers gradually raised their goals from self-improvement to improvement of the farmers' plight. In a determined effort to escape the clutches of the trusts, they established cooperatives for both consumers and producers. Their most ambitious experiment was an attempt to manufacture harvesting machinery, but this venture, partly as a result of mismanagement, ended in financial disaster.

Embattled Grangers also went into politics, enjoying their most gratifying success in the grain-growing regions of the upper Mississippi Valley, chiefly in Illinois, Wisconsin, Iowa, and Minnesota. There, through state legislation, they strove to regulate railway rates and the storage fees charged by railroads and by the operators of warehouses

The Grange Awakening the Sleepers. The farmer tries to arouse the apathetic public to the dangers of the onrushing railroad monopoly.

and grain elevators. Many of the state courts, notably in Illinois, were disposed to recognize the principle of public control of private business for the general welfare. But a number of the so-called Granger Laws were badly drawn, and they were bitterly fought through the high courts by the well-paid lawyers of the "interests." Following judicial reverses, most severely at the hands of the Supreme Court in the famous Wabash Railroad decision of 1886 (see p. 497), the Grangers faded rapidly in influence. But their organization has lived on as a vocal champion of farm interests, while brightening rural life with social activities.

Farmers' grievances likewise found a vent in the Greenback Labor party, which combined the inflationary appeal of the earlier Greenbackers with a program for improving the lot of labor. In 1878, the high-water mark of the movement, the Greenback-Laborites polled over a million votes and elected fourteen members of Congress. In the presidential election of 1880 the Greenbackers ran General James B. Weaver, an old Granger who was a favorite of the Civil War veterans and who possessed a remarkable voice and bearing. He spoke to perhaps a half-million citizens in a hundred or so speeches, but polled only 3 percent of the total popular vote.

The Passionate Populist Crusade

A striking manifestation of rural discontent, cresting in the late 1880s, came through the Farmers' Alliances, North and South, white and black. Like the Grangers, these groups sponsored picnics and other social gatherings; they bestirred themselves in politics; they organized cooperatives of various kinds; and they sought to break the strangling grip of the railroads and manufacturers. By about 1890 the members of the Farmers' Alliances probably numbered about 1 million hard-bitten souls, many of whom sang "Toilers Unite" and "Where Will the Farmer Be?"

A new grouping—the People's party—began to emerge spectacularly in the early 1890s. Better known as the Populists, and cynically dubbed the "Popocrats," these zealous folk attracted countless recruits from the Farmers' Alliances. The higher the foreclosure rate on mortgages, the deeper the anger of the farmers. Numerous whiskered prophets sprang forward to lead the Populists. Among these assorted characters loomed an eloquent red-haired "spellbinder," Ignatius Donnelly of Minnesota, who was three times elected to Congress.

The queen of the "calamity howlers" was undeniably Mary Elizabeth ("Mary Yellin' ") Lease, a tall, mannish woman who was called "the Kansas Pythoness." In 1890 she made an estimated 160 speeches. Upbraiding the moneyed aristocracy and denouncing the government "of Wall Street, by Wall Street, and for Wall Street," she reportedly cried that the Kansans should raise "less corn and more hell." They did. The big-city New York *Evening Post* snarled, "We don't want any more states until we can civilize Kansas." To many Easterners, complaint, not corn, was the chief crop of the Westerners.

Conservatives branded the Populists "Calamity Shouters," "Calamity Prophets," and "Calamity Howlers." In 1892 the Chicago *Tribune* much underestimated the appeal of the Populists when it sneered, "The calamity platform adopted by the Populists at Omaha might invite a limited measure of support in a droughty season or a grasshopper year."

Yet the Populists, despite their peculiarities, were not to be laughed aside. In deadly earnest, they were leading an impassioned crusade to relieve the misfortunes of the farmer. Smiles faded from Republican and Democratic faces alike as countless thousands of Populists sang, "Good-bye, My Party, Good-bye." Yawning Eastern plutocrats would have done well to heed these Western "hayseeds," for at long last the calloused and sunbaked sons of the prairies were marshaling their vast political strength. They would soon join their brother farmers in the South in a ferocious attack on the Northeastern citadels of power.

Mary E. Lease (1853–1933). She was so eloquent as to be called a "Patrick Henry in Petticoats." (Courtesy of the Kansas Historical Society.)

VARYING VIEWPOINTS

For at least two generations, historical writing about the American West was dominated by the Turner thesis. In a famous essay of 1893, "The Significance of the Frontier in American History," historian Frederick Jackson Turner argued that the American character had been uniquely shaped by the frontier experience. Europeans had been transformed into tough, inventive, and self-reliant Americans in the struggle to overcome the hazards of the wilderness, including distance, deserts, and Indians. Turner wrote just three years after the superintendent of the census had officially declared the frontier line to be no longer recognizable. Thus in part Turner's essay posed a provocative question: What forces might forge a distinctive national character now that the testing ground of the frontier had been plowed and tamed?

Turner's hypothesis is among the most important and stimulating yet proposed about the formative influences on American society. But as the frontier era recedes ever further into the past, scholars are less persuaded that the Turner thesis is an adequate explanation of the national identity. Americans are still different from Europeans and other peoples, even though Turner's frontier virtually disappeared nearly a century ago. The latest scholarship has also demonstrated that the West did not transform the rest of the country but rather was transformed by it, especially in its industrialization. Recent writers have also ceased to portray the Indians as just another obstacle for white civilization to overcome on its westward march. If any culture was transformed by the American frontier experience, it was Indian culture, which was altered almost beyond recognition by contact with the whites.

SELECT READINGS

Vivacious chapters appear in R. A. Billington, *Westward Expansion* (3rd ed., 1967). Walter Prescott Webb, *The Great Plains* (1931), is a classic. Native Americans are discussed in Wilcomb Washburn, *The Indian in America* (1975), and in Dee Brown's popularly written *Bury My Heart at Wounded Knee: An Indian History of the American West* (1970). Consult also R. K. Andrist, *The Long Death* (1964), W. H. Leckie, *The Military Conquest of the Southern Plains* (1963), and S. L. A. Marshall's military history, *Crimsoned Prairie: The War Between the United States and the Plains Indians* (1972). Two intriguing studies of cross-cultural perception are Robert F. Berkhofer, Jr., *The White Man's Indian* (1978), and Richard Drinnon, *Facing West: The Metaphysics of Indian-Hating and Empire-Building* (1980). For beef, see Lewis Atherton, *The Cattle Kings* (1961), P. Durham and E. L. Jones, *The Negro Cowboys* (1965), Robert Dykstra, *The Cattle Towns* (1968), and Gene M. Gressley, *Bankers and Cattlemen* (1966). On mining, consult Rodman Paul, *Mining Frontiers of the Far West, 1848–1880* (1963), and W. S. Greever, *The Bonanza West* (1963). The farmers' problems are examined in Fred A. Shannon, *The Farmer's Last Frontier* (1945), and Gilbert C. Fite, *The Farmer's Frontier* (1966). Two special studies of interest are Allan G. Bogue, *Money at Interest: The Farm Mortgage on the Middle Border* (1955), and the same author's *From Prairie to Corn Belt: Farming on the Illinois and Iowa Prairies in the Nineteenth Century* (1963). On the farmer's protest, see John D. Hicks's indispensable *The Populist Revolt* (1931); more recent studies are Richard Hofstadter's highly influential *The Age of Reform* (1955), Norman Pollack, *The Populist Response to Industrial America* (1962), and W. T. K. Nugent, *The Tolerant Populists: Kansas Populism and Nativism* (1963). Henry Nash Smith, *Virgin Land: The American West as Symbol and Myth* (1950), is a landmark study of particular interest to students of literature.

29

The Revolt of the Debtor, 1889–1900

You come to us and tell us that the great cities are in favor of the gold standard. We reply that the great cities rest upon our broad and fertile prairies. Burn down your cities and leave our farms, and your cities will spring up again as if by magic. But destroy our farms, and the grass will grow in the streets of every city in the country.

WILLIAM JENNINGS BRYAN, Cross of Gold Speech, 1896

The Return of the Republicans Under Harrison

Benjamin Harrison—stocky, heavily bearded, and dignified—was inaugurated President under weeping heavens on March 4, 1889. The outgoing Grover Cleveland obligingly held an umbrella over him. The incoming President was an honest and earnest party man, but unhappily he was brusque and abrupt. He could charm a crowd of 10,000 people with his oratory, but he would chill them individually with a clammy handshake.

He came to be known, rather unfairly, as "the White House Ice Chest."

James G. Blaine, uncrowned king of the party, received the coveted secretaryship of state as a consolation prize. Still burning with ambition, the "Plumed Knight" did not get along well with his chief. Harrison, admittedly a lesser figure, rather resented his headstrong subordinate.

During the recent presidential campaign, Harrison had made his polite bow to civil service reform. But the Republicans, after their four-year fast, clamored hungrily for the fleshpots of federal office. Harrison followed the strict letter of the civil service law, but beheaded many Democrats. To his credit, he appointed to the Civil Service Commission a bespectacled and violently energetic New Yorker, Theodore Roosevelt. This eager-beaver young politician got his position as a reward for his oratory in the recent campaign, but ironically his new job was to prevent crass spoilsmanship.

Speaker Thomas B. Reed (1839–1902). Although from the politically unimportant state of Maine, "Czar" Reed was regarded at his peak as presidential timber. Bitterly opposing the war with Spain and the acquisition of the Philippines, he retired from Congress in 1899 to practice law. (Library of Congress)

Republicans in the House of Representatives could hardly expect smooth sailing; they had only three votes more than the necessary quorum of 163 members. If the Democrats continued their practice of refusing to answer roll calls, the Republicans could muster a quorum only with difficulty. The Democrats were also prepared to make numerous delaying motions. These included time-consuming demands for a roll call to determine the presence of a quorum, even though one was obviously present. For their part, the Republicans were eager to get on with squandering money and thus safeguard the high tariff that was producing a surplus.

Into this explosive cockpit stepped the new Republican speaker of the House, Thomas B. Reed of Maine. A hulking figure who towered 6 feet 3 inches (1.91 meters), he had already made his mark as a masterful debater. Cool and collected, he spoke with a harsh nasal drawl, and wielded a verbal harpoon of sarcasm. One congressman who had declaimed that he would "rather be right than President," like Henry Clay, was silenced by Reed's rasping sneer that he would "never be either." Strong men cringed at "the crack of his quip."

Early in 1890 the redoubtable Reed undertook single-handedly to change the House rules. He believed that the majority should legislate, in accord with democratic practices, and not be crippled by a filibustering minority. He therefore ignored Democratic speakers who sprang to their feet and sought to establish the absence of a quorum. In piecing out quorums, he counted as present certain Democrats in the chamber who had not answered the roll and who, rule book in hand, furiously denied that they were legally present. For three days pandemonium rocked the House, while Reed held his ground, reputedly counting as present congressmen who were in the barber shop or on trains headed for home.

The gavel rule of "Czar" Reed finally prevailed. The Fifty-first or "Billion Dollar" Congress*—the

*By the 1980s Congress was appropriating an average of more than a billion dollars *a day*!

first in peacetime to appropriate approximately this sum—gave birth to a bumper crop of expensive legislative babies. When the Democrats won control of the House two years later, they paid Reed the compliment of adopting some of his reforms for speedier action.

Political Gravy for All

President Harrison, himself a Civil War general, was disposed to deal generously with his old comrades-in-arms. He appointed as commissioner of pensions James Tanner, who had lost both legs at Bull Run. A notorious pension lobbyist, Corporal Tanner promised to drive a six-mule team through the Treasury, and to wring "from the hearts of some the prayer, 'God help the surplus.' " His extravagance and ineptitude cost him his job in less than a year, but he cut a wide swath while there. A Treasury surplus has never been a problem since his day.

The "Billion Dollar" Congress cooperated by opening wide the federal purse in the Pension Act of 1890. It showered pensions on all Union Civil War veterans who had served for ninety days and who were now unable to do manual labor. Between 1891 and 1895 the host of pensioners was thus raised from 676,000 to 970,000, and by the time Harrison left office in 1893 the annual bill had shot up from $81 million to $135 million.

This policy of liberality toward old soldiers had special attractions for Republican politicians. It helped to solve the problem of the Treasury surplus—a problem that had bedeviled President Cleveland. It helped to save the protective tariff by making plausible, even necessary, the continuance of high customs duties. It helped to secure Republican votes, for the aging veterans of the G.A.R. (Grand Army of the Republic) were grateful to the G.O.P. (Grand Old Party) for its handouts.

President Harrison Disposes of Surplus. (*Puck*, 1892.)

"Czar" Reed's gavel, pounding imperiously, drove through Congress additional bills, conspicuous among which was the Sherman Anti-Trust Act of 1890. This pioneering law, though a feeble bludgeon, did something to quiet the mounting uproar against bloated corporations.

Noteworthy also was the Sherman Silver Purchase Act of 1890. The Western miners were acutely unhappy over the limited silver-purchase program under the Bland-Allison Law of 1878, and many of the silverites were demanding unrestricted government buying of the "beloved white metal." At the same time, many debt-burdened Western and Southern farmers were clamoring for the unlimited coinage of silver. They were convinced that the addition of an immense amount of metallic money would inflate the currency, and thus make for higher prices and easier debt payments. The "Gold Bug" East looked with conservative horror on any such tampering with the money supply, but hungered for the profits that might be reaped from a boost in the tariff schedules.

Thus the stage was set for a huge logrolling operation. Western silver agitators agreed to support a protective tariff, which they detested; Eastern protectionists agreed to support a silver bill, which they distrusted. As a part of the resulting Sherman Silver Purchase Act of 1890, the Treasury was to buy a total of 4.5 million ounces (127,800 kilograms) monthly—about all that was being mined—and pay for it in notes redeemable in either silver or gold. This new law, while boosting the price for the miners, would approximately double the minimum amount of silver that could be acquired under the old Bland-Allison Law.

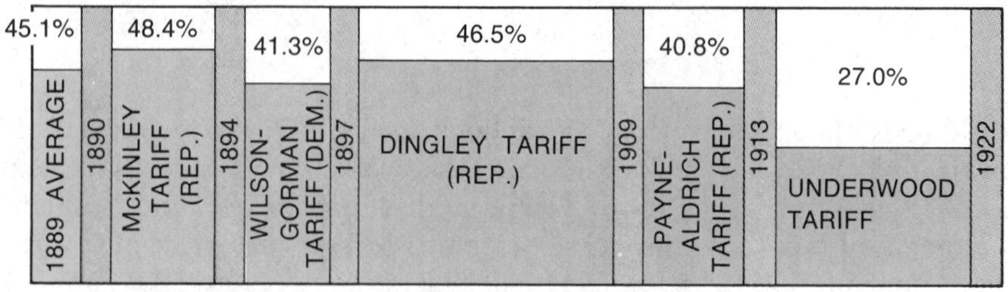

AVERAGE PERCENTAGE RATES ON DUTIABLE GOODS, 1890–1922

See p. 241 for earlier figures, p. 739 for later figures.

McKinley's Tariff Bill

High-protection Republicans, mistakenly claiming a mandate from the voters in the presidential election of 1888, prepared to push the tariff schedules higher. A bill was sponsored in the House by William McKinley of Ohio, who was soon to be dubbed "the high priest of high protection." Rates were boosted to the highest peacetime level yet—an average of 48.4 percent on dutiable goods. A bothersome surplus was disposed of by putting raw sugar on the free list and giving a bounty of two cents a pound to American sugar producers.

The McKinley Bill, by raising slightly the tariff duties on certain agricultural products, made a feeble attempt to quiet the outcries of the farmers. But the concession was a hollow one indeed. Few foreign growers of farm produce—wheat, corn, barley, potatoes—could hope to compete with the soil-rich Americans on their own ground.

These new duties on manufactured goods, as ill luck would have it, actually brought new woes to the farmer. Some Eastern manufacturers raised their prices even before the law went into effect. Tin peddlers—a number of them reportedly in the pay of the Democrats—went systematically from house to house in the Middle West, displaying their wares to the housewife. They would cleverly but dishonestly say that yesterday a pie pan sold for ten cents, but today for twenty-five cents--all because of the wicked new Republican tariff.

Sweeping tariff revisions, like the McKinley Act, have usually boomeranged against the party in power. Mounting discontent against "Bill" McKinley and the McKinley Bill, combined with other grievances, caused the voters to rise in their wrath, especially in the Middle Western farm belt. The congressional landslide of 1890 reduced the Republican membership of the House from 166 to a scant 88 members, as compared with 235 Democrats. Farmers' Alliance men were notably successful in the Southern and Western states, and the new Congress was to contain nine of their spokesmen. Even the highly publicized McKinley was swept out of office, partly because of a Democratic gerrymander* of his district. But he was elected governor of Ohio the next year, and remained in the limelight.

The Presidential Hopefuls of 1892

Malcontents among laborers and farmers, aroused to new fury by the McKinley Bill, were about to fuse into the Populist party early in 1892. Many of them were members of the old Farmers' Alliance. In the spirit of a camp-meeting revival they sang:

> Bring out the good old ballot, boys,
> We'll *right* our every *wrong*.

In July 1892, the Populists formally met at Omaha in their presidential nominating convention, which conservatives called a "mass meeting of maniacs." They uproariously nominated for the presidency the personable and eloquent old Greenbacker, General James B. Weaver.

The Populist platform, which received a forty-minute ovation, was a scorching summation of grievances. It horrified the Eastern conservatives by proclaiming that "tramps and millionaires" come from "the same prolific womb of govern-

---

*To gerrymander is to rearrange electoral districts in such a way as to submerge the voting strength of the opposition. In Massachusetts in 1812 one grotesquely shaped district resembled a salamander; hence the term "*gerry*mander," after Governor Gerry.

The Kansas Legislature, 1890. Rifle-bearing Populists seized the Kansas capitol after the election of 1890, to make good their claim that they had won at the polls. Republicans disagreed and eventually prevailed when sergeants-at-arms, shown here, restored order. (The Kansas State Historical Society, Topeka.)

mental injustice." It demanded the free and unlimited coinage of silver at the ratio of 16 to 1, as a means of increasing the currency in circulation. It urged a graduated income tax. It insisted on government ownership of the telephone and telegraph, and particularly of the railroad. The time had come, the Populists declaimed, "when the railroad corporations will either own the people or the people must own the railroads."

Several weeks earlier, in June 1892, the Republicans had gathered in Minneapolis. Renomination of the cold-fish Harrison was unavoidable, even though he was cordially disliked by the party bosses. Three days before the convention met, Secretary Blaine dramatically resigned from the Cabinet, as if to focus attention on himself. But the aging and ailing "Plumed Knight's" plume was drooping badly, and Harrison was easily renominated on a platform that vigorously upheld the protective tariff.

The Democratic Man of Destiny was the portly but energetic ex-President, Grover Cleveland. He had built up a profitable law practice in New York City, and after hobnobbing with a wealthy clientele, had become increasingly conservative in outlook. Yet such was his reputation that he was nominated at Chicago on the first ballot.

Unhorsing President Harrison

On the whole the presidential campaign of 1892 was clean, quiet, and creditable. Republicans cried, "Grover, Grover, all is over," while the Democrats came back with the chant:

> Grover! Grover!
> Four years more of Grover,
> Out they go, in we go,
> Then we'll be in clover.

A few faint appeals were made to the fast-fading Bloody Shirt. Among suggestive Republican songs were "When [General] Harrison Heard the Bugle's Call" and "How Will the Soldier Vote?" But the tariff, as in the preceding campaign, was the overshadowing issue. High-tariff Republicans chorused, "Hail Protection" and "Good-bye, Free

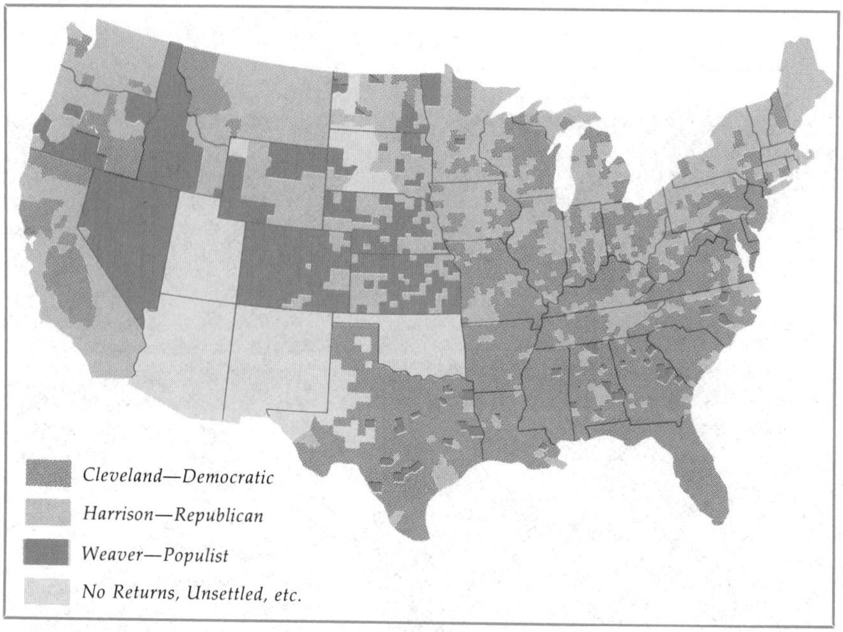

PRESIDENTIAL ELECTION OF 1892 (showing vote by county) Note the concentration of Populist strength in the semi-arid farming regions of the Western half of the country. (Compare with annual precipitation map on p. 532.)

Traders, Goodbye." Low-tariff Democrats countered with "Drive the High-Tariff Tinkers to the Wall" and "Free Wool to Make Our Breeches."

An epidemic of strikes then sweeping the country proved damaging to Harrison's cause: they eloquently refuted the shopworn Republican argument that high protection meant high wages. The most notorious outburst flared forth at Carnegie's Homestead plant near Pittsburgh, following a pay slash for the steelworkers. Company officials called in 300 armed Pinkerton detectives. Defiant strikers, armed with rifles and dynamite, forced their assailants to surrender after a pitched battle in which ten persons were killed and some sixty wounded. Troops were eventually summoned, and both the strike and the union were broken. But this unsavory episode—lead instead of bread—doubtless cost the Republicans thousands of votes.

With this unexpected boost from the Pinkerton Agency, Cleveland unhorsed Harrison. "Old Grover" polled 277 electoral votes to his opponent's 145, and 5,556,918 popular votes to 5,176,108. Cleveland, like Andrew Jackson, received a popular plurality three times, though he took office only twice.

The Populists made a remarkable showing. Singing "Good-bye, Party Bosses," they rolled up 1,041,028 popular votes and 22 electoral votes for General Weaver. They thus became one of the few third parties in American history to break into the electoral column. But their electoral votes came only from six Middle Western and Western states, four of which (Kansas, Colorado, Idaho, and Nevada) fell completely into the Populist basket. The new party failed to gain valuable allies when the indebted white farmers of the Solid South, though sorely tempted, refused to desert the Democratic camp in large numbers. They were fearful of losing political power to the blacks, for there was even a segregated Colored Farmers' National Alliance that claimed more than a million members.

A popular protest song of the 1890s among Western farmers was entitled "The Hayseed." One stanza ran:

I once was a tool of oppression,
And as green as a sucker could be,
And monopolies banded together
To beat a poor hayseed like me.

Southern blacks, tens of thousands of them attracted by Populist reforms, were heavy losers. When the white ruling class discovered that this vote could not be controlled, all remaining black suffrage in the South was virtually eliminated. More than a half-century was to pass before the blacks could again vote in considerable numbers. Accompanying this disfranchisement were more severe Jim Crow laws, backed up by atrocious lynchings and designed primarily to keep blacks segregated in public places, including hotels and restaurants.

"Old Grover" Cleveland Again

Grover Cleveland took office once again in 1893, the only President ever re-elected after defeat. He was the same old bull-necked and bull-headed Cleveland, with a little more weight, polish, conservatism, and self-assertiveness. He was still inclined to put his foot down rather than slide it down, to demand a whole loaf or none, to go his own resolute way rather than hold his nose and play ball with the politicians. But if it was the same old Grover Cleveland, it was not the same old country; the debtors were up in arms, and the advance shadows of panic were falling.

Cleveland's attorney general, Richard Olney, was a stocky and conservative Yankee, cut from the same piece of cloth as his stubborn and pugnacious chief. As a wealthy corporation lawyer associated with the railroads, he had no stomach for a vigorous prosecution of big business under the Interstate Commerce Act and the Sherman Anti-Trust Act. His record was generally one of weakness and deliberate failure, for he was not a man to "betray a trust." He cheerfully lost his cases on behalf of the government.

Hardly had Cleveland seated himself in the presidential chair when the devastating Panic of 1893 burst about his burly frame. Lasting for about four years, it was in some respects the worst of the century. Contributing causes were no doubt the splurge of overspeculation, labor disorders, and the current agricultural depression. Free-silver agitation had also damaged American credit abroad, and the usual pinch on American finances had come when European banking houses, after earlier failures, began to call in loans from the United States.

Distress was acute and widespread. About 8,000 American business houses collapsed in six months, and dozens of railroad lines went into the hands of receivers. Business executives "died like flies under the strain," wrote Henry Adams. Soup kitchens were set up for the unemployed, while gangs of hoboes ("tramps") wandered aimlessly about the country. Local charities did their feeble best, but the federal government, bound by the let-nature-take-its-course philosophy of the century, was unable to relieve the suffering masses.

Cleveland, who had earlier been bothered by a surplus, was now burdened with a deficit. Under the Sherman Silver Purchase Act, the Treasury was required to issue legal tender notes for the silver bullion that it bought. Owners of the paper currency would then present it for gold, and by law the notes had to be reissued. New holders would repeat the process, thus draining away gold in an "endless chain" operation.

Alarmingly, the gold reserve in the Treasury dropped below $100 million, which was popularly regarded as the safe minimum for supporting about $350 million in outstanding paper money. Cleveland saw no alternative but to halt the bleed-

> In his special message to Congress (1893) Cleveland said: "Unless Government bonds are to be constantly issued and sold to replenish our exhausted gold, only to be again exhausted, it is apparent that the operation of the silver-purchase law now in force leads in the direction of the entire substitution of silver for the gold in the Government Treasury, and that this must be followed by the payment of all Government obligations in depreciated silver."

ing away of gold by engineering a repeal of the Sherman Silver Purchase Act of 1890. For this purpose he summoned Congress into an extra session in the summer of 1893.

Unknown to the country, complications threatened from another quarter. A malignant growth had developed on the roof of Cleveland's mouth, and it had to be removed on a private yacht with extreme secrecy. If the President had died under the knife, his place would have been taken by the "soft money" vice-president, Adlai E. Stevenson—an eventuality that would have deepened the crisis.

In Congress the debate over the repeal of the silver act was meanwhile running its heated course. An eloquent young congressman from Nebraska, the thirty-three-year-old William Jennings Bryan, held the galleries spellbound for three hours as he championed the cause of free silver. The friends of silver announced that "hell would freeze over" before Congress passed the repeal measure. But an angered Cleveland used his office-giving power to break the filibuster in the Senate. He thus alienated the Democratic silverites and disrupted his party at the very outset of his administration.

Gold Shortages and Job Shortages

The hemorrhaging of gold from the Treasury was only partially stopped by the repeal of the Sherman Silver Purchase Act. Other currency was still being presented for redemption, and in February 1894, the gold reserve sank to a dismaying $41 million. The nation was in grave danger of going off the gold standard.

Again Cleveland was forced to act vigorously. As a champion of sound money, he could see no alternative but to sell government bonds for gold and deposit the proceeds in the Treasury. Two bond issues were floated in 1894, totaling over $100 million, but the "endless chain" operations continued relentlessly.

Early in 1895, Cleveland turned in desperation to J. P. Morgan, "the bankers' banker," and a Wall

West and South Feed the Country While Wall Street Milks It. A cartoon of the 1890s highly popular with Democrats and Populists.

Street syndicate. After tense negotiations at the White House, the bankers agreed to lend the government $65 million in gold. They were obviously in business for profit, so they charged a commission amounting to about $7 million. But they did make a significant concession when they agreed to obtain one-half of the gold abroad and take the necessary steps to dam it up in the leaky Treasury. The loan, at least temporarily, helped restore confidence in the nation's finances. Following one more public bond sale and a business upswing, the crisis was surmounted.

But the bond deal stirred up a storm. The Wall Street ogre, especially in the eyes of the silverites and other debtors, was a symbol of all that was wicked and grasping. Cleveland's secretive dealings with mighty "Jupiter" Morgan were savagely condemned as a "sellout" of the national government. But Cleveland was certain that he had done no wrong. Sarcastically denying that he was "Morgan's errand boy," he asserted: "Without shame and without repentance I confess my share of the guilt."

Ragged armies of the unemployed, victims of the depression, were meanwhile staging demonstrations. The most famous of these marches was that of "General" Jacob S. Coxey, a wealthy Ohio quarry owner, who started for Washington in 1894 with several score of men, accompanied by a swarm of newspaper reporters. His platform included a demand that the government relieve unemployment by an inflationary public works program, supported by some $500 million in legal tender notes to be issued by the Treasury. Coxey himself rode in a carriage with his wife and infant son, appropriately named Legal Tender Coxey, while his tiny "army" tramped along behind, singing:

> We're coming, Grover Cleveland,
> 500,000 strong,
> We're marching on to Washington
> to right the nation's wrong.

The "Commonweal Army" of Coxeyites finally straggled into the nation's capital. But the "invasion" took on the aspects of a comic opera when "General" Coxey and his "lieutenants" were arrested for walking on the grass. Other armies—"petitions in boots"—were less well behaved, and accounted for considerable disorder and pillage.

Cleveland Crushes the Pullman Strike

Violent flare-ups accompanied labor protests, notably in Chicago. Most frightening was the crippling Pullman strike of 1894. Eugene V. Debs, an impetuous but personally lovable labor leader, had helped organize the American Railway Union of about 150,000 members. The Pullman Palace Car Company, which maintained a model town near Chicago for its employees, was hit hard by the depression and cut wages about one-third. But it did not reduce rent for the company houses. The workers finally struck—in some places overturning Pullman cars—and paralyzed railway traffic from Chicago to the Pacific Coast.

This terrorism in Chicago was serious but not completely out of hand. At least this was the judgment of Governor Altgeld of Illinois, a friend of the downtrodden who had pardoned the Haymarket Square anarchists the year before (see p. 509). But Attorney General Olney, an arch-conservative and an ex-railroad attorney, urged the dispatch of federal troops. His legal grounds were that the strikers were interfering with the transit of the United States mail. Cleveland supported Olney with the ringing declaration, "If it takes the entire army and navy to deliver a postal card in Chicago, that card will be delivered."

To the delight of conservatives, the Pullman strike was crushed by bayonet-supported intervention from Washington. Debs and his leading associates, who had defied a federal court injunction to cease striking, were sentenced to six months' imprisonment for contempt of court. Ironically, the lean labor agitator spent much

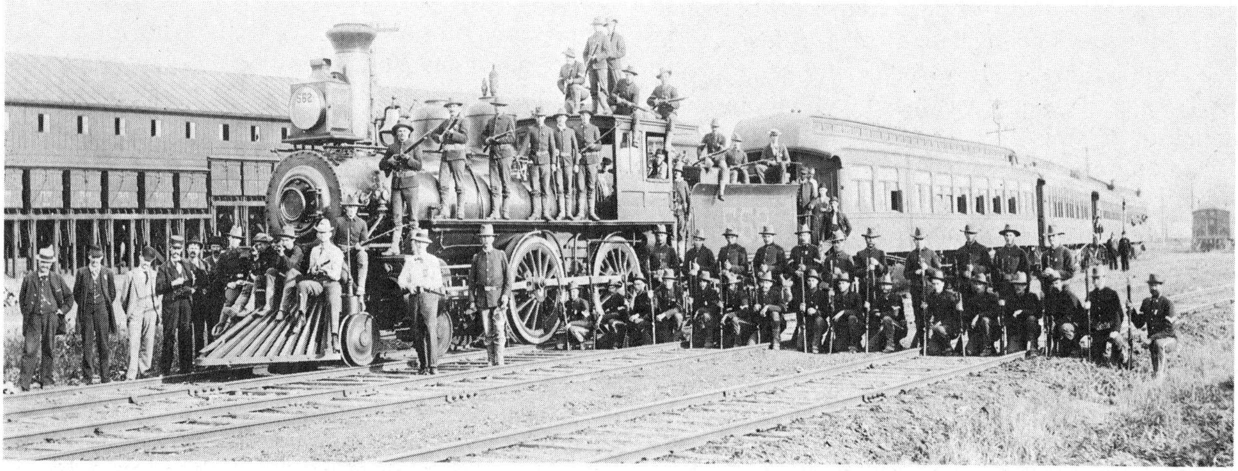

The Pullman Strike, 1894. These federal troops broke the back of the strike by force of arms. (Culver Pictures, Inc.)

After the Pullman strike collapsed, Debs said, "No strike has ever been lost." In 1897 he declared, "The issue is Socialism versus Capitalism. I am for Socialism because I am for humanity."

of his enforced leisure reading radical literature, which had much to do with his later leadership of the Socialist movement in America.

Embittered cries of "government by injunction" now burst from organized labor. This was the first time that such a legal weapon had been used conspicuously by Washington to break a strike, and it was all the more distasteful because defiant laborites who were held in contempt could be imprisoned without jury trial. Signs multiplied that employers were striving to smash labor unions by court action. Non-labor elements of the country, including the Populists and other debtors, were likewise incensed. They saw in the brutal Pullman episode further proof of an unholy alliance between Big Business and the courts.

Democratic Tariff Tinkering

The McKinley Tariff of 1890 had been designed to keep protection high and the surplus low. It succeeded remarkably in achieving both goals. By 1894 the Treasury was faced with an alarming deficit of $61 million.

In Congress the Democrats undertook to frame a tariff that would provide adequate revenue with moderate protection, as they had promised in the Cleveland-Harrison campaign of 1892. A bill aimed at securing these objectives was introduced in the House. As a concession to the Populists and other foes of "plutocracy," the measure included a tax of 2 percent on incomes over $4,000. Joseph H. Choate, a wealthy lawyer, growled, "Communistic, socialistic."

When the new tariff bill reached the Senate, it ran afoul of a swarm of lobbyists in the pay of Big Industry. After much buttonholing and vote trading, the Wilson-Gorman Bill was drastically revamped by the addition of over 630 amendments. The Sugar Trust stirred up a scandal when it inserted benefits to itself worth a sweet $20 million a year. As a result of such backstairs pressures, the Wilson-Gorman law of 1894 fell scandalously short of establishing a low tariff, even though it did reduce the existing McKinley rates from 48.4 percent to 41.3 percent on dutiable goods. (See chart, p. 544).

Cleveland was outraged by what he regarded as a gross betrayal of Democratic campaign pledges. In an angry outburst he denounced the bill as "party perfidy and party dishonor"—to the glee of the Republicans. But to veto the patchwork affair would leave the even higher McKinley Tariff on the books, so Cleveland grudgingly let the bill become law without his signature. The Wilson-Gorman hodgepodge at least had the redeeming feature of the income tax, which was highly popular among the masses.

But the income tax lasted less than a year. In 1895 the Supreme Court, by a five-to-four decision, struck down this part of the Wilson-Gorman Act.* The only popular feature of the unpopular tariff law thus perished under the judicial tomahawk. A chorus of denunciation rose from the Populists and other impoverished groups, who found further proof that the courts were only the tools of the plutocrats.

Democratic political fortunes naturally suffered. The tariff dynamite which had blasted the Republicans out of the House in 1890 now dislodged the Democrats, with a strong helping hand from the depression. Revitalized Republicans, singing "The Soup House" and "Times Are Mighty Hard," won the congressional elections of 1894 in a landslide, and now had 244 votes to 105 for the Demo-

*It violated the "direct tax" clause. See Art. I, Sec. IX, para. 4, Appendix. The 16th Amendment to the Constitution, adopted in 1913, permitted an income tax.

Uncle Sam: "It Won't Work Without a New Wheel." A specious argument for bimetallism. (W. H. Harvey, *Coin's Financial School Up to Date,* 1895.)

crats. The prospects of the Republicans for 1896 seemed roseate. They were openly boasting that they had only to nominate a "rag baby" or a "yaller dog," and they could put it in the White House. Such optimism misread the signs of the times.

Discontented debtors, especially the Populists, were turning in throngs to free silver as a cure-all. An enormously popular pamphlet, entitled *Coin's Financial School* (1894), was being distributed by the hundreds of thousands of copies. Written by William Hope Harvey, it was illustrated by clever woodcuts, one of which depicted the gold ogre beheading the beautiful silver maiden. In fiction parading as fact, the booklet showed how the "little professor"—"Coin" Harvey—overwhelmed the bankers and professors of economics with his brilliant sallies in behalf of free silver. The belief was gaining momentum among silverites and debtors that there was a foul conspiracy on foot, both nationally and internationally, to elevate gold above silver.

McKinley: Hanna's Fair-Haired Boy

The leading candidate for the Republican presidential nomination in 1896 was ex-Congressman McKinley of Ohio, sponsor of the ill-starred tariff bill of 1890. He had established a creditable Civil War record, having risen to the rank of major; he hailed from the electorally potent state of Ohio; and he could point to long years of honorable service in Congress, where he had made many friends by his kindly and conciliatory manner. Rather small in stature (5 feet 7 inches; 1.7 meters), and with a high forehead and a prominent chin, he added to his inches by his dignity and by his resemblance to Napoleon Bonaparte—a characteristic seized upon by the cartoonists. He was widely hailed as "the Napoleon of Protection" and "the Advance Agent of Prosperity."

As a presidential candidate, McKinley was peculiarly the creation of a fellow Ohioan, Marcus Alonzo Hanna. The latter had made his fortune in the iron business, and he now coveted the role of President-maker. He was personally attracted to McKinley; "I love McKinley," he once said. When the overgenerous Ohio congressman faced bankruptcy after unwisely endorsing a friend's notes for about $100,000, Hanna and his wealthy associates paid off the obligation.

Hanna, as a wholehearted Hamiltonian, believed that a prime function of government was to aid business. Honest, earnest, rough, and direct, he became the personification of Big Industry in politics. He was often cartooned, quite unfairly, as a bloated bully in a loud checkered suit with a dollar sign on each checker. As a conservative in business, he was a confirmed "standpatter," content not to rock the boat. He believed that in some measure prosperity "trickled down" to the laborer, whose dinner pail was full when business flourished. He trusted in trusts.

A hardfisted Hanna, although something of a novice in politics, organized his pre-convention campaign for McKinley with consummate skill and with a liberal outpouring of his own money. "Czar" Reed was a leading challenger. But his sarcastic tongue had made too many enemies, and he was too rigidly opposed to silver. The convention steamroller, well lubricated with Hanna's dollars, nominated McKinley on the first ballot at St. Louis in June 1896.

The Republican platform cleverly straddled the monetary question. It declared for the gold standard, even though McKinley's voting record in Congress had been embarrassingly friendly to silver. But the platform made a gesture toward the silverites when it came out for international bimetallism, or a worldwide gold-silver standard. The catch was that all the leading nations of the world would have had to agree to such a scheme, and this obviously they would not do. Additionally the platform condemned hard times and Democratic incapacity, while pouring praise on the protective tariff.

Hanna: That man Clay was an ass. It's better to be President than to be right!

Hanna Lampooned. This cartoon reflects Democratic and Populist resentment of the wealth and power of Republican Mark Hanna and his candidate, William McKinley. (Library of Congress)

Bryan: Silverite Messiah

Dissension riddled the Democratic camp. Cleveland no longer led his party; dubbed "the Stuffed Prophet," he was undeniably the most unpopular man in the country. Labor-debtor groups remembered too vividly the silver-purchase repeal, the Pullman strike, the backstairs Morgan bond deal. Ultraconservative in finance, Cleveland was now more a Republican than a Democrat on the silver issue.

Rudderless, the Democratic convention met in Chicago in July 1896, with the silverites in command. Shouting insults at the absent Cleveland, they refused, by a suicidal vote of 564 to 357, to endorse their own administration. They had the enthusiasm and the numbers; all they lacked was a leader.

A new Moses suddenly appeared in the person of William Jennings Bryan of Nebraska. Then only thirty-six years of age and known as "the Boy Orator of the Platte,"* he stepped confidently onto the platform before 15,000 people. His masterful presence was set off by handsome features, a smooth-shaven jaw, and raven-black hair. He radiated honesty, sincerity, and energy. He had a good mind but not a brilliant one; he was less a student of books than of human nature; and he possessed broad human sympathies. His was a great heart rather than a great head; a great voice rather than a great brain.

In Chicago the setting was made to order for a magnificent oratorical effort. Bryan could be sure of a sympathetic hearing, for as a congressman and a nationwide lecturer he had already emerged as one of the leading champions of free silver. A hush fell over the convention as he stood before it. With an organlike voice that rolled into the outer corners of the huge hall, he delivered a fervent plea for silver. Rising to supreme heights of eloquence, he thundered, "We will answer their demands for a gold standard by saying to them:

*One contemporary sneered that Bryan, like the Platte River, was "six inches deep and six miles wide at the mouth."

'You shall not press down upon the brow of labor this crown of thorns, you shall not crucify mankind upon a cross of gold.'"

The Cross of Gold speech was a sensation. Swept off its feet in a tumultuous scene, the convention nominated Bryan the next day on the fifth ballot. The platform declared for the unlimited coinage of silver at the ratio of 16 ounces of silver to 1 of gold, though the market ratio was about 32 to 1. This meant that the silver in a dollar would be worth about fifty cents.

Democratic "Gold Bugs," unable to swallow Bryan, bolted their party over the silver issue. Conservative Senator Hill of New York, when asked if he was a Democrat still, reportedly replied, "Yes, I am a Democrat still—*very* still." The Democratic minority, including Cleveland, charged that the Populist-silverites had stolen both the name and the clothes of their party. They nominated a lost-cause ticket of their own, and many of them, including Cleveland, hoped for a McKinley victory.

Populists were left out in the cold, for the Democratic majority had appropriated their main plank —"16 to 1," that "heaven-born ratio." The bulk of the confused "Popocrats," rather than submit to a hard-money McKinley victory, endorsed Bryan in their convention. Singing "The Jolly Silver Dollar of the Dads," they became in effect the "Demo-Pop" party. But many of the original Populists refused to support Bryan, and went down with their colors nailed to the mast.

Hanna Leads the "Gold Bugs"

Mark Hanna smugly assumed that he could make the tariff the focus of the campaign. But Bryan, a dynamo of energy, forced the free-trade issue into a back seat when he took to the stump in behalf of free silver. Sweeping through twenty-seven states and traveling 18,000 miles (29,000 kilometers), he made between five and six hundred speeches—thirty-six in one day—and even invaded the East, "the enemy's country." Vachel Lindsay caught the spirit of his oratorical orgy:

A Republican View of Bryan. A variant of this satire was "In Go(l)d We Trust." (New York *Press*, 1896.)

Prairie avenger, mountain lion,
Bryan, Bryan, Bryan, Bryan,
Gigantic troubadour, speaking like a siege gun,
Smashing Plymouth Rock with his boulders from
the West.*

Free silver became almost as much a religious as a financial issue. Hordes of fanatical free-silverites hailed Bryan as the Messiah to lead them out of the wilderness of debt. They sang, "We'll All Have Our Pockets Lined with Silver" and "No Crown of Thorns, No Cross of Gold."

Bryan created panic among Eastern conservatives with his threat of converting their holdings overnight into fifty-cent dollars. The "Gold Bugs" vented their alarm in abusive epithets, which ranged all the way from "fanatic" and "madman" to "traitor" and "murderer." "In God We Trust, with Bryan We Bust," the Republicans sneered, while one Eastern clergyman cried, "That platform was made in Hell."

Widespread fear of Bryan and the "silver lunacy" enabled "Dollar Mark" Hanna, now chairman of the Republican National Committee, to shine as a money raiser. He "shook down" the trusts and plutocrats, and piled up an enormous "slush fund" for a "campaign of education"—or of propaganda, depending on one's point of view. The Republicans amassed the most formidable

---

*Reprinted with permission of Macmillan Publishing Co., Inc., from *Collected Poems* by Vachel Lindsay. Copyright 1925 by Macmillan Publishing Co., Inc., renewed 1948 by Elizabeth C. Lindsay.

political campaign chest thus far in American history. At all levels—national, state, and local—it amounted to about $16 million, as contrasted with about $1 million for the poorer Democrats—roughly "16 to 1." With some justification, the Bryanites accused Hanna of "buying" the election, and of floating McKinley into the White House on a tidal wave of greenbacks. The Republicans definitely had the edge in money and mud.

Appealing to the Pocketbook Vote

With gold gushing into his money bags, Hanna waged a high-pressure campaign against silver. He distributed tens of millions of pamphlets, tracts, leaflets, and posters, many of them in the native languages of immigrant groups. He sent out hundreds of "spellbinders" onto the stump, where they engaged in the free and unlimited coinage of wordage. There was a maximum of shouting and a minimum of thinking, primarily because only a few trained economists were able to grasp fully the implications of silver-and-gold bimetallism—and even they disagreed. "The whole currency question," wrote the humorist "Mr. Dooley" (F. P. Dunne), "is a matter of lungs."

Republicans harped constantly on their promise of prosperity. Reminding the voters of Cleveland's "Democratic panic," they appealed to the "belly vote" with their prize slogan: "McKinley and the Full Dinner Pail." McKinley, though an effective orator, was no match for Bryan in the rough-and-tumble of stump speaking. He remained at his Ohio home, conducting a quiet and dignified "front porch" campaign. Stressing prosperity, he read calm and confident little speeches to delegations of visiting Republicans.

Bryan's cyclonic campaign, launched with irresistible enthusiasm, began to lose steam as the weeks passed. If the election had been held in August, instead of November, the golden-voiced "Peerless Leader" might well have won. But Hanna's splendid organization and far-flung campaign of "education" gradually began to tip the scales. Also, during the weeks just before the election, the price of wheat rose sharply, owing largely to crop failures abroad. Hostility to the Republican party in the vast wheat belt began to wane, even though agriculture generally remained depressed.

Fear probably was the strongest ally of Hanna, the worst enemy of Bryan, who allegedly had "silver on the brain." Republican businessmen placed contracts with manufacturers, contingent on the election of McKinley. A few factory owners, with thinly veiled intimidation, paid off their workers and told them not to come to work on Wednesday morning if Bryan won. Reports were also current that employers were threatening to pay their employees in fifty-cent pieces, instead of dollars, if Bryan triumphed. Such were some of the "dirty tricks" of the "Stop Bryan, Save America" crusade.

Money Talks. A reference to the common assumption that Hanna's lavish use of money swung the election. (Buffalo *Times,* 1896.)

Class Conflict: Plowholders versus Bondholders

Hanna's campaign methods paid off, for on election day McKinley triumphed decisively. The vote was 271 to 176 in the Electoral College, and 7,104,779 to 6,502,925 in the popular column. Responding to fear, hope, and excitement, an unprecedented outpouring of voters flocked to the polls. McKinley ran strongly in the populous East, where he carried every county of New England, and in the upper Mississippi Valley. Bryan's states, concentrated in the debt-burdened South and the

PRESIDENTIAL ELECTION OF 1896
(with electoral vote by state)
This election tolled the deathknell of the Gilded Age political system, with its razor-close elections, strong party loyalties, and high voter turnouts. For years after 1896 Republicans predominated, and citizens showed declining interest in either joining parties or voting.

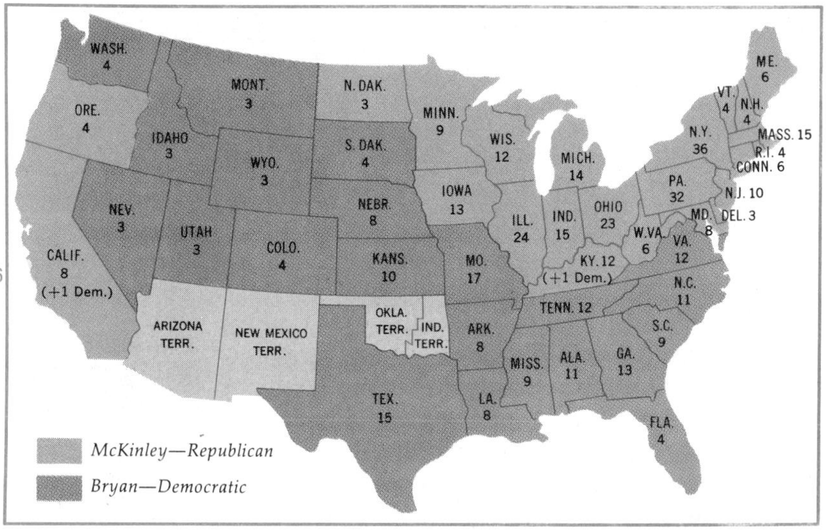

trans-Mississippi West, involved more acreage than McKinley's but less population—only the South and the desert, cynics said.

The free-silver election of 1896—probably the most significant since Lincoln's victories in 1860 and 1864—highlighted serious sectional cleavages. One basic reason for Bryan's defeat, despite his strength in the South and West, was his lack of appeal to the unmortgaged farmer and the urban laborer, especially in the East. Many an Eastern wage earner voted for his job and his full dinner pail, threatened as they were by free silver, free trade, and fireless factories.

Unhappily, the Bryan-McKinley battle likewise accentuated an ugly class conflict, probably the most serious since the election of Jefferson in 1800. Debtors, hard-pinched farmers, poorer folk, and other malcontents were for the most part pitted against the more prosperous pillars of society. On the surface, the election was the age-old story of the underprivileged many against the privileged few, of the indebted back country against the wealthier seaboard, of the country against the city, of the agrarians against the industrialists, of Main Street against Wall Street, of the nobodies against the somebodies. Bryan made an evangelical appeal to the radical foes of the social order, but there were simply not enough of them, not even enough Democrats.

In gold-standard England there was much relief over McKinley's victory. The London *Standard* commented, "The hopelessly ignorant and savagely covetous waifs and strays of American civilization voted for Bryan, but the bulk of the solid sense, business integrity, and social stability sided with McKinley. The nation is to be heartily congratulated."

As a matter of simple humanitarianism, the mortgage-crushed farmers deserved some relief from social and economic ills not of their own making. They did not regard themselves as "dishonest," especially when they cried out against having to pay back dearer dollars than those they had borrowed. Silver was a symbol—a misleading symbol—of their plight. Bryan himself believed that the basic issue was not free silver but free people—a free people seeking escape from the clutches of plutocracy.

The outcome was a resounding victory for Big Business, the big cities, middle-class virtues, and innate American conservatism. In a sense, Alexander Hamilton again triumphed from the grave. McKinley's election no doubt upheld the nation's financial honor and averted serious economic strains. But these dangers were grossly exaggerated by Hanna's propaganda mill, with its unwritten slogan, "In Gold We Trust." Even so, the smashing victory of 1896 insured a Republican grip on the White House for sixteen consecutive years.

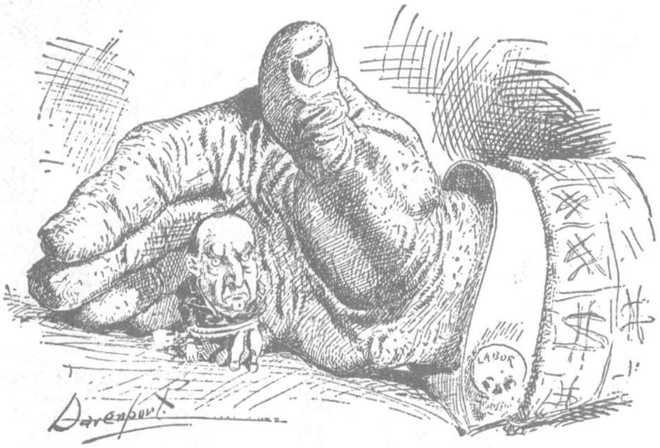

McKinley in the Palm of Hanna's Hand.
(New York *Journal,* 1896.)

Republican Standpattism Enthroned

An eminently "safe" McKinley took the inaugural oath in 1897. Though a man of considerable ability, he was an ear-to-the-ground politician who seldom got far out of line with majority opinion. His cautious, conservative nature caused him to shy away from the flaming banner of reform—or even of progressivism. Business was given a free rein, and the trusts, which had trusted him in 1896, were allowed to develop more mighty muscles without serious restraints.

McKinley, unlike Cleveland, worked smoothly in party harness. With impeccable white vest, he seemed never to perspire, even in cruelly muggy Washington. Able to get along well with Congress—he had served there for many years—he shone best at reconciling conflicting interests. Conciliatory and warm-handed, he would send an angry-faced man away beaming, sometimes wearing a carnation from the presidential desk. McKinley continued to maintain intimate relations with Hanna but he was by no means under the thumb of his mentor, despite Vachel Lindsay's cruel query:

> Where is McKinley, Mark Hanna's McKinley,
> His slave, his echo, his suit of clothes?

Not surprisingly, the new "standpat" Cabinet was both conservative and aged. The venerable Senator John Sherman of Ohio, now seventy-four years old and suffering from a serious loss of memory, was "kicked upstairs" into the post of secretary of state. Hanna coveted his Senate seat, and Sherman was induced to resign so that the governor of Ohio could reward McKinley's benefactor with the vacated place.

The tariff issue, which had played second fiddle to silver in the "Battle of '96," quickly forced itself to the fore. Cautious Republicans were reluctant to tackle legislation that would firmly establish the gold standard; there were still too many silverites left in Congress. But action on the current Wilson-Gorman law was not raising enough revenue to cover the annual Treasury deficits, and the Republican trusts had purchased additional protection by their lush contributions to Hanna's "slush fund."

In due course the Dingley Tariff Bill was jammed through the House in 1897, under the pounding gavel of the rethroned "Czar" Reed. The proposed new rates were high, but not high enough to satisfy the paunchy lobbyists, who once again descended upon the Senate. Over 850 amendments were tacked onto the overburdened bill. The resulting piece of patchwork finally established the average rates at 46.5 percent, substantially higher than the Democratic Wilson-Gorman Act of 1894, and in some categories even higher than the McKinley Act of 1890. (See chart, p. 558.)

Inflation Without Silver

Prosperity, long lurking around the corner, began to return with a rush in 1897, the first year of McKinley. The depression of 1893 had run its course, and farm prices rose. Paint-thirsty Middle

Western barns blossomed out in new colors, and the wheels of industry increased their hum. Republican politicians like crowing roosters causing the sun to rise, claimed credit for bringing in the sunlight of prosperity.

The Gold Standard Act, loudly demanded by hard-moneyites, was not passed by the Republicans until 1900, when many silverites had left Congress. It provided that the paper currency was to be redeemed freely in gold. Last-ditch silverites fought the bill with bitterness but without success. The cries of the inflationists, further choked by returning prosperity, gradually died away. Thus ended some twenty years of paternalistic attempts to "do something" for the debtor.

In retrospect, a controlled expansion of American currency in the 1880s and 1890s was clearly desirable. Prices were depressed, money was tight, and the volume of currency in circulation lagged far behind the increasing volume of business. Agrarian debtors therefore had a good cause: relief from social and economic hardship through an inflation of the dollar supply. But free silver, which aroused exaggerated fears, was a poor sword. By brandishing this tinseled weapon, Bryan actually defeated his own ends. The free-silver fixation not only discredited the case for needed currency expansion, but seriously set back the movement for agrarian reform.

Nature and science gradually provided an inflation that the "Gold Bug" East had fought so frantically to prevent. Electrifying discoveries of new gold deposits in Canada (Klondike), Alaska, South Africa, and Australia eased the pressure, as did the perfecting of the cheap cyanide process for extracting gold from low-grade ore. Moderate inflation thus took care of the currency needs of an explosively expanding nation, as its circulatory system greatly improved. The tide of "silver heresy" rapidly receded, and the "popocratic" fish were left gasping high and dry on a golden-sanded beach.

VARYING VIEWPOINTS

Populism seemed to pose the only organized opposition to the new economic and political order that settled massively into place in the 1890s. Thus the Populists became heroes to several generations of writers who disliked that new order and looked back longingly at America's agrarian past. John D. Hicks' *The Populist Revolt* (1931) sympathetically portrayed the embattled farmers as last-ditch defenders of a passing way of life, doomed to go down to defeat with "Boy Bryan" in 1896.

The Hicks point of view was the dominant one until about 1955, when it was sharply challenged by Richard Hofstadter in *The Age of Reform.* Hofstadter charged that Hicks and other writers had romanticized the Populists, who were themselves simply "harassed little country businessmen," not picturesque "calamity howlers" standing steadfast against the advance of commercial culture. Moreover, argued the city-born-and-bred Hofstadter, the Populist revolt was aimed not just at big business and high finance, but somewhat irrationally at urbanism, the East, and modernity itself.

Hofstadter thus exposed a "dark side" of Populism, which contained elements of anti-intellectualism, self-deception, and even anti-Semitism. This view has proved to be remarkably persuasive. Yet it, in turn, has been vigorously attacked by Norman Pollack's *The Populist Response to Industrial America* (1962), which tries to rehabilitate the Populists as critics of capitalism. Another challenger is Lawrence Goodwyn's *Democratic Promise: The Populist Movement in America* (1976), which focuses on the farmer's real grievances in the South.

SELECT READINGS

Valuable background can be found in the books by Shannon, Hicks, and Hofstadter cited in the previous chapter. A comprehensive survey is H. U. Faulkner, *Politics, Reform, and Expansion: 1890–1900* (1959). Harrison is fully portrayed in H. J. Sievers, *Benjamin Harrison, Hoosier Statesman* (1959), and the same author's *Benjamin Harrison: Hoosier President* (1968). For Cleveland, see titles by Nevins and Merrill cited in Chapter 26. Consult also J. Rogers Hollingsworth, *The Whirligig of Politics: The Democracy of Cleveland and Bryan* (1963). Paolo E. Coletta's biography of *William Jennings Bryan* (3 vols., 1964–1969) is rich in *and Bryan* (1963). The best book on McKinley in office is Lewis L. Gould, *The Presidency of William McKinley* (1980). Paolo E. Coletta's biography of *William Jennings Bryan* (3 vols., 1964–1969) is rich in detail. See also Paul W. Glad, *The Trumpet Soundeth: William Jennings Bryan and His Democracy, 1896–1912* (1960). Politics are handled in H. Wayne Morgan, *From Hayes to McKinley* (1969), R. D. Marcus, *Grand Old Party: Political Structure in the Gilded Age* (1971), and Clifton K. Yearley, *The Money Machines* (1970), about financing the political parties. The South gets special attention in T. Saloutos, *Farmer Movements in the South, 1865–1933* (1960), Sheldon Hackney, *Populism to Progressivism in Alabama* (1969), and in Lawrence Goodwyn, *Democratic Promise: The Populist Movement in America* (1976). Two intriguing analyses of the social bases of political change in this era are Paul Kleppner, *The Cross of Culture: A Social Analysis of Midwestern Politics* (1970), and Richard Jensen, *The Winning of the Midwest: Social and Political Conflict, 1888–1896* (1971). The election of 1896 is examined in Robert F. Durden, *The Climax of Populism: The Election of 1896* (1965), and S. L. Jones, *The Presidential Election of 1896* (1964). Also informative are P. W. Glad, *McKinley, Bryan, and the People* (1964), and H. W. Morgan, *William McKinley and His America* (1963).

30

The Path of Empire

We assert that no nation can long endure half republic and half empire, and we warn the American people that imperialism abroad will lead quickly and inevitably to despotism at home.

Democratic National Platform, 1900

Faint Stirrings of Imperialism

A momentous shift in American foreign policy occurred in the sunset decades of the 19th Century. The new directions roughly paralleled the far-reaching changes that were taking place in manufacturing, agriculture, and the social structure. America was becoming increasingly outward-looking as exports shot up, both in manufactured goods and agricultural products.

Before the Civil War, the United States had adopted two basic foreign policies regarding Europe. One was the isolationist creed of non-involvement and non-entanglement in foreign broils. It meant, in brief, "We'll keep out." The other was the Monroe Doctrine, which meant basically, "You keep out"—that is, of the Americas. The Republic had warned the non-American powers to stay away, partly because it valued its freedom from European despots, and partly because it wanted to continue its expansive Manifest Destiny without hindrance. In addition to these basic policies, the nation had made some halting progress toward the arbitration of international disputes, especially those with powerful European nations that could not be easily or profitably fought.

The Civil War, with its violent dislocations, naturally affected foreign policy. A spirit of isolation continued with full vigor, while the Monroe Doctrine emerged with new laurels after the ejection of the French intruders from Mexico in 1867. But the once-potent impulse of Manifest Destiny was dead. Too much blood and treasure had gone down the drain of Civil War; too much energy and enterprise were being poured into Reconstruction, Indian fighting, railroad building, and other outlets. From the end of the Civil War to the 1880s, the indifference of most Americans to the outside world was almost unbelievable.

In 1881 James G. Blaine, the "spirited" secretary of state, brought a refreshing new outlook to American foreign policy. He had visions of expanding the nation's economic and diplomatic interests into the Far East, the Pacific, and especially Latin America. As a warm admirer of the pioneer Pan-Americanist Henry Clay, he issued invitations to the Latin American republics for the first great Pan-American conclave, to be held in Washington. But the bullet that killed President Garfield blasted Blaine's plans, and his stodgy successor in the State Department rather abruptly canceled the project.

Blaine had nevertheless cast his seeds on fertile ground. One of his successors in the State Department gradually began to see the light regarding the "Big Sister" policy. The United States again issued invitations for the first general meeting of its kind, and eighteen American republics sent delegates to Washington in 1889. By a curious turn of the wheel, Blaine returned as secretary of state under Harrison, just in time to shine in the role of host. words, the First Pan-American Conference was a sensational success. But the concrete results were meager. The frock-coated delegates did little more than open a crack in the door for economic cooperation through reciprocal tariff reduction. They also set up a clearinghouse for information, ultimately known as the Pan-American Union, and later housed in a Carnegie-given marble palace in Washington. But the Washington conference itself was a trail-blazing beginning—the first of a long and increasingly important series of inter-American assemblages.

Blaine's Belligerent Diplomacy

The rising new spirit in America manifested itself in a series of diplomatic crises or near-wars in the late 1880s and early 1890s.

Seals were the bone of contention with Britain. The United States had acquired with Alaska the two tiny Pribilof Islands, the breeding place of some 4 million fur seals. Sealskin coats were then fashionable, and Canadian seal poachers found it profitable to range off America's islands outside the 3-mile (4.83-kilometer) limit. There they reddened the water with the indiscriminate slaughter of the sleek mammals.

Drastic action was needed to save the seals from going the way of the buffalo. In the late 1880s, American revenue vessels boldly seized several Canadian sealing craft on the high seas. The Canadians and British reacted angrily against this viola-

In the quarrel with Britain over seals that were allegedly American, Secretary James G. ("Jingo Jim") Blaine used undiplomatic language in his formal protests. One finds such pronouncements as, "The law of the sea is not lawlessness" and "One step beyond that which Her Majesty's Government has taken in this controversy and piracy finds its justification."

PROTECTING THE SEALS
Hunters took cruel advantage of the seals' vulnerability during mating season. Male seals could then be clubbed to death on dry land, and females were easily netted or shot as they cruised the waters off the breeding grounds for food.

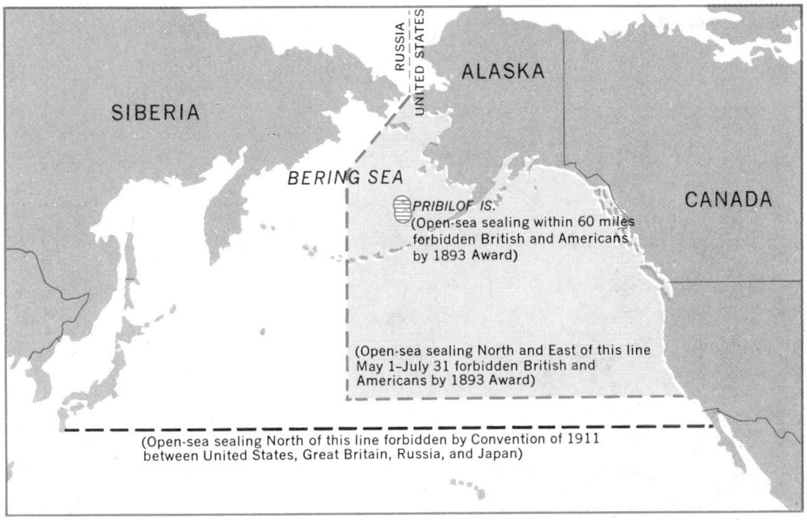

tion of freedom of the seas—ironically, a time-honored American principle.

Secretary Blaine, who inherited the quarrel, had a good ethical case but a poor legal one. Yet he strove energetically to persuade London that because the United States owned the breeding ground of the seals, it had some jurisdiction over the furry creatures outside the 3-mile (4.83-kilometer) line. The unrestrained slaughter, he also argued, was contrary to good public morals.

This dispute over seals was finally referred to an arbitral tribunal sitting at Paris in 1893. After due deliberation, the arbitrators decided every major legal point against the United States. But to safeguard the seals they set up a closed zone (which happened to be too small) and a closed season (which happened to be the wrong time of the year). The result was a resounding defeat for both the Americans and their seals, but something of a victory for international arbitration. The salvation of the disappearing herd was to come in 1911 by a different type of international agreement (p. 624)—a pioneering venture in saving "endangered species."

Other diplomatic controversies quickened the patriotic pulse. The United States skirted close to the brink of bloodshed with Germany in 1889, over the palm-shaded islands of Samoa. The Republic almost clashed with Italy in 1891, when eleven Italians were lynched in New Orleans, following a series of murders that seemed to point to the stiletto of the Sicilian Blackhanders. Diplomatic relations were severed; war impended. Ominously, the Italian navy, on paper at least, was much the stronger. But hostilities were happily averted when the United States, as a friendly gesture, agreed to pay $25,000 to Italy.

An even uglier clash in 1892 involved Chile. That string-bean-shaped republic had recently been convulsed by civil war, and the Washington government was accused of showing undue sympathy toward the faction that eventually lost. In an atmosphere of hostility, a party of sailors from an American warship, the *Baltimore,* was allowed shore leave at Valparaiso. A fight broke out in the True Blue saloon, and when order was restored, two American sailors were dead and nearly a score of others were injured. President Harrison, the aroused ex-soldier, made stern demands on Chile, and hostilities seemed inevitable. Alarm spread to the Pacific Coast of the United States, for Chile, as a Pacific naval power, boasted some formidable modern warships.

So enormous was the power of the United States, actual and potential, that Chile was finally forced to knuckle under and pay an indemnity of $75,000. The Chileans have never completely forgotten what to them was undue severity—using a sledgehammer to crush a butterfly. Although the ordinarily aggressive Blaine in this instance tried

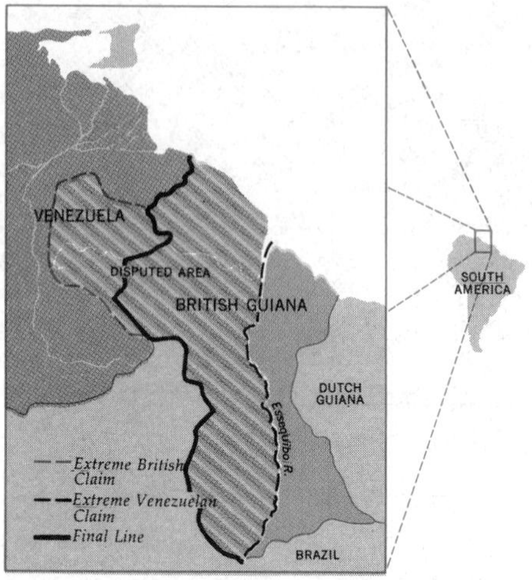

THE VENEZUELA–BRITISH GUIANA BOUNDARY DISPUTE

Secretary Olney's undiplomatic note to Britain read: "To-day the United States is practically sovereign on this continent, and its fiat is law upon the subjects to which it confines its interposition. . . . Its infinite resources combined with its isolated position render it master of the situation and practically invulnerable as against any or all other powers."

to restrain the anger of his chief, much of the goodwill he had so laboriously created at the recent Pan-American Conference went down the drain.

Monroe's Doctrine and the Venezuelan Squall

America's anti-British feeling, which periodically came to a head, flared forth ominously in 1895–1896 over Venezuela. For more than a half-century the jungle boundary between British Guiana and Venezuela had been in dispute. The Venezuelans, whose claims on the whole were extravagant, had repeatedly urged arbitration. But the prospect of a peaceful settlement faded when gold was discovered in the disputed area.

President Cleveland, a champion of righteousness and no lover of Britain, at length decided upon a strong protest. His no less pugnacious Secretary of State Olney was authorized to present to London a smashing note, which Cleveland later dubbed a "twenty-inch gun" blast. Olney declared in effect that the British, by attempting to dominate Venezuela in this quarrel and acquire more territory, were flouting the Monroe Doctrine. London should therefore submit the dispute to arbitration. Not content to stop here, Olney haughtily informed the number one naval power that the United States was now calling the tune in the Western Hemisphere.

British officials, unimpressed, took four months to prepare their reply. Preoccupied elsewhere, they were inclined to shrug off Olney's lengthy blast as just another twist of the Lion's tail designed to elicit cheers from Irish-American voters. When London's answer finally came, it flatly de-

The Real British Lion. A widespread American concept in the 1890s. (New York *Evening World*, 1895.)

nied the relevance of the Monroe Doctrine, while no less emphatically spurning arbitration. In short, the affair was none of America's business.

President Cleveland—"mad clear through," as he put it—sent a bristling special message to Congress. He urged an appropriation for a commission of experts, who would run the line where it ought to go. Then, he implied, if the British would not accept this rightful boundary, the United States would fight for it.

The entire country, irrespective of political party, was swept off its feet in an outburst of hysteria. War seemed inevitable, even though Britain had thirty-two warships of the battleship class to only five for America.

Fortunately, sober second thoughts prevailed on both sides of the Atlantic. The British, though vastly annoyed by their upstart cousins, had no real urge to fight. Canada was vulnerable to yet-to-be-raised American armies, and Britain's rich merchant marine was vulnerable to American commerce raiders. The European atmosphere was menacing, for Britain's traditional policy of "splendid isolation" was bringing insecure isolation. Russia and France were unfriendly; and Germany, under the saber-rattling Kaiser Wilhelm II, was about to challenge British naval supremacy.

The Venezuelan crisis had evidently passed its peak when the German Kaiser, blunderingly and unwittingly, increased chances of a peaceful solution. An unauthorized British raiding party of 600 armed men was captured by the Dutch-descended Boers in South Africa, and the Kaiser forthwith cabled his congratulations to the victors. Overnight, British anger against America was largely deflected to Germany. After further negotiations, London consented to arbitrate the Venezuelan dispute. The final decision, ironically, awarded the British the bulk of what they had claimed from the beginning.

America had skated close to the thin ice of a terrible war, but the results on the whole were favorable. The prestige of the Monroe Doctrine was immensely enhanced. Europe was irked by Cleveland's claim to domination in this hemisphere, and both Latin America and Canada were somewhat alarmed. But he had made his claim stick. Many Latin American republics were pleased by the determination of the United States to protect them, and when Cleveland died in 1908, some of them lowered their flags to half-mast.

"The World's Plunderers."
(Thomas Nast, *Harper's Weekly,* 1885.)

The chastened British, their eyes fully opened to the European peril, were now determined to cultivate Yankee friendship. They inaugurated an era of "patting the Eagle's head," which replaced a century or so of America's "twisting the Lion's tail." Growing numbers of Englishmen were willing to heed Alfred Lord Tennyson's earlier injunction:

> Be proud of those strong sons of thine
> Who wrench'd their rights from thee!

Inspiring the New Manifest Destiny

A heady new spirit of Manifest Destiny had begun to surge through American veins by the early 1890s. A reconstructed South was rising again;

and the nominal closing of the frontier indicated that old energies would have to be diverted into different channels. America was bursting with a sense of power generated by the vast increase in her population, wealth, and industrial productivity. "Expand or explode" was accepted as an elemental law, and many manufacturers were seeking new overseas markets for the contents of their bulging warehouses.

Other forces were stimulating overseas expansion. The lurid yellow press of Joseph Pulitzer and William R. Hearst was whetting the popular taste for excitement. The missionary-conscious churches were on the lookout for new overseas vineyards to till. Outward-looking advocates of a "large policy" were interpreting Darwinism to mean that the earth belonged to the energetic, the strong, the fit—that is, to the virile Americans. Jingoes, including the fight-thirsty young Theodore Roosevelt and the scholarly Congressman Henry Cabot Lodge, were whooping it up for expansion and, if need be, war.

A new steel navy was being pushed with vigor. It found a potent ally in the pen of Captain Alfred T. Mahan, who in 1890 published *The Influence of Sea Power upon History, 1660–1783.* His basic theme was that the twin prizes of victory and world dominion went to those nations that won and retained control of the sea—findings that were avidly read by Englishmen, Germans, and Japanese. Mahan thus unwittingly stimulated the fateful naval race that gained momentum at the turn of the century.

In the United States, the gospel according to Mahan eventually shaped the thinking of many large-minded Americans, especially those who perceived that overseas colonies would require naval protection. They came to believe that naval power and world power were Siamese twins. Red-blooded citizens redoubled their agitation for a mightier navy, while demanding an American-built Isthmian canal that could shuttle the nation's warships from the Atlantic to the Pacific and back.

New great-power alignments were jelling. Germany was emerging as the colossus of Europe, and as a latecomer in the colonial scramble was scooping up leavings from the banquet table of earlier diners. Japan's debut as a world power came when she gave anemic China a bad beating during 1894–1895, thereby exposing the weakness of the Chinese Empire to a predatory world. In 1898 the Germans, responding to a global spirit of grab, extorted a valuable leasehold from China at Shantung; and in the same year the Russians followed suit at Port Arthur.

A dangerous spirit of bellicosity stirred America by 1898. People craved new sensations, for many were bored with threadbare issues like the tariff and free silver. The nation had not fought a rousing war for over thirty years, and a restless younger generation was envious of the Civil War veterans, with their idealized tales of "tenting on the old camp ground."

War scares with Germany, Italy, Chile, and Britain had whetted the national appetite, while leaving it frustrated. If America was going to show the world that she was "some pumpkins," she might have to fight somebody. If she was going to play the colonial game, she would have to acquire overseas real estate, as the other powers were doing. The upsurge of the new Manifest Destiny became as irresistible as that of the old Manifest Destiny in the 1840s and 1850s.

Three-Power Schemings in Samoa

The broad-bosomed Pacific Ocean witnessed some of the first manifestations of the new Manifest Destiny. As early as 1878, the United States had secured rights to a naval base in Samoa, at the harbor of Pago Pago, where American sailors and whalers had found relaxation and refreshment of various kinds. Britain and Germany also became covetously interested in this idyllic archipelago; and Britons, Germans, and Americans frantically intrigued with the natives for commercial and strategic control.

Tension mounted to the breaking point between the Germans and Americans. On a memorable

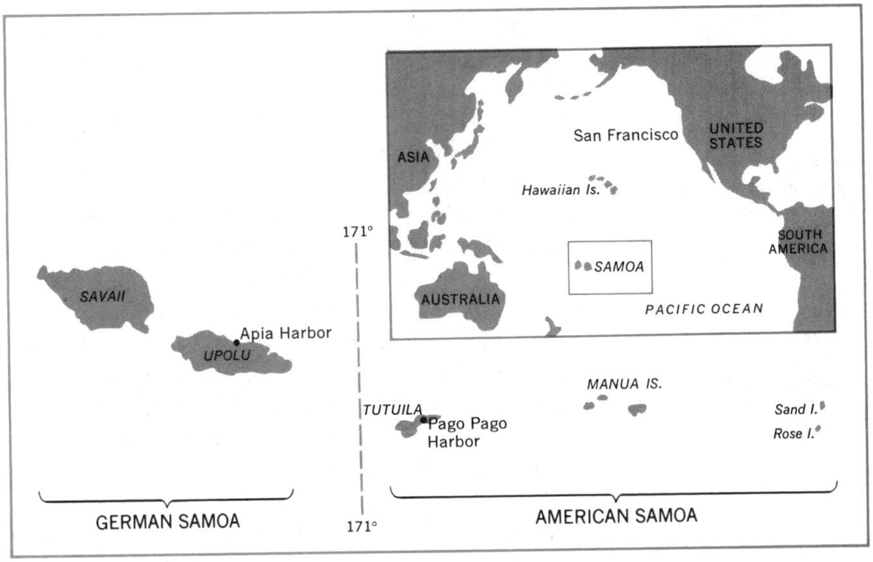

SAMOA, 1899
The location of Samoa in the Pacific Ocean is shown in the inserted small-scale map.

day in 1889, the crews of three German and three American men-of-war were glowering at each other over loaded guns. Hostilities might well have started then and there had not a frightful hurricane wrecked all six warships in Apia harbor, as the one British warship made it out to sea.

Stiffly bowing diplomats meanwhile had gathered at the Berlin Conference, meeting in the spring of 1889. Discussions went forward under the direction of the imperious Prince Bismarck, with the no less imperious Secretary Blaine cabling instructions from Washington to the American delegates. The solution finally adopted was a clumsy three-way protectorate, operated jointly by the Americans, Germans, and British. This awkward arrangement naturally drew wide criticism in America as a reckless departure from the non-entanglement warnings of the Founding Fathers.

The Samoan sequel was the familiar story of too many cooks overheating the broth. In 1899, ten years later, the islands were divided outright between Germany and America, with Britain being granted compensation elsewhere. A new mood was evidently coming over the American people when they were prepared to risk entanglement—even war—over these faraway islands.

Spurning the Hawaiian Pear

Enchanted Hawaii had early attracted the attention of Americans. In the morning years of the 19th Century, the breeze-brushed islands were a way station and provisioning point for Yankee shippers, sailors, and whalers. In 1820 came the first New England missionaries, who preached the twin blessings of Protestant Christianity and protective calico. They came to do good—and did well; their sons did even better. In some respects Honolulu took on the earmarks of a typical New England town.

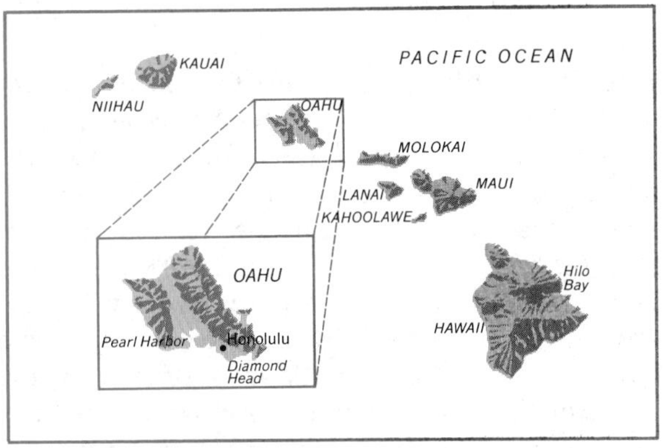

THE HAWAIIAN ISLANDS

Queen Liliuokalani (1838–1917). She was the last reigning Queen of Hawaii, whose opposition to reforms led to her dethronement. She wrote many songs, the most famous of which was *Aloha Oe* or *Farewell to Thee,* played countless times by Hawaiian bands for departing tourists. (Hawaii Public Archives.)

Americans gradually came to regard the Hawaiian Islands as a virtual extension of their own coastline. The State Department, beginning in the 1840s, sternly warned other powers to keep their grasping hands off. America's grip was further tightened in 1875 by a commercial reciprocity agreement, and in 1887 by a treaty with the native government guaranteeing priceless naval-base rights at spacious Pearl Harbor.

But trouble, both economic and political, was brewing in the languid insular paradise. Sugar culture, which had become immensely profitable, went somewhat sour in 1890 when the McKinley Tariff erected barriers against the Hawaiian product. White planters, mostly Americans, were further alarmed by the increasingly autocratic tendencies of dusky Queen Liliuokalani, who insisted that native Hawaiians should control Hawaii. Desperate whites, though only a tiny minority, organized a successful revolt early in 1893. It was openly assisted by American troops, who landed under the unauthorized orders of the expansionist American minister in Honolulu. "The Hawaiian pear is now fully ripe," he wrote exultantly to his superiors in Washington, "and this is the golden hour for the United States to pluck it."

Hawaii, like Texas of earlier years, seemed ready for annexation—at least in the eyes of the ruling American whites. An appropriate treaty was rushed to Washington. But before it could be railroaded through the Senate, the Republican President Harrison's term expired and the Democratic President Cleveland came in. "Old Grover," who set great store by "national honesty," suspected that his powerful nation had gravely wronged the deposed Queen Liliuokalani.

Cleveland abruptly withdrew the treaty from the Senate early in 1893 and then sent a special investigator to Hawaii. The subsequent probe revealed the damning fact that a majority of the Hawaiian natives did not favor annexation at all. But the white revolutionists were firmly in the saddle and Cleveland could not unhorse them without using armed force—a step which American public opinion would never have tolerated. Although the Queen could not be reinstated, the sugar-coated move for annexation had to be abandoned temporarily—until 1898.

The question of annexing Hawaii touched off the first full-fledged imperialistic debate in American experience. Cleveland was savagely criticized for trying to stem the New Manifest Destiny, and a popular jingle ran:

> . . . Liliuokalani,
> Give us your little brown hannie.

But Cleveland's motives, in a day of international land grabbing, were honorable both to himself and to his country. The Hawaiian pear continued to ripen for five more years.

Revolt in the Cuban Pesthouse

Cuba's masses, frightfully misgoverned, again rose against their Spanish oppressor in 1895. The roots of their revolt were partly economic, with partial origins in the United States. Sugar production—backbone of the island's prosperity—was crippled when the American tariff of 1894 restored high duties on the toothsome product.

Driven to desperation, the insurgents adopted a scorched-earth policy. They reasoned that if they did enough damage, Spain might be willing to move out. Or the United States might move in and help the Cubans win their independence. In pursuance of this destructive strategy, the *insurrectos* put the torch to cane fields and sugar mills; they even dynamited passenger trains.

American sympathies, ever on the side of patriots fighting for freedom, went out to the Cuban underdogs. Aside from pure sentiment, the United States had an investment stake of about $50 million in Cuba, and an annual trade stake of about $100 million. Moreover, Spanish misrule in Cuba menaced the shipping routes of the West Indies and the Gulf, and less directly the future Isthmian canal.

Fuel was added to the Cuban conflagration in 1896 with the coming of the Spanish General ("Butcher") Weyler. He undertook to crush the rebellion by herding many civilians into barbed-wire reconcentration camps, where they could not give assistance to the armed *insurrectos*. Lacking proper sanitation, these enclosures turned into deadly pestholes, in which the victims died like flies.

An outraged American public demanded action. Congress in 1896 overwhelmingly passed a resolution which called upon President Cleveland to recognize the belligerency of the revolted Cubans. But as the government of the insurgents consisted of hardly more than a few fugitive leaders under palm trees, Cleveland—an anti-jingoist and anti-imperialist—refused to budge. He defiantly remarked that if Congress declared war he would not, as commander-in-chief, issue the necessary order to mobilize the army.

The Mystery of the *Maine* Explosion

Atrocities in Cuba were made to order for the sensational new "yellow journalism." William R. Hearst and Joseph Pulitzer, then engaged in a titanic duel for circulation, attempted to outdo each other with screeching headlines and hair-raising "scoops." Lesser competitors zestfully followed suit.

Where atrocity stories did not exist, they were invented. Hearst sent the gifted artist Frederic Remington to Cuba to draw sketches, and when the latter reported that conditions were not bad enough to warrant hostilities, Hearst is alleged to have replied, "You furnish the pictures and I'll furnish the war." Among other outrages, Remington depicted Spanish customs officials brutally disrobing and searching an American woman. Most readers of Hearst's *Journal*, their indignation soaring, had no way of knowing that such tasks were performed by female attendants.

"Butcher" Weyler was removed in 1897, yet conditions steadily worsened. There was some talk in Spain of granting the restive island a type of self-government, but such a surrender was so bitterly opposed by many Spaniards in Cuba that they engaged in furious riots. Early in 1898 Washington sent the battleship *Maine* to Cuba, ostensibly for a "friendly visit" but actually to

Remington's Disrobing Propaganda. (New York *Journal*, 1897.)

protect and evacuate Americans if a dangerous flare-up should again occur.

This already explosive situation suddenly grew acute, on February 9, 1898, when Hearst sensationally headlined a private letter written by the Spanish minister in Washington, Dupuy de Lôme. The indiscreet epistle, which had been stolen from the mails, described President McKinley as an ear-to-the-ground politician who lacked good faith. The resulting uproar was so violent that de Lôme was forced to resign.

A tragic climax came a few days later, on February 15, 1898, when the *Maine* mysteriously blew up in Havana harbor, with a loss of 260 officers and men. Two investigations of the iron coffin were undertaken, one by United States naval officers, the other by Spanish officials, whom the Americans would not trust near the wreck. The Spanish commission announced that the explosion had been internal and presumably accidental; the American commission reported that the blast had been caused by a submarine mine. Washington, not unmindful of popular indignation, spurned Spanish proposals of arbitration.

The Spanish Brute. (From *Judge*.)

> Many Spaniards felt that accusations about their blowing up the *Maine* reflected on Spanish honor. One Madrid newspaper spoke up: "The American jingoes . . . imagine us capable of the most foul villainies and cowardly actions. Scoundrels by nature, the American jingoes believe that all men are made like themselves. What do they know about noble and generous feelings? . . . We should not in any way heed the jingoes: they are not even worth our contempt, or the saliva with which we might honor them in spitting at their faces."

Various theories have been advanced as to how the *Maine* was blown up. The least convincing explanation of all is that the Spanish officials in Cuba were guilty, for they were under the American gun, and Spain was far away. Not until 1976 did Admiral H. G. Rickover, under U.S. navy auspices, give what appears to be the final answer. He presented overwhelming evidence that the initial explosion had resulted from spontaneous combustion in one of the coal bunkers adjacent to a powder magazine. Ironically, this is essentially what the Spanish commission had concluded in 1898.

Red-blooded Americans, now war-mad, blindly accepted the least likely explanation. Lashed to fury by the yellow press, they leaped to the conclusion that the Spanish government had been guilty of intolerable treachery. The battle cry of the hour became:

> Remember the *Maine!*
> To hell with Spain!

Nothing would do but to hurl the "dirty" Bourbon flag from the hemisphere.

McKinley Unleashes the Dogs of War

A popular belief that professional diplomats cause wars is not borne out by the events of 1898. American negotiators, by patient persuasion, had induced the Madrid authorities to yield to the first two of Washington's basic demands, namely a revocation of reconcentration and an armistice in Cuba with the rebels.

But the American public was on fire for war, and the Cubans probably would have continued fighting. The cautious Chief Executive was condemned by jingoes as "Wobbly Willie" McKinley, while fight-hungry Theodore Roosevelt reportedly snarled that the "white-livered" occupant of the White House did not have "the backbone of a chocolate éclair." The President, whose shaken nerves required sleeping pills, was even being hanged in effigy. Many critics did not realize that backbone was needed to stay out of war, not to plunge into it.

McKinley's private desires clashed sharply with the public demands of the people. He did not want hostilities, for he had seen enough bloodshed as a major in the Civil War. Mark Hanna and Wall Street did not want war, for business might be unsettled. But a frenzied public, prodded by the yellow press, clamored for war to free the abused Cubans. The President, recognizing the inevitable, finally yielded and gave the people what they wanted.

But public pressures did not fully explain McKinley's course. He had no faith in Spain's promises regarding Cuba; she had made them and broken them before. He was certain that there would have to be a showdown sooner or later. He believed in the democratic principle that the people should rule, and he hesitated to deny the American masses what they demanded—even if it was not good for them. He also perceived that if he stood out against war, the Democrats would make political capital out of his stubbornness. Bryan might sweep into the presidency two years later under a banner inscribed "Free Cuba and Free Silver." The gold-standard McKinley was a staunch party man, and to him it seemed better to break up the remnants of Spain's once-glorious empire than to break up the Grand Old Party—especially since war seemed inevitable.

On April 11, 1898, McKinley sent his war message to Congress, urging armed intervention to free the oppressed Cubans. The legislators responded uproariously with what was essentially a declaration of war. In a burst of self-righteousness, they likewise adopted the hand-tying Teller Amendment. This proviso proclaimed to the world that when America had overthrown Spanish misrule, she would give the Cubans their freedom—a declaration that caused imperialistic Europeans to smile skeptically.

President William McKinley (1843–1901). Traditionally regarded as a pliant tool of Mark Hanna and Republican big business, he is now rated by historians as a reasonably able President. He was notably considerate toward his long-ailing wife, who suffered embarrassing seizures at state dinners. He would graciously cover her contorted face with a handkerchief. (Library of Congress)

Dewey's May Day Victory at Manila

The American people plunged into the war lightheartedly, like school children off to a picnic. Bands blared incessantly "There'll Be a Hot Time in the Old Town Tonight" and "Hail, Hail, the Gang's All Here," thus leading foreigners to believe that those were national anthems.

But such jubilation seemed premature to European observers. The regular army, commanded by corpulent Civil War oldsters, was unprepared for a war under tropical skies. It numbered only 2,100 officers and 28,000 men, as compared with some 200,000 Spanish troops in Cuba. The American navy, at least to transatlantic experts, seemed slightly less powerful than Spain's. European powers, moreover, were generally friendly to their Old World associate. The only conspicuous exception was the ally-seeking British, who were ardently wooing their giant daughter in the west.

Yet in one important respect Spain's apparent superiority was illusory. Her navy, though formidable on paper, was in wretched condition. It labored under the added handicap of having to operate thousands of miles from its home base. But the new American steel navy, now fifteen years old and ranking about fifth among the fleets of the world, was in fairly good trim, though the war was to lay bare serious defects.

The readiness of the navy owed much to two men: the easygoing Secretary Long and his bellicose subordinate, Assistant Secretary Theodore Roosevelt. The secretary hardly dared leave his desk for fear that his overzealous underling would stir up a hornet's nest. On February 25, 1898, while Long was away for a weekend, Roosevelt had cabled Commodore George Dewey, commanding the American Asiatic Squadron at Hong Kong, to descend upon Spain's Philippines in the event of war. McKinley subsequently confirmed these instructions, even though an attack in the faraway Far East seemed like a strange way to free nearby Cuba.

Dewey carried out his orders magnificently on May 1, 1898. Sailing boldly with his six warships at night into the fortified harbor of Manila, he trained his guns the next morning on the ten-ship Spanish fleet, one of whose craft was only a moored hulk without functioning engines. The entire collection of antiquated and overmatched vessels was quickly destroyed, with a loss of nearly 400 Spaniards killed and wounded, and without the loss of a single life in Dewey's fleet. An American consul who was there wrote that all the American sailors needed was cough drops for throats made raw by cheers of victory.

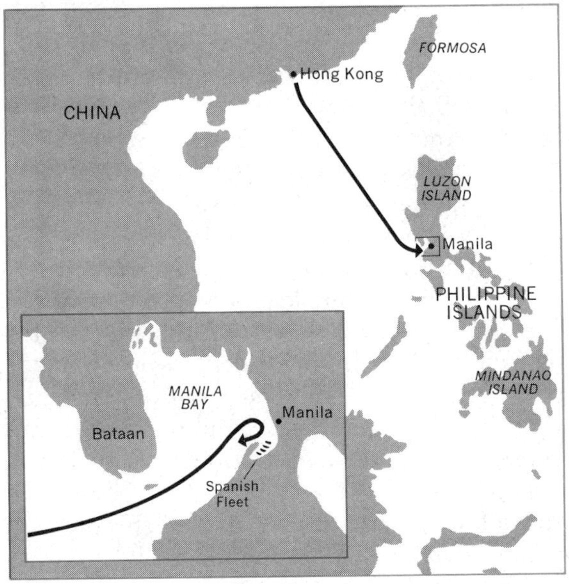

DEWEY'S ROUTE IN THE PHILIPPINES, 1898

Unexpected Imperialistic Plums

George Dewey, quiet and taciturn, became a national hero overnight. He was promptly promoted to the rank of admiral, as the price of flags rose sharply. An amateur poet blossomed forth with:

> Oh, dewy was the morning
> Upon the first of May,
> And Dewey was the Admiral,
> Down in Manila Bay.
> And dewy were the Spaniards' eyes,
> Them orbs of black and blue;
> And dew we feel discouraged?
> I dew not think we dew!

Yet Dewey was in a perilous position. He had destroyed the enemy fleet, but he could not storm the forts of Manila with his sailors. His nerves frayed, he was forced to wait in the steaming-hot bay while troop reinforcements were slowly assembled in America.

Foreign warships meanwhile had begun to gather in the harbor, ostensibly to safeguard their nationals in Manila. The Germans sent five vessels—a naval force more powerful than Dewey's—and their haughty admiral defied the American blockade regulations. After several disagreeable incidents, Dewey lost his temper and threatened the arrogant German with war "as soon as you like." Happily, the storm blew over. The British commander, by contrast, was conspicuously successful in carrying out London's new policy of friendliness. A false tale consequently spread that the British dramatically interposed their ships to prevent the Germans from blowing the Americans out of the water.

Long-awaited American troops, finally arriving in force, captured Manila on August 13, 1898. They collaborated with the Filipino insurgents, commanded by their well-educated, part-Chinese leader, Emilio Aguinaldo. Dewey, to his later regret, had brought this shrewd and magnetic revolutionist from exile in Asia, so that he might weaken Spanish resistance.

These thrilling events in the Philippines had meanwhile focused attention on Hawaii. An impression spread that America needed the archipelago as a coaling and provisioning way station, in order to send supplies and reinforcements to Dewey. The truth is that the United States could have used these island "Crossroads of the Pacific" without annexing them, so eager was the white-dominated Honolulu government to compromise its neutrality and risk the vengeance of Spain. But an appreciative American public would not leave Dewey in the lurch. A joint resolution of annexation was rushed through Congress and approved by McKinley on July 7, 1898.

The residents of Hawaii, granted American citizenship with annexation, received full territorial status in 1900. These events in the idyllic islands, though seemingly sudden, were but the culmination of nearly a century of Americanization by sailors, whalers, traders, and missionaries.

Emilio Aguinaldo (c. 1869–1964). Leader of the Philippine insurrection against American rule, Aguinaldo never became completely reconciled. After all his brushes with death, he died in Manila in 1964 in his ninety-fifth year.

The Confused Invasion of Cuba

Shortly after the outbreak of war, the Spanish government ordered a fleet of warships to Cuba. It was commanded by Admiral Cervera, who protested that his wretchedly prepared ships would court suicide. Four armored cruisers finally set forth (one without its main battery of guns), accompanied by six torpedo boats, three of which had to be abandoned en route.

Panic seized the Eastern seaboard of the United States, even though Cervera would obviously have to stop at a West Indian port to replenish his coal supply. American vacationers abandoned their seashore cottages, while nervous investors moved their securities to inland depositories. Demands for protection poured in on Washington from nervous citizens, and the Navy Department was forced to detach some useless old Civil War ships to useless places for morale purposes. (The power of a panicky and ignorant public opinion is a fearsome thing, and if Spain had been stronger the results could have been disastrous.) Cervera finally found refuge in bottle-shaped Santiago harbor, Cuba, where he was blockaded by the much more powerful American fleet.

Sound strategy seemed to dictate that an American army be sent in from the rear to drive out Cervera. Command of the invading force was entrusted to the grossly overweight General William R. Shafter, a leader so blubbery and gout-stricken that he had to be carried about on a door. The ill-prepared American conquerors were unequipped for war in the tropics, though amply provided with heavy woolen underwear and uniforms designed for sub-zero operations against the Indians.

The "Rough Riders," a part of the invading army, now charged onto the stage of history. This colorful regiment of volunteers, short on discipline but long on dash, consisted largely of Western cowboys and other hardy characters, with a sprinkling of ex-polo players and ex-convicts. Commanded by Colonel Leonard Wood, the group was organized principally by the glory-hungry Roosevelt, who had resigned from the Navy Department to serve as lieutenant colonel. Though totally without military experience, he used his strong political "pull" to secure his commission and to bypass physical standards. He was so near-sighted that as a safeguard he took along a dozen pairs of spectacles, cached in handy spots on his person or nearby.

> With a mixture of modesty and immodesty, Colonel Roosevelt wrote privately in 1903 of his "Rough Riders": "In my regiment nine-tenths of the men were better horsemen than I was, and probably two-thirds of them better shots than I was, while on the average they were certainly hardier and more enduring. Yet after I had had them a very short while they all knew, and I knew too, that nobody else could command them as I could."

About the middle of June a bewildered American army of 17,000 men finally embarked at congested Tampa, Florida, amid scenes of inde-

Colonel Theodore Roosevelt with Some of the "Rough Riders." Roosevelt later described his first encounter with the Spanish enemy: "Soon we came to the brink of a deep valley. There was a good deal of cracking of rifles way off in front of us, but as they used smokeless powder we had no idea as to exactly where they were, or who they were shooting at. Then it dawned on us that we were the target. The bullets began to come overhead, making a sound like the ripping of a silk dress, with sometimes a kind of pop. . . . We advanced, firing at them, and drove them off." (Library of Congress.)

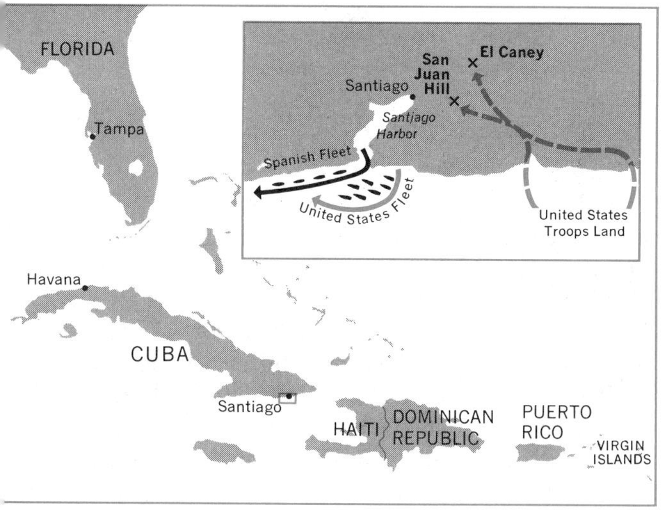

THE CUBAN CAMPAIGN, 1898

scribable confusion. The "Rough Riders," fearing that they would be robbed of glory, rushed one of the transports, and courageously held their place for almost a week in the broiling sun. About half of them finally got to Cuba without most of their horses, and the bowlegged regiment then came to be known as "Wood's Weary Walkers."

Shafter's landing near Santiago, Cuba, was made without serious opposition. Defending Spaniards, even more disorganized than the Americans, were unable to muster at this spot more than 2,000 men. Brisk fighting broke out on July 1 at El Caney and San Juan Hill, up which Colonel Roosevelt and his horseless "Rough Riders" charged, with strong support from two crack black regiments. They suffered heavy casualties, but the colorful colonel, having the time of his life, shot a Spaniard with his revolver, and rejoiced to see his victim double up like a jack rabbit. He later wrote a book on his exploits which, "Mr. Dooley" remarked, ought to have been entitled *Alone in Cubia* [*sic*].

Curtains for Spain in America

The American army, fast closing in on Santiago, spelled doom for the Spanish fleet. Admiral Cervera, again protesting against suicide, was flatly ordered to fight for the honor of the flag. The odds against him were heavy: the guns of the U.S.S. *Oregon* alone threw more metal than his four armored cruisers combined. After a running chase, on July 3, the foul-bottomed Spanish fleet was entirely destroyed, as the wooden decks caught fire and the blazing infernos were beached. About 500 Spaniards were killed, as compared with 1 for the Americans. "Don't cheer, men," admonished Captain Philip of the *Texas*, "the poor devils are dying." Shortly thereafter Santiago surrendered.

Hasty preparations were now made for a descent upon Puerto Rico before the war should end. The American army, commanded by the famed Indian-fighter General Nelson A. Miles, met little resistance, as most of the population greeted the invaders as liberating heroes. "Mr. Dooley" was led to refer to "Gin'ral Miles' Gran' Picnic an' Moonlight Excursion." By this time Spain had satisfied her honor and, on August 12, 1898, she signed an armistice.

If the Spaniards had held out a few months longer in Cuba, the American army might have melted away. The inroads of malaria, typhoid, dysentery, and yellow fever became so severe that hundreds were incapacitated—"an army of convalescents." Others suffered from odorous canned meat known as "embalmed beef." Fiery and insubordinate Colonel Roosevelt, who had no regular military career to jeopardize, was a ringleader in making "round robin"* demands on Washington that the army be moved before it perished. About 25,000 men, 80 percent of them ill, were transferred to chilly Long Island, where the light summer clothing finally arrived.

One of the worst scandals of the war was the high death rate from sickness, especially typhoid fever. This disease was rampant in the unsanitary training camps located in the United States. All told, nearly 400 men lost their lives to bullets; over 5,000, to bacteria and other causes.

* A "round robin" is signed in circular form around the edges of a document so that no one person can be punished as the first signer.

The "round robin" that Colonel Roosevelt and seven fellow officers signed read in part: "We . . . are of the unanimous opinion . . . that the army is disabled by malarial fever to the extent that its efficiency is destroyed, and that it is in a condition to be practically entirely destroyed by an epidemic of yellow fever. . . . The army must be moved at once, or perish. As the army can be safely moved now, the persons responsible for preventing such a move will be responsible for the unnecessary loss of many thousands of lives."

A "goat" had to be found, even though the American people themselves were basically to blame for the ineptitudes and blunders. They had insisted on plunging into war without adequate preparations. The victim of their wrath proved to be Secretary of War Alger, a wealthy lumberman, whom McKinley was finally forced to dismiss. He might have ranked as a competent secretary of war—if there had been no war.

McKinley Heeds Duty, Destiny, and Dollars

Late in 1898 the Spanish and American negotiators met in Paris, there to begin heated discussions. McKinley had sent five commissioners, including three senators, who would have a final vote on their own handiwork. War-racked Cuba, as expected, was freed from her Spanish overlords. The Americans had little difficulty in securing the remote Pacific island of Guam, which they had captured early in the conflict from astonished Spaniards who, lacking a cable, had not known that a war was on. They also picked up Puerto Rico, the last crumb of Spain's once magnificent American empire. It was to prove a difficult morsel for Uncle Sam to digest.

Knottiest of all was the problem of the Philippines, a veritable apple of discord. These lush islands not only embraced an area larger than the British Isles but contained a completely alien population of some 7 million souls. McKinley was confronted with a devil's dilemma. He did not feel that America could honorably give the islands back to Spanish misrule, especially after it had fought a war to free Cuba. And America would be turning its back upon its responsibilities in a cowardly fashion, he believed, if it simply pulled up anchor and sailed away.

Other alternatives open to McKinley were trouble-fraught. The ill-prepared native Filipinos, if left to govern themselves, might fall into anarchy. One of the major powers might then try to seize them, possibly aggressive Germany, and the result might be a world war into which the United States would be sucked. Seemingly the least of the evils consistent with national honor and safety was to acquire all the Philippines, and then perhaps give "the little brown brothers" their freedom later.

President McKinley, ever sensitive to public opinion, kept a carefully attuned ear to the ground. The rumble that he heard seemed to call for the entire group of islands. Zealous Protestant missionaries were eager for new converts from Spanish Catholicism*; and the invalid Mrs. McKinley, to whom her husband was devoted, expressed deep concern about the welfare of the Filipinos. Wall Street had generally opposed the war; but awakened by the booming of Dewey's guns, it was clamoring for profits in the Philippines. "If this be commercialism," cried Mark Hanna, then "for God's sake let us have commercialism."

A tormented McKinley, so he was later reported as saying, finally went down on his knees seeking divine guidance. An inner voice seemed to tell him to take all the Philippines and Christianize and civilize them. This solution apparently coincided with the demands of the American people as well as with the McKinley-Hanna outlook. The mixture of things spiritual and material in McKinley's reasoning was later slyly summarized by

* The Philippines were substantially Christianized by Catholics before the founding of Jamestown in 1607.

Uncle Sam's White Elephant.
(New York *Herald,* 1898.)

an historian: "God directs us—perhaps it will pay." Profits thus joined hands with piety.

Fresh disputes broke out with the Spanish negotiators in Paris, once McKinley had reached the thorny decision to keep the Philippines. Manila had been captured the day *after* the armistice was signed, and the islands could not properly be listed among the spoils of war. The deadlock was broken when the Americans at length agreed to pay Spain $20 million for this Philippine liability—one of the best bargains the Spaniards ever drove and their last great haul from the New World. Ex-Speaker "Czar" Reed sneered at America's having acquired millions of Malays, at three dollars a head, "in the bush."

America's Course (Curse?) of Empire

The signing of the pact of Paris—a trouble-fraught document—touched off one of the most impassioned debates of American history. Except for glacial Alaska and coral-reefed Hawaii, the Republic had hitherto acquired only contiguous territory on the continent. All previous acquisitions had been thinly peopled and capable of ultimate statehood. But in the Philippines the nation had on its hands a distant tropical area, thickly populated by Asiatics of alien race, tongue, religion, and governmental institutions.

An Anti-Imperialist League sprang into being to fight the McKinley administration's expansionist moves. The organization included some of the most prominent people in America, including the presidents of Stanford and Harvard Universities, the philosopher William James, and the novelist Mark Twain. The anti-imperialist blanket even stretched over such strange bedfellows as the labor leader Samuel Gompers and the steel titan Andrew Carnegie. "Goddamn the United States for its vile conduct in the Philippine Isles!" burst out the usually mild-mannered Professor James. The Harvard philosopher could not believe that America could "puke up its ancient soul in five minutes without a wink of squeamishness."

Anti-imperialists had still other arrows in their quiver. The Filipinos panted for freedom; and to annex them would violate the "consent of the governed" philosophy in the Declaration of Independence. Despotism abroad might well beget despotism at home. Finally, annexation would propel the United States into the political and military cauldron of the Far East.

Yet the expansionists or imperialists could sing a seductive song. They appealed to patriotism and to the glory of annexation—"don't let any dastard dishonor the flag by hauling it down." Stressing the opportunities for exploiting the islands, they played up possible trade profits. Manila, in fact, might become another Hong Kong. The richer the natural resources of the islands appeared to be, the less capable of self-government the Filipinos seemed to be. Rudyard Kipling, the British poet laureate of imperialism, urged America down the slippery path:

> Take up the White Man's burden—
> Ye dare not stoop to less—
> Nor call too loud on Freedom
> To cloak your weariness.

In short, the wealthy Americans must help to uplift (and exploit) the underprivileged, underfed, and underclad of the world.

In the Senate the Spanish treaty ran into such heated opposition that it seemed doomed to de-

The Expansion Rooster. (San Francisco *Chronicle*, 1900.)

feat. But at this juncture the silverite Bryan unexpectedly sallied forth as its champion. As a Democratic volunteer colonel whom the Republicans had kept out of Cuba, he apparently had no reason to help the McKinley administration out of a hole. But free silver was dead as a political issue. Bryan's foes assumed that he was preparing to fasten the stigma of imperialism on the Republicans, and then to sweep into the presidency in 1900 under the flaming banner of anti-imperialism.

Bryan could support the treaty on plausible grounds. He argued that the war would not officially end until America had ratified the pact. She already had the islands on her hands, and the sooner she accepted the document, the sooner she could give the Filipinos their independence. After Byran had used his personal influence with certain Democratic senators, the treaty was approved, on February 6, 1899, with only one vote to spare. But the responsibility, as Bryan had foreseen, rested primarily on the Republicans.

Perplexities in Puerto Rico and Cuba

Puerto Rico was a poverty-stricken island, the fertility of whose million inhabitants, including many blacks, outran that of their soil. By the Foraker Act of 1900 Congress accorded the Puerto Ricans a limited degree of popular government, and in 1917 granted them United States citizenship. Although the American regime worked wonders in education, sanitation, good roads, and other physical improvements, many of the inhabitants continued to clamor for independence. Many ultimately moved to New York City, where they added to the complexity of the melting pot.

A thorny legal problem was posed by the question: Did the Constitution follow the flag? Did American laws, including tariff laws, apply with full force to the newly acquired possessions, chiefly the Philippines and Puerto Rico? Beginning in 1901 with the Insular Cases, a badly divided Supreme Court decreed in effect that the flag outran the Constitution, and that the outdistanced document did not necessarily extend with full force to the new windfalls. Congress was thus left with a free hand to determine the degree of applicability. The Court had apparently modified its views somewhat under the pressure of public opinion as expressed in the presidential election of 1900. This shift led "Mr. Dooley" to quip that whether the Constitution followed the flag or not, the Supreme Court followed the "iliction returns."

Cuba, scorched and chaotic, presented another headache. An American military government, set up under the administrative genius of General Leonard Wood of Rough Rider fame, wrought miracles in government, finance, education, agriculture, and public health. Under his leadership a frontal attack was launched on yellow fever. Spectacular experiments were performed by Dr.

Uncle Sam: "By Gum, I Rather Like Your Looks." (Denver *Rocky Mountain News,* 1900.)

General Wood Cleans Up Cuba.
(Minneapolis *Tribune*, 1899.)

Walter Reed and others upon American soldiers, who volunteered as human guinea pigs; and the stegomyia mosquito was proved to be the lethal carrier. A cleanup of breeding places for mosquitoes wiped out yellow fever in Havana, while removing the recurrent fear of epidemics in cities of the South and the Atlantic seaboard.

The United States, honoring its self-denying Teller Amendment of 1898, withdrew from Cuba in 1902. Old World imperialists could scarcely believe their eyes. But the Washington government could not turn this rich and strategic island completely loose on the international sea; a grasping power like Germany might secure dangerous lodgment near America's soft underbelly. The Cubans were therefore forced to write into their own Constitution of 1901 the so-called Platt Amendment.

The hated restriction placed a severe hobble on the Cubans. They bound themselves not to impair their independence by treaty, or by contracting a debt beyond their resources. They further agreed that the United States might intervene with troops to restore order and to provide mutual protection. Finally, they promised to sell or lease needed coaling or naval stations, ultimately two and then only one (Guantánamo), to their powerful "benefactor." The United States is still there on about 28,000 acres under an agreement that can be revoked only by the consent of both parties.

New Horizons in Two Hemispheres

In essence the Spanish-American War was a kind of gigantic coming-out party. Despite a common misconception, the conflict did not cause the United States to become a world power. Dewey's thundering guns merely advertised the fact that the nation was already a world power.

The war itself was short (113 days), spectacular, low in casualties, and uninterruptedly successful—despite the bungling. American prestige rose sharply, and European powers grudgingly accorded the Republic more respect. In Germany, Prince Bismarck reportedly growled that there was a special Providence which looked after drunkards, fools, and the United States of America. At times it seemed as though not only Providence but the Spaniards were fighting on the side of the Yankees. So great in fact was America's good fortune that rejoicing citizens found in the victories further support—misleading support—for their indifference to adequate preparedness.

An exhilarating new spirit thrilled America. National pride was touched and cockiness was increased by what John Hay called a "splendid little war."* Enthusiasm over these triumphs made easier the rush down the thorny path of empire. America did not start the war with imperialistic motives, but after falling through the cellar door of imperialism in a drunken fit of idealism, she wound up with imperialistic and colonial fruits in her grasp. The much-criticized British imperialists were pleased, partly because of the new-found friendship, partly because misery loves company. But America's German rival was envious, and Latin American neighbors were deeply suspicious of Yankee greed.

By taking on the Philippine liability, the United States became a full-fledged Far Eastern power.

*Anti-imperialist William James called it "our squalid war with Spain."

> Three years after the Spanish-American War ended, a foreign diplomat in Washington remarked, "I have seen two Americas, the America before the Spanish American War and the America since."

Hereafter these distant islands were to be a "heel of Achilles"—a kind of indefensible hostage given to Japan, as the event proved in 1941. With singular shortsightedness, the Americans assumed dangerous commitments that they were later unwilling to defend by proper naval and military outlays.

But the lessons of unpreparedness were not altogether lost. Captain Mahan's big navyism seemed vindicated, and pride in the exploits of the navy brought popular support for more and better battleships. The inept Secretary Alger was succeeded in the War Department by a masterly organizer, Elihu Root, who established a general staff and founded the War College in Washington. His genius later paid dividends when the United States found itself involved in the World War of 1914–1918.

One of the happiest results of the conflict was the further closing of the "bloody chasm" between North and South. Thousands of patriotic Southerners had flocked to the Stars and Stripes, and the gray-bearded General Joseph ("Fighting Joe") Wheeler—a Confederate cavalry hero of about a thousand Civil War skirmishes and battles—was given a command in Cuba. He allegedly cried, in the heat of battle, "To hell with the Yankees! Dammit, I mean the Spaniards."

A no less gratifying result was the victory over disease. Without the conquest of yellow fever ("Yellow Jack"), which had helped ruin the French project in Panama, there might have been no Isthmian canal. The splendid pioneering work of Dr. Jesse W. Lazear, who lost his life, and Dr. James Carroll, who suffered a severe heart ailment, deserves unstinted praise. The unsung heroes of the test tube included United States soldiers who volunteered to be used as mosquito-bitten guinea pigs. They merit hardly less acclaim than war heroes like Admiral George Dewey and Colonel Theodore Roosevelt.

VARYING VIEWPOINTS

Imperialism has long been an embarrassing topic for students of American history, largely because of the Republic's own revolutionary origins and anticolonial tradition. Many writers discuss the dramatic overseas expansion of the 1890s as some kind of aberration—a sudden, singular, and short-lived departure from time-honored American principles and practices. Various excuses have been offered to explain this spasmodic lapse: the irresponsible behavior of the "yellow press"; the political strains imposed by the depression of the 1890s and the Populist upheaval; and the contagious scramble for imperial possessions by European powers during these years.

But recently some historians, notably William Appleman Williams and Walter LaFeber, have sought to ascribe American imperialism to deep-lying economic causes, especially the hunger for overseas markets. These scholars try to link the two most striking developments of the age: the amazing industrialization of America and the Republic's emergence as a great world power. They conclude that the explanation for expansion abroad is to be found in economic expansion at home. In essence, this approach takes a backward step toward the old-fashioned concept of the "Age of the Robber Barons," and seeks to apply that concept to foreign policy. Such a "revisionist" interpretation has been sharply challenged by scholars who argue that foreign policy is much too complex to be explained by economic factors alone.

SELECT READINGS

Refer to Morgan (on McKinley) cited in the previous chapter and Nevins (on Cleveland) cited in Chapter 26. Main outlines are sketched in F. R. Dulles, *America's Rise to World Power, 1898–1954* (1955), and in H. W. Morgan, *America's Road to Empire* (1965). Two general (and quite contrasting) interpretations of modern American foreign policy are G. F. Kennan, *American Diplomacy* (1951), and W. A. Williams, *The Tragedy of American Diplomacy* (1959). Consult also Williams' *The Roots of the Modern American Empire* (1969). See also E. R. May, *Imperial Democracy* (1961), and his *American Imperialism: A Speculative Essay* (1968), Walter LaFeber, *The New Empire* (1963), J. W. Pratt, *Expansionists of 1898* (1936), and W. A. Russ, *The Hawaiian Revolution* (1959) and *The Hawaiian Republic* (1961). Thoughtful perceptions are given in Robert Seager II, *Alfred Thayer Mahan* (1977), James L. Abrahamson, *America Arms for a New Century* (1981), and J. A. S. Grenville and G. E. Young, *Politics, Strategy, and American Diplomacy: Studies in Foreign Policy, 1873–1917* (1966). Milton Plesur, *America's Outward Thrust, 1865–1890* (1971), provides useful background to the "imperial" decade. On the war itself see Frank Freidel, *The Splendid Little War* (1958), and Walter Millis, *The Martial Spirit* (1931). Fascinating reading is H. G. Rickover, *How the Battleship* Maine *Was Destroyed* (1976). Helpful studies of the opponents of expansion are R. L. Beisner, *Twelve Against Empire: The Anti-Imperialists, 1898–1900* (1968), and E. Berkeley Tompkins, *Anti-Imperialism in the United States: The Great Debates, 1890–1920* (1970). Thomas McCormick sees a design for "informal" imperialism in *The China Market* (1967). D. F. Healey examines *The United States in Cuba, 1898–1902* (1963), while Leon Wolff paints a grim picture of American involvement in the Philippines in *Little Brown Brother* (1961). For more on the Philippine imbroglio, see P. W. Stanley, *A Nation in the Making: The Philippines and the United States, 1899–1921* (1975), and Richard E. Welch, Jr., *Response to Imperialism: The United States and the Philippine-American War, 1899–1902* (1979).

31

America on the World Stage, 1899-1909

I never take a step in foreign policy unless I am assured that I shall be able eventually to carry out my will by force.

THEODORE ROOSEVELT, 1905

"Little Brown Brothers" in the Philippines

Unhappily, the liberty-loving Filipinos were tragically deceived. They had assumed that they, like the Cubans, would be granted their freedom after the war. A clear-cut pledge by Congress to this effect probably would have averted the sorry sequel, but the Senate by the narrowest of margins refused to pass such a resolution. Bitterness toward the American troops continued to mount, and finally erupted into open insurrection on February 4, 1899, under Emilio Aguinaldo.

The war with the Filipinos, unlike the "splendid" little set-to with Spain, was sordid and prolonged. It involved more savage fighting, more soldiers killed in action, and far more scandal. Anti-imperialists redoubled their protests. In their view the United States, having plunged into war with

Spain to free Cuba, was now fighting 10,000 miles (16,100 kilometers) away to rivet shackles on a people who asked for nothing but liberty—in the American tradition.

As the ill-equipped Filipino armies were defeated, they melted into the jungle to wage a vicious guerrilla warfare. Many of the primitive natives used barbarous methods, and inevitably the infuriated American troops sank to their level. A brutal soldier song betrayed inner feelings:

> Damn, damn, damn the Filipinos!
> Cross-eyed kakiak ladrones!
> Underneath the starry flag
> Civilize 'em with a Krag [rifle],
> And return us to our own beloved homes.

Atrocity tales shocked and rocked the United States, for such methods did not reflect America's better self. Uncle Sam's soldiers were goaded to such extremes as the painful "water cure"—that is, forcing water down the victim's throat until he yielded information or died. Reconcentration camps were even established which strongly suggested those of "Butcher" Weyler in Cuba. America, having begun the Spanish war with noble ideals, now dirtied her hands. One New York newspaper published a reply to Rudyard Kipling's famous poem:

> We've taken up the white man's burden
> Of ebony and brown;
> Now will you kindly tell us, Rudyard,
> How we may put it down?

The backbone of the Filipino insurrection was finally broken in 1901, when Aguinaldo was captured by a clever if unsporting ruse. But sporadic fighting dragged on for many dreary months.

The problem of a government for the conquered islanders worried President McKinley who, in 1899, appointed a Philippine Commission to make appropriate recommendations. In its second year this body was headed by the future President, William H. Taft, an able and amiable lawyer-judge from Ohio who weighed about 350 pounds (159 kilograms). Forming a strong attachment for

Liberty Halts American Butchery in the Philippines. (*Life*, 1899.)

the Filipinos, he called them his "little brown brothers" and danced light-footedly with their tiny women. But among the American soldiers, sweatily combing the jungles, a different view of the insurgent prevailed:

> He may be a brother of Big Bill Taft,
> But he ain't no brother of mine.

McKinley's "benevolent assimilation" of the Philippines proceeded with painful slowness. Millions of American dollars were poured into the islands to improve roads, sanitation, and public health. Important economic ties, including trade in sugar, developed between the two peoples. American teachers—"pioneers of the blackboard"—set up an unusually good school system and helped make English a second language. But all this vast expenditure, which profited America little, was ill received. The Filipinos, who hated compulsory civilization, preferred less sanitation and more liberty. Like caged hawks, they beat against their gilded bars until they finally got their freedom, on the Fourth of July, 1946.

John Hay Defends China (and U.S. Interests)

Exciting events had meanwhile been brewing in faraway and enfeebled China. Following her defeat by Japan in 1894–1895, the imperialistic European powers, notably Russia and Germany, moved in. Like vultures descending upon a stranded whale, they began to tear away valuable leaseholds and economic spheres of influence from the Manchu government.

A growing group of Americans viewed the vivisection of China with alarm. Churches were worried about their missionary vineyards; manufacturers and exporters feared that Chinese markets would be monopolized by Europeans. An alarmed American public, openly prodded by the press and unofficially prodded by certain free-trade Britons, demanded that Washington do something. Secretary of State John Hay, a quiet but witty poet-novelist-diplomat with a flair for capturing the popular imagination, finally decided upon a dramatic move.

In the summer of 1899 Hay dispatched to all the great powers a communication soon known as the Open Door note. He urged them to announce that in their leaseholds or spheres of influence they would respect certain Chinese rights and the ideal of fair competition. In short, in their dealings with foreign traders the intruding powers would observe the Open Door. The principle was not new, for America had tried repeatedly to make it the basis of her commercial dealings with China in the 19th Century. But the phrase "Open Door" quickly caught the public fancy and gained wide acceptance.

John Hay (1838–1905). This gifted writer, poet, novelist, historian, and wit first attained some prominence as assistant private secretary to President Lincoln. He became a headline-catching secretary of state under President McKinley, notably with the Open Door. (Library of Congress.)

> The commercial interests of both Britain and America were imperiled by the power grabs in China, and a close understanding between the two powers would have helped both. Yet as Secretary Hay wrote privately in June 1900: "Every Senator I see says, 'For God's sake, don't let it appear we have any understanding with England.' How can I make bricks without straw? That we should be compelled to refuse the assistance of the greatest power in the world [Britain], *in carrying out our own policy,* because all Irishmen are Democrats and some [American] Germans are fools—is enough to drive a man mad."

Hay's proposal of this self-denying policy caused much squirming in the leading capitals of the world. It was like asking all men who do not have thieving designs to stand up and be counted. Italy alone accepted the Open Door unconditionally; she was the only major power that had no leasehold or sphere of influence in China. Britain, Germany, France, and Japan all accepted, but subject to the condition that the others acquiesce unconditionally. Russia, with covetous designs on China's Manchuria, in effect politely declined. But John Hay, rather than run the risk of a flat rejection, cleverly interpreted the Russian refusal as an acceptance, and proclaimed that the Open Door was in effect. Under such dubious midwifery was the infant born, and no one should have been surprised when the child proved to be sickly and relatively short-lived.

Hinging the Open Door in China

Open door or not, patriotic Chinese did not care to be used as a mat by the Europeans. In 1900 a super-patriotic group known as the "Boxers" broke loose with the cry "Kill Foreign Devils." Over 200 missionaries and other luckless whites were murdered, and a number of foreign diplomats were besieged in the capital, Peking.

A rescue force of some 18,000 soldiers, hastily assembled, arrived in the nick of time. This multination contingent consisted of Japanese, Russian, British, French, German, and American troops, with the American contribution some 2,500 men. Such participation in a joint military operation, especially in Asia, was plainly contrary to the nation's time-honored principles of non-entanglement and non-involvement. But America had not been a Far Eastern power in the days of the Founding Fathers.

The victorious allied invaders acted angrily and vindictively. They assessed prostrate China an excessive indemnity of $333 million, of which America's share was to be $24.5 million. When Washington discovered that this sum was much more than enough to pay damages and expenses, it remitted about $18 million. The Peking government, appreciating this gesture of goodwill, set aside the money to educate a selected group of Chinese students in the United States. These bright young men later played a significant role in the Westernization of the Orient.

The Boxer Rebellion, 1900. These U.S. troops helped to rescue the besieged Westerners in Peking. (National Archives.)

Secretary Hay now let fly another paper broadside, for he feared that the triumphant powers might use the Boxer outrages as a pretext for carving up China outright. His new circular note to the powers in 1900 announced that henceforth the Open Door would embrace the territorial integrity of China, in addition to her commercial integrity. Hay remembered his previous rebuff; this time he did not ask for formal acceptances.

Defenseless China was spared partition during these troubled years. But her salvation was probably not due to Hay's fine phrases, which the American people were reluctant to back up with fighting men. China owed her preservation far more to the strength of the competing powers; none of them could trust the others to gain an advantage.

Kicking "Teddy" Roosevelt Upstairs

President McKinley's renomination by the Republicans in 1900 was a foregone conclusion. He had piloted the country through a victorious war; he had acquired rich, though burdensome, real estate; he had established the gold standard; and he had brought the promised prosperity of the full dinner pail. "We'll stand pat!" was the poker-playing counsel of Mark Hanna. McKinley was renominated at Philadelphia on a platform that smugly endorsed prosperity, the gold standard, and overseas expansion.

An irresistible vice-presidential boom had developed for "Teddy" Roosevelt (TR), the cowboy-hero of San Juan Hill. Capitalizing on his war-born popularity, he had been elected governor of New York, where Thomas C. ("Easy Boss") Platt had found him headstrong and difficult to manage.

Platt and his cronies therefore devised a scheme to kick the colorful colonel upstairs into the vice-presidency.

This plot to railroad Roosevelt worked beautifully. Gesticulating wildly, he attended the nominating convention, where his Western-style cowboy hat made him stand out like a white crow. He had no desire to die of slow rot in the vice-presidential "burying ground," but he was eager to prove that he could get the nomination if he wanted it. He finally gave in when, to the accompaniment of cries of "We Want Teddy," he received a unanimous vote, except for his own. A frantic Hanna reportedly moaned that there would be only one heartbeat between that wild-eyed "madman"—"that damned cowboy"—and the presidency of the United States.

William Jennings Bryan, now a colonel also, was the odds-on choice of the Democrats, meeting at Kansas City. He was not a shooting-war hero, but he had run the risks of disease and "embalmed beef" in army camps, where he had contracted typhoid fever. The free-silver issue was now as dead as an abandoned mine, but Bryan, a slave to consistency, forced a silver plank down the throats of his protesting associates. He thus helped crucify himself on a cross of silver. The Democratic platform proclaimed, as did Bryan,

Two Views of the Rough Rider as Vice-President. *(Left,* Washington *Times; right,* Washington *Post.)*

that the "paramount" issue was Republican overseas imperialism.

Imperialism or Bryanism in 1900?

Campaign history partially repeated itself in 1900. McKinley, the soul of dignity, sat safely on his front porch, as before. Bryan, also as before, took to the stump in a cyclonic campaign, assailing both imperialism and Republican-fostered trusts.

The super-energetic, second-fiddle Roosevelt out-Bryaned Bryan. He toured the country with revolver-shooting cowboys, and his popularity cut heavily into Bryan's support in the Middle West. Flashing his magnificent teeth and pounding his fist fiercely into his palm, Roosevelt denounced all dastards who would haul down Old Glory.

Bryanites loudly trumpeted their "paramount" issue of imperialism. Lincoln, they charged, had abolished slavery for 3.5 million Africans; McKinley had re-established it for 7 million Malayans. But the question of imperialism was actually stale; it had been agitating the novelty-loving American people for more than two years. The Republic had the Philippines on its hands anyhow, and the real question was not "Should it keep them?" but "What should it do with them in the future?" Besides, anti-imperialists like Bryan were merely encouraging the Filipinos to resist.

Republicans responded by charging that "Bryanism," not imperialism, was the paramount issue. By this accusation they meant that Bryan would rock the boat of prosperity, once he got into office with his free-silver lunacy and other dangerous ideas. The voters were much less concerned about imperialism than about "Four Years More of the Full Dinner Pail" and "Let Well Enough Alone." Prosperity at home seemed more important than freedom abroad. When the smoke cleared off, McKinley had triumphed by a much wider margin than in 1896: 7,207,923 to 6,358,133 popular votes, and 292 to 155 electoral votes.

Victory for the Republicans was not a mandate for or against imperialism, legend to the contrary. The confused voters were not asked to decide

"Four More Years of Full Dinner Pails."
Contemporary cartoon.

this issue but, basically, to select either McKinley or Bryan. Many citizens who favored Bryan's anti-imperialism feared his free silver; many who favored McKinley's "sound money" hated his imperialism. One citizen wrote to ex-President Cleveland: "It is a choice between evils, and I am going to shut my eyes, hold my nose, vote, go home and disinfect myself." If there was any mandate at all it was for the two Ps: prosperity and protection. Content with good times, the country anticipated four more years of a full dinner pail crammed with fried chicken. And "Boss" Platt of New York gleefully looked forward to inauguration day, when he would see Roosevelt "take the veil" as Vice-President.

TR: Brandisher of the Big Stick

Kindly William McKinley had scarcely served another six months when, in September 1901, he was murdered by a deranged anarchist. Roosevelt became President at age forty-two, the youngest thus far in American history. Knowing that he had a reputation for impulsiveness and radicalism, he sought to reassure the country by proclaiming that he would carry out the policies of his predecessor. Cynics sneered that he would indeed carry them out—to the garbage heap.

What manner of man was Theodore Roosevelt, the red-blooded blue blood? Born into a wealthy and distinguished New York family, he had fiercely built up his spindly, asthmatic body by a stern and self-imposed routine of exercise. Graduating from Harvard with Phi Beta Kappa honors, he published at the age of twenty-four the first of some thirty volumes of muscular prose. Then came busy years, which involved duties as a ranch owner and bespectacled cowboy ("Four Eyes") in the Dakotas, followed by various political posts. When fully developed, he was a barrel-chested 5 feet 10 inches (1.76 meters), with prominent teeth, squinty eyes, droopy mustache, and piercing voice.

The Rough Rider's high-voltage energy was electrifying. Believing that it was better to wear out than to rust out, he would shake the hands of some 6,000 persons at one stretch, or ride horseback many miles in a day as an example for portly cavalry officers. Not surprisingly, he gathered about him a group of athletic, tennis-playing cronies, who were popularly dubbed "the Tennis Cabinet."

Incurably boyish and bellicose, Roosevelt loved a fight—"an elegant row." He never ceased to preach the virile virtues and to denounce civilized softness, with its pacifists and other "flubdubs" and "mollycoddles." An ardent champion of military and naval preparedness, he adopted as his pet proverb, "Speak softly and carry a Big Stick, [and] you will go far." If a statesman had the Big Stick, he could work his will among foreign nations without shouting; if he lacked it, shouting would do no good. TR had both a Big Stick and a shrill voice.

Wherever Roosevelt went, there was a great stir. At a wedding he eclipsed the bride; at a funeral the corpse. Shockingly unconventional, he

Theodore Roosevelt. Roosevelt gives a speech in North Carolina in 1902. (The Bettmann Archive.)

loved to break hoary precedents—the hoarier the better. He was a colossal egoist, and his self-confidence merged with self-righteousness. So sure was he of the correctness of his convictions that he impetuously branded people liars who disagreed with him. As a true cosmopolite, he loved people and mingled with all ranks of men, from Catholic cardinals to professional prize fighters, one of whom blinded a Rooseveltian eye in a White House bout.

An outspoken moralizer and reformer, Roosevelt preached righteousness from the White House pulpit. John Morley, a British author, found him an interesting combination of St. Paul and St. Vitus. Yet he was an opportunist who would compromise rather than butt his head against a stone wall. He was, in reality, much less radical than his blustery actions would indicate. A middle-of-the-roader, he stood just a little left of center, and bared his mule-like molars at liberals and reactionaries alike.

Roosevelt rapidly developed into a master politician with an idolatrous personal following. TR—as he was called—had an enormous popular appeal, partly because the common man saw in him a fiery champion. A magnificent showman, he was always front-page copy; and his cowboyism, his bear shooting, his outsize teeth, and his pince-nez glasses were ever the delight of the cartoonist. Though a staunch party man, he detested many of the dirty-handed bosses; but he learned, as Cleveland never did, to hold his nose and work with them.

Above all, Roosevelt was a direct-actionist. He believed that the President should lead; and although he made mistakes, he kept things noisily moving—generally forward. Never a lawyer, he condemned the law and the courts as too slow. He had no real respect for the delicate checks and balances among the three branches of the government. Finding the Constitution too rigid, he would on occasion ignore it; finding Congress too rebellious, he tried a mixture of coercion and compromise on it.

TR finally developed his extraordinary "stewardship theory," which, critics charged, must have made Jefferson and others writhe in their graves. The President, so he felt, may take any action in the general interest that is not specifically forbidden by the laws and the Constitution. Wallace Irwin noted:

> The Constitution rides behind
> And the Big Stick rides before,
> (Which is the rule of precedent
> In the reign of Theodore.)*

Colombia Blocks the Canal

Foreign affairs absorbed much of Roosevelt's bullish energy. Having traveled extensively in Europe, he enjoyed a far more intimate knowledge of the

---

*From "The Ballad of Grizzly Gulch," in *At the Sign of the Dollar* (1903). Reprinted by permission of the author.

outside world than most of his predecessors.

The Spanish-American War had emphasized the need of constructing the long-talked-about canal, through which only printer's ink had ever flowed. Anxious Americans had learned a dramatic object lesson when the battleship *Oregon,* stationed on the Pacific Coast at the outbreak of hostilities, made a full-speed dash around South America to join the fleet in Cuban waters. Alarmists speculated on what might have happened if she had not arrived in time for the Battle of Santiago, and if the Spanish fleet had been stronger. An Isthmian canal would plainly augment the strength of the navy by increasing its mobility. Such a waterway would also make easier the defense of such recent acquisitions as Puerto Rico, the Philippines, and Hawaii, while facilitating the operations of the American merchant marine.

Initial obstacles in the path of the canal builders were legal rather than geographical. By the terms of the ancient Clayton-Bulwer Treaty, concluded with Britain in 1850, the United States could not secure exclusive control over such a route. But by 1901 America's British cousins were willing to yield ground. Confronted with an unfriendly Europe and bogged down in the South African Boer War, they conceded the Hay-Pauncefote Treaty in 1901. It not only gave the United States a free hand to build the canal, but conceded the right to fortify it as well.

The Battleship *Oregon.*
(Naval Photographic Center.)

Legal barriers now removed, the next question was: Where should the canal be dug? Many American experts favored the Nicaraguan route, but the agents of the old French Canal Company were eager to salvage something from the costly failure at S-shaped Panama. Represented by a young, energetic, and unscrupulous engineer, Philippe Bunau-Varilla, the New Panama Canal Company suddenly dropped the price of its holdings from $109 million to the fire-sale price of $40 million.

The Nicaragua-versus-Panama issue was hotly debated in Congress, where a serious objection to Nicaragua was its volcanic activity. Providentially for Bunau-Varilla, Mount Pelée, on the West Indian island of Martinique, blew its top in May 1902, and wiped out some 30,000 souls. The clever Frenchman hastily secured ninety Nicaraguan postage stamps, each bearing a picture of the country's most fearsome volcano, and sent one to each senator. Hanna delivered a persuasive Senate speech, in which he stressed the engineering advantages of the Panama route. In June 1902, Congress finally accepted his views.

The scene now shifted to Colombia, of which Panama was an unwilling part. A treaty highly favorable to the United States was negotiated in Washington with the agent of the Colombian government in Bogotá. It granted the lease of a 6-mile-wide (9.66-kilometer) zone in perpetuity, in return for $10 million and an annual payment of $250,000. But when the pact was submitted to the Bogotá Senate, it was unanimously rejected. The Isthmian strip was regarded as one of Colombia's most valuable natural assets, and many Colombians felt that they were not getting enough money. Evidence later unearthed indicates that if Washington had been willing to pay an additional $15 million, the pact would have been approved.

Roosevelt was infuriated by his setback at the hands of what he called those "dagoes." Frantically eager to be elected President "in his own right" in 1904, he was anxious to "make the dirt fly" to impress the voters. "Damn the law," he reportedly cried in private, "I want the canal

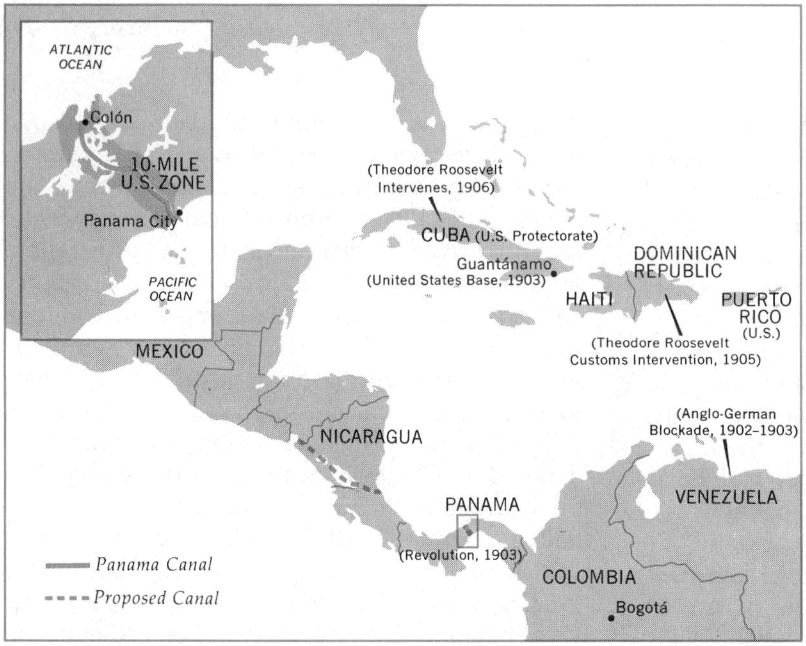

BIG STICK IN THE CARIBBEAN
In 1901 Roosevelt declared: "If a man continually blusters . . . a big stick will not save him from trouble; and neither will speaking softly avail, if back of the softness there does not lie strength, power. . . . If the boaster is not prepared to back up his words his position becomes absolutely contemptible."

built!" He assailed "the blackmailers of Bogotá" who, like armed highwaymen, were blocking the onward march of civilization. He failed to point out that the Senate of the United States also rejects treaties.

Uncle Sam Creates Puppet Panama

Impatient Panamanians, who had rebelled numerous times, were ripe for another revolt. They had counted on a wave of prosperity to follow construction of the canal, and they feared that the United States would now turn to the Nicaraguan route. Scheming Bunau-Varilla was no less disturbed by the prospect of losing the company's $40 million. Working hand in glove with the Panama revolutionists, he raised a tiny "patriot" army consisting largely of members of the Panamanian fire department, plus 500 "bought" Colombian troops—for a reported price of $100,000.

The Panama revolution occurred on November 3, 1903, with the incidental killing of a Chinese civilian and a donkey. Colombian troops were gathered to crush the uprising, but American naval forces would not let them cross the Isthmus. Roosevelt justified this highly questionable interference by a strained interpretation of the treaty of 1846 with Colombia. (This pact obligated Washington to maintain the "perfect neutrality" of the Isthmus, obviously against outsiders.)

Roosevelt moved rapidly to make steamy Panama a virtual outpost of the United States. Three days after the uprising, he hastily extended the right hand of recognition. Fifteen days later, Bunau-Varilla, who was now the Panamanian minister despite his French citizenship, signed the Hay–Bunau-Varilla treaty in Washington. The price of the canal strip was left the same, but the zone was widened from 6 to 10 miles (9.66 to 16 kilometers). The French company gladly pocketed its $40 million from the United States Treasury.

Roosevelt, it seems clear, did not actively plot to tear Panama from the side of Colombia. But the conspirators knew of his angrily expressed views, and they counted on his using the Big Stick to prevent Colombia from intervening. Yet the Rough Rider became so indiscreetly involved in the affair as to create the impression that he had been a secret party to the intrigue.

Unhappily the United States suffered a black eye as a result of Roosevelt's "cowboy diplomacy." European imperialists, who were old hands at this

TR Intervenes in Panama. (The Bettmann Archive.)

sort of thing, could now raise their eyebrows sneeringly at America's superior moral pretensions—and they did.

Completing the Canal and Appeasing Colombia

The so-called rape of Panama marked an ugly downward lurch in Uncle Sam's relations with Latin America. Much fear had already been aroused by the recent seizure of Puerto Rico and by the Yankee stranglehold on Cuba. The fate of Colombia, when she dared defy the Colossus of the North, indicated that her weak sister republics were not safe. The era of the bullying "Big Brother" policy was definitely launched.

Roosevelt heatedly defended himself against all charges of evildoing. He claimed that he had received a "mandate from civilization" to start the canal, and that Colombia had wronged the United States by not permitting herself to be benefited. To deal with these "blackmailers," he insisted, was like "nailing currant jelly to the wall."

But TR was not completely candid. He failed to point out that the Nicaragua route was about as feasible, and that it was available without a revolu-

tion. Yet this alternative would have involved some delay, and the presidential election of 1904 was fast approaching.

Active work was begun on "making the dirt fly" in 1904, but grave difficulties were encountered, ranging from labor troubles to landslides. The organization was finally perfected under an energetic but autocratic West Point engineer, Colonel George Washington Goethals. At the outset, sanitation proved to be more important than excavation. Colonel William C. Gorgas, the quiet and determined exterminator of yellow fever in Havana, ultimately made the Canal Zone "as safe as a health resort."

Americans finally succeeded where Frenchmen had failed. In 1914 the colossal canal project was completed at an initial cost of about $400 million,

Roosevelt in Panama. He visited the Panama Canal construction site in 1906 to see "the dirt fly." He was the first President to leave the United States for foreign soil. (Theodore Roosevelt Collection, Harvard College Library.)

I□II□II□II□II□II□II□II□II□II□II□II□II□II□II□II□II□II□

In 1911 Roosevelt made a costly boast in a speech in Berkeley, California: "I am interested in the Panama Canal because I started it. If I had followed traditional, conservative methods I would have presented a dignified state paper . . . to Congress and the debates on it would have been going on yet; but I took the Canal Zone and let Congress debate; and while the debate goes on the Canal does also."

I□II□II□II□II□II□II□II□II□II□II□II□II□II□II□II□II□II□I

just as World War I was breaking out. The whole enterprise, in the words of the English writer James Bryce, was "the greatest liberty Man has ever taken with Nature."

Roosevelt as ex-President continued to exult over this geographical surgery. He was at pains to point out that even though debate went on over his "rape" of Panama, ships went through the canal. Colombia had offered to arbitrate her grievance, but the United States, though often preaching arbitration, declined to risk a decision at the hands of foreigners. Subsequent Democratic Congresses, willing to do penance for the Republican sins of Roosevelt, attempted to apologize to Colombia and to indemnify her for her loss. But the still-violent Rough Rider cried that this would be done over his dead body, and as long as he was alive his friends in the Senate defeated the proposed treaty.

Oil provided an unexpected lubricant. Gushers of liquid "black gold" were discovered in Colombia, and would-be exploiters from Yankeeland were getting the cold shoulder. Roosevelt had died in 1919, and in 1921 the United States Senate acted. Suddenly troubled by a tender conscience, it approved a heart-balm treaty, which granted Colombia $25 million without an apology. But such a sum is in itself an apology. The tragedy is that in 1903 about half this so-called canalimony, in addition to the original $10 million, would probably have averted the scandal.

Roosevelt and Venezuelan Vexations

Tropical Venezuela lay in the iron grip of dictator Cipriano Castro, whom Roosevelt privately branded "an unspeakably villainous little monkey." Castro had defaulted on his nation's indebtedness to certain European powers, and late in 1902 Britain took the lead in inducing Germany to join in collecting the debts. Roosevelt had no serious objections: he believed that misbehaving republics might properly be "spanked."

Spanking proved effective. The Germans sank two Venezuelan gunboats, and with unnecessary ruthlessness bombarded a town early in 1903. Dictator Castro hastened to accept an arbitration proposal that he had earlier spurned, and Washington was glad to transmit his acceptance to the European powers.

Opinion in the United States, less acquiescent, was now angrily aroused against this ironfisted intervention. The British ringleaders, fearful of ruining the newly won American friendship, pulled in their horns, leaving Germany to bear the full brunt of Yankee disapproval. The European powers finally accepted arbitration of their monetary claims in 1903, and the unhappy affair was patched up.

The Monroe Doctrine no doubt gained muscle

Monroe Doctrine, A Live Wire. (New York *Herald*, by permission of the New York *Sun*, Inc.)

as a result of the Venezuela episode. A resentful American public had served warning that it would frown upon European powers which, with mailed fist, set out to "spank" the weak Latin American neighbors.

TR's Perversion of Monroe's Doctrine

Defaulted debts also concerned the revolution-rent Dominican Republic, whose "chronic wrongdoing" Roosevelt deplored. He feared that the Germans or other Europeans might come as bill collectors. If they came, they might stay; if they stayed, they would violate the Monroe Doctrine; if they violated the Monroe Doctrine, the United States might have to fight them.

TR therefore evolved a devious policy of "preventive intervention," better known as the Roosevelt corollary of the Monroe Doctrine. Under it Americans would intervene themselves, take over the customhouses, pay off the debts, and keep the troublesome powers on the other side of the Atlantic. The United States had a moral obligation to do so, Roosevelt argued, because it would not permit the European nations themselves to intervene in the bankrupt banana republics. In short, no outsiders could push the Latin nations around except Uncle Sam, Policeman of the Caribbean.

This new brandishing of the Big Stick in the Caribbean became effective in 1905. It was formalized by a Dominican treaty two years later, after Roosevelt had engaged in a "glorious" quarrel with the Senate. Dominican officials, who had raked in much juicy graft, were not happy over such interference, and they acquiesced only after some judicious arm-twisting from Washington. But from a debt-collecting point of view, the customhouse intervention was a success.

Roosevelt's corollary, though tacked onto the Monroe Doctrine, bore only a strained relation to the original dictum of 1823. Monroe had in effect said to the European powers, "Thou shalt not intervene." TR changed this warning to mean, "We shall intervene to prevent you from intervening." The Roosevelt doctrine was actually so radical as to be a completely new policy, but it gained readier acceptance by being associated with the honored name of Monroe. Yet in its own right the corollary had considerable merit as a defensive stroke.

Roosevelt wrote to a correspondent in February 1904: "I have been hoping and praying for three months that the Santo Domingans would behave so that I would not have to act in any way. I want to do nothing but what a policeman has to do. . . . As for annexing the island, I have about the same desire to annex it as a gorged boa-constrictor might have to swallow a porcupine wrong-end-to."

Roosevelt's rewriting of Monroe's doctrine had its dark side. It probably did more than any other one step to promote the "Bad Neighbor" policy begun in these years. As time wore on, the new corollary was used to justify wholesale interventions and repeated landings of the Marines, all of which helped turn the Caribbean into a "Yankee lake." Latin Americans mistakenly cursed the unoffending Monroe, when they should have cursed the offending Roosevelt. To them it seemed as though the Monroe Doctrine, far from providing a shield, was a cloak behind which the United States sought to strangle them. Wallace Irwin slyly criticized the new interventionism:

Here's a bumper to the doctrine of Monroe, roe, roe,
  And the neighbors whom we cannot let alone;
Through the thirst for diagnosis we're inserting
    our proboscis
  Into everybody's business but our own.*

The shadow of the Big Stick likewise fell on Cuba in 1906. Revolutionary disorders brought an appeal from the Cuban president and, "necessity

*From "Monroe Doctrinings," in *Random Rhymes and Odd Numbers* (The Macmillan Company, copyright 1906). Reprinted by permission of the publisher.

being the mother of intervention," United States Marines were landed. These police forces were withdrawn temporarily in 1909, but in Latin American eyes the episode was but another example of the creeping power of the Colossus of the North.

The Big Stick in Two Hemispheres

Booted and spurred, Roosevelt had meanwhile been charging into the Canada-Alaska boundary controversy. America's vast northern neighbor had, for several years, seriously disputed the line between herself and the Alaska panhandle. Washington contended that under the original Russo-American treaty of 1824, the boundary should follow the snake-like windings of the coast. The Canadians argued that the line should be run straighter, leaving the heads of the deeper inlets in their hands. Finally in 1903 a treaty was concluded between London and Washington. It referred the controversy to six "impartial justices of repute," three Americans appointed by President Roosevelt and three British subjects—two Canadians and one Briton—named by their King.

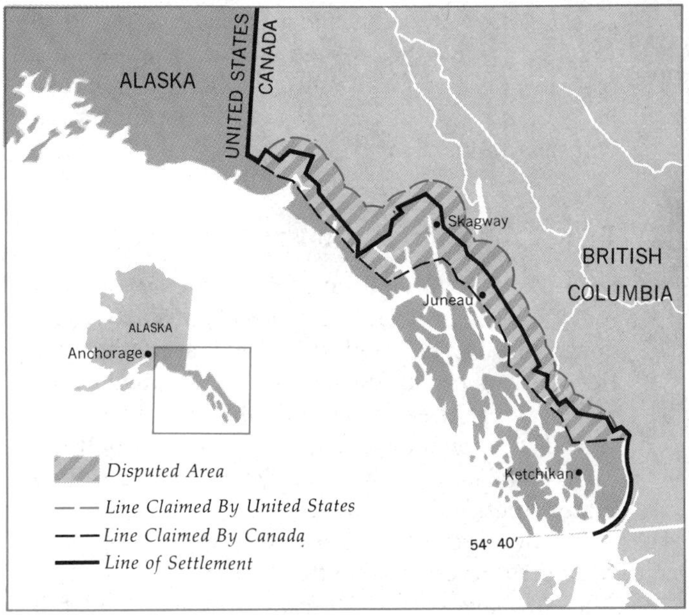

THE ALASKAN BOUNDARY SETTLEMENT, 1903

The so-called Alaska boundary arbitration actually created disputes. Roosevelt, cocksure as usual, convinced himself that the Canadian claims were "an outrage pure and simple." Behind the scenes, he displayed his Big Stick, threatening that if America lost he would seize what was properly hers with troops. The key British arbitrator, faced with the awful responsibility of starting a war, may have been unduly swayed. At length the tribunal voted four to two—the two being Canadians—in favor of the basic American contention, although narrowing somewhat the coastal strip. The Canadians were deeply angered, perhaps more so by the British, who had betrayed them, than by Roosevelt, who had browbeaten them.

A bigger storm had meanwhile been brewing in North Africa over French-protected Morocco, at which the imperial-minded Germans were casting covetous eyes. In 1905 the Kaiser landed there and made a saber-rattling speech. Overnight an international storm blew up, involving France and Britain as the chief adversaries of Germany. At the prompting of the Kaiser, Roosevelt consented to help arrange for an international conference at Algeciras, Spain, in 1906.

Two American delegates were sent to the parley on Morocco, despite the non-entanglement warnings of the Founding Fathers. Roosevelt privately took the side of France, partly because he distrusted the Kaiser, whom he dubbed "that autocratic zigzag." When deadlock developed at Algeciras, the President flourished his Big Stick at the erratic German ruler and, in his own words, gently "stood him on his head." As the German army was not ready to march, the Kaiser backed down and suffered something of a diplomatic defeat.

But why should America be embroiling herself in Morocco? Her trade and investment stake—the Open Door—was negligible. Roosevelt in effect was developing a further new interpretation of the Monroe Doctrine. He evidently believed that he was justified in intervening in overseas crises that might touch off globe-girdling hostilities, because

TR Upholds the World. The large button on his chest proclaims "My Policies." (New York *World*.)

such a conflagration probably would suck his nation in. His timely intervention may possibly have prevented worldwide war from breaking out in 1906 rather than in 1914.

The Second Hague Disarmament Conference met in 1907. Although officially called by the Czar, as before, it was actually initiated by Roosevelt, who responded to the proddings of American public opinion. Nothing was accomplished in the area of arms reduction, owing largely to the opposition of militaristic Germany to disarmament and arbitration. But the Conference did adopt some useful regulations on such subjects as international debt collection, humane warfare, and the rights and obligations of neutrals. Although the United States was represented at The Hague—another step away from isolation—the war-loving Roosevelt, deep in the Japanese crisis, was rather indifferent to the sessions.

Underdog Sympathy in the Russo-Japanese War

The Russian Bear, having lumbered across Asia, was seeking to bathe his frostbitten paws in the ice-free ports of China's Manchuria, particularly Port Arthur. In Japanese eyes, Manchuria and Korea in Czarist hands were pistols pointed at Japan's strategic heart. Russian troops had invaded Manchuria during the Boxer outburst of 1900, and despite solemn promises were not withdrawing. The Czar was obviously stalling until his trans-Siberian railroad could be finished, as it would be in a few months. With the clock ticking against them, the Japanese suddenly began war in 1904 by a devastating surprise attack on the Russian fleet at Port Arthur.

On paper, American sympathies should have gone out to Russia, for she was a traditional friend of long standing. During the 19th Century the United States had managed to get along unusually well with her, primarily because of a common bitterness against Britain, and also because Americans had little to do with the Russians. But by the sunset of the century the ancient grudge against Mother England was evaporating, and the Yankees were coming into direct contact with Russia as she menaced their Open Door interests in China. The American people were also repelled by this naked imperialism, and especially by Czarist despotism, as highlighted by shocking descriptions of Siberian prison camps in American magazines of the 1880s and 1890s. Worst of all were the terrible massacres of Russian Jews, which broke out anew with frightful fury at the time of the Russo-Japanese War.

FAR EAST, 1904–1905

Tiny Japan had a sentimental claim to American sympathy, for she was peculiarly the protégé of the United States. The Americans had forced open her gates to Western civilization, and they had taken great pride in the speed with which she had acquired a veneer of Occidental culture. As between Russia and Japan, Russia seemed to be the big bully and Japan the underdog—and American hearts went out to the Japanese. The Russians resentfully reminded America how they had seemingly stood by her during the dark days of her Civil War—though for selfish reasons, as is now known.

Roosevelt Engineers the Peace of Portsmouth

Undersized but efficient, the Japanese administered a humiliating series of beatings to the inept Russians in Manchuria and on the sea. But as the war dragged on, Japan began to run short of men and yen—a weakness she did not want to betray to the enemy. The Tokyo officials therefore approached Roosevelt in the deepest secrecy, and asked him to take steps that would bring the peace negotiators together.

Although Roosevelt did not relish the thankless role of umpire, he felt that a speedy end of the war was to America's interests. Either Japan or Russia might collapse, thus upsetting the balance of power in the Far East. The surviving combatant would then become dominant, to the jeopardy of America's commercial, missionary, and other interests.

Under Roosevelt's vigorous shepherding, the Japanese and Russian delegates gathered near Portsmouth, New Hampshire, in 1905. The politely bowing Orientals, on the basis of their victories, presented stern demands. They asked for a huge indemnity and for all of the island of Sakhalin, which commands the Amur River—the Mississippi of Siberia.

Roosevelt at Portsmouth Conference. TR meets with the two Russian and two Japanese delegates, 1905. Roosevelt wrote that dealing with U.S. senators was a tough job, but dealing with these peace envoys was even tougher. He had to be "polite and sympathetic and patient in explaining for the hundredth time something perfectly obvious . . . when I really want to give utterance to whoops of rage and jump up and knock their heads together." (The Bettmann Archive.)

> There is a curious modernity about what Roosevelt wrote to a British friend in May 1905: "I like the Russian people, but abhor the Russian system of government and I cannot trust the word of those at the head."

Agreement at Portsmouth was difficult. Roosevelt encountered stubbornness in both the Japanese and Russians; in disgust he branded the Czar "a preposterous little creature." After he had blustered behind the scenes, the Japanese grudgingly gave ground. They abandoned their claims for an indemnity, and agreed to accept half of Sakhalin. But they strengthened their preeminent position in Korea, and displaced Russia as the dominant foreign power in Manchuria.

Brickbats rained upon the President, "the honest broker," from both sides. The Russians, accusing him of being a Jewish "Rosenfelt," insisted that they could have whipped their foe. The Japanese, whose expectations had been raised, felt robbed of their indemnity. Throughout Japan, Roosevelt's portrait was turned to the wall. But he found some solace in the Nobel Peace Prize of 1906, which he largely deserved, despite his glorification of war.

Two historic friendships withered on the windswept plains of Manchuria. That between Russia and America, already strained, fell upon more evil days. That between Japan and America entered upon a more troubled phase. The United States had emerged in 1898 as a great power, with crucial interests in the Far East. During 1904–1905 Japan likewise emerged as a great power, with conflicting ambitions. Uncle Sam could no longer pat his bright little protégé on the head and show him off. Japan and America were now rivals; and feelings of suspicion, fear, and jealousy were bound to supplant the one-time happy relationship. To many Americans, the Nipponese were getting too big for their kimonos.

Japanese Laborers in California

The population of America's Pacific Coast was directly affected by the Russo-Japanese War. A new restlessness came to the rice paddies of Japan, largely as a result of the dislocations and tax burdens caused by the recent conflict. Numerous Japanese laborers, with their wives and numerous children, began to pour into the spacious valleys of California. By 1906 there were approximately 70,000 Japanese on the Pacific Coast.

Nervous Californians, confronted by another "yellow peril," were fearful of being drowned in an Oriental sea. Seizing upon a new variant of the old anti-Chinese slogan, they cried, "The Japanese must go." The Eastern part of the United States, indifferent to the prolific Japanese, did not share the alarm of the Pacific Coast.

A showdown on the Japanese influx came in 1906. Following the frightful earthquake and fire of that year in San Francisco, the local school authorities, pressed for space, decreed that Oriental children should attend a special school. This edict, though aimed at overage Japanese "boys," was designed basically to advertise to the rest of the nation the alarm of California over the inflow of cheap foreign labor.

Instantly, the Japanese school incident brewed an international crisis. The people of Japan, highly sensitive on questions of race, regarded this discrimination as an insult to them and their beloved children. On both sides of the Pacific, irresponsible war talk sizzled in the yellow press—the real "yellow peril." Roosevelt, who as a Rough Rider had welcomed shooting, was less happy over the prospect of California's stirring up a war which all the other states would have to fight. He therefore invited the entire San Francisco Board of Education, headed by a bassoon-playing mayor under indictment for graft, to come to the White House.

TR finally broke the deadlock, but not until he had waved his Big Stick and bared his big teeth. The Californians were induced to repeal the offensive school order and to accept what came to be known as "the Gentlemen's Agreement." This secret understanding was worked out, during 1907–1908, by an exchange of diplomatic notes between Washington and Tokyo. The Japanese, for their part, agreed to stop the flow of laborers to the American mainland by witholding passports. Caucasian Californians, their fears allayed, henceforth slept easier.

The World Cruise of the Great White Fleet

Roosevelt, who loved grand flourishes, dreamed up a fantastic one, partially for the benefit of Japan. Though not a coward, he was afraid that the Japanese thought him afraid. He suspected that his intercession between California and Japan was being interpreted in Tokyo as prompted by fear of the Nipponese. On paper, the American navy was then second among the navies of the world, thanks to his zeal for preparedness, and that of Japan was fifth. Partly to impress the Japanese with the potency of the Big Stick, he daringly decided to send the entire battleship fleet out to the Pacific Coast, and subsequently from there all the rest of the way around the world.

"Isn't It a Daisy?" Uncle Sam admires his battleship fleet. (Philadelphia *Record.*)

Pained protests arose from American critics. They charged that the mad scheme would provoke war; that the fleet would break down or be sunk; and that the Eastern seaboard would be stripped of its defenders. But Roosevelt stood firm, and late in 1907 the sixteen smoke-belching battleships started from Virginia waters. Their commander pointedly declared that he was ready for "a feast, a frolic, or a fight."

The Great White Fleet—to the accompaniment of cannonading champagne corks—received a series of tumultuous outpourings. At South American ports the Yankee warships were greeted with heartwarming rejoicing, for to many they were the effective teeth of the Monroe Doctrine against European invasion. The flotilla finally reached the Pacific Coast in safety, and then steamed on to Hawaii, New Zealand, and Australia. After the customary cheers, the ships headed for Japanese waters, where alarmists claimed that secret mines were planted. If war had broken out, the American fleet would have been lost because the neutral ships supplying coal would have had to withdraw.

As events turned out, an overwhelming reception in Japan was the high point of the trip. Tens of thousands of kimonoed school children had been trained to wave tiny American flags and sing "The Star-Spangled Banner"—reportedly in English. In the happy diplomatic atmosphere created by the visit of the fleet, the Root-Takahira agreement of 1908 was reached with Japan. Both powers solemnly pledged themselves to respect each other's territorial possessions in the Pacific, and to uphold the Open Door in China. The once fight-thirsty Roosevelt, who thus went out of his way to avoid a fight with Japan, regarded the battleship cruise as his most important contribution to peace.

After visiting the Mediterranean, the fleet steamed into home waters early in 1909, just in time to usher out the Roosevelt regime in a blaze of glory. Unquestionably the spectacular voyage—the Big Stick in action—popularized and accelerated American naval preparedness, while probably stimulating worldwide navalism. The Monroe Doctrine was correspondingly strengthened against European intervention. Finally, this breathtaking demonstration wrote another chapter in America's emergence as a great power, and in the development of international-mindedness in its people. "Join the Navy and See the World" was a potent recruiting slogan that grew out of the cruise.

VARYING VIEWPOINTS

Disagreement marks historical appraisals of America's emergence as a great power at the turn of the 20th Century. On the one hand, historians have praised the maturing of the Republic, which was now able to take its place among the arbiters of the world's destinies. On the other hand, many writers have tried to define America's new role in distinctive terms. They argue that the United States did not enter the great power game as just another player, but introduced a new style of diplomatic play, and perhaps even a new set of rules.

Judgments clash about these alleged innovations. An older school of thought stresses the idealism that America brought to the world arena. More recently, "New Left" revisionists have charged that America's contribution to international life was the self-serving notion of "informal empire," typified by a worldwide Open Door doctrine. This strategy shunned formal territorial possession but sought economic dominance of foreign raw materials, markets, and investments.

Historians disagree further about the motivating impulses of American diplomacy. Recent "revisionists" have tended almost exclusively to emphasize domestic economic factors in explaining American foreign policy. The United States sought foreign markets, the argument goes, to solve the problems of domestic overproduction and recurring business depressions. Other scholars respond that international politics can only be properly understood in an international context. They argue that Theodore Roosevelt, for example, acted not for narrow domestic reasons but because he realistically perceived that if the United States did not hold its own against the other powers, it would soon risk being pushed around in its own hemisphere, despite the Monroe Doctrine.

SELECT READINGS

Broad outlines appear in F. R. Dulles, *America's Rise to World Power* (1955). More detailed is H. K. Beale, *Theodore Roosevelt and the Rise of America to World Power* (1956). H. F. Pringle's biography of *Theodore Roosevelt* (1931) is anecdotal and antagonistic. More analytical and sympathetic are J. M. Blum, *The Republican Roosevelt* (new ed., 1977), W. H. Harbaugh, *Power and Responsibility* (1961), and G. W. Chessman, *Theodore Roosevelt and the Politics of Power* (1969). Especially good on the youthful T. R. are Edmund Morris, *The Rise of Theodore Roosevelt* (1979), and David McCullough, *Mornings on Horseback* (1981). For the Open Door, consult A. W. Griswold, *The Far Eastern Policy of the United States* (1938), Marilyn B. Young, *The Rhetoric of Empire: America's China Policy, 1895–1901* (1968), and G. F. Kennan, *American Diplomacy* (1951). On relations with Japan see Raymond Esthus, *Theodore Roosevelt and Japan* (1966), the same author's *Theodore Roosevelt and the International Rivalries* (1970), Charles E. Neu, *An Uncertain Friendship: Theodore Roosevelt and Japan, 1906–1909* (1967) and his *The Troubled Encounter: The United States and Japan* (1975). Also valuable are two books by Akira Iriye, *Across the Pacific* (1967) and *Pacific Estrangement: Japanese and American Expansion, 1897–1911* (1972). Both naval and political history are keenly handled in W. R. Braisted, *The United States Navy in the Pacific, 1897–1909* (1958). On the treatment of the Japanese in the United States, see Roger Daniels, *The Politics of Prejudice* (1962).

32

Progressivism and the Republican Roosevelt

When I say I believe in a square deal I do not mean . . . to give every man the best hand. If the cards do not come to any man, or if they do come, and he has not got the power to play them, that is his affair. All I mean is that there shall be no crookedness in the dealing.

THEODORE ROOSEVELT, 1905

Progressive Roots

Nearly 76 million Americans greeted the new century in 1900. Of them, almost 1 in 7 was foreign-born. In the fourteen years of peace that remained before the Great War of 1914 engulfed the globe, 13 million more migrants would carry their bundles down the gangplanks to the Land of Promise.

Hardly had the 20th Century dawned on the racially mixed American people than they were convulsed by a reform movement, the like of which the nation had not seen since the 1840s. The new crusaders, who called themselves "progressives," waged war on many evils, notably monopoly, corruption, inefficiency, and social

Life on the Lower East Side of New York City. "Street Arabs" often slept wherever they could. Many families counted themselves lucky to share a single room, no matter how squalid. (Jacob A. Riis Collection, Museum of the City of New York.)

injustice. The progressive army was large, multicolored, and widely deployed, but it had a single battle cry: "Strengthen the State." The "real heart of the movement," explained one progressive reformer, was "to use the government as an agency of human welfare."

The ground swell of the new reformist wave went far back—to the Greenback Labor party of the 1870s and the Populists of the 1890s, to the mounting unrest throughout the land as grasping industrialists concentrated more and more power in fewer and fewer hands. An outworn philosophy of hands-off individualism seemed increasingly out of place in the modern machine age. Social and economic problems were now too complex for the designedly feeble Jeffersonian organs of government. Progressive theorists were insisting that society could no longer afford the luxury of a limitless hands-off policy (laissez-faire). The people, through government, must substitute mastery for drift.

Well before 1900 perceptive politicians and writers had begun to pinpoint targets for the progressive attack. Bryan, Altgeld, and the Populists loudly branded the "bloated trusts" with the stigma of corruption and wrongdoing. In 1894 Henry Demarest Lloyd charged headlong into the Standard Oil Company with his book entitled *Wealth against Commonwealth.* Eccentric Thorstein Veblen assailed the new rich with his prickly pen in *The Theory of the Leisure Class* (1899), a savage attack on "predatory wealth" and "conspicuous consumption."

Other pen-wielding knights likewise entered the fray. The keen-eyed and keen-nosed Danish immigrant Jacob A. Riis, a reporter for the New York *Sun,* shocked middle-class Americans in 1890 with *How the Other Half Lives.* His account was a damning indictment of the dirt, disease, vice, and misery of the rat-gnawed human rookeries known as New York slums. The book deeply influenced a future New York City police commissioner, Theodore Roosevelt. Novelist Theodore Dreiser used his blunt prose to batter promoters and profiteers in *The Financier* (1912) and *The Titan* (1914).

Socialists, now swelling in numbers, must take high rank among the caustic critics of existing injustices. Many of them were European immigrants who decried "bloody capitalism," and they began to register appreciable strength at the ballot boxes as the new century dawned. They received much of their inspiration from abroad, where countries like Germany were launching daring experiments in state socialism. In faraway Australia and New Zealand, socialist reforms were also being undertaken which attracted much notice in America.

The Socialists found a gifted ally in young Jack (John Griffith) London, the bastard, ill-educated "oyster pirate" of San Francisco Bay, who became a prolific writer of novels. Steeped in Darwin and in Marx and other German thinkers, London was deeply concerned with the class struggle and with the clash between the civilized brain and primitive force. His stirring tales, such as *The Call of the Wild* (1903) and *The Sea Wolf* (1904), owed their popularity chiefly to their exciting plots. But on a higher level they were closely related to the current reformist agitation.

Raking Muck with the Muckrakers

Beginning about 1902 the exposing of evil became a flourishing industry among American publishers. A group of aggressive ten- and fifteen-cent popular magazines surged to the front, notably *McClure's, Cosmopolitan, Collier's,* and *Everybody's.* Waging fierce circulation wars, they dug deep for the dirt that the public loved to hate.

> In his Muckraker speech (1906), Roosevelt said: "Now, it is very necessary that we should not flinch from seeing what is vile and debasing. There is filth on the floor and it must be scraped up with the muck-rake; and there are times and places where this service is the most needed of all the services that can be performed. But the man who never does anything else, who never thinks or speaks or writes, save of his feats with the muck-rake, speedily becomes, not a help to society, not an incitement to good, but one of the most potent forces for evil."

Enterprising editors financed extensive research and encouraged pugnacious writing by their bright young reporters, whom President Roosevelt branded as "Muckrakers" in 1906. Annoyed by their excess of zeal, he compared the mudslinging magazine dirt-diggers to the figure in Bunyan's *Pilgrim's Progress* who was so intent on raking manure that he could not see the celestial crown dangling overhead.

Despite presidential scolding, these Muckrakers boomed circulation, and some of their most scandalous exposures were published as best-selling books. The reformer-writers ranged far, wide, and deep in their crusade to lay bare the muck of iniquity in American society. In 1902 a brilliant New York reporter, Lincoln Steffens, launched a series of articles in *McClure's* entitled "The Shame of the Cities." He fearlessly unmasked the corrupt alliance between Big Business and municipal government. Steffens was followed in the same magazine by Ida M. Tarbell, a quiet spinster who published a devastating but factual exposé of the Standard Oil Company. (Her father had been ruined by the oil interests.) Fearing legal reprisals, the muckraking magazines went to great pains and expense to check their material—paying as much as $3,000 to verify a single Tarbell article. R. S. Baker, who attacked assorted abuses, was successfully sued for $15,000 and costs, but his case was a noteworthy exception.

Muckrakers fearlessly tilted their pen-lances at varied targets. They assailed the malpractices of life insurance companies and tariff lobbies. They roasted the Beef Trust, the "Money Trust," the railroad barons, and the corrupt amassing of American fortunes. Thomas W. Lawson, an erratic speculator who had himself made $50 million on the stock market, laid bare the practices of his accomplices in "Frenzied Finance." This series of articles, appearing in 1905–1906, rocketed the circulation of *Everybody's*. Lawson, by fouling his own nest, made many enemies among his rich associates, and he died a poor man.

David G. Phillips shocked an already startled nation by his series in *Cosmopolitan* entitled "The Treason of the Senate" (1906). He boldly charged that seventy-five of the ninety senators did not represent the people at all but the railroads and trusts. This withering indictment, buttressed by facts, impressed President Roosevelt. Phillips continued his slashing attacks through novels, and was fatally shot in 1911 by a deranged young man whose family he had allegedly maligned.

Some of the most effective fire of the Muckrakers was directed at social evils. The ugly list included the immoral "white slave" traffic in women, the rickety slums, and the appalling number of industrial accidents. The sorry subjugation of blacks was spotlighted in Ray Stannard Baker's *Following the Color Line* (1908), while the abuses of child labor were brought luridly to light by John Spargo's *The Bitter Cry of the Children* (1906).

Vendors of potent patent medicines (often heavily spiked with alcohol) likewise came in for bitter criticism. These conscienceless vultures sold incredible quantities of adulterated or habit-forming drugs, while "doping" the press with lavish advertising. Muckraking attacks in *Collier's* were ably

Child Workers. The boy is already a veteran coal miner. Two young girls tend a thread-winding machine. (*Left,* International Museum of Photography at George Eastman House; *right,* Library of Congress.)

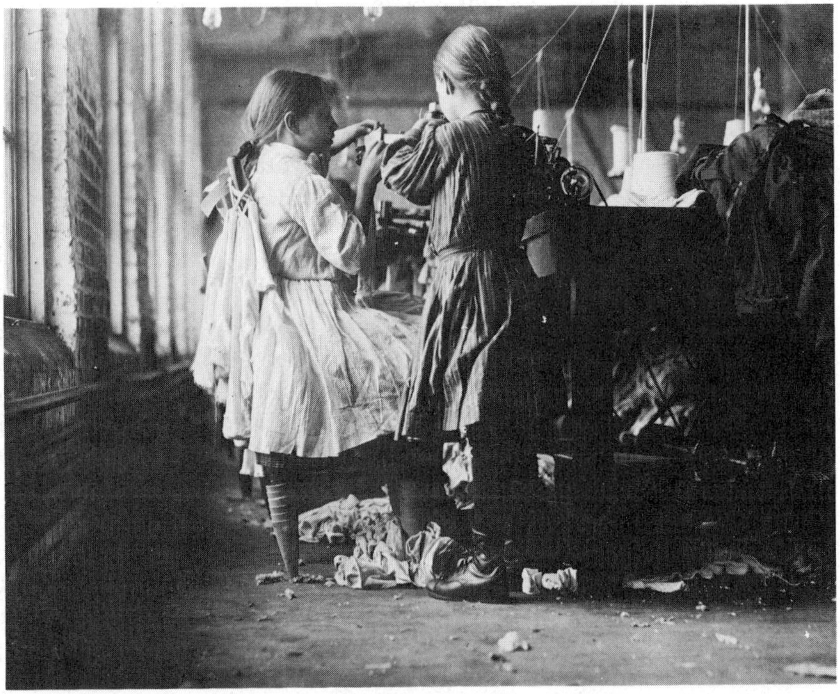

reinforced by Dr. H. W. Wiley, chief chemist of the Department of Agriculture, who with his famous "Poison Squad" performed experiments on himself.

Full of sound and fury, the Muckrakers signified much about the nature of the progressive reform movement. They were long on lamentation and short on sweeping remedies. To right social wrongs they counted on publicity and an aroused public conscience, not drastic political change. They sought not to overthrow capitalism but to cleanse it. The cure for the ills of American democracy, they earnestly believed, was more democracy.

> Ex-President Roosevelt wrote of reform in 1913: "It is vitally necessary to move forward and to shake off the dead hand, often a fossilized dead hand, of the reactionaries; and yet we have to face the fact that there is apt to be a lunatic fringe among the votaries of any forward movement."

Political Progressivism

Progressive reformers were mainly middle-class men and women who felt themselves squeezed from above and below. They sensed pressure from the new giant corporations, the restless immigrant hordes, and the aggressive labor unions. The progressives simultaneously sought two goals: to use state power to curb the trusts, and to stem the socialist threat by generally improving the common person's conditions of life and labor. Progressives emerged in both major parties, in all regions, and at all levels of government. The truth is that progressivism was less a minority movement and more a majority mood.

One of the first objectives of progressives was to regain the power that had slipped from the hands of the people into those of the "interests." These ardent reformers pushed for direct primary elections so as to undercut power-hungry party bosses. They favored the "initiative" so that voters could directly propose legislation themselves, thus bypassing the boss-bought state legislatures. Progressives also agitated for the "referendum." This device would place laws on the ballot for final approval by the people, especially laws that had been railroaded through a compliant legislature by free-spending agents of Big Business. The "recall" would enable the voters to remove faithless elected officials, particularly those who had been bribed by bosses or lobbyists.

Rooting out graft also became a prime goal of earnest progressives. A number of the state legislatures passed corrupt-practices acts, which limited the amount of money that a candidate could spend for his election. Such legislation also restricted huge gifts from corporations, for which the donors would expect special favors. The secret Australian ballot was likewise being introduced more widely in the states to counteract boss rule. Bribery was less feasible when the briber could not tell if he was getting his money's worth from the bribed.

Direct election of United States senators became a favorite goal of progressives, especially after the Muckrakers had exposed the scandalous tie-in between greedy corporations and Congress. By 1900 the Senate contained so many rich men that it was often sneered at as "the Millionaires' Club." Too many of the prosperous solons, elected as they then were by trust-dominated legislatures, heeded the voice of their "masters" rather than that of the masses.

A constitutional amendment to bring about the popular election of senators had rough sledding in Congress, for the plutocratic members of the Senate were happy with existing methods. But a number of states established primary elections in which the voters expressed their preferences for the Senate. The local legislatures, when choosing senators, found it politically wise to heed the voice of the people. Partly as a result of such pressures, the 17th Amendment to the Constitution,

> In 1908 President Roosevelt wrote prophetically: "Personally I believe in woman's suffrage, but I am not an enthusiastic advocate of it, because I do not regard it as a very important matter. I am unable to see that there has been any special improvement in the position of women in those states in the West that have adopted woman's suffrage, as compared with those states adjoining them that have not adopted it. I do not think that giving the women suffrage will produce any marked improvement in the condition of women. I do not believe that it will produce any of the evils feared, and I am very certain that when women as a whole take any special interest in the matter they will have suffrage if they desire it."

approved in 1913, established the direct election of senators. (See Appendix.) But the expected improvement in caliber was slow in coming.

Woman suffrage, the goal of feminists for many decades, likewise received powerful new support from the progressives early in the 1900s. Political reformers believed that the distaff vote would elevate the political tone; foes of the saloon felt that they could count on the support of enfranchised females. The "suffragists," crying "Votes for Women" and "Equal Suffrage for Men and Women," protested bitterly against "Taxation without Representation." Many of the states, especially the more liberal ones in the West, gradually extended the vote to women. But by 1910 nationwide female suffrage was still a decade away; and a suffragist could still be sneeringly defined as "One who has ceased to be a lady and has not yet become a gentleman."

Progressivism in the Cities and States

Progressives scored some of their most impressive gains in the cities. Frustrated by the inefficiency and corruption of machine-oiled city government, many localities followed the pioneering example of Galveston, Texas. In 1901 it had appointed expert-staffed commissions to manage urban affairs. Other communities adopted the city-manager system, also designed to take politics out of municipal administration. Some of these "reforms" obviously valued efficiency more highly than democracy, as control of civic affairs was further removed from the hands of the people.

Urban reformers likewise attacked "slumlords," juvenile delinquency, and wide-open prostitution (vice-at-a-price), which flourished in red-light districts unchallenged by bribed police. Public-spirited city-dwellers also moved to halt the corrupt sale of franchises for streetcars and other public utilities.

Progressivism naturally bubbled up to the state level, notably in Wisconsin, which became a yeasty laboratory of reform. The governor of the state, pompadoured Robert M. ("Fighting Bob") La Follette, was an undersized but overengined crusader who emerged as the most militant of the progressive Republican leaders. After a desperate fight with entrenched monopoly, he reached the governor's chair in 1901. Routing the lumber and

Mr. La Follette's Strongest Card. Reform government in Wisconsin. (Reprinted Courtesy of the Chicago *Tribune*.)

railroad "interests," he wrested considerable control from the crooked corporations and returned it to the people. He also perfected a scheme for regulating public utilities, while laboring in close association with experts on the faculty of the state university at Madison.

Other states marched steadily toward the progressive camp, as they undertook to regulate railroads and trusts, chiefly through public utilities commissions. Oregon was not far behind Wisconsin, and California made giant-boot strides under the stocky Hiram W. Johnson. Elected Republican governor in 1910, this dynamic prosecutor of grafters helped break the dominant grip of the Southern Pacific Railroad on California politics and then, like La Follette, set up a political machine of his own. Heavily whiskered Charles Evans Hughes, the able and fearless reformist Republican governor of New York, had earlier gained national fame as an investigator of malpractices by gas and insurance companies and by the coal trust.

In these and other states, fired-up progressives tackled head-on a whole array of social problems. One of the most remarkable features of this era was the energy and confidence with which reformers did battle with a host of evils. They finally secured the enactment of safety and sanitation codes for industry, and closed certain harmful trades to juveniles. Progressives further protected the toiler with workingman's compensation laws, thus relieving the injured laborer from the burden of lawsuits to prove negligence on the part of the employer. The reformers also secured laws setting maximum hours and minimun wages.

Steaming and unsanitary sweatshops were a public scandal in many cities. The issue was thrust into the public eye in 1911, when a fire at the Triangle Shirtwaist Company in New York City incinerated 146 women workers, mostly girls. Lashed by the public outcry, the legislature of New York and later other legislatures passed laws regulating the hours and conditions of toil in such firetraps. Prisons and "reform" schools likewise came under sharp scrutiny, as the public increasingly accepted the view that these penal institutions were primarily for reformation rather than punishment.

But crusaders for these humane measures did not always have smooth sailing. One dismaying setback came in 1905, when the Supreme Court invalidated a New York law establishing a ten-hour day for bakers. Yet the reformist progressive wave finally washed up into the judiciary, and in 1917 the Court upheld a ten-hour law for factory workers. Gradually the concept of the employer's responsibility to society was replacing the old dog-eat-dog philosophy of unregulated free enterprise.

Corner saloons, with their shutter doors, naturally attracted the ire and fire of progressives. Alcohol was intimately connected with prostitution in red-light districts, with the drunken voter, with crooked city officials dominated by "booze" interests, and with the blowsy "boss" who counted poker chips by night and miscounted ballots by day (including the "cemetery vote"). By 1900 cities like New York and San Francisco had one saloon for about every 200 people.

Anti-liquor campaigners received powerful support from several militant organizations, notably the Woman's Christian Temperance Union (W.C.T.U.). Saintly Frances E. Willard, one of its founders, would fall on her knees in prayer on saloon floors. She found a vigorous ally in the

Temperance Women Sing Outside Saloon. *(Frank Leslie's Illustrated Newspaper,* Feb. 21, 1874. By permission of the Houghton Library, Harvard University.)

Anti-Saloon League, which was aggressive, well organized, and well financed. The Prohibition party, which had put a presidential ticket in the field as early as 1872, was similarly snowballing strength.

Caught up in the crusade, some states and numerous counties passed "dry" laws which controlled, restricted, or abolished alcohol. The big cities were generally "wet," for they had a large immigrant vote accustomed in the Old Country to the free flow of wine and beer. When World War I erupted in 1914, nearly one-half of the population lived in "dry" territory, and nearly three-fourths of the total area had outlawed the saloon. (See map, p. 698.) Demon Rum was groggy, and he was to be floored—temporarily—by the 18th Amendment in 1919.

TR's Square Deal for Labor

Theodore Roosevelt, though something of an imperialistic busybody abroad, was touched by the progressive wave at home. Like other reformers, he feared that the "public interest" was being submerged in the drifting seas of indifference. Everybody's interest was nobody's interest. Roosevelt decided to make it his. His sportsman's instincts spurred him into demanding a "square deal" for capital, labor, and the public at large. Broadly speaking, his program embraced three Cs: control of the corporations, consumer protection, and conservation of natural resources.

The "square deal" for labor received its acid test in 1902, when a crippling strike broke out in the anthracite coal mines of Pennsylvania. Some 140,000 besooted workers, many of them illiterate immigrants, had long been frightfully exploited and accident-riddled. They demanded, among other improvements, a 20 percent increase in pay and a reduction of the working day from ten to nine hours.

Unsympathetic mine owners, confident that a chilled public would react against the miners, refused to arbitrate or even negotiate. One of their spokesmen, the multimillionaire George F. Baer, reflected the high-and-mighty attitude of certain ungenerous employers. Workers, he wrote, would be cared for "not by the labor agitators, but by the Christian men to whom God in His infinite wisdom has given the control of the property interests of this country." Closed minds meant closed mines.

As coal supplies dwindled, factories and schools were forced to shut down, and even hospitals felt the icy grip of winter. Desperately seeking a solution, Roosevelt summoned representatives of the striking miners and the mine owners to the White House. He was vastly annoyed by the "extraordinary stupidity and bad temper" of the "wooden-headed gentry" who operated the mines. As he later confessed, if it had not been for the dignity of his high office, he would have taken one of them "by the seat of the breeches" and "chucked him out of the window."

Roosevelt finally resorted to his trusty Big Stick when he threatened to seize the mines and operate them with federal troops. Faced with this first-time-ever threat to use federal bayonets against capital, rather than labor, the owners grudgingly consented to arbitration. A compromise decision ultimately gave the miners a 10 percent pay boost and a working day of nine hours. But their union was not officially recognized as a bargaining agent.

Keenly aware of the mounting antagonisms between capital and labor, Roosevelt urged Congress to create a new Department of Commerce and Labor. This goal was achieved in 1903. (Ten years later the agency was split into two.) An important arm of the newly born Department of Commerce and Labor was the Bureau of Corporations, which was authorized to probe businesses engaged in interstate commerce. The Bureau was highly useful in helping to break the stranglehold of monopoly, and in clearing the road for the era of "trust busting."

New Railroad Restrictions

Americans love bigness but hate monopoly, and Roosevelt shared their prejudices. The bite of the much-ballyhooed Sherman Anti-Trust Act of 1890 had proved almost completely toothless, and "trustification" was spreading at an alarming rate.

The Sherman Anti-Trust Law Returns from the Dead. (Bartholomew in the Minneapolis *Journal.*)

The President, who habitually hurled harsh words at the "predatory rich," was distressed by the sinister power and wealth of the trusts. To him free enterprise did not mean freedom for the wealthy to exploit the poor.

"Trusts" rapidly came to be a fighting word. Roosevelt believed that these gigantic organizations, with their efficient tools of production, were here to stay. He concluded that there were "good" trusts, with public consciences, and "bad" trusts, with unbridled greed and lust for power. Yet the less discriminating public began to cry with increasing vigor, "Smash the trusts." Thrown on the defensive, the monopolists countered by insisting that success in business was not a crime, and that prosecution under anti-trust laws was often persecution. But there was clearly a crying need for judicious regulation—for policing rather than punishing.

Similarly the many-webbed railroads, grown arrogant like the trusts, were sorely in need of restraint. The Interstate Commerce Act of 1887, tossed as a feeble sop to the public, had proved almost completely ineffective. Railroad barons could endlessly appeal all decisions on rates to the federal courts—a process that might take ten years.

Under the spurs of the ex-cowboy, Congress passed effective railroad legislation, beginning with the Elkins Act of 1903. This curb was aimed primarily at the rebate evil, which had now become so rampant that some operators actually welcomed regulation. Heavy fines could henceforth be imposed, not only on the railroads that gave rebates but also on the shippers who accepted them. Within a few years a number of railroads and manufacturers were convicted under the new law and suffered painful penalties. A spectacular case hit the headlines in 1907, when Judge Kenesaw Mountain Landis found the Standard Oil Company guilty on 1,462 counts of accepting rebates. He thereupon fined the offending corporation an unprecedented $29,240,000. But a higher court set aside his judgment, which seemed more like vengeance than justice.

Much more effective than the Elkins Act in restraining the railroads was the Hepburn Act of 1906. Free passes, with their hint of bribery, were severely restricted. The once-infantile Interstate Commerce Commission was expanded, and its reach was extended to include express companies, sleeping-car companies, and pipelines. For the first time the Commission was given real molars when it was authorized, on complaint of shippers, to nullify existing rates and establish maximum rates.

Though backed by an exasperated public, the Hepburn Act lost some of its proposed teeth in the congressional machinery. The House passed it by the overwhelming margin of 346 to 7, but in the more conservative Senate the railroad lobby rallied for a last-ditch stand. The lobbyists finally secured a compromise proviso to the effect that rate decisions might be appealed to the federal courts. But pending court action, the Commis-

> Roosevelt preached: "The man who advocates destroying the trusts by measures which would paralyze the industries of the country is at least a quack, and at worst an enemy to the Republic."

sion's rates would stand, and the burden of proof that those rates were unfair rested squarely with the carriers.

TR: Trust Buster with a Padded Stick

Roosevelt, as a trust buster, first burst into the headlines in 1902 with an attack on certain railroads. In a spectacular move he authorized his attorney general to file suit under the Sherman Anti-Trust Act against the Northern Securities Company. This gigantic corporation was a holding company, of which J. P. Morgan was the chief financier and "Empire Builder" James J. Hill was the leading organizational genius. These Napoleonic planners sought to achieve a virtual monopoly of the railroads of the Northwest, and potentially of an even vaster area. Roosevelt was thus challenging the most regal potentates of the industrial aristocracy.

The railway promoters appealed to the highest tribunal. Early in 1904, by a 5-to-4 decision, the Supreme Court held that the Northern Securities Company violated the Sherman Anti-Trust Act and must be dissolved. This decision jolted the financial world and angered Big Business, but greatly enhanced TR's reputation as a trust smasher.

Roosevelt's Big Stick crashed down on other giant monopolies, as he initiated over forty legal proceedings against them. The Supreme Court in 1905 declared the Beef Trust illegal, and the heavy hand of justice fell upon monopolists handling sugar, fertilizer, harvesters, and other key commodities.

Much mythology has inflated Roosevelt's reputation as a trustbuster. The Rough Rider understood the political popularity of monopoly-smashing, but he did not consider it sound economic policy. Combination and integration, he felt, were the hallmarks of the age, and to try to stem the tide of economic progress by political means he considered the rankest folly. Bigness was not necessarily badness; so why punish success? Roosevelt's real purpose in assaulting the Goliaths of industry was symbolic: to prove conclusively that the government, not private business, ruled the country. He believed in regulating, not fragmenting, the Big Business combines. The threat of dissolution, he felt, might make the moguls of monopoly more amenable to federal regulation—as it did.

The Sow That Breeds the Litter. In Populist eyes the Wall Street Money Trust bred and fattened the other trusts, while the little pig representing the people lay dead. (W. H. Harvey, *Coin's Financial School up to Date,* 1895.)

In truth, Roosevelt never swung his trust-crushing stick with maximum force. In many ways, the huge industrial behemoths were healthier—though perhaps more "tame"—at the end of Roosevelt's reign than they had been before. His successor, William Howard Taft, actually "busted" more trusts than TR did. In one celebrated instance in 1907, Roosevelt even gave his personal blessing to J. P. Morgan's plan to have U.S. Steel absorb the Tennessee Coal and Iron Company, without fear of anti-trust reprisals. When Taft then launched a suit against U.S. Steel in 1911, the political reaction from TR was explosive.

Caring for the Consumer

Roosevelt backed a noteworthy measure in 1906 that benefited both corporations and consumers. Big meat packers were being shut out of certain European markets because some American meat—from the small packinghouses, claimed the giants—had been found to be tainted. Foreign governments were even threatening to ban all American meat imports by throwing out the good beef with the bad botulism.

At the same time, American consumers hungered for safer canned products. Their appetite for reform was whetted by Upton Sinclair's sensational novel *The Jungle,* published in 1906. Sinclair intended his revolting tract to focus attention on the plight of the workers in the big canning factories, but instead he appalled the public with his description of disgustingly unsanitary food products. (As he put it, he aimed for the nation's heart, but hit its stomach.) The book described in nauseating detail the filth, disease, and putrefaction in Chicago's damp, ill-ventilated slaughterhouses. Many readers, including Roosevelt, were so sickened that for a time they found meat unpalatable. The President was moved by the loathsome mess in Chicago to appoint a special investigating commission, whose cold-blooded report almost outdid Upton Sinclair's novel. It related how piles of poisoned rats, rope ends, splinters, and other debris were scooped up and canned as potted ham. A cynical jingle ran:

> Mary had a little lamb,
> And when she saw it sicken,
> She shipped it off to Packingtown,
> And now it's labeled chicken.

Backed by a nauseated public, Roosevelt induced Congress to pass the Meat Inspection Act of 1906. It decreed that the preparation of meat shipped over state lines would be subject to federal inspection from corral to can. Although the largest packers resisted certain features of the act, they grudgingly accepted it as an opportunity to drive their smaller, fly-by-night competitors out of business. At the same time, they could receive the government's seal of approval on their exports. As a companion to the Meat Inspection Act, the Pure Food and Drug Act of 1906 was designed to prevent the adulteration and mislabeling of foods and drugs.

Earth Control

Pushful Americans, assuming that their natural resources were inexhaustible, had looted and polluted their vast domain with unparalleled speed and greed. The West especially was eager to accelerate the process, for it believed that rapid expansion "built up the country" and increased prosperity by pushing up land values. As for being worried about the future, common frontier queries were, "Why preserve the wilderness when we've been fighting it for years?" and "What has posterity ever done for us?" But long before the end of the 19th Century, far-visioned men could see that such a squandering of the nation's birthright would have to be halted or America would sink from resource-richness to despoiled squalor.

A feeble step in the right direction had come under President Hayes in 1877, when Congress passed the Desert Land Act. The federal government agreed to sell up to 640 acres at $1.25 an acre, provided that the purchaser would reclaim the thirsty soil in three years. This pioneering law led to some irrigation and much fraud. Witnesses would swear that they had seen the land being irrigated—which often meant that a bucket of water had been poured on it.

An aroused Congress, faced with the end of the frontier, had finally made a major move toward conservation. In the law of 1891 it authorized the President to set aside public forest lands for

> In his annual message to Congress (1907), Roosevelt declared prophetically, "We are prone to speak of the resources of this country as inexhaustible; this is not so. The mineral wealth of the country, the coal, iron, oil, gas, and the like, does not reproduce itself, and therefore is certain to be exhausted ultimately; and wastefulness in dealing with it to-day means that our descendants will feel the exhaustion a generation or two before they otherwise would."

national reserves. Under Presidents Harrison, Cleveland, and McKinley some 46 million acres of magnificent trees were rescued from the lumberman's saw and preserved for a grateful posterity.

Congress had further grappled with the reclamation problem in 1894, when it approved the Carey Act. Arid federal lands in the West would be ceded to individual states, provided that the state in each instance would cause the land to be irrigated and settled upon. This forward-looking measure, through the happy marriage of desert and water, led to the cultivation of about a million barren acres.

A new day in the history of conservation dawned with the advent of Roosevelt. He looked upon the crusade, though still in the creeping stage, as one phase of the fight against predatory corporations. Huntsman, naturalist, rancher, lover of the great out-of-doors, he was appalled by the pillaging of timber and mineral resources. By 1900 only about a quarter of the virgin forests remained erect, three-fourths of them in private hands. Lumbermen had already logged off most of the virgin timber from Maine to Michigan, and the sharp thud of their axes was beginning to split the silence in the great fir forests of the Pacific slope. Roosevelt proceeded to set aside in federal reserves some 125 million acres, or almost three times the acreage thus saved from the saw by his three predecessors. He similarly earmarked millions of acres of coal deposits, as well as water resources useful for irrigation and power. To set a shining example, in 1902 he banned Christmas trees from the White House.

> Gifford Pinchot, a foremost conservationist in the Roosevelt administration, wrote: "The object of our forest policy is not to preserve the forests because they are refuges for the wild creatures of the wilderness, but the making of prosperous homes. Every other consideration comes as secondary. . . . The test of utility . . . implies that no lands will be permanently reserves which can serve the people better in any other way."

Loggers in the State of Washington, 1912. It took the sweat and skill of many men to conquer a giant Douglas Fir like this one. An axe-wielding "sniper" had rounded the edges of this log so that a team of oxen, driven by a "bull-whacker," could more easily drag it out of the woods along a "skid road." "Skid road" (sometimes corrupted as "skid row") was also a name for the often-sleazy sections of logging towns, where loggers spent their time in the off-season. (Culver Pictures, Inc.)

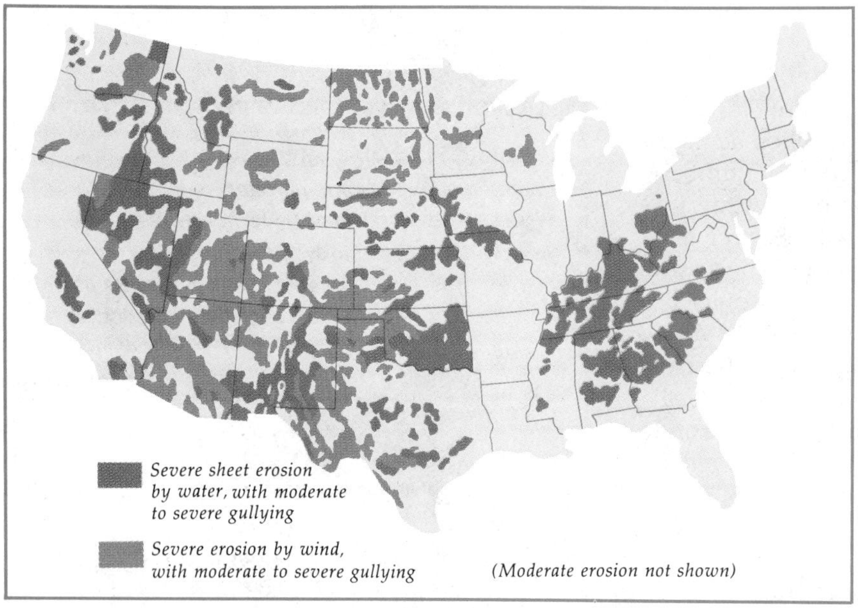

THE EXTENT OF EROSION, 1934

Note the extensive wind erosion in the Southwest, which was dubbed the "Dust Bowl" in the 1930s. Mechanized farmers had "busted" the sod of the Southern plains so thoroughly that they literally broke the back of the land. Tons of dust blew out of the Dust Bowl in the 1930s and blotted the sun from the skies as far away as New York. A Kansas newspaperman reported in 1935 that in his dust-darkened town "Lady Godiva could ride through streets without even the horse seeing her."

But the dynamic TR's concept of conservation went beyond the simple sentiment of "woodman-spare-that-tree." Intelligent use, not esthetic preservation, was Roosevelt's first priority. Under him, professional foresters and engineers developed a policy of multiple-use resource management. They sought to combine recreation, sustained-yield logging, watershed protection, and summer stock-grazing on the same expanse of federal land.

Rational use of resources meant large-scale and long-term planning, as well as efficient administrative techniques. Roosevelt's conservation program, like many of his business policies, meant working hand in glove with the biggest resource users. The one-man-and-a-mule logger, or the one-man-and-a-dog sheepherder, could not be counted upon to cooperate with the new resources bureaucracy. The little fellow was inevitably shouldered aside, in the interests of efficiency, by the combined strength of big business and big government.

Roosevelt Champions Conservation

Roosevelt, though by far the noisiest, was not the first conservationist. Other zealots before him had broken important ground, notably Gifford Pinchot, head of the federal Division of Forestry and a red-blooded member of TR's "Tennis Cabinet." But Roosevelt seized the banner of leadership, and charged into the fray with all the weight of his prestige, his energy, his firsthand knowledge, and his slashing invective.

The thirst of the desert still unslaked, Congress responded to the whip of the Rough Rider by passing the Newlands Act of 1902. Washington was authorized to collect money from the sale of public lands in the sun-baked Western states, and then use these funds for the development of irrigation projects. Settlers repaid the cost of reclamation from their now-productive soil, and the money was put into a revolving fund to finance more such enterprises. The giant Roosevelt Dam, constructed in Arizona on the Salt River, was appropriately dedicated by ex-President Roosevelt in 1911.

Roosevelt's most dramatic single move toward conservation came in 1908, when he summoned the Conference of Governors to Washington. The group consisted of prominent governors, justices of the Supreme Court, selected members of Congress, and celebrities like Bryan, Cleveland, and Carnegie. One encouraging result was to inspire the governors to carry on the good work at home.

High Point for Conservation. Conservationist Roosevelt and famed naturalist-conservationist John Muir visit Glacier Point, on the rim of Yosemite Valley, California. In the distance are Yosemite Falls; a few feet behind Roosevelt is a sheer drop of 3,254 feet. (Historical Pictures Service, Chicago.)

Eighteen months later, forty-one states had set up active conservation commissions.

Conservation, including reclamation, was probably Roosevelt's most enduring tangible achievement. The Isthmian canal would have been dug sooner or later, but lands that are eroded and resources that are raped do not readily come back. The super-active President took conservation out of the conversation stage, threw the force of his colorful personality behind it, dramatized it, and aroused public opinion to a constructive crusade. Conservation under Roosevelt became almost a religion; its more truly scientific stages were to come in later decades.

> Campaigning in Kansas in 1910, ex-President Roosevelt said, "Of all the questions which can come before this nation, short of its existence in a great war, there is none which compares in importance with the great central task of leaving this land even a better land for our descendants than it is for us, and training them into a better race to inhabit the land and pass it on. Conservation is a great moral issue, for it involves the patriotic duty of insuring the safety and continuance of the nation."

Elected President "In His Own Right"

Roosevelt looked forward to the election of 1904 with keen concern. Resenting the sneering title "His Accidency," he was eager to secure popular endorsement by election under his own colors. He was undeniably the idol of the masses—the children's "Teddy Bear" honored his bear-shooting exploits—but the conservative Republican bosses regarded him as an unmanageable maverick. They pined for a standpatter like Mark Hanna, his only possible rival, who, as "Roosevelt luck" would have it, died early in 1904.

The "Cowboy President" was nominated at Chicago in 1904 by acclamation. As an antidote to his presumed radicalism, the delegates chose for Vice-President a frigid standpatter from Indiana, Charles W. Fairbanks—dubbed "Icebanks." The platform likewise offset Roosevelt's wild tendencies by upholding tariff protection and the gold standard, while letting the trusts off with a verbal slap on the wrist.

Radical Bryan Democrats, twice led down to defeat by the "Peerless Leader," were unhorsed at the St. Louis convention. The hardbitten conservative wing, now back in the saddle, loudly demanded a "safe and sane" candidate. Eastern "safe-and-saners" managed to nominate the colorless Judge Alton B. Parker, an impeccably respectable New York lawyer of high character. As a vote getter of considerable power in his home state, "Parker the Silent" was actually more liberal than his reactionary followers represented him to be.

The Democratic platform reflected the unhappiness of the party over Roosevelt's usurpations of legislative and judicial functions. It flayed his administration as "spasmodic, erratic, sensational, spectacular, and arbitrary." No reference was made to the silver issue, though Parker angered the Bryanites by sending a telegram to the convention in which he came out bluntly for the gold standard.

The ensuing canvass proved tame. Judge Parker, hitting at Rough Riderism, demanded a "government of law, not of men." He finally injected some fireworks when he accused the Republicans of collecting campaign funds from corporations which expected favors in return. Roosevelt promptly cried "liar," but a subsequent congressional investigation proved that the charge had considerable validity. The Standard Oil Company contributed a lubricant of $125,000.

Full dinner pails added luster to the Republican cause, but the overshadowing issue was TR's Big Stick personality—"Theodore Roosevelt, one and indivisible." His popularity was not dimmed by loose charges that while in Cuba he had shot a Spaniard in the back; and his worshipful following sang lustily, "Three Cheers for the Rough Rider" and "We Want Teddy for Four Years More."

Anti-TR Election Cartoon.
(New York *World,* 1904.)

The colorful cowboy clattered home in a canter, and proved to be the first "accidental" President to succeed himself. The electoral count was 336 to 140; the popular count, 7,623,486 to 5,077,911. Roosevelt's avalanche even swept down into the border state of Missouri. The painfully pedestrian Parker proved to be the worst-beaten major candidate since Horace Greeley was snowed under in 1872. Many pro-silver Bryanites, protesting Parker's stand for gold, boycotted the polls.

This victory was a glorious personal triumph for the strenuous President and "my policies." The voters clearly preferred Roosevelt, the impetuous candidate of the conservative party, to Parker, the conservative candidate of the impetuous party. In his hour of elation the "dee-lighted" winner announced that he regarded his partial first term of three and one-half years as a full term, and that under no circumstances would he be a candidate for a third term. This was a tactical blunder, for the power of the king wanes when the people know that he will be dead in four years.

"The Roosevelt Panic" of 1907

Prosperity suffered a sharp setback in 1907, when a short but punishing panic descended. It was partly a reaction to worldwide economic trends, partly the result of the billions of dollars in corporation stock that had glutted the market. Centering heavily in Wall Street, the financial flurry was known as "the Rich Man's Panic," and was featured by frightened "runs" on banks. Suicides and criminal indictments were common.

The financial world hastened to blame Roosevelt for the panic. It cried that this "quack," "demagogue," and "crazy man" had unsettled industry by his boat-rocking tactics. Conservatives damned him as "Theodore the Meddler," and branded the current distress "the Roosevelt Panic." The hot-tempered President lashed back at his critics when he accused "certain malefactors of great wealth" of having deliberately engineered

Taft Campaigning. A powerful voice was a political necessity in the pre-electronic age. (United Press International Photo)

the monetary crisis to force the government to relax its assaults on trusts.

Fortunately, the Panic of 1907 paved the way for long-overdue fiscal reforms. Precipitating a currency shortage, the flurry laid bare the need for a more elastic medium of exchange. In a crisis of this sort, the hard-pressed banks were unable to increase the volume of their money, and those with ample reserves were reluctant to lend to their less fortunate sisters. Congress in 1908 responded to existing pressures by passing the Aldrich-Vreeland Act, which authorized National Banks to issue emergency currency backed by various kinds of collateral. The path was thus smoothed for the epochal Federal Reserve Act of 1913.

The Taft-Bryan Presidential Sweepstakes of 1908

Roosevelt was still so immensely popular in 1908 that he could easily have won a second presidential nomination, and almost certainly the election. Although at loggerheads with Congress and hated by big business, he almost hypnotized the masses. The Benéts have captured his appeal:

> T.R. is spanking a Senator,
> T.R. is chasing a bear,
> T.R. is busting an Awful Trust
> And dragging it from its lair.
>
> They're calling T.R. a lot of things
> —The men in the private car—
> But the day-coach likes exciting folks
> And the day-coach likes T.R.*

Roosevelt did not really want to leave the White House; he had enjoyed a "bully time" in the presidential goldfish bowl. But he felt bound by his impulsive post-election promise after his victory in 1904.

The departing President naturally sought a successor who would carry out "my policies"—that is, the forward-looking Roosevelt program. The man of his choice was his amiable, ample-girthed, and huge-framed (6 feet tall; 1.83 meters) secretary of war, William Howard Taft, a moderate progressive. Taft had made an admirable record under TR as an administrator in subordinate capacities. As an heir apparent, he had often been called upon to "sit on the lid"—all 350 pounds (159 kilograms) of him—when Roosevelt was absent.

Big-stick methods were much in evidence at the Republican convention of 1908 in Chicago. Roosevelt, wielding his enormous influence backstage, had lined up enough delegates behind his handwritten platform and hand-picked candidate. He also employed the convention machinery—the "steam roller"—to push Taft's nomination through on the first ballot, thus heading off a possible stampede to himself. The Republican (Roosevelt) platform, pointing with pride in all directions and praising TR's policies, declared against monopoly, while promising both tariff revision and currency reform.

Three weeks later, in July 1908, the Democrats

*"Theodore Roosevelt" from *A Book of Americans* by Rosemary & Stephen Vincent Benét. Copyright, 1933, by Rosemary & Stephen Vincent Benét. Copyright renewed ©, 1961, by Rosemary Carr Benét. Reprinted by permission of Brandt & Brandt Literary Agency, Inc.

TR Engineers Taft's Nomination at Chicago.
(Harding in the Brooklyn *Eagle*, 1908.)

met at mile-high Denver, in the heart of the silver country. The Bryanites, who had returned to the driver's seat, had no stomach for another drubbing under a stodgy candidate like Judge Parker. Twice-beaten Bryan, the hardy quadrennial, was nominated with uproarious enthusiasm on the first ballot. His platform condemned the flighty personal rule of Roosevelt, as well as the alleged stranglehold of the trusts on American life.

The campaign of 1908 was even duller in some ways than that of 1904, though both the portly Taft and the balding "Boy Orator" took to the stump. Taft, who read cut-and-dried speeches to large crowds, made a fence-straddling effort to present himself as a progressive in the West and a conservative in the East. Four Ps helped the Republican ticket: prosperity, progressivism, prosecution of the trusts, and personalities—Taft and Roosevelt, largely Roosevelt. The progressive Bryan, attempting to capitalize on the President's popularity, endorsed many Rooseveltian policies. Alleging that they had been stolen from him, he not illogically represented himself as the logical man to carry them out.

A prosperous country was quite content to accept the stable leadership of Taft—the man so emphatically endorsed by Roosevelt, who in a sense was running again. "Shall the people rule?" cried the silver voice of Bryan. They decided to do so with solid Judge Taft, who polled 321 electoral votes to 162 for the "Peerless Leader." The victor's popular count was 7,678,908 to 6,409,104. Bryan garnered fewer votes than in 1896, despite the increase in population, though he fared much better than the colorless Parker four years earlier. The Socialists amassed a surprising tally of 420,793 for Eugene V. Debs, the "hero" of the Pullman strike of 1894.

Bryan, apostle of lost causes, was finished as a presidential possibility. Yet a number of ideas that he sponsored were seized upon and put into operation by the Republicans. He once quipped that he was the only man who could rule the nation by losing the presidency.

The Rough Rider Thunders Out

Roosevelt, ever in the limelight, left early in 1909 for a lion hunt in Africa. His numerous enemies clinked glasses to the toast "Health to the Lions." But the savage beasts failed to "do their duty." To an ex-President all the rest of life is an anticlimax, and the tragedy of Roosevelt is that he left his office too young, at the age of fifty, when still bursting with energy. Ex-Presidents are usually some-

> Roosevelt, who preached the doctrine of the "strenuous life," practiced it until almost the end. In 1913 he sent a political message on a still-preserved phonograph recording to the Boy's Progressive League: "Don't flinch, don't foul, and hit the line hard."

thing of a problem, and here was one who did not take kindly to the role of private citizen.

Roosevelt was branded by some in his day as a wild-eyed radical, but his reputation as an eater of errant industrialists now seems inflated. He fought many a sham battle, and the number of laws that he inspired was certainly not in proportion to the amount of noise he emitted. He was often under attack from the reigning business lords, but the more enlightened of them knew that they had a friend in the White House. Roosevelt should be remembered first and foremost as the cowboy who started to tame the bucking bronco of adolescent capitalism, and thus ensured it a long adult life.

TR's enthusiasm and perpetual youthfulness, like an overgrown Boy Scout's, appealed to the young of all ages. "You must always remember," a British diplomat cautioned his colleagues, "that the President is about six." As a kind of umpire, he served as a political lightning rod to protect capitalists against popular indignation—and against socialism, which Roosevelt regarded as "ominous." He strenuously sought the middle road between unbridled individualism and paternalistic socialism.

Several other contributions of Roosevelt lasted beyond his presidency. First, he greatly enlarged the power and prestige of the presidential office—and masterfully developed the technique of using the Big Stick of publicity as a political bludgeon. Second, he helped to direct and make respectable the progressive movement. His Square Deal, in a sense, was the grandfather of the New Deal later launched by his fifth cousin, Franklin D. Roosevelt.

Finally, to a greater degree than any of his predecessors, TR opened the eyes of the American people to the fact that they lived in the same world with other nations. As a great power they had fallen heir to responsibilities—and had been seized by ambitions—from which there was no escaping.

VARYING VIEWPOINTS

Debate about progressivism has revolved around a question that is simple to ask but devilishly difficult to answer: Who were the progressives? It was once taken for granted that progressive reformers were simply the heirs of the Jeffersonian-Jacksonian-Populist reform tradition; they were the oppressed and downtrodden common people who finally erupted in wrath and demanded their due. In his influential *Age of Reform,* Richard Hofstadter debunked that view. Progressive leaders, he argued, were middle-class people whose pocketbooks were not threatened by emerging industrialism but whose social status was jeopardized. "Status anxiety" thus prompted these people to become reformers, and their psychological motivation tended to render many of their efforts quirky and ineffectual.

By contrast, "New Left" writers, notably Gabriel Kolko, argue that progressivism was dominated by older business elites who successfully perverted "reform" to their own conservative ends. Still other scholars, such as Samuel P. Hays and Robert H. Wiebe, suggest that the progressives were members of a newly emergent social class possessed of the new techniques of scientific expertise and organizational know-how. In this view, progressivism was not a struggle of the people *versus* the "interests," nor a confused campaign by status-threatened reformers, nor a conservative coup d'état. The movement was simply an effort to rationalize and modernize many social institutions ("reform without a fight"). Yet the argument that progressives paved the way to a scientific, bureaucratic future is severely qualified by Otis Graham's study showing that less than half the surviving progressives approved the later reforms of the New Deal. Where did the progressives—and progressivism—go?

SELECT READINGS

Perceptive interpretations are Samuel P. Hays, *The Response to Industrialism, 1885–1914* (1957), Robert H. Wiebe, *The Search for Order* (1967), and Richard Hofstadter, *The Age of Reform* (1955). More detailed are Eric Goldman, *Rendezvous with Destiny* (rev. ed., 1956), George Mowry, *The Era of Theodore Roosevelt* (1958), Otis Graham, *The Great Campaigns: Reform and War in America, 1900–1928* (1971), and the same author's *Encore for Reform: The Old Progressives and the New Deal* (1967). Valuable analyses of progressivism at the state level include Mowry's *The California Progressives* (1951), Richard McCormick's exceptionally good *From Realignment to Reform: Political Change in New York State, 1893–1910* (1981), and David Thelen's study of Wisconsin, *The New Citizenship* (1972). David Chalmers analyzes *The Muckrake Years* (1974). The government's relation to the economy is scrutinized in W. Letwin, *Law and Economic Policy in America* (1965), Grant McConnell, *Private Power and American Democracy* (1966), and in Albro Martin, *Enterprise Denied: Origins of the Decline of American Railroads* (1971). Two especially provocative views of this issue are James Weinstein, *The Corporate Ideal in the Liberal State* (1968), and Gabriel Kolko, *The Triumph of Conservatism* (1963). Consult also Robert Wiebe, *Businessmen and Reform* (1962), and Alfred D. Chandler, *The Visible Hand* (1977). On pure food and drugs, see O. E. Anderson, *The Health of a Nation* (1958), and J. H. Young, *Toadstool Millionaires* (1961). Other social issues of importance are treated in J. H. Timberlake, *Prohibition and the Progressive Movement* (1963), David J. Rothman, *Conscience and Convenience: The Asylum and its Alternatives in Progressive America* (1980), Roy Lubove, *The Progressives and the Slums* (1962), Allen F. Davis, *Spearheads for Reform: The Social Settlements and the Progressive Movement, 1890–1914* (1967), R. H. Bremner, *From the Depths: The Discovery of Poverty in the United States* (1956), and Jack Holl, *Juvenile Reform in the Progressive Era* (1971). On conservation, see Samuel P. Hays, *Conservation and the Gospel of Efficiency* (1959), Elmo Richardson, *The Politics of Conservation* (1962), and James Penick, Jr., *Progressive Politics and Conservation* (1968).

33

William Howard Taft and the Progressive Revolt

I am in this [Progressive] fight for certain principles, and the first and most important . . . is . . . "Thou shalt not steal." Thou shalt not steal a nomination. Thou shalt neither steal in politics nor in business. Thou shalt not steal from the people the birthright of the people to rule themselves.

THEODORE ROOSEVELT, in Chicago, 1912

Taft: A Round Peg in a Square Hole

William Howard Taft, with his ruddy complexion and upturned mustache, was inaugurated in 1909 during one of the worst sleet storms of the century. He inspired widespread confidence. "Everybody loves a fat man," the saying goes, and the jovial Taft, with "mirthquakes" of laughter bubbling up from his abundant abdomen, was personally popular. He had graduated second in his class at Yale, and had established an admirable reputation as a lawyer and judge, though widely regarded as hostile to labor unions. He had been a trusted administrator under Roosevelt–in the Philippines, at home, and in Cuba, where he had served capably as a "trouble shooter."

But "good old Will" suffered from fatal political

handicaps. "Appointed" by Roosevelt, he followed the noise, bluster, and showmanship of TR; and any successor was bound to seem a pale anticlimax. Taft could not rush into controversies with gnashing teeth; he could not brand men liars, and then dash off to shoot bears. Instead, he played a little golf, at a time when this pastime was a "dude's game," and his bulging figure looked ridiculous in a golfing outfit.

Roosevelt believed in a government by men—at least by one man, himself. Taft was an ingrained legalist who believed in a government by laws rather than by men. With his careful legal training, he cringed at the alleged Rooseveltian dictum: "Damn the law!" He searched the statutes to find authority for his proposed actions; Roosevelt had scanned them, if at all, to see if there was anything to stop his actions.

President William H. Taft (1857–1930). A conservative lawyer-judge, Taft was handicapped by following the dominating Theodore Roosevelt. About two weeks after taking over the presidency, he wrote to "My dear Theodore," that "When I am addressed as 'Mr. President,' I turn to see whether you are not at my elbow." (Brown Brothers.)

Roosevelt had led the conflicting elements of the Republican party by the sheer force of his personality. Taft, though talented in other ways, had none of the arts of a dashing political leader, and none of Roosevelt's zest for the fray. "Politics make me sick" is the refrain that runs through his private letters. A better lieutenant than leader, he had permitted himself to be pushed into the presidential "prison" by his ambitious wife and brothers; his own ambition was for membership on the Supreme Court. Recoiling from the clatter of controversy, he generally adopted an attitude of passivity toward Congress. He was a poor judge of public opinion; and his candor made him a chronic victim of "foot-in-mouth" disease.

"Peaceful Bill" Taft was no doubt a mild progressive, but at heart he was more wedded to the status quo than to change. Carried along on the coattails of Roosevelt's vigorous progressivism, he at first seemed to be more progressive than he actually was. The heavy responsibilities of the presidency sobered him, so that at times he appeared to be downright reactionary.

Taft's official family at the outset was packed with standpatters, including some who suffered from hardening of the intellectual arteries. The Cabinet—an ultra-conservative body—was dominated by prosperous lawyers. It contained no representative of the party's "insurgent" wing, which was on fire for reform of current abuses. The leading Cabinet member was an able corporation lawyer, Secretary of State Philander C. Knox, known as "Sleepy Phil" because of his weak-kneed prosecution of the trusts as attorney general under McKinley.

The Payne-Aldrich Tariff Betrayal

Agitation for a sharp reduction of the high Dingley Tariff of 1897 had gained momentum during the "reign" of Roosevelt. But the Rough Rider had been much too adroit, despite his apparent rashness, to tackle this dynamite-laden issue. Outcries for reform finally became so overwhelming that the Republican platform of 1908 "unequivocally"

Taft the Golfer Hits Tariff Ball. Actually, he flubbed the ball. Contemporary cartoon.

pledged a tariff revision, without saying whether the revision would be up or down. Taft interpreted this promise to mean a substantial reduction, and forthrightly announced that he would strive toward that goal.

This clamor for tariff revision was but one aspect of the current progressive crusade. Many progressives considered the protective tariff to be "the Mother of Trusts," and regarded the existing Dingley Act as contributing to the high cost of living. Impassioned spokesmen for the agricultural Middle West argued further that tariff walls hampered the importation of cheap manufactured goods, and at the same time hurt the sale of American farm surpluses abroad. But the hidebound Old Guard Republicans, many of them well-fed beneficiaries of protection, were content to let the high Dingley Tariff stand. "Aren't all our fellows happy?" asked one of their leaders, the shrewd, cynical, cigar-chewing speaker of the House, Joseph G. ("Uncle Joe") Cannon.

But tariff revision could not be sidestepped. A transparently honest Taft, true to his promises, called Congress into special session in March 1909. The so-called Payne Bill, as approved by the House, provided for modest reductions. But these proved distasteful to the Senate, then dominated by a coterie of reactionaries. This group was brilliantly led by multimillionaire Senator Aldrich of Rhode Island, who, though personally charming, was dictatorial. With an arrogant display of power, the senatorial Old Guard engineered 847 changes in the Payne Bill, some 600 of which were revisions upward. As a feeble sop to the public, hides and a few other items, including sea moss and canary-bird seed, were put on the free list. "Mr. Dooley" was prompted to remark that "Practically ivrything nicissry to existence comes in free." Actually, the duties were reduced from 46.5 to 40.8 percent. (See chart on p. 558.)

When it became evident that the Payne-Aldrich Bill would bring no substantial downward revision, alarm and anger swept through the grain-growing Middle West. Frustrated farmers increased their cries for a high tariff on Western agricultural produce and lowered duties on Eastern manufactured articles. A group of a half-dozen or so Middle Western senators, led by stumpy and grim-faced "Battling Bob" La Follette of Wisconsin, fought the Payne-Aldrich Bill tooth and nail. Unable to prevent its passage, they at least advertised its fraud to the entire country. But the senatorial insurgents did not emerge empty-handed. They did force into the measure a pioneering 1 percent tax on corporation profits, and they did give added impetus to the move for attaching an income-tax amendment to the federal Constitution.

The Payne-Aldrich hodgepodge put Taft on an awkward spot. He could point to some slight reductions and to other redeeming features, including provision for a fact-finding Tariff Commission. But the measure seemed like a flagrant betrayal of his promise to reduce the tariff substantially. If he signed the Payne-Aldrich Bill, he would solemnize that betrayal. If he vetoed it, he would disrupt a party that was showing dangerous signs of breaking into insurgent and conservative factions. After much hand-wringing, Taft signed.

Taft's subsequent campaign for the new tariff was most ill-advised. He might well have said that while the law was bad, it was the best he could wheedle from Congress. But instead he went out on a speaking tour and vigorously defended the

Taft Pleads for Lower Tariff. TR glares from the wall, and the Big Stick gathers cobwebs. One congressman wrote that Taft was "a well-meaning man who was born with two left feet." (Johnson in the Philadelphia *North American*, 1909.)

Payne-Aldrich monstrosity. At Winona, Minnesota, he went overboard and insisted that the measure was "the best bill that the Republican Party ever passed." In the midst of the resulting uproar, he floundered into hotter water by explaining lamely that he had dictated the speech hurriedly between railroad stations.

Conservation Controversies Under Taft

Taft was a genuine friend of conservation, and his contributions compared rather favorably with his predecessor's, in fact, eclipsed them in some categories. He set up the Bureau of Mines to conserve mineral resources and to safeguard human resources. He secured authority from Congress to rescue from private exploitation millions of acres of coal lands in Wyoming and Montana—a procedure that Roosevelt had rather questionably exercised on his own responsibility. Taft also withdrew water-power sites from private exploitation, in pursuance of legislation passed by Congress in 1910.

The President's praiseworthy steps toward conservation were largely erased in the public mind by the violent Ballinger-Pinchot quarrel, which erupted in 1909. The storm center was Secretary of the Interior Ballinger, an expert on land law from the state of Washington. Roosevelt, prone to be contemptuous of statutes, had achieved much of his success in conservation by stretching existing laws to the limit—and even beyond. Ballinger, a lawyer troubled by legal scruples, reversed this process when he threw open to private exploitation water-power sites in Wyoming and Montana that had been arbitrarily withdrawn under Roosevelt. Valuable coal lands in Alaska were likewise opened to giant corporations, also in accordance with the strict letter of the law.

Ballinger's retreat scandalized ardent Rooseveltian conservationists. The Rough Rider might have burst out, "Damn the law—these natural resources must be preserved for the people!" Spearheading the criticism was a former member of Roosevelt's Tennis Cabinet, Gifford Pinchot, chief of the Division of Forestry of the Department of Agriculture. In the resulting free-for-all Taft, who was a stickler for administrative efficiency, felt compelled to uphold Secretary Ballinger and dismiss Pinchot for insubordination. A subsequent congressional investigation cleared Ballinger, amid angry cries of "whitewash" from the Rooseveltites. A minority report, dictated partly by Republican insurgents, condemned Secretary Ballinger.

Unhappily the bad taste left by the Ballinger uproar lingered. Taft was much too loyal to desert a subordinate under fire, so he kept the secretary on for a year and a half after the storm broke. Later revelations indicate that the berated Ballinger was on sounder legal ground than many critics believed. But at that time Taft seemed to be handing over to greedy interests those natural resources that TR had so spectacularly rescued. The whole unsavory episode widened the growing rift between the President and the ex-President, one-time bosom friends.

The Insurgent Uprising of 1910

The reformist wing of the Republican party was now up in arms. It had been aroused mostly by the unpopular Payne-Aldrich Tariff and by White House support for Ballinger. Taft was being pushed increasingly into the company of the standpat Old Guard. Its leading mouthpiece in the House of Representatives was the coarse and profane "Uncle Joe" Cannon, who occupied the driver's seat of the well-oiled House machinery. Becoming insufferably dictatorial, he denied places on important committees to members who were so bold as to grumble against his practices.

Republican insurgents in the House, many of them Roosevelt worshipers, were all set to stage a spectacular uprising. Led by George W. Norris of Nebraska, they made the exciting discovery that by joining hands with the Democrats they could outvote the standpat Republicans and curb the tyrannical Cannon. Accordingly, in March 1910, they engineered a memorable revolt against "Cannonism." After tense sessions, one of which lasted about thirty hours, they gained the upper hand. Specifically, they took away Cannon's privilege of appointing the all-important Rules Committee, made that body elective by the House, and excluded the speaker from it. Cannon, who had blocked reform legislation, now lost his arbitrary power to decide what bills could be presented to the full House and voted on.

The Common People Await Teddy's Return.
(Herbert Johnson's Scrapbook.)

Insurgents had looked in vain to the White House for aid in their fight against Cannon. The breach between the President and the Republican progressives widened in the struggle to pass the Mann-Elkins Act of 1910, designed to strengthen the Interstate Commerce Commission. Taft had backed a mildly progressive measure, but the insurgents took the bit in their teeth and ran away with the bill, enacting far stronger restrictions than the cautious President wanted. Infuriated, he turned openly on the rebels, determined to purge them in the upcoming congressional elections.

By the spring of 1910 the Grand Old Party was split wide open, owing in part to the clumsiness of Taft. A popular jingle voiced the longing of many Rooseveltians for their hero's return from Africa:

> Teddy, come home and blow your horn,
> The sheep's in the meadow, the cow's in the corn.
> The boy you left to 'tend the sheep
> Is under the haystack fast asleep.

A suspicious "Teddy" returned triumphantly to New York in June 1910, and shortly thereafter stirred up a tempest. He had already heard enough from talebearers to suspect that Taft was carrying out "my policies"—on a stretcher. Unable to keep silent, he took to the stump and at Osawatomie, Kansas, shocked the Old Guard with a flaming speech. The doctrine that he proclaimed—popularly known as "the New Nationalism"—urged the national government to increase its power in order to correct crying social and political abuses. This doctrine was Hamiltonian centralization for social betterment, preached, conservatives thought, by a "wild man."

Mounting dissension within Republican ranks was further exposed by the congressional elections in November 1910. In a victory of landslide proportions, the Democrats emerged with 228 seats, leaving the once-haughty Republicans with only 161. Symptomatic of the radical trend of the times was the election of a Socialist representative, Austrian-born Victor L. Berger of Milwaukee.* The Republicans, by virtue of holdovers, retained the Senate, 51 to 41, but the insurgents in their midst were numerous enough to make that hold precarious.

Taft the Trust Buster

Oddly enough, the floundering President had meanwhile been gaining some fame as a smasher of monopoly. The ironical truth is that colorless Taft caused ninety legal proceedings to be brought against the trusts during his four years, as compared with some forty-four for Roosevelt in seven and one-half years. But the statistics are misleading, for TR had generated the anti-trust momentum, and some of his cases were more important than Taft's.

By happenstance the most sensational judicial victories of the Taft regime came during 1911, in two cases that had been initiated under Roosevelt. The Supreme Court ordered the dissolution of the mighty Standard Oil Company, which was judged to be a combination in restraint of trade under the Sherman Anti-Trust Act of 1890. At the same time the Court handed down its famous "rule of reason," namely, that the government should prosecute only those combinations suspected of an "unreasonable" restraint of trade. Two weeks later, in May 1911, the Supreme Court no less dramatically ordered the dissolution of the gigantic American Tobacco Company. But in neither case did the militant progressives feel that the breakup was as effective as it ought to be. For his part, Taft dealt judiciously with what he called "the curse of bigness," for he declared that "mere size is no sin against the law."

"Upset," 1911. Supreme Court decision upsets Standard Oil (*Jersey Journal* cartoon, by permission.)

Wall Street "interests" received another rude jolt in 1912–1913. The Pujo Committee, authorized by the now-Democratic House of Representatives, undertook a prolonged probe of the so-called Money Trust. "The greatest monopoly in this country is the money monopoly," asserted Dr. Woodrow Wilson, a fast-rising political star in New Jersey. The Pujo investigators were to find that banking houses dominated by the Morgan and Rockefeller interests held 341 directorships in corporations worth over $22 billion.

The Stillborn Canadian Reciprocity of 1911

Bad luck pursued Taft into foreign affairs, especially those involving Canada. For many decades this big but weak northern sister had been seeking a reciprocal tariff arrangement. Her aim was to lower duties on goods coming from the Yankees, in return for corresponding concessions by her wealthy neighbor. With unusual zeal, Taft threw himself squarely behind this scheme. Reciprocal tariff reductions might quiet the critics who were condemning the distasteful Payne-Aldrich Tariff, and perhaps restore some of his lost luster.

In 1911 a formal agreement was signed with Canada, and Taft summoned Congress in special session to approve it. But far from gaining popularity, he merely stirred up a hornet's nest. The lumbermen and grain farmers of the Middle

*He was finally denied his seat in 1919, during a wave of anti-Red hysteria.

West, where the Republican insurgents were entrenched, cried out against the loss of their tariff protection against Canadian products. They accused Taft of having "sold out" to the trusts. Many industrialists in truth welcomed free raw materials from Canada, as well as tariff-free new markets for their finished products. But Taft, at last aroused to the point of applying whip and spur, drove the trade agreement through Congress. He left behind a long trail of bruised, battered, and bitter feelings.

Champions of reciprocity in Canada, who at first had hailed the agreement with delight, now began to cool off. The new Democratic speaker of the House, Champ Clark of Missouri, alarmed the Canadians when he suggested, in a highly publicized speech, that reciprocity would be a step toward the inevitable annexation of America's northern neighbor. Taft himself rather clumsily revealed the imperialistic claws of the measure by remarking that under it Canada would become a mere economic satellite of the United States.

Suspicious Canadians had no desire to be a backdoor lumber camp or, worse yet, to be annexed to their powerful neighbor. Many of them cried in alarm, "No truck or trade with the Yankees." A heated special election in Canada, in which the basic issue was the British Union Jack versus Old Glory, was won by the anti-reciprocity party. The agreement with Washington was thereupon repudiated. A tactless Taft, after all his perspiring exertions, had nothing to show but failure.

Speaker Clark's explosive speech in the House favoring reciprocity reads in part: "I am for it because I hope to see the day when the American flag will float over every square foot of the British–North American possessions clear to the North Pole. They are people of our blood. They speak our language. Their institutions are much like ours. They are trained in the difficult art of self-government."

The Dollar Goes Abroad as a Diplomat

The brand of "Dollar Diplomacy" was stamped, somewhat unfairly, on the foreign affairs of the Taft administration. This concept was two-sided: (1) using foreign policy to protect Wall Street dollars invested abroad, and (2) using Wall Street dollars to uphold foreign policy. The first aspect was grossly overplayed by Taft's critics; the second aspect was widely misunderstood.

Though ordinarily lethargic, Taft bestirred himself to use the lever of American investments to boost American diplomacy. Washington warmly encouraged Wall Street bankers to pump their surplus dollars into foreign areas of strategic concern to the United States, especially in the Far East and in the regions that might menace the Panama Canal. Otherwise investors from rival powers, say, Germany, might take advantage of financial chaos and secure a lodgment inimical to Uncle Sam's interests, both physical and commercial. New York bankers would thus strengthen American defenses and foreign policies, while bringing further prosperity to their homeland—and to themselves.

The Almighty Dollar thus came to supplant the Big Stick. A peace-loving Taft was not nearly so enthusiastic for military preparedness as the pugnacious TR, and did not push battleship construction with vigor. The navy, unable to keep up with Britain and Germany in their frantic race, dropped from second to third place, just ahead of France.

China's Manchuria was the object of Taft's most spectacular effort to pump the reluctant dollar into the Far Eastern theater. Ambitious little Japan and imperialistic Russia, recent foes, controlled the railroads of this strategic province. Taft saw in the Manchurian railway monopoly a possible strangulation of Chinese economic interests, and a consequent slamming of the Open Door in the faces of American merchants. In 1909 Secretary of State Knox blunderingly proposed that a group of American and foreign bankers buy the Manchurian railroads, and then turn them over to China under a self-liquidating arrangement. Both Japan and Russia, unwilling to be jockeyed out of their dominant position, bluntly rejected Knox's overtures. Again Taft was showered with ridicule.

Another dangerous trouble spot was the revolution-riddled Caribbean—now virtually a Yankee lake. Hoping to head off trouble, Washington urged Wall Street bankers to pump dollars into the financial vacuums in Honduras and Haiti to keep out foreign funds. The United States, under the Monroe Doctrine, would not permit foreign nations to intervene, and consequently it had some moral obligation to interfere financially to prevent economic and political chaos.

Again necessity was the mother of armed Caribbean intervention. Sporadic disorders in palm-fronded Cuba, Honduras, and Santo Domingo brought American forces in the days of Taft. A revolutionary upheaval in Nicaragua, perilously close to the nearly completed canal, resulted in the landing of 2,500 marines in 1912. (See map, p. 643.)

A luckless Taft could point to a few diplomatic triumphs, even though the Big Stick did gather cobwebs. The age-old dispute over the smelly Newfoundland fisheries was finally settled in 1912, when an Anglo-American pact set up a permanent arbitral board. In the previous year an agreement signed by four nations—the United States, Britain, Japan, and Russia—rescued America's North Pacific seal herd. These furry creatures had dwindled from about 4 million to 120,000, but within thirty-five years the new multi-power safeguards raised the figure to around the 3 million mark. (See map, p. 561.)

"Where Will He Land?" (Steele in the Denver *Post*, February 1912.)

The Taft-Roosevelt Rupture

The insurgent uprising in Republican ranks had meanwhile been blossoming into a full-fledged revolt. Early in 1911 the National Progressive Republican League was formed, with the fiery, white-maned Senator La Follette of Wisconsin its leading candidate for the Republican presidential nomination. The assumption was that Roosevelt, an anti–third termer, would not permit himself to be "drafted."

But the restless Rough Rider began to change his views about third terms as he saw Taft, hand in glove with the hated Old Guard, discard "my policies." In February 1912, Roosevelt formally wrote to seven state governors that he was willing to accept the Republican nomination. His reasoning was that the third-term tradition applied to three *consecutive elective* terms. Exuberantly he cried, "My hat is in the ring!" and "The fight is on and I am stripped to the buff!"

Roosevelt forthwith seized the Progressive banner, while La Follette, who had served as a convenient pathbreaker, was protestingly elbowed aside. Girded for battle, the Rough Rider clattered into the presidential primaries then being held in many states. He shouted through half-clenched teeth that the President had fallen under the thumb of the reactionary bosses, and that although Taft "means well, he means well feebly." The once-genial Taft, now in a fighting mood, retorted by branding the Roosevelt supporters as "emotionalists and neurotics." He reportedly declared, "Even a rat in a corner will fight," thus leaving the impression that he would act just like any other cornered animal.

As the fight thickened, Roosevelt allowed himself to be carried away by his progressive zeal for increased popular control of government. He strenuously advocated the "recall," or removal, of judges who might be anti-reformist or "interest-controlled." What was more shocking, he came out flatly for the recall of judicial decisions. This scheme, though not as radical as pictured, was a first-class blunder. It alienated many mild progressives, who now feared more than ever that they had a wild man on their hands.

Yet Roosevelt, on the surface, seemed to be sweeping all before him. Still the popular idol, he carried most of the presidential primaries in the states that held them. He even captured Taft's Ohio. But the portly President, who had the smooth-running party machinery behind him, was successful in lining up delegates from the Solid South—an area where the Republican ticket had not won an electoral vote for decades.

A Taft-Roosevelt explosion was near in June 1912, when the Republican convention met in Chicago. The Rooseveltites, who were about 100 delegates short of winning the nomination, challenged the right of some 250 Taft delegates to be seated. Most of these contests were arbitrarily settled in favor of Taft, whose supporters held the throttle of the convention steamroller. The Roosevelt adherents, crying "fraud" and "naked theft," in the end refused to vote.

Taft triumphed, though ironically he won renomination by the same steamroller tactics that TR had used in his behalf four years earlier. But the Republican platform, bending to the breeze of progressive doctrine, favored trust control and currency reform—without going overboard for them. Roosevelt, the good sportsman, proved to be a poor loser. Having tasted for once the bitter cup of defeat, he was on fire to lead a third-party crusade.

Roosevelt the Take-Back Giver. (Knecht in the Evansville [Indiana] *Courier.*)

The Emergence of Dr. Thomas Woodrow Wilson

Office-hungry Democrats—the "outs" since 1897—were jubilant over the disruptive Republican brawl at Chicago. The party in power, the adage runs, is seldom defeated; it splits into factions and defeats itself.

If the Democrats were to keep abreast of the times and win, they would have to come up with an outstanding reformist leader. Fortunately for them, one appeared in Dr. Woodrow Wilson, once a mild conservative but now a militant progressive. Beginning professional life as a brilliant academic lecturer on government, he had risen in 1902 to the presidency of Princeton University, and there he had achieved some sweeping educational reforms. In the interests of promoting higher education, he had also battled to abolish the snobbish eating clubs and fuse their members with the rest of the student body. But here he had suffered defeat at the hands of the wealthy alumni.

Wilson's final struggle at Princeton involved the proposed graduate school. He was eager to build it in the physical center of the university, and thus elevate the intellectual life of the undergraduates. But the equally stubborn Dean West insisted on locating the structure on the outskirts, where the serious graduates would not be debased by undergraduate frivolity. Dean West finally secured a handsome bequest, with authority to build the school where he chose. From then on Princeton was not big enough for both the president and the dean.

By 1910 Wilson had emerged as the potential governor of New Jersey. His name was nationally known, largely because his spirited campaign for educational reform chimed in with current progressive thinking. The Democrats of boss-ridden New Jersey, needing a respectable candidate for the governorship, offered the nomination to Dr. Wilson. They reasoned that if they should have the good luck to win, they could privately lead the bespectacled professor around by his long academic nose, while using him as a show-window "front."

Wilson accepted the New Jersey nomination in 1910, and then put on a tremendous fighting campaign. "God! Look at that man's jaw," exclaimed one observer. In a series of eloquent speeches, Wilson boldly assailed the trusts in a state that was known as "the Mother of Trusts," including Standard Oil of New Jersey. He passionately advocated political and social reforms that would return the state government to the people, and thus break the iron grip of selfish minorities and "predatory" interests.

The "Schoolmaster in Politics," riding the crest of the progressive wave, was swept into the governorship. Demanding "pitiless publicity" for wrongdoing, he turned against the bewildered bosses and routed them. He then drove through the legislature a sheaf of forward-looking measures—reforms that were tailored to make reactionary New Jersey one of the more liberal states. Filled with righteous indignation, Wilson was at his best. He revealed irresistible reforming zeal, burning eloquence, superb powers of leadership, and a refreshing habit of appealing over the heads of the scheming bosses to the sovereign people. Now a figure of national eminence, Wilson was being widely mentioned for the presidency.

Contemporary Caricature of Wilson. He looked like the professor he had been, and he never completely lost the professorial manner. In a speech in 1919, Wilson declared: "Sometimes people call me an idealist. Well, that is the way I know I am an American. America is the only idealistic nation in the world."

When the Democrats met at Baltimore in 1912, Wilson enjoyed impressive support, though lacking a majority of the delegates. The front-running contender was the speaker of the House, Champ Clark of Missouri. An experienced legislator and a popular orator of the old-fashioned school, he had displayed only moderately progressive tendencies. The intellectual level of some of his back-country followers is indicated by their popular song: "They Gotta Quit Kickin' My Dawg Aroun'." Clark polled a majority of the votes on some of the early ballots, though falling short of the required two-thirds, while Wilson ran a strong second.

Wilson's cause was unexpectedly supported by the old war-horse, Bryan. Presumably willing to have lightning strike him a fourth time, he was present as a delegate from Nebraska pledged to vote for Champ Clark. But when the formidable New York delegation, with its Wall Street connections, suddenly turned to Clark, Bryan no less dramatically switched to Wilson. He proclaimed that he could not support a candidate of the moneyed interests. This spectacular shift possibly helped Wilson. But by then Clark had shot his bolt, and the Princetonian received the nomination on the forty-sixth ballot. The Democratic platform pointed up Wilson's limited liberalism by coming out emphatically for reforms, including anti-trust legislation, monetary changes, and tariff reduction.

The "Bull Moose" Campaign of 1912

Surging events had meanwhile been thrusting Roosevelt to the fore as a candidate for the presidency on a third-party Progressive Republican ticket. The fighting ex-cowboy, angered by his recent rebuff, was eager to lead the charge. A pro-Roosevelt Progressive convention, with about 2,000 delegates from forty states, assembled in Chicago during August 1912. Roosevelt was applauded tumultuously as he cried in a vehement speech, "We stand at Armageddon, and we battle for the Lord!" The hosanna spirit of a revival meeting suffused the convention, while the hoarse delegates sang "Onward, Christian Soldiers" and "Battle Hymn of the Republic." William Allen White, the caustic Kansas journalist, later wrote, "Roosevelt bit me and I went mad."

Fired-up Progressives entered the campaign with both righteousness and high enthusiasm. Their platform—a "Covenant with the People"—endorsed thoroughgoing reforms and struck at "invisible" government. Roosevelt boasted that he felt "as strong as a bull moose," and hence the bull moose took its place with the jackass and the elephant in the American political zoo. As one poet whimsically put it:

> I want to be a Bull Moose,
> And with the Bull Moose stand
> With antlers on my forehead
> And a Big Stick in my hand.

Roosevelt and Taft were bound to slit each other's political throats; by dividing the Republican vote they guaranteed a Democratic victory. In truth the only question, said one cynic, was which corpse would get the more flowers in the form of ballots. The two antagonists tore into each other as only former friends can. "Death alone can take me out now," cried the once-jovial Taft, as he branded Roosevelt a "dangerous egotist" and a "demagogue." Roosevelt, fighting mad, assailed Taft as a "fathead" with the brain of a "guinea pig."

Despite the clashing personalities, the overshadowing question of the 1912 campaign was which of two varieties of progressivism would prevail—Roosevelt's New Nationalism or Wilson's New Freedom. Both men favored a more active governmental role in economic and social affairs, but they disagreed sharply over specific strategies. Roosevelt preached the theories spun out by the progressive thinker Herbert Croly in his book, *The Promise of American Life* (1910). Croly and TR both favored continued consolidation of trusts

GOP Divided by Bull Moose Equals Democratic Victory. (*Puck*, 1912.)

Wilson Campaigning, 1912. (Brown Brothers.)

and labor unions, paralleled by the growth of powerful regulatory agencies in Washington. Roosevelt and his "Bull Moosers" also campaigned for woman's suffrage and a broad program of social welfare, including minimum wage laws and "socialistic" social insurance. Clearly the Progressives looked forward to the kind of activist welfare state that Franklin Roosevelt's New Deal would one day make a reality.

Wilson's New Freedom, by contrast, looked backward to an older era of small enterprise. The Democrats shunned social welfare proposals and pinned their economic faith to competition. The keynote of Wilson's campaign was not regulation but fragmentation of the big industrial combines, chiefly by means of a vigorous enforcement of the anti-trust laws.

The campaign of 1912 provided abundant color and drama. Political vocalizers hailed Roosevelt with such songs as "We're Ready for Teddy Again" and "The Moose Is Loose," and sang with soulful dedication:

> We will follow Roosevelt,
> Follow! Follow!
> Anywhere! Everywhere,
> We will follow on.

Taft's adherents denounced Roosevelt's dictatorial ambitions in songs like "Teddy Must Be King," while gladsome Democrats sang "Row, Row, Woodrow" and "Wilson—That's All." The heat of the campaign cooled a bit when, in Milwaukee, Roosevelt was shot in the chest by a fanatic. The Rough Rider suspended active campaigning for more than two weeks after delivering, with Bull Moose gameness and a bloody shirt, his scheduled speech.

Woodrow Wilson: A Minority President

Ex-Professor Wilson won handily, with 435 electoral votes and 6,293,454 popular votes. Back in Princeton, Dean West is said to have groaned, "My God, I've made Wilson President of the United States."

"Bull Moose" Roosevelt was the lively corpse that got the more ballot-box flowers. The totals for him stood at 88 electoral votes and 4,119,538 popular votes. Taft carried only two states, Utah and Vermont, with 8 paltry electoral votes, while gathering 3,484,980 popular votes.

The election figures are fascinating. Wilson, with only 41 percent of the popular vote, was clearly a minority President, though his party won a majority in Congress. His popular total was actually smaller than Bryan had amassed in any of his three defeats, despite the increase in population. Taft and Roosevelt together polled over a million and a quarter more votes than the Democrats. Progressivism rather than Wilson was the runaway winner. Though the Democratic total obviously included many conservatives in the Solid South, still the combined Progressive vote for Wilson and Roosevelt exceeded the tally of the more conservative Taft. To the Progressive tally must be added some support for the Socialist candidate, hardy Eugene V. Debs, who rolled up 900,672 votes, or more than twice as many as he had netted four years earlier. Starry-eyed Socialists dreamed of being in the White House within eight years.

Mortified Republicans were now free to engage

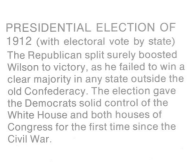

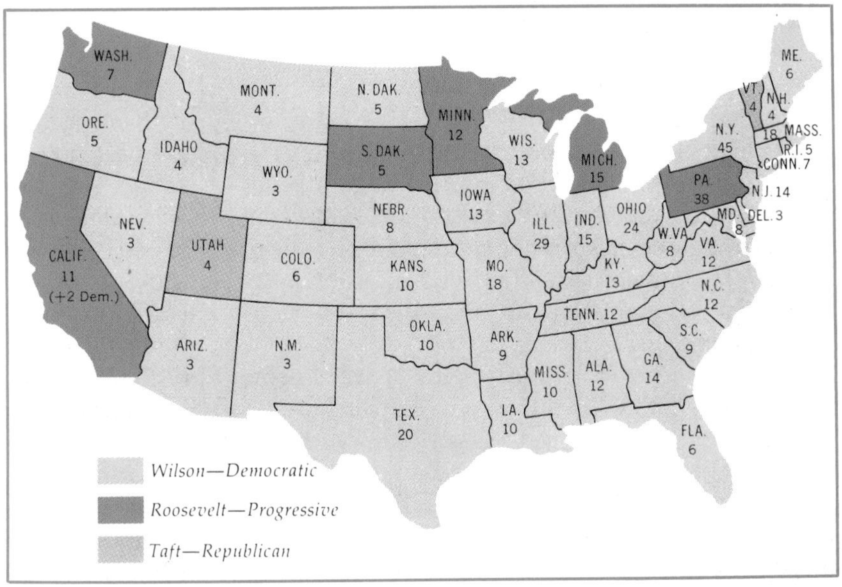

PRESIDENTIAL ELECTION OF 1912 (with electoral vote by state) The Republican split surely boosted Wilson to victory, as he failed to win a clear majority in any state outside the old Confederacy. The election gave the Democrats solid control of the White House and both houses of Congress for the first time since the Civil War.

in some sorrowful second-guessing. If they had united behind the progressive Roosevelt, they might well have won; if they had united behind the conservative Taft, they might well have lost. But in this event they would have kept their ranks intact, and might have triumphed four years later, instead of losing again.

Roosevelt's lone-wolf course was tragic both for himself and for his former Republican associates. Until 1912 he had set great store by party loyalty; now he had brought untold woes upon himself and his party. Perhaps, to rephrase William Allen White, he had bitten himself and gone mad. The Progressive party, which was primarily a one-man show, had no future because it had elected few candidates to state and local offices. Without patronage plums to hand out to the faithful workers, death by slow starvation was inevitable. Yet the Progressives made a tremendous showing for a hastily organized third party, and helped spur the enactment of many of their pet reforms by the Wilsonian Democrats.

Taft in Retrospect

An aura of bumble, fumble, and stumble clung to Taft, who left the White House in 1913 after the worst defeat yet suffered by an incumbent. His personal humiliation, combined with the disruption of his party, caused many critics to regard him as a flat failure.

The Presidential Vote, 1912

Candidate	*Party*	*Electoral Vote*	*Popular Vote*	*Approximate Percentage*
Woodrow Wilson	Democratic	435	6,293,454	41%
Theodore Roosevelt	Progressive	88	4,119,538	27
William H. Taft	Republican	8	3,484,980	23
Eugene V. Debs	Socialist	—	900,672	6
E. W. Chafin	Prohibition	—	206,275	1
A. E. Reimer	Socialist-Labor	—	28,750	.2

This indictment of Taft is unfair. His achievements in conservation and trust busting were substantial, if lacking in fireworks. In addition, the Mann-Elkins Act of 1910 brought the railroads under a tighter governmental rein, and rather belatedly extended the authority of the Interstate Commerce Commission to the telegraph and cable companies.

Gratifying strides toward better government were made under Taft. Civil service reform received a strong boost, particularly as more postmasters were added to the classified service. Congress, for its part, enacted significant reform legislation in 1910 and 1911. New laws were specifically designed to give publicity to the campaign funds of congressmen and to set limits to their political outlays, albeit ineffectively. Finally, a higher degree of administrative efficiency came in 1913, when Congress separated the Department of Commerce and Labor into two departments.

The wondrous West continued to develop. A needed stimulus came when Congress revised the Homestead Act, in 1909 and again in 1912, to square with the realities of farming in arid regions. New Mexico and Arizona were welcomed in 1912 as the forty-seventh and forty-eighth stars. Taft showed his judicial bent when he held up the admission of Arizona until an objectionable provison for the recall of judges was removed from her constitution. (Once in the Union, Arizona reinstated this radical provision; and there was then nothing that the President or Congress could do about it.)

Wilson and Taft. The outgoing President greets the incumbent at Wilson's inauguration, 1913. (Library of Congress)

Additional legislative landmarks dotted the four Taft years. The Postal Savings Bank Act of 1910, in the teeth of bitter opposition from the bankers, belatedly provided facilities like those found in many European countries. A parcel-post system, similar to foreign models, was likewise approved in 1912, but not until the express companies had fought it hammer and tongs. An impressive total of some 700 million parcels flooded through the post office during 1913, the first year of operation. Finally, the 16th Amendment, making lawful a federal income tax, was formally riveted to the federal Constitution in February 1913. (See Appendix.)

All these measures add up to a commendable record of cautious progress, even though some of them were routine or were enacted primarily by Democratic votes. Taft, the amiable misfit, was not only unlucky but a victim of his times. Despite his mildly reformist tendencies, progressive sentiment was sweeping so rapidly past his rotund figure that he seemed to be standing still.

Taft's remaining life was fruitful. He taught law for eight pleasant years at Yale University, and in 1921 became chief justice. This exalted post, which he had long coveted, was one for which he was admirably fitted by training and temperament, and in which he was successful. His eight years on the Supreme Bench were among the happiest of his life, just as the four years of his "sentence" in the Big White Jail had proved to be the most unhappy.

VARYING VIEWPOINTS

Both Theodore Roosevelt and Woodrow Wilson called themselves progressives, and some contemporary commentators claimed that they were no more different than Tweedledum and Tweedledee. But despite their similarities, the two leading candidates in 1912 clashed on several important points, especially regarding the proper relation of the government to the private economy. Roosevelt preached continuous administrative control, while Wilson believed in stiff anti-trust measures. The Rough Rider also endorsed a broad range of social welfare measures, including workman's compensation and unemployment insurance. But Wilson shunned such programs because they violated his small-government principles and his devotion to states' rights.

Differences such as these point up a difficult problem in all discussions of progressivism: How can the historian generalize about a movement that promoted such inconsistent, even contradictory, views? Did only one of the two candidates represent "true" progressivism? Was there any common element that linked both Roosevelt and Wilson as co-participants in a "progressive movement"? The term "progressive" has been so warped and worn in the effort to stretch it over so many people and policies that some historians have urged abandoning the word altogether.

SELECT READINGS

Several of the titles cited in the previous chapter are relevant, especially those by Goldman, Hofstadter, Hays, Wiebe, Kolko, and Mowry. Consult also Mowry's *Theodore Roosevelt and the Progressive Movement* (1946). Sympathetic biographical coverage is H. F. Pringle, *The Life and Times of William Howard Taft* (2 vols., 1939), which should be supplemented by Donald Anderson, *William Howard Taft* (1973), and Paolo Coletta, *The Presidency of William Howard Taft* (1973). John Braeman examines another important figure from this era in *Albert Beveridge* (1971). The Ballinger-Pinchot feud is described in James Penick, Jr., *Progressive Politics and Conservation* (1968). Walter V. Scholes and Marie V. Scholes examine *The Foreign Policies of the Taft Administration* (1970). Russell B. Nye gives valuable background on the insurgent movement in *Midwestern Progressive Politics* (1951). See also James Holt, *Congressional Insurgents and the Party System, 1909–1916* (1968), and Norman Wilensky, *Conservatives in the Progressive Era: The Taft Republicans of 1912* (1965). Socialism is analyzed in James Weinstein, *The Decline of Socialism in America, 1912–1925* (1967), and in Ray Ginger, *The Bending Cross: A Biography of Eugene Victor Debs* (1949). On the radical and colorful "Wobblies," see Melvyn Dubofsky, *We Shall Be All: A History of the Industrial Workers of the World* (1969). The rise of Wilson is described in A. S. Link, *Wilson: The Road to the White House* (1947), and in John M. Mulder, *Woodrow Wilson: The Years of Preparation* (1978).

34

Woodrow Wilson and the New Freedom

This is not a day of triumph; it is a day of dedication. Here muster not the forces of party, but the forces of humanity. . . . I summon all honest men, all patriotic, all forward-looking men, to my side. God helping me, I will not fail them, if they will but counsel and sustain me!

THOMAS WOODROW WILSON, Inaugural Address, 1913

Wilson: The Idealist in Politics

(Thomas) Woodrow Wilson, the second Democratic President since 1861, looked like the ascetic intellectual he was, with his clean-cut features, pinched-on eyeglasses, and trim figure (5 feet 11 inches and 179 pounds; 1.8 meters, 81.2 kilograms). Born in Virginia shortly before the Civil War, and reared in Georgia and the Carolinas, the professor-politician was the first man from one of the seceded Southern states to reach the White House since Zachary Taylor, sixty-four years earlier.

The impact of Dixieland on young "Tommy"

Wilson was profound. His upbringing in the burned-out South caused him to sympathize with the gallant attempt of the Confederacy to win its independence in 1861–1865. His later ideal of self-determination for minority peoples, the world over, was no doubt partly inspired by these youthful impressions. Wilson was not only born a Southern Democrat, but he developed into a Democrat steeped in the ultra-liberal Jeffersonian tradition. Like Jefferson, a fellow Virginian, he had strong faith in the judgment of the masses—if they were properly informed.

Son of a Presbyterian minister, Wilson was reared in an atmosphere of extreme piety. He believed devoutly in the power of prayer and in the presence of a personal God. At heart a clergyman, he later used the presidential pulpit to preach his inspirational political sermons.

Wilson was not only a born reformer but an idealist who could radiate righteous indignation. Moved by a stern sense of duty when he saw wrongdoing, he would become "angry for the right." As an earnest Christian who habitually read his Bible and prayed in the bosom of his family, he hated war so intensely that he became a pacifist at heart. Such tendencies were reinforced by his boyhood years in Yankee-gutted Georgia.

A moving orator, Wilson could rise on the wings of spiritual power to soaring eloquence. Yet he was inclined, professor-like, to be more in touch with his subject than with his audience. Skillfully using a persuasive voice, he relied not on arm waving but on sincerity and moral appeal. As a lifelong student of finely chiseled words, he turned out to be a "phraseocrat" who coined many noble epigrams. Someone has remarked that he was born halfway between the Bible and the dictionary, and never got away from either.

A profound student of government, Wilson believed that the Chief Executive should play a dynamic role. He was convinced that Congress could not function properly unless the President, like a kind of prime minister, got out in front and provided leadership. Somewhat paradoxically, this reserved professor of theoretical politics became an astute practical politician. He was often dramatically effective, both as governor and as President, in appealing over the heads of legislators to the sovereign people.

President Woodrow Wilson (1856–1924). A realist-idealist, Wilson wrote some six years before coming to the White House: "The President is at liberty, both in law and conscience, to be as big a man as he can." Fighting desperately later for the League of Nations and breaking himself down, he said: "I would rather fail in a cause that I know some day will triumph than to win in a cause that I know some day will fail." (New-York Historical Society, New York City.)

Splendid though Wilson's intellectual equipment was, he suffered from serious defects of personality. Though jovial and witty in private, he could be cold and standoffish in public. Incapable of unbending and acting the showman, like "Teddy" Roosevelt, he lacked the common touch. He loved humanity in the mass rather than the individual in person. His academic background caused him to feel most at home with scholars, although he had to work wry-facedly with politicians. An austere and somewhat arrogant intellectual, he looked down his nose through pince-nez glasses upon lesser minds, including journalists. He was especially intolerant of stupid senators, whose "bungalow" minds made him "sick."

Wilson's burning idealism—especially his desire to reform ever-present wickedness—drove him forward faster than lesser spirits were willing to go. When concentrating on one problem, he would neglect others; he had what he described as "a single-track mind." His sense of moral righteousness was such that he found compromise difficult: black was black, wrong was wrong, and one should never compromise with wrong. His Scotch Presbyterian ancestors had passed on to him an inflexible stubbornness. When convinced that he was right, he would break before he would bend, unlike Theodore Roosevelt. He tended to make personal enemies of his political foemen; and if he was forced to choose between principle and friend, the friend had to go.

"All Ready in the Event of Possible Hostilities," 1913. Bryan as peace-dove secretary of state. (Courtesy of Philadelphia *Inquirer*.)

Bryan and Offices for Deserving Democrats

Wilson's inaugural address, delivered before a vast crowd on March 4, 1913, reflected high idealism and deep dedication. It foreshadowed a program of reform designed to achieve the New Freedom of the average man—freedom from exploitation by Big Business and high finance. Wilson forthwith proceeded to push his proposals with unflagging zeal. Few Presidents have come to the White House with a clearer program or one destined to be more completely achieved.

Wilson's Cabinet inspired no great confidence. It was composed largely of "unknowns," principally because the Democrats had been out of power for sixteen years. The sons of the Confederacy had again captured Washington. Five Cabinet members were Southern-born, including the North Carolina newspaperman-politician Josephus Daniels, who became "managing editor of the Navy." He gained considerable ill will by banning alcohol from American warships. The handsome, vibrant, thirty-one-year-old Franklin D. Roosevelt of New York, who had a passion for ships, was made assistant secretary of the navy.

Bryan, three-time loser, fell heir to the secretaryship of state—the highest appointive post available. He was totally without experience as a diplomat, as were most secretaries during those years, and he knew little international law. The New York *Sun* thought that he was about as well suited for his position as a "merman to play football." But he was the liberal leader of a strong element in the Democratic party. The new President, though distrusting Bryan's intellectual furnishings, simply could not leave him out of the Cabinet. As "Mr. Dooley" said, it would be better for Wilson to have Bryan "in his bosom than on his back."

Bryan proved to be something of a problem child, even though he added liberal strength. His reformist zeal even ran to the abolition of liquor at official functions—"grape juice diplomacy." His activities as a political spoilsman unfortunately hampered Wilson's earnest efforts to promote the merit system. Bryan had incurred many political debts over the years, for millions of Democrats had voted for him in three elections.

He now eagerly sought gravy jobs for "deserving Democrats"—as he called them. This inept phrase rasped "resolute Republicans," who had been doing the same thing for years and who now responded with hypocritical jeers.

Yet Bryan turned out to be a more useful Cabinet member than cynics had predicted. Buttonholing his Democratic friends in Congress, he used his charm and immense personal influence to speed on its way Wilson's bulging portfolio of reform legislation. An ardent lover of peace, like Wilson, he bestirred himself energetically to negotiate some thirty conciliation treaties. These agreements bound the signatory nations not to begin hostilities for a year after a dispute broke out, by which time their anger presumably would have evaporated. The "cooling-off" or "wait a bit" treaties embodied the ancient axiom, "When angry count fifty, when very angry count a hundred." These pacts might have amounted to more if the Great War had not wrapped Europe in flames in 1914.

More influential than any regular member of the Cabinet was another Southerner, Colonel (honorary) Edward M. House. This smallish, self-effacing Texan, who had helped elect Wilson, was a skilled politician and wire-puller. With a judicious rather than a profound mind, he aspired to no formal office but enjoyed the thrill that came from being the power behind the throne. For nearly seven years he was Wilson's most intimate adviser—a one-man Kitchen Cabinet.

Wilson Tackles the Tariff

Seeking New Freedoms that would free the people from monopoly, Wilson promptly prepared for an all-out assault on what he called "the triple wall of privilege." He meant, of course, the tariff, the trusts, and the archaic system of banking and currency. The first barrier was the unpopular Payne-Aldrich Tariff, which badly needed revamping.

Wilson met the tariff issue head-on, early in 1913, with refreshing decisiveness. First he summoned Congress into special session. Then he prepared an eloquent message against special privilege. But he did not send it over to the Capitol to be read loudly by a bored clerk, as had been the invariable rule since Jefferson's day in 1801. Instead, he appeared before a joint session of Congress and presented the appeal himself with characteristic poise and effectiveness. This precedent-shattering episode further highlighted Wilson's determination to provide aggressive leadership, and to achieve closer cooperation between the President and Congress. Strangely enough, Theodore Roosevelt, the precedent smasher, had not revived the personal appearances of George Washington and John Adams. Wilson remarked smilingly as he rode away from Capitol Hill, "I think we put one over on Teddy that time."

As usual, the new Underwood Tariff Bill ran the familiar gauntlet. Providing for a substantial reduction of existing rates, it passed the House without a serious hitch. But progress was stormy when it reached the Senate, which contained many "tools" of the "special interests." A swarm of lobbyists—"the third house of Congress"—were reportedly about to disembowel the bill, as they had done repeatedly in the past.

This tariff crisis sharply challenged Wilson's leadership. He promptly issued a fighting appeal to the people, with the objective of building up

Schoolmaster Wilson. He lays down the law to Congress at the outset. (New York *Tribune*, 1913.)

"The Funeral Oration," 1913. Wilson buries commercial prosperity with his tariff message. A Republican view. (Courtesy of the Philadelphia *Inquirer.*)

a backfire against the scheming lobbyists. The masses, he insisted, had no agents in Washington to look after their welfare, but the predatory interests did have. Public opinion, aroused by Wilson's eloquence and "pitiless publicity," is believed to have caused the lobbyists to become more discreet. The Senate finally approved the new tariff bill late in 1913, after six months of windy debate.

Fruits of Freer Trade

The Underwood-Simmons Tariff was not a free-trade measure; nor was it really a low-tariff law. Wilson favored not free trade but freer opportunity. Average annual rates were chopped down from 40.8 to 27 percent. All told, the law reduced the duties on more than 900 items, and enlarged the free list by including such basic products as raw wool and steel rails. Increases were tacked on to more than eighty commodities, principally luxuries, and chiefly for revenue. Though still definitely protective, the new measure achieved the first genuine tariff reduction since the Civil War, and thus redeemed Democratic pledges of revision. (See chart, p. 552.)

Significantly, the Underwood Act was also a landmark in tax legislation. Under authority recently granted by the 16th Amendment, Congress included a graduated levy, beginning with incomes of $3,000 for single persons and $4,000 for married couples. A married man earning $5,000 would pay about $10. Such painlessly low rates were raised in 1916, owing to the World War emergency, and the next year revenue from the income tax shot ahead of that from the tariff. This gap since then has been vastly widened, to the accompaniment of growing complaints.

The Underwood Tariff, though acidly criticized, was a giant step toward correcting injustices. It decreased the indirect burden on the poor by lowering the customs duties, and increased the direct burden on the rich by enacting an income tax. Southern Democrats were delighted to shift a part of the tax load onto the backs of their Yankee brethren, many of whom were Big Business Republicans. Northern capitalists, complaining that they had now lost the Civil War, declared that they were the victims of class legislation and sectional discrimination.

Experts regard the Underwood Act as one of the best-balanced tariff measures ever to pass Congress. But how well it would have worked in normal times will never be known. The titanic World War erupted in 1914, before the new law had been on the books a year. One unhappy result of European blockades was a sharp reduction of anticipated imports and hence customs revenue.

Wilson Battles the Bankers

A second bastion of the "triple wall of privilege" was the banking and currency system, now outgrown. The country's financial structure, still creaking along under the Civil War National Banking Act, revealed glaring defects. Its most serious shortcoming, as laid bare by the Panic of 1907, was the inelasticity of the currency. The amount of money in circulation was heavily concentrated in Wall Street, and could not be speedily expanded in times of financial stress into areas that were badly pinched.

In 1908 Congress had authorized an investigation by the National Monetary Commission, headed by a reactionary banker, Senator Aldrich. Three years later it recommended a gigantic central bank, with numerous branches. This institution would in effect be the Third Bank of the United States. Wall Street financiers would assume the role of long-departed Nicholas Biddle, who in ghostly form struck terror into the hearts of the Bryanites. They feared that through such a monster bank the "Money Trust" would concentrate even more power in the hands of a favored few.

For their part, Democratic currency reformers were fired up by recent hearings held by a House committee. Headed by Congressman Arsène Pujo, it had traced the tentacles of the "money monster" into the hidden vaults of American banking and business. President Wilson's confidant, Louis D. Brandeis, a progressive-minded Massachusetts attorney, further fanned the flames of reform with his incendiary though scholarly book, *Other People's Money and How the Bankers Use It* (1914).

Aroused Democrats, with Wilson leading the attack, prepared to battle the bankers. In June 1913, in a second dramatic appearance before both Houses of Congress, the President delivered a stirring plea for genuine banking reform. The legislative machinery then began to grind. Standpat Republicans fought vigorously for a huge private bank with fifteen branches, close to the "Money Trust." But liberal Democrats, with Bryan lobbying behind the scenes, demanded a decentralized bank, in government hands, not in those of private moneychangers.

Secretary of the Treasury McAdoo recalled in his autobiography (1931) that many bankers and experts had fought the Federal Reserve Act: "I found that they could take the same set of facts and reach two diametrically opposite conclusions. For example, Forgan [a Chicago banker] estimated that the currency would be contracted to the extent of $1,800,000,000, while Senator Elihu Root, using the same data, predicted an inflation of at least $1,800,000,000."

"His Alibi." (New York *World,* 1913.)

Deadlock rapidly developed in Congress. Representative Carter Glass of Virginia, chief sponsor of the administration's banking bill, spoke dejectedly to Wilson of resignation. "Damn it, don't resign, old fellow," rejoined the President in one of his rare outbursts of profanity; "outvote them." The embattled Bryan Democrats finally triumphed over the bankers, and the epochal Federal Reserve Act was signed late in 1913.

Though complex, the Federal Reserve System was efficient. At its head in Washington sat the Federal Reserve Board, appointed by the President. The vesting of such arbitrary power in an inner group alarmed the moneyed men, who naturally distrusted the "politicians." To achieve a compromise between centralization and decentralization, the country was divided into twelve districts, each with a centralized bank owned by the member banks. One result was centralization within decentralization. A network of inter-

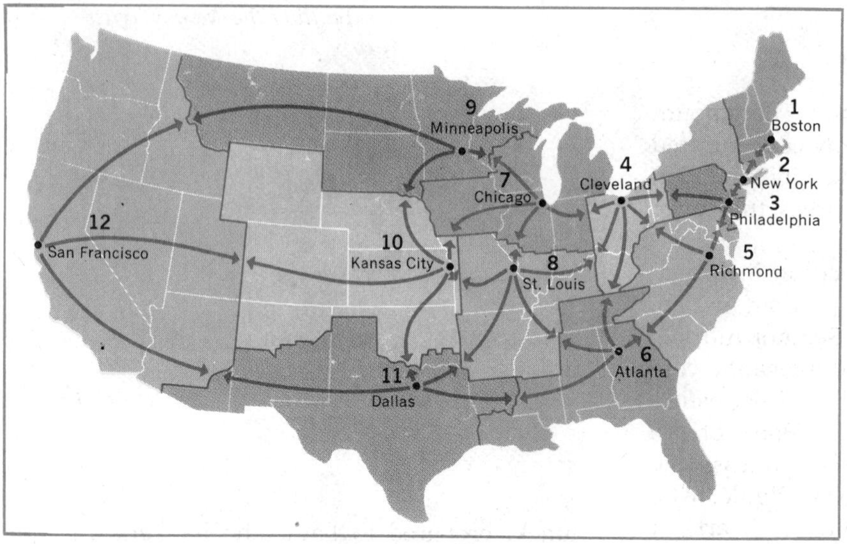

POSSIBLE INTERFLOW OF TWELVE FEDERAL RESERVE DISTRICTS AND BANKS
Alaska and Hawaii are included in the Twelfth District.

connecting financial pipelines radiated from each of the twelve Federal Reserve reservoirs, and these speeded the flow of currency and credit to the areas suffering serious financial drought. Congress thus met the long-felt need for a free-flowing currency.

The Federal Reserve Act also tightened the rein on existing institutions. All National Banks were required to join the new system, and others were at liberty to do so, once they had complied with its regulations. The twelve Federal Reserve Banks, which could be used as depositories for government funds, were actually bankers' banks. They dealt not with private individuals but with banking institutions.

An ingenious arrangement provided for expanding the paper money in time of emergency. The Federal Reserve Board was empowered to issue Federal Reserve currency backed by commercial paper—such as the promissory notes of businessmen—held by the member banks in various localities. Thus the amount of money in circulation could be quickly increased to meet the legitimate needs of business.

The Federal Reserve Act, which absorbed and ultimately ended the hoary independent treasury system of President Van Buren, was a red-letter achievement. It carried the nation with flying banners through the financial crises of the World War of 1914–1918. Many bankers who at first had viewed the Federal Reserve System with alarm were finally won over completely.

The President Tackles the Trusts

Without pausing for breath, Wilson pushed toward the last rampart in the "triple wall of privilege"—the trusts. He would thus achieve another of his New Freedoms—freedom from monopoly—and also restore free competition. Early in 1914 he again went before Congress in a personal appearance that still carried drama. His plea this time was for legislation that would loosen the strangling grip of special privilege.

Nine months and thousands of words later, Congress responded with the Federal Trade Commission Act of 1914. The new law empowered the President, through a bipartisan commission of five men, to turn a searchlight on industries engaged in interstate commerce, such as the meat packers. The commission was expected to crush monopoly in the cradle by careful investigation, followed by "cease and desist" orders where warranted. These presumably would root out harmful practices, including price discrimination, unfair competition, false advertising, misbranding, adulteration, and bribery and threats.

But this legislation alone could not cut the knot

of monopoly. The trusts had further entrenched themselves through interlocking directorates, which involved the same person serving on different boards of directors. Astute industrialists were now resorting more and more to the device known as the holding company, whose chief business was to hold the stocks or securities of other companies and derive income from them. A corporation produced a useful commodity like harvesters; a holding company produced profits.

The Clayton Anti-Trust Act of 1914 attempted to come to grips with these evils. It forbade practices that lessened competition, created monopoly, or resulted in objectionable price discrimination. It also restricted various types of interlocking directorates and holding companies, provided that they involved monopoly. All this sounded impressive on paper, but actually the Clayton Act suffered from loopholes and other weak spots. While a definite improvement on the old Sherman Anti-Trust Act of 1890, it disappointed the more zealous foes of monopoly.

Simultaneously the Clayton Act conferred certain benefits, long overdue, on organized labor. The outworn Sherman Anti-Trust Act, toothless though it was in restraining trusts, had been effective in crushing labor organizations. Conservative courts had unexpectedly held that monopolistic unions, like monopolistic corporations, fell under the restraints of the Sherman Act. A classic case in 1908 involved the striking hatters of Danbury, Connecticut. In 1912 they were assessed triple damages of more than $250,000, which resulted in the loss of their savings and homes. The Clayton Act presumably exempted labor and agricultural organizations from anti-trust prosecution, while specifically sanctioning such frowned-upon weapons as strikes and peaceful picketing. The new law also prohibited court injunctions in labor disputes, except in cases which involved "irreparable injury" to property.

But the gains of labor were illusory. Overtrustful workingmen greeted the new law with enthusiasm, partly because it legally lifted human labor from the category of "a commodity or article of commerce." Samuel Gompers, with unjustified praise, even hailed the act as the Magna Charta of labor.

"Vindicated," 1914. (Fitzpatrick in the St. Louis *Post-Dispatch*.)

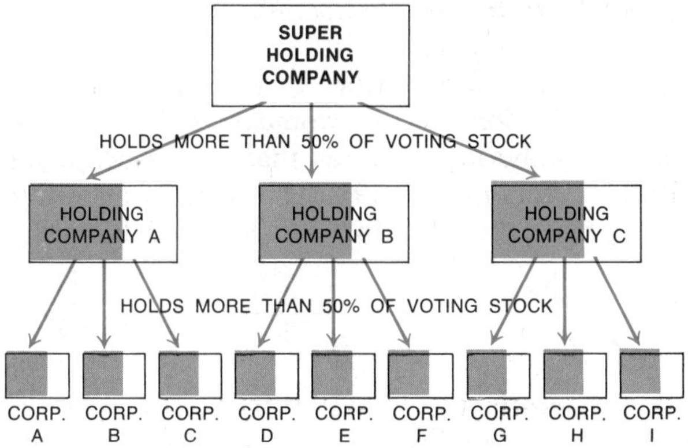

ORGANIZATION OF HOLDING COMPANIES

It should be borne in mind that the voting stock of a corporation is often only a fraction of the total stock.

But conservative courts in later years, invoking restrictive clauses in the law, often clipped the wings of organized labor.

The trusts, thus partially curbed by Wilsonian legislation, gradually faded from the headlines. Corporations on the whole were inclined to obey the restraining "cease and desist" orders issued by the Federal Trade Commission. Broad-minded courts, for their part, were disposed to follow the "rule of reason," and punish only those combines guilty of unreasonable restraints on trade. The coming of the Great War with Germany in 1917 caused big industry to seem less wicked. With full-scale production desperately needed, Washington was apt to relax prosecutions and wink at technical violations of the anti-trust laws. But the commission lives on as a powerful agency designed to keep business competition free and fair.

Democratic Doldrums

President Wilson, ramming an impressive sheaf of bills through Congress, was almost irresistible during his first eighteen months. For once, the creed of a political party was matched by deed. The "Schoolmaster President" achieved these legislative victories largely by sheer power of leadership, with a strong assist from the Democratic party machinery and the still-vibrant spirit of progressivism. Displaying an unbending backbone, he held Congress in session for over seventy-two weeks. Critics sneered that Professor Wilson was like the teacher, ruler in hand, who sternly keeps the students after school until they have completed their assignments.

But after the initial brilliant successes the Wilsonian spell began to wear off. Ever the idealist, the Princetonian was eager to spur the country into self-improvement more speedily than it wanted to go.

Economic depression further dampened the reformist mood. During the latter part of 1913 and much of 1914, a business recession laid a blighting hand on American industrial life. The dread specter of unemployment again stalked through the land. "Generals" Coxey and Kelly, with down-at-the-heel hoboes and other malcontents, again mobilized "armies" for a descent upon Washington. High-protection Republicans blamed the depression on the Underwood Tariff, which was admitting the handiwork of "cheap foreign labor." Scenting political danger, Wilson moved to appease businessmen by making conservative appointments to the new Federal Reserve Board and Federal Trade Commission.

World War I, erupting in the summer of 1914, first deepened and then dispelled the depression. The shock resulting from the European blowup, which caused the New York Stock Exchange to close, threatened financial disaster. But gradually orders began to pour in from Europe for American bread and bullets. Business perked up, and before long the nation was basking in the sunlight of unprecedented prosperity.

But before war-boom days fully arrived, the voters had vented some discontent at the polls. The mid-term congressional elections, held in November 1914, reduced the margin of the Democratic majority in the House from 147 to 25. But this setback cannot correctly be interpreted as a repudiation of Wilson. His election in 1912 had been a three-party affair. The congressional canvass of 1914 was the first straight-out two-party contest under Wilson; and as he won a clear majority in the House, the result could be hailed as a victory for the Democrats.

Wilson also read the election results as a victory for progressive forces. He could perceive that re-election in 1916 would hinge on his successful gathering of votes that had gone to the Bull Moosers back in 1912. Hence he turned away from his rightward drift of 1914 and backed a

A potent slogan used by the Democrats in their successful mid-term elections (1914) was: "War in the East! Peace in the West! Thank God for Wilson!"

series of measures dear to progressive and populistic hearts.

Triumphs for the Toilers

Fretful farmers were generally neglected by probusiness Republican regimes, but the Democratic Congress had enough momentum left to provide them with some relief. The Federal Farm Loan Act of 1916 made credit available to farmers at low rates of interest—a reform that had been demanded long before by the Populists. Notable among the several other attempts at rural relief was the Warehouse Act of 1916, which authorized loans on the security of staple crops. This was also a populistic scheme. Other laws provided for aid in constructing highways and in establishing agricultural extension work in the colleges.

Laboring men, already benefited by the Clayton Act, received additional aid as the wave of progressive reform continued to foam forward. Common sailors, who had been treated with extreme brutality from cat-o'-nine-tail days onward, were now given welcome relief. The La Follette Seaman's Act of 1915, sponsored by "Fighting Bob" La Follette of Wisconsin, required decent wages, treatment, and food. But while helping mariners, the law hurt the merchant marine. Standards were pushed so high that American shipping suffered in competition with the low-paying tramp steamers of the world.

Other enlightened social reforms were signed by Wilson's busy pen. Notable among them was the Workingmen's Compensation Act of 1916, which granted assistance to federal civil service employees during periods of disability. In the same year Wilson approved an act restricting child labor on products flowing into interstate commerce. But this badly needed safeguard was struck down by the standpat Supreme Court as an invasion of states' rights. Gratifying progress finally came only in the 1930s under the New Deal.

Railroad workers, numbering about 1.7 million, were not sidetracked. An imminent strike on the railways threatened a crippling nationwide tie-up in 1916, with a consequent blow at the administration's belated attempts to launch a defense program. The organized Railroad Brotherhoods, pinched by the mounting cost of living, spurned mediation. Wilson then moved. In another surprise appearance before Congress, he urged sweeping concessions to the workers. The response was the Adamson Act of 1916, which established an eight-hour day for all employees on trains in interstate commerce, with extra pay for overtime. Ex-Professor Wilson, though earning the gratitude of the Brotherhoods, was assailed in business circles for his abject "surrender" to union officials.

Wilson further won the enmity of Big Business and endeared himself to progressives in January 1916. He then nominated for the Supreme Court the reformer Louis D. Brandeis—the "people's attorney" and the first Jew to be called to the High Bench.

But Wilson's progressivism had its limits, and it

"Too Cowed [Proud] to Fight," 1916. Congress passes Adamson Eight-Hour Act. (Harding in the Brooklyn *Eagle*.)

clearly stopped short of better treatment for blacks. The Southern-bred Wilson actually presided over accelerated segregation in the federal bureaucracy. When a delegation of black leaders called on him to protest this policy, he virtually froze them out of his office.

Undoing Dollar Diplomacy

The quiet scholar-President, dedicated to New Freedoms, recoiled from the aggressive foreign policies of his predecessors. As a lover of peace and a hater of imperialism, he was repelled by the Big Stickism of Roosevelt. As an implacable foe of the big-money interests, he detested the so-called Dollar Diplomacy of Taft. He was convinced that little good could come out of Wall Street.

Wilson had been in office only a week when, in sensational fashion, he declared war on Dollar Diplomacy in Latin America. He announced that his administration would not support American bankers and other "interests" in that area, even though some of them had invested funds there as a result of Taft's promptings.

Shifting his attack from Latin America to the Far East, Wilson further shocked the financial world just a week later, in mid-March 1913. He proclaimed that he would give no special assistance to American bankers who, under the proddings of Taft, had rather reluctantly embarked upon a six-nation loan in China. Wilson believed that this scheme, designed to finance a strategic Chinese railroad, encroached on the sovereignty of China. Worse yet, it might entangle the United States. The bankers, shivering from this Wilsonian bucket of cold water, pulled out of the project the next day. One critic snarled, "Dollar Diplomacy was at least better than none at all."

But Wilson soon found, especially in Nicaragua, that his noble ideals clashed with political realities. An incomplete treaty with this banana republic, negotiated under Taft's Dollar Diplomacy, offered attractive strategic advantages. Bryan therefore proceeded to press for this highly favorable new pact. It placed Nicaragua even more securely within the orbit of the United States by granting a perpetual option on a Nicaraguan canal route, together with a ninety-nine-year lease on sites for bases near both ends. The pact was so sweeping as to make Taft's Dollar Diplomacy, in the words of one critic, look like mere "ten-cent diplomacy."*

Anti-Imperialism Becomes Wilsonian Imperialism

Revolution-rent Haiti likewise forced Wilson to eat his anti-imperialistic words. The climax of disorders came in 1914–1915, when an outraged populace literally tore to pieces the brutal Haitian president. In both years Wilson was reluctantly forced to dispatch marines to protect American lives and property. In 1916 Washington concluded a treaty with Haiti which provided for United States supervision of finances and police, and which made the French-speaking republic a protectorate of the Colossus of the North. Sovereignty-loving Haitians resented the presence of the Yankees; and various uprisings occurred, in which hundreds of rebels were killed.

To Wilson's distress, the story of Santo Domingo seemed like a carbon copy of the Haitian intervention. Serious outbursts in the island republic brought the leathernecked marines in 1916, and the debt-cursed land came under the shadow of the American eagle's wings. Increasingly the Caribbean Sea, with its vital approaches to the now-completed Panama Canal, was taking on the earmarks of a Yankee preserve.

The purchase of the Danish West Indies (the Virgin Islands), concluded in 1917, tightened the grip of the Yankee in these shark-infested waters. Washington was forced to pay the war-inflated price of $25 million, its costliest territorial addition. This fancy figure reflected the fear that these isles might be occupied by the Germans for submarine bases, with disastrous results to American shipping. Uncle Sam thus acquired an expensive Carib-

*The pact, completed in 1916, was terminated by mutual agreement in 1971.

THE UNITED STATES IN THE CARIBBEAN
This map explains why many Latin Americans accused the United States of turning the Caribbean Sea into a Yankee lake. It also suggests that Uncle Sam was much less "isolationist" in his own back yard than he was in faraway Europe or Asia.

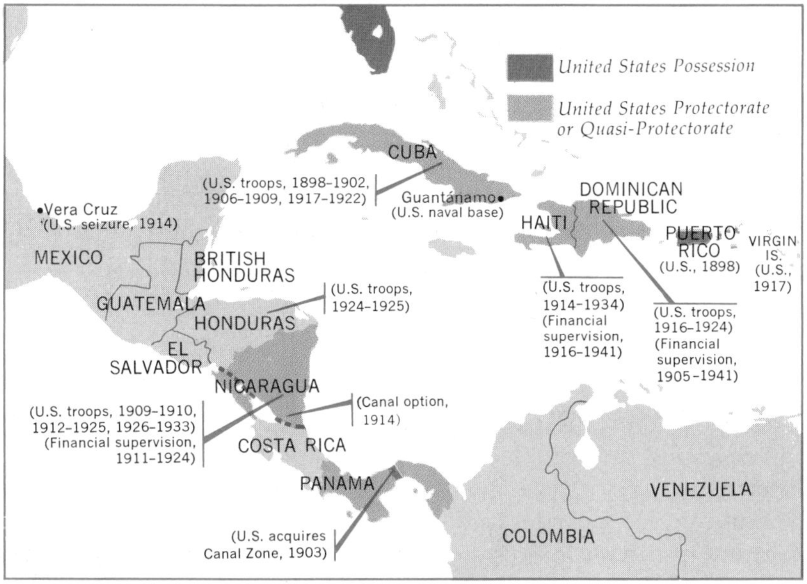

bean "poorhouse"—three main islands and some fifty islets, peopled by about 20,000 impoverished blacks.

An embarrassed Wilson, now a prisoner of circumstances, had meanwhile changed his views of 1913 on the six-power loan to China. Impelled by American self-interest and the stern realities of international politics during the World War, he did an about-face in 1917. Bewildered Wall Street bankers were now strongly urged to go back into the dubious enterprise. Thus the idealist-President, instead of reversing Taft's Dollar Diplomacy, succeeded in reversing himself.

In the midst of these flip-flops, Wilson and his Democratic following did succeed in steering their traditional course regarding the Philippines. Ever since Bryan's heyday, the Democrats had favored cutting loose from this burdensome overseas liability. The Filipinos, who panted for complete freedom, were immensely heartened in 1916 when the Democratic Congress passed the Jones Act. It granted the boon of virtual territorial status, and declared flatly that the United States would grant independence as soon as a "stable government" could be established. That happy day came thirty-six years later.

"A New Sentry in the Caribbean Sea," 1916. Uncle Sam sits on the three main Virgin Islands. (Courtesy of Dayton *News.*)

Wilson Demands Fair Play for Japan and Britain

The menacing clouds of a crisis with Japan had meanwhile appeared in 1913. California's legislature, seeking to discourage the procreative and acquisitive Japanese, was drafting legislation to debar them from owning land in the Golden State. Tokyo, ever sensitive to slights, lodged vigorous protests, which touched off nasty talk of war. At fortress Corregidor, in the Philippines, American gunners were kept on an around-the-clock alert for six weeks.

Wilson was deeply concerned. As a good Christian he deplored discrimination against the Japanese in California. As a peace lover, he regretted action by one state that might involve all of the other forty-seven in a bloody conflict. Desperately seeking to avert a clash, he dispatched Secretary Bryan to California to plead with the legislature. The law that finally passed softened the slap somewhat by not mentioning the Japanese by name, but it prevented Oriental ownership of land by discriminating against "aliens ineligible to citizenship." Nevertheless, Wilson's intercession and Bryan's friendliness helped calm Tokyo, and the crisis was surmounted.

The Japanese, already imperialistic-minded, took advantage of the European conflagration to present to Peking, in 1915, their "Twenty-one Demands." If accepted, these would impinge severely upon China's sovereignty and slam shut the Open Door. Under vigorous protests from Washington, Tokyo finally toned down some of its more offensive terms.

Nearer home, the disputed Panama Canal Tolls Act of 1912 caused Wilson sleepless nights. This law, passed by Congress in the dying months of the Taft regime, specifically exempted American coastwise ships from paying tolls. The Hay-Pauncefote Treaty with Britain in 1901 had granted America a free hand to build and fortify the canal—provided that she would open it to *all* nations on the same tolls-paying terms. Washington interpreted this pact to mean all *other* nations; the British interpreted it to mean *all* nations, including the United States. London consequently lodged emphatic protests.

Wilson was thus squeezed between international morality and political expediency. The exemption for American ships was popular, especially among the Irish-Americans, who cheered any twisting of the Lion's tail. But the more Wilson read the treaty, the more convinced he was that America was breaking a promise to London, no matter what the government's hairsplitting lawyers argued. As a Southern gentleman, he believed that a nation of honor, like a man of honor, should keep its promise—all the more so if it was powerful enough to prevail. The nation was too big to act small.

> Wilson, according to his secretary J. P. Tumulty, spoke of resigning and making an "appeal to the people" if he did not win on the canal tolls. "In case of failure in this matter," Tumulty quotes Wilson as saying, "I shall go to the country, after my resignation is tendered, and ask it to say whether America is to stand before the world as a nation that violates its contracts as mere matters of convenience, upon a basis of expediency."

Appearing before Congress in March 1914, Wilson made a moving plea for a repeal of the exemption. The House and Senate, after a stormy debate, grudgingly granted his request. Grateful Britons, possibly as a result of a tacit understanding, continued to support Wilson's faltering Mexican policy. So it was that less than two weeks before the eruption of World War I, the last serious dispute with London was settled. This fact had an important bearing on the pro-British attitude that prevailed in America at the onset of the conflict.

Revolution Below the Rio Grande

Rifle bullets whining across the southern border served as a constant reminder that all was not quiet in Mexico. Under the three-decade dictatorship of Porfirio Díaz—"Díazpotism"—the natural resources of Mexico had been exploited by foreign investors in oil, railroads, and mines. By 1913

American capitalists had optimistically sunk about a billion dollars into this underdeveloped but richly endowed country, and about 50,000 American citizens had taken up residence south of the Rio Grande.

This surface calm to the south merely concealed the combustibles of revolution. For if Mexico was rich, the Mexicans were poor. Most of the 15 million inhabitants—predominantly peons—were landless, while a handful of wealthy landowners and foreign capitalists monopolized the wealth. Little wonder that the masses began to agitate for reform, under the leadership of men like Francisco Madero, a California-educated visionary.

A blowup began in 1910, and the next year the aging Díaz fled the country to escape revolutionary vengeance. President Madero, his successor, proved utterly incapable of controlling the swirling forces thus unleashed. The revolution took an ugly turn in February 1913, less than two weeks before Wilson entered the White House, when Madero was murdered by a conscienceless clique. It included General Huerta, a full-blooded Indian, who a few days earlier had made himself ruler.

President Wilson, to whom Taft gladly passed on the Mexican muddle, was at the outset presented with a giant-sized headache. The turmoil in Mexico inevitably led to the destruction of American lives and property, and to an angry outcry in the United States for armed intervention. Prominent among those beating the tom-toms for war was the influential chain-newspaper publisher William R. Hearst, whose views presumably were colored by his ownership of a Mexican ranch larger than the state of Rhode Island.

Yet Wilson stood firm against intervention. As a peace lover, he was opposed to violent methods, especially in behalf of the greedy "interests" that he distrusted. He persuasively justified his stand in a speech at Mobile, Alabama, in October 1913, when he declared that it was "perilous" to determine foreign policy "in the terms of material interest." For good measure, he went on to proclaim that the United States would never take "one additional foot of territory by conquest."

Uncle Sam Refuses Huerta's Blood-Drenched Hand. Republican journalist George Harvey wrote: "What legal or moral right has a President of the United States to say who shall or shall not be President of Mexico?" (New York *Daily Tribune*, 1913.)

This reassuring promise was widely heralded as a retreat from the interventionist twist given the Monroe Doctrine by Theodore Roosevelt.

General-President Huerta, though bloody-handed, brought a semblance of order to Mexico. His government was gradually recognized by a number of foreign powers, especially after he had shown a tolerant attitude toward their investors. Washington would normally have granted recognition also, for traditional policy had been to recognize firmly entrenched (de facto) governments, whether established by bullets or ballots.

But Wilson, dead set against recognizing "government by murder," put idealism above traditionalism. Committed to the New Freedom at home, he would not be a party to crushing freedom abroad. He steadfastly refused to extend the right hand of fellowship to that "desperate brute" Huerta, who seemingly did not have the support of the Mexican masses. "I am going to teach the South American republics to elect good men," the ex-schoolmaster assured a visiting Briton.

Not content with merely holding the line, Wilson next undertook to drive "the unspeakable Huerta" from office. In 1914 he lifted an earlier embargo on arms so that munitions could flow to Huerta's

I◻II◻II◻II◻II◻II◻II◻II◻II◻II◻II◻II◻II◻II◻II◻II◻II◻I

Congressman Humphrey voiced Republican complaints against Wilson's Mexican policy in 1916: "It is characterized by weakness, uncertainty, vacillation, and uncontrollable desire to intermeddle in Mexican affairs. He has not had the courage to go into Mexico nor the courage to stay out. . . . I would either go into Mexico and pacify the country or I would keep my hands entirely out of Mexico. If we are too proud to fight, we should be too proud to quarrel. I would not choose between murderers."

I◻II◻II◻II◻II◻II◻II◻II◻II◻II◻II◻II◻II◻II◻II◻II◻II◻I

principal rivals, white-bearded Venustiano Carranza and swarthy Francisco ("Pancho") Villa. Drawing a sharp distinction between the poor peons and their ruthless rulers, Wilson insisted that he was trying to help the Mexican people shake off their tyrants. Over in Germany, Emperor Wilhelm II sneered, "Morality [is] all right, but what about the dividends?"

Wilson's policy of "watchful waiting," as he called it, was condemned by Big Business Republicans and other American investors. "Wrathfully waiting," they preferred the brass-knuckled stability that would come with a "strong man" like Huerta. Pressure upon Wilson for forcible intervention mounted, especially when dozens of Americans were killed during recurrent disorders. The President's course was branded as "deadly drifting," while Theodore Roosevelt jeered, "He kissed the blood-stained hand that slapped his face."

American Meddling and Muddling in Mexico

The Mexican volcano erupted at the Atlantic seaport of Tampico, in April 1914, when a small party of American sailors was arrested and taken from a United States navy launch plainly displaying the Stars and Stripes. Although the captives were promptly released with expressions of regret, the hotheaded American admiral demanded a formal apology and a salute of twenty-one guns. Huerta defiantly refused to salute the flag of a nation that did not even recognize him as the ruler of Mexico.

Wilson, heavy-hearted but stubbornly determined to eliminate Huerta, went before Congress to ask for authority to use force in Mexico. After two days of heated debate, permission was granted, on April 22, 1914. But one day earlier, Wilson had ordered naval units, which were seeking to intercept a German merchant ship carrying arms to Huerta, to capture the city of Vera Cruz. The marines and sailors gained their objective, which cost the lives of 19 Americans and some 200 Mexicans, to say nothing of the wounded. War hysteria swept the United States, and a full-dress shooting conflict seemed inevitable.

At this critical juncture Wilson was rescued from a point of no return. The ABC Powers—Argentina, Brazil, and Chile—fearful of another Mexican War, tendered their good offices. Washington promptly and gratefully accepted. The upshot was a meeting at Niagara Falls, in mid-1914, at which the five nations concerned were represented. Although the immediate results were inconclusive, the United States was able to show to the world its determination not to crush Mexico.

Huerta at length collapsed under the pressures from within and without. Resigning in July 1914, and fleeing to Spain, he was soon succeeded by his arch-rival, strong-willed Venustiano Carranza. Wilson's "watchful waiting," though savagely condemned, was successful at least to this extent.

The sinister figure of "Pancho" Villa had meanwhile stolen the spotlight. A bloodthirsty combination of bandit and Robin Hood, he emerged as the chief rival of President Carranza, whom Wilson reluctantly supported with shipments of arms. Villa showed his contempt and hatred for the "gringos" in January 1916, when his followers killed eighteen United States citizens in cold blood at Santa Ysabel, Mexico. The culminating outrage occurred in March 1916, when Villistas shot up Columbus, New Mexico, leaving behind seventeen dead Americans and many others injured, but suffering heavier losses themselves.

Pancho Villa with His Rag-Tag Army in Mexico, c. 1916. His daring, impetuosity, and horsemanship made Villa a hero to the masses of northern Mexico. Yet he proved to be a violent and poorly directed force against social abuses, and he was assassinated in 1923. (Brown Brothers.)

General John J. ("Black Jack")* Pershing, a grim-faced and ramrod-erect veteran of the Cuban and Philippine campaigns, was ordered to break up the bandit band. His hastily organized force of several thousand horse-borne troops penetrated deep into rugged Mexico with surprising speed, mauled the Villistas, and narrowly missed capturing Villa. President Carranza permitted the invasion with reluctance, and only after a face-saving agreement that would permit Mexico to invade the United States under reversed conditions.

*So called from his earlier service as an officer with the crack black 10th Cavalry.

Pershing's expedition—"the perishing expedition," it was dubbed—at length ran into a blind alley. In the face of clashes with the suspicious Carranzista forces and imminent war with Germany, the invading army was withdrawn early in January 1917.

But the seemingly fruitless foray into Mexico was not without consequence. The confused mobilization of American troops, including the National Guard, advertised military weaknesses and helped spur the preparedness movement. The Germans were not impressed with America's armed strength, and the spectacle of the frustrated Pershing expedition was before them when they decided to push Wilson into war with their all-out submarine attacks.

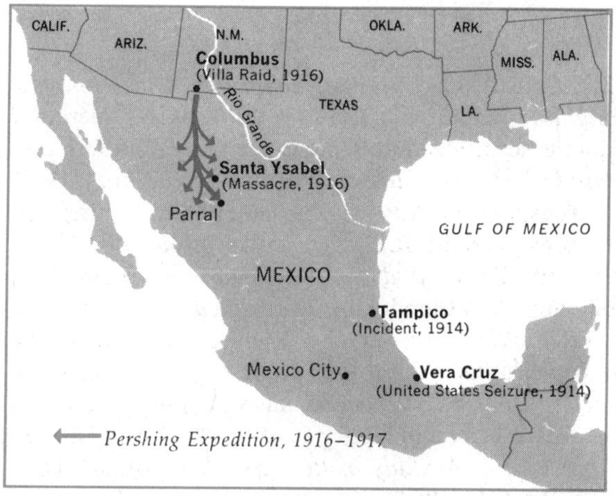

THE UNITED STATES AND MEXICO, 1914–1917

Wilsonian Winnings in Mexico

Wilson's Mexican policy, despite charges of spinelessness, had much to commend it. Elevating human rights above property rights, in the spirit of the New Freedom, the idealist-moralist in the White House strove to leave the masses of Mexico free to reap the fruits of their own revolution. And this they did in the troubled decades that lay ahead.

In dealing with Mexico, Wilson proved to be as much a man of vision as a visionary. He kept his hands free for more pressing crises elsewhere, especially those involving the German submarines. He avoided the vexations and bloodshed of a full-fledged war—a conflict that would have soaked up vast amounts of blood and money. He resisted the clamor for taking over all Mexico—an operation that would have resembled the Philippine vexation, only many times multiplied.

Wilsonian righteousness, despite serious blunders, emerged reasonably clean from the Mexican muddle. "We can afford," the President had told Congress in 1913, "to exercise the self-restraint of a really great nation which realizes its own strength and scorns to misuse it." Even though America's interests elsewhere required a modified use of Dollar Diplomacy, Wilson still tried to steer his stormy course by the far-off stars of idealism.

VARYING VIEWPOINTS

Wilson's achievement in realizing his New Freedom reforms in 1913 and 1914 undeniably constitutes one of the most noteworthy examples of presidential leadership. Yet the precise character of Wilson's accomplishment remains something of a puzzle. Some historians conclude that Wilson, having beaten Roosevelt in the election, proceeded to implement Roosevelt's program. These scholars point especially to the New Nationalist flavor of the Federal Reserve Act and the Federal Trade Commission. Other analysts claim that the Clayton Anti-Trust Act faithfully followed Wilson's campaign pledges and reflected his "real" political beliefs. Still other critics, noting especially Wilson's appointment of businessmen to the new governmental bodies, charge that the rhetoric of progressive reform was simply a cloak for the consolidation of conservative rule. This debate again illustrates the difficulty of defining "progressive." More generally, the controversy highlights the problem of assessing the meaning of "reform" in the American system of democratic capitalism.

SELECT READINGS

See the titles by Goldman, Hofstadter, Hays, Wiebe, and Kolko cited in the two preceding chapters. A comprehensive overview is A. S. Link, *Woodrow Wilson and the Progressive Era, 1910–1917* (1954); more detailed is the same author's *Wilson: The New Freedom* (1956). William E. Leuchtenburg puts Wilson in a wider context in *The Perils of Prosperity, 1914–1932* (1958). Biographies of Wilson include Link's five-volume *Wilson* (1947–1965), and those by John A. Garraty, Arthur Walworth, and John M. Blum. Particularly interesting is Alexander and Juliette George's psychological study, *Woodrow Wilson and Colonel House* (1956). For a sharply constrasting view, see Edwin A. Weinstein, *Woodrow Wilson: A Medical and Psychological Biography* (1981). Consult also William Diamond, *The Economic Thought of Woodrow Wilson* (1943). Wilson's secretary of state is scrutinized in Paolo Coletta, *William Jennings Bryan: Progressive Politician and Moral Statesman* (1969). Various aspects of Wilson's Mexican policy are interestingly presented in R. E. Quirk, *An Affair of Honor: Woodrow Wilson and the Occupation of Vera Cruz* (1962), and C. C. Clendenen, *The United States and Pancho Villa* (1961). Consult also Robert Freeman Smith, *The United States and Revolutionary Nationalism in Mexico, 1916–1932* (1972). Social and intellectual currents are described in Henry F. May, *The End of American Innocence: A Study of the First Years of Our Own Time, 1912–1917* (1959).

35

The Road to World War I

Property can be paid for; the lives of peaceful and innocent people cannot be. The present German submarine warfare against commerce is a warfare against mankind.

WOODROW WILSON, War Message, April 2, 1917

Thunder Across the Sea

Europe's powder magazine, long smoldering, blew up in the summer of 1914, when the flaming pistol of a Serb patriot killed the heir to the throne of Austria-Hungary. An outraged Vienna government forthwith presented a stern ultimatum to neighboring Serbia, and war seemed inevitable. Austria-Hungary hoped to localize the conflict between herself and the Serbians, while Germany most ill-advisedly gave her Austro-Hungarian ally a blank-check promise of support.

An explosive chain reaction followed. Tiny Serbia, backed by her powerful Slav neighbor, Russia, refused to bend the knee sufficiently. The Russian Czar began to mobilize his ponderous war machine, menacing Germany on the east. At the same time his ally, France, was confronting Germany on the west. The Germans in alarm suddenly struck at France through unoffending Belgium; their objective was to knock their ancient enemy out of the war so that they would have a free hand to repel Russia. Great Britain, her coastline jeopardized by the assault on Belgium, was sucked into the conflagration on the side of France.

Almost overnight most of Europe was involved in a fight to the death. On one side were arrayed the Central Powers: Germany and Austria-Hungary—and later Turkey and Bulgaria. On the other side were the Allied Powers, principally France, Britain, and Russia—and later Japan and Italy. The network of alliances on which the peace of Europe had been precariously balanced seemed to be pulling the nations into the slippery abyss, much like falling mountain climbers tied to the same rope.

Americans were stunned and bewildered, though not completely surprised. For something like two decades alarmists had predicted a European upheaval, but previous crises had all been surmounted. The cry of "wolf, wolf" had been raised so many times that the American people could hardly believe that the dread beast was at last on the loose. They instinctively thanked God for the ocean moats, and self-righteously congratulated themselves on having had ancestors wise enough to emigrate from the hell pits of Europe. America felt strong, snug, smug, and secure.

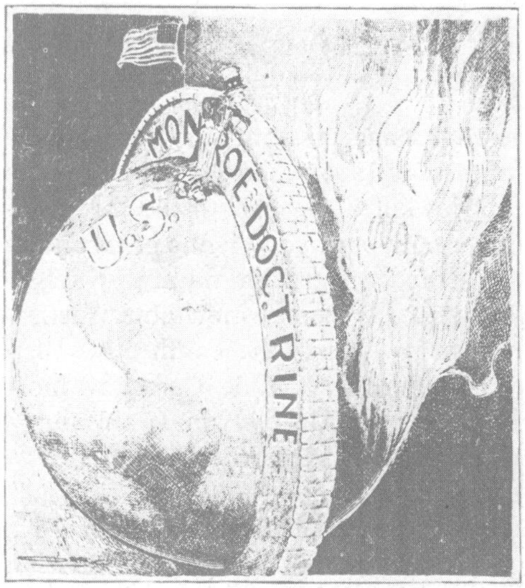

"The Great Wall," 1914. The Monroe Doctrine is depicted as a protective shield. (Courtesy of Nashville *Tennessean.*)

President Wilson promptly issued the routine proclamation of neutrality, and later warned his countrymen to be neutral in both thought and deed. At heart pro-Ally, he was a lifelong admirer of British civilization and a rather frequent summer visitor to the British Isles. But outwardly he kept his sympathies in check, at least during the early stages of the conflict.

Most Americans, though earnestly desiring to stay out of the blood bath, on the whole sympathized strongly with the Allied camp. Perhaps half of the American people, who now numbered about 100 million, traced their lineage back to British or Canadian sources. A hundred different cultural and economic ties bound the Republic to Great Britain, while Anglo-American diplomatic relations had recently risen to a new level of friendliness.

But enthusiasm for the Allies would have been much less warm if bleeding France had not been in their ranks. The hearts of many Americans went out to their traditional friend, and a few volunteers entered her armed services, notably the aviation unit known as the Lafayette Escadrille. France had helped to win independence, and Americans felt that they owed her an unrepayable debt. Robert Underwood Johnson prayed:

> Forget us, God, if we forget
> The sacred sword of Lafayette!

The fate of Belgium deepened pro-Ally sentiment in America. This tiny nation, by an act of unprovoked aggression, had been largely flattened by the German streamroller. Countless Belgians were facing starvation when boyish-faced Herbert Hoover, a spectacularly successful mining engineer who happened to be in London, was chosen to form a relief organization. The young master organizer, then only forty years of age, did a magnifi-

Herbert Hoover as a Young Mining Engineer. As a Stanford undergraduate, he had shown administrative aptitude as manager of the football team. (Crandall Collection, Hoover Institution, Stanford, California.)

cent job of feeding the Belgians. He was aided by generous gifts from fellow Americans, whose hearts naturally went with their donations.

Wellsprings of Anti-German Feeling

When war flamed across Europe, the German-Americans comprised the largest single foreign-born group. Counting persons with at least one foreign-born parent, transplanted peoples from the Central Powers numbered about 11 million. Countless thousands of German-Americans and other pro-German "hyphenated" Americans, many of whom had emigrated only physically, expressed noisy sympathy for the Fatherland. They were enthusiastically abetted by numerous Irish-Americans, who naturally cheered any foe of their ancient enemy, Great Britain.

But the American people as a whole were anti-German from the outset. Germany, as a chip-on-the-shoulder newcomer among the powers, had discriminated against America's allegedly diseased pork, and had collided with American expansionist ambitions in Samoa and at Manila Bay. Elbowing for "a place in the sun," the Germans had joined the imperialistic scramble in China, the East Indies, the Pacific, and Africa. Their low-priced goods, bearing the fearsome trademark "Made in Germany," had displaced those of many foreign competitors, including Yankees.

The Germans, moreover, seemed born to the sword. They had recently overtaken the United States in the naval race, and their magnificent army of goose-steppers was reputed to be the most formidable in Europe. In short, the Germans were identified in the American mind with navalism, militarism, and saber-rattling jingoism. And their Emperor, Kaiser Wilhelm II, seemed to be the embodiment of the dangers of German aggression, arrogant autocracy, and decaying monarchism. With villainous upturned mustaches, and a sinister withered arm which suggested degeneracy, he antagonized an America that was traditionally anti-monarchical.

Principal Foreign Elements in the United States (Census of 1910)
(TOTAL U.S. POPULATION: 91,972,266)

Country of Origin		*Foreign-Born*	*Natives with Two Foreign-Born Parents*	*Natives with One Foreign-Born Parent*	*Total*
Central Powers	Germany	2,501,181	3,911,847	1,869,590	8,282,618
	Austria-Hungary	1,670,524	900,129	131,133	2,701,786
Allied Powers	Great Britain	1,219,968	852,610	1,158,474	3,231,052
	(Ireland)*	1,352,155	2,141,577	1,010,628	4,504,360
	Russia	1,732,421	949,316	70,938	2,752,675
	Italy	1,343,070	695,187	60,103	2,098,360
TOTAL (for all foreign countries, including those not listed)		13,345,545	12,916,311	5,981,526	32,243,282

*Ireland was not yet independent.

The Kaiser Ravishes Belgium. He had little to do with the so-called atrocities, but propagandists made him the archvillain of the war. (New York *World,* 1914.)

Germany sank even lower in American esteem in 1914, when she seemingly provoked the war with calculated malice. It mattered not that the other powers, as historians were later to prove, shared much of the blame. Germany's guilt seemed beyond dispute when she assaulted "poor little Belgium," whose neutrality she and the other powers had solemnly guaranteed by treaty as far back as 1839. The misdeed took on a more evil aspect when the German Chancellor blunderingly dismissed the neutrality pact as a mere "scrap of paper."

Paper Bullets

America was the richest and most powerful of the neutrals. Her open aid, or at least her sympathy, was well worth cultivating.

Allied propagandists, especially the British, enjoyed unusual success in the United States. They were careful to use the tactics of the gentle wooer, partly because they could be sure of a sympathetic hearing. Moreover, most of the transatlantic stories were filtered through British cables, and the scissors of the censors sheared away versions harmful to the Allied cause.

Allied agents drenched the United States with tales of German savagery—tales that stressed the inhuman submarine warfare and the abuse of Belgium. Charges of "Hunnish" barbarity were strengthened by atrocity stories, many of which later proved false. Among these hoaxes were a "crucified Canadian," a "corpse factory" where Germans supposedly converted human bodies into soap, Belgian babies with their hands amputated, and Belgian maidens with their breasts slashed off.

Atrocities always occur in large-scale wars—and on both sides. Most of this conflict was fought on non-German soil, and the inevitable clashes with civilians dyed the German villains a deeper black. Many Americans even came to believe that the green-clad German warriors thundered through Belgium with babies impaled on their bayonets. The Allies, for their part, were careful not to publicize the rapes and other barbarities committed by their own soldiers.

The brutal execution of Edith Cavell by the Germans in Belgium was one of the worst blunders of the war. Their victim, an English nurse behind German lines, had helped scores of convalescent Allied soldiers to escape so that they might fight another day. Her death before a firing squad was legally defensible, but it was incredibly stupid, for she was a woman and a nurse. The shock to the civilized world was reinforced by such effective propaganda as the American motion picture entitled "Edith Cavell, the Woman the Germans Shot."

German propaganda in America fell on much less fertile ground. A hostile reception was almost certain, owing to the long background of Teutonic friction and blundering. German suitors for America's favor, moreover, were inclined to use the crude embrace of the caveman, without sufficient finesse. And what little they did accomplish was largely undone by the ruthlessness of the militarists in the Fatherland.

A dispute persists as to the effectiveness of Allied propaganda. No one can deny that there was a vast amount of it, but no one can measure its effects with precision. Most Americans were undoubtedly pro-Ally from the beginning, and atrocity tales from overseas merely confirmed their existing prejudices. Allied propaganda, though partly fictional, was generally based on facts, notably the invasion of Belgium, the shooting of Edith Cavell, and the sinking of the *Lusitania*.

Pro-Ally sentiment in America deepened as the anxious neutrality period lengthened. Ardent Allied sympathizers declared that only a "moral eunuch" could be neutral in thought, as Wilson had urged. The feeling took root that Britain was "fighting our fight," and that a person was not "100 percent American" unless he was pro-Ally. But the great majority still fervently hoped that they could stay out of the terrible war.

The Fatherland, the chief German-American propaganda newspaper in the United States, cried, "We [Americans] prattle about humanity, while we manufacture poisoned shrapnel and picric acid for profit. Ten thousand German widows, ten thousand orphans, ten thousand graves bear the legend 'Made in America.' "

America Earns Blood Money

When Europe burst into flames in 1914, the United States was still bogged down in the business recession of 1913–1914. The British and French hastened to place huge orders for war materials, and soon American industry pulled itself out of the morass of hard times onto a peak of wartime prosperity.

As the war machine in Europe chewed up munitions, the Allies began to exhaust their credits in the United States. If the nation were not to be plunged back into the dreary days of depression, so the argument ran, American bankers would have to lend huge sums of money to the Allied governments. The Wilson administration at first frowned upon these loans, for they seemed like a flagrant act of unneutrality. But such objections rapidly faded before the prospect of renewed economic distress.

Private enterprise, notably the Wall Street firm of J. P. Morgan and Company, came to the rescue. Largely through bond sales in the United States, American agencies were able to advance to the Allies during the period of neutrality the enormous sum of $2.3 billion. At the same time, Wall Street lent only $27 million to the blockaded Germans, who were regarded as poor risks. Thus the Americans were not only selling munitions to the Allied camp—munitions that were making thousands of German widows and orphans—but were providing the necessary money.

Germany and Austria-Hungary protested bitterly against the immense trade in munitions, for America was becoming the chief arsenal of the Allies. But this profitable if bloody business was undoubtedly legal. The Germans themselves, as neutrals, had earlier sold military hardware for a profit. Washington made it clear to Germany and Austria-Hungary that America was showing no favoritism: she would be delighted to make money out of them also, if they would only come and

U. S. Exports to Belligerents, 1914–1916

Belligerent	*1914*	*1915*	*1916*	*Percentage Relation of 1916 Figure to 1914 Figure*
Britain	$594,271,863	$911,794,954	$1,526,685,102	257%
France	159,818,924	369,397,170	628,851,988	393
Italy*	74,235,012	184,819,688	269,246,105	364
Germany	344,794,276	28,863,354	288,899	0.08

*Italy joined the Allies in April 1915.

get the munitions. The catch was that the British blockade prevented deliveries.

Germany Attempts to Stop Arms Shipments

German-American groups, raising loud but futile protests, demanded that Washington forbid all shipments of arms abroad. Such a stoppage would have been entirely lawful. But by the time Congress came to grips with the explosive issue, the so-called merchants of death were reaping lush profits—and the new prosperity was too precious to be cast aside.

An American embargo on munitions would have been a heaven-sent boon to the Germans. They had built up their vast war machine with adequate stockpiles of military supplies, knowing well that, in the face of a British blockade, they probably could not import armaments from abroad. The sea-controlling Allies had amassed less formidable stockpiles, partly because they knew that they could count on supplementary arms from neutrals, including the United States.

A stoppage of American munitions would have been a signal victory for the Germans, a stunning defeat for the Allies. Whether America did something or nothing about halting arms shipments, she would appear to be unneutral. So she followed the profitable path of doing nothing—a course that was all the easier because her heart was with the Allies. Economically she was thus bound closer and closer to the Allied war chariot by the golden chains of trade.

German and Austrian secret agents, under orders to interrupt the flow of munitions, resorted to violence. They fomented strikes in the arms factories, and plotted fires, explosions, and other acts of sabotage. Suspicious Americans saw a sinister German hand in the wrecking of the New Jersey Black Tom munitions plant, which blew up in 1916 with a loss of $22 million. Two German attachés in Washington, as well as the Austro-Hungarian ambassador, were implicated in such underhanded schemes and were forced to leave the country in 1915.

In the end German plottings backfired badly. In August 1915, Dr. Albert, a key German agent, absent-mindedly left his briefcase on a New York elevated car. It was promptly picked up by an American Secret Service agent, and some of the documents relating to industrial sabotage were published in the newspapers. The American imagination was further filled with images of German spies—men with short-cropped square heads and rolls of fat on the backs of their bull necks. Thus American opinion, already ill-disposed, was further turned against the Kaiser and his Fatherland.

Britain's Blockade of Germany

Diplomatic relations with Britain, despite America's pro-Ally bias, were not all smooth sailing. The global struggle, as during the Napoleonic Wars, involved a contest for sea power. And the United States, as earlier, was the most flourishing neutral carrier. The naval blockade, which was still Britain's most potent offensive weapon, was bound to bruise American shippers.

Early in the war, the British inaugurated their slow-strangulation blockade of Germany. Among other steps, they proclaimed the North Sea a military zone and proceeded to mine it heavily. Neutral ships approaching the European coast were forced to stop at the neck of the British bottle for inspection and—if approved—for their sailing directions through the deadly mined area. They would not be approved, naturally, if they carried contraband of war. The British, arbitrarily redefining contraband, included foodstuffs, cotton, and other items not hitherto regarded as directly useful in waging war. American farmers and manufacturers, feeling the pinch, raised cries of protest.

London likewise redefined blockade. A close-in blockade of the German coasts by warships, in the old-fashioned style, was rendered risky by modern long-range guns and by lurking submarines. Alleging "unusual" or "peculiar" conditions in this conflict, the British would force American ships off the high seas into their ports. There a leisurely search could be undertaken, sometimes with X-ray photographs, to inspect cargo for con-

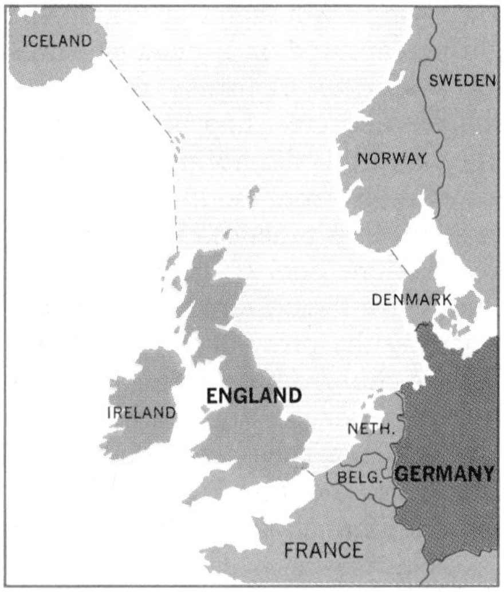

BRITISH MILITARY AREA
(declared November 3, 1914)

cealed contraband. This highly irregular procedure, quite different from the usual offshore blockade sanctioned by international law, evoked emphatic protests from Washington. But since the British paid for many of the cargoes thus confiscated, the edge was taken off the complaints of the shippers, especially those from the cotton-producing South.

The British also arbitrarily expanded the doctrine of continuous voyage, as interpreted by the United States during the Civil War. (See p. 400.) Germany's neutral neighbors, like Holland and Denmark, suddenly began to purchase from the United States enormous quantities of hitherto little-used goods. Imports of American lard into Denmark during the first few months of the war, for example, rose from virtually zero to 22 million pounds (10,000 metric tons). Obviously, some of these commodities were slipping into Germany through the neutral "conduit pipes." The British therefore limited such imports to their pre-war proportions, and confiscated or diverted the rest. A loud squawk arose from American merchants, but again such complaints were partially quieted when London ultimately provided monetary compensation.

> The British-born secretary of the interior, Franklin Lane, wrote privately in May 1915, "There isn't a man in the Cabinet who has a drop of German blood in his veins, I guess. Two of us were born under the British flag. I have two cousins in the British army, and Mrs. Lane has three. . . . Yet each day that we meet we boil over somewhat, at the foolish manner in which England acts. Can it be that she is trying to take advantage of the war to hamper our trade . . . ?"

These annoying British practices violated American traditions, especially freedom of the seas. America in 1914–1915 had a powerful navy—the third strongest in the world. If she had used it to escort her merchant ships, the British would have been forced to abandon their objectionable practices, at least against the United States. They simply could not afford to quarrel with their overseas munitions depot.

Why did America fail to take a stronger stand? Her sympathies, including those of the Wilson administration, were with the Allies, and she did not want to drive them into a corner. The American ambassador in London, editor-writer Walter H. Page, was bewitched by the British—the one race that had "guts." He therefore deliberately removed the sting from some of the official protests from Washington. In addition, American shippers could file claims and collect damages later, even though they might not make as juicy profits as they would have reaped if left alone. Finally, German tactics, especially with the submarine, were so inhumane as to eclipse British offenses.

The German Periscope Emerges

Germany did not tamely consent to being starved out by an illegal blockade—or one she regarded as illegal. Retaliating against the British for mining the North Sea, Berlin announced a submarine war area around the British Isles. The Germans were

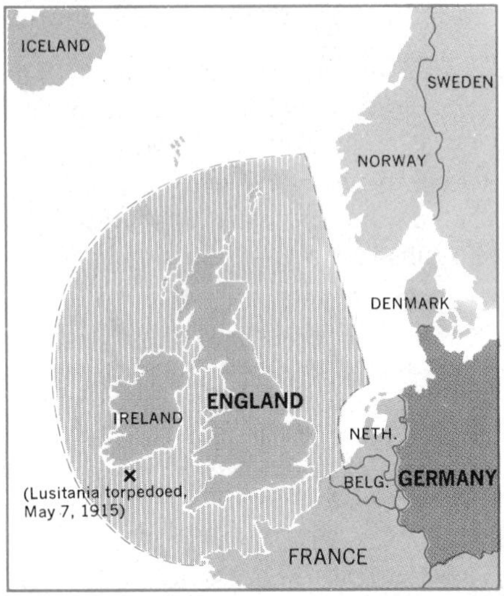

GERMAN SUBMARINE WAR ZONE
(declared February 4, 1915)

markedly inferior to Britain in their surface navy, but they had developed the murderous new submarine to a high pitch of efficiency. They therefore proclaimed, in February 1915, that they would use their cigar-shaped marauders to sink all enemy merchant ships within the proscribed submarine zone.

German U-boat attacks posed a clear threat to the United States. Although Berlin officials declared that they would try not to sink *neutral* shipping, they conceded that mistakes probably would occur. Their aim was partly to frighten away neutral merchant ships, and thus tighten the counterblockade of Britain. But President Wilson, outraged by the submarine menace, ringingly warned Germany that she would be held to "strict accountability" for any attacks on American vessels or citizens.

The submarine, as a commerce destroyer, was a weapon so new that existing international law could not be made to fit it. In the days of the sailing vessel, the rule had been that a warship, upon stopping a merchantman, must first of all dispatch a boarding party to ascertain its nationality and its cargo. If the victim was an enemy vessel—or a neutral vessel carrying contraband of war to the enemy—it might be captured or, if need be, sunk. But destruction could not rightfully take place until the passengers and crew had been put in a position of safety—and this did not mean in small boats hundreds of miles from land.

But the old sailing-ship practices were dangerous in the new machine age. If the fragile submarine emerged to give the customary warning, it might be rammed by the prow of the merchantman or sunk by one shot from a 6-inch gun. After some disastrous experiences, the Germans became extremely cautious. They concluded that if they were going to use their potent new weapon at all, they had better launch their torpedoes first and write diplomatic notes later. They argued that if the antique rules of international law did not fit their modern weapons, the "unusual" or "peculiar" conditions of the war justified changing the rules.

Beleaguered Britons, who had done some rule changing of their own regarding blockades, heatedly replied that the rules could not be changed in the middle of the game. They insisted that if the submarine could not be used according to the rules, then the submarine, not the rules, ought to be scrapped. In short, the Germans were invited to withdraw their terrible new weapon—and lose the war.

The *Lusitania's* Last Trip, May 1915

German U-boats began their deadly work on schedule. From February to early May 1915, they sank about ninety ships of various kinds in the war zone. The grisly toll included one British passenger steamer, with the loss of an American life.

Then, on May 7, 1915, stark tragedy struck the England-bound *Lusitania.* This crack passenger liner, a four-funneled British Cunarder, was torpedoed without the conventional warning off the coast of Ireland and sank in eighteen minutes. The death roll numbered 1,198 persons, 128 of whom were Americans. Many of the victims were women and children.

The salient facts about the *Lusitania* are clear. She had no mounted guns and was unresisting. She was carrying 4,200 cases of small-arms ammunition, as well as other munitions of war. Yet the nature of the cargo had no bearing whatever on the rule—long established in international law—that an "innocent" passenger ship must be warned in advance of sinking.

Countless Germans, quite understandably, rejoiced over the destruction of this death-dealing cargo. One unauthorized German even struck off a fanciful medal showing the *Lusitania* bristling with huge cannon. But the United States, as well as much of the rest of the civilized world, was swept by a wave of shock and anger. This act of "mass murder" was condemned as "piracy," and the New York *Nation* branded the deed as one for which "a Hun would blush, a Turk be ashamed." "Damnable! Damnable! Absolutely hellish!" cried "Billy" Sunday, the acrobatic evangelist. The eastern part of the nation, closer to the war, seethed with talk of fighting. But the rest of the country showed a strong distaste for hostilities.

Wilson, the peace lover, set his jaw against leading a disunited nation into war. He well remembered the mistake in 1812 of his fellow Princetonian, James Madison. Instead, by a series of increasingly strong notes, he attempted to bring the German war lords sharply to book.

But Wilson's hand was weakened, and the Germans were pleased, by evident signs of disunity. The pacifist Secretary Bryan dramatically resigned rather than sign a protest that might spell shooting.

> The American ambassador in Berlin reflected a German point of view on the *Lusitania* when he cabled, "Anyway, when Americans have reasonable opportunity to cross the ocean [on American ships] why should we enter a great war because some American wants to cross on a [British] ship where he can have a private bathroom or because Americans may be hired to protect by their presence cargoes of ammunition? . . . Nor can English passenger ships sailing with orders to ram submarines and often armed be put quite in the category of altogether peaceful merchantmen."

***The Lusitania* Leaving New York on Her Last Voyage, 1915.** The *Lusitania* was not conventionally armed, but the Germans regarded her as a belligerent blockade-runner carrying neutral American passengers as "shields" to protect her cargo of munitions. Her captain had orders to ram and destroy on sight any enemy submarine. (U.S. Signal Corps, National Archives.)

Theodore Roosevelt, again athirst for war, assailed the "flubdubs" and "mollycoddles" who recoiled from fighting. He angrily condemned the "weasel words" of that word-lover in the White House, who had sent toothless note "No. 11,765, Series B."

Yet Wilson, sticking to his verbal guns, made some diplomatic progress. A new crisis developed in August 1915, when another British liner, the *Arabic,* was sunk with a loss of two Americans. Berlin, responding to outraged protests from Washington, reluctantly agreed not to sink unarmed and unresisting passenger ships *without warning.* By thus partially muzzling the submarine, Wilson won a gratifying diplomatic victory—at least temporarily.

Pressures for Preparedness

Alert citizens had already recognized the need for strengthening the nation's military muscles, for the day might come when America would be sucked into the conflict. The navy was strong, but the army, numbering about 100,000 regulars, was weak. It ranked about fifteenth among the armies of the world, in the same bracket with Persia. In 1915 the secretary of war reported with alarm that he had only a two-day supply of ammunition for the artillery, much of which was obsolete.

Conspicuous among the champions of arming were Colonel Theodore Roosevelt and General Leonard Wood, old-time Rough Riders and now apostles of preparedness. They were largely instrumental in establishing, beginning in 1915, a number of summer training camps for officers, notably the one at Plattsburg, New York. Equipment was so short that trainees sometimes drilled with broomsticks in place of rifles. But even these feeble measures were opposed by the pro-German elements, by confirmed isolationists, and by pacifists. A song that caught the current mood was "I Didn't Raise My Boy to Be a Soldier."

President Wilson, still a pacifist at heart, revealed little enthusiasm at the outset for preparedness. His views were generally shared by Secretary Bryan, who proclaimed in 1915 with incredible naiveté that if war should come the President would issue a call and "the sun would go down on a million men in arms." But after repeated sinkings of merchant ships by German U-boats, Wilson gradually edged toward active preparedness. In December 1915—fifteen long months after war had broken out in Europe—he belatedly urged Congress to roll up its sleeves for defense. Public pressures backed him up. Highlighting the popular agitation was a series of monster parades, one of which was led down Pennsylvania Avenue by a flag-holding Wilson.

The culmination of the preparedness campaign was a series of stopgap measures passed by Congress, notably the National Defense Act of June 1916. It was designed to beef up the regular army to 175,000 officers and men, and the National Guard to 450,000 officers and men, with provision for an officers' reserve corps. These increases were a promising step forward, but totally inadequate to meet the storm that was brewing.

Naval preparedness fared better, for the fleet was traditionally regarded as the first line of de-

The President Leads a Preparedness Parade. After the *Lusitania* sinking in May 1915, Wilson dropped his opposition to an American military buildup. In 1916 he toured the country to urge support for preparedness. (Brown Brothers.)

fense. President Wilson, early in 1916, called for "incomparably the greatest navy in the world." Congress responded, in August 1916, with a grant of $313 million for new construction—the largest defense appropriation that it had yet passed. Emphasis was mistakenly on big battleships—"white elephants of the sea"—rather than on the smaller and badly needed anti-submarine craft. War ended in Europe before a single new capital ship was completed.

The Council of National Defense, designed to coordinate industry and defense, was likewise created. It consisted of six Cabinet officers and seven unpaid civilians, all of whom did yeoman work in helping to unsnarl the tangled skeins of the national economy as war impended.

An expanded merchant marine, which was urgently needed for naval auxiliary purposes, also claimed attention. In September 1916, Congress created the Shipping Board and appropriated $50 million for the purchase or construction of urgently needed craft. This program likewise proved to be based upon a shocking underestimate of requirements.

Germany Muzzles the U-Boat—Temporarily

Anti-travel legislation was meanwhile being urged, because the only sure way to prevent the killing of Americans on the high seas was to keep them out of submarine-infested waters. Early in 1916 two resolutions came before Congress, each of them designed to prohibit citizens from sailing on armed belligerent merchant ships or passenger liners into the danger zones. Both proposals commanded an impressive amount of support in Congress and throughout the country. They were passed in essence in the 1930s—one war too late.

But Wilson, ever the stubborn idealist, was alarmed by these weak-kneed proposals. He argued that if America surrendered her technical rights to sail on belligerent vessels, she would soon be forced to make other concessions. Before long the whole "fine fabric" of international law would break down, as much of it already had. Wilson earnestly believed that to yield such rights, even slightly, would be dishonorable.

These two "scuttle" resolutions in Congress were finally sidetracked, as Wilson brandished his presidential club. American citizens continued to sail into the danger zones, where they had a perfect right to go. But when killed, they were just as dead as if they had been wrong.

An alarming new crisis developed with Germany in March 1916, after she had honored the *Arabic* "muzzling" pledge for six months. A French cross-channel passenger steamer, the *Sussex,* was struck by a German torpedo, with some loss of life and serious injuries to several Americans. This attack, at least outwardly, seemed like a deliberate violation of earlier assurances by Berlin.

Infuriated by the *Sussex* assault, Wilson went out on a limb. He informed the Germans, in angered phrases, that they must renounce the inhuman practice of sinking merchantmen without warning. Otherwise he would have to break diplomatic relations—an almost certain prelude to war.*

Germany grudgingly accepted Wilson's *Sussex* ultimatum, thereby agreeing not to sink passenger ships and merchantmen without proper warning. But Berlin attached a long string to its acceptance: America would have to persuade the Allies to respect international law in their unlawful blockade. This, obviously, was something that Washington could not or would not do. Wilson promptly accepted the German pledge, without accepting the "string." He thus won another temporary but precarious diplomatic victory—precarious because Germany could pull the string whenever she chose, and the President would have to sever relations.

Wilson Runs on an Anti-War Ticket (1916)

As the presidential year 1916 loomed, the Bull Moose Progressives of 1912 rallied once again around Roosevelt. Meeting in Chicago in their

---

*One alternative was to accept a safe-conduct arrangement with Germany for American shipping, but such a concession, though offered by the Germans, Wilson rejected.

"swan song" convention, they uproariously renominated the Rough Rider. But Roosevelt, who hated Wilson and all his works, had no stomach for leading another hopeless cause that would again split the Republicans and insure the re-election of the pacifistic professor. He therefore declined the nomination. In doing so he sounded the death knell of the Progressive party, amid angry charges by Bull Moosers that he had betrayed them for his own selfish purposes.

The Republican convention also met in Chicago at the same time, with admirers of Roosevelt shouting, "Teddy, Teddy, Everybody's for Teddy." But Old Guard Republicans detested the renegade who had ruptured the party in 1912. Instead, they drafted Charles Evans Hughes, a vigorous, outwardly cold, and highly intellectual justice of the Supreme Court who had been loftily remote from the party split of 1912. His character was unimpeachable; his liberal achievements as governor of New York appealed to progressives; and his record as a member of the Supreme Court did not antagonize the Old Guard. The Republican platform condemned the Democratic tariff, Democratic assaults on the trusts, and Wilson's wishy-washiness in dealing with both Mexico and Germany.

Wilson, the dominant Democrat, was nominated by acclamation in St. Louis. The most popular theme of the convention was that he had refused to fight at every provocation. In this wildly cheering assemblage, further inspiration was found for the slogan "He Kept Us Out of War."

The richly bewhiskered Hughes ("an animated feather duster") left the bench for the stump, and there he was not at home. In some speeches he assailed Wilson for not having stood up to the Kaiser more menacingly; in other areas, where the German-American vote was vital, he took a less bellicose line. This fence-straddling operation led to the jeer, "Charles Evasive Hughes." Wilson ignored him on the theory that one should not try to murder a man who is committing suicide.

Roosevelt, frothing for war, was a dubious asset to the Republicans. In a series of skin-'em-alive speeches against Wilson, he alienated many German-American voters, whom Hughes badly needed for victory. TR not only flayed that "damned Presbyterian hypocrite Wilson" but privately sneered at Hughes as a "bearded ice-

A Wilson Campaign Truck, 1916. The re-elected President would soon have to eat the slogan about keeping out of war. (United Press International photo.)

PRESIDENTIAL ELECTION OF 1916
(with electoral vote by state)
Wilson was so worried about being a lame-duck President in a time of great international tensions that he drew up a plan whereby Hughes, if victorious, would be appointed Secretary of State, Wilson and the Vice-President would resign, and Hughes would thus succeed immediately to the Presidency.

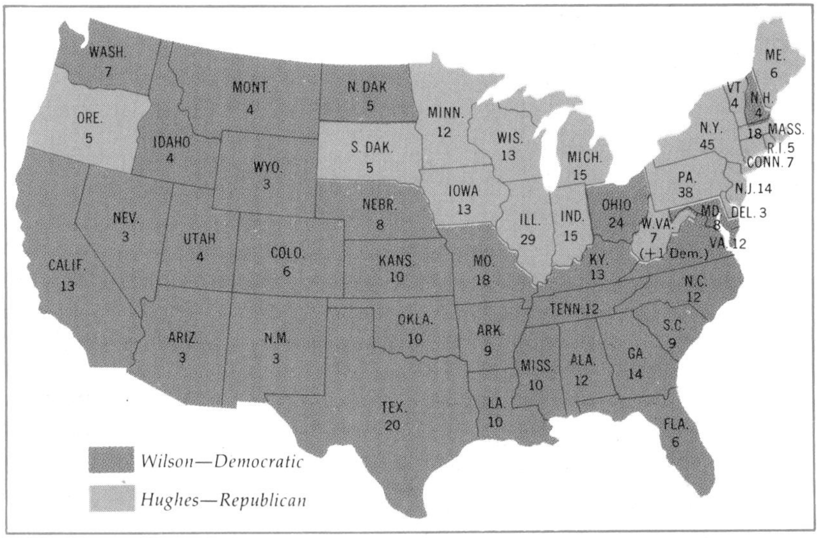

berg" and as a "whiskered Wilson"—the only difference between the two men being "a shave."

Democratic organizers, concentrating their fire on doubtful districts, played up the pro-Wilson slogan "He Kept Us Out of War." Orators warned the voters that by electing Hughes the nation would be electing a fight—with a certain frustrated Rough Rider leading the charge. A Democratic advertisement appealing to workingmen read:

> You Are Working;
> —Not Fighting!
> Alive and Happy;
> —Not Cannon Fodder!
> Wilson and Peace with Honor?
> or
> Hughes with Roosevelt and War?

The West Turns the Tide for Wilson

On election day Hughes, looking like a surefire winner, swept the East. This section contained a heavy concentration of voters who were anti-labor, anti-progressive, and pro–big business. Wilson went to bed that night prepared to accept defeat, while New York newspapers displayed huge portraits of "THE PRESIDENT-ELECT—CHARLES EVANS HUGHES."

But the rest of the country turned the tide. Middle Westerners and Westerners, attracted by Wilson's progressive reforms and anti-war policies, flocked to the polls for the President. War-boom prosperity also helped his cause. The final result, in doubt for several days, hinged on California, which Wilson carried by some 3,800 votes out of about a million cast. The Golden State was lost to Hughes by the blunders of his managers, notably the snub known as the "forgotten handshake." Though in the same hotel, Hughes had inadvertently failed to meet California's favorite son, the fiery progressive, Governor Hiram W. Johnson, TR's running mate in 1912.

Wilson barely squeaked through, with a final vote of 277 to 254 in the Electoral College, and 9,129,606 to 8,538,221 in the popular column. The pro-labor Wilson, who had backed the eight-hour law for railroad men, received strong working-class support. His liberal reform program also won the votes of many ex-Progressives; the defeat of the Republicans stemmed largely from their failure to lure enough wayward Bull Moosers back into their camp. Wilson had not specifically promised to keep the country out of war, but probably enough people relied on such implicit assurances to insure his victory. The outcome could be written largely in terms of four Ps: peace, prosperity, progressivism, and pro-laborism.

During the 1916 campaign J. A. O'Leary, the head of a pro-German and pro-Irish organization, sent a scorching telegram to Wilson condemning him for having been pro-British in approving war loans and ammunition traffic. Wilson shot back an answer: "Your telegram received. I would feel deeply mortified to have you or anybody like you vote for me. Since you have access to many disloyal Americans and I have not, I will ask you to convey this message to them." President Wilson's devastating and somewhat insulting response probably won for him more votes than it lost.

Germany's Brutal U-Boat Challenge

Wilson, desperately seeking peace, now undertook the role of world mediator. He perceived that the surest way to keep America out of the titanic conflict was to bring it to an end before his nation was sucked in. In the hope of securing a negotiated peace, he bluntly called upon the belligerents, in December 1916, to state their war aims. The Allied response was fuller and franker than that of the Germans, although the Allied leaders were privately annoyed by the efforts of the President to smoke them out. Like the Germans, they cherished secret imperialistic objectives that could not stand the pitiless light of publicity.

But Wilsonian mediation was foredoomed to failure. The simple truth is that by this time so much blood and treasure had been squandered that politicians could not face their people without the fruits of victory. Each side still hoped for a knockout blow.

Undaunted, Wilson next went before the Senate, on January 22, 1917, to deliver one of his most moving addresses. It was an open appeal to world opinion. To the dismay of the Allies, he realistically declared that a victor's peace would not bring peace. "It must be a peace without victory," he insisted. "Only a peace between equals can last."

Germany's war lords answered Wilson with a blow of the mailed fist. Astounding both him and the civilized world, they announced on January 31, 1917, that they were going to reopen their submarine campaign. This time they would sink *all* merchant ships, including America's, found within the stipulated danger zone. The Germans would permit the United States to send one merchant ship a week (no contraband) to and from England, if properly marked and following a prescribed route on prescribed days. To Wilson, this was an insulting restriction on freedom of the seas.

American dealings with both Britain and Germany were then such as to increase the force of the U-boat bombshell. Ever since the *Sussex* pledge, some eight months earlier, relations with Berlin had been outwardly calm, while those with the Allies had been stormy. Ironically, both Germany and America were contending for freedom of the seas, each in its own way. Especially irritating to Americans was Britain's practice of searching neutral mails for enemy correspondence, allegedly with an eye to trade secrets. London also legally but offensively blacklisted German-tainted firms in the United States—firms with which His Majesty's subjects were forbidden to trade. Even the pro-Ally Wilson burst out that the "poor boobs" in England got on his nerves.

Regarding the British blacklist Wilson wrote to Colonel House (July 23, 1916), "I am, I must admit, about at the end of my patience with Great Britain and the Allies. This blacklist business is the last straw. . . . It is becoming clear to me that there lies latent in this policy the wish to prevent our merchants getting a foothold in markets which Great Britain has hitherto controlled and all but dominated." In later years House stated improbably that if it had not been for Germany's submarine offenses, war might have come with Britain instead of Germany.

The momentous U-boat declaration came as no sudden impulse. Fighting in Europe was stalemated on barbed-wire entanglements and in mud-choked trenches; delay meant that the noose of the British hunger blockade was drawing tighter around the necks of 65 million Germans. Germany's naval experts, now boasting more than 100 U-boats, were confident that an all-out submarine campaign would knock Britain out of the war in a few months—as it almost did.

Berlin officials recognized that the U-boat proclamation was a virtual declaration of war. But what of it? America had no formidable army, owing in part to Wilson's delay in backing an effective preparedness drive. Even if she had trained a powerful military force, she could not have transported and supplied it with the ships that she had. Seemingly she was already helping the Allies about as much as she could with shipments of war materials. The conflict would presumably be over, with Germany crowned the victor, before America the Unready could throw her full weight into the scales.

The Submarine Causes a Break with Berlin

Wilson, his high hopes for peace torpedoed by the U-boat announcement, was in the position of a poker player whose bluff has been called. In his *Sussex* ultimatum he had proclaimed in effect that if the German militarists should again open their ruthless submarine warfare, he would have to sever relations. This he reluctantly did on February 3, 1917, when the German ambassador in Washington was handed his passport. There was no other way out—unless a proud, patriotic, and powerful America was to be humiliated in the eyes of the world.

Yet Wilson still nursed one flickering hope for peace. Despite evidence to the contrary, he could not bring himself to believe that the Germans would carry out their threat to sink American ships. Determined not to lead his people into war prematurely, he insisted on awaiting actual "overt" acts by German U-boats against American lives and property.

The issue of arming defenseless American merchantmen now thrust itself forward. As ships continued to cling to port, piled-up surpluses clogged the docks and economic paralysis began to grip the country. Mobs of irate housewives in New York demonstrated angrily for food. Wilson thereupon asked Congress for authority to arm American merchantmen. But a small band of antiwar senators, conspicuously from the German-populated areas of the Middle West, helped to engineer a filibuster until Congress adjourned, March 3, 1917. Professor Wilson sternly lectured the "little group of willful men" who had rendered a great nation "helpless and contemptible." Then, finding the authority in an almost forgotten law, he sent a few American ships to sea armed with defensive guns.

Meanwhile the Zimmermann note, hardly less sensational than the U-boat declaration itself, had blazed into the headlines on March 1, 1917. Its author, the German foreign secretary, had secretly outlined a course of action pending a shooting war with America. Germany would seek to arrange a German-Mexican alliance, holding out to anti-Yankee Mexico the inducement of recovering Texas, New Mexico, and Arizona. Japan was also to be invited to join in the scheme. Hitherto the Pacific Coast had been lukewarm toward war. But this clumsy German note, intercepted and passed on by British agents, helped arouse the entire nation.

War by Act of Germany

Those long-dreaded "overt" acts finally came in mid-March 1917. Four unarmed American merchantmen were sunk on the high seas by German U-boats, with a loss of thirty-six lives. As one Philadelphia newspaper observed, the "difference between war and what we have now is that now we aren't fighting back."

In the same March 1917, the bitter prospect of fighting Germany was sweetened by news from

The U.S.S. *Illinois.* This was one of four unarmed American merchantmen sunk by Germany in mid-March 1917. Photo taken from the German submarine (foreground). (Courtesy Department of the Navy.)

Russia. An epochal upheaval suddenly overthrew Czarist tyranny and established a liberal but short-lived provisional government. The American people could now look forward to fighting foursquare for democracy on the side of the Allies, without the black sheep of Russian despotism in the Allied fold.

A reluctant Wilson, unable to escape the pressure of "overt" acts, finally summoned Congress into special session. Pale and erect, he stood before the hushed joint session, on the evening of April 2, 1917, to read an inspired document. In solemn tones he declared that America had no quarrel with the German people, but only with their "military masters." By making war on all mankind they would not permit others to live in peace. Wilson then asked Congress to recognize the state of war "which has thus been *thrust* upon it." "It is a fearful thing," he concluded, to lead the nation into war, but "the right is more precious than peace."

On Good Friday, April 6, 1917, Congress responded with its fateful war resolution, acknowledging the fact that war had been "thrust" upon the Republic. Debate was brief but heated, with the count 82 to 6 in the Senate, and 373 to 50 in the House. The pro-war vote reflected a substantial degree of unity, especially in the industrial and financial East, which had developed a strong stake in the success of the Allied cause.

The dissenters were concentrated in the South and Middle West, notably in Wisconsin, Illinois, Missouri, and Minnesota. There the German-Americans were numerous and vocal. One of their senatorial spokesmen, "Fighting Bob" La Follette of Wisconsin, stirred up a storm of protest when he shouted, "I say Germany has been patient with us." Senator Norris of Nebraska declared that the nation was going to war "at the command of gold" and that "the dollar sign" was about to be sewn on the American flag. Additional members of Congress probably would have voted against war if they had dared defy the whirlwind of popular indignation.

"I Dare You To Come Out." The Kaiser defies American rights, national honor, freedom of the seas, and international law. (Richards in the Philadelphia *North American,* 1917.)

Why War Came to America

Why were the American people finally dragged into the conflagration, despite their two and one-half years of determination to stay out?

The German U-boat was undoubtedly the precipitant. In a figurative sense, America's war declaration bore the well-known trademark "Made in Germany." Take away the submarine and the United States might have stayed out.

Choosing the right foe was not difficult. British and other Allied restrictions on American commerce were galling but endurable; claims for damages could be collected later. But Germany resorted to the mass killing of civilians; and there was no adequate monetary recompense for taking life. One Boston newspaper luridly concluded that while the Allies were "a gang of thieves," the Germans were "a gang of murderers." Many Americans were so deeply disturbed by the U-boat, and by its threat to freedom of the seas, that at the outset they proposed to fight a limited-liability war. They would pull out as soon as the Germans agreed to respect America's rights on the high seas.

But in pointing the finger of accusation solely at the blood-spattered submarine, the American people overlooked their own share of responsibility. Undeniably, the United States was in some degree to blame for inviting these ruthless reprisals. The Germans found it easier to resort to their last desperate throw of the dice because of America's seemingly unfriendly policies. She was sending munitions in vast quantities to their foes; she was advancing credits for such purchases; and she was acquiescing in the "unusual" British blockade that was slowly starving the Fatherland, all the while condemning the German counter-blockade. Bryan charged that the United States had failed to hold the scales of neutrality even—assuming that this was possible.

Once the "overt" acts came, the American people accepted the verdict of war with considerable enthusiasm. At heart they were pro-Ally. They were bound closely to the British and French by profitable golden threads, which were in danger of being cut off by ruthless German tactics. Repelled by German frightfulness, Americans swallowed Allied propaganda the more avidly. They finally came to believe, as one American newspaper put it: "ENGLAND'S DEFEAT OUR DEFEAT."

Fear of Germany's militaristic and monarchical threat to democracy was a clincher. Many Americans assumed that if the Kaiser won the war he would dash across the Atlantic, with millions of spike-helmeted soldiers. Hunnish "slitters of babies' throats" would brush aside the Monroe Doctrine, and then crush precious liberties under a Prussian boot heel. Even if there should be no immediate German assault, the triumph of the Kaiser would badly upset the long-established European balance of power. The United States would then, as many apprehensive Americans believed, be placed in ultimate jeopardy.

Dangers of a future attack, either directly or by way of Latin America, appear to have been more grave than those of an immediate invasion. Naval and military difficulties hampering a prompt overseas assault were immense. But countless Americans accepted such an attack as an alarming possibility. They preferred to fight in 1917, when

On March 20, 1917, shortly after the news of the sinking of three American ships had arrived, President Wilson met with his Cabinet. Secretary of the Navy Daniels recorded in his diary: "All declared for war except Burleson [postmaster general] and I, and the President said, 'Burleson, you and Daniels have not spoken.' Burleson said he thought we were already at war [which was true], and that unless President called Congress the people would force action. The President said, 'I do not care for popular demand. I want to do right, whether popular or not.' . . . President was solemn, very sad!!"

they had European allies afloat, than to wait until they might have to face the wrath of the German militarists alone.

The American people were not duped into war by profit-seeking connivers. They were not dragged in, as later charged, by Wall Street bankers, propagandists, sloganeers, weaponeers, and munitioneers. Although loans for the Allies were not inexhaustible, the munitions makers were reaping obscene profits, unhampered by government restrictions and wartime excess-profits taxes. Their unpublished slogan might well have been "Neutrality Forever."

As the crisis developed early in 1917, America's entrance into the war became inevitable. Desperate German militarists, with confidence in their U-boats, had concluded that they had more to gain than to lose by making the United States an open enemy. Certain defeat was too high a price for them to pay for America's continued "neutrality."

VARYING VIEWPOINTS

President Wilson in his war message claimed that Germany had thrust war upon the United States—that the Kaiser's U-boats had finally pushed a proud nation too far. That remained the "official" version of explaining America's entry into the conflict. But in the war's disappointing aftermath, some critics wondered if Wilson's historic departure from traditional non-intervention in European wars had been worthwhile. Should America have entered the fray? Was the Republic sucked into the conflict for the wrong reasons? Writers like Walter Millis and Charles C. Tansill raised these questions with disturbing intensity during the isolation-inclined 1930s. They argued that America's entry had been a tragic mistake. The public had been duped by British propaganda, and Wilson had been blinded by his own stubborn moralism. Worse still, these dissenters concluded, America seemed to have fought more to make the world safe for the House of Morgan's loans than to make it safe for democracy.

Those views lost popularity when the United States went to war again in 1941 with the old enemy. Then a different school of thought took command, stressing the real strategic danger that a victorious Germany would have posed in 1917, and hence justifying Wilson's decision for war. In fact, scant evidence has been unearthed to prove either that Wilson had a firm grasp of America's economic stake in an Allied victory, or that he had finely calculated his country's long-run security interests. Thus the submarine remains the villain of the piece, though the nagging question persists: Precisely why did Wilson insist on "strict accountability" for the U-boat attacks?

SELECT READINGS

Comprehensive descriptions of the road to war can be found in Ernest May, *The World War and American Isolation, 1914–1917* (1959), and Daniel M. Smith, *The Great Departure: The United States and World War I, 1914–1920* (1965). Consult also Ross Gregory, *The Origins of American Intervention in the First World War* (1971), John M. Cooper, Jr., *The Vanity of Power: American Isolation and the First World War, 1914–1917* (1969), and Patrick Devlin, *Too Proud to Fight: Woodrow Wilson's Neutrality* (1975). Sharply critical of Wilson's leadership are Walter Millis, *The Road to War* (1935), Charles C. Tansill, *America Goes to War* (1938), and T. A. Bailey and P. B. Ryan, *The Lusitania Disaster* (1975), which disposes of many myths. For the European background see Laurence Lafore, *The Long Fuse* (1965), and Fritz Fischer, *Germany's Aims in the First World War* (1967). Arthur Link takes a broad view in *Woodrow Wilson: Revolution, War, and Peace* (1979), and provides more detail in the relevant volumes of his biography, *Wilson* (5 vols., 1947–1965). Robert E. Osgood keenly analyzes Wilson's diplomacy in *Ideals and Self-Interest in America's Foreign Relations* (1953), as does Edward Buehrig in *Woodrow Wilson and the Balance of Power* (1955).

36

The War to End War, 1917–1918

The world must be made safe for democracy. Its peace must be planted upon the tested foundations of political liberty. We have no selfish ends to serve. We desire no conquest, no dominion. We seek no indemnities for ourselves, no material compensation for the sacrifices we shall freely make.

WOODROW WILSON, War Message, April 2, 1917

Wilsonian Idealism Enthroned

Destiny dealt cruelly with Woodrow Wilson. The lover of peace, as fate would have it, was forced to lead a hesitant and peace-loving nation into war. It fell to the scholarly Wilson, deeply respectful of American traditions, to shatter one of the most sacred of those traditions by entangling America in a distant European war.

How could the President arouse his countrymen to shoulder this unprecedented burden? For more than a century, they had prided themselves on their isolation from the periodic outbursts of militarized

Anti-German Propaganda. (Trustees of the Imperial War Museum, London.)

violence that afflicted the Old World. Since 1914, their pride had been reinforced by the lush profits gained through neutrality. German U-boats had now undeniably shoved a reluctant America into the abyss, but Wilson could whip up no enthusiasm, especially in the landlocked Middle West, by fighting merely to make the world safe against the submarine. He would have to proclaim more glorified aims.

Wilson's burning idealism led him instinctively to an inspired decision. Radiating the spiritual fervor of his Presbyterian ancestors, he declared the twin goals of "a war to end war" and a crusade "to make the world safe for democracy." Flourishing the sword of righteousness, Wilson virtually hypnotized the nation with his lofty ideals. He contrasted the selfish war aims of the other belligerents, allied and enemy alike, with America's shining altruism. America, he preached, did not fight for the sake of riches or territorial conquest. The Republic sought only to shape an international order in which democracy could flourish without fear of power-crazed autocrats and militarists.

In Wilsonian idealism, the personality of the President and the necessities of history were perfectly matched. The high-minded Wilson genuinely believed in the principles he so eloquently intoned. And probably no other appeal could have successfully converted the American people from their historic hostility to involvement in European squabbles. Americans, it seemed, could be either isolationists or crusaders, but nothing in between.

Wilson's appeal worked—perhaps too well. Holding aloft the torch of idealism, the President fired up the public mind to a fever pitch. "Force, force to the utmost, force without stint or limit," he cried, while the country responded less elegantly with "Hang the Kaiser" and "To Hell with the Hapsburgs and Hohenzollerns"—the ruling houses of Austria-Hungary and Germany.

The entire nation, catching the frenzied spirit of a religious revival, burst into song. This was undoubtedly America's singingest war. Most memorable was George M. Cohan's spine-tingling "Over There":

Over there, over there.
Send the word, send the word over there,
That the Yanks are coming, the Yanks are coming,
The drums rum-tumming ev'rywhere.

Fourteen Potent Wilsonian Points

Wilson quickly came to be recognized as the moral leader of the Allied cause and the spokesman for it. His early speeches, though eloquent, were rather vague and overlong. Advisers urged him to boil down his main objectives into inspiriting, placard-like paragraphs that would be effective propaganda. This he did admirably in his Fourteen Points Address, delivered on January 8, 1918, before an enthusiastic Congress. A primary purpose was to keep reeling Russia in the war. The general effect was to inspire the drooping Allies to mightier efforts, while demoralizing the war-weary enemy nations by holding out alluring promises to their dissatisfied minorities.

The first five of the Fourteen Points were broad in scope. (1) A proposal to abolish secret treaties pleased liberals of all countries. (2) Freedom of the seas appealed to the Germans, as well as to Americans who distrusted British sea power. (3) A removal of economic barriers among nations was comforting to Germany, which feared post-war vengeance. (4) Reduction of armament burdens was gratifying to taxpayers everywhere. (5) An adjustment of colonial claims in the interests of both the natives and the great powers concerned was reassuring, especially to those people who hated both imperialism and colonialism.

Other points among the fourteen proved no less seductive. They held out the promise of partial or full independence to oppressed minority groups, such as the Poles, millions of whom lay under the heel of Germany and Austria-Hungary. The capstone point, Number Fourteen, foreshadowed the League of Nations—a hope-fraught international organization that was to provide a system of collective security. Wilson earnestly hoped that this new scheme would effectively guarantee the political independence and territorial integrity of all countries, whether large or small.

"The Message," 1918. Wilson's Fourteen Points address gives hope to oppressed peoples. (Courtesy of Omaha *World-Herald.*)

In subsequent addresses, hardly less lofty, Wilson clarified and supplemented his original Fourteen Points. The list finally came to number about twenty-three. With flaming phrases Wilson declared for a just, permanent, and open peace, while stressing the desirability of consulting subject peoples in the forthcoming treaty settlements. This last point—the self-determination "dynamite"—stirred anew many unrealizable hopes.

The so-called Fourteen Points proved to be a mighty engine of propaganda, for they undoubtedly undermined the enemy's "will to victory." In China, a translated volume of Wilson's speeches became a best seller. In lonely huts in the mountains of Italy, candles burned before poster-portraits of the revered American prophet. In Poland, starry-eyed university men would meet on the streets, clasp hands, and utter only one word, "Wilson."

Yet Wilson's appealing points, though raising hopes the world over, were not everywhere applauded. Certain leaders of the Allied nations, with an eye to territorial booty, were less than enthusiastic. Hard-nosed Republicans at home grumbled, and some of them openly sneered at the "fourteen commandments" of "God Almighty Wilson."

A Nation's Factories Go to War

War began for America with dismal days. On land the Allies definitely were not winning, and on sea the silent submarines took a frightful toll in April and May of 1917. During the most dismaying weeks, merchant ships were being sunk at the rate of nine a day, and at one time England had grain supplies for only six weeks. The tide turned only when the British reluctantly adopted the convoy system and the Allies managed to perfect other anti-sub devices.

Victory was no foregone conclusion, and at best would involve a herculean effort. It would

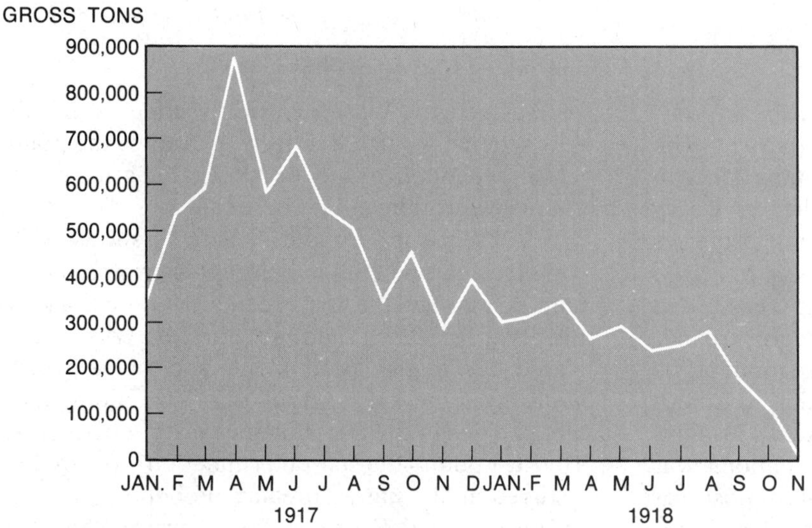

MERCHANT TONNAGE SUNK BY GERMAN U-BOATS
(January 1917–November 1918) The British Prime Minister, David Lloyd George, prophetically told an American audience that victory "was to be found in one word, ships, in a second word, ships, and a third word, ships."

be achieved only if the country could unsnarl its red tape, reorganize its mighty industrial plant, and retool itself for fighting—while time still permitted. The struggle was a global conflict, which had to be fought as much with big smokestacks as with big guns. "It is not an army that we must train for war," proclaimed Wilson; "it is a nation."

Unfortunately, towering obstacles confronted economic mobilizers. Sheer ignorance was among the biggest roadblocks. No one knew precisely how much steel or explosive powder the country was capable of producing. Old ideas also proved to be liabilities, as traditional fears of big government hamstrung efforts to orchestrate the economy from Washington. States'-rights Democrats and businessmen alike balked at federal economic controls, even though the embattled nation could ill afford the free-wheeling, hit-or-miss chaos of the peacetime economy.

Late in the war, and after bruising political battles, Wilson succeeded in imposing some order on this economic confusion. In March, 1918, he appointed lone-eagle stock speculator Bernard Baruch to head the War Industries Board. Through delicate negotiations with various industries, the silver-thatched Baruch cleared up many of the worst economic bottlenecks, and by war's end the military production program was flowing fairly smoothly. But the War Industries Board had only feeble formal powers, and it was disbanded within days after the Armistice. Even in the midst of a globe-girdling crisis, the American preference for *laissez-faire* and for a weak central government proved amazingly strong.

Women on the Home Front. The war brought many women, including this tractor-driver, into jobs previously reserved for men. (BBC Hulton Picture Library.)

Perspiring workers were urged to put forth their best efforts, spurred by the slogan "Labor Will Win the War." Women were encouraged to enter industry and also agriculture, where they were called "farmerettes." The old saying took on a new twist: "A Woman's Place Is in the War." Tens of thousands of Southern blacks were drawn to the North by the magnet of war industries—the large-scale beginnings of a "Southernization" of immense sociological significance. A New Jersey anti-loafing law required all ablebodied males to be regularly employed in some useful occupation, and a "Work or Fight" rule was issued by the War Department in 1918. Fortunately for the Allied cause, Samuel Gompers and his powerful American Federation of Labor gave loyal support to the war effort.

Yet labor harbored grievances. Admittedly, the wages of 1914 had nearly doubled by 1918, and many manual laborers could sport gaudy silk shirts. But inflationary prices, boosted by the war, feverishly kept pace with the wage scale. The pinch of H.C.L.—"high cost of living"—was felt in every modest American home. Not even the call of patriotism and Wilsonian idealism could stifle all labor disputes; and during the conflict there were some 6,000 strikes, most of them mercifully brief. The National War Labor Board, with ex-President Taft as co-chairman, was finally established as the supreme court for labor disputes. More than 1,000 cases came before it.

Some of the most crippling labor sabotage was engineered by the left-wing Industrial Workers of the World (I.W.W.s), popularly known as the "I Won't Works" or "Wobblies." As transient laborers in such industries as fruit and lumber, the "Wobblies" were victims of some of the worst working conditions in the country. When they protested, many of them were arrested, beaten up, or run out of town. Advocating "one big industrial union" and proclaiming "An injury to one is an injury to all," they chanted:

> The hours are long, the pay is small,
> So take your time and buck them all.

Hooverizing on Food and Fuel

Members of the War Trade Board became the leading "economic warriors" of the United States. By issuing the proper licenses to maritime shippers, they controlled exports and imports. The Board also continued the Allied practice of rationing imports of the neutral countries adjacent to Germany, and published a "blacklist" of enemy-tainted firms in neutral countries with which American citizens were forbidden to trade. Ironically, Washington had vigorously opposed both rationing and blacklisting in its protests to London during its years of neutrality. But these weapons, though disagreeable, could be employed within the framework of international law.

"Fuel Will Win the War" was another popular appeal. The Fuel Administration was headed by Harry A. Garfield, president of Williams College and a son of the murdered President. Spurred by the slogan "Mine More Coal," production was ultimately increased by about two-fifths. Despite these heroic efforts, the chilled public schools of New York had to close during one critical period for lack of coal, and certain factories were temporarily shut down.

Significant economies in fuel were achieved by voluntary self-sacrifice. There were "heatless Mondays" and "lightless nights," the latter produced by turning off electrical displays. "Daylight saving time," conceived much earlier by Benjamin Franklin, was introduced to conserve power. Similar efforts were made to economize on petroleum, including the voluntary "gasless Sundays."

COAL
Buy early
Save money
Help the Railroads
Aid the Fighters
Prevent heatless days
U.S. FUEL ADMINISTRATION

Typical Appeal To Mine Coal

Food Administrator Hoover Mobilizes His Army. (Darling in the Des Moines *Register,* 1917.)

Food was an even more pressing problem. As the larder of democracy, America not only had to feed herself but produce enough surplus for her allies. By a happy inspiration, the man chosen to head the Food Administration was the Quaker-humanitarian Herbert C. Hoover, already world-famous for his success in saving starving Belgium. A letter, which bore the sole address: "Miracle Man, Washington, D.C.," was promptly delivered to him.

A superb organizer, Hoover mobilized the nation for less waste and more production. "Food Will Win the War—Don't Waste It" became a favorite slogan, as the Food Administration waged a whirlwind propaganda campaign through posters, billboards, newspapers, pulpits, and movies. Loyal citizens were urged to "use all leftovers," to observe "the gospel of the clean plate," and to practice "the patriotism of the lean garbage can." "Full Garbage Pails," the slogan ran, "Mean Empty Dinner Pails." Even children, when eating apples, were urged to be "patriotic to the core."

Hoover deliberately avoided issuing ration cards, as was done in Europe. In common with other American war administrators, he preferred to rely on voluntary compliance, rather than on formal edicts. Thanks to the super-heated patriotic wartime spirit, this scheme worked. "To Hooverize" became a synonym for "to economize." In order to save food for export, Hoover proclaimed wheatless Mondays and Wednesdays, meatless Tuesdays, and porkless Thursdays and Saturdays—all on a voluntary basis. Curious and unappetizing substitutes were found in wheatless bread ("Victory bread"), sugarless candy, and vegetarian lamb chops. A popular verse ran:

My Tuesdays are meatless,
My Wednesdays are wheatless,
I'm getting more eatless each day.
My coffee is sweetless,
My bed it is sheetless,
All sent to the Y.M.C.A.

Food surpluses were piled up in still other ways. The country soon broke out in a rash of vegetable "Victory gardens," as perspiring patriots hoed their way to victory in backyards or on vacant lots. Congress severely restricted the use of foodstuffs for manufacturing alcoholic beverages, and the war-born spirit of economy and self-denial helped accelerate the wave of prohibition that was sweeping the country. Many leading brewers were German or German-descended, and this taint made the drive against alcohol all the more popular.

Hoover's work was sensationally successful. Farm products were increased one-fourth, and food shipments to the hard-pressed Allied coun-

Food Administration Poster. (Hoover Institution, Stanford University, California.)

tries mounted to three times America's prewar exports.

America's Bridge of Boats

The Atlantic Ocean was in some respects Germany's most effective ally. An anxious question was: Could America transport enough troops and supplies, in view of scanty shipping and grievous losses to submarines, to turn the tide of battle? "Ships, Ships, and More Ships" was the desperate call of the Allies.

The Shipping Board, farsightedly created in 1916, was supplemented in 1917 by the Emergency Fleet Corporation. These two agencies bestirred themselves mightily to increase available tonnage. Among other steps, enemy merchant ships in American harbors were seized and put into operation, despite efforts by their crews to wreck the machinery. Conspicuous among these craft was the gigantic German *Vaterland* which, renamed the *Leviathan,* served as a mighty transatlantic troop carrier. Neutral ships tied up in American harbors were at length requisitioned, with compensation to the owners. In this haul were eighty-seven Dutch vessels.

Miracles in Shipbuilding.
(BBC Hulton Picture Library.)

More vital was a gigantic drive to construct new tonnage. A few concrete vessels were launched, including one appropriately named *Faith.* A wooden-ship program was undertaken, yet after months of war, birds were still nesting in the trees from which the vessels were to be hammered. Prefabricated steel ships were built for the first time on a large scale, with much of the construction undertaken in shipyards on the Great Lakes, far distant from the sea. The accent was on speed, and the staccato of the riveters ("Rivets Are Bayonets—Drive Them Home") announced that "The Ships Are Coming." One frantically built vessel was launched in twenty-seven days.

Although the huge ships-for-victory program was painfully slow in gathering momentum, ship construction finally far outran tonnage destruction by the U-boats. Long before the war ended the nation was laying down two keels for every one lost. On a glorious July 4, 1918, ninety-five vessels were launched in the various American yards. All told, the Shipping Board built and delivered in 1918 a total of 533, many of which splashed into the water after the Armistice. The largest shipyard, the Hog Island plant near Philadelphia, alone had some 80 miles (129 kilometers) of railroads. When the war ended there were 350,000 workers in 341 shipyards—or two times the shipbuilding capacity of the rest of the world.

America's railroads, which fed the transatlantic "bridge of ships," creaked badly. No two lines were organized quite alike, and the thirty-odd systems were soon working at cross-purposes. So serious became the snarl that, in December 1917, Wilson placed the entire network under government control. Director general of railroads was the tall, hawk-nosed secretary of the treasury, William G. McAdoo, who had married Wilson's daughter Eleanor in the White House and who was dubbed "the Crown Prince."

Washington ran the railroads at a loss, partly because it kept the rates low and the financial guarantee to the owners high. Economy was no object. Speed and the winning of the war were the major aims, and here McAdoo succeeded, even though he incurred a deficit of $862 million. But the charge that he had "McAdoodled" the railroads was thereafter used as a strong argument against government ownership. Washington likewise took over the telephones, the telegraphs, and the cables.

"Over the Top" with Dollars

Tax burdens added to the other unpleasant war burdens. The conflict was fantastically expensive, judged by previous American experience, and in the closing stages cost $44 million a day. About one-third of this total outlay was handled by a pay-as-you-go policy. Increased taxes brought increased revenue through the income tax, the corporation tax, the excess profits tax, the luxury taxes—the so-called nuisance taxes on theater tickets and similar items.

Most of the money for financing victory was borrowed directly from the citizen in huge bond "drives." The Treasury, in line with its policy of making the war a personal effort, abandoned the Civil War practice of marketing bonds through profit-taking banking houses. Bonds were issued in denominations as low as $50, and Thrift Stamps could be purchased by children for as little as twenty-five cents. The appeal was to both profit and patriotism. Interest rates were relatively low but the bond purchaser could proudly display a button on his lapel to prove that he was neither un-American nor pro-German.

Four great Liberty Loan drives, followed by a Victory Loan drive in 1919, netted the impressive total of $21,448,120,300. About 65 million persons contributed from their savings to make "silver bullets." The drives involved much emotional appeal through monster parades and slogans like "Halt the Hun" and "Remember: It's Cheaper to Win Than to Lose." All five of the huge loans were oversubscribed—"went over the top," in the current trench-warfare phrase. Cities and regions vied with one another in competitive outbursts of patriotism.

Hanging the Kaiser—A Favorite Sport. (*Life*, 1918.)

Pressures of various kinds, patriotic and otherwise, were used to sell bonds. The unfortunate German-American who could not display a Liberty Bond button might find his house bedaubed with yellow paint. A number of luckless persons, suspected of being pro-German, were roughly handled, and there was at least one instance of a man who signed for a bond with a rope around his neck.

The Red Cross and other private agencies of benevolence simultaneously staged smaller drives of their own. Slogans that they used with great effectiveness were "Give Until It Hurts" and "Think What You Can Afford to Give—Then Double It."

Creel Manipulates Minds

Mobilizing the mind for war, both in America and abroad, was an urgent task facing the Washington authorities. For this purpose, the Committee on Public Information was created. It was headed by a youngish journalist, George Creel, who, though outspoken and tactless, was gifted with zeal and imagination. His job was to "sell" America on the war, and "sell" the world on Wilsonian war aims.

The Creel organization, employing 150,000 workers at home and overseas, proved that words were weapons. It sent out an army of 75,000 "Four-Minute Men"—often longer-winded than that—who delivered countless speeches containing much "patriotic pep."

Creel's propaganda took varied forms. Posters were splashed on billboards in the "Battle of the Fences," as artists "rallied to the colors." Millions of leaflets and pamphlets, which contained the most pungent Wilsonisms, were showered like confetti upon the world. Special propaganda booklets with red-white-and-blue covers were distributed by the millions, some of them attempting to prove that Germany had started the war with diabolical intent. Hang-the-Kaiser "movies," with such titles as *The Kaiser, the Beast of Berlin* and *To Hell with the Kaiser,* revealed the "Hun" in his bloodiest colors. Arm-waving song leaders by the thousands led huge audiences in songs that poured scorn on the enemy and glorified the "boys" in uniform.

Creel was unsurpassed as a propagandist. In a sense he typified American war mobilization, which relied more on aroused passion and voluntary compliance than on formal laws. But he rather oversold the ideals of Wilson, and led the world to expect too much. When the President proved to be a mortal and not a god, the resulting disillusionment at home and abroad was disastrous. Paper bullets can be overdone.

America's most noteworthy contribution to the "science" of warfare was in "mobilizing the mind of the world." Regrettably, some of Creel's techniques were later copied by the master propagandists serving Adolf Hitler and other dictators.

Enforcing Loyalty and Stifling Dissent

A potential source of internal danger was the formidable group of German-Americans. They numbered over 8 million, counting those with at least one parent foreign-born, out of a total population of 100 million. Before America entered the war, an official in the German Foreign Office boasted that there were 500,000 German army reservists in the United States. The American ambassador proudly retorted that there were 500,001 lamp posts on which they could be hanged.

German-Americans, on the whole, proved to be gratifyingly loyal. Hundreds of thousands of them not only bought Liberty Bonds but fought bravely under the Stars and Stripes. Yet rumor-mongers were quick to spread tales of spying and sabotage: even trifling epidemics of diarrhea were blamed on German agents. A few German-Americans were tarred, feathered, and beaten; and in one extreme case a German Socialist in Illinois was lynched by a drunken mob.

As emotion mounted, hate hysteria swept the nation against Germans and things Germanic. Orchestras found it unsafe to present German-composed music, like that of Wagner or Beethoven; and the brilliant Austro-Hungarian violinist, Fritz Kreisler, was forbidden to play in New Jersey. The

"Making His Dollars Fight," 1917. A German-American is forced to buy bonds. (Courtesy Baltimore *American*.)

teaching of the German language was shortsightedly discontinued in many high schools and colleges. Sauerkraut became "Liberty cabbage," hamburg or hamburger steak became "Liberty steak," German measles became "Liberty measles," and dachshunds became "Liberty pups," that is, if one were unpatriotic enough to own them.

Both the Espionage Act of 1917 and the Sedition Act of 1918 reflected current fears. These twin measures were inspired partly by hatred of the Germans, partly by a desire to prevent obstruction of the war effort. Over 1,900 prosecutions were undertaken under both laws.

Socialists fell under strong suspicion of pro-Germanism, for a majority went on record as opposing this "capitalistic war." A minority, stirred by patriotic impulses, seceded from the party. But Eugene V. Debs, kingpin Socialist, continued to speak out violently against American participation. Convicted in 1918 under the Espionage Act, he was sentenced to ten years in a federal penitentiary. After he had served about two years, President Harding granted him a Christmas-present pardon.

A number of I.W.W.s were likewise prosecuted during the war under the Espionage Act. In 1918 William D. ("Big Bill") Haywood, a one-eyed giant of a man, and ninety-nine associates were convicted. Haywood himself received a twenty-year sentence. (His ashes were later buried in the Kremlin with those of other famous revolutionaries.) In all, there were 1,532 arrests under the Sedition Act for disloyal utterances, 65 for threats against Wilson, and 10 for sabotage.

Censorship of a mild sort was occasionally imposed on the press. A Socialist newspaper, *The Masses* (New York), was denied second-class mailing privileges, and at one time an issue of the liberal New York *Nation* was held up.

These prosecutions form an ugly chapter in the history of American civil liberty. Though flouting traditional freedoms, they seemed justified by the national emergency. With the dawn of peace, presidential pardons were rather freely granted, and the nation gradually got back on even keel. Yet a few victims lingered behind bars into the 1930s.

The Navy Brought Them Over

Already cleared for action, the navy got into the war first—though belatedly. Early in May 1917, an initial flotilla of six destroyers arrived in Ireland for desperately needed anti-submarine operations.

All in all, the American sailors had their hands full. They helped the British battleships hem in the German high-seas fleet; they played a leading role in laying down a 230-mile (370-kilometer) mine barrage from Scotland to Norway, designed to bottle the deadly U-boats in the North Sea. This gigantic operation, involving 70,000 contact mines, was a not-too-successful scheme of young Assistant Secretary of the Navy Franklin D. Roosevelt, who even this early "thought big."

Simultaneously the navy assisted in tightening the British blockade noose around Germany. America did not violate international law flagrantly, but she did cooperate with the British in enforcing practices against the neutrals to which she had strongly objected while herself a neutral.

Navy Recruiting Poster, World War I.
(Courtesy Department of the Navy.)

The navy's muscles, though strong, bulged in the wrong places. Wilson's naval preparedness act of 1916 had authorized huge battleships, which were almost useless for anti-submarine operations. After America's entry into the conflict the construction of capital ships was halted, and in the first nine months of 1918 no fewer than eighty-three smaller destroyers were launched. A popular cry was "Help Muzzle the Mad Dogs of the Sea." Responding to the call, the navy did yeoman work by destroying German U-boats with depth bombs and other devices.

Most spectacular of the navy's achievements was the escorting to France of scores of troop transports, American and Allied. More than 2 million soldiers were taken "over there," but only one Europe-bound transport was torpedoed. Six troopless vessels were lost on their way home.

"Yanks" to the Rescue in France

Long regarded as quickly expandable, the army was more of a problem than the navy. The nation, in every one of its major conflicts, had been confronted with two tasks: first to raise an army, and second to fight the war. This emergency was no exception.

Most citizens, at the outset, did not dream of sending a mighty force to France. As far as fighting went, America would use her navy to uphold freedom of the seas. She would continue to ship war materials to the Allies and supply them with loans, which finally totaled nearly $10 billion. But in April and May of 1917, the European associates laid their cards on the table. They confessed that they were not only scraping the bottom of their money chests but, more ominously, of their manpower barrels. A huge American army would have to be raised, trained, and transported, or the whole Western Front would collapse.

Some kind of token force was necessary at once for European morale. The command of the American Expeditionary Forces (A.E.F.) was entrusted to efficient and stubborn General John J. ("Black Jack") Pershing, who had chased Villa in Mexico. On the Fourth of July, 1917, he led a tiny, ill-trained force of khaki-clad Americans through the streets of Paris, amid frenzied cries of "Vive l'Amérique." One of Pershing's close subordinates, touching on the debt-to-France theme, proclaimed, "Lafayette, we are here."

The ill-prepared "Yanks" were coming—slowly. Not until October 23, 1917, nearly seven months after Congress had formally declared hostilities, did the first small detachments of American troops see battle action. "We are at war but not in it," ran a current quip.

Fight-thirsty Theodore Roosevelt, still dreaming of Rough Rider days despite his nearly sixty years, was eager to raise a volunteer division and take it to France. Such a unit would have bolstered Allied morale, but it would also have drawn off the cream of American military leadership. This conflict was a global struggle, with no place for Rough Rider heroics, and Wilson icily rebuffed Roosevelt's offer. It was probably the bitterest disappointment of the ex-President's eventful life.

Making Plowboys into Doughboys

Conscription was the only answer to the need for raising an immense army with all possible speed. Wilson disliked a draft, as did many other Americans with Civil War memories; such forcible methods were alien to basic traditions. What would be gained, many citizens asked, if the nation militarized itself in order to defeat a militaristic Germany? But Wilson finally accepted and eloquently supported conscription as a disagreeable and temporary necessity.

The proposed draft bill immediately ran into a barrage of criticism in Congress. Champ Clark of Missouri, deploring compulsion, cried out that there was "precious little difference between a conscript and a convict." Prophets of doom predicted that on draft-registration day the streets would run red with blood. At length Congress—six weeks after declaring war—grudgingly got around to passing conscription.

A Universal Draft. The pre-war song "I Didn't Raise My Boy To Be a Soldier" was changed to "I Didn't Raise My Boy To Be a Slacker," which in turn inspired the cruel parody: "I Didn't Raise My Dog To Be a Sausage." (Chopin in the San Francisco *Examiner,* 1917.)

As later amended, the draft act was a true "selective service" law. It required the registration of all males between the ages of eighteen and forty-five. No "draft dodger" could purchase his exemption or hire a substitute, as in the easy-going days of the Civil War. The "selective" idea was that the government would "select" the draftee for duty in those places where he would be most useful. As a result, there were many exemptions for men in key industries, such as shipbuilding. Among those exempted was Jack Dempsey, soon to be the "slacker" heavyweight boxing champion.

The draft machinery, on the whole, worked effectively. Registration day proved to be a day of patriotic pilgrimages to flag-draped registration centers, and there was no shedding of blood, as gloomily predicted. Despite precautions, some 337,000 "slackers" escaped the draft and about 4,000 conscientious objectors were excused.

New wrinkles were added to the old services. Provision was made for training army and navy officers in the colleges, but in general this program creaked badly. For the first time women were admitted to the armed forces: some 11,000 to the navy and 269 to the marine corps.

The draft slipped promptly into high gear, as the singing of "Johnny, Get Your Gun" became the inspiration of the hour. Within a few frantic months the army was increased from about 200,000 men to over 4 million. The green draftees ("rookies") were herded into hastily built wooden camps, where they were given heavy doses of high-pressure training. As the popular song ran:

> They marched me twenty miles a day
> to fit me for the war—
> I didn't mind the first nineteen
> but the last one made me sore.

Yet morale was excellent, thanks largely to the ideals of defending democracy and ending war. The hastily trained men, eager to "lick" the Kaiser, were on fire to get "across the pond." After six months of concentrated effort, the "doughboys" might be shipped overseas, singing "Good-bye Broadway, Hello France." Upon arrival, they were supposedly given about two more months of training before seeing front-line action. But so great was the urgency that too many doughboys went into the trenches scarcely knowing how to handle a rifle, much less a bayonet.

Fighting in France—Belatedly

Russia's collapse underscored the need for haste. The communistic Bolsheviks, after seizing power, ultimately removed their beaten country from the "capitalistic" war early in 1918. This sudden defection released hundreds of thousands of battle-tested German veterans for the front in France. In the western theater, for the first time in the war, the Germans were developing a dangerous superiority in manpower.

Berlin's calculations as to American tardiness were surprisingly accurate. Germany had counted on knocking out Britain in six months, long before America could get into the struggle. No really effective American fighting force reached France until about a year after Congress declared war. Berlin had also reckoned on the inability of the Americans to transport their army, assuming that they were able to raise one. Here again the German predictions were not far from the mark. Over half of the tonnage for transports was diverted by Britain and her European allies from other pressing tasks, although the United States scraped together about 46 percent of the needed shipping.

France gradually began to bustle with American "doughboys." The first trainees to reach the front were used as replacements in the Allied armies, and were generally deployed in quiet sectors with the British and French. Enormous supply depots, as well as quarters for officers and men, were constructed in France. Here sprawled an amazing 225 miles (362 kilometers) of American barracks and 127 miles (204 kilometers) of hospital wards. The newcomers soon made friends with the French girls—or tried to—and one of the most sung-about women in history was the fabled "Mademoiselle from Armentières." One of the printable stanzas ran:

> She was true to me, she was true to you,
> She was true to the whole damned army, too.

Much of America's equipment—in certain categories all of it—was borrowed from the Allies. The list included a large proportion of light artillery, howitzers, tanks, airplanes, and rifles. One explanation is that the American war-production program had lagged dangerously in spots. In addition the Allies, with depleted manpower, preferred to use the available shipping for troops and provide the equipment themselves.

"Lafayette, We Are Here." The "doughboys" arrive in France. (Culver Pictures, Inc.)

Haste made waste. Hundreds of millions of dollars spent on American artillery were largely thrown away. The Browning machine gun was an excellent weapon, but it was developed too late to be of significant use. An aircraft program was wastefully ineffective to the point of scandal, although the whole effort involved little outright graft. Among other bottlenecks, strikes by the I.W.W. interrupted processing of the lightweight spruce wood, although the day was saved by a government-sponsored union, the L.L.L.L. (Loyal Legion of Loggers and Lumbermen). Altogether, America produced only 12,000 aircraft, not all of which were combat planes.

American airmen—"Cavaliers of the Clouds"—hung up an enviable record in France. In the end the United States could boast twenty-two "aces," or men who had netted five or more enemy craft. The leading hero was indestructible Captain Edward V. ("Eddie") Rickenbacker, later prominent in commercial aviation, whose bag was twenty-two airplanes and three balloons.

America Helps Hammer the "Hun"*

The dreaded German drive on the Western Front exploded in the spring of 1918. Spearheaded by about half a million troops, the enemy rolled forward with terrifying momentum. So dire was the peril that the Allied nations for the first time united under a Supreme Commander, the quiet French Marshal Foch, whose axiom was: "To make war is to attack." Until then the Allies had been fighting imperfectly coordinated actions.

At last the ill-trained "Yanks" were finally coming—and not a moment too soon. Late in May 1918,

*In 1900 the Kaiser had himself used this term in urging German troops to behave like Huns in crushing the Chinese rebels ("Boxers").

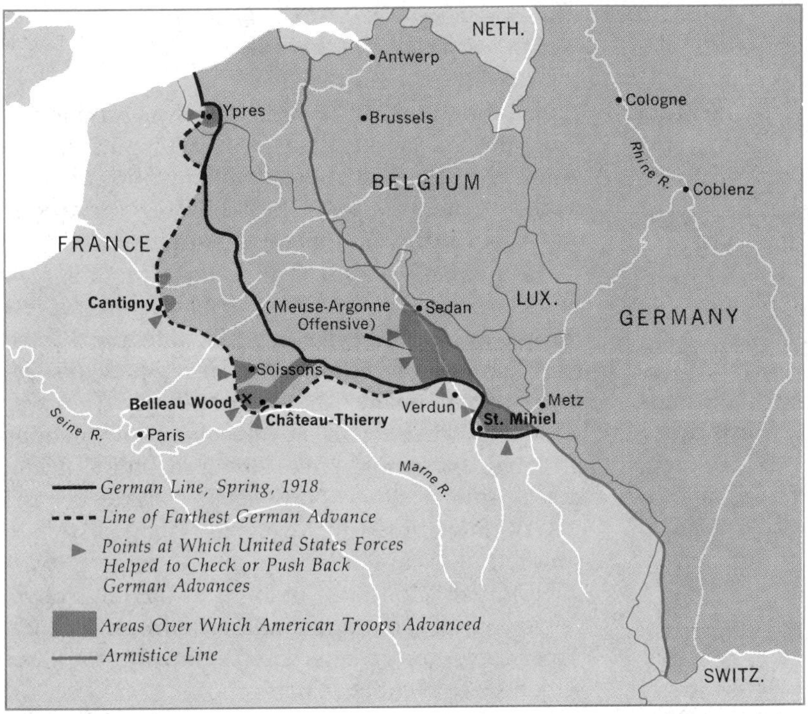

MAJOR U.S. OPERATIONS IN FRANCE, 1918

One "doughboy" recorded in his diary his baptism of fire at St. Mihiel: "Hiked through dark woods. No lights allowed, guided by holding on the pack of the man ahead. Stumbled through underbrush for about half mile into an open field where we waited in soaking rain until about 10:00 p.m. We then started on our hike to the St. Mihiel front, arriving on the crest of a hill at 1:00 a.m. I saw a sight which I shall never forget. It was the zero hour and in one instant the entire front as far as the eye could reach in either direction was a sheet of flame, while the heavy artillery made the earth quake."

the forward-rolling Germans, smashing to within 40 miles (64 kilometers) of Paris, threatened to knock out France. Newly arrived American troops, numbering fewer than 30,000, were thrown into the breach at Château-Thierry, where they played a dramatic role in helping to stem the tide. In June the United States marines cleared the Germans from bloody Belleau Wood. The victory was so heroic that appreciative Frenchmen renamed the place "Bois de Marins" (Marine Woods). The lean and mean marines, ever cocky, could boast in their posters, "First in the Fight."

American weight in the scales was now being felt. By July 1918, the awesome German drive had spent its force, and keyed-up American boys participated in a Foch counter-offensive in the Second Battle of the Marne. This engagement marked the beginning of a German withdrawal that was never effectively reversed. As proof of mounting strength, seven American divisions (about 189,000 men) fought in the Second Battle of the Marne, as compared with sixty Allied divisions. In September 1918, nine American divisions (about 243,000 men) joined four French divisions to dislodge the Germans from the St. Mihiel salient, a German dagger in France's flank.

The Americans, dissatisfied with merely bolstering the British and French, had meanwhile been demanding a separate army. Pride, patriotism, and morale all required that the "Yanks" have their own command, assigned to a specific fighting front. The French, on the contrary, insisted that the American boys be used merely as replacements. But General Pershing, jut-jawed and offense-minded, fought a winning battle against the Allied leaders. The Americans were finally assigned a front of eighty-five miles (137 kilometers), stretching northwestward from the Swiss border to meet the French lines.

As a part of the last mighty Allied assault, involving several million men, Pershing's army undertook the Meuse-Argonne offensive, from September 26 to November 11, 1918. One objective was to cut the German railroad lines feeding the Western Front. This battle, the most titanic thus far in American history, lasted forty-seven days and engaged 1.2 million American troops. With especially heavy fighting in the rugged Argonne Forest, the killed and wounded mounted to 120,000, or 10 percent of the Americans involved. The slow progress and severe losses from machine guns resulted in part from inadequate training, in part from dashing open-field tactics, with the bayonet liberally employed. Tennessee-bred Alvin C. York, a member of an anti-war religious sect, became a hero when he single-handedly killed 20 Germans and captured 132 more.

Victory was in sight—and fortunately so. The slowly advancing American armies in France were eating up their supplies so rapidly that they were in grave danger of running short. But the battered Germans, although their own soil was not being invaded, were ready to raise their arms and cry "Kamerad" ("Comrade"). Their allies were deserting them; the British blockade was causing critical food shortages; and the German armies were reeling under the sledgehammer blows of the Allies. Propaganda leaflets, containing seductive Wilsonian promises, were raining upon their crumbling lines from balloons, shells, and rockets.

At the Front. An American gunner fires a British-made light machine gun. (National Archives.)

The Fourteen Points Disarm Germany

Berlin was now ready to hoist the white flag. Warned of imminent defeat by the generals, it turned to the presumably softhearted Wilson in October 1918, seeking a peace based on the Fourteen Points. In stern responses, the President made it clear that the Kaiser must be thrown overboard before an armistice could be negotiated. War-weary Germans, whom Wilson had been trying to turn against their "military masters," took the hint. The Kaiser was forced to flee to Holland, where he lived out his remaining twenty-three years, "unwept, unhonored, and unhung."

As events proved, the Fourteen Points served better for propaganda than for peacemaking. Allied leaders, whose territorial ambitions were embodied in secret treaties, feared that Wilson's lofty ideals would tie their hands. But they urgently needed the support of rich Uncle Sam for post-war reconstruction. Mystery man Colonel House, speaking for Wilson, hinted at a separate German-American treaty if the Allies were not reasonable. They finally agreed, with feet-dragging reluctance, to negotiate a peace based on the Fourteen Points. But they insisted on two reservations: one on freedom of the seas that would safeguard British naval power, and one on reparations that would assure France of collecting compensation for damage inflicted by the invading "Hun."

The exhausted Germans were through. They laid

> Theodore Roosevelt, referring to Wilson's practice of drafting diplomatic notes on his own typewriter, telegraphed several senators (October 24, 1918): "Let us dictate peace by the hammering guns and not chat about peace to the accompaniment of clicking typewriters. The language of the fourteen points and the subsequent statements explaining or qualifying them are thoroughly mischievous." Roosevelt favored unconditional surrender.

German "Repentance." A prophetic reflection of the view that the failure to smash Germany completely would lead to another world war. (Dallas *News*, 1918.)

down their arms after the Allies had solemnly assured them that the peace treaty would be based on the Fourteen Points—with the two exceptions noted. The Armistice was formally signed at eleven o'clock on the eleventh day of the eleventh month of 1918, and an eerie, numbing silence fell over the Western Front. War-taut America burst into a delirium of around-the-clock rejoicing, as streets were jammed with laughing, whooping, milling, dancing masses. The war to end wars had ended.

The Harvest from Global War

Beyond doubt the war effort of the aroused Western giant had been prodigious. America got into the fray, belatedly and awkwardly but full of dash and enthusiasm, just in time to help turn the tide to victory. More than 4 million citizen-soldiers donned uniforms. The total casualties were 320,000, of which 116,000 were deaths, including losses from disease. Yet these gory tolls were minor when bracketed with those suffered by Britain, France, and Russia. As compared with other American wars, death from disease was generally reduced. An exception was the terrible influenza epidemic of 1918, which took a worldwide toll of some 10 million lives, mostly civilians. The ultimate

Day of Jubilation. Helmet-tossing U.S. soldiers greet Armistice in front-line France. Tantalizing reports of the war's approaching end circulated for several days before the official Armistice on November 11. One battle-weary "doughboy" wrote in his diary that on November 10 "the papers show a picture of the Kaiser entitled 'William the Lost,' and stating that he has abdicated. Rumor at night that Armistice was signed. Some fellows discharged their arms in the courtyard, but most of us were too well pleased with dry bunk to get up." (Courtesy U.S. Army.)

AMERICAN LIFE IN PAINTING 1865-Present

Prisoners from the Front, 1866, by Winslow Homer (1836–1910)

Throughout his long career, Homer excelled at painting distinctively American scenes and gained wide reknown as perhaps America's most "typical" artist. This painting, shown at the Paris International Exposition of 1867, reflects Homer's first-hand observations of the Civil War. The Union officer somewhat disdainfully asserts his command of the situation; the beaten Confederates, their arms not yet entirely laid down, exhibit an out-at-the-elbows pride and defiance. *The Metropolitan Museum of Art. Gift of Mrs. Frank B. Porter, 1922.*

The Strike, 1886, by Robert Koehler (1850–1917)

Scenes like this were becoming more typical of American life in the late 19th Century, as industrialism advanced spectacularly and sometimes ruthlessly. Here an entire community of men, women, and children—many of them apparently immigrant newcomers—challenges the power of the "boss." The scene is tense but orderly, though violence seems to be imminent, as one striker reaches for a rock. *Collection of Lee Baxandall. Color photograph courtesy Local 1199, Drug and Hospital Union, New York.*

The Buffalo Hunt, 1890, by Frederic Remington (1861–1909)

A New Yorker who first went west at the age of nineteen as a cowboy and ranch cook, Remington became the foremost artist of the vanishing way of life of the old Far West. Once a common sight on the high plains, the kind of buffalo kill that Remington records here was a great rarity by the time he painted this scene in 1890. The once vast herds of bison had long since been reduced to a pitiful few by the white man's rifles. *Detail, Courtesy of the Buffalo Bill Historical Center, Cody, Wyoming.*

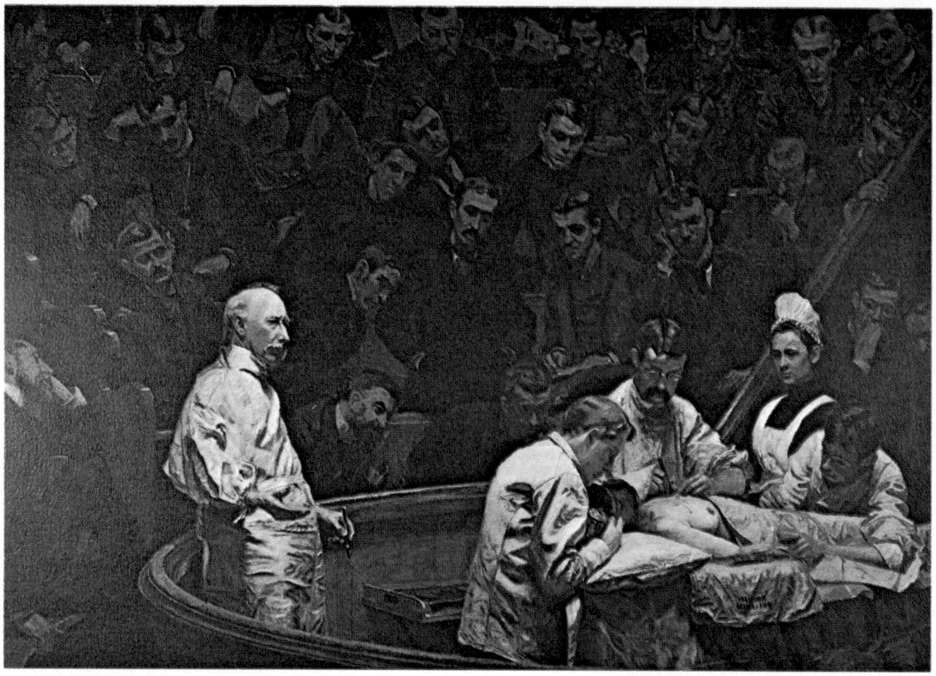

Agnew Clinic, 1889
by Thomas Eakins (1844–1916)

Walt Whitman wrote that Eakins was that rare artist who saw what was, rather than what ought to be. His paintings manifest a frank, sometimes brutal, realism. This depiction of Dr. David H. Agnew's surgical clinic at the University of Pennsylvania was considered too vivid, for it showed the partially nude body of a woman. Note the intentness of the medical-student spectators, who were pioneers in a dawning age of "scientific" medicine. *University of Pennsylvania School of Medicine.*

Hairdresser's Window, 1907
by John Sloan (1871–1951)

Sloan grew up in the Philadelphia of Eakins' day and, like Eakins, he painted with raw candor everyday scenes. The swarming life of New York City had a special appeal to his artistic eye. He was a prominent member of the so-called Ashcan School, a group of artists in the progressive period who relentlessly depicted vulgar and even comic scenes like this one portraying a bleached blonde hairdresser bleaching the hair of a client. *Wadsworth Atheneum, Hartford, Connecticut* (Ella Gallup Sumner and Mary Catlin Sumner Collection).

The Thankful Poor, 1895, by Henry O. Tanner (1859–1937)

Tanner loomed large among American black artists. He had studied with Eakins in Philadelphia and had learned from him to approach his subjects with unsentimental honesty. The unadorned simplicity of this painting of a poor black man and child gives it a quiet and moving power. *Private Collection.*

Mary Cassatt

Mother and Child, c. 1890
by Mary Cassatt (1845–1926)

Another Philadelphian, Cassatt pursued almost her entire artistic career in Paris and was the only American invited to exhibit with the French Impressionists. She was perhaps America's greatest woman painter. Her favorite motif was a mother and child, a subject she portrayed with great sensitivity and warmth. Compare the compassionate and affectionate quality of this painting of a woman with Willem de Kooning's *Woman I. Courtesy the Wichita Art Museum. The Roland P. Murdock Collection.*

Migration, c. 1932, by William Gropper (1897–)

The Great Depression of the 1930s prompted many artists to wield their brushes in the cause of social justice. One of the most active of the "social realists" was William Gropper, a professional caricaturist whose paintings often have a cartoon-like quality. Some critics have complained that Gropper produced only visual clichés and that his painting is more propaganda than art. But the power of Gropper's convictions is apparent in this stark portrayal of a family in the 1930s being blown out of the Dust Bowl. *Gift of Oliver B. James, University Art Collections, Arizona State University, Tempe, Arizona.*

The Subway, 1950
by George Tooker (1920–)

The paintings of Tooker, a Harvard-educated New Yorker, reflect the loneliness and anxiety of much modern urban life. Here he draws on surrealistic techniques to emphasize the hard angularity of the urban environment and the fear and isolation of the people who inhabit it. Compare this chilling contemporary view of human existence, and the underlying philosophy it represents, with the 18th-Century perspective seen in Copley's *Revere* and Stuart's *Skater* (previous color section). *Egg tempera on composition board, 18 × 36 inches. Collection of Whitney Museum of American Art. Juliana Force Purchase.*

Woman, I, 1950–1952
by Willem de Kooning (1904–   )

Born in Holland, de Kooning has pursued much of his career in the United States. He thus reversed the usual direction of artistic migration, and symbolizes America's artistic coming-of-age relative to Europe. Painting with a furious technique, he depicts exaggerated, horrifying images of modern life. Compare his portrayal of a woman here with Mary Cassatt's treatment of the same subject in *Mother and Child. Oil on canvas, 6 ft. 3⅞ in. × 58 in. Collection, The Museum of Modern Art, New York.*

MECHA Mural, 1974, by student artists directed by Sergio O'Cadiz

People have scribbled on walls since time immemorial, but in the 1960s and 1970s mural painting emerged as a new form of American folk art. Drab buildings and bare fences, often in minority inner-city neighborhoods, were turned into huge canvases. This mural incorporates many Mexican-American and Mexican themes, including the United Farm Workers' bird symbol and a skeleton, a frequent motif in Mexican art. *Courtesy of Santa Ana College, Rancho Santiago Community College District: Preston Mitchell, photographer, La Mirada, CA.*

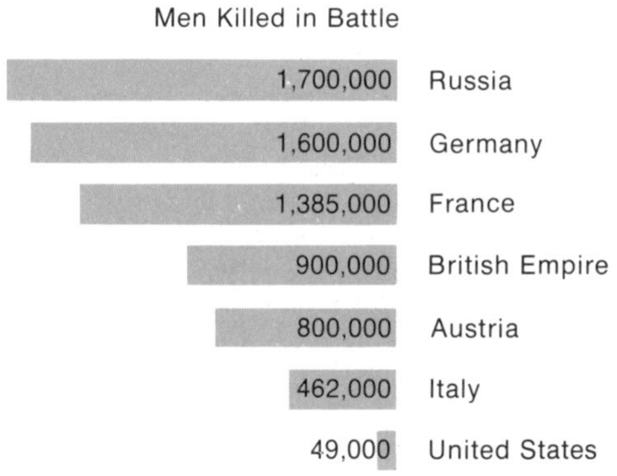

APPROXIMATE COMPARATIVE LOSSES IN WORLD WAR I

cost of the war to the United States was staggering, roughly $112 billion, including nearly $75 billion in veterans' benefits.

American operations were not confined solely to France; small detachments fought in Belgium, Italy, and notably Russia. The United States, hoping to keep stores of munitions from falling into German hands when Bolshevik Russia quit fighting, contributed some 5,000 troops to an Allied invasion of North Russia at Archangel. Wilson likewise sent nearly 10,000 troops to Siberia as a part of an Allied expedition, which included more than 70,000 Japanese. Major American purposes were to prevent Japan from getting a stranglehold on Siberia, to rescue some 45,000 marooned Czechoslovak troops, and to snatch military supplies from Red Bolshevik control. Sharp fighting at Archangel and in Siberia involved casualties on both sides, including several hundred Americans. The Communist rulers of Soviet Russia have never allowed their people to forget these "capitalistic" interventions.

The War of 1917–1918 exposed some chronic ailments in American society. Despite abundant warning time, the nation was flatfootedly unprepared for its leap into global war. Mobilization relied more on patriotic emotionalism than on the cool majesty of the laws. Hysteria swept the land, and many ancient injustices were glaringly revealed.

Black Soldier Hero of World War I. (United Press International photo.)

More than 300,000 black men were drafted to fight in a war to make the world safe for a democracy that they did not fully enjoy. (Lynchings and race riots during these decades were continuing at an appalling pace.) About two-thirds of the black draftees, often to their discontent, were assigned to labor battalions and other non-combat units. Their morale was not helped by vicious race riots, especially the one in East St. Louis in 1917, during which some forty blacks and eight whites lost their lives. Various kinds of discrimination against the draftees made for inflamed feelings, notably in the South. In 1917 thirteen black soldiers were hanged for murder after being provoked into striking back and killing seventeen whites at Houston, Texas. Nevertheless, black combat units did reach France, some of which fought with distinction, especially the 369th regiment, dubbed by Germans "Hell Fighters."

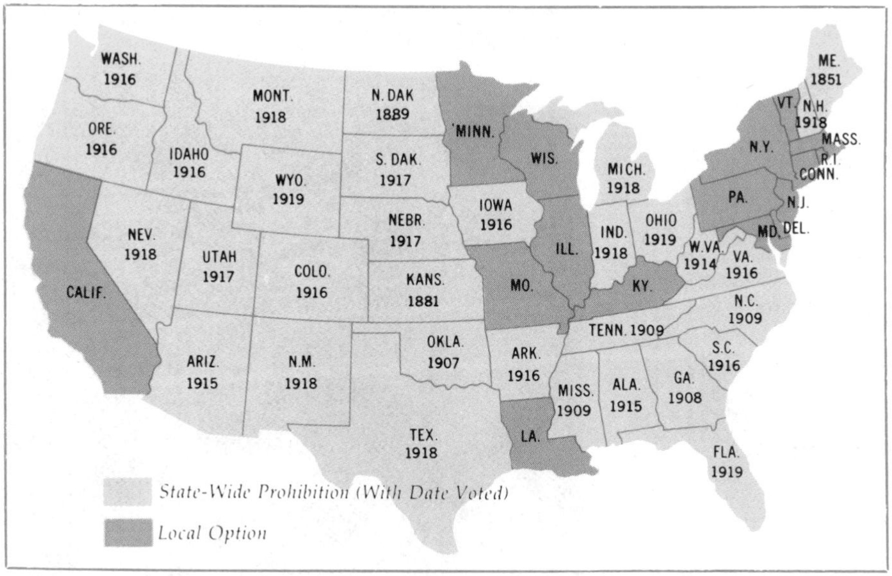

PROHIBITION ON THE EVE OF THE 18TH AMENDMENT, 1919

The 18th Amendment was ratified by the essential 36th state (Nebraska) on January 16, 1919. Thirsty soldiers returning from France complained that while they had been abroad making the world safe for democracy, their countrymen had made America unsafe for drinkers.

No lasting grade-A war heroes, black or white, emerged from this conflict. Stern-faced General Pershing did not radiate the glamor that one associates with presidential timber. The traditional glory of arms was overshadowed by barbed wire, metal monsters called tanks, lethal poison gas, mud, rats, and lice ("cooties"). Master organizer Herbert Hoover, the so-called Knight of the Lean Garbage Can, became the outstanding hero—and he was a civilian.

Prohibition was one of two major constitutional amendments floated through by the war emergency. The need for conserving grain and other foodstuffs, combined with an idealistic spirit of self-sacrifice, brought ratification of the 18th Amendment in 1919. (See Appendix.) Most of America had already been voted dry by state action, but the constitutional amendment achieved —on paper—the dream of a saloonless nation.

Woman suffrage, regarded as essential to national unity, was likewise stimulated by the conflict. President Wilson had hitherto opposed it ("He Kept Us Out of Suffrage"), but at last he supported this concession as "a vitally necessary war measure." "Votes for women" achieved a final triumph when, in 1920, the 19th Amendment was written into the Constitution. (See Appendix.) In politics, so the witticism went, the rolling pin now replaced the steamroller. But a sharp elevation of moral tone, so confidently predicted, did not follow the new amendment. Women tended to vote the same way as men.

Suffragists Picket the White House, 1917. Militant feminists sometimes handcuffed themselves to the White House fence to dramatize their appeal to the President. (Library of Congress.)

Constitutional changes were overshadowed by economic dislocations. Swollen war industries brought bulging pay envelopes, but the invisible hand of inflation reached greedily into them. (Prices nearly doubled between 1916 and 1920). Despite burdensome war taxes, a new crop of profiteers emerged, and the select American millionaire group shot up from 16,000 to 20,000.

But the conflict, despite problems, vindicated American democracy. The German militarists had sneered at America's ability to gird herself for battle while there was yet time. The Republic astonished them—and to some extent itself—when it finally managed to mount a mighty crusade for victory. Democracy, after all, did not seem so spineless and inept.

VARYING VIEWPOINTS

Many historians have suggested that World War I killed the progressive movement with an overdose of super-patriotism and repression, thus paving the way for the reactionary decade of the 1920s. Such a view powerfully reinforced the isolationism of many citizens in the 1930s. They feared that another conflagration would cripple the New Deal, just as the First World War had suffocated the earlier reform campaign. But other critics have pointed out that World War I in fact helped to fulfill many progressive aspirations, including labor gains, woman suffrage, prohibition, and especially a stronger federal government. The war thus poses in yet another form the vexing question of the character of progressivism. Frustratingly, the conflict constitutes a cramped historical laboratory in which to test the various hypotheses, since American belligerency lasted only nineteen months.

SELECT READINGS

The home front is emphasized in David M. Kennedy, *Over Here: The First World War and American Society* (1980). Economic mobilization is covered in Robert Cuff, *The War Industries Board* (1973), Daniel R. Beaver, *Newton D. Baker and the American War Effort* (1966), and Charles Gilbert, *American Financing of World War I* (1970). On labor, see Frank L. Grubbs, Jr., *The Struggle for Labor Loyalty* (1968), and David Brody, *Labor in Crisis: The Steel Strike of 1919* (1965). Politics are treated in Seward Livermore, *Politics is Adjourned: Woodrow Wilson and the War Congress, 1916–1918* (1966). American propaganda efforts are colorfully portrayed in J. R. Mock and C. Larson, *Words That Won the War* (1939), and S. L. Vaughn, *Holding Fast the Inner Lines: Democracy, Nationalism, and the Committee on Public Information* (1980). The abuse of civil liberties is luridly described in H. S. Peterson and G. C. Fite, *Opponents of War, 1917–1918* (1957), more soberly analyzed in H. N. Scheiber, *The Wilson Administration and Civil Liberties, 1917–1921* (1960), Paul L. Murphy, *World War I and The Origin of Civil Liberties in the United States* (1979), and Zechariah Chafee, *Free Speech in the United States* (1941). Military operations are recounted in H. A. DeWeerd, *President Wilson Fights His War* (1968), and Edward M. Coffman, *The War to End All Wars: The American Military Experience in World War I* (1968). Consult also A. E. Barbeau and Florette Henri, *Unknown Soldiers: Black American Troops in World War One* (1974). On Wilson's foreign economic policies, see Jeffrey Safford, *Wilsonian Maritime Diplomacy* (1978), and Burton Kaufman, *Efficiency and Expansion: Foreign Trade Organization in the Wilson Administration* (1974). Useful monographs are George F. Kennan, *Soviet-American Relations, 1917–1920* (2 vols., 1956, 1958), and Betty M. Unterberger, *America's Siberian Expedition, 1918–1920* (1956). Some of the war's literary impact is assessed in Stanley Cooperman, *World War I and the American Novel* (1966).

37

Making and Unmaking the Peace

Dare we reject it [the League of Nations] and break the heart of the world?

WOODROW WILSON, 1919

Wilson Steps Down from Olympus

As the war in Europe crashed to a close, Woodrow Wilson towered at the peak of his popularity and power. No other man had ever occupied so dizzy a pinnacle as moral leader of the world; no other man had ever been presented with so breathtaking an opportunity as a peacemaker.

Success seemed assured. Superb as a war leader, Wilson now had behind him the prestige of victory and the economic resources of the mightiest nation on earth. But regrettably his sureness of touch gradually deserted him, and he began to make a series of tragic fumbles.

His first error was the "October Appeal." The war crisis had brought an enforced political truce, and the popular slogan had been "Politics Is Adjourned." Republicans had generally supported the Democratic program for victory, although many diehards had protested against the dictatorial practices of "Kaiser" Wilson. The congressional elections of November 1918 were imminent, and the President believed that his hands would be strengthened at the Paris peace table if the voters should return a Democratic majority. Urged by anxious politicians, he reverted to his "appeal habit" by publicly calling for a Democratic Congress.

Republicans responded with a bitter cry that the political truce had been broken. Politics, in fact, had never been "adjourned"; partisanship had merely simmered below the surface, with Theodore Roosevelt more than simmering. To avoid being branded unpatriotic, Republicans had widely assailed Wilson for not fighting the war more fiercely and efficiently.

On election day the voters tramped to the polls and, by a rather narrow margin, returned a Republican Congress. Whether the result was materially influenced by Wilson's appeal cannot be determined with certainty. But having staked his prestige on the outcome, he suffered a grievous loss of face. At the Paris peace table, he was the only one of the leading statesmen not entitled to be present—that is, on the basis of a legislative majority under a cabinet form of government.

Wilson next infuriated Republicans by announcing that he was going to Paris to help make the peace. At that time no President had ever journeyed to Europe, though Theodore Roosevelt had visited Panama in 1906 to see "the dirt fly." Wilson's critics charged that he had developed a God-complex—a desire, as ex-President Taft put it, "to hog the whole show." The egoist-idealist in the White House was needed at home, so Republicans argued, to grapple with reconstruction. In the hurly-burly of the Peace Conference, this "mushy sentimentalist" would be overwhelmed and "bamboozled." But in Washington, at one end of a wire, he presumably could make his decisions quietly, calmly, and effectively.

The President Snubs the Senate

Renewed outcries burst from Republican lips when Wilson announced the five-man American peace commission. It consisted of himself; the quiet and faithful Colonel House, his second self; Secretary of State Lansing; a military adviser, General T. H. Bliss; and a little-known Republican, ex-career diplomat Henry White. In addition, there were scores of technical advisers, chiefly scholars from quiet campuses whom ex-Professor Wilson regarded as "his kind."

Republicans, now the majority party on the basis of the recent congressional elections, insisted that they were not represented at all. Henry White, though a Republican, was so minor a one as to be negligible. Republicans had been good enough to fight in the war, they complained; then why should they not have a real place at the peace table? Humorist Will Rogers had Wilson tell them, "We'll split 50–50—I will go and you fellows can stay."

Wilson also snubbed the Senate in making up the peace commission, even though the jealous solons would have to approve the treaty. He did not ask their advice, partly because he had little respect for the "pygmy-minded" senators. He did not put a single one of them on the peace commission, although there was ample precedent for doing so.

The Peace Delegation—A Republican View. *Left to right:* Wilson, House, Lansing, White, Bliss, Baruch, Hoover, Creel. (*Harvey's Weekly,* 1919.)

Choosing a Republican senator presented a problem, for the logical one was slender and aristocratically bewhiskered Henry Cabot Lodge of Massachusetts, Ph.D., Harvard. His mind, quipped one critic, was like the soil of his native New England, "naturally barren but highly cultivated." As the author of many books, Lodge had been known as "the scholar in politics" until Wilson appeared on the scene. The two men came to hate each other passionately and blindly.

But Wilson, in ignoring the Senate, seems to have been primarily preoccupied with global problems. He was like the baseball player, as someone has said, who knocked the ball into the left-field bleachers and then forgot to touch home plate.

The brutal truth is that certain Republican leaders were out to knife Wilson—that "drum major of civilization." He had trampled heavily on the corns of business tycoons with his New Freedom reforms, and the Republican leaders wanted to turn back the clock to the golden days of McKinley standpattism. Wilson must not be permitted to conclude a triumphant peace. If he did, he might—unspeakable thought!—feel that he had to be re-elected for a third term to carry out its provisions.

An Idealist Battles the Imperialists in Paris

Woodrow Wilson, the great prophet arisen in the West, received tumultuous welcomes from the masses of France, England, and Italy late in 1918 and early in 1919. They saw in his idealism the promise of a better world. "Vive l'Amérique!" and "Vive le Président," cried the French, while the Italians no less enthusiastically hailed "Il Presidente." In Milan, Wilson responded to the tears and cheers by throwing kisses with both hands. But the statesmen of France and Italy were careful to keep the new messiah at arm's length from worshipful crowds. He might so arouse the people as to overthrow their leaders and upset finespun imperialistic plans.

Almost from the outset, the Paris Conference of great and small nations fell into the hands of an inner clique, known as the Big Four. Such inner-sanctum diplomacy was inevitable because the confused multi-power gathering was too unwieldy. But behind-the-scenes secrecy seemed to violate the first—and one of the most popular—of the Fourteen Points: "Open Covenants Openly Arrived At." The frustrated journalists were infuriated by secret covenants secretly connived at.

Wilson in Dover, England, 1919. Hailed by many Europeans in early 1919 as the Savior of the Western world, Wilson was a fallen idol only a few months later, when his own countrymen repudiated the peace treaty he had helped to craft. (National Archives.)

"The Race." Russian Bolshevism seems to be forging ahead of the peace negotiators at Paris. (Fitzpatrick in the St. Louis *Post-Dispatch*.)

The Big Four proved to be both a powerful and a colorful body. Wilson, representing the richest and freshest great power, more or less occupied the driver's seat. He was joined by genial Premier Vittorio Orlando of Italy and by the brilliant Prime Minister David Lloyd George of Britain. Perhaps the most realistic of the quartet was cynical, hard-bitten Premier Georges Clemenceau of France, the seventy-eight-year-old "organizer of victory" known as "the Tiger."

Speed was urgent when the Conference opened on January 18, 1919. Europe seemed to be slipping into anarchy; the red tide of Communism was licking westward from Bolshevist Russia. A current saying in Paris was "Better a bad treaty today than a good treaty four months hence."

What problem should be tackled first? Wilson had come to Paris with his primary long-run goal the League of Nations, designed as a world parliament to avert future wars. All countries would be represented in the Assembly and the great powers additionally would have seats in the Council. But the rest of the Big Four—all Old World realists—were lukewarm at best about the visionary Wilsonian scheme. They were far more eager to carve up the territorial spoils, as prearranged in secret treaties.

Thoroughly aroused, Wilson opposed with all his Scotch Presbyterian stubbornness any imperialistic parceling out of the booty. Such a division would be an outrageous violation of Point Five, relating to colonies. He finally forced the acceptance of a compromise between naked imperialism and Wilsonian idealism. The victorious powers would not receive the conquered territory outright, but only as trustees or "mandatories" of the League of Nations. Strategic Syria, for example, was awarded to France, and oil-rich Iraq to Britain. This half-loaf solution, as applied to certain underdeveloped areas, proved to be little more than the old pre-war imperialism, thinly disguised.

Meanwhile Wilson had been serving as midwife for the League of Nations. The idea was not original with him; other planners in America had been working on it, as had certain far-visioned British and French thinkers. But Wilson, embracing the scheme with characteristic enthusiasm, made it peculiarly his own. Chosen chairman of the committee that drafted the League Covenant, he labored earnestly on it after conference hours. In ten high-pressure sessions, he drove the document through in reasonably complete form, though it still needed polishing.

Wilson's next task was to get the draft accepted by the entire Conference. Many members, eager to grapple with immediate problems, argued that the League of Nations should be dealt with last. Then, some intriguers hoped, it would be sidetracked, lest it interfere with imperialistic ambitions. But Wilson gained a signal victory in mid-February 1919 when he not only won acceptance of the League Covenant by a committee but persuaded the Conference to make it an integral part of the final peace treaty. At one time he spoke so eloquently for his adopted brainchild that even the hard-boiled newspaper reporters forgot to take notes.

Grave concern was expressed by General Bliss, one of the five American peace commissioners (December 18, 1918): "I am disquieted to see how hazy and vague our ideas are. We are going to be up against the wiliest politicians in Europe. There will be nothing hazy or vague about their ideas."

The Senate Warns Wilson

Wilson, who had done remarkably well for an amateur diplomat, now had to leave the Paris battlefield for a time. Domestic duties required a quick trip back to America, to sign bills passed by Congress and to attend to other pressing business.

An ugly storm was brewing in the Senate. Certain Republican solons were sharpening their knives for Wilson; they distrusted the "League of Denationalized Nations" and the "League of Nations Claptrap." To them the new scheme was either a useless "sewing circle" or an overpotent "super-state." Senator Lodge, jealous and embittered, was active in rallying his Republican following. His ranks were joined by a dozen or so isolationists, mostly Republicans, who were known as "the Battalion of Death." This small group of "irreconcilables" or "bitter-enders" was headed by rabble-rousing orators, notably Senator William E. Borah of Idaho and Senator Hiram W. Johnson of California.

Bitterness against Wilson flared forth ominously in early March 1919 when Senate Republicans published a Round Robin. This was a sensational manifesto signed by thirty-nine Republican senators or senators-elect—enough to defeat the treaty.

"Seein' Things." (Brooklyn *Eagle*, 1919.)

They proclaimed, for all the world to know, that the Senate would not approve the League of Nations in its existing imperfect form.

Fighting mad, Wilson struck back. On the eve of his return to Paris, he defiantly announced in a New York speech that the League would be inseparably tied into the treaty. The senators could not cut it out without killing the whole pact—and they dared not, he was confident, break the heart of the world.

The Round Robin, a virtual stab in the back for Wilson, delighted his Allied adversaries in Paris. They were now in a stronger bargaining position. The President would have to come back and beg—as he subsequently did—for changes in the Covenant that would safeguard the Monroe Doctrine and other heritages so precious to the senators.

Frustrated France Demands Security

Next came the grim battle with the French, who above all sought security against another periodic German invasion. Hardheaded Premier Clemenceau, who remembered that steel bayonets and not paper ideals had repelled the enemy, sneered at the Fourteen Points. "God gave us His Ten Commandments," he reportedly remarked, "and we broke them. Wilson gave us his Fourteen Points—we shall see."

Clemenceau demanded the German Rhineland as a buffer, even though the acquisition of several million Germans by France would be a flagrant violation of self-determination. The heated dispute was complicated by French demands for the coal-rich Saar Valley, inhabited almost solidly by Germans.

At the peak of the French crisis, in early April 1919, Wilson was prostrated by influenza. Burning with a temperature of 103° (39.4°C), he lay in his bedroom racked by fits of coughing. To every demand of Clemenceau, seated with the rest of the Big Four in the outer chamber, he returned a defiant "no." His patience exhausted, he finally took steps to order the presidential liner, the

George Washington, to be readied for his return. French newspapers jeered that he was going home to mother.

The Conference was saved when the French deadlock was broken by compromise. Germany's coveted Saar Basin would remain under the League of Nations for fifteen years, and then a vote of the population would determine its fate.* France yielded her demands for the Rhineland buffer state in return for a Security Treaty, signed by Wilson and Lloyd George. By its terms both America and Britain agreed to come to the defense of the French in the event of a future attack by the German invader. This pact was quickly pigeonholed by the United States Senate, which shied away from all entangling alliances.

For France, which still bore the marks of the Hunnish invader, the outcome was supremely disillusioning. Deprived of both the Rhineland and a feeling of security, she was forced to drink the bitter dregs of betrayal.

Italy and Japan Defy Self-Determination

A clash now loomed with Italy, which demanded the key port of Fiume, near the head of the Adriatic Sea. Unfortunately, this landlocked harbor happened to be the most valuable seaport of the newly created nation of Yugoslavia. The city itself was inhabited predominantly by Italians, but the Yugoslavs were more numerous in the outskirts. To turn over these foreigners to Italy, like cattle in a pasture, would be a glaring violation of self-determination. Wilson, true to principle, fought valiantly for an acceptable alternative. But when the Italian delegates proved stubborn, he reverted to old habits and on April 23, 1919, issued a spectacular appeal over their heads to the masses of Italy.

Wilson's maneuver fell flat, for the Italian delegates went home in a huff. Their people, at heart more interested in booty than in ideals, turned savagely against the once-worshiped "Il Presidente." Yet Wilson, while not completely winning his point, kept the Italians from winning theirs—at least temporarily. The result was a hollow victory for self-determination.

> Colonel House, one of the five American delegates, wrote (April 22, 1919), "The whole world is speculating as to whether the Italians are 'bluffing' or whether they really intend going home and not signing the Peace unless they have Fiume. It is not unlike a game of poker."

The next crucial struggle was with the Japanese, who had been shrewdly biding their time. When war broke out in 1914, Japan had joined the Allies and had seized Germany's holdings on China's Shantung peninsula, as well as the German islands in the Pacific. The overcrowded Japanese were naturally eager to keep all these spoils. Their persistence was rewarded when they were allowed to

Japan Allegedly Using League to Grab China. (San Francisco *Chronicle*.)

*The Saar population voted overwhelmingly to rejoin Germany in 1935.

retain the strategic Pacific islands, though only as a mandate from the League of Nations.*

As for German rights in Shantung, Wilson opposed the Japanese claims with set jaw. To turn the fortunes of some 30 million Chinese over to the tender mercies of Japan would be an intolerable violation of self-determination. The politely bowing delegates from Nippon threatened to walk out, and if they had joined the absent Italians, the Peace Conference might well have dissolved.

In the end Wilson, with a wry face, was forced to accept a compromise on Shantung. Japan would keep Germany's economic holdings, and later return the strategic peninsula to China. The Chinese delegates in Paris, outraged, refused to sign the treaty. This whole solution smelled so much of old-time imperialism as to cause Clemenceau to jeer that Wilson "talked like Jesus Christ but acted like Lloyd George."

The Peace Treaty That Brought a New War

A completed Treaty of Versailles, after more weeks of wrangling, was handed to the Germans in June 1919—almost literally on the point of a bayonet. They had given up their arms on the strength of assurances that they would be granted a peace based on the Fourteen Points, with two reservations. A careful analysis of the treaty shows that only about four of the twenty-three original Wilsonian points and subsequent principles were fully honored. Loud and bitter cries of betrayal burst from German throats—charges that Adolf Hitler vehemently reiterated during his meteoric rise to power.

Wilson, of course, was guilty of no conscious betrayal. But the Allied powers were torn by conflicting aims, many of them sanctioned by secret treaties. There had to be compromise at Paris—or there would be no agreement. Faced with hard realities, Wilson was forced to compromise away some of his less-cherished Fourteen Points in order to salvage the more precious League of Nations. He was much like the mother who had to throw her sickly younger children to the pursuing wolves in order to save her sturdy firstborn son.

A troubled Wilson was not happy with the results. Greeted a few months earlier with frenzied acclaim in Europe, he was now a fallen idol, condemned alike by disillusioned liberals and frustrated imperialists. He was keenly aware of some of the injustices that had been forced into the treaty. But he was hoping that the League of Nations—a potent League with America as a leader—would iron out the inequities.

The Treaty of Versailles, hammered out in a madhouse of clashing ambitions, was clearly vulnerable to criticism. One of its chief weaknesses was that it fell between two stools. It tried to establish a lasting peace, while at the same time punishing the fallen foe. It was too harsh for a peace of accommodation, and too "soft"—thanks in part to Wilson—for a peace of vengeance. The victor may have peace, and he may have vengeance, but he can hardly hope to get both from the same treaty.

Yet the richly condemned Peace of Versailles had much to commend it. Not the least among its merits was its liberation of millions of minority peoples, such as the Poles, from the yoke of an alien dynasty. All the chaotic circumstances considered, the marvel is that any kind of an acceptable pact was signed.

Much—almost everything—depended on the good faith of the men and nations that carried out the treaty. If they had acted in the spirit intended, the results might well have been less tragic. Disappointing though Wilson's handiwork was, he saved the pact from being an old-time peace of imperialism. His critics to the contrary, the settlement was almost certainly a fairer one because he had gone to Paris.

The Domestic Parade of Prejudice

At home in America, breakers loomed. Wilson returned, early in July 1919, in an uncompromising mood; privately he vowed that he would give no

*In due time the Japanese illegally fortified these islands—the Marshalls, Marianas, and Carolines—and used them as bases against the United States in World War II.

"Pilgrim Landing in America, 1919." (Harding in the Brooklyn *Eagle*, 1919.)

"nosegays" to the senators whom he scorned. But the nation's temper had been changing while the wheels of the Peace Conference were grinding. The people had been emotionally aroused to march on to Berlin and hang the Kaiser—or perhaps boil him in oil. Wilson had brought a deep feeling of frustration by negotiating a cease-fire before fiery patriots could enjoy their fun. Colonel Theodore Roosevelt, still full of fight at the time of the Armistice, had bitterly condemned all the "peace twaddle."

Victory also brought an emotional letdown and economic readjustments. The citizenry, keyed up overlong to a spirit of self-sacrifice, were suffering the inevitable "slump in idealism." It was deepened by a feeling of disillusionment that was reflected in the slogan, "No More Parades." The world was not "safe for democracy," and just after the costly "war to end war" there were some twenty wars of varying dimensions raging all over the world. America had asked for nothing at the Paris Conference except peace. Instead of that, she was getting nothing but ingratitude from the Allies whom she had strained herself to help—while of course defeating a common enemy.

Disillusion kept pace with demobilization. Jobless "Yanks," pouring back by the hundreds of thousands, added to the national discontent. Sailing to France convinced that the French had wings and the Germans horns, they had been repelled by the ever-present manure piles and the "gouging" of French shopkeepers. The Germans of the Rhineland—especially the blonde girls—seemed so much cleaner and nicer than the French. Perhaps, some of the "doughboys" thought, America had fought the wrong foe. Prolonged delays in getting back to "God's country" had likewise bred nasty tempers among American soldiers. Common complaints were "Let Europe stew in her own juice" and "Lafayette, we are still here." A popular song ran:

> We drove the Boche [Hun] across the Rhine,
> The Kaiser from his throne.
> Oh, Lafayette, we've paid our debt,
> For Christ's sake, send us home.

Super-patriots in America, with their strong isolationist convictions, raised a furious outcry against entanglement. Revering the memory of Washington, Jefferson, and Monroe, they were hostile to a newfangled "League of Notions." Why fly the glorious Stars and Stripes below the flag of some internationalized super-state? One rhymester wrote sneeringly to the tune of "My Country 'Tis of Thee":

> Our foreign countries, thee,
> Lands of the chimpanzee,
> Thy names we love. . . .

The Treaty of Versailles, one of the least perused and most abused in history, was showered with brickbats from all sides. Rabid Hun-haters, regarding the pact as not harsh enough, voiced their discontent. Professional liberals, like the editors of the New York *Nation,* thought it too harsh—and a gross betrayal to boot. German-Americans, Italian-Americans, and other "hyphenated" Americans were aroused because the peace settlement was not sufficiently favorable to their native lands.

Irish-Americans, traditional twisters of the British Lion's tail, denounced the League. They felt that with the additional votes of the five Dominions it gave Britain undue influence; and they feared that it could be used to force the United States to crush any rising for Irish independence. Crowds of Irish-American zealots hissed and booed Wilson's name.

Wilson's Tour and Collapse (1919)

Despite mounting discontent, the President had reason to feel optimistic. When he brought home the treaty, with the "Wilson League" firmly riveted in as Part I, a strong majority of the people still seemed favorable. At this time—early July 1919—Senator Lodge had no real hope of defeating the pact. His strategy was merely to amend it in such a way as to "Americanize," "Republicanize," or "senatorialize" it. The Republicans could then claim political credit for the changes.

One potent weapon that Lodge could wield was delay, for delay would confuse and divide public opinion. As chairman of the powerful Senate Committee on Foreign Relations, he read the entire 264-page treaty aloud, even though it had been printed. At one time only the senator and a clerk occupied the committee room. Protracted hearings were also held by the committee, and dozens of people of various nationalities aired their grievances.

"Going to Talk to the Boss." (Chicago *News*, 1919.)

The treaty was in danger of being drowned in a sea of words.

Wilson fretted increasingly as the hot summer of 1919 wore on. The bulky pact was bogged down in the Senate, while the nation was drifting into confusion and apathy. He therefore decided to go to the country in a spectacular speechmaking tour. He would appeal over the heads of the Senate to the sovereign people—as he often had in the past.

This strenuous barnstorming campaign was undertaken in the face of protests by physicians and friends. Wilson had never been robust; he had entered the White House nearly seven years before with a stomach pump and with headache pills for his neuritis. His frail body had begun to sag under the strain of partisan strife, a global war, and a hectic peace conference. But he declared that he was willing to die, like the "doughboys" whom he had sent into battle, for the sake of the new world order.

The presidential tour, begun in September 1919, got off to a rather lame start. The Middle West received Wilson lukewarmly, partly because of strong German-American influence. Trailing after him like bloodhounds came two "irreconcilable" senators, Borah and Johnson, who used their stump-speaking talents in the same cities a few days later. Hat-tossing crowds responded to the attacks on Wilson by crying, "Impeach him, impeach him!"

But the reception was different in the Rocky Mountain region and on the Pacific Coast. These areas, which had elected Wilson in 1916, welcomed him with heartwarming outbursts. The high point—and the breaking point—of the return trip was at Pueblo, Colorado, September 25, 1919. Wilson, with tears coursing down his cheeks, pleaded for the League of Nations as the only real hope of preventing future wars. That night he collapsed from physical and nervous exhaustion.

Wilson was whisked back in the "funeral train" to Washington, where several days later a stroke paralyzed one side of his body. During the next few weeks he lay in a darkened room in the White House, as much a victim of the war as the un-

Wilson and His Advisers, c. 1920. After his stroke in 1919, the sickly Wilson met only occasionally with his Cabinet. (The Bettmann Archive.)

known soldier buried at Arlington. For seven and one-half months he did not meet his Cabinet. Who really ran the government is still something of a mystery, although at times Mrs. Wilson sifted the few papers that were brought to his attention—"boudoir government." As the tragedy unfolded, second-guessers pointed out that Wilson should never have left Washington. Instead, they argued, he should have tried to work out a compromise with the headstrong senators, difficult though that course might have been.

Wilson Rejects the Lodge-Reserved Treaty

Senator Lodge, coldly calculating, was now at the helm. After failing to amend the treaty outright, he finally came up with fourteen formal reservations to it—a sardonic slap at Wilson's Fourteen Points. These safeguards reserved the rights of the United States under the Monroe Doctrine and the Constitution, and otherwise sought to protect American sovereignty. Senator Lodge and other critics were especially alarmed by Article X of the League because it *morally* bound the United States to aid any member victimized by external aggression. A jealous Congress wanted to reserve to itself the constitutional war-declaring power. But in general the Lodge reservations merely restated the obvious. If the treaty had been approved with them attached, they probably would have been largely forgotten, as so often happens with reservations.

But Wilson, hating Lodge, saw red at the mere suggestion of the *Lodge* reservations. He was quite willing to accept somewhat similar reservations sponsored by his faithful Democratic followers, but he insisted that the Lodge reservations "emasculated" the entire pact. The truth is that ten of them applied to the League, and only four rather harmlessly to the main body of the treaty.

Public sentiment had meanwhile been shifting. By late November 1919—two months after Wilson's collapse—popular opinion apparently favored some kind of reservations, whether of the Democratic or of the Lodge stripe. But Wilson, lying in his secluded and darkened sickroom, still had faith that he could get the treaty accepted without reservations. His bedside attendants, fearful of shocking him into a relapse, dared not tell him the disagreeable truth.

Though too feeble to lead, Wilson was still strong enough to obstruct. When the day finally came for the voting in the Senate, he sent word to all true Democrats to vote *against* the treaty with the odious Lodge reservations attached. He hoped that when these were cleared away, the path would be open for ratification without reservations, or with only mild Democratic reservations.

Loyal Democrats in the Senate, on November 19, 1919, blindly did Wilson's bidding. Combining with the "irreconcilables," mostly Republicans, they rejected the treaty with the Lodge reservations appended, 55 to 39. Then the Democrats tried to ram through the pact without any reservations, but mustered only 38 votes to 53. The irreconcilable "Battalion of Death," delighted with the turn of events, had now joined hands with the regular Republicans.

Defeat Through the Lodge-Wilson Deadlock

The nation was too deeply shocked to accept the verdict as final. About four-fifths of the senators professed to favor the treaty, with or without reservations, yet a simple majority could not agree on a single proposition. So strong was public indignation that the Senate was forced to act a second time. In March 1920, the treaty was brought up again, with the Lodge reservations tacked on.

There was only one possible path to success. Unless the Senate approved the pact with the Lodge reservations, the entire document would be rejected. But the sickly Wilson, still sheltered behind drawn curtains and blind to disagreeable realities, again sent word to all loyal Democrats to vote down the treaty with the obnoxious Lodge reservations. When he signed this letter, he signed the death warrant of the treaty as far as America was concerned.

This time the count was closer. A total of twenty-one realistic Democrats, seeing that the choice was now the reserved pact or none at all, joined forces with the Lodge Republicans. A total of twenty-three loyal Democrats sided with the "Battalion of Death" to cast negative votes. On a fateful March 19, 1920, the treaty netted a simple majority but failed of the necessary two-thirds majority by a count of 49 yeas to 35 nays.

Who defeated the treaty? The Lodge-Wilson personal feud, traditionalism, isolationism, Southern sectionalism, disillusionment, and partisanship all entered the confused picture. Lodge maneuvered astutely to prevent another rupture in the party ranks like the Taft-Roosevelt rift of 1912. But Wilson himself must bear a substantial share of the responsibility. As stubborn as when fighting Dean West at Princeton over the graduate school, he refused to accept a half-loaf. He asked for all or nothing—and got nothing. One Democratic senator angrily charged that the President had strangled his own brainchild with his own palsied hands

Senator Hitchcock, the Democratic leader, later told of one of his brief visits to Wilson and his suggestion of compromise with Lodge.

"'Let Lodge compromise,' he replied.

'Well, of course,' I added, 'he must compromise also, but we might well hold out the olive branch.'

'Let Lodge hold out the olive branch,' he retorted, and that ended it for that day, for he was too sick a man to argue with in the presence of his anxious doctor and his more anxious wife.'"

rather than let the Senate straighten its crooked limbs. Isolationist Republicans jeeringly rewrote the 1916 slogan to read: "He Kept Us Out of Peace." One cynic said that Wilson was left "without a League to stand on."

Preparing the "Solemn Referendum" of 1920

Wilson had his own pet solution for the deadlock, and this partly explains why he refused to compromise on Lodge's terms. He proposed to settle the treaty issue in the forthcoming presidential campaign of 1920 by appealing to the people—the old appeal habit again—for a "solemn referendum." This was sheer folly, for a true mandate on the League in the noisy arena of politics was a clear impossibility.

Republican delegates were jubilant when they met in Chicago in June 1920. Wilson was broken and discredited; the wayward Bull Moosers had wandered back into camp. The Old Guard, spearheaded by the Senate clique, was back in the saddle. Again the saying was current, as in 1896, that all the Republicans had to do was nominate a rag baby or a yellow dog. The platform that the party bosses devised was a masterpiece of ambiguity—a teeter-totter rather than a platform. It appealed to Republicans who favored the League, like ex-President Taft, and to Republicans who derided it, like Senators Borah and Johnson.

The political woods were full of presidential hopefuls. Colorful General Leonard Wood, whom Wilson had snubbed during the war, was the front-running candidate for the nomination. He was opposed, among others, by Senator Johnson of California, who had gained much notoriety by his unbridled assaults on the League.

As the leading contestants killed one another off, the political weather vane began to veer toward genial Senator Warren G. Harding of Ohio. A group of Senate bosses, meeting rather casually in the historic "smoke-filled" Room 404 of the Hotel Blackstone, informally decided on the affable and malleable Ohioan. Their fair-haired boy was a prosperous, back-slapping, small-town newspaper editor of the "folksy" type, quite the opposite of Wilson, who had earlier noted the senator's "disturbingly dull" mind. Harding had further increased his acceptability by urging a return to "normalcy"—something that the country ardently desired. Despite grave doubts as to his mentality and morality, certain cigar-chomping bosses helped to engineer his nomination.

When it came to the vice-presidency, the perspiring delegates rebelled against domination by the party wheelhorses. Taking the bit in their teeth, they nominated a frugal, grim-faced native of Vermont, Governor Calvin ("Silent Cal") Coolidge of Massachusetts. He had commended himself to the conservative delegates by his recent role, much overrated, in breaking a policemen's strike in Boston.

The Democrats, for the first time in the history of presidential conventions, met in breeze-swept San Francisco. Wilson, ill though he was, secretly angled for a third nomination. But all such maneuvers fell flat. His son-in-law, lanky "Crown Prince" McAdoo, was a leading contender who suffered from the increasing public distaste for both Wilson and his in-laws. At length the convention turned to a wealthy Ohio newspaper editor, the earnest and energetic Governor James M. Cox. The platform came out strongly for the League of Nations, as did the nominee. The vice-presidential nomination went to young Franklin D. Roosevelt, a tall, handsome, vibrant, thirty-eight-year-old New Yorker who had gained some fame as assistant secretary of the navy.

> Shortly after the Boston police strike was actually broken despite his own apathy, Coolidge sent a ringing telegram to Samuel Gompers, president of the American Federation of Labor: "There is no right to strike against the public safety by anybody, anywhere, any time."

The Solemn Muddlement of 1920

As campaigns go, this one was rather listless, for the threadbare League issue had been under constant debate for over a year. The Socialist New York *Call* thought that the League of Nations was as "vital as a dead cat in a gutter." A confused Harding, initially kept on his front porch by the party bosses, made a number of contradictory statements about the League. His most consistent theme was that if elected he would work for a vague Association of Nations—*a* league but not *the* League.

Harding's following was badly divided. A group of thirty-one celebrities, mostly Republicans and including Hoover, Root, and Hughes, signed a statement declaring that the election of Harding was the surest way to get America into a reserved League. Bitter-end isolationists like Borah and Johnson insisted, on the contrary, that his election was the surest way to keep out. Republican slogans were "Let's Have Done with Wiggle and Wobble" and "Back to Normalcy."

When the sloganeering and the shouting ended, Harding was swept into the presidency by a tremendous tidal wave of ballots. The long-frustrated females, given the vote several months earlier by the 19th Amendment, swelled the totals with woman power. Harding polled 16,152,200 votes to 9,147,353 for Cox, thus amassing a prodigious plurality of 7,004,847. The electoral count was 404 to 127. Eugene V. Debs, federal prisoner No. 9653 at

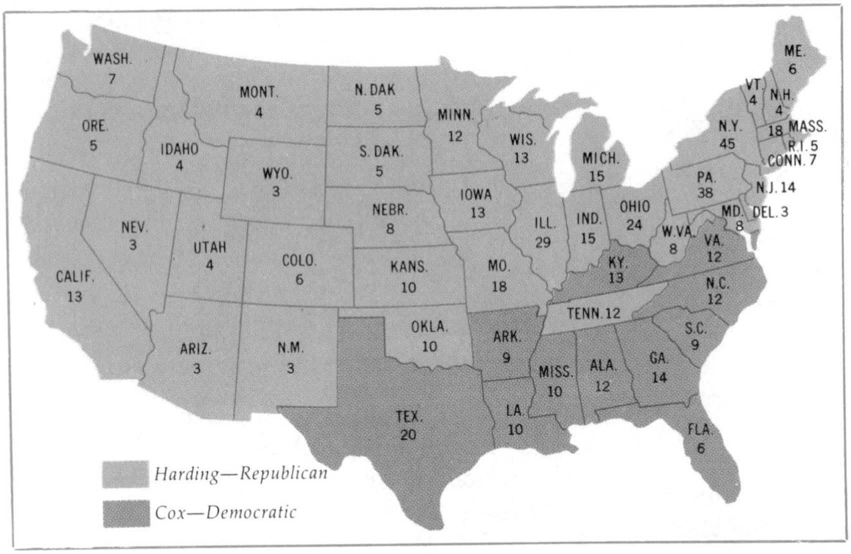

PRESIDENTIAL ELECTION OF 1920 (with electoral vote by state) Cox rashly claimed that "traitors" would vote Republican. But Harding and Coolidge ran successfully as small-town boys who had made good. Harding celebrated his 55th birthday on election day, and the voters presented him with the largest victory margin to date in an American presidential election.

the Atlanta Penitentiary, rolled up the largest vote for the Socialist party in its history—919,799. Much of this left-wing support was doubtless a protest against the ineffective, second-rate Cox and the befuddled, stuffed-shirt Harding. "Thank God only one of them can be elected" was a cynical saying.

Was Harding's smashing victory a popular mandate against the League of Nations? The isolationist Republican wing gloatingly insisted that Wilson had asked for a "solemn referendum"—and now he had it. But there were so many issues that the outcome could not be a clear endorsement of any one proposal. If the electorate had been asked to vote on the League with reservations, they probably would have approved it. But they were never given such an opportunity.

Yet the election of 1920 had deeper meanings. The pendulum had swung back, and the Republicans, normally the majority since the Civil War, were returned to power. A crippled ghost candidate named Wilson, rather than an energetic Cox, had been running. Public desire for a change found vent in a resounding repudiation of "high and mighty" Wilsonism; in fact, "Down with Wilson" was a common slogan of the period. People were tired of professional highbrowism, star-reaching idealism, bothersome do-goodism, moral overstrain, and constant self-sacrifice. Eager to lapse back into "normalcy," they were willing to accept a second-rate President—and they got a third-rate one. It was election "by disgust," with "General Grouch" the winner.

Harding's election, combined with Wilson's rejection, pronounced the death sentence of the League in America. Republican isolationists continued to insist that the election returns were a sweeping mandate against this "super-state," and politicians increasingly shunned the League as they would have shunned a leper. To them the "solemn referendum" looked like a deliberate recall. There is simply no arguing with a suffocating plurality of 7 million votes.

A living legend, Wilson died three years later, with admirers kneeling in the snow outside his

"He Did It!" (Copyright Los Angeles *Times.* Reprinted by permission.)

Washington home. One unsparing critic, the newspaperman William Allen White, wrote:

> God gave him a great vision.
> The devil gave him an imperious heart.
> The proud heart is still.
> The vision lives.

The Betrayal of Great Expectations

America's spurning of the League was tragically short-sighted. The Republic had helped to win a costly war, but it blindly kicked the fruits of victory under the table. Whether a strong international organization would have averted World War II in 1939 will always be a matter of dispute. But there can be no doubt that the orphaned League of Nations was undercut at the start by the refusal of the mightiest power on the globe to join it. The Allies themselves were largely to blame for the new world conflagration that flared up in 1939, but they found a convenient justification for their own timorous shortcomings by pointing an accusing finger at Uncle Sam.

The ultimate collapse of the Treaty of Versailles must be laid, at least in some degree, at America's doorstep. This complicated pact, tied in with the four other peace treaties through the League Covenant, was a top-heavy structure designed to rest on a four-legged table. The fourth leg, the United States, was never put into place. This rickety structure teetered crazily for over a decade, and then crashed in ruins—a debacle which played into the hands of the German demagogue Adolf Hitler.

America lost moral face by her preach-and-run policy. She claimed advantages and opportunities without duties or responsibilities; she wanted peace—without having to pay for it. Her desertion of her war partners, even granting their imperialistic aims, marked the first serious breach in the ranks of the Allies. This fatal secession indirectly facilitated the ascent of Hitler and his brown-shirted bullies.

The Reparations Commission is a case in point. It had been created under the Treaty of Versailles with the understanding that America would exercise an important moderating influence. When she abdicated, the French secured a dominant voice. The result was an astronomical, trouble-breeding reparations bill of some $32 billion, presented to the Germans virtually at pistol point. Although most of it was never paid, it contributed richly to the continuing economic chaos in Germany and elsewhere in Europe. These dangerous dislocations in turn were fuel for the propaganda machine that would promote the rise of Adolf Hitler, a misbegotten child of the Treaty of Versailles.

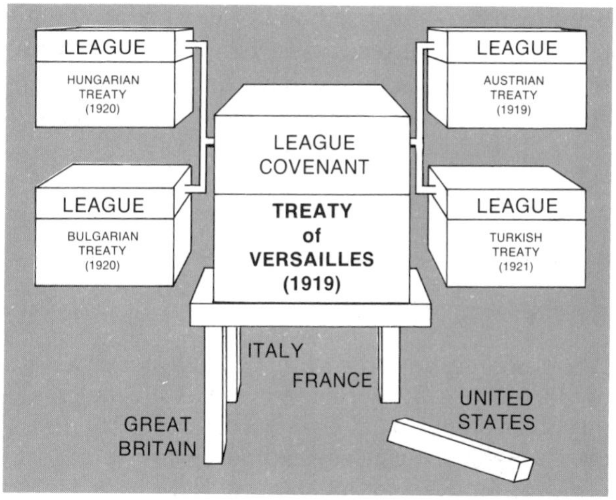

INTERLOCKING TREATY STRUCTURE

No less ominous events were set in motion when the Senate spurned the Security Treaty with France. The French, fearing that a new generation of Germans would follow in their fathers' goose-steps, undertook to build up a powerful military force. Predictably resenting the presence of strong French armies, Germany began to rearm illegally. This witches' cauldron of uncertainty and suspicion brewed an intoxicant which helped inflame the fanatical following of dictator Hitler.

The United States, as the tragic sequel proved, hurt its own cause when it buried its head in the sands. Granted that the conduct of its Allies had been disillusioning, it had its own ends to serve by carrying through the Wilsonian program. It would have been well advised if it had resolutely assumed its war-born responsibilities, and had resolutely played the role of global leader into which it had been thrust by the iron hand of destiny. In the interests of its own security, if for no better reason, the United States should have used its enormous strength to shape world-shaking events. Instead, it permitted itself to drift along aimlessly and dangerously toward the abyss of a second and even more bloody international disaster.

VARYING VIEWPOINTS

Was Woodrow Wilson a starry-eyed idealist or a hard-nosed realist? For more than half a century, this question has hung over discussions of the President's wartime diplomacy and peacemaking, especially his proposal for a League of Nations. Wilson's detractors charge that the American leader naively tried to impose his own high-minded legal and moral concepts on international affairs, which often do not operate according to the rules of law and morality. Some "New Left" writers have claimed that Wilson's diplomacy revealed an objectionable purpose of another kind: a thrust to open the world to American economic penetration.

Wilson's defenders usually emphasize that his lofty principles were tempered by pragmatism. They stress the give-and-take character of some of his proposals, such as mandates for former colonial territories. Apologists also point out that the League did embody the modern, and presumably "realistic," concept of "collective security." Recently, writers such as Arno Mayer and N. Gordon Levin, Jr., have attempted to rehabilitate Wilson. They credit him with an immensely sophisticated grasp of the way certain "ideals," such as free trade, reduced armaments, and political stability, would benefit both the world and the profit margins of American businessmen. To them Wilson now appears to be a far-seeing visionary who perceived the compatibility of his high principles with this country's own material interests.

SELECT READINGS

The problems are treated sketchily in A. S. Link, *Woodrow Wilson: Revolution, War, and Peace* (1979); they are discussed in detail in T. A. Bailey, *Woodrow Wilson and the Lost Peace* (1944) and *Woodrow Wilson and the Great Betrayal* (1945). Herbert Hoover, *The Ordeal of Woodrow Wilson* (1958), is a somewhat personalized account which is also revealing of ex-President Hoover. Detailed studies are Paul Birdsall, *Versailles Twenty Years After* (1941), Ferdinand Czernin, *Versailles, 1919* (1964), Harold Nicolson, *Peacemaking, 1919* (1933), S. P. Tillman, *Anglo-American Relations at the Paris Peace Conference of 1919* (1961), Inga Floto, *Colonel House in Paris: A Study of American Policy at the Paris Peace Conference 1919* (1973), L. E. Gelfand, *The Inquiry: American Preparations for Peace, 1917–1919* (1963), R. N. Stromberg, *Collective Security and American Foreign Policy* (1963), N. Gordon Levin, Jr., *Woodrow Wilson and World Politics* (1968), A. J. Mayer, *Political Origins of the New Diplomacy* (1959), and the same author's *Politics and Diplomacy of Peacemaking* (1967). Consult also Arthur Walworth, *America's Moment: 1918* (1977), and Michael J. Hogan, *Informal Entente: The Private Structure of Co-operation in Anglo-American Economic Diplomacy, 1918–1928* (1977). Lodge is somewhat rehabilitated in J. A. Garraty, *Henry Cabot Lodge* (1953), and especially in W. C. Widenor, *Henry Cabot Lodge and the Search for an American Foreign Policy* (1980). Useful monographs are Ralph A. Stone, *The Irreconcilables: The Fight Against the League of Nations* (1970), and W. M. Bagby, *The Road to Normalcy: The Presidential Campaign and Election of 1920* (1962).

38

American Life in the "Roaring Twenties"

America's present need is not heroics but healing; not nostrums but normalcy; not revolution but restoration; . . . not surgery but serenity.

WARREN G. HARDING, 1920

Insulating America from the Radical Virus

Bloodied by the war and disillusioned by the peace, Americans turned inward in the 1920s. Shunning diplomatic commitments to foreign countries, they also denounced "radical" foreign ideas, condemned "un-American" life-styles, and clanged shut the immigration gates against foreign peoples. They partly sealed off the domestic economy from the rest of the world, and plunged headlong into a dizzying decade of home-grown prosperity.

Hysterical fears of Red Russia continued to color American thinking for several years after the Bolshevik revolution of 1917, which spawned a tiny Communist party in America. Tensions were heightened by an epidemic of strikes that convulsed the Republic at war's end, many of them the result of high prices and frustrated union-organizing drives. Upstanding Americans jumped to the conclusion that labor troubles were fomented by bomb-and-whisker Bolsheviks. A general strike in Seattle in 1919, though modest in its demands and orderly in its methods, prompted a call from the mayor for federal troops, to head off "the anarchy of Russia." Fire-and-brimstone evangelist "Billy" Sunday struck a responsive chord when he described a Bolshevik as "a guy with a face like a porcupine and a breath that would scare a pole cat. . . . If I had my way, I'd fill the jails so full of them that their feet would stick out the window."

The "Big Red Scare" of 1919–1920 resulted in a nationwide crusade against left-wingers whose Americanism was suspect. Attorney General A. Mitchell Palmer, who perhaps "saw Red" too easily, earned the title of "the Fighting Quaker" by his excess of zeal in rounding up suspects. They ultimately totaled about 6,000. This drive to root out radicals was redoubled in June 1919, when a bomb shattered both the nerves and the Washington home of Palmer. "The Fighting Quaker" was thereupon dubbed "the Quaking Fighter."

Other events highlighted the Red Scare. Late in December 1919, a shipload of 249 alleged alien radicals was deported on the *Buford* ("Soviet Ark") to the "workers' paradise" of Russia. One zealot cried, "My motto for the Reds is S.O.S.–ship or shoot." Hysteria was temporarily revived in September 1920, when a still-unexplained bomb blast in Wall Street killed thirty-eight persons and wounded several hundred others.

Various states joined the pack in the outcry against radicals. In 1919–1920 a number of legislatures, reflecting the anxiety of "solid" citizens, passed criminal syndicalism laws. These anti-Red statutes, some of which were born of the war, made unlawful the mere *advocacy* of violence to secure social change. Critics protested that mere words were not criminal deeds, that there was a great gulf between throwing fits and throwing bombs, and that "free screech" was for the nasty as well as the nice. Violence was done to traditional American concepts of free speech as I.W.W.s and other radicals were vigorously prosecuted. The hysteria went so far that in 1920 five members of the New York legislature, all lawfully elected, were denied their seats simply because they were Socialists.

The Red Scare was a godsend to conservative businessmen, who used it to break the backs of the fledgling unions. Labor's call for the "closed," or all-union, shop was denounced as "Sovietism in disguise." Employers, in turn, hailed their own antiunion campaign for the "open" shop as "the American Plan."

Anti-Redism and anti-foreignism were reflected in a notorious case regarded by liberals as a "judicial lynching." Nicola Sacco, a shoe-factory worker, and Bartolomeo Vanzetti, a fish peddler, were convicted in 1921 of the murder of a Massachusetts paymaster and his guard. The jury and judge were probably prejudiced in some degree against the defendants because they were Italians, atheists, anarchists, and draft dodgers.

Liberals and radicals the world over rallied to the defense of the two aliens doomed to die. The

Bolsheviks Hide under the Stars and Stripes.
(Philadelphia *Inquirer*, 1919.)

> An author-soldier (Guy Empey) applauded the "deportation delirium" when he wrote: "I believe we should place them [the Reds] all on a ship of stone, with sails of lead, and that their first stopping place should be hell."

case dragged on for six years until 1927, when the condemned men were electrocuted. Communists and other radicals were thus presented with two martyrs in the "class struggle," while many American liberals hung their heads. The evidence against the accused, though damaging, betrayed serious weaknesses. If the trial had been held in an atmosphere less surcharged with anti-Redism, the outcome might well have been only a prison term.

Hooded Hoodlums of the KKK

A new Ku Klux Klan, spawned by the post-war reaction, mushroomed fearsomely in the early 1920s. Despite the familiar sheets and hoods, it more closely resembled the anti-foreign "nativist" movements of the 1850s than the anti-black night riders of the 1860s. It was anti-foreign, anti-Catholic, anti-black, anti-Jewish, anti-pacifist, anti-Communist, anti-internationalist, anti-evolutionist, anti-bootlegger, anti-gambling, anti-adultery, and anti–birth control. It was also pro–Anglo Saxon, pro–"native" American, and pro-Protestant. In short, the besheeted Klan betokened an extremist, ultra-conservative uprising against many of the forces of diversity and modernity that were transforming American culture.

As reconstituted, the Klan spread with astonishing rapidity, especially in the Middle West and the "Bible Belt" South. At its peak in the mid-1920s, it enrolled about 5 million dues-paying members and wielded potent political influence. It capitalized on the typically American love of excitement, adventure, and joining, to say nothing of the adolescent love for secret ritual. "Knights of the Invisible Empire" included among their

KKK Parade of 40,000 Men in Washington, 1925. (United Press International photo.)

officials Imperial Wizards, Grand Goblins, King Kleagles, and other horrendous "kreatures." The most impressive displays were "konclaves" and huge flag-waving parades. The chief warning was the burning of the fiery cross. The principal weapon was the lash, supplemented by tar and feathers. Rallying songs were "The Fiery Cross on High," "One Hundred Percent American," and "The Ku Klux Klan and the Pope" (against kissing the Pope's toe). One brutal slogan was, "Kill the Kikes, Koons, and Katholics."

This reign of hooded horror, so repulsive to the best American ideals, collapsed rather suddenly in the late 1920s. Decent people at last recoiled from the orgy of ribboned flesh and terrorism, while scandalous embezzling by Klan officials launched a congressional investigation. The bubble was punctured when the movement was exposed, not as a crusade, but as a vicious racket based on a ten-dollar initiation fee. At bottom, the KKK was an alarming manifestation of the intol-

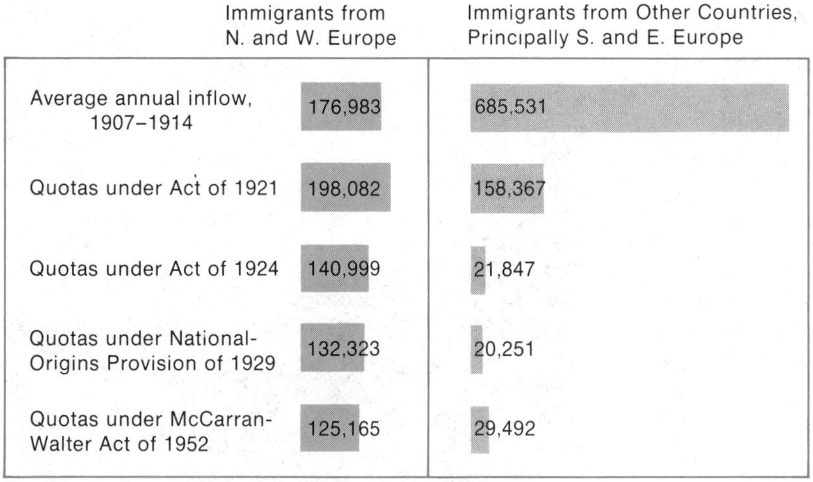

Immigrants from
N. and W. Europe
Immigrants from Other Countries,
Principally S. and E. Europe
Average annual inflow,
1907–1914
176,983
685,531
Quotas under Act of 1921
198,082
158,367
Quotas under Act of 1924
140,999
21,847
Quotas under National-
Origins Provision of 1929
132,323
20,251
Quotas under McCarran-
Walter Act of 1952
125,165
29,492

ANNUAL IMMIGRATION AND THE QUOTA LAWS

erance and prejudice so common in the anxiety-plagued minds of the 1920s. America needed no such cowardly apostles, whose white sheets concealed dark purposes.

Stemming the Foreign Flood

Isolationist America of the 1920s, ingrown and provincial, had little use for the immigrants who began to flood into the country again as peace settled soothingly on the war-torn world. Some 800,000 stepped ashore in 1920–21, about two-thirds of them from southern and eastern Europe. "One-hundred-percent Americans," gagging at the sight of this resumed "new immigration," cried that the famed poem at the base of the Statue of Liberty was all too literally true: they claimed that a sickly Europe was indeed vomiting on America "the wretched refuse of its teeming shore."

Congress temporarily plugged the breach with the Emergency Quota Act of 1921. Newcomers from Europe were restricted in any given year to a definite quota, which was set at 3 percent of the persons of their nationality who had been living in the United States in 1910. This national-origins system was relatively favorable to the immigrants from Southern and Eastern Europe, for by 1910 immense numbers of them had already arrived.

This stopgap legislation of 1921 was replaced, after more mature reflection, by the Immigration Act of 1924. Quotas for foreigners were cut from 3 percent to 2 percent. The national-origins base was shifted from the census of 1910 to that of 1890,

The Only Way To Handle It. (Library of Congress.)

"Two-Faced Uncle Sam." After the face-slapping Immigration Act of 1924, the Japanese regarded Uncle Sam as a fiend wearing the mask of a gentleman. (Tokyo *Miyako,* 1924.)

> A recognized expert on American immigration, Henry P. Fairchild, wrote in 1926, "The typical immigrant of the present does not really live in America at all, but, from the point of view of nationality, in Italy, Poland, Czecho-Slovakia, or some other foreign country."

when comparatively few South Europeans had arrived.* Great Britain and Northern Ireland, for example, could send 65,721 a year as against 5,802 for Italy. South Europeans bitterly condemned the device as unfair and discriminatory—a triumph for the "nativist" belief that blue-eyed and fair-haired North Europeans were of better blood. The purpose was clearly to freeze America's existing racial composition, which was largely North European. A flagrantly discriminatory section of the Immigration Act of 1924 slammed the door absolutely against Japanese immigrants. Mass "Hate America" rallies erupted in Japan, and one Japanese superpatriot expressed his outrage by committing suicide near the American Embassy in Tokyo. Exempt from the quota system were Canadians and Latin Americans.

The quota system effected an epochal departure in American practice. It recognized that the nation was filling up and that a "No Vacancy" sign was needed. Immigration henceforth died down to a comparative trickle; the famed melting pot henceforth would operate primarily on the foreigners already present. By 1931, probably for the first time in American experience, more foreigners left than arrived. Quotas thus caused America to sacrifice something of her tradition of freedom and opportunity, as well as much of her color and variety.

The Prohibition "Experiment"

One of the last peculiar spasms of the progressive reform movement was prohibition, loudly supported by crusading churches and by women. The arid new order was authorized in 1919 by the 18th Amendment (see the *Constitution*, p. xvii, at the end of the book), as implemented by the Volstead Act passed by Congress later that year. Together these laws made the world "safe for hypocrisy."

The legal abolition of alcohol was fairly popular in the Middle West, and especially so in the South. Southern whites were eager to keep stimulants out of the hands of the blacks, lest they burst out of "their place." But despite the overwhelming ratification of the "dry" amendment, strong opposition persisted in the larger Eastern cities. Concentrated colonies of "wet" foreign-born peoples hated to abandon their Old World drinking habits. Yet most Americans assumed that prohibition had come to stay. Everywhere there were last wild flings, as the nation prepared to enter upon a permanent "alcoholiday."

But prohibitionists were naive in the extreme. They overlooked the tenacious American tradition of strong drink and of weak control by the central government, especially over private lives. They

*Five years later the Act of 1929, using 1920 as the quota base, virtually cut immigration in half by limiting the total to 152,574 a year. In 1965 Congress abolished the national-origins quota system.

forgot that the federal authorities had never satisfactorily enforced a law where the majority of the people—or a strong minority—were hostile to it. They ignored the fact that one cannot make a crime overnight out of something that millions of people have never regarded as a crime. Law makers could not legislate away a thirst.

Peculiar conditions hampered the enforcement of prohibition. Profound disillusionment over the aftermath of the war raised serious questions as to the wisdom of further self-denial. Slaking thirst became a cherished personal liberty, and many ardent wets believed that the way to bring about repeal was to violate the law on a large enough scale. Hypocritical, hip-flasked legislators spoke or voted dry while privately drinking wet. ("Let us strike a blow for liberty" was an ironic toast.) Frustrated soldiers, returning from France, complained that prohibition had been "put over" on them while they were "over there." Grimy workingmen bemoaned the loss of their cheap beer, while pointing out that the idle rich could buy all the illicit alcohol they wanted. Flaming youth of the Jazz Age thought it "smart" to swill bootleg liquor—"liquid tonsillectomies." Millions of older citizens likewise found forbidden fruit fascinating, especially when they engaged in "bar hunts."

Prohibition might have started off on a better foot if there had been a larger army of enforcement officials. But the state and federal agencies were understaffed, and their snoopers, susceptible to bribery, were underpaid. The public was increasingly distressed as scores of persons, including innocent bystanders, were killed by quick-triggered dry agents.

Prohibition simply did not prohibit. The old-time "men only" corner saloons were replaced by thousands of "speakeasies," each with its tiny grilled window through which the thirsty spoke softly before the barred door was opened. Hard liquor, especially the cocktail, was drunk in staggering volume by both sexes. Largely because of the difficulties of transporting and concealing bottles, beverages of high alcoholic content were popular. Foreign rumrunners, often from the West Indies,

Federal Agents Destroy Booze in Brooklyn.
(The Bettmann Archive, Inc.)

had their inning, and countless cases of liquor leaked down from Canada. The zeal of American prohibition agents on occasion strained diplomatic relations with Uncle Sam's northern neighbor.

"Home brew" and "bathtub gin" became popular, as law-evading adults engaged in "alky cooking" with toy stills. The worst of the homemade "rotgut" produced blindness, even death. The affable bootlegger worked in silent partnership with the friendly undertaker.

Yet the "noble experiment" was not entirely a failure. Bank savings increased, and absenteeism in industry decreased, presumably because of the newly sober ways of formerly soused bar-flies. On the whole, probably less liquor was consumed than in the days before prohibition, though strong drink continued to be available. As the legendary tippler remarked, prohibition was "a darn sight better than no liquor at all."

The Golden Age of Gangsterism

Prohibition spawned shocking crimes. The lush profits of illegal alcohol led to bribery of the police, many of whom were induced to see and smell no evil. Violent gang wars broke out in the big cities between rivals seeking to corner the rich market in booze. Rival triggermen used their sawed-off shotguns and chattering "typewriters" (machine guns) to "erase" bootlegging competitors who were trying to "muscle in" on their "racket." In the gang wars of the 1920s in Chicago, about 500 low characters were murdered. Arrests were few and convictions were even fewer, as the button-lipped gangsters "covered" for one another with the underworld's code of silence.

Chicago was by far the most spectacular example of lawlessness. In 1925 "Scarface" Al Capone, a grasping and murderous booze distributor, began six years of gang warfare which netted him millions of blood-spattered dollars. He zoomed through the streets in an armor-plated car with bulletproof windows. A Brooklyn newspaper quipped:

> And the pistols' red glare,
> Bombs bursting in air
> Give proof through the night
> That Chicago's still there.

Capone, though branded "Public Enemy Number One," could not be convicted of the cold-blooded massacre, on St. Valentine's Day in 1929, of seven disarmed members of a rival gang. But after serving most of an eleven-year sentence in a federal penitentiary for income-tax evasion, he was released as a syphilitic wreck.

"The King Still Reigns," 1930. Gangster Al Capone, headquartered in Chicago, was reported as saying: "Everybody calls me a racketeer. I call myself a business man. When I sell liquor, it's bootlegging. When my patrons serve it on a silver tray on Lake Shore Drive, it's hospitality." (Courtesy of Baltimore *Sun*.)

Gangsters rapidly moved into other profitable and illicit activities: prostitution, gambling, and narcotics. Honest merchants were forced to pay "protection money" to the organized thugs; otherwise their windows would be smashed, their trucks overturned, or their employees or themselves beaten up. Racketeers even invaded the ranks of local labor unions as organizers and promoters. Organized crime had come to be one of the nation's most gigantic businesses. By 1930 the annual "take" of the underworld was estimated to be from $12 billion to $18 billion—several times the income of the Washington government.

Criminal callousness sank to new depths in 1932 with the kidnapping for ransom, and eventual murder, of the infant son of aviator-hero Charles A. Lindbergh. The entire nation was inexpressibly shocked and saddened, causing Congress in 1932 to pass the so-called Lindbergh Law making interstate abduction in certain circumstances a death-penalty offense.

Monkey Business in Tennessee

Education in the 1920s continued to make giant bootstrides. More and more states were requiring young people to remain in school until age sixteen or eighteen, or until graduation from high school. The proportion of seventeen-year-olds who finished high school almost doubled in the 1920s, to more than one in four.

The most revolutionary contribution to educational theory during these yeasty years was made by mild-mannered Professor John Dewey, who served on the faculty of Columbia University from 1904 to 1930. By common consent one of America's few front-rank philosophers, he set forth the principles of "learning by doing" that formed the foundation of so-called progressive education with its greater "permissiveness." He believed that the workbench was as essential as the blackboard, and that "education for life" should be a primary goal of the teacher.

This new emphasis on creating socially useful adults rendered many schools more attractive. No longer was the schoolhouse a kind of juvenile jail, from which the pupils burst at the end of the year chanting, as young Dewey had when a youngster in Vermont, "Good-bye school, good-bye teacher, damned old fool."

Science also scored wondrous advances in these years. A massive public-health program, launched by the Rockefeller Foundation in the South in 1909, had virtually wiped out the ancient affliction of hookworm by the 1920s. Better nutrition and health care helped to increase the life expectancy of a new-born infant from fifty years in 1901 to fifty-nine years in 1929.

Yet both science and education in the 1920s were subjected to unfriendly fire from Fundamentalists. These old-time religionists charged that the teaching of Darwinian evolution was destroying faith in God and the Bible, while contributing to the moral breakdown of youth in the Jazz Age. Numerous attempts were made to secure laws prohibiting the teaching of evolution, "the bestial hypothesis," in the public schools, and three Southern states adopted such shackling measures. The trio included Tennessee, in the heart of the so-called Bible Belt South, which, ironically enough, was a last refuge of New England Puritanism.

The stage was set for the memorable "Monkey Trial" at the hamlet of Dayton, eastern Tennessee, in 1925. A likable high school biology teacher, John T. Scopes, was indicted for teaching evolution. Batteries of newspapermen, armed with notebooks and cameras, descended upon the quiet town to witness the spectacle, as did hundreds of gaping "yokels" from the nearby hills. Scopes was defended by nationally known lawyers, while William Jennings Bryan, an ardent Presbyterian Fundamentalist, joined the prosecution. Taking the stand as an expert on the Bible, Bryan was made to appear foolish by the famed criminal lawyer, Clarence Darrow. Five days after the trial was over, Bryan died of apoplexy, no doubt brought on by the heat and strain.

"Gathering Data for the Tennessee Trial." Bryan finds no proof of evolution in the zoo. (New York *World,* 1925.)

> The bombastic Fundamentalist evangelist W. A. ("Billy") Sunday declared in 1925, "If a minister believes and teaches evolution, he is a stinking skunk, a hypocrite, and a liar."

This historic clash between theology and biology proved inconclusive. Scopes, the forgotten man of the drama, was found guilty and fined $100. But the supreme court of Tennessee, while upholding the law, set aside the fine on a technicality.* The Fundamentalists at best won only a hollow victory, for the absurdities of the trial cast ridicule on their cause. Increasing numbers of Christians

*The Tennessee law was not formally repealed until 1967.

were coming to reconcile the revelations of religion with the findings of modern science, and church membership continued to mount.

The Mass Consumption Economy

Prosperity—real, sustained, and widely shared—put much of the "roar" into the twenties. The economy kicked off its war harness in 1919, faltered a few steps in the recession of 1921–1922, and then sprinted forward for nearly seven years. Both the recent war and Treasury Secretary Andrew Mellon's tax policies favored the rapid expansion of capital investment. Ingenious machines, powered by relatively cheap energy from newly tapped oil fields, dramatically increased the productivity of the laboring man. Assembly-line production reached such perfection in Henry Ford's famed Rouge River plant near Detroit that a finished automobile emerged every ten seconds.

Great new industries suddenly sprouted forth. Supplying electrical power for the humming new machines became a giant business in the 1920s. Above all the automobile, once the horseless chariot of the rich, now became the carriage of the common man. By 1930, Americans owned almost 30 million cars.

The nation's deepening "love affair" with the automobile headlined a momentous shift in the character of the economy. American manufacturers seemed to have mastered the problems of production; their worries now focused on consumption. Could they find the mass markets for the goods they had contrived to spew forth in such profusion?

Responding to this need, a new arm of American commerce came into being: advertising. By persuasion and ploy, allure and sexual suggestion, advertisers sought to make Americans chronically discontented with their paltry possessions, and to want more, more, more. A founder of this new "profession" was Bruce Barton, prominent New York partner in a Madison Avenue firm. In 1925 Barton published a best seller, *The Man Nobody Knows*, setting forth the seductive thesis that Jesus Christ was the greatest adman of all time. "Every advertising man ought to study the parables of Jesus," Barton preached. "They are mar-

The Ford Assembly Line: Making the Model T, 1914. First introduced in 1913, Ford's "assembly line system" was based on the principle of "taking the work to the man," rather than moving workers and tools around on the factory floor. By 1914 this revolutionary technique had cut the average labor time needed to build a Model T chassis from twelve and one-half to one and one-half hours. (Courtesy of Ford Motor Company.)

velously condensed, as all good advertising should be." Barton even had a good word to say for Christ's executive ability: "He picked up twelve men from the bottom ranks of business and forged them into an organization that conquered the world."

In this commercialized atmosphere, even sports were becoming a big business. Ballyhooed by the "image-makers," home-run heroes like George H. ("Babe") Ruth were far better known than most statesmen. The fans bought tickets in such numbers that "Babe's" hometown park, Yankee Stadium, became known as "the house that Ruth built." In 1921 the slugging heavyweight champion, Jack Dempsey, knocked out the dapper French light-heavyweight, Georges Carpentier. The Jersey City crowd in attendance had paid more than a million dollars—the first in a series of million-dollar "gates" in the golden 1920s.

Buying on credit was another innovative feature of the post-war economy. "Possess today and pay tomorrow" was the message directed at buyers. Once-frugal descendants of Puritans went ever deeper into debt to own all kinds of new-fangled marvels—refrigerators, vacuum cleaners, and especially cars and radios—now. Prosperity thus accumulated an overhanging cloud of debt, and the economy became increasingly vulnerable to disruptions of the credit structure.

"Babe" Ruth: The "Sultan of Swat."
(Brown Brothers.)

Putting America on Rubber Tires

A New Industrial Revolution slipped into high gear in America in the 1920s. Thrusting out steel tentacles, it changed the daily life of the people in unprecedented ways. Machinery was the new messiah—and the automobile was its principal prophet.

Of all the inventions of the era, the automobile cut the deepest mark. It heralded an amazing new industrial system, based on assembly-line methods and mass-production techniques.

Americans adapted rather than invented the gasoline engine; Europeans can claim the original honor. By the 1890s a few daring American inventors and promoters, including Henry Ford and Ransom E. Olds (Oldsmobile), were developing the infant automotive industry. By 1910 there were sixty-nine companies, with a total annual production of 181,000 units. The early contraptions were neither speedy nor reliable. Many a stalled motorist, profanely cranking his balky car, had to endure the jeer "Get a horse" from the occupants of a passing dobbin-drawn carriage.

An enormous industry sprang into being, as Detroit became the motorcar capital of America. The mechanized colossus owed much to the stopwatch efficiency techniques of Frederick W. Taylor, a prominent inventor, engineer, and tennis player, who sought to eliminate waste motion. His epitaph reads: "Father of Scientific Management."

Best known of the new crop of industrial wizards was Henry Ford, who more than any other man put America on rubber tires. His high and hideous Model T ("Tin Lizzie") was cheap, rugged, and reasonably reliable, though rough and clat-

Henry Ford in His First Car, Built in 1896. He has been called "Father of the Traffic Jam." (Courtesy of Ford Motor Company.)

tering. The parts of Ford's "flivver" were highly standardized, but the behavior of this "rattling good car" was so individualized that it became the butt of numberless jokes.

Lean and silent Henry Ford, who was said to have wheels in his head, erected an immense personal empire on the cornerstone of his mechanical genius, though his associates provided much of the organizational talent. Ill-educated, this multimillionaire mechanic was socially and culturally narrow; "History is bunk," he once testified. But he devoted himself with one-track devotion to the gospel of standardization. After two early failures, he grasped and applied fully the techniques of assembly-line production—"Fordism." He is supposed to have remarked that the purchaser could have his automobile any color he desired—

> Efficient Henry Ford was accused of invading privacy in 1922, when this notice was posted in his Detroit factory: "From now on it will cost a man his job . . . to have the odor of beer, wine or liquor on his breath, or to have any of these intoxicants on his person or in his home. The Eighteenth Amendment is a part of the fundamental laws of this country. It was meant to be enforced. Politics has interfered with the enforcement of this law, but so far as our organization is concerned, it is going to be enforced to the letter."

just as long as it was black. So economical were his methods that in the mid-20s he was selling the Ford roadster for $260—well within the purse of a thrifty workingman.

The flood of Fords was phenomenal. In 1914 the "Automobile Wizard" turned out his five hundred thousandth Model T. By 1930 his total had risen to 20 million, or, on a bumper-to-bumper basis, more than enough to encircle the globe. A national newspaper and magazine poll conducted in 1923 revealed Ford to be the people's choice for the presidential nomination in 1924. By 1929, when the Great Bull Market collapsed, there were 26 million motor vehicles registered in the United States. This figure, averaging 1 for every 4.9 Americans, represented far more automobiles than existed in all the rest of the world.

The Advent of the Gasoline Age

The impact of the self-propelled carriage on various aspects of American life was tremendous. A gigantic new industry emerged, dependent on steel, but displacing steel from its kingpin role. Employing directly or indirectly about 6 million people by 1930, it was a major prop of the nation's prosperity. Thousands of new jobs, moreover, were created by supporting industries. The lengthening list would include rubber, glass, and fabrics, to say nothing of thousands of service stations and garages. America's standard of living, responding to this infectious prosperity, rose to an enviable level.

New industries boomed lustily; older ones grew sickly. The petroleum business experienced an explosive development. Hundreds of oil derricks shot up in California, Texas, and Oklahoma, as these states expanded wondrously and the new frontier became an industrial frontier. The once-feared railroad octopus, on the other hand, was hard hit by the competition of passenger cars, buses, and trucks. An age-old story was repeated: one industry's gains were another industry's pains.

Other effects were widely felt. Speedy marketing of perishable foodstuffs, such as fresh fruits, was accelerated. A new prosperity enriched outlying farms, as city dwellers were provided with produce at attractive prices. Countless new roads ribboned out to meet the demand of the American motorist for smoother and faster highways, often paid for by taxes on gasoline. The Era of Mud ended as the nation made haste to construct the finest network of hard-surfaced roadways in the world. Lured by new seductiveness in advertising, and encouraged by the perfecting of installment-plan buying, countless Americans with short purses acquired the habit of riding as they paid.

Zooming motorcars were agents of social change. At first a luxury, they rapidly became a necessity. Essentially devices for needed transportation, they soon developed into a badge of freedom and equality—a necessary prop for self-respect. To some, ostentation seemed more important than transportation. Leisure hours could now be spent more pleasurably, as tens of thousands of cooped-up souls responded to the call of the open road on joyriding vacations. Women were further freed from clinging-vine dependence on males. Isolation among the sections was broken down, while the less attractive states lost population at an alarming rate. America was becoming a nation of nomads.

Other social by-products of the automobile were visible. Autobuses made possible the consolidation of schools, and to some extent of churches. The trend toward hivelike urbanization was partially slowed. City workers could now live in the suburbs ("suburbia") and commute by motorcar or bus to railroad stations, there to catch the 7:52 for work.

The demon machine, on the other hand, exacted a terrible toll by catering to the American mania for speed. Citizens were becoming statistics. Not counting the hundreds of thousands of injured and crippled, the one millionth American had died in a motor accident by 1951—more than all those killed on all the battlefields of all the nation's wars to that date. "The public be rammed" seemed to be the motto of the new age.

Virtuous home life partially broke down as joyriders of all ages forsook the ancestral hearth for the wide open spaces. The morals of flaming youth sagged correspondingly—at least in the judgment of their elders. Even the disgraceful crime waves of the 1920s and 1930s were partly stimulated by the motorcar, for gangsters could now make quick getaways.

Yet no sane American would plead for a return of the old horse and buggy, complete with fly-

A Farewell to the Horse as Early as 1899. New York City was home to some 150,000 horses at the turn of the century. Each creature produced several pounds of manure a day. Horse "dumplings" littered nearly every street, attracting flies and emitting stench. In dry weather the traffic ground the manure to dust, which blew in sickening clouds about the city. (Davenport in the New York *Journal*.)

breeding manure. The automobile contributed notably to improved air and environmental quality, despite its later notoriety as a polluter. Life might be cut short on the highways, and smog might poison the air, but the automobile brought more convenience, pleasure, and excitement into people's lives than almost any other single invention.

Man Develops Wings

Gasoline engines also provided the power which enabled man to fulfill his age-old dream of sprouting wings. After near-successful experiments by others with heavier-than-air craft, the Wright brothers, Orville and Wilbur, performed "the Miracle at Kitty Hawk," North Carolina. On a historic day—December 17, 1903—Orville Wright took aloft a feebly engined plane that stayed airborne for 12 seconds and 120 feet (37 meters). Thus the Air Age was launched by two obscure bicycle repairmen.

As aviation gradually got off the ground, the world slowly shrank. The public was made increasingly air-minded by unsung heroes—often martyrs—who appeared as stunt fliers at fairs and other public gatherings. Airplanes—"flying coffins" —were used with marked success for various purposes during the Great War of 1914–1918. Shortly thereafter private companies began to operate passenger lines with airmail contracts, which were in effect a subsidy from Washington. The first transcontinental airmail route was established from New York to San Francisco in 1920.

In 1927 modest and skillful Charles A. Lindbergh, the so-called Flyin' Fool, electrified the world by the first solo west-to-east conquest of the Atlantic. Seeking a prize of $25,000, the lanky stunt flier courageously piloted his single-engined plane, "The Spirit of St. Louis," from New York to Paris in a grueling 33 hours and 39 minutes.

Lindbergh's exploit swept Americans off their feet. Fed up with the cynicism and debunking of the Jazz Age, they found in this wholesome and handsome youth a genuine hero. They clasped the

Lindbergh and His "Spirit of St. Louis." (National Archives.)

fluttering "Lone Eagle" to their hearts much more warmly than the bashful young man desired. In the words of Angela Morgan:

> Lad, you took the soul of me
> That long had lain despairing,
> Sent me Heaven-faring
> Gave me wings again.*

"Lucky Lindy" received an uproarious welcome in the "hero canyon" of lower Broadway, as 1,800 tons of ticker tape and other improvised confetti showered upon him. Lindbergh's achievement—it was more than a "stunt"—did much to dramatize and popularize flying, while giving a strong boost to the infant aviation industry.

The impact of the airship was tremendous. It provided the soaring American spirit with yet another dimension. At the same time, it gave birth to a giant new industry. Unfortunately, the accident rate in the pioneer stages of aviation was

---

*"Lindbergh," in *The Spirit of St. Louis,* ed. Charles Vale (George H. Doran Company, 1927).

high, though hardly more so than on the early railroads. But by the 1930s and 1940s, travel by air on regularly scheduled airlines was markedly safer than on many overcrowded highways.

Man's new wings also increased the tempo of an already breathless civilization. The floundering railroad received another sharp setback through the loss of passengers and mail. A lethal new weapon was given to the gods of war; and with the coming of city-busting aerial bombs men could well debate whether the conquest of air was a blessing or a curse. The Atlantic was shriveling to about the size of the Aegean Sea in the days of Socrates, while isolation behind ocean moats was becoming a bygone dream.

The Radio Revolution

The speed of the airplane was far eclipsed by the speed of radio waves. Guglielmo Marconi, an Italian, invented wireless telegraphy in the 1890s, and his brainchild was used for long-range communication during World War I.

Next came the voice-carrying radio, a triumph of many minds. A red-letter day was posted in November 1920, when the Pittsburgh station KDKA broadcast the news of the Harding landslide. Later miracles were achieved in transatlantic wireless photographs, radiotelephones, and television. In harmony with American free enterprise, radio programs were generally sustained by bothersome "commercials," as contrasted with the drabber government-owned systems of Europe.

Like other marvels, the radio not only created a new industry, but added richness to the fabric of American life. More joy was given to leisure hours, and many children who had been lured from the fireside by the automobile were brought back by the radio. The nation was better knit together. Various sections heard Americans with standardized accents, and countless millions "tuned in" on perennial comedy favorites like "Amos 'n' Andy." Advertising was further perfected as an art.

Educationally and culturally, the radio made a significant contribution. Sports were further stimulated. Politicians had to adjust their speaking techniques to the new medium, and millions rather than thousands of voters heard their pleas. A host of listeners swallowed the gospel of their favorite newscaster, or were even ringside participants in world-shaking events. Finally, the music of famous artists and symphony orchestras was beamed into countless homes. Television, which came into its own after World War II ended in

> Radio came in with a bang in the winter of 1921–1922. A San Francisco newspaper reported a discovery that countless citizens were making, "There is radio music in the air, every night, everywhere. Anybody can hear it at home on a receiving set, which any boy can put up in an hour."

Radio Listeners and Lookers in the 1920s.
(Brown Brothers.)

1945, did much of what radio did, only more graphically.

Hollywood's Filmland Fantasies

The flickering movie was the fruit of numerous geniuses, including Thomas A. Edison. As early as the 1890s this novel contraption, though still in crude form, had attained some popularity in the naughty peep-show penny arcades. The real birth of the moving picture came in 1903, when the first story sequence reached the screen. This breathless melodrama—*The Great Train Robbery*—was featured in the five-cent theaters, popularly called "nickelodeons." Spectacular among the first full-length classics was D. W. Griffith's *The Birth of a Nation,* which glorified the Ku Klux Klan of Reconstruction days and defamed the blacks. White Southerners would fire their six-shooters at the silver screen during the attempted "rape" scene.

A fascinating industry was thus launched. Hollywood, in southern California, quickly became the movie capital of the world, for it enjoyed a maximum of sunshine and other advantages. Early producers featured nudity and heavy-lidded female vampires ("vamps"), and an outraged public forced the screen magnates to set up their own rigorous code of censorship. The motion picture really arrived during the World War of 1914–1918, when it was used as an engine of anti-German propaganda. Specially prepared "hang the Kaiser" films aided powerfully in selling war bonds and in boosting morale.

A new era began in 1927 with the success of the first "talkie"—*The Jazz Singer,* starring the white performer Al Jolson in blackface. The age of the "silents" was ushered out as theaters everywhere were "wired for sound." At about the same time reasonably satisfactory color films were being produced.

Movies eclipsed all other new forms of amusement in the phenomenal growth of their popularity. Tens of thousands of actors and "extras" were employed in the cardboard cities behind Hollywood's high wooden fences, to say nothing of additional thousands engaged in exhibiting the films and selling noisy popcorn. Movie "stars" of the first pulchritude commanded much larger salaries than the President of the United States, in some cases as much as $100,000 for a single picture. Many actors and actresses were far more widely known than the nation's political leaders.

The "movie habit" rapidly created a nation of "cinemaniacs." By 1930 weekly admissions totaled 100 million—a large number of them "repeaters"—in a population of 122,775,000. Many of the moviegoers were openmouthed children, much of whose education, not all of it wholesome, was derived from this new type of textbook.

Other social consequences of the silver screen were incalculable. Attendance at movie "palaces" provided an escape from drab reality; filmland became the standard for taste, styles, songs, and morals. Newsreels, travelogues, and other informative "shorts" offered infinite possibilities for education, but they constituted only a tiny part of the total offering. Two by-products of the industry were the cheap movie magazine and the no less cheap keyhole commentator, both unduly concerned with the foibles and "sex-capades" of the "stars."

Nor did the influence of the moving picture end here. It almost exterminated vaudeville, and robbed the footlighted theater of much patronage. It no doubt hurt attendance at religious services.

> In the face of protests against sex in the movies, the industry appointed a "Movie Czar," Will H. Hays, who issued the famous "Hays Code" in 1934. As he stated in a speech, "This industry must have toward that sacred thing, the mind of a child, toward that clean virgin thing, that unmarked slate, the same responsibility, the same care about the impressions made upon it, that the best clergyman or the most inspired teacher of youth would have."

Like the radio and the motorcar, it contributed to the further standardization of America, for the mass of the people idolized the same actors and heard the same "hit" tunes. Hollywood dominated not only the domestic but the foreign movie market, and regrettably provided potent anti-American propaganda. Movie-makers placed an unwholesome overemphasis on the idle rich, the plush boudoir, the glowering gangster, and the quick-shooting cattle rustler.

The Delirious Decade

Far-reaching changes in life-styles and values paralleled the dramatic upsurge of the economy. The census of 1920 revealed that for the first time a majority of Americans no longer lived in the countryside, but in urban areas. Women found new opportunities for employment in the booming cities, though they tended to cluster in a few low-paying jobs (such as retail clerking and office typing) that quickly became classified as "women's work." An organized birth-control movement, led by fiery feminist Margaret Sanger, openly championed the use of contraceptives. A National Women's Party began in 1923 to agitate for an Equal Rights Amendment to the Constitution.* To some defenders of traditional ways, it seemed that the world had suddenly gone mad.

Even the churches were affected. The Fundamentalist champions of the old-time religion lost ground to the Modernists, who liked to think that God was a "good guy" and the universe a pretty chummy place.

Some churchmen tried to fight the Devil with worldly weapons. Competing with joy-riding automobiles and golf links, they turned to quality entertainment of their own, including wholesome moving pictures for young people. One uptown House of the Lord in New York advertised on a billboard: "Come to Church: Christian Worship Increases Your Efficiency."

*The campaign for an Equal Rights Amendment (ERA) was still stalled short of success six decades later.

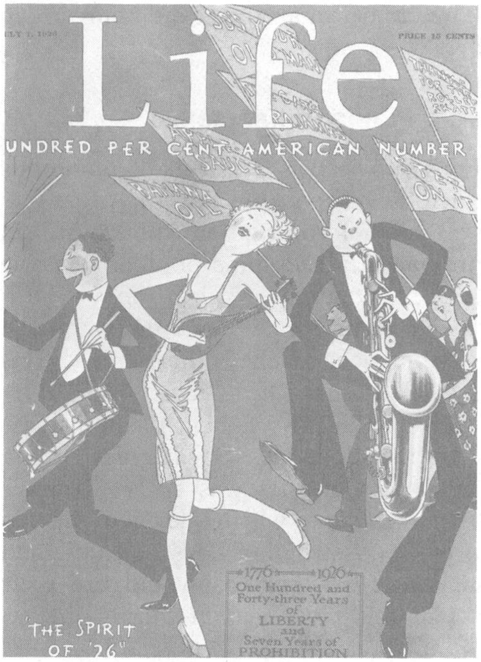

Slap-Happy 1926 on Magazine Cover.
(Courtesy of The New-York Historical Society, New York City.)

Even before the war, one observer thought the chimes had "struck sex o'clock in America," and the 1920s witnessed what many old-timers thought was a veritable erotic eruption. Advertisers exploited sexual allure to sell everything from soap to car tires. Once-modest maidens now proclaimed their new freedom as "flappers" in bobbed tresses and dresses. Young women appeared with hemlines elevated, stockings rolled, breasts taped flat, cheeks rouged, and lips a "crimson gash" that held a dangling cigarette. Thus did the "flapper" symbolize a yearned-for, devil-may-care independence (some said wild abandon) in American women. Still more adventuresome females shocked their elders when they sported the new one-piece bathing suits.

Justification for this new sexual frankness could be found in the recently translated writings of Sigmund Freud. This Viennese physician appeared to argue that sexual repression was responsible for a variety of nervous and emotional ills. Thus not pleasure alone, but health, demanded sexual gratification and liberation.

Many taboos flew out the window as sex-conscious Americans let themselves go. As unknowing Freudians, teenagers pioneered the sexual frontiers. Glued together in syncopated embrace, they danced to jazz music squeaking from phonographs. In an earlier day a kiss had been the equivalent of a proposal of marriage. But in the new era exploratory young folk sat in darkened movie houses or took to the highways and byways in automobiles—branded "houses of prostitution on wheels" by straitlaced elders. There youthful "neckers" and "petters" poached upon the forbidden territory of each other's bodies.

If the flapper was the goddess of the "Era of Wonderful Nonsense," jazz was its sacred music. With its virtuoso wanderings and tricky syncopation, jazz moved up from New Orleans along with the migrating blacks during World War I. Tunes like W. C. Handy's "St. Louis Blues" became instant classics, as the wailing saxophone became the trumpet of the new era. Blacks gave birth to jazz, but the entertainment industry soon spawned all-white bands—notably Paul Whiteman's. Caucasian impresarios cornered the profits, though not the creative soul, of America's most native music.

Literary Liberation

Likewise in literature an older era seemed to have ground to a halt with the recent war. By the dawn of the 1920s, most of the custodians of an aging genteel culture had died—Henry James in 1916, Henry Adams in 1918, and William Dean Howells (the "Dean of American literature") in 1920. A few novelists who had been popular in the previous decades lingered on, notably the well-to-do, cosmopolitan New Yorker Edith Wharton and the Virginia-born Willa Cather, esteemed for her stark but sympathetic portrayals of pioneering on the prairies.

But in the decade after the war, a new generation of writers burst upon the scene. Many of them hailed from ethnic and regional backgrounds different from that of the Protestant New Englanders who traditionally had dominated American cultural life. The newcomers exhibited the energy of youth, the ambition of excluded outsiders, and, in many cases, the smoldering resentment of ideals

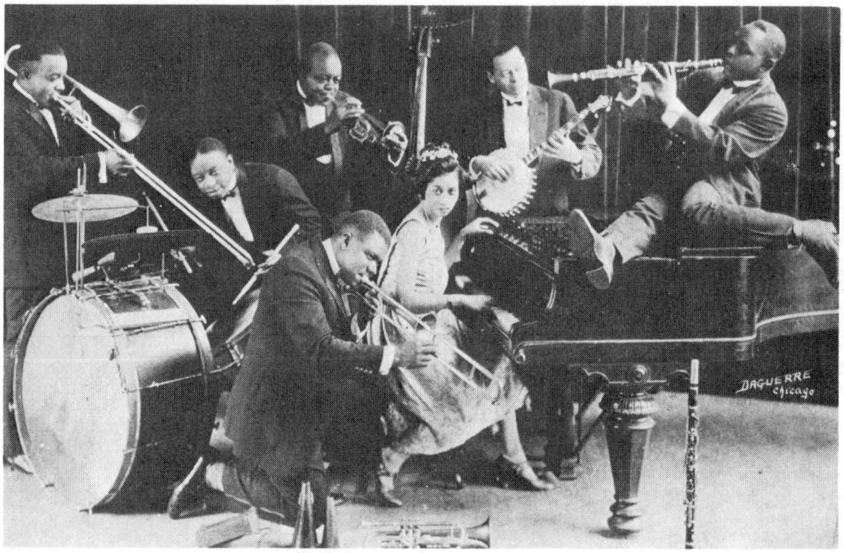

King Oliver's Creole Jazz Band, Early 1920s. Joseph "Joe" King Oliver arrived in Chicago from New Orleans in 1918. His band became the first important black jazz ensemble, and made Chicago's Royal Garden Cafe a magnet for jazz lovers. Left to right: Honoré Dutrey, trombone; Baby Dodds, drums; King Oliver, coronet; Lil Hardin, piano; Bill Johnson, banjo; and Johnny Dodds, clarinet. Kneeling in the foreground is the young Louis Armstrong. (Historical Pictures Service, Chicago)

betrayed. They bestowed on American literature a new vitality, imaginativeness, and artistic quality.

A patron saint of many young authors was Henry L. Mencken, the "Bad Boy of Baltimore," who admired their critical attitude toward American society. But few went so far in their fault-finding as Mencken himself. Little escaped his acidic wit. In the pages of his green-covered monthly *American Mercury* he wielded a slashing rapier as much as a pen. He assailed marriage, patriotism, democracy, prohibition, Rotarians, and the middle-class American "booboisie." The South he contemptuously dismissed as "the Sahara of the Bozart" (a bastardization of *beaux-arts*, French for the fine arts), and he scathingly attacked do-gooders as "Puritans." Puritanism, he jibed, was "the haunting fear that someone, somewhere, might be happy."

The war had jolted many young writers out of their complacency about traditional values and literary standards. With their pens they probed for new codes of morals and understanding, as well as fresh forms of expression. F. Scott Fitzgerald, a handsome Minnesota-born Princetonian then only twenty-four years old, became an overnight celebrity when he published *This Side of Paradise* in 1920. The book became a kind of Bible for the young. It was eagerly devoured by aspiring flappers and their ardent wooers, many of whom affected an air of bewildered abandon toward life. Catching the spirit of the hour (often about 4 A.M.), Fitzgerald found "All gods dead, all wars fought, all faiths in man shaken." He followed this melancholy success with *The Great Gatsby* (1925), a brilliant evocation of the glamour and cruelty of an achievement-oriented society. Theodore Dreiser's masterpiece of 1925 explored much the same theme: *An American Tragedy* dealt with the murder of a pregnant working girl by her socially ambitious young lover.

Ernest Hemingway, who had seen action on the Italian front in 1917, was among the writers most affected by the war. He responded to pernicious propaganda and the overblown appeal of patriotism by devising his own lean, word-sparing style. Hemingway spoke with a voice that was to have many imitators but no real equals. In *The Sun Also Rises* (1926), he told of disillusioned, spiritually numb American expatriates in Europe. In *A Farewell to Arms* (1929), he crafted one of the finest novels in any language about the war experience. A troubled soul, he finally blew out his brains with a shotgun blast in 1961.

F. Scott Fitzgerald and His Wife, Zelda. They are shown here in the early days of their marriage. (Historical Pictures Service, Chicago.)

Other writers turned to a critical probing of American small-town life. Sherwood Anderson dissected various fictional personalities in *Winesburg, Ohio* (1919), finding them all in some way warped by their cramped psychological surroundings. But the chief chronicler of Midwestern life was spindly, red-haired, heavy-drinking Sinclair Lewis, a hotheaded journalistic product of Sauk

In *A Farewell to Arms* (1929), Ernest Hemingway wrote: "I was always embarrassed by the words sacred, glorious, and sacrifice and the expression in vain. . . . There were many words that you could not stand to hear and finally only the names of places had dignity. Certain numbers were the same way and certain dates and these with the names of the places were all you could say and have them mean anything. Abstract words such as glory, honor, courage, or hallow were obscene beside the concrete names of villages, the numbers of roads, the names of rivers, the numbers of regiments, and the dates." (Courtesy of Charles Scribner's Sons.)

Centre, Minnesota. A master of satire, he sprang into prominence in 1920 with *Main Street,* the story of one woman's unsuccessful war against provincialism. In *Babbitt* (1922) he affectionately pilloried George F. Babbitt, a prosperous, vulgar, middle-class real estate broker who slavishly conformed to the respectable materialism of his group. The word "Babbittry" was quickly coined to describe his all-too-familiar life-style.

William Faulkner, a dark-eyed, pensive Mississippian, penned a bitter war novel in 1926, *Soldier's Pay.* He then turned his attention to a fictional chronicle of an imaginary, history-rich Deep South county. In powerful books like *The Sound and the Fury* (1929) and *As I Lay Dying* (1930), Faulkner peeled back layers of time and consciousness from the constricted souls of his ingrown Southern characters.

Faulkner said in 1956: "The writer's only responsibility is to his art. He will be completely ruthless if he is a good one. He has a dream. It anguishes him so much he must get rid of it. He has no peace until then. Everything goes by the board: honor, pride, decency, security, happiness, all to get the book written."

Nowhere was innovation in the 1920s more obvious than in poetry. Ezra Pound, a brilliantly erratic Idahoan who deserted America for Europe, rejected what he called "an old bitch civilization, gone in the teeth," and proclaimed his doctrine: "Make It New." He strongly influenced Missouri-born and Harvard-educated T. S. Eliot, who took up residence in England. In "The Waste Land" (1922), Eliot produced one of the most impenetrable but influential poems of the century. Robert Frost, a San Francisco–born poet, wrote hauntingly about his adopted New England. The most daringly innovative of all was e. e. cummings, who relied on unorthodox diction and peculiar typesetting to produce startling poetical effects.

On the stage, Eugene O'Neill, a New York dramatist and Princeton dropout of globe-trotting background, laid bare Freudian notions of sex in plays like *Strange Interlude* (1928). A prodigious playwright, he authored more than a dozen productions in the 1920s, and won the Nobel Prize in 1936.

O'Neill arose from New York's Greenwich Village, which before and after the war was a seething cauldron of writers, painters, musicians, actors, and other would-be artists. After the war, a black cultural renaissance also took root uptown in Harlem, led by such gifted writers as Claude McKay and Langston Hughes, and jazzmen like Louis Armstrong. They proudly exulted in their black culture. Although many whites frequented the black jazz joints, black writers were yet to win a wide audience among white readers.

Architecture also married itself to the new materialism and functionalism. The era of machinery continued to lure droves of people to the cities; by 1920 over one-half of the population lived in urban areas. Long-range city planning was being intelligently projected, and architects like Frank Lloyd Wright were advancing the

In the play, *The Emperor Jones* (1920), O'Neill has a former black Pullman porter and ex-convict say: "For de little stealin' dey gits you in jail soon or late. For de big stealin' dey makes you emperor and puts you in de Hall o' Fame when you croaks. If dey's one thing I learns in ten years on de Pullman cars listenin' to de white quality talk, it's dat same fact."

theory that buildings should grow from their sites and not slavishly imitate Greek and Roman importations. The Machine Age outdid itself in New York City when it thrust upward the cloud-brushing Empire State Building, 102 stories high. Dedicated in 1931, "The Empty State Building" towered partially vacant during the depressed 1930s.

Wall Street's Big Bull Market

The boom of the Golden Twenties showered genuine benefits on Americans, their incomes and living standards assuredly rose, but there always seemed to be something fantastic about it all. People sang, somewhat incredulously:

My sister she works in the laundry,
My father sells bootlegger gin,
My mother she takes in the washing,
My God! how the money rolls in!

Signals abounded that the economic joy ride might end in a crash; even in the best years of the 1920s several hundred banks failed annually. This something-for-nothing craze was well illustrated by real estate speculation, especially the fantastic Florida boom that culminated in 1925. Numerous underwater lots were sold to eager purchasers for preposterous sums. The whole wildcat scheme collapsed when the peninsula was devastated by a West Indian hurricane, which belied advertisements of a "soothing tropical wind."

The stock exchange provided even greater sensations. Speculation ran wild, and an orgy of boom-or-bust trading pushed the bull market up to dizzy peaks. "Never sell America short" and "Be a bull on America" were favorite catchwords, as Wall Street gamblers gored one another and fleeced greedy lambs. The stock market became a veritable gambling den.

As the 1920s lurched forward, everybody seemed to be buying stocks "on margin"—that is, with a small down payment. Barbers, stenographers, and elevator boys cashed in on "hot tips" picked up while on duty. One valet was reported to have parlayed his wages into a quarter of a million dollars. "The cash register crashed the Social Register" as rags-to-riches Americans eagerly worshiped at the altar of the ticker-tape machine. So powerful was the intoxicant of quick profits that few heeded the voices raised in certain quarters to warn that this kind of tinsel prosperity could not last forever.

Little was done by Washington to curb money-mad speculators. In the wartime days of Wilson,

"Just Like Water off a Duck's Back." (Columbus *Dispatch*, 1929.)

the national debt had rocketed from the 1914 figure of $1,188,235,400 to the 1921 peak of $23,976,250,-608. Conservative principles of money-management pointed to a diversion of surplus funds to reduce this financial burden.

A businesslike move toward economic sanity was made in 1921, when a Republican Congress created the Bureau of the Budget. Its director was to assist the President in preparing careful estimates of receipts and expenditures for submission to Congress as the annual budget. This reform, long overdue, was designed in part to prevent haphazardly extravagant appropriations.

The burdensome taxes inherited from the war were especially distasteful to Secretary of the Treasury Mellon, as well as to his fellow millionaires. Their theory was that such high levies forced the rich to invest in tax-exempt securities, rather than in the factories that provided prosperous payrolls. The Mellonites also argued, with considerable persuasiveness, that high taxes not only discouraged business but also brought a smaller net return to the Treasury than moderate taxes.

Seeking to succor the "poor" rich man, Mellon helped engineer a series of tax reductions from 1921 to 1926. Congress followed his lead by repealing the excess profits tax, abolishing the gift tax, and reducing excise taxes, the surtax, the income tax, and estate taxes. In 1921 a wealthy man with an income of $1 million had paid $663,000 in income taxes; in 1926 he paid about $200,000. Mellon's spare-the-rich policies thus shifted much of the tax burden from the wealthy to the middle-income groups.

Mellon, the "greatest secretary of the treasury since Hamilton," remains a controversial figure. True, he reduced the national debt by $10 billion—from about $26 billion to $16 billion. But foes of the emaciated multimillionaire charged that he should have bitten a larger chunk out of the debt, especially while the country was pulsating with prosperity. He was also accused of indirectly encouraging the bull market. If he had absorbed more of the national income in taxes, there would have been less money left for frenzied speculation. His refusal to do so typified the single-mindedly pro-business regime that dominated the political scene throughout the postwar decade.

VARYING VIEWPOINTS

Just as the 1920s have seemed to mark a "great divide" in political history, so has the decade been depicted as a watershed in the history of American society and culture. These colorful years witnessed the shift from a capital-goods to a consumer-goods economic base; a climax to the festering feud between old-stock Americans and immigrants; and repeated confrontations between wets and dries, religious Fundamentalists and Modernists, the literary Old Guard and the avant-garde, the countryside and the city. Historians have generally concluded that the forces of progress triumphed in this decade over the forces of tradition. The census finding in 1920 that a majority of Americans now lived in "urban" areas is often cited as a summary symbol of the changes on which that triumph rested.

But the modern, transformative character of the 1920s has perhaps been exaggerated. The Great Depression amply demonstrated that familiar problems of the business cycle remained. Mounting evidence points to the persistence of ethnic identities and cultural traits. Folklore to the contrary, prohibition *did* diminish the consumption of alcohol by Americans. Recent events have demonstrated the continued vitality of "old-time religion." And rural culture, manifested in widespread suspicion of cities and the popularity of "country western" music, still lives.

SELECT READINGS

The best introduction to the 1920s is William Leuchtenburg, *The Perils of Prosperity, 1914–1932* (1958). Frederick Lewis Allen, *Only Yesterday* (1931) is an evocative recollection of the texture of life in the decade. Equally informative are R. S. and H. M. Lynd's classic sociological studies, *Middletown* (1929) and *Middletown in Transition* (1937). Robert K. Murray, *Red Scare* (1955) is authoritative; on the same subject, see Stanley Coben, *A. Mitchell Palmer* (1963). Immigration restriction is dealt with in John Higham, *Strangers in the Land* (1955). Paul A. Carter, *Another Part of the Twenties* (1977) also deals with immigration and ethnicity. The standard work on the revived Klan is David M. Chalmers, *Hooded Americanism* (rev. ed. 1981). Also valuable is Kenneth T. Jackson, *The Ku Klux Klan in the City, 1915–1930* (1967). Prohibition is handled in Andrew Sinclair, *Era of Excess: A Social History of the Prohibition Movement* (1962), Joseph R. Gusfield, *Symbolic Crusade* (1963), and Norman H. Clark's highly readable *Deliver Us From Evil* (1976). On a related subject, see Humbert S. Nelli, *The Business of Crime* (1976). Revealing on the Scopes trial are Ray Ginger, *Six Days or Forever?* (1958), and L. W. Levine's sensitive study of William Jennings Bryan, *Defender of the Faith* (1965). On the economy, see G. H. Soule, *Prosperity Decade* (1947), Alfred D. Chandler, *Strategy and Structure: Chapters in the History of Industrial Enterprise* (1962), Irving Bernstein, *The Lean Years: A History of the American Worker, 1920–1933* (1960), and Daniel Nelson, *Frederick Winslow Taylor and the Rise of Scientific Management* (1980). On advertising, consult Stuart Ewen, *Captains of Consciousness* (1976). Movies are featured in Lary May, *Screening Out the Past: The Birth of Mass Culture and the Motion Picture Industry* (1980) and in Robert Sklar, *Movie-Made America* (1975). The "youth culture" is the subject of Paula Fass, *The Damned and the Beautiful: American Youth in the 1920s* (1977). Changing sexual attitudes are analyzed in David M. Kennedy, *Birth Control in America: The Career of Margaret Sanger* (1970). Gilbert Osofsky describes the background of the "Harlem Renaissance" in *Harlem: The Making of a Ghetto, 1890–1930* (1966). See also David Lewis, *When Harlem was in Vogue* (1981). Two stimulating literary histories are Frederick J. Hoffman, *The Twenties: American Writing in the Postwar Decade* (1955), and Alfred Kazin, *On Native Grounds* (1942). David M. Kennedy, *Over Here: The First World War and American Society* (1980), pays special attention to the literature that emerged from the war experience.

39

The Politics of Boom and Bust, 1920-1932

We in America today are nearer to the final triumph over poverty than ever before in the history of any land. We have not yet reached the goal—but . . . we shall soon, with the help of God, be in sight of the day when poverty will be banished from this nation.

HERBERT HOOVER, 1928

The Republican "Old Guard" Returns

Handsome President Harding, with erect figure (6 feet; 1.83 meters), broad shoulders, high forehead, bushy eyebrows, and graying hair, was one of the best-liked men of his generation. An easy-going, warmhanded first-namer, he exuded graciousness and love of people. So kindly was his nature that he would brush off ants rather than crush them.

Yet the amiable, smiling exterior concealed a weak, flabby interior. With a mediocre mind, Harding quickly found himself beyond his depth in the Presidency. "God! What a job!" was his anguished cry on one occasion.

President Warren G. Harding (1865–1923). After his death it was revealed that he had been an unfaithful husband. Harding's father was rumored to have said that if Warren had been born a girl she would have been "in trouble" much of the time because of an inability to say "no." (Brown Brothers.)

Harding, like Grant, was unable to detect moral halitosis in his evil associates, and he was soon surrounded by his poker-playing, shirt-sleeved cronies of the "Ohio Gang." "A good guy," Harding was "one of the boys." He hated to hurt people's feelings, especially those of his friends, by saying "no"; and designing political leeches capitalized on this weakness. The difference between George Washington and Warren Harding, ran a current quip, was that while Washington could not tell a lie, Harding could not tell a liar. He "was not a bad man," said one Washington observer. "He was just a slob."

Candidate Harding, who admitted his scanty mental furnishings, had promised to gather about him the "best minds" of the party. Charles Evans Hughes—masterful, imperious, incisive, brilliant—brought to the secretaryship of state a dominating if somewhat conservative leadership. The new secretary of the treasury was a lean and elderly Pittsburgh aluminum king, Andrew W. Mellon, multimillionaire collector of the paintings that are now displayed in Washington as his gift to the nation. Chubby-faced Herbert Hoover, famed feeder of the Belgians and "Hooverizer," became secretary of commerce. An energetic businessman and engineer, he raised his second-rate Cabinet post to first-rate importance, especially in drumming up foreign trade for American manufacturers.

But the "best minds" of the Cabinet were largely offset by two of the worst. Senator Albert B. Fall of New Mexico, a scheming anti-conservationist, was appointed secretary of the interior. As guardian of the nation's natural resources, he resembled the wolf hired to protect the sheep. Harry M. Daugherty, a small-town lawyer but a big-time crook in the "Ohio Gang," was supposed to prosecute wrongdoers as attorney general.

GOP Reaction at the Throttle

Well-intentioned but weak-willed, Harding was a perfect "front" for enterprising industrialists. A McKinley-style old order settled heavily back into place at war's end, crushing the reform seedlings that had sprouted in the progressive era. A blowsy, nest-feathering crowd moved into Washington and proceeded to hoodwink Harding, whom many regarded as an "amiable boob."

This new Old Guard hoped to improve on the old business doctrine of *laissez-faire*. Their plea was not simply for government to keep hands off business, but for government to help guide business along the path to profits. They subtly and effectively achieved their ends by putting the courts and the administrative bureaus into the safekeeping of fellow standpatters. Harding initiated these practices and set the tone of Republican economic policies for the rest of the decade.

The Supreme Court was a striking example of this trend. Harding lived less than three years as President, but to him fell the task of appointing four of the nine justices. Several of his choices were or became deep-dyed reactionaries, and they held the dike against popular currents for nearly two decades. Harding's fortunate choice for chief justice was ex-President Taft, who not only performed his duties ably but surprisingly was more liberal than some of his cautious associates.

In the first years of the 1920s the Supreme Court axed progressive legislation. It killed a federal child-labor law, stripped away many of labor's hard-won gains, and rigidly restricted governmental intervention in the economy. In the landmark case of *Adkins* v. *Children's Hospital* (1923), the Court invalidated a minimum-wage law for women. Its strained ruling was that because females now had the vote (19th Amendment), they could no longer be protected by special legislation.

Corporations, under Harding, could once more relax and expand. Anti-trust laws were often ignored, circumvented, or feebly upheld by friendly prosecutors in the attorney general's office. The Interstate Commerce Commission, to single out one agency, came to be dominated by men who were personally sympathetic to the managers of the railroads. Harding reactionaries might well have boasted, "We care not what laws the Democrats pass as long as we are permitted to administer them."

Big industrialists, striving to lessen competition, now had a free hand to set up trade associations. Cement manufacturers, for example, would use these agencies to agree upon standardization of product, publicity campaigns, and a united front in dealing with the railroads and labor. Although many of these associations ran counter to the spirit of existing anti-trust legislation, their formation was encouraged by Secretary Hoover. His sense of engineering efficiency was shocked by the waste resulting from cutthroat competition.

> Mr. Justice Holmes, wryly dissenting in the *Adkins* case, said: "It would need more than the 19th Amendment to convince me that there are no differences between men and women, or that legislation cannot take those differences into account."

The Aftermath of War

Wartime government controls on the economy were swiftly dismantled. The War Industries Board disappeared with almost indecent haste. With its passing, progressive hopes for more government regulation of big business evaporated.

Washington likewise returned the railroads to private management in 1920. Reformers had hoped that wartime government operation of the lines might lead to their permanent nationalization. Instead, Congress passed the Esch-Cummins Transportation Act of 1920, which encouraged private consolidation of the railroads and pledged the Interstate Commerce Commission to guarantee their profitability. The new philosophy was not to save the country from the railroads, as in the days of the Populists, but to save the railroads for the country.

The federal government also tried to pull up anchor and get out of the shipping business. The Merchant Marine Act of 1920 authorized the Shipping Board, which controlled about 1500 vessels, to dispose of much of the hastily built wartime fleet at bargain-basement prices. The board operated the remaining vessels without conspicuous success. Under the LaFollette Seaman's Act of 1915, American shipping could not thrive in competition with foreigners, who all too often provided their crews with wretched food and starvation wages.

Labor, suddenly deprived of its wartime crutch of friendly government support, limped along badly in the postwar decade. A bloody strike in the steel industry was ruthlessly broken in 1919, partly by exploiting ethnic and racial divisions among the steelworkers, and partly by branding the strikers as dangerous "Reds." The Railway Labor Board, a successor body to the wartime labor boards, ordered a wage cut of 12 percent in 1922, provoking a two-month strike. It ended when Attorney General Daugherty, who fully shared Harding's big-business bias, clamped on the strikers one of the most sweeping injunctions in American history. Unions wilted in this hostile political environment, and membership dropped by nearly 30 percent between 1920 and 1930.

Vicious race riots also rocked the Republic in the years following the Great War. The prospect of fat pay envelopes in smoking war plants had sucked thousands of blacks out of the South into such northern industrial cities as New York and Chicago. The war thus kicked off an historic exodus that redistributed America's black population, with lasting social and political effects. But in the immediate post-war period, blacks were brutally taught that the North was not a Promised Land. A racial reign of terror descended on Chicago in the summer of 1919, leaving twenty-three blacks and fifteen whites dead. Clashes also inflamed Knoxville, Omaha, Washington, and other cities.

Needy veterans were among the few nonbusiness groups to reap lasting gains from the war. Congress in 1921 generously created the Veterans' Administration, authorized to operate hospitals and provide vocational rehabilitation for the disabled.

Non-disabled veterans, unwilling to be slighted, quickly organized into pressure groups. Noteworthy was the American Legion, founded in Paris in 1919 by Colonel Theodore Roosevelt, Jr. Legionnaires met periodically to renew old hardships and let off steam in good-natured horseplay. The Legion soon became distinguished for its militant patriotism, rock-ribbed conservatism, and zealous anti-radicalism.

The Legion also became notorious for its aggressive lobbying for veteran's benefits. The chief grievance of the former "doughboys" was monetary—they wanted their "dough." The former servicemen demanded "adjusted compensation" to make up for the wages they had "lost" when they turned in their work clothes for military uniforms during the Great War.

Critics denounced this demand as a holdup "bonus," but the millions of veterans deployed heavy political artillery. They browbeat Congress into passing a bonus bill in 1922, which Harding promptly vetoed. Re-forming their lines, the repulsed veterans gathered for a final attack. In 1924 Congress again hoisted the white flag and passed the Adjusted Compensation Act. It gave every former soldier a paid-up insurance policy due in twenty years—adding about $3.5 billion to the total cost of the war. Penny-pinching Calvin Coolidge sternly vetoed the measure, but Congress overrode him, leaving the veterans with their loot.

America Seeks Benefits without Burdens

Making peace with the fallen foe was the most pressing problem left on Harding's doorstep. The United States, having rejected the Treaty of Versailles, was still technically at war with Germany, Austria, and Hungary nearly three years after the Armistice.

Peace was finally achieved by lone-wolf tactics. In July 1921, Congress passed a simple joint resolution that declared the war officially ended. This declaration, and the subsequent peace treaties with Germany, Austria, and Hungary, formally reserved to the United States all the rights and privileges conferred upon it by the repudiated Versailles settlement.

Isolation was enthroned in Washington. The Harding administration, with the Senate "irreconcilables" holding a hatchet over its head, continued to regard the League of Nations as a thing unclean. Harding at first refused even to support the League's world health program. But the new world body was much too important to be completely ignored. "Unofficial observers" were sent to its seat in Geneva, Switzerland, to hang around like detectives shadowing a suspected criminal.

Harding could not completely turn his back on the outside world, especially the Middle East, where a sharp rivalry developed between America and Britain for oil-drilling concessions. Remem-

"Harding's Way out of the War," 1921. As for the League of Nations, Harding declared in 1923 that it was "as dead as slavery. . . . Let it rest in the deep grave." (Fitzpatrick in the St. Louis *Post-Dispatch*.)

bering that the Allies had floated to victory on a flood of oil, experts recognized that liquid "black gold" was to be as necessary as blood in the battles of tomorrow. Secretary Hughes at length secured for American oil companies the right to share in the exploitation of the sandy region's oil riches.

Disarmament was one international issue on which Harding, after much indecision, finally seized the initiative. He was prodded by businessmen unwilling to dig deeper into their pockets for money to finance the ambitious naval building program started during the war. A deadly contest was shaping up with Britain and Japan, who watched with alarm as the oceans filled with American vessels. Britain still commanded the world's largest navy, but the clatter of American riveters proclaimed that the United States would soon overtake her. Tensions ran especially high in the Far East, where the Japanese were growing increasingly restive. Anxieties were further heightened by a long-standing Anglo-Japanese alliance (signed in 1902), which apparently obligated the British to join with Japan in the event of war between Japan and the United States.

Ship-Scrapping at the Washington Conference

Public agitation in America, fed by these worries, brought about the headline-making Washington "Disarmament" Conference in 1921–1922. Invitations went to all the major naval powers—except Bolshevik Russia, whose government the United States refused officially to recognize. The double agenda included naval disarmament and the situation in the Far East.

At the outset, Secretary Hughes startled the delegates, who were expecting the usual diplomatic fence-straddling, with a comprehensive, concrete plan for declaring a ten-year "holiday" on construction of battleships and even for scrapping some of the huge dreadnoughts already built or being built. He proposed that the scaled-down navies of America and Britain should enjoy parity in battleships and aircraft carriers, with Japan on the small end of a 5–5–3 ratio. This arrangement sounded to the sensitive Japanese ambassador like "Rolls-Royce, Rolls-Royce, Ford."

Complex bargaining followed in the wake of Hughes's proposals. The Five-Power Naval Treaty of 1922 embodied Hughes's ideas on ship ratios, but only after face-saving compensation was offered to the insecure Japanese. The British and Americans both conceded that they would refrain from fortifying their Far Eastern possessions, including the Philippines. The Japanese were not subjected to such restraints in their possessions. In addition, a four-power treaty replaced the Anglo-Japanese alliance. The new pact bound Britain, Japan, France, and the United States to preserve the status quo in the Pacific—another concession to the jumpy Japanese. Finally, the Washington Conference gave chaotic China—"the Sick Man of the Far East"—a shot in the arm with the Nine-Power Treaty of 1922, whose signatories agreed to nail wide open the Open Door in China.

When the final gavel banged, the Hardingites

	Battleships	Battleship Tonnage	Aircraft Carrier Tonnage
U. S.	18	525,000	135,000
Britain	22	525,000	135,000
Japan	10	315,000	81,000
France	7	175,000	60,000
Italy	6	175,000	60,000

LIMITS IMPOSED BY WASHINGTON CONFERENCE
The pledge of the British and Americans to refrain from fortifying their Far Eastern possessions, while Japan was allowed to fortify hers, was the key to the naval limitation treaty. The United States and Great Britain thus won a temporary victory, but later paid a horrendous price when they had to dislodge the well-entrenched Japanese from the Pacific in World War II.

boasted with much fanfare—and some justice—of their globe-shaking achievement in disarmament. But their satisfaction was somewhat illusory. No restrictions had been placed on small warships, and the other powers churned ahead with the construction of cruisers, destroyers, and submarines, while penny-pinching Uncle Sam lagged dangerously behind. Congress also pointedly declared that it was making no commitment to the use of armed force or any kind of joint action when it ratified the Four-Power Treaty. These reservations, in effect, rendered the treaty a dead letter. Ominously, Americans seemed content to rely for their security on words and wishful thinking, rather than on weapons and hardheaded realism.

A similar sentimentalism welled up later in the decade, when Americans clamored for the "outlawry of war." The conviction spread that if quarreling nations would only take the pledge to foreswear war as an instrument of national policy, swords could be beaten into plowshares. Calvin Coolidge's secretary of state, Frank B. Kellogg, who later won the Nobel Peace Prize for his role, was lukewarm about the idea. But after petitions bearing more than 2 million signatures cascaded into Washington, he signed with the French foreign minister in 1928 the famed Kellogg-Briand Pact. Officially known as the Pact of Paris, it was ultimately ratified by sixty-two nations.

As for the burdens of armament, the New York *Independent,* a prominent magazine, noted in January 1921 that the country was "more afraid of the tax collector than of any more distant foe."

This new parchment peace was delusory in the extreme. Defensive wars were still permitted, and what scheming aggressor could not cook up an excuse of self-defense? Lacking both muscles and teeth, the pact was a diplomatic derelict—and virtually useless in a showdown. Yet it accurately—and dangerously—reflected the American mind in the 1920s, which was all too ready to be lulled into a false sense of security. This mood took even deeper hold in the ostrichlike neutralism of the 1930s.

Hiking the Tariff Higher

A comparable lack of realism afflicted foreign economic policy in the 1920s. Businessmen, short-sightedly obsessed with the dazzling prospects in the prosperous home market, sought to keep that market to themselves by flinging up high, virtually unclimbable, tariff walls around the United States. They were spurred into action by their fear of a flood of cheap goods from recovering Europe, especially in the brief but sharp recession of 1921–1922.

In 1921, less than three months after Harding's inauguration, Congress passed the hastily formulated Emergency Tariff Act. It raised duties on certain agricultural products, including wool and sugar, and clamped an embargo on German dyestuffs.

Emergency legislation was followed the next year by the more comprehensive Fordney-McCumber Tariff Law of 1922. Glib lobbyists once more descended upon Congress and helped boost schedules from the average of 27 percent under Wilson's Underwood Tariff of 1913 to an average of 38.5 percent, which was almost as high as Taft's Payne-Aldrich Tariff of 1909. (See graph, p. 739.) More important was the acceleration of the trend toward high protection. Duties on farm produce were increased, and the principle was proclaimed that the general rates were designed to equalize the cost of American and foreign production. A promising degree of flexibility was introduced for the first time when the President was authorized, with the advice of the fact-finding Tariff Commission, to reduce or increase duties by as much as 50 percent.

Presidents Harding and Coolidge, true to their big-industry sympathies, were far more friendly to tariff increases than to reductions. In six years they authorized thirty-two upward changes, including on their list vital commodities like dairy products, chemicals, and pig iron. During the same period the White House ordered only five reductions. These included mill feed and such trifling items as bobwhite quail, paintbrush handles, phenol, and cresylic acid.

"It Works Both Ways," 1921.
(Courtesy of Dallas *News.*)

The high-tariff course thus charted by the Republican regimes set off an ominous chain reaction. European producers felt the squeeze, for the American tariff walls prolonged the post-war chaos. An impoverished Europe needed to sell its manufactured goods to the United States, particularly if it hoped to achieve economic recovery and to pay its huge war debt to Washington. America needed to give foreign nations a chance to make a profit from her so that they could buy her manufactured articles and repay debts. International trade, Americans were slow to learn, is a two-way street. In general, they could not sell to others in quantity unless they bought from them in quantity—or lent them more American dollars.

Erecting tariff walls was a game that two could play. The American example spurred European nations, throughout the feverish 1920s, to pile up higher barriers themselves. These artificial obstacles were doubly bad: they hurt not only American-made goods but the products of neighboring European countries as well. The whole vicious circle further deepened the international economic distress, providing one more rung on the ladder by which Adolf Hitler scrambled to power.

The Stench of Scandal

Loose morality and get-rich-quickism of the Harding era manifested themselves spectacularly in a series of scandals.

Early in 1923 Colonel Charles R. Forbes, onetime deserter from the army, was caught with his hand in the till and resigned as head of the Veterans' Bureau. An appointee of the gullible Harding, he and his accomplices looted the government to the tune of about $200 million, chiefly in connection with the building of veterans' hospitals. He was sentenced to two years in a federal penitentiary.

Most shocking of all was the Teapot Dome scandal, an affair which involved priceless naval oil reserves at Teapot Dome (Wyoming) and Elk Hills (California). In 1921 the slippery secretary of the interior, Albert B. Fall, induced his careless colleague, Secretary of the Navy Denby, to transfer these valuable properties to the Interior Department. President Harding indiscreetly signed the secret order. Fall then quietly leased the lands to oilmen Harry F. Sinclair and Edward L. Doheny, but not until he had received a bribe ("loan") of $100,000 from Doheny and about three times that amount in all from Sinclair.

Teapot Dome, no tempest in a teapot, finally came to a whistling boil. Details of the crooked transaction gradually began to leak out in March 1923, two years after Harding took office. Fall, Sinclair, and Doheny were indicted the next year, but the case dragged through the courts until 1929. Finally Fall was found guilty of taking a bribe and was sentenced to one year in jail. By a curious quirk of justice, the two bribe givers were acquitted while the bribe taker was convicted, although Sinclair served several months in jail for having "shadowed" jurors and for refusing to testify before a Senate committee.

The oily smudge from Teapot Dome polluted the prestige of the Washington government. Right-thinking citizens wondered what was going on when public officials could sell out the nation's vital resources, especially those reserved for the United States navy. The acquittal of Sinclair and Doheny undermined faith in the courts, while giving further currency to the cynical sayings, "You can't put a million dollars in jail" and "In America everyone is assumed guilty until proven rich."

Other scandals erupted, two of them involving suicides. Persistent reports as to the underhanded doings of Attorney General Daugherty brought a Senate investigation in 1924 of the illegal sale of pardons and liquor permits. Forced to resign,

"Gushing," 1924. The Teapot Dome Scandal spewed out oily crooks. (Fitzpatrick in the St. Louis *Post-Dispatch.*)

the accused official was tried in 1927 but was released after a jury twice failed to agree. During the trial, Daugherty hid behind the trousers of the now-dead Harding by implying that persistent probing might uncover crookedness in the White House.

Harding was mercifully spared the full revelation of these iniquities, though his worst suspicions were aroused. While the scandals were beginning to break, he embarked upon a speechmaking tour across the country all the way to Alaska. On the return trip he died in San Francisco, on August 2, 1923, of pneumonia and thrombosis. His death may have been hastened by a broken heart resulting from the disloyalty of designing friends. Mourning millions, not yet fully aware of the graft in Washington, expressed genuine sorrow.

The brutal fact is that Harding was not a big enough man for the presidency—as he himself privately admitted. Such was his weakness that he tolerated persons and conditions which subjected the Republic to its worst disgrace since the days of President Grant.

Calvin Coolidge: A Yankee in the White House

News of Harding's death was sped to Vice-President Coolidge, then visiting at the New England farmhouse of his father. By the light of two kerosene lamps the elder Coolidge, a justice of the peace, used the old family Bible to administer the presidential oath to his son.

This homespun setting was symbolic of Coolidge. Quite unlike Harding, the stern-faced Vermonter, with his thin nose and tightly set lips, embodied the New England virtues of honesty, morality, industry, and frugality. As a youth, his father reported, he seemed to get more sap out of a maple tree than did any of the other boys. Practicing a rigid economy in both money and words, "Silent Cal" came to be known in Washington conversational circles for his brilliant flashes of silence. His dour, serious visage prompted the acid observation that he had been "weaned on a pickle."

Coolidge seemed to be a crystallization of the commonplace. A painfully shy individual of average height (5 feet 10 inches; 1.77 meters), he was blessed with only mediocre powers of leadership. He would occasionally flash a dry wit in private; but his speeches, delivered in a nasal New England twang, were invariably boring. A staunch apostle of the status quo, he was no knight in armor riding forth to tilt at wrongs. His only horse, in fact, was an electric-powered steed on which he took his exercise. True to Republican philosophy, he became the "high priest of the great god Business." He believed that "the man who builds a factory builds a temple" and "the man who works there worships there."

The hands-off temperament of "Cautious Cal" Coolidge suited the times perfectly. His thrifty, cheeseparing nature caused him to sympathize fully with Secretary of the Treasury Mellon's efforts to reduce both taxes and debts. No foe of industrial bigness, he let business have its head.

The Cash Register Chorus. Business croons its appreciation of "Coolidge Prosperity." (Courtesy, *St. Louis Post-Dispatch* and the State Historical Society of Missouri)

Farm-Bred Coolidge Revisits Vermont. (Harvard College Library.)

"Coolidge luck" held during his five and a half prosperity-blessed years.

Ever a profile in caution, Coolidge slowly gave the Harding regime a badly needed moral fumigation. Yet he did not expel shady characters with undue haste, nor did he strain himself in tracking down crooks. Teapot Dome had scalded the Republican party badly, but so transparently honest was the vinegary Vermonter that the scandalous oil did not rub off on him.

In his easygoing prosecution of offenders, Coolidge adjusted comfortably to the relaxed moral standards of the time. The public, though at first shocked by scandal, quickly simmered down; and an alarming tendency developed in certain quarters to excuse some of the wrongdoers on the grounds that "they had gotten away with it." Some critics even condemned the government prosecutors for continuing to rock the boat. America's moral sense was evidently being dulled by prosperity.

"The Man with the Hoe." (Courtesy of Muskogee [Oklahoma] *Phoenix.*)

Frustrated Farmers

Sun-bronzed farmers were caught squarely in a boom-and-bust cycle in the post-war decade. While the fighting had raged, they had raked in money hand over gnarled fist; by the spring of 1920 the price of wheat had shot up to an incredible three dollars a bushel. But peace brought an end to government-guaranteed high prices and to massive purchases by other nations, as foreign production reentered the stream of world commerce.

Machines also threatened to plow the farmer under an avalanche of his own over-abundant crops. The gasoline-engine tractor was working a revolution on American farms. This steel mule was to cultivation and sowing what the McCormick reaper was to harvesting. A blue-denimed husbandman no longer had to plod after the horse-drawn plow with high-footed gait. He could sit erect on his chugging mechanical chariot and turn under and harrow many acres in a single day. He could grow bigger crops on larger areas, using fewer horses and hired hands. The wartime boom had encouraged him to bring vast new tracts under cultivation, especially in the "wheat belt" of the upper Midwest. But such improved efficiency and expanded agricultural acreage helped to pile up more price-dampening surpluses. A withering depression swept through agricultural districts in the 1920s, when one farm in four was sold for debt or taxes.

As a plaintive song of the period ran:

> No use talkin', any man's beat,
> With 'leven-cent cotton and forty-cent meat.

Schemes abounded for bringing relief to the hard-pressed farmers. A bipartisan "farm bloc" from the agricultural states sprouted up in Congress in 1921, and succeeded in driving through some helpful laws. Noteworthy was the Capper-Volstead Act, which exempted farmers' marketing cooperatives from anti-trust prosecution. The farm bloc's favorite proposal was the McNary-Haugen Bill, pushed energetically from 1924 to 1928. It sought to keep agricultural prices high by authorizing the government to buy up surpluses and sell them abroad. Losses to the government were to be made up by a special tax on the farmers. Congress twice passed the bill, but frugal Calvin Coolidge twice vetoed it. Farm prices stayed down, and the farmers' political temperatures stayed high, reaching fever pitch in the election of 1924.

A Three-Way Race to the White House in 1924

Self-satisfied Republicans, chanting "Keep Cool and Keep Coolidge," nominated "Silent Cal" for the Presidency at their convention in Cleveland in the simmering summer of 1924. Squabbling Democrats had more difficulty choosing a candidate when they met in New York's sweltering Madison Square Garden. Reflecting many of the cultural tensions of the decade, the party was hopelessly split between "wets" and "drys", urbanites and farmers, Fundamentalists and modernists, northern liberals and southern standpatters, immigrants and old-stock Americans. In one symptomatic spasm of discord, the conventioneers failed by just one vote to pass a resolution condemning the Ku Klux Klan.

Deadlocked for an unprecedented 102 ballots, the convention at last turned wearily, sweatily, and unenthusiastically to John W. Davis. A wealthy corporation lawyer connected with the Wall Street banking house of J. P. Morgan and Company, the polished nominee was no less conservative than cautious Calvin Coolidge.

The field was now wide open for a liberal candidate. White-pompadoured Senator ("Fighting Bob") LaFollette of Wisconsin, perennial aspirant to the Presidency and now sixty-nine years of age, sprang forward to lead a new progressive grouping. He gained the endorsement of the American Federation of Labor and enjoyed the support of the shrinking Socialist party, but his major constituency was made up of the price-pinched farmers. LaFollette's new Progressive party, fielding only a presidential ticket, with no candidates for local office, was a head without a body. It proved to be only a shadow of the robust progressive coalition of pre-war days. Its platform called for government ownership of railroads and relief for farmers, lashed out at monopoly and anti-labor injunctions, and urged a constitutional amendment to limit the Supreme Court's power to invalidate laws passed by Congress.

LaFollette turned in a respectable showing, polling nearly five million votes. But "Cautious Cal" and the oil-bespattered Republicans slipped easily back into office, overwhelming Davis, 15,725,016 votes to 8,386,503. The electoral count

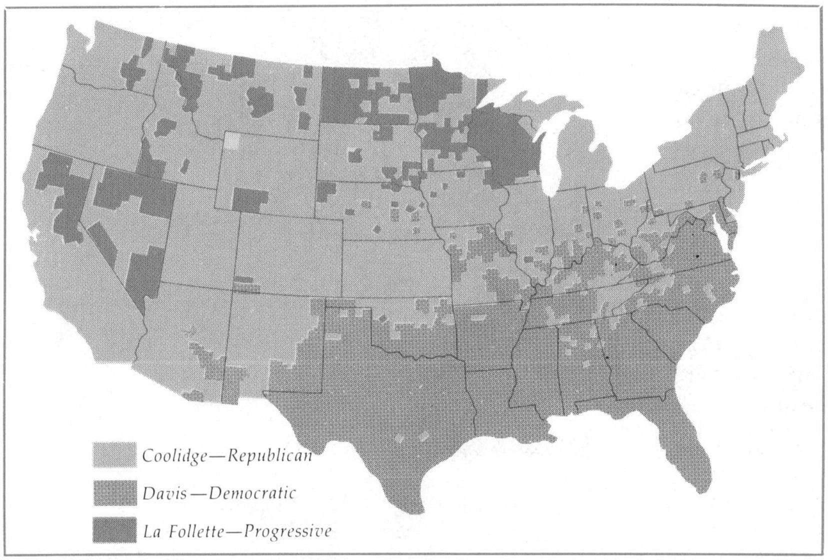

PRESIDENTIAL ELECTION OF 1924 (showing popular vote by county). Note the concentration of LaFollette's votes in the old Populist strongholds of the Middle West and the mountain states. His ticket did especially well in the grain-growing districts battered by the post-war slump in agricultural prices.

stood at 382 for Coolidge, 136 for Davis, and 13 for LaFollette, all from his home state of Wisconsin. As the so-called conscience of the calloused 1920s, LaFollette injected a badly needed liberal tonic into a decade drugged on prosperity. But times were too good for too many for his reforming message to carry the day.

Foreign Policy Flounderings

Isolation continued to reign in the Coolidge era. Despite presidential proddings, the Senate proved unwilling to allow America to adhere to the World Court—the judicial arm of the still-suspect League of Nations. Coolidge only half-heartedly—and unsuccessfully—pursued further naval disarmament after the loudly trumpeted agreements worked out at the Washington Conference in 1922.

A glaring exception to Uncle Sam's inward-looking indifference to the outside world was his armed interventionism in the Caribbean and Central America. American troops were withdrawn (after an eight-year stay) from the Dominican Republic in 1924, but they remained in Haiti from 1914 to 1934. President Coolidge in 1925 briefly removed American bayonets from troubled Nicaragua, where they had glinted intermittently since 1909, but in 1926 he sent them back, 5,000 strong, and they stayed until 1933. American oil companies clamored for a military expedition to Mexico in 1926 when the Mexican government began to assert its sovereignty over oil resources. Coolidge kept cool and defused the Mexican crisis with some skillful diplomatic negotiating. But his mailed-fist tactics elsewhere bred sore resentments south of the Rio Grande, where critics loudly assailed "*Yanqui* imperialism."

Overshadowing all other foreign-policy problems in the 1920s was the knotty issue of international debts, a complicated tangle of private loans, Allied war debts, and German reparations payments. Almost overnight, World War I had reversed the international financial position of the United States. In 1914 America had been a debtor nation in the sum of about $4 billion; by 1922 she had become a creditor nation in the sum of about $16 billion. The Almighty Dollar rivaled the pound sterling as the financial giant of the world. American investors loaned some $10 billion to foreigners in the 1920s, though even this huge river of money could not fully refloat the war-shelled world economy. Americans, bewitched by lucrative investment opportunities in their domestic economy, did not lend nearly so large a fraction of their national income overseas as had the British in the pre-war period.

The key knot in the debt tangle was the $10 billion that the United States Treasury had loaned to the Allies during and immediately after the war. Uncle Sam held their I.O.U.'s—and he wanted to be paid. The Allies, in turn, protested that the demand for repayment was grossly unfair. The French and the British pointed out, with much justice, that they had held up a wall of flesh and bone against the common foe until America the Unready had finally entered the fray. America, they argued, should write off her loans as war costs, just as the Allies had been tragically forced to write off the lives of millions of young men. The debtors also complained that the real effect of their borrowed dollars had been to fuel the boom in the already

"Harmony in Europe," 1932. (Courtesy of Detroit *News.*)

roaring wartime economy in America, where nearly all their purchases had been made. And the final straw, protested the Europeans, was that America's post-war tariff walls made it almost impossible for them to sell the goods to earn the dollars to pay their debts.

Unravelling the Debt Knot

Uncle Sam's tightfisted insistence on getting his money back helped to harden the hearts of the Allies against conquered Germany. The French and the British demanded that the Germans make enormous reparations payments, totaling some $32 billion, as compensation for war-inflicted damages. The Allies hoped to settle their debts to America with the money received from Germany. The French, seeking to extort lagging reparations payments, sent troops into Germany's industrialized Ruhr Valley in 1923. Berlin responded by permitting its currency to inflate astronomically. At one point in October 1923, a loaf of bread cost 480 million marks, or about $120 million in preinflation money. German society teetered on the brink of mad anarchy, and the whole international house of financial cards threatened to flutter down in colossal chaos.

Sensible statesmen now urged that war debts and reparations alike be drastically scaled down or even canceled outright. But to Americans such proposals smacked of "welshing" on a debt. "We went across, but they won't come across," cried a prominent politician. Scrooge-like, Calvin Coolidge turned aside suggestions of debt cancellation with a typically terse question: "They hired the money, didn't they?" The Washington administration proved especially unrealistic in its dogged insistence that there was no connection whatever between debts and reparations.

Reality finally was partly recognized in the Dawes Plan of 1924. Negotiated largely by Charles Dawes, about to be Coolidge's running mate, it

Pundit Walter Lippmann wrote in the New York *World* (1926): "International debts are like bills submitted to pay for the damage done on a wild party by one's grandfather. The payment seems to the debtor like pure loss, and when it is paid by one nation to another it seems like tribute by the conquered to the conqueror. Money borrowed to build a railroad earns money to pay for itself. But money borrowed to fight a war produces nothing."

ASPECTS OF THE FINANCIAL MERRY-GO-ROUND, 1921–1933
Great Britain, with a debt of over $4 billion owed to the U.S. Treasury, had a huge stake in proposals for inter-Allied debt cancellation, but France's stake was even larger. Less prosperous than Britain in the 1920s, and more battered by the war, which had been fought on her own soil, France owed nearly $3.5 billion to the United States, and additional billions to Britain.

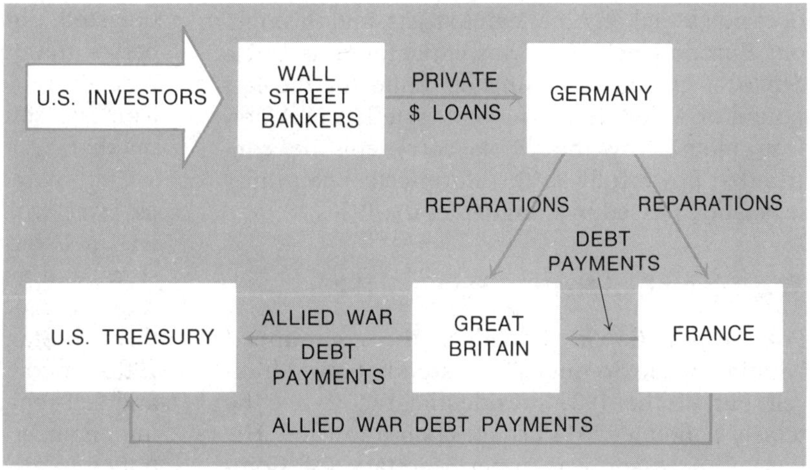

"Our Collections from France." (Fitzpatrick in the St. Louis *Post-Dispatch.*)

rescheduled German reparations payments and opened the way for further American private loans to Germany. The whole financial cycle now became still more complicated, as American bankers loaned money to Germany, Germany paid reparations to France and Britain, and the former Allies paid war debts to the United States. Clearly the source of this monetary merry-go-round was the flowing well of American credit. When that well dried up after the Great Crash in 1929, the tangled jungle of international finance quickly turned into a desert. President Herbert Hoover declared a one-year debt moratorium in 1931, and before long all the debtors had defaulted—except "honest little Finland," which struggled along making payments until the last of her debt was erased in 1976.

Uncle Sam never did get his money, but he harvested a lush crop of ill will. Irate French crowds on occasion attacked American tourists, and throughout Europe Uncle Sam was caricatured as Uncle Shylock, greedily whetting his knife for the last pound of Allied flesh. The bad taste left in American mouths by the whole sorry episode contributed powerfully to the storm-cellar neutrality legislation passed by Congress in the 1930s.

The Triumph of Herbert Hoover, 1928

Poker-faced Calvin Coolidge, the tight-lipped "Sphinx of the Potomac," apparently bowed himself out of the 1928 presidential race when he tersely announced: "I do not choose to run." His logical successor was super-Secretary (of Commerce) Herbert Hoover, unpopular with the political bosses, but the much-admired darling of the masses, who asked "Hoo but Hoover?" He was nominated on a platform that clucked contentedly over prosperity and prohibition.

Still-squabbling Democrats nominated Alfred E. Smith, four-time governor of New York and one of the most colorful personalities in American politics. He was a wise-cracking, glad-handing liberal who suffered from fatal political handicaps. "Al(cohol)" Smith was soakingly and drippingly "wet" at a time when the country was still devoted to the "noble experiment" of prohibition. To a nation that had only recently moved to the city, native New Yorker Smith seemed too abrasively urban. He was a Roman Catholic in an overwhelmingly Protestant—and unfortunately prejudiced—land. Many dry, rural, and fundamentalist Democrats gagged on his candidacy, and they saddled the wet Smith with a dry running mate and a dry platform. Jauntily sporting a brown derby and a big cigar, Smith, "the Happy Warrior," tried to carry alcohol on one shoulder and water on the other. But his effort was doomed from the start.

Radio figured prominently in this campaign for the first time, and it helped Hoover more than Smith. The New Yorker had more personal sparkle, but he could not project it through the radio (which in his Lower East Side twang he pronounced "radd-dee-o," grating the ears of many listeners). Iowa-born Hoover, with his double-breasted dignity, came out of the microphone better than he went in. Decrying un-American "socialism" and preaching "rugged individualism," he sounded both grass-rootish and statesmanlike.

Chubby-faced, ruddy-complexioned Herbert Hoover, with his painfully high starched collar, was a living example of the American success story, and an intriguing mixture of two centuries. As a poor orphan boy who had worked his way through Stanford University, he had absorbed the 19th-Century copybook maxims of industry, thrift, and self-reliance. As a fabulously successful mining engineer and a brilliant businessman, he had honed to a high degree the efficiency doctrines of the progressive era.

A small-town boy from Iowa and Oregon, he had traveled and worked abroad extensively. Long years of self-imposed exile had deepened his determination, abundantly supported by national tradition, to avoid foreign entanglements. His experiences abroad had further strengthened his faith in American individualism, free enterprise, and small government.

With his unshaken dignity, Hoover was a far cry from the ordinary back-slapping politician. Though a citizen of the world and loaded down with international honors, he was shy, standoffish, and stiff. Personally colorless in public, he had been accustomed during much of his life to giving orders to subordinates and not to soliciting votes. Never before elected to public office, he was thin-skinned in the face of criticism, and he did not adapt himself readily to the necessary give-and-take of political accommodation. His real power lay in his integrity, his humanitarianism, his passion for assembling the facts, his efficiency, his talents for administration, and his ability to inspire loyalty in close associates. They called him "the Chief."

As befitted America's newly mechanized civilization, Hoover was the ideal businessman's candidate. A millionaire in his own right, he recoiled from anything suggesting socialism, paternalism, or "planned economy." Yet as secretary of commerce he had exhibited some progressive instincts. He endorsed labor unions and supported federal regulation of the new radio broadcasting industry. He even flirted for a time with the idea of government-owned radio, similar to the British Broadcasting Corporation (B.B.C.).

Hoover Meets Members of the Press.
(Hoover Institution on War, Revolution and Peace.)

"Fine Opportunity for a Modern Engineer."
(Darling in the Des Moines *Register,* 1929.)

As bands blared Smith's theme song, "The Sidewalks of New York," the campaign sank into the sewers below the sidewalks. Despite the best efforts of Hoover and Smith, below-the-belt tactics were employed to a disgusting degree by lower-level campaigners. Religious bigotry raised its hideous head over Smith's Catholicism. An irresponsible whispering campaign claimed that "A Vote for Al Smith Is a Vote for the Pope," and that the White House, under Smith, would become a branch of the Vatican—complete with "Rum, Romanism, and Ruin." Hoover's attempts to quash such "smears" were in vain.

The proverbially Solid South—"one hundred percent American" and a stronghold of Protestant

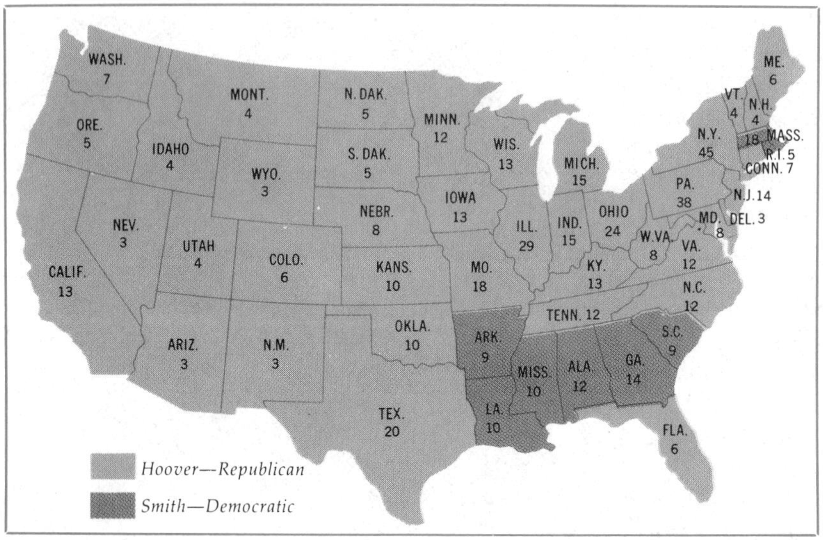

PRESIDENTIAL ELECTION OF 1928
(with electoral vote by state)

Smith, despite his defeat, managed to poll almost as many votes as the victorious Coolidge had in 1924. By attracting to the party an immense urban or "sidewalk" vote, the breezy New Yorker foreshadowed Roosevelt's New Deal victory in 1932, when the Democrats patched together the Solid South and the urban North. A cruel joke had Smith cabling the Pope a single word after the election: "Unpack."

Ku Klux Klanism—shied away from "city slicker" Al Smith. It might have accepted a Catholic, or a wet, or the descendant of Irish grandparents, or an urbanite. But a mixture of Catholicism, wettism, foreignism, and liberalism brewed on the sidewalks of New York was too bitter a dose for Southern stomachs. Smith's theme song was a constant and rasping reminder that his upbringing had not been convincingly American.

Hoover triumphed in a landslide. He bagged 21,391,381 popular votes to 15,016,443 for his embittered opponent, while rolling up an electoral count of 444 to 87. A huge Republican majority was returned to the House of Representatives. Tens of thousands of dry Southern Democrats—"Hoovercrats"—rebelled against Smith, and Hoover proved to be the first Republican candidate in fifty-two years, except for Harding's Tennessee victory in 1920, to carry a state that had seceded. He swept five states of the former Confederacy, as well as all the Border States.

President Hoover's First Moves

Prosperity in the late 1920s smiled broadly as the Hoover years began. Soaring stocks on the bull market continued to defy the laws of financial gravitation. But two immense groups of citizens were not getting their share of the riches flowing from the national horn of plenty: the unorganized wage earners and especially the disorganized farmers.

Hoover's administration, in line with its philosophy of promoting self-help, responded to the outcry of the farmers with legislative aspirin. The Agricultural Marketing Act, passed by Congress in June 1929, was designed to help the farmers help themselves, largely through producers' cooperatives. It set up a Federal Farm Board, with a revolving fund of half a billion dollars at its disposal. Money was lent generously to farm organizations seeking to buy, sell, and store agricultural surpluses.

In 1930 the Farm Board itself created both the Grain Stabilization Corporation and the Cotton Stabilization Corporation. The prime goal was to bolster sagging prices by buying up surpluses. But the two agencies were soon suffocated by an avalanche of farm produce, as wheat dropped to fifty-seven cents a bushel and cotton to five cents a pound.

Farmers had meanwhile clutched at the tariff as a possible straw to help keep their heads above the waters of financial ruin. During the recent presidential campaign, Hoover, an amateur in politics, had been stampeded into a politically unwise pledge. He had promised to call Congress into special session to consider agricultural relief and, specifically, to bring about "limited" changes in the tariff. These hope-giving assurances no doubt won many votes for Hoover in the Middle Western farm belt.

The Hawley-Smoot Tariff of 1930 followed the well-worn pattern of legislative horse trading. It started out in the House as a fairly reasonable protective measure, designed to assist the farmers. But by the time the high-pressure lobbyists had pushed it through the Senate, it had acquired about a thousand amendments. It thus turned out to be the highest protective tariff in the nation's peacetime history. The average duty on nonfree goods was raised from 38.5 percent, as established by the Fordney-McCumber Act of 1922, to nearly 60 percent.

"Mr. Hoover: Leave It to Willie." The flexible clause was designed to curb the tariff. Acid-tongued H. L. Mencken called Hoover "a fat Coolidge." (Omaha *World-Herald.* By permission.)

To angered foreigners, the Hawley-Smoot Tariff was a blow below the trade belt. It seemed like a declaration of economic warfare on the entire outside world. It reversed a promising worldwide trend toward reasonable tariffs and widened the yawning trade gaps. It plunged both America and other nations deeper into the terrible depression which had already begun. It increased international financial chaos, and forced the United States further into the bog of economic isolationism.

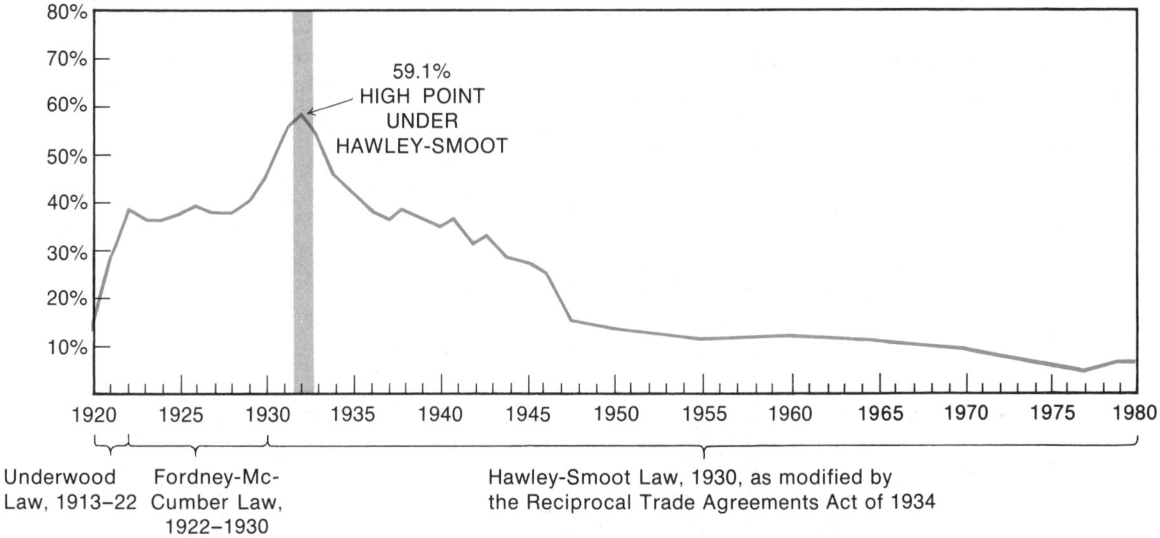

TARIFF TRENDS, 1920–1980
Average annual percentage rates on dutiable goods.

And economic isolationism, both at home and abroad, was playing directly into the hands of a wild-eyed German demagogue, Adolf Hitler.

The Great Crash Ends the Golden Twenties

When Herbert Hoover confidently took the presidential oath on March 4, 1929, there were few black clouds on the economic horizon. The "Long Boom" seemed endless, with the painful exception of the debt-blanketed farm belt. America's productive colossus—stimulated by the automobile, radio, movie, and other new industries—was roaring along at a dizzy speed that suggested a permanent plateau of prosperity. Few people sensed that it might smother its own fires by pouring out too much.

The speculative bubble was actually near the bursting point. Prices on the stock exchange continued to spiral upward and create a fool's paradise of paper profits, despite Hoover's early but fruitless efforts to curb speculation through the Federal Reserve Board. A few prophets of disaster were bold enough to raise warning voices, but they were drowned out by the mad chatter of the ticker-tape machine.

A catastrophic crash came in October 1929. It was partially triggered by the British, who raised their interest rates in an effort to bring back capital lured abroad by American investments. Foreign investors and wary domestic speculators began to dump their "insecurities," and an orgy of selling followed. Tensions built up to the panicky "Black Tuesday" of October 29, 1929, when 16,410,030 shares of stocks were sold in a save-who-may scramble. Wall Street became a wailing wall as gloom and doom replaced boom, and suicides increased alarmingly. A current "sick joke" had hotel room clerks ask registrants, "For sleeping or jumping?"

Losses, even in blue-chip securities, were fantastic. By the end of 1929—two months after the initial crash—stockholders had lost $40 billion in paper values, or more than the total cost of World War I to the United States. Typical prices of stocks are given in the table below.

Selected Stock Prices, Sept.–Nov. 1929

Stocks	*Adjusted High Price*	*Low Price*
	Sept. 3, 1929	*Nov. 13, 1929*
American Can	$181⅞	$ 86
General Electric	396¼	168⅛
Montgomery Ward	137⅞	49¼

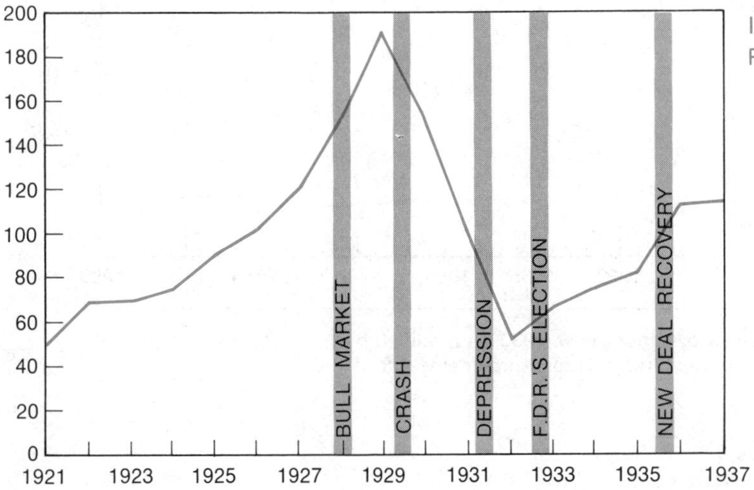

INDEX OF COMMON STOCK PRICES (1926 = 100)

The stock-market collapse heralded a business depression, at home and abroad, which was the most prolonged and withering in American or world experience. No other industrialized nation suffered so severe a setback. By the end of 1930 about 6 or 7 million workers in the United States were jobless; two years later the figure had about doubled. Hungry and despairing men pounded pavements in search of non-existent jobs ("We're firing, not hiring"). Where employees were not discharged, wages and salaries were often slashed. A current jingle ran:

> Mellon pulled the whistle,
> Hoover rang the bell
> Wall Street gave the signal
> And the country went to hell.

The misery and gloom were incalculable, as forests of dead chimneys stood starkly against the sky. Over 5,000 banks collapsed in the first three years of the depression, carrying down with them the life savings of tens of thousands of widows and retired citizens. Countless thousands of honest, hardworking people lost their homes and farms to the forecloser's hammer. Bread lines formed, soup kitchens dispensed food, and apple sellers stood shivering on street corners trying to peddle their wares for five cents. Foreign trade faded badly, for the worldwide depression dried up purchasing power. As cash registers gathered cobwebs, the song "My God, How the Money Rolls In" was replaced with "Brother, Can You Spare a Dime?"

Hooked on the Horn of Plenty

What caused the Great Depression? One basic explanation was overproduction by both farm and factory. Ironically, the depression of the 1930s was one of abundance, not want. It was the "Great Glut" or the "Plague of Plenty."

The nation's ability to produce goods had clearly outrun its capacity to consume or pay for them. Too much money was going into the hands of a few wealthy people, who in turn invested it in factories and other agencies of production. Not enough was going into salaries and wages, where revitalizing purchasing power could be more quickly felt.

Other maladies were at work. Overexpansion of credit through installment-plan buying overstimulated production. Paying on so-called easy terms caused many a consumer to plunge in beyond his depth. Normal technological unemployment, resulting from new labor-saving machines, also added its burden to the abnormal unemployment of the "threadbare thirties."

This already bleak picture was further darkened by economic anemia abroad. Britain and the Continent had never fully recovered from the upheaval of World War I. Depression in America was given a further downward push by a chain-reaction financial collapse in Europe, following the failure in 1931 of a prominent Vienna banking house. A drying up of international trade, moreover, had been hastened by the shortsighted Hawley-Smoot Tariff of 1930. European uncertainties over reparations, war debts, and defaults on loans owed to America caused tensions that reacted unfavorably on the United States. Many of these conditions had been created or worsened by Uncle

Farm Depression and Industrial Expansion in the 1920s. (Fitzpatrick in the St. Louis *Post-Dispatch*.)

Sam's own narrow-visioned policies, but it was now too late to unscramble the omelet.

As if man-made disasters were not enough, a terrible drought scorched the Mississippi Valley in 1930. Thousands of farms were sold at auction for taxes, though in some cases kind neighbors would intimidate prospective buyers, bid one cent, and return the property to its original owner. Farm tenancy or rental—a species of peonage—was spreading at an alarming rate among both whites and blacks.

By 1930 the depression had become a national calamity. Through no fault of their own, a host of industrious citizens had lost everything. They wanted to work—but there was no work. The blighting effect of all this dazed despair on the spirit was incalculable and long lasting. America's "uniqueness" no longer seemed so unique or her manifest destiny so manifest. Hitherto the people had grappled with storms, trees, stones, and other physical obstacles. But the depression was a baffling wraith they could not grasp. Initiative and self-respect were stifled, as panhandlers begged for food or "charity soup." In extreme cases "ragged individualists" slept under "Hoover blankets" (old newspapers), fought over the contents of garbage cans, or cooked their findings in old oil drums in tin-and-paper shantytowns cynically named "Hoovervilles." The very foundations of America's social structure trembled.

> Shivering men sold apples on the street corners of the big cities at five cents apiece. Hoover, in his *Memoirs* (1952), claims that the apple growers shrewdly and profitably capitalized on "the sympathy of the public for the unemployed." He further states, with obvious exaggeration, "Many persons left their jobs for the more profitable one of selling apples. When any left-winger wishes to indulge in scathing oratory, he demands, 'Do you want to return to selling apples?'"

Rugged Times for Rugged Individualists

Hoover's exalted reputation as a wonder-worker and efficiency engineer crashed about as dismally as the stock market. He doubtless would have shone in the prosperity-drenched Coolidge years, when he had foreseen the abolition of poverty and poorhouses. But damming the Great Depression proved to be a task beyond his engineering talents.

The perplexed President was thus impaled on the horns of a cruel dilemma. As a deservedly famed humanitarian, he was profoundly distressed by the widespread misery about him. Yet as a "rugged individualist," deeply rooted in an earlier era of free enterprise, he shrank from the heresy of government handouts. Convinced that industry, thrift, and self-reliance were the virtues that had made America great, he feared that a government

A San Francisco Bread Line in 1933. (Dorothea Lange Collection, The Oakland Museum.)

doling out doles would weaken, perhaps destroy, the national fiber.

Hoover had deep faith in the efficiency of the industrial machine, which itself was undamaged by depression. From time to time he would attempt to encourage the public by issuing optimistic statements, which often were followed by a fresh decline. He was accused of saying, although he did not use these precise words, that prosperity was hovering just around the corner. "Hoovering," critics jibed.

As the depression nightmare steadily worsened, relief by local government agencies broke down. Hoover was finally forced to turn reluctantly from his doctrine of log-cabin individualism and accept the proposition that the welfare of the people in a nationwide depression is a direct concern of the national government.

The President at last worked out a compromise between the old hands-off philosophy and the "soul-destroying" direct dole then being used in England. He would assist the hard-pressed railroads, banks, and rural credit corporations, in the hope that if financial health were restored at the top of the economic pyramid, unemployment would be relieved at the bottom on a trickle-down basis.

Partisan critics sneered at the "Great Humanitarian"—he who had fed the faraway Belgians but would not use federal funds to feed needy Americans. Hostile commentators remarked that he was willing to lend government money to the big bankers, who allegedly had plunged the country into the mess. He would likewise lend money to agricultural organizations to feed pigs—but not people. Pigs, cynics noted, had no character to undermine.

Blaming Hoover. The once-popular President became an object of ridicule after 1929. (The Bettmann Archive, Inc.)

Hoover spoke approvingly in a campaign speech in 1928 of "the American system of Rugged Individualism." In 1930 he referred to Cleveland's 1887 veto of a bill to appropriate seed grain for the drought-stricken farmers of Texas: "I do not believe that the power and duty of the General Government ought to be extended to the relief of individual suffering. . . . The lesson should be constantly enforced that though the people support the Government the Government should not support the people."

Much of this criticism was unfair. Though continued suffering seemed to belie the effectiveness of Hoover's measures, his efforts probably prevented a more serious collapse than did occur. And his expenditures for relief, revolutionary for that day, paved the path for the enormous federal outlays of his New Deal successor, Franklin Roosevelt. Hoover proved that the old bootstrap-pulling techniques would no longer work in a crisis of this magnitude, especially where people lacked boots.

Herbert Hoover: Pioneer for the New Deal

President Hoover, in line with his "trickle-down" philosophy, at last recommended that Congress vote immense sums for useful public works. Though at heart an anti-spender, he secured from

Congress appropriations totaling $2.25 billion for such projects. To alarmists, the Washington ship of state seemed in danger of sinking in a red-ink sea of unbalanced budgets and mounting debts. Hoover warned, "Prosperity cannot be restored by raids on the public treasury."

Most imposing of the public enterprises was the gigantic Hoover Dam on the Colorado River. Voted by Congress in the days of Coolidge, it was begun in 1930 under Hoover and completed in 1936 under Roosevelt. It succeeded in creating a huge man-made lake for purposes of irrigation, flood control, and electric power.

But Hoover sternly fought all schemes that he regarded as "socialistic." Conspicuous among them was the Norris Muscle Shoals Bill, designed to dam the Tennessee River and ultimately embraced by Franklin Roosevelt's Tennessee Valley Authority. Hoover emphatically vetoed this measure, primarily because he opposed the government's selling electricity in competition with its own citizens in private companies.

Early in 1932 Congress, responding to Hoover's belated appeal, established the Reconstruction Finance Corporation (R.F.C.). With an initial working capital of half a billion dollars, this agency became a government lending bank. It was designed to provide indirect relief by assisting insurance companies, banks, agricultural organizations, railroads, and even hard-pressed state and local governments. But to preserve individualism and character, there would be no loans to individuals from this "billion-dollar soup kitchen."

"Pump-priming" loans by the R.F.C. were no doubt of widespread benefit, though the organization was established many months too late for maximum usefulness. Projects that it supported were largely self-liquidating, and the government as a banker actually profited to the tune of many millions of dollars. Giant corporations so obviously benefited from this assistance that the R.F.C. was dubbed—rather unfairly—"the millionaires' dole." The irony is that the thrifty and individualistic Hoover had sponsored the project, though with initial reluctance. It actually had a strong New-Dealish flavor.

Hoover's administration also provided some indirect benefits for labor. After stormy debate, Congress passed the Norris–La Guardia Anti-Injunction Act in 1932, and Hoover signed it. The measure outlawed "yellow dog" (anti-union) contracts, and forbade the federal courts to issue injunctions to restrain strikes, boycotts, and peaceful picketing.

The truth is that Herbert Hoover, despite criticism of his "heartlessness," did inaugurate a significant new policy. In previous panics the masses had been forced to "sweat it out." Slow though Hoover was to abandon this 19th-Century bias, by the end of his term he had traveled a long way toward government assistance for needy citizens—a road that Franklin Roosevelt was to take all the way.

Hoover's woes, one should note, were increased by a hostile Congress. At critical times during his first two years, the Republican majority proved highly uncooperative. Friction worsened during his last two years. A depression-cursed electorate, rebelling in the congressional elections of 1930, so reduced the Republican majority that Democrats controlled the new House and almost controlled the Senate. Insurgent Republicans could—and did—combine with opposition Democrats to harass Hoover. Some of the President's troubles were deliberately manufactured by congressmen who, in his words, "played politics with human misery."

Routing the Bonus Army in Washington

Many veterans of World War I were numbered among the hard-hit victims of the depression. Industry had secured a "bonus"—though a dubious one—in the Hawley-Smoot Tariff. So the thoughts of the former "doughboys" naturally turned to what the government owed them for their services in 1917–1918, when they had "saved" democracy. A drive developed for the premature payment of the deferred bonus voted by Congress in 1924 and payable in 1945.

Hoover was icily unsympathetic to a bonus. As a sound-money man, he emphatically opposed all suggestions from pressure groups for further un-

The Battle of Anacostia Flats. Troops using tear gas laid waste the BEF encampment, 1932. (United Press International photo.)

balancing the budget and inflating the currency. But a vote-conscious Congress proved more responsive. It passed a bill in 1931 enabling veterans to borrow up to 50 percent on their bonus (adjusted compensation), instead of 22 percent. This concession would impose an additional burden on the Treasury, already in the red, of from $1 billion to $2 billion. Hoover's vigorous veto was so much wasted ink.

Thousands of impoverished veterans, both of war and unemployment, were now prepared to move on to Washington, there to demand of Congress the immediate payment of their *entire* bonus. The "Bonus Expeditionary Force" (B.E.F.), which mustered about 20,000 souls, converged on the capital in the summer of 1932. These supplicants promptly set up unsanitary public camps and erected shacks on vacant lots—a gigantic "Hooverville." They thus created a menace to the public health, while attempting to intimidate Congress by their presence in force. After the pending bonus bill had failed in Congress by a narrow margin, Hoover arranged to pay the return fare of about 6,000 bonus marchers. The rest refused to decamp, though ordered to do so.

Following riots that cost two lives, Hoover responded to the demands of the Washington authorities by ordering the army to evacuate the unwanted guests. Though Hoover charged that the "Bonus Army" was led by Reds and riff-raff, in fact only a sprinkling of them were former convicts and Communist agitators. The eviction was carried out by General Douglas MacArthur with bayonets and tear gas, and with far more severity than Hoover had planned. A few of the former soldiers were injured as the torch was put to their pathetic shanties in the inglorious "Battle of Anacostia Flats." An eleven-month-old "bonus baby" allegedly died from exposure to tear gas.

This brutal episode brought down additional condemnation on the once-popular Hoover, who by now was the most loudly booed man in the country. The Democrats, not content with his vulnerable record, employed professional "smear" artists to drive him from office. Cynics sneered that the "Great Engineer" had in a few months "ditched, drained, and damned the country." The existing panic was unfairly branded "the Hoover Depression." In truth, Hoover had been oversold as a superman—and the public grumbled when his magician's wand failed to produce rabbits. The time was ripening for the Democratic party—and Franklin D. Roosevelt—to cash in on Hoover's calamities.

Japanese Militarists Attack China

The Great Depression, which brewed enough distress at home, added immensely to difficulties abroad.

Rampaging Japan stole the Far Eastern spotlight. In September 1931, the Japanese imperialists, noting that the Western world was badly mired down in depression, lunged into Manchuria. Alleging provocation, they rapidly overran the coveted Chinese province, and proceeded to bolt shut the Open Door in the conquered area.

Peaceful peoples were stunned by this act of naked aggression. It was a flagrant violation of the League of Nations covenant, as well as of various other international agreements solemnly signed by Tokyo. Far-visioned observers feared that unless the major powers, acting through the League of Nations, could force Japan to disgorge, the League would perish. Failure would kill collective security, and wipe out the best hope of averting another global conflagration.

Meeting in Geneva, the League was eager to strengthen itself by luring Uncle Sam into its camp. In response to an urgent invitation, an American sat for the first time, though unofficially, with the Council of the League during its discussions of the Manchurian crisis. An American also served on the firsthand investigating commission appointed by the League.

But intervention by the League availed nothing. Its five-man commission of probers reported in 1932 that the Japanese incursion was unjustified. But this condemnation, instead of driving Japan out of Manchuria, merely drove Japan out of the League. Another nail was thus hammered into the coffin of collective security.

Numerous red-blooded Americans, though by no means a majority, urged strong measures,

"The Light of Asia," 1933. Japan sets fire to treaty commitments. (Reprinted with permission of Washington *Daily News.*)

ranging from boycotts to blockades. Possibly a tight blockade by the League, backed by the United States, would have brought Japan sharply to book. But Hoover reflected the isolationist sentiments of most Americans, who wanted no part of the Far Eastern mess. One newspaper remarked that America did not "give a hoot in a rain barrel" about who controlled Manchuria.

The League was handicapped in taking two-fisted action by the non-membership of the United States. Washington flatly rebuffed initial attempts in 1931 to secure American cooperation in applying economic pressures. But Secretary of State Stimson, who was much more internationalist-minded than Hoover, indicated that the United States probably would not interfere with a League embargo. The next year Stimson was more eager to take vigorous steps, but the President cautiously restrained him.

Washington in the end decided to fire only paper bullets at the Japanese aggressors. The so-called Hoover-Stimson doctrine, proclaimed in 1932, declared that the United States would not recognize any territorial acquisitions achieved by force. Righteous indignation—or a preach-and-run policy—would substitute for vigorous initiatives.

> Hoover later wrote of his differences with Secretary Stimson over economic boycotts: "I was soon to realize that my able Secretary was at times more of a warrior than a diplomat. To him the phrase 'economic sanctions' was the magic wand of force by which all peace could be summoned from the vasty deep. . . . Ever since Versailles I had held that 'economic sanctions' meant war when applied to any large nation."

This verbal slap on the wrist from America did not deter the march of the Japanese militarists. Smarting under a Chinese boycott, they bombed Shanghai in 1932, with shocking losses to the civilians. Outraged Americans launched informal boycotts of Japanese goods, chiefly dime-store knickknacks. But there was no real sentiment for armed intervention among a depression-ridden people who remained strongly isolationist during the 1930s. President Hoover, who fully shared their views, believed that boycotts and embargoes spelled bayonets and bombs.

In a broad sense, collective security died and World War II was born in 1931 on the windswept plains of Manchuria. The League members had the economic and naval power to halt Japan, but lacked the courage to act. One reason—though not the only one—was that they could not count on America's support. Even so, the Republic came closer to stepping into the chill waters of internationalism than American prophets would have dared to predict in the early 1920s.

Hoover Pioneers for the Good Neighbor Policy

Hoover's arrival at the White House brought a more hopeful turn to relations with the southern neighbors. The new President was deeply interested in the colorful lands below the Rio Grande; shortly after his election in 1928 he had undertaken a goodwill tour of Latin America—on an American battleship.

World depression gave birth to a less aggressive attitude in the United States toward weak Latin neighbors. Following the stock-market collapse of 1929, Americans had less money to invest abroad. As millions of dollars' worth of investments in Latin America went sour, many Yankees felt that they were more preyed upon than preying. Economic imperialism—so called—became much less popular in the United States than it had been in the Golden Twenties.

As an advocate of international goodwill, Hoover strove to abandon the interventionist twist given to the Monroe Doctrine by Theodore Roosevelt. In 1932 he negotiated a new treaty with the French-speaking republic of Haiti, and this pact, later supplanted by an executive agreement, provided for the complete withdrawal of American bayonets by 1934. Further pleasing omens came early in 1933, when the last marine "leathernecks" sailed away from the banana republic of Nicaragua after an almost continuous stay of some twenty years.

Herbert Hoover, the Engineer in Politics, thus happily engineered the foundation stones of the "Good Neighbor" policy. Upon them rose an imposing edifice in the days of his successor, Franklin Roosevelt.

VARYING VIEWPOINTS

Many American historians have been "liberals," and this political preference has strongly colored writing about the 1920s. The decade is often depicted as a rude interruption of the supposedly continuous reform surge that pulsated from progressivism to the New Deal. In this view, Harding's "normalcy" was not normal at all, and the conservatism of Coolidge and Hoover appeared as some kind of aberration. The three Republican Presidents are seen as constituting a reactionary interlude in the forward march of liberal reform that is supposedly the main theme of American society in the present century. Such an interpretation is conspicuous in John D. Hicks's *Republican Ascendancy*.

Yet in recent years many questions have been raised about this judgment. As historians increasingly distinguish progressivism from the New Deal, they naturally ask what, if anything, the 1920s "interrupted." And when "New Left" critics in the 1960s pooh-poohed the reform character of progressivism and of the New Deal itself, they implicitly suggested that the 1920s carried forward the essentially *conservative* course of modern American history.

Herbert Hoover's changing historical reputation illustrates these trends. He was widely criticized, for four decades after his Presidency, as a callous incompetent and a head-in-the-sand, doctrinaire, *laissez-faire* conservative. But Hoover was partly rehabilitated in the 1970s when skepticism about big, activist government spread in the wake of Vietnam and the Watergate scandals. Hoover's historical standing will probably continue to serve as a kind of barometer of attitudes toward government. And debate continues as to whether the 1920s represented the last chapter in the history of a dying conservative order, or simply another episode, however dramatic, in the ongoing saga of a highly individualistic, business-oriented society.

SELECT READINGS

A lively introduction to the post-war decade is Burl Noggle, *Into the Twenties: The United States from Armistice to Normalcy* (1974). On Harding, see Andrew Sinclair's favorable *The Available Man* (1965), Francis Russell's critical *The Shadow of Blooming Grove* (1968), and R. K. Murray's balanced *The Harding Era* (1969). Consult also Murray's *The Politics of Normalcy: Government Theory and Practice in the Harding-Coolidge Era* (1973). Burl Noggle looks at the chief scandal of the period in *Teapot Dome* (1962). David M. Kennedy, *Over Here: The First World War and American Society* (1980) discusses post-war race relations and demobilization, as well as the international economic aftermath of the war, a subject treated at greater length in Joan Hoff Wilson, *American Business and Foreign Policy, 1920–1933* (1971). For the background to the Washington disarmament conference, consult Roger Dingman, *Power in the Pacific: The Origins of Naval Arms Limitation, 1914–1922* (1976). For the Conference itself, see T. H. Buckley, *The United States and the Washington Conference, 1921–1922* (1970). Other foreign policy topics are covered in L. E. Ellis, *Frank B. Kellogg and American Foreign Relations, 1925–1929* (1961), and R. H. Ferrell, *Peace in Their Time: The Origins of the Kellogg-Briand Pact* (1952). The Democratic party is analyzed in David Burner, *The Politics of Provincialism* (1967). Biographies of Coolidge include W. A. White's cynical and amusing *A Puritan in Babylon* (1938) and D. R. McCoy's scholarly *Calvin Coolidge: The Quiet President* (1967). The complicated international financial tangle of the 1920s is deftly discussed in Herbert Feis, *The Diplomacy of the Dollar* (1950) and in the early chapters of Charles Kindleberger, *The World in Depression* (1973). The drama of the 1928 election is captured in Allan J. Lichtman, *Prejudice and the Old Politics: The Presidential Election of 1928* (1979), and in Ocsar Handlin, *Al Smith and His America* (1958). The best brief biography of Hoover is Joan Hoff Wilson, *Herbert Hoover, Forgotten Progressive* (1975). Brilliantly unsympathetic toward Hoover is A. M. Schlesinger, Jr., *The Crisis of the Old Order, 1919–1933* (1957). More favorable is David Burner, *Herbert Hoover: A Public Life* (1979). See also A. U. Romasco, *The Poverty of Abundance* (1965) and Jordan A. Schwarz, *The Interregnum of Despair: Hoover, Congress, and the Depression* (1970). Hoover's own *American Individualism* (1922) is thought-provoking, while his memoirs are marred by excessive self-justification: *The Cabinet and the Presidency, 1920–1933* (1952), and *The Great Depression, 1929–1941* (1952). On the Depression itself, consult J. K. Galbraith's breezy *The Great Crash, 1929* (1955), Peter Temin's trenchant *Did Monetary Factors Cause the Great Depression?* (1976), and Lester V. Chandler's comprehensive *America's Greatest Depression* (1970). On foreign affairs consult R. H. Ferrell, *American Diplomacy in the Great Depression* (1957), E. E. Morison, *Turmoil and Tradition: A Study of the Life and Times of Henry L. Stimson* (1960), Armin Rappaport, *Henry L. Stimson and Japan, 1931–1933* (1963), and Donald M. Dozer, *Are We Good Neighbors? Three Decades of Inter-American Relations, 1930–1960* (1959).

40

The Great Depression and the New Deal

The country needs and . . . demands bold, persistent experimentation. It is common sense to take a method and try it. If it fails, admit it frankly and try another. But above all, try something.

FRANKLIN D. ROOSEVELT, 1932 campaign speech

FDR: A Politician in a Wheelchair

Voters were in an ugly mood as the presidential campaign of 1932 neared. Countless factory chimneys remained ominously cold, while more than 11 million unemployed workers and their families sank ever deeper into the pit of poverty. The "chicken in every pot" of 1928 had seemingly laid a discharge slip in every pay envelope.

Herbert Hoover, sick at heart, was renominated by the Republican convention in Chicago without great enthusiasm. Not to run him again would be a suicidal confession of failure. The platform indulged in extravagant praise of Republican anti-depression policies, while halfheartedly promising to repeal national prohibition and return control of liquor to the states.

The rising star in the Democratic firmament was Governor Franklin Delano Roosevelt of New York, a fifth cousin of Theodore Roosevelt. Like the Rough Rider, he had been born to a wealthy New York family, had graduated from Harvard, had been elected as a kid-glove politician to the New York legislature, had served as governor of the Empire State, had been nominated for the vice-presidency (though not elected), and had served capably as assistant secretary of the navy. Though both men were master politicians, adept with the colorful phrase, FDR was suave and conciliatory, while TR was pugnacious and denunciatory.

Infantile paralysis, while putting steel braces on Franklin Roosevelt's legs, put additional steel into his soul. Until 1921, when the dread disease struck, young Roosevelt—tall (6 feet 2 inches; 1.88 meters), athletic, classic-featured, and as handsome as a Greek god—impressed observers as charming and witty yet at times a supercilious and arrogant "lightweight." But suffering humbled him and brought him down to the level of common clay. In courageously fighting his way back from complete helplessness to a hobbling mobility, he schooled himself in patience, tolerance, compassion, and strength of will. He once remarked that after trying for two years to wiggle one big toe, all else seemed easy.

Roosevelt's political appeal was amazing. His commanding presence and his golden speaking voice, despite a sophisticated accent, combined to make him the premier American orator of his generation. He could turn on charm in private conversations as one would turn on a faucet. As a popular depression governor of New York, he had sponsored heavy state spending to relieve human suffering. Though favoring frugality, he believed that money, rather than humanity, was expendable. He revealed a deep concern for the plight of the "forgotten man"—a phrase he used in a 1932 speech—although he was assailed by the rich as a "traitor to his class."

Exuberant Democrats met in Chicago in June 1932 and speedily nominated Roosevelt. Al Smith felt entitled to a second chance; and a beautiful friendship wilted when he was elbowed aside for Franklin Roosevelt.* The Democratic platform came out more flat-footedly than the Republican for repeal of prohibition, assailed the so-called Hoover depression, and promised not only a balanced budget but sweeping social and economic reforms. Roosevelt flew daringly through stormy weather to Chicago to accept the nomination in person. He electrified the delegates and the public with these words: "I pledge you, I pledge myself to a new deal for the American people."

> In his successful campaign of 1928 for the governorship of New York, Roosevelt had played down alleged Democratic "socialism": "We often hear it said that government operation of anything under the sun is socialistic. If that is so, our postal service is socialistic, so is the parcel post which has largely taken the place of the old express companies; so are the public highways which took the place of the toll roads."

Presidential Hopefuls of 1932

In the campaign that followed, Roosevelt seized the offensive with a slashing attack on the Republican Old Dealers. In all, he traveled about 25,000 miles (40,000 kilometers). He was especially eager to prove that he was not an invalid ("Roosevelt Is Robust"), and to display his magnificent torso and radiant personality to as many voters as possible.

Roosevelt consistently preached a New Deal for the "forgotten man," but he was annoyingly vague and somewhat contradictory. Many of his speeches were "ghost-written" by the "Brains Trust" (popularly the "Brain Trust"), a small group of reform-minded intellectuals. They were pre-

*In supporting the crippled Roosevelt for office in 1928, Al Smith had said, "The governor of New York does not have to be an acrobat."

Roosevelt and Happy Days. (Wide World Photos.)

dominantly youngish college professors, who, as a kind of Kitchen Cabinet, later authored much of the New Deal legislation. Roosevelt rashly promised a balanced budget and berated heavy Hooverian deficits, amid cries of "Throw the Spenders Out!" and "Out of the Red with Roosevelt." All this was to make ironical reading in later months.

The high spirits of the Democrats found vent in the rallying cry "Everything Will Be Rosy with Roosevelt" and in the catchy air "Happy Days Are Here Again." This theme song fitted FDR's indestructible smile, his jauntily angled cigarette holder, his breezy optimism, and his promises to do something even at the risk of bold experimentation.

Grim-faced Herbert Hoover remained in the White House, conscientiously battling the depression through short lunches and long hours. Out on the firing line his supporters halfheartedly cried, "The Worst Is Past," "It Might Have Been Worse," and "Prosperity Is Just Around the Corner." Faint blushes of returning prosperity did become visible in the early months of the campaign, but these gradually faded as election day neared. Hoover never ceased to insist that the uncertainty and fear produced by Roosevelt's impending victory plunged the nation back into the depression.

With the campaign going badly for the Republicans, a weary and despondent Hoover was persuaded to take to the stump. He stoutly reaffirmed his faith in American free enterprise and individual initiative, and gloomily predicted that if the Hawley-Smoot Tariff were repealed, the grass would grow "in the streets of a hundred cities." Such down-at-the-mouthism contrasted sharply with Roosevelt's tooth-flashing optimism and sparkling promises.

The Humiliation of Hoover in 1932

Hoover had been swept into office on the rising tide of prosperity; he was swept out by the receding tide of depression. The flood of votes totaled 22,821,857 for Roosevelt and 15,761,841 for Hoover; the electoral count stood at 472 to 59. In all, the loser carried only six rock-ribbed Republican states.

One striking feature of the election was the beginning of a heavy shift of blacks, traditionally grateful to the Republican party of Lincoln, over to the Roosevelt camp. As the "last hired and first fired," the blacks had been among the worst sufferers from the depression. Beginning with the election of 1932, they were to comprise, notably in the great urban centers of the North, a vital element in the Democratic party.

Hard times unquestionably ruined the Republicans, for the electoral upheaval in 1932 seems to have been more anti-Hoover than pro-Roosevelt. Democrats had only to harness the national grudge and let it pull them to victory. "A Vote for Roosevelt Is a Vote against Hoover," ran the saying. An overwhelming majority appear to have voiced a demand for a change: *a* new deal rather than *the* New Deal, for the latter was only a gleam in the eyes of its sponsors. Any upstanding Democratic candidate probably could have won.

The pre-inauguration "lame duck" period now ground slowly to an end. Hoover, though defeated and repudiated, continued to be President for four long months, until March 4, 1933. But he was helpless to embark upon any long-range policies without the cooperation of Roosevelt—and the victorious President-elect proved rather uncooperative. Hoover at length succeeded in arranging two meetings with him to discuss the war-debt muddle. But Roosevelt, who airily remarked to the press, "It's not my baby," fought shy of assuming responsibility without authority. As Hoover privately confessed, he was trying to bind his successor to an anti-inflationary policy that would have made impossible many of the later New Deal experiments. But in politics the winner, not the loser, calls the tune.

With Washington deadlocked, the vast and vaunted American economic machine clanked to a virtual halt. One worker in four tramped the streets, feet weary and hands idle. Banks were locking their doors all over the nation, as people nervously stuffed paper money under their mattresses. Hooverites, then and later, accused Roosevelt of deliberately permitting the depression to worsen, so that he could emerge the more spectacularly as a savior.

FDR and the Three R's: Relief, Recovery, Reform

Great crises often call forth gifted leaders; and the hand of destiny tapped Roosevelt on the shoulder. On a dreary inauguration day, March 4, 1933, his vibrant voice, broadcast nationally from a bullet-proof stand, provided the American people with inspirational new hope. He denounced the "money changers" who had brought on the calamity, and declared that the government must wage war on the Great Depression as it would wage war on an armed foe. His clarion note was: "Let me assert my firm belief that the only thing we have to fear is fear itself."

Roosevelt moved decisively. Now that he had full responsibility, he boldly declared a nationwide banking holiday, March 6–10, as a prelude to opening the banks on a sounder basis. He then summoned the overwhelmingly Democratic Congress into special session to cope with the national emergency. Members stayed at their task for the so-called Hundred Days (March 9 – June 16, 1933), hastily grinding out an unprecedented basketful of remedial legislation. Some of it seemed related to earlier progressivism, but mostly these new measures sought to deal with a desperate emergency.

Roosevelt's New Deal program was sparked by three R's—relief, recovery, and reform. Short-range goals were relief and immediate recovery, especially in the first two years. Long-range goals were permanent recovery and reform of current abuses, particularly those that had produced the boom-and-bust catastrophe. The three-R objectives often overlapped and got in one another's way. But amid all the haste and topsy-turvyism, the gigantic New Deal program lurched forward.

Firmly ensconced in the driver's seat, Roosevelt cracked the whip. A green Congress so fully shared the panicky feeling of the country that it was ready to rubber-stamp bills drafted by White House advisers—measures that Roosevelt called "must legislation." More than that, Congress gave the President extraordinary blank-check powers: some of the laws that it passed expressly delegated legislative authority to the Chief Executive. One senator complained that if FDR asked Congress "to commit suicide tomorrow, they'd do it."

Roosevelt was delighted to accept executive leadership, and Congress responded to it, although he did not always know precisely where he was going. He was inclined to do things by intuition—off the cuff. He was like the quarterback, as he put it, whose next play depends on the success of the previous play. So desperate was the mood of an action-starved public that movement, even in the wrong direction, seemed better than no movement at all.

The frantic Hundred Days Congress passed

Principal New Deal Acts During Hundred Days Congress, 1933
(ITEMS IN PARENTHESES INDICATE SECONDARY PURPOSES.)

Recovery	*Relief*	*Reform*
FDR closes banks, March 6, 1933		
Emergency Banking Relief Act, March 9, 1933		
(Beer Act)	(Beer Act)	Beer and Wine Revenue Act, March 22, 1933
(CCC)	Unemployment Relief Act, March 31, 1933, creates Civilian Conservation Corps (CCC)	
FDR orders gold surrender, April 5, 1933		
FDR abandons gold standard, April 19, 1933		
(FERA)	Federal Emergency Relief Act, May 12, 1933, creates Federal Emergency Relief Administration (FERA)	
(AAA)	Agricultural Adjustment Act (AAA), May 12, 1933	
(TVA)	(TVA)	Tennessee Valley Authority Act (TVA), May 18, 1933
		Federal Securities Act, May 27, 1933
Gold-payment clause repealed, June 5, 1933		
(HOLC)	Home Owners' Refinancing Act, June 13, 1933, creates Home Owners' Loan Corporation (HOLC)	
National Industrial Recovery Act, June 16, 1933, creates National Recovery Administration (NRA), Public Works Administration (PWA)	(NRA; PWA)	(NRA)
(Glass-Steagall Act)	(Glass-Steagall Act)	Glass-Steagall Banking Reform Act, June 16, 1933, creates Federal Deposit Insurance Corporation

For later New Deal measures, see p. 757.

"The Galloping Snail." A jeer at the "assembly-line" bills rammed through Congress. (Thomas in the Detroit *News*. By permission.)

many essentials of the New Deal "three Rs," though important long-range measures were added in later sessions. These reforms, already foreshadowed by the Democratic platform of 1932, were generally in tune with the Bull Moose–New Freedom tradition. Many of them were long overdue, sidetracked by World War I and the Old Guard reaction of the 1920s. The New Dealers, sooner or later, embraced such progressive ideas as unemployment insurance, old-age insurance, minimum-wage regulations, and restrictions on child labor. Many of these forward-looking measures had already been adopted a generation or so earlier by the more enlightened countries of Western Europe. A few such reforms had been accepted on a limited basis by some of the states, chiefly during the progressive era. But in the area of social welfare the United States, in the eyes of many Europeans, remained a "backward nation."

Roosevelt Tackles Money and Banking

Banking chaos cried aloud for immediate action. Congress pulled itself together, and in an incredible eight hours had the Emergency Banking Relief Act of 1933 ready for Roosevelt's busy pen. The new law clothed the President with power to regulate banking transactions and foreign exchange, and to reopen solvent banks.

Roosevelt, the master showman, next turned to the radio to deliver the first of his thirty famous "Fireside Chats." As some 35 million people hung on his soothing words, he gave assurances that it was now safer to keep money in a reopened bank than "under the mattress." Confidence returned with a gush, and the banks began to unlock their doors.

The Emergency or Hundred Days Congress buttressed public reliance on the banking system by enacting the memorable Glass-Steagall Banking Reform Act. This measure provided for the Federal Deposit Insurance Corporation, which insured individual deposits up to $5,000 (later raised). Thus ended the disgraceful epidemic of bank failures, which dated back to the "wildcat" days of Andrew Jackson.*

Roosevelt moved swiftly elsewhere on the financial front, seeking to protect the melting gold reserve and to prevent panicky hoarding. He ordered all private holdings of gold to be surrendered to the Treasury in exchange for paper currency, and then took the nation off the gold standard. The Emergency Congress responded to his recommendation by canceling the gold-payment clause in all contracts and authorizing repayment in paper money. A "managed currency" was well on its way.

Early in 1934 Roosevelt reduced the value of the gold content of the dollar to 59.06 cents, in accordance with authority granted by Congress. His theory was that this tinkering with the currency would stimulate business through controlled inflation. Prices did rise somewhat, but not in proportion to the change in the value of the currency. Alarmed conservatives, like the now "unhappy warrior" Al Smith, assailed "the baloney dollar" and accused the government of robbing the people

*When FDR was inaugurated in 1933, not a single Canadian bank had failed.

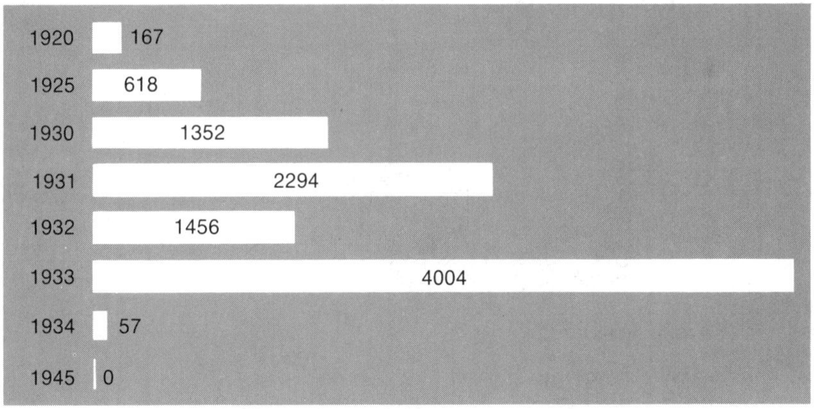

BANK FAILURES AND THE BANKING ACT OF 1933

of forty cents on every dollar they owned. Actually, the purchasing power of the newly shrunken dollar was not substantially inferior to that of the old, except in purchases from foreigners.

Creating Jobs for the Jobless

Overwhelming unemployment, perhaps even more than banking, clamored for prompt remedial action. Roosevelt had no hesitancy about using federal money to assist the unemployed, and at the same time to "prime the pump" of industrial recovery. A farmer has to pour a little water into a dry pump to start the flow.

The Hundred Days Congress responded to Roosevelt's spurs when it created the Civilian Conservation Corps (CCC), which proved to be perhaps the most popular of all the New Deal "alphabetical agencies." This law provided employment in fresh-air government camps for about 3 million uniformed young men, many of whom might otherwise have been driven into criminal habits. Their work was useful—including reforestation, fire fighting (forty-seven lost their lives), flood control, and swamp drainage. The recruits were required to help the old folks by sending home most of their pay. Both human resources and natural resources were thus conserved, though there were minor complaints of "militarizing" the nation's youth. Critics charged that CCC "soldiers" would later claim pensions for exposure to poison ivy.

The first major effort of the new Congress to grapple with the millions of adult unemployed was the Federal Emergency Relief Act. Its chief aim was immediate relief rather than long-range recovery. The resulting Federal Emergency Relief Administration (FERA) was handed over to zealous Harry L. Hopkins, a rail-thin, shabbily dressed, chain-smoking New York social worker who had earlier won Roosevelt's friendship and who became one of his most influential advisers. Hopkins' agency finally granted about $3 billion to the

Reliefers Receive Free Federal Potatoes in Cleveland. (Wide World Photos.)

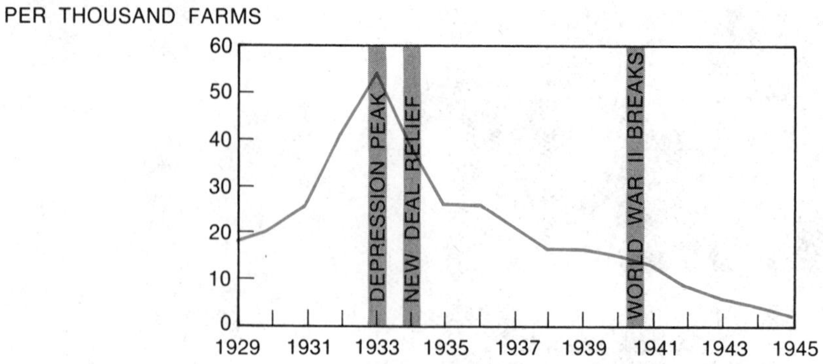

FARM FORECLOSURES AND DEFAULTS, 1929–1945

states for direct dole payments or preferably for wages on work projects.*

Immediate relief was also given two large and hard-pressed special groups by the Hundred Days Congress. One section of the Agricultural Adjustment Act made available many millions of dollars to help farmers meet their mortgages. Another law created the Home Owners' Loan Corporation (HOLC). Designed to refinance mortgages on nonfarm homes, it ultimately assisted about a million badly pinched households—and bailed out mortgage-holding banks.

Harassed by the continuing plague of unemployment, FDR himself established the Civil Works Administration (CWA) late in 1933. As a branch of the Federal Emergency Relief Administration, it also fell under the direction of Hopkins. Designed to provide purely temporary jobs during the cruel winter emergency, it served a useful purpose. Tens of thousands of jobless were employed at leaf raking and other make-work tasks, which were dubbed "boondoggling." As this kind of labor put a premium on shovel-leaning slow motion, the scheme was widely criticized. "The only thing we have to fear," scoffers remarked, "is work itself."

Direct relief from Washington to needy families helped pull the nation through the ghastly winter of 1933–1934. But the disheartening persistence of unemployment and suffering demonstrated that emergency relief measures must be not only continued but supplemented. One danger signal was the appearance of various demagogues, notably a magnetic "microphone Messiah," Father Coughlin, a Catholic priest in Michigan who began broadcasting in 1930 and whose slogan was "Social Justice." His anti–New Deal harangues to some 40 million radio fans finally became so anti-Semitic, Fascistic, and demagogic that he was silenced in 1942 by his superiors.

Also notorious among the new brood of agitators were those who capitalized on popular discontent to make pie-in-the-sky promises. Most conspicuous of these men was a United States senator, Huey P. ("Kingfish") Long of Louisiana, whose brassy, rabble-rousing talents publicized

Frances Perkins (1882–1965). The first woman Cabinet member, she served as secretary of labor under Roosevelt. She was subjected to much undeserved criticism from male businessmen, laborites, and politicians. They sneered that FDR kept her in labor for many years. (Print from Franklin D. Roosevelt Library; owned by UPI.)

*A boast attributed to Hopkins in 1938 was: "We will spend and spend, tax and tax, and elect and elect."

Later Major New Deal Measures, 1933–1939
(ITEMS IN PARENTHESES INDICATE SECONDARY PURPOSES.)

Recovery	*Relief*	*Reform*
(CWA)	FDR establishes Civil Works Administration (CWA), Nov. 9, 1933	
Gold Reserve Act, Jan. 30, 1934, authorizes FDR's devaluation, Jan. 31, 1934		
		Securities and Exchange Commission (SEC) authorized by Congress, June 6, 1934
(Reciprocal Trade Agreements)	(Reciprocal Trade Agreements)	Reciprocal Trade Agreements Act, June 12, 1934
(FHA)	National Housing Act, June 28, 1934, authorizes Federal Housing Administration (FHA)	(FHA)
(Frazier-Lemke Act)	Frazier-Lemke Farm Bankruptcy Act, June 28, 1934	
(Resettlement Administration)	FDR Creates Resettlement Administration, April 30, 1935	
(WPA)	FDR creates Works Progress Administration (WPA), May 6, 1935, under act of April 8, 1935	
(Wagner Act)	(Wagner Act)	(Wagner) National Labor Relations Act, July 5, 1935
		Social Security Act, August 14, 1935
		Public Utility Holding Co. Act, Aug. 26, 1935
(Soil Conservation Act)	Soil Conservation and Domestic Allotment Act, Feb. 29, 1936	
(USHA)	(USHA)	U.S. Housing Authority (USHA) established by Congress, Sept. 1, 1937
(Second AAA)	Second Agricultural Adjustment Act, Feb. 16, 1936	
(Fair Labor Standards)	(Fair Labor Standards)	Fair Labor Standards Act, June 25, 1938
		Reorganization Act, April 3, 1939
		Hatch Act, Aug. 2, 1939

his "Share Our Wealth" program, with "Every Man a King." Every family was to receive $5,000, supposedly at the expense of the prosperous. Fear of his becoming a Fascist dictator ended when he was shot by an assassin in the Louisiana state capitol in 1935.

Another Pied Piper was gaunt Dr. Francis E. Townsend of California, a retired physician whose savings had recently been wiped out. He attracted the pathetic support of perhaps 5 million "senior citizens" with his fantastic plan. Each oldster sixty years of age or over was to receive $200 a month, provided that he spent it within the month. One estimate had the scheme costing one half of the national income.

Partly to quiet the groundswell of unrest produced by such crackbrained proposals, Congress authorized the Works Progress Administration (WPA) in 1935. The objective was employment on useful projects. Launched under the supervision of the ailing but energetic Hopkins, this remarkable agency ultimately spent about $11 billion on thousands of public buildings, bridges, and hard-surfaced roads. It controlled crickets in Wyoming and built a monkey pen in Oklahoma City. Critics sneered that WPA meant "We Provide Alms," but the fact is that over a period of eight years nearly 9 million persons were given jobs.

We work all day
For the WPA.
Let the market crash,
We collect our cash.

Agencies of the WPA also found part-time occupations for needy high school and college students, and for such unemployed white-collar workers as actors, musicians, and writers. John Steinbeck, future Nobel Prize novelist, counted dogs in his California county. Cynical taxpayers condemned lessons in tap dancing, as well as the painting of scenes on post office walls. But much precious talent was nourished, self-respect was preserved, and more than a million pieces of art were created, many of them publicly displayed.

Depression Art. This mural "Work, the American Way," was painted under the auspices of the Works Progress Administration, c.1939. (WPA Photographs, Archives of American Art, Smithsonian Institution.)

A Helping Hand for Industry and Labor

A daring attempt to stimulate a nationwide comeback was initiated when the Emergency Congress authorized the National Recovery Administration (NRA). This ingenious scheme was by far the most complex and far-reaching effort by the New Dealers to combine immediate relief with long-range recovery and reform. Triple-barreled, it was designed to assist industry, labor, and the unemployed.

Individual industries—over 200 in all—were to work out codes of "fair competition," under which hours of labor would be reduced so that employment could be spread over more people. A ceiling was placed on the maximum hours of labor; a floor was placed under wages to establish minimum levels.

Labor, under the NRA, was granted additional benefits. Workers were formally guaranteed the right to organize and bargain collectively through representatives *of their own choosing*—not through handpicked agents of the company's choosing. The hated "yellow dog" or anti-union contract was expressly forbidden, and certain safeguarding restrictions were placed on the use of child labor.

Industrial recovery through the NRA fair codes

would at best be painful, for these called for self-denial by both management and labor. Patriotism was appealed to by mass meetings and monster parades, which included 200,000 marchers on New York City's Fifth Avenue. A handsome Blue Eagle was designed as the symbol of the NRA, and merchants subscribing to a code displayed it in their windows with the slogan "We Do Our Part." A newly formed professional football team was christened the Philadelphia Eagles. Such was the enthusiasm for the NRA that for a brief period there was a marked upswing of business activity, although Roosevelt had warned, "We cannot ballyhoo our way to prosperity."

But the high-flying Blue Eagle gradually fluttered to earth. Too much self-sacrifice was expected of labor, industry, and the public for such a scheme to work. Critics began to brand NRA "National Run Around" and "Nuts Running America," symbolized by what Henry Ford called "that damn Roosevelt buzzard." A new "Age of Chiselry" dawned as certain unscrupulous businessmen ("chiselers") publicly displayed the blue bird on their windows but secretly violated the codes. Complete collapse was imminent when, in 1935, the Supreme Court shot down the dying eagle in the famed Schechter "sick chicken" decision. The learned justices *unanimously* held that Congress could not "delegate legislative powers" to the executive. They further declared that congressional control of interstate commerce could not properly apply to a local fowl business, like that of the Schechter brothers in Brooklyn and New York. Roosevelt was incensed by this "horse and buggy" interpretation of the Constitution, but actually the Court helped him out of a bad jam.

The same act of Congress that hatched the blue-eagled NRA also authorized the Public Works Administration (PWA), likewise intended both for industrial recovery and for unemployment relief. The agency was headed by the secretary of the interior, acid-tongued Harold L. Ickes, a free-swinging ex–Bull Mooser. Long-range recovery was the primary purpose of the new agency, and in time over $4 billion was spent on some 34,000 projects, which included public buildings, highways, and parkways. One spectacular achievement was the Grand Coulee Dam on the Columbia River —the largest structure erected by man since the Great Wall of China. Speed was essential if the jobless were to be put back to work, but "Honest Harold" Ickes was so determined to prevent waste and extravagance that he blocked maximum relief.

Big Business Holds the Line Against NRA. (Knott in the Dallas *News*, 1933.)

Special stimulants aided the recovery of one segment of business—the liquor industry. The imminent repeal of the prohibition amendment afforded an opportunity to raise needed federal revenue and at the same time to provide some employment. Prodded by Roosevelt, the Hundred Days Congress in one of its earliest acts legalized light wine and beer with an alcoholic content (presumably non-intoxicating) not exceeding 3.2% by weight, and levied a tax of $5 on every barrel so manufactured. Disgruntled drys, unwilling to acknowledge the breakdown of law and order begotten by bootlegging, damned Roosevelt as "a 3.2% American." Prohibition was officially repealed by the 21st Amendment late in 1933 (see Appendix)—and the saloon returned.

Paying Farmers Not to Farm

Ever since the war-boom days of 1918 the horny-handed farmers had suffered from low prices and overproduction, especially in grain. During the depression these conditions became desperate as countless mortgages were foreclosed, as corn was burned for fuel, and as embattled bands of farmers tried to prevent shipment of crops to glutted markets. In Iowa several counties had to be placed under martial law.

"Eliza Crossing the Ice." Business crosses the ice of New Deal alphabetical agencies. (Courtesy San Francisco *Chronicle.*)

A radical new approach to farm recovery was embraced when the Emergency Congress established the Agricultural Adjustment Administration (AAA). Through "artificial scarcity" this agency was to establish "parity prices" for basic commodities. "Parity" was the price set for a product that gave it the same real value, in purchasing power, that it had enjoyed during the period from 1909 to 1914. The AAA would eliminate price-depressing surpluses by paying growers to reduce their crop acreage. The millions of dollars needed for these payments were to be raised by taxing processors of farm products, such as flour millers, who in turn would shift the burden to consumers.

Unhappily, the AAA got off to a wobbly start. It was begun after much of the cotton crop for 1933 had been planted, and balky mules, trained otherwise, were forced to plow under countless young plants. Several million squealing pigs were purchased and slaughtered. Much of their meat was distributed to persons on relief, but some of it was used for fertilizer. This "sinful" destruction of food, at a time when thousands of citizens were hungry, increased condemnation of the American economic system by many left-leaning critics.

"Subsidized scarcity" did have the effect of raising farm income, but the whole confused enterprise met with acid criticism. Farmers, food processors, consumers, and taxpayers were all in some degree unhappy. Paying the farmers not to farm actually increased unemployment, at a time when other New Deal agencies were striving to decrease it. When the Supreme Court finally killed the AAA in 1936 by declaring its regulatory taxation provisions unconstitutional, loud rejoicing was heard among foes of the plow-under program.

Quickly recovering from this blow, the New Deal Congress hastened to pass the Soil Conservation and Domestic Allotment Act of 1936. The withdrawal of acreage from production was now achieved by paying the farmer to plant soil-conserving crops, like soybeans, or to let his land lie fallow. With the emphasis thus on conservation, the Supreme Court placed the stamp of its approval on the revamped scheme.

The Second Agricultural Adjustment Act of 1938, passed two years later, was a more comprehensive substitute, although it continued conservation payments. If the grower observed acreage restrictions on specified commodities like cotton and wheat, he would be eligible for parity payments. Other provisions of the new AAA were designed to give farmers not only a fairer price but a more substantial share of the national income. Both goals were partially achieved.

Dust Bowls and Black Blizzards

Dame Nature meanwhile had been providing some unplanned scarcity. Late in 1933 a prolonged drought struck the states of the trans-Mississippi Great Plains. Rainless weeks were followed by furious, whining winds, while the sun was darkened by millions of tons of powdery topsoil torn from once-fertile areas. Despondent citizens sat on front porches with protective masks on their

Novelist Steinbeck relates that when the "Okies" and "Arkies" reached California, they found the big growers unwilling to pay more than twenty-five cents an hour for work in the fields. One owner is made to say, "A Red is any son-of-a-bitch that wants thirty cents an hour when we're paying twenty-five!"

faces, watching the farms swirl by. Some of the dust darkened faraway Boston.

Burned and blown out of the Dust Bowl, tens of thousands of refugees fled their ruined acres. In five years about 350,000 Oklahomans and Arkansans—"Okies" and "Arkies"—trekked to southern California in "junkyards on wheels." The dismal story of these human tumbleweeds was realistically portrayed in John Steinbeck's best-selling novel *The Grapes of Wrath* (1939), which proved to be the *Uncle Tom's Cabin* of the Dust Bowl.

Zealous New Dealers, sympathetic toward the soil tillers, made various other efforts to relieve their burdens. The Frazier-Lemke Farm Bankruptcy Act, passed in 1934, made possible a suspension of mortgage foreclosures for five years,

Dust Bowl Refugees. Family of "Okies" in California. (Library of Congress.)

but it was voided the next year by the Supreme Court. A revised law, limiting the grace period to three years, was unanimously upheld. In 1935 the President set up the Resettlement Administration, charged with the task of removing near-farmless farmers to better land. And more than 200 million young trees were successfully planted on the bare prairies as windbreaks by the young men of the Civilian Conservation Corps, even though one governor jeered at trying to "grow hair on a bald head."

Battling Bankers and Big Business

Reformist New Dealers were determined from the outset to curb the "money changers" who had played fast and loose with gullible investors before the Wall Street crash of 1929. The Hundred Days Congress passed the "Truth in Securities Act" (Federal Securities Act), which required promoters to transmit to the investor sworn information regarding the soundness of their stocks and bonds. An old saying was thus reversed to read: "Let the seller beware," although the buyer might never read the fine print.

In 1934 Congress took further steps to protect the public against fraud, deception, and inside manipulation. It authorized the Securities and Exchange Commission (SEC), which was designed as a watchdog administrative agency. Stock markets henceforth were to operate more as trading marts and less as gambling casinos.

New Dealers likewise directed their fire at public-utility holding companies, those super-super-corporations. Citizens had seen one of these incredible colossi collapse during the spring of 1932, when Chicagoan Samuel Insull's multibillion-dollar financial empire crashed. Possibilities of controlling, with a minimum of capital, a half-dozen or so pyramided layers of Big Business suggested to Roosevelt "a ninety-six-inch dog being wagged by a four-inch tail." The Public Utility Holding Company Act of 1935 finally delivered a "death sentence" to this type of fatty growth, except where it might be deemed economically needful.

The TVA Harnesses the Tennessee River

Inevitably, the sprawling electric-power industry attracted the fire of New Deal reformers. Within a few decades it had risen from nothingness to a colossus with an investment of $13 billion. As a public utility, it reached directly and regularly into the pocketbooks of millions of consumers for vitally needed services. Ardent New Dealers accused it of gouging the public with excessive rates, especially since it owed its success to having secured, often for a song, priceless waterpower sites from the public domain.

The tempestuous Tennessee River provided New Dealers with a rare opportunity. With its tributaries, the river drained a badly eroded area about the size of England, and one containing some 2.5 million of the most poverty-stricken people in America. The federal government already owned valuable properties at Muscle Shoals, where it had erected plants for needed nitrates in World War I. By developing the hydroelectric potential of the entire area, Washington could combine the immediate advantage of putting thousands of people to work with a long-term project for reforming the power monopoly.

An act creating the Tennessee Valley Authority (TVA) was passed in 1933 by the Hundred Days Congress. This far-ranging enterprise was largely a result of the steadfast vision and unflagging zeal of Senator George W. Norris of Nebraska, after whom one of the mighty dams was named. From the standpoint of "planned economy," the TVA was by far the most revolutionary of all New Deal schemes.

This new agency was determined to discover precisely how much the production and distribution of electricity cost, so that a "yardstick" could be set up to test the fairness of rates charged by private companies. Utility corporations lashed back at this entering wedge of governmental control, charging that the low cost of TVA power was due to dishonest bookkeeping and the absence of taxes. Critics complained that the whole dream was "creeping socialism in concrete."

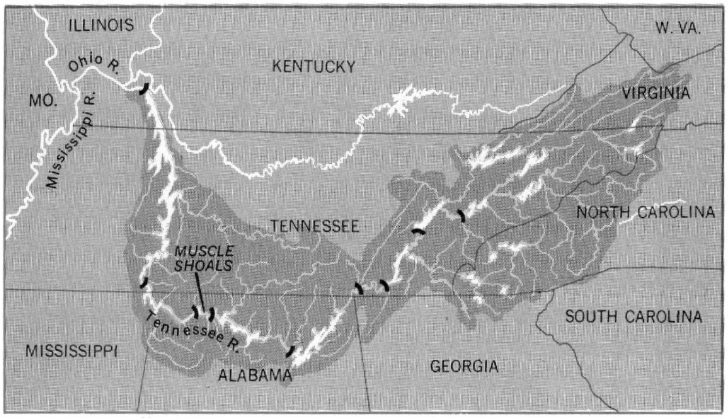

TVA AREA

Only the nine dams on the Tennessee River are shown here. There are more than twenty on the tributaries.

But the New Dealers, shrugging off such outcries, pointed a prideful finger at the amazing achievements of the TVA. The gigantic project had brought to the area not only full employment and the blessings of cheap electric power, but low-cost housing, abundant cheap nitrates, the restoration of eroded soil, reforestation, improved navigation, and flood control. Rivers ran blue instead of brown; and a once poverty-cursed area was being transformed into one of the most flourishing regions in the country. Foreigners were greatly impressed with the possibilities of similar schemes in their own lands, and exulting New Dealers agitated for parallel enterprises in the

In flooding the Tennessee valleys to build the dams, the TVA authorities had to provide new houses for the lowland poor folk. According to one account, "When Ezra Hill saw the plans for the home which was to replace his old one in the flood area, he pointed to the place on the print showing the circles and ovals of bathroom fixtures. 'What's all this? . . . I won't have it! I guess a privy [outside] is still good enough for me.' "

valleys of the Columbia and Missouri Rivers. But conservatives in Congress, growing bolder, confined this particular type of socialism to the Tennessee Valley.

Housing Reform and Social Security

Gratifying beginnings had meanwhile been made by the New Deal in housing construction. To speed recovery and better homes, Roosevelt set up the Federal Housing Administration (FHA) as early as 1934. The building industry was to be stimulated by small loans to householders, both for improving their dwellings and completing new ones. So popular did the FHA prove to be that it was one of the few "alphabetical agencies" to outlast the Age of Roosevelt.

Congress bolstered the program in 1937 by authorizing the United States Housing Authority (USHA)—an agency designed to lend money to states or communities for low-cost construction. Though units for about 650,000 low-income persons were started, new building fell tragically short of needs. New Deal efforts to expand the project ran head-on into vigorous opposition from real-estate promoters, builders, and landlords ("slumlords"), to say nothing of anti–New Dealers who attacked what they considered down-the-rathole spending. Nonetheless, for the first time in a century the slum areas in America ceased growing and even shrank.

Incomparably more important was the success of New Dealers in the field of unemployment insurance and old-age pensions. Their greatest victory was the epochal Social Security Act of 1935—one of the most complicated and far-reaching laws ever to pass Congress. To cushion future depressions, the measure provided for federal-state unemployment insurance. To provide security for old age, specified categories of retired workers were to receive regular payments from Washington, ranging from $10 to $85 a month (later raised) and financed by a payroll tax on both employers and employees. Provision was also made for the blind, cripples, delinquent children, and other dependents.

Republican opposition to the sweeping new legislation was bitter. "Social Security," insisted Hoover, "must be builded upon a cult of work, not a cult of leisure." The GOP national chairman falsely charged that every worker would have to wear a metal dog tag for life.

Social Security was largely inspired by the example of some of the more highly industrialized nations of Europe. In the agricultural America of an earlier day, there had always been farm chores for all ages, and the large family had cared for its own dependents. But in an urbanized economy, at the mercy of boom-and-bust cycles, the government was now recognizing its responsibility for the welfare of its citizens. By 1939 over 45 million persons were eligible for Social Security benefits, and in subsequent years further categories of workers were added and the payments to them were periodically increased.

A New Deal for Unskilled Labor

The NRA Blue Eagles, with their call for collective bargaining, had been a godsend to organized labor. As New Deal expenditures brought some slackening of unemployment, labor began to feel more secure and hence more self-assertive. A rash of walkouts occurred in the summer of 1934, including a paralyzing general strike in San Francisco (following a "Bloody Thursday") which was broken only when outraged citizens resorted to vigilante tactics.

When the Supreme Court axed the Blue Eagle, a Congress sympathetic to labor unions undertook to fill the vacuum. The fruit of its deliberations was the Wagner or National Labor Relations Act of 1935. This trail-blazing law created a powerful new National Labor Relations Board for administrative purposes, and reasserted the right of labor to engage in self-organization and to bargain collectively through representatives of its own choice. The Wagner Act proved to be one of the real

"The Great Divide," 1936. Steel industry as a factor in splitting labor. Note the industrial unions going left, the craft unions, right. (Fitzpatrick in the St. Louis *Post-Dispatch.*)

milestones on the rocky road of the American labor movement.

Under the encouragement of a highly sympathetic National Labor Relations Board, a host of unskilled workers began to organize themselves into effective unions. The leader of this drive was beetle-browed, domineering, and melodramatic John L. Lewis, boss of the United Mine Workers. In 1935 he succeeded in forming the Committee for Industrial Organization (CIO) within the ranks of the skilled-craft American Federation of Labor. But skilled workers, ever since the days of the ill-fated Knights of Labor in the 1880s, had shown only lukewarm sympathy for the cause of unskilled labor, especially blacks. In 1936, following inevitable friction with the CIO, the older federation suspended the upstart unions associated with the newer organization.

Nothing daunted, the rebellious CIO moved on a concerted scale into the huge automobile industry. Late in 1936 the workers resorted to a revolutionary technique (earlier used in both Europe and America) known as the sit-down strike: they refused to leave the factory buildings of General Motors at Flint, Michigan, and thus prevented the importation of strikebreakers. Conservative respecters of private property were scandalized. The CIO finally won a resounding victory when its union, after heated negotiations, was recognized by General Motors as the sole bargaining agency for its employees.

General Motors Sitdown Strikers, Flint, Michigan, 1937. Strikers like these sometimes kept their spirits up with the song "Sit Down":

> When the boss won't talk
> Don't take a walk;
> Sit down, sit down.

(United Press International photo.)

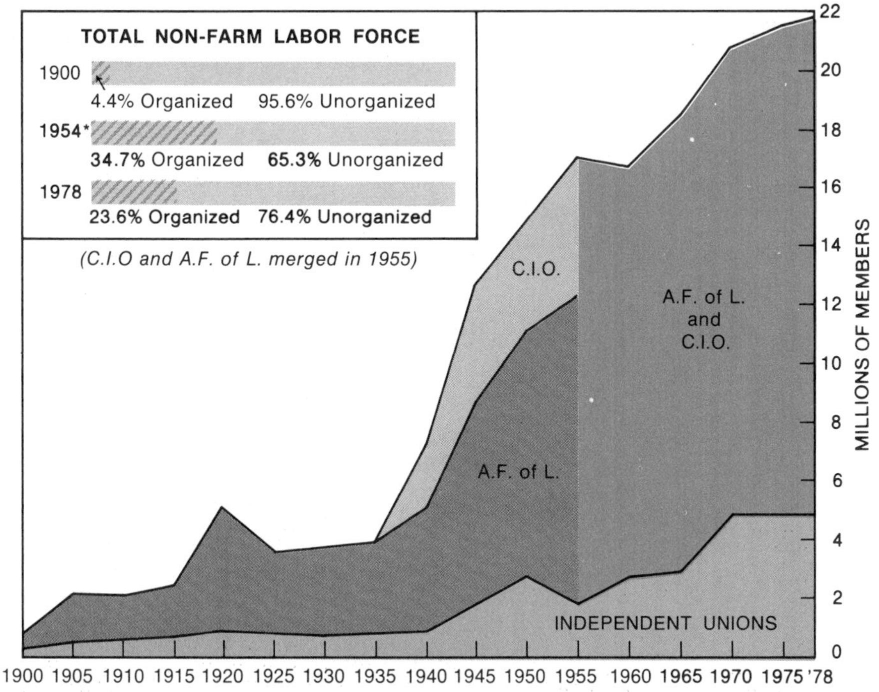

THE RISE OF ORGANIZED LABOR, 1900–1978
*The high point of organized labor, in percentage terms, was in 1954.

Roosevelt's "Coddling" of Labor

Unskilled workers now pressed their advantage. The United States Steel Company, hitherto an impossible nut for labor to crack, averted a costly strike when it voluntarily granted rights of unionization to its CIO-organized employees. But the "Little Steel" companies fought back savagely. Citizens were shocked in 1937 by the Memorial Day massacre at the plant of the Republic Steel Company in South Chicago. There, in a bloody fracas, police fired upon pickets and workers, leaving the area strewn with several score dead and wounded.

A better deal for labor continued when Congress, in 1938, passed the memorable Fair Labor Standards Act (Wages and Hours Bill). Industries involved in interstate commerce were to set up minimum-wage and maximum-hour levels. Though not immediately established, the specific goals were forty cents an hour (later raised) and a forty-hour week. Labor by children under sixteen was forbidden; under eighteen, if the occupation was dangerous. These reforms were bitterly though futilely opposed by many industrialists, especially by those Southern textile manufacturers who had profited from low-wage labor.

In later New Deal days, labor unionization flourished like crabgrass; "Roosevelt wants you to join a union" was the rallying cry of professional organizers. The President received valuable support at ballot-box time from labor leaders and many appreciative workingmen. One mill worker remarked that Roosevelt was "the only man we ever had in the White House who would know that my boss is a s.o.b." FDR was indeed the "forgotten man's" man.

The CIO surged forward, breaking completely with the AF of L in 1938. On that occasion the *Committee* for Industrial Organization was formally reconstituted as the *Congress* of Industrial Organizations (the new CIO), under the high-handed presidency of John L. Lewis. By 1940 the CIO could claim about 4 million members in its constituent unions, including some 200,000 blacks. Nevertheless bitter and annoying jurisdictional feuding, involving strikes, continued with

John L. Lewis (1880–1969). Lewis became a miner and worked his way up to the presidency of the United Mine Workers of America. He once remarked of strikebreaking soldiers, "You can't dig coal with bayonets."

the AF of L. At times labor seemed more bent on costly civil war than on its age-old war with management.

Landon Challenges "the Champ" in 1936

As the presidential campaign of 1936 neared, the New Dealers were on top of the world. They had achieved considerable progress, and millions of "reliefers" were grateful to their bountiful government. The exultant Democrats, meeting in Philadelphia, pushed through the renomination of Roosevelt in a brief rubber-stamp ceremony. Their platform stood squarely on the record of the New

The Republicans, assembling in Cleveland, were hard pressed to find someone to feed to "the Champ." They finally settled on the colorless and mildly liberal Governor Alfred M. Landon of the Sunflower State of Kansas, a wealthy oil man, whose chief claim to distinction was that he had balanced the budget of his state in an era of unbalanced budgets. The Republican platform, though promising relief benefits that would cost many millions, condemned the New Deal of Franklin "Deficit" Roosevelt–its radicalism, experimentation, confusion, and "frightful waste." Popular watchwords were "Defeat the New Deal and Its Reckless Spending," "Let's Get Another Deck," "Life, Liberty, and Landon," and "Let's Make It a Landon-Slide."

Landon–"the Kansas Coolidge"–was honest, sincere, homespun, "common-sensical," and as American as cherry pie. But he had a poor radio voice and seemed schoolboyish on the stump. Surrounded by imitation Kansas sunflowers, he stressed "deeds, not deficits," and condemned New Deal highhandedness. Though opposing the popular Social Security Act, he advocated just enough reform to cause the Democrats to retort that he would continue the New Deal–a secondhand New Deal–in his own way. He was, they sneered, "the poor man's Hoover."

Democrats denounced the GOP as the party of the Big Moneyed Interests and the Big Depression, and amid loud choruses of boos cried, "Remember Hoover!" The embittered ex-President called for "a holy crusade for liberty." A group of wealthy Republicans and conservative Democrats had in 1934 formed the American Liberty League to fight "socialistic" New Deal schemes, and they vented their reactionary spleen against "that man" Roosevelt, "the New Dealocrat." But they hurt their own cause by becoming a made-to-order target for FDR. His dander aroused, he took to the stump and denounced the "economic royalists" who sought to "hide behind the flag and the

> Three days before the 1936 election Roosevelt sounded positively dictatorial in his speech at New York's Madison Square Garden: "I should like to have it said of my first Administration that in it the forces of selfishness and of lust for power met their match. I should like to have it said of my second Administration that in it these forces met their master."

Constitution." "I welcome their hatred," he proclaimed.

A landslide overwhelmed Landon, as the demoralized Republicans carried only two states, Maine and Vermont. This dismal showing caused political wiseacres to make the old adage read: "As Maine goes, so goes Vermont."* The popular vote was 27,751,597 to 16,679,583; the electoral count was 523 to 8—the most lopsided in 116 years. Democratic majorities, riding in on Roosevelt's magic coattails, were again returned to Congress. Jubilant Democrats could now claim more than two-thirds of the seats in the House, and a like proportion in the Senate.

The battle of 1936, perhaps the most bitter since Bryan's in 1896, partially bore out Republican charges of class warfare. Even more than in 1932, the needy economic groups were lined up against the so-called greedy economic groups ("Tories"). CIO units contributed generously to FDR's campaign chest. Many left-wingers turned to Roosevelt, as the customary third-party protest vote sharply declined. The blacks, several million of whom had also enjoyed welcome relief checks, had by now largely shaken off their traditional allegiance to the Republican party. To them, Lincoln was "finally dead." He continued to be, even though the Democrats were more interested in black votes than in black rights.

FDR won primarily because he appealed to the "forgotten man," whom he never forgot. Some of the President's support was only pocketbook-deep: "reliefers" were not going to bite the hand that doled out the government checks. No one, as Al Smith remarked, "shoots at Santa Claus." But Roosevelt in fact had forged a powerful and enduring coalition of the South, the blacks, the urbanites, and the poor.

*Maine, which traditionally held its state elections in September, was long regarded as a political weather vane. Hence the expression "As Maine goes, so goes the nation."

Eleanor Roosevelt Voting at Hyde Park, November, 1936. Mrs. Roosevelt was certainly the most visible and probably the most energetic of all the First Ladies. Among varied activities, she wrote a daily newspaper column and traveled and lectured widely while promoting many causes. (Franklin D. Roosevelt Library.)

Nine Old Men on the Supreme Bench

Bowing his head to the sleety blasts, Roosevelt took the presidential oath on January 20, 1937, instead of the traditional March 4. The 20th Amendment to the Constitution, sponsored by Senator Norris of TVA fame, had been ratified in 1933. (See Appendix.) It swept away the post-election "lame duck" session of Congress, and shortened by six weeks the awkward period before inauguration.

Flushed with victory, Roosevelt interpreted his re-election as a mandate to continue New Deal reforms. But in his eyes the cloistered old men on the Supreme Bench, like fossilized stumbling blocks, stood stubbornly in the pathway of progress. In nine major cases involving the New Deal, the Roosevelt administration had been defeated seven times. The Court was ultra-conservative, and six of the nine oldsters in black were over seventy. As luck would have it, not a single member had been appointed by FDR in his first term.

Roosevelt—his "Dutch up"—viewed with mounting impatience what he regarded as the obstructive conservatism of the Court. Some of these

Old Guard appointees were hanging on with a senile grip, partly because they felt it their patriotic duty to curb the "socialistic" tendencies of that radical in the White House. Roosevelt believed that the voters in three successive elections—the presidential elections of 1932 and 1936 and the mid-term congressional elections of 1934—had returned a smashing verdict in favor of his program of reform. Democracy, in his view, meant rule by the people. If the American way of life was to be preserved, Roosevelt argued, the Supreme Court ought to get in line with the supreme court of public opinion.

Roosevelt finally hit upon a Court scheme that he regarded as "the answer to a maiden's prayer." When he sprang it on a shocked nation, early in 1937, he caught the country and Congress completely by surprise. One basic reason was that the proposition had never been mentioned in the recent campaign. Roosevelt bluntly asked Congress for legislation to permit him to add a new justice to the Supreme Court for every member over seventy who would not retire. The maximum membership could then be fifteen. Roosevelt pointed to the necessity of injecting vigorous new blood, for the Court, he alleged, was far behind in its work. This charge, which turned out to be false, brought heated accusations of dishonesty. At best, Roosevelt was headstrong and not fully aware of the fact that the Court, in popular thinking, had become something of a sacred cow.

The Supreme Court Under Pressure. FDR regarded the justices as horse-and-buggy legalists. (Seibel in the Richmond *Times-Dispatch*, 1937.)

The Court Changes Course

Congress and the nation were promptly convulsed over the scheme to "pack" the Supreme Court with a "dictator bill," which one critic called "too damned slick." Franklin "Double-crossing" Roosevelt was savagely condemned for attempting to break down the delicate checks and balances among the three branches of the government. He was accused of grooming himself as a dictator by trying to browbeat the judiciary. In the eyes of countless citizens, mostly Republicans but including many Democrats, basic liberties seemed to be in jeopardy. "God Bless the Supreme Court" was a fervent prayer.

The Court had meanwhile not been unaware of the ax hanging over its head. Whatever his motives, Mr. Justice Roberts, formerly regarded as conservative, began to vote on the side of his liberal colleagues. "A switch in time saves nine"

> In a radio address (March 1937), Roosevelt expressed some startling thoughts about the Supreme Court: "We have . . . reached the point . . . where we must take action to save the Constitution from the Court and the Court from itself. We must find a way to take an appeal from the Supreme Court to the Constitution itself. We want a Supreme Court which will do justice under the Constitution—not over it."

was the classic witticism inspired by this change. By a 5 to 4 decision the Court, in March 1937, upheld the principle of a state minimum wage for women, thereby reversing its stand on a different case a year earlier. In succeeding decisions, a Court more sympathetic to the New Deal upheld the National Labor Relations Act (Wagner Act) and the Social Security Act. Roosevelt's "Court packing" scheme was further undermined when Congress voted full pay for justices over seventy who retired, whereupon one of the oldest conservative members resigned, to be replaced by a New Dealer, Mr. Justice Black.

Congress finally passed a court reform bill, but this watered-down version applied only to the lower courts. Roosevelt, the master politician, thus suffered his first major legislative defeat at the hands of his own party in Congress. Americans have never viewed lightly a tampering with the Supreme Court by the President, no matter how popular he may be. Yet in losing this battle, Roosevelt incidentally won his campaign. The Court, as he had hoped, became markedly more friendly to New Deal reforms. Furthermore, a succession of deaths and resignations enabled him to make nine appointments to the tribunal—more than any of his predecessors since George Washington. Father Time "unpacked" the Court.

Yet in a sense FDR lost both the Court battle and the war. He so aroused conservatives of both parties in Congress that few New Deal reforms were passed after 1937, the year of the fight to "pack" the Supreme Court.

The Twilight of the New Deal

From 1933 to 1937 the country had been gradually inching its way out of the depression, largely because of the billions of dollars injected by Congress into the economic bloodstream. Although millions of dejected souls remained unemployed, gratifying gains had been registered. "We planned it that way," remarked Roosevelt cheerily.

But in 1937 a sharp recession set in which hit bottom in 1938. The President's critics, branding this setback "the Roosevelt Depression," asserted that if FDR could plan upward spirals he must also have planned the downward dip. This particular recession was probably due to an overrapid cutting back of "pump-priming" spending by Washington.

Undiscouraged, Roosevelt had meanwhile been pushing the remaining measures of the New Deal. Early in 1937 he urged Congress—a Congress growing more conservative—to authorize a sweeping reorganization of the national administration in the interests of streamlined efficiency. But the issue became tangled up with his presumed dictatorial ambitions in regard to the Supreme Court, and he suffered another stinging defeat. Two years later, in 1939, Congress partially relented and in the Reorganization Act gave him limited powers for administrative reforms, including the key new Executive Office in the White House.

The New Dealers were accused of having the richest campaign chest in history; and in truth government relief checks had a curious habit of coming in bunches just before ballot time. To remedy such practices, which tended to make a farce of free elections, Congress adopted the much-heralded Hatch Act of 1939. It debarred federal administrative officials, except the highest policy-making officers, from active political campaigning and soliciting. It also forbade the use of government funds for political purposes, as well as the collection of campaign contributions from persons receiving relief payments. The Hatch Act was broadened in 1940 to place limits on campaign contributions and expenditures, but such clever ways of getting around it were found that on the whole the legislation proved disappointing.

By 1938 the New Deal had clearly lost most of its early momentum. Magician Roosevelt could find few spectacular new reform rabbits to pull out of his tall silk hat. In the congressional elections of 1938 the Republicans, for the first time, cut heavily into the unwieldy New Deal majorities in Congress, though failing to gain control of either house. The international crisis which came to a boil in 1938–1939 shifted public attention away from domestic reform, and no doubt helped save the political hide of the Roosevelt "spendocracy." The New Deal, for all practical purposes, had shot its bolt.

New Deal or Raw Deal?

Foes of the New Deal condemned its alleged waste, incompetence, confusion, contradictions, and cross-purposes, as well as the chiseling and graft in the alphabetical agencies—"alphabet soup," sneered Al Smith. Roosevelt had done nothing, cynics said, that an earthquake could not have done better. Critics deplored the employment of "crackpot" college professors, leftist "pinkos," and outright Communists. Such subversives, it was charged, were trying to make America over in the Bolshevik-Marxist image under "Rooseveltski." The Hearst newspapers assailed

> The Red New Deal with a Soviet seal
> Endorsed by a Moscow hand,
> The strange result of an alien cult
> In a liberty-loving land.

Roosevelt was further accused by conservatives of being Jewish ("Rosenfeld"), and of tapping too many bright young Jewish leftists ("The Jew Deal") for his "Drain Trust."

Hardheaded businessmen, who "had met a payroll," were shocked by the leap-before-you-look, try-anything-once spirit of Roosevelt, the jolly improviser. They accused him of confusing noise and movement with progress. Humorist Will Rogers, the rope-twirling "poet lariat" of the era, remarked that if Roosevelt were to burn down the Capitol, people would say, "Well, we at least got a fire started, anyhow."

"Bureaucratic meddling" and "regimentation" were also bitter complaints of anti–New Dealers; and in truth bureaucracy did blossom. The federal government, with its hundreds of thousands of employees, became incomparably the largest single business in the country, as the states faded farther into the background. Unhappily, many of the ill-trained newcomers to the political payroll represented a setback for greater efficiency.

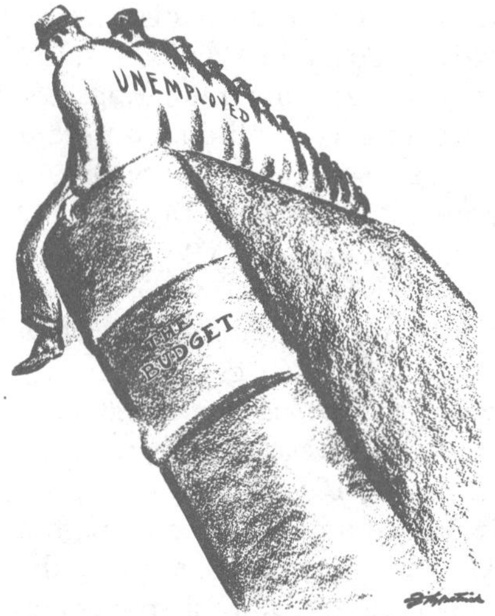

"Keeping It Out of Balance," 1935.
(Fitzpatrick in the St. Louis *Post-Dispatch.*)

Promises of budget balancing, to say nothing of other promises, had flown out the window—so foes of the New Deal pointed out. The national debt had skyrocketed from the already enormous figure of $19,487,000,000 in 1932 to $40,440,000,000 by 1939. America was becoming, its critics charged, a "handout state" trying to squander itself into prosperity—U.S. stood for "unlimited spending." Such lavish benefactions were undermining the old virtues of thrift and initiative. Ordinary Americans, once self-reliant citizens, were getting a bad case of the "gimmies": their wishbones were becoming larger than their backbones. In the 19th Century, hard-pressed workers went West; now they went on relief.

Business was bitter. Accusing the New Deal of

> A basic objective of the New Deal was featured in Roosevelt's second inaugural address (1937): "I see one-third of a nation ill-housed, ill-clad, ill-nourished. . . . The test of our progress is not whether we add more to the abundance of those who have much; it is whether we provide enough for those who have too little."

fomenting class strife in a once middle-class America, conservatives insisted that the laboring man and the farmer—especially the big operator—were being pampered. Why "soak the successful"? Countless businessmen, especially Republicans, declared that they could pull themselves out of the depression if they could only get the federal government—an interventionist Big Government—off their backs. Private enterprise, they charged, was being stifled by "planned economy," "planned bankruptcy," "creeping socialism," and the philosophy "Washington can do it better," with a federal pill for every ill. States' rights were being ignored, while the government was competing in business with its own citizens, under a "dictatorship of Do-gooders."

The aggressive leadership of Roosevelt—"one-man super-government"—also came in for denunciation. Heavy fire was especially directed at his attempts to browbeat the Supreme Court and to create a "dummy Congress." He had even tried in the 1938 elections, with backfiring results, to "purge" members of Congress who would not lockstep with him. The three senators whom he publicly opposed were all triumphantly re-elected.

The most damning indictment of the New Deal was that it had failed to cure the depression. Afloat in a sea of red ink, it had merely administered aspirin, sedatives, and Band-Aids. Many economists believed that better results would have been achieved by much greater deficit spending. Despite some $20 billion poured out in six years of deficit spending and lending, of leaf raking and pump priming, the gap was not closed between production and consumption. There were even more mountainous farm surpluses under Roosevelt than under Hoover. Millions of dispirited men were still unemployed in 1939, after six years of drain, strain, and pain. Not until World War II blazed forth in Europe with Hitler—the greatest pump primer of all—was the unemployment headache solved. The sensational increase in the national debt was caused by World War II, not the New Deal. The national debt was only $40 billion in 1939 but $258 billion in 1945.

FDR's Balance Sheet

New Dealers staunchly defended their record. Admitting that there had been some waste, they pointed out that relief—not economy—had been the primary object of their multi-front war on the depression. Conceding also that there had been some graft, they argued that it had been trivial in view of the immense sums spent and the obvious need for haste.

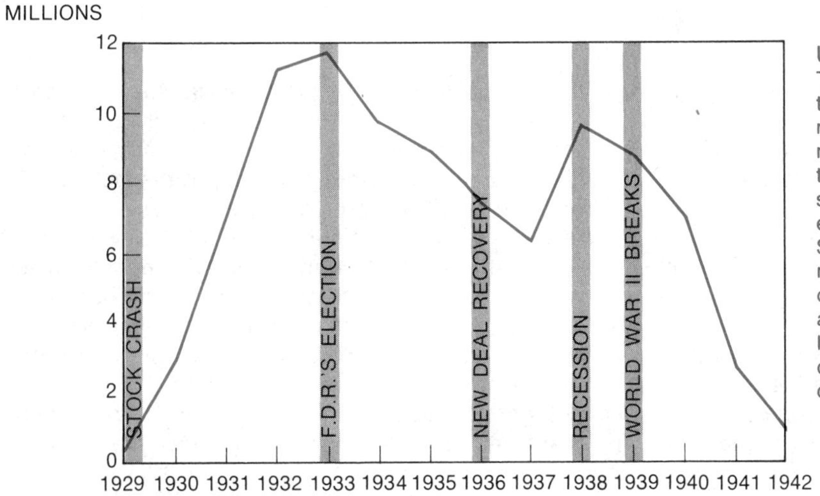

UNEMPLOYMENT, 1929–1942

UNEMPLOYMENT, 1929–1942
These cold figures can only begin to suggest the widespread human misery caused by mass unemployment. One man wrote to a newspaper in 1932: "I am forty-eight; married twenty-one years; four children, three in school. For the last eight years I was employed as a Pullman conductor. Since September, 1930, they have given me seven months part-time work. Today I am an object of charity. . . . My small, weak, and frail wife and two small children are suffering and I have come to that terrible place where I could easily resort to violence in my desperation."

Apologists for Roosevelt further declared that the New Deal had relieved the worst of the crisis in 1933. It promoted the philosophy of "balancing the human budget," and accepted the principle that the federal government was bound to prevent mass hunger and starvation by "managing" the economy. The Washington regime was to be used, not feared. America's economic system was kept from collapse; a fairer distribution of the national income was achieved; and the citizens were enabled to retain their self-respect. "Nobody is going to starve" was Roosevelt's promise.

Though hated by business tycoons, FDR should have been their patron saint, so his admirers claimed. He deflected popular resentments against business, and may have saved the American system of free enterprise. Roosevelt's quarrel was not with capitalism but with capitalists; he purged American capitalism of some of its worst abuses so that it might be saved from itself. He may even have headed off a more radical swing to the left by a mild dose of what was mistakenly condemned as "socialism." The head of the American Socialist party, when once asked if the New Deal had carried out the Socialist program, reportedly replied that it had indeed—on a stretcher.

A grim quip of the times was: "Roosevelt doesn't hate rich men. He only wants to skin them."

Roosevelt, like Jefferson, provided reform without a bloody revolution—at a time when some foreign nations were suffering armed uprisings and when many Europeans were predicting either communism or fascism for America. He was upbraided by the left-wing radicals for not going far enough; by the right-wing conservatives for going too far. Choosing the middle road, he has been called the greatest American conservative since Hamilton. He was in fact Hamiltonian in his espousal of big government, but Jeffersonian in his concern for the forgotten man. Demonstrating anew the value of powerful presidential leadership, he exercised that power to relieve the erosion of the nation's greatest physical resource—its people. He helped preserve democracy in America at a time when democracies abroad were disappearing down the sinkhole of dictatorship. And in playing this role he unwittingly girded the nation for its part in the titanic war that hung on the horizon—a war in which democracy the world over would be at stake.

VARYING VIEWPOINTS

The New Deal has stirred hot debate since its beginnings in 1933. Some contemporaries like Herbert Hoover, and some historians like Edgar E. Robinson, condemned Roosevelt's program as a "socialistic" break from American traditions. But until recently the great majority of historians have approved the political values of the New Deal and have praised its accomplishments.

Yet even pro-Roosevelt scholars disagree about the relation of the New Deal to the past. Arthur M. Schlesinger, Jr., for example, portrays the New Deal as a dramatic climax to the Populist-progressive reform campaigns. He consequently tends to play down the role of the depression in stimulating reforms. Yet Richard Hofstadter, in his *Age of Reform,* while favorable to the New Deal, sees it as a bold response to a unique situation, and hence a departure from the old reform tradition. In the last decade or so, several younger "New Left" historians have revived the "old left" criticism that the New Deal was neither bold nor innovative, but simply a conservative holding action to shore up sagging capitalism. The consensus seems to be somewhere in the middle. As William Leuchtenburg has put it, the New Deal engineered a "half-way revolution," neither outright socialistic nor simply conservative, but one that significantly transformed American life.

SELECT READINGS

A masterly summation is W. E. Leuchtenburg, *Franklin D. Roosevelt and the New Deal, 1932–1940* (1963). Briefer and more critical of the limitations of reform is Paul Conkin, *The New Deal* (rev. ed., 1975). A readable biography is J. M. Burns, *Roosevelt: The Lion and the Fox* (1956). More detailed is Frank Freidel, *Franklin D. Roosevelt* (4 vols., 1952–1973). A sympathetic and perceptive family portrait is Joseph P. Lash, *Eleanor and Franklin* (1971). Brilliantly pro-FDR are the three volumes of Arthur M. Schlesinger, Jr.'s: *Age of Roosevelt: The Crisis of the Old Order* (1957), *The Coming of the New Deal* (1959), and *The Politics of Upheaval* (1960). Less favorable is E. E. Robinson, *The Roosevelt Leadership* (1955). See also Richard Hofstadter, *The Age of Reform* (1955). John M. Blum, *From the Morgenthau Diaries* (3 vols., 1959–1967), gives the perspective of an important New Deal insider. The views of other contemporaries may be found in Frances Perkins, *The Roosevelt I Knew* (1946) and R. G. Tugwell, *In Search of Roosevelt* (1972). Biographies of other key figures include T. H. Williams, *Huey Long* (1969), Melvyn Dubofsky and Warren Van Tine, *John L. Lewis* (1977), Jordan A. Schwarz, *The Speculator: Bernard Baruch in Washington, 1917–1965* (1981), and Michael E. Parrish, *Felix Frankfurter* (Vol. I, 1982). On the relation of the old progressives to the New Deal, consult Otis L. Graham, Jr., *An Encore for Reform* (1967), and Ronald L. Feinman, *Twilight of Progressivism: The Western Republican Senators and the New Deal* (1981). The social impact of the depression is vividly etched in Studs Terkel, *Hard Times* (1970), in Ann Banks, *First-Person America* (1980), and in contemporary novels like John Steinbeck's *Grapes of Wrath* (1939). Of special interest is Lois Scharf, *To Work and to Wed: Female Employment, Feminism, and the Great Depression* (1980). Labor is dealt with in Irving Bernstein, *Turbulent Years* (1970), and in Peter Friedlander, *The Emergence of a U.A.W. local, 1936–1939* (1975). Ellis Hawley, *The New Deal and the Problem of Monopoly* (1966) is a superb analysis of the conflicting currents of economic policy in the Roosevelt administration. James Patterson, *The New Deal and the States* (1969) examines the local impact of the Roosevelt measures, as does Charles H. Trout, *Boston, the Great Depression, and the New Deal* (1977). Indians receive special attention in Graham D. Taylor, *The New Deal and American Indian Tribalism* (1980), and in Kenneth R. Philp, *John Collier's Crusade for Indian Reform* (1977). On blacks, see Harvard Sitkoff, *A New Deal for Blacks* (1978). Especially good on intellectual history are Richard H. Pells, *Radical Visions and American Dreams: Culture and Social Thought in the Depression Years* (1973) and Daniel Aaron, *Writers on the Left* (1961). Mel Piehl, *The Catholic Worker and the Origins of Catholic Radicalism in America* (1982) is a particularly sensitive treatment. Special topics are treated in Donald Worster, *Dust Bowl: The Southern Plains in the 1930s* (1979), M. N. Penkower, *The Federal Writers' Project* (1977), Norris Hundley, Jr., *Water and the West* (1975), James T. Patterson, *Congressional Conservatism and the New Deal* (1967), Frank Freidel, *F. D. R. and the South* (1965), Thomas K. McCraw, *TVA and the Power Fight, 1933–1939* (1971), Roy Lubove, *The Struggle for Social Security, 1900–1935* (1968), and Paul L. Murphy, *The Constitution in Crisis Times, 1918–1969* (1972).

41

Franklin D. Roosevelt and the Shadow of War

The epidemic of world lawlessness is spreading. When an epidemic of physical disease starts to spread, the community approves and joins in a quarantine of the patients in order to protect the health of the community against the spread of the disease. . . . There must be positive endeavors to preserve peace.

FRANKLIN D. ROOSEVELT, Chicago Quarantine Speech, 1937

The London Conference and Soviet Recognition

The sixty-six-nation London Economic Conference, meeting in the summer of 1933, revealed how intimately Roosevelt's early foreign policy was entwined with his schemes for domestic recovery. This distinguished assemblage, to which America sent delegates, had as its major purpose a frontal attack on the global depression. It was particularly eager to stabilize national currencies on a worldwide front; and to such a course Washington had apparently committed itself in advance.

But Roosevelt began to have second thoughts.

He evidently believed that his gold-juggling policies were stimulating faint blushes of returning prosperity. An international agreement on currency might tie his hands; and, as an astute politician, he was unwilling to sacrifice probable recovery at home for possible recovery abroad. While vacationing on a cruiser in the North Atlantic, he dashed off a radio message to London, scolding the Conference for trying to stabilize currencies, and urging it to turn to more basic economic ills.

Roosevelt's bombshell message blew the rug from under the London Conference. The delegates adjourned empty-handed, amid cries of American bad faith. The Conference, in any event, probably would have failed to produce a wonder drug for the world's economic maladies. But the devil-take-the-hindmost attitude of Roosevelt plunged the world even deeper into the morass of narrow isolationism and extreme nationalism. This unfortunate trend, as fate would have it, played directly into the hands of power-mad dictators.

"Just Another Customer," 1933. The U.S. recognizes Russia. (Courtesy of the Dallas *News.*)

Less spectacular than Roosevelt's torpedoing of the London Conference was his formal recognition of the Soviet Union, late in 1933. Disagreeable though the thought might be to conservative Americans, the Bolshevik government had fastened itself securely on the backs of the Russian masses, and had won recognition from other great powers. There was a certain unreality in America's refusing to recognize, after sixteen long years, the official existence of the Moscow government—a regime representing 160 million people and holding sway over one-sixth of the earth's land surface. Washington's cold-shoulder treatment, moreover, had not caused the Soviet Union to collapse, or induced the Bolsheviks to abandon their insidious propaganda for world revolution.

Why did Roosevelt extend the right hand of recognition? He was first of all an outspoken liberal, not bound by the conservatism of his Republican predecessors. Hitler was on the rise in Germany, land-hungry Japan was on the rampage in the Far East, and many Americans believed that the recognition of Moscow might bolster the Russians against the Nipponese. Finally, a depression-ridden United States was willing to gamble that an enriching trade would develop with the Soviet Union. Profits promote partnerships.

Horse-trading negotiations with the Russians were concluded in Washington during November 1933. The Soviets formally promised, among other assurances, to refrain from revolutionary propaganda in America. They promptly broke this pledge. Large-scale trade with the U.S.S.R. did not develop, primarily because a huge American loan, which the Russians had expected, was not granted. Russia was regarded as a poor credit risk. Uncle Sam was to some extent duped by Moscow, but at least he was now on official speaking terms—or name-calling terms—with the rulers of the largest and most populous of the white nations. Roosevelt remarked that while Russia was not yet "housebroken," it was still a good breed of dog. Dissenting conservatives condemned "Bolshevik Butchers" and "Profits Stained with Blood."

Freedom for (from?) the Filipinos

The Great Depression, otherwise a blight, actually brightened hopes for Philippine independence. McKinley's imperialistic dream bubble in the Far East had burst, and American taxpayers were eager to throw overboard their expensive tropical liability. Organized labor clamored for the exclusion of low-wage Filipinos, while American producers of sugar and other products were eager to restrict competition from the Philippines.

In 1934 Congress, remembering its earlier promises of Philippine independence, responded to the prodding of such self-seeking groups. It passed a bill under which the potentially rich islands were to become free, but only after a ten-year period of economic and political tutelage. Uncle Sam's military establishments were to be relinquished, but naval bases were to be reserved for future discussion–and retention.

Rather than freeing the Philippines, the American people tried to free themselves *from* the Philippines. With a selfish eye to their own welfare, they imposed upon the Filipinos economic terms so ungenerous as to threaten the islands with prostration. American isolationists, moreover, rejoiced to be rid of this Far Eastern heel of Achilles–so vulnerable to Japanese attack. Yet these turn-tail-and-run tactics, though applauded by anti-colonialists in Eastern Asia, cost America "face" in the Far East. Abandoning the Filipinos did nothing to discourage the barefaced aggressions of the Japanese militarists.

Good-Neighborism Under FDR

A refreshing new era in relations with Latin America was heralded when Roosevelt ringingly proclaimed in his inaugural address, "I would dedicate this nation to the policy of the Good Neighbor."

Old-fashioned intervention by bayonet in the Caribbean had not paid off, except in an evil harvest of resentment, suspicion, and fear. The Great Depression had cooled off Yankee economic aggressiveness, as thousands of investors in Latin American "securities" became sackholders rather than stockholders. There were now fewer dollars to be protected by the rifles of the hated marines.

Roosevelt has generally received extravagant credit for the Good Neighbor policy. Actually, the retreat from economic imperialism in Latin America had already been foreshadowed under Harding and Coolidge, and particularly under Hoover. But FDR went the whole way, partly because of his liberal tendencies, and partly because global politics were shifting. With warthirsty dictators seizing power in Europe and Asia, he was eager to line up the Latin Americans to help defend the Western Hemisphere. Embittered neighbors would be potential tools of transoceanic aggressors.

President Roosevelt made clear at the outset that he was going to renounce armed intervention, particularly the vexatious corollary of the Monroe Doctrine devised by his cousin, Theodore Roosevelt. Late in 1933, at the Seventh Pan-American Conference in Montevideo, the United States delegation formally accepted non-intervention.

Deeds followed words. The last marines embarked from Haiti in 1934. In the same year restive Cuba was released from the hobbles of the Platt Amendment, under which Uncle Sam had been free to intervene, although the naval base at Guantánamo was retained. Tiny Panama received a similar uplift in 1936, when the leading strings of Washington were partially unfastened.

President-elect Hoover, during his goodwill trip to Latin America (1928–1929), repeatedly referred in speeches to "good neighbor" and "good neighbors." In Uruguay he declared, "I have hoped that I might by this visit symbolize the courtesy of a call from one good neighbor to another, that I might convey the respect, esteem and desire for intellectual and spiritual co-operation." Roosevelt did not invent the phrase "Good Neighbor."

The hope-inspiring Good Neighbor policy, with the accent on consultation and non-intervention, received its acid test in Mexico. A seizure of Yankee oil properties in 1938, under the constitution of 1917, brought vehement demands for armed intervention from American investors. But Roosevelt successfully resisted the clamor, and a settlement was finally threshed out in 1941, even though the oil companies lost much of their original stake.

Spectacular success crowned Roosevelt's Good Neighbor policy. His earnest attempts to inaugurate a new era of friendliness, though hurting some Yankee bondholders, paid rich dividends in goodwill among the peoples to the south. No other citizen of the United States has ever been held in such high esteem in Latin America during his lifetime. Roosevelt was cheered with tumultuous enthusiasm when, as a "traveling salesman for peace," he journeyed to the special Inter-American Conference at Buenos Aires in 1936. The Colossus of the North now seemed less a vulture and more an eagle.

Secretary Hull's Reciprocal Trade Agreements

Intimately associated with Good Neighborism, and also popular in Latin America, was the reciprocal trade policy of the New Dealers. Its chief architect was high-domed Secretary of State Cordell Hull, a homespun Tennessean of the low-tariff school. Like Roosevelt, he believed that trade was a two-way street; that a nation can sell abroad only as it buys abroad; that tariff barriers choke off foreign trade; and that trade wars beget shooting wars.

Responding to the Hull-Roosevelt leadership, Congress passed the Reciprocal Trade Agreements Act in 1934. Designed in part to lift American export trade from the depression doldrums, this far-visioned measure was aimed at both relief and recovery. At the same time it would put into active operation the low-tariff policies of the New Dealers. (See chart, p. 739.)

The Trade Agreements Act avoided the dangerous uncertainties of a wholesale tariff revision; it merely whittled down the most objectionable schedules of the Hawley-Smoot law by amending them. Roosevelt was empowered to lower existing rates by as much as 50 percent, provided that the other country involved was willing to respond with similar reductions. The resulting pacts, moreover, were to become effective without the formal approval of the Senate. This novel feature not only insured speedier action, but sidestepped the twin evils of logrolling and high-pressure lobbying in Congress.

Secretary Hull, whose zeal for reciprocity was unflagging, succeeded in negotiating pacts with twenty-one countries by the end of 1939. During these same years American foreign trade increased appreciably, all presumably in part as a result of the Hull-Roosevelt policies. Trade agreements undoubtedly bettered economic and political relations with Latin America, and proved to be an influence for peace in a war-bent world.

The Reciprocal Trade Agreements Act, with modifications, was renewed periodically by Congress—but invariably in the teeth of heated pro-

"One of Our Quaint Ideas About Foreign Trade." (Fitzpatrick in the St. Louis *Post-Dispatch.*)

tests from high-tariff Republicans. James G. Blaine, Republican secretary of state of yesteryear, had fathered the reciprocal trade policy. But dyed-in-the-wool Republicans were inclined to shun the Blaine baby in Democratic diapers. Manufacturers were not alone in their opposition; they were joined by many Middle Western farmers who were hurt by lowered duties on meat and other foreign imports. But a majority of the New Deal Congress felt that the interests of special groups, however important, should be sacrificed to those of the nation as a whole.

The Rome-Berlin Axis. Hitler and Mussolini meet. (Wide World Photos.)

Impulses Toward Storm-Cellar Isolationism

Post-1918 chaos in Europe, followed by the Great Depression, fostered the ominous concept of totalitarianism. The individual was nothing; the state was everything. Communist Russia led the way, with the crafty and ruthless Joseph Stalin finally emerging as dictator. Blustery Benito Mussolini, a swaggering Fascist, seized the reins of power in Italy during 1922. And Adolf Hitler, a fanatic with a toothbrush mustache, plotted and harangued his way into control of Germany in 1933 with liberal use of the "Big Lie."

Hitler was the most immediately dangerous, because he combined tremendous power with impulsiveness. A frustrated Austrian painter, with hypnotic talents as an orator and a leader, he had secured control of the Nazi party by making political capital of the Treaty of Versailles and the depression-spawned unemployment. He was thus a misbegotten child of the shortsighted post-war policies of the victorious Allies, including the United States. The desperate German people had fallen in behind the new Pied Piper, for they saw no other hope of escape from the plague of economic chaos and national disgrace. In 1936 the Nazi Hitler and the Fascist Mussolini allied themselves in the Rome-Berlin Axis.

International gangsterism was likewise spreading in the Far East, where the Nipponese were on the make. Like Germany and Italy, Japan was a so-called "have-not" power. Like them, she resented the ungenerous Treaty of Versailles. Like them, she demanded additional space for her teeming millions, condemned to a potted-plant existence.

Japanese navalists were not to be denied. Determined to find a place in the Asiatic sun, Tokyo gave notice in 1934 of the termination of the twelve-year-old Washington Naval Treaty. A year later at London, the Japanese torpedoed all hope of effective naval disarmament. Upon being denied complete parity, they walked out on the multi-power conference and accelerated their construction of giant battleships.

Jut-jawed Mussolini, seeking both glory and empire in Africa, brutally attacked Ethiopia in 1935 with bombers and tanks. The brave defenders, armed with spears and ancient firearms, were speedily crushed. Members of the League of Nations could have caused Mussolini's war

Mussolini's thirst for national glory in primitive Ethiopia is indicated by his remark in 1940, "To make a people great it is necessary to send them to battle even if you have to kick them in the pants." (The Italians were notoriously unwarlike.) In 1934 Mussolini proclaimed in a public speech, "We have buried the putrid corpse of liberty."

machine to creak to a halt—if they had only dared to embargo oil. But when the League quailed rather than risk global hostilities, it merely signed its own death warrant.

Isolationism, long festering in America, received a strong boost from these alarms abroad. Though disapproving of the dictators, Americans still believed that their encircling seas conferred a kind of mystic immunity. They were continuing to suffer the disillusionment born of their participation in World War I, which they now regarded as a colossal blunder. They likewise cherished bitter memories of the ungrateful and defaulting debtors. As early as 1934 a spiteful Congress had passed the Johnson Debt Default Act. which prevented debt-dodging nations from borrowing further in the United States. If attacked again by aggressors, these delinquents could "stew in their own juice." A Middle Western farmer reportedly said, "I don't give a darn what happens to them fellers as long as it don't happen to me."

Mired down in the Great Depression, Americans had no real appreciation of the revolutionary forces being harnessed by the dictators. The "have-not" powers were out to become "have" powers. Americans were not so much afraid that totalitarian aggression would cause trouble as they were fearful that they might be drawn into it. Strong nationwide agitation welled up for a constitutional amendment to forbid a declaration of war by Congress—except in case of invasion—unless there was first a favorable popular referendum. With a mixture of seriousness and frivolity, a group of Princeton University students began to agitate in 1936 for a bonus to be paid to the Veterans of Future Wars (V.F.W.s) while still alive.

Congress Legislates Neutrality

As the gloomy 1930s lengthened, an avalanche of lurid articles and books poured from American presses condemning the munitions manufacturers as war-fomenting "merchants of death." A Senate committee, headed by Senator Nye of North Dakota, was appointed in 1934 to investigate the "blood business." By sensationalizing evidence regarding America's entry into World War I, the senatorial probers tended to shift the blame away from the German submarine onto the American bankers and arms manufacturers. As the munitions-makers had obviously made money out of the war, many a naive soul leaped to the illogical conclusion that these soulless scavengers had caused the war in order to make money. This kind of reasoning suggested that if the profits could only be removed from the arms traffic—"one hell of a business"—the country could keep out of any world conflict that might erupt in the future.

Responding to overwhelming popular pressure, Congress made haste to legislate the nation out of war. Action was spurred by the danger that Mussolini's Ethiopian assault would plunge the world into a new bloodbath. The Neutrality Acts of 1935, 1936, and 1937, taken together, stipulated that *when the President proclaimed* the existence of a foreign war, certain restrictions would automatically go into effect. No American could legally sail on a belligerent ship, or sell or transport munitions to a belligerent, or make loans to a belligerent.

This head-in-the-sands legislation marked in effect an abandonment of the traditional policy of freedom of the seas—a policy for which America had professedly fought two full-fledged wars and several undeclared wars. The Neutrality Acts, so called, were specifically tailored to keep the nation out of a conflict like World War I. If they had been in effect at that time, America probably would not

"The Jig-Saw Puzzle," 1939.
(Cassel in the Brooklyn *Eagle*.)

have been sucked in—at least not in April 1917. Congress was one war too late with its legislation. What had seemed dishonorable to Wilson seemed honorable and desirable to a later disillusioned generation.

Storm-celler neutrality proved to be tragically shortsighted. America falsely assumed that the decision for peace or war lay in her own hands, not in those of the satanic forces already unleashed in the world. Prisoner of her own fears, she failed to recognize that she should have used her enormous power to control international events in her own interest. Instead, she remained at the mercy of events controlled by the dictators.

Statutory neutrality, though of undoubted legality, was of dubious morality. America served notice that she would make no distinction whatever between the brutal aggressor and his innocent victims. By striving to hold the scales even, she actually overbalanced them in favor of the dictators who had armed themselves to the teeth. By declining to use her vast industrial strength to aid her democratic friends and defeat her totalitarian foes, she helped spur the aggressors along their blood-spattered path of conquest.

America Dooms Loyalist Spain

The Spanish Civil War of 1936–1939—a proving ground and dress rehearsal in miniature for World War II—was a painful object lesson in the folly of neutrality-by-legislation. Spanish rebels, who rose against the left-leaning republican government in Madrid, were headed by Fascistic General Francisco Franco. Generously aided by his fellow conspirators, Hitler and Mussolini, he undertook to overthrow the established Loyalist regime, which in turn was assisted on a smaller scale by the Soviet Union. This pipeline from Communist Moscow chilled the natural sympathies of many Americans, especially those of Roman Catholic faith.

Washington continued official relations with the Loyalist government. In accordance with previous American practice, this regime should have been free to purchase desperately needed munitions in the United States. But Congress, with the encouragement of Roosevelt and with only one dissenting vote, amended the existing neutrality legislation so as to apply an arms embargo to both Loyalists and rebels. "Roosevelt," remarked dictator Franco, "behaved in the manner of a true gentleman." FDR later regretted being so gentlemanly.

Uncle Sam thus sat on the sidelines while Franco, abundantly supplied with arms and men by his fellow dictators, strangled the republican government of Spain. The democracies, including the United States, were so determined to stay out of war that they helped to condemn a fellow democracy to death. In so doing, they further encouraged the dictators to take the dangerous

Claude Bowers, the U.S. ambassador in Spain, deplored neutrality and favored support for the defeated Loyalists. When he returned to America and met with Roosevelt, the President's first words were, "We've made a mistake. You've been right all along." At least this is what Bowers states in his memoirs.

road which led over the precipice of World War II.

Such peace-at-any-price-ism was further cursed with illogic. While determined to stay out of war, America declined to build up her armed forces to a point where she could deter the aggressors. In fact, she allowed her navy to decline in relative strength. She had been led to believe that huge fleets cause huge wars; she was also trying to spare the complaining taxpayer during the grim days of the Great Depression. When President Roosevelt repeatedly called for preparedness, he was branded a warmonger. Not until 1938, the year before World War II exploded, did Congress come to grips with the problem when it passed a billion-dollar naval construction act. The calamitous story was repeated of too little—and that too late.

Appeasing Japan and Germany

Sulfurous war clouds had meanwhile been gathering in the tension-taut Far East. In 1937 the Japanese militarists, at the Marco Polo Bridge near Peking, touched off the explosion that led to a full-dress invasion of China. In a sense this attack was the curtain raiser of World War II.

Roosevelt declined to invoke the recently passed neutrality legislation, noting that the so-called China incident was not an officially declared war. If he had put the existing restrictions into effect, he would have cut off the tiny trickle of munitions on which the Chinese were desperately dependent. The Japanese, of course, could continue to buy mountains of war supplies in the United States.

In Chicago—unofficial isolationist "capital" of America—Roosevelt delivered his sensational "Quarantine Speech" in the autumn of 1937. Alarmed by the recent aggressions of Italy and Japan, he called for "positive endeavors" to "quarantine" the aggressors—presumably by economic embargoes. One immediate result was a cyclone of protest from isolationists and other foes of involvement; they feared that a moral quarantine would lead to a shooting quarantine. Startled by this angry response, Roosevelt sought by less direct means to curb the dictators.

America's isolationist mood deepened, especially in regard to China. In December 1937, Japanese aviators bombed and sank an American gunboat, the *Panay,* in Chinese waters, with a loss of two killed and thirty wounded. In the days of 1898, when the *Maine* went down, this outrage might have provoked war. But after Tokyo hastened to make the necessary apologies and pay a proper indemnity, the American public breathed a deep sigh of relief. Japanese militarists were thus encouraged to vent their anger against the "superior" white race by subjecting American civilians in China, both male and female, to humiliating slappings and strippings.

More immediately menacing was Adolf Hitler. In 1935 he had openly flouted the Treaty of Versailles by introducing compulsory military service in Germany. The next year he boldly marched into the demilitarized German Rhineland, likewise contrary to the detested treaty, while France and Britain looked on in an agony of indecision. Lashing his following to a frenzy, Hitler undertook to persecute and then liquidate the Jewish population in the areas under his control. In the end, he wiped out about 6 million innocent victims, mostly in gas chambers. Calling upon his people to sacrifice butter for guns, he whipped the new

Nazi Occupation of Czechoslovakia, 1939.
(Eastfoto.)

German air force and mechanized ground divisions into the most devastating military machine the world had yet seen.

Suddenly, in March 1938, Hitler bloodlessly occupied German-speaking Austria, his birthplace. The democratic powers, wringing their hands in despair, prayed that this last grab would satisfy his passion for conquest.

But Hitler could not stop. Later in 1938 he continued his "war of nerves" by his bullying demands for the German-inhabited Sudetenland of his neighbor, tiny Czechoslovakia. The leaders of Britain and France, eager to appease Hitler, sought frantically to bring the dispute to the conference table. President Roosevelt, also deeply alarmed, kept the wires hot with personal messages, to both Hitler and Mussolini, urging a peaceful settlement.

A conference was finally arranged in Munich, Germany, in September 1938. The Western European democracies, badly unprepared for war, betrayed Czechoslovakia to Germany when they consented to the shearing away of the Sudetenland. They hoped—and these hopes were shared by the American people—that the concessions at the conference table would appease the power-lust of Hitler and bring "peace in our time." Indeed, he publicly promised that the Sudetenland "is the last territorial claim I have to make in Europe."

"Appeasement" of the dictators, symbolized by the ugly word "Munich," turned out to be merely surrender on the installment plan. It was like giving a cannibal a finger in the hope of saving an arm. In March 1939, scarcely six months later, Hitler suddenly erased the rest of Czechoslovakia from the map, contrary to his solemn promises. The democratic world was again stunned.

Hitlerian Belligerency and U.S. Neutrality

Joseph Stalin, the sphinx of the Kremlin, was a key to the peace puzzle. In the summer of 1939 the British and French were busily negotiating with Moscow, hopeful of securing a mutual-defense treaty that would halt Hitler. But mutual suspicions proved insuperable. Almost overnight the Soviet Union astounded the watching world by signing, on August 23, 1939, a non-aggression treaty with the German dictator.

The notorious Hitler-Stalin pact was epochal. It meant that the Nazi German leader now had a green light to make war on Poland and the Western democracies, without fearing a stab in the back from Russia—his Communist arch foe. Consternation struck those wishful thinkers in Western Europe who had fondly hoped that Hitler might be egged upon Stalin so that the twin menaces would bleed each other to death. It was as plain as the mustache on Stalin's face that the wily Soviet dictator was plotting to turn his German accomplice against the Western democracies. The two warring camps would then kill each other off—and leave Stalin bestriding Europe like a colossus.

World War II was only hours away. Hitler, intensifying the pressure, demanded from neighboring Poland a return of the areas wrested from Germany after World War I. Failing to secure satisfaction, he sent his mechanized divisions crashing into Poland at dawn on September 1, 1939.

Britain and France, honoring their commitments to Poland, promptly declared war. At long last they perceived the folly of continued appeasement. But they were powerless to aid Poland, which succumbed in three weeks to Hitler's smashing strategy of terror. Stalin, as prearranged secretly in his fateful pact with Hitler, came in on the kill for his share of old Russian Poland. Long-dreaded World War II was now fully launched, and the long truce of 1919–1939 had ended.

President Roosevelt speedily issued the routine proclamations of neutrality. The American people were overwhelmingly anti-Nazi and anti-Hitler; they fervently hoped that the democracies would win; they fondly believed that the forces of righteousness would again triumph, as in 1918. But they were desperately determined to stay out: they were not going to be "suckers" again.

Neutrality promptly became a heated issue in the United States. Ill-prepared Britain and

European War Narrows the Atlantic.
(Courtesy of the Washington *Star*.)

France urgently needed American airplanes and other weapons, but the Neutrality Act of 1937 raised a sternly forbidding hand. Roosevelt summoned Congress in special session, shortly after the invasion of Poland, to consider a lifting of the arms embargo. After six hectic weeks of debate, a makeshift law emerged.

The Neutrality Act of 1939 provided that henceforth the European democracies might buy American war materials, but only on a "cash and carry" basis. This meant that they would have to transport the munitions in their own ships, after paying for them in cash. America would thus avoid loans, war debts, and the torpedoing of American arms-carriers. While Congress thus loosened former restrictions in response to interventionist cries, it added others in response to isolationist fears. Roosevelt was now authorized to proclaim danger zones into which American merchant ships would be forbidden to enter.

This unneutral neutrality law clearly favored the democracies against the dictators—and was so intended. As the British and French navies controlled the Atlantic, the European aggressors could not send their ships to buy America's munitions. The United States not only improved its moral position, but simultaneously helped its economic position. An overseas demand for war goods brought a sharp upswing from the recession of 1937–1938, and ultimately solved the decade-long unemployment crisis. (See chart, p. 789.)

Aftermath of the Fall of France

The months following the collapse of Poland, while France and Britain marked time, were known as the "phony war." An ominous silence fell on Europe, as Hitler shifted his victorious divisions from Poland for a knockout blow at France. Inaction during this anxious period was relieved by the Soviets, who wantonly attacked neighboring Finland in an effort to secure strategic buffer territory. The debt-paying Finns, who had a host of admirers in America, were speedily granted $30 million by an isolationist Congress for *non-military* supplies. But despite heroic resistance, Finland was finally flattened by the Russian steamroller.

An abrupt end to the "phony war" came in April 1940, when Hitler, again without warning, overran his weaker neighbors, Denmark and Norway. Hardly pausing for breath, the next month he launched an unannounced assault on Holland and Belgium, followed by a paralyzing blow at France. By late June, France was forced to surrender, but not until Mussolini had pounced on its rear for a jackal's share of the loot. Only by the so-called

In 1924, while briefly imprisoned, Hitler prepared a remarkable book, *Mein Kampf* (*My Struggle*), which brazenly set forth his objectives and techniques. He was a past master of the "Big Lie." As he wrote: "The primitive simplicity of their minds [the masses] renders them a more easy prey to a big lie than a small one, for they themselves often tell little lies but would be ashamed to tell big ones." He also said, "The victor will never be asked if he told the truth" and "Success is the sole earthly judge of right and wrong."

miracle of Dunkirk did the British manage to evacuate to England the bulk of their shattered and partially disarmed army. The crisis providentially brought forth an inspired leader in Prime Minister Winston Churchill, the bulldog-jawed orator who nerved his people to fight off the fearful air bombings of their cities.

France's sudden collapse shocked Americans out of their daydreams. Stout-hearted Britons, singing "There'll Always Be an England," were all that stood between Hitler and the end in Europe of constitutional government. If Britain went under, Hitler would have at his disposal the workshops, shipyards, and slave labor of Western Europe. He might even have the powerful British fleet as well. This frightening possibility, which seemed to pose a dire threat to American security, steeled the American people to a tremendous effort.

Roosevelt moved with electrifying energy and dispatch. He called upon an already debt-burdened nation to build huge airfleets and a two-ocean navy, which could also check Japan. Congress, jarred out of its apathy toward preparedness, within a year appropriated the astounding sum of $37 billion. This figure was more than the total cost of fighting World War I.

Pro-British Propaganda. This patriotic poster was put out by the Committee to Defend America by Aiding the Allies. (Trustees of the Imperial War Museum, London.)

"Just So There'll Be No Misunderstanding." Hitler and Mussolini are warned not to seize orphaned colonies in America. (Ray in the Kansas City *Star*.)

Congress also passed a conscription law, approved September 6, 1940. Under this measure—the first peacetime draft in American history—provision was made for training each year 1.2 million troops and 800,000 reserves. The act was later adapted to the requirements of a global war.

The Latin American bulwark likewise needed bolstering. Holland, Denmark, and France, all crushed under the German jackboot, had orphaned colonies in the New World. Would these fall into German hands? At the Havana Conference of 1940 the United States, by implication, agreed to share with its twenty sister republics the responsibility of upholding the Monroe Doctrine. This ancient dictum, hitherto unilateral, had been a bludgeon brandished only by the hated Yankee colossus. Now multilateral, it was to be wielded by twenty-one pairs of American hands—at least in theory.

Bolstering Britain with the Destroyer Deal (1940)

Before the fall of France, Washington had generally observed a technical neutrality. But now Americans had to choose between neutrality and unneutral assistance to Britain before she fell under the heel of Hitler. Neutrality quickly went into the ash can.

Roosevelt at first arranged to transfer surplus federal arms to private American concerns ("dummies"), through which the weapons could be sent to bomb-blasted Britain. Thus airplanes, rifles, mortars, artillery, and ammunition were shipped in a technically legal way.

Advocates of aid to England formed propaganda groups, the most potent of which was the Committee to Defend America by Aiding the Allies. Its argument was double-barreled. To interventionists, it could appeal for direct succor to the British by such slogans as "Britain Is Fighting Our Fight." To the isolationists, it could appeal for assistance to the democracies by "All Methods Short of War," so that the terrible conflict would be kept in faraway Europe.

The isolationists, both numerous and sincere, were by no means silent. Determined to avoid bloodshed at all costs, they organized the America First Committee and proclaimed, "England Will Fight to the Last American." They contended that America should concentrate what strength she had to defend her own shores, lest a victorious Hitler, after crushing Britain, successfully assault her. Their basic philosophy was "The Yanks Are Not Coming," and their most effective speechmaker was the famed aviator Colonel Charles A. Lindbergh who, ironically, had narrowed the Atlantic in 1927.

Britain was in critical need of destroyers, for German submarines were again threatening to starve her out with attacks on shipping. Roosevelt moved boldly when, on September 2, 1940, he agreed to transfer to Great Britain fifty old-model, four-funnel destroyers left over from World War I. In return, the British promised to hand over to the United States eight valuable defensive base sites, stretching from Newfoundland to South America. These strategically located outposts were to remain under the Stars and Stripes for ninety-nine years.

Transferring fifty destroyers to a foreign navy was a highly questionable disposal of government property, despite a strained interpretation of existing legislation. The exchange was achieved by a simple presidential agreement, without so much as a "by your leave" to Congress. Applause burst from the aid-to-Britain advocates, many of whom had been urging such a step. But condemnation arose from "America Firsters" and other isolationists, as well as from anti-administration Republicans. Some of them approved the transfer but decried Roosevelt's secretive and high-handed methods. Yet so grave was the crisis that the President was unwilling to submit the scheme to the uncertainties and delays of a full-dress debate in Congress.

Shifting warships from a "neutral" United States

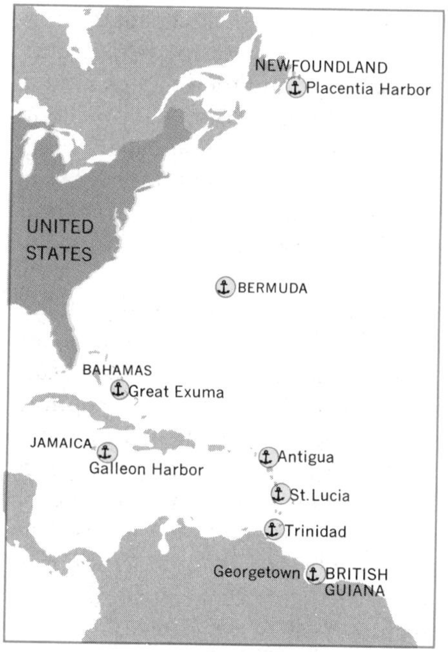

DESTROYER DEAL BASES

to a belligerent Britain was, beyond question, a flagrant violation of neutral obligations—at least neutral obligations that had existed before Hitler's barefaced aggressions rendered dangerous such old-fashioned concepts of fair play. Public opinion polls demonstrated that a majority of Americans were determined, even at the risk of armed hostilities, to provide the battered British with "all aid short of war."

> The old-line Republican bosses were not happy over having a recent Democrat head their ticket. Ex-Senator James Watson reportedly told Willkie to his face, "You have been a Democrat all your life. I don't mind the church converting a whore, but I don't like her to lead the choir the first night."

FDR Shatters the Two-Term Tradition (1940)

A distracting presidential election, as fate decreed, came in the midst of this crisis. The two leading Republican aspirants were round-faced and flat-voiced Senator Robert A. Taft of Ohio, son of the ex-President, and an energetic boy-wonder, lawyer-prosecutor Thomas E. Dewey of New York. But in one of the miracles of American political history, the Philadelphia convention was swept off its feet by an interventionist latecomer, Wendell L. Willkie, a German-descended son of Hoosier Indiana. This dynamic lawyer—tousle-headed, long-lipped, broad-faced, and large-framed—had until recently been a Democrat and the head of a huge public-utilities corporation. A complete novice in politics, he had rocketed from political nothingness in a few short weeks. His great appeal lay in his personality, for he was magnetic, transparently sincere, and honest in a homespun, Lincolnesque way.

With the galleries in Philadelphia wildly chanting "We Want Willkie," the delegates finally accepted this political upstart as the only candidate who could possibly beat Roosevelt. The Republican platform condemned FDR's alleged dictatorship, as well as the costly and confusing zigzags of the New Deal. Willkie, an outstanding liberal, was not so much opposed to the New Deal as to its extravagances and inefficiencies. Democratic critics branded him "the rich man's Roosevelt" and "the simple barefoot Wall Street lawyer."

While the rumor-pot boiled, Roosevelt delayed to the last minute the announcement of his decision to challenge the sacred two-term tradition. Despite what he described as his personal yearning for retirement, he avowed that in so grave a crisis he owed his experienced hand to the service of his country and humanity. The Democratic delegates in Chicago, realizing that only with "the Champ" could they defeat Willkie, drafted him by a technically unanimous vote. "Better a Third Term than a Third-Rater" was the war cry of many Democrats.

Burning with sincerity and energy, Willkie launched out upon a whirlwind, Bryanesque campaign in which he delivered over 500 speeches. At times his voice became a hoarse croak. The country was already badly split between interventionists and isolationists, and Willkie might have widened the breach dangerously by a violent attack on Roosevelt's aid-to-Britain policies. But seeing eye to eye with FDR on the necessity of bolstering the democracies, he refrained from assailing the President's interventionism, though objecting to his methods.

In the realm of foreign affairs, there was not much to choose between the two candidates. Both promised to stay out of the war; both promised aid to the victims of aggression; both promised to strengthen the nation's defenses. Yet Willkie, with a mop of black hair in his eyes, hit hard at Rooseveltian "dictatorship" and the third term. His enthusiastic followers cried, "Win with Willkie," "No Fourth Term Either," and "There's No Indispensable Man."

Roosevelt, busy at his desk with mounting problems, made only a few speeches. Stung by taunts that he was leading the nation by the back door into the European slaughterhouse, he repeatedly denied any such intention. His most specific state-

PRESIDENTIAL ELECTION OF 1940
(with electoral vote by state)
Willkie referred to Roosevelt only as "the third-term candidate." On election eve, FDR hinted that Communists and Fascists were among Willkie's supporters. Despite these campaign conflicts, the two men respected each other. FDR later asked Willkie to serve as his emissary abroad, and even suggested that they run together on a coalition ticket in 1944.

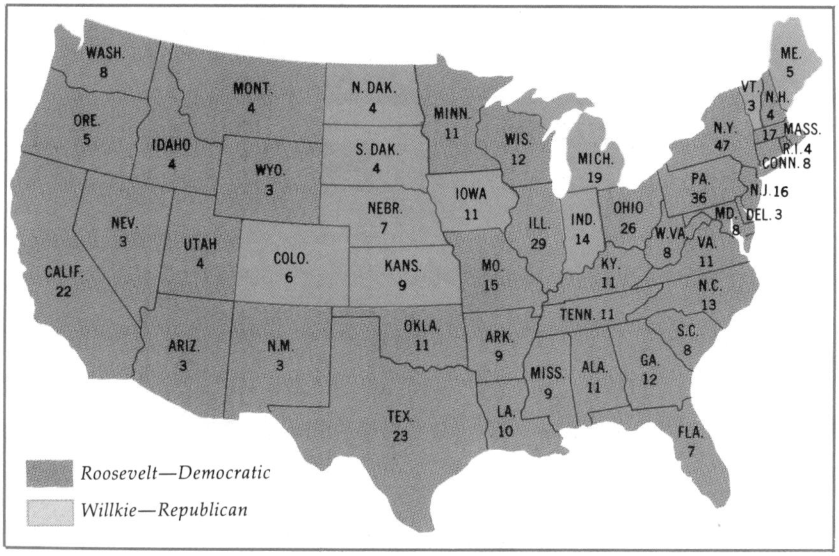

ment was at Boston, where he emphatically declared, "Your boys are not going to be sent into any foreign wars"—a pledge that later came back to plague him. He and his henchmen vigorously defended the New Deal, as well as all-out preparations for the defense of America and aid to the Allies.

1940 Campaign Poster. Roosevelt made political hay out of his New Deal reforms—and his defense policies. (Courtesy, Franklin D. Roosevelt Library)

Roosevelt triumphed in an unprecedented turnout of the voters, although Willkie ran a strong race. The popular total was 27,244,160 to 22,305,198, and the electoral count was 449 to 82. This contest was much less of a walkaway than in 1932 or 1936; Democratic majorities in Congress remained about the same.

Jubilant Democrats hailed their triumph as a mandate to abolish the two-term tradition. But the truth is that Roosevelt won in spite of the third-term handicap. Voters generally felt that, should war come, the experienced hand of the tried leader was needed at the helm. Less appealing was the completely inexperienced hand of the well-intentioned Willkie, who had never held public office.

The hoary argument that one should not change horses in the middle of a stream was strong, especially in an era of war-spawned prosperity. Roosevelt might not have won if there had not been a war crisis. On the other hand, he probably would not have run if foreign perils had not loomed so ominously. In a sense, his opponent was Adolf Hitler, not Willkie.

Congress Passes the Landmark Lend-Lease Law

By late 1940 embattled Britain was nearing the end of her financial tether; her credits in America were being rapidly consumed by insatiable war orders. But Roosevelt, who had bitter memories of

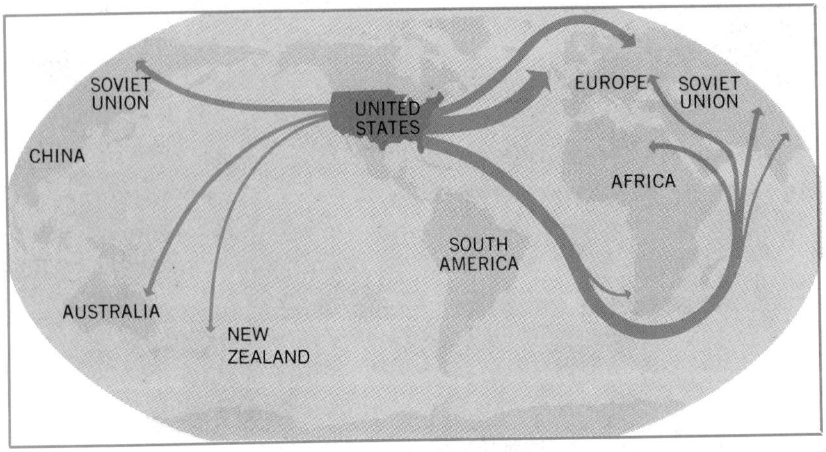

MAIN FLOW OF LEND-LEASE AID (width of arrows indicates relative amount) **The proud but desperate British Prime Minister, Winston Churchill, declared in early 1941: "Give us the tools and we will finish the job." Lend-lease eventually provided the British and other Allies with $50 billion worth of "tools."**

the wrangling over the Allied debts of World War I, was determined, as he put it, to eliminate "the silly, foolish, old dollar sign." He finally hit on the scheme of lending or leasing American arms to the reeling democracies. When the shooting was over, to use his comparison, the guns and tanks could be returned, just as one's next-door neighbor would return a length of garden hose when a threatening fire was put out. But isolationist Senator Taft retorted that lending arms was like lending chewing gum: "You don't want it back." Who wants a chewed-up tank?

The lend-lease bill, patriotically numbered 1776, was entitled "An Act Further to Promote the Defense of the United States." Sprung on the country after the election was safely over, it was praised by the administration as a device that would keep the nation out of the war, rather than get it in. The underlying concept was "Send guns, not sons" or "Billions, not bodies." America, so Roosevelt promised, would be the "arsenal of democracy." She would send a limitless supply of arms to the victims of aggression, who in turn would finish the job and keep the war on their side of the Atlantic. Accounts would be settled by returning the used weapons or their equivalents when the war was ended.

Lend-lease was heatedly debated throughout the land and in Congress. Most of the opposition came, as might be expected, from isolationists and anti-Roosevelt Republicans. The scheme was assailed as "the blank-check bill" and, in the words of isolationist Senator Wheeler, as "the new Triple-A bill"—a measure designed to "plow under every fourth American boy." Nevertheless lend-lease was finally approved in March 1941 by sweeping majorities in both houses of Congress.

Lend-lease was one of the most momentous laws ever to pass Congress; it was a challenge hurled squarely into the teeth of the Axis dictators. America pledged herself, to the extent of her vast resources, to bolster those nations that were indirectly defending her by fighting aggression. When the gigantic operation ended in 1945, she had sent about $50 billion worth of arms and equipment—much more than the cost to her of World War I—to those nations fighting aggressors. The passing of lend-lease was in effect an economic declaration of war; a shooting declaration could not be very far around the corner.

By its very nature, lend-lease marked the abandonment of any pretense of neutrality. It was no destroyer deal arranged privately by Roosevelt. It was universally debated, over drugstore counters and cracker barrels, from California to Maine; and the sovereign citizen at last spoke through convincing majorities in Congress. Most people probably realized that they were tossing the old concepts of neutrality out the window. But they also recognized that they would play a suicidal game if they bound themselves by the oxcart rules of the 19th Century—especially while the aggressors themselves openly spurned international obligations. Lend-lease would admittedly involve a grave risk of war, but most Americans were prepared to take that chance rather than see Britain collapse and then face the dictators alone.

Lend-lease had the somewhat incidental result of gearing the nation's own factories for all-out war production. The enormously increased capacity thus achieved helped to save America's own skin when, at long last, the shooting war burst around her head.

Hitler himself evidently recognized lend-lease as an unofficial declaration of war. Until then, Germany had avoided attacking American ships; memories of Uncle Sam's decisive intervention in 1917–1918 were still fresh in German minds. But after the passing of lend-lease there was less point in trying to curry favor with the United States. On May 21, 1941, the *Robin Moor,* an unarmed American merchantman, was torpedoed and destroyed by a German submarine in the South Atlantic, outside a war zone. The sinkings had started, but on a limited scale.

Hitler's Assault on Russia Spawns the Atlantic Charter

Two globe-shaking events marked the course of World War II before the assault on Pearl Harbor in 1941. One was the fall of France; the other was Hitler's invasion of Russia.

The scheming dictators, Hitler and Stalin, had been uneasy yoke-fellows under the ill-begotten pact of 1939. As masters of the double-cross, neither trusted the other. They engaged in prolonged dickering in a secret attempt to divide potential territorial spoils between them, but Stalin gagged on dominant German control of the Balkans. Hitler thereupon decided to crush his co-conspirator, seize the oil and other resources of Russia, and then have a free hand to snuff out Britain. He assumed that his all-conquering armies would subdue the "Mongol half-wits" of Russia in a few short weeks.

Out of a clear sky, on June 22, 1941, Hitler launched a devastating attack on his Soviet neighbor. This timely assault was an incredible stroke of good fortune for the democratic world—or so it seemed at the time. The two menaces could now slit each other's throats on the icy steppes of Russia. Or they would if the Soviets did not speedily collapse, as many military experts predicted.

> Senator Harry S Truman (later President) had a common reaction to Hitler's invasion of Russia in 1941: "If we see that Germany is winning, we ought to help Russia, and if we see Russia is winning, we ought to help Germany, and that way let them kill as many as possible."

Sound American strategy seemed to dictate speedy aid to Russia while she was still afloat. Roosevelt immediately promised assistance, and backed up his words by making some military supplies available. Several months later, interpreting the lend-lease law to mean that the defense of Russia was essential for the defense of the United States, he extended $1 billion in lend-lease—the first installment on an ultimate total of $11 billion. Meanwhile the valor of the Red Army, combined with the white paralysis of an early Russian winter, had halted the Hitlerian invaders at the gates of Moscow.

With the collapse of the Soviets still a dread possibility, the drama-charged Atlantic Conference was held in August 1941. British Prime Minister Winston Churchill, with cigar embedded in his cherubic face, secretly met with Roosevelt on a warship off the foggy coast of Newfoundland. This was the first of a series of history-making conferences between the two statesmen for the discussion of common problems, including the menace of Japan in the Far East.

The most memorable offspring of this get-together was the eight-point Atlantic Charter. It was formally accepted by Roosevelt and Churchill, and endorsed by the Soviet Union later that year. Suggestive of Wilson's Fourteen Points, the new covenant outlined the aspirations of the democracies for a better world at war's end.

"Unexpected Guest," 1941. Russia joins the democracies, Britain and America. (Courtesy Detroit *News.*)

Surprisingly, the Atlantic Charter was rather specific. While opposing imperialistic annexations, it promised that there would be no territorial changes contrary to the wishes of the inhabitants (self-determination). It further affirmed the right of a people to choose their own form of government and, in particular, to regain the governments abolished by the dictators. Among various other goals, the Charter declared for disarmament and a peace of security, pending "a permanent system of general security" (a new League of Nations).

Liberals the world over took heart from the Atlantic Charter, as they had taken heart from Wilson's comparable Fourteen Points. It was especially gratifying to subject populations, like the Poles, who were then ground under the iron heel of a conqueror. But the agreement was roundly condemned in the United States by isolationists and others hostile to Roosevelt. What right, they charged, had "neutral" America to confer with belligerent Britain on common policies? Such critics missed the point: the nation was no longer neutral.

U.S. Destroyers and Hitler's U-Boats Clash

Lend-lease shipments of arms to Britain on British ships were bound to be sunk by German wolf-pack submarines. If the intent was to get the munitions to England, not to dump them into the ocean, the freighters would have to be escorted by American warships. Britain simply did not have enough destroyers. The dangerous possibility of being "convoyed into war" had been mentioned in Congress during the lengthy debate on lend-lease, but administration spokesmen had brushed the idea aside. Their strategy was to make only one commitment at a time.

The fateful decision to convoy was taken in July 1941. Roosevelt, by virtue of his authority as commander-in-chief of the armed forces, issued orders to the navy to escort lend-lease shipments to Iceland. The British would then shepherd them the rest of the way.

Inevitable clashes with submarines ensued on the Iceland run, even though Hitler's orders were to strike American warships only in self-defense. In September 1941, the U.S. destroyer *Greer,* provocatively trailing a German U-boat, was attacked by the undersea craft, without damage to either side. Roosevelt then proclaimed a shoot-on-sight policy. On October 17, the escorting destroyer *Kearny,* while engaged in a battle with U-boats, lost eleven men when it was crippled but not sent to the bottom. Two weeks later the destroyer *Reuben James* was torpedoed and sunk off southwestern Iceland, with the loss of more than 100 officers and men.

Neutrality was still inscribed on the statute books, but not in American hearts. Congress, responding to public pressures and confronted with a shooting war, voted in mid-November 1941 to pull the teeth from the now-useless Neutrality Act of 1939. Merchant ships could henceforth be legally armed, and they could enter the com-

A Damaged U.S.S. *Kearny (left)* Towed into Iceland Port. (U.S. Army Signal Corps Photo, courtesy Navy Department.)

bat zones with munitions for Britain. Americans braced themselves for wholesale attacks by Hitler's submarines.

Heading for the Surprise Assault at Pearl Harbor

The blowup came, not in the Atlantic, but in the faraway Pacific. This explosion should have surprised no close observer, for Japan, since September of 1940, had been a formal military ally of Nazi Germany—America's shooting foe in the North Atlantic.

Japan's position in the Far East had grown more perilous by the hour. She was still mired down in the costly and exhausting "China incident," from which she could extract neither honor nor victory. Her war machine was fatally dependent on immense shipments from the United States of steel, scrap iron, oil, and aviation gasoline. Such assistance to the Japanese aggressor was highly unpopular in America. But Roosevelt had resolutely held off an embargo, lest he goad the Tokyo warlords into a descent upon the oil-rich and weakly defended Dutch East Indies.

Washington, late in 1940, finally imposed the first of its embargoes on Japan-bound supplies. This blow was followed in mid-1941 by a "freezing" of Nipponese assets in the United States and a cessation of all shipments of gasoline and other sinews of war. As the oil gauge dropped, the squeeze on Japan grew steadily more nerve-racking. Protracted delay was on the side of the United States. Japanese leaders were faced with two painful alternatives. They could either knuckle under to the Americans, or break out of the embargo ring by a desperate attack on the oil supplies and other riches of Southeast Asia. The ticking of the clock, while soothing to American ears, drove the Japanese to madness.

Final tense negotiations with Japan took place in Washington during November and early December of 1941. The State Department insisted that the Japanese clear out of China but, to sweeten the pill, offered to renew trade relations on a limited basis. Japanese imperialists, after waging a bitter war against the Chinese for more than four years, were unwilling to lose face by withdrawing at the behest of the United States. Faced with capitulation or continued conquest, they chose the sword. They had to put up or shut up, as the American press noted. They put up, believing that the war had been forced on them.

Officials in Washington, having "cracked" the top secret code of the Japanese, knew that Tokyo's decision was for war. But the United States, as a democracy committed to public debate and action by Congress, could not shoot first. Roosevelt, misled by Japanese ship movements in the Far East, evidently expected the blow to fall on British Malaya or perhaps on the Philippines. No one in high authority in Washington seems to have believed that the Japanese were either strong enough or foolhardy enough to lash out at Hawaii.

But the paralyzing blow struck Pearl Harbor, while Tokyo was deliberately prolonging negotiations in Washington. Japanese bombers, winging in from distant aircraft carriers, attacked without warning on the "Black Sunday" morning of December 7, 1941. It was a date, as Roosevelt told Congress, "which will live in infamy." About 3,000 casualties were inflicted on American personnel; many aircraft were destroyed; the battleship fleet was virtually wiped out when all eight of the craft were sunk or otherwise immobilized; and numerous small vessels were damaged or destroyed. Fortunately for America, the three priceless aircraft carriers happened to be outside the harbor.

An angered Congress, the next day, officially recognized the war that had been "thrust" upon the United States. The roll call in the Senate and House lacked only one vote of unanimity. Germany and Italy, allies of Japan, spared Congress the indecision of debate by declaring war on December 11, 1941. This challenge was formally accepted on the same day by a unanimous vote of both Senate and House. The unofficial war, of many months' duration, was now official.

The Battleship *West Virginia* Wrecked at Pearl Harbor.
(U.S. Navy photo.)

America's Transformation from Bystander to Belligerent

Japan's hara-kiri gamble in Hawaii paid off only in the short run. True, the Pacific fleet was largely destroyed or immobilized, but the sneak attack aroused and united America as almost nothing else could have done. To the very day of the blowup, a strong majority of Americans still wanted to keep out of war. But the bombs that pulverized Pearl Harbor blasted the isolationists into silence. The only thing left to do, growled isolationist Senator Wheeler, was "to lick hell out of them."

But Pearl Harbor was not the full answer to the question as to why the United States went to war. This treacherous attack was but the last explosion in a long chain reaction. Following the fall of France, Americans were confronted with a devil's dilemma. They desired above all to stay out of the conflict; yet they did not want Britain to be knocked out. They wished to halt Japan's conquests in the Far East—conquests that menaced not only American trade and security but international peace as well. To keep Britain from collapsing, the Roosevelt administration felt compelled to extend the unneutral aid that invited attacks from German submarines. To keep Japan from expanding, Washington undertook to cut off vital Japanese supplies and invite possible retaliation. Rather than let democracy die and dictatorship rule supreme, a strong majority of citizens were evidently determined to support a policy that might lead to war. It did.

Clearheaded Americans had come to the conclusion that no nation was safe in an era of inter-

Roosevelt's war message to Congress began with these famous words: "Yesterday, December 7, 1941—a date which will live in infamy—the United States of America was suddenly and deliberately attacked by naval and air forces of the Empire of Japan."

national anarchy. Appeasement—the tactic of throwing the weaker persons out of the sleigh to the pursuing wolves—had been tried, but it had merely whetted dictatorial appetites. Power-drunk dictators had flouted international law and decency. Pursuing the philosophy that might makes right, they had cynically negotiated non-aggression treaties with their intended victims, merely to lull them into a false sense of security. Most Americans were determined to stand firm—and let war come if it must—because they were convinced that with ruthless dictators on the loose the world could not long remain half enchained and half free.

VARYING VIEWPOINTS

After World War II ended in 1945, many historians were convinced that tragedy could have been averted if only the United States had awakened earlier from its isolationist illusions. These scholars condemned the policies and attitudes of the 1930s as a "retreat from responsibility." Much historical writing about the 1930s in the post-war period contained the strong flavor of medicine to ward off another infection by the isolationist virus. Yet in the wake of the Vietnam disaster, some historians began to suspect that there had been an overdose of the internationalist tonic—or that the prescription had been adulterated. The appeasement "lessons" of the 1930s could not properly be applied to any and all subsequent situations. Ho Chi Minh was not Hitler and Vietnam was not Nazi Germany, yet American policy-makers frequently defended their actions in Southeast Asia by making dubious comparisons with the pre–World War II decade. The reaction to this use (or misuse) of history has not spawned a "new isolationism" among historians, but has prompted a renewed effort to understand the 1930s on their own terms, rather than construing the events of those years as timeless lessons for posterity.

SELECT READINGS

Indispensable and comprehensive is Robert Dallek, *Franklin D. Roosevelt and American Foreign Policy, 1932–1945* (1979). A useful brief survey is J. E. Wiltz, *From Isolation to War, 1931–1941* (1968). More specialized is Lloyd Gardner, *Economic Aspects of New Deal Diplomacy* (1964). Isolationism is ably handled in Selig Adler, *The Isolationist Impulse* (1957), Manfred Jonas, *Isolationism in America, 1935–1941* (1966), and two books by Robert A. Divine, *The Illusion of Neutrality* (1962) and *The Reluctant Belligerent* (1965). Consult also the classic (and semi-official) volumes of W. L. Langer and S. E. Gleason, *The Challenge to Isolation* (1952) and *The Undeclared War* (1953), as well as Wayne S. Cole, *America First: The Battle Against Intervention, 1940–1941* (1953). R. E. Sherwood, *Roosevelt and Hopkins* (1948), is a readable account of Roosevelt's diplomacy, as is J. M. Burns, *Roosevelt: The Soldier of Freedom* (1970). See also J. W. Pratt, *Cordell Hull, 1933–1944* (2 vols., 1964). On Good Neighborism consult Irwin F. Gellman, *Good Neighbor Diplomacy* (1979). The Spanish problem is dealt with in Allen Guttmann, *The Wound in the Heart: America and the Spanish Civil War* (1962). For the Far East, see Dorothy Borg, *The United States and the Far Eastern Crisis of 1933–1938* (1964), W. L. Neumann, *America Encounters Japan* (1962), P. W. Schroeder, *The Axis Alliance and Japanese-American Relations, 1941* (1958), and R. J. C. Butow, *Tojo and the Coming of the War* (1961). Warren F. Kimball analyzes *The Most Unsordid Act: Lend Lease, 1939–1941* (1969). The preliminaries to the war with Japan are well presented in Herbert Feis, *The Road to Pearl Harbor* (1950), and Roberta Wohlstetter, *Pearl Harbor: Warning and Decision* (1962). Charles A. Beard extravagantly blames FDR for manipulating the country into war in *President Roosevelt and the Coming of the War, 1941* (1948). A spirited rebuttal is Basil Rauch, *Roosevelt from Munich to Pearl Harbor* (1950).

42

America in World War II

Never before have we had so little time in which to do so much.

FRANKLIN D. ROOSEVELT, 1942

The Allies Trade Space for Time

America was plunged into the inferno of World War II with the most stupefying and humiliating military defeat in her history. In the dismal months that ensued, the democratic world teetered on the edge of disaster.

Japan's fanatics forgot that when one stabs a king, one must stab to kill. A wounded but still potent American giant pulled himself out of the mud of Pearl Harbor, grimly determined to avenge the bloody treachery. "Get Hirohito first" was the cry that rose from millions of infuriated Americans, especially on the Pacific Coast. These outraged souls regarded America's share in the global conflict as a private war of vengeance in the Pacific with the European front a kind of holding operation.

But Washington, cooperating with the British, had earlier and wisely adopted the grand strategy of "getting Hitler first." If America diverted her main strength to the Pacific, Hitler might crush both Russia and Britain, and then emerge unconquerable in Fortress Europe. But if Germany was knocked out first, the combined Allied forces could be concentrated on Japan, and her daring game of conquest would be up. Meanwhile enough American strength would be sent to the Pacific to prevent the Nipponese from digging in too deeply.

The get-Hitler-first strategy was retained. But it encountered much ignorant criticism from two-fisted Americans who, according to opinion polls, at one time constituted a plurality. Aggrieved protests were also registered by shorthanded American commanders in the Pacific, and by Chinese and Australian allies. But Roosevelt, a competent strategist in his own right, was able to resist these pressures.

Given time, the Allies seemed bound to triumph. But would they be given time? True, they had on their side the great mass of the world's population, but the wolf is never frightened by the number of the sheep. The United States was the mightiest military power on earth—potentially. But wars are won with bullets, not blueprints. Indeed, America came perilously close to losing the war to the well-armed aggressors before she could begin to throw her full weight into the scales.

Time, in a sense, was the most-needed munition. Expense was no limitation. The overpowering problem confronting America was to retool herself for all-out war production, while praying that the dictators would not meanwhile crush the democracies. Haste was all the more imperative because the highly skilled German scientists might turn up with unbeatable secret weapons—as they almost did.

America's task was far more complex and backbreaking than during World War I. She had to feed, clothe, and arm herself, as well as transport her forces to regions as far separated as Britain and Burma. More than that, she had to send a vast amount of food and munitions to her hard-pressed allies, who stretched all the way from Russia to Australia. Could the American people, reputedly "gone soft," measure up to this colossal responsibility? Was democracy "rotten" and "decadent," as the dictators sneeringly proclaimed?

Unity at Home and Abroad

National unity was no worry, thanks to the electrifying blow by the Japanese at Pearl Harbor. The cynical aggressions of the dictators had laid naked the issue of survival. This time America was not out to make the world safe for democracy, but to make the world safe—for decency. The handful of strutting pro-Hitlerites in the United States melted away, while millions of Italian-Americans and German-Americans loyally supported the nation's war program. Communists and sympathetic "fellow travelers" had denounced the Anglo-French "imperialist war" before Hitler attacked Stalin in 1941, but they now clamored for an all-out assault on the Axis powers. There was no witch-hunting persecution of dissenting groups, as in World War I.

About 110,000 Japanese-Americans, concentrated on the Pacific Coast, provided a painful exception. The Washington top command, fearing that they might act as saboteurs for the Mikado in case of invasion, decided to herd them together in concentration camps, though about two-thirds of them were American-born citizens. This brutal precaution turned out to be unnecessary, for the loyalty and combat record of the Japanese-Ameri-

> American song titles aimed at the Japanese after Pearl Harbor were "Goodbye, Momma, I'm Off to Yokohama," "We Are the Sons of the Rising Guns," "Oh, You Little Son of an Oriental," "To Be Specific, It's Our Pacific," and "The Sun Will Soon Be Setting on the Land of the Rising Sun."

American Citizen of Japanese Ancestry Awaits Relocation. (Library of Congress.)

A young Japanese-American recorded in his diary on May 3, 1942, some of his first impressions of his hastily thrown-together "detention center": "I saw a soldier in a tall guardhouse near the barbed wire and did not like it because it reminds me of a concentration camp."

cans, especially those from Hawaii, proved to be admirable.* Partial financial compensation after the war did something to recompense these uprooted citizens for their sufferings and losses.

Black Americans generally supported the war effort, despite the disillusionment of World War I. Though resenting inequalities, including segregated blood banks for the wounded, they saw no future in Hitler's cremation-camp "final solution." Nearly 700,000 black draftees were serving in the army at the war's end, or about one-ninth of the total. Less discriminated against than in World War I, they were still generally assigned to service branches rather than combat units. But some of them saw bloody action in Europe and the Pacific.

As during 1917–1918, tens of thousands of black civilians migrated from the South to the North and West to work in war industries, and explosive tensions developed over employment, housing, and segregated facilities. Responding to such pressures, Roosevelt issued an executive order forbidding discrimination in defense industries. He also established the Fair Employment Practices Commission (FEPC), designed to monitor compliance with his edict. Despite such well-meaning efforts, in 1943 vicious race riots erupted in Los Angeles, New York, and Detroit. In the Michigan city alone, twenty-five blacks and nine whites lost their lives, to say nothing of the injured.

World War II was no idealistic crusade, as in 1917–1918. The appropriate agencies in Washington did make some effort to propagandize abroad with the Atlantic Charter, as well as with other hope-giving Rooseveltian pronouncements. But the accent was on action. Americans realized that they had before them a dirty job, and that the only way out was forward. They did their killing coldly, methodically, calculatingly, efficiently. It was not a singing war, as in 1917–1918. "Praise the Lord and Pass the Ammunition" enjoyed some vogue, as did "God Bless America." But the latter was a song of consecration rather than of excitation.

An unexpected degree of unity was also achieved among the Allies, thanks in part to the jolting effect of Pearl Harbor. On January 1, 1942, the representatives of twenty-six countries, including the United States, signed in Washington the Declaration of the United Nations. This group, which formed the nucleus of the yet-unborn

*A future U.S. senator of Japanese ancestry from Hawaii, Daniel Inouye, lost an arm in Italy while fighting with a much-decorated Japanese-American unit.

United Nations Organization, pledged itself to fight foursquare, under the principles of the Atlantic Charter, and not to make separate peaces.

Latin American nations, their largest sister republic the victim of a treacherous attack, rallied behind the once-hated Colossus of the North. The one conspicuous exception was Fascist-inclined Argentina, with its large Italian and German population and with its burning jealousy of rich Uncle Sam, a competitor in beef and grain. Yet the Good Neighbor policy of the 1930s reaped a happy harvest during these anxious years. Pan-Americanism became more a fact than a phrase, as the Yankees spent billions of dollars in Latin America for tin, nitrates, and other urgently needed materials.

Aid to the ever-suspicious Soviets claimed a high priority. Dedicated to the destruction of capitalism through Communism, the Russians accepted distrustfully the vast amount of munitions provided by their American stepbrothers-in-arms. Lend-lease materials from the United States in time made up only about 10 percent of the total military equipment of the Soviet Union. But these contributions came in the form of desperately needed trucks, automobiles, military aircraft, and other equipment, without which the Russians probably could not have smashed their way to Berlin.

"The Three Musketeers," FDR, Stalin, and Churchill. (Drawn by Manning in the Phoenix *Arizona Republic;* reprinted by permission of the McNaught Syndicate, Inc.)

Smokestacks Go to War

America was already partially geared for a war economy when the arousing blow fell at Pearl Harbor. Allied orders for munitions, plus lend-lease operations and defense appropriations, had all contributed to the chassis of a mighty war-production machine. But at the outset the nation was only ankle-deep in the conflict.

Vital materials were in dangerously short supply, partly because the Republic had failed to stockpile enough needed commodities. When the Japanese overran British Malaya and the Dutch East Indies, shortly after Pearl Harbor, they snapped America's lifeline of natural rubber, and cut off most of her essential tin and quinine. Supplements or substitutes for these critical items, especially rubber, were urgently needed—and eventually were found. Most spectacular of all was the creation of a huge synthetic rubber industry, which had to be started from scratch. After much fumbling, it was brought into production just in the nick of time by "Rubber Czar" William M. Jeffers, president of the Union Pacific Railroad.

First things had to come first. The War Production Board, under genial Donald M. Nelson, vice-president of Sears, Roebuck and Company, halted non-essential building in order to conserve materials for war purposes. Priorities were set up for most industries. "Dollar-a-year men" in Washington again worked at a desperate pace, and as the red tape slowly unwound they did not even have time, quipsters said, for a nervous breakdown.

Rationing goods to the consumer was undertaken on a huge scale for the first time in American experience, as more dollars pursued fewer products. Voluntary "Hooverizing," as in 1917–1918, was not enough, for a cynical remark in grocery stores was, "I'm just stocking up before the hoarders get here." Ration tickets were issued for butter, meat, gasoline, and other necessities; and on the whole the system worked. But a minority of selfish souls patronized illegal sellers of goods, known as "black marketeers" and "meatleggers."

A booming wartime economy eventually boosted

prices about 30 percent, as the sneaky hand of inflation robbed every pay envelope. Among various agencies, the Office of Price Administration was set up, and it helped to keep rents and commodity prices within reasonable bounds by placing ceilings on them.

"What Price Ceiling?" 1942. Labor costs rise before controls are imposed. (Los Angeles *Times,* copyright Los Angeles *Times.* Reprinted by permission.)

America's Prodigies of Production

Labor, which felt the pinch of mild inflation, had to be kept happy if production quotas were to be attained. The AF of L and the CIO were among the important groups that joined in no-strike pledges, with the understanding that the government would hold the lid on the cost of living. Yet prices continued to inch upward, and a rash of strikes broke out, some of them "wildcat" strikes not authorized by union leaders. Noteworthy among the troublemaking groups were the United Mine Workers, who several times were called out on strike against the coal operators by their crusty and iron-willed leader, John L. Lewis. The accident-ridden miners, who harbored genuine grievances, finally won coveted concessions after Lewis had defied Washington and had temporarily jeopardized the war effort.

Threats of lost production through strikes became so serious that Congress, in June 1943, passed the Smith-Connally Anti-Strike Act. It authorized the seizure and operation by the federal government of tied-up industries. Strikes against any industry thus operated were made a criminal offense. Under the Smith-Connally Act, Washington seized and ran the coal mines and, for a brief period, the railroads. Yet work stoppages, dangerous though they were, actually accounted for less than 1 percent of the total working time of the nation's laboring force during the war—a record better than blockaded Britain's. American workers, on the whole, were commendably efficient.

Agricultural production was one of the miracles of these anxious years. Though shorthanded because the armed services drained manpower, the farmers rolled up their sleeves and produced bumper crops. Providentially, as in 1917–1918, weather conditions were unusually favorable. Farm income, despite price controls, more than doubled, as countless mortgages were joyously paid off. The blue-jeaned farmers had probably never before been so prosperous, though they had to labor long hours to provide "food for freedom." Their sweat was supplemented, as in 1917–1918, by countless volunteer green-thumbers, who hopefully planted "victory gardens" in back yards and vacant lots.

The Battle of Production was clearly won by 1943. Unemployment became only a bad dream, as such agencies as the Civilian Conservation Corps and the Works Progress Administration received an "honorable discharge." President Roosevelt, in fact, declared that "Dr. New Deal" had given way to "Dr. Win the War." But the abounding prosperity was in some degree misleading. The inflation squeeze, though fairly well controlled, was pinching white-collar workers and others on fixed incomes.

Warriors, Women, and War Bonds

All told, the armed services enrolled more than 15 million men and women. The draft was tightened after Pearl Harbor, as millions of young men were plucked from their homes and clothed in "G.I." (government issue) outfits. Scores of training camps peppered the land, while the education of officer material went forward rapidly in the colleges. With an eye to the long pull, draft deferments were often granted to key workers in industry and agriculture, as in World War I.

Women desk-warriors came into their own. They had been used sparingly in 1917–1918, but now some 216,000 of them were efficiently employed for non-combat duties, chiefly clerical. Best known of these "women in arms" were the WAACS (army), WAVES (navy), marines, and SPARS (coast guard).

The "War for Survival" of 1941–1945, more than that of 1917–1918, was an all-out conflict. Old folks came out of retirement "for the duration" to serve in industry or as air-raid wardens in civilian defense. Western Union telegraph "boys" were often elderly men. Women were drawn from the home into war work, even into the heavier industries such as shipbuilding, where "Rosie the Riveter" won laurels. Rosie also helped to build tanks and airplanes, and when the war ended she was in no hurry to put down her tools. Rosie and millions of her sisters wanted to keep on working, and many of them did. The war thus touched off a revolution in the roles of women in American society.

Poster appeals and slogans urging women to enlist in the WAACs (Women's Army Auxiliary Corps) were "Speed Them Back, Join the WAAC," "I'd Rather Be with Them—than Waiting for Them," "Back the Attack, Be a WAAC! For America Is Calling," and (a song throwback to World War I) "The WAACs and WAVES Will Win the War, Parlez Vous."

Shipbuilding, as in 1917–1918, was pressed at a frantic pace in an effort to outrace the deadly submarine. The output of the shipyards, partly as a result of the use of prefabricated materials, was no less phenomenal than that of the industrial plants. A leading miracle-man shipbuilder was Henry J. Kaiser, who was dubbed "Sir Launchalot": one of his ships was assembled within five days, complete with life belts and coat hangers. In 1943 alone American shipyards produced a formidable navy. Long before the shooting stopped, the United States had incomparably the mightiest merchant fleet the world had ever seen.

The conflict proved to be prodigiously expensive. The wartime bill mounted to more than $330 billion—ten times the direct cost of World War I and twice as much as *all* previous federal spending since 1776. The national debt skyrocketed from $48,961,000,000 in 1941 to $258,682,000,000 in 1945. When production finally slipped into high gear, the war was costing about $250 million dollars a day.

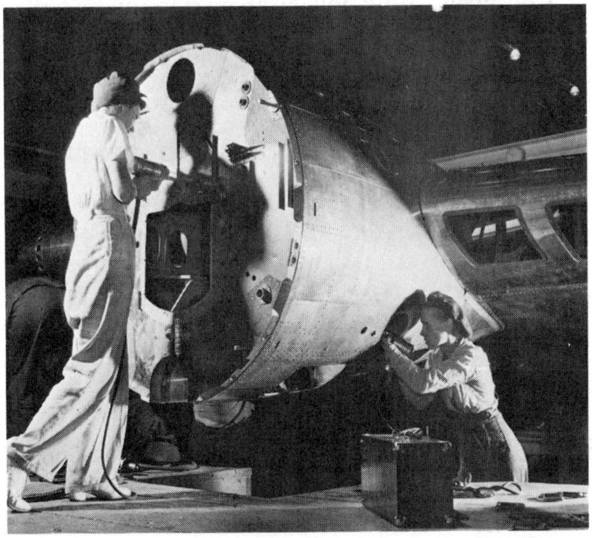

Women Riveters in California Aircraft Plant. (National Archives.)

BILLIONS OF DOLLARS

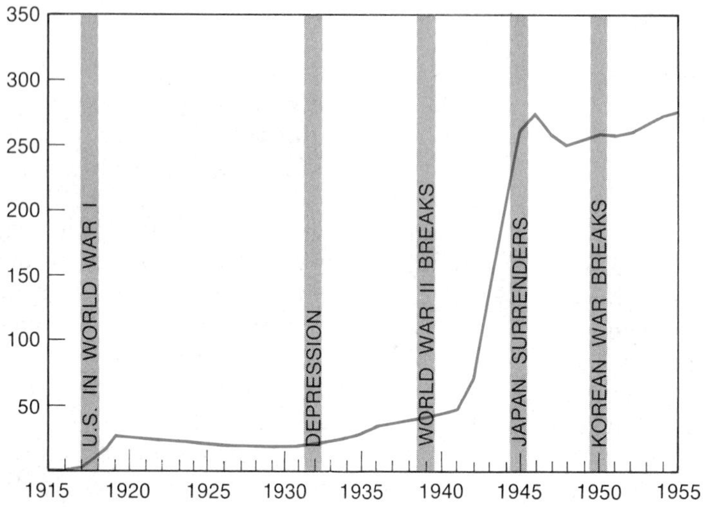

NATIONAL DEBT, 1915–1955
Inflation and continuing budget deficits sent the national debt level over $1 trillion in the 1980s, when more than 9 percent of federal expenditures went for interest payments on that huge sum. But as this chart clearly shows, World War II provided the first massive boost to the mushrooming debt.

This flood of war-born deficit dollars—not the relatively modest rivulet of New Deal spending—at last swept the plague of unemployment from the land. War, not enlightened social policy, cured the depression. As the post-war economy continued to depend dangerously on military spending for its health, many observers saw in the years 1941–1945 the origins of a "warfare-welfare state."

Roosevelt would have preferred to follow a pay-as-you-go policy in financing the war, but the costs were simply too gigantic. The income-tax net now caught more people than ever before and then dipped more deeply into their pockets; maximum tax rates rose as high as 90 percent. Still, only about two-fifths of war costs were paid from current revenues.

The bulk came from borrowing. Altogether, the government launched eight high-pressure War Bond drives, all of them oversubscribed. An effective new wrinkle was added when regular deductions, with the consent of the workers, were lifted from pay envelopes for bond purchases.

Slogans backed the bond-buying blitz, including, "Get in the Scrap or Buy a Share of America," "If You Can't Go Over, Come Across," "Back the Attack—Buy More than Ever Before," "Let's Go—for the Knockout Blow," "Let's Pave the Road to Rome with War Bonds," "The Most I Can Sell, Is the Least I Can Do," "They Give Their Lives—You Lend Your Money," "You've Done Your Bit. Now Do Your Best!" Song writers did their bit with "Dig Down Deep," "Get Aboard the Bond Wagon," and "I Paid My Income Tax Today"—surely the only song ever written about the income tax.

The Rising Sun in the Pacific

Early successes of the efficient Japanese militarists were breathtaking: they realized that they would have to win quickly or lose slowly. Seldom, if ever, has so much been conquered so rapidly with so little loss.

Simultaneously with the assault on Pearl Harbor, the Japanese launched widespread and uniformly successful attacks on various Far Eastern bastions. These included the American outposts of Guam, Wake, and the Philippines. In a dismayingly short time, the Nipponese invader seized not only the British-Chinese port of Hong Kong but also British Malaya, with its critically important supplies of rubber and tin.

Nor did the Nipponese tide stop there. The undersized but overambitious soldiers of the Emperor, plunging into the snake-infested jungles of Burma, cut the famed Burma road. This was the route over which the United States had been trucking a trickle of munitions to the armies of the Chinese Generalissimo Chiang Kai-shek, who was still resisting the Japanese invader in China. Thereafter intrepid American aviators were forced to fly a handful of war supplies to Chiang "over the hump" of the towering Himalaya Mountains from the India-Burma theater. Meanwhile the Japanese had lunged southward against the oil-rich Dutch East Indies. The jungle-matted islands speedily fell to the assailant, after the combined British, Australian, Dutch, and American naval and air forces had been smashed at an early date by their numerically superior foe.

Better news came from the Philippines, which succeeded dramatically in slowing down the Mikado's warriors for five months. The Japanese promptly landed a small but effective army, and General Douglas MacArthur, the statuesque American commander, withdrew to a strong defensive position at Bataan, not far from Manila. There about 20,000 American troops, supported by a much larger force of ill-trained Filipinos, held off violent Japanese attacks until April 9, 1942. The defenders, reduced to eating mules and monkeys, heroically traded their lives for time in the face of hopeless odds. They grimly joked while vainly hoping for reinforcements:

> We're the battling bastards of Bataan;
> No Mamma, no Papa, no Uncle Sam. . . .

Before the inevitable American surrender, General MacArthur was ordered by Washington to depart secretly for Australia, there to head resistance against the Japanese. Leaving by motorboat and airplane, he proclaimed, "I shall return." After the battered remnants of his army had hoisted the white flag, they were treated with vicious cruelty in the infamous 85-mile (137-kilometer) Bataan death march. The island fortress of Corregidor, in Manila Harbor, held out until May 6, 1942, when it surrendered and left Japanese forces in complete control of the Philippine archipelago.

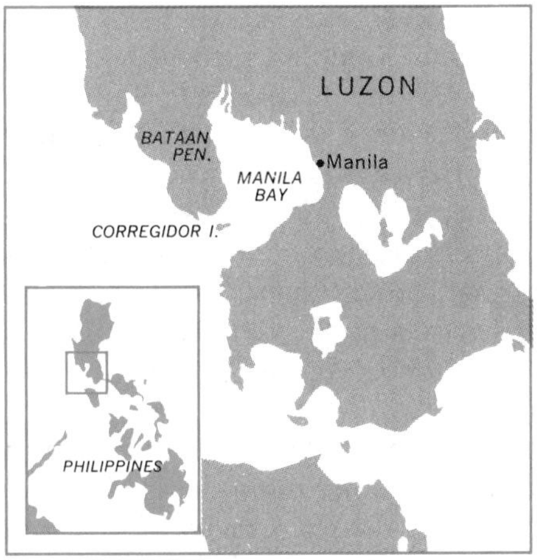

CORREGIDOR–BATAAN

Japan's High Tide at Midway

The aggressive warriors from Nippon, making hay while the Rising Sun shone, pushed relentlessly southward. They invaded the turtle-shaped island of New Guinea, north of Australia, and landed on the Solomon Islands, from which they threatened Australia itself. Their onrush was finally checked by a crucial naval battle fought in the Coral Sea, in May 1942. An American carrier task force, with Australian support, inflicted heavy losses on the victory-flushed Nipponese. For the first time in history the fighting was all done by carrier-based aircraft, and neither fleet saw or fired a shot directly at the other.

Japan next undertook to seize Midway Island, more than 1,000 miles (1,600 kilometers) northwest of Honolulu. From this strategic base, it could launch devastating assaults on Pearl Harbor, and perhaps force the weakened American Pacific fleet into destructive combat. An epochal naval battle was fought near Midway, June 3–6, 1942. Admiral Chester W. Nimitz, a high-grade naval strategist, directed a smaller but skillfully maneuvered carrier force, under Admiral Raymond A. Spruance, against the powerful invading fleet. The fighting was all done by aircraft, and the Japanese broke off action after losing four vitally important carriers.

The smashing success at Midway, combined with the Battle of the Coral Sea, turned the tide of Japan's conquest. But the thrust of the Nipponese into the eastern Pacific did net them America's fog-girt islands of Kiska and Attu, in the Aleutian archipelago, off Alaska. This easy conquest aroused fear of an invasion of the United States from the northwest. Much American strength was consequently diverted to the defense of Alaska, including the construction of the "Alcan" highway through Canada.

Yet the Japanese imperialists, overextended in 1942, suffered from "victory disease." Their appetites were bigger than their stomachs. If they had only dug in and consolidated their gains, they would have been much more difficult to dislodge.

American Leapfrogging Toward Tokyo

Following the heartening victory at Midway, the United States for the first time was able to seize the initiative in the Pacific. In August 1942, American ground forces gained a toehold on Guadalcanal Island, in the Solomons, in an effort to protect the lifeline from America to Australia through the Southwest Pacific. An early naval defeat inflicted by the Japanese shortened American supplies dangerously, and for weeks the United States troops held onto the malarial island only by their fingernails. After four desperate sea battles for naval control, the Japanese troops evacuated Guadalcanal in February 1943.

American and Australian forces, under General MacArthur, meanwhile had been hanging on grimly to the southeastern tip of New Guinea, the last buffer protecting Australia. The scales of war gradually began to tip as the American navy, including submarines, inflicted lethal losses on Japanese supply ships and troop carriers. Conquest of the north coast of New Guinea was completed by August 1944, after General MacArthur

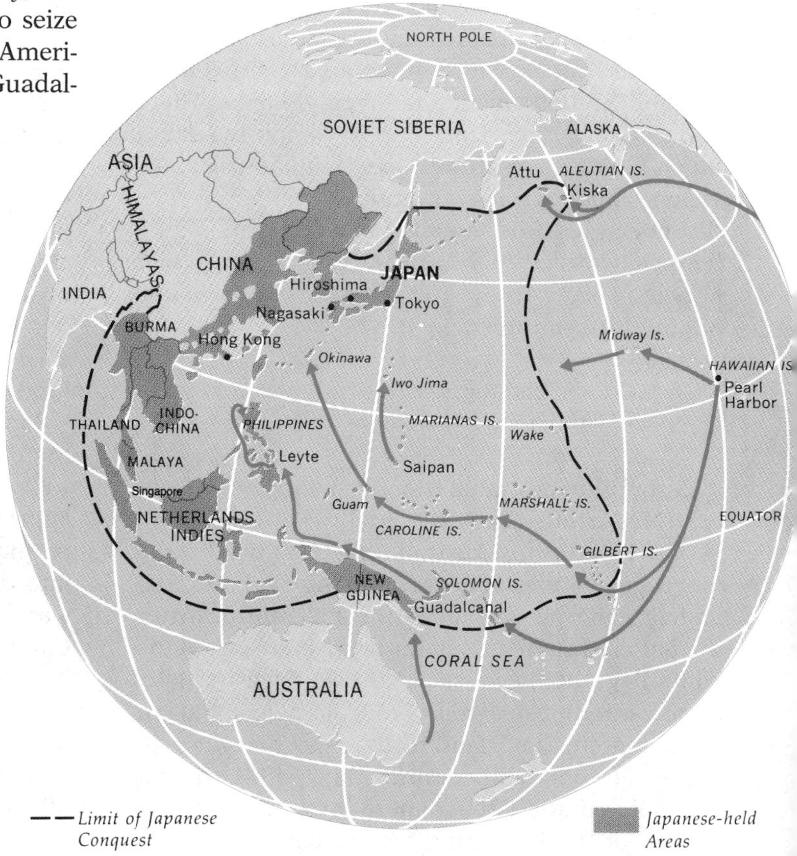

UNITED STATES THRUSTS IN THE PACIFIC, 1942–1945

American strategists had to choose among four proposed plans for waging the war against Japan:
1. Defeating the Japanese in China by funneling supplies over the Himalayan "hump" from India;
2. Carrying the war into Southeast Asia (a proposal much favored by the British, who could thus regain Singapore);
3. Heavy bombing of Japan from Chinese air bases;
4. "Island-hopping" from the South Pacific to within striking distance of the Japanese home islands. This strategy, favored by General Douglas MacArthur, was the one finally emphasized.

The U.S.S. *Bunker Hill* Hit by Two Japanese Suicide Planes in Pacific War, May 11, 1945. (National Archives.)

had fought his way westward through green jungle hells. This hard-won victory was the first leg on the long return journey to the Philippines.

The United States navy, with marines and army divisions doing the meat-grinder fighting, had meanwhile been leapfrogging the Japanese islands in the Pacific. Old-fashioned strategy dictated that the American forces, as they drove toward Tokyo, should reduce the fortified Japanese outposts on their flank. This course would have taken many bloodstained months, for the holed-in defenders were prepared to die to the last man in their caves. The new strategy of island hopping ("leapfrogging") called for bypassing some of the most heavily fortified Japanese posts, capturing nearby islands, setting up airfields on them, and then neutralizing the enemy bases through heavy bombing. Deprived of supplies from the homeland, the Mikado's outposts would slowly wither on the vine—as they did.

Brilliant success crowned the American attacks on the Japanese island strongholds in the Pacific, where Admiral Nimitz skillfully coordinated the efforts of naval, air, and ground units. In May and August of 1943, Attu and Kiska in the Aleutians were easily retaken. In November 1943, "bloody Tarawa" and Makin, both in the Gilbert Islands, fell after suicidal resistance. In January and February 1944, the key outposts of the Marshall group succumbed after savage fighting.

Especially prized islands were the Marianas, of which America's conquered Guam was one. They were spacious enough to provide abundant airfields for American super-bombers, and they were close enough to Japan to permit round-trip bombing. After fanatical resistance, the major islands fell to the American attackers in July and August 1944. With these unsinkable aircraft carriers now available, the first sustained air attacks on Japan were launched by giant bombers in November 1944.

The Allied Halting of Hitler

Early setbacks for America in the Pacific were paralleled in the Atlantic. Hitler had entered the war with a formidable fleet of ultra-modern submarines, which ultimately operated in "wolf packs" with frightful effect, especially in the North Atlantic, the Caribbean, and the Gulf of Mexico. During ten months of 1942 more than 500 merchantmen were reported lost—111 in June alone—as ship destruction far outran construction.

The tide of subsea battle turned with agonizing slowness. Old techniques, such as escorting convoys of merchantmen and dropping depth bombs from destroyers, were strengthened by air patrol, radar, and the bombing of submarine bases. "Keep 'Em Sailing" was the motto of oil-begrimed merchant seamen, hundreds of whom perished as unsung heroes in icy seas.

Not until the spring of 1943 did the Allies clearly have the upper hand against the U-boat. If they had not won the Battle of the Atlantic, Britain would have been forced under, and a second front could not have been launched from her island springboard. Victory over the undersea raiders was nerve-rackingly narrow. When the war ended, Hitler was about to mass-produce a fearsome new submarine—one that could remain under water indefinitely and cruise at seventeen knots when submerged.

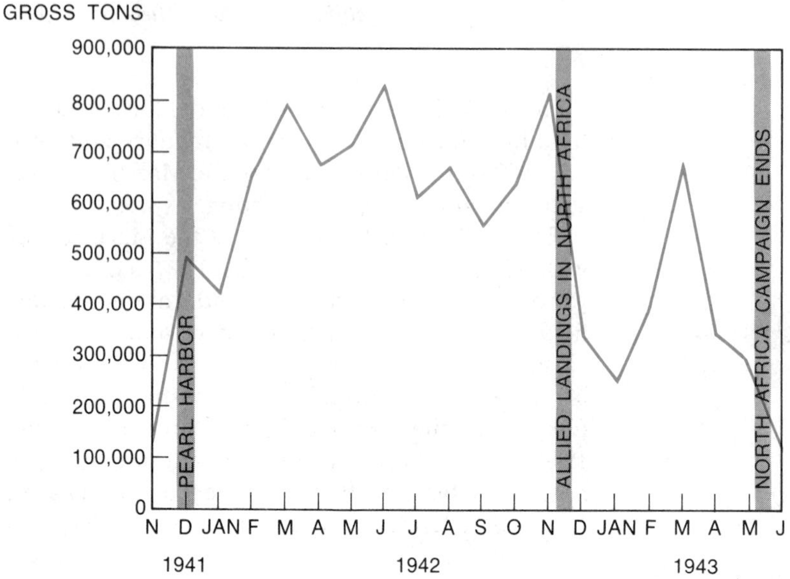

MERCHANT TONNAGE SUNK BY U-BOATS (November 1941–June 1943)
In early 1942, the U-boats stalked America's Atlantic coast. They picked off night-traveling, coast-hugging ships silhouetted against the lights from coastal cities that had failed to impose effective black-outs. Eventually the submarine menace was contained by electronic detection techniques (especially radar), and by airborne anti-submarine patrols operating from "baby flattops," small escort aircraft carriers.

Meanwhile, the turning point of the land-air war against Hitler had come late in 1942. The British, who had launched a 1,000-plane raid on Cologne in May, were now cascading bombs, with American help, on German cities. The Germans under Marshal Rommel—"the Desert Fox"—had driven across the hot sands of North Africa into Egypt, perilously close to the Suez Canal. A breakthrough would have spelled disaster for the Allies. But late in October 1942, the British General Montgomery delivered a withering attack at El Alamein, west of Cairo. With the aid of several hundred hastily shipped American Sherman tanks, he speedily drove the enemy back to Tunisia, more than 1,000 miles (1,600 kilometers) away.

On the Soviet front, the unexpected successes of the Red Army gave a new lift to the Allied cause. In September 1942, the Russians halted the German steamroller at rubble-bestrewn Stalingrad, graveyard of Hitler's hopes. More than a score of invading divisions, caught in an icy noose, later surrendered or were "mopped up." In November 1942, the resilient Russians unleashed a crushing counter-offensive, which was never seriously reversed. A year later, Stalin had regained about two-thirds of the blood-soaked Russian motherland wrested from him by the Teutonic invader.

Prime Minister Churchill observed in a speech (May 1943): "The proud German Army has by its sudden collapse, sudden crumbling and breaking up . . . once again proved the truth of the saying, 'The Hun [German] is always either at your throat or at your feet.' "

American Troops Entering Cologne, March 1945.
(H. Armstrong Roberts.)

The North African Second Front

Soviet leaders meanwhile had never ceased to clamor for an Anglo-American second front—a demand stridently supported by the few American Communists. Red divisions were doing practically all of the mud-and-blood fighting against Hitler's armies, and Moscow insisted that the Allies get into the war and drain off their fair share of the invader's strength. Russian officials did not regard the American operations in the Pacific as helpful, nor did they look upon the Allied aerial blasting of Germany as an adequate second front.

Many Americans were eager to begin a diversionary invasion of France in 1942 or in 1943, while Russia was still afloat. Fears prevailed that the Soviets, unable to hold out against Germany, might make a separate peace, as they had in 1918, and leave the western Allies to face the fury of Hitler alone. The British, remembering their fearful losses in 1914–1918, were not enthusiastic about a frontal assault on German-held France. It might end in complete disaster. They preferred to attack Hitler's Fortress Europe through the "soft underbelly" of the Mediterranean, while gathering strength for a cross-channel thrust.

An invasion of French-held North Africa was a compromise second front. It seemed less risky than a premature descent upon the coast of France, yet it would serve as a partial answer to the demands of the Russians for a diversion. If successful, it would open the Axis-dominated Mediterranean to lifeline communication with India and other parts of Asia.

The highly secret Allied attack on North Africa, launched in November 1942, was headed by a gifted and easy-smiling American general, Dwight D. ("Ike") Eisenhower, a master of organization and conciliation. As a joint Allied operation ultimately involving some 400,000 men (British, Canadian, French, and chiefly American), the invasion was the mightiest waterborne effort up to that time in history. About 850 ships of various sorts were employed.

At the outset, the surprise landing in North Africa was highly successful. The neutralized French, both anti-Hitler and pro-Ally, put up only a token resistance. After savage fighting with the Germans, who inflicted one sharp setback on the green Americans, the remnants of the German-Italian army were finally trapped in Tunisia. Some 266,000 dazed survivors surrendered in May 1943.

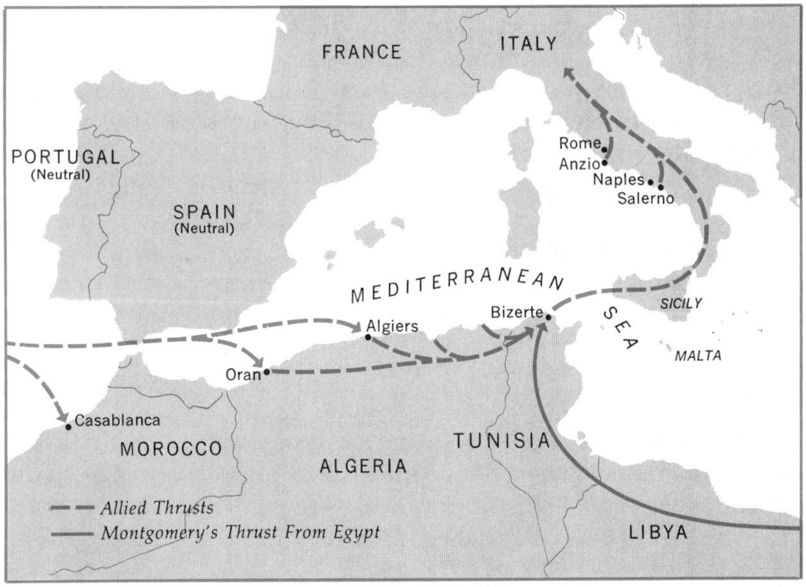

ALLIED THRUSTS IN NORTH AFRICA AND ITALY, 1942–1945

Victory came fairly swiftly to the Allies in North Africa, but attacking the "soft underbelly" of Europe proved to be a delusion in Italy, where the rugged terrain favored the German defenders. They put up a bitter resistance on the landing beaches and made the Allies pay dearly for every yard gained as they retreated slowly up the mountainous spine of the Italian peninsula.

The North African campaign, though redeeming one continent, in itself was not conclusive. It was not the beginning of the end, but "the end of the beginning." Certain Russian spokesmen scoffed at this second-rate second front, but valuable lessons were learned for the full-fledged invasion of France.

At a Washington press conference (May 25, 1943), visiting Prime Minister Churchill was asked how collapsing Italy should be treated. He replied, "All we can do is to apply the physical stimuli which we have at our disposal to bring about a change of mind in these recalcitrant persons. Of this you may be sure: we shall continue to operate on the Italian donkey at both ends, with a carrot and with a stick."

The Rough Road to Rome

New blows were now planned by the Allies. At Casablanca, in newly occupied French Morocco, President Roosevelt, who had boldly flown the Atlantic, met in a historic conference with Winston Churchill in January 1943. The Big Two agreed to step up the Pacific war, invade Sicily, increase pressure on Italy, and insist upon an "unconditional surrender" of the enemy—a phrase earlier popularized by General Grant during the Civil War. Such an unyielding policy would presumably hearten the ultra-suspicious Soviets, who professed to fear separate Allied peace negotiations. It would also forestall charges of broken armistice terms, such as had come after 1918.

Yet "unconditional surrender" proved to be one of the most controversial moves of the war. The main criticism was that it steeled the enemy to fight to a last-bunker resistance, while discouraging anti-war groups in Germany from revolting. Although there was no doubt some truth in these charges, no one can prove that "unconditional surrender" either shortened or lengthened the war. But by helping to destroy the German government utterly, the harsh policy immensely complicated the problems of reconstruction.

The victorious Allied forces—American, British, and Canadian—now turned against the not-so-soft underbelly of Europe. Sicily fell, in August 1943, after sporadic but sometimes bitter resistance. Shortly before the conquest of the island, Mussolini was deposed and a new Rome government was set up. Italy surrendered unconditionally early in September 1943, while Allied troops were pouring onto the toe of the Italian boot. President Roosevelt, referring to the three original Axis accomplices—Germany, Italy, and Japan—joked grimly that it was now one down and two to go. Two years later Mussolini, together with his attractive mistress, was brutally lynched by his own people. Both bodies were ingloriously hung up by the heels for public display.

But if Italy dropped out of the war, the Germans did not drop out of Italy. Hitler's well-trained troops resisted the Allied invaders with methodical and infuriating stubbornness. The luckless Italians, turning their coats, declared war on Germany in October 1943. "Sunny Italy" proceeded to belie her name, for in the snow-covered and mud-caked mountains of her elongated peninsula occurred some of the muddiest, bloodiest, and most frustrating fighting of the war.

For many months Italy seemed to be a dead end. After a touch-and-go assault on the Anzio beachhead, Rome was taken on June 4, 1944. Two days later, when the tremendous cross-channel invasion of France began, Italy became a kind of sideshow. But the Allies, with limited manpower, continued to fight their way slowly and painfully into northern Italy. On May 2, 1945, only five days before Germany's official surrender, several hundred thousand Axis troops in Italy laid down their arms and became prisoners of war.

The Italian campaign, though agonizingly slow, was by no means fruitless. It opened the Mediterranean, diverted some German divisions from the blazing Russian and French fronts, and provided

Allies Landing in Normandy, June 6, 1944. Nine-foot ocean swells on invasion day made loading the assault landing craft, such as the one pictured here, treacherous business. Many men were injured or tossed into the sea as the bathtub-like amphibious vessels bobbed wildly up and down alongside the troop transports. As the vulnerable boats churned toward the beach, some officers led their tense, grim-faced troops in prayer. One major quoted from Shakespeare's *Henry V:*
"He that outlives this day, and comes safe home
Will stand a tip-toe when this day is named."
(Wide World Photos.)

air bases for bombing assaults on German Austria and southern Germany.

Eisenhower's D-Day Invasion of France

The Russians had never ceased their clamor for an all-out second front, and the time rapidly approached for the coordination of promised efforts. Marshal Joseph Stalin, with a careful eye on Russian military operations, balked at leaving the Soviet Union. President Roosevelt, who jauntily remarked in private, "I can handle that old buzzard," was eager to confer with him. The President seemed confident that Rooseveltian charm could woo the hardened conspirator of the Kremlin from his nasty Communist ways.

Teheran, the capital of Iran (Persia), was finally chosen as the meeting place. To this ancient city Roosevelt riskily flew, after a stopover conference in Cairo with Britain's Churchill and China's Chiang Kai-shek regarding the war against Japan. At Teheran the discussions among Stalin, Roosevelt, and Churchill—from November 28 to December 1, 1943—progressed smoothly. Perhaps the most important achievement was agreement on broad plans, especially those for launching Russian attacks on Germany from the east simultaneously with the prospective Allied assault from the west.

Preparations for the cross-channel invasion of France were gigantic. Britain's fast-anchored isle virtually groaned with munitions, supplies, and troops, as nearly 3 million fighting men were readied. As the United States was to provide most of the Allied warriors, the overall command was entrusted to an American, General Eisenhower. He had already distinguished himself in the North African and Mediterranean campaigns, not only for his military capacity but also for his gifts as a conciliator of clashing Allied interests.

French Normandy, farther but less heavily fortified than other beaches, was pinpointed for the invasion assault. On D-Day, June 6, 1944, the enormous operation, which involved some 4,600 vessels, unwound. Stiff resistance was encountered from the Germans, who had been misled by a feint into expecting the blow to fall farther north. The Allies quickly achieved mastery

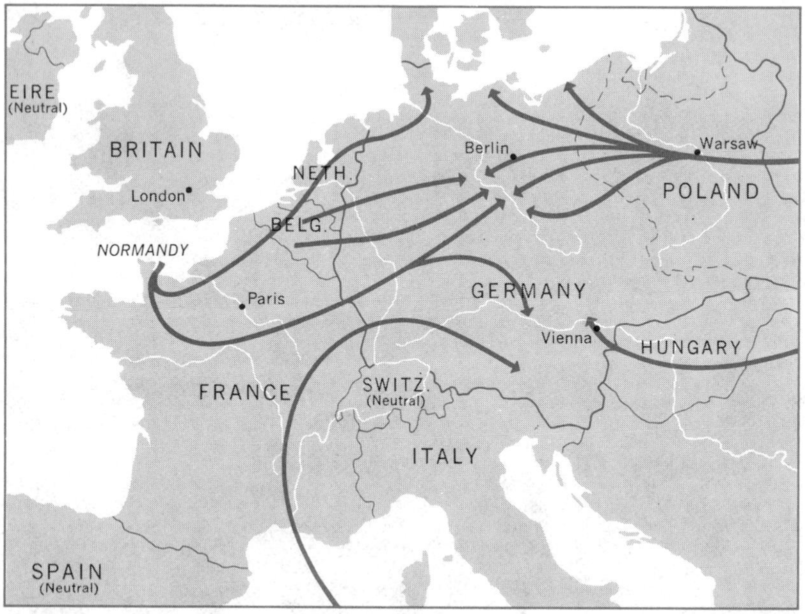

FINAL ALLIED THRUSTS IN EUROPE, 1944–1945
General Eisenhower held back his forces and permitted the oncoming Russians to capture Berlin, with the loss of about 100,000 Soviet soldiers. He argued with considerable force that because Roosevelt and Churchill had already assigned Berlin and its environs to the Soviets, American blood should not be shed unnecessarily.

of the air over France. They were thus able to block reinforcements by crippling the railroads, while worsening German fuel shortages by bombing gasoline-producing plants.

The Allied beachhead, at first clung to with fingertips, was gradually enlarged, consolidated, and reinforced. After desperate fighting, the invaders finally broke out of the German iron ring at the base of the Normandy peninsula. Most spectacular were the lunges across France by American armored divisions, brilliantly commanded by blustery and profane General George S. ("Blood 'n' Guts") Patton. The retreat of the German defenders was hastened when an American-French force landed in August 1944 on the southern coast of France and swept northward. With the assistance of the French "underground," Paris was liberated in August 1944, amid exuberant manifestations of joy and gratitude.

Allied forces rolled irresistibly toward Germany,

G.I.'s Help To Liberate Paris. Here they are greeted by grateful French people. Some Europeans eventually soured on the presence of so many American "saviors." A British parody of the First World War American marching song, "Over There," went:

Over-paid
Over-fed
And over here.

(United Press International photo.)

and many of the Americans encountered places, like Château-Thierry, familiar to their fathers in 1918. "Lafayette, we are here again," proclaimed some of the American soldiers jocosely. The first important German city (Aachen) fell to the Americans in October 1944, and the days of Hitler's "Thousand-Year Reich" seemed to be numbered.

FDR: The Fourth-Termite of 1944

The presidential campaign of 1944, which was bound to divert energy from the war program, came most awkwardly as the titanic conflict roared to its climax. But the normal electoral processes continued to function, despite some loose talk of suspending them "for the duration."

Victory-starved Republicans met in Chicago with hopeful enthusiasm. They quickly nominated the short, mustached, and dapper Thomas E. Dewey, popular vote-getting governor of New York. Regarded as a liberal, he had already made a national reputation as a prosecutor of grafters and racketeers in New York City. His shortness and youth—he was only forty-two—had caused Harold Ickes to sneer that the candidate had cast his diaper into the ring. To offset Dewey's mild internationalism, the convention nominated for the vice-presidency a strong isolationist, handsome and white-maned Senator John W. Bricker of Ohio. Yet the platform called for an unstinted prosecution of the war, and for the creation of a new international organization to maintain peace.

Franklin Roosevelt, obviously ageing under the strain, was the "indispensable man" of the Democrats. No other major figure was available, and the war was apparently grinding to its grand finale. He was nominated at Chicago on the first ballot by acclamation. But in a sense he was the "forgotten man" of the convention for, in view of his age, an unusual amount of attention was focused on the vice-presidency.

The scramble for the vice-presidential plum turned into something of a free-for-all. Henry A. Wallace, onetime "plow 'em under" secretary of agriculture, had served four years as Vice-President and desired a renomination. But conservative Democrats distrusted him as an ill-balanced and unpredictable liberal.* A "ditch Wallace" move developed tremendous momentum, despite the popularity of Wallace with large numbers of voters and many of the delegates. With Roosevelt's blessing, the vice-presidential nomination finally went to smiling and self-assured Senator Harry S Truman of Missouri ("the new Missouri Compromise"). Hitherto inconspicuous, he had recently attained national visibility as the efficient chairman of a Senate committee conducting an investigation of wasteful war expenditures. Nobody had much against him or on him.

> During the bitter campaign of 1944, Roosevelt's pre–Pearl Harbor policies came under sharp attack from Congresswoman Clare Boothe Luce (the "Blonde Bombshell"), who violently charged Roosevelt with having "lied us into war because he did not have the political courage to lead us into it."

Roosevelt Defeats Dewey

A dynamic Dewey took the offensive, for Roosevelt was too busily involved in directing the war to spare much time for speechmaking. The vigorous young "crime buster," with his beautiful baritone voice and polished diction, denounced the tired and quarrelsome "old men" in Washington. He proclaimed repeatedly that after "twelve long years" of New Dealism it was "time for a change." As for the war, Dewey would not alter the basic strategy but would fight it better—a type of "me-tooism" ridiculed by the Democrats. The fourth-term issue did not figure prominently, now that the ice had been broken by Roosevelt's third term.

---

*Wallace had incurred much ridicule when he declared in a 1942 speech, "The object of this war is to make sure that everybody in the world has the privilege of drinking a quart of milk a day." Cynics shortened this to "milk for the Hottentots."

Dewey vs. FDR. The people return a verdict. (Courtesy Washington *Evening Star.*)

But "Dewey-eyed" Republicans, half-humorously, professed to fear fifth and sixth terms by the "lifer" in the White House.

In the closing weeks of the campaign, Roosevelt left his desk for the stump. He was stung by certain Republican charges, including alleged aspersions on his pet Scottie dog, Fala. He was also eager to show himself, even in chilling rains, to spike well-founded rumors of failing health.

Substantial assistance came from the new Political Action Committee of the CIO, which was organized to get around the law banning the direct use of union funds for political purposes. Zealous CIO members, branded as Communists by the Republicans, rang countless doorbells and asked, with pointed reference to the recent depression, "What were you doing in 1932?" At times Roosevelt seemed to be running again against Hoover.

Roosevelt, as customary, won a sweeping victory: 432 to 99 in the Electoral College; 25,602,504 to 22,006,285 in the popular totals. Elated, he quipped that "the first twelve years are the hardest." As in every one of his previous three campaigns, he was opposed by a majority of the newspapers, which were owned chiefly by Republicans. His popular majority declined from 1940, partly because of the absence of many soldiers. Younger people tended to support Roosevelt; and consequently a Democratic Congress had passed a law making it possible for service personnel to vote. But only about one-fourth of them did so, and their absentee ballots did not affect the result materially.

It seems clear that Roosevelt won primarily because the war was going well. A winning pitcher is not ordinarily taken out. Foreign policy was a decisive factor with untold thousands of voters, who concluded that Roosevelt's experienced hand was needed in fashioning a future organization for world peace. The dapper Dewey, whom Ickes reportedly dubbed "the little man on top of the wedding cake," had spoken smoothly of international cooperation, but his isolationist running mate, Bricker, had implanted serious doubts. The Republican party was still suffering from the taint of isolationism fastened on it by the Hardingites.

The Last Days of Hitler

By mid-December 1944, the month after Roosevelt's fourth-term victory, Germany seemed to be wobbling on her last legs. The Soviet surge had penetrated eastern Germany. Allied aerial "blockbusters," making the "rubble bounce" on an around-the-clock schedule, were falling like giant hailstones on cities, factories, and transportation arteries. The German western front seemed about to buckle under the sledgehammer blows of the Americans and their allies.

Hitler then staked everything on one last throw of his reserves. Secretly concentrating a powerful force, he hurled it, on December 16, 1944, against the thinly held American lines in the heavily befogged and snow-shrouded Ardennes forest. Caught off guard, the outmanned Americans were driven back, and the key Belgian port of Antwerp was menaced. The ten-day penetration was finally halted after the 101st Airborne Division had stood firm at the vital bastion of Bastogne. The commander, Brigadier General A. C. McAuliffe, defiantly answered the German demand for surrender with one word, "Nuts." Reinforcements were rushed up, and the last-gasp

Hitlerian offensive was at length bloodily stemmed in the Battle of the Bulge.

In March 1945, forward-driving American troops reached Germany's Rhine River, where, by incredibly good luck, they found one strategic bridge undemolished. Pressing their advantage, General Eisenhower's troops reached the Elbe River in April 1945. There, a short distance south of Berlin, American and Russian advance guards dramatically clasped hands, amid cries of *"Amerikanskie tovarishchi"* (American comrades). The conquering Americans were horrified to find blood-bespattered and still-stinking concentration camps, where the German Nazis had engaged in scientific mass murder of "undesirables," including an estimated 6 million Jews. These horrors, for once, far exceeded the lurid reports of propagandists.

The vengeful Russians, clawing their way forward from the east, reached Berlin in April 1945. After desperate house-to-house fighting, followed by an orgy of pillage and rape, they captured the bomb-shattered city. Adolf Hitler, after a hasty marriage to his mistress, committed suicide in an underground bunker, April 30, 1945.

American and Russian Soldiers Meet in Germany, 1945. Such friendly sights soon became rare as mutual suspicion deepened. (U.S. Army photo.)

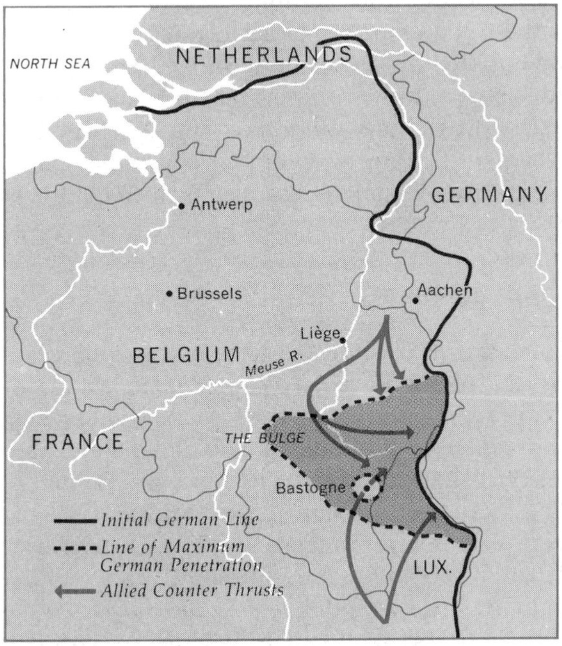

BATTLE OF THE BULGE

Tragedy had meanwhile struck the United States. President Roosevelt, while relaxing at Warm Springs, Georgia, suddenly died from a massive cerebral hemorrhage on April 12, 1945. The crushing burden of twelve years in the White House had finally taken its toll. Knots of confused and leaderless citizens gathered to discuss the future anxiously, as a bewildered and unbriefed Vice-President Truman took the helm.

On May 7, 1945, what was left of the German government surrendered unconditionally. The next day was officially proclaimed V-E Day—Victory in Europe Day—and it was greeted with frenzied rejoicing in the Allied countries.

Japan Dies Hard

Japan's rickety bamboo empire meantime was tottering to its fall. American submarines—"the silent service"—were sending the Japanese merchant marine to the bottom so fast that they were running out of prey. All told, these underseas craft destroyed 1,042 ships, or about 50 percent of Nippon's entire life-giving merchant fleet.

Giant bomber attacks were more spectacular. Launched from Saipan and other captured Marianas, they were reducing the enemy's fragile cities to cinders. The massive fire-bomb raid on Tokyo, March 9–10, 1945, was annihilating. It destroyed over 250,000 buildings, gutted a quarter of the city, and killed an estimated 83,000 persons—a loss comparable to that later inflicted by atomic bombs.

General MacArthur was also on the move. Completing the conquest of jungle-cursed New Guinea, he headed northwest for the Philippines, en route to Japan, with 600 ships and 250,000 men. In a scene well staged for the photographers, he splashed ashore at Leyte Island, on October 20, 1944, with the summons: "People of the Phillippines, I have returned. . . . Rally to me."

Nippon's navy—still menacing—now made one last-chance effort to destroy MacArthur by wiping out his transports and supply ships. A gigantic clash at Leyte Gulf, fought on the sea and in the air, was actually three battles (October 23–26, 1944). The Americans won all of them, though the crucial engagement was almost lost when Admiral William F. ("Bull") Halsey was decoyed away by a feint.

Japan was through as a sea power: it had lost about sixty ships in the greatest naval battle of all time. American fleets, numbering more than 4,000 vessels, now commanded Asiatic seas. Several battleships, raised from the mud of Pearl Harbor, were finding belated but sweet revenge.

Overrunning Leyte, MacArthur next landed on the main Philippine island of Luzon, in January 1945. Manila was his major objective; the ravaged city fell in March, but the Philippines were not conquered until July. Victory was purchased only after bitter fighting against holed-in Japanese, who took a toll of over 60,000 American casualties.

America's iron ring was tightening mercilessly around Nippon. The tiny island of Iwo Jima, needed as a roosting place for damaged American bombers returning from Japan, was captured in March 1945. This desperate twenty-five-day assault cost over 4,000 American dead.

Okinawa, a well-defended Japanese island, was next on the list: it was needed for closer bases from which to blast and burn enemy cities and industries. Fighting dragged on from April to June of 1945. Nipponese soldiers, fighting with cornered-rat courage from their caves, finally sold Okinawa for 80,000 American casualties, while suffering far heavier losses themselves.

The Flag Raising at Iwo Jima. Atop Mt. Suribachi, press photographer Joe Rosenthal snapped this dramatic picture, probably the most famous of the war. (National Archives.)

The American navy, which covered the invasion of Okinawa, sustained severe damage. Japanese suicide pilots, in an exhibition of mass hara-kiri for their god-emperor, crashed their bomb-laden planes onto the decks of the invading fleet. All told, they sank over thirty ships and badly damaged scores more. The navy farsightedly had developed floating dry docks and other time-saving new techniques, all of which helped it to keep up the pressure.

Atomic Awfulness

Strategists in Washington were meanwhile planning an all-out invasion of the main islands of Japan—an invasion that presumably would cost hundreds of thousands of American (and Japanese) casualties. Tokyo, recognizing imminent defeat, had secretly sent peace feelers to Russia, which had not yet entered the Far Eastern war. But bomb-scorched Japan still showed no outward willingness to surrender *unconditionally*.

The Potsdam conference, held near Berlin in July 1945, sounded the death knell of the Japanese.

The Hiroshima Holocaust.
(Official U.S. Air Force photo.)

There President Truman, still new on his job, met in a seventeen-day parley with Joseph Stalin and the British leaders. The conferees issued a stern ultimatum to Japan: surrender or be destroyed. American bombers showered the grim warning on Japan in tens of thousands of leaflets, but no encouraging response was forthcoming.

America had a fantastic ace up her sleeve. Early in 1940, after Hitler's wanton assault on Poland, Roosevelt was persuaded by American and exiled scientists, notably German-born Albert Einstein, to push ahead with gigantic preparations for unlocking the secret of an atomic bomb. Congress, at Roosevelt's blank-check request, blindly made available nearly $2 billion. Many military minds were skeptical of this "damned professor's nonsense," but fear of well-known German scientific progress provided an additional spur.

The huge atomic project was pushed feverishly forward, as American know-how and industrial power were combined with the most advanced scientific knowledge. Much technical skill was provided by British and Continental scientists, some of whom ironically had been forced to flee the torture chambers of the dictators. Finally, in the desert near Alamogordo, New Mexico, on July 16, 1945, the experts detonated the first awesome atomic device.

With Japan still refusing to surrender, the Potsdam threat was fulfilled. On August 6, 1945, a lone American bomber dropped one atomic bomb on the military-base city of Hiroshima, Japan. In a blinding flash of death, followed by a funnel-shaped cloud, about 180,000 persons were left killed, wounded, or missing. Some 70,000 of them were dead or presumed dead.

Two days later, on August 8, Stalin entered the war against Japan, exactly on the deadline date previously agreed upon with his allies. Regrouped Soviet armies speedily overran the depleted Japanese defenses in Manchuria and Korea in a six-day "victory parade" which involved several thousand Russian casualties. Stalin was evidently determined to be in on the kill, lest he lose a voice in the final division of Japan's holdings.

Fanatically resisting Japanese, though facing atomization, still did not surrender. American airmen, on August 9, dropped a second atomic bomb on the naval-base city of Nagasaki, home of the fictional "Madame Butterfly." The explosion took a horrible toll of about 80,000 persons killed or missing.

Japan could endure no more. On August 10, 1945, Tokyo sued for peace on one condition: that Hirohito, the bespectacled Son of Heaven, be allowed to remain on his ancestral throne as nominal Emperor. Despite their "unconditional surrender" policy, the Allies accepted this condition on August 14. The Japanese, though losing face, saved both their exalted ruler and what was left of their native land.

The formal end came, with dramatic force, on September 2, 1945. Official surrender ceremonies were conducted by General MacArthur on the battleship *Missouri* in Tokyo Bay. At the same time Americans at home hysterically celebrated V-J Day—Victory in Japan Day—after the most horrible war in history had ended in a mushrooming atomic cloud.

The Allies Triumphant

World War II proved to be terribly costly. American forces suffered some 1 million casualties, about one-third of which were deaths. Compared with other wars, the proportion killed by wounds and disease was sharply reduced, owing in part to the use of blood plasma and of miracle drugs, notably penicillin. Yet heavy though American losses were, the Russian allies suffered casualties many times greater—perhaps 20 million persons killed.

America was fortunate in emerging with its mainland virtually unscathed. Two Japanese submarines, using shells and bombers, had rather harmlessly attacked the California and Oregon coast, and a few balloons, incendiary and otherwise, had drifted across the Pacific. But that was about all. Much of the rest of the world was bomb-pocked, rubble-strewn, and impoverished. Yet America's natural resources, magnificent though they were, had been seriously depleted by the ravenous war machine.

This complex conflict was the best-fought war in America's history. Though unprepared for it at the outset, the nation was better prepared than for the others, partly because she had begun to buckle on her armor about a year and

Johnny Comes Marching Home. Newport News, Virginia, 1945. Hero's welcomes greeted most returning "G.I.'s," in contrast to the non-welcome later accorded veterans of the Vietnam War. (Photo by U.S. Army Signal Corps.)

a half before the war officially began. She was actually fighting German submarines in the Atlantic months before the final explosion in the Pacific at Pearl Harbor. In the end, she proved herself to be resourceful, tough, adaptable—able to accommodate herself to the tactics of an enemy who was relentless and ruthless.

American military leadership proved to be of the highest order. A new crop of war heroes emerged in brilliant generals like Eisenhower, MacArthur, and Marshall (chief of staff), and in imaginative admirals like Nimitz and Spruance. President Roosevelt and Prime Minister Churchill, as kindred spirits, collaborated closely in planning overall strategy. "It is fun to be in the same decade with you," FDR once cabled the British leader.

Industrial leaders were no less skilled, for marvels of production were performed almost daily. Assembly lines proved no less important than battle lines; and victory went again to the side with the big smokestacks. The enemy was almost literally smothered in an avalanche of bayonets, bullets, bazookas, and bombs. Hitler and his Axis co-conspirators had chosen to make war with machines, and the ingenious Yankees could ask for nothing better. From 1940 to 1945, American factories rolled out an incredible 300,317 airplanes. As Winston Churchill remarked, "Nothing succeeds like excess."

Hermann Göring, a Nazi leader, had sneered, "The Americans can't build planes—only electric iceboxes and razor blades." Democracy had given its answer, as the dictators, despite long preparation, were overthrown and discredited. It is true that an unusual amount of direct control was exercised over the individual by the Washington authorities during the war emergency. But the American people preserved their precious liberties without serious impairment.

VARYING VIEWPOINTS

The United States emerged militarily triumphant in 1945, but one event threatened to tarnish the crown of moral victory: the atomic bombing of Japan. America is the only nation ever to have used an atomic weapon in war, and some critics noted cynically that the bomb was dropped, not on European enemies, but on people of a non-white race. A few scholars, notably Gar Alperovitz, have further charged that the holocaust at Hiroshima and Nagasaki was not the final shot of World War II, but the first salvo in the Cold War. Alperovitz notes that the Japanese were already defeated in the summer of 1945 and were attempting to arrange a *conditional* surrender. President Truman ignored those attempts and unleashed his horrible new weapon, so the argument goes, not only to defeat Japan but also to frighten the Russians into less aggressive behavior.

Could the use of the atomic bomb have been avoided? The fact is that few policymakers even asked that question at the time, as Martin J. Sherwin's studies have made clear. American leaders wanted to end the war as quickly as possible, for a variety of reasons, and the bomb undoubtedly hastened the devastating conclusion. It also strengthened the American hand against the Russians, but that was not the *primary* reason for the fateful decision to proceed with the nuclear incineration of two Japanese cities. Nevertheless, remorse and misgivings about those horrible bomb-bursts continue to plague the nation's conscience.

SELECT READINGS

A scholarly discussion of the home front is John M. Blum, *V Was for Victory: Politics and American Culture During World War II* (1976). Consult also Richard Polenberg, *War and Society: The United States, 1941–1945* (1972). On women, see W. Chafe, *The American Woman: Her Changing Social, Economic, and Political Roles, 1920–1970* (1972); on the internment of the Japanese-Americans, consult Roger Daniels, *Concentration Camps U.S.A.: Japanese Americans and World War II* (1971). Also interesting is Allan M. Winkler, *The Politics of Propaganda: The Office of War Information, 1942–1945* (1978). The military history of the war is capably handled in A. R. Buchanan, *The United States and World War II* (2 vols., 1964). The naval side is treated in S. E. Morison, *The Two-Ocean War* (1963), a condensation of his multivolume official history. See also R. F. Weigley, *Eisenhower's Lieutenants: The Campaigns of France and Germany, 1944–1945* (1981). High strategy is developed in K. R. Greenfield, *American Strategy in World War II* (1963). A good introduction to wartime diplomacy is Gaddis Smith, *American Diplomacy During the Second World War* (1965). More detailed are Herbert Feis's three volumes: *Churchill, Roosevelt, Stalin* (2nd ed., 1967), *Between War and Peace: The Potsdam Conference* (1960), and *The Atomic Bomb and the End of World War II* (1966). Also valuable are R. Dallek's work, cited in the preceding chapter, Robert Divine, *Roosevelt and World War II* (1969), James M. Burns, *Roosevelt: The Soldier of Freedom* (1970), Christopher Thorne, *Allies of a Kind: The United States, Britain, and the War against Japan* (1978). John L. Gaddis, *The United States and the Origins of the Cold War, 1941–1947* (1972), and two "revisionist" works that are highly critical of American policy: Gabriel Kolko, *The Politics of War: The World and United States Foreign Policy, 1943–1945* (1968), and Lloyd Gardner, *Architects of Illusion: Men and Ideas in American Foreign Policy, 1941–1949* (1970). On the atomic bomb, see R. G. Hewlett and O. E. Anderson, Jr., *The New World* (1962), M. Sherwin, *A World Destroyed: The Atomic Bomb and the Grand Alliance* (1975), and Gar Alperovitz's questionable critique of American nuclear strategy, *Atomic Diplomacy* (1965).

43

Harry S Truman and the Cold War

I believe that it must be the policy of the United States to support free peoples who are resisting subjugation by armed minorities or by outside pressures.

HARRY S TRUMAN, "Truman Doctrine" Message, 1947

Truman: the "Gutty" Man from Missouri

Trim and owlishly bespectacled Harry S Truman, with his graying hair and friendly, toothy grin, was called "the average man's average man." Even his height—5 feet 9 (1.75 meters)—was average. The first President in many years without a college education, he had farmed, served as an artillery officer in France during World War I, and failed as a haberdasher. He then tried his hand at precinct-level Missouri politics, through which he rose from a judgeship to the United States Senate. Though a protégé of a notorious political machine in Kansas City, he had managed to keep his own hands clean.

The roof caved in on Truman with Roosevelt's sudden death. Problems were overpowering, and the firm-mouthed new President approached his tasks with becoming humility. Gradually gaining confidence to the point of cockiness, he displayed courage, decisiveness, and a willingness to fight. Though amateurish as a public speaker at first, he finally developed into one of the most effective "give 'em hell" speakers of his generation.

Yet by degrees the defects of Truman's common clay became painfully apparent. A smallish man suddenly thrust into an overwhelming job, he was inclined to go off half-cocked or stick mulishly to some wrongheaded notion. On occasion, he would dash off hot-tempered and highly indiscreet s.o.b. letters. Worst of all, he permitted designing old associates of the "Missouri gang" to gather around him and, like Grant, was stubbornly loyal to them when they were caught with the cream on their whiskers. "To err is Truman" was a cynical explanation.

President Harry S Truman (1884–1972). When his Republican opponents complained that he was giving them "hell," he replied, "I don't give 'em hell, I just tell the truth and they think it's hell." (Harry S Truman Library.)

This was the man on whom Roosevelt's oversize mantle fell in April 1945, when victory over Hitler was in view. Truman's most pressing task was to follow through and win both the war and the peace. Fortunately, he developed a surprising capacity to seize the tiller with bold hand in time of crisis. If he was sometimes small in small things, he was often big in the big things. A motto on the White House desk read, "The buck stops here." A favorite saying of his was, "If you can't stand the heat, get out of the kitchen."

Yalta: Bargain or Betrayal?

Vast and silent, the Soviet Union continued to be the Great Enigma. The conference at Teheran in 1943, where Roosevelt had first met Stalin on a man-to-man basis, had done something to clear the air, but much had remained unsettled.

A final fateful conference of the Big Three had taken place in February 1945 at Yalta. At this former Czarist resort on the relatively warm shores of the Black Sea, Stalin, Churchill, and the fast-failing Roosevelt reached momentous agreements, after pledging their faith with vodka. Final plans were laid for smashing the buckling German lines and shackling the beaten Axis foe. Stalin agreed that Poland, with revised boundaries, should have a representative government based on free elections—a pledge that he soon broke. Bulgaria and Romania were likewise to have free elections—a promise also flouted. The Big Three further announced that they had decided to hold a multipower conference, this time in San Francisco, for the purpose of fashioning a new international organization for peace.

Of all the painful decisions at Yalta, the most controversial concerned the Far East. The atomic bomb had not yet been tested, and Washington strategists expected frightful American casualties in the projected assault on Japan. From Roosevelt's standpoint it seemed highly desirable that Stalin should enter the Far Eastern war, pin down Japanese troops in Manchuria and Korea, and lighten American losses. Russian casualties had already been enormous, and the Soviets presumably needed inducements to bring them into the Far Eastern conflagration.

Horse-trader Stalin was in a position at Yalta to exact a high price. He agreed to attack Japan within two to three months after the collapse of Germany; and he later redeemed his pledge in full. In return, the Soviets were promised the southern half of Sakhalin Island, lost by Russia to Japan in 1905, and Japan's Kurile Islands as well. The Soviet Union was also granted joint control over the railroads of China's Manchuria and, in a revival of Czarist imperialism, received special privileges in the two key seaports of that area, Dairen and Port Arthur. These concessions evidently would give Stalin control over vital industrial centers of America's weakening Chinese ally.

Russia's last-minute entry into the war against Japan was hailed in America with delight. But critics quickly concluded that Stalin's aid had not been needed, and that in any case his desire to grab his share of the spoils would have brought him into the conflict without concessions. Foes of the dead Roosevelt charged angrily that he had sold Chiang Kai-shek down the river when he conceded control of China's Manchuria to Stalin. The consequent undermining of Chinese morale, so the accusation ran, contributed powerfully to Chiang's overthrow by the Communists four years later.

Defenders of the departed Roosevelt were not silent. They argued that if Stalin had kept his promise to support free elections in Poland and the liberated Balkans, the sorry sequel would have been different. Actually, Russian troops had then occupied much of eastern Europe, and a war to throw them out was unthinkable. Apologists for Roosevelt also contended that Stalin, with his mighty Red Army, could have secured much more of China, and that the Yalta conference really set limits to his ambitions. Stalin did pledge himself to make a treaty of friendship and alliance with Chiang's government, and he carried through his promise later in 1945.

"Uncorked at Last!" Secret Yalta papers released ten years later, 1955. (The Albany, New York, *Knickerbocker News.* By permission.)

A myth of the "empty chair" took root—especially in the Soviet Union—that Russian-American relations would not have gone sour if Roosevelt had only lived. The truth is that several weeks before his death, he was shocked to learn that Moscow was about to violate its free-election pledges at Yalta concerning Poland and the Balkans. He died knowing that his charm and generous treatment had failed to lure the Russian Communists away from their menacing imperial designs and their goal of world revolution.

Birth Pangs of the United Nations

As flags wept at half-mast, the United Nations Conference met in San Francisco, on the scheduled April 25, 1945, despite Roosevelt's dismaying death thirteen days earlier. Groundwork had been laid for the historic gathering over a period of several years. The sobered Republicans, in sharp contrast with 1919, had shown a strong disposition to go along with Democratic leadership. Roosevelt, in turn, had displayed more tact than Wilson. He had chosen both Democrats and Republicans for the American delegation, and in addition had included senators on it. He had also avoided Wilson's mistake of riveting the new world organization to the dead weight of an unpopular peace treaty.

With a drizzling rain outside, the delegates from nearly fifty nations assembled in the classically styled San Francisco War Memorial Opera House. The United Nations Charter, as finally whipped together after nine weeks of hectic debate, bore strong resemblances to the old League of Nations Covenant. Two kingpin bodies were set up. One was the Security Council, dominated by the Big Five powers—the United States, Russia, Britain, France, and China. The other was the Assembly, which could be controlled by the smaller countries. A new International Court of Justice was patterned after the old World Court under the League of Nations.

The response of the Senate to the United Nations Charter in 1945 contrasted strikingly with its chilly reception of the League of Nations Covenant in 1919. One senator cried, "Can you not still see the blood on the floor?" After a brief flurry of debate, the final vote was taken on July 28, 1945. Impressed by an overwhelmingly favorable public opinion, the senators approved the document by a vote of 89 to 2.

"Wearied and Getting Nowhere." (Bishop in the St. Louis *Star-Times*, 1947.)

The U.N.'s Early Successes and Failures

The United Nations, which ultimately erected its permanent glass home in New York City, soon disappointed the hopes of those who had cried for One World. The Soviet bloc, a suspicious and outvoted minority, deliberately employed obstructionist tactics. As time passed, the conviction deepened that the Russians had not joined the U.N. in good faith. Evidently they had entered with the intention of snarling it up, and of using it as a megaphone for their incendiary propaganda. Particularly harsh were their wild charges of "warmongering" against America and her "capitalistic" associates.

The built-in big-power veto in the Security Council proved to be a near-fatal stumbling block. At San Francisco this device had been adopted in the expectation that it would be used sparingly, but the Soviets invoked it routinely to block any action that might thwart their schemes to expand Russian power and ideology. Within a few years they had wielded this potent hatchet scores of times.*

Despite these setbacks, the U.N. could point to success in varied theaters. It played a praiseworthy role in helping to preserve peace in Iran, in Kashmir (India), in Indonesia, and elsewhere. It was largely instrumental in creating the new Jewish state of Israel, and in temporarily dampening the subsequent hostilities that broke out between the Jews and their resentful Arab neighbors.

Under the Trusteeship Council, the U.N. set up trust territories that resembled the old League of Nations mandates. In 1947 the United States insisted on—and received as a trustee—the strategic Japanese-mandated islands in the Pacific. These insular outposts, already dearly purchased with American blood, were deemed essential to America's future defense plans.

*By the 1970s, roles were reversed and the United States found itself obliged to use the veto rather freely.

Another significant agency of the U.N. was the Economic and Social Council. Elected by the General Assembly, it achieved substantial gains in world health and in social, cultural, and economic betterment. Prominent among its far-reaching arms was the United Nations Educational, Scientific, and Cultural Organization (UNESCO), which sought to promote a more wholesome understanding among the nations. But certain ultra-nationalistic groups in the United States condemned the experiment as internationalist and un-American.

Far more disheartening was the failure of the U.N. to tame the awesome new technology of the atom. United States delegate Bernard Baruch proposed a promising plan in 1946 to the Atomic Energy Commission of the U.N. He called for an international agency to inspect all nuclear facilities to prevent the manufacture of weapons. Once the inspection machinery was working smoothly, the United States would destroy its own atomic arsenal and end its monopoly. But the suspicious Soviets refused to tie their hands with any such agreement. They wanted the United States to disarm first, and rejected the idea of inspection. They did not want capitalist "spies" snooping around Mother Russia, and they evidently expected to make their own city-wrecking bombs in due course. As the atomic clock ticked ominously away, the Russians came ever nearer their goal.

> Bernard Baruch, in presenting his plan for the control of atomic energy to the United Nations, in June, 1946, said, "We are here to make a choice between the quick and the dead. That is our business. Behind the black portent of the new atomic age lies a hope which, seized upon with faith, can work our salvation. If we fail, then we have damned every man to be the slave of fear. Let us not deceive ourselves; we must elect world peace or world destruction."

America Retools for Peace

After the war ended with an atomic bang, America was again confronted with the familiar pattern of demobilization. Millions of men and women in the armed forces had to be put back into civilian clothes—a process that went forward fairly rapidly. Congress made generous financial provision for readjustment to non-military life. Several million ex-service men and women, whose schooling in many instances had been interrupted, took advantage of the educational benefits provided by Congress in the so-called G.I. Bill of Rights. Colleges during the post-war years were crowded to the blackboards, as more than a million eager veterans entered halls of higher learning.

But the demobilization of laurel-laden warriors was conducted with indecent haste, and without proper regard for America's new power position. When the enemy collapsed, the Republic had the most potent striking force ever assembled—and it was relatively fresh. To wipe it out would create a power vacuum into which the aggressive men of Moscow would be tempted to move. Yet tremendous pressure converged on Washington from sweethearts, parents, and children ("Bring-Daddy-Back-Home Clubs"). These earnest souls were loudly supported by homesick and mutinous G.I.s themselves, who staged noisy "I wanna go home" demonstrations all the way from Germany to India. They warned home congressmen, "No boats, no votes." The shortsighted views of the American people finally prevailed, and the costly tools of victory were tossed away. "Nothing recedes like success," ran a perverted proverb.

On other fronts, economic demobilization lurched forward. War factories and other installations owned by the government were disposed of at fire-sale prices, partly in the misplaced hope that there could never be another war. Price controls were removed, except for rents, although not until President Truman had waged a slam-bang losing fight with Congress for continued restrictions. Manufacturers and retailers were eager to get back to the old law of "supply and demand"—

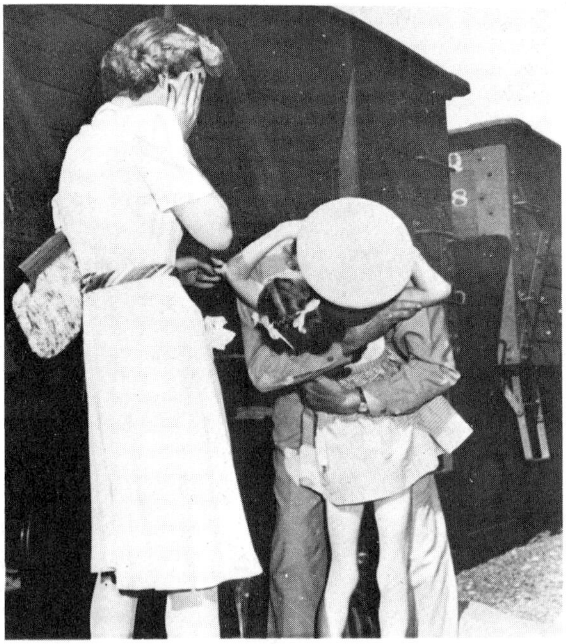

Daddy Comes Home. (Wide World Photos, Inc.)

and they did. With rationing ended, demand outran supply; people were tired of substituting liver for steak. By December 1946, prices were about one-third higher than in the previous year.

Inflationary pressures were almost irresistible. During the war automobiles, refrigerators, stoves, and other appliances had been in short supply, owing chiefly to the ravenous appetite of the munitions industries for scarce metals. When the shooting stopped, the people had amassed fat savings—an estimated $44 billion—and they were starved for consumer goods. With the purchasers bidding competitively, and with the government making heavy shipments of supplies to devastated Europe, prices were bound to soar.

Labor Tramps Ahead

The "working stiff" was pinched by the inflationary spiral, which had about halved the purchasing power of the depression dollar. During the war he had been restrained from striking by high wages and high-pressure patriotism. But when the fighting ended and overtime pay was sharply reduced, he was in a rebellious mood, especially when he saw management raking in profits from the pent-up demand.

An epidemic of strikes swept the country, and during 1946 alone some 4.6 million laborers downed their tools for varying periods. Especially crippling were the work stoppages in such industries as steel and motorcar manufacturing. Stark drama unfolded in the bituminous coal industry when iron-willed John L. Lewis, defying a court injunction in 1946, led out his faithful miners. Deaths from accidents were high, and lethal "black lung" was common. The strikers were forced to return to their pits, but not until a federal court had fined Lewis $10,000 and the union a whopping $3.5 million (later reduced).

Embattled laborers were usually successful in winning wage increases, largely because the order-swamped manufacturers could pass the additional costs on to the consumer. But as prices continued to creep upward, further rounds of strikes resulted, followed by new price rises—in a dog-chasing-its-tail cycle. Yet employment continued full, and during the early post-war years the economy provided the amazing total of 60 million jobs.

Labor, on the whole, registered significant gains during these feverish post-war years. The workers,

> John L. Lewis, leader of the accident-cursed coal miners, told a House Labor Committee (April 1947): "If we must grind up human flesh and bones in an industrial machine . . . then, before God, I assert that those who consume coal, and you and I who benefit from that service . . . owe protection to those men first, and we owe security to their families after, if they die. I say it! I voice it! I proclaim it! And I care not who in heaven or hell oppose it!"

newly New Deal unionized, were winning vacation allowances, old-age pensions, and other unaccustomed welfare benefits. A trail-blazing contract, signed by giant General Motors in 1948, included a clause to the effect that wages would rise and fall automatically with the rise and fall of the cost-of-living index.

Underprivileged black laborers, to an increasing degree, were sharing the war-spawned prosperity. Southern congressmen were blocking President Truman's recommendations for a national fair employment practices law and for civil rights legislation. But the plight of black "second-class citizens" was being generally improved by state legislation and changing public attitudes. Symptomatic of a new day for Afro-Americans was the breaking of the color bar in big-league baseball. Amid less controversy than predicted, the Brooklyn Dodgers led the way in 1947, when they signed a star black second baseman, Jack Roosevelt ("Jackie") Robinson, a former college football player.

"Where Does He Fit In?" Doubts about the Taft-Hartley Act, 1949 (The Albany, New York, *Knickerbocker News.* By permission.)

Labor Curbs and Housing Programs

The growing power of organized workingmen had meanwhile proved deeply disturbing to many conservatives. Asserting that Big Labor was now as much a menace as Big Business had ever been, die-hard industrialists demanded a showdown. The Republicans gained control of Congress in 1947, for the first time in fourteen years, and proceeded to call the tune. Balding, blunt-spoken Robert A. Taft of Ohio, son of the former President and one of the Republican big guns of the Senate, became co-sponsor of a controversial new labor law known as the Taft-Hartley Act. It was passed in June 1947, over President Truman's vigorous veto.

The new Taft-Hartley law promptly became a storm center. Partly designed to protect the public, this piece of legislation contained a number of provisions that caused labor leaders to condemn the entire act as a "slave labor law." Especially irksome were the provisions outlawing the closed (all-union) shop, while making unions liable for damages resulting from jurisdictional disputes among themselves. Union leaders were also required to take a non-Communist oath, though employers were not forced to do so. Despite labor's pained outcries, Taft-Hartleyism, while annoying, did not cripple the labor movement. The AF of L by 1950 could boast 8 million members and the CIO 6 million.

Wretched housing was another grievance of labor, as indeed of much of the population. New construction had been slowed or halted by the war, while at the same time the country had experienced a baby boom. Tens of thousands of migrant workers, moreover, had hived around war industries. This trend was most conspicuous in the northern industrial areas, like Detroit, and on the Pacific Coast, notably in California, which experienced a spectacular increase of population.

In response to Truman's persistent proddings, Congress finally tackled the housing problem.

Laws were passed in 1948 and 1949 to provide federally financed construction, despite the outraged protests of real-estate promoters and other vested interests. But these measures, though promising steps forward, fell far short of pressing needs. Hundreds of thousands of additional structures would have to be built if the nation was going to wipe out its disgraceful slums and provide homes to match its fabulous wealth.

Reconstruction and De-Nazification

At the close of the war America, rich and unscarred, had a moral obligation to help her less fortunate sisters—or so many of her citizens felt. "It is now 11:59 on the clock of starvation," warned Herbert Hoover.

Aid of a non-military nature continued to flow to Europe, even though the end of the shooting brought an abrupt end to lend-lease. The United States simply could not afford to see the ravaged peoples of Europe fall prey to creeping Communism. Wealthy Uncle Sam carried the heavy end of the log in financing short-term relief, chiefly through the United Nations Relief and Rehabilitation Administration (UNRRA). This organization did life-saving work from 1943 to 1947 by providing succor for many destitute countries in both Europe and Asia. Official relief was supplemented by personal gifts, particularly the private packages of food and clothing sent by Americans to starving families in Europe under the auspices of CARE (Cooperative for American Remittances to Europe).

Displaced persons—"D.P.s," or "Delayed Pilgrims," they were called—numbered several million unfortunates uprooted by the war. Large numbers of them were anti-Communists who did not dare return to their Red-dominated homelands. America had room for many of these rootless souls, but Congress moved slowly and halfheartedly in the face of possible unemployment, maladjustment, and the importation of dangerous foreign doctrines. An act as finally passed in 1948—expanded in 1950—made provision for the admission of 205,000 carefully selected persons in two years.

Two wartime associates received special attention. The prostrate Philippines, in accordance with the act of Congress in 1934, were formally awarded independence in 1946 on America's Independence Day—July 4. The United States agreed to provide substantial financial assistance, and in return received leases on more than a score of military, naval, and air-base sites.

Impoverished Britain was grudgingly voted a low-interest loan in 1946 of $3.75 billion. Much opposition was registered, especially on the floor of Congress, by the isolationists, the anti-British,

Former President Truman wrote in 1956: "The American approach to world affairs was best demonstrated by the manner in which we treated conquered nations. . . . We set up the means to feed and clothe and take care of the physical needs of the people. We rehabilitated the conquered nations instead of attempting to keep them conquered and prostrate. . . . This was something new in the history of nations."

War Refugees. Italian civilians were fed at the American Red Cross center in Lucca, Italy. This was probably their first meal in some time. (U.S. Army photograph.)

and the economy-minded, who feared that the money would never be repaid. A cynical jingle ran:

> There will always be a U.S.A.
> If we don't give it away.

Germany presented especially thorny problems. Policy-makers in Washington were determined that she should not rise in her industrial and military might, again to menace the peace of the world. Multiple goals were therefore adopted: de-Nazification, de-militarization, de-industrialization, and democratization. Some Hitler-haters in America, remembering that an industrialized Germany had been an aggressor, were determined to reduce the German Fatherland to a potato patch. But in the end less harsh courses were adopted, partly because Germany was the key to the economic recovery of Europe.

De-Nazification involved punishing Nazi German leaders for war crimes. The Allies joined in trying twenty-two leading culprits at Nuremberg, Germany, during 1945–1946, with Associate Justice Robert H. Jackson of the United States Supreme Court serving as a special prosecutor. Accusations included committing crimes against the laws of war and humanity, and plotting aggressions contrary to solemn treaty pledges.

"Witnesses for the Prosecution," 1945.
(Fitzpatrick in the St. Louis *Post-Dispatch.*)

Justice, new style, was harsh. In 1946, nineteen of the accused Nazis were convicted: twelve were sentenced to the gallows and seven to jail terms. "Foxy Hermann" Göring, whose blubbery chest had once blazed with ribbons, cheated the hangman by swallowing a hidden cyanide capsule a few hours before his scheduled execution. The trials of scores of small-fry Nazis continued for several years. Legalistic critics in America condemned these proceedings as judicial lynchings, for the victims were tried for offenses that had not been clear-cut crimes when the war began. In any event, future aggressors were warned that they might expect the noose instead of the halo—that is, if they lost.

Russian Roadblocks to Peace in Germany and Japan

Allied efforts to make a peace treaty with Germany and Austria speedily ran onto the rocks of Soviet obstruction. Germany and Austria, as previously agreed, were arbitrarily broken into four military zones, and one of them was assigned to each of the Big Four powers: France, Britain, America, and Russia. But the ever-suspicious Russians did not work well in multi-power harness. Besides, they were eager to bleed Germany with heavy reparations—in money, goods, and factories—and leave her so desperately impoverished that her people would fall prey to the seductive promises of Soviet Communism. Moreover, a weak and Sovietized Germany would forestall another Hitler-like invasion.

An ominous gulf between the Russians and the Western Allies gradually widened. The Soviet zone in eastern Germany was turned into a Communist puppet, even though the three-power Potsdam agreement of 1945 had stipulated that the German Reich was to be treated as an economic whole. Moscow was reluctant to conclude multi-power settlements with Germany and Austria, lest these two conquered nations wriggle out from

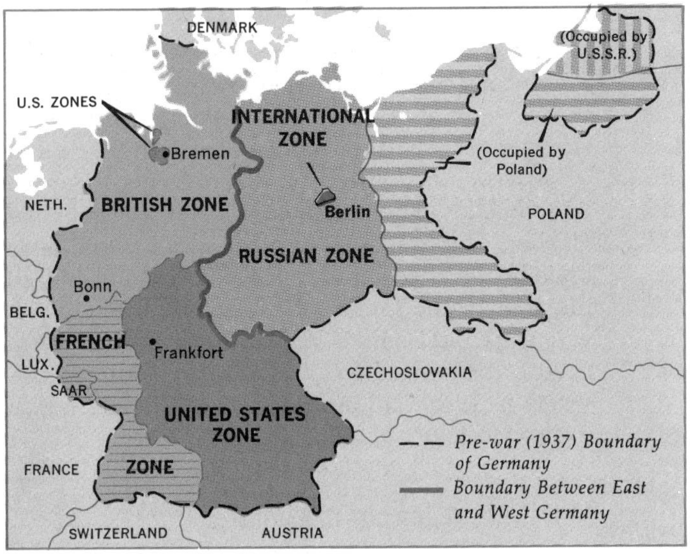

POST-WAR PARTITION OF GERMANY

under the Soviet heel. But there were no insuperable obstacles to peace pacts with Italy, Bulgaria, Hungary, Romania, and Finland; and treaties were formally signed with these defeated countries in 1947.

Reconstruction in Japan was simpler than in Germany, primarily because it was largely a one-man show. The occupying American army, under the supreme Allied commander, five-starred General Douglas MacArthur, sat in the driver's seat. In the teeth of violent protests from the Soviet officials, he went inflexibly ahead with his program for the democratization of Japan. Following the pattern in Germany, top Japanese "war criminals" were tried in Tokyo from 1946 to 1948. Eighteen of them were sentenced to prison terms and seven were hanged.

General MacArthur, as a kind of Yankee Mikado, enjoyed phenomenal success. He made a tremendous impression on the Japanese with his aloof, Greek-god bearing; and the vanquished sons of Nippon cooperated with their conqueror to an astonishing degree. They were clever enough to see that good behavior and the adoption of democracy would speed the end of the occupation—as it did. A MacArthur-dictated constitution was adopted in 1946, renouncing militarism and introducing Western ways of democratic government.

The non-Communist powers, fed up with Soviet obstruction, at length concluded a separate treaty with Japan at San Francisco in 1951—six years after the surrender ceremonies. With passions cooled, it was essentially a "soft peace," designed to help the Nipponese get back on their sandaled feet and stand as a bulwark against Communism in Eastern Asia.

Crystallizing the Cold War

The wartime "Grand Alliance" of America, Britain, and Russia was a misbegotten child of necessity, but it raised hopes of peaceful cooperation after the common enemy was crushed. When Hitler fell, a vast reservoir of goodwill existed in the United States for the resolute Russians. Although distrusted as Communists, they had helped save American skins while saving their own. If the men in the Kremlin had only sung a sweeter tune, they might have borrowed billions of American dollars to help rebuild their shattered motherland.

Instead of milking America, the Russian rulers kicked her in the teeth. Habitually suspicious and dedicated to world Communism since 1917, they cried "capitalist encirclement"—even though the United States was demobilizing with indecent haste. But the Russians professed to fear Western subversion and American atomic bombs. To consolidate their revolutionary base, they clanged

> Former Prime Minister Churchill, in a highly controversial speech at Fulton, Missouri (March 1946), warned of Communist Russia's expansiveness: "From Stettin in the Baltic to Trieste in the Adriatic an iron curtain has descended across the Continent."

down an "iron curtain" across central Europe from the Baltic to the Adriatic. Nations like Poland and Hungary virtually disappeared from Western sight behind Moscow's Communist shield.

Apologists for the Soviets charged that the Americans themselves were at fault. The officials in Washington were too fearful of the spread of Communism, too haughty, too eager to use their wealth to boost themselves into permanent control of the world's economy, and too insensitive to Russian fears of yet another stab into the Red heartland across the windswept plains of Eastern Europe.

The disagreeable truth seems to be that the Cold War was in some sense inevitable. Communist Russia and capitalistic America were both historically isolated to some degree from the world and were unfamiliar with each other. They suddenly found themselves staring eyeball to eyeball over the prostrate body of ravaged Europe—a Europe that had been the traditional center of international affairs. Mutual suspicion and hostility were evidently unavoidable.

One of the first Soviet thrusts was directed at oil-rich Iran in 1946. In an effort to secure oil concessions similar to those already obtained by the English and Americans, Stalin broke an agreement to remove his troops from Iran's northernmost province. Instead, he used them to aid a pro-Soviet separatist movement. Truman sent off a stinging protest, and Stalin backed down.

Arrogant Capitalist. The Communists stereotyped Truman with moneybags and atomic bombs, defiantly backed by the West European capitalistic statesmen. (From the Soviet satirical magazine *Krokodil.*).

Moscow's iron-fisted policy in Eastern Europe and the Middle East wrought a psychological Pearl Harbor. The eyes of Americans were jarred wide open by the Kremlin's refusal to become a civilized member of the family of nations. Wartime goodwill evaporated into a cloud of dark distrust. "I'm tired of babying the Soviets," wrote Truman privately in 1946, and attitudes on both sides began to harden icily.

Marshaling Marshall Dollars

Truman, backed by an aroused public opinion, formally adopted a "get-tough-with-Russia" policy in 1947. His first dramatic move was triggered by word that Britain, heavily burdened, could no longer bear the financial and military load of defending Greece against Communist pressures. If Greece fell, Turkey would presumably collapse and the strategic Eastern Mediterranean would be lost to the free world.

In a surprise appearance, the President went before Congress, on March 12, 1947, and urged it to support what came to be known as the Truman Doctrine. America, he felt, should attempt to halt or "contain" Communist aggression wherever it threatened free peoples. Specifically, he asked Congress to appropriate $400 million for the economic and military bolstering of both Greece and Turkey. The legislators, reflecting the changed public mood, responded with lopsided votes of approval. American aid was rushed to the troubled spots, and Greece and Turkey, Truman believed, were saved from the clutches of Communism. His critics contended that he had over-reacted by lending unlimited support to right-wing elements, including dictators.

Truman's counter-moves against outside aggression actually proved far too limited in scope. Western Europe—especially Italy, France, and

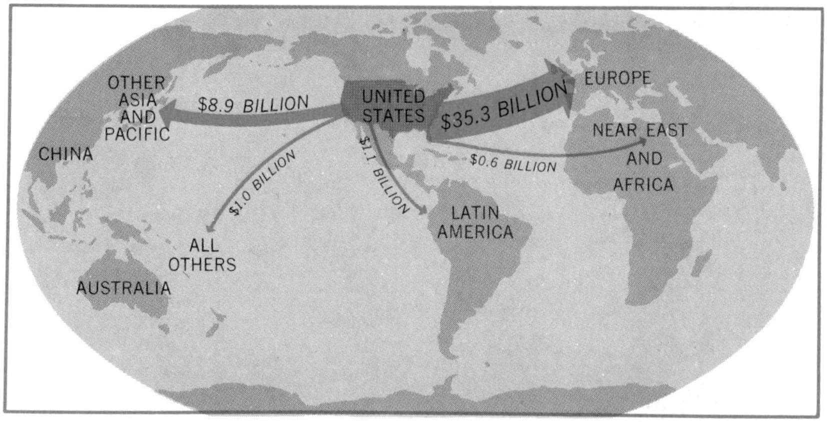

UNITED STATES FOREIGN AID, MILITARY AND ECONOMIC, 1945–1954
Marshall Plan aid swelled the outlay for Europe. Note the emphasis on the "developed" world, with relatively little aid going to what are now called "third world" countries.

Germany—was still suffering from the hunger and economic chaos spawned by the war. These key nations were in grave danger of being taken over from the inside by the "stomach Communists"—that is, by desperate people to whom any change would seem a change for the better.

Secretary of State George C. Marshall, the most distinguished desk-general of the recent war, was delegated to step into the breach. In a commencement address at Harvard University on June 5, 1947, he virtually invited the countries of Europe to get together and work out plans for their economic recovery. If they did so, Washington might help them with adequate financial assistance, pending that day when they could support themselves and consequently strengthen American policy.

"Where To?" Truman Doctrine, 1947. (Courtesy of Richmond *Times-Dispatch*.)

The democratic nations of Europe rose to the life-giving bait with enthusiasm and, in July 1947, a conference was held in Paris to thrash out details. The Soviets spurned a priceless opportunity to snarl the Marshall Plan hopelessly when they walked out of the conference. They branded the whole scheme an "imperialist" plot, cooked up by the Wall Street "Knights of the Dollar" for "the enslavement of Europe."

The next move was up to Congress, which had to vote the money. As outlined by President Truman, the plan was to spend billions of dollars (ultimately $12.5 billion) over four years in sixteen cooperating countries. Uncle Sam was already tax-burdened and debt-ridden, and critics of the Marshall scheme, chiefly old-line isolationists, branded it "The Martial Plan," "Operation Rathole," and "The Share-the-American-Wealth Plan."

Finally, in April 1948, Congress voted the initial appropriation—with evident reluctance. A few voices were raised to say that as good Samaritans Americans owed help to their needy neighbors and recent allies. But the clincher turned out to be the naked aggression of Soviet Communism. The Marshall Plan appropriation was languishing in Congress when a Communist coup in Czechoslovakia, involving the suicide (or murder?) of its

"American Motor of the Latest Type." The conquering Truman uses U.S. moneybags to induce dollar-hungry European nations to draw the U.S. capitalistic chariot. (From the Soviet satirical magazine *Krokodil.*)

foreign minister, provided a frightening new object lesson in how a democracy could be enchained overnight.

Truman's Marshall Plan on the whole proved to be a spectacular success. The billions voted by Congress were administered by the Economic Cooperation Administration, headed by Paul G. Hoffman, former president of the Studebaker automobile corporation. Life-giving American dollars pumped a blood transfusion into the economic veins of the anemic Western European nations, and within a few years most of them were approaching or even exceeding their pre-war production output. The Communist parties in Italy and France lost some ground, and these two keystone countries were saved from the westward thrust of Communism. And both America and Europe were spared another great depression, as the Marshall Plan planners had hoped.

America Begins to Rearm

The struggle to stem Soviet Communism resulted in what came to be known as "the Cold War." It was not war—yet it was not peace. The alarming tactics of the Kremlin completely banished the dreams of tax-weary Americans that guns could be beaten into automobiles.

The Soviet menace spurred the unification of the armed services, as well as the creation of a huge new national security apparatus. Congress in 1947 passed the National Security Act, creating the Department of Defense. The Department was to be housed in the sprawling Pentagon building on the banks of the Potomac, and to be headed by a new Cabinet officer, the secretary of defense. Under him, but now without Cabinet status, were the civilian secretaries of the navy, the army (replacing the old secretary of war), and the air force (a recognition of the rising importance of air power). The uniformed heads of each service were brought together as the Joint Chiefs of Staff. Unification was a large and necessary step toward more efficient military management, but it did not end inter-service rivalry, as reflected in the annual football contests between the academies at West Point, Annapolis, and Colorado Springs.

The National Security Act also established a National Security Council to advise the President on security matters, and a Central Intelligence Agency to coordinate the government's foreign fact-gathering. The "Voice of America," authorized by Congress in 1948, began beaming American radio broadcasts behind the Iron Curtain. In the same year Congress enacted the nation's first peacetime military draft, providing for the conscription of selected young men from nineteen to twenty-five years of age. The overshadowing presence of the Selective Service System shaped millions of young people's educational, marital, and career plans in the following quarter-century. One shoe at a time, a war-weary America was reluctantly returning to a war footing.

Ferreting Out Alleged Communists

One of the most active Cold War fronts was at home, where a new anti-Red chase was in full cry. Many nervous citizens feared that Communist spies, paid with Moscow gold, were undermining the government and treacherously misdirecting foreign policy. In 1947 Truman launched a massive "loyalty" program. The attorney general drew up a list of ninety supposedly disloyal organizations, none of which was given the right to prove its innocence. A Loyalty Review Board investigated more than 3 million federal employees, some 3,000 of whom either resigned or were dismissed, none under formal indictment.

Individual states likewise became intensely security-conscious. Loyalty oaths in increasing numbers were demanded of employees, educational and otherwise. Disagreeable incidents involving freedom of speech and teaching burst into the headlines. The gnawing question for many earnest Americans was: could the nation continue to enjoy traditional freedoms in the face of a ruthless international conspiracy known as Soviet Communism?

In 1949 eleven Communists were brought before a New York jury for violating the Smith Act of 1940, the first peacetime anti-sedition law since 1798. Hiding behind the very Constitution they were attempting to destroy, the defendants were convicted of advocating the overthrow of the American government by force, and were sent to prison.

The House of Representatives in 1938 had established a Committee on Un-American Activities to investigate "subversion." In 1948 committee member Richard M. Nixon, an ambitious Red-catcher, led the chase after Alger Hiss, a prominent ex–New Dealer and a distinguished member of the "Eastern Establishment." Accused of being a Communist agent in the 1930s, Hiss demanded the right to defend himself. He dramatically met his chief accuser before the Un-American Activities Committee in August 1948. Hiss denied everything, but was convicted of perjury in 1950 and sentenced to five years in prison.

In his inaugural address, January 1949, Truman said: "Communism is based on the belief that man is so weak and inadequate that he is unable to govern himself, and therefore requires the rule of strong masters. . . . Democracy is based on the conviction that man has the moral and intellectual capacity, as well as the inalienable right, to govern himself with reason and justice."

In February 1950, Senator Joseph R. McCarthy, a Wisconsin Republican, spectacularly charged that there were scores of known Communists in the Department of State. He proved utterly unable to substantiate his accusation, and many Americans, including President Truman, began

Feelings Run High over Communist Subversives. Demonstrators for and against convicted atomic spies Julius and Ethel Rosenberg parade in front of the White House in 1953. For details, see p. 834. (United Press International photo.)

to fear that the Red-hunt was turning into a witch-hunt. In 1950 Truman vetoed the McCarran Internal Security Bill, which among other provisions authorized the President to arrest and detain suspicious persons during an "internal security emergency." Critics protested that the bill smacked of police-state, concentration-camp tactics. But the congressional guardians of the Republic's liberties enacted the bill over Truman's veto.

The Berlin Airlift and NATO

The Cold War had meanwhile come perilously close to flaring into a hot war in the rubble heap known as Berlin. Lying deep within the Soviet zone of Germany (see map, p. 843), this democratic isle in a Red sea had been broken into four sectors, each of which was occupied by troops of one of the four great powers. Yet no provision had been made for guaranteeing joint control of the roads and railroads approaching Berlin through the Soviet-controlled zone. In 1948, following angry controversies over German currency reform and four-power control, the Russians sprang the trap. They abruptly choked off land and water routes to Berlin, no doubt reasoning that the Allies would be starved out.

Rather than turn tail and run, the British and Americans, chiefly Americans, organized a gigantic airlift in the midst of trigger-finger tension. For nearly a year intrepid aviators, summer and winter, flew in the necessities of the Berliners, including coal—expensive coal. At its peak the airlift ("Operation Vittles") was ferrying some 4,500 tons of supplies a day to more than 2 million people, at the rate of one plane every three minutes. The Berliners, though former enemies, were heartened and grateful.

Moscow, taken aback, was sobered by the determination of the Allies to stand firm. The democracies at length won an impressive moral victory when the Russians, their fingers burned by an Allied counter-blockade, formally lifted their ban on surface shipments in May 1949.

Two Germanies thus emerged from the Soviet-engineered deadlock: the Communist-dominated East Germany and the democratically organized West Germany. The government of the West German Republic was formally and hopefully set up in 1949 at the historic Rhine city of Bonn, birthplace of Beethoven.

Berliners Watch Incoming U.S. Relief Airplane, 1948. (Walter Sanders, *Life Magazine,* © 1948 Time, Inc.)

Soviet menaces meanwhile had been forcing the divided democracies of Western Europe into an unforeseen degree of unity, both economic and political. In 1948, Britain, France, Belgium, the Netherlands, and Luxembourg signed a path-breaking defensive alliance at Brussels. A security-seeking America, despite a deep-seated prejudice against peacetime entanglements, was drawn irresistibly toward the new grouping.

The alliance negotiations reached their climax in Washington. There, on April 4, 1949, the representatives of twelve nations, with white-tie pageantry, signed the historic North Atlantic Pact. It stipulated that an attack on one member by an aggressor would be an attack on all, and that the signatories would then take such action as they deemed necessary, including "armed force."

Would the United States Senate, despite a strongly favorable public opinion, reject the treaty? Last-ditch isolationists insisted that the scheme was a dangerous involvement which would cause the Republic to become a kind of helpless tail to the European kite. But security came before tradition, and the Senate registered its approval, on July 21, 1949, by a vote of 82 to 13.

The pact was truly epochal. Uncle Sam did not assume a hard-and-fast commitment to rush to the aid of any one of the signatories assaulted by Soviet Russia—but there was clearly a moral commitment. Due notice was served on the government in Moscow that it attacked at its peril, and preparations were pushed by the North Atlantic Treaty Organization (NATO) to build up an army for defensive purposes. Membership was boosted to fourteen in 1952 by the inclusion of Greece and Turkey; to fifteen in 1955 by the addition of West Germany.

It seemed evident to Americans that the free nations would have to stand together, or they would be picked off one by one—in daisy-plucking fashion. A willingness to join a peacetime military alliance, despite hoary tradition, revealed a tormenting concern over Soviet aggressions. The Cold War had forced the nation to face cold facts.

Democratic Dissensions and Divisions in 1948

Republican prospects had seldom looked rosier as the presidential campaign of 1948 neared. The GOP could point happily to the congressional elections of 1946, when the voters, responding to the slogan "Had Enough?" had elected a Republican Congress. Seemingly the country was fed up with New Deal spending, high prices, and "High-Tax Harry" Truman.

Jubilant Republicans, meeting in Philadelphia, departed sharply from previous practice. They noisily renominated a warmed-over candidate, the once-defeated Thomas E. Dewey, governor of New York, still as debonair as if he had stepped out of a bandbox. The platform listed in detail the shortcomings of the New Deal, and revived the threadbare theme that it was "time for a change." "Save What's Left" became a popular Republican slogan.

Democratic politicos, also gathering in Philadelphia, worked up no real enthusiasm for their hand-me-down President, Harry S Truman. An effort had been made to draft war-hero Dwight D. Eisenhower, and when he continued to turn a deaf ear, the "dump Truman" movement collapsed. The peppery President, unwanted but undaunted, was then chosen in the face of violent opposition from the Southern delegates. They were alienated by his strong stand in favor of civil rights for blacks, who now mustered many votes in the big-city ghettos of the North. The song "I'm Just Wild about Harry" became "I'm Just Mild about Harry."

Truman's nomination split the party wide open. Embittered Southern Democrats from thirteen states, like their fire-eating forebears of 1860, next met in their own convention, in Birmingham, Alabama, with Confederate flags brashly in evidence. Amid scenes of heated defiance, these "Dixiecrats" nominated Governor J. Strom Thurmond of South Carolina on a States' Rights party ticket.

To add to the confusion within Democratic

Democratic Split Raises GOP Hopes. (Bishop in the St. Louis *Star-Times.* 1948.)

ranks, former Vice-President Henry A. Wallace threw his hat into the ring. Having parted company with the administration over its get-tough-with-Russia policy, he was nominated at Philadelphia by the new Progressive party—a bizarre collection of disgruntled ex–New Dealers, starry-eyed pacifists, progressives, well-meaning liberals, and Communist-fronters, who chanted:

> One, two, three, four,
> We don't want another war.

Wallace, a vigorous if misguided liberal, assailed Uncle Sam's "dollar imperialism" from the stump. Drenched with rotten eggs in hostile cities, this so-called Pied Piper of the Politburo took what appeared to be a pro-Soviet line that undoubtedly weakened America's diplomatic posture. In these perilous times preaching peace with the Soviets was unpopular.

Truman Achieves the "Miracle" of 1948

Truman's chances seemed desperate. A party is ordinarily doomed when it splits in half; this time it had split three ways. It had been in power for sixteen long years, had made many well-publicized mistakes, had incurred a host of enemies, and had lost the Congress to the Republicans in 1946. The Democrats were vulnerable, moreover, to the charge of "Communist coddling."

Dewey, riding a "Victory Special" train, fell victim to overconfidence, especially after the public-opinion polls and the political experts had him winning in a walk. To many voters he seemed cold, smug, superior, arrogant, and evasive. Noncommittal in the extreme, he engaged in dispensing soothing-syrup generalities, including "Our future lies before us." Democrats jeered that GOP spelled "Grand Old Platitudes." But Dewey's strategy was basically sound: If victory is certain, why tie one's hands by making any more positive commitments than one has to?

Harry Truman—"the forgotten man"—was seemingly left almost alone, with inadequate money and few active supporters. But his instincts as a "gut-fighter" were aroused on behalf of his forward-looking program for civil rights, improved labor benefits, and health insurance. Rolling up his sleeves, he put on a furious, free-swinging, one-man campaign. Touring the country and showing his "folksy" personality to advantage, he delivered some 300 "give 'em hell" speeches at numerous whistle-stops. He condemned the Taft-Hartley "slave labor" law, and lashed out at the "notorious" record of the "do nothing," "good for nothing," Republican Eightieth Congress—the "worst in history." That body, he shouted to a roaring mass of 100,000 people in Iowa, had "stuck a pitchfork in the farmer's back." He airily waved aside the findings of the pollsters as "sleeping polls," designed to lull the voters to sleep. The crowds, growing increasingly large and enthusiastic, cried back, "Pour it on 'em, Harry!"

Only a Republican genius, it was said, could lose this election; and "President" Dewey succeeded brilliantly in snatching defeat from the jaws of

Presidential Election of 1948

Candidates	*Popular Vote*	*Electoral Vote*
Truman (Democratic)	24,105,812	303 (chiefly South, Middle West, and West)
Dewey (Republican)	21,970,065	189 (chiefly New England, Middle Atlantic states)
Thurmond (States' Rights Democratic)	1,169,063	39 (Ala., Miss., La., S.C.)
Wallace (Progressive)	1,157,172	0

"That Ain't the Way I Heard It!" Truman wins. (United Press International photo.)

victory. Truman swept to a stunning triumph, to the complete bewilderment of the politicians, pollsters, prophets, and pundits. The chagrined Chicago *Tribune* had overconfidently run off an edition with the headline "DEWEY DEFEATS TRUMAN." The statistical results, as shown in the table on the facing page, are most revealing. To make victory all the sweeter, the Democrats regained control of Congress, fully prepared to continue New Deal spending under "Roosevelt's fifth term."

Why the sensational upset? High among the reasons must rank Republican overconfidence, fed by the poll-takers and reflected in the light turnout, smaller than in 1940. Farmers found Truman's promises of price supports more reassuring than Dewey's; labor opposed the Republican-sponsored Taft-Hartley law; and the massed black vote in the large Northern cities naturally turned to Truman as a result of his pro–civil rights stand. The country was prosperous, and government checks were still flowing out from the Treasury to various voters. Finally, Truman's lone-wolf, never-say-die campaign won him the support of many Americans who admired "guts." No one wanted him, someone remarked, except the mass of the voters.

New Dealers Become Fair Dealers

Smilingly confident, Truman sounded a clarion note, in the fourth point of his inaugural address, when he called for a "bold new program" ("Point Four"). The plan was to lend American money and technical aid to underdeveloped lands to help them help themselves. Truman wanted to spend millions to keep underprivileged peoples from becoming Communists, rather than to spend billions to shoot them after they had become Communists. This far-seeing program was officially launched in 1950, and it brought badly needed assistance to impoverished countries, notably in Latin America, Africa, the Near East, and the Far East.

A Fair Deal, aimed at helping poverty-stricken peoples at home, was fully outlined in Truman's annual message to Congress in January 1949. The President issued an appeal for a sweeping program that would embrace badly needed housing, full employment, higher minimum wages, better price supports for farmers, new TVAs for other major river valleys, and an extension of Social Security. This Fair Deal program went further in some respects than the New Deal itself, and the Republicans condemned these "Fear Deal" proposals as designed to create a socialistic and spendthrift "welfare state."

The Fair Dealers, despite Truman's zeal, achieved only a small part of their program. A filibuster by Southern members of the Eighty-first Congress—the "eighty-worst"—blocked a federal anti-poll tax law and a fair employment practices act. But in 1949 Congress, bowing to inflation, did boost the minimum wage to 75 cents an hour from the 40 cents set in 1940. Progress was also made toward slum clearance and public housing in the Housing Act of 1949. Perhaps the greatest success of Truman's Fair Deal came in the Social Security Act of 1950, which broadened the old-age insurance benefits of the original law of 1935. It added some 9.7 million beneficiaries to the 35 million already covered.

The Nuclear Arms Race and China's Collapse

President Truman shocked the nation by announcing in September 1949 that the Soviets had exploded an atomic bomb—approximately three years earlier than many experts had thought possible. American strategists since 1945 had counted on keeping the Soviets in line by threats of a one-sided aerial attack with nuclear weapons. America's monopoly of this lethal weapon may in fact have restrained the Russians from launching out on a course of armed aggression. But atomic bombing was now a game that two could play.

The stunning success of the Soviet scientists was presumably due, at least in part, to the cleverness of Communist spies in stealing American secrets. Notorious among those Americans and Britishers who had allegedly "leaked" atomic data to Moscow were two American citizens, Julius and Ethel Rosenberg. They were convicted in 1951 of espionage, and after prolonged appeals went to the electric chair in 1953—the only people in American history ever executed in peacetime for espionage. Their sensational trial and electrocution, combined with fear of the A-bomb, rallied public support for look-under-the-bed congressional Red-hunters.

Bad news of a different sort came in 1949 with the catastrophic fall of China to the Communists. Since the end of the war, and even earlier, Washington had halfheartedly supported the Nationalist government of Chiang Kai-shek in his bitter civil war with the Communists. But the generalissimo gradually began to forfeit the confidence of his people, owing to the ineptitude and corruption within his regime. Communist armies swept south overwhelmingly, and late in 1949 Chiang was forced to flee with the remnants of his once-powerful force to the last-hope island of Formosa (Taiwan).

The collapse of Nationalist China was a depressing defeat for America and her allies in the Cold War—the worst to date. At one fell swoop nearly one-fourth of the world's population—some 500 million souls—was swept into the Communist camp. The Republicans, seeking "goats" who had "lost China," assailed President Truman and his bristly mustached, British-appearing secretary of state, Dean Acheson. They insisted that Democratic agencies, wormy with Communists, had deliberately withheld aid from Chiang Kai-shek so that he would fall. Democrats heatedly replied that when a regime has forfeited the support of its people, no amount of outside help will save it. Truman, the argument ran, did not "lose" China because he never had China to lose. Chiang himself had never had all China.

The horrifying race in "city-busting" weapons continued at a stepped-up pace. If force was the only language that the Soviets respected, then weakness in the democratic world would invite disaster. Late in 1952, after tests in the South Pacific, word leaked out that an American hydrogen device, many times more lethal than the atomic bomb, had been exploded. The assumption was that the Soviets would soon have one also—and the next year they claimed that they did. If the Cold War should blaze into a hot war, perhaps there would be no world left for the Communists to communize or the democracies to democratize—a sobering thought that may have given pause to both camps. Peace through mutual terror might yet come to be the last best hope of mankind.

> In August 1949, Secretary of State Acheson explained publicly why America had "dumped" Chiang Kai-shek: "The unfortunate but inescapable fact is that the ominous result of the civil war in China was beyond the control of the government of the United States. Nothing that this country did or could have done within the reasonable limits of its capabilities could have changed that result; nothing that was left undone by this country has contributed to it. It was the product of internal Chinese forces, forces which this country tried to influence but could not."

VARYING VIEWPOINTS

Who was to blame for starting the Cold War? For nearly a generation after World War II, American historians generally agreed that the suspicious and grasping Soviets were almost solely responsible. This "orthodox" appraisal fitted comfortably with the traditional view of the United States as a God-blessed land with an idealistic foreign policy. But in the 1960s a revisionist interpretation began to flower, powerfully reinforced by revulsion against American atrocities in Vietnam. "New Left" revisionists like the Kolkos attempted to reverse the orthodox view. They argued that the Soviets had only defensive intentions at the end of World War II, and that the United States had behaved aggressively and irresponsibly. Some critics pointed the accusing finger at Truman. They alleged that he had abandoned Roosevelt's conciliatory approach and had adopted a bullying attitude, bolstered by the atomic bomb. More radical revisionists sought the roots of American "aggression" before Truman's time in long-standing policies of economic expansion.

The revisionist criticism has compelled the recognition that the United States did have vital interests at stake in post-war diplomacy, and that policy-makers pursued those interests with vigor. But is self-interest necessarily immoral? Is security a one-way street? Can the blame ever be exclusively with one side in a complex international dispute? Some critics charge that the revisionist argument is stamped with its own brand of American provincialism, since it portrays the entire post-war world as shaped preponderantly by America's counter-revolutionary "imperialism." And so long as Soviet archives are closed, Russian intentions will remain a matter of conjecture.

SELECT READINGS

See the titles cited in the preceding chapter by Gaddis, Gardner, Alperovitz, Sherwin, Feis, and Kolko. Consult also Feis's *From Trust to Terror: The Onset of the Cold War, 1945–1950* (1970), which defends American policy, and Joyce and Gabriel Kolko's *The Limits of Power: The World and United States Foreign Policy, 1945–1954* (1972), which roundly condemns Washington's actions. Useful surveys of the diplomatic history of the period, all of them in varying degrees critical of American policy, are Stephen Ambrose, *Rise to Globalism: American Foreign Policy, 1938–1976* (rev. ed., 1976), Walter LaFeber, *America, Russia, and the Cold War, 1945–1980* (4th ed., 1980), and D. Yergin, *Shattered Peace* (1977). Among the few useful books on the Russian side is Vojtech Mastny, *Russia's Road to the Cold War* (1979). Broader accounts that include discussion of domestic events are Eric Goldman, *The Crucial Decade—and After: America, 1945–1960* (1961), A. L. Hamby, *Beyond the New Deal: Harry S Truman and American Liberalism* (1973), B. J. Bernstein, ed., *Politics and Policies of the Truman Administration* (1970), and Robert J. Donovan, *Conflict and Crisis: The Presidency of Harry S Truman* (1977). Various aspects of foreign policy are analyzed in D. S. Clemens, *Yalta* (1970), C. L. Mee, *Potsdam* (1975), B. Kuklick, *American Policy and the Division of Germany* (1972), T. A. Bailey, *The Marshall Plan Summer* (1978), W. P. Davison, *The Berlin Blockade* (1958), and R. E. Osgood, *NATO: The Entangling Alliance* (1962). The Asian side is treated in Akira Iriye, *The Cold War in Asia* (1974), H. Feis, *The China Tangle* (1953), Tang Tsou, *America's Failure in China, 1941–1950* (1963), F. S. Dunn, *Peace-Making and the Settlement with Japan* (1963), and Kazuo Kawai, *Japan's American Interlude* (1960). On the "Red scare" at home, see R. M. Freeland, *The Truman Doctrine and the Origins of McCarthyism* (1971). Valuable personal reflections by policy-makers include Truman's own *Year of Decisions* (1955) and *Years of Trial and Hope* (1956), G. F. Kennan, *Memoirs, 1925–1950* (1967), Dean Acheson, *Present at the Creation* (1969), and Charles Bohlen, *Witness to History* (1973). They should be supplemented by Hugh De Santis's probing study of the professional foreign service, *The Diplomacy of Silence* (1980). The implications of the election of 1948 are examined in Samuel Lubell, *The Future of American Politics* (1952). Aspects of domestic Communism are developed in D. A. Shannon, *The Decline of American Communism: A History of the Communist Party of the United States since 1945* (1959), Joseph R. Starobin, *American Communism in Crisis, 1943–1957* (1972), and K. M. Schmidt, *Henry A. Wallace: Quixotic Crusade, 1948* (1960).

44

Korea and the Eisenhower Era

The attack upon Korea makes it plain beyond all doubt that Communism has passed beyond the use of subversion to conquer independent nations and will now use armed invasion and war.

HARRY S TRUMAN, June 27, 1950

The Korean Volcano Erupts (1950)

Korea, the Land of the Morning Calm, heralded a new and more ominous phase of the Cold War—a shooting phase—in June 1950.

When Japan collapsed in 1945, Russian troops had accepted the Japanese surrender north of the 38th parallel on the Korean peninsula, and American troops had done likewise south of that line. Both superpowers professed to want the reunification of Korea, but each helped to set up rival regimes above and below the parallel.

By 1949, when the Russians and Americans had both withdrawn their forces, the entire peninsula was a bristling armed camp, with two hostile regimes eyeing each other suspiciously. Secretary of State Acheson seemed to wash his hands of the dispute early in 1950, when he declared in a memorable speech that Korea was outside the essential United States defense perimeter in the Pacific.

The explosion came on June 25, 1950. Spearheaded by Soviet-made tanks, North Korean army columns rumbled across the 38th parallel. Caught flat-footed, the South Korean forces were shoved back southward to a dangerously tiny defensive area around Pusan, their weary backs to the sea.

President Truman sprang quickly into the breach, for he remembered that the old League of Nations had died from inaction. The invasion seemed to provide devastating proof of a fundamental premise in Washington's foreign policy: that even a slight relaxation of America's guard was an invitation to Communist aggression somewhere. Truman took full advantage of temporary Russian absence from the United Nations Security Council on June 25, 1950, when he obtained a unanimous condemnation of North Korea as an aggressor. The Council also called upon all U.N. members, including the United States, to "render every assistance" to restore peace. Two days later, without consulting Congress, Truman ordered American air and naval units to support South Korea. Before the week was out, he also ordered General Douglas MacArthur's Japan-based troops into action alongside the beleaguered South Koreans.

"History Doesn't Repeat Itself." Truman and the U.N. rush to the rescue over the League of Nations' grave. (Low in the London *Daily Herald*, 1950. Reprinted by special permission; world copyright reserved.)

Officially, the United States was simply participating in a United Nations "police action." But in fact the United States made up the overwhelming bulk of the U.N. contingents, and General MacArthur, appointed U.N. commander of the entire operation, took his orders from Washington, not from the Security Council.

The Military Seesaw in Korea

Rather than fight his way out of the southern Pusan perimeter, MacArthur launched a daring amphibious landing behind the enemy's lines at Inchon. This bold gamble, on September 15, 1950, succeeded brilliantly; within two weeks the North Koreans had retreated pell-mell behind the "sanctuary" of the 38th parallel. Truman's avowed intention was to restore South Korea to its former borders, but the pursuing South Koreans had already crossed the 38th parallel, and there seemed little point in permitting the North Koreans to regroup and come again. The U.N. Assembly tacitly authorized a crossing by MacArthur, whom President Truman ordered northward, provided that there was no intervention in force by the Chinese or Soviets.

The Americans thus raised the stakes in Korea, and in so doing, they quickened the fears of another potential player in this dangerous game. Red Chinese spokesmen had publicly warned that they would not sit idly by and watch hostile troops approach the strategic Yalu River boundary between Korea and China. But MacArthur poohpoohed all predictions of an effective intervention by the Chinese, and reportedly boasted that he would "have the boys home by Christmas."

MacArthur guessed wrong. In November 1950 hordes of Chinese "volunteers" fell upon his rashly overextended lines and hurled the U.N. forces reeling back down the peninsula. The fighting now sank into a frostbitten stalemate on the icy terrain near the 38th parallel.

An imperious MacArthur, humiliated by this rout, pressed for drastic retaliation. He favored a blockade of the China coast and bombardment of

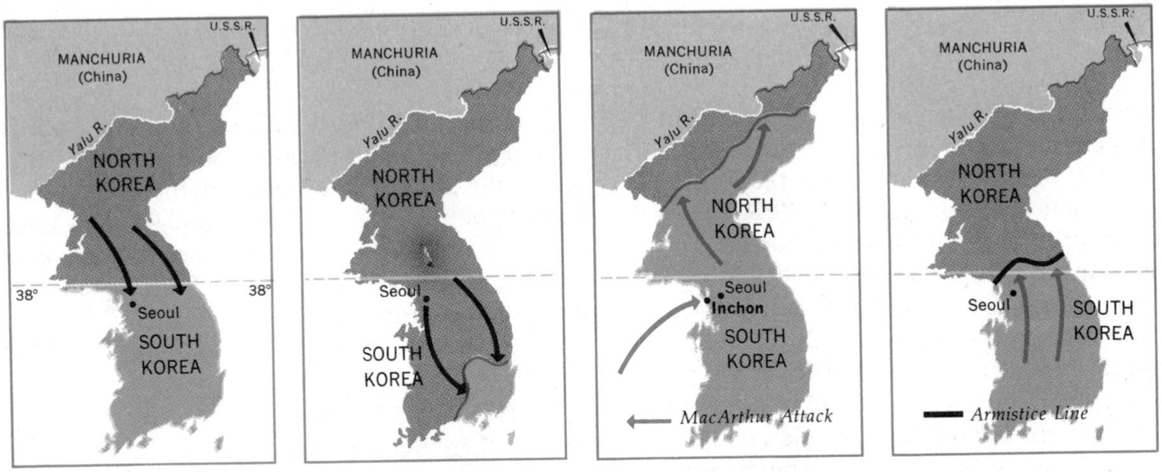

June 25, 1950 | Sept. 14, 1950 | Nov. 25, 1950 | July 27, 1953

THE SHIFTING FRONT IN KOREA

Chinese bases in Manchuria. But Washington policy-makers, with anxious eyes on Russia, refused to enlarge the already costly conflict. The chairman of the joint chiefs of staff declared that a wider clash in Asia would be "the wrong war, at the wrong place, at the wrong time, and with the wrong enemy." Europe, not Asia, was the administration's first concern; and Russia, not China, loomed as the more threatening foe.

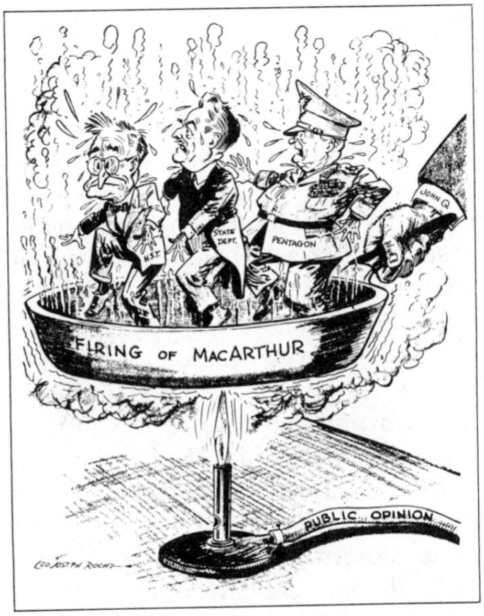

Truman Takes the Heat. (Courtesy, Buffalo *Courier Express;* photo by Barry Donahue.)

Two-fisted General MacArthur felt that he was being asked to fight with one hand tied behind his back. He sneered at the concept of a "limited war," and insisted that "there is no substitute for victory." When the general began to take issue publicly with presidential policies, Truman had no choice but to remove the insubordinate MacArthur from command (April 11, 1951). The imperious war hero returned to an uproarious welcome, while Truman was condemned as a "pig," an "imbecile," a "Judas," and an appeaser of "Communist Russia and Communist China." In July 1951, truce discussions began in a rude field tent near the firing line, but were almost immediately snagged on the issue of prisoner exchange. They dragged on unproductively for nearly two years—while men continued to die.

The Advent of Eisenhower

Democratic prospects in the forthcoming presidential election of 1952 were blighted by the military deadlock, the clash with MacArthur, war-bred inflation, and the whiffs of scandal from the White House. Dispirited Democrats, convening in Chicago, nominated a reluctant Adlai E. Stevenson, the witty, eloquent, and idealistic governor of Illinois. Republicans headed off a determined attempt by the isolationist wing of their party to nominate "Mr. Republican," Ohio Senator Robert

The Republicans' Choice, 1952. Nominee Eisenhower and his vice-presidential running mate Nixon greet the delegates. (Wide World Photos, Inc.)

A. Taft. Instead, they enthusiastically chose General Dwight D. Eisenhower on the first ballot. As something of a concession to the hard-line anti-Communist Taft supporters, the convention selected as "Ike's" running mate California Senator Richard M. Nixon, who had distinguished himself as a merciless Red-hunter.

Eisenhower was already the most popular American of his time, as "I Like Ike" buttons everywhere testified. His ruddy face, captivating grin, and glowing personality made him a perfect candidate in the dawning new age of television politics. He had an authentic hero's credentials as wartime supreme commander of the Allied forces in Europe, army chief of staff after the war, and the first supreme commander of NATO from 1950 to 1952. He had also been "civilianized" by a brief term as president of Columbia University, from 1948 to 1950.

Striking a grandfatherly, non-partisan pose, Eisenhower left the rough campaigning to Nixon, who relished pulling no punches. The vice-presidential candidate lambasted his opponents with charges that they had cultivated corruption, caved in on Korea, and coddled Communists. He particularly blasted the intellectual ("egghead") Stevenson as "Adlai the appeaser," with a "Ph.D. from [Secretary of State] Dean Acheson's College of Cowardly Communist Containment."

Nixon himself faltered when reports surfaced of a secretly financed "slush fund" he had tapped while holding a seat in the Senate. Eisenhower seriously considered dropping him from the ticket, but a scared Nixon went on national television with a theatrical appeal filled with self-pity, during which he referred to the family cocker spaniel,

PRESIDENTIAL ELECTION OF 1952 (with electoral vote by state)
A Democrat quipped that "If the voters liked the Republicans the way they liked Ike, the two-party system would be in bad shape." Fortunately for Democrats, Eisenhower scored a personal, not a party, victory. Republicans won minuscule majorities in Congress, majorities that disappeared in the congressional elections two years later.

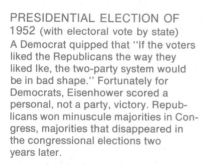

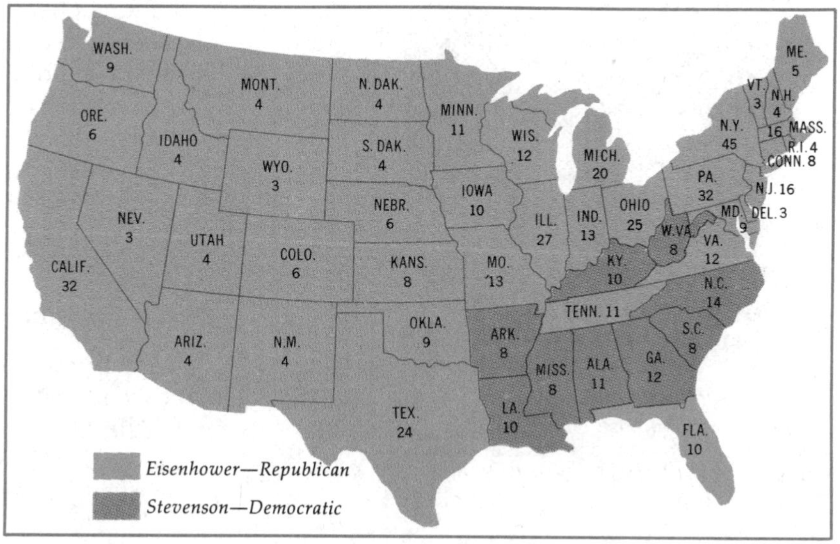

Checkers. This "Checkers speech" was so heart-tugging as to save him his place on the ticket.

The outcome of the presidential election was never really in doubt. Given an extra prod by Eisenhower's last-minute pledge to go personally to Korea to end the war, the voters massively declared for "Ike." He garnered 33,936,234 votes to Stevenson's 27,314,992. He cracked the Solid South wide open, ringing up 442 electoral votes to 89 for his opponent. "Ike" not only ran far ahead of his ticket, but managed to pull enough Republicans into office on his military coattails to insure GOP control of the new Congress by a paper-thin margin.

"Ike" Takes Command

True to his campaign pledge, President-elect Eisenhower undertook a flying three-day visit to Korea in December 1952. But even a glamorous "Ike" could not immediately budge the peace negotiations off dead center. Seven long months later, after Eisenhower had threatened to use atomic weapons, an armistice was finally signed but was repeatedly violated in succeeding decades.

Korean War Scene. Grief-stricken American soldier whose buddy has been killed is being comforted, while a medical corpsman fills out casualty tags. (U.S. Army photograph.)

The brutal and futile fighting had lasted three years. About 54,000 Americans lay dead, joined by perhaps more than a million Chinese, North Koreans, and South Koreans. Tens of billions of American dollars had been poured down the Asian sinkhole. Yet this terrible toll in blood and treasure bought only a return to the conditions of 1950; Korea remained divided at the 38th parallel. Americans took what little comfort they could from the fact that Communism had been "contained" and that the blood-letting had been "limited" to something less than full-scale global war.

With the Korean flames outwardly extinguished, Eisenhower began to gather the reins of government more securely into his hands. His political hero was Herbert Hoover, and he set out to restore the conservative regime of Hoover's day. His Cabinet, critics jibed, consisted of "eight millionaires and a plumber"—and the "plumber," Labor Secretary Martin Durkin, soon resigned. Defense Secretary Charles Wilson, former president of General Motors, declared that "what was good for the country was good for General Motors, and vice versa"—perhaps the most concise statement ever of Big Business Republicanism.

Remembering his military experience, "Ike" proceeded to set up a neat organizational scheme in the White House, relying on his Cabinet and staff much as a general relies on his junior officers. Such a setup, critics charged, had little to do with the political realities of the presidency. Democratic Congressman Sam Rayburn quipped: "No, won't do. Good man, but wrong business."

The Menace of McCarthyism

One of the first problems Eisenhower had to contend with was the swelling popularity and fearful power of Senator Joseph R. McCarthy, the anti-Communist "crusader." McCarthy had burst upon the national scene in February 1950

Exposing "Reds." Senator McCarthy makes a point at the army-McCarthy hearings in 1954 while army counsel Joseph Welch ponders a reply. McCarthy declared in a speech in 1951: "Let me assure you that regardless of how high-pitched becomes the squealing and screaming of those left-wing, bleeding-heart, phony liberals, this battle is going to go on." (United Press International photo.)

when he reportedly charged in a public speech that Secretary of State Dean Acheson was knowingly employing 205 Communist party members in the Department of State. Pressed to reveal the names, McCarthy at first conceded that there were only 57 genuine Communists, and in the end failed to find even one. His Republican colleagues nevertheless realized the political usefulness of this kind of attack on the Democratic administration. Even the supposedly fair-minded Senator Robert Taft urged McCarthy: "If one case doesn't work, try another." Ohio's Senator John Bricker reportedly said, "Joe, you're a dirty s.o.b., but there are times when you've got to have an s.o.b. around, and this is one of them."

McCarthy flourished in the seething Cold War atmosphere of suspicion and fear. He was not the first nor even the most effective anti-Red, but he was the most ruthless, and did the most damage to American traditions of fair play and free speech. Elected to the Senate on the basis of a trumped-up war-hero record ("Congress needs a tail-gunner"), McCarthy was just an obscure junior senator until he exploded his bombshell announcement in 1950 of Communists in the State Department. For the next four years "low-blow Joe" proved a master at manipulating the media and playing upon the anxieties of politicians and the public. The careers of countless officials, writers, actors, and others were ruined after McCarthy had "named" them, often unfairly, as Communists or Communist sympathizers.

As McCarthy's accusations spread ever more widely, his rhetoric grew bolder. Democrats, he charged, "bent to the whispered pleas from the lips of traitors." General George Marshall, former army chief of staff and ex–secretary of state, was denounced as "part of a conspiracy so immense and an infamy so black as to dwarf any previous venture in the history of man."

Statesmen trembled in the face of such onslaughts, especially when opinion polls showed that a majority of the American people approved of McCarthy. Further, his intervention in certain key senatorial elections brought resounding defeat for his enemies. Eisenhower at first tried to stay out of McCarthy's way, saying, "I will not get in the gutter with that guy." Trying to appease the brash demagogue from Wisconsih, Eisenhower allowed him, in effect, to control personnel policy at the State Department. One baleful result was severe damage to the morale and effectiveness of the professional Foreign Service.

McCarthy finally bent the bow too far. The nominal end of the Korean War partly cooled the feverish atmosphere in which he had thrived. When

Curiously, the Senate "condemned" McCarthy, not for assailing fellow Americans, but for failing to cooperate with a Senate investigating committee regarding matters which "affected the honor of the Senate and instead, repeatedly abused members who were trying to carry out assigned duties, thereby obstructing the constitutional processes of the Senate. . . ." On the other hand, a Fort Worth, Texas, newspaper wrote, "Joe McCarthy was slowly tortured to death by the pimps of the Kremlin."

he attacked the United States army, he at last met his match. The embattled military men fought back in thirty-five days of televised hearings in the spring of 1954. Up to 20 million Americans at a time watched in fascination as a boorish, surly McCarthy publicly cut his own throat by parading his essential meanness and irresponsibility. A few months later the Senate formally condemned him for "conduct unbecoming a member."

Three years later, unwept and unsung, McCarthy died. But "McCarthyism" has passed into the English language as a label for the dangerous forces of unfairness and fear that a democratic society can unleash only at its peril. The senator actually hurt his alleged cause by causing Americans to be more afraid of the supposed Communists in their midst than of the real Communists in Moscow.

The Blacks Surge Forward

Black Americans had racked up only a few minor gains since New Deal days. President Truman in 1948 had ended segregation in the federal service and had ordered "equality of treatment and opportunity" in the armed forces. The military brass had at first protested that "the army is not a sociological laboratory," but manpower shortages in Korea forced the integration of combat units, without the predicted loss of effectiveness. Yet Congress stubbornly resisted passing civil rights legislation, and President Eisenhower showed no real signs of interest in the racial issue. Within the government, initiative thus passed to the Supreme Court.

Breaking the path for civil rights advances was broad-jawed Chief Justice Earl Warren, former governor of California. Elevated to the Supreme Bench by Eisenhower, Warren shocked the President and other traditionalists with his active judicial intervention in previously tabooed social issues. Publicly snubbed and privately criticized by Eisenhower, Warren persisted in encouraging the Court to apply his straightforward populist principles to its interpretation of the Constitution: in short, legislation by the judiciary, in default of legislation by Congress.

The unanimous decision of the Warren Court in *Brown* v. *Board of Education of Topeka, Kansas* in May 1954 was epochal. In a forceful opinion, the learned justices ruled that segregation in the public schools was "inherently unequal" and thus unconstitutional. The uncompromising sweep of the decision startled conservatives like an exploding time bomb, for it reversed a decision of the Supreme Court in 1896. Desegregation, the justices insisted, must go ahead with "all deliberate speed."

The Border States generally made reasonable efforts to comply with this ruling, but in the Deep

In the desegregation decision of 1954, the Supreme Court quoted approvingly from a lower court: "Segregation of white and colored children in public schools has a detrimental effect upon the colored children. The impact is greater when it has the sanction of the law; for the policy of separating the races is usually interpreted as denoting the inferiority of the Negro group. A sense of inferiority affects the motivation of a child to learn. Segregation . . . has a tendency to retard the educational and mental development of Negro children. . . ."

South die-hards organized "massive resistance" against the Court's attack on the sacred principle of "separate but equal." More than 100 southern congressmen and senators signed a "Declaration of Constitutional Principles" in 1956, pledging their unyielding resistance to desegregation. Several states diverted public funds to hastily created "private" schools, for there the integration order was more difficult to apply. Throughout the South, White Citizens' Councils, sometimes with fire and hemp, thwarted attempts to make integration a reality. Ten years after the Court's momentous ruling, fewer than 2 percent of the eligible blacks in the Deep South states were sitting in classrooms with whites.

Integration at Little Rock. A white mob jeers angrily at the first black students entering Central High School, 1957. (Wide World Photos, Inc.)

Crisis at Little Rock

The Eisenhower administration was little inclined toward promoting integration. But in September 1957, "Ike" was forced to act. Orval Faubus, Arkansas governor, mobilized the National Guard to prevent nine black students from enrolling in Little Rock's Central High School. Faced with this direct challenge to federal authority, Eisenhower sent in troops to escort the children to their classrooms.

In the same year (1957) Congress passed the first Civil Rights Act since Reconstruction days. It set up a permanent Civil Rights Commission to investigate violations of civil rights, and authorized federal injunctions to protect voting rights. A feeble piece of legislation, this act was only tepidly endorsed by President Eisenhower, who did not believe that mere laws could change people's hearts.

Blacks meanwhile had been taking the civil rights movement into their own hands. On a historic day in December 1955, Mrs. Rosa Parks, a

Martin Luther King, Jr., and His Wife Coretta Arrested. King and his wife were arrested for the first time in Montgomery, Alabama, in 1955 while organizing a bus boycott. (Charles Moore, Black Star.)

college-educated black seamstress, boarded a bus in Montgomery, Alabama, took a seat in the "whites only" section, and refused to give it up. The incident touched off a year-long black boycott of the city buses, while catapulting to prominence the chief organizer, the Reverend Martin Luther King, Jr. The discipline and dignity of the boycotters, plus the inspirational leadership of Martin Luther King, Jr., heralded a new era of confidence and power for the South's restive blacks.

Eisenhower Republicanism at Home

The balding, sixty-two-year-old General Eisenhower had entered the White House in 1953 pledging his administration to a philosophy of "dynamic conservatism." "In all those things which deal with people, be liberal, be human," he advised. But when it came to "people's money, or their economy, or their form of government, be conservative." Observers noted that this balanced, middle-of-the-road course harmonized with the depression-haunted and war-weary mood of the times. Some critics condemned "Ike's" presidency as a case of "the bland leading the bland."

Above all, Eisenhower strove to balance the federal budget and guard the Republic from what he called "creeping socialism." His budget-chopping ax fell painfully on the necks of 183,000 federal employees, and on certain red-inked sections of Truman's proposed budget. True to his small-government philosophy, Eisenhower supported the transfer of control over offshore oil fields from the federal government to the states. "Ike" also tried to curb the TVA by encouraging a private power company to build a generating plant to compete with the massive public utility spawned by the New Deal. Speaking of the TVA, Eisenhower reportedly said, "By God, if ever we could do it, before we leave here, I'd like to see us *sell* the whole thing, but I suppose we can't go that far." "Ike's" secretary of health, education, and welfare condemned free distribution of Salk anti-polio vaccine as "socialized medicine." Secretary of Agriculture Ezra Taft Benson grappled manfully with the soaring costs of farm price supports. Yet prosperity remained beyond the next furrow for most farmers, despite mountains of surplus grain, bought by the government and stored in silo-shaped containers at a cost to taxpayers of nearly $2 million a day. Benson tried to get the government off the farm and return to "free-market" conditions—but he only succeeded in spending more money than any previous secretary of agriculture.

A Popular President. "Ike" exuded grandfatherly goodwill. (Dwight D. Eisenhower Library.)

Eisenhower Republicans obviously could not unscramble all the eggs that had been fried by New Dealers and Fair Dealers for twenty long years. In many ways, "Ike" accepted and even advanced New Dealish programs. During his presidency, Social Security benefits were extended and the minimum wage raised to $1.00 an hour. In a public works project that dwarfed anything the New Deal had ever dreamed of, Eisenhower also backed a $27 billion plan to build 42,000 miles (67,600 kilometers) of sleek, fast, interstate highways.

Despite his good intentions, Eisenhower managed to balance the budget only three times in his eight years in office, and in 1959 he incurred the biggest peacetime deficit thus far in American history. Yet critics blamed his fiscal timidity for aggravating several business recessions during the decade, especially the sharp downturn of 1957–1958, which left more than 5 million workers jobless. Economic troubles helped to revive the Democrats, who regained control of both houses of Congress in 1954. Unemployment jitters also helped to spark the merger of the AF of L and the CIO in 1955.

A "New Look" in Foreign Policy

Mere "containment" of Communism was condemned in the 1952 Republican platform as "negative, futile and immoral." Incoming Secretary of State John Foster Dulles promised not merely to stem the Red tide but to "roll back" its gains and "liberate captive peoples." At the same time, the new administration promised to balance the budget by cutting military spending.

How were these two contradictory goals to be reached? Dulles answered with a "policy of boldness" in early 1954. The genial General Eisenhower would relegate the army and the navy to the back seat and build up an air fleet of super-bombers with city-busting nuclear bombs. These fearsome weapons would be equipped to inflict "massive retaliation" on the Russians if they got out of hand. The advantages of this new policy were thought to be its paralyzing nuclear impact and its cheaper price tag when compared with conventional forces—"more bang for the buck."

"Do These Men Look Like Slave Workers?" A view of Russia's Khrushchev. (Little in the Nashville *Tennessean.* By permission.)

Both aspects of the touted "new look" in foreign policy were delusions. In 1956 the Hungarians rose up against their Soviet masters, and appealed in vain to the United States for aid. Embittered Hungarian freedom fighters naturally accused Uncle Sam of "welshing" when the chips were down. To his dismay, Eisenhower also discovered that the aerial and atomic hardware necessary for "massive retaliation" was staggeringly expensive. Military costs shot skyward. In 1960, as Eisenhower was about to leave office, he sagely but ironically warned against the dangerous growth of a "military-industrial complex" that his own policies had nurtured.

The Vietnamese Nightmare

Europe, thanks to the Marshall Plan and NATO, seemed reasonably secure by the early 1950s, but East Asia was a different can of worms. Nationalist movements had sought for years to throw off the French colonial yoke in Indochina. The Vietnamese leader, goateed Ho Chi Minh, had tried to appeal personally to Woodrow Wilson in Paris as early as 1919 to support self-determination for the peoples of Southeast Asia. Franklin Roosevelt had likewise inspired hope among Asian nationalists.

Cold War events dampened the dreams of anticolonial Asian peoples. Their leaders—including Ho Chi Minh—became increasingly Communist while the United States became increasingly anti-Communist. By 1954, American taxpayers were financing nearly 80 percent of the costs of a bottomless French colonial war in Indochina. Uncle Sam's share amounted to about $1 billion a year.

Despite this massive aid, French forces continued to crumble under guerrilla onslaughts. In March 1954, a key French garrison was trapped hopelessly in the fortress of Dien Bien Phu. The new "policy of boldness" was now put to the test.

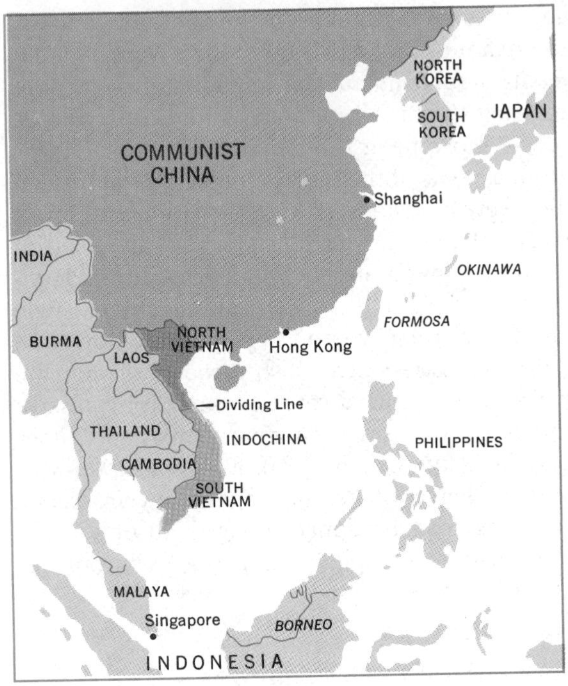

THE FAR EAST, 1955–1956

Secretary Dulles, Vice-President Nixon, and the chairman of the joint chiefs of staff favored intervention with American bombers to help bail out the beleaguered French. But Eisenhower, correctly fearing British non-support, held back.

Dien Bien Phu fell, and a multi-nation conference at Geneva roughly halved the two Vietnams at the 17th parallel, supposedly temporarily. The victorious Ho Chi Minh in the north consented to this arrangement on the assurance that Vietnam-wide elections would be held within two years. In the south, a pro-Western government under Ngo Dinh Diem was soon entrenched at Saigon. The Vietnamese never held the promised elections, primarily because the Communists seemed certain to win, and Vietnam remained a dangerously divided country.

Eisenhower promised economic and military aid to the conservative Diem regime, provided that it undertook certain social reforms. Change came at a snail's pace, but American aid continued, as Communist guerrillas heated up their campaign against Diem. The Americans had evidently backed a losing horse, but could see no easy way to call off their bet. Secretary Dulles, in a vain attempt to prop up his shaky policy in Vietnam, engineered the organization of the eight-member Southeast Asia Treaty Organization (SEATO), including the United States, Britain, and France. Pieced together in late 1954, it was but a pale imitation of NATO and, as events were to prove, a frail prop on which to lean for the security of South Vietnam.

A False Lull in Europe

The United States had initially backed the French in Indochina, in part to win French approval of a plan to rearm Western Germany. Despite French fears, the Germans were finally welcomed into the NATO fold in 1955, with an expected contribution of half a million troops. In the same year, the East European countries and the Soviets signed the Warsaw Pact, creating a Red military counterweight to the newly bolstered NATO forces in the West.

Despite these hardening military lines, the Cold War seemed to be thawing a bit in 1955. In May the Soviets rather surprisingly agreed to end the occupation of Austria, though only after exacting a stiff price. A summit conference in July produced little progress on the burning issues, but it bred a conciliatory "spirit of Geneva" that caused a modest blush of optimism to pass over the face of the Western world. Hopes rose further the next year when Soviet Communist party boss Nikita Khrushchev, a burly ex–coal miner, publicly denounced the bloody excesses of Joseph Stalin, the dictator dead since 1953.

Violent events late in 1956 ended the post-Geneva lull. When the liberty-loving Hungarians struck for their freedom, they were ruthlessly overpowered by Soviet tanks. While the Western world looked on in horror, Budapest was turned into a slaughterhouse, and thousands of refugees fled in panic for the Austrian border. The United States eventually altered its immigration laws to admit 30,000 Hungarian fugitives.

Storm over Suez

The Suez crisis proved even more explosive than that in Hungary. President Nasser of Egypt, an ardent Arab nationalist, was seeking funds to build an immense dam on the upper Nile for urgently needed irrigation and power. America and Britain tentatively offered financial help, but when Nasser began to flirt openly with the Communist camp, Secretary of State Dulles dramatically withdrew the dam offer. Thus slapped in the face, Nasser promptly regained face by nationalizing the Suez Canal, owned chiefly by British and French stockholders.

Nasser's stroke placed a razor's edge at the jugular vein of Western Europe's oil supply. Secretary Dulles labored strenuously to ward off armed intervention, which was forbidden by the U.N. charter. But America's apprehensive British and French allies, after deliberately keeping Washington in the dark and coordinating their blow with one from Israel, staged a joint assault on Egypt late in October 1956. They were evidently determined to internationalize the canal and eliminate Nasser as a potential Middle Eastern Hitler.

For a breathless week the world teetered on the edge of the abyss. President Eisenhower, reluctantly siding against Britain and France, honored the non-aggression commitment of the U.N. charter and supported a cease-fire resolution. Russia, which for once voted with the Americans, threatened to pour "volunteers" into Egypt. Bending to such pressures, Britain, France, and Israel resentfully withdrew their troops, and for the first time in history a U.N. police contingent was sent to maintain order.

As the United Nations emerged with new laurels, the North Atlantic Treaty Organization (NATO) tottered. Britain and France were angered by America's willingness to turn against old friends and join the Soviet "butchers of Budapest." The United States, irritated by the behind-the-back aggression of its NATO allies, rather grudgingly supplied them with oil during the five months when the Suez Canal was being cleared of sunken ships.

Increasing Communist pressures on the oil-rich Middle East prompted Washington to seek a new protective parasol. The instrument seized upon was the so-called Eisenhower Doctrine, approved overwhelmingly by Congress in March 1957. It formally empowered the President to extend economic and military aid to the nations of the Middle East, provided that they desired it and were threatened by aggression from a Communist-controlled country.

Secretary Dulles, determined "to go to the brink," took a strong position in the Far East as well as in the Middle East in 1958. Chinese Communists began to shell the tiny Nationalist-held island of Quemoy, to which Chiang Kai-shek had rashly committed about one-third of his entire Formosan army. Washington, brandishing the big stick of the Seventh Fleet, backed him in his determination to hang on. At the same time, Dulles partially quieted Communist fears by flying to Formosa and inducing Chiang to renounce the use of force in regaining the Chinese mainland.

The Voters Still Like "Ike" in 1956

Blood-spattered Budapest and Suez provided the backdrop for the elections of 1956. Despite a heart attack in 1955 and a major abdominal operation in 1956, Eisenhower still enjoyed the public's confidence and affection. He and Vice-President Nixon were unanimously renominated by a jubilant Republican convention in San Francisco. Democrats, for their part, dutifully offered up Adlai Stevenson for a second time. Voters were thus presented with two warmed-over candidates—the first such match-up since 1900.

Democrats charged that the only order the magnetic ex-general had ever given was to mark time. They carped at Republican stand-pattism, at Eisenhower's shaky health (though Stevenson was

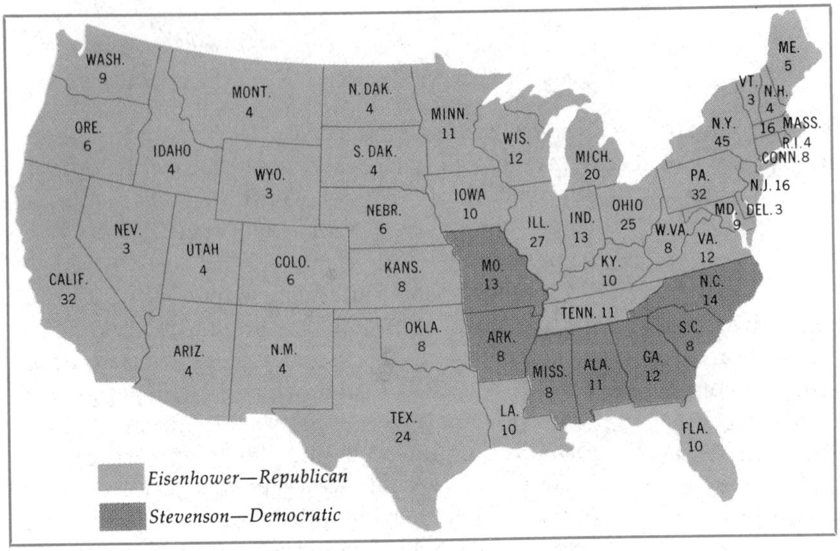

PRESIDENTIAL ELECTION OF 1956 (with electoral vote by state)
Eisenhower made even deeper inroads than he had in 1952 into the traditional bastion of Democratic strength, the once-solid South. Louisiana went Republican for the first time since Reconstruction days in 1876.

to die first), and at the dubious moral character of "Tricky Dick" Nixon. In response, the GOP preened itself on being the party of peace, prosperity, and happiness. The biggest Republican asset remained "Ike's" irrepressible grin.

The election was a resounding personal endorsement of Eisenhower. He piled up an enormous majority of 35,590,472 votes to Stevenson's 26,022,752; in the Electoral College the count was 457 to 73. "Any jockey would look good riding Ike," crowed the GOP national chairman. But the general's coattails this time were not so stiff or so broad. He failed to win for his party either house of Congress—the first time since Zachary Taylor's election in 1848 that a winning President had left such a losing ticket behind him. The country remained heavily Democratic; but Eisenhower remained widely beloved. Voters were especially reluctant to abandon the old war-horse when events abroad threatened to spark off World War III at a push of the button.

Round Two for "Ike"

In fragile health, Eisenhower began his second term as a part-time President. Critics charged that he had his hands on his golf clubs, fly rod, and shotgun more often than on the levers of power. He seemed to rely more than ever on trusted lieutenants like Secretary of State Dulles and presidential assistant Sherman Adams, the tough-minded ex-governor of New Hampshire who had publicly condemned Democratic corruption.

Adams' chickens came home to roost in 1958, when a House investigation revealed that he had accepted expensive gifts from a Boston industrialist, on whose behalf he had thrice mildly interceded with federal agencies. Adams was forced to leave the White House under a dark cloud of scandal. Secretary Dulles, who had traveled half a million miles by air, died of cancer in 1959. His successor, Christian A. Herter, did not enjoy the President's confidence to the same degree. Shorn of his two most trusted aides, "Ike" in his last years did less golfing and more governing.

A key area in which the President bestirred himself was labor legislation. A drastic labor-reform bill in 1959 grew out of recurrent strikes in critical industries and scandalous revelations of gangsterism in high unionist echelons. In particular, fraud and brass-knuckle tactics tainted the Teamsters Union. The millionaire Teamster chief, "Dave" Beck, invoked the Fifth Amendment against self-incrimination 209 times before a Senate investigating committee in 1957 to avoid telling what he had done with $320,000. He was later sentenced to prison for embezzlement. When his union defiantly elected the tough-fisted James

R. Hoffa as his successor, the AF of L–CIO expelled the Teamsters. The Senate committee finally reported that in fifteen years union officials had stolen or misappropriated some $10 million. Hoffa later was jailed for jury tampering, served a part of his sentence, and then disappeared—evidently the victim of the gangsters with whom he had consorted.

Legislation was clearly needed to prevent collective bargaining from becoming collective bludgeoning. Teamster boss Hoffa threatened to defeat for re-election those congressmen who dared to vote for a "tough" labor bill. Eisenhower responded with a dramatic television appeal, and Congress in 1959 passed the Landrum-Griffin Act. It was designed to bring labor leaders to book for financial shenanigans and to prevent bully-boy tactics. Seizing the opportune moment, anti-laborites also forced into the bill prohibitions against "secondary boycotts" and certain kinds of picketing.

The Race with Russia into Space

Soviet scientists astounded the world on October 4, 1957, by lofting into orbit around the globe a beep-beeping "baby moon" (Sputnik I), weighing 184 pounds (83.5 kilograms). A month later they topped their own ace by sending aloft a larger satellite (Sputnik II), weighing 1,120 pounds (507 kilograms) and carrying a dog.

This amazing scientific breakthrough shattered American self-confidence. The Soviets had long been trying to convince the uncommitted nations that the shortcut to superior industrial production lay through Communism—and the Sputniks bolstered their claim. America had seemingly taken a back seat in scientific achievement. Envious "backward" nations laughed at Uncle Sam's discomfiture, all the more so because the Soviets were occupying outer space while American troops were occupying the high school in Little Rock.

Military implications of these man-made satellites proved sobering. If the Russians could fire heavy objects into outer space, they certainly could reach America with intercontinental ballistic missiles. Old-soldier Eisenhower, adopting a father-knows-best attitude toward the Soviet "gimmick," remarked that it should not cause "one iota" of concern. Others, chiefly Republicans, blamed the Truman administration for having spent more for supporting peanuts than for supporting a missile program at an early date. Agonizing soul-searching led to the conclusion that while the United States was well advanced on a broad scientific front, including color television, the Soviets had gone all-out for rocketry. Experts testified that America's manned bombers were still a powerful deterrent, but heroic efforts were needed if the alleged "missile gap" was not to widen.

"Rocket fever" swept the nation. After humiliating and well-advertised failures (the Russians concealed theirs), the Americans regained some prestige four months after the initial Soviet triumph. They managed to put into orbit a grapefruit-sized satellite weighing 2.5 pounds (1.14 kilograms).

The Sputnik spur led to a critical comparison of the American educational system, already under fire as too easygoing, with that of the Soviet Union. A strong move developed to replace "frills" with solid subjects—to substitute square root for square dancing. Congress rejected demands for federal scholarships, but late in 1958 the National Defense and Education Act (NDEA) authorized $887 million in loans to needy college students and in grants for the improvement of teaching the sciences and languages. Exploring space between the ears seemed necessary if America was going to "catch up with the Russians" in exploring outer space.

Nuclear Bombs, Lebanon, and Berlin

The fantastic race toward nuclear annihilation continued unabated. Emboldened by his Sputniks, Premier Khrushchev boasted openly that he would shower rockets on America. Humanity-minded scientists urged that nuclear tests be stopped before the atmosphere became so polluted as to produce generations of deformed monsters. The Soviets, after completing an intensive series of exceptionally "dirty" tests, proclaimed a suspension in March 1958, and urged the Western world to follow. Beginning in October 1958, Washington did halt both underground and atmospheric testing. But all attempts to regularize such suspensions by proper inspection sank on the reef of mutual suspicions. "Bargain-basement bombs" were meanwhile in the making, with every prospect that lesser powers would soon join the exclusive nuclear club.

Thermonuclear suicide seemed nearer in July 1958, when both Egyptian and Communist plottings threatened to engulf Western-oriented Lebanon. After its president had called for aid under the Eisenhower Doctrine, the United States boldly landed several thousand troops (ultimately about 14,000) and helped restore order without taking a single life. This energetic action, in the teeth of Soviet condemnation and threats, served notice that Washington was unwilling to travel the well-rutted road to appeasement.

Khrushchev, no doubt feeling his missile-muscles, deliberately provoked an even more ominous crisis over Berlin—"a bone in the throat," he said—in November 1958. Annoyed by this pro-Western oasis in a Communist desert, he gave the three Western powers (Britain, France, the United States) six months in which to pull their troops out of West Berlin. The Soviet East German satellite would then take over, and if the West resisted, Moscow would rush to the aid of its puppet. This could only mean World War III. But Eisenhower and Dulles, again remembering the perils of appeasement, staunchly refused to yield well-established rights. The six-month deadline passed almost unnoticed.

In a radio-television address, at the time of the Lebanon invasion, Eisenhower said: "I am well aware of the fact that landing . . . troops . . . could have some serious consequences. That is why this step was taken only after the most serious consideration and broad consultation. . . . It was required to support the principles of justice and international law upon which peace and a stable international order depend."

Goodwill Diplomacy and the Spy Plane

Eisenhower took his cue from the highly publicized tours of Khrushchev when he embarked upon a whirlwind, eleven-nation, goodwill trip in December 1959, all the way from Europe to India. Early in 1960 he staged a repeat performance in Latin America. Grinning his way through showers of confetti and shouts of "Eekay" (Ike), he scored a great personal triumph. He no doubt generated goodwill, but Democratic critics charged that stagecraft was no substitute for statecraft.

The burly Khrushchev, seeking new propaganda laurels, was eager to meet with Eisenhower and pave the way for a "summit conference" with Western leaders. Despite grave misgivings as to any tangible results, the President invited him to America in 1959. Arriving in New York, Khrushchev appeared before the U.N. General Assembly and dramatically resurrected the ancient Soviet proposal of complete disarmament. But he offered no practical means of achieving this end. He then journeyed out to the Pacific Coast and returned by way of Iowa, where he approvingly patted a prize pig. But the smiling, kewpie-doll exterior concealed a steely, bellicose interior, which occasionally erupted in bullying denunciations.

A noteworthy result of this tour was a meeting at Camp David, the President's rustic retreat in Maryland. Khrushchev emerged saying that his ultimatum for the evacuation of Berlin would be extended indefinitely. The relieved world gave prayerful but premature thanks for the "spirit of Camp David."

The Paris "summit conference," scheduled for May 1960, turned out to be an incredible fiasco.

"What's So Funny?" Premier Khrushchev gloats over Ike's spying discomfiture. (Copyright 1960 by Herblock in *The Washington Post.*)

Both Moscow and Washington had publicly taken a firm stand on the burning Berlin issue, and neither could risk a public backdown. Then, on the eve of the conference, an American U–2 spy plane was shot down deep in the heart of Russia. After bungling bureaucratic denials in Washington, "honest Ike" took the unprecedented step of assuming personal responsibility. Professing to be insulted by his "fishy friend," Khrushchev stormed into Paris filling the air with invective. He demanded that Eisenhower not only apologize for the spy flights but punish those responsible for them. The President obviously would not punish himself, so the conference collapsed before it could get off the ground.

Khrushchev's "diplomacy by tantrum" virtually ended Eisenhower's "diplomacy by goodwill tour." Moscow abruptly canceled its invitation to Eisenhower to visit Russia. Violent demonstrations in Japan forced the President, with much loss of face, to abandon a trip to the Flowery Kingdom during his Far Eastern tour. America's slipping prestige thus received yet another body blow.

Cuba's Castroism Spells Communism

An ill-timed "goodwill" tour by Vice-President Nixon through South America in 1958 reaped a harvest of spit and spite. After being stoned, spat upon, and shouted down at Lima (Peru), Nixon narrowly escaped serious injury from a mob in Caracas (Venezuela). Decent Latin Americans were apologetic, but one of their leaders explained that since the masses could not vent their anger by spitting on the United States, they spat on the Vice-President of the United States. Latin Americans bitterly resented Uncle Sam's lavishing billions of dollars on Europe, while doling out only millions to the poor relations to the south. Liberals everywhere were outraged by Washington's willingness to support—even decorate—bloody dictators who would insure the sanctity of dollar investments.

Most ominous of all was the Communist beachhead in Cuba. The iron-fisted dictator Batista had encouraged huge investments of American capital, and Washington in turn had given him some support. When black-bearded Dr. Fidel Castro engineered a revolution early in 1959, he denounced the Yankee imperialists and began to expropriate valuable American properties in pursuing a land-distribution program. Washington, finally losing patience, released Cuba from "imperialistic slavery" by cutting off the heavy imports of Cuban sugar. Castro retaliated against this "imperialistic aggression" with further wholesale confiscations of Yankee property, and in effect made his left-wing dictatorship an economic and military satellite of Moscow. Washington broke diplomatic relations with Cuba early in 1961.

"We Stand on Our Own Two Feet." Soviets support Castro. (Don Hesse in the St. Louis *Globe-Democrat.*)

Americans talked seriously of invoking the Monroe Doctrine before the Russians set up a Communist base only 90 miles (145 kilometers) from their shores. Khrushchev angrily proclaimed that the Monroe Doctrine was dead, and indicated that he would shower missiles upon the United States if it attacked his good friend Castro.

The Cuban revolution, which Castro sought to "export" to his neighbors, brought other significant responses. At San José, Costa Rica, in August 1960, the United States induced the Organization of American States to condemn (unenthusiastically) Communist infiltration into the Americas. President Eisenhower, whom Castro dubbed "the senile White House golfer," hastily proposed a long-deferred "Marshall Plan" for Latin America. Congress responded to his recommendation with an initial authorization of $500 million. The Latin Americans had Castro to thank for attention which many of them regarded as too little and too late.

The "Kitchen Debate." Vice-President Nixon, on a goodwill visit, and Soviet Premier Khrushchev wage an impromptu discussion on the nature of free government at the American exhibition in Moscow, 1959. (Photograph by Elliott Erwitt, Magnum Photos, Inc.)

Kennedy Challenges Nixon for the Presidency

Republicans faced up to the presidential campaign of 1960 without great optimism, for they had taken a bad beating in the mid-term congressional elections of 1958. Voters had been especially disturbed by the recession of 1957–1958, farm problems, and foreign tensions. Not only had the Republicans suffered the heaviest losses in the history of Senate elections, but the casualties were especially heavy among ultra-conservative Republican senators. A crestfallen Eisenhower was dismayed that his "New Republicanism" had not taken root.

Vice-President Nixon was the Republican heir apparent. To many, he was a gifted party leader; to others, a ruthless opportunist. The "old" Nixon had been a no-holds-barred campaigner, especially in assailing Democrats and left-wingers. The "new" Nixon was represented as a mature, seasoned statesman. More in the limelight than any earlier Vice-President, he had shouldered heavy new responsibilities and had traveled globally as a "trouble shooter" in various capacities. He had vigorously defended American democracy in a famous "kitchen debate" with Khrushchev in Moscow in 1959. His supporters, flourishing a telling photograph of this finger-pointing episode, claimed that he alone knew how to "stand up to" the Russians.

Liberal and personable Governor Nelson A. Rockefeller of New York had thrown his hat into the ring, but had withdrawn it in the face of strong support by the "regulars" for the safe-and-sane Nixon. But the Rockefeller revolt did force a more liberal platform upon the Republican convention, to the acute dissatisfaction of the stand-pat wing of the party. Nixon was nominated unanimously on the first ballot in Chicago. His running mate was handsome Henry Cabot Lodge, Jr., of Massachusetts (grandson of Woodrow Wilson's arch-foe), who had served conspicuously for seven years as American representative to the United Nations.

By contrast, the Democratic race for the presidential nomination started as a free-for-all. Supporters of Adlai Stevenson cried, "We're Madly for Adlai," but hard-headed politicians shied away from a two-time loser. John F. Kennedy, a tall (6 feet; 1.83 meters), youthful, dark-haired, and tooth-flashing millionaire senator from Massachusetts, won impressive victories in the primaries. He then scored a first-ballot triumph in Los Angeles over his closest rival, Senator Lyndon B. Johnson, the Senate majority leader from Texas. A disappointed South was not completely appeased when Johnson accepted second place on the ticket in an eleventh-hour marriage of convenience. Kennedy's challenging acceptance speech called upon the American people for sacrifices to achieve their potential greatness, which he hailed as the New Frontier.

The Presidential Issues of 1960

Bigotry, as was inevitable, showed its snarling face. Senator Kennedy was a Roman Catholic, the first to be nominated since Al Smith's ill-starred campaign in 1928. Smear artists revived the ancient charges about the Pope's controlling the White House. Kennedy pointed to his fourteen years of service in Congress, denied that he would be swayed by Rome, and asked if some 40 million Catholic Americans were to be condemned to second-class citizenship from birth.

Kennedy's Catholicism aroused misgivings in the Protestant, Bible-belt South, which was ordinarily Democratic. "I fear Catholicism more than I fear Communism," declaimed one Baptist minister in North Carolina. But the religious issue largely canceled itself out. If many Southern Democrats supported Nixon because of Kennedy's Catholicism, many Northern Republicans supported Kennedy because of the bitter attacks on their Catholic faith.

Also vital was the international crisis, which focused attention on the "experience" of the candidates. Republicans harped on the fact that both Nixon and Lodge were old hands at talking back to Moscow. (Slogan: "They Understand What Peace Demands.") The forty-seven-year-old Nixon emphasized the youth, immaturity, and naiveté of his forty-three-year-old opponent.

Kennedy struck back by attacking the do-

> Candidate Kennedy, in a speech to a Houston group of Protestant ministers (Sept. 12, 1960), declared, "I believe in an America where the separation of church and state is absolute—where no Catholic prelate would tell the President, should he be a Catholic, how to act, and no Protestant minister would tell his parishioners for whom to vote . . . and where no man is denied public office because his religion differs from the President who might appoint him or the people who might elect him."

John F. Kennedy Campaigning for the Presidency, 1960.
(Photograph by Henri Dauman, Magnum Photos, Inc.)

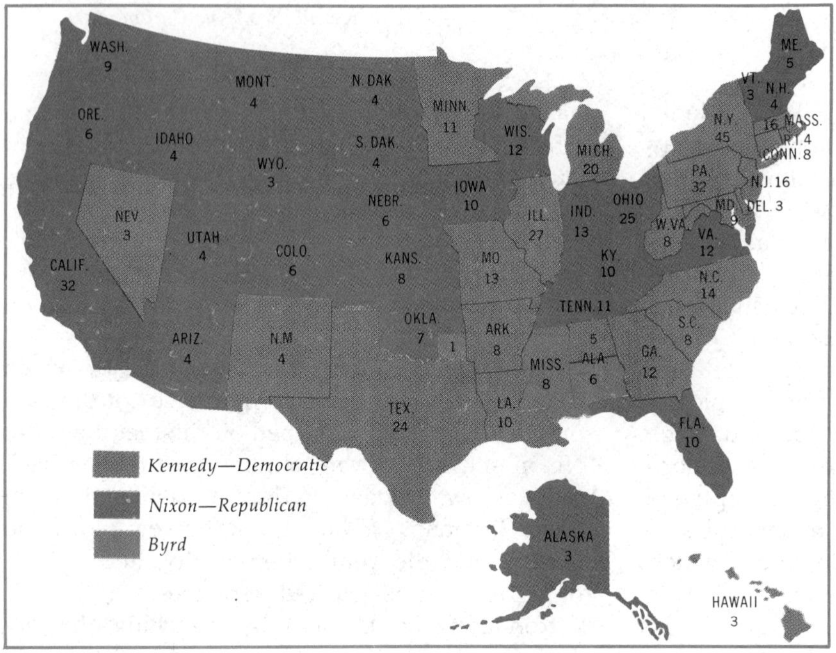

PRESIDENTIAL ELECTION OF 1960 (with electoral vote by state) Kennedy owed his hairbreadth triumph to his victories in 26 of the 40 largest cities—and to Lyndon Johnson's strenuous campaigning in the South, where Kennedy's Catholic religion may have been a hotter issue than his stand on civil rights.

nothingism of the Eisenhower administration in the face of alarming Soviet progress. He insisted that the Russians, with their nuclear bombs and Sputniks, had gained on America in prestige and power. Nixon, forced to defend the dying administration, replied that the nation's prestige had not slipped, although Kennedy was causing it to do so by his unpatriotic talk. The aged but amazingly energetic Eisenhower, stung by these gloom-and-doom reflections on his stewardship, took to the stump in the closing days of the campaign. He thereby prompted the Democrats to charge that he was trying to carry Nixon "piggyback" into the White House.

Television may well have tipped the scales. Nixon agreed to meet Kennedy in four so-called debates—probably a strategic error. The little-known senator may have gained just by showing up to share the huge viewing audience the Vice-President commanded. The contestants crossed words in millions of living rooms before audiences estimated at 60 million or more. Nobody "won" the debates. But Kennedy at least held his own and did not suffer by comparison with the more "experienced" Nixon. Many viewers found Kennedy's glamor and vitality far more appealing than Nixon's tired and pallid appearance.

Kennedy squeezed through by the rather comfortable margin of 303 electoral votes to 219, but with the breathtakingly close popular margin of only 118,574 votes out of over 68 million cast. Like Franklin Roosevelt, Kennedy ran well in the large industrial centers, where he had strong support from laborites, Catholics, and blacks. (He had solicitously telephoned the pregnant Mrs. Martin Luther King, Jr., whose husband was then imprisoned in Georgia for a sit-in.)

Although losing a few seats, the Democrats swept both houses of Congress by wide margins, as was a foregone conclusion. The possibility of another Republican President handcuffed by an opposition Congress definitely hurt Nixon. Many voters were weary of government by deadlock. John Fitzgerald Kennedy—the youngest man and the first Catholic to be elected President—was free to set out for his New Frontier, provided that the die-hard conservatives in his party would join the wagon train.

An Old General Fades Away

President Eisenhower, the aging "dynamic" conservative, continued to enjoy extraordinary popularity to the final curtain. Despite Democratic jibes about "eight years of golfing and goofing," of "putting and puttering," he was universally admired and respected for his dignity, decency, sincerity, goodwill, and moderation.

Pessimists had predicted that Eisenhower would be a seriously crippled "lame duck" during his second term, owing to the barrier against reelection erected by the 22nd Amendment, ratified in 1951. (See Appendix.) In truth, he displayed more vigor, more political know-how, and more aggressive leadership during his last two years than ever before. For an unprecedented six years, from 1955 to 1961, Congress remained in Democratic hands, yet he established unusual control over it. He wielded the veto 169 times, and only twice was he overridden by the required two-thirds vote.

America was generally prosperous, despite pockets of poverty and unemployment, recurrent recessions, and perennial farm problems. The budget was in balance, the Treasury showed a surplus, and the up-creep in prices was being slowed. To the north the vast St. Lawrence waterway project, constructed jointly with Canada and completed in 1959, had turned the cities of the Great Lakes into bustling ocean seaports.

In his Farewell Address on radio and television, Jan. 17, 1961, Eisenhower warned against a potent new menace: "This conjunction of an immense military establishment and a large arms industry is new in the American experience. . . . In the councils of government, we must guard against the acquisition of unwarranted influence, whether sought or unsought, by the military-industrial complex."

"Old Glory" could now proudly display fifty stars. Alaska attained statehood in 1959, as did Hawaii. Alaska, though gigantic, was thinly populated and non-contiguous, but these objections were overcome in a Democratic Congress that expected Alaska to vote Democratic. Hawaii had ample population (largely of Oriental descent), advanced democratic institutions, and more acreage than Rhode Island, Delaware, or Connecticut.

Though a crusading general, Eisenhower as President mounted no moral crusade for civil rights or related issues. Yet he obviously was not another "honest Harding," and he had done far more than grin away problems and tread water. As a Republican President he had further woven the reforms of the Democratic New Deal and Fair Deal into the fabric of national life. He had acquitted himself far better than any other professional military man in the White House, including his fellow West Pointer, General Grant, the only other Republican ever to serve two full terms. He had ended one war and avoided all others. As the decades lengthened, appreciation of him grew.

"What's So Lame [Duck] about It?" Ike's goodwill tours. (Alexander in *The Evening and Sunday Bulletin.*)

VARYING VIEWPOINTS

Liberal historians, reflecting a Democratic bias that is widespread in academic circles, have written about the 1950s as the time of the "great postponement." These critics condemn Eisenhower as visionless and passive, and lament the failure of the decade to carry forward vigorously the programs of the New Deal. But to other scholars the Eisenhower era has begun to appear in a more favorable light. It looms as an island of calm between the noisy clashes of the Truman years and the convulsive upheavals of the 1960s. "Ike's" easygoing leadership looks more attractive when compared with the consequences of Kennedy's youthful charisma and Johnson's restless dynamism. Eisenhower has also been rehabilitated by those historians who stress his wisdom in restraining his more hawkish advisers at the time of Dien Bien Phu—in sharp contrast to Lyndon Johnson's later military intervention in Vietnam. General Eisenhower, the former warrior, presided over eight years of peace. This achievement can be claimed for no other President since the end of World War II. Yet he left behind the combustibles of conflict.

SELECT READINGS

The era is surveyed readably in E. F. Goldman, *The Crucial Decade—and After: America, 1945–1960* (1961), William Manchester, *The Glory and the Dream: A Narrative History of America, 1932–1972* (1974), W. Leuchtenburg, *A Troubled Feast: American Society since 1945* (1973), and more succinctly in Charles C. Alexander, *Holding the Line: The Eisenhower Era, 1952–1961* (1975). The Korean War is discussed in David Rees, *Korea: The Limited War* (1964), and in J. W. Spanier, *The Truman-MacArthur Controversy and the Korean War* (2nd ed., 1965). Eisenhower's own memoirs are rather bland: *Mandate for Change, 1953–1956* (1963) and *Waging Peace, 1956–1961* (1965). G. W. Reichand, *The Reaffirmation of Republicanism: Eisenhower and the Eighty-third Congress* (1975), praises the President's political skills. Robert A. Divine, *Eisenhower and the Cold War* (1981), praises his diplomatic restraint. A lively "inside account" of "Ike's" administration is E. J. Hughes, *Ordeal of Power* (1963). More comprehensive is Herbert S. Parmet, *Eisenhower and the American Crusades* (1972). The man who twice lost to "Ike" is sympathetically portrayed in J. B. Martin, *Stevenson of Illinois* (1976). The Red hunts are described in Earl Latham, *The Communist Controversy in Washington* (1966), Richard Rovere, *Senator Joe McCarthy* (1959), and Robert Griffith, *The Politics of Fear* (1970), which focuses on the Senate. M. P. Rogin analyzes *McCarthy and the Intellectuals* (1967). The Rosenberg case is examined in W. and M. Schneir, *Invitation to an Inquest* (1968); the Hiss case, in Allen Weinstein, *Perjury* (1978). The background and consequences of the Supreme Court's 1954 desegregation decision are ably presented in Richard Kluger, *Simple Justice: The History of* Brown *v.* Board of Education *and Black America's Struggle for Equality* (1976). See also Anthony Lewis, *Portrait of a Decade* (1964), N. V. Bartley, *The Rise of Massive Resistance* (1969), and D. L. Lewis, *King: A Critical Biography* (1970). Townsend Hoopes, *The Devil and John Foster Dulles* (1973), is perceptive on the controversial secretary of state. Consult also Herman Finer, *Dulles over Suez* (1964). For the debates over strategic arms, see Urs Schwarz, *American Strategy* (1966), Henry Kissinger, *Nuclear Weapons and Foreign Policy* (1957), and Herman Kahn's chilling *On Thermonuclear War* (1960). The origins of the Vietnam debacle are traced in Henry Brandon, *Anatomy of Error* (1969), A. M. Schlesinger, Jr., *The Bitter Heritage* (1967), and Frances FitzGerald's sensitive *Fire in the Lake* (1972). Consult also David Halberstam's anecdotal and informative *The Best and the Brightest* (1972). On the election of 1960, see T. H. White's colorful *The Making of the President, 1960* (1961).

45

The Stormy Sixties

In the final analysis it is their war. They are the ones who have to win it or lose it . . . the people of Vietnam.

JOHN F. KENNEDY, September 1963

Kennedy's New Frontier Spirit

Hatless and topcoatless in the 22° F chill (−5° C), youthful John F. Kennedy delivered a stirring inaugural address on January 20, 1961. Tall, elegantly handsome, speaking crisply and with atаccato finger jabs at the air, Kennedy personified the glamor and vigor of the new administration. The youngest President ever elected, he assembled one of the youngest Cabinets, including his thirty-five-year-old brother Robert as attorney general. "Bobby," the President quipped, would find the experience useful when he began to practice law. Business whiz Robert S. McNamara left the presidency of the Ford Motor Company to take over the Defense Department. Along with other youthful, talented advisers, they made up an inner circle of "the best and the brightest" men around the President.

The Youngest President. In his inaugural address, Kennedy struck a stern note: "Let every nation know, whether it wishes us well or ill, that we shall pay any price, bear any burden, meet any hardship, support any friend, oppose any foe to assure the survival and the success of liberty." (United Press International photo.)

From the outset Kennedy inspired high expectations, especially among the young. His challenge of a "New Frontier" quickened patriotic pulses. He brought a warm heart to the Cold War when he proposed the Peace Corps, an army of idealistic and mostly youthful volunteers to bring American skills to underdeveloped countries. He summoned citizens to service with his clarion call to "ask not what your country can do for you: ask what you can do for your country."

Himself Harvard-educated, Kennedy and his Ivy League lieutenants (heavily from Harvard) radiated confidence in their abilities. The President's personal grace and wit won him the deep affection of many of his countrymen. In an unprecedented gesture, he invited white-maned poet Robert Frost to speak at his inaugural ceremonies. The old Vermont versifier shrewdly took stock of the situation. "You're something of Irish and I suppose something of Harvard," he told Kennedy—and advised him to be more Irish than Harvard.

The European Time Bomb

A few months after settling into the White House, the new President met Soviet Premier Khrushchev at Vienna, in June 1961. Kennedy sought cooperation, but the tough-talking Russian adopted a belligerent attitude, threatening to make a treaty with East Germany and cut off Western access to Berlin. Visibly shaken, the President refused to be bullied. Upon returning, he requested an increase in the military budget, and called up reserve troops for the possible defense of Berlin. The Soviets backed off from their most bellicose threats but suddenly began to construct the Berlin Wall in August 1961. A barbed-wire and concrete barrier, it was designed to plug the heavy population drain from East Germany to West Germany. But to the free world the "Wall of Shame" looked like a gigantic enclosure around a concentration camp.

The Barbed-Wire and Brick Berlin Wall, 1962. (United Press International photo.)

Kennedy meanwhile turned his attention to Western Europe, now miraculously prospering after the tonic of Marshall Plan aid and the growth of the American-encouraged Common Market, or commercial union. He finally secured passage of the Trade Expansion Act in 1962, authorizing tariff cuts of up to 50 percent to promote trade with Common Market countries. This legislation led to the so-called Kennedy Round of tariff negotiations, concluded in 1967, and to a significant expansion of European-American trade.

But not all of Kennedy's ambitious designs for Europe were realized. American policy-makers were dedicated to an economically and militarily united "Atlantic Community," with Uncle Sam the dominant partner. But they found their way blocked by towering, stiff-backed President Charles de Gaulle of France. The Frenchman was suspicious of American intentions in Europe, and on fire to recapture the *gloire* of Napoleonic France. With a haughty *"non"* he vetoed British application for Common Market membership in 1963. He likewise dashed cold water on an American proposal to develop a multinational nuclear arm within NATO. De Gaulle deemed the Americans unreliable in a crisis, so he tried to preserve French freedom of action by developing his own small atomic force ("farce," jibed his critics). Despite the perils of nuclear proliferation or Soviet domination, De Gaulle demanded an independent Europe, free of Yankee influence.

Foreign Flare-Ups and "Flexible Response"

Special problems for American foreign policy emerged from the worldwide de-colonization of European overseas possessions after World War II. The African Congo received its independence from Belgium in 1960 and immediately exploded in violence. The United Nations sent in a peacekeeping force, to which Washington contributed much money but no manpower. Critics complained that increasingly Uncle Sam was picking up the tab for United Nations operations, while the organization itself was becoming dominated by the numerous newcomer nations from once-colonial Asia and Africa.

Sparsely populated Laos, freed of its French colonial overlords in 1954, was festering dangerously by the time Kennedy came into office. The Eisenhower administration had drenched this jungle kingdom with dollars, but failed to cleanse the country of an aggressive Communist element. A Red Laos, many observers feared, would be a river on which the influence of Communist China would flood into all of Southeast Asia.

As the Laotian civil war raged, Kennedy's military advisers seriously considered sending in American troops. But the President found that he had insufficient forces to put out the fire in Asia and still honor his commitments in Europe. Kennedy thus sought a diplomatic escape hatch in the fourteen-power Geneva conference which agreed on the neutralization of Laos in 1962.

These "brush-fire wars" intensified the pressure for a shift away from Secretary Dulles' dubious doctrine of "massive retaliation." Kennedy felt hamstrung by the knowledge that in a crisis he had the Devil's choice between humiliation or nuclear incineration. With Defense Secretary McNamara, he pushed the strategy of "flexible response"—that is, developing an array of military "options" that could be precisely matched to the scope and importance of the crisis at hand. To this end, Kennedy increased spending on conventional military forces and launched the Special Forces (Green Berets). They were an elite anti-guerrilla outfit trained to survive on snake meat and to kill with scientific finesse.

Stepping into the Vietnam Quagmire

The doctrine of "flexible response" seemed sane enough but it contained lethal logic. It potentially lowered the level at which diplomacy would give way to shooting. It also provided a mechanism for a progressive, and possibly endless, stepping-up of the use of force. Vietnam soon presented a grisly demonstration of these dangers.

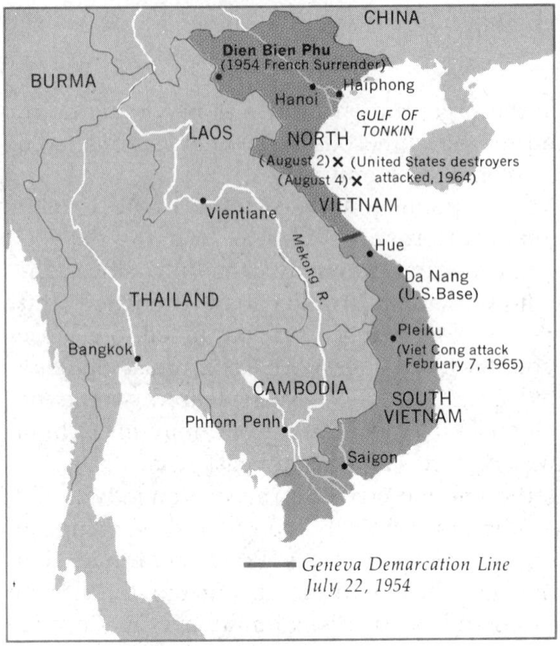

VIETNAM AND SOUTHEAST ASIA

"Backbone." U.S. supports South Vietnam. (Copyright © 1964, The Chicago *Sun-Times*. Reprinted courtesy of The Chicago *Sun-Times* and Bill Mauldin.)

The conservative Diem government in Saigon, despite a deluge of American dollars, had ruled shakily since the partition of Vietnam in 1954. Anti-Diem agitation, spearheaded by the local Communist Viet Cong and encouraged by the Red regime in the north, noisily threatened to topple the pro-American government from power. In a fateful decision late in 1961, Kennedy ordered a sharp increase in the number of "military advisers" (U.S. troops) in South Vietnam.

American troops had allegedly entered Vietnam to foster political stability—to help protect Diem from the Communists long enough to allow him to enact basic social reforms favored by the Americans. But the Kennedy administration eventually despaired of the reactionary Diem, and encouraged a successful coup against him in November 1963. Ironically, the United States thus contributed to a long process of political disintegration that its original policy had meant to prevent. Kennedy still told the South Vietnamese that it was "their war," but he had made dangerously deep political commitments. By the time of his death, he had ordered more than 15,000 American men into the far-off Asian slaughter pen. A graceful pullout was becoming increasingly difficult.

Cuban Confrontations

Uncle Sam regarded Latin America as his backyard, but his southern neighbors feared and resented the powerful Colossus of the North. President Kennedy extended the warm hand of friendship with the Alliance for Progress (*Alianza para el Progresso*), hailed as a Marshall Plan for Latin America. A primary goal was to help the Good Neighbors close the ghastly gap between the calloused rich and the wretched poor, and thus quiet Communist agitation. But results were disappointing; there was little alliance and even less progress. American handouts had little positive impact on Latin America's staggering social problems.

Kennedy also struck below the border with the mailed fist. He had inherited from the Eisenhower administration a CIA-backed scheme to topple Fidel Castro from power by invading Cuba with anti-Communist exiles. Trained and armed by Americans in Central America and supported by American air power, the invaders would trigger a popular uprising and sweep to victory—or so the planners predicted.

On a fateful April 17, 1961, some 1,200 exiles

landed at Cuba's Bay of Pigs. Kennedy had decided from the outset against *direct* intervention, and the ancient aircraft of the anti-Castroites were no match for Castro's air force. In addition, no popular uprising greeted the invaders. With the invasion bogged down at the Bay of Pigs, Kennedy stood fast in his decision to keep hands off, and the bullet-riddled band of anti-Castroites surrendered. Most of them rotted for two years in Cuban jails, but were eventually "ransomed" for some $62 million worth of American drugs and other supplies. Kennedy manfully assumed full responsibility for the failure, remarking that "victory has a hundred fathers, and defeat is an orphan."

The Bay of Pigs blunder naturally pushed Castro even further into the Soviet embrace. Wily Chairman Khrushchev lost little time taking full advantage of his Cuban comrade's position just 90 miles (145 km) off Florida's coast. In October 1962, the aerial photographs of American spy planes revealed that the Russians were secretly and speedily installing nuclear-tipped missiles in Cuba. The Soviets evidently intended to use these devastating weapons to shield Castro and to blackmail the United States into backing down in Berlin and other trouble spots.

Kennedy and Khrushchev now began a nerve-racking game of "nuclear chicken." The President flatly rejected air force proposals for a "surgical" bombing strike against the missile-launching sites.

"It Certainly Was Loaded!" The Bay of Pigs affair. (Reprinted with permission of the Minneapolis *Star*.)

Instead, on October 22, 1962, he ordered a naval "quarantine" of Cuba and demanded immediate removal of the threatening missiles. He also served notice on Khrushchev that any attack on the United States from Cuba would be regarded as coming from the Soviet Union, and would trigger nuclear retaliation against the Russian heartland.

For an anxious week Americans waited while Soviet ships approached the patrol line established by the United States navy off Cuba. Seizing or sinking a Russian vessel on the high seas would unquestionably be regarded by the Kremlin as an act of war. The world teetered breathlessly on the brink of global atomization.

In this tense eyeball-to-eyeball confrontation, Khrushchev finally flinched. On October 28, he agreed to a partially face-saving compromise, by which he would pull the missiles out of Cuba. The United States in return agreed to end the quarantine and not invade the island.

Fallout from the Cuban missile crisis was considerable. A humiliated Khrushchev was ultimately hounded out of the Kremlin and became an "unperson." The Democrats did better than expected in the mid-term elections of November 1962—allegedly because the Republicans were "Cubanized." Kennedy, apparently sobered by the appalling risks he had just run, pushed harder for a nuclear test-ban treaty with the Soviet Union. After prolonged negotiations in Moscow, a pact prohibiting trial nuclear explosions in the atmosphere was signed in late 1963. Another barometer indicating a thaw in the Cold War was the installation (August 1963) of a Moscow-Washington "hot line," permitting immediate teletype communication in case of crisis.

Most significant was Kennedy's speech at the American University, Washington, D.C., in June 1963. The President urged Americans to abandon a view of Russia as a Devil-ridden land filled with fanatics, and instead to deal with the world "as it is, not as it might have been had the history of the last eighteen years been different." Kennedy thus tried to lay the foundations for a realistic policy of peaceful coexistence with the Soviet

Russia Throws Monkey Wrench into U.N. Proceedings. (Cartoon by Fletcher in the Sioux City, Iowa *Journal*.)

Union. The Cold War appeared to be thawing, at least by a few degrees.

The New Frontier at Home

Kennedy had come into office with narrow Democratic majorities in Congress. Southern members of his own party threatened to team up with Republicans and lay the ax to New Frontier proposals such as medical assistance for the aged and increased federal aid to education. Kennedy won a first round in his campaign for a more cooperative Congress when he forced an expansion of the all-important House Rules Committee, dominated by conservatives who could have bottled up his entire legislative program. Despite this victory, the New Frontier did not expand swiftly. Key medical and education bills remained stalled in Congress.

Another vexing problem was the economy. Kennedy had campaigned on the theme of "getting the country moving again" after the recessions of the Eisenhower years. While his advisers debated the best kind of economic medicine to apply, the President tried to hold the line against crippling inflation. His administration helped negotiate a non-inflationary wage agreement in the steel industry in early 1962. The assumption was that the companies for their part would keep the lid on prices.

Almost immediately, steel management announced significant price increases, thereby seemingly demonstrating bad faith. The President erupted in wrath, remarking that his father had once said that "all businessmen were sons of bitches." He called the "big steel" men onto the White House carpet, and unleashed his Irish temper. Overawed, the steel operators backed down, as S.O.B. buttons were worn, meaning "Sons of Business" or "Save Our Business."

The steel episode provoked fiery attacks by Big Business on the New Frontier, but Kennedy soon appealed to believers in free enterprise when he announced his support of a general tax cut bill.

John H. Glenn Ready for Space Flight, 1962. (NASA.)

He rejected the advice of those who wished greater government spending, and chose to stimulate the economy by slashing taxes and putting more money directly into private hands. When he announced his policy before a Big Business group, one observer called it "the most Republican speech since McKinley."

For economic stimulus, as well as for military strategy and scientific prestige, Kennedy also promoted a multi-billion-dollar project to land a man on the moon. When skeptics objected that the money could best be spent elsewhere, Kennedy "answered" them in a speech at Rice University in Texas: "But why, some say, the moon? . . . And they may well ask, why climb the highest mountain? Why, thirty-five years ago, fly the Atlantic? Why does Rice play Texas?"

Dr. Martin Luther King, Jr. In 1964, King wrote: "Nonviolent resistance paralyzed and confused the power structures against which it was directed." (Flip Schulke, Black Star.)

The Black Revolutionary Outburst

Kennedy had campaigned with a strong appeal to black voters, but he proceeded gingerly to redeem his promises. He had given a pledge to eliminate racial discrimination in federally funded housing projects "with a stroke of the pen." But it took him nearly two years to find the right pen.

Before long Kennedy was caught up in a convulsive racial revolution. Aroused blacks, impatient at the snail's pace of school desegregation in the Deep South, had begun to force the integration issue in new ways. A "sit-in" at a Woolworth lunch counter in Greensboro, North Carolina, in February 1960 had swelled into a wave of further sit-ins, lie-ins, wade-ins, and pray-ins to compel equal treatment for blacks in restaurants, transportation, employment, housing, and voter registration. The most distinguished leader of this movement was the Reverend Martin Luther King, Jr., a young, bell-voiced clergyman from Atlanta. He preached Christian love and embraced the non-violent tactics of India's Mohandas Gandhi. Not surprisingly, he was awarded the Nobel Peace Prize in 1964.

In the spring of 1963, King launched a campaign against discrimination in Birmingham, Alabama. A fascinated world watched television screens as peaceful demonstrators were repeatedly repelled by the police with fire hoses, attack dogs, and electric cattle prods.

Integrating the Southern universities almost brought wholesale slaughter. Some of them desegregated painlessly, but the University of Mississippi became a volcano. A twenty-nine-year-old air force veteran, James Meredith, encountered violent opposition when he attempted to register in October 1962. In the end President Kennedy was forced to send in 400 federal marshals and 3,000 troops. Two men died and scores were injured, but Meredith doggedly attended classes. He ultimately graduated—with a sheepskin that cost two lives and some 4 million taxpayer dollars.

In Alabama, Governor George Wallace stood in the doorway to prevent two black students from entering the State University in June 1963. "Segregation now! Segregation tomorrow! Segregation forever!" he shouted. But he soon yielded to federal pressures and let the students pass.

"We Shall Overcome." Martin Luther King, Jr., leads a peaceful demonstration from Selma to Montgomery in March 1965. (Photograph by Bruce Davidson, Magnum Photos, Inc.)

Jolted by these racial confrontations, President Kennedy went on television, June 11, 1963, and called the situation a "moral crisis." He pleaded for new civil rights legislation to protect black citizens. In August, Martin Luther King, Jr., led 200,000 demonstrators, mostly black, on a peaceful "March on Washington" to demand more governmental action in the struggle for racial equality.

Still the violence continued. On the very night of Kennedy's stirring television appeal, a white gunman shot down Medgar Evers, a Mississippi civil rights worker. In September 1963, an explosion blasted a Baptist church in Birmingham, killing four black girls who had just finished their lesson, "The Love That Forgives." By the time of Kennedy's death, his civil rights bill was making little legislative headway. Frustrated blacks were growing increasingly impatient.

The Killing of Kennedy

Violence haunted America in the mid-60s, and it stalked grotesquely onto center stage on November 22, 1963. While riding in an open limousine in downtown Dallas, President Kennedy was shot in the brain by a concealed rifleman and died within seconds. As a stunned nation nursed its grief, the tragedy grew still more unbelievable. The alleged assassin, a furtive figure named Lee Harvey Oswald, was himself shot to death in front

Lyndon Johnson Sworn in on Air Force One. Kennedy's widow stands on Johnson's left in this dramatic scene just moments after the assassination. (Wide World Photos, Inc.)

of the television cameras by a self-appointed avenger, Jack Ruby. So bizarre were the events surrounding the two murders that even an elaborate official investigation conducted by Chief Justice Warren could not quiet all doubts and theories about what had really happened.

Vice-President Johnson was promptly sworn in as President on a waiting airplane and flown back to Washington with Kennedy's body. Though he mistrusted "the Harvards," Johnson retained most of the bright Kennedy team. He managed a dignified and efficient transition, pledging continuity with his predecessor's policies.

For several days, the nation was steeped in sorrow. Not until then did many Americans realize how fully their young, vibrant President and his bewitching wife had cast a spell over them. Chopped down in his prime after only slightly more than 1,000 days in the White House, he was acclaimed more for the ideals he had enunciated and the spirit he had kindled than for the concrete goals he had achieved. He had laid one myth to rest forever—that a Catholic could not be trusted with the presidency of the United States. Mass was celebrated only once in the White House—the day of his funeral.

The LBJ Brand on the Presidency

The torch had now passed to craggy-faced Lyndon Baines Johnson, a Texan who towered 6 feet 3 inches (1.91 meters). The new President hailed from the populist hill country of west Texas, whose people had first sent him to Washington as a twenty-nine-year-old congressman in 1937. Franklin D. Roosevelt was a political "Daddy" to him, Johnson claimed, and he had supported New Deal measures down the line. But when LBJ lost a Senate race in 1941, he learned the sobering lesson that liberal political beliefs did not necessarily win elections. He trimmed his sails to the right, and squeezed himself into a Senate seat in 1948 with a questionable 87-vote margin—hence the ironic nickname, "Landslide Lyndon."

Entrenched in the Senate, Johnson developed into a legislative wheeler-dealer. He became the Democratic majority leader in 1954, wielding power second only to that of Eisenhower in the White House. He could move mountains or checkmate men as the occasion demanded, using what came to be known as the "Johnson treatment"—a flashing display of back-slapping, flesh-pressing, and arm-twisting that overbore friend and foe alike.

As President, Johnson quickly shed the conservative coloration of his Senate years to reveal a still-living liberal underneath. He rammed Kennedy's stalled tax cut and civil rights bills through Congress, and added proposals of his own for a billion-dollar "War on Poverty." Johnson voiced special concern for Appalachia, where the sickness of the soft-coal industry had left tens of thousands of mountain folk on the human slag heap.

Johnson's nomination by the Democrats in 1964 was a foregone conclusion; he was chosen by acclamation in Atlantic City as his birthday present. He had dubbed his domestic program the "Great Society"—a sweeping set of New Dealish economic and welfare measures aimed at transforming the American way of life. His proposals sprawled so completely over the middle of the road as to leave mostly gutters for the extreme right and the extreme left.

Johnson Battles Goldwater in 1964

Thanks to the tall Texan, the Democrats stood foursquare on their most liberal platform since Truman's Fair Deal days. The Republicans, convening in San Francisco's Cow Palace, nominated box-jawed Senator Barry Goldwater of Arizona, a bronzed and bespectacled champion of rock-ribbed conservatism. The stage was thus set for a historic clash of political principles.

Goldwater's forces had galloped out of the Southwest to ride roughshod over the moderate Republican "Eastern Establishment." Insisting that the GOP offer "a choice not an echo," Goldwater attacked the federal income tax, the Social

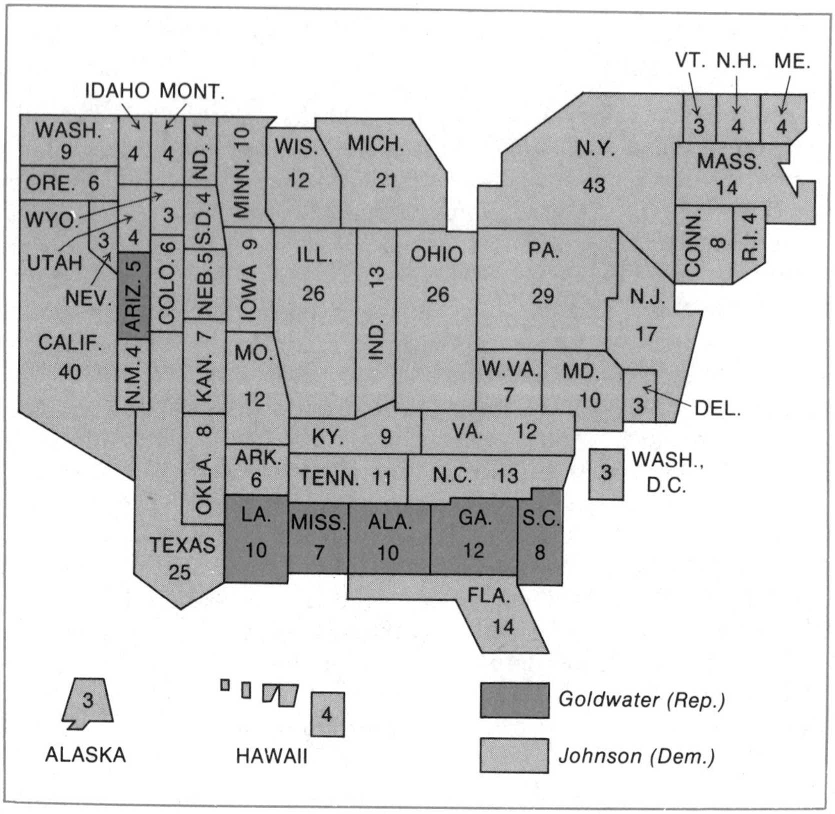

PRESIDENTIAL ELECTION OF 1964

States distorted according to number of electoral votes indicated on each state. In New Orleans, toward the end of the campaign, a gutsy Johnson displayed his commitment to civil rights when he told a story about an old senator who once said of his deep-South constituents: "I would like to go back down there and make them just one more Democratic speech. . . . The poor old State, they haven't heard a Democratic speech in 30 years. All they hear at election time is Negro, Negro, Negro!" Johnson's open voicing of sentiments like this contributed heavily to his losses in the traditionally Democratic "Solid South."

Security system, the Tennessee Valley Authority, civil rights legislation, the nuclear test-ban treaty, and, of course, the Great Society. His fiercely dedicated followers proclaimed: "In Your Heart You Know He's Right," which prompted the Democratic response, "In Your Guts You Know He's Nuts." Goldwater warmed right-wing hearts when he announced that "extremism in the defense of liberty is no vice. And . . . moderation in the pursuit of justice is no virtue."

Goldwater radiated sincerity and charm, but he could not rise above his handicaps. He was clearly a minority candidate, and his aggressive "rightism" repelled millions of his own fellow Republicans. The Arizonan also habitually "shot from the lip," notably when he urged that American field commanders be given discretionary authority to use tactical nuclear weapons. Democrats gleefully exploited the image of Goldwater as a trigger-happy cowboy who would "Barry us" in the debris of World War III. This terrifying prospect loomed larger in the closing weeks of the campaign, when Russia's leader, Khrushchev, was sacked and Red China exploded its first nuclear bomb. In such a jittery atmosphere, voters shied away from the six-gun style of the Republican candidate.

Johnson cultivated the image of a resolute statesman by seizing upon the Tonkin Gulf episode early in August 1964. Unbeknown to the American public or Congress, U.S. navy ships had been cooperating with South Vietnamese gunboats in provocative raids along the coast of North Vietnam. Two of these American destroyers were reportedly fired upon by the North Vietnamese on August 2 and 4, although exactly what happened remains unclear. Johnson later reportedly quipped, "For all I know, the Navy was shooting at whales out there."

Johnson promptly called the attacks "unprovoked," and moved swiftly to make political hay out of this episode. He ordered a "limited" retaliatory air raid against the North Vietnamese bases, proudly proclaiming that he sought "no wider war"—thus implying that the trigger-happy Goldwater did. Johnson also used the incident to spur congressional passage of the all-purpose Tonkin Gulf Resolution. With only two dissenting votes in both houses, the lawmakers virtually abdicated their war-declaring powers and handed the President a blank check to use further force in Southeast Asia.

The towering Texan rode to a spectacular victory in November 1964. The voters were herded into Johnson's column by fondness for the Kennedy legacy, faith in Great Society promises, and fear of Goldwater. A stampede of 43,129,484 Johnson votes trampled the Republican ticket, with its 27,176,873 supporters. The tally in the Electoral College was 486 to 52. Goldwater carried only his native Arizona and five other states—all of them, significantly, in racially restless Dixieland. This cracking of the once solidly Democratic South afforded the Republicans about the only faint light in an otherwise bleak political picture. Johnson's record-breaking 61 percent of the popular vote swept lopsided Democratic majorities into both houses of Congress. The inept Goldwater proved to be not so much a candidate as a catastrophe, as some observers predicted that the Grand Old Party was stumbling down the road to the Federalist-Whig cemetery.

The Great Society Congress

Johnson's victory temporarily smashed the conservative coalition of Southern Democrats and Northern Republicans. A wide-open legislative road stretched before the Great Society programs, as the President skillfully ringmastered his 2-to-1 Democratic majorities. Congress poured out a flood of legislation, comparable only to the output of the New Dealers in the Hundred Days Congress of 1933. Fiscal orthodoxy flew out the window and planned deficits came in the door, as Johnson at last delivered on long-delayed Democratic promises of social reform. The Office of Economic Opportunity, the front line of the Great Society's War on Poverty, had its appropriation doubled to nearly $2 billion. Congress granted more than $1 billion to redevelop the gutted hills of Appalachia, and voted a slightly greater amount for aid to elementary and secondary education. Yet the end results proved that poverty could not be papered over with greenbacks.

Johnson neatly avoided the thorny question of separation of church and state by channeling educational aid to students, not schools, thus allowing funds to flow to hard-pressed parochial institutions. (Catholic John F. Kennedy had not dared to touch this prickly issue.) With a keen eye for the dramatic, LBJ signed the education bill in the humble one-room Texas schoolhouse that he had attended as a boy. He also delighted in knowing that all "these Harvards" were working for him, a graduate of Southwest Texas State Teachers' College in San Marcos.

Other landmark laws flowed from Johnson's "hip pocket Congress." Medicare for the elderly became a reality in 1965. Although it was a bitter pill for the American Medical Association to

An LBJ Speech. By the end of his term, he was so unpopular that he could find nonheckling audiences only on military bases or on navy ships. (Wally McNamee photographer; The Washington *Post*.)

swallow, the system was welcomed by millions of older Americans who were being pushed into poverty by skyrocketing medical costs.

A tireless Johnson also prodded the Congress into creating two new Cabinet offices: the Department of Transportation and the Department of Housing and Urban Development (HUD). He named the first black Cabinet member in the nation's history, noted economist Robert C. Weaver, to be secretary of housing and urban development. Other noteworthy laws established a National Endowment for the Arts and Humanities, designed to lift the level of American cultural life, and still others sweepingly reformed the long-criticized quota system for immigrants.

The Black Revolution Explodes

In Johnson's native South, the walls of segregation were crumbling, but not fast enough for long-suffering blacks. The Civil Rights Act of 1964 gave the federal government more muscle to enforce school-desegregation orders and to prohibit racial discrimination in all kinds of public accommodations and employment. But the problem of voting rights remained. In Mississippi, which had the largest black minority of any state, only about 5 percent of eligible blacks were registered to vote. The lopsided pattern was similar throughout the South. Ballot-denying devices like the poll tax, literacy tests, and bare-faced intimidation still barred black people from the political process.

Beginning in 1964, opening up the polling booths became the chief goal of the black movement in the South. The 24th Amendment, ratified in January 1964, abolished the poll tax in federal elections. (See Appendix.) Blacks joined hands with white civil rights workers—many of them student volunteers from the North—in a massive voter-registration drive in Mississippi during the "Freedom Summer" of 1964. Singing "We Shall Overcome," they zealously set out to soothe generations of white anxieties and black fears.

But events soon blighted bright hopes. In late June 1964, one black and two white civil rights workers disappeared in Mississippi. Their badly beaten bodies were later found buried beneath an earthen dam. FBI investigators eventually arrested twenty-one white Mississippians in connection with the killings, including the local sheriff. But white juries refused to convict whites for these murders. In August, an integrated "Mississippi Freedom Democratic party" delegation was denied its seat at the national Democratic convention. Only a handful of black Mississippians had succeeded in registering to vote.

Early in 1965 Dr. Martin Luther King, Jr., resumed the voter-registration campaign in Selma, Alabama, where blacks made up 50 percent of the population but only 1 percent of the voters. State troopers with tear gas and whips assaulted King's demonstrators as they marched peacefully to the state capital at Montgomery. A Boston Unitarian minister was killed, and a few days later a white Detroit woman was shotgunned to death by Klansmen on the highway near Selma.

As the nation recoiled in horror before these violent scenes, President Johnson, speaking in soft Southern accents, delivered a memorable address on television. What happened in Selma, he insisted, concerned all Americans, "who must overcome the crippling legacy of bigotry and injustice." Then, in a stirring adaptation of the anthem of the civil rights movement, the President concluded: "And we shall overcome." Following words with deeds, Johnson speedily shepherded through Congress the landmark Voting Rights Act of 1965, signed into law on August 6. It outlawed literacy tests and sent federal voter registrars into several Southern states. Johnson later capped his legislative record on civil rights when he persuaded Congress in 1968 to pass the long-delayed Open Housing Bill, though the results were disappointing.

Black Rage

The Voting Rights Act of 1965 marked the end of an era in the troubled history of the black movement—the era of civil rights campaigns, focused on the South, and led by peaceable moderates like Martin Luther King, Jr. Just five days after President Johnson signed the new voting law, a bloody riot exploded in Watts, a fairly respectable black ghetto in Los Angeles. Enraged blacks burned and looted their neighborhoods for nearly a week. When the smoke finally cleared, thirty-one blacks and three whites lay dead, more than 1,000 persons had been injured, and hundreds of buildings stood charred and gutted.

Increasingly, violent voices began to be heard in the black movement, and its leadership divided dangerously between advocates of peaceful or militant tactics. Rising bitterness was highlighted by the career of Malcolm X, a brilliant Black Muslim preacher who favored black separatism and condemned the "blue-eyed white devils." In early 1965, he was cut down by black gunmen while speaking to a large crowd in New York City.

The moderation of Martin Luther King, Jr., came under heavy fire from younger black radicals in June 1966. King and Trinidad-born Stokely Carmichael of the Student Non-Violent Coordinating Committee (SNCC) vowed to resume a voter registration march through Mississippi, after its originator, James Meredith, had been gunned down along a Mississippi highway. (He was the same black man who had gained entrance to the University of Mississippi in 1962.) Sharp disagreements almost immediately flared forth, as Carmichael urged giving up peaceful demonstrations and pursuing "Black Power."

James Meredith Shot During March to Jackson, Mississippi, 1966. (Wide World Photos, Inc.)

The phrase frightened many whites, and their fears deepened when Carmichael was quoted as saying that Black Power "will smash everything Western civilization has created." Level-headed advocates of Black Power intended the slogan to describe a broad-front effort to *exercise* the political rights gained by the civil rights movement. But for a time Black Power seemed simply a justification for pillage and arson. City-shaking riots erupted in Newark, New Jersey, in the summer of 1967, taking 25 lives, and in Detroit, Michigan, where federal troops restored order after 43 people had died in the streets. Black rioters blindly burned down their own neighborhoods, attacking not so much white people as the symbols of white domination. These included the landlord's property, policemen, and even firemen, who had to battle blacks chanting "Burn, baby, burn."

Riotous tactics angered white Americans, who now threatened to retaliate with their own "backlash" against ghetto arsonists and killers. Inner-city anarchy baffled many Northerners, who had considered racial problems a purely "Southern" question. But the black movement had moved North—as had nearly half the nation's black people. In the North the Black Power movement now focused less on civil rights and more on economic demands. Black unemployment, for example, was nearly double that for whites. These oppressive new problems seemed even less likely to be solved peaceably than the struggle for voting rights in the South.

Despair deepened when the magnetic and moderate voice of Martin Luther King, Jr., was forever silenced by a sniper's bullet in Memphis, Tennessee, on April 4, 1968. This outrage triggered a nationwide orgy of ghetto-gutting and violence that cost over forty lives.

Rioters noisily made news, but thousands of other blacks quietly made history. Their voter registration in the South had shot upward, and by the late 1960s there were several hundred black

"You Don't Understand Boy—You're Supposed To Just Shuffle Along." (From *Straight Herblock*, Simon and Schuster, 1964.)

elected officials in the Old South. Cleveland, Ohio, and Gary, Indiana, had elected black mayors. By 1972 nearly half of the Southern black children sat in integrated classrooms. Actually, more schools in the South were integrated than in the North. About a third of black families had risen economically into the ranks of the middle class—though an equal proportion remained below the "poverty line."

Combatting Communism in Two Hemispheres

Violence at home eclipsed Johnson's legislative triumphs, while foreign flare-ups threatened his political life. Discontented Dominicans rose in revolt against their military government in April 1965. Johnson speedily announced that the Dominican Republic was the target of a Castro-like coup by "Communist conspirators," and he dispatched American troops, ultimately some 25,000, to protect American lives and restore order. But the evidence of a Communist takeover was fragmentary at best. Johnson was widely condemned, at home and in Latin America, for his temporary reversion to the officially abandoned "gunboat diplomacy." Critics charged that the two-fisted Texan was far too eager to back right-wing regimes with bayonets.

At about the same time, Johnson was floundering deeper into the monsoon mud of Vietnam. Viet Cong guerrillas attacked an American air base at Pleiku, South Vietnam, in February 1965. The President immediately ordered retaliatory bombing raids against military installations in North Vietnam, and for the first time ordered attacking U.S. troops to land. By the middle of March 1965, the Americans had "Operation Rolling Thunder" in full swing—regular full-scale bombing attacks against North Vietnam. Before 1965 ended, some 184,000 American troops were involved, most of them slogging through the jungles and rice paddies of South Vietnam searching for guerrillas clad in black pajamas. When Barry Goldwater was asked what he would be doing differently in Vietnam if he were President, he replied that he would be doing the same thing—only "catching hell"

Marines Splash Ashore in South Vietnam. (Naval Photographic Center.)

for it. Many Americans complained that they had voted for Johnson but had got Goldwater.

Johnson had now taken the first fateful steps down a slippery path. He and his advisers believed that a fine-tuned, step-by-step increase in American force would drive the enemy to defeat with a minimum loss of life on both sides. But the President reckoned without due knowledge of the toughness, resiliency, and dedication of the local Viet Cong and their North Vietnamese allies. Aerial bombardment actually strengthened the Communists' will to resist. The enemy matched every increase in American firepower with more men and more wiliness in the art of guerrilla warfare.

The South Vietnamese themselves were meanwhile becoming spectators in their own war, as the fighting became increasingly Americanized. Corrupt and collapsible governments succeeded each other in Saigon with bewildering rapidity. Yet American officials continued to talk of defending a faithful democratic ally. Washington spokesmen also defended America's action as a test of Uncle Sam's "commitment" and of the reliability of his numerous treaty pledges to resist Communist encroachment. If the United States were to cut and run from Vietnam, claimed pro-war "hawks," other nations would doubt America's word, crumble under Communist pressure, and drive America's first line of defense back to Waikiki Beach, in Hawaii, or even to the coast of California. Persuaded by such panicky thinking, Johnson steadily raised the military stakes in Vietnam. By 1968 he had poured more than half a million men into Southeast Asia, and the annual bill for the war was exceeding $30 billion. Yet the end was nowhere in sight.

Vietnam Vexations

America could not defeat the enemy in Vietnam, but she seemed to be defeating herself. World opinion grew increasingly hostile; the blasting of an underdeveloped country by a mighty superpower struck many critics as obscene. Several nations expelled American Peace Corps volunteers. Disgusted European allies complained that they were being neglected militarily and punished economically, as America exported war-bred inflation to her trading partners. Haughty Charles de Gaulle, ever suspicious of American reliability, ordered NATO off French soil in 1966.

Overcommitment in Southeast Asia also tied America's hands elsewhere. Capitalizing on American distractions in the Orient, the Soviet Union expanded its influence in the Mediterranean area, especially in Egypt. Tiny Israel humiliated the Russian-backed Egyptians in a devastating six-day war in June 1967, but the Middle East remained a packed powder keg that the war-plagued Americans could not defuse.

The United States proved equally helpless when the North Koreans seized a U.S. intelligence ship, the *Pueblo*, in January 1968, evidently in international waters. They imprisoned the crew of some eighty men for eleven months. This humiliating episode angered red-blooded Americans, but it provoked no military response at a time when one Asiatic war was more than enough.

Domestic discontent also festered as the Vietnamese entanglement dragged on. Anti-war demonstrations had begun on a small scale with campus "teach-ins" in 1965, and gradually these protests mounted to tidal-wave proportions. As the long arm of the military draft dragged more and more young men off to the Asian slaughter pen, resistance stiffened. Thousands of draft registrants fled to Canada; others publicly burned their draft cards. Hundreds of thousands of marchers filled the streets of New York, San Francisco, and other cities, chanting "Hell no, we won't go," and "Hey, hey, LBJ, how many kids did you kill today." Countless citizens felt the pinch of war-spawned inflation. Many Americans also felt pangs of conscience at the spectacle of their countrymen burning peasant huts and blistering civilians with ghastly napalm.

Opposition in Congress to the Vietnam involvement centered in the influential Senate Committee

Anti-War Demonstration in San Francisco, 1969. Public opinion gradually but inexorably turned against the war. In 1965, polls showed that only 15% of Americans favored withdrawal from Vietnam. But by 1969, 68% of those interviewed indicated that they considered the war a "mistake," and by 1970, a majority supported withdrawal of U.S. troops. (Peter Lake, Black Star.)

on Foreign Relations, headed by a former Rhodes scholar, Senator Fulbright of Arkansas. A constant thorn in the side of the President, he staged a series of widely viewed televised hearings in 1966 and 1967, during which prominent personages aired their views, largely anti-war. Gradually the public came to feel that it had been lied to about the causes and "winnability" of the war. A yawning "credibility gap" opened between the government and the people. New flocks of anti-war "doves" were hatching daily.

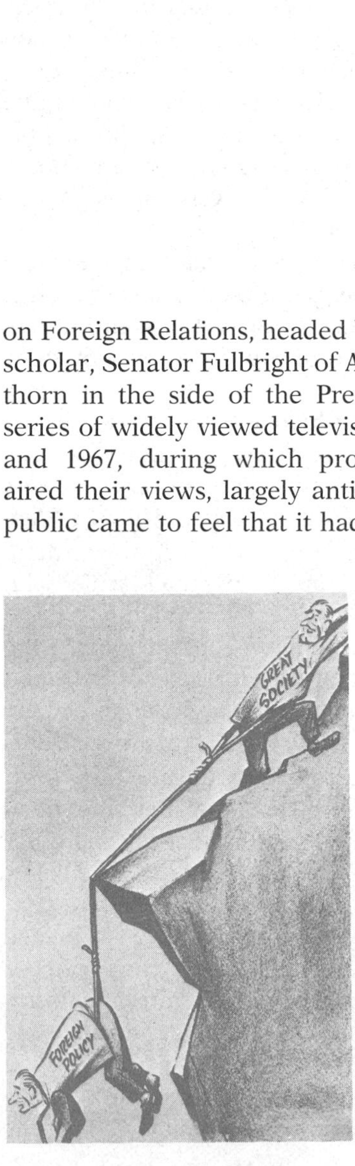

"Onward and Upward." Johnson's hopes for a Great Society were constantly dragged down by the grim demands of the Vietnam War. (Crawford for the NEA. Reproduced by permission of the Newspaper Enterprise Association.)

Even within the administration, doubts were deepening about the wisdom of the war. When Defense Secretary McNamara expressed increasing unease at the course of events, he was quietly eased out of the Cabinet. Johnson did announce "bombing halts" in early 1966 and early 1967, supposedly to lure the enemy to the peace table. But Washington did not pursue its "peace offensive" with much energy, and the other side did not respond with encouragement. Both sides used the bombing pauses to funnel more troops into South Vietnam.

By early 1968 the brutal and futile struggle had become the longest and most unpopular foreign war in the nation's history. More bombs had been dropped on Vietnam than on all enemy territory in World War II. Evidence mounted that America had been entrapped in an Asian civil war, fighting against highly motivated rebels who were striving to overthrow an oppressive regime. Yet Johnson clung to his basic strategy of stepping up the pressure bit by bit. He stubbornly assured doubting

"It's Hopeless." A Chinese cartoonist views Vietnam.

Americans that he could see "the light at the end of the tunnel." He would "save" Vietnam by destroying it.

Vietnam Topples Johnson

Hawkish illusions that the struggle was about to be won were shattered by a blistering Communist offensive launched in late January 1968, during Tet, the Vietnamese New Year. At a time when the Viet Cong guerrillas were supposedly licking their wounds, they suddenly and simultaneously mounted savage attacks on twenty-seven key South Vietnamese cities, including the capital, Saigon. Although eventually beaten off with heavy losses, they demonstrated anew that victory could not be gained by Johnson's strategy of gradual escalation. With an increasingly insistent voice, American public opinion demanded a speedy end to the war. Opposition grew so vehement that President Johnson could feel the very foundations of government shaking under his feet.

American military leaders responded to the Tet attacks with a request for 200,000 more troops. The largest single increment yet, this addition would have swollen American troop strength in Vietnam to about the three-quarter-million mark. The size of the request staggered many policy-makers. Former Secretary of State Dean Acheson reportedly advised the President that "the Joint Chiefs of Staff don't know what they're talking about." Johnson himself now began to doubt seriously the wisdom of continuing on his raise-the-stakes course.

The President meanwhile was being sharply challenged from within his own party. Eugene McCarthy, a little-known Democratic senator from Minnesota, had emerged as a contender for the 1968 Democratic presidential nomination. He

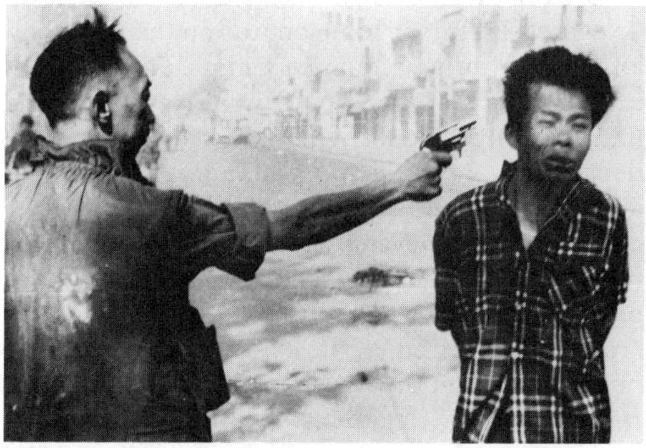

Justice on a Saigon Street, 1968. South Vietnamese police chief executes suspected Viet Cong guerrilla. (Wide World Photos, Inc.)

Robert F. Kennedy Campaigning, 1968. Kennedy shakes hands with supporters during motorcade in downtown Hammond, Indiana. (United Press International photo.)

gathered a small army of anti-war college students as campaign workers. Going "clean for Gene," with shaven faces and shortened locks, these idealistic recruits of the "Children's Crusade" invaded the key presidential primary state of New Hampshire to ring doorbells. On March 12, 1968, their efforts gave McCarthy an incredible 42 percent of the Democratic votes and 20 of the 24 convention delegates. President Johnson was on the same ballot, but only as a write-in candidate. Four days later Senator Robert F. Kennedy of New York, the murdered President's younger brother and by now himself a "dove" on Vietnam, threw his hat into the ring.

These startling events abroad and at home were not lost on LBJ. The country might explode in greater violence if he met the request of the generals for more troops. His own party was dangerously divided on the war issue. He might not even be able to win renomination after his relatively poor showing in New Hampshire. Yet he remained committed to victory in Vietnam. How could he salvage his blind-alley policy?

Johnson's answer came in a bombshell address on March 31, 1968. He announced on nationwide television that he would finally apply the brakes to the escalating war. He would freeze American troop levels and gradually shift more responsibility to the South Vietnamese themselves. Aerial bombardment of the enemy would be drastically scaled down. Then in a dramatic plea to unify a dangerously divided nation, Johnson startled his vast audience by firmly declaring that he would not be a candidate for the presidency in 1968.

Johnson's "abdication" had the effect of preserving the military status quo. He had held the "hawks" in check, while offering himself as a sacrifice to the militant "doves." The United States could thus maintain the maximum *acceptable* level of military activity in Vietnam with one hand, while trying to negotiate a settlement with the other.

North Vietnam responded somewhat encouragingly three days later, when it expressed a willingness to talk about peace. After a month of haggling over the site, the adversaries agreed to meet in Paris. But progress was glacially slow, as prolonged bickering developed over the very shape of the conference table.

The Presidential Sweepstakes of 1968

Summer in 1968 was one of the hottest political seasons in the nation's history. Johnson's heir apparent for the Democratic nomination was his liberal Vice-President, Hubert H. Humphrey, a former druggist, college teacher, mayor, and senator. Loyally supporting LBJ's Vietnam policies through thick and thin, he received the support of the party apparatus, dominated as it was by the White House. Senators McCarthy and Kennedy meanwhile dueled in several state primaries, with Kennedy's bandwagon gathering ever-increasing speed. But on June 5, 1968, the night of an exciting victory in the California primary, Kennedy was shot to death by a young Arab immigrant resentful of the candidate's pro-Israeli views.

Surrounded by bitterness and frustration, the Democrats met in Chicago in late August 1968. Angry anti-war zealots, deprived by an assassin's bullet of their leading candidate, streamed menacingly into Chicago. Mayor Daley responded by arranging for barbed-wire barricades around the convention hall ("Fort Daley"), as well as thousands of police and National Guard reinforcements. Many demonstrators baited the men in blue as "pigs." Other militants, chanting "Ho, Ho, Ho Chi Minh," shouted obscenities and hurled bags and cans of human filth at the police lines. As people the world over watched on television, the exasperated "peace officers" broke into a "police riot," clubbing and manhandling innocent and guilty alike. Acrid tear gas fumes hung heavy over the city, and even drifted up to candidate Humphrey's hotel suite. Hundreds of people were arrested and scores hospitalized, but no one was killed except, as cynics said, the Democratic party and its candidate.

Richard Nixon on the Campaign Trail, 1968. (United Press International photo.)

Humphrey steamrollered to the nomination on the first ballot. The dovish McCarthyites failed even to secure an anti-war platform plank. Instead, the Humphrey forces, echoing the President, rammed through their own declaration that armed force would be relentlessly applied until the enemy showed more willingness to negotiate.

Democratic Presidential Hopeful Hubert Humphrey and Inquiring Reporters, 1968. (Wide World Photos, Inc.)

Scenting victory as the Democrats divided, the Republicans had jubilantly convened in plush Miami Beach, Florida, early in August 1968. Richard M. Nixon, the former Vice-President whom John F. Kennedy had narrowly defeated eight years earlier, arose from his political grave to win the nomination. Nixon, with a "loser's image," was fighting history. Not since 1840 had a candidate won the presidency for a first term after a previous electoral defeat for that office. But Nixon had doggedly entered and won several Republican primaries. As a "hawk" on Vietnam and a right-leaning middle-of-the-roader on domestic policy, he could please the Goldwater conservatives and was acceptable to party moderates. He appealed to white Southern voters and to the "law and order" element when he tapped as his vice-presidential running mate Maryland's Governor Spiro T. Agnew, noted for his tough stands against blacks and dissidents. The Republican platform called for victory in Vietnam and a strong anti-crime policy.

A "spoiler" third-party ticket—the American Independent party—added color and confusion

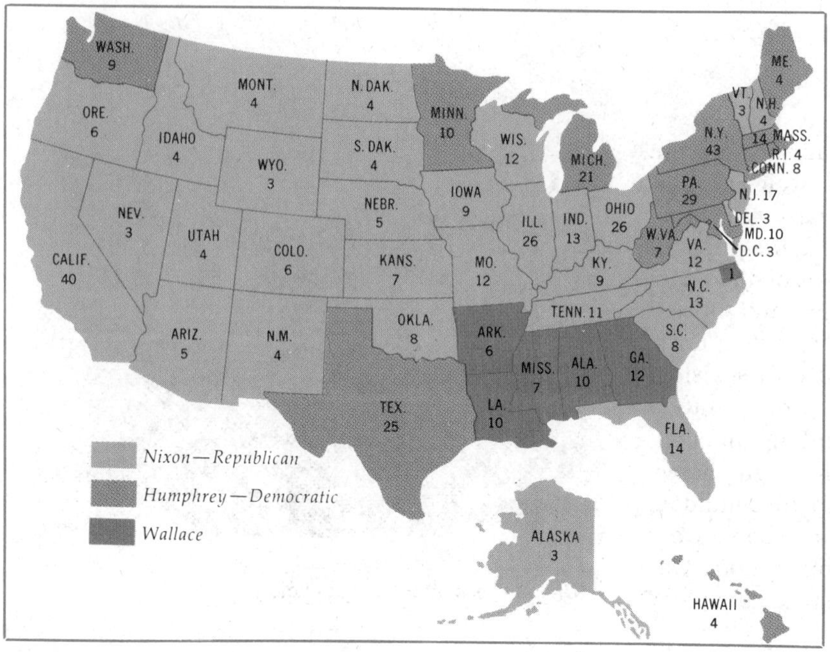

PRESIDENTIAL ELECTION OF 1968 (with electoral vote by state)
George Wallace won in 5 states, and he denied a clear majority to either of the two major-party candidates in 25 other states. A shift of some 50,000 votes might well have thrown the election into the House of Representatives, giving Wallace the strategic bargaining position that he sought.

to the campaign. It was headed by a scrappy ex-pugilist, George C. Wallace, former governor of Alabama. Wallace jabbed repeatedly at "pointy-headed bureaucrats," and he taunted hecklers as "bums" who needed a bath. Speaking behind a bullet-proof screen, he called for prodding the blacks into their place, with bayonets if necessary. He and his running mate, former Air Force General Curtis LeMay, also proposed smashing the North Vietnamese to smithereens by "bombing them back to the Stone Age."

The Triumph of Nixon

Vietnam proved a less crucial issue than expected. Between the positions of the Republicans and the Democrats there was little to choose. Both candidates were committed to keeping on with the war until the enemy would settle for an "honorable peace," which seemed to mean an "American victory." The millions of "doves" had no place to roost, and many refused to vote at all. Humphrey, scorched by the LBJ brand, went down to defeat as a loyal prisoner of his chief's policies, despite Johnson's last-minute effort to bail him out by announcing a *total* bombing halt.

Nixon, who had lost a cliff-hanger to Kennedy in 1960, won one in 1968. He garnered 302 electoral votes, with 43.4 percent of the popular tally (31,785,480), as compared with 191 electoral votes and 42.7 percent of the popular votes (31,275,166) for Humphrey. Not since Woodrow Wilson in 1912 had the victor received so small a percentage. Nixon was also the first President-elect since 1848 not to bring in on his coattails at least one House of Congress for his party in an initial presidential election. He carried not a single major city, thus attesting to the continuing urban strength of the Democrats, who also won about 95 percent of the black vote. Nixon had received no clear mandate to do anything. He was a minority President who owed his election to divisions over the war and protest against high taxes, the unfair draft, crime, and rioting.

Wallace did more poorly than expected. Yet he won an impressive 9,906,473 popular votes and 45 electoral votes, all from five states of the Deep South, four of which the Republican Goldwater had carried in 1964. "Why waste your vote?" was an argument that sent many of Wallace's followers over into the ranks of the major parties. Even so, he remained a formidable force, for he had amassed the largest third-party popular vote in American history.

The Obituary of Lyndon Johnson

Talented but tragedy-struck Lyndon Johnson returned to his Texas ranch in January 1969. His party was defeated and his "me too" Hubert Humphrey was repudiated. His popularity remained low in the opinion polls, although it had risen somewhat after his "great renunciation"—ironically one of his most popular acts.

Yet Johnson's legislative leadership for a time had been remarkable. No President since Lincoln had worked harder or done more for civil rights. None had shown more compassion for the poor, the ill-educated, and the black. Johnson seemed to suffer from a kind of inferiority complex about his own arid cultural background, and he strove furiously to prove that he could be a great "people's President" in the image of his idol, Franklin Roosevelt. His legislative achievements in his first three years in office indeed invited comparison with those of the New Deal.

But by 1966 Johnson was already sinking into the Vietnam quicksands. The Republicans had made gains in Congress, and a white "backlash" had begun to form against the black movement. Great Society programs began to wither on the vine, as soaring war costs sucked tax dollars into the military machine. Johnson had promised both guns and butter, but could not keep that promise. Ever-creeping inflation blighted the prospects of prosperity, and the War on Poverty met resistance as stubborn as the Viet Cong and also suffered defeat. Great want persisted alongside great wealth.

Johnson had crucified himself on the cross of Vietnam. The Asian quagmire engulfed his noblest intentions. Committed to some degree by his two predecessors, he had chosen to defend the American foothold and enlarge the conflict rather than be run out. He was evidently persuaded by his brightest advisers, both civilian and military, that a "cheap" victory was possible. It would be achieved by massive aerial bombing and large, though limited, troop commitments. His decision not to escalate the fighting further offended the "hawks," and his refusal to back off altogether antagonized the "doves." Like the Calvinists of colonial days, luckless Lyndon Johnson was damned if he did and damned if he did not.

VARYING VIEWPOINTS

Why did the United States become so deeply immersed in the Vietnam quagmire? Three different explanations have been proposed. The first, appraising Vietnam in the context of the Cold War "containment" policy, portrays the Southeast Asian war as simply another instance of American response to the menace of the Communist "monolith." Had the United States refused to resist the enemy in Vietnam, other nations would have lost faith in America's "will" and ultimately the United States would have been fighting alone on its own Pacific beaches. A worldwide cycle of Communist aggression would thus have been encouraged, just as Hitler had been encouraged by the "appeasers" at Munich in 1938.

The second explanation does not question the anti-Communist thrust of American foreign policy, but holds that Vietnam was a mistaken application of that policy. We should have known better, this argument goes, than to have taken over from the French their unwinnable war against a colonial people seeking to throw overboard Western control. Precisely *why* American policy-makers did *not* know better is not so clearly explained.

The third explanation is the "New Left" revisionist view. It maintains that the Vietnam involvement was but the logical (and near-fatal) consequence of an "imperialistic" foreign policy. In this view, America feels that it must resist all left-leaning challenges to the existing world order, in order to preserve the capitalist system. Significantly, this interpretation bears some resemblance to the "official" defense of American policy. But "New Left" proponents reverse the "official" value judgment by holding that American capitalism is not worth preserving.

SELECT READINGS

The tumultuous decade of the sixties is treated in the books by Manchester and Leuchtenburg cited in the previous chapter. Consult also W. L. O'Neill, *Coming Apart: An Informal History of America in the 1960s* (1971), and Richard Polenberg's history of the entire post-war period, *One Nation Divisible: Class, Race, and Ethnicity in the United States Since 1938* (1980). On Kennedy, see Theodore C. Sorenson, *Kennedy* (1965), and Arthur M. Schlesinger, Jr., *A Thousand Days* (1965), both appreciative accounts by insiders. More critical is H. Fairlie, *The Kennedy Promise* (1973). Other useful biographies include Arthur M. Schlesinger, Jr., *Robert F. Kennedy and His Times* (1978), Warren I. Cohen, *Dean Rusk* (1980), and H. S. Parmet, *Jack: The Struggles of John F. Kennedy* (1980). Seymour Harris is informative on *Economics of the Kennedy Years* (1964), as is Jim F. Heath, *John F. Kennedy and the Business Community* (1969). On the Justice Department and civil rights, see V. Navasky, *Kennedy Justice* (1971). For the Bay of Pigs consult Tad Szulc and K. E. Meyer, *The Cuban Invasion* (1962); for the Cuban missiles, Elie Abel, *The Missile Crisis* (1966), R. F. Kennedy, *Thirteen Days* (1969), and Graham Allison, *Essence of Decision* (1971). Roger Hilsman, *To Move a Nation* (1967), favorably discusses Kennedy's foreign policies; more critical is R. J. Walton, *Cold War and Counter-Revolution: The Foreign Policy of John F. Kennedy* (1972). Kennedy's assassination is scrutinized, not entirely satisfactorily, in *The Official Warren Commission Report* (1964). Gripping reading is W. Manchester, *Death of a President* (1967). R. E. Evans and R. Novak, *Lyndon B. Johnson: The Exercise of Power* (1966), provides valuable background on the President's pre-White House career. P. Geyelin, *Lyndon B. Johnson and the World* (1966), is a survey of foreign policy. Eric Goldman, *The Tragedy of Lyndon Johnson* (1969), is a sympathetic yet critical account of the Johnson presidency. In the same vein, with a psychoanalytic touch, is Doris Kearns, *Lyndon B. Johnson and the American Dream* (1976). Johnson's own memoir, *The Vantage Point* (1971), is marred by excessive self-justification. The conditions that called forth Great Society programs are movingly described in Michael Harrington, *The Other America: Poverty in the United States* (1962). For the operation of the Great Society programs, see J. C. Donovan, *The Politics of Poverty* (1967), and S. A. Levitan and R. Taggart, *The Promise of Greatness* (1976). The racial upheavals of the decade are perceptively put into context by Charles Silberman, *Crisis in Black and White* (1964). *The Report of the National Advisory Commission on Civil Disorders* (1968) is a mine of information. Consult also R. M. Fogelson, *Violence as Protest* (1971). Equally useful on the racial issue are Clayborne Carson, *In Struggle: SNCC and the Black Awakening of the 1960s* (1981), Carl M. Brauer, *John F. Kennedy and the Second Reconstruction* (1977), and W. H. Chafe, *Civilities and Civil Rights: Greensboro, North Carolina, and the Black Struggle for Freedom* (1980). On "New Left" radicals, consult Kirkpatrick Sale, *SDS* (Students for a Democratic Society) (1973), Sara Evans, *Personal Politics* (1979), and Todd Gitlin, *The Whole World is Watching: Mass Media in the Making and Unmaking of the New Left* (1980). Howard Zinn admiringly describes *SNCC: The New Abolitionists* (1964). On Vietnam, see the titles cited in the preceding chapter by Brandon, Schlesinger, Halberstam, and FitzGerald. Consult also G. H. Kahin and J. W. Lewis, *The United States in Vietnam* (rev. ed., 1967), Theodore Draper, *Abuse of Power* (1967), Townsend Hoopes, *The Limits of Intervention* (1969), and *The Pentagon Papers*, published in various editions in 1971. For a defense of American policy, see W. W. Rostow, *The Diffusion of Power* (1972). Presidential elections are described in continuing installments of T. H. White's *The Making of the President, 1964* (1965) and *The Making of the President, 1968* (1969).

46

The Rise and Fall of Richard Nixon

In all my years of public life, I have never obstructed justice. People have got to know whether or not their President is a crook. Well, I'm not a crook; I earned everything I've got.

RICHARD NIXON, 1973 speech

Nixonian Beginnings

Inaugurated on January 20, 1969, a calm and confident President Nixon urged a people torn with dissension over Vietnam and racism to lower their voices and "stop shouting at one another." Elected as a plurality President by only a 43 percent minority and confronted by a strongly Democratic Congress, he obviously could launch no reformist crusade. His early moves were characterized by coolness and caution. The basic political strategy was not to move too far to the right or left, but to enlarge the "silent center," while courting further Republican support in the South. To this end Nixon soft-pedaled civil rights and desegregation, openly opposed school busing to achieve racial balance, and gave the blacks, who had voted overwhelmingly against him, only token representation

President Richard M. Nixon. Reversing Kennedy's inaugural plea to "bear any burden," Nixon told Congress in February 1970: "America cannot—and will not—conceive all the plans, design all the programs, execute all the decisions and undertake all the defense of the free nations of the world." (White House photo.)

in high office. His attorney general, a former New York law partner, was grim-faced John N. Mitchell, who could be expected to fulfill Republican promises of law and order. (In 1975 he was sentenced to a prison term for having violated the law.)

Nixon gave high priority to the task of cooling down the overheated economy, which had produced the insidious inflationary spiral of the "soaring sixties." Living costs were rising so alarmingly as to inspire serious talk of wage-price controls. In the early stages of his administration, Nixon tackled the problem in part by cutting back on government expenditures and defense contracts, with a consequent rise in unemployment. His purpose was to halt inflation by producing a recession that was mild enough not to qualify as a depression. But creating unemployment proved easier than stemming inflation, which, when combined with stagnation, produced alarming "stagflation."

Jet-plane diplomacy characterized Nixon's early months, and he was soon the most airborne President in history. Within weeks of his inauguration he embarked on an eight-day tour of European capitals, and in July 1969 he made a flying visit to Asia, returning by way of Communist Romania. The new President clearly prided himself on his expertise in foreign affairs. He appointed a figurehead secretary of state and held the reins of diplomacy tightly in the White House. Critics accused Nixon of believing that the nation could look after itself domestically and that the President's job was to tend exclusively to foreign affairs.

The surface of the moon was the scene of a fantastic episode in Russian-American rivalry in July 1969. An unmanned Soviet spacecraft crashed futilely into the moon-dust, but two American astronauts for the first time planted human footprints on the moonscape. This astounding venture had been launched by President Kennedy in 1961, and the price tag turned out to be about $24 billion. Critics charged that the money could better have been spent for needed projects here on earth. But the moon-glow surrounding this astonishing feat inflated the national pride and impressed peoples the world over.

On the Moon. Astronaut Aldrin poses with a stretched U.S. flag on the windless moon. His companion, Armstrong, said, as he stepped from the spacecraft, "That's one small step for man; one giant leap for mankind." (Photo taken by Armstrong. Courtesy NASA.)

A New Team on the Supreme Bench

Nixon had lashed out during the campaign at the "permissiveness" of the Supreme Court presided over by Chief Justice Earl Warren. For nearly two decades the Warren Court's "judicial activism" had rankled conservatives. "Government-by-the-judiciary" made even some liberals uneasy.

Following his appointment in 1953, the jovial Chief Justice Warren had led the Court into a series of decisions that drastically affected civil rights, the criminal law, the practice of religion, and the structure of political representation. The decisions of the Supreme Court under Warren reflected its deep concern for the individual, no matter how lowly. In 1963 it held (*Gideon* v. *Wainwright*) that all defendants in serious criminal cases were entitled to legal counsel, even if they were too poor to afford it. More controversial were the rulings in two cases—*Escobedo* (1964) and *Miranda* (1966)—which ensured the right of the accused to remain silent and to enjoy other protections when accused of a crime. In this way safeguards were erected against confessions extorted under the rubber hose and other torture. Critics of these decisions were loud in their condemnation of "crook coddling," and demanded that the courts handcuff criminals, not the "cops."

Nor did the Court shy away from explosive religious issues. In two shocking decisions, in 1962 and 1963, it voted against required prayers and Bible reading in the public schools. These rulings were based on the 1st Amendment, which required the separation of church and state, but they seemed to put the justices in the same bracket with atheistic Communists. Cynics predicted that the "old goats in black coats" would soon be erasing "In God We Trust" from all coins.

Infuriating to many Southerners was the determination of the Court, following the school desegregation decision of 1954, to support black people in civil rights cases. Five Southern state legislatures officially nullified the "sociological" Supreme Court decision, but they in turn were overruled by the high tribunal. In general, it held that the states could not deny to blacks the rights that were extended to white people. States'-rights Southerners complained bitterly that the Warren Court was not interpreting the Constitution but rewriting it, at the expense of states' rights. It was acting more like a legislative and not enough like a judicial body.

The Warren Court also developed the philosophy that where the states permitted notorious evils to persist, it should step in. Of special concern was the overrepresentation in state legislatures of cow-pasture agricultural areas, especially where urban areas were bursting their boundaries. Adopting the principle of one-man-one-vote, the Court intervened in 1962 and again more emphatically in 1964. It ruled that the state legislatures, both upper and lower Houses, would have to be reapportioned according to the human population, irrespective of cows. States'-righters and assorted right-wingers raised anew the battle cry, "Impeach Earl Warren." But the legislatures grudgingly went ahead with reapportionment.

From 1954 onward the Court came under endless criticism, the bitterest since New Deal days. Its foes made numerous but unsuccessful efforts to clip its wings through bills in Congress or through constitutional amendments. But the Court reflected perhaps not so much its own philosophy as the necessity of grappling with stubborn social problems spawned by mid-century tensions. The black-robed justices were evidently determined to protect the rights of the individual, white or black, Communist or criminal, against the tyranny of the majority, even if the individuals in some cases were "not very nice people."

Fulfilling recent campaign promises, President Nixon undertook to change the Court's philosophical complexion. Taking advantage of several vacancies, he sought appointees who would strictly interpret the Constitution, cease "meddling" in social and political questions, and not coddle radicals or criminals. The Senate in June 1969 speedily confirmed his nomination of white-maned Warren E. Burger of Minnesota to succeed the retiring Earl Warren as chief justice. But the successive nominations of two Southern judges, both vulner-

"You Mean These Apply To The Riff-Raff Too?" (From *The Herblock Gallery,* Simon and Schuster, 1968.)

able to charges of racism and mental mediocrity, were narrowly defeated amid bitter accusations. Nixon tried again with less offensive candidates, and before the end of 1971 the Court counted four conservative Nixon appointments out of nine members.

Vietnamizing the Vietnam War

At the outset, President Nixon enjoyed gratifying success in quieting the public uproar over Vietnam. His announced policy was to withdraw the 540,000 American troops in South Vietnam over an extended period. The South Vietnamese, with American money, weapons, training, and advice, could then gradually take over the burden of fighting their own war. In pursuance of this objective, Nixon flew to Midway Island in June 1969, there to confer with President Thieu of South Vietnam. Following top-secret discussions, Nixon announced the scheduled withdrawal of the initial contingent of 25,000 troops.

The so-called Guam Doctrine or Nixon Doctrine thus evolved. It embraced the concept that the United States would honor its existing defense commitments, but that henceforth Asiatics would have to fight their own wars without the support of large bodies of American ground troops.

As for Vietnam, Nixon's policy was not so much to end the conflict as to "Vietnamize" it by gradually turning it over to South Vietnam. His hope was that in time the North Vietnamese would be willing to end this seemingly endless war. Meanwhile it would continue without American troops but with American support—aerial, naval, financial, and advisory. But even this much involvement was distasteful to American "doves," many of whom demanded a withdrawal that was prompt, complete, unconditional, and irreversible.

Opposition to the bottomless war entered upon a new phase in October 1969, when the protesters staged a massive national Vietnam moratorium. In contrast to previous outbursts of violence, it featured peaceful, almost prayerful, demonstrations by several million people. An estimated 100,000 jammed the Boston Common, and some 50,000 filed by the White House carrying lighted candles.

Undaunted, Nixon launched his own home-front counter-offensive. On November 3, 1969, he delivered a dramatic televised appeal to the great "silent majority." The response was overwhelmingly favorable to his gradual Vietnamization, and his poll-popularity, which had been sagging, rose sharply. In harsher tones than Nixon, Vice-President Agnew lashed out at the "misleading" news media and the "effete corps of impudent snobs" who demanded quick withdrawal from Vietnam.

Disgust with the bloody mess in Vietnam was further deepened by shocking reports, especially those involving the massacre of innocent women and children by American troops in the village of My Lai. Only one officer, an obscure Lieutenant Calley, was convicted by a U.S. military court of murder (some twenty victims). His sentence was progressively lightened from twenty to ten years, and he was ultimately paroled. By January 1970, the Vietnam conflict had become the longest in

"Cold War? Not for Some." (Brimrose in the Portland *Oregonian.* By permission.)

American history, and with over 40,000 killed and over 250,000 wounded, the third most costly foreign war in the nation's experience.

By early 1970 the Vietnam issue had become partially eclipsed by such burning domestic problems as inflation, racism, and pollution. Some of the tensions had been eased, especially on the college campuses, by reducing the draft calls and by shortening the period of draftability, on a lottery basis, from eight years to one year.

Cambodianizing the Vietnam War

For several years the North Vietnamese and Viet Cong had been using "neutral" Cambodia, bordering South Vietnam on the west, as a springboard for troops, weapons, and supplies. Suddenly, on April 29, 1970, without consulting Congress, Nixon ordered American forces, joining with the South Vietnamese, to clean out these hornets' nests. In announcing his bold stroke, he assured the nation that the incursion would be limited to the borderland area. He further declared that the American (but not South Vietnamese) troops would be speedily withdrawn, and that the "boys" would be brought home on schedule.

> At a press conference in May 1970, President Nixon explained why he had called student rioters "bums." He stated that he had always upheld the right of non-violent dissent, but "when students on university campuses burn buildings, when they engage in violence, when they break up furniture, when they terrorize their fellow students and terrorize the faculty, then I think 'bums' is perhaps too kind a word to apply to that kind of person."

News of the Cambodian invasion hit the already restless campuses like a bombshell. Students nationwide angrily responded with wholesale rock throwing, window smashing, and arson. At Kent State University, in Ohio, National Guardsmen fired into an angry crowd, killing four and wounding many more; at Jackson State College, in Mississippi, the highway patrol discharged volleys at a student dormitory, killing two black students. The nation fell prey to turmoil as rioters and arsonists convulsed the land.

Nixon's assurances that he was invading Cambodia to save lives and shorten American involvement was evidently persuasive with the great "silent majority." In the short run, at least, the stroke was a mild success, for it resulted in the capture of some stores of weapons, ammunition, and rice. But the larger objective of eliminating the enemy base was not achieved. The American troops were withdrawn on June 29, 1970, after only two months, and with assurances to Cambodia of continued aerial, naval, and financial support.

Supporters of Nixon argued that he had gained at least eight months for the South Vietnamese to strengthen themselves, but many of the immediate results were disturbing. Communist forces, in reaction, overran large areas of Cambodia, while threatening the remainder. Bitterness in America between the "hawks" and "doves" deepened, as right-wing groups physically assaulted leftists. Disillusionment among the blacks with "whitey's war" increased ominously in the armed forces. The youth of America, further aroused, were only slightly mollified when Congress, in June 1970, passed a law of dubious constitutionality which lowered the voting age to eighteen. The Senate (though not the House) overwhelmingly repealed the Gulf of Tonkin blank check given President Johnson by Congress in 1964, while seeking other ways to restrain Nixon.

Congressional Politics and Anti-War Agitation

Veto hatchet in hand, Nixon continued to be at odds with Congress throughout his troubled years. Both houses, strongly Democratic, shied away from heaping political credit on the President by enacting his programs. For his part, Nixon opposed, at least initially, an unbalanced budget and an increased national debt. When he disapproved of what he regarded as "budget busting" legislation, he would impound billions of dollars appropriated by Congress for specific purposes, even over his veto. Other Presidents had occasionally failed to spend surplus money, but Nixon engaged in this practice repeatedly and on an enormous scale, despite a series of court decisions overruling him. Impoundment was but one glaring example of his presidential expansion of constitutional powers at the expense of the legislative branch.

With Congress often in a balky mood, Nixon enjoyed scant success in 1970 with his legislative program, and none at all in his attempts to overhaul the scandalously ineffective welfare system. One landmark law turned the nation's mail over to a federal but independent U.S. Postal Service, which proved less efficient and more expensive than its predecessor.

Nixon was grimly determined to secure the election of a Republican Congress and defeat "obstructionists" of both parties. In the autumn of 1970 he embarked upon a nationwide barnstorming tour against the "rising tide of terrorism," and his effort was undoubtedly the most far-flung ever undertaken by an incumbent President in a mid-term election. He encountered boisterous heckling from "thugs and hoodlums" opposed to the Vietnam War. In San Jose, California, a small but violent group of "hippie"-type "bums" shouted epithets and threw eggs and stones that narrowly missed injuring him. Decent Democrats, who bitterly resented Nixon's accusations of violence and criminality, charged that such demonstrations were staged by Republican "dirty tricksters" to discredit their opponents and the anti-war movement. Whatever the truth, in November the President could claim a victory of sorts at the polls. He did not dislodge the Democratic majority in Congress, but the Republicans won nine extra seats in the House of Representatives and two in the Senate. The Republican cause was doubtless hurt by declining employment, rising prices, spiraling inflation, and the slow-motion withdrawal of troops from the Vietnam death trap.

Public demonstrations against the Asian war crested again in late April and early May 1971, when mass rallies and marches once more erupted from coast to coast. Belligerent "doves" attempted to shut down the government in Washington by

The War at Home. Anti-war students clash with police in Ann Arbor, Michigan, in 1970. (Ken Hamblin, Black Star.)

blocking bridges, streets, and intersections with their bodies, stalled cars, and other objects. In subsequent clashes with the authorities, scores of demonstrators suffered injuries, as did some police. Thousands of activists and spectators alike were arrested and held a day or so in the football stadium of the Washington Redskins. The detention of citizens without charge was clearly a violation of their constitutional rights, but the authorities argued that pressing dangers took clear priority over individual liberties. President Nixon, stout champion of law and order, had no sympathy with "pampering punks" and "coddling criminals."

New combustibles fueled the fires of anti-war discontent in June 1971. The New York *Times* began publishing a top-secret study of America's involvement in the Vietnam War, prepared by officials in the Pentagon. These purloined Pentagon Papers laid bare the miscalculations, blunders, and deceptions of the Kennedy and Johnson administrations, especially the provoking of the North Vietnamese in 1964 into the attack in the Gulf of Tonkin. The individual most responsible for this leak to the press was Dr. Daniel Ellsberg, who had worked on these same papers in the Pentagon and who subsequently photocopied them. Despite his breach of the law in thus exposing the state secrets, he evidently believed that his patriotic duty required him to reveal to the public the cynicism and trickery involved. He was subsequently indicted for theft and conspiracy, but his case was finally dismissed because of a counter-illegality by the prosecuting Washington government.

New Directions in China and Nixonomics

The two great Communist powers, Red China and Red Russia, were now at each other's throats over their clashing interpretations of Marxism. Balance-of-power strategy dictated that the United States should play off one antagonist against the other, rather than face both united, especially if Washington expected to enlist the aid of both the Soviet Union and China in pressuring North Vietnam into peace.

The burdensome Vietnam War was intimately related to President Nixon's increasing interest in Red China, a chief supplier of the North Vietnamese Communists. For some while the administration had been making conciliatory noises through the Bamboo Curtain toward Peking, especially in regard to easing official trade restrictions. The Chinese responded by inviting American table tennis players to China, where, as expected, the visitors suffered a sound beating by the world champions. "Ping-Pong diplomacy" thus led to a further relaxation of tensions, and in July 1971, Nixon startled a huge television audience by announcing that he had accepted with pleasure an invitation to visit Red China the next year. This unexpected move, which was bound to infuriate Republican right-wingers and other conservatives, presented a sharp contrast to Nixon's previous record. He owed his early rise in politics to being one of the most persistent and consistent Communist baiters in American public life—"a card-carrying anti-Communist."

America had long blackballed Red China as a prospective member of the United Nations, but now Nixon neatly reversed himself and endorsed a two-China policy. This course involved the admission of mainland China and the continued membership of offshore China (Taiwan), a charter member. But many of the less-developed countries of the United Nations were happy to slap the rich and capitalistic Uncle Sam by welcoming a Communist regime. They gleefully joined the majority in the Assembly that voted to admit Red China and expel tiny Taiwan on October 25, 1971. One Tanzanian delegate danced an impromptu jig in the aisle.

The health of American foreign relations was intimately related to the health of the American economy, particularly the drooping dollar. It was officially devalued in 1972 and again in 1973. In the area of "Nixonomics," as in the overseas theater, the President executed some spectacular flipflops. Although his distaste for economic controls was well known, in August 1971 he announced with fanfare his New Economic Policy, which included an initial wage-price freeze for ninety days in an effort to hold down the fast-spiraling inflation. (Price-fixing had not been undertaken since the Korean War in 1951.) All these changes came at a time when the nation's balance of trade was showing a distressing deficit, and the once Almighty Dollar was being pounded down and scorned in the world markets, as American tourists quickly discovered. The national debt continued to mount alarmingly as Nixon backed away from his balance-the-budget philosophy.

Nixon in Peking and Moscow

An airborne President and his party, including Mrs. Nixon, made a historic visit to China during the last eight days of February 1972. Between glass-clinking toasts, Nixon engaged in extended conferences with Chairman Mao and Premier Chou En-lai, and walked on the fabled Great Wall of China. A joint statement issued at the end did little more than reaffirm the fixed positions of both powers, although the United States declared its "ultimate" objective to be withdrawal of its armed forces and installations from offshore China (Taiwan). Diplomatically the visit only established a face-to-face dialogue between both nations, while opening the door for more extended contacts, including possible formal recognition. The Russians were obviously displeased to see Nixon snuggling up to their sworn enemy; and America's valuable Japanese ally, which had not been consulted in advance, experienced a severe loss of face, known as the "Nixon shock" (*shokku*).

As was true of the earlier Peking visit, Dr. Henry A. Kissinger, Nixon's special adviser on national security affairs, had prepared the path to Moscow. Smiling, bespectacled, and German-accented, he had reached America as a youth when his parents fled Hitler's anti-Jewish persecutions. Becoming a brilliant professor of government at Harvard, he subsequently served Nixon with numerous intercontinental flights ("shuttle diplomacy"), and with a high degree of tireless diplomatic skill and per-

Balancing Act. Nixon treads delicately between the two Communist super-powers in 1973, holding some of the wheat with which he enticed both into détente. (© Ranan R. Lurie)

sistence. In 1969 he began to meet secretly with North Vietnamese officials in Paris to negotiate an end to the war in Vietnam.

President Nixon's extended talks in Moscow featured an unprecedented television address to the Russian (and American) people. The visit not only heralded an era of relaxed tensions called détente but resulted in a number of significant agreements late in May 1972. A primary goal was to cut the colossal costs of the frantic race in nuclear arms. The first major achievement was a treaty, subsequently approved by the Senate, which limited each nation to two defensive clus-

> Dr. Kissinger implausibly denied that the U.S. was making advances to China for the purpose of pressuring Russia. "We are pursuing our policy . . . on the ground that a stable peace . . . is difficult to envisage if 800 million people are excluded from a dialogue with the most powerful nation in the world."

ters of anti-ballistic missiles, each with 100 units. The second significant pact was an executive agreement to freeze long-range nuclear missiles, built or building, at their existing levels for a period of five years. Known as the SALT agreement (for Strategic Arms Limitation Talks), this accord was a long-overdue first step toward ending the arms race. Subsequent SALT steps were to follow in future years.

The SALT agreement proved controversial in America. The Russians deployed bigger and more powerful weapons, and they could ultimately add a larger number of independently targeted warheads to each monster. Clearly the bankrupting race in nuclear arms would continue in certain categories. But one result of the eased relations with food-short Russia was the great grain deal of July 1972—a three-year arrangement by which the food-rich United States agreed to sell at least $750 million worth of wheat, corn, and other cereals. Using clever capitalistic tricks, the Russian Communists bought up the desired grain in America quietly and cheaply. As a consequence, prices for the now scarce commodity rose sharply and American bread-eaters were forced to pay millions of dollars more than if there had been no "great grain steal." For the first time in decades, the United States could see the end of its stored surplus of cereals.

McGovern Challenges Nixon

Vietnam was bound to be a burning issue in President Nixon's campaign for re-election. Nearly four years had passed since he had promised, as a presidential candidate, to end the war and "win" the peace. Yet in the spring of 1972 the fighting escalated anew to alarming levels when the North Vietnamese, heavily equipped with foreign tanks, burst through the demilitarized zone (DMZ) separating the two Vietnams. Nixon reacted promptly by launching massive bombing attacks on strategic centers in North Vietnam, including Hanoi, the capital. Gambling heavily on foreign forbearance, he also ordered the dropping of contact mines to blockade the principal harbors of North Vietnam. Either Russia or China or both could have responded explosively, but neither did, and the North Vietnamese offensive finally ground to a halt.

The vexatious Vietnam issue was bound to have a political impact at home. During a grueling fight in the Democratic primaries, Senators Humphrey and Muskie, running mates on the same presidential ticket four years earlier, undercut each other, and Governor George C. Wallace of Alabama was almost killed when shot and paralyzed by a deranged young man in Maryland. Ultraliberal Senator George McGovern of South Dakota, the earnest and indefatigable "Prairie Populist," managed to line up enough delegates to insure his lopsided nomination at the Miami convention of the Democrats in July 1972. Dedicated as he was to pulling the remaining 30,000 or so American troops out of Vietnam in ninety days, he issued a clarion call in his speech of acceptance, "Come Home America!"

McGovern undoubtedly had the backing of the large and respectable anti-war element in the Democratic party, with its leaning toward liberalism and idealism. He also appealed to the racial minorities, the feminists, the youth, and the leftists. But in enlisting this oddly assorted following McGovern managed to snub and alienate the traditional backbone of his party, as well as numerous independents. The recent revolt of youth had brought a hasty enactment and ratification of the 26th Amendment (1971), which lowered the voting age to eighteen years, and McGovern was counting on about three-fourths of the youthful vote. Less than half of the group from 18 to 21 bothered to go to the polls or even to register, and the percentage of their support for McGovern was disappointing to him.

Late the next month, August 1972, the exultant Republicans, all set to renominate Nixon and Agnew, also met in Miami. There they chanted "Four More Years, Four More Years," as they acclaimed their leader's so-called triumphs for peace in China and Russia. They condemned the

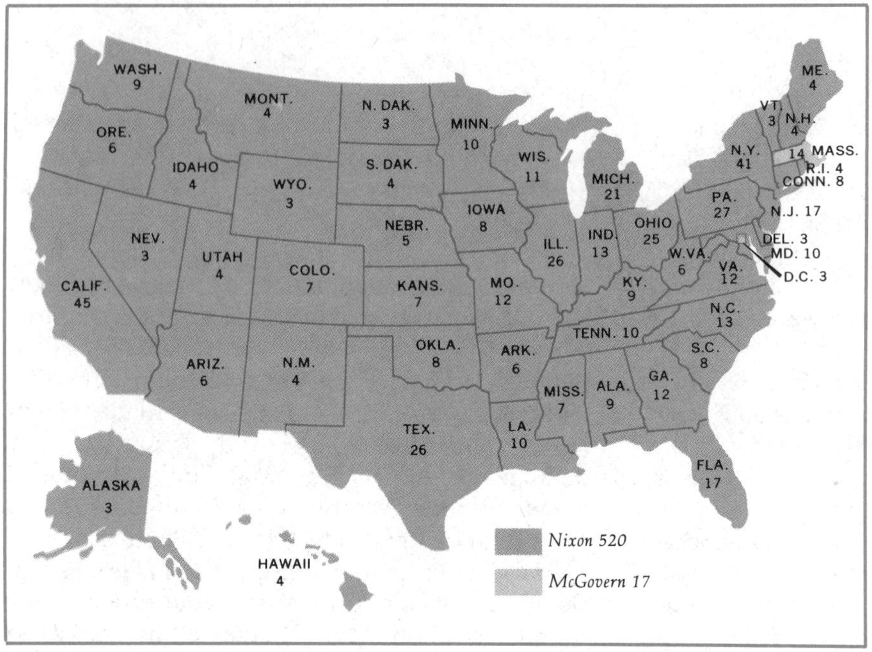

PRESIDENTIAL ELECTION OF 1972
Nixon buried McGovern in this election, but when his administration soon thereafter began to sink in a swamp of scandals, bumper stickers appeared in Boston proclaiming "Don't blame me, I'm from Massachusetts."

"crackpot" welfare schemes of McGovern, his proposed slashing of defense funds, and his alleged intention of reducing America to a "second-class power." They demanded a negotiated "peace with honor" rather than a "peace with surrender" in Vietnam. Using eye-catching charts, they showed how Nixon (in nearly four years) had wound down "the Democratic war" in Vietnam from some 540,000 troops to about 30,000, with more to come home shortly. There was no boasting about a concurrent windup of aerial and naval forces, which now totaled about 100,000 men. Outside the convention hall, police arrested some 300 of the most militant anti-war demonstrators.

McGovern's candidacy was probably doomed from the outset. The nominee hastily tapped Senator Eagleton of Missouri as his running mate, after several other invitees had declined. Word soon leaked out that Eagleton, over a period of years, had received psychiatric care, including shock treatments. McGovern loyally declared that he was behind Eagleton "1,000 percent," but soon concluded that it would be better to dump him. This he arranged to do, in favor of the Catholic Sargent Shriver, former President Kennedy's brother-in-law. This act of expediency shattered one of McGovern's best assets—a reputation for decisiveness, candor, and credibility.

The Nixon Landslide of 1972

President Nixon subsequently remarked that "the election was over the day he (McGovern) was nominated." This statement was probably true, because the Democratic party had already torn itself to pieces in the bitter primary fights. Their candidate only made matters worse by dumping Eagleton and proposing impractical schemes for curing economic malfunctioning. They included his soon-withdrawn proposal of $1,000 for every American (more than $200 billion). His strongest talking point was his promise to bring the boys home from the blood-soaked jungle trap in Vietnam. Even this appeal was largely canceled out when, twelve days before the balloting, the high-flying Dr. Kissinger returned from the Vietnam negotiations in Paris to proclaim that "peace is at hand." He explained that a few minor details would be settled in "three or four days." The Democrats could only reply lamely that if peace was at hand, it should have come four years and thousands of casualties sooner.

The Republican landslide of November 1972 was superficially awesome, despite a relatively light turnout of voters. Many were discouraged by the public-opinion polls, which with uncanny accuracy predicted the lopsided victory. Nixon swept every state except Massachusetts and the non-state District of Columbia, piling up 520 to 17 electoral votes and a popular majority of 47,167,319 to 29,168,509, or an almost unprecedented 60.7 percent. Although in a sense the victor won by default, Nixon claimed a mandate for his policies—past, present, and future. But if it was a mandate, it was not for his party; Nixon rode back into office on the crest of the loneliest landslide in the history of the presidency. The Republicans not only failed to recapture Congress but gained only twelve new seats in the House and lost two in the Senate—an unexampled rebuke to the head of the ticket in a presidential victory of this magnitude. Many voters, deluded into thinking that the war in Vietnam had just ended, regarded the candidates as a choice of evils. Much of the pro-Nixon vote was a vote by disgruntled Democrats against McGovern, as further attested by the election of a majority of Democratic state governors.

Nixon's success at the polls was partially attributable to his legislative program in 1972. He had approved a revenue-sharing bill which provided for a return of $30.2 billion in federal revenues to the state and local governments over a period of five years. The assumption was that these funds would assist the localities with such social-service problems as mass transit, education, and housing. Congress increased Social Security benefits by raising the contributions of employees and employers by 20 percent, and by providing for automatic increases when the cost of living rose more than 3 percent in any calendar year.

Bombing North Vietnam to the Peace Table

The dove of peace, "at hand" in Vietnam just before the balloting, took flight after the election, when Nixon refused to be stampeded into accepting terms that had obvious loopholes. After the fighting on both sides had again escalated, he launched a furious two-week bombing ("the Christmas blitz") of North Vietnam. To outsiders, this appeared to be an iron-handed effort to drive the North Vietnamese back to the conference table. The attack was the heaviest of the war and resulted in substantial losses of America's big B-52 bombers. Evidently this merciless pounding had the desired effect, because the North Vietnamese negotiators returned to Paris and agreed to cease-fire arrangements on January 23, 1973, nearly three months after peace was prematurely proclaimed. The terms were sweeping. The United States within sixty days would withdraw its remaining 27,000 or so troops, but would be allowed to provide South Vietnam with replacements for worn-out weapons. Prisoners of war on both sides would be released, including some 560 Americans. The government of South Vietnam would be permitted to remain under the autocratic President Thieu, with American support. Other stipulations called for a future election, which the Communists expected would enable them to take over the entire country. Oddly enough, the North Vietnamese were permitted to retain some 145,000 troops in South Vietnam, where they could be used to spearhead a powerful new offensive when the time seemed ripe. Ominously, the North Vietnamese still occupied about 30 percent of South Vietnam.

President Nixon hailed the face-saving cease-fire agreements as "peace with honor." What he evidently meant was that the United States had not simply withdrawn completely, as McGovern had advocated, and left American prisoners and all of South Vietnam to the Communists. Nixon did not want to be charged with having lost a war, with consequent weakened credibility. The nation had poured into this Asian quagmire more than 50,000 American lives, to say nothing of some 300,000 casualties and well over 100 billion taxpayer dollars. The President felt that the United States should emerge on its feet rather than on its knees. Yet America was heavily committed to sustaining indefinitely an independent but authoritarian South Vietnam with additional billions of dollars in financial assistance, military supplies, advisers, and long-range aerial support. Such was the high cost of leaving.

Repeated Republican boasts that Nixon had ended the war rang hollow, because the cease-fire agreements were daily violated, heavy fighting continued, and at least 50,000 Vietnamese, North and South, were reportedly killed during the year following "peace with honor." In a sense there were no winners or losers—just victims. The long list included draft-dodgers and deserters, for whom the "doves" raised a mounting cry for amnesty.

Watergate Woes

Nixon did not have long to enjoy his recent electoral triumph of November 1972, for it was soon sullied by a flood of so-called Watergate scandals. On June 17, 1972, some two months before his renomination, a bungled burglary had occurred in the Democratic headquarters, located in the Watergate apartment-office complex in Washington. Five men were arrested inside the building with electronic "bugging" equipment in their possession. They were working for the Republican Committee for the Re-election of the President—popularly known as CREEP—which had managed to raise tens of millions of dollars, often by secretive, unethical, or unlawful means. Large corporate contributions, some in the range of $100,000 or more, resembled bribes or extortion money paid in the expectation of future or continued favors from the Nixon administration. CREEP had also engaged in a "dirty tricks" campaign of unethical espionage and sabotage, including faked documents, directed against Democratic candidates in the campaign of 1972.

The Watergate break-in proved to be only the tip of an iceberg in a slimy sea of corruption that made the Grant and Harding scandals look almost respectable. A number of prominently placed White House aides and advisers were forced to resign. Many were involved in a criminal obstruction

"The Ancient Mariner." Nixon troubled by Watergate albatross. (Courtesy SCRAWLS and the Palm Beach *Post.*)

of justice through tangled cover-ups or payment of hush money. By early 1974, twenty-nine people had been indicted, had pleaded guilty, or had been convicted of Watergate-related crimes. Additionally, about ten corporations had been convicted of making illegal contributions. Other guilty persons and companies surfaced in the months ahead.

The scandal in Washington also provoked the improper or illegal use of the Federal Bureau of Investigation and the Central Intelligence Agency. Even the Internal Revenue Service was called upon by Nixon's aides to audit or otherwise harass political opponents and others who had fallen into disfavor. A White House "enemies list" turned up which included innocent citizens who were to be hounded or prosecuted in various ways—as though the government were the persecutor rather than the protector and servant of the people. In the name of national security, Nixon's aides had authorized a burglary of the files of Dr. Daniel Ellsberg's psychiatrist, so great was the determination to convict the man who had "leaked" the Pentagon Papers. This was the most notorious exploit of the White House "plumbers unit," created to plug up leaks of confidential information that might be useful to foreign powers.

A select Senate committee, headed by the aging Senator Sam Ervin of North Carolina, conducted a prolonged and widely televised series of hearings in 1973–1974. John Dean III, a former White House lawyer with a remarkable memory, testified glibly and at great length as to the involvement of the top echelons in the White House, including the President, in the cover-up of the Watergate break-in. Dean in effect accused Nixon of the crime of obstructing justice, but the committee then had only the unsupported word of Dean against White House protestations of innocence.

The Great Tape Controversy

A bombshell exploded before Senator Ervin's committee in July 1973 when a former presidential aide reported the presence in the White House of "bugging" equipment, installed under the President's authority. Nixon's conversations, in person or on the telephone, had been recorded on tape without notifying the other parties that electronic eavesdropping was taking place.

Nixon had emphatically denied prior knowledge of the Watergate burglary or involvement in the cover-up. Now Dean's sensational testimony could be checked against the White House tapes, and the Senate committee could better determine who was telling the truth. But for months Nixon flatly refused to produce the taped evidence, partly on the grounds that he would weaken the presidential office for his successors (and himself). He took refuge behind various principles, including separation of powers and executive privilege (confidentiality). But all of them were at least constitutionally dubious, especially when used to cover up crime or obstruct justice. A common conclusion was that if Nixon were innocent, he would strengthen the presidency by promptly making available the evidence that would prove his innocence. Not to do so was widely (and correctly) interpreted as a confession of guilt or a defiant affirmation that the President held himself above the law.

"Tapeworm." Republican elephant suffers from a strange disease. (Robert Graysmith, San Francisco *Chronicle*, by permission.)

The anxieties of the White House deepened when Vice-President Agnew, whom Nixon had lifted from relative obscurity in 1968, was forced to resign in October 1973. Although evidently not involved in the Watergate-related crimes, he was accused of taking bribes or "kickbacks" from Maryland contractors while governor and also as Vice-President. The case against him proved so overwhelming that, rather than go to jail, he pleaded "no contest" to a charge of income-tax evasion. His plea in these circumstances amounted to an admission of guilt. Fined $10,000 and placed on three-year probation, he fell even further when disbarred as a lawyer.

President Nixon himself was now in danger of being removed by the impeachment route, so Congress invoked the 25th Amendment (see Appendix) to replace Agnew with a twelve-term congressman from Michigan, Gerald ("Jerry") Ford. As a former football star at the University of Michigan, he had achieved fame in college for brawn rather than brains, but his record in public life was politically respectable and his financial affairs proved to be above suspicion at a time when unquestioned honesty was in short supply. He was hailed as "Mr. Clean."

Ten days after Agnew's resignation came the famous "Saturday Night Massacre" (October 20,

1973). Archibald Cox, a Harvard law professor appointed as a special prosecutor by Nixon in May, had been assured of a free hand in securing relevant tapes and other documents from the White House. After encountering stubborn resistance, he finally issued a subpoena for what he required. Nixon thereupon fired Cox, and then accepted the resignations of the attorney general and the deputy attorney general because they would not fire Cox.

The outraged public outcry, especially as expressed in a flood of telegrams to the White House, brought such strident demands for impeachment or resignation that Nixon backed down. Although he agreed to comply with demands for tapes and documents from the new special prosecutor and the House Judiciary Committee, such materials were forthcoming only partially and after foot-dragging delays. Word gradually leaked out of the White House that some of the tapes were missing, that others had never been recorded, and that portions of key conversations had been mysteriously blotted out, perhaps deliberately "sanitized."

The House Judiciary Committee now faced up more resolutely to an investigation of impeachment charges. Such activity intensified after revelations that Nixon's income-tax returns in recent years had benefited from astonishingly large but unallowable deductions, some of which more than suggested fraud.

The Secret Bombing of Cambodia

As if Watergate were not enough, the constitutionality of Nixon's continued aerial battering of Cambodia came under increasing fire. In July of 1973 America was shocked to learn that the U.S. air force had already secretly conducted some 3,500 bombing raids against North Vietnamese positions in Cambodia. They had begun in March 1969, and had continued for some fourteen months prior to the open American incursion in May 1970. Evidently the Cambodian government proved cooperative and President Nixon had privately notified a few hawkish leaders of Congress whose approval could be expected. But perhaps the most disturbing feature of these sky forays was that while they were going on, American officials, including the President, were avowing that Cambodian neutrality was being respected. Countless Americans began to wonder what kind of representative government they had if they were fighting a war which they knew nothing about and would have opposed if they had known of its existence.

> The Washington *Post* (July 19, 1973) carried this news item: "American B-52 bombers dropped about 104,000 tons of explosives on Communist sanctuaries in neutralist Cambodia during a series of raids in 1969 and 1970. . . . The secret bombing was acknowledged by the Pentagon the Monday after a former Air Force major . . . described how he falsified reports on Cambodian air operations and destroyed records on the bombing missions actually flown."

Defiance followed secretiveness. Nixon's large-scale bombing of Communist forces in Cambodia after the Vietnam cease-fire had gone into effect in 1973 was in the open, and was carried on in the teeth of furious public opposition. Many Americans, especially after Vietnam, abhorred the philosophy of destroying a country in order to save it from Communism. Such bombing assaults grew more devastating in the early summer of 1973, and were designed to help the rightist Cambodian government against Cambodian Communists. Nixon stretched his war-making powers (he had no war-declaring powers under the Constitution) when he argued that crushing the Communists in Cambodia was one way of supporting the Vietnam cease-fire, to which the United States was a party.

A clear majority in both Houses of Congress favored an end to the bombing, but repeated efforts to achieve a stoppage by adding amendments to essential appropriations bills fell before the President's veto pen. There were always enough hawkish votes in the House, at least one-third plus one, to prevent Congress from overriding the Nixonian negative. But appropriations were running short, the power of the purse finally prevailed, and in June 1973, the President was forced to accept a compromise. He would reluctantly end the bombing and other military operations in Cambodia on August 15—some six weeks later—and thereafter would seek congressional approval of any future activity in that blasted country. Yet he and Dr. Kissinger both regarded this enforced cessation of bombing as an act of great weakness that would undermine "the prospect for world peace."

"Henry Kissinger, Diplomat with a Global Vision." Born in Germany, Kissinger never lost his German accent. A brilliant Harvard professor, he first served as Nixon's adviser on national security affairs and then as secretary of state. (Robert Graysmith, San Francisco *Chronicle*, by permission.)

The "New Isolationism"

The "doves" in Congress had long opposed the expansion of war-making powers by Presidents Johnson and Nixon, especially in Indochina. Johnson had operated under authority hastily voted by Congress in the blank-check Tonkin Gulf resolution; Nixon no longer enjoyed this sanction because Congress had repealed it in June 1971. Then, after failing eight times to override Nixon's veto, Congress finally mustered enough votes to pass its own restriction on the war-making powers in November 1973. Under the new law the President was required to report to Congress within 48 hours after committing troops to a foreign conflict or "substantially" enlarging American combat units in a foreign country. Such a limited authorization would have to end within sixty days unless Congress extended it for thirty more days.

Compelling Nixon to end the bombing of Cambodia in August 1973 was but one manifestation of what came to be called the "New Isolationism." It was largely a child of the ugly war in Vietnam and the subsequent "peace" that demanded open-ended monetary and other material support. The detested draft ended in January 1973, although retained on a standby basis. Future members of the armed forces were to be well-paid volunteers—a change that greatly eased tensions among the youth, especially in the colleges. Insistent demands arose in Congress for reducing American armed forces abroad, especially since some 300,000 remained in Europe more than a quarter of a century after Hitler's downfall. The argument often heard was that the Western European countries, with more population than the Soviet Union, ought by now to be willing and able to provide for their own defense against the forces of Communism. But President Nixon, fearful of a weakened hand in the high-stakes game of power politics, headed off all serious attempts at troop reduction. The patchwork North Atlantic Treaty Organization continued to function, with some of the fifteen members unreliably dragging their feet.

Dr. Kissinger, Nixon's adviser on national security affairs, proclaimed in April 1973 "the Year of Europe," with a stronger NATO alliance occupying center stage. Such hopes were dashed, yet 1973 turned out to be "the Year of Kissinger," for the German-born émigré officially became secretary of state in September 1973—a post that he had already virtually held. The next month he was awarded one-half of the $122,000 Nobel Peace Prize for his role in negotiating the Paris accords which had brought a "cease-fire" to Vietnam—a cease-fire that had already claimed some 50,000 lives. The other half went to the chief North Vietnamese negotiator at Paris, Le Duc Tho. He refused his share for the reason that "peace" had never come to Vietnam.

Invaded Israel and American Aid

The long-rumbling Middle East erupted anew in October 1973, when the rearmed Syrians and Egyptians unleashed crushing surprise attacks on Israeli forces. They were obviously seeking to regain the extensive territory lost in the so-called Six Day War of 1967. The Israelis, though attackers in the earlier conflict, were caught off guard while celebrating their most sacred holiday, Yom Kippur. Battles flamed furiously on both fronts as the Egyptians stormed across the Suez Canal and attacked Israeli fall-back positions.

Israel was caught in a desperate bind, pinched as she was between Syria on the north and Egypt on the south. Few observers believed that her vengeful Arab enemies, if overwhelmingly victorious, would stop at regaining only lost land. Secretary Kissinger hastily flew to Moscow in a last-ditch effort to restrain the Soviets, who had provided the attackers with the great bulk of their tanks, aircraft, and other sophisticated weapons. Nixon promptly placed America's nuclear forces on a precautionary alert when he learned, whether correctly or not, that the Russians were poised to fly combat troops into the Suez area. The deterrent effect of the President's bomb-rattling is unknown, but in any event the Russians did not intervene and America's NATO allies drew back in alarm. The Israelis suffered such heavy losses of arms in the initial surprise onslaught that Nixon ordered a gigantic airlift of nearly $2 billion in war materials, which undoubtedly saved the day. Included was a gift of 1,000 tanks.

At a crucial phase of the fighting along the Suez Canal, the Israelis executed a brilliant thrust across the waterway to the rear of the enemy, thereby threatening destruction of the Egyptian armies and the capture of Cairo. This successful strategic stroke, combined with American intervention and diplomatic assistance, ended the fighting on the Israeli-Egyptian front. The combatants were gradually disentangled, as the Israelis withdrew to a new defense line somewhat farther back from the canal. An uneasy peace settled over the Syrian front seven bloody months later, after intense negotiations during which Secretary Kissinger shuttled back and forth from Damascus to Jerusalem for thirty-two days.

The Arab Oil Embargo

America's policy of backing Israel against her oil-rich neighbors exacted a heavy penalty. Late in October 1973, the Arab countries suddenly clamped an embargo on oil for the United States and other Israel-supporting countries. The oil-thirsty American people, numbering about 6 percent of the world's population but consuming some 30 percent of its energy, derived only about 6 percent of their petroleum supply from Arab lands. But this deficiency was enough to create a fuel crisis. The United States, though abundantly forewarned by experts, overnight discovered that the age of cheap and abundant oil had ended. Nixon, though opposing rationing, enthroned an energy czar, and the American people suffered through a long winter of lowered thermostats and speedometers. Lines of automobiles at service

"Hat in Hand." (Editorial cartoon by Lou Grant of the Oakland *Tribune*. Copyright, Los Angeles *Times* Syndicate. Reprinted with permission.)

stations lengthened as tempers shortened and an incipient business recession deepened.

The "energy crisis" suddenly energized a number of long-deferred projects. The costly pipeline from northern to southern Alaska received congressional sanction in 1974, over the protests of conservationists and environmentalists, who feared oil spills and the destruction of flora and fauna, including caribou. President Nixon also urged a crash program to make America self-sufficient in energy by the target date 1980. Proposals multiplied for utlizing energy from the sun, wind, geothermal sources, and untapped coal deposits, of which the United States had more than half of the world's known reserves—or enough to last for an estimated several hundred years. Yet heavy coal consumption would increase air pollution. The result was that agitation mounted for relaxing standards for clean air and water, as well as for pushing ahead with more nuclear power stations, despite their ever-present threat of catastrophic radioactivity.

Nixon, the Law-and-Order Man.
(Douglas Marlette, The Charlotte *Observer*.)

The Arab "blackmail" embargo, partially leaky, was lifted in March 1974, after five months of anxiety, and after the Egypt-Israeli cease-fire had taken effect. Countless Americans, especially those in big gas-gulping cars, reverted thoughtlessly to their speeding and other wasteful practices. The Middle Eastern sheiks had about quadrupled their price of crude oil, and their inevitable accumulation of tens of billions of dollars jeopardized the American balance of trade and payments. And despite the resumed flow of Middle Eastern oil, the country continued to be plagued in 1974 by double-digit inflation, high unemployment, and the growing realization that the cost of energy was headed ever upward.

Impeachment Politics

Political tribulations added to the nation's cup of woe in 1974. The continuing impeachment inquiry cast damning doubts on President Nixon's truthfulness and moral integrity. The impeachment investigation reached a new climax on April 29, 1974, when Nixon belatedly responded to the demand of the House Judiciary Committee for forty-two tapes by making a dramatic appearance on television. Exuding confidence, and with a huge pile of manuscript folders at his elbow, he staged a virtuoso performance. He announced that he was not submitting the requested Watergate tapes to the House, but only typed transcripts of those portions that he, though under investigation, deemed relevant to the impeachment proceedings. He further declared that "everything that is relevant" was revealed, including some material not subpoenaed, and that this mass of documentary evidence would further prove his innocence. He also stated that the "rough" language thus submitted would embarrass him, but that he was including it because he had "nothing to hide."

Publication of the bulky transcripts in one printed volume stirred up a storm of criticism. Readers, including congressmen, quickly perceived that Nixon had not provided the tapes or even the contents of all the forty-two requested. He had, in fact, cut out substantial portions of those presented. Much of the "rough" language had been replaced with the phrases "expletive deleted" or "characterization deleted." In one uncensored passage Nixon described President Truman as an "old bastard" whom many had admired for "standing by people . . . who were guilty as hell." Even more shocking to many readers was the low tone of the White House conversations: cynical, amoral, vindictive, self-serving, and conspiratorial. Some of the President's former defenders were reminded of the secret plottings of gangsters. The once-popular Nixon slogan was modified to read, "Four More Years—Two Off for Good Behavior."

A releasing of the tapes deepened grave suspicions about the President's role in the Watergate cover-up and related crimes. Nixon temporarily rode out the storm by what he called "stonewalling," that is, by flatly refusing to turn over any more tapes to the investigators. The issue of withholding "confidential" evidence was finally brought directly to the Supreme Court.

The Unmaking of a President

Nixon meanwhile diverted some attention from the impeachment probe by embarking on two spectacular tours, the first to the Middle East in mid-June 1974, and the second to the Soviet Union later that month.

He returned from his modest foreign triumphs to suffer a series of disastrous setbacks. On July 24, 1974, the Supreme Court unanimously ruled that he had no right, under executive privilege, to withhold from the special prosecutor those portions of the sixty-four tapes that involved relevant criminal activity. Nixon reluctantly agreed to comply with this decision.

The House Judiciary Committee pressed ahead with its articles of impeachment. The key vote came late in July 1974, when the committee adopted the first article, which charged obstruction of "the administration of justice," including Watergate-related crimes. The count was 27 to 11, with all of the Democrats and nearly half of the Republican members voting for impeachment. Two other articles were later approved by the committee accusing Nixon of having abused the powers of his office and of having shown contempt of Congress by ignoring lawful subpoenas for relevant tapes and other evidence. Insiders were certain that at least the first of the articles of impeachment would pass the Democratic House by wide margins. The President would then have to subject himself and the nation to a long and disruptive trial in the Senate, all the while hoping that a two-thirds vote for conviction could not be mustered.

Seeking to soften the impact of inevitable disclosure, Nixon voluntarily took a step, on August 5, 1974, that had a devastating effect on what remained of his credibility. He now made public

Pushing for Impeachment. An angry and disillusioned public grew increasingly impatient with the President's evasions in 1974. (United Press International photo.)

The Last Goodbye. Nixon lifts off in a White House helicopter for the last time as President on August 9, 1974. (Wide World Photos, Inc.)

three subpoenaed tapes of conversations with his chief aide on June 23, 1972. One of them had him giving orders, six days after the Watergate break-in, to use the Central Intelligence Agency to hold back an investigation by the Federal Bureau of Investigation. Last-ditch defenders of Nixon had hitherto claimed that there was no direct evidence of a crime—no "smoking pistol." Now Nixon's own tape-recorded words convicted him of having been an active party to the attempted cover-up, in itself the crime of obstructing justice. More than that, he had solemnly told the American people on television that he had known nothing of the Watergate cover-up until about nine months later.

The public backlash proved to be overwhelming. Republican leaders in Congress concluded that the guilty and unpredictable Nixon was a loose cannon on the deck of the ship of state. They frankly informed the President that his impeachment by the full House and removal by the Senate were foregone conclusions. They made it clear that he would best serve his nation, his party, and himself by resigning with honor, or a semblance of it. If convicted by the Senate he would lose all his normal retirement benefits; if he resigned he could retain them—more than $150,000 a year—and retire in royal splendor.

Left with no better choice, Nixon choked back his tears and announced his resignation in a dramatic television appearance on August 8, 1974. In this Farewell Address he admitted having made some "judgments" that "were wrong" but insisted that he had always acted "in what I believed at the time to be the best interests of the nation." Unconvinced, countless Americans would change the song "Hail to the Chief" to "Jail to the Chief."

The nation had survived a wrenching constitutional crisis, which proved that the impeachment machinery forged by the Founding Fathers could work when public opinion overwhelmingly demanded that it be made to work. The principles were strengthened that no person is above the law and that the President must be held to strict accountability for his acts. Democracy was still flourishing when the sovereign people could force out of office the powerful head of the mightiest nation without firing a single shot. The United States of America, on the eve of its 200th birthday as a republic, had given an impressive demonstration of self-discipline and self-government to the rest of the world.

The First Unelected President

Gerald Rudolph Ford, the first person to be made President solely by a vote of Congress, entered the blackened White House, in August 1974, under serious handicaps. He was widely—and unfairly—suspected of being little more than a dim-witted former football player. President Johnson had sneered that "Jerry" was so lacking in brainpower that he could not walk and chew gum at the same time. Worse, Ford had been selected, not elected, Vice-President, following Spiro Agnew's resignation in disgrace. An odor of illegitimacy hung about this President without precedent. Yet long-time congressman Ford had many friends on Capitol Hill, and for a time enjoyed a political "honeymoon."

Then, out of a clear sky, Ford granted a complete pardon to Nixon for any crimes he may have committed as President, discovered or undiscovered. Nixon gratefully accepted this gift without acknowledging his guilt, although Ford insisted

How Long Will Nixon Haunt the GOP? Doubts about Ford's pardon of Nixon clouded his brief presidency. (Joseph A. Smith as printed in *Newsweek*, September 23, 1974. Collection of the artist)

President Ford in the Oval Office. The first unelected president, Ford also served one of the shortest terms—less than two and one-half years. He helped the country to recover from the trauma of Watergate, but the voters nevertheless denied him election in his own right in 1976. (Courtesy, Ford Library. Photo by David Hume Kennerly)

that Nixon's very acceptance amounted to a confession of wrongdoing. The fallen Nixon continued to live in kingly retirement, while many subordinates who had carried out his commands languished in prison.

In issuing the "unpardonable pardon," Ford explained that Nixon and his family had already suffered enough; that the former President was in dangerously poor health (which he was); that passions had been so widely aroused that no fair trial was possible; and that only a full pardon could restore "domestic tranquillity" to the passion-torn nation. All these explanations seemingly testified to Ford's compassion, but Democrats particularly were outraged. They wanted iron-toothed justice, even vengeance. They heatedly charged, without persuasive evidence, that Ford was carrying out a "buddy deal" that had been cooked up when Nixon nominated him for the Vice-Presidency. Lingering suspicions about the pardon deal cast a dark shadow over Ford's prospects of being elected President in his own right in 1976.

His honeymoon now ended, Ford hit rough weather in the heavily Democratic Congress. A serious recession inspired several billion-dollar spending bills intended to reduce unemployment. Fearing the inflationary effects of these huge appropriations, Ford vetoed them. In all, he laid his veto ax to more than fifty bills during his brief term in office. Attacking the inflation problem, Ford launched a Whip Inflation Now campaign (complete with WIN buttons), but it failed to get off the ground. Inflation did drop from the double-digit range of 12 percent to about 5 percent by the end of 1976, but the improvement turned out to be only temporary. Unemployment remained stubbornly high—about 7 percent by the time Ford vacated the White House in January 1977.

Ford's Foreign Affairs

The so-called détente with Russia that Nixon had crafted went haltingly forward. Hopes for a more civilized world rose modestly in July 1975 when President Ford joined leaders from 34 other nations in Helsinki, Finland, to sign several sets of historic accords. One group of agreements officially wrote an end to World War II by finally legitimizing the Soviet-dictated boundaries of Poland and other East European countries. In return, the Soviets put their signatures to a "third basket" of agreements, guaranteeing more liberal exchanges of people and information between East and West, and protecting certain basic "human rights." The Helsinki accords helped to kindle small dissident movements in Eastern Europe and even in Russia itself, but the Soviets soon poured ice water on these sputtering flames of freedom. Russian restrictions on Jewish emigration had already, in December 1974, prompted the U.S. Congress to add punitive restrictions to a U.S.–Russian trade bill.

West Europeans, especially the West Germans, cheered the Helsinki conference as a milestone of détente, but in the United States critics increasingly charged that détente was proving to be a one-way street, with American grain and technology flowing across the Atlantic to Russia, and with little of comparable importance flowing back. American conservatives cried that the Soviet Communists were not only preparing to "bury us," but that unwary Americans were supplying the shovels.

Détente was also conspicuously two-faced. Soviet ships and planes hauled great quantities of arms and military technicians to pro-Communist forces around the globe, while Cuba's Castro, with Moscow's blessing, dispatched thousands of troops to Africa. Such ill-concealed activity dashed hopes of establishing diplomatic relations with Cuba.

Despite these difficulties, Ford at first clung stubbornly to détente. Unwilling to offend the Russians, he refused to receive at the White House the distinguished Russian writer Alexander Solzhenitsyn, who had been exiled by the Kremlin for exposing wholesale Soviet brutalities. Conservatives heaped abuse on Ford for this act of calculated rudeness, and they denounced détente with mounting fury. Even the prestigious Henry Kissinger came under attack as one of the chief architects of détente, and his power began to fade like a burned-out comet. By the end of his term Ford was refusing even to pronounce the word *détente* in public, and the thaw in the Cold War was threatening to prove chillingly brief.

Victory for North Vietnam

Early in 1975, the North Vietnamese gave full throttle to their long-expected drive southward. President Ford urged Congress to vote still more weapons for Vietnam, but his plea was in vain, and without the crutch of massive American aid,

Vietnam Refugees, 1975. Thousands of South Vietnamese citizens who had supported the U.S. presence in the war against North Vietnam crowded onto every available form of transportation leaving the country. Fearing massive reprisals by the Communists, they were willing to leave everything they owned and go anywhere, as long as it was out of the Communists' reach. (Official U.S. Navy Photograph)

the South Vietnamese quickly and ingloriously collapsed.

The dam burst so rapidly that the remaining Americans had to be frantically evacuated by helicopter, the last of them on April 29, 1975. Also rescued were about 140,000 South Vietnamese, most of them so dangerously identified with the Americans that they feared a bloodbath by the victorious Communists. President Ford compassionately admitted these people to the United States, where they added further seasoning to the melting pot.

America's longest, most frustrating war thus ended, not with a bang, but with a whimper. In a technical sense the Americans had not lost the war; their client nation had. The United States had fought the North Vietnamese to a standstill and had then withdrawn its troops in 1973, leaving the Vietnamese to fight their own war, with generous shipments of costly American aircraft, tanks, and other munitions. President Thieu of South Vietnam complained bitterly that the United States had not done or sent enough. Yet the estimated cost to America was $118 billion in current outlays and some 56,000 dead and 300,000 wounded. The American people had in fact provided just about everything, except the will to win—and that could not be injected by outsiders.

Technicalities aside, the United States had lost more than a war. It had lost face in the eyes of foreigners, pride in itself, confidence in its military prowess—and much of the economic muscle that had made possible its world leadership since World War II. One of the toughest tasks facing the Ford administration was to find a cure, both at home and abroad, for the crippling symptoms of the "post-Vietnám syndrome."

In mid-May 1975, about six weeks after the breakneck pullout from Vietnam, Washington applied some strong but strange medicine to its ailing foreign-policy image. Cambodian Communists provided the opportunity when they seized

Passing the Buck. A cruel, satirical view of where responsibility for the Vietnam debacle should be laid. (© 1975, Jules Feiffer. Reprinted with permission of Universal Press Syndicate.)

the *Mayaguez,* an unarmed American merchant ship, and captured its thirty-nine crew members. Scarcely pausing for clarification or negotiation, Ford dispatched American forces to free the American sailors. The rescuers succeeded—but only after losing about as many lives as they presumably saved.

This swift, two-fisted strike proved a tonic to the American public, who were still smarting from their recent rout in Vietnam, but its effects were short-lived. Americans reluctantly came to realize that their power as well as their pride had been wounded in Vietnam, and that recovery would be slow and painful.

VARYING VIEWPOINTS

Richard Nixon may well be the most controversial political personality in recent American history. He built his career on the most inflammatory issues of the day, from Red-chasing in the 1940s to the Vietnam War in the 1960s, and the Watergate episode ended his public life with the most explosive constitutional crisis in over a century. Ever combative and resourceful, he antagonized his enemies and cultivated his followers with unremitting energy and skill. Hence there are few "objective" accounts of the Nixon years; passion still guides the pens of most writers (including Nixon himself), producing assessments that are either bitterly critical or aggressively apologetic. Thus it may be some time before historians can make a balanced appraisal of Nixon's role. The stain of Watergate, for example, has almost blotted from the record Nixon's initiatives in foreign policy, especially toward China. Whatever the final judgment, it seems that historians will be unforgiving of the wounds that Watergate inflicted on the American body politic. Trust in elected leaders is an essential but fragile ingredient in a democracy, and that trust was badly undermined by the Watergate revelations.

SELECT READINGS

Nixon's intriguing personality is examined in Gary Wills, *Nixon Agonistes: The Crisis of the Self-Made Man* (1970), and in Fawn Brodie, *Richard Nixon: The Shaping of His Character* (1981). Rowland Evans, Jr., and Robert D. Novak discuss *Nixon in the White House: The Frustration of Power* (1971). Theodore White continues his chronicle of presidential electioneering in *The Making of the President, 1972* (1973); White registers his disillusion with Nixon in *Breach of Faith* (1975). The Democratic loser in 1972 is analyzed in Robert S. Anson, *McGovern* (1972). R. M. Scammon and Ben J. Wattenberg look at underlying changes in the electorate in the 1960s in *The Real Majority* (1970). Valuable background on American foreign policy in the Nixon years can be found in David P. Calleo and Benjamin Rowland, *America and the World Political Economy* (1973). See also Richard J. Barnet, *Roots of War* (1972), and, on multinational corporations, Richard J. Barnet and R. E. Muller, *Global Reach* (1974). Incisive assessments of Nixon's initiatives in foreign policy include Henry Brandon, *The Retreat of American Power* (1973), Robert E. Osgood et al., *Retreat from Empire? The First Nixon Administration* (1973), and R. W. Tucker, *A New Isolationism* (1972). On the Paris peace negotiations, see Gareth Porter, *A Peace Denied* (1975). Restrospectives on Vietnam include George C. Herring, *America's Longest War* (1979), L. H. Gelb and R. K. Betts, *The Irony of Vietnam: The System Worked* (1979), Guenter Lewy, *America in Vietnam* (1978), and William Shawcross's chilling account of Cambodia, *Sideshow* (2nd ed., 1981). Shawcross is vigorously rebutted in Henry Kissinger's rich memoir, *White House Years* (1979). The Middle East is the focus of W. B. Quandt, *Decade of Decision: American Policy toward the Arab-Israeli Conflict, 1967–1976* (1977). Arthur M. Schlesinger, Jr., traces the growth of *The Imperial Presidency* (1973). The Watergate crisis is vividly described in two books by Carl Bernstein and Robert Woodward, *All the President's Men* (1974) and *The Final Days* (1976). Jonathan Schell, *The Time of Illusion* (1976), assesses the impact of the crisis on the nation's spirit and institutions. Many of the fallen President's former men have written of their involvement in the Watergate affair, including Jeb Stuart Magruder, John Dean, John Erlichman, and H. R. Haldeman. Nixon himself has produced a lengthy volume, *RN: The Memoirs of Richard Nixon* (1978). "Jerry" Ford, the first appointed President, is analyzed by his former press secretary in J. F. ter Horst, *Gerald Ford and the Future of the Presidency* (1974). For a sharply critical view, see Clark Mollenhoff, *The Man Who Pardoned Nixon* (1976). Consult also Richard Reeves, *A Ford, Not a Lincoln* (1975), and Ford's own *A Time to Heal: The Autobiography of Gerald R. Ford* (1979). Nixon's and Ford's controversial secretary of state is the subject of several books: David Landau, *Kissinger: The Uses of Power* (1972), Stephen R. Graubard, *Kissinger: Portrait of a Mind* (1973), Bernard and Marvin Kalb, *Kissinger* (1974), and Bruce Mazlish, *Kissinger: The European Mind in American Policy* (1976). On the final collapse of South Vietnam, see the esposé by ex-CIA agent Frank Snepp, *Decent Interval* (1977).

47

The Carter Interlude and the Reagan Revolution

As the first man from the Deep South in 130 years to be President of this nation, I say that these people in white sheets do not understand our region and what it's been through. . . . They do not understand what our country stands for.

PRESIDENT JIMMY CARTER,
responding to the interruption of his speech
by Ku Klux Klansmen in Tuscumbia, Alabama,
Labor Day, 1980.

The Bicentennial Campaign

America's 200th birthday, in 1976, fell on a presidential election year—a fitting coincidence for a proud democracy. Gerald Ford energetically sought nomination for the presidency in his own right. After a bruising contest with his chief rival, former movie actor and former California governor Ronald Reagan, Ford won the Republican nomination by a narrow margin at the Kansas City convention.

The Democratic standard bearer was fifty-one-year-old James Earl Carter, Jr., a dark-horse candidate who galloped out of obscurity during

Carter Campaigning in California, 1976.
(Tony Korody, Sygma.)

the long primary-elections season. A graduate of the Naval Academy, he had come home from the sea to manage his family's peanut-farming business in Plains, Georgia, a state which he had subsequently served as governor from 1971 to 1975. Flashing a toothy smile and insisting on humble "Jimmy" as his first name, this born-again Baptist touched many people with his down-home sincerity. He ran against the memory of Nixon and Watergate as much as he ran against Ford, and his most effective campaign pitch was his promise that "I'll never lie to you." Untainted by ties with a corrupt and cynical Washington, he attracted voters as an outsider who would clean the disorderly house of "Big Government." He also appealed to the Deep South, the once-rebellious section that had not been represented in the White House since Zachary Taylor's presidency in 1849–1850, 126 years earlier.

As the campaign entered its final stretch, the two candidates faced off in a series of nationally televised debates, the first such encounters since the Kennedy-Nixon exchanges in 1960. Ford flubbed badly in front of the cameras when he stated emphatically that Poland and other Soviet satellites in Eastern Europe were not groaning under Moscow's thumb. He thus alienated a large part of the sizeable Polish-American vote, and raised disturbing doubts about his grasp of foreign affairs.

Carter squeezed out a narrow victory on election day, with 51 percent of the popular vote. The electoral count stood at 297 to 240. The winner swept every state except Virginia in his native South. Especially important were the votes of blacks, 97 percent of whom cast their ballots for Carter. Ford, the former football star, took his disappointing loss with sporting grace. Carter, with equal grace, paid generous tribute to his opponent when in his inaugural address he warmly thanked Ford for helping to heal the wounds the nation had suffered because of Watergate.

The Carter Honeymoon

After the colorful inaugural ceremonies of January 20, 1977, Jimmy Carter waved off the official black limousine and walked, hand-in-hand with his wife Rosalyn, down Pennsylvania Avenue to his new home at the White House. This act symbolized his determination to maintain the common touch. Carter's Cabinet choices reflected his desire to broaden his political base, as well as reward his political supporters. Carter named Patricia Harris as Secretary of Housing and Urban Development, Juanita Kreps as Secretary of Commerce, civil rights activist Andrew Young as Ambassador to the United Nations, and Cyrus Vance, a former Kennedy-Johnson Pentagon official, as Secretary of State. Carter's vice-president, former Minnesota Senator Walter ("Fritz") Mondale, provided a link to the northern, liberal wing of the party. The new President's popularity remained exceptionally high during his first few months in office, even when he courted public disfavor by courageously keeping his campaign promise to pardon 10,000 draft evaders of the Vietnam War era.

Carter also enjoyed hefty Democratic majorities in both houses of Congress. Hopes ran high that the stalemate of the Nixon-Ford years between a Republican White House and a Democratic Capitol Hill would now be ended. At first, Carter enjoyed notable political success. Congress granted his request to create a new Cabinet-level Department of Energy. Calling the American tax system "a disgrace to the human race," Carter also proposed tax reform and reduction. Congress eventually obliged him, in part, with an $18 billion tax cut in 1978.

But Carter's honeymoon did not last long. An inexperienced outsider, he had campaigned against the Washington "establishment," and never quite made the transition to being an insider himself. He repeatedly rubbed congressional fur the wrong way, especially by failing to consult adequately with the leaders. Critics charged that he isolated himself in a shallow pool of fellow Georgians, whose ignorance of the ways of Washington compounded the problems of their greenhorn chief. Before his first year in office was finished, Carter lost the services of one of the ablest of these advisers, Budget Director Bert Lance. Flamboyant and talented, Lance attracted attention for his cracker-barrel wit ("If it ain't broke, don't fix it"), and, unfortunately, for his wheeling and dealing while a bank director in Georgia. After lengthy and embarrassing hearings, which revealed Carter's inability to protect his friend, Lance resigned in late 1978.

"Don't worry, Bert, you're no trouble to me at all!"

Carter's Sea of Troubles. Carter was forced to deal with the Lance affair simultaneously with a number of tricky foreign and domestic issues. (© Renault/Rothco)

President Jimmy Carter's Inaugural Walk, 1977. (J. P. Laffont and Owen Franken, Sygma.)

Carter's Humanitarian Diplomacy

As a committed Christian, President Carter displayed from the outset an overriding concern for "human rights" as the guiding principle of his foreign policy. He verbally lashed the dictatorial regimes of Cuba and Uganda, among others, and cut foreign aid to the repressive governments in Uruguay, Argentina, and Ethiopia. But he stopped short of punitive actions against other offending nations, such as South Korea or the Philippines, presumably because they were too vital to American security to risk insulting. In the African nations of Rhodesia (later Zimbabwe) and South Africa, Carter championed the oppressed black majority, whose cause was also eloquently defended by United Nations Ambassador Andrew Young.

The nightmarish nuclear arms race with the Soviet Union continued to cause jitters, especially because the limitations on intercontinental ballistic missiles, embodied in the SALT agreements signed by President Nixon, were due to expire in late 1977. Carter in February 1977 publicly called for renewing the SALT accords and extending them to include real reductions in nuclear armaments, not just limitations on their growth. The Soviets gave these proposals a frosty reception, though both sides agreed to honor the SALT treaty even after it formally expired. Meanwhile, the world shuddered along, hoping for some salvation from the horror of nuclear holocaust.

Carter had better luck with two treaties designed to turn over to Panama complete ownership and control of the Panama Canal by the year 2000. Bloody Yankee-go-home riots had erupted on the Isthmus in 1964, and Presidents Johnson, Nixon, Ford, and Carter all favored releasing Panama from the yoke of 19th-Century imperialism dating back to Theodore Roosevelt and 1903. Conservatives bitterly opposed relinquishing control over the canal. Ronald Reagan rode the campaign trail in 1976 declaring that "we bought it, we paid for it, it's ours, and we are going to keep it." The two treaties, insuring the continuing neutrality of the canal and handing its ownership over to the Panamanians by the end of the century, squeaked through the Senate with only one vote to spare for the necessary two-thirds majority (68 to 32). The United States thus made partial amends for Theodore Roosevelt's "Big Stick" tactics near the dawn of the century.

ROTHCO

Historical Double-Take. Many Americans who looked back reverently to Roosevelt's "Rough Rider" diplomacy were outraged at the Panama "give-away." But the Carter administration, looking to the future, argued persuasively that relinquishing control of the canal would be healthy for U.S.-Latin American relations. (© Valtman/Rothco)

Camp David, the woodsy presidential retreat in the Maryland mountains, provided the scene of Carter's most spectacular foreign policy achievement. By August 1978 relations between Egypt and Israel had deteriorated so far that another blowup in the misery-drenched Middle East seemed imminent. So grave was the danger that Carter courageously risked humiliating failure by inviting President Anwar Sadat of Egypt and Prime Minister Menachem Begin of Israel to a summit conference at the rustic Camp David hideaway.

Skillfully serving as go-between, Carter after thirteen days persuaded the two visitors to sign an accord (September 17, 1978) that held considerable promise of peace. Israel agreed in principle to withdraw from territory conquered in the 1967 war, and Egypt in return promised to respect Israel's borders. Both parties pledged themselves to sign a formal peace treaty within three months. When that deadline passed with no treaty signed, Carter again displayed admirable fortitude by flying in person to the Middle East in March 1979 to bring the suspicious neighbors to final agreement. The President crowned this diplomatic success by resuming full diplomatic relations with China in early 1979, after a nearly thirty-year interruption.

Despite these dramatic accomplishments, trouble stalked Carter's foreign policy. Overshadowing all international issues was the ominous reheating of the Cold War with Russia. Détente fell into

The Signing of the Camp David Agreement, September 17, 1978. Anwar Sadat of Egypt, Jimmy Carter of the United States, and Menachem Begin of Israel put their signatures to the historic accord that brought hopes of peace to the war-torn Middle East. (© Sygma)

disrepute as thousands of Cuban troops, assisted by Soviet advisors, appeared in Angola, Ethiopia, and elsewhere in Africa to support revolutionary factions. Negotiations with Moscow over the SALT II agreement remained stalled in the face of this Soviet military meddling. Also worrisome was the apparent confusion about foreign policy within the Carter administration. Ambassador Young repeatedly embarrassed the White House with his outspoken views, including his claim that Cuban troops were a stabilizing element in Africa. He committed one indiscretion too many in 1979 when he intervened without authority in the delicate Middle East situation, and was forced to submit his resignation. In the administration's innermost circles, the dovish Secretary of State, Cyrus Vance, seemed always at odds with the hawkish National Security Advisor, Polish-born Zbigniew Brzezinski. "Who's in charge here" was a question repeatedly raised by the President's foreign-policy critics, whose numbers were growing.

Carter Tackles the Ailing Economy

Adding to Carter's mushrooming woes was the failing health of the economy. Inflation had afflicted the nation since the 1960s, when Lyndon Johnson had badly strained the country's economic muscles by trying simultaneously to fight a costly war in Vietnam and to fight poverty at home with his "Great Society" programs. Prices rose feverishly, increasing at a rate of more than 10 percent a year by 1974 ("double-digit" inflation). Crippling oil-price hikes from the Organization of Petroleum Exporting Countries (OPEC) in 1974 dealt the reeling economy another body blow. A stinging recession brought the inflation rate down temporarily during Gerald Ford's presidency, but virtually from the moment of Carter's inauguration prices resumed their dizzying ascent. OPEC nearly doubled its petroleum charges in 1979, helping to drive American inflation well above 13 percent. The soaring bill for imported oil pushed America's balance of payments deeply into the red (an unprecedented $40 billion in 1978), as Americans paid more for foreign products than they were able to earn from selling their own goods overseas.

Yawning deficits in the federal budget, reaching nearly $60 billion in 1980, further aggravated the economy's inflationary ailments. Americans with fixed incomes—mostly elderly persons or workers without a strong union to go to bat for them—

suffered from shrinking real incomes, as their dollars diminished in purchasing power. People with money to lend pushed interest rates ever higher, hoping to protect themselves from being repaid in badly depreciated dollars. The "prime rate," the rate of interest that banks charged their very best customers, vaulted to an unheard-of 20 percent in early 1980. The high cost of borrowing money shoved small businesses to the wall and strangled the construction industry, heavily dependent on loans to finance new housing and other projects.

From the outset, Carter diagnosed America's economic disease as stemming primarily from the nation's costly dependence on foreign oil. Accordingly, one of the first acts of his presidency was a dramatic appeal to Congress, and to the American people watching on television, to embark on an energy crusade that he called "the moral equivalent of war." He called for legislation to improve energy conservation, especially by curtailing the manufacture of large, gas-guzzling automobiles. But these proposals, in April 1977, ignited a blaze of indifference among the American people. They had already forgotten the long gasoline lines of 1973, when OPEC had first imposed an oil embargo. Public apathy and congressional hostility smothered Carter's hopes of quickly initiating an energetic energy program.

"Hello There, Have You Thought About the Energy Crisis Today?" Carter opposes gas-guzzling cars. (Robert Graysmith, The San Francisco *Chronicle*.)

Rats Desert a Sinking Ship. (Douglas Borgstedt, Copley News Service.)

Carter's Energy Woes

Events in far-away Iran jolted Americans out of their complacency about energy supplies in 1979. The imperious Mohammed Reza Pahlevi, Shah of Iran, had long ruled his oil-rich land with a will of steel. His repressive regime finally provoked a backlash, and the Shah was forced into globe-wandering exile in January 1979. Violent revolution, spearheaded by Muslim fundamentalists, engulfed Iran in the wake of the Shah's departure, and the crippling chaos soon spread to the country's oil fields. As Iranian oil stopped flowing into the stream of world commerce, petroleum prices resumed their steep rise, and shortages appeared. Americans once again found themselves waiting impatiently in long lines at their local gas stations, or allowed to buy gasoline only on specified days.

1979 Gas Line in New England. Scenes like this, repeated in all parts of the country, painfully impressed upon Americans the reality of the energy crisis. (© Michael Gordon/Picture Group)

These disquieting disruptions pained the American people, and presented Carter with both problems and opportunities. The shock of rising oil prices and tightening oil supplies spurred inflation and threatened to stifle the economy. On the other hand, the suddenness and seriousness of the crisis vividly underscored the President's contention that the nation had to adopt a comprehensive energy program. Seeking to take political advantage of the calamity, Carter began in April 1979 to lift price controls from domestically produced oil, a move designed both to curtail consumption and increase production. At the same time, he called for a massive "windfall profits" tax on the increased revenues that domestic oil producers would enjoy as a result of rising prices.

As the oil crisis deepened, President Carter sensed the rising temperature of popular discontent, and sought ways to advance still further toward his energy goals. He promised a major speech on the energy question, to be delivered on July 5, 1979—but when the date approached, Carter abruptly and mysteriously cancelled his address and retreated to the presidential mountain hideaway at Camp David, Maryland. There he remained largely out of public view for ten days. Like a royal potentate of old, summoning the wise men of the realm for their counsel in a time of crisis, Carter called in over 100 leaders from all walks of life to give him their views. Yet true to his folksy image, he ended his consultations by going to a nearby small town and soliciting the advice of

Carter Seeks Advice. A self-professed man of the people, Carter frequently betook himself to humble homes and modest town halls to listen to the voices of average Americans. Here he visits with a steelworker's family in Carnegie, Pennsylvania, in July, 1979. (Associated Press photo)

some ordinary Americans in their modest living room. Meanwhile, the nation waited anxiously for the results of these extraordinary deliberations.

Carter came down from the mountaintop on July 15, 1979, and revealed his thoughts to the American people in a remarkable television address. His listeners expected to hear about an energy program, but before he got to that point, Carter delivered a kind of old-fashioned "jeremiad." He chided his countrymen for falling into a "moral and spiritual crisis," and for being too concerned with "material goods." He spoke somberly about the "malaise" afflicting the country. His over-all message seemed to be that he was trying hard to be a good leader, but that the people were irresponsibly refusing to be led.

Finally, Carter arrived at his energy proposals. He boldly called for a ten-year, $140 billion dollar federal program. Its centerpiece was to be a government-backed Energy Security Corporation, whose chief function would be to develop synthetic fuels ("synfuels") to replace costly foreign oil. Included also were proposals to impose limits on foreign oil imports and to encourage the substitution of coal for oil, especially by electrical utility companies.

Carter's address stunned and even perplexed the nation, and he let drop another shoe a few days later. In a bureaucratic massacre of almost unprecedented proportions, he fired four Cabinet secretaries. At the same time he circled the wagons of his Georgian advisers more tightly about the White House by reorganizing and expanding the power of his personal staff. Critics began to wonder aloud whether Carter, the professed man of the people, was losing touch with the popular mood of the country.

Foreign Affairs and the Iranian Imbroglio

Hopes for a less dangerous world rose slightly in June 1979, when President Carter met with Soviet leader Leonid Brezhnev in Vienna to sign the long-stalled SALT II agreements, limiting the levels of lethal strategic weapons in the Russian and American arsenals. Yet from the outset Carter faced an uphill battle in trying to persuade the United States Senate to approve the SALT II treaty. Conservative critics of the President's defense policies remained deeply suspicious of the Soviet Union, which they regarded as the Wicked Witch of the East. Carter had already outraged them by his opposition to several high-technology weapons systems, including a new strategic bomber (the "B-1"), a $2-billion-dollar nuclear aircraft carrier, and deadly neutron bombs for deployment in Europe. Accusing Carter of being soft on the Soviets and careless in his concern for American security, these hard-liners unsheathed their long knives to carve up the SALT treaty when it came to the Senate for debate in the summer of 1979. Their hand was strengthened when news reports broke that a Soviet "combat brigade" was stationed in Castro's Cuba.

Two-Way SALT Talks. The grim specter of nuclear holocaust haunted the SALT II talks between Carter and Russian Leader Leonid Brezhnev in Vienna in June, 1979. (© Uluschak/Rothco)

Political earthquakes in the petroleum-rich Persian Gulf region finally buried all hopes of ratifying the SALT treaty. The Western world depended heavily on the Gulf nations for oil, the black milk from Mother Earth that nourishes all modern, industrial economies. Yet this vital lifeline lay dangerously close to the Soviet Union. The prospect that political turmoil in the region might provide an excuse for the Soviet Army to march in and seize control of essential oil supplies caused nightmares throughout the Western world.

Nightmare seemed to become reality on November 4, 1979, when a howling mob of rabidly anti-American Muslim militants stormed the United States Embassy in Teheran, Iran and took all its occupants hostage. The captors then demanded that the American authorities ship back to Iran the exiled Shah, who had arrived in the United States two weeks earlier for medical treatment. The shaky Iranian government, barely visible through the smoke of revolution and religious upheaval then rocking the country, refused to intervene against the militants. Ayatollah Ruhollah Khomeini, the white-bearded Muslim holy man who inspired the revolutionaries, even accused the United States of masterminding an attack on the sacred Muslim city of Mecca. Vicious anti-American riots exploded in Muslim communities from the Middle East to the Philippines, taking two American lives in Pakistan.

World opinion hotly condemned the diplomatic felony in Iran, while Americans agonized both over the fate of the hostages and the stability of the entire Persian Gulf region. The Soviet army then aroused the West's worst fears on December 27, 1979, when it blitzed into the mountainous nation of Afghanistan, next door to Iran, and appeared to be poised for a thrust at the oil-jugular of the Gulf.

"History teaches, perhaps, very few clear lessons. But surely one such lesson learned by the world at great cost is that aggression, unopposed, becomes a contagious disease."
President Jimmy Carter, addressing the nation on January 4, 1980, about the Soviet invasion of Afghanistan.

President Carter reacted vigorously to these alarming events. He slapped an embargo on the export to Russia of grain and high-technology machinery, and called for a boycott of the upcoming Olympic Games in Moscow. He proposed the creation of a "Rapid Deployment Force" to respond to suddenly developing crises in far-away places, and requested that young people (including women) be made to register for a possible military draft. The President proclaimed that the United States would "use any means necessary, including force," to protect the Persian Gulf against Soviet incursions. He grimly conceded that he had misjudged the Russians, and the SALT treaty became a dead letter in the Senate. Meanwhile, the Soviet army met unexpectedly stiff resistance in Afghanistan, and bogged down in a nasty guerilla war that

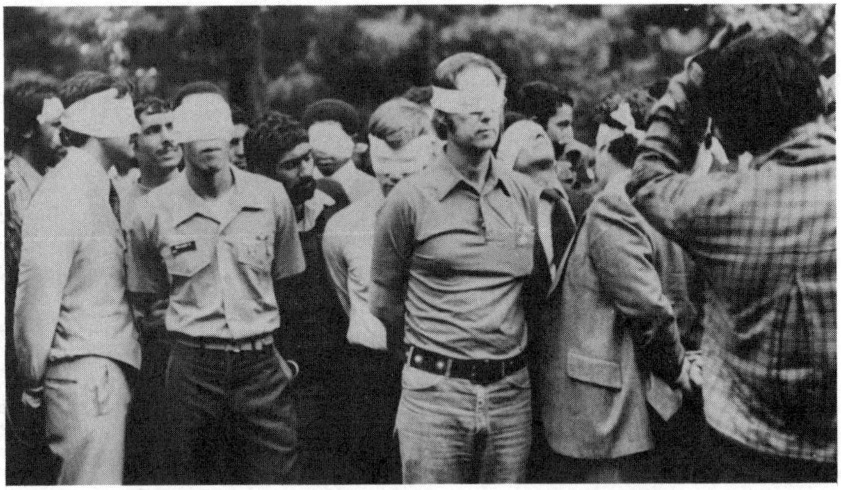

Blindfolded American Hostages Displayed by Iranian Militants, November, 1979. Humiliating scenes like this one were telecast on American television during the hostages' 444 days of captivity. (© 1981 Sipa Press from Black Star)

came to be called "Russia's Vietnam." But though the Russian bear was stalled in Afghanistan, the crisis in Iran ground on.

The Iranian Hostage Humiliation

The Iranian hostage episode was Carter's—and America's—bed of nails. The captured Americans languished in cruel captivity, while the nightly news broadcasts in the United States showed humiliating scenes of Iranian mobs burning the American flag and spitting upon effigies of Uncle Sam. Americans at home displayed yellow ribbons—a traditional sign of longing for absent loved ones—to show their concern for their captive countrymen. The Washington government refused to accede to the militants' demand to return the Shah and his fabled wealth to Iran. Carter froze billion of dollars of Iranian assets in the United States, and called upon other countries to follow his example and curtail trade with the offending revolutionary regime.

Carter at first tried to apply economic sanctions and the pressure of world public opinion against the Iranians, while waiting for the emergence of a stable government with which to negotiate. But the political upheaval in Iran rumbled on endlessly, and the President's frustration grew. The Iranians released a few of the prisoners, but in April 1980 the Ayatollah Khomeini declared that the hot-headed militants, rather than the formal government, would retain custody of the 52 remaining hostages. Carter responded by giving the go-ahead to a daring rescue mission. A highly trained commando team, flying specially outfitted aircraft and stealthily evading radar detection, penetrated deep into Iran's sandy interior. From a pre-arranged staging area, the rescuers planned to swoop down upon the occupied embassy compound, liberate the captive Americans, and spirit them out of the country. The plan required tick-tock perfect timing to succeed, and when equipment failures prevented some members of the team from reaching their destination, the mission had to be scrapped. As the commandos withdrew in the dark desert night, two of their aircraft collided, killing eight of the would-be rescuers.

This disastrous failure of the rescue raid proved anguishing for Americans. The episode seemed to underscore the nation's helplessness and even incompetence in the face of a mortifying insult to the national honor. The raid also triggered the resignation of Secretary of State Cyrus Vance, apparently because he disapproved of the administration's abandonment of diplomatic efforts to end the hostage deadlock. As for the luckless Shah, he died at last in Egypt in July 1980, after shuttling from one sick bed to another in America and Panama for several tormented months. Despite the Shah's death, the stalemate with Iran dragged on throughout the rest of Carter's term in office, providing an embarrassing backdrop to the President's embattled struggle for re-election.

Other embarrassments also bedevilled Carter. When the American delegate to the U.N. in March 1980 joined in the unanimous Security Council condemnation of Israel's policy of establishing settlements in occupied Arab territories, Carter disavowed the vote, declaring that his ambassador had made a mistake. Flabbergasted critics cried

This cartoon makes cruel sport of Carter's failed rescue mission in Iran and the embarassing antics of his brother, Billy. (© Taylor/Rothco)

out against Carter's mismanagement of the nation's affairs. Accusations of incompetence stung Carter deeply, for he had campaigned on a pledge to run an administration "as competent as the American people." He entitled his official autobiography *Why Not the Best?*, to which his adversaries now responded "We got the worst." The President's beer-drinking, bad-boy brother Billy caused him further grief in the summer of 1980 when it was revealed that he had accepted a large "loan" from the government of Libya, whose fanatical leader, Colonel Muammar Qaddafi, preached ugly anti-Americanism and supported international terrorism. An "ABC" (Anybody But Carter) movement gathered steam as the 1980 election season approached.

The Election of Ronald Reagan, 1980

Disaffection with Carter ran deep even in his own party. His fiscal conservatism, as well as his removal of regulatory controls from major industries (such as the airlines), prompted the charge that he was a Republican wolf clothed as a Democratic sheep. Liberal inheritors of the Democratic New Deal tradition grew especially restless. They found their champion in Senator Edward Kennedy of Massachusetts, the last survivor of the assassin-plagued Kennedy brothers. In late 1979 Kennedy declared his intention to contest Carter's renomination. But Kennedy was handicapped from the outset by lingering suspicions about his involvement in a 1969 automobile accident on Chappaquiddick Island, Massachusetts, in which a young woman assistant was drowned when his car went off a bridge.

While Kennedy and Carter noisily slugged it out in a series of bruising primary elections, Republicans proceeded in gentlemanly fashion to select their presidential nominee. Ronald Reagan, perennial darling of the right wing, easily outdistanced his rivals and secured the nomination he had sought for over a decade. Liberal Republican John Anderson, a well-groomed and well-spoken Congressman from Illinois, proved unable to march

Senator Edward Kennedy Campaigning in Miami, in November, 1979. Democratic liberals rallied to the charismatic Kennedy, but they proved insufficiently strong to stop Jimmy Carter's renomination. (© Robert Emerson / Picture Group)

rightward to the beat of Reagan's drum. He bolted the party to launch his own independent presidential bid. But his candidacy, aimed at voters slightly left of center, worried Carter much more than it did Reagan.

The hour of the conservative right seemed at last to have arrived. Census figures confirmed that the average American was older than in the stormy 1960s, and much more likely to live in the South or West, the traditional bastions of the "old right." The conservative cause drew added strength from the emergence of a "new right" movement, partly in response to the "counter-cultural" protests of the 1960s. Spearheading the new right were evangelical Christian groups like the Moral Majority, which was composed of a dedicated minority of believers who enjoyed startling success as political fund-raisers and organizers. New right supporters tackled "social" issues such as abortion, the Equal Rights Amendment, pornography, and homosexual rights—all of which they passionately de-

President Reagan. The oldest man ever elected to the Presidency, Reagan displayed youthful vigor both on the campaign trail and in office. (© 1980 Dennis Brack from Black Star)

nounced. Together, the old and new right added up to a powerful political combination.

Ronald Reagan was well suited to lead this gathering conservative crusade. An actor turned politician, he enjoyed enormous popularity with his crooked grin and aw-shucks manner. He had grown up in a small Illinois town, the son of a ne'er-do-well, impoverished Irish father with a fondness for the bottle. Reagan got his start in life in the depressed 1930s as a sports announcer for an Iowa radio station. Good looks and a way with words landed him acting jobs in Hollywood, where he became a B-grade star in the 1940s. He displayed a flair for politics as president of the Screen Actors Guild in the McCarthy era of the early 1950s, when he helped to purge communists and other suspected "reds" from the film industry. In 1954 he became a spokesman for the General Electric Corporation at a salary of some $150,000 per year. In that position he began to abandon his New Deal-ish political views and increasingly to preach a conservative, anti-government line. Reagan's huge visibility and growing skill at promoting the conservative cause made him attractive to a group of wealthy California businessmen, who helped to launch his political career as Governor of California from 1966 to 1974.

Memories of Chappaquiddick and the country's conservative mood killed Kennedy's candidacy. A badly battered Jimmy Carter, his party divided and in disarray, was left to do battle with Ronald Reagan. The Republican candidate proved to be a formidable campaigner. He used his professional acting skills to great advantage in a series of televised "debates" with the colorless Carter. Reagan attacked the incumbent's fumbling performance in foreign policy and blasted the "big government" philosophy of the Democratic party (a philosophy that Carter did not fully share). Carter countered ineffectively with charges that Reagan was a trigger-happy Cold Warrior who might push the country into nuclear war.

Carter's spotty record in office was no defense against Reagan's popular appeal. On election day, the Republican rang up a spectacular victory, bagging over 51 percent of the popular vote, while 41 percent went to Carter and 7 percent to Anderson. The electoral count stood at 489 for Reagan and 49 for Carter (Anderson failed to gain a single electoral vote). Carter managed to win only six states and the District of Columbia, a defeat almost as crushing as George McGovern's loss to Richard Nixon in 1972. He was the first elected president to be unseated by the voters since Herbert Hoover was ejected from office in 1932. Equally startling, the Republicans gained control of the Senate for the first time in twenty-five years. Leading Democratic liberals, including Senator George McGovern, had been "targeted" for defeat by well-heeled new right groups. They went down like dead timber in the conservative windstorm that swept the country.

Carter showed dignity in defeat, delivering a thoughtful farewell address that stressed his ef-

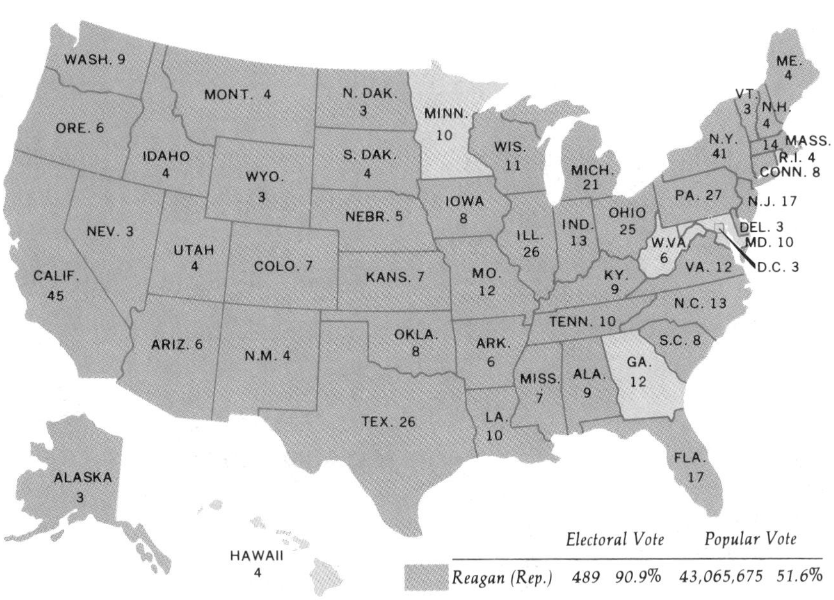

	Electoral Vote		Popular Vote	
Reagan (Rep.)	*489*	*90.9%*	*43,065,675*	*51.6%*
Carter (Dem.)	*49*	*9.1%*	*34,733,785*	*41.7%*
Anderson (Ind.)	*0*	*0.0%*	*5,559,773*	*6.7%*

THE 1980 ELECTION. This map graphically displays Reagan's landslide victory over both Carter and Anderson.

forts to scale down the deadly arms race, to promote human rights, and to protect the environment. In one of his last acts in office, he signed a bill preserving some 100 million acres of Alaskan land for national parks, forests, and wildlife refuges. An unusually intelligent, articulate, and well-meaning president, he had been hampered by his lack of managerial talent, and had been badly buffeted by events beyond his control, such as the soaring price of oil and the galling insult of the continuing hostage crisis in Iran. If he was correct in believing that the country was suffering from a terrible "malaise," he never found the right medicine to cure the disease.

One of Jimmy Carter's former speechwriters commented on Carter's sometimes puzzling personality in 1979: The president, he said, displayed "a combination of arrogance, complacency, and—dread thought—insecurity at the core of his mind and soul. . . . He holds explicit, thorough positions on every issue under the sun . . . but he has no large view of the relations between them. . . . He fails to project a vision larger than the problem he is tackling at the moment. . . . [Yet] with his moral virtues and his intellectual skills, he is perhaps as admirable a human being as has ever held the job."

President Carter. Hard-working and high-minded, Carter was beset by foreign and economic problems during his presidency. Defeated in 1980 by Ronald Reagan, Carter became the fifth president since Eisenhower's day to fail to serve two full terms in office. (Official White House photo)

The Reagan Revolution

Reagan's arrival in Washington was triumphal. His old show-business friends helped to make the inaugural ceremonies extravagantly colorful. The Iranians contributed to the festive mood by releasing the hostages on Reagan's inauguration day, January 20, 1981, after 444 days of captivity. The new President, a hale and hearty 69-year-old, was devoted to fiscal fitness. He went vigorously into action on his first day in office by declaring a hiring freeze on federal employees, and soon after he announced plans to slash some 37,000 jobs from the federal payrolls. Reagan also placed a freeze on implementing new economic regulations, which he believed throttled business and stifled economic growth.

Reagan assembled a conservative cabinet of the "best and the rightest." They included former Nixon chief of staff and former NATO commander Alexander Haig as Secretary of State, and a highly controversial Coloradan, James Watt, as Secretary of the Interior. Watt was a product of the "Sagebrush Rebellion," a fiercely anti-Washington movement that had sprung up to protest federal control over the rich mineral and timber resources in the western states. Environmentalists howled loudly about Watt's schemes to hobble the Environmental Protection Agency, and to permit oil drilling in scenic places. After bitter protests, they succeeded in halting Watt's plan to allow oil exploration off the California coastline. Watt blithely rebuffed critics by saying that "I make lots of mistakes because I make lots of decisions."

Republican conservatives scored a double victory in 1980, winning control of both the White House and the Senate. Aided by conservative Democratic "boll weevils," they also dominated the House of Representatives, and a new era of conservatism seemed to dawn in the nation's capital. (© 1980, Jim Borgman/King Features Syndicate.)

The American Hostages Return from Iran, January 20, 1981. In a pointed insult to Jimmy Carter, the Iranians released the hostages on the day he left office. (Sygma)

A major goal of Reagan's political career was to reduce the size of the government by shrinking the federal budget and slashing taxes. He declared that "Government is not the solution to our problem. Government is the problem." Years of New Deal–style tax-and-spend programs, he quipped, had created a federal government that reminded him of the definition of a baby as a creature who was all appetite at one end, with no sense of responsibility at the other.

With religious zeal and remarkable effectiveness, Reagan set out to persuade Congress to legislate his policies into law. He proposed a new federal budget that necessitated cuts of some $35 billion dollars, mostly in social programs like food stamps and federally funded job-training centers. Reagan worked naturally in harness with the Republican majority in the Senate, but to get his way in the Democratic House, he undertook some old-fashioned politicking. He especially wooed a group of mostly Southern conservative Democrats (dubbed "boll weevils") who abandoned their own party's leadership to follow the president.

Then on March 6, 1981, a deranged gunman shot the President as he was leaving a Washington hotel. A .22-caliber bullet penetrated beneath Reagan's left arm and collapsed his left lung. (Within one year, cranks or fanatics wounded or killed not only Reagan, but also musician John Lennon, Egyptian President Anwar Sadat, and even Pope John Paul II.) With admirable courage and grace, and with impressive physical resilience for a man his age, Reagan recovered rapidly from his violent ordeal. Twelve days after the attack, he walked out of the hospital and returned to work. When he appeared a few days later on national television to address the Congress and the public on his budget, the outpouring of sympathy and support was enormous.

In his inaugural address, Ronald Reagan summoned Americans to "an era of national renewal." He explained that "It will be my intention to curb the size and influence of the federal establishment and to demand recognition of the distinction between the powers granted to the federal government and those reserved to the states or to the people. . . . Now so there will be no misunderstanding, it is not my intention to do away with the government. It is rather to make it work—work with us, not over us; to stand by our side, not ride on our back. . . . Can we solve the problems confronting us? The answer is an unequivocal and emphatic yes. To paraphrase Winston Churchill, I did not take the oath I have just taken with the intention of presiding over the dissolution of the world's strongest economy."

Reagan's budget cuts fell almost exclusively on social programs, while the military budget was scheduled to increase substantially. (© Mazzotta/Rothco)

The Battle of the Budget

Swept along on a tide of presidential popularity, Congress swallowed Reagan's budget proposals, approving expenditures of some $695 billion, with a projected deficit of about $38 billion. To hit those financial targets, drastic surgery was required on existing programs. Congress only nicked the Defense Department's budget, but plunged its scalpel deeply into social programs. Wounded Democrats wondered if the president's intention was to cut the budget or to gut the budget.

Reagan's triumph amazed political observers, especially defeated Democrats. The new President had descended upon Washington like an avenging angel of conservatism, kicking up a blinding whirlwind of political change. He sought nothing less than the dismantling of the welfare state, and the reversal of the political evolution of the preceding half century. His impressive performance demonstrated the power of the presidency with a skill not seen since Lyndon Johnson's day. Out the window went the textbooks that had concluded, largely on the basis of the stalemate of the 1970s, that the White House had been eclipsed by a powerful, uncontrollable Congress.

Reagan hardly rested to savor the sweetness of his victory. Part two of his economic program called for deep tax cuts, amounting to 25 percent across-the-board reductions over a period of three years. Once again, Reagan displayed his skill as a performer and a persuader in a highly effective television address in July 1981, when he pleaded for congressional passage of the tax-cut bill. Democrats, he quipped, "had never met a tax they didn't hike." Thanks largely to the continued defection of the "boll weevils" from the Democratic camp, the President again had his way. In August, 1981, Congress approved a set of sweeping tax reforms that lowered individual tax rates, virtually eliminated federal estate taxes, and created new tax-free savings plans for small investors. Reagan's "supply-side" economic advisers assured him that the combination of budgetary discipline and tax reduction would stimulate new investment and dramatic gains in productivity.

But somehow things did not work out that way. Investors remained wary about the inflation rate and hesitated to put their money in new long-term ventures, as the President's men had expected. The automobile industry, once the brightest jewel in America's industrial crown, was turning in its dimmest performance in history. Battling against Japanese imports, major automakers reported losses in the hundreds of millions of dollars. The stock market continued to sag, interest rates remained stubbornly high, and the unemployment rate approached nearly 9 percent by early 1982. More people were out of work than at any time since the Great Depression of the 1930s. Fuming and frustrated Democrats angrily charged that the President's brutal budget cuts slashed especially cruelly at the poor and the handicapped, and that his tax cuts favored the well-to-do. They accused Reagan of trying to make those Americans with the frailest shoulders carry the heaviest burden in the fight for fiscal reform.

Beset by a limping economy and a yawping pack of Democratic critics, the president's popularity began to sag. Setting aside his nice-guy image,

The Supreme Court Goes Co-ed. Sandra Day O'Connor, the first woman Justice in the Court's history, with President Ronald Reagan, who appointed her, and Chief Justice Warren Burger. (United Press International photo)

Reagan also showed in the late summer of 1981 that his bite was worse than his bark, when he fired thousands of striking air traffic controllers and prohibited them from ever again holding any federal job. Organized labor was dumbfounded at these mailed-fist tactics.

But the President "stole a march" on his liberal critics, and partially disarmed the feminists who opposed his stand against abortion, when in July 1981 he nominated Sandra Day O'Connor to be a justice of the Supreme Court of the United States. A brilliant Stanford Law School graduate and public-spirited Arizona judge, O'Connor appealed to the President in part because she sympathized with his views on abortion, as he had taken care to ascertain. When she was sworn in on September 25, 1981, she became the 102nd justice and the first woman to ascend to the high bench in the Court's 191-year history. Ironically, it had fallen to the most conservative President in half a century to appoint a woman to the Court, as liberals had long desired.

Reagan's Tough Foreign Policy

Hard as nails toward the Soviet Union in his campaign speeches, Reagan saw no reason to change his tune after he arrived in the White House. In one of his first presidential news conferences he claimed that the Soviets were "prepared to commit any crime, to lie, to cheat," in pursuit of their goal of world conquest. Critics wondered how the President could fulfill his promise to negotiate a new arms agreement with the Russians when he had publicly painted them as so dishonest. Bafflement deepened when Reagan lifted Jimmy Carter's grain embargo against the offensive Soviets, even though they remained embattled in Afghanistan. In tones reminiscent of the Carter years, questioners asked if the Reagan administration even had a consistent foreign policy.

Europe flinched at the prospect of a re-heated Cold War. Détente had brought both peace of mind and prosperity to West Europeans, and they turned a deaf ear to what they regarded as Reagan's out-dated battle cry. They appeared to listen more attentively to the siren call of Russian leader Leonid Brezhnev, who talked alluringly of removing Soviet missiles from Western Russia and striking lucrative trade deals with the Europeans. A shudder ran through Western Europe in October 1981 when Reagan seemed to endorse the concept that the United States might fight the Russians in a "limited" nuclear war on European soil. Scrambling to stop the downward slide in America's relationship with her European allies, Reagan proposed new arms-control talks with the Russians in a speech that was telecast live to Europe on November 18, 1981. Negotiations actually began in Geneva within a few days, though progress was slow.

Relations with Russia nosedived again the following month. The government of Poland, needled for over a year by a popular movement of working people organized into a massive union called "Solidarity," clamped martial law on the troubled country. Reagan saw the heavy fist of the Kremlin inside this Polish iron glove, and he imposed economic sanctions on Poland and Russia alike. Notably absent from the mandated measures was a resumption of the grain embargo, which would have pinched the pocketbooks of too many American farmers.

The volatile Middle Eastern pot continued to boil ominously. Prospects for a peaceful resolution of the decades-old Arab-Israeli conflict were dealt a severe blow in October 1981 when extremist Egyptian nationalists gunned down the courageous and peace-seeking president of Egypt, Anwar Sadat. Israel badly strained its bonds of friendship with the United States by continuing to allow new settlements to be established in the oc-

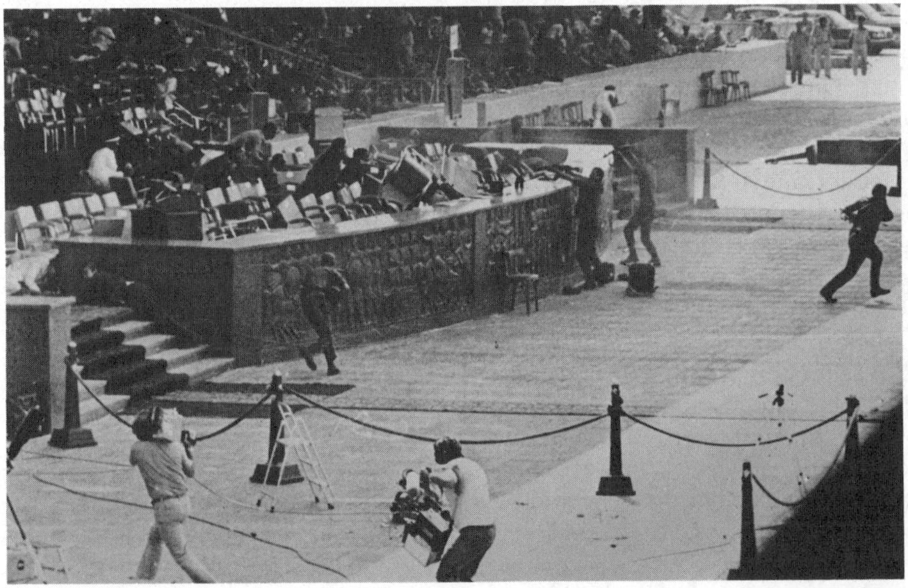

The Assassination of Anwar Sadat, October, 1981. The Egyptian President's violent death at the hands of Muslim extremist Egyptian army officers blighted hopes for peace in the Middle East. (Makram Karim/*Al Akbar*/Gamma/Liaison)

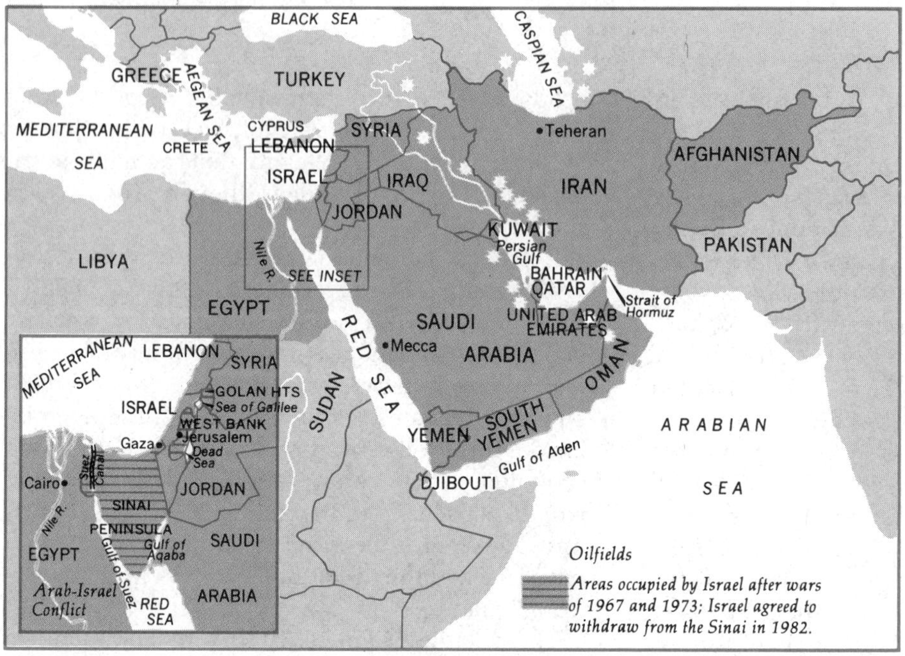

THE MIDDLE EAST.
A combination of political instability and precious petroleum resources has made the region from Egypt to Afghanistan an "arc of crisis."

cupied territory of the Jordan River's West Bank. Israel further inflamed world opinion when it forsook diplomacy and sent fighter-bombers to destroy a nuclear facility in Iraq. Many Americans also resented Israeli attempts to block the sale to Saudi Arabia of an $8.5 billion package of advanced weaponry, including the sophisticated AWACS (Airborne Warning and Command System) radar.

Elsewhere in the Arab world, Libya continued to be a thorn in American flesh. Colonel Qaddafi viciously denounced America and supplied oil-derived dollars to international terrorist groups. Soviet-built Libyan fighter planes attacked U.S. Navy aircraft on maneuvers in the Mediterranean Sea in August 1981, resulting in the loss of two of the Libyan jets. Soon thereafter rumors circulated that Libya had sent assassination squads into the United States to kill the President and other leaders. No firm evidence of such a menace ever materialized, but in early 1982 Washington prohibited the import of Libyan oil to the United States and embargoed all exports to the belligerent North African nation.

Central America, in America's own backyard, also rumbled menacingly in the early months of the Reagan administration. A leftist revolution had deposed the long-time dictator of Nicaragua in 1979. President Carter had tried to ignore the anti-American rhetoric of the revolutionaries, and to establish good diplomatic relations with them. But Reagan took their rhetoric at face value, and hurled back at them some hot language of his own. He accused the Nicaraguans of turning their country into a forward base for Soviet and Cuban military penetration of all of Central America. Brandishing photographs taken from high-flying spy planes, administration spokesmen claimed that Nicaraguan leftists were shipping weapons to revolutionary forces in tiny El Salvador, torn by violence since a coup in 1979. Reagan sent American military "advisers" to El Salvador in February 1981, and many Americans feared that the stage was being set for another bloody American involvement resembling Vietnam.

As his first year in office closed, Reagan appeared to have lost the head of political steam that had propelled him to such striking successes in his early months in the White House. "Supply-side" economics seemed to be a beautiful theory murdered by a gang of brutal facts. As the administration's economic forecasts proved breathtakingly mistaken, estimates of the possible federal deficit climbed toward the stupefying sum of $100 billion. To make matters worse, Reagan called for a massive armaments buildup that was to cost $1.5 trillion dollars over a five-year period. Critics complained that it was impossible to cut taxes, vastly increase defense spending, and balance the budget, all at the same time.

But Reagan showed few signs of retreating from his strongly held views, despite the pleadings of his fellow Republicans who feared for their political lives if the economy failed to revive. Like the Democratic "boll weevils," a group of liberal Republicans known as "gypsy moths" began to fly away from their party. Observers expected Reagan to respond to these realities by postponing his tax cuts or scaling back his arms expenditures, but instead the President used his State of the Union message in January 1982 to announce a program of "New Federalism." He proposed a dramatic shifting of duties from Washington to the states, who would bear a larger proportion of welfare costs in exchange for Washington's assumption of greater responsibility for medical-care programs. Governors were at first cool to this proposed swap, and many critics regarded it as simply a distraction from the problems of the still-stumbling economy. Whether the "Reagan revolution" would really amount to a "national renewal" was a question whose answer lay in the lap of the future.

The New Federalism. Critics complained that Reagan's proposals to shift welfare costs to the states amount to "passing bucks" that didn't exist. (© Liederman/Rothco)

CENTRAL AMERICA AND THE CARIBBEAN.
This region of historical importance to the United States experienced dramatic political upheavals in the late 1970s and early 1980s.

VARYING VIEWPOINTS

Jimmy Carter's presidency was widely judged to have been a failure, but opinions differ about how to explain what went wrong. Some critics blame Carter's personality. They charge that he was ill-prepared for high office, indecisive, and inept at politicking, either on Capitol Hill or on television. Carter's defenders point to the disastrous effects of events largely beyond the President's control, such as the jolting oil-price hikes of 1979, Soviet behavior in Afghanistan, and the mortifying hostage ordeal in Iran. Still other observers, mostly on the right, ascribe Carter's difficulties to his own Democratic party's continuing commitment to the liberal policies of Franklin Roosevelt's New Deal and Lyndon Johnson's Great Society. And some analysts maintain that American society has simply become ungovernable, by anyone, given the proliferation of "single-interest" constituencies and the national breakdown of political and cultural consensus.

Any assessment of the implications of Ronald Reagan's sweeping victory in 1980 must begin with an appraisal of the causes of Carter's failure. Did Reagan's victory simply represent a reaction against Carter's personality? Did it express national frustration with the limping economy and the lingering hostage crisis? Or did it represent a permanent swerve to the right in the country's political mood, a repudiation of the New Deal tradition? And was Reagan's smashing initial success with Congress a fluke or did it signal a new era of effective—and conservative—presidential leadership?

SELECT READINGS

Jimmy Carter wrote his own biography, *Why Not the Best?* (1975), which should be supplemented with David Kucharsky, *The Man from Plains* (1976). Sharply critical are Clark R. Mollenhoff, *The President Who Failed: Carter out of Control* (1980), and Joseph A. Califano, Jr. (whom Carter fired from the Cabinet), *Governing America: An Insider's Report from the White House and the Cabinet* (1981). Consult also Haynes Johnson, *In the Absence of Power: Governing America* (1980), and Laurence H. Shoup, *The Carter Presidency and Beyond* (1980). Michael Tanzer provides useful background on one of the Carter administration's top priorities in *The Energy Crisis* (1975). The debate on Panama spawned two noteworthy books: Walter LaFeber's pro-withdrawal *The Panama Canal: The Crisis in Historical Perspective* (1978), and Paul B. Ryan's anti-withdrawal *The Panama Canal Controversy* (1977). George Lenczowski illuminates Carter's Middle East diplomacy in *The Middle East in World Affairs* (4th ed., 1980). On the SALT negotiations, see Thomas W. Wolfe, *The SALT Experience* (1979) and Strobe Talbott, *Endgame: The Inside Story of Salt II* (1979). The catastrophe in Iran is described in Michael Ledeen and William Lewis, *Debacle: The American Failure in Iran* (1981), in Barry M. Rubin, *Paved with Good Intentions: The American Experience and Iran* (1980), and in Pierre Salinger, *America Held Hostage* (1981). Ronald Reagan is profiled in Bill Bayorsky, *Ronald Reagan: His Life and Rise to the Presidency* (1981), and in Hedrick Smith, et al., *Reagan the Man, the President* (1981). Alan Crawford analyzes the political currents that carried Reagan to victory in *Thunder on the Right: The "New Right" and the Politics of Resentment* (1980). For a discussion of the intellectual side of the new right, see Peter Steinfels, *The Neoconservatives: The Men Who Are Changing America's Politics* (1979).

48

The American People Since World War II

America stands at this moment at the summit of the world.

WINSTON CHURCHILL, 1945

The Post-War Baby Boom

The American people, 140 million strong, cheered the blinding atomic climax of World War II in 1945. But when the shouting died away, countless men and women began to worry about the future. Four fiery years of global war had not driven from their minds the painful memories of twelve desperate years of the Great Depression.

The decade of the 1930s had left deep scars. Joblessness and insecurity had pushed up the suicide rate and had depressed the marriage and birthrates. Breadless bread-winners had often felt a nagging sense of guilt about their helplessness, despite abundant evidence that the economic system, not individual initiative, had broken down. Grim-faced observers were warning that the war had only temporarily lifted the pall of economic stagnation, and that peace would only bring back the depression. Homeward-bound G.I.s, so the gloomy prediction ran, would step out of the chow lines of the army and back into the breadlines of the unemployed.

But these dreary forecasts did not take into account the breathtaking vitality of the post-war economy or the resiliency of the American spirit. Confident young men and women tied the nuptial knot in record numbers at war's end, and they set in immediately to fill the nation's empty cradles. They thus touched off an explosive "baby boom" that lasted more than a decade, adding more than 50 million persons to the nation's population by the end of the 1950s. The soaring birthrate finally leveled off in the 1960s, and by 1972 had declined below the point necessary to sustain existing population figures—or "zero population growth" (ZPG). If the trend persisted, the American population would climb only modestly above its 1980 level of about 226 million.

This boom-and-bust cycle of births begot a bulging wave along the American population curve. As the oversized post-war generation grew to maturity, it was destined to strain and even distort certain aspects of American life. Elementary school enrollments, for example, swelled to nearly 34 million pupils in 1970. Then began a steady decline, as the onward-marching age group left in its wake closed schools and unemployed teachers. The maturing babies of the post-war boom also had an economic impact. As tykes and toddlers, they made up a lucrative market for manufacturers of canned food and other baby products. But in the 1970s the leading baby-food company, faced with shrinking sales, added new product lines like shampoo to its offerings.

The multitude of youngsters between the ages of fifteen and twenty-four increased by more than 11 million in the ten years after 1960—a mushroom growth that laid the basis for the much-ballyhooed "youth culture." By the 1960s affluent American adolescents were estimated to be spending over $20 billion a year, much of it for "teen" clothes and rock music. But in the 1970s the most popular jeans maker was marketing clothes with a fuller cut for those former college "kids" who could no longer squeeze into their size 30 Levi's. Predictions were that the impact of the post-war generation would continue to ripple through American society well into the next century, as its members passed into job markets and eventually into retirement.

Gray Power

Retirement was increasingly likely to be a lengthier experience for Americans, who were living longer. A person born at the dawn of the century could expect to survive less than fifty years, but a white male born in the 1980s could anticipate a lifespan of about seventy years. Yet his white female counterpart would probably outlive him by eight years. (The figures were slightly lower for nonwhites.) Women had long shown superior powers of survival over men, and the life-expectancy gap between men and women widened as the 20th Century lengthened. The census of 1950 recorded that women for the first time made up a majority of Americans, thanks largely to greater feminine durability. Miraculous medical advances lengthened and strengthened lives. Noteworthy were the development of antibiotics after 1940 and Dr. Jonas Salk's discovery in 1953 of a vaccine against a dreaded crippler, polio.

Longer lives spelled more older people. One American in nine was over sixty-five years of age as the 1980s began, and projections were that one of every six people would be in the "sunset years" by 2030, as the median age rose toward forty. This ageing of the population as a whole raised problems of a political, social, and economic nature. Elderly persons took a cue from youthful protesters of the 1960s and organized into groups like the "Gray Panthers" to lobby for governmental favors. In 1977 the "wrinkled radicals" scored a major victory when the California legislature abolished mandatory retirement at age sixty-five, and in 1978 the federal Congress passed similar legislation.

These triumphs for "senior citizens" symbolized the fading of the "youth culture" that had colored the American scene in the preceding three decades. Such changes also highlighted the growing pains of the Social Security system, established in

Senior Citizen for Lower Prices.
(Owen Franken; Stock, Boston.)

1935 in part to provide income for retired workers. Forty years later benefits had risen so high, and the ratio of active workers to retirees had dropped so low, that drastic adjustments were necessary. By the year 2000 there would be one retired person for every two workers. Congress steeply increased mandatory Social Security contributions in 1977, and many workers paid higher Social Security taxes (a maximum of $2271 by 1983) than income taxes. Extending the working lifetime of still-active oldsters was one way of easing the financial pressure on the Social Security system.

Sick Cities and Sprawling Suburbs

Young or old, Americans tended increasingly to lead solitary lives. Families had fewer members, thanks in part to the spreading use of effective birth-control techniques like "the pill," first developed in the 1950s. A poll in 1975 revealed that a majority of Americans considered two or fewer children per family to be the ideal. One person in every thirteen lived alone in 1979, and fewer than half the nation's households were occupied by more than two people.

Fluid neighborhoods proved less able to sustain long-term relationships among persons and families, as an average of more than 30 million Americans changed residences in every year since the Second World War. Between 1975 and 1979 four out of every ten people moved to a different house.

If they were white, the footloose tended to move to the suburbs, which expanded after World War II at a rate nearly double that of overall population growth. There millions of Americans lived in dispersed houses, often commuting to work or driving to the store alone in their private automobiles. (Some commentators, trying to put the best face on things, described the car as the modern person's "Walden Pond"—the only solitary refuge from the crowded hubbub of everyday life.)

"White flight" left the inner cities black, brown, and broke. Poorer residents, largely non-whites, filled in behind the departing white middle class, and tax-paying businesses fled with their affluent customers from downtown shops to "satellite" shopping centers. Despite black economic gains following the massive civil rights drives of the 1960s, the population of the green suburbs remained nearly 95 percent white. Close to 60 percent of American blacks were central-city dwellers by the early 1980s, while fewer than 25 percent of whites still inhabited the urban core. America was becoming a nation of black metropolises surrounded by white "greenbelts," thus adding a vivid and vexatious racial element to the age-old conflict between city and country.

America's "alabaster cities" of song and story grew more sooty and less safe in the era after World War II. Pollution, arson, and robbery were among the curses of urban life. Killjoys claimed that breathing smoggy urban air every day was equivalent to smoking several packs of lung-blackening cigarettes daily. Striking policemen, firemen, garbage collectors, and mass-transit drivers demonstrated to urbanites how vulnerable they were to damaging disruptions of their daily routines.

"The Thinker." (Osrin in the Cleveland *Plain Dealer.*)

But worst of all was the plague of lawlessness. The rate of violent crimes committed in the cities increased threefold in the dozen years after 1960, and was growing again in the 1980s. Murder victims fell at the rate of one every 24 minutes in 1981. Burglaries occurred every ten seconds; every seven minutes a woman was raped. Desperate citizens often set up vigilante patrols to protect their neighborhoods. Frightened urbanites cowered like nightly prisoners in their locked and bolted apartments. A long and grisly series of murders of black youths terrorized residents of Atlanta, Georgia, in the early 1980s, saddening an outraged nation.

The Smiling Sunbelt

The woes of the decaying cities in the industrial North not only pushed many families into the suburbs, but forced a goodly number of people to leave the region altogether. In the three decades after 1950, the population of the North increased at only half the rate of the South and West. Especially striking was the galloping growth of the "Sunbelt"—a fifteen-state area stretching in a smiling crescent from Virginia through Florida and Texas to Arizona and California. In the 1950s California alone accounted for one-fifth of the nation's population growth, and by 1963 had outdistanced New York as the most populous state, with approximately 20 million people.

The South and the Southwest were a new frontier for Americans after World War II. These modern pioneers came in search of a more temperate climate, lower taxes, cheaper energy, bigger paychecks, and smaller crowds. Jobs they found in plenty, especially in the California electronics industry, in the aerospace complexes in Florida and Texas, and in huge military installations. Southern congressmen, especially powerful chairmen of committees, proved adept at securing lucrative defense contracts for their region.

Cascading dollars from Washington indeed accounted for much of the Sunbelt's new prosperity, even though Southern and Western politicians led the cry against government spending. In 1976 the South and the West collected nearly $22 billion more from the federal Treasury than they paid in, while the once-dominant Northeast and Midwest (the "frostbelt") sent almost 30 billion more dollars to Washington than they received. Embittered Northerners, realizing that they were being milked of locally needed tax dollars to nourish the "new South," rallied political support with a sarcastic slogan, "The North shall rise again."

The South still lagged behind the rest of the country in income and population, but it was rapidly closing the gap. Southern real wage rates reached near equality with the national average by the mid-1970s. And black people, once hounded from the South by prejudice and poverty, were for the first time returning in numbers to the land of their ancient bondage. They came because of the improved racial climate after the civil-rights successes of the 1960s, and, like whites, because of the increasing availability of jobs.

These dramatic shifts of wealth and population further broke the historic grip of the North on the nation's political life. All the elected occupants of the White House since Kennedy's day have hailed from Sunbelt states, and the region's congressional representation is increasing with rising population levels. A political free-for-all was taking shape as robust Sunbelters elbowed for their place

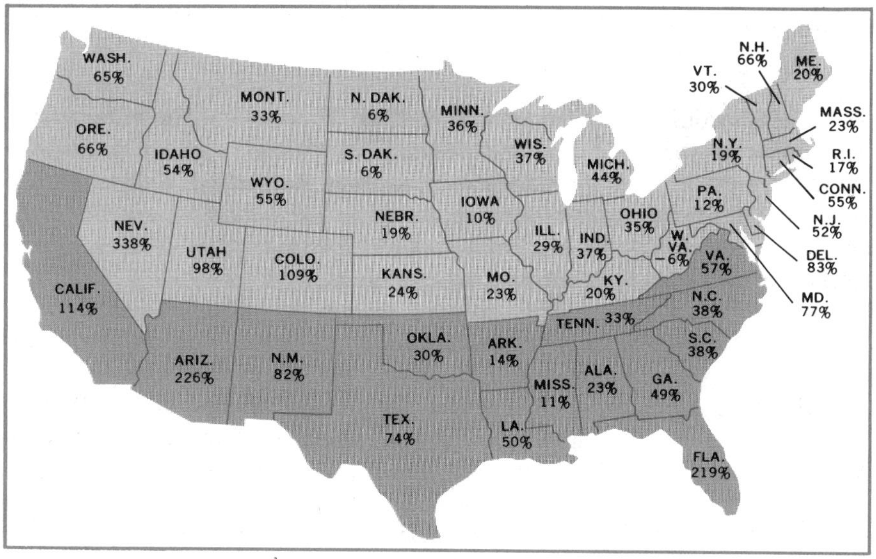

POPULATION INCREASE IN THE SUNBELT STATES: 1950–1979

States with figures higher than 50% were growing faster than the national average. Note that "Sunbelt" is a loose geographical concept, as some deep-South states had very little population growth, while the mountain and Pacific states were booming.

at the Washington gravy trough, while aroused Northerners sought to muscle them aside in pursuit of federal dollars for their troubled cities.

Economic Ferment

The faltering economy in the early post-1945 years threatened to confirm the worst predictions of the doom-sayers who foretold another Great Depression. Real gross national product in 1946 and 1947 slumped sickeningly from its wartime peak and began to climb only haltingly in 1948. Not until 1950 did real national production and income regain the levels of World War II. Then, beginning in 1951, the American economy surged onto a dazzling plateau of sustained growth. National income nearly doubled in the 1950s and again in the 1960s. It shot through the trillion dollar mark in 1973 and touched 2.5 trillion (in inflated dollars) in 1980. Americans, some 6 percent of the world's people, enjoyed about 40 percent of the world's wealth.

Ominously, much of this glittering prosperity rested on the underpinning of colossal military budgets, thus leading some critics to speak of a "permanent war economy." The economic upsurge of 1951 was fueled by massive appropriations for the Korean War, and throughout the 1950s the spending of the Department of Defense accounted for about 10 percent of gross national product. Pentagon dollars primed the pumps of high-technology industries like aerospace, plastics, and electronics—areas in which the United States reigned supreme. The military budget also financed much scientific research and development ("R and D"—hence the name of one of the most famous "think tanks," the Rand Corporation). This systematic scientific pioneering amounted to the "institutionalization of invention." Technological research teams stimulated the economy with new products and processes, such as transistors and micro-circuits, just as lone inventors like Alexander Graham Bell and Thomas Edison had done in an earlier day.

The seemingly insatiable demand of the growing economy for energy led to a sixfold increase in the country's electricity-generating capacity in the quarter-century after 1945. Spidery grids of electrical cables carried the pent-up power of coal, oil, or falling water to activate the tools of workers. By the 1970s they could produce nearly twice as much in an hour's work as they had in the 1940s.

The Problems of Plenty

Even more spectacular were advances in agricultural productivity, which increased nearly fourfold in the post-war decades. The one-farm farmer became an endangered species as consolidation produced giant agribusinesses with costly machinery. Thanks largely to mechanization and to rich new fertilizers, one farmworker in the 1980s could produce food for over fifty people, compared with about fifteen in the 1940s. Farmers whose forebears had busted sod with oxen or horses now plowed their fields seated in air-conditioned tractor cabs, listening on their stereophonic headsets to weather forecasts or the latest Chicago commodities market quotations. Once the mighty backbone of the agricultural Republic, farmers made up less than 3 percent of the American population by the 1980s—yet they fed much of the world.

The booming economy created more than 24 million new jobs in the post-war decades, but relatively few of them were on assembly lines. The fastest-growing employment opportunities were in service occupations, notably medical care, communications, teaching, merchandising, and finance. Growing most lustily of all was bureaucratic government, which by the early 1980s employed nearly one in five working Americans. Contrary to popular belief, federal payrolls held fairly steady, while employees working for state and local governments have more than tripled

Bossy's New Home. A large commercial dairy farm in Pennsylvania. (Grant Heilman Photography.)

since World War II. The days of the enterprising lone businessman, including "mom and pop" grocery stores, seemed numbered. Self-employed persons accounted for less than 8 percent of the labor force in the 1980s, down from over 30 percent at the beginning of the century.

The growing group of white-collar workers proved less inclined to join labor unions than their blue-collar cousins. Strikes in the 1970s by teachers, firefighters, and police forces, and in 1981 by air traffic controllers, stirred fear and resentment among the general public. But the percentage of workers who belonged to unions was slipping steadily downward. Organized labor had lost much of its crusading zeal. It also alienated many of its liberal friends in the 1960s when it appeared to obstruct the advance of black people into higher-paid occupations. And it lost the confidence of countless rank-and-file members after a series of revelations of corruption (especially in the use of pension funds) and even murder involving union officials.

As the gusher of post-war prosperity continued to pour forth wealth, Americans drank deeply from the gilded goblet. Millions of depression-pinched souls sought to make up for the deprivations of the blighted 1930s. They determined to "get theirs" while the getting was good. They tried to spend away the memory of the impoverished pre-war past, and gave little heed to the future. Lack of cash was no obstacle, as buying on credit became intoxicatingly popular. The indebtedness of American consumers skyrocketed from a mod-

David Riesman, in *The Lonely Crowd* (abridged edition,1960), said: "One thing that has happened . . . is a rise in the expectations held of life by many Americans who have risen above subsistence. This is the American form of 'the revolution of rising expectations,' of which the motto is 'If things are good, why aren't they better still?'"

est $6 billion at the end of World War II to over $300 billion by the opening of the 1980s. Thrift flew out the window, as the lure of the "good life" led the American people ever deeper into the red.

As the median income of an American family rose in the early 1980s above $19,000 per year, the struggle intensified to "keep up with the Joneses." A people who had once considered a chicken in every pot as the standard of comfort and security now hungered for two cars in every garage, swimming pools, vacation homes, and gas-guzzling "recreation vehicles."

Manhattan's Lower East Side, 1977. The persistence of poverty amidst plenty baffled policy-makers and angered critics in post-war America. (Bob Adelman.)

Economic Storm Clouds

A rising tide lifts all boats, and the post-war river of riches lifted most Americans to new heights of consumption. But the golden flood of prosperity actually obscured persistent inequalities in American society. The richest 20 percent of Americans in the 1980s still raked in nearly half the nation's income. This privileged position had changed little over the course of the century, despite progressive and New Deal reforms and the widespread prosperity of the post-1945 period. Nor was there significant change in the relative position of the poorest 20 percent of Americans. They continued to receive less than 5 percent of the national income, just as they had before the 1930s. Black families, on the whole, earned 40 percent less than white families, and Chicanos, Puerto Ricans, and Native Americans fared more poorly still. Twenty-five million Americans remained mired in poverty in the 1980s—a depressing indictment of the inequities still afflicting the world's richest superpower.

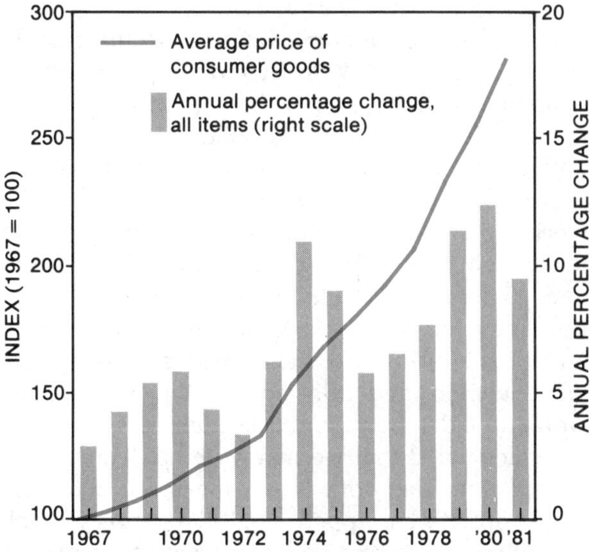

The History of the Consumer Price Index, 1967–1981. This graph shows both the annual percentage of inflation and the absolute increase in 1967 dollars. (Statistical Abstract of the United States)

Other ugly problems lurked behind the glittering veil of America's wealth. Inflation made illusory the increases in money income, as the value of the dollar was more than halved in the fifteen years after 1967. Prices rocketed skyward in response to the costs of the Vietnam War, to mushrooming bills for imported oil, and to a worldwide shortage of food in the early 1970s. Yet creeping inflation had stalked the American economy for two decades before the dramatic upsurge of the 1970s.

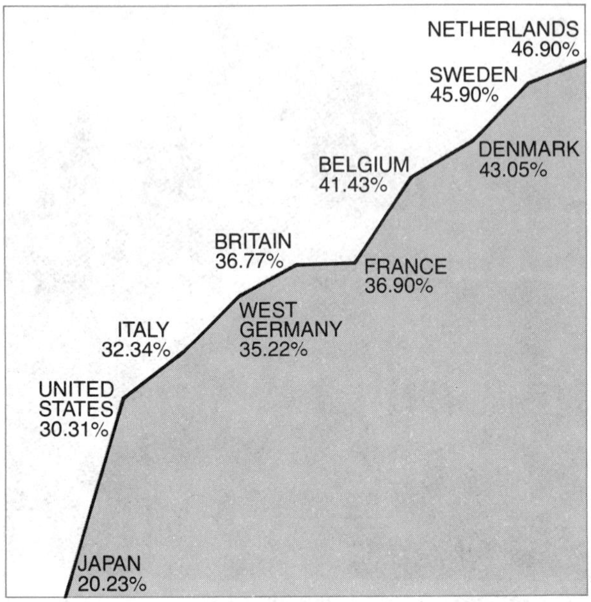

COMPARATIVE TAX BURDENS
Percentage of GNP paid as taxes in major industrial countries, 1975.

Some economists concluded that inflation was built into the system—constituting the most troublesome question confronting economic policy-makers since an earlier generation grappled with the Great Depression.

Critics continued to assail the lopsided distribution of resources in moneyed America. They charged that the post-war explosion of prosperity had produced a troublesome combination of private opulence and public privation. Americans had color televisions in their homes, but garbage in their streets. They ate rich food, but breathed foul air. They had built over 200 million private automobiles since World War II, but only two new metropolitan systems of mass transportation. The only public "service" for which Americans seemed willing to be taxed was national defense. The United States remained the land of individualism, at least economically. Despite increasing howls of protest from taxpayers, Americans gave a smaller percentage of their gross national product to the tax collector than in almost any other advanced, industrialized nation.

Most worrisome of all was the rapid exhaustion of the oil and gas fields that furnished most of the country's energy. By the early 1980s the United States, once a major oil exporter, was importing nearly one-half its petroleum supply, much of it from the Middle East. Industrialism feeds on energy; without fuels, the whole painfully built structure of the modern economy will collapse. All industrialized countries looked anxiously to the next century, searching for a new energy base to replace the petroleum-fired economy of the 20th Century. Nuclear power plants afforded one possible and partial answer, but they aroused deep fears about their vulnerability to accident, conversion to military use, or the danger of terrorist blackmail. Whatever the solution, it was bound to be costly.

Woman Power

Of all the beneficiaries of post-war prosperity, none reaped greater rewards than women. More than ever, urban offices, factories, and shops provided a bonanza of employment for female workers. During World War II, more than 5 million women took the places of the departing GIs, even in heavy industries like shipbuilding. To a remarkable extent, they stayed at their jobs after the war. Women had made up less than 20 percent of the work force in the early part of the century, but at the conclusion of World War II they comprised over 25 percent of the labor pool. Two out of every three new jobs in the 1960s went to women. By the end of the 1970s two wage-earners in every five were women, and fully half of the working-age women held jobs outside the home.

Cynics noted that women were the "new immigrants" into the work force—the latest cheap labor supply to be tapped by all-devouring capitalism. Women did receive lower wages than men in corresponding jobs, and they tended to be employed in a few low-skill, low-prestige occupations. (Though they made up more than half the population, women in 1980 accounted for less than 15 percent of lawyers and judges, and less than 12 percent of physicians.) Some observers also charged that families in which both parents worked were subjected to painful stress, much as the peasant families of the immigrants had been wrenched out of their familiar routine by contact with urban industrialism.

But whatever its origins, the new employment prospect for women set off a groundswell of social and psychological changes that mounted to tidal proportions in the 1970s. When Betty Friedan in 1963 published her runaway bestseller, *The Feminine Mystique,* she spoke in rousing accents to millions of able, educated women who applauded her indictment of the stifling boredom of suburban housewifery. Many of those women were already working, though they struggled against the guilt and frustration of leading an "unfeminine" life. Friedan gave focus and fire to their feelings, and the modern woman's movement was launched. Traditional feminine roles were everywhere questioned. Women's liberationists ("libbers") picketed the Miss America pageant, burned their bras, condemned advertisements that "demeaned women," and insisted that men help with housework and babysitting. Some men feared, with exaggeration, that the hand that rocked the cradle was turning into the hand that cradled the rock. Even the English language came under attack as "sexist." Mrs. and Miss gave way to Ms., chairman to chairperson, and he and she to he/she or (s)he.

The New (Working) Woman. Many previously all-male occupations—and some brand-new ones—were opened to women in the 1960s and 1970s. (Photo: Suzanne Arms—Jeroboam.)

> Betty Friedan, in *The Feminine Mystique* (1963), said: "If I am right, the problem that has no name stirring in the minds of so many American women today is not a matter of loss of femininity or too much education, or the demands of domesticity. . . . It may well be the key to our future as a nation and a culture. We can no longer ignore that voice within women that says: 'I want something more than my husband and my children and my home. . . . ' And work can now be seen as the key to the problem that has no name."

Despite ridicule from "male chauvinists," the women's cause made notable headway. The Civil Rights Act of 1964 prohibited sexual discrimination by employers. Within a few years several major corporations, including American Telephone and Telegraph, were forced to give back wages to female employees who had not been receiving equal pay for equal work, and to abolish hiring and promotion practices that discriminated against women. President Johnson signed an executive order in 1965 that required employers on federal contracts to take "affirmative action" to insure that more women and underprivileged minorities were hired. Congress in 1972 sent to the states for ratification the Equal Rights Amendment to the Constitution.* Commonly called ERA, it would guarantee sexual equality as part of the

*See Appendix, proposed Article XXVII of the Constitution.

highest law of the land, though a stiff opposition, including many women, threatened to block final passage. Despite bitter criticism from Roman Catholics and other "right-to-life" groups, the Supreme Court in 1973 upheld a woman's right to an abortion during the early months of pregnancy.

Forward-looking feminists overturned the barriers that guarded many a citadel of masculinity. Many all-male strongholds, including Yale and Princeton, opened their doors to women undergraduates, and even West Point, Annapolis, and the Air Force Academy fell to the forces of the feminist revolution. By 1980 the armed services counted some 19,000 women officers, including a handful of brigadier generals and rear admirals, and the United Mine Workers reported that several hundred women miners were descending daily into the nation's coal pits and mineshafts.

Leaders of women's liberation felt that they still had a long way to go as the United States passed through the 1980s. But many women looked back with pride on the gains achieved since World War II. Though prosperity made possible much of the redefinition of the traditional feminine role, women themselves claimed much of the credit. In countless "rap" sessions and consciousness-raising groups, they had massively overhauled American sexual values and the distribution of masculine and feminine functions. Women were made more resilient and men more sensitive to the problems of womanhood. Family life changed as "egalitarian marriages," childless marriages, and "trial marriages" became ever more common. The emerging new role of women promised one day to add up to a revolution comparable to the coming of industrialism or the emancipation of the slaves.

In Black America

Black people also scored notable advances in the post-war period, though they too still had a long hill to climb before reaching equality. Blatant segregation in public facilities was rapidly becoming a relic of the past, and the number of black elected officials in the 1970s climbed toward the 4,000 mark, including hundreds in the Old South, eighteen congresspersons and senators, and the mayors of Atlanta, Washington, and Los Angeles. By 1970 the black-white income gap had been partially closed, as black families were earning on the average about 64 percent of the income of their white counterparts. But black economic gains had flowed in large part from general prosperity, rather than any basic redistribution of the nation's wealth or permanent eradication of oppression. When the economy faltered in the early 1970s, the racial income gap began to widen again. Blacks once more suffered from the age-old stigma of being "the last hired and the first fired." Black unemployment was nearly double that of whites, and among black teenagers more than one in three found it almost impossible to land any kind of job.

Women headed more than a third of black families, or three times the rate for whites. Understandably, a majority of these husbandless and jobless women depended on welfare to feed their children. As sociologists increasingly emphasized the importance of the home environment for success in school, it became clear that many fatherless, impoverished black children continued to suffer from educational handicaps that were difficult to overcome. As the 1980s began, black youths still typically had about one year less schooling than whites and were less than half as likely to earn a college degree.

Education remained the principal fighting front for blacks still struggling for their share of the American dream. Public-school integration eventually went forward in the South after the Supreme Court's epochal desegregation decision of 1954, even though one white child in ten had taken refuge in the South's rapidly expanding private schools.

The North was soon transformed into the main educational battleground. There segregated schools often resulted not from overt discrimination but from segregated residential patterns. Many white parents had moved to new neighborhoods, often in the suburbs, to provide better schools for their children. Now they felt deeply

White Backlash. "Soiling of Old Glory." Anti-busing demonstration in Boston, April 1976. (Stanley Forman, Boston *Herald American*.)

threatened by court-ordered busing that seemed to deprive them unfairly of their hard-bought advantages. Violent confrontations shook cities like Boston, where school officials tried to achieve racial balance by busing. A new wave of "white flight" swept many metropolitan areas, as families fled not just to more distant suburbs but to private schools. In some Northern cities, the public-school system was being virtually abandoned to black pupils.

White anxiety about advancing minorities was also evident in higher education. Many colleges and professional schools initiated special admissions programs for minority groups in the 1960s, and college enrollments by blacks shot up. But by the 1970s white students who had been denied admission raised to new heights the cry of "reverse discrimination." They charged that their rights had been violated by admissions officers who in some cases put more weight on ethnic background than on ability or achievement.

One white Californian, Allan Bakke, made headlines in 1978 when the United States Supreme Court, by the narrowest margin (5–4), upheld his claim that his application to medical school had been turned down because of an admissions program that partially favored minority people. The Court declared that preference in admissions could not be given to members of any group, minority or majority, on the basis of ethnic or racial identity alone. Among the dissenters on the sharply divided bench was the Court's only black justice, Thurgood Marshall. He warned in an impassioned opinion that the majority decision might sweep away years of progress by the civil rights movement. But many civil rights supporters took cheer from the Court's concession that ethnic and racial background might still be taken into account in admissions decisions, even if strict quotas were now deemed unconstitutional.

Ethnic Pride

Subgroups of various ethnic backgrounds grew more self-conscious in post-war America. The fire under the melting pot seemed to have flickered out by the 1960s, and observers spoke of the "unmeltable ethnics." Descendants of European immigrants, long thought to have been fused into the national amalgam, began to assert their unalloyed separateness. Ethnic stereotyping became a hazardous occupation, and dialect jokes fell into serious disrepute. Afro-Americans rediscovered their ancestral roots and proclaimed that black was beautiful. New immigrant groups proudly displayed their distinctiveness, as newcomers poured into the country in the highest numbers since the 1920s (over 800,000 "legals" in 1980). In a striking departure from the historic pattern of immigration, Europe contributed far fewer people than did Asia and Latin America.

Indians, as the oldest Americans, had seen their culture largely wiped out by white Europeans in the 19th Century, and they had been nearly neglected to death in the 20th Century. But in the 1960s almost 1 million Native Americans shared in the general awakening of "cultural nationalism." They aggressively asserted their rich heritage, and forced white Americans to recognize the desperate plight of the Indian—often jobless, reservation-bound, and illiterate.

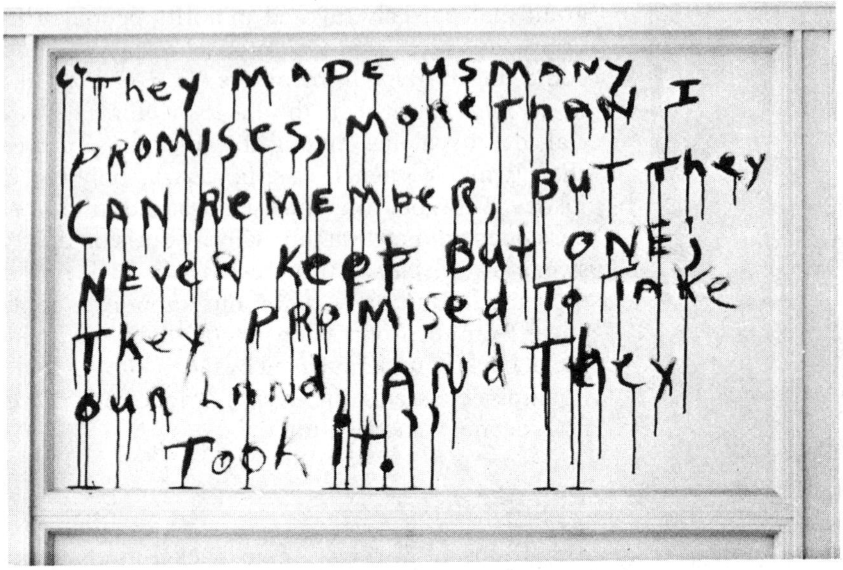

The Indians' Lament. A sign painted by demonstrators on the wall of the Bureau of Indian Affairs office in Washington, D. C. (Steve Northup, Camera 5.)

Militant members of the American Indian Movement (AIM) seized the Indian Bureau in Washington in 1972. The following year heavily armed Indians occupied the ghost-haunted village of Wounded Knee, South Dakota (see p. 535), and held it for more than two months, amidst national publicity. Lawyers replaced warriors as various tribes sought, with some success, to secure multimillion-dollar payments for land "stolen" by the whites. One Indian lawsuit pointed to a legal technicality in an old treaty that seemed to warrant the return to tribal possession of nearly half the state of Maine.

Brown Power

Hispanic-Americans were another neglected minority suddenly thrust into the headlines after World War II. This diverse group numbered at least 14 million by the early 1980s, including about 2 million Puerto Ricans in the Northeast, and about 1 million Cubans, mostly in Florida. The largest contingent of Spanish-stock Americans were Chicanos, or Mexican-Americans, concentrated in the Southwest. Census takers reported more than 6 million Chicanos in the country, but illegal immigrants probably doubled that figure. More than a million Mexicans were reportedly crossing the border illegally every year.

The original Mexican-Americans were an "old" minority. Like the Indians, they had inhabited immense parts of the continent, especially Texas and California, well before the white "Anglos" arrived on the scene. At the time of the American Revolution, Spanish-Mexican culture was already more than 250 years old, and a chain of thriving mission settlements linked Mexico City with Monterey Bay in present-day central California. Like the Indians, the original Spanish-speaking settlers in the Southwest became Americans by conquest, not consent.

But the great majority of Chicanos came to the United States as immigrants. As many as a million may have fled northward during the years of the Mexican Revolution, 1910–1920. They concentrated in urban *barrios,* or neighborhoods, making Los Angeles the urban center with the second largest Mexican population in the world (after Mexico City). Mexican-Americans suffered the regrettably familiar discrimination and abuse afforded other immigrant groups in American cities. In June 1943, young "zoot-suit" clad Chicanos in

Los Angeles were viciously attacked by Anglo sailors who cruised the streets in taxi-cabs, searching for victims. Brawling erupted into full-scale rioting and spread to other southern California cities, as well as to Chicago, Detroit, and Philadelphia. Order was restored only after the Mexican ambassador made a special plea, pointing out that such "race riots" were grist for Nazi propaganda mills.

The United States also offered employment in agriculture for Mexico's masses of restless poor people. Between 1942 and 1964, 5 million Mexican *braceros,* or seasonal workers, found work on farms and ranches in Texas and California under a program jointly administered by the governments of Mexico and the United States. *Braceros* worked hard as "stoop laborers" for low pay, lived in tumble-down shanties for a few days or weeks, then moved on to the next harvest. Because they were aliens and were always on the move, they proved almost impossible to organize into a union that might press for better wages and working conditions. Ending the *bracero* program thus was the necessary precondition for the formation of the United Farm Workers Organizing Committee (UFWOC), set up in 1963 by soft-spoken César Chavez.

Robert Kennedy Breaks Bread with César Chavez, 1968. The Chicano organizer of farm workers was ending a 23-day protest fast. (United Press International photo.)

> In 1968 the House Committee on Education and Labor reported that "the strike for recognition, with all its disastrous consequences, has largely become a thing of the past . . . in all industries but agriculture. There, the law of the jungle which generally prevailed 33 years ago [before the Wagner Labor Relations Act] still exists." It was this "jungle" that Cesar Chavez and the United Farm Workers tried to civilize.

Chavez soon made *la huelga* (the strike) a household word in much of the country, as a UFWOC strike against grape-growers led to a nation-wide consumers' boycott of table grapes. After years of struggle, Chavez won significant concessions from the growers, though the Teamsters' Union later challenged his leadership in the fields.

Chavez and other Chicano leaders also strove to organize the political power of their people. Mexican-American votes gave John F. Kennedy his winning edge in the crucial state of Texas in 1960, and Robert F. Kennedy made a point of befriending Chavez during the presidential primary race in California in 1968. All these gains invigorated ethnic consciousness and pride. Chicano influence seemed likely to grow, as suggested by the increasing presence of Spanish-language ballots and TV broadcasts. Spanish-stock Americans, newly confident and organized, might well become the nation's largest ethnic minority, outnumbering even blacks, sometime in the 1980s.

Cultural Contradictions

Fast-paced changes everywhere shook the pillars of tradition in the anxious post-war age. The family, once a haven of refuge from the cruel world, was suffering heavy blows. By the 1980s divorces annually totaled half the number of marriages. Seven times more children were affected by divorce than at the turn of the century, and kids who commuted between separated parents were becoming commonplace. The child-rearing function of the family dwindled as youngsters spent more time with "parent-substitutes" at day-care centers and schools, or with television, the new "electronic babysitter." Estimates were that the average child at age sixteen had watched up to 15,000 hours of TV, more time than was spent with parents or teachers.

Parents had become so uncertain how to raise their children in a rapidly changing world that many of them turned for advice to books, especially Dr. Benjamin Spock's *The Common Sense Book of Baby and Child Care,* first published in 1945. Millions of American youngsters in the following decades were raised on "the gospel according to Spock." The good doctor urged a natural, relaxed attitude toward child-rearing. He stressed parental "permissiveness" and de-emphasized strict rules and schedules for infants. Critics blamed him for breeding softness and disrespect for authority into an entire generation of American young people, including draft resisters in the Vietnam War era.

Whatever the cause, a newly negative attitude toward all kinds of authority seemed to pervade post-war American society. Not only the family, but other traditional institutions like the schools and the churches seemed to be losing their ability to define values and shape behavior. No matter what the topic, conventional wisdom or inherited ideas came under fire. "Trust no one over thirty" was a popular sneer in the 1960s.

> Historian Theodore Roszak wrote in 1969: "It would hardly seem an exaggeration to call what we see arising among the young a 'counter culture': meaning, a culture so radically disaffiliated from the mainstream assumptions of our society that it scarcely looks to many as a culture at all, but takes on the alarming appearance of a barbarian intrusion."

> As a tough motorcycle-gang leader, Marlon Brando, in the film *The Wild One* (1954), summed up the anarchic impulses of the decade when he was asked, "What are you rebelling against?" His reply: "What d'ya got?"

Disrespect for authority had deep historical roots in American culture, but it burst into full bloom in the 1950s. "Beat" poets like Allen Ginsberg and novelists like Jack Kerouac voiced dark disillusion with the materialistic beliefs of the "establishment." The attractive young actor James Dean, in movies like *Rebel Without a Cause* (1955), expressed the restless frustration of many young people.

The disillusion of the young reached crisis proportions in the tumultuous 1960s. Prompted by seething resentment against the war in Vietnam, many sons and daughters of the baby-boom generation turned to mind-bending drugs, tuned in to "acid rock," and dropped out of "straight" society. Some explored Oriental religions. Others "did their own thing" in communes or "alternate" institutions. Beflowered women in trousers and long-haired men with earrings heralded the rise of a self-conscious "counterculture" mortally opposed to traditional American ways.

Strait-laced guardians of respectability denounced the self-indulgent romanticism of the "flower children" as the beginning of the end of modern civilization. Sympathetic observers hailed the "greening" of America—the replacement of materialism and imperialism by a new consciousness of human values. But the upheavals of the 1960s could be largely attributed to three Ps: the youthful population bulge, protest against the Vietnamese War, and the apparent permanence of prosperity. As the decade flowed into the 1970s, the flower children grew older and had children of their own, the war ended, and a chilling recession blighted the bloom of prosperity. Young people in the 1970s seemed more concerned with finding a

A Youth Commune. An "alternative" life style. (Dennis Stock, Magnum Photos, Inc.)

job in the system than with tearing it down. The "counterculture" appeared in retrospect to be not the road to the future but an historical blind alley.

Beyond the 1960s

Yet some residues from the frothy 1960s remained. Opinion polls revealed that millions of Americans now regularly puffed marijuana. Sexual attitudes seemed drastically altered, as increasing numbers of men and women engaged in premarital intimacies. Legal sanctions against obscenity and pornography withered away, and nudity became almost obligatory on stage and screen. Even old taboos against homosexuality were crumbling as "gays" emerged from their closets and loudly demanded sexual tolerance.

A wave of religious fervor also seemed to roll out of the spiritually conscious 1960s. Church membership climbed toward record levels, and over 95 percent of adults in 1971 stated a religious preference. "Born-again" Christians abounded, including peanut-farmer Jimmy Carter of Georgia. The country was still predominantly Protestant, though Roman Catholics accounted for nearly 37 percent of churchgoers in the early 1980s. Even in the tradition-bound Catholic Church, the liberal reforms launched in the 1960s endured. Clerics abandoned their Roman collars and Latin lingo, folk-songs replaced Gregorian chants, and meatless Fridays became ancient history. But some cynics complained that changes like these proved that the churches, unable to defeat the Devil, had embraced him.

Modern America provided many diversions to compete with the churches for the national soul. At

> Speaking in 1961, Newton Minow urged his hearers to sit at length before a television screen. "I can assure you," he said, "that you will observe a vast wasteland. You will see a procession of game shows, violence, audience participation shows, formula comedies about totally unbelievable families, blood and thunder, mayhem, violence, sadism, murder, Western badmen, Western goodmen, private eyes, gangsters, more violence, and cartoons. And, endlessly, commercials—many screaming, cajoling and offending."

the close of World War II, less than half of American households were equipped with telephones; three decades later more than 95 percent had television sets, most of them color. Pre–World War II Americans had consistently mentioned reading as their favorite leisure-time activity. By the 1970s they overwhelmingly told pollsters that watching TV was their favorite indoor sport. Many newspapers folded as the public increasingly turned to the electronic eye for its view of the world. Some critics charged that Americans were not only reading less, but also understanding less. The average television news broadcast emitted far fewer words than could be printed on a single page of newspaper.

Politics also felt the impact of television, as the line between show business and the public business became blurred. Candidates who appeared to good advantage on the screen had a competitive edge. Some former film and sports stars even parlayed their media images into political careers, notably ex-actor Ronald Reagan of California. Political scientists argued that one especially troublesome tendency of the mass media was to obliterate local "intermediary" organizations, including political parties themselves, in favor of direct (usually one-way) communication between politicians and the public. Ominously, there was a direct relationship between the amount of money that candidates could raise and their effectiveness on television. These developments opened the door wide for demagoguery, deception, or the denial of a local voice in the political process.

Standard amusements also beguiled post-war Americans. Televised professional football grew so spectacularly in popularity during the 1960s that it rivaled baseball as the national sport, at least for spectators. Horseracing still attracted larger crowds than any other American sporting activity, followed far behind by collegiate football, now a big business. An increasing number of Americans shunned the spectator's role altogether. Seeking to "get away from it all" (and from each other), they flocked to the ski slopes, hiking trails, or jogging paths.

The Life of the Mind

Despite the mind-sapping chatter of the "boob tube," Americans in the post-war era were better educated than ever before. The GI Bill of Rights paid the college fees of millions of veterans in the 1940s and 1950s, thus stimulating a vast expansion of higher education. By the end of the 1970s colleges were graduating nearly a million degree-holders a year, and one person in four in the eighteen-to-twenty-four-year-old age group was enrolled in an institution of higher learning.

This expanding mass of educated persons lifted the economy to more advanced levels while creating consumers for "high culture." Americans annually made some 300 million visits to museums in the 1980s, and boasted about a thousand opera companies and 1,500 symphony orchestras. Despite television, Americans bought books in record numbers, especially after the "paperback explosion" of the 1960s, when more than a million volumes a day were being sold. Increasingly, educated Americans read the lamentations of writers who protested against the affluent post-war society that had made possible these very gains in mass education and culture.

> Yale psychiatrist Kenneth Keniston in 1971 said: "It is absolutely unprecedented in world history to have 75 percent of an age group with at least a high school education. We're very much into a kind of society that has never existed before. No one can guess the full impact of these wide educational gains. But they certainly mean that a large segment of society will be more literate, more capable of dealing with complexity, less attached to the traditional pieties. And social conflicts do flow from increased education. A person attached to traditional concepts accepts the idea of law and order, for instance. The college-educated person is more likely to ask, 'Is the law a just law?' "

Harvard sociologist David Riesman criticized post-war Americans as conformists in *The Lonely Crowd* (1950), as did William H. Whyte, Jr., in *The Organization Man* (1956). The novelist Sloan Wilson explored a similar theme in *The Man in the Gray Flannel Suit* (1955). Harvard economist John Kenneth Galbraith questioned the relation between private enterprise and the public good in a series of books beginning with *The Affluent Society* (1958) and extending to *Economics and the Public Purpose* (1973). Collusion at the highest levels of the "military-industrial complex" was the subject of *The Power Elite* (1956), an influential piece of modern-day muckraking by radical sociologist C. Wright Mills, who became a hero to the "New Left" in the 1960s. Futurologist Daniel Bell pointed to disturbing trends that might spell the doom of the post-war social and economic order in *The Coming of Post-Industrial Society* (1973) and *The Cultural Contradictions of Capitalism* (1976).

The Power of the Pen

In fiction-writing, some of the pre–World War II "realists" continued to ply their trade, notably Ernest Hemingway in *The Old Man and the Sea* (1952). A Nobel laureate in 1954, Hemingway was dead by his own duckgun in 1961. John Steinbeck, another pre-war writer who persisted in graphic portrayals of American society, received the Nobel Prize for literature in 1962, the seventh American to be so honored.

Brutal realism also characterized the earliest novels that portrayed soldierly life in World War II, such as Norman Mailer's *The Naked and the Dead* (1948) and James Jones's *From Here to Eternity* (1951). But as time passed, realistic writing fell from favor. Authors tended increasingly to write of the war and other topics in fantastic and even psychedelic prose. Joseph Heller's *Catch-22* (1961) dealt with the improbable antics and anguish of American airmen in the wartime Mediterranean. A savage satire, it made readers hurt when they laughed. The supercharged imagination of Kurt Vonnegut, Jr., poured forth works of puzzling complexity in sometimes impenetrably inventive prose.

Pennsylvania-born John Updike described the white middle class at bay in books like *Rabbit Run* (1960) and *Couples* (1968), as did Massachusetts-bred John Cheever in *The Wapshot Chronicle* (1957) and *The Wapshot Scandal* (1964). Louis Auchincloss wrote elegantly of upper-class New Yorkers, and Gore Vidal contributed a series of sometimes impish and always iconoclastic novels, including *Myra Breckinridge* (1968), about a reincarnated transsexual. Together, these writers constituted the rear guard of an older, WASP* elite that had long dominated American writing.

Writers on the Margin

The most striking development in post-war American letters was the rise of younger authors who represented the "marginal" regions and ethnic groups now coming into their own. The South boasted a literary renaissance, led by the veteran Mississippi author William Faulkner, who was made a Nobel recipient in 1950. Fellow Mississippians Walker Percy and Eudora Welty grasped the falling torch from the failing Faulkner, who died in 1962. Tennessean Robert Penn Warren immortalized Louisiana politico Huey Long in *All the King's Men* (1946). Flannery O'Connor wrote perceptively of her native Georgia, and Virginian William Styron confronted the harsh history of his home state in a controversial fictional representation of an 1831 slave rebellion, *The Confessions of Nat Turner* (1967).

Books by black authors also made the best-seller lists, beginning with Richard Wright's chilling portrait of a black Chicago killer in *Native Son* (1940). Ralph Ellison depicted the black person's quest for personal identity in *Invisible Man* (1952), one of the most moving novels of the post-war era. James Baldwin won plaudits as a novelist and essayist, particularly for his sensitive reflections on the racial question in *The Fire Next Time* (1963). Black

*White Anglo-Saxon Protestant.

William Faulkner, 1955. Faulkner had often written of defeat and of the inescapable burdens of history. But in his Nobel Prize speech in 1950 he declared: "I decline to accept the end of man. . . . I believe that man will not merely endure: he will prevail." (Wide World Photos, Inc.)

nationalist LeRoi Jones, who changed his name to Imamu Amiri Baraka, crafted powerful plays like *Dutchman* (1964). Native Americans too achieved literary recognition, as Kiowa author N. Scott Momaday won a Pulitzer Prize for his portrayal of Indian life in *House Made of Dawn* (1968).

Especially bountiful was the outpouring of books by Jewish novelists. Some critics quipped that a knowledge of Yiddish was becoming necessary to understand much of the dialogue presented in modern American novels. J. D. Salinger painted an unforgettable portrait of a sensitive, upper-class, Anglo-Saxon adolescent in *Catcher in the Rye* (1951), but other Jewish writers found their favorite subject matter in the experience of lower- and middle-class Jewish immigrants. Philip Roth wrote comically about young New Jersey suburbanites in *Goodbye, Columbus* (1959) and penned an uproarious account of a sexually obsessed middle-aged New Yorker in *Portnoy's Complaint* (1969). Chicagoan Saul Bellow contributed masterful sketches of Jewish urban and literary life in landmark books like *The Adventures of Augie March* (1953), *Herzog* (1962), and *Humboldt's Gift* (1975). Bellow became the eighth American Nobel laureate for literature in 1977.

Cultural Landmarks

Poetry also flourished in the post-war era, though poets too were often highly critical, even deeply despairing, about the shape of American life. Older poets were still active, including cantankerous Ezra Pound, jailed after the war in a U.S. army detention center near Pisa, Italy, for alleged collaboration with the Fascist enemy. Connecticut insurance executive Wallace Stevens and New Jersey pediatrician William Carlos Williams continued after 1945 to pursue "second careers" as prolific poets. But younger poets were coming to the fore. Pacific Northwesterner Theodore Roethke wrote lyrically about the land until his death by drowning in Puget Sound in 1963. Robert Lowell, descended from a long line of patrician New Englanders, sought to apply the wisdom of the Puritan past to the perplexing present in allegorical poems like *For the Union Dead* (1964). Troubled Sylvia Plath penned the moving verses of *Ariel* (1966) and a disturbing novel, *The Bell Jar* (1963), but her career was cut short when she took her own life in 1963. Another brilliant poet of the period, John Berryman, ended it all in 1972 by leaping from a Minneapolis bridge onto the frozen bank of the Mississippi River. Poetry seemed to be a dangerous occupation in modern America. The life of the poet, it was said, began in sadness and ended in madness.

Playwrights were also active, especially Tennessee Williams with his series of sordid dramas about psychological misfits. Noteworthy were *A Streetcar Named Desire* (1947) and *Cat on a Hot Tin Roof* (1955). Arthur Miller brought to the stage searching probes of American values, notably in *Death of a Salesman* (1949). In the 1960s Edward Albee exposed the snarling underside of middle-class life in

Who's Afraid of Virginia Woolf? (1962). The preeminent American playwright of the 1970s appeared to be Neil Simon, who specialized in clever comic confections.

New York became the art capital of the world after World War II, as well-heeled Americans supported a large number of painters and sculptors. The Ford Foundation also became a major patron of the arts, as did the federal government after the creation of the tax-supported National Foundation for the Arts in 1965. The open, tradition-free American environment seemed especially congenial to the experimental mood of much modern art. Jackson Pollock pioneered abstract expressionism in the 1940s and 1950s, flinging paint on huge canvases stretched on his studio floor. Realistic representation went out the window, as artists like Pollock and Willem de Kooning strove to create "action paintings" that expressed the painter's individuality and made the viewer a creative participant in defining the painting's "meaning." Pop artists in the 1960s, notably Andy Warhol, depicted every-day items of consumer culture, such as soup-cans. Robert Rauschenberg made elaborate collages out of objects like cardboard boxes and newspaper clippings. Claes Oldenburg tried to stun viewers into a new visual awareness with unfamiliar versions of familiar objects, such as giant plastic sculptures of pillow-soft telephones.

Architecture also benefited from the building boom of the post-war era. Old master Frank Lloyd Wright produced strikingly original designs, as in the round-walled Guggenheim Museum in New York. Louis Kahn employed stark geometric forms and basic building materials like brick and concrete to make beautiful, simple buildings. Eero Saarinen, the son of a Finnish immigrant, contributed a number of imaginative structures, including two Yale University residential colleges that evoked the atmosphere of an Italian hill town. In the 1970s Atlanta architect John Portman designed huge building complexes, such as Detroit's Renaissance Center, that suggested spaciousness even in the midst of crowded cities.

Detroit's Renaissance Center. This magnificent building complex was designed by architect John Portman. (Courtesy John Portman & Associates; photo by Alexandre Georges.)

The American Prospect

The American spirit surged with vitality as the nation headed toward the last decade of the 20th Century, but grave problems still plagued the Republic. The economic growth that had made the American dream a near reality for so many people seemed in danger of a permanent slow-down. Energy costs were headed skyward, and a new sensitivity to the environmental price of "progress" placed hobbles on business expansion. Some Americans, soured on the false satisfactions of wealth, welcomed the prospect of a "no-growth" economy. But enlarging the economic pie had historically been the American way of appeasing the appetites of various groups for a richer life. Because of fabulous growth, Americans had happily been spared bitter battles over the distribution of a relatively fixed supply of this world's goods. "No-growth" would change the rules of the political

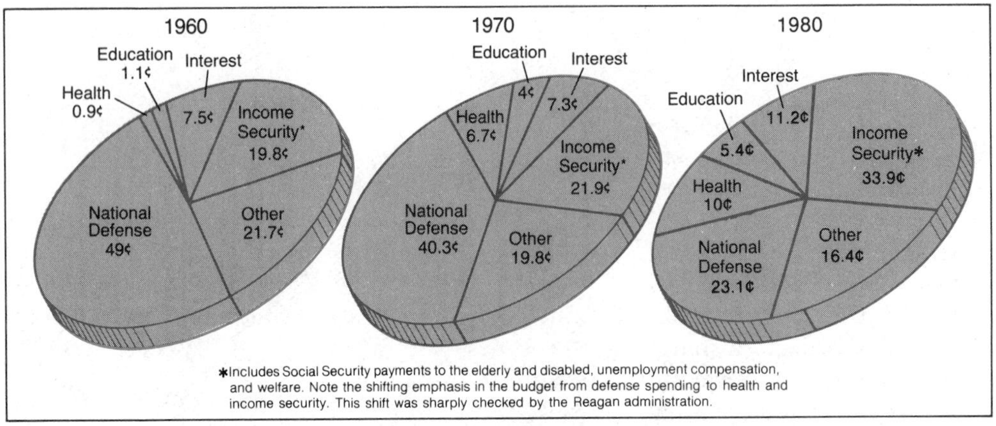

THE FEDERAL BUDGET DOLLAR AND HOW IT IS SPENT, BY MAJOR CATEGORY

game with consequences that no one could foresee. And for the great majority of the world's aspiring peoples who still plowed with oxen and nightly went to bed hungry, "no-growth" seemed a cruel joke perpetrated by the privileged few who had already grown fat and happy.

"Can we afford tomorrow?" was a question that came increasingly often to the lips of many Americans, despite the enormous wealth of their society. As incomes shot up, so did expectations, pushing still higher the level of living that most people found minimally acceptable. Expenditures for health care, for example, had risen incredibly since World War II, amounting to nearly 10 percent of the gross national product by 1980. The largest single supplier of goods and services to gigantic General Motors was not the U.S. Steel Corporation but the Blue Cross and Blue Shield health plans. Proposals for a federal national health insurance program were thus being pushed to the top of the political agenda.

> Peter Passell and Leonard Ross, in *The Retreat from Riches* (1973), wrote: "The process of slowing growth is more likely to cause unnecessary ulcers than it is to alter our materialist values. . . . Twenty more years of growth could do for the poor what the Congress won't do. . . . Quite simply, growth is the only way in which America will ever reduce poverty."

The staggering problem, as usual, was the price tag, estimated to be in the neighborhood of hundreds of billions of dollars. As early as 1973 the budget of the Department of Health, Education, and Welfare had surpassed that of the Department of Defense. Soon thereafter a majority of Americans seemed to conclude that they were no longer willing to foot the bill for further government "benefits." After four decades of advancing New Deal–style programs, a counter-current took hold. Jimmy Carter campaigned successfully in 1976 against the bloated bureaucracy in Washington, and a leading rival for the nomination was California's Governor Jerry Brown, who preached that "small is beautiful." In Brown's home state in 1978 Californians staged a "tax revolt" (known by its ballot title of "Proposition 13") that drastically slashed property taxes and forced painful cuts in government services. Californians thus touched off a "tax quake" that soon jolted other state capitals and even rocked the pillars of Congress in faraway Washington, D.C. In 1980, Ronald Reagan rode that same political shock wave to presidential victory, and proceeded to shake the "welfare state" to its very foundations. For the time being, at least, Americans apparently wanted more private goods and fewer public services.

America was once a revolutionary force in a world of conservatism; it is now a conservative force in a world of revolutionism. This century has witnessed the Communist revolution, anti-colonial revolutions, and revolutions against ignorance, racism, sexism, and poverty. Everywhere, especially in the Third World, is the "Revolution of Rising Expectations." The United States has resisted many of these movements in the outside world, and at home Americans thus far have managed to adjust to drastic social changes without undergoing shattering social upheavals. But as the human family grows at an alarming rate on a shrinking planet, the prospects for prolonged social peace may not be promising.

The task of steering a safe passage into a nuclearized future is the overshadowing mission confronting the American people in the closing decades of the present century—in many ways "the American century." At the same time, new opportunities beckon in outer space, in the laboratory, and in the unending quest for social justice, individual fulfillment, and international peace. The challenges facing the Americans are formidable, at home and abroad, but so is the Republic. As the 20th Century approaches its sunset, the people of the United States can still proudly claim, in the words of Lincoln, that they and their heritage represent "the last best hope of earth."

VARYING VIEWPOINTS

No epoch in American history has witnessed so many bewildering changes as the era after World War II. Abundance has boosted millions of Americans into the comfortable ranks of the middle classes. At the same time, the spectacle of affluence has kindled the desires of the less privileged to share in a piece of the American pie. Wide margins of wealth have permitted the society to satisfy those desires, at least in part, without any paralyzing confrontations. But historical appraisals of these developments also include a negative aspect, as indicated in the titles of the books about the period by Carl Degler and William Leuchtenburg. Prosperity has been prodigious, but it seems to have spawned new social problems almost as rapidly as it has resolved old ones. It has fostered a consumer culture that is often too wasteful, too fast-paced, and too destructive of cherished values. It has perhaps promised more than can ever be delivered.

Many critics are claiming that the post-war epoch has already ended. They argue that as economic growth slows down and as the competition among groups for relatively scarce social goods becomes more intense, America will enter a new and unpredictable period in her history. That transformation will perhaps be comparable in its impact to the passing of the frontier phase in the late 19th Century.

SELECT READINGS

Lucid overviews can be found in Carl N. Degler, *Affluence and Anxiety: America since 1945* (2nd ed., 1975), and William Leuchtenburg, *A Troubled Feast: American Society since 1945* (1973). For a comprehensive account by a British observer, see Godfrey Hodgson, *America in Our Time* (1976). John Brooks, *The Great Leap* (1966), highlights the rapid transformation of American society after World War II. The early post-war years are brought to life in Eric Goldman, *The Crucial Decade and After—America, 1945–1960* (1961). The 1960s get special attention in David Burner et al., *A Giant's Strength: America in the 1960s* (1971), and in William L. O'Neill, *Coming Apart: An Informal History of America in the 1960s* (1971). The problems of the cities are examined in Blake McKelvey, *The Emergence of Metropolitan America, 1915–1966* (1968). A provocative discussion may be found in Jane Jacobs, *The Death and Life of Great American Cities* (1961). Suburbia is the subject of Herbert J. Gans, *The Levittowners* (1967), and of Robert C. Wood, *Suburbia: Its People and Their Politics* (1959). The beleaguered educational system is perceptively analyzed in Charles Silberman, *Crisis in the Classroom* (1970), and the implications of the home environment for performance in school are persuasively presented in Christopher Jencks, *Inequality* (1972). Harold G. Vatter gives a valuable account of *The United States Economy in the 1950s* (1963). Edward Denison argues that improved education is the key to economic growth in *The Sources of Economic Growth in the United States* (1962). See the same author's *Accounting for United States Economic Growth, 1929–1969* (1974). The agricultural sector is discussed in Edward Higbee, *Farms and Farmers in an Urban Age* (1963). The rise of the "sunbelt" is dramatically portrayed in Kirkpatrick Sale, *Power Shift* (1975). Several authors have examined the question of the distribution of wealth: Herman Miller, *Rich Man, Poor Man* (1971), Gabriel Kolko, *Wealth and Power in America* (rev. ed., 1964), and Robert Lampman, *The Share of the Top Wealth-Holders in National Wealth* (1962). The evolving social participation of women is clearly spelled out by William Henry Chafe in *The American Woman: Her Changing Social, Economic, and Political Roles, 1920–1970* (1972) and in the same author's more theoretical *Women and Equality: Changing Patterns in American Culture* (1977). Consult also Juanita Kreps, *Sex in the Marketplace* (1971), regarding women in the work force, and G. G. Yates, *What Women Want: The Ideas of the Movement* (1975). Several ethnic minority groups are examined in Daniel P. Moynihan and Nathan Glazer, *Beyond the Melting Pot* (1963). Consult also Andrew Levison, *The Working-Class Majority* (1974). On blacks, see S. A. Levitan et al., *Still a Dream: The Changing Status of Blacks Since 1960* (1975). On Mexican-Americans, see Matt S. Meier and Feliciano Rivera, *The Chicanos* (1972), and Jacques Levy, *Cesar Chavez* (1975). Oscar Lewis movingly depicts the problems of Puerto Ricans in *La Vida* (1966). For Indians, consult S. A. Levitan, *Indian Giving: Federal Programs for Native Americans* (1975). Bernard Rosenberg and D. M. White, eds., *Mass Culture* (1957), is especially interesting on the 1950s. The emergence of a "youth culture" in the 1960s is illuminated in three studies by Kenneth Keniston: *The Uncommitted* (1965), *Young Radicals* (1968), and *Youth and Dissent* (1971). Popular books indicating the mood of the 1960s include Theodore Roszak, *The Making of a Counter-Culture* (1969), and Charles Reich, *The Greening of America* (1970). Ronald Berman offers a critical view of the developments of the decade in *America in the Sixties* (1968). Richard Goodwin gives an eloquent summing-up of the cultural ferment of the Vietnam era in *The American Condition* (1974). The political side of the "counter-culture" is treated in Irwin Unger, *The Movement* (1974). Consult also Kirkpatrick Sale, *SDS* (Students for a Democratic Society) (1973). A French observer, Jean-François Revel, offers an interesting commentary in *Without Marx or Jesus: The New American Revolution Has Begun* (1971). The often inflammatory upheavals of the period are put into historical context in H. D. Graham and T. Gurr, *Violence in America* (1969), and in Robert Fogelson, *Violence as Protest* (1971). Sexual changes are scrutinized in Daniel Yankelovich, *The New Morality* (1974), Morton Hunt, *Sexual Behavior in the 1970s* (1974), and Paul Robinson, *The Modernization of Sex* (1976). John W. Aldridge, *After the Lost Generation* (1951), looks at the earliest post–World War II writers. On post-war literature in general, see Tony Tanner, *City of Words* (1971), and Alfred Kazin, *Bright Book of Life* (1973). On the arts, consult Edward Lucie-Smith, *Late Modern: The Visual Arts Since 1945* (1969). The prospect of future economic growth is seriously questioned in D. H. Meadows et al., *The Limits to Growth* (1973), and M. Mesarovic and Eduard Pestel, *Mankind at the Turning Point* (1974). Equally gloomy is Robert L. Heilbroner, *An Inquiry into the Human Prospect* (1974). For less pessimistic predictions, see John Maddox, *The Doomsday Syndrome* (1972), and Peter Passell and Leonard Ross, *The Retreat from Riches* (1973). Also intriguing on the 1960s is Morris Dickstein, *The Gates of Eden: American Culture in the Sixties* (1977). For acid comment on the 1970s see Christopher Lasch, *The Culture of Narcissism* (1979). On the baby boom and its implications, consult Richard A. Easterlin, *Birth and Fortune: The Impact of Numbers on Personal Welfare* (1980), and Landon Y. Jones, *Great Expectations: America and the Baby Boom Generation* (1980).

DECLARATION OF INDEPENDENCE
In Congress, July 4, 1776

The Unanimous Declaration of the Thirteen United States of America

[Bracketed material in color has been inserted by the authors. For adoption background, see pp. 104–105.]

When, in the course of human events, it becomes necessary for one people to dissolve the political bands which have connected them with another, and to assume, among the powers of the earth, the separate and equal station to which the laws of nature and of nature's God entitle them, a decent respect to the opinions of mankind requires that they should declare the causes which impel them to the separation.

We hold these truths to be self-evident: That all men are created equal; that they are endowed by their Creator with certain unalienable rights; that among these are life, liberty, and the pursuit of happiness; that, to secure these rights, governments are instituted among men, deriving their just powers from the consent of the governed; that whenever any form of government becomes destructive of these ends, it is the right of the people to alter or to abolish it, and to institute new government, laying its foundation on such principles, and organizing its powers in such form, as to them shall seem most likely to effect their safety and happiness. Prudence, indeed, will dictate that governments long established should not be changed for light and transient causes; and accordingly all experience hath shown that mankind are more disposed to suffer, while evils are sufferable, than to right themselves by abolishing the forms to which they are accustomed. But when a long train of abuses and usurpations, pursuing invariably the same object, evinces a design to reduce them under absolute despotism, it is their right, it is their duty, to throw off such government, and to provide new guards for their future security. Such has been the patient sufferance of these colonies; and such is now the necessity which constrains them to alter their former systems of government. The history of the present King of Great Britain is a history of repeated injuries and usurpations, all having in direct object the establishment of an absolute tyranny over these states. To prove this, let facts be submitted to a candid world.

He has refused his assent to laws, the most wholesome and necessary for the public good. [See royal veto, p. 84.]

He has forbidden his governors to pass laws of immediate and pressing importance, unless suspended in their operation till his assent should be obtained; and, when so suspended, he has utterly neglected to attend to them.

He has refused to pass other laws for the accommodation of large districts of people [by establishing new counties], unless those people would relinquish the right of representation in the legislature, a right inestimable to them, and formidable to tyrants only.

He has called together legislative bodies at places unusual, uncomfortable, and distant from the depository of their public records, for the sole purpose of fatiguing them into compliance with his measures. [E.g., removal of Massachusetts Assembly to Salem, 1774.]

He has dissolved representative houses repeatedly, for opposing, with manly firmness, his invasions on the rights of the people. [E.g., Virginia Assembly, 1765.]

He has refused for a long time, after such dissolutions, to cause others to be elected; whereby the legislative powers, incapable of annihilation, have returned to the people at large for their exercise; the state remaining, in the mean time, exposed to all the dangers of invasions from without and convulsions within.

He has endeavored to prevent the population [populating] of these states; for that purpose obstructing the laws for naturalization of foreigners; refusing to pass others to encourage their migration hither, and raising the conditions of new appropriations of lands. [E.g., Proclamation of 1763, p. 57.]

He has obstructed the administration of justice, by refusing his assent to laws for establishing judiciary powers.

He has made judges dependent on his will alone, for the tenure of their offices, and the amount and payment of their salaries. [See Townshend Acts, p. 90.]

He has erected a multitude of new offices, and sent hither swarms of officers to harass our people and eat out their substance. [See enforcement of Navigation Laws, p. 90.]

He has kept among us, in times of peace, standing armies, without the consent of our legislatures. [See pp. 86, 90.]

He has affected to render the military independent of, and superior to, the civil power.

He has combined with others to subject us to a jurisdiction foreign to our constitution, and unacknowledged by our laws, giving his assent to their acts of pretended legislation:

For quartering large bodies of armed troops among us [see Boston Massacre, pp. 86, 90];

For protecting them, by a mock trial, from punishment for any murders which they should commit on the inhabitants of these states [see 1774 Act, pp. 92, 93];

For cutting off our trade with all parts of the world [see Boston Port Act, p. 92];

For imposing taxes on us without our consent [see Stamp Act, p. 87];

For depriving us, in many cases, of the benefits of trial by jury;

For transporting us beyond seas, to be tried for pretended offenses;

For abolishing the free system of English laws in a neighboring province [Quebec], establishing therein an arbitrary government, and enlarging its boundaries, so as to render it at once an example and fit instrument for introducing the same absolute rule into these colonies [Quebec Act, p. 93];

For taking away our charters, abolishing our most valuable laws, and altering fundamentally the forms of our governments [E.g., in Massachusetts, p. 92];

For suspending our own legislatures, and declaring themselves invested with power to legislate for us in all cases whatsoever [see Stamp Act repeal, p. 89].

He has abdicated government here, by declaring us out of his protection and waging war against us. [Proclamation, p. 102.]

He has plundered our seas, ravaged our coasts, burned our towns, and destroyed the lives of our people. [E.g., the burning of Falmouth (Portland), p. 102.]

He is at this time transporting large armies of foreign mercenaries [Hessians, p. 102] to complete the works of death, desolation, and tyranny already begun with circumstances of cruelty and perfidy scarcely paralleled in the most barbarous ages, and totally unworthy the head of a civilized nation.

He has constrained our fellow-citizens, taken captive on the high seas [by impressment], to bear arms against their country, to become the executioners of their friends and brethren, or to fall themselves by their hands.

He has excited domestic insurrection among us [i.e., among slaves], and has endeavored to bring on the inhabitants of our frontiers the merciless Indian savages, whose known rule of warfare is an undistinguished destruction of all ages, sexes, and conditions.

In every stage of these oppressions we have petitioned for redress in the most humble terms; our repeated petitions have been answered only by repeated injury. [E.g., pp. 100, 102.] A prince, whose character is thus marked by every act which may define a tyrant, is unfit to be the ruler of a free people.

Nor have we been wanting in our attentions to our British brethren. We have warned them, from time to time, of attempts by their legislature to extend an unwarrantable jurisdiction over us. We have reminded them of the circumstances of our emigration and settlement here. We have appealed to their native justice and magnanimity; and we have conjured them, by the ties of our common kindred, to disavow these usurpations, which would inevitably interrupt our connections and correspondence. They, too, have been deaf to the voice of justice and of consanguinity [blood relationship]. We must, therefore, acquiesce in the necessity which denounces [announces] our separation, and hold them, as we hold the rest of mankind, enemies in war, in peace friends.

We, therefore, the representatives of the United States of America, in General Congress assembled, appealing to the Supreme Judge of the world for the rectitude of our intentions, do, in the name and by the authority of the good people of these colonies, solemnly publish and declare, That these United Colonies are, and of right ought to be, FREE AND INDEPENDENT STATES; that they are absolved from all allegiance to the British crown, and that all political connection between them and the state of Great Britain is, and ought to be, totally dissolved; and that, as free and independent states, they have full power to levy war, conclude peace, contract alliances, establish commerce, and do all other acts and things which independent states may of right do. And for the support of this declaration, with a firm reliance on the protection of Divine Providence, we mutually pledge to each other our lives, our fortunes, and our sacred honor.

[Signed by] JOHN HANCOCK [President]

[and fifty-five others]

CONSTITUTION OF THE UNITED STATES OF AMERICA

[Boldface headings and bracketed explanatory matter and marginal comments (both in color) have been inserted for the reader's convenience. Passages that are no longer operative are printed in italic type.]

PREAMBLE

On "We the people," see p. 236n.

We the people of the United States, in order to form a more perfect union, establish justice, insure domestic tranquillity, provide for the common defense, promote the general welfare, and secure the blessings of liberty to ourselves and our posterity, do ordain and establish this CONSTITUTION for the United States of America.

Article I. Legislative Department

Section I. Congress

Legislative power vested in a two-House Congress. All legislative powers herein granted shall be vested in a Congress of the United States, which shall consist of a Senate and a House of Representatives.

Section II. House of Representatives

1. The people elect representatives biennially. The House of Representatives shall be composed of members chosen every second year by the people of the several States, and the electors [voters] in each State shall have the qualifications requisite for electors of the most numerous branch of the State Legislature.

2. Who may be representatives. No person shall be a Representative who shall not have attained to the age of twenty-five years, and been seven years a citizen of the United States, and who shall not, when elected, be an inhabitant of that State in which he shall be chosen.

See 1787 compromise, p. 132.

See 1787 compromise, p. 133.

3. Representation in the House based on population; census. Representatives and direct taxes[1] shall be apportioned among the several States which may be included within this Union, according to their respective numbers, *which shall be determined by adding to the whole number of free persons, including those bound to service for a term of years* [apprentices and indentured servants], *and excluding Indians not taxed, three-fifths of all other persons* [slaves].[2] The actual enumeration [census] shall be made within three years after the first meeting of the Congress of the United States, and within every subsequent term of ten years, in such manner as they shall by law direct. The number of Representatives shall not exceed one for every thirty thousand, but each State shall have at least one Representative; *and until such enumeration shall be made, the State of New Hampshire shall be entitled to choose three, Massachusetts eight, Rhode Island and Providence Plantations one, Connecticut five, New York six, New Jersey four, Pennsylvania eight, Delaware one, Maryland six, Virginia ten, North Carolina five, South Carolina five, and Georgia three.*

4. Vacancies in the House are filled by election. When vacancies happen in the representation from any State, the Executive authority [governor] thereof shall issue writs of election [call a special election] to fill such vacancies.

---

[1] Modified in 1913 by the 16th Amendment re income taxes (see p. 630).

[2] The word "slave" appears nowhere in the Constitution; "slavery" appears in the 13th Amendment. The three-fifths rule ceased to be in force when the 13th Amendment was adopted in 1865 (see p. 404 and Amendments below).

See Chase and Johnson trials, pp. 171, 448–449; Nixon trial preliminaries, pp. 895–897.

5. The House selects its Speaker; has sole power to vote impeachment charges (i.e., indictments). The House of Representatives shall choose their Speaker and other officers; and shall have the sole power of impeachment.

Section III. Senate

1. Senators represent the states. The Senate of the United States shall be composed of two Senators from each State, *chosen by the legislature thereof,*[1] for six years; and each Senator shall have one vote.

2. One-third of Senators chosen every two years; vacancies. *Immediately after they shall be assembled in consequence of the first election, they shall be divided as equally as may be into three classes. The seats of the Senators of the first class shall be vacated at the expiration of the second year, of the second class at the expiration of the fourth year, and of the third class at the expiration of the sixth year,* so that one-third may be chosen every second year; *and if vacancies happen by resignation or otherwise, during the recess of the legislature of any State, the Executive* [governor] *thereof may make temporary appointments until the next meeting of the legislature, which shall then fill such vacancies.*[2]

3. Who may be Senators. No person shall be a Senator who shall not have attained to the age of thirty years, and been nine years a citizen of the United States, and who shall not, when elected, be an inhabitant of that State for which he shall be chosen.

4. The Vice-President presides over the Senate. The Vice-President of the United States shall be President of the Senate, but shall have no vote, unless they be equally divided [tied].

5. The Senate chooses its other officers. The Senate shall choose their other officers, and also a President *pro tempore,* in the absence of the Vice-President, or when he shall exercise the office of President of the United States.

See Chase and Johnson trials, pp. 171, 448–449.

6. The Senate has sole power to try impeachments. The Senate shall have the sole power to try all impeachments. When sitting for that purpose, they shall be on oath or affirmation. When the President of the United States is tried, the Chief Justice shall preside:[3] and no person shall be convicted without the concurrence of two-thirds of the members present.

7. Penalties for impeachment conviction. Judgment in cases of impeachment shall not extend further than to removal from office, and disqualification to hold and enjoy any office of honor, trust or profit under the United States: but the party convicted shall nevertheless be liable and subject to indictment, trial, judgment and punishment, according to law.

Section IV. Election and Meetings of Congress

1. Regulation of elections. The times, places and manner of holding elections for Senators and Representatives shall be prescribed in each State by the legislature thereof; but the Congress may at any time by law make or alter such regulations, except as to the places of choosing Senators.

2. Congress must meet once a year. The Congress shall assemble at least once in every year, and such meeting *shall be on the first Monday in December, unless they shall by law appoint a different day.*[4]

---

[1] Repealed in favor of popular election in 1913 by the 17th Amendment.

[2] Changed in 1913 by the 17th Amendment.

[3] The Vice-President, as next in line, would be an interested party.

[4] Changed in 1933 to January 3 by the 20th Amendment (see p. 767 and below).

Section V. Organization and Rules of the Houses

1. Each House may reject members; quorums. Each house shall be the judge of the elections, returns and qualifications of its own members, and a majority of each shall constitute a quorum to do business; but a smaller number may adjourn from day to day, and may be authorized to compel the attendance of absent members, in such manner, and under such penalties, as each house may provide.

See "Bully" Brooks case, p. 370.

2. Each House makes its own rules. Each house may determine the rules of its proceedings, punish its members for disorderly behavior, and with the concurrence of two-thirds, expel a member.

3. Each House must keep and publish a record of its proceedings. Each house shall keep a journal of its proceedings, and from time to time publish the same, excepting such parts as may in their judgment require secrecy; and the yeas and nays of the members of either house on any question shall, at the desire of one-fifth of those present, be entered on the journal.

4. Both Houses must agree on adjournment. Neither house, during the session of Congress, shall, without the consent of the other, adjourn for more than three days, nor to any other place than that in which the two houses shall be sitting.

Section VI. Privileges of and Prohibitions upon Congressmen

1. Congressional salaries; immunities. The Senators and Representatives shall receive a compensation for their services, to be ascertained by law and paid out of the treasury of the United States. They shall in all cases except treason, felony and breach of the peace, be privileged from arrest during their attendance at the session of their respective houses, and in going to and returning from the same; and for any speech or debate in either house, they shall not be questioned in any other place [i.e., they shall be immune from libel suits]

2. A Congressman may not hold any other federal civil office. No Senator or Representative shall, during the time for which he was elected, be appointed to any civil office under the authority of the United States, which shall have been created, or the emoluments whereof shall have been increased, during such time; and no person holding any office under the United States shall be a member of either house during his continuance in office.

Section VII. Method of Making Laws

See 1787 compromise, p. 132.

1. Money bills must originate in the House. All bills for raising revenue shall originate in the House of Representatives; but the Senate may propose or concur with amendments as on other bills.

President Nixon, more than any predecessors, "impounded" billions of dollars voted by Congress for specific purposes, because he disapproved of them. The courts generally failed to sustain him, and his impeachment foes regarded wholesale impoundment as a violation of his oath to "faithfully execute" the laws.

2. The President's veto power; Congress may override. Every bill which shall have passed the House of Representatives and the Senate, shall, before it become a law, be presented to the President of the United States; if he approve he shall sign it, but if not he shall return it with his objections to that house in which it shall have originated, who shall enter the objections at large on their journal, and proceed to reconsider it. If after such reconsideration two-thirds of that house shall agree to pass the bill, it shall be sent, together with the objections, to the other house, by which it shall likewise be reconsidered, and, if approved by two-thirds of that house, it shall become a law. But in all such cases the votes of both houses shall be determined by yeas and nays, and the names of the persons voting for and against the bill shall be entered on the journal of each house respectively. If any bill shall not be returned by the President within ten days (Sundays excepted) after it shall have been presented to him, the same shall be a law, in like manner as if he had signed it, unless the Congress by their adjournment prevent its return, in which case it shall not be a law [this is the so-called pocket veto].

3. All measures requiring the agreement of both Houses go to President for approval. Every order, resolution, or vote to which the concurrence of the Senate and House of Representatives may be necessary (except on a question of adjournment) shall be presented to the President of the United States; and before the same shall take effect, shall be approved by him, or being disapproved by him, shall be repassed by two-thirds of the Senate and House of Representatives, according to the rules and limitations prescribed in the case of a bill.

Section VIII. Powers Granted to Congress

Congress has certain enumerated powers:

1. It may lay and collect taxes. The Congress shall have power to lay and collect taxes, duties, imposts, and excises, to pay the debts and provide for the common defense and general welfare of the United States; but all duties, imposts and excises shall be uniform throughout the United States;

2. It may borrow money. To borrow money on the credit of the United States;

3. It may regulate foreign and interstate trade. To regulate commerce with foreign nations, and among the several States, and with the Indian tribes;

For 1798 naturalization, see p. 161.

4. It may pass naturalization and bankruptcy laws. To establish an uniform rule of naturalization, and uniform laws on the subject of bankruptcies throughout the United States;

5. It may coin money. To coin money, regulate the value thereof, and of foreign coin, and fix the standard of weights and measures;

6. It may punish counterfeiters. To provide for the punishment of counterfeiting the securities and current coin of the United States;

7. It may establish a postal service. To establish post offices and post roads;

8. It may issue patents and copyrights. To promote the progress of science and useful arts by securing for limited times to authors and inventors the exclusive right to their respective writings and discoveries;

See Judiciary Act of 1789, p. 143.

9. It may establish inferior courts. To constitute tribunals inferior to the Supreme Court;

10. It may punish crimes committed on the high seas. To define and punish piracies and felonies committed on the high seas [i.e., outside the three-mile limit] and offenses against the law of nations [international law];

11. It may declare war; authorize privateers. To declare war,[1] grant letters of marque and reprisal,[2] and make rules concerning captures on land and water;

12. It may maintain an army. To raise and support armies, but no appropriation of money to that use shall be for a longer term than two years;[3]

13. It may maintain a navy. To provide and maintain a navy;

14. It may regulate the army and navy. To make rules for the government and regulation of the land and naval forces;

See Whiskey Rebellion, p. 147.

15. It may call out the state militia. To provide for calling forth the militia to execute the laws of the Union, suppress insurrections, and repel invasions;

---

[1] Note that the President, though he can provoke war (see the case of Polk, p. 267) or wage it after it is declared, cannot declare it.

[2] Papers issued private citizens in wartime authorizing them to capture enemy ships.

[3] A reflection of fear of standing armies earlier expressed in the Declaration of Independence.

16. It shares with the states control of militia. To provide for organizing, arming, and disciplining the militia, and for governing such part of them as may be employed in the service of the United States, reserving to the States respectively the appointment of the officers, and the authority of training the militia according to the discipline prescribed by Congress;

17. It makes laws for the District of Columbia and other federal areas. To exercise exclusive legislation in all cases whatsoever, over such district (not exceeding ten miles square) as may, by cession of particular States, and the acceptance of Congress, become the seat of government of the United States,[1] and to exercise like authority over all places purchased by the consent of the legislature of the State, in which the same shall be, for the erection of forts, magazines, arsenals, dock-yards, and other needful buildings;—and

Congress has certain implied powers:

This is the famous "Elastic Clause"; see p. 146.

18. It may make laws necessary for carrying out the enumerated powers. To make all laws which shall be necessary and proper for carrying into execution the foregoing powers, and all others powers vested by this Constitution in the government of the United States, or in any department or officer thereof.

Section IX. Powers Denied to the Federal Government

See 1787 slave compromise, p. 133.

1. Congressional control of slave trade postponed until 1808. *The migration or importation of such persons as any of the States now existing shall think proper to admit shall not be prohibited by the Congress prior to the year 1808; but a tax or duty may be imposed on such importation, not exceeding $10 for each person.*

See Lincoln's unlawful suspension, p. 420.

2. The writ of habeas corpus[2] may be suspended only in case of rebellion or invasion. The privilege of the writ of habeas corpus shall not be suspended, unless when in cases of rebellion or invasion the public safety may require it.

3. Attainders[3] and ex post facto laws[4] forbidden. No bill of attainder or ex post facto law shall be passed.

4. Direct taxes must be apportioned according to population. No capitation [head or poll tax], or other direct, tax shall be laid, unless in proportion to the census or enumeration herein before directed to be taken.[5]

5. Export taxes forbidden. No tax or duty shall be laid on articles exported from any State.

6. Congress must not discriminate among states in regulating commerce. No preference shall be given by any regulation of commerce or revenue to the ports of one State over those of another; nor shall vessels bound to, or from, one State, be obliged to enter, clear, or pay duties in another.

See Lincoln's unlawful infraction, p. 420.

7. Public money may not be spent without congressional appropriation; accounting. No money shall be drawn from the treasury, but in consequence of appropriations made by law; and a regular statement and account of the receipts and expenditures of all public money shall be published from time to time.

---

1 The District of Columbia, 10 miles square, was established in 1791 with a cession from Virginia (see p. 144).

2 A writ of habeas corpus is a document that enables a person under arrest to obtain an immediate examination in court to ascertain whether he is being legally held.

3 A bill of attainder is a special legislative act condemning and punishing an individual without a judicial trial.

4 An ex post facto law is one that fixes punishments for acts committed before the law was passed.

5 Modified in 1913 by the 16th Amendment (see p. 630, and Amendments below).

8. Titles of nobility prohibited; foreign gifts. No title of nobility shall be granted by the United States: and no person holding any office of profit or trust under them, shall, without the consent of the Congress, accept of any present, emolument, office, or title, of any kind whatever, from any king, prince, or foreign state.

Section X. Powers Denied to the States

Absolute prohibitions on the states:

On contracts, see Fletcher *v.* Peck, *p. 212.*

1. The states are forbidden to do certain things. No State shall enter into any treaty, alliance, or confederation; grant letters of marque and reprisal [i.e., authorize privateers]; coin money; emit bills of credit [issue paper money]; make anything but gold and silver coin a [legal] tender in payment of debts; pass any bill of attainder, ex post facto,[1] or law impairing the obligation of contracts, or grant any title of nobility.

Conditional prohibitions on the states:

Cf. Confederation chaos, p. 125.

2. The states may not levy duties without the consent of Congress. No State shall, without the consent of the Congress, lay any imposts or duties on imports or exports, except what may be absolutely necessary for executing its inspection laws: and the net produce of all duties and imposts, laid by any State on imports or exports, shall be for the use of the treasury of the United States; and all such laws shall be subject to the revision and control of the Congress.

3. Certain other federal powers are forbidden the states except with the consent of Congress. No State shall, without the consent of Congress, lay any duty of tonnage [i.e., duty on ship tonnage], keep [non-militia] troops or ships of war in time of peace, enter into any agreement or compact with another State, or with a foreign power, or engage in war, unless actually invaded, or in such imminent danger as will not admit of delay.

Article II. Executive Department

Section I. President and Vice-President

1. The President the chief executive; his term. The executive power shall be vested in a President of the United States of America. He shall hold his office during the term of four years,[2] and, together with the Vice-President, chosen for the same term, be elected as follows:

See 1787 compromise, p. 133.

See 1876 Oregon case, p. 461.

2. The President is chosen by electors. Each State shall appoint, in such manner as the legislature thereof may direct, a number of electors, equal to the whole number of Senators and Representatives to which the State may be entitled in the Congress; but no Senator or Representative, or person holding an office of trust or profit under the United States, shall be appointed an elector.

A majority of the electoral votes needed to elect a President. *The electors shall meet in their respective States, and vote by ballot for two persons, of whom one at least shall not be an inhabitant of the same State with themselves. And they shall make a list of all the persons voted for, and of the number of votes for each; which list they shall sign and certify, and transmit sealed to the seat of government of the United States, directed to the President of the Senate. The President of the Senate shall, in the presence of the Senate and House of Representatives, open all the certificates, and the votes shall then be counted. The person having the greatest number of votes shall be the President, if such number be a*

---

[1] For definitions, see footnotes 3 and 4 on preceding page.

[2] No reference to re-election; for anti-third term 22d Amendment, see below.

See Burr-Jefferson disputed election of 1800, p. 164.

majority of the whole number of electors appointed; and if there be more than one who have such majority, and have an equal number of votes, then the House of Representatives shall immediately choose by ballot one of them for President; and if no person have a majority, then from the five highest on the list the said house shall in like manner choose the President. But in choosing the President the votes shall be taken by States, the representation from each State having one vote; a quorum for this purpose shall consist of a member or members from two-thirds of the States, and a majority of all the States shall be necessary to a choice. In every case, after the choice of the President, the person having the greatest number of votes of the electors shall be the Vice-President. But if there should remain two or more who have equal votes, the Senate shall choose from them by ballot the Vice-President.[1]

See Jefferson as Vice-President in 1796, p. 158.

3. Congress decides time of meeting of Electoral College. The Congress may determine the time of choosing the electors and the day on which they shall give their votes; which day shall be the same throughout the United States.

To provide for foreign-born like Alexander Hamilton, born in the British West Indies.

4. Who may be President. No person except a natural-born citizen, *or a citizen of the United States at the time of the adoption of this Constitution,* shall be eligible to the office of President; neither shall any person be eligible to that office who shall not have attained to the age of thirty-five years, and been fourteen years a resident within the United States [i.e., a legal resident]

Modified by Amendments XX and XXV below.

5. Replacements for President. In case of the removal of the President from office or of his death, resignation, or inability to discharge the powers and duties of the said office, the same shall devolve on the Vice-President, and the Congress may by law provide for the case of removal, death, resignation, or inability, both of the President and Vice-President, declaring what officer shall then act as President, and such officer shall act accordingly, until the disability be removed, or a President shall be elected.

6. The President's salary. The President shall, at stated times, receive for his services a compensation, which shall neither be increased nor diminished during the period for which he shall have been elected, and he shall not receive within that period any other emolument from the United States, or any of them.

7. The President's oath of office. Before he enter on the execution of his office, he shall take the following oath or affirmation:—"I do solemnly swear (or affirm) that I will faithfully execute the office of the President of the United States, and will to the best of my ability preserve, protect and defend the Constitution of the United States."

Section II. Powers of the President

See Cabinet evolution, p. 142.

1. The President has important military and civil powers. The President shall be commander in chief of the army and navy of the United States, and of the militia of the several States, when called into the actual service of the United States; he may require the opinion, in writing, of the principal officer in each of the executive departments, upon any subject relating to the duties of their respective offices, and he shall have power to grant reprieves and pardons for offenses against the United States, except in cases of impeachment.[2]

2. The President may negotiate treaties and nominate federal officials. He shall have power, by and with the advice and consent of the Senate, to make treaties, provided two-thirds of the Senators present concur; and he shall nominate, and by and with the advice and consent of the Senate, shall appoint ambassadors, other public ministers and consuls, judges of the Supreme Court, and all other officers of the United States, whose appointments are

---

1 Repealed in 1804 by the 12th Amendment (for text, see Amendments below).

2 To prevent the President's pardoning himself or his close associates, as was feared in the case of Richard Nixon. See pp. 896–897.

For President's removal power, see pp. 448–449.

not herein otherwise provided for, and which shall be established by law: but the Congress may by law vest the appointment of such inferior officers, as they think proper, in the President alone, in the courts of law, or in the heads of departments.

3. The President may fill vacancies during Senate recess. The President shall have power to fill up all vacancies that may happen during the recess of the Senate, by granting commissions which shall expire at the end of their next session.

Section III. Other Powers and Duties of the President

For President's personal appearances, see p. 635.

Messages; extra sessions; receiving ambassadors: execution of the laws. He shall from time to time give to the Congress information of the state of the Union, and recommend to their consideration such measures as he shall judge necessary and expedient; he may, on extraordinary occasions, convene both houses, or either of them, and in case of disagreement between them, with respect to the time of adjournment, he may adjourn them to such time as he shall think proper; he shall receive ambassadors and other public ministers; he shall take care that the laws be faithfully executed, and shall commission all the officers of the United States.

Section IV. Impeachment

See Johnson's acquittal, p. 449; also Nixon's near impeachment, pp. 896–897.

Civil officers may be removed by impeachment. The President, Vice-President and all civil officers[1] of the United States shall be removed from office on impeachment for, and on conviction of, treason, bribery, or other high crimes and misdemeanors.

Article III. Judicial Department

Section I. The Federal Courts

See Judicial Act of 1789, p. 143.

The judicial power belongs to the federal courts. The judicial power of the United States shall be vested in one Supreme Court, and in such inferior courts as the Congress may from time to time ordain and establish. The judges, both of the Supreme and inferior courts, shall hold their offices during good behavior, and shall, at stated times, receive for their services a compensation which shall not be diminished[2] during their continuance in office.

Section II. Jurisdiction of Federal Courts

1. Kinds of cases that may be heard. The judicial power shall extend to all cases, in law and equity, arising under this Constitution, the laws of the United States, and treaties made, or which shall be made, under their authority;—to all cases affecting ambassadors, other public ministers and consuls;—to all cases of admiralty and maritime jurisdiction;—to controversies to which the United States shall be a party;—to controversies between two or more States;—*between a State and citizens of another State;*[3]—between citizens of different States;—between citizens of the same State claiming lands under grants of different States, and between a State, or the citizens thereof, and foreign states, citizens or subjects.

2. Jurisdiction of the Supreme Court. In all cases affecting ambassadors, other public ministers and consuls, and those in which a State shall be party, the Supreme Court shall have original jurisdiction.[4] In all the other cases before mentioned, the Supreme Court shall have appellate jurisdiction,[5] both as to law and fact, with such exceptions, and under such regulations, as the Congress shall make.

---

[1] I.e., all federal executive and judicial officers, but not members of Congress or military personnel.

[2] In 1978, in a case involving federal judges, the Supreme Court ruled that diminution of salaries by inflation was irrelevant.

[3] The 11th Amendment (see Amendments below) restricts this to suits by a state against citizens of another state.

[4] I.e., such cases must originate in the Supreme Court.

[5] I.e., it hears other cases only when they are appealed to it from a lower federal court or a state court.

3. Trial for federal crime is by jury. The trial of all crimes, except in cases of impeachment, shall be by jury; and such trial shall be held in the State where the said crimes shall have been committed; but when not committed within any State, the trial shall be at such place or places as the Congress may by law have directed.

Section III. Treason

1. Treason defined. Treason against the United States shall consist only in levying war against them, or in adhering to their enemies, giving them aid and comfort. No person shall be convicted of treason unless on the testimony of two witnesses to the same overt act, or on confession in open court.

See Burr trial, p. 177.

2. Congress fixes punishment for treason. The Congress shall have power to declare the punishment of treason, but no attainder of treason shall work corruption of blood, or forfeiture except during the life of the person attainted.[1]

Article IV. Relations of the States to One Another

Section I. Credit to Acts, Records, and Court Proceedings

Each state must respect the public acts of the others. Full faith and credit shall be given in each State to the public acts, records, and judicial proceedings of every other State.[2] And the Congress may by general laws prescribe the manner in which such acts, records, and proceedings shall be proved [attested], and the effect thereof.

Section II. Duties of States to States

1. Citizenship in one state is valid in all. The citizens of each State shall be entitled to all privileges and immunities of citizens in the several States.

2. Fugitives from justice must be surrendered by the state to which they have fled. A person charged in any State with treason, felony, or other crime, who shall flee from justice, and be found in another State, shall on demand of the executive authority [governor] of the State from which he fled, be delivered up, to be removed to the State having jurisdiction of the crime.

This stipulation is sometimes openly flouted. In 1978 Governor Jerry Brown of California, acting on humanitarian grounds, refused to surrender to South Dakota an American Indian, Dennis Banks, who was charged with murder in an armed uprising.

3. Slaves and apprentices must be returned. *No person held to service or labor in one State, under the laws thereof, escaping into another, shall, in consequence of any law or regulation therein, be discharged from such service or labor, but shall be delivered up on claim of the party to whom such service or labor may be due.*[3]

Basis of fugitive slave laws; see pp. 350–351.

Section III. New States and Territories

1. Congress may admit new states. New States may be admitted by the Congress into this Union; but no new State shall be formed or erected within the jurisdiction of any other State; nor any State be formed by the junction of two or more States, or parts of States, without the consent of the legislatures of the States concerned as well as of the Congress.[4]

E.g., Maine (1820); see pp. 209–210.

2. Congress regulates federal territory and property. The Congress shall have power to dispose of and make all needful rules and regulations respecting the territory or other property belonging to the United States; and nothing in this Constitution shall be so construed as to prejudice any claims of the United States, or of any particular State.

---

[1] I.e., punishment only for the offender; none for his heirs.
[2] E.g., a marriage valid in one is valid in all.
[3] Invalidated in 1865 by the 13th Amendment (for text see Amendments below).
[4] Loyal West Virginia was formed by Lincoln in 1862 from seceded Virginia. This act was of dubious constitutionality and was justified in part by the wartime powers of the President. See pp. 390–391.

Section IV. Protection to the States

United States guarantees to states representative government and protection against invasion and rebellion. The United States shall guarantee to every State in this Union a republican form of government, and shall protect each of them against invasion; and on application of the legislature, or of the executive [governor] (when the legislature cannot be convened), against domestic violence.

See Cleveland and the Pullman strike, pp. 549–550.

Article V. The Process of Amendment

The Constitution may be amended in four ways. The Congress, whenever two-thirds of both houses shall deem it necessary, shall propose amendments to this Constitution, or, on the application of the legislatures of two-thirds of the several States, shall call a convention for proposing amendments, which, in either case, shall be valid to all intents and purposes, as part of this Constitution, when ratified by the legislatures of three-fourths of the several States, or by conventions in three-fourths thereof, as the one or the other mode of ratification may be proposed by the Congress; provided *that no amendments which may be made prior to the year one thousand eight hundred and eight shall in any manner affect the first and fourth clauses in the ninth section of the first article;*[1] and that no State, without its consent, shall be deprived of its equal suffrage in the Senate.

Article VI. General Provisions

This pledge honored by Hamilton, p. 143.

1. The debts of the Confederation are taken over. All debts contracted and engagements entered into, before the adoption of this Constitution, shall be as valid against the United States under this Constitution, as under the Confederation.

2. The Constitution, federal laws, and treaties are the supreme law of the land. This Constitution, and the laws of the United States which shall be made in pursuance thereof; and all treaties made, or which shall be made, under the authority of the United States, shall be the supreme law of the land; and the judges in every State shall be bound thereby, anything in the Constitution or laws of any State to the contrary notwithstanding.

3. Federal and state officers bound by oath to support the Constitution. The Senators and Representatives before mentioned, and the members of the several State legislatures, and all executive and judicial officers, both of the United States and of the several States, shall be bound by oath or affirmation to support this Constitution; but no religious test shall ever be required as a qualification to any office or public trust under the United States.

Article VII. Ratification of the Constitution

See 1787 irregularity, p. 134.

The Constitution effective when ratified by conventions in nine states. The ratification of the conventions of nine States shall be sufficient for the establishment of this Constitution between the States so ratifying the same.

Done in Convention by the unanimous consent of the States present, the seventeenth day of September in the year of our Lord one thousand seven hundred and eighty-seven and of the Independence of the United States of America the twelfth. In witness whereof we have hereunto subscribed our names.

[Signed by]

G° WASHINGTON
Presidt and Deputy from Virginia
[and thirty-eight others]

[1] This clause, re slave trade and direct taxes, became inoperative in 1808.

AMENDMENTS TO THE CONSTITUTION

Amendment I. Religious and Political Freedom

For background of Bill of Rights, *see p. 143.*

Congress must not interfere with freedom of religion, speech or press, assembly, and petition. Congress shall make no law respecting an establishment of religion,[1] or prohibiting the free exercise thereof; or abridging the freedom of speech, or of the press; or the right of the people peaceably to assemble, and to petition the government for a redress of grievances.

Amendment II. Right to Bear Arms

The people may bear arms. A well-regulated militia being necessary to the security of a free State, the right of the people to keep and bear arms [i.e., for military purposes] shall not be infringed.[2]

Amendment III. Quartering of Troops

See Declaration of Independence and British quartering above.

Soldiers may not be arbitrarily quartered on the people. No soldier shall, in time of peace, be quartered in any house without the consent of the owner, nor in time of war, but in a manner to be prescribed by law.

Amendment IV. Searches and Seizures

A reflection of colonial grievances against Crown.

Unreasonable searches are forbidden. The right of the people to be secure in their persons, houses, papers, and effects, against unreasonable searches and seizures, shall not be violated, and no [search] warrants shall issue but upon probable cause, supported by oath or affirmation, and particularly describing the place to be searched, and the persons or things to be seized.

Amendment V. Right to Life, Liberty, and Property

When witnesses refuse to answer questions in court, they routinely "take the Fifth Amendment."

The individual is guaranteed certain rights when on trial and the right to life, liberty, and property. No person shall be held to answer for a capital, or otherwise infamous crime, unless on a presentment [formal charge] or indictment of a grand jury, except in cases arising in the land or naval forces, or in the militia, when in actual service in time of war or public danger; nor shall any person be subject for the same offense to be twice put in jeopardy of life or limb; nor shall be compelled in any criminal case to be a witness against himself, nor be deprived of life, liberty, or property, without due process of law; nor shall private property be taken for public use [i.e., by eminent domain] without just compensation.

Amendment VI. Protection in Criminal Trials

See Declaration of Independence above.

An accused person has important rights. In all criminal prosecutions, the accused shall enjoy the right to a speedy and public trial, by an impartial jury of the State and district wherein the crime shall have been committed, which district shall have been previously ascertained by law, and to be informed of the nature and cause of the accusation; to be confronted with the witnesses against him; to have compulsory process [subpoena] for obtaining witnesses in his favor, and to have the assistance of counsel for his defense.

---

1 In 1787 "an establishment of religion" referred to an "established church," or one supported by all taxpayers, whether members or not. But the courts have often acted under this article to keep religion, including prayers, out of the public schools.

2 The courts, with "militia" in mind, have consistently held that the "right" to bear arms is a limited one.

Amendment VII. Suits at Common Law

The rules of common law are recognized. In suits at common law, where the value in controversy shall exceed twenty dollars, the right of trial by jury shall be preserved, and no fact tried by a jury shall be otherwise re-examined in any court of the United States, than according to the rules of the common law.

Amendment VIII. Bail and Punishments

Excessive fines and unusual punishments are forbidden. Excessive bail shall not be required, nor excessive fines imposed, nor cruel and unusual punishments inflicted.

Amendment IX. Concerning Rights Not Enumerated

Amendments IX and X were bulwarks of Southern states' rights before the Civil War.

The people retain rights not here enumerated. The enumeration in the Constitution, of certain rights, shall not be construed to deny or disparage others retained by the people.

Amendment X. Powers Reserved to the States and to the People

A concession to states' rights, p. 146.

Powers not delegated to the federal government are reserved to the states and the people. The powers not delegated to the United States by the Constitution, nor prohibited by it to the States, are reserved to the States respectively, or to the people.

Amendment XI. Suits against a State

The federal courts have no authority in suits by citizens against a state. The judicial power of the United States shall not be construed to extend to any suit in law or equity, commenced or prosecuted against one of the United States by citizens of another State, or by citizens or subjects of any foreign state. [Adopted 1798.]

Amendment XII. Election of President and Vice-President

Forestalls repetition of 1800 electoral dispute, p. 164.

See 1876 disputed election, pp. 460–463.

See 1824 election, pp. 223–224.

1. Changes in manner of electing President and Vice-President; procedure when no presidential candidate receives electoral majority. The electors shall meet in their respective States, and vote by ballot for President and Vice-President, one of whom, at least, shall not be an inhabitant of the same State with themselves; they shall name in their ballots the person voted for as President, and in distinct ballots the person voted for as Vice-President, and they shall make distinct lists of all persons voted for as President, and of all persons voted for as Vice-President, and of the number of votes for each, which lists they shall sign and certify, and transmit sealed to the seat of government of the United States, directed to the President of the Senate;—the President of the Senate shall, in the presence of the Senate and House of Representatives, open all the certificates and the votes shall then be counted;—the person having the greatest number of votes for President shall be the President, if such number be a majority of the whole number of electors appointed; and if no person have such majority, then from the persons having the highest numbers not exceeding three on the list of those voted for as President, the House of Representatives shall choose immediately, by ballot, the President. But in choosing the President, the votes shall be taken by States, the representation from each State having one vote; a quorum for this purpose shall consist of a member or members from two-thirds of the States, and a majority of all the States shall be necessary to a choice. And if the House of Representatives shall not choose a President whenever the right of choice shall devolve upon them, before *the fourth day of March*[1] next following, then the Vice-President shall act as President, as in the case of the death or other constitutional disability of the President.

2. Procedure when no vice-presidential candidate receives electoral majority. The person having the greatest number of votes as Vice-President shall be the Vice-President, if such

[1] Changed to January 20 by the 20th Amendment (for text, see Amendments below).

number be a majority of the whole number of electors appointed; and if no person have a majority, then from the two highest numbers on the list the Senate shall choose the Vice-President; a quorum for the purpose shall consist of two-thirds of the whole number of Senators, and a majority of the whole number shall be necessary to a choice. But no person constitutionally ineligible to the office of President shall be eligible to that of Vice-President of the United States. [Adopted 1804.]

Amendment XIII. Slavery Prohibited

For background, see pp. 403–404.

Slavery forbidden. 1. Neither slavery[1] nor involuntary servitude, except as a punishment for crime whereof the party shall have been duly convicted, shall exist within the United States, or any place subject to their jurisdiction.

2. Congress shall have power to enforce this article by appropriate legislation. [Adopted 1865.]

Amendment XIV. Civil Rights for Ex-slaves,[2] etc.

For background, see p. 440.

For corporations as "persons," see p. 490.

1. Ex-slaves made citizens; U.S. citizenship primary. All persons born or naturalized in the United States, and subject to the jurisdiction thereof, are citizens of the United States and of the State wherein they reside. No State shall make or enforce any law which shall abridge the privileges or immunities of citizens of the United States; nor shall any State deprive any person of life, liberty, or property, without due process of law; nor deny to any person within its jurisdiction the equal protection of the laws.

Abolishes three-fifths rule for slaves, Art. I, Sec. II, para. 3.

2. When a state denies citizens the vote, its representation shall be reduced. Representatives shall be apportioned among the several States according to their respective numbers, counting the whole number of persons in each State, excluding Indians not taxed. But when the right to vote at any election for the choice of Electors for President and Vice-President of the United States, Representatives in Congress, the executive and judicial officers of a State, or the members of the legislature thereof, is denied to any of the male inhabitants of such State, being twenty-one years of age and citizens of the United States, or in any way abridged, except for participation in rebellion, or other crime, the basis of representation therein shall be reduced in the proportion which the number of such male citizens shall bear to the whole number of male citizens twenty-one years of age in such State.

Leading ex-Confederates denied office. See p. 438.

3. Certain persons who have been in rebellion are ineligible for federal and state office. No person shall be a Senator or Representative in Congress, or Elector of President and Vice-President, or hold any office, civil or military, under the United States, or under any State, who, having previously taken an oath, as a member of Congress, or as an officer of the United States, or as a member of any State legislature, or as an executive or judicial officer of any State, to support the Constitution of the United States, shall have engaged in insurrection or rebellion against the same, or given aid or comfort to the enemies thereof. But Congress may, by a vote of two-thirds of each house, remove such disability.

The ex-Confederates were thus forced to repudiate their debts and pay pensions to their own veterans, plus taxes for the pensions of Union veterans, their conquerors.

4. Debts incurred in aid of rebellion are void. The validity of the public debt of the United States, authorized by law, including debts incurred for payment of pensions and bounties for services in suppressing insurrection or rebellion, shall not be questioned. But neither the United States nor any State shall assume or pay any debt or obligation incurred in aid of insurrection or rebellion against the United States, or any claim for the loss or emancipation of any slave; but all such debts, obligations, and claims shall be held illegal and void.

---

[1] The only explicit mention of slavery in the Constitution.

[2] Occasionally an offender is prosecuted under the 13th Amendment for keeping an employee or other person under conditions approximating slavery.

5. Enforcement. The Congress shall have power to enforce, by appropriate legislation, the provisions of this article. [Adopted 1868.]

Amendment XV. Suffrage for Blacks

For background, see p. 442.

Black males are made voters. 1. The right of citizens of the United States to vote shall not be denied or abridged by the United States or by any State on account of race, color, or previous condition of servitude.

2. The Congress shall have power to enforce this article by appropriate legislation. [Adopted 1870.]

Amendment XVI. Income Taxes

For background, see pp. 550, 630.

Congress has power to lay and collect income taxes. The Congress shall have power to lay and collect taxes on incomes, from whatever source derived, without apportionment among the several States, and without regard to any census or enumeration. [Adopted 1913.]

Amendment XVII. Direct Election of Senators

Senators shall be elected by popular vote. 1. The Senate of the United States shall be composed of two Senators from each State, elected by the people thereof, for six years; and each Senator shall have one vote. The electors in each State shall have the qualifications requisite for electors of [voters for] the most numerous branch of the State legislatures.

2. When vacancies happen in the representation of any State in the Senate, the executive authority of such State shall issue writs of election to fill such vacancies: Provided, that the Legislature of any State may empower the executive thereof to make temporary appointments until the people fill the vacancies by election as the Legislature may direct.

3. This amendment shall not be so construed as to affect the election or term of any Senator chosen before it becomes valid as part of the Constitution. [Adopted 1913.]

Amendment XVIII. National Prohibition

For background, see p. 684.

The sale or manufacture of intoxicating liquors is forbidden. 1. *After one year from the ratification of this article the manufacture, sale, or transportation of intoxicating liquors within, the importation thereof into, or the exportation thereof from the United States and all territory subject to the jurisdiction thereof, for beverage purposes, is hereby prohibited.*

2. *The Congress and the several States shall have concurrent power to enforce this article by appropriate legislation.*

3. *This article shall be inoperative unless it shall have been ratified as an amendment to the Constitution by the legislatures of the several States, as provided by the Constitution, within seven years from the date of the submission thereof to the States by the Congress.* [Adopted 1919; repealed 1933 by 21st Amendment.]

Amendment XIX. Woman Suffrage

For background, see p. 684.

Women guaranteed the right to vote. 1. The right of citizens of the United States to vote shall not be denied or abridged by the United States or by any State on account of sex.

2. The Congress shall have power to enforce this article by appropriate legislation. [Adopted 1920.]

Amendment XX. Presidential and Congressional Terms

Shortens lame-duck periods by modifying Art. I, Sec. IV, para. 2.

1. Presidential, vice-presidential, and congressional terms of office begin in January. The terms of the President and Vice-President shall end at noon on the 20th day of January, and the terms of Senators and Representatives at noon on the 3d day of January, of the years in which such terms would have ended if this article had not been ratified; and the terms of their successors shall then begin.

2. New meeting date for Congress. The Congress shall assemble at least once in every year, and such meeting shall begin at noon on the 3d day of January, unless they shall by law appoint a different day.

3. Emergency presidential and vice-presidential succession. If, at the time fixed for the beginning of the term of the President, the President-elect shall have died, the Vice-President-elect shall become President. If a President shall not have been chosen before the time fixed for the beginning of his term, or if the President-elect shall have failed to qualify, then the Vice-President-elect shall act as President until a President shall have qualified; and the Congress may by law provide for the case wherein neither a President-elect nor a Vice-President-elect shall have qualified, declaring who shall then act as President, or the manner in which one who is to act shall be selected, and such persons shall act accordingly until a President or Vice-President shall have qualified.

4. The Congress may by law provide for the case of the death of any of the persons from whom the House of Representatives may choose a President whenever the right of choice shall have devolved upon them, and for the case of the death of any of the persons from whom the Senate may choose a Vice-President whenever the right of choice shall have devolved upon them.

5. Sections 1 and 2 shall take effect on the 15th day of October following the ratification of this article.

6. This article shall be inoperative unless it shall have been ratified as an amendment to the Constitution by the Legislatures of three-fourths of the several States within seven years from the date of its submission. [Adopted 1933.]

Amendment XXI. Prohibition Repealed

For background, see p. 759.

1. 18th Amendment repealed. The eighteenth article of amendment to the Constitution of the United States is hereby repealed.

2. Local laws honored. The transportation or importation into any State, Territory, or Possession of the United States for delivery or use therein of intoxicating liquors, in violation of the laws thereof, is hereby prohibited.

3. This article shall be inoperative unless it shall have been ratified as an amendment to the Constitution by conventions in the several States, as provided in the Constitution, within seven years from the date of the submission thereof to the States by the Congress. [Adopted 1933.]

Amendment XXII. Anti-Third Term Amendment

Sometimes referred to as the anti–Franklin Roosevelt amendment.

Presidential term is limited. 1. No person shall be elected to the office of President more than twice, and no person who has held the office of President, or acted as President, for more than two years of a term to which some other person was elected President shall be elected to the office of President more than once. But this article shall not apply to any person holding the office of President when this article was proposed by the Congress [i.e., Truman], and shall not prevent any person who may be holding the office of President, or acting as President, during the term within which this article becomes operative [i.e., Truman] from holding the office of President or acting as President during the remainder of such term.

2. This article shall be inoperative unless it shall have been ratified as an amendment to the Constitution by the legislatures of three-fourths of the several States within seven years from the date of its submission to the States by the Congress. [Adopted 1951.]

Amendment XXIII. District of Columbia Vote

Designed to give the District of Columbia three electoral votes and to quiet the century-old cry of "No taxation without representation." Yet the District of Columbia still has only one non-voting member of Congress.

1. Presidential Electors for the District of Columbia. The District constituting the seat of Government of the United States shall appoint in such manner as the Congress may direct:

A number of electors of President and Vice-President equal to the whole number of Senators and Representatives in Congress to which the District would be entitled if it were a State, but in no event more than the least populous State; they shall be in addition to those appointed by the States, but they shall be considered for the purposes of the election of President and Vice-President, to be electors appointed by a State; and they shall meet in the District and perform such duties as provided by the twelfth article of amendment.

2. Enforcement. The Congress shall have the power to enforce this article by appropriate legislation. [Adopted 1961.]

Amendment XXIV. Poll Tax

Designed to end discrimination against blacks and other poor folk. An aspect of the civil rights crusade under President Lyndon Johnson. *See p. 868.*

1. Payment of poll tax or other taxes not to be prerequisite for voting in federal elections. The right of citizens of the United States to vote in any primary or other election for President or Vice-President, for electors for President or Vice-President, or for Senator or Representative in Congress, shall not be denied or abridged by the United States or any State by reason of failure to pay any poll tax or other tax.

2. Enforcement. The Congress shall have the power to enforce this article by appropriate legislation. [Adopted 1964.]

Amendment XXV. Presidential Succession and Disability[1] (1967)

1. Vice-President to become President. In case of the removal of the President from office or of his death or resignation, the Vice-President shall become President.[2]

2. Successor to Vice-President provided. Whenever there is a vacancy in the office of the Vice-President, the President shall nominate a Vice-President who shall take office upon confirmation by a majority vote of both Houses of Congress.

Gerald Ford was the first "appointed President." *See pp. 891–901.*

3. Vice-President to serve for disabled President. Whenever the President transmits to the President pro tempore of the Senate and the Speaker of the House of Representatives his written declaration that he is unable to discharge the powers and duties of his office, and until he transmits to them a written declaration to the contrary, such powers and duties shall be discharged by the Vice-President as Acting President.

---

[1] Passed by a two-thirds vote of both Houses of Congress in July 1965; ratified by the requisite three-fourths of the state legislatures, February 1967, or well within the seven-year limit.

[2] The original Constitution (Art. II, Sec. I, para. 5) was vague on this point, stipulating that "the powers and duties" of the President, but not necessarily the title, should "devolve" on the Vice-President. President Tyler, the first "accidental President," assumed not only the powers and duties but the title as well.

4. Procedure for disqualifying or requalifying President. Whenever the Vice-President and a majority of either the principal officers of the executive departments or of such other body as Congress may by law provide, transmit to the President pro tempore of the Senate and the Speaker of the House of Representatives their written declaration that the President is unable to discharge the powers and duties of his office, the Vice-President shall immediately assume the powers and duties of the office as Acting President.

Thereafter, when the President transmits to the President pro tempore of the Senate and the Speaker of the House of Representatives his written declaration that no inability exists, he shall resume the powers and duties of his office unless the Vice-President and a majority of either the principal officers of the executive department[s] or of such other body as Congress may by law provide, transmit within four days to the President pro tempore of the Senate and the Speaker of the House of Representatives their written declaration that the President is unable to discharge the powers and duties of his office. Thereupon Congress shall decide the issue, assembling within forty-eight hours for that purpose if not in session. If the Congress, within twenty-one days after receipt of the latter written declaration, or, if Congress is not in session, within twenty-one days after Congress is required to assemble, determines by two-thirds vote of both Houses that the President is unable to discharge the powers and duties of his office, the Vice-President shall continue to discharge the same as Acting President; otherwise, the President shall resume the powers and duties of his office.

Amendment XXVI. Lowering Voting Age (1971)

A response to the current revolt of youth, *see pp. 884ff.*

1. Ballot for eighteen-year-olds. The right of citizens of the United States, who are eighteen years of age or older, to vote shall not be denied or abridged by the United States or by any State on account of age.

2. Enforcement. The Congress shall have power to enforce this article by appropriate legislation.

Amendment XXVII. Sex Equality (Sent to States, 1972)

See pp. 930–932 for background.

1. Women's rights guaranteed. Equality of rights under the law shall not be denied or abridged by the United States or by any State on account of sex.

2. Enforcement. The Congress shall have the power to enforce, by appropriate legislation, the provisions of this article.

3. Timing. This amendment shall take effect two years after the date of ratification.

[The original time limit on ratification was due to expire on March 22, 1979, but Congress, in a controversial move, extended the deadline to June 30, 1982. Yet ratification remained stalled on the expiration of that date, because only 35 of the necessary 38 states had given their approval.]

Growth of U.S. Population and Area

Census	Population of United States	Increase over the Preceding Census: Number	Percent	Land Area (Sq. Mi.)	Pop. per Sq. Mi.
1790	3,929,214			867,980	4.5
1800	5,308,483	1,379,269	35.1	867,980	6.1
1810	7,239,881	1,931,398	36.4	1,685,865	4.3
1820	9,638,453	2,398,572	33.1	1,753,588	5.5
1830	12,866,020	3,227,567	33.5	1,753,588	7.3
1840	17,069,453	4,203,433	32.7	1,753,588	9.7
1850	23,191,876	6,122,423	35.9	2,944,337	7.9
1860	31,433,321	8,251,445	35.6	2,973,965	10.6
1870	39,818,449	8,375,128	26.6	2,973,965	13.4
1880	50,155,783	10,337,334	26.0	2,973,965	16.9
1890	62,947,714	12,791,931	25.5	2,973,965	21.2
1900	75,994,575	13,046,861	20.7	2,974,159	25.6
1910	91,972,266	15,997,691	21.0	2,973,890	30.9
1920	105,710,620	13,738,354	14.9	2,973,776	35.5
1930	122,775,046	17,064,426	16.1	2,977,128	41.2
1940	131,669,275	8,894,229	7.2	2,977,128	44.2
1950	150,697,361	19,028,086	14.5	2,974,726 *	50.7
1960 †	179,323,175	28,625,814	19.0	3,540,911	50.6
1970	203,235,298	23,912,123	13.3	3,536,855	57.5
1980	226,504,825	23,269,527	11.4	3,536,855	64.0

* As remeasured in 1940; shrinkage offset by increase in water area.
† First year for which figures include Alaska and Hawaii.

Admission of States

(SEE P. 137 FOR ORDER IN WHICH THE ORIGINAL THIRTEEN ENTERED THE UNION.)

Order of Admission	State	Date of Admission	Order of Admission	State	Date of Admission
14	Vermont	March 4, 1791	33	Oregon	Feb. 14, 1859
15	Kentucky	June 1, 1792	34	Kansas	Jan. 29, 1861
16	Tennessee	June 1, 1796	35	West Virginia	June 20, 1863
17	Ohio	March 1, 1803	36	Nevada	Oct. 31, 1864
18	Louisiana	April 30, 1812	37	Nebraska	March 1, 1867
19	Indiana	Dec. 11, 1816	38	Colorado	Aug. 1, 1876
20	Mississippi	Dec. 10, 1817	39	North Dakota	Nov. 2, 1889
21	Illinois	Dec. 3, 1818	40	South Dakota	Nov. 2, 1889
22	Alabama	Dec. 14, 1819	41	Montana	Nov. 8, 1889
23	Maine	March 15, 1820	42	Washington	Nov. 11, 1889
24	Missouri	Aug. 10, 1821	43	Idaho	July 3, 1890
25	Arkansas	June 15, 1836	44	Wyoming	July 10, 1890
26	Michigan	Jan. 26, 1837	45	Utah	Jan. 4, 1896
27	Florida	March 3, 1845	46	Oklahoma	Nov. 16, 1907
28	Texas	Dec. 29, 1845	47	New Mexico	Jan. 6, 1912
29	Iowa	Dec. 28, 1846	48	Arizona	Feb. 14, 1912
30	Wisconsin	May 29, 1848	49	Alaska	Jan. 3, 1959
31	California	Sept. 9, 1850	50	Hawaii	Aug. 21, 1959
32	Minnesota	May 11, 1858			

Presidential Elections*

Election	Candidates	Parties	Popular Vote	Electoral Vote
1789	GEORGE WASHINGTON	No party designations		69
	John Adams			34
	Minor Candidates			35
1792	GEORGE WASHINGTON	No party designations		132
	John Adams			77
	George Clinton			50
	Minor Candidates			5
1796	JOHN ADAMS	Federalist		71
	Thomas Jefferson	Democratic-Republican		68
	Thomas Pinckney	Federalist		59
	Aaron Burr	Democratic-Republican		30
	Minor Candidates			48
1800	THOMAS JEFFERSON	Democratic-Republican		73
	Aaron Burr	Democratic-Republican		73
	John Adams	Federalist		65
	Charles C. Pinckney	Federalist		64
	John Jay	Federalist		1
1804	THOMAS JEFFERSON	Democratic-Republican		162
	Charles C. Pinckney	Federalist		14
1808	JAMES MADISON	Democratic-Republican		122
	Charles C. Pinckney	Federalist		47
	George Clinton	Democratic-Republican		6
1812	JAMES MADISON	Democratic-Republican		128
	DeWitt Clinton	Federalist		89
1816	JAMES MONROE	Democratic-Republican		183
	Rufus King	Federalist		34
1820	JAMES MONROE	Democratic-Republican		231
	John Q. Adams	Independent Republican		1
1824	JOHN Q. ADAMS (Min.)†	Democratic-Republican	108,740	84
	Andrew Jackson	Democratic-Republican	153,544	99
	William H. Crawford	Democratic-Republican	46,618	41
	Henry Clay	Democratic-Republican	47,136	37
1828	ANDREW JACKSON	Democratic	647,286	178
	John Q. Adams	National Republican	508,064	83
1832	ANDREW JACKSON	Democratic	687,502	219
	Henry Clay	National Republican	530,189	49
	William Wirt	Anti-Masonic }	33,108	7
	John Floyd	National Republican }		11
1836	MARTIN VAN BUREN	Democratic	762,678	170
	William H. Harrison	Whig }		73
	Hugh L. White	Whig }		26
	Daniel Webster	Whig }	736,656	14
	W. P. Mangum	Whig }		11
1840	WILLIAM H. HARRISON	Whig	1,275,016	234
	Martin Van Buren	Democratic	1,129,102	60
1844	JAMES K. POLK (Min.)†	Democratic	1,337,243	170
	Henry Clay	Whig	1,299,062	105
	James G. Birney	Liberty	62,300	

* Candidates receiving less than 1 percent of the popular vote are omitted. Before the 12th Amendment (1804), the Electoral College voted for two presidential candidates, and the runner-up became Vice-President. Basic figures are taken primarily from *Historical Statistics of the United States, 1789–1945* (1949), pp. 288–290; *Historical Statistics of the United States, Colonial Times to 1957* (1960), pp. 682–683; and *Statistical Abstract of the United States, 1969* (1969), pp. 355–357.

† "Min." indicates minority President—one receiving less than 50 percent of all popular votes.

Presidential Elections (Continued)

Election	Candidates	Parties	Popular Vote	Electoral Vote
1848	ZACHARY TAYLOR	Whig	1,360,099	163
	Lewis Cass	Democratic	1,220,544	127
	Martin Van Buren	Free Soil	291,263	
1852	FRANKLIN PIERCE	Democratic	1,601,274	254
	Winfield Scott	Whig	1,386,580	42
	John P. Hale	Free Soil	155,825	
1856	JAMES BUCHANAN (Min.)*	Democratic	1,838,169	174
	John C. Fremont	Republican	1,341,264	114
	Millard Fillmore	American	874,534	8
1860	ABRAHAM LINCOLN (Min.)*	Republican	1,867,198	180
	Stephen A. Douglas	Democratic	1,379,434	12
	John C. Breckinridge	Democratic	854,248	72
	John Bell	Constitutional Union	591,658	39
1864	ABRAHAM LINCOLN	Union	2,213,665	212
	George. B. McClellan	Democratic	1,802,237	21
1868	ULYSSES S. GRANT	Republican	3,012,833	214
	Horatio Seymour	Democratic	2,703,249	80
1872	ULYSSES S. GRANT	Republican	3,597,132	286
	Horace Greeley	Democratic and Liberal Republican	2,834,125	66
1876	RUTHERFORD B. HAYES (Min.)*	Republican	4,036,298	185
	Samuel J. Tilden	Democratic	4,300,590	184
1880	JAMES A. GARFIELD (Min.)*	Republican	4,454,416	214
	Winfield S. Hancock	Democratic	4,444,952	155
	James B. Weaver	Greenback-Labor	308,578	
1884	GROVER CLEVELAND (Min.)*	Democratic	4,874,986	219
	James G. Blaine	Republican	4,851,981	182
	Benjamin F. Butler	Greenback-Labor	175,370	
	John P. St. John	Prohibition	150,369	
1888	BENJAMIN HARRISON (Min.)*	Republican	5,439,853	233
	Grover Cleveland	Democratic	5,540,309	168
	Clinton B. Fisk	Prohibition	249,506	
	Anson J. Streeter	Union Labor	146,935	
1892	GROVER CLEVELAND (Min.)*	Democratic	5,556,918	277
	Benjamin Harrison	Republican	5,176,108	145
	James B. Weaver	People's	1,041,028	22
	John Bidwell	Prohibition	264,133	
1896	WILLIAM MC KINLEY	Republican	7,104,779	271
	William J. Bryan	Democratic	6,502,925	176
1900	WILLIAM MC KINLEY	Republican	7,207,923	292
	William J. Bryan	Democratic; Populist	6,358,133	155
	John C. Woolley	Prohibition	208,914	
1904	THEODORE ROOSEVELT	Republican	7,623,486	336
	Alton B. Parker	Democratic	5,077,911	140
	Eugene V. Debs	Socialist	402,283	
	Silas C. Swallow	Prohibition	258,536	
1908	WILLIAM H. TAFT	Republican	7,678,908	321
	William J. Bryan	Democratic	6,409,104	162
	Eugene V. Debs	Socialist	420,793	
	Eugene W. Chafin	Prohibition	253,840	

* "Min." indicates minority President—one receiving less than 50 percent of all popular votes.

Presidential Elections (Continued)

Election	Candidates	Parties	Popular Vote	Electoral Vote
1912	WOODROW WILSON (Min.)*	Democratic	6,293,454	435
	Theodore Roosevelt	Progressive	4,119,538	88
	William H. Taft	Republican	3,484,980	8
	Eugene V. Debs	Socialist	900,672	
	Eugene W. Chafin	Prohibition	206,275	
1916	WOODROW WILSON (Min.)*	Democratic	9,129,606	277
	Charles E. Hughes	Republican	8,538,221	254
	A. L. Benson	Socialist	585,113	
	J. F. Hanly	Prohibition	220,506	
1920	WARREN G. HARDING	Republican	16,152,200	404
	James M. Cox	Democratic	9,147,353	127
	Eugene V. Debs	Socialist	919,799	
	P. P. Christensen	Farmer-Labor	265,411	
1924	CALVIN COOLIDGE	Republican	15,725,016	382
	John W. Davis	Democratic	8,386,503	136
	Robert M. La Follette	Progressive	4,822,856	13
1928	HERBERT C. HOOVER	Republican	21,391,381	444
	Alfred E. Smith	Democratic	15,016,443	87
1932	FRANKLIN D. ROOSEVELT	Democratic	22,821,857	472
	Herbert C. Hoover	Republican	15,761,841	59
	Norman Thomas	Socialist	881,951	
1936	FRANKLIN D. ROOSEVELT	Democratic	27,751,597	523
	Alfred M. Landon	Republican	16,679,583	8
	William Lemke	Union, etc.	882,479	
1940	FRANKLIN D. ROOSEVELT	Democratic	27,244,160	449
	Wendell L. Willkie	Republican	22,305,198	82
1944	FRANKLIN D. ROOSEVELT	Democratic	25,602,504	432
	Thomas E. Dewey	Republican	22,006,285	99
1948	HARRY S TRUMAN (Min.)*	Democratic	24,105,812	303
	Thomas E. Dewey	Republican	21,970,065	189
	J. Strom Thurmond	States' Rights Democratic	1,169,063	39
	Henry A. Wallace	Progressive	1,157,172	
1952	DWIGHT D. EISENHOWER	Republican	33,936,234	442
	Adlai E. Stevenson	Democratic	27,314,992	89
1956	DWIGHT D. EISENHOWER	Republican	35,590,472	457
	Adlai E. Stevenson	Democratic	26,022,752	73
1960	JOHN F. KENNEDY (Min.)*	Democratic	34,226,731	303
	Richard M. Nixon	Republican	34,108,157	219
1964	LYNDON B. JOHNSON	Democratic	43,129,484	486
	Barry M. Goldwater	Republican	27,178,188	52
1968	RICHARD M. NIXON (Min.)*	Republican	31,785,480	301
	Hubert H. Humphrey, Jr.	Democratic	31,275,166	191
	George C. Wallace	American Independent	9,906,473	46
1972	RICHARD M. NIXON	Republican	45,767,218	520
	George S. McGovern	Democratic	28,357,688	17
1976	JIMMY CARTER	Democratic	40,828,657	297
	Gerald R. Ford	Republican	39,145,520	240
1980	RONALD W. REAGAN	Republican	43,201,220	489
	Jimmy Carter	Democratic	34,913,332	49
	John B. Anderson	Independent	5,581,379	0

* "Min." indicates minority President—one receiving less than 50 percent of all popular votes.

Presidents and Elected Vice-Presidents

Term	*President*	*Vice-President*
1789–1793	George Washington	John Adams
1793–1797	George Washington	John Adams
1797–1801	John Adams	Thomas Jefferson
1801–1805	Thomas Jefferson	Aaron Burr
1805–1809	Thomas Jefferson	George Clinton
1809–1813	James Madison	George Clinton (d. 1812)
1813–1817	James Madison	Elbridge Gerry (d. 1814)
1817–1821	James Monroe	Daniel D. Tompkins
1821–1825	James Monroe	Daniel D. Tompkins
1825–1829	John Quincy Adams	John C. Calhoun
1829–1833	Andrew Jackson	John C. Calhoun (resigned 1832)
1833–1837	Andrew Jackson	Martin Van Buren
1837–1841	Martin Van Buren	Richard M. Johnson
1841–1845	William H. Harrison (d. 1841) John Tyler	John Tyler
1845–1849	James K. Polk	George M. Dallas
1849–1853	Zachary Taylor (d. 1850) Millard Fillmore	Millard Fillmore
1853–1857	Franklin Pierce	William R. D. King (d. 1853)
1857–1861	James Buchanan	John C. Breckinridge
1861–1865	Abraham Lincoln	Hannibal Hamlin
1865–1869	Abraham Lincoln (d. 1865) Andrew Johnson	Andrew Johnson
1869–1873	Ulysses S. Grant	Schuyler Colfax
1873–1877	Ulysses S. Grant	Henry Wilson (d. 1875)
1877–1881	Rutherford B. Hayes	William A. Wheeler
1881–1885	James A. Garfield (d. 1881) Chester A. Arthur	Chester A. Arthur
1885–1889	Grover Cleveland	Thomas A. Hendricks (d. 1885)
1889–1893	Benjamin Harrison	Levi P. Morton
1893–1897	Grover Cleveland	Adlai E. Stevenson
1897–1901	William McKinley	Garret A. Hobart (d. 1899)
1901–1905	William McKinley (d. 1901) Theodore Roosevelt	Theodore Roosevelt
1905–1909	Theodore Roosevelt	Charles W. Fairbanks
1909–1913	William H. Taft	James S. Sherman (d. 1912)
1913–1917	Woodrow Wilson	Thomas R. Marshall
1917–1921	Woodrow Wilson	Thomas R. Marshall
1921–1925	Warren G. Harding (d. 1923) Calvin Coolidge	Calvin Coolidge
1925–1929	Calvin Coolidge	Charles G. Dawes
1929–1933	Herbert C. Hoover	Charles Curtis
1933–1937	Franklin D. Roosevelt	John N. Garner
1937–1941	Franklin D. Roosevelt	John N. Garner
1941–1945	Franklin D. Roosevelt	Henry A. Wallace
1945–1949	Franklin D. Roosevelt (d. 1945) Harry S Truman	Harry S Truman
1949–1953	Harry S Truman	Alben W. Barkley
1953–1957	Dwight D. Eisenhower	Richard M. Nixon
1957–1961	Dwight D. Eisenhower	Richard M. Nixon
1961–1965	John F. Kennedy (d. 1963) Lyndon B. Johnson	Lyndon B. Johnson
1965–1969	Lyndon B. Johnson	Hubert H. Humphrey, Jr.
1969–1974	Richard M. Nixon	Spiro T. Agnew; Gerald R. Ford
1974–1977	Gerald R. Ford	
1977–1981	Jimmy Carter	Walter F. Mondale
1981–	Ronald Reagan	George Bush

INDEX

Abilene (Kansas), 529
Abolitionism, 121; reasonable, 338–39; in South, 341. *See also* Slavery
Abolitionist(s), 327, 346, 352, 403; John Brown, 368–69, 377–78, 385; extremism among, 342–43; Horace Greeley, 311, 382, 404; and Kansas-Nebraska Act, 362; and Mexican war, 272; militant, 339–40, 341; moderate, 340; newspapers, 367; reputation of, 344; Charles Sumner, 369–70, 439
Abortion, 918, 932
Acadia, 48
Acadians, 51
Acheson, Dean, 834, 836–37, 841, 873
Act of Toleration, 15
Adams, Abigail, 121, 158
Adams, Charles Francis, 413, 414
Adams, Henry, 165, 189, 192, 201, 453, 518, 547, 717
Adams, John, 63, 91, 121, 122–23, 195, 224; and American Navy, 163–64; and Boston Tea Party, 92; characterized, 156; at Continental Congress, 94; death of, 182; and Declaration of Independence, 104; French missions of, 115, 159, 160–61; Hamilton's attack on, 163; law profession of, 66; and "midnight judges," 169; presidency of, 157–58, 165; and public opinion, 162; quoted, 67, 72, 81, 108, 160, 161, 320; vice-presidency of, 142
Adams, John Quincy, 195, 207, 230, 246, 340, 380; election of, 223–24, 228; and Florida, 215; in House of Representatives, 231; presidency of, 224–26; as secretary of state, 214, 216, 217, 219–20
Adams, Samuel, 59, 69, 91, 95, 106, 131; at Continental Congress, 94; and ratification of Constitution, 135
Adams, Sherman, 848
Adamson Act, 641
Adjusted Compensation Act, 726
Adkins v. *Children's Hospital,* 725
Admiralty courts, 88
Adolphus, King Gustavus, 35
Advertising, 60, 82, 709–10
"Affirmative action," 931
Afghanistan, Soviet invasion of, 911–12, 919
Africans, in colonial America, 62–63, 65, 66
Afro-Americans, 65, 336, 436, 933. *See also* Blacks; Freedmen; Slavery
Agassiz, Louis, 314
Agnew, Spiro T., 875, 882, 887, 891, 898
Agricultural Adjustment Acts, 753, 756, 757, 760
Agricultural Adjustment Administration (AAA), 760
Agricultural Marketing Act, 738
Agriculture; canal system's impact on, 285–86; in colonial America, 66; free farms, 374; grain industry, 531–32, 759; and McCormick's mechanical reaper, 281–82, 397; mechanization of, 535; in Middle Colonies, 38, 66; overproduction problem, 732–33, 759–60; pattern of American production (1860), 283; post-World War II, 927–28; scientific, 331–32; in South, 431–32, 491; during World War II, 798. *See also* Farmers
Aguinaldo, Emilio, 571, 580, 581
Aircraft carriers, 801, 803
Airplanes, 713–14
Air traffic controllers, firing of striking, 918
Alabama, 413, 414, 415, 419
Alabama, 276; Reconstruction in, 444; slavery in, 337
Alamo, 248
Alaska, 200, 216, 449–50; Japanese threat to, 802; pipeline project in, 895; statehood for, 855
Alaska boundary arbitration, 592
Albany, 38
Albany Congress, 51–52
Albee, Edward, 940–41
Albert, H. E., 654
Alcan highway, 802
Alcoholism, 315–17. *See also* Temperance movement
Alden, John, 23
Alden, Priscilla, 23
Aldrich, Sen. N. W., 619, 637
Aldrich, T. B., 501
Aldrich-Vreeland Act, 613
Alexander I, Czar, 195, 218
Alger, Horatio, 511–12
Alger, Sec. R. A., 574, 578
Alien Laws, 161, 162, 163, 169
Allen, Ethan, 101, 127
Alliance for Progress, 860. *See also* Latin America
Allies (World War I), 650, 653, 662, 679; and Versailles Treaty, 692, 699; war debt of, 734–36
Allies (World War II), 794–95; triumph of, 814–15
Alperovitz, Gar, 815
Altgeld, John P., 495, 549, 599
"America Firsters," 785. *See also* Isolationism
American Expeditionary Forces (A.E.F.), 677
American Federation of Labor (AF of L), 495–96, 671, 733, 764, 765–66; growth of, 822; merger with CIO, 845; during World War II, 798
American Independent party, 875–76
American Indian Movement (AIM), 934. *See also* Indians, American
American Legion, 726
American Medical Association, 867–68
American Peace Society, 315
American Protective Association, 502
American Railway Union, 549
American Red Cross, 517, 674
American Revolution, 48; impact of, 120; roots of, 81–83; second, 427; views of, 98
American Revolutionary War: beginnings of, 95; British position in, 95–96; campaigns of, 107–108, 112–14; colonial army in, 97–98; colonial position in, 96–97; consequences of, 117, 119–20; economic changes after, 122–23; French assistance in, 110–11, 112, 114; social changes after, 120–22; and Treaty of Paris, 115–16; as world war, 111–12
American Society for the Prevention of Cruelty to Animals, 517
American System, 204, 223
American Telephone and Telegraph, 931
American Temperance Society, 316
American Tobacco Company, 491, 622
Americas, *see* New World
Ames, Fisher, 138, 158
Amnesty Act, 457–58
Amusement, business of, 519–20. *See also* Leisure activity
Anacostia Flats, Battle of, 745
Anarchism, 501
Anderson, John, 913, 914
Anderson, Sherwood, 718
Andros, Sir Edmund, 29–30, 46
Anglican Church, *see* Church of England
Anglo-French intercolonial wars, 46–49, 51. *See also* France
Anglo-Spanish wars, in Carolinas, 16. *See also* Spain
Angola, 907
Annapolis, Naval Academy at, 327
Anne, Queen of England, 46
Anthony, Susan B., 308, 317–18, 515
Antietam, Battle of, 402–403, 413
Anti-Federalists, 134–35, 139, 149–51. *See also* Federalists
Anti-foreignism, 501, 502, 702; of early 1800s, 300–301; in 1856 presidential campaign, 371
Anti-Imperialist League, 575
Antin, Mary, 500
Anti-polygamy laws, 305
Anti-Saloon League, 516–17, 605
Anti-slavery societies, 338, 367. *See also* Abolitionist(s)
Anti-trust legislation: Clayton Act, 639–40, 648; Sherman Act, 490, 543, 547, 605–606, 607, 622, 639
Anti-war movement, 871–73, 882
Anzio, 806
Apache Indians, 525
Appalachia, 333–34, 865, 867
Appleby, John F., 535

Appomattox Court House, 409, 425
Arabic, 658, 659
Arab world, oil embargo of, 894–95, 908. *See also* Middle East
Arbitration, international, 561
Architecture: antebellum, 319–20; in colonial America, 74; late 19th-century, 518–19; in machine age, 719–20; 20th-century, 941. *See also* Arts
Ardennes Forest, 810
Argentina, 797, 905
Aristocracy: in America, 221–22; of colonial America, 63–64; planter, 330–31. *See also* Social classes
Arizona, statehood for, 532, 630
Arkansas: Reconstruction in, 444; secession of, 390
Ark Royal, 11
Armada, Spanish, 10–11
Armed Neutrality, 111
Armed services: unification of, 828; women in, 932
Armistice, of World War I, 682
Armour, Philip, 488, 529
Arms limitation, 700. *See also* Nuclear weapons
Armstrong, Louis, 717, 719
Army, American: colonial, 97–98; and Mexican War, 271; after War of 1812, 203. *See also specific wars*
Arnold, Benedict, 101, 102, 103, 108–109, 112, 114
Aroostook War, 259–60
Arthur, Chester A., 463, 464, 465–67
Arthur, T. S., 316
Articles of Confederation, 97, 123–26, 129–30, 135, 138
Artisans, of colonial America, 64, 66
Arts: antebellum, 319–20; music, 320–21; in late 19th century, 517–19; national literature 203, 321–22; in 20th century, 940–41; WPA subsidy of, 758. *See also* Literature
Ashbury, Francis, 303
Ashburton, Lord, 260
Assembly-line production, 710, 711. *See also* Industry
Associated Press, 510
Association, The, 94, 126
Astor, John Jacob, 289
Atchison, Topeka, and Santa Fe Railroad, 479
Atlanta (Georgia), 406, 432; murders of black youths in, 926
Atlantic Charter, 789–90, 796, 797
Atlantic Conference, 789
Atomic bomb, 813, 815, 834. *See also* Nuclear weapons
Attucks, Crispus, 90
Auchincloss, Louis, 939
Audubon, John J., 314
Austerlitz, Battle of, 178
Austin, Stephen, 247
Australia, 120
Austria, Nazi occupation of, 782
Austrian Succession, War of, 49
Autobuses, 712
Automobiles, 709, 710–11, 712–13, 716
Automobile industry: post-World War II strikes in, 821; union in, 764
Aviation, 713–14
AWACS (Airborne Warning and Command System), 920
Axis powers, 778, 795. *See also* Hitler; Mussolini
Aztecs, 5, 7

Baby boom, post-war, 923–24. *See also* Population increase
Bache, Benjamin Franklin, 157
Bacon, Nathaniel, 14, 15
Bacon's Rebellion, 14
Baer, George F., 605
Bahamas, 5
Bailey, James A., 519
Baker, Ray Stannard, 600–601
Bakke decision, 933
Balboa, Vasco Nuñez, 6
Baldwin, James, 939
Ballinger, Sec. R. A., 620, 621
Baltimore, 561
Baltimore, Lord (Cecelius Calvert), 14, 15
Baltimore (Maryland), 140; railroad strike in, 463
Baltimore and Ohio Company, 286, 287
Bamboo Curtain, 885
Bancroft, George, 327
Banking: in colonial America, 84; Federal Reserve System, 636–38; National Banking System, 417; and Panic of 1873, 458. *See also* Economy
Banking holiday, 652
Bank of the United States (B.U.S.): creation of, 147; expiration of, 189–90, 203, 208; Hamilton's proposal for, 145, 146; during Jackson's presidency, 241–43, 244; during Jefferson's presidency, 169; Jefferson's view of, 146; and panic of 1819, 207; Second, 203, 205
Bankruptcy, in 1880s, 535–36
Baptists, 70, 121, 301, 302–303, 505. *See also* Religion
Baraka, Imamu Amiri, 940
Barbados, 24
Barbed wire, 532, 537
Barnum, Phineas T., 306, 321, 519
Barton, Bruce, 709–10
Barton, Clara, 517
Baruch, Bernard M., 670, 820
Baseball, 520, 822, 938; in antebellum America, 306
Basketball, 520
Bastogne, 810
Bataan death march, 801
Batista, Fulgencia, 851
Baton Rouge (Louisiana), 45
Baxter, Richard, 69
Bay of Pigs, 861
Beard, Charles A., 139, 386, 427
Bear Flag Republic, 269. *See also* California
Beaver, 67, 217. *See also* Fur trade
Beck, Dave, 848
Beecher, Henry Ward, 493, 515
"Beef barons," 529
Beef Trust, 601, 607
Beer and Wine Revenue Act, 753
Beer brewing, 300
Begin, Menachem, 906, 907
Belgium, 650–51, 652–53, 783
Belknap, Sec. W. W., 456–57
Bell, Alexander Graham, 484–85, 927
Bell, Daniel, 939
Bell, John, 379, 380
Bellamy, Edward, 511
Bellow, Saul, 940
Benét, Rosemary, 482, 613
Benét, Stephen Vincent, 482, 613
Bennett, James Gordon, 311
Benson, Ezra Taft, 844
Benton, Sen. Thomas H., 266
Berger, Victor L., 622
Bergh, Henry, 517
Berkeley, Gov., 14, 18
Berlin: airlift, 830–31; crisis, 850; fall of, 811; wall, 858
Berlin Conference (1889), 565
Berryman, John, 940
Bessemer process, 486. *See also* Steel industry
Bible, 69, 504. *See also* Religion
Bible Belt, 703, 708
Bible Commonwealth, 23–24
Bicentennial Campaign, 903–904
Bicycles, 520
Biddle, Nicholas, 242, 243, 244, 254, 637
Biglow Papers, 325
Bill of Rights, 143, 146, 161
Birkbeck, Morris, 293
Birmingham (Alabama), 863, 864
Birth control, 310, 515, 716, 925
Birthrate, in colonial America, 60. *See also* Population growth
Bismarck, Otto von, 565, 577
Bison, 526–27
Black, Justice Hugo, 769
Black Ball Line, 289
Black Codes, 434–36, 441. *See also* Reconstruction
"Black Friday," 455
"Black gold," 487
Black Hawk, 246
"Black ivory," 121, 335. *See also* Slavery
"Black Legend," 8
Blacklisting: by employers, 493–94; as weapon of war, 662, 671
Black movement, 868–70, 877
Black Muslims, 869
Black Power, 869
Blacks: in American Revolution, 95, 121; and Black Codes, 434–36, 441; and Carter administration, 904; congressional representation of, 439; and Constitution, 133; as cowboys, 530; in Democratic party, 751, 767; early emancipationists, 32, 37; education for, 507; and Emancipation Proclamation, 403–405; in Farmer's Alliance, 546; and Indian Wars, 524; introduced into colo-

nies, 13; and labor unions, 494, 496; music of, 321, 717; post-1815, 249–50, 261, 367–69; in post-World War II economy, 822; poverty among, 929; power of vote, 454; revolutionary outburst of, 863–64; in southern legislatures, 445–46; in Spanish-American War, 573; status in colonies, 62–63; suffrage for, 439, 442, 547; and Supreme Court decisions, 842; in 20th century, 601, 932–33; in Union armies, 395–96; urban migration of, 925; in Vietnam war, 883–84; voter registration for, 868–70; in War of 1812, 192; in war industries, 671; during Wilson's administration, 642; and women's movement, 515; in World War I, 683; in World War II, 796; writers, 939–40; youths, murder of, in Atlanta, 926. *See also* Freedmen; Reconstruction; Slavery; South
Black Warrior, 359
Blackwell, Elizabeth, 318
Blaine, James G., 460, 471, 545, 778; and election of 1884, 467–68, 469; as secretary of state, 465, 542, 560–62, 565
Bland, Richard P., 459
Bland-Allison Act, 459, 543
Blenheim, Battle of, 49
Bliss, Gen. T. H. 687, 689
Blockade, naval: during Civil War, 390, 398–400, 419; during War of 1812, 195, 197; during World War I, 654–55, 663, 676. *See also* Submarine warfare
Blockade-running, 399–400
"Bloody Shirt," waving of, 454, 460, 465, 468, 472, 545
Bloomer, Amelia, 318
Blue Cross/Blue Shield, 942
Blue Eagles, NRA, 763
Blue laws, 31, 38
Board of Trade, 83
Bolívar, Simón, 226
Bolshevism, 701–702. *See also* Communism
Bonaparte, *see* Napoleon Bonaparte
Bonds: government, 547, 548; war, 674, 800
Bondsmen, black, 334–36
Bonn, 830
Bonus army, 744–45
Bonus Bill (1817), 205
Books, 509; in colonial America, 74; paperback explosion, 938; popularity of, 511–14. *See also* Literature
Boom towns, 528–29
Boone, Daniel, 57
Booth, Edwin T., 306
Booth, John Wilkes, 306, 424
Booth, Junius Brutus, 305–306
Bootleggers, 706, 759
Borah, William E., 690, 694, 697
Border States, 390–91, 403. *See also* Civil War
Boston (Massachusetts), 23, 24, 29, 31, 61, 69; committees of correspondence in, 91; and Era of Good Feelings, 206; evacuation of, 103; and "Intolerable Acts," 92; Irish immigration to, 299; police strike in, 697; population of, 140; school desegregation in, 933; sewage system in, 298; transcendentalism in, 322
Boston Associates, 278, 280
Boston "Massacre," 90–91
Boston Port Act, 92, 93, 94
Boston Tea Party, 91–92, 96
"Bounty boys," 416
Bowditch, Nathaniel, 313
Bowers, Claude, 780
Bowie, James, 247, 248
Boxer Rebellion, 583
Boxing, 520
Boycott, black, 844
Boycott handbill, 89
Bracero program, 935
Braddock, Gen. Edward, 52, 53, 55
Bradford, William, 23, 39
Brain Trust, FDR's, 750–51
Brandeis, Louis D., 637, 641
Brando, Marlon, 936
Brandywine, Battle of, 109
Brazil: and Portuguese exploration, 4, 6; sugar industry in, 33
"Bread Colonies," 38
Bréboeuf, Jean de, 44
Breckinridge, John C., 379, 380
Brezhnev, Leonid, 910, 919
Bricker, John W., 809, 810, 841
Britain, *see* Great Britain
British Broadcasting Corporation (B.B.C.), 737
British West Indies, 16, 225–26. *See also* West Indies
Broadcloth Mob, 341
Brock, Isaac, 190
Brook Farm, 319
Brooklyn (New York), 36
Brooks, Rep. P. S., 369, 370
Brown, Gov. J. E., 398
Brown, Jerry, 942
Brown, John, 368–69, 377–78, 385
Brown, Moses, 275
Brown v. *Board of Education of Topeka, Kansas*, 842
Brown Power, 934–35
Brownson, Orestes, 299
Bryan, William Jennings, 548, 557, 599, 610, 665, 708; and election of 1896, 554–55; and election of 1900, 584–85; and election of 1908, 614; and election of 1912, 626–27, 628; quoted, 541; as secretary of state, 634–35, 642, 657, 658; and silver issue, 552–53; and Spanish treaty, 576; support for Wilson, 626–27
Bryant, William Cullen, 322
Bryce, James, 590
Brzezinski, Zbigniew, 907
Buchanan, James, 290, 356, 369, 371, 384; election of, 372; presidency of, 373–74; and secession, 382–83
Buena Vista, 269
Buffalo (New York), 288, 526–27
Bulgaria, 817
Bulge, Battle of, 811
Bull Moose campaign, 627–28
Bull Moose party, 659–60
Bull Run, Battles of, 400–401, 402
Bunau-Varilla, Philippe, 587, 588
Bundling, 60–61
Bunker (Breed's) Hill, Battle of, 96, 101–102, 107
Bunyan, John, 69
Bureau of the Budget, creation of, 721
Bureau of Corporations, 605
Bureau of Indian Affairs, 245, 934
Bureau of Mines, 620
Burger, Warren E., 881
Burgoyne, Gen. John, 108–109
Burke, Edmund, 86, 92
Burleson, Postmaster General, 665
Burma road, 801
Burnaby, Andrew, 56
Burnside, Gen. Ambrose E., 407
Burr, Aaron, 164, 165, 177
Business: of amusement, 519–20; and Coolidge presidency, 731; early 19th century, 279; and farming, 282; vs. farm interests, 555; government regulation of, 484, 490; and law, 550; mining, 529; post-Civil War, 455; and progressivism, 602; and Republican party, 724; and T. Roosevelt's administration, 607; and Wilson's administration, 641. *See also* Commerce; Economy; Trade
Busing, 933. *See also* Desegregation; Education
Butler, Sen. A. P. 370
Butler, Gen. Benjamin F., 392, 449, 454n
Byrd family, 13, 75, 105

Cabinet, presidential, 142; of John Adams, 158; Carter's, 904; Cleveland's, 470; Eisenhower's, 840; evolution of, 143; FDR's, 751; Grant's, 456; Harding's, 724; Jackson's, 234, 235, 244; Kennedy's, 857; Lincoln's, 388–89; McKinley's, 556; Reagan's, 916; Taft's, 618; Tyler's, 258; Washington's, 142–43; Wilson's, 634–35, 695
Cable, transatlantic, 289–90. *See also* Communication
Cables, war takeover of, 674
Cabot, John, 6
Cabral, Pedro, 4
Cadillac, Antoine, 44
"Cajuns," 51
Calhoun, John C., 207, 227, 271, 331; and Bonus Bill, 205; last formal speech, 351; and "Tariff of Abominations," 228; and Tariff of 1816, 204, 226; vice-presidency of, 234, 235
California, 265, 266–67; admission to statehood, 349; discovery of gold in, 348–49, 528; and Japan, 643–44; Japanese laborers in, 595–96; Japanese school incident in, 595
Callender, James, 162
Calley, Lt. William, 892
Calvin, John, 20, 74
Calvinism, 20–21, 32, 69, 302. *See also* Religion
Cambodia: invasion of, 883; secret bombing of, 892–93

Camels, 360
Cameras, 517
Cameron, Sec. Simon, 388
Camp, Walter C., 520
Camp David accords, 906
Canada, 46, 120; abortive invasions of, 102, 109, 189–90; and Alaska boundary arbitration, 592; British invasion of, 52; defeat of French in, 54; establishment of Dominion, 414; and fishing rights, 214; French in, 41–43, 45, 93; as Indian base, 186; Irish-American invasions of, 414; missionaries in, 43–44; Pitt's strategy for, 53–54; planned invasion of, 187–88; and Prohibition, 706; rebellion in, 251, 259; and seal issue, 560–61; tariff arrangements with, 622–23; and Vietnam War, 871; after War of 1812, 199–200
Canal system, 205, 235, 284–86, 287. *See also* Transportation
Canning, George, 217, 218, 225–26, 246
Cannon, Joseph G., 619, 621
Cape Hatteras, 17
Capone, Al, 707
Capper-Volstead Act, 732
Captains of Industry, 484, 489, 497
CARE (Cooperative for American Remittances to Europe), 823
Carey Act, 609
Caribbean: and dollar diplomacy, 624; French islands in, 43; and Monroe Doctrine, 218, 219; and New England trade, 67; and T. Roosevelt's foreign policy, 591; and War of Jenkins' Ear, 49; and Wilson's diplomacy, 642–43. *See also specific countries.*
Carmichael, Stokely, 869
Carnegie, Andrew, 485, 486–87, 488, 532, 575, 610; contributions to libraries, 510
Carolinas: American Revolutionary War in, 112–13; colonization of, 15–17; early map of, 17. *See also* North Carolina; South Carolina
Caroline, 259, 260
Carpentier, Georges, 710
"Carpetbaggers," 443. *See also* Reconstruction
Carranza, Venustiano, 646, 647
Carroll, Charles, 286
Carroll, James, 578
Carruth, W. H., 504
Carter, Billy, 913
Carter, James Earl, Jr. (Jimmy), 914–15, 919, 937, 942; and American hostages in Iran, 911, 912, 915; disaffection with, 912–13; economic policy of, 907–908; election of, 903–904; energy policy of, 908–910; foreign policy of, 910–12; humanitarian diplomacy of, 905–907; presidency of, 904–905, 915, 922; quoted, 903, 911
Carter, Rosalyn, 904
Cartwright, Peter, 303
Carver, George Washington, 507
Casablanca Conference, 806
Cass, Lewis, 347, 348
Castro, Cipriano, 590
Castro, Fidel, 851, 852, 860–61, 899
Casualties: of Vietnam War, 883, 889; of World War I, 682; of World War II, 811–14
Cather, Willa, 717
Catherine the Great, 111
Catholic Church, liberal reforms in, 951. *See also* Roman Catholics
Catholics, *see* Roman Catholics
Cattle industry, 529–30. *See also* Meat-packing industry
Cavalier tradition, 13, 330–31
Cavell, Edith, 652, 653
Censorship, during World War I, 676
Central America, British in, 357
Central Intelligence Agency (CIA), 828, 860, 890, 897
Central Pacific Railroad, 478–79
Central Powers, 650, 651
Cervera, Admiral, 571, 573
Champlain, Samuel de, 42–43
Chancellorsville, Battle of, 408
Chapultepec, 272
"Charity Colony," 17
Charles I, of England, 13, 21, 23, 27, 28
Charles II, of England, 14, 27, 28, 29, 35, 45–46; and Carolinas, 15–16
Charleston (South Carolina), 15–16, 61, 63, 140, 432; fall of, 112–13
Chase, Sec. Salmon P., 388, 422, 423
Chase, Samuel, 171
Château-Thierry, 680, 809
Chautauqua movement, 506–507
Chavez, César, 935
Checks and balances, 133, 223
Cheever, John, 939
Cherokee Indians, 225, 245. *See also* Indians, American
Chesapeake, 179, 189, 194
Cheyenne (Wyoming), 529
Chiang Kai-shek, 801, 807, 818, 834, 847
Chicago (Illinois), 285, 297; gang wars of, 707; growth of, 503; Haymarket Square episode, 495; 1968 Democratic Convention at, 875
Chicanos, 929, 934–35
Child labor, 280, 601, 641; New Deal restrictions on, 754, 758, 765. *See also* Labor
Chile, hostilities with, 561
China, 2, 3; fall of, 834; Japanese invasion of, 745–47, 781; and Open Door policy, 582, 583; six-power loan to, 642, 643. *See also* Far East policy
China, People's Republic of: diplomatic relations with, 906; and Korean War, 837–38; nuclear tests of, 866; and Vietnam War, 885
Chinese-Americans: discrimination against, 502; labor threat of, 463–64; railroad labor of, 478
Chivington, J. M., 524, 525
Choate, Joseph H., 550
Choctaw, 245. *See also* Indians, American
Cholera, 314
Chou En-lai, 886
Christian Science, 505–506
Churchill, Winston, 784, 788, 789, 804, 814; at Casablanca, 806; Iron Curtain speech, 825; quoted, 923; at Teheran, 807; at Yalta, 817
Church of Christ, Scientist (Christian Science), 505–506
Church of England, 9, 18, 21, 71, 72, 121
Church of Jesus Christ of Latter-Day Saints, *see* Mormons
Churches: in colonial America, 71–72; in 19th-century America, 301–304; after Revolution, 121. *See also* Religion; *specific denominations*
Church and state, 26, 121, 164
Cincinnati (Ohio), 281, 297
Circus, 519
Cities: crime and corruption in, 503–504, 926; growth of, 297; migration to, 503, 534; problems of, 298, 925–26; progressivism in, 603–605; and railroads, 481; and spread of education, 507. *See also* Towns
City planning, 519, 719
Civilian Conservation Corps (C.C.C.), 753, 755, 761, 798
Civil liberties, during war, 676, 815
Civil rights, and Nixon administration, 879
Civil Rights Act, 462, 843, 868, 931
Civil Rights Bill, 440, 441
Civil Rights Commission, 843
Civil rights movement, 843, 868. *See also* Blacks; Desegregation
Civil service, and Jackson presidency, 233
Civil Service Commission, 466, 542
Civil service reform, 460; of Arthur's administration, 466–67; and President Garfield, 464; during Grant's administration, 458
Civil War: attack on Fort Sumter, 389–90; blacks in, 395–96; blockade, 398–400; casualties of, 344, 425; consequences of, 425–26; Copperheadism, 421; costs of, 344, 425; diplomacy during, 411–12; and Emancipation Proclamation, 403–405; European position, 391–92; historical views of, 386, 410, 427; and King Cotton, 397, 419; military campaigns, 400–403, 405–409; North's position, 393–95; piracy during, 413–14; and role of Daniel Webster, 236; secession, 381–83; soldiers of, 415–16; South's position, 392–93, 394
Civil Works Administration, 756, 757
Claflin, Tennessee. 514–15
Clark, Champ, 625, 626, 627, 677
Clark, George Rogers, 113, 116, 262
Clark, William, 176
Clay, Henry, 187, 207, 296, 347, 357, 396, 560; and Bank of U.S., 241, 242; and election of 1824, 223–24; and election of 1832, 243, 244; and internal improvements, 205, 235; and Missouri Compromise, 209, 211; as presidential candidate, 223, 244, 261, 263–64; as secretary of state, 224, 226; and slavery issue, 351, 353; and Tariff of 1832, 239; and Treaty of Ghent, 195; and Tyler presidency, 256–57; and War Hawks, 185, 204
Clayton Anti-Trust Act, 639–40, 648
Clayton-Bulwer Treaty, 357–58, 587
Clemenceau, Georges, 689, 690, 692

Clemens, Samuel, *see* Twain, Mark
Clergymen, in colonial America, 66. *See also* Religion
Clermont, 284
Cleveland, Grover, 477, 541, 566, 585, 609, 610; and Cuban revolt, 567; election of, 468–69; and election of 1888, 472; and election of 1892, 545, 546; first administration of, 469–71, 472–73; quoted, 502, 547; and regulation of railroads, 483; second administration of, 547–50; and Venezuelan crisis, 562–63
Cleveland (Ohio), 285
Clinton, Gov. DeWitt, 197, 284, 288
Clipper ships, 290–91. *See also* Transportation
Clothing industry, 278. *See also* Textile industry
Coal industry, post-World War II strikes in, 821. *See also* Miners
Cobbett, William, 153
Cochran, Thomas, 427
"Cod, sacred," 31, 32
Cody, William F. ("Buffalo Bill"), 519, 526
Coexistence, policy of, 861
Cohan, George M., 668
Cohens v. *Virginia,* 212
Cold Harbor, Battle of, 409
Cold War, 825–26, 828; attitudes toward, 835; and McCarthyism, 841; thaw in, 846, 861–62
Collective security, 746, 747
Colleges, 509; in colonial America, 72–73; growth of, 308; numbers of graduates, 508; in post-Civil War era, 507–508. *See also* Education; Universities
Collier's, 600, 601–602
Colombia: appeasement of, 589–90; and Panama Canal issue, 586–88
Colonial America: agriculture in, 66; aristocracy of, 63–64; churches established in, 71–72; culture of, 73–75; education in, 72–73; ethnic groups in, 61–63; industry in, 66–68; life-styles in, 77–79; and mercantilism, 83–86; newspapers in, 75; politics in, 75–77; population of, 59–63; professional men in, 66; religion in, 69–72; slavery in, 62–63, 65–66; social structure of, 63–65; study of, 79; trade in, 67, 68; transportation in, 68–69
Colonies: early American, 39, 55–56; English, 8–10; Middle, 38–39; original American, 16, 59; plantation, 18; Spanish, 8. *See also* France; Great Britain; Spain
Colonization: of Carolinas, 15–17; of Connecticut, 26–27; of Georgia, 16, 17–18; of Maryland, 14–15, 16; of Massachusetts, 16, 23; of New England, 22–24, 26–27; of Rhode Island, 16, 26; of Virginia, 12–14, 16
Colorado, statehood for, 532
Columbia convention, 239, 240
Columbia River, 176, 262–63
Columbian Exposition, 519
Columbus, Christopher, 3, 4–5, 6
Combine, 535
Commerce: and cables, 289–90; exports, 331; imports, 145, 228. *See also* Economy; Tariffs; Trade
Commerce, Department of, 630
Commerce and Labor, Department of, 605
Committee to Defend America by Aiding the Allies, 785
Committee for Industrial Organization (CIO), 764, 765. *See also* Congress of Industrial Organizations
Committee on Public Information, 674–75
Committee for the Re-election of the President, 890
Committee on Un-American Activities, 829
Committees of correspondence, 91
Common Market, 859
Common Sense, 103–104, 321
"Commonweal Army," 549
Commonwealth v. *Hunt,* 281
Communication: advances in, 274; Atlantic cable, 289–90; overland stages, 291; telegraph, 279, 291, 311. *See also* Transportation
Communism, 501; in China, 834; fear of, 828–30
Communist parties: in America, 701; in postwar Europe, 828
Communistic experiments, 319
Compact theory, 162–63
Compromise of 1820 (Missouri Compromise), 209–11, 361, 362, 373
Compromise of 1850, 349, 353–54, 355
Compromise of 1877, 461–63
Comstock, Anthony, 515
Comstock Law, 515
Comstock Lode, 528
Concentration camps, 811
Conestoga wagons, 282
Confederate States of America, 382; European support for, 391–92; leaders of, 430–31; piracy of, 413–14; presidency of, 397–98; war chances of, 393. *See also* Reconstruction
Confederation: creation of, 123–26; critical conditions of, 129–30
Congo, 859
Congregational Church, 25, 70, 71, 72, 121, 301, 303; government, democracy in, 31. *See also* Religion
Congress, U.S.: "Billion Dollar," 542–43; Continental, 94–95, 97; 51st, 542–43; Great Society, 867–68; Hundred Days, 752–54, 755, 756, 758, 759, 760, 761, 762; logrolling in, 144; Republican 80th, 832; Second Continental, 100, 101, 123; and Stamp Act, 88; Twelfth, 185; and Vietnam War, 871–72, 884. *See also* House of Representatives; Senate
Congress of Industrial Organizations (CIO), 765–66; growth of, 822; merger with AF of L, 845; during World War II, 798, 810
Congressional Committee on the Conduct of the War, 422
Conkling, Sen. Roscoe, 460, 463, 464, 465
Connecticut: character of, 30; colonization of, 16, 26–27; royal charter for, 29. *See also* New England
Conquistadores, Spanish, 6–8
Conscientious objectors, 678
Consciousness-raising groups, 932
Conscription: and Vietnam War, 871, 883, 893; during World War I, 677–78; pre-World War II, 784; during World War II, 799; post-World War II, 828
Conservation movement, 534, 608–11; and energy crisis, 908; and Taft presidency, 620
Conservatism: of Constitution framers, 133–34, 138–39; Federalist, 165
Conservatives, 504
Constitution, 172, 193, 194, 467
Constitution, federal: central government under, 135; conservative framers of, 133–34, 138–39; drafting of, 132–33; first, 125–26; ratification of, 134–38; unwritten, 142
Constitutional amendments: Bill of Rights, 143, 146, 161; 1st, 881; 12th, 158n, 223; 13th, 404; 14th, 440, 441, 442, 443, 448, 490; 15th, 444–45, 448; 16th, 630, 636; 17th, 602–603; 18th, 517, 605, 684, 705, 711; 19th, 684, 697; 20th, 767; 21st, 759; 22nd, 157n, 855; 24th, 868; 25th, 891; 26th, 887
Constitutional Union party, 379
Constitutions, state, 120
Consumers, protection for, 607–608
Continental Congress, 94–95, 97; Second, 100, 101, 123
Continuous voyage, doctrine of, 655
Contraction, policy of, 459
Convention of 1800 (France), 160
Convoy system: of World War I, 669; of World War II, 790. *See also* Navy
Conwell, Russell, 489–90
Coogler, J. G., 512
Cooke, Jay, & Company, 417, 458
Coolidge, Calvin, 697, 698, 736, 747; and Adjusted Compensation Act, 726; and election of 1924, 733–34; foreign policy of, 734; presidency of, 731–32; on tariff, 729; and war debt, 735
Cooper, James Fenimore, 203, 295, 322
Cooperatives, farmers', 732. *See also* Grange
Copley, John S., 74
Copperheads, 421, 422
Copyright law, 259, 509–10
Coral Sea, Battle of, 801, 802
Corbett, Jim, 520
Cornbury, Lord, 76
Corn Laws, 289
Cornwallis, Gen. Charles, 113, 114
Coronado, Francisco, 6, 7
Corporations, 493–94, 942; dummy homesteaders of, 531; government regulation of, 490. *See also* Business
Corregidor, surrender of, 801
Corruption: in cities, 503–504; after Civil War, 455; of Grant era, 456–57; and railroads, 482–83. *See also* Watergate scandals
Cortes, Hernando, 7
Cosmopolitan, 600, 601
Cotton, 275–76, 289, 329–31, 374, 491, 492;

during Civil War, 397; dependence on, 332; exports, 331
Cotton, John, 24, 25
Cotton gin, 276, 329
Cotton Stabilization Corporation, 738
Coughlin, Father Charles E., 756
Council of National Defense, 659
Counterculture, of 1960s, 936–37
Covered wagons, 263
Cowboys, 529–30
Cox, Archibald, 892
Cox, James M., 697, 698
Coxey, Gen. Jacob S., 548–49, 640
Craftsmen, in colonial America, 68
Crane, Stephen, 513–14
Crawford, William H., 223
Crazy Horse, 525
Credit, public, 143–44, 146
Crédit Mobilier Construction Company, 456, 478, 482
Crédit Mobilier scandal, 456, 465
Creeks, 5, 245. *See also* Indians, American
Creel, George, 675
CREEP, 890
Creole, 259
Cresswell, Nicholas, 88
Crèvecoeur, Michel de, 61
Crime: and automobile, 712; in cities, 503–504, 926; organized, 707; during Prohibition era, 706–707
Crimean War, 315, 359, 374
Crittenden, Sen. John J., 383, 391
Crittenden Compromise, 383–84
Croats, immigration of, 499
Crockett, Davy, 222, 247, 248
Croly, Herbert, 627
Cromwell, Oliver, 13
Crops, cash, 535. *See also* Agriculture
Croquet, 520
Crusades, and early exploration, 2
Cuba, 357, 576–77, 624, 776, 899, 905; Castro's revolution in, 851–52; invasion of, 571–73, 860–61; landing of marines in, 591–92; and manifest destiny, 358–59; and Paris peace settlement, 55; revolt in, 566–67
Cuban missile crisis, 861
Cubans, in America, 934
Cumberland Road, 208, 283
cummings, e. e., 719
Currency: American dollar, 908; during American Revolutionary War, 97; in colonial America, 84; Confederate, 417–18; greenback plan, 454, 458, 538–39; paper money, 141; printing-press, 417; state-issued, 129, 130. *See also* Banking; Silver issue
Cushman, Charlotte, 306
Custer, George A., 524, 525
Customs duties, of post-Revolutionary era, 144–45. *See also* Tariffs
Cyanide process, of gold extraction, 557
Czechoslovakia, 782, 827–28

Daguerre, Louis, 320
Daley, Richard, 875
Dance, in colonial America, 78
Daniels, Sec. Josephus, 634, 665
Dare, Virginia, 9
Darrow, Clarence, 708
Dartmouth College v. *Woodward,* 213
Darwin, Charles, 489, 504
Daugherty, Harry M., 724, 726, 730
Daughters of Liberty, 89
Davis, Jefferson, 246, 331, 357, 385, 425, 457; pardon of, 430–31; president of Confederacy, 382, 397–98, 402, 421; as secretary of war, 360
Davis, John W., 733–34
Davis, Justice David, 461
Dawes, Charles, 735
Dawes Act, 472, 527
Dawes Plan, 735–36
Daylight saving time, 671
D-Day, 807–809
Dean, James, 936
Dean, John, III, 891
Death penalty, in colonial America, 37
Debates, presidential: Carter-Ford, 904; Kennedy-Nixon, 854
Debs, Eugene V., 549–50, 614, 628, 676, 697–98
Debtors' prisons, 207, 315
Decatur, Stephen, 159
Declaration of Independence, 65, 68, 104–105, 121, 335; signers of, 63, 64, 286
Declaratory Act, 89
Deere, John, 281
Deerfield (Massachusetts), 48
Defense, Department of, 828, 857, 917, 927, 942
de Gaulle, Charles, 859, 871
Degler, Carl, 943
de Kooning, Willem, 941
DeLancey family, 35
Delaware, 16, 38
de la Warr, Lord, 38
Demobilization, after World War II, 820–21
Democracy: in colonial America, 25, 77; and Constitution, 133, 134, 139; economic vs. political, 122, 296; on frontier, 296–97; and impeachment politics, 897; Jacksonian, 207, 221–37; of numbers, 222; oligarchy of, 330; Poet Laureate of, 324; social, 121
Democratic party: blacks in, 751, 767; post-Civil War, 454; and union, 369. *See also* Elections; Political Parties
Democratic-Republicans, 149–51, 157–58, 168–69
Democrats, 250; Copperhead, 421, 422; and election of 1860, 378–80; and Kansas-Nebraska Act, 362–63; Peace, 422; Southern, 831; War, 422
Demo-Pop party, 553
Dempsey, Jack, 677, 710
De-Nazification, 824
Denby, Sec. Edwin, 730
Denmark, 783
Deportation, of alien radicals, 702
Depression: of 1870s, 458–59, 483, 494; of 1890s, 486, 556; of 1913–14, 640; and war, 800; post-World War I, 709. *See also* Economy; Great Depression; Panic
Desegregation, 842, 863, 932; and Nixon administration, 879. *See also* Blacks; Education
Deserters, 890
Desert Land Act, 608
Des Moines (Iowa), 45
De Soto, Hernando, 6–7
Détente, 886, 899, 906–907, 919
Detroit (Michigan), 44, 190, 285; race riots in, 796, 869
Dewey, Commodore George, 569–70, 571, 577, 578
Dewey, John, 707–708
Dewey, Thomas E., 786, 809–10, 831–33
Dey of Algiers, 128, 132
Diaz, Bartholomeu, 3
Díaz, Porfirio, 644, 645
Dickens, Charles, 259, 280, 295
Dickinson, Emily, 512
Diem, Ngo Dinh, 846, 860
Dien Bien Phu, 845–46
Dingley Tariff Bill, 556, 618–19
Diphtheria, 66
Diplomacy: dollar, 623–24, 642; "grape juice," 634; humanitarian, 905–907; ping pong, 885; shuttle, 886. *See also* Foreign policy
Disarmament: Hague Conference, 593; Kellogg-Briand Pact, 728; after World War I, 727–28. *See also* Nuclear weapons
Discovery: history of, 18; principal voyages of, 6. *See also* Explorers
Disease: and American Indians, 526; influenza epidemic, 682; and modern science, 708; during Spanish-American War, 573; yellow fever, 573, 574, 576–77, 578
Displaced persons, 823
District of Columbia, 144, 349–50, 354. *See also* Washington, D.C.
Divorce Bill, 252–53
Divorce rates, 515, 516, 935–36
Dix, Dorothea, 315
Dixiecrats, 831
Dodge City, 529
Doheny, Edward L., 730
Dollar, fall of, 908. *See also* Currency
Dollar Diplomacy, 623–24, 642
Domestic feminism, 310
Dominican Republic, 591, 870
Dominion of New England, 29, 30, 46
Donnelly, Ignatius, 539
"Doughboys," 677, 679, 680, 694
Douglas, Stephen A., 351, 369, 370, 373, 441; and Compromise of 1850, 353; on Crittenden Compromise, 384; death of, 422; and election of 1860, 378, 380; Kansas-Nebraska scheme of, 361–62; -Lincoln debates, 375–77
Douglass, Frederick, 334, 338, 395, 451
Dow, Neal S., 317
Draft-dodgers, 678, 871, 890. *See also* Conscription
Draftees, of Civil War, 415–16
Drake, Sir Francis, 10–11

"Drake's Folly," 487
Dred Scott decision, 373–74
Dreiser, Theodore, 514, 600, 718
Drew, "Uncle Daniel," 482
Drought, 536, 742; and New Deal, 760–61
DuBois, W. E. B., 451, 507
Duke, James Buchanan, 491
Dulles, John Foster, 845, 846, 847, 848, 859
Dunkirk, evacuation of, 784
Dunne, F. P., as Mr. Dooley, 554, 573, 576, 619, 634
Dunning, William A., 451
Duquesne, Fort, 50–51, 52
Durkin, Martin, 840
Dust Bowl, 610, 760–61
Dutch, in New World, 33–36
Dutch Reformed Church, 20, 33
Dwight, Timothy, 164

Eagleton, Thomas, 888
Eakins, Thomas, 518
East Germany, 830
East India Company: British, 92; Dutch, 33
East Indies, Dutch in, 33
Eastman, George, 517
Eaton, Peggy, 234–35
Economic Cooperation Administration, 828
Economy: continental, 288–89; and education, 938; growth in, 292; inequality in, 289; mass consumption, 709–10; plantation, 351; post-Civil War, 431–32, 446; post-World War II, 927–30; after Revolutionary War, 122–23; of South, 332; wartime, 797–98. *See also* Depression; Inflation; Panic; Recession
Edict of Nantes, 41, 43
Edison, Thomas A., 485, 509, 518, 715, 927
Eddy, Mary Baker, 505–506
Education: for adults, 308–309; for blacks, 507, 932; in colonial America, 72–73; expansion of, 938; higher, 308–309; and national government, 225; in 1920s, 707–708; in Northwest, 126; public, 506–507; public school system 306–308; in Puritan Massachusetts, 32; after Revolution, 122; and slavery, 338; for women, 507–508. *See also* Colleges; Schools; Universities
Education system: and baby boom, 924; criticism of, 849
Edward VI, of England, 10
Edwards, Jonathan, 70, 74, 335
Egypt: and Camp David accord, 906; and Yom Kippur War, 894. *See also* Middle East
Einstein, Albert, 813
Eisenhower, Dwight D., 61, 831, 846, 852, 854; election of, 839–40; foreign policy of, 845; as general, 805, 807, 811, 814; goodwill trip of, 850, 851; and integration, 842, 843; in Korea, 840; and McCarthyism, 841; presidency of, 844–45, 848, 855, 856; quoted, 855; renomination of, 847–48; and Suez crisis, 847; and U-2 spy plane, 851
Eisenhower Doctrine, 847, 850
Elderly: gray power, 924–25; medical care for, 867–68. *See also* Population increase
Elections, congressional: of 1798, 162; of 1865, 438; of 1866, 441; of 1894, 550–51; of 1910, 621–22; of 1914, 640; of 1918, 687; of 1938, 769; of 1958, 852; of 1970, 884
Elections, presidential: of 1800, 164–65; of 1812, 197; of 1820, 211; of 1824, 223–24; of 1828, 230, 231; of 1832, 243–44; of 1836, 250; of 1840, 230–31, 254–55; of 1844, 263–65; of 1848, 347–48; of 1852, 355–57; of 1856, 371–73; of 1860, 378, 380–81; of 1864, 422–24; of 1868, 454; of 1872, 457–58; of 1876, 460–63; of 1880, 464–65; of 1884, 467–69; of 1888, 471–73, 544; of 1892, 544–47; of 1896, 551–56; of 1900, 584–85; of 1904, 611–12; of 1908, 613–14; of 1912, 627–28, 629; of 1916, 659–61; of 1920, 697–98; of 1924, 733–34; of 1928, 736–38; of 1932, 750–52; of 1936, 767; of 1940, 786–87; of 1944, 809–10; of 1948, 831–33; of 1952, 838–40; of 1956, 847–48; of 1960, 852–54; of 1964, 856–67; of 1968, 874–76; of 1972, 887–89; of 1976, 903–904; of 1980, 913–15
Electoral College, 133, 158, 222–23
Electoral Commission, of 1877, 462
Electoral Count Act, 461
Electric light, 485
Electric power industry, 762, 927
Elevated cars, electric-powered, 503
Elevator, 518
Eliot, Charles W., 509
Eliot, T. S., 719
Elizabeth I, Queen of England, 10, 11
Elkins Railroad Act, 606
Ellison, Ralph, 939
Ellsberg, Daniel, 885, 890
El Salvador, 920
Emancipation Proclamation, 392, 396, 403–405
Embargo Act, 179–81
Emergency Banking Relief Act, 753, 754
Emergency Fleet Corporation, 673
Emergency Quota Act, 704
Emergency Tariff Act, 729
Emerson, Ralph Waldo, 38, 274, 293, 296, 309, 378, 484; abolition sentiments of, 354; "Concord Hymn," 95; quoted, 313, 329, 348, 362; "Self-Reliance," 295; on slavery, 333; transcendentalism of, 322–23; and Unitarian movement, 302; on utopias, 319; on Daniel Webster, 352
Empey, Guy, 703
Empire State Building, 720
Employees, federal, 233, 280. *See also* Civil Service
Endangered species, 561
Energy, Department of, 905
Energy conservation, 908
Energy crisis, 895, 909, 930
Energy Security Corporation, 910
England, *see* Great Britain
Entertainment industry, 717
Environmental Protection Agency, 916
Epidemics, 314
Episcopal Church, 121, 303, 505. *See also* Church of England; Religion
Equal Rights Amendment (ERA), 716, 913, 931–32
Era of Good Feelings, 201, 205–207, 220; second, 354
"Era of Good Stealings," 454–56
Erie Canal, 205, 284–86
Ervin, Sen. Samuel J., 891
Esch-Cummins Transportation Act, 725
Escobedo decision, 881
Espionage Act, 676
Ethiopia, 778–79, 905, 907
Ethnic groups in colonial America, 61–63. *See also* Immigration
Ethnic pride, 933–34
Europe: and colonization of America, 18; and Confederacy, 391; and New World developments, 58. *See also specific countries*
Europeans: Americanization of, 18; in colonial America, 39. *See also* Immigration
Evers, Medgar, 864
Everett, Edward, 320
Everybody's, 600, 601
Evolution, controversy over, 504, 708–709. *See also* Religion
Excise tax: Jefferson's elimination of, 169; of post-Revolutionary era, 144–45. *See also* Tariffs; Taxation
Executive Office, 769
Ex parte Milligan, 442
Explorers: English, 7–8; French, 45; Jesuit, 44; Portuguese, 3–4; Spanish, 4–8

Factory system, 275, 276; after American Revolution, 181; after Civil War, 430; during Civil War, 418; growth of, 277; and labor, 279–80; and working classes, 497. *See also* Manufacturing
Fairbanks, Charles W., 611
Fairchild, Henry P., 705
Fair Deal Program, 833
Fair Employment Practices Commission (FEPC), 796
Fair Labor Standards Act, 757, 765
Fall, Sen. Albert B., 724, 730
Fallen Timbers, Battle of, 155
Family, changing, 309–10, 935–36
Far East, exports of, 2
Far East policy, 577–78; and Boxer Rebellion, 583; and dollar diplomacy, 623–24; Nixon's, 882–83, 885, 886; Open Door, 582, 583; Peace of Portsmouth, 594–95; Wilson's, 642
Farmers: of colonial America, 64; as debtors, 535–36; decrease in numbers, 928; federal legislation for, 641; government subsidization of, 760, 844; and Great Depression, 741; migration of, 534; organized, 538, 539; pioneer, 281–82; and post-war economic order, 732–33; problems of, 536–37; and surpluses, 771. *See also* Agriculture
Farmers' Alliances, 539, 544, 546
Farming: dry, 532; Western, 531–32. *See also* Agriculture

Farragut, Adm. David G., 406, 423–24
Faubus, Orval, 843
Faulkner, William, 719, 939, 940
Federal Bureau of Investigation (FBI), 868, 890, 897
Federal Deposit Insurance Corporation, 753, 754
Federal Emergency Relief Act, 753, 755
Federal Emergency Relief Administration, 753, 755–56
Federal Farm Board, 738
Federal Farm Loan Act, 641
Federal government, land owned by, 534, 609
Federal Housing Administration (FHA), 757, 763
Federalist, The, 137, 321
Federalists, 134–35, 136, 154; and Alien and Sedition Laws, 161–62; "Blue Light," 197; as constructionists, 205; demise of, 165, 205; Hamiltonian, 148–49, 151, 152, 163; and Hartford Convention, 197–98; historical view of, 166; and Louisiana Purchase, 175; New England, 188–89, 199; on war with Britain, 155, 199
Federal Reserve Act, 613, 638, 648
Federal Reserve Board, 637, 638, 640, 740
Federal Reserve System, 637–38
Federal Securities Act, 753, 761
Federal Trade Commission, 638, 640, 648
Federal Trade Commission Act, 638
Feminist movement, 121, 310, 317–18, 514, 515. *See also* Women
Ferdinand, King of Spain, 4
Fertilizer Trust, 537
Feudalism, industrial, 536; in New France, 43
Field, Cyrus, 289–90
"Fifty-Niners," 419
Fillmore, Pres. Millard, 353, 356, 371, 372
Finland, 736, 783
"Fireside chats," 754
Fish, Hamilton, 456
Fishing: Canadian, 214; in colonial America, 67; in New England, 32
Fisk, "Jubilee Jim," 455, 482
Fitzgerald, F. Scott, 718
Fitzgerald, Zelda, 718
Five Power Naval Treaty, 727
Fletcher v. *Peck,* 212–13
Flexible response, doctrine of, 859
Florida: acquisition of, from Spain, 215–16; annexation of, 56; discovery of, 6; and Paris peace settlement, 55; Reconstruction in, 444; and Treaty of 1818, 214–15
Florida Purchase Treaty, 216
"Flower children," 936
Flying Cloud, 290
Foch, Marshal, 679, 680
Food Administration, 672
Football, 520, 938
Foraker Act, 576
Forbes, Col. Charles R., 729–30
Force Acts, 447
Force Bill, 240
Ford, Gerald R., 891, 903, 904; foreign policy of, 899–901; and Nixon pardon, 898–99; presidency of, 897–99
Ford, Henry, 709, 710–11, 759
Ford Foundation, 941
Fordney-McCumber Tariff Law, 729, 739
Foreign aid, during American Revolution, 96, 105, 109
Foreign policy, 578; of John Quincy Adams, 225–26; Carter's, 910–12; during Civil War, 411–12; Coolidge's, 734; Eisenhower's, 845; Ford's, 899–901; Good Neighbor, 747, 776–77, 797; Harding's, 727–28; imperialism, 559–60; of Andrew Jackson, 246–47; Kennedy's, 859; Mexican, 646–48; Nixon's, 882–83, 885, 886, 892–94; Reagan's, 918–21; post-Revolutionary, 127–28; T. Roosevelt's, 586–87, 597; Taft's, 622–24; and War of 1812, 214; "watchful waiting," 646; Wilson's, 642–44. *See also* Far East Policy; France; Great Britain; Spain
Foreign Service, 841
Formosa, 834
Forrest, Edwin, 305
"Forty-Eighters," 300
Foster, Stephen C., 321
Founding Fathers: identification of, 131–32; non-interventionist policies of, 176. *See also specific people*
Four-Power Treaty, 728
Fourteen Points, 668–69, 688, 690, 692, 695; peace based on, 681–82
Fourth of July, 296
France: aid to American colonies from, 97; and American Revolution, 110–11, 112, 114; American soldiers in, 677, 678–81; Canadian colonization of, 41–43, 45, 93; and Civil War, 411–12; D-Day invasion of, 807–809; and Embargo Act, 181; fall of, 783–84, 789; and Jackson presidency, 246–47; mercantilism of, 85–86; New World colonization by, 44–45; in North American struggle, 45–47; in Ohio Valley, 50–51; at Paris Peace Conference, 690–91; security treaty with, 691, 699; and Suez crisis, 847; unofficial fighting with, 158–60; war debt of, 735–36; at war with England, 178; in World War I, 650, 677
Franco, Gen. Francisco, 780
Franco-American Treaty of 1778, 153, 158
Franklin, Benjamin, 39, 61, 64, 70, 73, 135, 671; and Albany Congress, 52; as ambassador to France, 96, 109, 110, 115; and American Revolutionary War, 97, 105; cartoons by, 51, 52, 55; and Declaration of Independence, 105; library established by, 75; as literary figure, 74, 321; and peace negotiations, 115; at Philadelphia Convention, 130–31, 132; quoted, 66, 69, 86, 105, 134, 142; scientific contributions of, 74–75
Franklin, Williams, 105
Frazier-Lemke Farm Bankruptcy Act, 757, 761
Frederick the Great, 49, 51
Fredericksburg, Battle of, 407–408
Freedmen, 334; enfranchised, 443–45; post-Civil War, 432–33. *See also* Blacks; Slavery
Freedmen's Bureau, 434–35, 440, 441
Freedom of the seas, 662. *See also* Blockade
Freeport Doctrine, 378
Free-silver, *see* Silver; Silver issue
Free-Soil party, 251, 341, 347–48
Frémont, John C., 269, 371–72
French and Indian War, 48, 51, 52, 55, 56, 57
French Revolution, impact of, 152–53, 216
French war(s): map of, in North America, 50; undeclared, 48
Freud, Sigmund, 716–17
Friedan, Betty, 931
Frontenac, Comte de, 47
Frontier: character of, 295–96; colonial, 82; end of, 533–34, 608; farmers on, 281; and Indian barrier, 522–24; Kentucky, 57; leisure activity on, 77–78; life on, 294–95; patricians on, 63–64; "permanent," 245; railroads on, 477; as state of mind, 534–35; Tennessee, 57
Frost, Robert, 719, 858
Fuel crisis, 894. *See also* Energy crisis
Fugitive slave law, 350, 352, 354–55, 362, 365, 366
Fulbright, Sen. William J., 872
Fuller, Margaret, 318
Fulton, Robert, 284
Fundamentalists, 504, 708, 716. *See also* Religion
Fundamental Orders, 26–27
Fur trade: of Middle Colonies, 38; in New England, 27; of New France, 43, 44; in Ohio Valley, 50; post-Revolutionary, 127

Gabriel, 338
Gadsden, James, 360
Gadsden Purchase, 360
Gag resolution, 342
Galbraith, John Kenneth, 939
Gallatin, Albert, 169
Galveston (Texas), 603
Gama, Vasco da, 3
Gambling, 707
Gangsterism, 706–707; and automobile, 712; international, 778. *See also* Corruption
Garfield, Harry A., 671
Garfield, James A., 286, 314; assassination of, 465, 466; and Crédit Mobilier scandal, 465; election of, 464–65; presidency of, 465
Garland, Hamlin, 5o9
Garrison, William Lloyd, 339–40, 341, 355
Gas lines, 894–95, 908, 909
Gasoline age, advent of, 711–13
Gates, Gen. Horatio, 109
General Incorporation Law, 279
General Motors, 764, 822, 840, 942
Genêt, Edmond Charles, 154, 157
Geneva Conference, 859
Gentlemen's Agreement, 595–96
George, Henry, 494, 511
George I, of England, 46
George II, of England, 46
George III, of England, 46, 104, 105, 129, 155, 180; and American Revolutionary War, 95, 96, 102, 113, 114; characterized, 91; end of rule of, 115; and Loyalists, 107;

quoted, 116; statue erected to, 89
Georgia, 81; colonization of, 16, 17–18; early map of, 17; Reconstruction in, 444; slavery in, 337; Union conquest of, 406–407; and War of Jenkins' Ear, 49
Germain, Lord George, 114
German-Americans, 499; and anti-German sentiment, 651–52; in colonial America, 61; immigration of, 298, 300–301, 320; and Versailles Treaty, 693–94; during World War I, 654, 675–76; during World War II, 795
Germantown, Battle at, 109
Germany: Britain's blockade of, 654–55; and colonialism, 218; and Fourteen Points, 681; immigration from, 298, 300–301, 320; and imperialism, 563, 564; in NATO, 846; partition of, 825, 830; reparations bill for, 734, 735–36; and Samoa, 564–65; and Soviet-American relations, 824–25; in World War I, 650. *See also* Cold War; World War II
Geronimo, 525
Gerrymander, 544 and n
Gettysburg, Battle of, 408
Ghent, Treaty of, 195–97, 200, 277
"Ghost Dance" cult, 527
Ghost towns, 477, 529
Gibbons, Cardinal James, 505
Gibbons v. *Ogden*, 212
G.I. Bill of Rights, 820, 938
Gibraltar, Rock of, 115
Gideon v. *Wainwright*, 881
Gilbert, Sir Humphrey, 8–9
Gilded Age, 459, 473, 555
Ginsberg, Allen, 936
Gladden, Washington, 505
Glass, Carter, 637
Glass-Steagall Banking Reform Act, 753, 754
Glenn, John H., 862
Glidden, Joseph F., 532
Glorious Revolution (1688), 29, 30
Godey's Lady's Book, 309
Godkin, Edwin L., 511
Goethals, George Washington, 589
Gold, California discovery of, 348–49. *See also* Currency
"Gold Bugs," 543, 553–54, 557. *See also* Silver issue
Gold Reserve Act, 757
Gold standard, 548, 583, 753
Gold Standard Act, 557
Goldwater, Barry, 865–67, 870–71
Gompers, Samuel, 495–96, 575, 639, 671, 697
Good Neighbor policy: FDR's, 776–77; Hoover's, 747; during World War II, 797
Goodwyn, Lawrence, 557
Gordon, N. P., 335
Gorgas, Col. William C., 589
Gorges, Sir Ferdinando, 27
Göring, Hermann, 814–15, 824
Gould, Jay, 455, 482, 493
Government: attitudes toward, 748; centralization of, 135; legitimacy of, 133; and railroads, 483; separation of powers in, 171. *See also* Federal government; Representative government
Governors, colonial, 76
Grady, Henry W., 491
Graham, Otis, 615
Grain deal, 887
Grain industry, 532, 759
Grain Stabilization Corporation, 738
Grand Army of the Republic (G.A.R.), 459, 471, 543
Grand Canyon, 6
Grand Coulee Dam, 759
Grand Old Party (GOP), 543, 621
Grange, 483, 538
Grant, Ulysses Simpson, 271, 392, 405–406, 408–10, 423, 855; election of, 454; as politician, 453–54; presidency of, 456–59; and third nomination, 460
Grasse, Admiral de, 114
Graveyard art, 60
Gray, Asa, 314
Gray, Capt. Robert, 262
Gray power, 924–25
Great Awakening, 70; Second, 302, 303, 308, 339. *See also* Religion
Great Britain 58, 152–53; American colonies of, 55–56; and American Revolution, 111–17; army of, 96; blockade of Germany by, 654–55; in Central America, 357; during Civil War, 404, 411–12, 414; destroyer deal for, 785–86; early colonization of, 8–10; Embargo Act, 181; impressment of seamen by, 178–79, 188, 196–97; Jamestown colony of, 11–12; kings of (1689–1820), 46; mercantilism of, 83–86; New World exploration by, 7–8; in North American struggle, 45–47, 52, 53–55; North American territory of (1713), 48; and October 1929 crash, 740; and Panama Canal, 644; post-war loan for, 823–24; Proclamation of 1763, 57; and seal issue, 560–61; Stuart dynasty in, 28, 45; and Suez crisis, 847; and Treaty of Ghent, 195–97; Tudor rulers of, 10; war debt of, 735–36; at war with France, 178; war of words with, 258–59; in World War I, 650. *See also* World War II
"Great Compromise," 132
Great Depression, 497; causes of, 740–42; impact of, 923; world-wide, 741
Great Lakes, 190–91, 200
Great Northern Railroad, 479, 480
Great Salt Lake, 217
Great Society, 865, 867–68, 877, 907
Great White Fleet, 596–97
Greece, 826, 831
Greeks, immigration of, 499
Greeley, Horace, 311, 382, 404, 457, 510, 612
Greenback Labor party, 459, 538–39, 599
Greenback movement, 538
Greene, Gen. Nathanael, 113
Green Mountain Boys, 127
Greer, 790
Grenville, George, 87–88
Grenville, Treaty of, 155
Griffith, D. W., 715
Griffith, John, 600
Grimké sisters, 318
Griswold, Roger, 162
Gross national product, post-World War II, 927
Grundy, Rep. Felix, 186
Guadalcanal Island, 802
Guadalupe-Hidalgo, Treaty of, 270
Guam, 574, 800, 803
Guam Doctrine, 882
Guantánamo, 577, 776
Guerrière, 194
Guiteau, Charles J., 465
Gulf of Tonkin, 866–67, 885, 893
Gunboats, 172
Guthrie (Oklahoma), 533

Hague Disarmament Conference, Second, 593
Haig, Alexander, 916
Haiti, 624, 642, 747, 776
Hale, Edward Everett, 421
"Half-Breed" faction, of Republican party, 460, 464, 465
"Half-Way Covenant," 32
Hall, Basil, 332
Halsey, Harlan F., 511
Halsey, William F., 812
Hamilton, Alexander, 123, 181, 275, 321, 555; attack on Adams, 163; conflict with Jefferson, 145–47, 148; death of, 177; leadership of, 149; military command of, 160; monetary policies of, 143–45, 146–47, 148, 157; at Philadelphia Convention, 130, 131; political philosophy of, 137, 212; on Quebec Act, 93; quoted, 140; and ratification of Constitution, 137, 138; as secretary of Treasury, 142–43; and Whiskey Rebellion, 147
Hamilton, Andrew, 75
Hamiltonians, 148–49, 151, *See also* Federalists
Hammond, Sen. James H., 336, 383
Hancock, John 85, 95, 131
Hancock, Winfield S., 464–65
Handy, W. C., 717
Hanna, Marcus Alonzo, 551–52, 555–56, 569, 574, 583, 611; on T. Roosevelt, 584; and "Gold Bugs," 553–54
Hanoi, bombing of, 887. *See also* North Vietnam
Harding, Warren G., 676, 747; death of, 703, 731; election of, 697–98; foreign policy of, 727–28; presidency of, 723–25, 726, 730; quoted, 701; scandals in administration of, 729–30; on tariff, 729
"Hardmoney" men, 458, 459
Harlem, New York, 36
Harpers Ferry, 377, 378
Harris, Patricia, 904
Harrison, Benjamin, 545, 546, 609; election of, 471–72; presidency of, 541–43
Harrison, William Henry, 186, 191, 199, 250, 257, 472; election of, 253–54; as Indian fighter, 208; presidency of, 256–57

Harte, Bret, 513, 529
Hartford (Connecticut), 26
Hartford Convention, 197–98
Harvard College, 8, 32, 63, 73, 122, 343, 507, 509
Harvester, 535. *See also* Reaper
Harvester Trust, 488, 537
Harvey, William Hope, 551
Hatch Act, 508, 757, 769
Havana Conference of 1940, 784
Hawaii, 565–66; annexation of, 471; statehood for, 855
Hawley-Smoot Tariff, 739, 741, 744, 751
Hawthorne, Nathaniel, 326
Hay, John 577, 582, 583
Hay-Bunau-Varilla Treaty, 588
Hayes, Lucy Webb, 463
Hayes, Rutherford B., 460–61, 462–64, 608
Haymarket Square episode, 495
Hayne, Sen. Robert Y., 235–36, 239
Hay-Pauncefote Treaty, 587, 644
Hays, Samuel P., 615
Hays, Will H., 715
Haywood, William D., 676
H.C.L. (high cost of living), 671
Health care, expenditures for, 942
Health, Education, and Welfare (HEW), Department of, 942
Hearst, William Randolph, 510, 564, 567, 568, 645
Heller, Joseph, 939
"Hell fighters," 683
Hell Gate, 36
Helper, Hinton R., 366–67
Helsinki accords, 899
Hemingway, Ernest, 513, 718, 719, 939
Henrich, A. P., 321
Henry VII, of England, 6, 10
Henry VIII, of England, 9–10
Henry, Patrick, 66, 94, 106, 131, 136, 138–39
Hepburn Act, 606
Herter, Christian A., 848
Hessians, in American Revolutionary War, 101–102, 103, 107
Hickok, James B. ("Wild Bill"), 529–30
Hicks, John D., 557, 747
Higginson, Thomas Wentworth, 512
"High culture," 938
High schools, 506, 508, 707. *See also* Schools
Highway system, in early 1800s, 282–83. *See also* Transportation
Hill, Ezra, 762
Hill, James J., 480, 607
"Hillbillies," 333
Hirohito, Emperor, 814
Hiroshima, 813, 815
Hispanic-Americans, 934, 935
Hiss, Alger, 829
Historians, American, 327
Hitchcock, Sen. Gilbert M., 696
Hitler, Adolf, 675, 692, 699, 729, 740, 771; his control of Nazi party, 778; halting of, 803–804; his invasions of Austria, Czechoslovakia, and Poland, 782, 783; his invasion of Russia, 789; last days of, 810–11; and lend lease, 789; liquidation of Jews by, 781; *Mein Kampf,* 783; and Spanish Civil War, 780. *See also* World War II
Ho Chi Minh, 793, 845, 846
Hoe, Richard, 311
Hoffa, James R., 848–49
Hoffman, Paul G., 828
Hofstadter, Richard, 557, 615, 772
Holding company, 639. *See also* Corporations
Holidays, in colonial America, 78; Fourth of July, 296; Thanksgiving Day, 22
Holland, 783
Holmes, Oliver Wendell, 314, 325, 415, 725
Home Owners' Loan Corp. (H.O.L.C.), 753, 756
Home Owners Refinancing Act, 753
Homer, Winslow, 518
Homestead Act, 374, 419, 438, 439, 530–31, 533, 603. *See also* Land Acts
Homosexuality, 937
Honduras, 624
Hone, Philip, 244, 252, 281, 314
Hooker, Gen. Joseph, 407–408
Hooker, Rev. Thomas, 26
Hoover, Herbert, 684, 697, 725, 763, 772, 823, 840; and Bonus army, 744–45; election of, 736–38; and election of 1932, 751–52; Good Neighbor policy of, 747, 776; and great crash, 740–43; and Manchurian crisis, 746–47; and New Deal, 743–44; presidency of, 738–40, 747–48; quoted, 723, 742, 743, 746; renomination of, 749; as secretary of commerce, 724; and war debt, 736; during World War I, 650–51, 672
Hoover Dam, 744
Hoover-Stimson doctrine, 746
Hoovervilles, 742, 745
Hopkins, Harry L., 755–56, 758
Hopkinson, Francis, 136
Horseracing, 938
Horseshoe Bend, Battle of, 192, 199
Hostages, American, in Iran, 911, 912, 915, 916
Hot line, 861
House, Col. Edward M., 635, 662, 681, 687, 691
House of Burgesses, in Virginia, 13, 63–64, 91. *See also* Legislatures
House of Representatives, 171, 621; and election deadlocks, 223–24; establishment of, 132; gag resolution in, 342; and Tariff of 1816, 204; and Tariff of 1828, 227; and Tariff of 1832, 239; and Tariff of 1833, 240; and Tariff of 1846, 265; war vote in (1812), 187. *See also* Congress; Elections, congressional; Reed, Thomas B.; Senate, U.S.
Housing: post-war, 822–23; urban, 503
Housing Act, 833
Housing Authority, U.S. (USHA), 757, 763
Housing and Urban Development (HUD), Department of, 868
Houston, Sam, 247–49
Howard, Oliver O., 435n
Howe, Elias, 278
Howe, Gen. William, 107, 108, 109
Howells, William Dean, 513, 717
Hudson, Henry, 33
Hudson River School, 320
Hudson's Bay Company, 217, 262, 266
Huerta, Gen. Victoriano, 645–46
Hughes, Charles Evans, 604, 660–61, 697; as secretary of state, 724, 727
Hughes, Langston, 719
Huguenots, 20, 41, 42, 43, 45
Hull, Cordell, 777
Hull, Gen. William, 190
Humphrey, Congressman, 646
Humphrey, Hubert H., 874, 875, 876, 877, 887
Hun, 675, 679–81. *See also* Germany; World War I
Hungary, uprising in, 845, 846–47
Huntington, Collis, P., 478, 479
Hurons, 43. *See also* Indians, American
Hutchinson, Anne, 25, 26
Hydrogen bomb, 834. *See also* Nuclear weapons
Hymnology, 321

Ickes, Harold L, 759, 809, 810
Idaho, statehood for, 532
Illinois, 361, 362; agrarian reform in, 538
Illiteracy, decline of, 506
Immigrants; attraction for, 500; and temperance movement, 605. *See also specific immigrant groups*
Immigration, 520; to American colonies, 61–62; and Civil War, 394–95; during colonial period, 82; in early 20th century, 598; and factory system, 281; German, 298, 300–301, 320; government regulation of, 502–503; historical view of, 311; involuntary, 65; Irish, 298–301; Japanese, 705; and labor conditions, 493; legislation restricting, 704–705; new, 499; and railroad companies, 481–82; to South, 332–33; from South Europe, 499–501; and westward expansion, 245. *See also* Quota system
Immigration Act, 704–705
Impeachment, 895–96
Imperialism, 577, 578; and election of 1900, 584–85; in foreign policy, 559–60; at Paris Peace Conference, 689; Wilsonian, 642–43; *Yanqui,* 734. *See also* Foreign policy
Impressment, 178–79, 188, 196–97
Incas, 5, 7
Income: of blacks, 932; family, 929; farm, 536; national, 927. *See also* Economy
Income tax, federal, 545, 630, 636. *See also* Taxation
Independent Treasury Bill, 252–53, 265
Indian Reorganization Act, 527–28
Indians, American: attitudes toward, 527; buffer state for, 195; citizenship for, 527; discovery of, in New World, 5–6; ethnic pride of, 933–34; and French and Indian War, 51, 52; and frontiers, 295; and fur

trade, 43–44; in North Carolina, 8, 15; Ohio River lands relinquished by, 199; population of, 528; reservations of, 526; transplantation of, 245–46; tribes at time of European colonization, 5; in Virginia, 12, 14; wars with, 524–26; and westward migration, 185–86; 522–24. *See also specific tribes*
Indochina, 845
Indonesia, 819
Industrialization: mechanization, 484–85; and South, 490–92; and standard of living, 492; and steel, 486; of West, 540
Industrial-military complex, 845, 855, 939
Industrial Revolution, 145, 274, 276, 279, 419, 484, 492, 710
Industrial Workers of the World (I.W.W.s), 671, 676, 679, 702
Industry: assembly-line methods in, 277; automobile, 710–11; aviation, 713–14; and canal system, 285; coal, 821; in colonial America, 66–68; film, 715–16; mass production in, 709; mechanization in, 274; in Middle Colonies, 38–39; New Deal regulation of, 765; in New England, 31–32, 204; petroleum, 485–86, 487–88, 712; after Revolution, 123; during F. Roosevelt administration, 758–59; war, 685; and War of 1812, 199, 204; women in, 484, 485, 492, 515; during World War I, 669–71; during World War II, 795, 797–99. *See also* Business; Economy; Factory system; Manufacturing
Inflation, 929–30; and Carter administration, 907; controlled, 754; and energy crisis, 895; post-World War I, 685; post-World War II, 821; during Revolutionary War, 122; without silver, 556–57; stagflation, 880; taxation by, 417–18; during Vietnam War, 871. *See also* Depression; Economy, Panic
Influenza epidemic, 682
Ingersoll, Robert G., 504–505
Inness, George, 518
Insanity, 315
Insull, Samuel, 761
Integration, 932. *See also* Blacks; Desegregation; Education
Inter-American Conference at Buenos Aires, 777
Internal Revenue Service, 890
International Court of Justice, 819
Interstate Commerce Act of 1887, 472, 483, 484, 490, 547, 606
Interstate Commerce Commission, 483–84, 606–607, 621, 630, 725
Intolerable Acts, 92–94
Inventions, 484–85; agricultural, 535; electrical, 485
Invisible Empire of the South, *see* Ku Klux Klan
Iowa: agrarian reform in, 538; martial law in, 760
Iran: American hostages in, 911, 912, 915, 916; Muslim revolution in, 908; Soviet troops in, 826; and U.N., 819
Ireland, immigration from, 298–301
Irish-Americans, 499, 644; and British policy, 460; and campaign of 1884, 469; and Chinese labor, 463; railroad labor of, 478; and Versailles Treaty, 694; vote of, 472
"Ironclad oaths," 493
Ironclads, 400. *See also* Navy
Iron Curtain, 825–26
Iron tramp steamers, 291
Iroquois Confederacy, 4, 5, 43, 47. *See also* Indians, American
Irving, Washington, 34, 36, 203, 321–22
Irwin, Wallace, 586, 591
Isabella, Queen of Spain, 4
Isolationism, 559, 734; attitudes toward, 793; economic, 739–40; illusion of, 220; impact of Pearl Harbor on, 792–93; and Manchurian crisis, 746–47; "new," 893–94; post-World War I, 701, 704; pre-World War II, 779, 781, 785; storm-cellar, 736, 778–79, 780
Israel, 919–20; and Camp David accord, 906; Six-Day War, 871; and U.N., 819; Yom Kippur War, 894
Italian-Americans: and Versailles Treaty, 693–94; during World War II, 795
Italians, immigration of, 499
Italy: Allied invasion of, 806–807; and colonialism, 218; Ethiopia invaded by, 778–79; and Far East trade, 2–3; at Paris Peace Conference, 691
Iwo Jima, 812

Jackson, Andrew, 62, 165, 207, 264, 293, 332; and Bank of U.S., 241–42, 244, 417; and Battle of Horseshoe Bend, 199; and Battle of New Orleans, 192–93; Cabinet crises of, 234–35; campaign of, 228–30; diplomacy of, 246–47; election of, 223, 228; and election of 1824, 223, 224; historical view of, 255; as Indian fighter, 208, 215, 222, 245; Indian policy of, 245; and nullification, 239, 240; political philosophy of, 222; presidency of, 231–33, 250–51; quoted, 221, 238, 247; re-election of, 243–44; and spoils system, 233–34; and states' rights, 236–37; and Texas issue, 249
Jackson, Helen Hunt, 527
Jackson, Rachel (Mrs. Andrew), 229
Jackson, Justice Robert H., 824
Jackson, Gen. Thomas J. ("Stonewall"), 392, 400, 402, 408
Jacksonianism, 255
Jackson State College, anti-war demonstrations at, 883
Jamaica, 59
James, Henry, 514, 717
James, William, 509, 514, 575, 577n
James I, of England, 11, 12, 13, 21, 28
James II, of England, 28, 29, 38, 45–46, 47
Jamestown (Virginia), 11–12
Japan: atomic bombing of, 813, 815; Manchurian invasion by, 745–47; Pacific expansion of, 800–801; at Paris Peace Conference, 691–92; and Peace of Portsmouth, 594–95; pre-World War II embargo, 791; reconstruction in, 825; trade with, 358; and war with Russia, 593–94; as world power, 564; in World War II, 800–802, 811–14
Japanese: discrimination against, 643–44; immigration quota for, 705; as labor threat, 595–96
Japanese-Americans, during World War II, 795–96
Jay, John, 45, 128, 137, 149, 155–56, 321; and Treaty of Paris, 115
"Jayle birds," 65
Jay's Treaty, 155–56, 158, 197
Jazz Age, 713, 717
Jeffers, William M., 797
Jefferson, Thomas, 121, 123, 144, 158, 313, 329; on John Adams, 158; anti-navalism of, 179; architecture of, 308, 320; back-country support for, 148; on Bank of U.S., 146; conflict with Hamilton, 145–47, 148; death of, 182; and election of 1800, 164–65; embargo of, 179–81; on independence, 104–105; on Andrew Jackson, 232; and Kentucky Resolutions, 162–63; and Louisiana Purchase, 173–77; on Chief Justice Marshall, 170; military policy of, 171–72; political leadership of, 149–51; political philosophy of, 125; popularity of, 181–82; presidency of, 167–69; quoted, 31, 119, 120, 129, 130, 131, 149, 150, 167, 168, 175, 182; re-election of, 177; as secretary of state, 142, 143; on slavery, 65, 209, 210, 330; and Supreme Court, 170–71, 212; vice-presidency of, 158, 162; whispering campaign against, 164
Jeffersonians, 148, 149–51, 152, 154, 155–56, 165
Jenkins, Capt. Robert, 49
Jenkins' Ear, War of, 49
Jeremiads, 32
Jesuits, in New France, 44
Jewish-Americans: 99; growth in numbers of, 505; writers among, 940
Jewish populations: immigration of, 500–501; mass murder of, 811; Nazi persecution of, 781; Russian, 593; Soviet restrictions on emigration of, 899
Jim Crow laws, 547
Jogues, Father Isaac, 44
John Paul II, Pope, 917
Johns Hopkins University, 508
Johnson, Pres. Andrew, 334, 423, 425, 431, 434, 445; and Congress, 439–42; and impeachment, 448–49; presidency of, 436–38; and Reconstruction plans, 440
Johnson, Hiram W., 604, 661, 690, 694, 697
Johnson, Lyndon B., 853, 854, 856, 864, 897–98, 907; "abdication" of, 874; on affirmative action, 931; and civil rights movement, 868–69; election of, 865–67; legislation produced by, 867–68; presidency of, 865, 877; succession of, 865; Vietnam policy of, 870–71, 872–73
Johnson, Robert Underwood, 650
Johnson, Samuel, 60
Johnson, William T., 334n
Johnson Debt Default Act, 779

Joint-capital ventures, 279
Joint-stock companies, 9, 11. *See also* Business
Jolson, Al, 715
Jones, James, 939
Jones, John Paul, 113
Jones, LeRoi, 940
Jones Act, 643
Joseph, Chief, 525, 526
Josephson, Matthew, 497
Journalism, 310–11, 322, 510; reform, 510–11; yellow, 510, 564, 567, 569. *See also* Literature; Newspapers
Journals, anti-slavery, 370
Judicial review, 170, 211
Judiciary, Federalist packing of, 169–70. *See also* Supreme Court
Judiciary Acts, 143, 169–70
Junius, 76

Kahn, Louis, 941
Kaiser, Henry J., 799
Kansas, 361; admission to statehood of, 369; North-South contest for, 367–69
Kansas City, 529
Kansas-Nebraska Bill, 361–63, 375
Kashmir, and U.N., 819
Kearney, Denis, 463
Kearneyites, 463
Kearny, 790, 791
Kearny, Stephen W., 269
Keitt, Rep. L. M., 343
Kelley, Oliver H., 538
Kellogg, Sec. Frank B., 728
Kellogg-Briand Pact, 728
Kelly, "General," 640
Kelly, William, 486
Keniston, Kenneth, 938
Kennedy, Edward M. (Ted), 913, 914
Kennedy, John F., 169, 853, 856, 935; and Berlin crisis, 860–62; election of, 854; foreign policy of, 859; killing of, 864–65; New Frontier of, 857–58, 862–63; presidency of, 862–63; quoted, 857, 858; and racial revolution, 863–64; and Vietnam, 860
Kennedy, Robert, 857, 874, 935
Kent State University, anti-war demonstration at, 883
Kentucky, 61, 140–41, 420
Kentucky Resolutions, 162–63, 170, 236
Kerouac, Jack, 936
Key, D. M., 462
Key, Francis Scott, 192
Khomeini, Ayatollah Ruhollah, 911, 912
Khrushchev, Nikita, 846, 849, 850, 852, 861, 866; diplomacy of, 851; and Kennedy, 858; Nixon debate with, 852
King, Coretta, 843, 854
King, Martin Luther, Jr., 843, 844, 863, 864, 868, 869
King George's War, 48
King Wheat, 535
King William's War, 47–48
Kipling, Rudyard, 295, 575, 581
Kissinger, Henry A., 886, 888, 893–94, 899
"Kitchen Cabinet," 234
Knickerbocker Group, 321, 322
Knights of Labor, 494–95
Know-Nothing party, 301, 371
Knox, Henry, 142
Knox, Philander C., 618, 623–24
Kolko, Gabriel, 615, 835
Kolko, Joyce, 835
Korea: invasion of South by North, 836–37; police action in, 837–38
Kreisler, Fritz, 675
Kreps, Juanita, 904
Ku Klux Klan, 446–48, 703–704, 715, 903

Labor: attitudes toward, 496; in colonial America, 67–68; during Eisenhower era, 848–49; and factory system, 279–80; gains for, 280; Japanese, 595–96; laws, 604; in New England mills, 277; Northern vs. Southern, 342; organized, 496, 928; post-World War I strikes, 725–26; and Pullman strike, 549–50; and F. Roosevelt administration, 758–59, 763–66; scarcity of, 275; slavery, 336, 426; unions, 281, 492–94; and Wilson administration, 641. *See also* Business; Factory systems; Manufacturing; Slavery; Unions; Workers
Labor, Department of, 630
Labor Day, 496
Ladd, William, 315
Lafayette Escadrille, 650
Lafayette, Marquis de, 96, 105
LaFeber, Walter, 578
La Follette, Robert M., 603–604, 619, 624, 664; as presidential candidate, 733–34
La Follette Seaman's Act, 641, 725
Laird Rams, 414
Laissez-faire, 599, 670, 724; during Cleveland's administration, 470. *See also* Business; Tariffs
Lamar, Mirabeau Buonaparte, 268
Lame duck, 164
Lancaster turnpike, 282
Lance, Bert, 905
Land: federal control of, 534, 609; free, 530–31, after Revolution, 124. *See also* Frontier
Land Acts, 207, 208. *See also* Homestead Act
Land-grant colleges, 508
Land grants, and railroad construction, 477
Landis, Kenesaw Mountain, 606
Landon, Alfred M., 766, 767
Land Ordinance of 1785, 126
Landrum-Griffin Act, 849
Land speculation, and panic of 1819, 207
Lane, Franklin, 655
Lanier, Sidney, 512
Lansing, Sec. Robert, 687
Laos, civil war in, 859
La Salle, Sieur de, 44–45
Latin America: Alliance for Progress, 860; and FDR, 776–77; and Mexican War, 272; Marshall Plan for, 852, 860; and Monroe Doctrine, 218, 219; Wilson on, 642; during World War II, 797; post-World War II, 851. *See also specific countries*
Laud, Archbishop William, 23
"Law and order," 875
Law profession, in colonial America, 66
Lawrence, Captain James, 194, 199
Lawson, Thomas W., 601
Lazarus, Emma, 502
Lazear, Jesse W., 578
League of Augsburg, War of, 48
League of Nations, 689, 690, 692, 697–98, 746; American attitudes toward, 726; and Ethiopian invasion, 778–79; later attitudes toward, 734; rejection of, 698–99
Lease, Mary Elizabeth, 539
Leather-Stocking tales, 322
Leather Trust, 488
Leaves of Grass, 324
Lebanon, 850. *See also* Middle East
Lecompton Constitution, 369, 377, 378
Le Duc Tho, 894
Lee, Richard Henry, 104
Lee, Robert E., 25, 271, 392, 394, 407, 434; and Battle of Antietam, 402, 403; and Battle of Chancellorsville, 408; surrender of, at Appomattox Court House, 409–10, 425; and Wilderness Campaign, 408–409
Legal Tender Act, 458n
Legislatures: black-and-white, 445–46; of colonial America, 75–77, 82; delay tactics of, 542. *See also* Congress; House of Representatives
Leisure activity, 519–20, 938; in colonial America, 77–78; effect of automobile on, 709, 710–711, 712–13, 716; entertainment industry, 717; on frontier, 77–78, 305–306; movies, 485, 715–16; radio 714–15, 716; sports and resorts, 306, 710, 714, 822
LeMay, Gen. Curtis, 876
Lend-Lease law, 787–89
Lennon, John, 917
Leuchtenberg, William, 772, 943
Levin, N. Gordon, Jr., 700
Lewis, John L., 764, 765, 766, 798, 821
Lewis, Meriwether, 176, 262
Lewis, Sinclair, 718–19
Lexington, Battle of, 95
Leyte Island, 812
Liberia, 336
Liberty Bonds, 675
Liberty Loan drives, 674
Liberty party, 264
Libraries: in colonial America, 75; spread of, 510. *See also* Education; Literature
Libya, 913, 920
Life expectancy, in antebellum America, 314; in early 20th century, 708, 924. *See also* Population growth
Life-styles: in colonial America, 77–79; on frontier, 294–95, 305–306; of 1920s, 716–17; post-World War II, 835–38; of slaves, 336–38
Lightning, 290
Liliuokalani, Queen, 566
Limited war, concept of, 838. *See also* Vietnam War

Lincoln, Abraham, 236, 246, 344, 363, 429, 445, 453; assassination of, 306, 424–25; on black soldiers, 396; and Border States, 391; Cabinet of, 388–89; critics of, 405; and Crittenden Compromise, 383–84; -Douglas debates, 375–77; early history of, 375; election of, 379–81, 382; Emancipation Proclamation, 396, 403–405; and Fort Sumter, 389–90; Gettyburg Address, 408, 426; inaugural speech, 387, 429; and Gen. McClellan, 401; martyrdom of, 424–25; and Mexican War, 268; presidency of, 387–88, 398; quoted, 268, 278, 306, 337, 365, 387, 411; re-election of, 422–24; and slavery, 337, 341, 343, 377, 391; and Mrs. Stowe, 366; war preparations of, 390, 420
Lincoln, Gen. Benjamin, 129
Lincoln, Mary Todd, 375
Lind, Jenny, 320–21
Lindbergh, Charles, A., 707, 713, 785
Lindbergh Law, 707
Lindsay, Vachel, 553, 556
Lippman, Walter, 735
Liquor industry, 759. *See also* Temperance movement
Lister, Joseph, 509
Literacy, increase in, 511. *See also* Education; Literature
Literacy test, 502
Literature, 509; anti-slavery, 365–67; colonial, 74; of early 1800s, 322–26; Knickerbocker Group, 321, 322; landmarks in, 511–14; national, 203, 321–22; of 1920s, 717–20; post-World War II, 939–40; and transcendentalism, 322–24; WPA subsidy of, 758
Little Big Horn, Battle of, 525
Little Rock (Arkansas), 843
Livingston, Robert R., 173, 174, 175, 177
Livingston family, 35
L.L.L.L. (Loyal Legion of Loggers and Lumbermen), 679
Lloyd, Henry Demarest, 599
Lloyd George, David, 670, 689, 691
Locke, John, 322
Lockouts, 493
Lodge, Henry Cabot, 564, 688, 690, 694, 695, 696
Lodge, Henry Cabot, Jr., 852
Logrolling, congressional, 144
Lôme, Dupuy de, 568
London, Jack, 514, 600
London Economic Conference (1933), 774–75
Lone Star Republic, 248, 260–61, 262, 267. *See also* Texas
Long, Sen. Huey P., 756–58, 939
Long, Sec. John D., 570
Long Drive, 529–30, 532
Longfellow, Henry Wadsworth, 23, 324–25, 510
Long Island, Battle of, 107
Lookout Mountain, Battle of, 406
Los Angeles, race riots in, 796
Louis XIV, of France, 41–42, 44, 46, 48
Louis XVI, of France, 110, 113, 153
Louisbourg, Fort, 49, 54
Louisiana, 44; and Paris peace settlement, 55; Reconstruction in, 444; slavery in, 337; Spanish in, 56. *See also* New Orleans
Louisiana Purchase, 128, 160, 173–77
L'Ouverture, Toussaint, 173
Lovejoy, Rev. Elijah P., 341
Lovejoy, Rep. Owen, 412
Lowell, James Russell, 268, 272, 325, 339, 385, 412
Lowell, Robert, 940
Loyalists, 95; of American Revolution, 105–106; exodus of, 106–107, 120; and treaty of peace, 127; in War of 1812, 200
Loyalty program, 828–29
Luce, Clare Booth, 809
Lumber industry, and conservation, 609–10. *See also* Conservation movement
Lumbering, in colonial America, 68, 78
Lusitania, sinking of, 653, 656–58
Luther, Martin, 9
Lyceums, 309, 323
Lynchings, 447, 547, 683. *See also* Blacks
Lyon, Mary, 308
Lyon, Matthew, 161, 162

McAdoo, William, 637, 673–74, 697
MacArthur, Gen. Douglas, 745, 801, 802–803, 812, 814, 825; firing of, 838; and Korean War, 837–38
McAuliffe, Gen. A. C., 810
McCarran Internal Security Bill, 830
McCarthy, Sen. Eugene, 873–74
McCarthy, Sen. Joseph R., 829, 840–42
McCarthyism, menance of, 840–42
McClellan, George B., 401–402, 403, 407; as presidential candidate, 423–24
McClure's, 600
McCormick, Cyrus, mechanical reaper of, 276, 281–82, 397, 419
McCulloch v. *Maryland,* 212, 241
Macdonough, Thomas, 191, 199
McGovern, Sen. George, 887–89, 914
McGuffey, William H., 307–308
McKay, Claude, 719
McKay, Donald, 290
McKinley, William, 490, 544, 568, 609; death of, 585; election of, 551–52, 554; and election of 1900, 583–85; and imperialism, 574–75; and Philippine Commission, 581; presidency of, 556; and Spanish-American War, 568–69, 571
McKinley Act, 556
McKinley Tariff, 544, 550–51, 566
McLeod, Alexander, 259
McNamara, Robert S., 857, 859, 872
McNary-Haugen Bill, 732
Macon's Bill No. 2, 184–85
Madero, Francisco, 645
Madison, James, 123, 136–37, 182, 202, 321, 657; and Bonus Bill, 205; at Philadelphia Convention, 131; presidency of, 184–85, 192, 205, 277; quoted, 173; and Virginia Resolution, 162; and War of 1812, 188, 189, 192, 198. *See also Marbury* v. *Madison*
Magazines, 203, 309, 510–11, 513; early 20th century, 600–602; movie, 715. *See also* Journalism; Literature
Magellan, Ferdinand, 6
Mahan, Alfred T., 564, 578
Mailer, Norman, 939
Maine, 567–68
Maine: admission to statehood, 210; boundary dispute, 259–60; colonization of, 27
Maine Law, 317
Malcolm, John, 92
Malcolm X, 869
Manchurian crisis, 745–47
Man without a Country, The, 421
Manhattan Island, 33, 34
Manifest Destiny, 263–65, 271, 272, 357, 358–59; New, 560, 563–64
Manila, Dewey's victory at, 569–70. *See also* Philippines
Man on the Moon project, 863, 880
Mann, Horace, 307
Mann-Elkins Act, 621, 630
Manufacturing: in colonial America, 67–68, 85, 275, 277–78; in 1860, 393; in New England, 204, 276–77. *See also* Factory system; Industry
Mao Tse-tung, 886
Maps, Battle of the, 260
Marbury, Wiliam, 170
Marbury v. *Madison,* 170, 211, 236
Marconi, Guglielmo, 714
Marco Polo Bridge, 781
Marcy, Sen. William L., 233
Marianas, 803
Maria Theresa, Empress of Austria, 49
Marine Corps, U.S., 159, 271
Marines: in Cuba, 592; in Haiti, 642; women in, 799
Market, labor, 493. *See also* Labor
Marne, Second Battle of, 680
Marriage, 515, 932; ratio of divorce to, 516, 935
Marshall, George C., 814, 827, 841
Marshall, John, 136–37, 159, 236; as chief justice, 170, 171, 177, 211–12; major decisions, 212–14
Marshall, Thurgood, 933
Marshall Plan, 827–28, 859; for Latin America, 852, 860
Mary, Queen of England, 10
Maryland, 14; and Articles of Confederation, 124; colonization of, 14–15, 16. *See also* Border States
Mason, Lowell, 321
Massachusetts: colonization of, 16, 23–24; committees of correspondence in, 91; and Fugitive Slave Act, 355; and "Intolerable Acts," 92; and ratification of Constitution, 135–36; religious intolerance in, 24–26; revolution in, 86; royal charter for, 30. *See also* Boston; New England
Massachusetts Bay Colony, 23–26, 27
Mass production, 277, 484; and mass consumption, 709–11. *See also* Factory system
Maury, Matthew F., 313

Maximilian, Archduke Ferdinand, 412
Mayaguez, 900–901
Mayans, 5
May Day strikes, 495
Mayer, Arno, 700
Mayflower, 21, 22
Mayflower Compact, 22
Meade, Gen. George G., 408
Meat industry, 488
Meat Inspection Act, 608
Meat-packing industry, 529, 607–608
Mechanization, 274–75. *See also* Factory system
Media, magazines, 510–11, 513, 600–602, 715. *See also* Books; Newspapers; Television
Medical schools, 66, 509
Medicare, 867–68
Medicine, in antebellum America, 314
Mellon, Sec. Andrew W., 709, 721, 724, 731
Melville, Herman, 295, 326
Memorial Day massacre, 765
Mencken, Henry L., 718, 739
Mercantilism, 83–84; vs. free trade, 246; menace of, 86; merits of, 84–86; theory of, 83. *See also* Trade
Merchant Marine, U.S., 157, 178, 290, 641, 659
Merchant Marine Act, 725
Meredith, James, 863, 869
Merrimack, 400
Mesabi range, 484
Mestizos, 8
Methodists, 18, 121, 301, 302–303. *See also* Religion
Metropolitan Opera House (New York), 518
Metternich, Prince, 219
Meuse-Argonne offensive, 680–81
Mexican-Americans, 934–35. *See also* Chicanos
Mexican Revolution, 644–48, 934
Mexican War, 266–72
Mexico: and American petroleum investment, 734; immigration from, 935; oil properties in, 777; peace settlement with 270; revolution in, 644–48, 934; and Texas question, 247–49, 260–62, 267; Wilson's policy in, 646–48
Mexico City, 269
Middle class, of colonial America, 64; stability of, 498–99. *See also* Social classes
Middle Colonies, 38–39; agriculture in, 38, 66; and British embargo, 55; government in, 76
Middle East, 726–27, 919–20; Six-Day War in, 871; and Suez crisis, 847; Yom Kippur War in, 894
Middlemen, 537
"Middle passage," 335. *See also* Slavery
Middle West, 703, 760–61, 764. *See also* Grange
"Midnight judges," 169–70
Midway Island, naval battle of, 801–802
Migration: Puritan, 23–24, 28; westward, 185–86, 530–34. *See also* Frontier; Immigration
Miles, Gen. Nelson A., 573
Military, British, 90, 96. *See also* Army
Military academies, in South, 331
Military-industrial complex, 845, 855, 939
Military Reconstruction Act, 442, 443
Militiamen, 189
Mill, John Stuart, 294
Miller, Arthur, 940
Miller, William, 303
Millionaires, 289, 418–19, 484, 488–90, 508, 544; industrial, 490; and railroads, 482; in steel industry, 486–87; after World War I, 685
Millis, Walter, 666
Mills, C. Wright, 939
Miners, 494, 764, 798, 821
Minimum wage, 754, 833, 844
Mining, in West, 528–29
Minnesota, 260; agrarian reform in, 538
Minorities: Brown Power, 934–35; and education, 933; elderly, 924–25; European, 500–501; Japanese school incident, 595. *See also* Blacks; Immigrants; Indians; Spanish-Americans; Women
Minow, Newton, 937
Minstrel shows, 321
"Minute Men," 95, 100
Miranda decision, 881
Missile gap, 849
Missionaries, in New France, 43–44
Missionary Ridge, 406
Mississippi, 212, 276, 318; Reconstruction in, 444; slavery in, 337
Mississippi Freedom Democratic party, 868
Mississippi River, 281, 286, 289; discovery of, 7; navigation of, 156; steamboats on, 284; value of, 173, 176
Missouri, 298–209
Missouri Compromise, 209–11, 301, 362, 373
Missouri River, 176, 214
Mitchell, John N., 880
Mobility: American, 534; post-World War II, 925
Moby Dick, 326
Model T, 709, 710–11
Modernists, 504, 716
Molasses Act, 68
Momaday, N. Scott, 940
Mondale, Walter ("Fritz"), 904
Money Trust, 601, 622, 637
Monitor, 400
Monk, Maria, 301
Monopoly, 490, 638; oil, 488; of railroads, 483, 607. *See also* Trusts
Monroe, James, 173, 174, 175, 198, 205, 215; foreign policy of, 214; presidency of, 205–206; quoted, 202; re-election of, 211
Monroe Doctrine, 217–20, 261, 426, 559, 560, 645, 665, 695; TR's interpretation of, 591–92; and Venezuelan crisis, 562–63. *See also* Latin America
Montana, statehood for, 532
Montcalm, Marquis de, 47, 54
Montgomery, Gen. Richard, 102
Montgomery, Marshal B. L., 804
Montgomery Ward, 535
Monticello (Virginia), 150, 320
Montreal, 52, 53, 54, 56
Moral Majority, 913
Morgan, Angela, 713
Morgan, J. Pierpont, 485, 486, 487, 505, 548, 607
Morgan, J. P., and Company, 653, 733
Morison, Samuel Eliot, 39
Morley, John, 586
Mormons, 522, 523, 532; Utah settlement of, 304–305
Morocco, 592
Morrill Act, 508
Morrill Tariff Act, 416–17
Morris, Gouverneur, 132
Morris, Roger, 122
Morse, Samuel F. B., 279
Mott, Lucretia, 317
Mount Holyoke Seminary, 308
Movie industry, origins of, 715–16
Movies, 485; talking, 715
Mower reaper, 281–82, 397, 419
Muckraking, 600–602, 939
Mudslingers, of 1884, 467–69
Mudslinging, 163–64, 229
Mugwumps, 468, 469
Munich agreements, 782
Munitions, World War I sales, 653–54
Museums, 938
Music, 320–21; jazz, 717; and radio, 714; WPA subsidy of, 758
Muskets, production of, 277
Muskie, Sen. Edmund, 887
Mussolini, Benito, 778–79, 780, 783, 806
My Lai, 882

Nagasaki, 813, 815
Naismith, James, 520
Napoleon Bonaparte, 160, 177, 178, 181; exile of, 200; and Louisiana Purchase, 173–75; and Madison's import policies, 185; and War of 1812, 188
Napoleon III, of France, 412–413
Narcotics, 707
Nassau, 399, 400
Nasser, Gamal Abdel, 847
Nast, Thomas, 456, 462
Nation, Carrie A., 516, 517
National American Women's Suffrage Association, 515
National Association for the Advancement of Colored People (NAACP), 507
National Banking Act, 636–37
National Banking System, 417. *See also* Banking
National character, Turner's hypothesis of, 540
National debt, 145; congressional assumption of, 143–44, 148; during Jefferson's presidency, 169; liquidation of, 245; after New Deal, 770; during Nixon presidency, 886; during World War II, 799
National Defense Act, 658
National Defense and Education Act (NDEA), 849

National Endowment for the Arts and Humanities, 868
National Foundation for the Arts, 941
National Grange of the Patrons of Husbandry, *see* Grange
National health insurance, proposals for, 942
National Housing Act, 757
National Industrial Recovery Act, 753
Nationalism: Asian, 845; industrial, 203–205; judicial, 211–212; new, 621; of South, 210, 385; after War of 1812, 202–203, 205. *See also* Unity
Nationalist China, collapse of, 834
National Labor Relations Act, 757, 763–64, 769
National Labor Relations Board, 764
National Labor Union, 484
National Monetary Commission, 637
National Progressive Republican League, 624
National Prohibition party, 516
National Recovery Administration (NRA), 753, 758–59, 763
National Security Act, 828
National Security Council, 828
National War Labor Board, 671
National Women's Party, 716
Native Americans, 5–6, 929, 933. *See also* Indians, American; *and specific tribes*
Nativism, 501, 502. *See also* Ku Klux Klan
NATO (North Atlantic Treaty Organization), 830–31, 839, 846, 847, 871, 893
Naturalization Law, 169
Naval Academy (Annapolis), 327
Naval stores, 68
Navies: German, 655–56; Japanese, 778. *See also* Submarine warfare
Navigation Laws, 29, 30, 83, 85–87, 91, 122, 127. *See also* Mercantilism
Navy, British, 11, 46, 153, 178, 193–94, 195
Navy, Russian, 414–15
Navy, U.S., 159; during Arthur's administration, 467; early, 113, 191; Great White Fleet, 596–97; ironclads in, 400; Jefferson's, 172; and Mexican War, 271; 19th-century buildup of, 564; during Spanish-American War, 570; in War of 1812, 193, 203; during World War I, 655, 658–59, 676–77; during World War II, 799, 801, 803, 812. *See also* Army
Nazis, 811, 824
Nebraska, 360, 361; farm bankruptcies in, 536
Necessity, Fort, 51
Negroes, *see* Blacks
Nelson, Donald M., 797
Nelson, Horatio, 177–78
Neutrality: congressional legislation of, 779–80; and lend-lease, 788. *See also* Isolationism
Neutrality Acts, 779–80, 782–83
Neutrality Proclamation, 153–54
Nevada, statehood for, 528
New Amsterdam, 33–34, 35
Newark, race riots in, 869
New Deal, 615, 628, 922; criticism of, 770–71; Indian, 527–28; justification for, 771–72; and labor unionization, 765; three Rs of, 752–54; twilight of, 769–70
New Economic Policy, 886
New England: birthrate in, 160; and British embargo, 55; colonization of, 22–24, 26–27; conscience of, 30–32; Dominion of, 29, 30, 46; education in, 72, 73; and Embargo Act, 180, 181; factories in, 276–77; historians from, 327; industry in, 31–32, 204; manufacturing in, 204, 393; map of settlements in (1650), 22; and sectionalism, 199, 235; social stratification in, 63; town-meeting government in, 76; transcendentalism in, 322; and War of 1812, 188–89, 197–98; way of life in, 32; and westward expansion, 286
New England Confederation, 27–28, 29, 34
New England Emigrant Aid Company, 367
New England Primer, 32, 69
New Federalism, 921
Newfoundland, 9, 48, 214; and fisheries dispute, 624
New France, 43–45, 46
New Freedom, 627, 628, 634, 638, 645, 648
New Frontier, 853, 854, 857–58, 862–63
New Hampshire, 16, 27, 136, 137. *See also* New England
New Harmony (Indiana), 319
New Haven (Connecticut), 27
New Jersey: colonization of, 16, 38–39; factories in, 276; small-state plan of, 132
Newlands Act, 610
New Left, 877
"New Lights," 70
New Mexico, 349, 360; statehood for, 532, 630
New Nationalism, 627–28, 648
New Netherland, 33–34, 35. *See also* New York; New York City
New Orleans, 45, 173, 175, 288; Battle of, 192–93; and Paris peace settlement, 55; population of, 297; Spanish in, 56; Union seizure of, 406
Newport (Rhode Island), 63
Newspapers: anti-Jackson, 229; in colonial America, 75; of early 1800s, 310–11; invention of linotype, 510; during Monroe's presidency, 206; political cartoons in, 456, 462; political role of, 456, 457; sensationalism of, 510; socialist, 676. *See also* Journalism; Media
New Sweden, 34–35
New World, 42; discovery of Indians in, 5–6; indirect discoverers of, 2–3; Quakers in, 36–38. *See also* France; Great Britain; Portugal; Spain
New York: colonization of, 16, 38–39; Dutch influence in, 35–36; factories in, 276; growth of, 503; Jewish immigration to, 501; race riots in, 796; and ratification of Constitution, 137, 138; saloons in, 604
New York City, 33, 61, 285, 288; as capital, 142; draft riots in, 415–16; and Irish immigration, 299; population of, 140, 297; water supply in, 298
New York Customs House, 463
New York Philharmonic Orchestra, 320
New York Stock Exchange, 640
Nez Percé Indians, 525, 526
Niagara, Fort, 195
Niagara Falls Conference, 646
Nicaragua, 357, 587, 642, 734, 747, 920
Nicaragua route, 588, 589
Nimitz, Adm. Chester W., 801, 803, 814
Nine Power Treaty, 727
Nixon, Richard M., 829, 839, 846, 847–48, 875; "Checkers speech" of, 839–40; in China, 885–86; election of, 876; and election of 1960, 852–54; energy policy of, 895; jet-plane diplomacy of, 880; pardon of, 898; presidency of, 879–80, 901; quoted, 879; re-election of, 887–89; resignation of, 896–97; in Russia, 886; and secret bombing of Cambodia, 892–93; in South America, 851; and Supreme Court, 881–82; and tape controversy, 891–92; and Vietnam War, 882–85, 886, 887, 889–90, 892–94; and Watergate scandal, 890–92, 895–97, 901
Nixon Doctrine, 882
Nominating conventions, national, 223, 243. *See also* Elections
Non-conformists, 21
Non-importation agreements, 88–89
Non-Intercourse Act (1809), 180, 184
Normalcy, 697, 698
Normal schools, 506
Normandy, Allied invasion of, 807–808
Norris, Frank, 514
Norris, Sen. George W., 621, 664, 762, 767
Norris-La Guardia Anti-Injunction Act, 744
Norris Muscle Shoals Bill, 744
Norsemen, in New World, 2
North: anti-slavery agitators in, 209; anti-slavery societies in, 338; and black suffrage, 444–45; and Compromise of 1850, 353; desegregation battles in, 932–33; and Dred Scott decision, 373; enlistees of, 416; free blacks in, 334; industrialization in, 277–78; and Missouri Compromise, 210; moral position of, 405; slavery in, 335; war advantages of, 410; at war's beginning, 393–95; war economy of, 416–17; war strategy of, 398–99; wartime prosperity in, 418–19. *See also* South
North, Lord, 91, 95–96, 110, 114, 115
North Africa: and T. Roosevelt's foreign policy, 592; in World War II, 805–806
North American maps: after 1763, 54; before 1754, 54
North American Review, 203, 309
North Atlantic Pact, 830–31
North Atlantic Treaty Organization, *see* NATO
North Carolina: colonization of, 15, 16–17; Indians in, 8, 15; and ratification of Constitution, 137–38; Reconstruction in, 444; secession of, 390
North Dakota, statehood for, 532
Northern Pacific Railroad, 479, 531
Northern Securities Company, 607
North Korea, 836–37
North Vietnam, 874, 885; bombing of, 870,

889; victory of, 899–900. *See also* Vietnam War
Northwest Ordinance, 124, 126–27
Norway, 783
Nova Scotia, 48, 49, 51
Novels, 512–14. *See also* Books; Literature
Nuclear weapons, 834; atomic bomb, 813, 815; Carter policy on, 906; international inspection of, 820; Soviet, 834; test-ban treaty, 849–50, 861, 886–87
Nullification, 225, 425; Calhoun's doctrine of, 235; in 1832, 341; and New England, 198; in South Carolina, 238–40; theory of, 228
Nuremberg trials, 824
Nutmeg, 30

Oakley, Annie, 519–20
Oberlin College, 308
O'Connor, Flannery, 939
O'Connor, Sandra Day, 918
October Appeal, 686–87
Office of Economic Opportunity (OEO), 867
Office of Price Administration, 798
Ogallala (Nebraska), 529
Ogden, Peter Skene, 217
Oglethorpe, James, 17, 49
Ohio, 140–41; electoral power of, 460, 551
"Ohio fever," 207
Ohio Valley, 50–51
Oil: embargo, 894–95, 908; imports, limits on, 910; industry, 485–86, 487–88, 712; Iranian, 908; in Pennsylvania, 419; price hikes, 907, 908–909
Okinawa, 812
Oklahoma: Apache settlement in, 525; Indian Territory of, 523; statehood for, 532, 533
Old-age insurance, 754
Oldenburg, Claes, 941
"Old Hickory," 231. *See also* Jackson, Andrew
Olds, Ransom E., 710
O'Leary, J. A., 662
Oliver, King, 717
Olney, Richard S., 483–84, 547, 549, 562
Olympic Games, American boycott of, 911
O'Neal, Peggy, 234–35
Oneida Colony, 319
O'Neill, Eugene, 719, 720
Open Door doctrine, 582, 583, 592, 593, 597, 746
Open Housing Bill, 868
Operation Rolling Thunder, 870
Opposition, legitimate, 182. *See also* Democracy; Government
Order of the Star-Spangled Banner, 301
Oregon, U.S.S., 573, 587
Oregon Country, 214, 217, 262; claim to, 176; settlement for, 265–66
Organization of American States (OAS), 852
Organization of Petroleum Exporting Countries (OPEC), 907, 908
Orlando, Vittorio, 689
Osceola, 246
Ostend Manifesto, 359
O'Sullivan, John L., 256
Oswald, Lee Harvey, 864–65
Otis, James, 66
Owen, Robert, 319

Pabst, Frederick, 300n
Pacific Ocean, new Manifest Destiny in, 564–65
Pacific Railraod, 359–60. *See also* Railroads
Pacific Railroad Act, 438
Pact of Paris, 728
Page, Walter H., 655
Pageot, Alphonse, 247
Pahlevi, Mohammed Reza (Shah of Iran), 908, 911, 912
Paine, Robert Treat, 152
Paine, Thomas, 100, 108, 131, 157, 301; *Common Sense,* 103–104, 321
Painting: antebellum, 320; colonial, 73–74; late 19th-century, 518; post-World War II, 941. *See also* Arts
Palmer, A. Mitchell, 702
Palmerston, Prime Minister, 413
Panama Canal, 586–90, 906
Panama Canal Tolls Act, 644
Panama Congress (1826), 226
Panama republic, 776; creation of, 588–89; treaty with, 906
Pan-American Conference: first, 560, 562; seventh, 776. *See also* Latin America
Pan-Americanism, 226, 560, 797
Pan-American Union, 560
Panay, 781
Panic: of 1819, 207; of 1837, 252, 259; of 1857, 374–75; of 1873, 458–59, 463; of 1893, 496, 547; of 1907, 612–13, 636. *See also* Depression; Economy
Paris, liberation of, 808
Paris, Pact of (1898), 575
Paris, peace settlement at (1736), 55–56
Paris, Treaty of (1783), 115–16
Paris Peace Conference (1919), 687–92
Paris Peace Talks (1968), 874
Parker, Alton B., 611–12
Parker, Theodore, 344
Parkman, Francis, 327
Parks, Rosa, 843–44
Parochial institutions, federal funds for, 867
Partisanship, of Jefferson era, 182. *See also* Political parties
Passell, Peter, 942
Pasteur, Louis, 509
Patent system, 278, 279
Patriots, of American Revolution, 105–106. *See also* Loyalists
Patronage, 459
Patrons of Husbandry, *see* Grange
Patroonships, in New Netherland, 34
Patton, Gen. George S., 808
Payne-Aldrich Tariff, 618–20, 621, 635, 729
Peace Corps, 858, 871
Peale, Charles W., 74, 320
Pearl Harbor, 566; attack on, 791–92; impact of attack on, 796
Pendleton Act of 1883, 466, 467
Peninsular Campaign, 402
Penn, William, 36–38
Pennsylvania: colonization of, 16, 36–39; factories in, 276; Germans in, 61; and ratification of Constitution, 135, 138; University of, 73, 242
Pension legislation, 470–71, 543
Pentagon Papers, 885, 890
People's party, 539. *See also* Populists
Percy, Walker, 939
Perkins, Frances, 756
"Permissiveness," 707
Perry, Commodore Matthew C., 358
Perry, Oliver Hazard, 190–91, 199
Pershing, Gen. John J., 647, 677, 680, 684
Personal liberty laws, 355
"Pet banks," 244, 252, 253
Petigru, James L., 390
Petroleum industry, 485–86, 487–88, 712
Philadelphia (frigate), 159
Philadelphia, 37, 61, 282, 286; anti-Catholic riots in, 301; First Church in, 39; growth of, 503; Independence Hall in, 123; national government in, 125; population of, 140, 297; "White House," 144
Philadelphia Convention, 130–33
Philanthropy: organized, 517; private, 508
Philip, Capt. John W., 573
Philip, King (Indian chief), 28
Philip II, of Spain, 10–11
Philippine Commission, 581
Philippines, 800, 801; acquisition of, 574–75; independence for, 581, 776, 823; insurrection in, 580–81; Jones Act, 643
Phillips, David G., 601
Phillips, Ulrich B., 344
Phillips, Wendell, 339, 403
Phips, William, 61
Phonograph, 485, 518
"Phony war," 783
Physicians, in colonial America, 66
Pickett, Gen. George E., 408
Pierce, Franklin, 361, 369, 370, 404–405; Cuban policy of, 359; election of, 355–57; presidency of, 357–58
Pierpont, John, 355
Pike, Zebulon M., 176
Pilgrims, 21–23. *See also* Puritanism
Pilgrim's Progress, 69
Pillsbury, John S., 532
Pinchot, Gifford, 609, 610, 620
Pinckney Treaty, 156
Pinkerton's Detective Agency, 401, 546
Pioneers, 294–95; Mormon, 304. *See also* Frontier
Piracy: and American privateers, 113–14; Barbary coast, 172; of Confederacy, 413–14; English, 10; North African, 128, 171, 203; in North Carolina, 17
Pitt, William, 51, 53–54, 56, 95
Pittsburgh, 51; railroad strike in, 463; steel industry in, 486, 491–92
"Pittsburgh plus" pricing system, 491–92
Pizarro, Francisco, 7
Plagues, 66, 314. *See also* Disease
Plains Indians, 523, 526. *See also* Indians,

American
Plantation(s): colonies, 18; degeneration of, 490–91; tobacco and, 13. *See also* Cotton; Economy; South
Plath, Sylvia, 940
Platt, Thomas C., 583–84, 585
Platt Amendment, 577, 776
Playwrights, 940–41
Plow, steel, 281
Plutocracy, 483, 489, 490
Plymouth Colony, 21–23
Pocahontas, 12
Poe, Edgar Allan, 325–26
Poetry, 940
Poland, 692, 782, 783, 817, 919
Poles, immigration of, 499
Political parties: birth of, 148; evolution of, 151. *See also* Third parties; Two-party system
Politics: in colonial America, 75–77; during Civil War, 422; of impeachment, 895–96; and railroads, 482–83. *See also* Elections
Polk, James K., 219, 261, 347; and California, 266–67, 269; election of, 263–65; and Mexican War, 267–68, 272; presidency of, 265–66
Pollack, Norman, 557
Pollock, Jackson, 941
Pollution, 925
Polo, Marco, 3
Polygamy, 303, 523, 532. *See also* Mormons
Ponce de León, Juan, 6
Pontiac (Indian chieftain), 56
Pony Express, 291
Poor, attitudes toward, 489–90. *See also* Social classes
Poor Richard's Almanack, 66, 69
Pope, Gen. John, 402
"Popocrats," 539
Popular sovereignty, doctrine of, 346–47, 373
Population growth: of Afro-Americans, 336; of American colonies, 59–60; among American Indians, 528; and industrialization, 498; and national policy, 154; and peace, 943; post-Civil War, 454; post-World War II, 923–24; in South, 926; urban, 140; and westward expansion, 263, 297–98. *See also* Immigration
Populist party, 539, 544, 546
Populists, 480, 490, 539, 550, 551, 599; in election of 1892, 544, 546–47; historical view of, 557, 578
Portman, John, 941
Port Royal, 48
Portsmouth, Peace of, 594–95
Portugal: New World exploration by, 3–4; New World territory of, 6
Postal Savings Bank Act, 630
Postal service: air, 713; in colonial America, 69; independent, 884
Potsdam Conference, 812–13, 824
Pound, Ezra, 719, 940
Poverty, wealth and, 289
Powderly, Terence V., 495
Powhatan Confederacy, 6. *See also* Indians, American
Pragmatism, 509, 700
Predestination, doctrine of, 20–21. *See also* Calvinism
Presbyterians, 20, 70, 71, 72, 301, 303. *See also* Religion
Prescott, William H., 327
Presidency: leadership of, 648; power of, 615; stewardship theory of, 586
Press, appeal of, 509–10
Press gangs, 178–79
Pribilof Islands, 560
Prices, post-World War II, 929
Primogeniture, 121
Princeton University, 625–26
Printing presses, in colonial America, 75. *See also* Newspapers
Prison system, 315
Privateers, American, 113–14, 194–95. *See also* Piracy
Proclamation of 1763, 57
Progressive party, 660, 733, 832
Progressivism, 615; in cities and states, 603–605; effect of World War I on, 685; and election of 1912, 628; and election of 1924, 733; origins of, 598–600; political, 602–603; and presidency, 631
Prohibition, 517, 684, 705–706; crime and, 706–707; repeal of, 759. *See also* Temperance movement
Prohibition party, 605
Promoters, after Civil War, 455
Propaganda: Allied, 652–53, 665, 666; Cold War, 828; of "gold bugs," 553; during World War I, 674–75, 681; pre-World War II, 785
Prophet, the, 186
Proposition 13, 942
Prosperity, 709, 927; impact of, 929, 943
Prostitution, 707
Protectionism, 204, 226; Cleveland's view of, 471–72; trend toward, 729. *See also* Tariffs
Protestantism, 505. *See also* Religion
Protestant Reformation, 9, 11, 20, 21. *See also* Religion
Protest movement, of blacks, 863–64. *See also* Blacks
Providence (Rhode Island), 26
Public-health program, 708
Public libraries, 510
Public opinion, on aid to Britain, 786
Public school systems, 300, 306–308. *See also* Education; Schools
Public Utility Holding Co. Act, 757, 761
Public Works Administration, 753, 759
Pueblo, 871
Pueblos, 5. *See also* Indians, American
Puerto Ricans, 929, 934
Puerto Rico, 574; citizenship in, 576; invasion of, 573
Pujo, Arsène, 637
Pujo Committee, 622
Pulitzer, Joseph, 510, 564, 567
Pullman Palace Car Company, 549
Pullman Palace Cars, 481
Pullman strike, 549–50
Pure Food and Drug Act, 608
Puritanism, Puritans, 18, 20–21, 30–31; experiment of, 39; migration of, to West Indies, 23–24; and 19th-century reform, 314–15; textbooks of, 32

Quakers, 24, 26, 39, 317, 325; in New Jersey, 38; in New Netherland, 33; in Pennsylvania, 36–38, 55
Quartering Act, 87
Quebec, 42, 52, 53; Battle of, 54; fall of, 56. *See also* Canada
Quebec Act, 93–94, 102
Queen Anne's War, 48
Quemoy, 847
Quincy, Josiah, 93
Quinine, 797
Quota system, 704–705; reform of, 868. *See also* Immigration

Race prejudice, in antebellum North, 334
Race riots: of 1965, 869; during World War I, 683; post-World War I, 726; during World War II, 796. *See also* Blacks
Races, in colonial America, 61–63. *See also* Blacks; Immigration; Indians, American
Radicals, 492; American outcry against, 701–703
Radio, 714–15, 716. *See also* Media
Railroad Brotherhoods, 641
Railroads, 286–88; and buffalo hunting, 526–27; consolidation of, 481–82; and corruption, 482–83; extension of, 479–80; and farm income, 537; government regulation of, 605–607; government subsidy of, 476–77; and immigration, 481–82; and Indian warfare, 526; and industrialization, 481; and Interstate Commerce Act, 473; Pacific, 359–60, 438; regulation of, 483–84; setbacks for, 712, 714; strikes, 463; transcontinental, 359–60, 477–79; and Western agriculture, 531; and World War I, 673–74. *See also specific railroads;* Transportation
Railway, electric, 484
Railway Labor Board, 725
Raleigh, Sir Walter, 1, 8, 9, 15
Rand Corporation, 927
Randolph, John, 156, 180, 185, 224, 227, 277
Rape, 317
"Rapid Deployment Force," 911
Rationing, wartime, 671, 672, 797
Rauschenberg, Robert, 941
Rauschenbush, Walter, 505
Rayburn, Sen. Sam, 840
Reagan, Ronald, 903, 906, 938, 942; budget proposals of, 916, 917; economic program of, 917–18; election of, 913–15; foreign policy of, 918–21; presidency of, 916–17, 922; quoted, 917; shooting of, 917
Reaper, McCormick's, 276, 281–82, 397, 419
Recession: of 1913–1914, 640, 653; of 1920s, 709; of 1937–1938, 769, 783; Nixon-Ford, 899. *See also* Depression; Economy
Reciprocal Trade Agreements, 777–78

Reciprocal Trade Agreements Act, 757, 777–78
Reconstruction, 429–31; end of, 463, 464; heritage of, 450–51; historical view of, 451; and lynching, 447; proposals and plans, 440; southern, by state, 444; by sword, 442–43
Reconstruction Finance Corporation (R.F.C.), 744
Recovery, of New Deal. 752–54
Redcoats, 90, 95, 96
Red Cross, 517, 674
Red Scare, 702, 828–30
Reed, Thomas B., 542–43, 551–52, 556, 575
Reed, Walter, 576–77
Reform: agrarian, 538; in antebellum America, 314–15; banking, 637; Jeffersonian, 169; in journalism, 510–11; of New Deal, 752–54; New Freedom, 648; of Progressives, 598–600, 603–605; social, 641; urban, 603. *See also* Abolitionism; Suffrage; Temperance movement
Refrigerator cars, 484, 529
Refugees, relief for, 823. *See also* Quota system
Relief, of New Deal, 752–54
Religion: in American colonies, 16, 17–18; in antebellum America, 301–304; "born-again" Christians, 937; in colonial America, 69–72; in colonial Rhode Island, 26; diversity in, 303–304; fundamentalists, 504, 708, 716; impact of Darwinism on, 504; in Massachusetts Colony, 24–26; in Middle Colonies, 39; ole-time, 708; in plantation economies, 18; and Supreme Court 881; variety of, 505–506. *See also* Great Awakening; *specific denominations*
Religious Society of Friends, *see* Quaker
Remington, Frederic, 567
Renaissance, 3
Reorganization Act, 757, 769
Reparations Commission, 699
Representative government: in colonial America, 75–77, 82; colonial attitudes toward, 25; of colonial New England, 28; in New Amsterdam, 33; in Pennsylvania, 37; and Philadelphia Convention, 132; of Pilgrims, 22; in Virginia, 13. *See also* Government; Legislatures
"Repressive Acts," 92, 93
Republican party, 363; and Big Business, 724; blacks in, 451; in 1856, 372; in 1860, 379; and election of 1880, 464–65; and election of 1916, 660; insurgent uprising in, 621–22; Liberal, 457–58; origin of, 454; post-Reconstruction, 454; radical, 438–39; "Stalwart" faction in, 460, 464, 465. *See also* Elections; Political parties
Republicans: Democratic, 149–51, 157–58; Jeffersonian, 148, 149–51, 152, 203; National, 250; National vs. Democratic, 228; Radical, 438–39
Republic Steel Company, 765
Research and development, government subsidy of, 927
Reservations, Indian, 526
Resettlement Administration, 757, 761
Resorts, fashionable, 306. *See also* Leisure activity
Resumption Act, 458
Reuben James, 790
Revels, Hiram R., 443
Revere, Paul, 28, 45, 73, 89, 91
Revolution: of colonial America, 81–83; of 1800 (Jeffersonian), 164–65, 169; of 1828 (Jacksonian), 230–31; transportation, 288. *See also* American Revolution; Industrial Revolution
Rhett, Senator, 343
Rhineland, 690, 691
Rhode Island, 17; colonization of, 16, 26; and ratification of Constitution, 137–38; royal charter for, 29. *See also* New England
Rhodesia, 905
Richmond (Virginia), 432. *See also* Confederate States of America
Rickenbacker, Edward V., 679
Rickover, Adm. H. G., 568
Riesman, David, 928, 939
Riis, Jacob A., 600
Rio Grande River, 249, 267
Riots, anti-war, 884–85; draft 415–16. *See also* Anti-war movement; Race riots
Road system: of early 1800s, 205; and Jackson presidency, 235; and national government, 225; and westward expansion, 208, 283. *See also* Transportation
Roanoke colony, 9
Robards, Rachel, 229
Robber barons, 578
Roberts, Justice Owen J., 768
Robin Moor, 789
Robinson, Edgar E., 772
Robinson, Jack Roosevelt (Jackie), 822
Rochambeau, Comte de, 112, 114
Rochester (New York), 285
Rockefeller, John D., 415, 485–86, 487–88, 489, 505, 508
Rockefeller, Nelson A., 852
Rockefeller Foundation, 708
Rocketry, 849
Roethke, Theodore, 940
Rogers, Will, 687, 770
Rolfe, John, 12
Roman Catholics, 300–301, 937; in colonial America, 72, 93–94; discrimination against, 502; growth in numbers of, 505; immigration of, 501; in Maryland, 14–15; in New France, 43–44; as presidential candidates, 736, 737, 853–54. *See also* Religion
Romania, 817
Rome-Berlin Axis, 778
Rommel, Field Marshal Erwin, 804
Roosevelt, Eleanor, 767
Roosevelt, Franklin D., 36, 615, 676, 738, 743, 744, 745, 865; and banking, 754–55, 761; at Casablanca, 806; and Churchill, 814; death of, 811; election of, 750–51; and election of 1940, 786–87; fourth election of, 809–10; Good-Neighborism under, 776–77; and industry, 758–59; and labor, 758–59, 763–66; presidency of, 752–811; Quarantine Speech, 774, 781; quoted, 749, 750, 766, 770, 774, 792, 794; re-election of, 767; renomination of, 766; and Supreme Court, 767–69; three R's of, 752–54; and unemployment, 755–58; as vice-presidential candidate, 697; war message of, 792; in Wilson's Cabinet, 634; at Yalta Conference, 817–18. *See also* New Deal
Roosevelt, Theodore, 36, 86, 542, 564, 600, 658, 687, 692; American Legion founded by, 726; as assistant secretary of navy, 570; conservation of, 609–11, 620; and consumer protection, 607–608; cowboy diplomacy of, 588–89; and election of 1904, 611–12; and election of 1912, 624–25, 627–28, 629; and election of 1916, 549–61; foreign policy of, 586–87, 597; and Monroe Doctrine, 591–92; muckraker speech of, 600; Nobel Peace Prize for, 595; and Panama Canal, 587–88, 589, 590; and Panic of 1907, 612; and Peace of Portsmouth, 594–95; presidency of, 585–97, 615; preventive intervention of, 591; progressivism of, 618, 631; quoted, 580, 588, 590, 591, 595, 598, 602, 603, 606, 608, 611, 614, 617; and "Rough Riders," 572–73; in Spanish-American War, 569, 578; square deal for labor from, 605; and Taft, 617–18, 621; as trust buster, 605–607; and Venezuela, 590–91; vice-presidency of, 583–84; and World War I, 677, 681
Roosevelt Dam, 610
Root, Elihu, 578, 637, 697
Root-Takahira agreement, 596
Rosenberg, Ethel, 834
Rosenberg, Julius, 834
Ross, E. A., 502
Ross, Leonard, 942
Roszak, Theodore, 936
Roth, Phillip, 940
"Rough Riders," 572–73
Roundheads, 13
Round Robin, 573, 574, 690
Rousseau, Jean-Jacques, 110
Royal African Company, 63
"Royal veto," 84
Rubber, during World War II, 797
Rubber tires, 710
Ruby, Jack, 865
Ruffin, Edmund, 331–32, 434
Rush-Bagot disarmament agreement, 200
Russia: and Alaska, 449–50; and Civil War, 391, 414–15; in New World, 216–17, 218, 219; in Oregon, 262; and Peace of Portsmouth, 594–95; revolution in, 664, 678; U.S. troops in, 683; in World War I, 649. *See also* Cold War; Détente; Soviet Union
Russo-American Treaty of 1824, 219
Russo-Japanese War, 593–94, 595
Ruth, George Herman ("Babe"), 61, 710

Saarinen, Eero, 941
Sacagawea (Shoshone Indian woman), 176

Sacco, Nicola, 702–703
Sackville-West, Sir Lionel, 472
Sadat, Anwar, 906, 907, 917, 919
Safety-valve theory, of frontier, 534
Saigon, evacuation of, 900. *See also* North Vietnam; Vietnam; Vietnam War
Sailor-snatching, 179. *See also* Impressment
St. Bartholomew's Day, 41
Saint-Gaudens, Augustus, 518
St. Lawrence River, 42
St. Lawrence waterway, 855
St. Leger, Col. Barry, 108, 109
St. Mihiel (France), 680
St. Valentine's Day massacre, 707
Salem (Massachusetts), 31
Salinger, J. D., 940
Salk, Jonas, 924
SALT (Strategic Arms Limitation Talks), 887, 906; II, 907, 910, 911
Salvation Army, 505
Samoa, 561, 564–65
Sand Creek, massacre at, 524
San Francisco (California), 266–67, 349; earthquake and fire in, 595; general strike in, 763; saloons in, 604
Sanger, Margaret, 716
Santa Anna, Gen., 248–49, 250, 261, 360; and Mexican War, 269, 270, 272
Santa Fe trail, 269
Santiago, Battle of, 573, 587
Santo Domingo, 173–74, 624; marines dispatched to, 642
Saratoga, Battle of, 109, 110
Sargent, John Singer, 518
"Saturday Night Massacre," 891–92
Savannah, 290
Savannah (Georgia), 17, 172, 407
Saudi Arabia, 920
"Scalawags," 443. *See also* Reconstruction
Scalps, bounties for, 52, 113
Schechter decision, 759
Schenectady (New York), 48
Schlesinger, Arthur M., Jr., 237, 255, 772
Schools: in colonial America, 72–73; tax-supported, 506; teach-training, 506. *See also* Education
Schlitz, Joseph, 300n
Schurz, Carl, 300, 395, 432
Science: advances in (1920s), 708; in colonial America, 74–75; 19th-century American, 313–14. *See also* Education
Scopes, John T., 708
Scotch-Irish, in colonial America, 61–62. *See also* Immigration
Scott, Dred, *see* Dred Scott decision
Scott, Michael, 196
Scott, Sir Walter, 331
Scott, Gen. Winfield, 199, 269–70, 356, 390
Screen Actors Guild, 914
Seal issue, 560–61, 624
Seaman's Act, 641, 725
Secession, 381–83, 385, 390, 425. *See also* Nullification; South
Sectionalism, 206; of New England, 199, 235; and slavery, 208–209; Southern, 235. *See also* Middle Colonies; New England; North; South
Securities and Exchange Commission (SEC), 757, 761
Security: attitudes toward, 835; collective, 746, 747
Security Council, U.N., 819
Security Treaty, 691, 699
Sedition Act, 161, 162, 163, 169, 676
Segregation, 842, 863–64. *See also* Blacks; Desegregation; Education
Selective Service law, 677–78. *See also* Conscription
Selective Service System, 828
Self-determination, 385, 691–92
Self-government, 139. *See also* Democracy; Representative government
Selma (Alabama), 868
Seminoles, 246. *See also* Indians, American
Senate, U.S., 171; establishment of, 132; as Millionaires Club, 602; and slavery issue, 351–53; and Watergate investigation, 891; Wilson's snub of, 687–88. *See also* Congress; House of Representatives; *specific treaties*
Seneca Falls (New York), Woman's Rights Convention at, 318. *See also* Feminist movement; Women
"Senior citizens," 924–25. *See also* Elderly
Separatists, 21–22
Serbia, 649
Servants, indentured, 14, 64–65
Seven Years' War, 51, 86. *See also* French and Indian War
Seward, William H., 371, 379, 412, 450; as secretary of state, 388, 389; on slavery, 352–53
Sewing machine, 278, 419. *See also* Textile industry
Sexual attitudes, 515, 937; revolution in, 520, 716–17; and women's movement, 932
Seymour, Horatio, 454
Shafter, Gen. William R., 572, 573
Shah of Iran, *see* Pahlevi, Mohammed Reza
Shakers, 319
Shakespeare, William, 11, 305
Shannon, 194
Shantung peninsula, German holdings on, 691–92
Sharecropping, in South, 536. *See also* Farmers
Shawnee Mission, 368
Shays, Capt. Daniel, 129, 132, 133
Shays's Rebellion, 129, 149
Sheffield, Lord, 127, 132
Sheridan, Gen. Philip H., 424, 524
Sherman, John, 524, 556
Sherman, William Tecumseh, 396, 406–407, 424, 457
Sherman Anti-Trust Act, 490, 543, 547, 605–606, 607, 622, 639
Sherman Silver Purchase Act, 543, 547–48
Sherwin, Martin J., 815
Shiloh, Battle of, 406
Shipbuilding, 38; clipper ships, 290–91; in colonial America, 67; in New England, 32; subsidies for, 86; during World War I, 673; during World War II, 799
Shipping, *see* Merchant Marine
Shipping Board, 659, 673, 725
Sholes, Christopher, 484
Shriver, Sargent, 888
Sicilian Blackhanders, 561
Sigel, Franz, 395
Silliman, Benjamin, 313–14
Silver: coinage of, 458–59, 543; free, 545, 547, 548, 551, 552–53, 555, 557, 584; inflation without, 556–57. *See also* Banking; Currency
Silver issue: and election of 1896, 553, 555; and election of 1904, 612
Simms, William Gilmore, 325
Simon, Neil, 941
Sinclair, Harry F., 730
Sinclair, Upton, 608
Singer, Issac, 278
Sioux Indians, 523, 524. *See also* Indians, American
Sioux War, 524–25
Sitting Bull, 525
Skyscrapers, 503, 518, 520
Slater, Samuel, 275, 280
Slaveowners, 333, 336, 337
Slavery, 206; and abolition movement, 32, 344; in colonial America, 62–63, 65–66; and Constitution, 133; cotton and, 276, 329; and Emancipation Proclamation, 403–405; extension of, 346, 347, 363; indentured servants, 64–65; indirect effects of, 331; institution of, 334–36; introduction in America, 13; in Kansas, 367–68; life style on plantation, 336–38; Lincoln on, 391; in Maryland, 14–15; and Mexican War, 272; in New England, 31; Quakers and, 37; and religious denominations, 303; revolts against, 65–66, 338; and Revolutionary War, 121; and sectional balance, 208–209; in South Carolina, 16; and Texas annexation, 249–50, 261. *See also* Abolitionism; Blacks; Freedmen
Slidell, John, 267
Slovaks, immigration of, 499
Slums, 298, 299, 503
Smallpox, 66, 314
Smith, Adam, 83
Smith, Alfred E., 750, 754–55, 767, 770; presidential candidacy of, 736, 737–38
Smith, Capt. John, 12
Smith, Joseph, 304
Smith, Sydney, 235, 321
Smith Act, 827
Smith-Connally Anti-Strike Act, 798
Social changes, after American Revolution, 120–22. *See also* Frontier
Social classes: of antebellum South, 333–34; in early America, 14; and Jacksonian presidency, 237; middle class, 498–99; and New Deal, 771; of post-Revolutionary era, 142; underprivileged vs. privileged, 555
Socialism, 501; of New Deal, 772; utopian, 511

Socialist movement, 492, 550, 600
Socialist party, 698, 733, 772
Socialists: and election of 1908, 614; and election of 1912, 628; and Red Scare, 702; during World War I, 676
Social Security Acts, 757, 763, 769, 833
Social Security system: benefits of, 844, 889; and Gray Power, 924–25
Social structure, 32; in colonial America, 63–65
Soil Conservation and Domestic Allotment Act, 757, 760
Solzhenitsyn, Alexander, 899
Sons of Liberty, 89
South: anti-slavery sentiment in, 338, 341; black suffrage in, 439, 442, 547; colonization of, 11–18; and Compromise of 1850, 353, 354; county government in, 76; and Cuba, 358–59; and desegregation, 843–44; and Dred Scott decision, 373; economic discrimination against, 491–92; effects of war in, 419, 433–34; enlistees of, 416; and industry, 490–92; integration in, 870; King Cotton in, 329–30, 332, 374; Ku Klux Klan in, 446–48; and Missouri Compromise, 210; moral position of, 405; and 1928 election, 737–38; population increase in, 926; racial composition of, 63; Reconstruction in, 444, 445–46; Republican party in (1964), 867; Revolutionary War in, 103; social stratification in, 63–64; and Tariff of 1828, 227–28; after war, 431–32; at war's beginning, 392–93; war economy of, 417–18. *See also* North
South Africa, 905
South Carolina: appeasement of, 240; colonization of, 15–16; nullification in, 238–40; Reconstruction in, 444; secession of, 381–82, 390; slavery in, 65, 337; and Tariff of Abominations, 227, 228, 238
South Dakota, statehood for, 532
Southeast Asia Treaty Organization (SEATO), 846
Southern Pacific Railroad, 479, 490, 604
Southey, Robert, 49
South Korea, *see* Korea
South Vietnam, *see* Vietnam
Soviet bloc, 819. *See also* Cold War
Soviet Union: atomic bomb of, 834; and Berlin, 830; Czechoslovakia takeover of, 827–28; German front, 804; German nonaggression treaty with, 782; Hitler's invasion of, 789; and Hungarian uprising, 845, 846–47; invasion of Afghanistan by, 911–12, 919; Iron Curtain policy of, 825–26; and Nixon diplomacy, 886–87; post-war relations between U.S. and, 818, 824–25; Reagan's policy on, 918–19; recognition of, 775; and SALT II, 910; Sputnik, 849; war declared on Japan, 813; as World War II ally, 797. *See also* Cold War; Détente; Russia
Space: and Man on the Moon project, 863, 880; race with Russia into, 849
Spain: *conquistadores* of, 6–8; and Cuban revolt, 566–67; explosion of *Maine*, 567–68; and Florida secession, 215–16; mercantilism of, 85–86; New World empire of, 6, 8; New World exploration by, 4–5, 7; in North American struggle, 45–47; in Oregon, 262; and Pinckney Treaty, 156
Spanish-American pact of 1819, 216
Spanish-Americans, 934–35
Spanish-American Treaty of 1795, 215
Spanish-American War, 570–74, 577; Dewey's victory at Manila, 569–70; navy during, 467; origins of, 569
Spanish Armada, 10–11
Spanish Civil War, 780
Spanish-Mexican settlements, 522
Spanish Succession, War of, 48
Spargo, John, 601
SPARS, 799
Speakeasies, 706
Special Forces (Green Berets), 859
Spice Islands (Indonesia), 2
Spock, Benjamin, 936
Spoils system, 233, 234, 466; and William Jennings Bryan, 634–35; during Garfield's presidency, 464, 465; during Hayes' administration, 463
Sports, 938; in antebellum America, 306; commercialism of, 710; late 19th-century, 520; and radio, 714. *See also* Leisure activity
"Spot" resolutions, 268
Sprague, F. J., 484
Spruance, Adm. Raymond A., 801, 814
Sputnik, 849
Square Deal, 615
Stagecoaches, 68, 291
Stagflation, 880
Stalin, Joseph, 778, 782, 804, 807, 813, 846; and Hitler's invasion of Russia, 789; and Soviet troops in Iran, 826; at Yalta Conference, 817–18
Stalingrad, 804
Stamp Act Congress (1765), 88
Stampp, Kenneth, 451
Stamp tax, 86–89
Standard of living, and automobile, 711–12
Standard Oil Company of Ohio, 485–86, 488, 492, 606, 612, 622
Standish, Capt. Myles, 22, 23
Standpattism, 556, 688
Stanford, Leland, 478, 479, 508
Stanton, Sec. Edwin M., 388, 398, 400, 424, 448–49
Stanton, Elizabeth Cady, 317, 318, 515
"Star-Spangled Banner, The" 192
Statehood, achievement of, 126
States, post-Revolution debts of, 144
States, progressivism in, 603–605
States' rights, 130; and Bank of U.S., 148; and Civil War, 421; and Jackson's presidency, 236–37; and New Deal, 770; Supreme Court and, 212, 213; and Virginia and Kentucky Resolutions, 163; and Warren Court, 881
States' Rights party, 831
Statue of Liberty, 502
Steamboats, 208, 284, 288, 298
Steamships, transoceanic, 298
Stedman, E. C., 378
Steel industry, 484, 485, 486–87; and inflation, 862; monopoly in, 607; post-World War II strikes in, 821; strikes in, 546, 765; union in, 765
Steffens, Lincoln, 600
Stein, Gertrude, 293
Steinbeck, John, 758, 761, 939
Stephens, Alexander, 379, 438
Steuben, Baron von, 98, 109
Stevens, Rep. Thaddeus, 439–40, 444, 449, 451
Stevens, Wallace, 940
Stevenson, Adlai E. (I), 548
Stevenson, Adlai (II), 838, 840, 847–48, 853
Stewardship theory, of presidency, 586
Stimson, Sec. Henry, 746
Stock market: during crash of 1929, 740–41; in early 1920s, 720–21; and SEC, 761
"Stock watering," 482
Stockyards, 529
Stone, Lucy, 318
Stoughton, William, 20
Stowe, Harriet Beecher, 310, 316, 339, 359, 365–66
Strategic Arms Limitation Talks, *see* SALT
Strikebreakers, 493, 495
Strikes, 280, 281, 496, 763; and cities, 925; in coal mines, 605; in 1892, 546; and fear of Communism, 701–702; against grape-growers, 935; May Day, 495; post-World War II, 821; Pullman, 549–50; sit-down, 764; in steel industry, 546, 765, 821; during World War II, 798. *See also* Labor; Unions
Stuart, Gilbert, 320
Stuart kings, 28, 45
Student Non-Violent Coordinating Committee (SNCC), 869
Stuyvesant, Peter, 34, 35
Styron, William, 939
Submarine warfare: German, 655–59, 662–63; in Pacific, 811; of World War II, 789, 790–91, 803
Subsidized scarcity, 760
Suburbs, 925, 926. *See also* Cities; Housing
Subways, 503
Suez crisis, 847
Suffrage: for blacks, 439, 442, 443–45, 547; in colonial America, 120; Jefferson's view of, 150; manhood, 164, 213, 221–22, 223, 230, 296, 307; for women, 317, 318, 515, 603, 684
Suffragists, 603, 684
Sugar Act, 86, 88
Sugar embargo, 851
Sugar industry: in Cuba, 566–67; in Hawaii, 566
Sugar Trust, 488, 550
Sullivan, John L., 520
Sullivan, Louis H. 518
Summit conference, Eisenhower-Khrushchev, 850–51

Sumner, Charles, 369–70, 439
Sumner, William Graham, 489, 509
Sumter, Fort, 389–90
Sunbelt states, 926–27
Sunday, W. A. (''Billy''), 504, 657, 702, 708
Supreme Court, 162, 163, 211, 442–43; on abortion, 932; *Bakke* decision, 933; *Brown* decision, 842; defining power of, 220; desegregation decision, 932; *Dred Scott* decision, 373–74; and farm interests, 538; and FDR, 767–69; first woman justice of, 918; and Jackson presidency, 232; and Jefferson presidency, 170–71; and labor laws, 604; La Follette's attacks on, 733; and Legal Tender Act, 458n; *Miranda* decision of, 881; and monopolies, 622; during Nixon presidency, 881–82; packing of, 768, 769; on Puerto Rico, 576; and railroad regulation, 483, 607; reactionaries in, 724–25; *Schechter* decision of, 759; and Social Security Act, 769; states' rights curbed by, 212; and Tenure of Office Act, 448–49; and Wilson-Gorman Act, 550
Sussex, 659, 662, 663
Swartwout, Samuel, 234
Sweatshops, 604
Sweden, in colonial America, 34–35
Swift, Gustavus, 488, 529
Symphony orchestras, 518, 938
Synthetic fuels, 910
Syracuse (New York), 285

Taft, Sen. Robert A., 786, 788, 822, 838–39, 841
Taft, William H., 581, 607, 624, 625, 687, 697; conservation of, 620; election of, 613–614; foreign policy of, 622–24; and Payne-Aldrich Tariff, 619–20; presidency of, 617–18, 629–30; as Supreme Court justice, 630, 725; as trust buster, 622; during World War I, 671
Taft-Hartley Act, 822, 832, 833
Talleyrand, 159, 160
Tallmadge amendment, 208
Tammany, Chief, 37
Tammany Hall, 37, 299
Taney, Chief Justice Roger B., 373
Tanner, James, 543
Tansill, Charles C., 666
Tarbell, Ida M., 600
Tariff, 86; of Abominations, 226–27, 228, 235, 238; during Cleveland's presidency, 471; Dingley, 554, 618–19; of 1816, 204, 277; of 1832, 238–39; of 1833, 240; of 1842, 265; of 1846, 265, 417; of 1857, 374, 385, 416; and election of 1888, 472–73; and election of 1892, 545; Emergency Tariff Act, 729; and farm income, 537; Hawley-Smoot, 739; Kennedy Round negotiations, 859; McKinley, 544, 550–51, 566; Payne-Aldrich, 618–20, 621, 635; Underwood (Underwood-Simmons), 635–36; Wilson on, 635–36. *See also* Trade
Taverns, 69, 134, 158, 287
Taxation: colonial attitudes toward, 88, 89; for education, 307; graduated income, 545, 630, 636; by inflation, 417–18; without representation, 24; spare-the-rich policies, 721; during World War I, 674. *See also* Income Tax
Taylor, Frederick W., 710
Taylor, Zachary, 267, 269, 347–48, 349, 353, 632, 848, 904
Teamsters' Union, 848–49, 935
Teapot Dome scandal, 730, 732
Tea tax, 90, 91–92
Tecumseh, Chief, 186, 191
Teheran Conference, 807
Telegraph, 279, 291, 311; war takeover of, 674
Telegraphy, wireless, 714
Telephones, 938; invention of, 484–85; war takeover of, 674
Television, 714–15; and Carter-Ford debates, 904; McCarthy hearings on, 842; and national elections, 854; and politics, 938. *See also* Media
Teller Amendment, 569, 577
Temperance movement, 300, 316–17, 463, 516–17, 604–605. *See also* Prohibition
Tennessee, 61; admission to statehood, 140–41; evolution controversy in, 708–709; Reconstruction in, 444; secession of, 390
Tennessee Coal and Iron Company, 607
Tennessee Valley Authority (TVA), 744, 762–63, 844
Tennessee Valley Authority Act (TVA), 753
Ten Nights in a Barroom, 305, 316
''Tennis Cabinet,'' 585, 620
Tennyson, Alfred Lord, 563
Tenure of Office Act, 448, 449
Terre Haute (Indiana), 45
Tet offensive, 873
Texas, 268; annexation of, 251, 260–62, 267; and Compromise of 1850, 349; controversy over, 247–50; and public opinion, 249; Reconstruction in, 444. *See also* Reconstruction
Textile industry, 279; in America, 275–76; and Civil War, 397; mechanization in, 274; in New England, 276–77; and slavery, 340; in South, 491, 492
Thackeray, William, 321–22
Thames, Battle of the, 191, 199, 253
Thanksgiving Day, 22
Theater, 305–306, 320, 519, 715
Thieu, Nguyen Van, 882, 889, 900
Third parties, 244; American Independent party, 875–76; Bull Moose party, 659–60; Constitutional Union party, 379; in election of 1924, 733–34; Free Soil party, 251, 341, 347–48; Greenback Labor party, 459, 538–39, 599; Know-Nothing party, 301, 371; Liberal Republican party, 457–58; Liberty party, 264; National Prohibition party, 516; Populist party, 539, 544, 546; States' Rights party, 831. *See also* Elections; Political parties
Third World, 943
Thoreau, Henry David, 323
Three Emperors, Battle of the, 178
''Three-fifths compromise,'' 133
''Three-hundred-dollar men,'' 415
Thurmond, J. Strom, 831
Ticonderoga, Fort, 101
Tilden, Samuel J., 456, 460–61
Tillman, Ben, 446
Tin, 797
Tippecanoe, Battle of, 186
Tobacco, 491; in colonial America, 65, 66, 85, 86; economy of, 1–13; European introduction of, 12; in Maryland, 14; and plantation system, 18; in Virginia, 12–13, 85, 86
Tobacco Trust, 488
Tocqueville, Alexis de, 296, 311, 317
Tokyo, bombing of, 812
Tonkin Gulf episode, 866–67, 885, 893
Tordesillas, Treaty of, 6
Tories, 105, 106. *See also* Loyalists
Toronto (Ontario), 192
Totalitarianism, 778. *See also* Communism
Town meeting, 25, 31, 76, 77
Towns: ghost, 477, 529; of Wild West, 529. *See also* Cities
Townsend, Francis, 758
Townshend, ''Champagne Charley,'' 90
Townshend Acts, 90, 91
Tractors, 732
Trade: American foreign, 289; in colonial America, 67, 68; with Far East, 358; free, 700; and mercantilism, 83–84; post-Revolutionary, 127–28, 145, 149; routes with the East, 4; with Soviet Union, 775; triangular, 67. *See also* Tariff
Trade Expansion Act, 859
Tradesmen, of colonial America, 64
Trade unions, 281
Trafalgar, Battle of, 177–178
''Trail of Tears,'' 245
Transcendentalism, 322–24
Transportation: advances in, 274; automobile, 709, 710–11, 712–13, 716; bicycle, 520; canal system, 284–86; in colonial America, 68–69; of early 1800s, 205, 282–83; importance of, 292; Pacific Railroad, 359–60; railroads, 286–88; river, 284; in South, 432; transatlantic, 82; and Union, 288–89; and westward expansion, 208. *See also* Airplanes; Railroads
Transportation, Department of, 868
Travis, W. B., 248
Treasury, federal: and Allied war debts, 734; and Cleveland, 471, 547; during Eisenhower era, 855; gold reserve in, 547; in post-Revolutionary era, 143, 148. *See also* National Debt; Silver issue
Treaties, with American Indians, 524. *See also specific treaties*
Treaty of 1818, 214, 262
Trent affair, 412
Trenton, battle at, 107
Triangle Shirtwaist Company, 604
Tripoli, Pasha of, 171
Tripolitan War, 171–72
Trist, Nicholas P., 270

Trowbridge, J. T., 424
Truman, Harry S, 789, 811; and atomic bomb 813, 815, 834; China policy of, 852; and demobilization, 820; election of, 831–33; Korean policy of, 836–37; loyalty program of, 828–29; and Marshall Plan, 827–28; Point Four program of, 833; at Potsdam Conference, 812–13; presidency of, 816–17; quoted, 816, 829, 836; and Red Scare, 847–48; segregation policy of, 842; and Soviet relations, 826; as vice-presidential candidate, 809
Truman Doctrine, 816, 826
Trumbull, John, 73–74, 320
Trust busting, 492, 605–607, 622
Trusts, 485–86, 488, 490; and TR, 605–607; and Taft, 622; and Wilson, 638–40
Trust territories, 819
Truth, Sojourner, 339
Tubman, Harriet, 350
Tudor rulers, 10
Tumulty, J. P., 644
Turgot, Anne Robert Jacques, 141
Turkey, 826, 831
Turner, Frederick Jackson, 237, 522, 540
Turner, Nat, 338, 341
Turnpikes, 282, 287. *See also* Transportation
Twain, Mark, 291, 296, 331, 459, 506, 512–13, 529, 575
Tweed Ring, 455–56, 504
Two-party system: origins of, 148–49; and slavery issue, 346. *See also* Third parties
Tyler, Pres. John, 253, 257–58, 261, 321
Typewriter, 484

U-2 spy plane, 851
U-boat attacks, 656, 658, 659, 662–63, 665, 666. *See also* Submarine warfare
Uganda, 905
Uncle Tom's Cabin, 305, 316, 339, 359, 365–66, 367, 392
"Unconditional surrender," 806, 814
Underground Railroad, 349–51, 355, 385, 388
Underwood (Underwood-Simmons) Tariff Bill (Act), 635–36, 729
Unemployment: attitudes toward, 494; among blacks, 869, 932; in 1890s, 548–49; and New Deal, 755–58, 763; 1929–1942, 771; and Nixon-Ford recession, 899; pre-Civil War, 374; after World War I, 693; and World War II, 783, 798, 800. *See also* Depression; Labor; Workers
Unemployment insurance, 754
Unemployment Relief Act, 753
Union Pacific Railroad, 456, 478–79, 797
Union party, 422
Unions, 492–94; AF of L, 495–96; during Eisenhower era, 848–49; and immigrant threat, 502; membership of, 928; organization of, 494–95; organized crime in, 707; Teamsters, 848–49, 935; for unskilled workers, 764; after World War II, 821–22. *See also* Labor; Workers
Unitarians, 302, 303, 323. *See also* Religion
United Farm Workers Organizing Committee (UFWOC), 935
United Mine Workers, 764, 766, 798, 932
United Nations, 796–97; beginnings of, 818–20; China in, 885; Educational, Scientific and Cultural Organization (UNESCO), 820; Khrushchev at, 850; Relief and Rehabilitation Administration (UNRRA), 823; and Suez crisis, 847
United States Steel Corporation, 487, 607, 765, 942
Unity: and Democratic party, 369; end of, 385; and Louisiana Purchase, 177; and transportation system, 288–89; Daniel Webster on, 236. *See also* Nationalism
Universities: minorities in, 933; in post-Civil War era, 507–508; Spanish, 8; state-supported, 308; women in, 932. *See also* Colleges; Education; *specific universities*
Updike, John, 939
Urban centers: and industrialization, 498; migration to, 503. *See also* Cities
Urbanization, 520; effect on women, 515; overrapid, 297–98; speed-up of, 484
Uruguay, 905
U.S.S.R., *see* Russia; Soviet Union
Utah, 349; settlement of, 304–305; statehood for, 305, 523, 532
Utopias: early 19th century, 327; wilderness, 318–19

Vallandigham, Clement L., 421
Valley Forge, 67, 97, 98, 109
Values, small-town, 520
Van Buren, Martin, 36, 249, 254, 280, 348; election of, 250; and election of 1848, 348; presidency of, 251–52; renomination of, 253; as secretary of state, 234, 235
Vance, Cyrus, 904, 907, 912
Vanderbilt, Cornelius, 480–81, 482, 486
Vanderbilt, William H., 476, 482
Vanzetti, Bartolomeo, 702–703
Vaudeville, 519, 715
Veblen, Thorstein, 599
V-E Day, 811
Venezuela, and European monetary claims, 590–91
Venezuelan crisis, 562–63
Vermont: admission to statehood, 141; manhood suffrage in, 222. *See also* New England
Verranzano, Giovanni da, 6
Versailles, Treaty of, 692, 693; collapse of, 699; and Senator Lodge, 695; rejection of, 695–96
Vesey, Denmark, 338
Veterans: Civil War, 532, 539, 543; of World War I, 726, 744–45; of World War II, 820
Veterans' Administration, creation of, 726
Vetoes, presidential: Eisenhower's 855; Ford's, 899; Andrew Jackson's, 232; Andrew Johnson's, 440, 441, 443
Vicksburg, Battle of, 406
Victory gardens, 672, 798
Victory Loan drive, 674
Vidal, Gore, 939
Vienna, Congress of, 196
Viet Cong, 860, 870, 871, 873, 877
Vietnam, 793, 845–46, 856; American atrocities in, 835; American troops in, 870–71; "ceasefire," 893–94; early commitment to, 859–60; partition of, 846
Vietnamization, 882–83
Vietnam War: Cambodianizing, 883–84; end of, 899–901; justification for, 877; opposition to, 871–73, 882, 884–85
Villa, Francisco ("Pancho"), 646, 647, 677
Villard, Henry, 479
Vinland, 2
Virginia: aristocratic origins of, 13; colonization of, 12–14, 16; House of Burgesses in, 13, 63–64, 91; large-state plan of, 132; and ratification of Constitution, 136–37; Reconstruction in, 444; revolution in, 86; secession of, 390; tobacco economy of, 12–13, 85, 86; University of, 308, 320
Virginia Company of London, 11–12, 13
Virginia Military Institute, 392
Virginia Resolutions, 162–63
Virgin Islands, 642
V-J Day, 814
"Voice of America," 828
Volstead Act, 705
Voltaire, François, 41, 121
Volunteers, of Civil War, 415–16
Vonnegut, Kurt, Jr., 939
Vote: for blacks, 439; for laborers, 280. *See also* Suffrage
Voting Rights Act, 868

WAACS, 799
Wabash case, 483, 538
Wade, Sen, Benjamin, 448, 449
Wage-price controls, 880
Wages and Hours Bill, 765
Wagner Act, 757, 763–64, 769, 935
Wake Island, 800
Walden, 323
Walker, David, 339
Walker, Robert J., 265
Walker Tariff, 417
Wallace, George, 863, 876, 887
Wallace, Henry A., 809, 832
Wallace, Gen. Lewis, 511
Walpole, Horace, 54
Waltham (Massachusetts), 276
War bonds, 674, 800
War College, 578
Warehouse Act, 641
War of 1812, 48, 172, 181; abortive invasion of Canada, 189–90; Battle of New Orleans, 192–93; British blockade, 195, 197; burning of Washington, D.C., 192; debate over, 201; effects of, 202; and Hartford Convention, 197–98; naval duels, 190, 191, 193–94; opposition to, 188–89, 197; privateers in, 194–95; results of, 198–201; and Treaty of Ghent, 195–97; vote on, in House of Representatives, 187
War Hawks, 183–84, 196
Warhol, Andy, 941

War Industries Board, 670, 725
War Labor Board, National, 671
Warner, Charles Dudley, 512–13
War on Poverty, 865, 877
War Production Board, 797
Warren, Earl, 842, 865, 867, 881
Warren, Robert Penn, 939
Wars: Anglo-French intercolonial, 47–49, 51; Anglo-Spanish, 16; Indian, 524–26. *See also* American Revolutionary War; Civil War; Mexican War; *specific wars*
Warsaw Pact, 846
War Trade Board, 671
Washington, Booker T., 338, 507
Washington (D.C.), 167; burning of, 192, 199; civil rights march on, 864; in early 1800s, 203; Vietnam moratorium in, 882
Washington, George, 66, 129, 148, 159–60, 293, 329; and American Revolutionary War, 98, 385; and Bank of United States, 146–47; at Continental Congress, 94; diversions of, 78; drafting of, 101; early history of, 50–51; Farewell Address of, 156–57; and French and Indian War, 51, 52; isolationism of, 166; and Jefferson contrasted, 168; leadership of, 96, 123; military defeats of, 109; military strategy of, 112, 114; military victories of, 107–108, 112; and militia, 55, 95; Neutrality Proclamation of, 153–54; at Philadelphia Convention, 130, 131; Philadelphia "White House" of, 144; portraits of, 74, 320; pro-Federalist regime of, 141–43; his proposal for national university, 225; quoted, 98; and ratification of Constitution, 135, 136–37; re-election of, 156; and voluntary retirement, 182; and Whiskey Rebellion, 147
Washington, Martha, 101, 221
Washington, statehood for, 532
Washington Disarmament Conference, 727–28, 734
Washington Naval Treaty, 778
Watergate scandals, 890–92, 895–97, 901
Waterloo, 196, 200
Watson, James, 786
Watt, James, 916
Watts riot, 869
WAVES, 799
Wayne, Gen. ("Mad Anthony"), 155
Wealth, gospel of, 488–90
Wealth and poverty, 289
Weaponry, for World War I, 679, 684. *See also* Nuclear weapons
Weapons systems, Carter's opposition to high-technology, 910
Weaver, Gen. James B., 480, 539, 544, 546
Weaver, Robert C., 868
Weaving, 276. *See also* Textile industry
Webster, Daniel, 221, 254, 321, 344, 356, 396; and Bank of U.S., 243; and Sen. Hayne, 235–36; quoted, 144, 236, 346; as secretary of state, 260; Seventh of March speech of, 346, 351–52; and states' rights, 213; on tariffs, 204, 226; and Tyler presidency, 256–57; on union, 340, 353, 357
Webster, Noah, 307
Webster-Ashburton treaty, 260
Weld, Theodore Dwight, 339
Welfare question, 292
"Welfare state," 942
Wellington, Duke of, 196
Welles, Sec. Gideon, 400
Welty, Eudora, 939
Wesley, John, 18
West, 293–94; and Bank of U.S., 243, cattle industry in, 529–30; and conservation movement, 608–609; economic growth of, 532–34; expansion of, 207–208; Indian barrier to, 522–24; mining industry in, 528–29; Oregon settlement, 262, 263; settlement of, 530–32; wildcat currency in, 244. *See also* Frontier, Sectionalism
West, Benjamin, 74
West, Dean, 625–26, 628
West Germany, 830
West Indian Company, Dutch, 33
West Indies: black slaves from, 62; British, 16, 225–26; French, 53, 68, 110, 153, 155; and Paris peace settlement, 55; post-Revolutionary trade with, 127, 128; Puritan migration to, 23–24; undeclared hostilities in, 160
West Point (Military Academy), 271
West Virginia, 390
Weyler, General, 567, 581
Wharton, Edith, 717
Wheat, 282, 531–32, 535
Wheatley, Phillis, 74
Wheeler, Sen. Burton K., 788, 792
Wheeler, Gen. Joseph, 578
Whigs, 98, 105, 253–54; Clay candidacy of, 263–64; demise of, 355–57; and election of 1848, 347; history viewed by, 98; origins of, 250; during Tyler presidency, 257–58
Whip Inflation Now (WIN) campaign, 899
Whiskey, excise on, 145
Whiskey Rebellion, 147–48, 158
Whiskey Ring, 456
Whistler, James, 518
White, Henry, 687
White, John, 8, 15
White, William Allen, 627, 629, 699
White Citizens' Councils, 843
Whitefield, George, 70
White flight, 925, 933
Whiteman, Paul, 717
"White slave" traffic, 601
Whitman, Walt, 324, 512
Whitney, Eli, 276, 277, 329, 484
Whittier, John Greenleaf, 45, 325, 352, 367, 372
Whyte, William H., 939
Wiebe, Robert H., 615
Wigglesworth, Michael, 30
Wilderness Campaign, 408–409
Wild West, image of, 534
"Wild West" shows, 519–20
Wiley, H. W., 602
Wilhelm II (Kaiser), 563, 646, 651, 681, 682
Willamette Valley, 262, 263
Willard, Emma, 308
Willard, Frances E., 516, 604
William and Mary, of England, 28, 29, 46, 47
Williams, Roger, 26
Williams, Tennessee, 940
Williams, William Appleman, 578
Williams, William Carlos, 940
Willkie, Wendell L., 786–87
Wilmot, David, 272
Wilmot Proviso, 272, 347, 351
Wilson, Charles, 840
Wilson, Sloan, 939
Wilson, Woodrow, 508, 622, 625–27, 640–41, 845; character of, 626, 633–34; death of, 698–99; diplomacy of, 700; election of, 628, 659–61; and Federal Reserve System, 636–38; foreign policy of, 642–44; Fourteen Points program of, 668–69, 681–82; and labor legislation, 641; Mexican policy of, 645, 646–48; as minority President, 628–29; October Appeal of, 686–87; at Paris Peace Conference, 687–92; policy toward blacks of, 642; progressivism of, 631; quoted, 632, 649, 662, 667, 686; Southern background of, 632–33; speechmaking tour of, 694; stroke paralyzing, 694–95; on tariff, 635–36; and Treaty of Versailles, 692, 696; and trusts, 638–40; and U.S. neutrality in World War I, 650, 653; and woman suffrage, 684; during World War I, 656, 657–58, 662, 663, 664, 665, 666, 667–68
Wilson-Gorman Act, 550, 556
"Windfall profits" tax, 909
Winthrop, John, 23, 25
Wisconsin, 300; agrarian reform in, 538
Wise, Governor, 377–78
Witchcraft persecutions, 31
Wobblies, 671
Wolfe, Gen. James, 54, 55
Women: and alcoholism, 316, 317; in armed forces, 678; black, 932; during Civil War, 419; education for, 507–508; effect of automobile on, 712; emergence of, 515–16; employment for (1920s), 716; "flappers," 716; on frontier, 294; higher education for, 308; in industry, 484, 485, 492, 515; in labor force, 280; and labor unions, 494; life span of, 924; minimum-wage law for, 725, 769; 19th century revolt of, 309–10, 317–18; and progressivism, 603; and sexual attitudes, 515; Southern, 419, 434; suffrage for, 317, 318, 684; in World War I, 671; in World War II, 799, 930
Women's Christian Temperance Union (W.C.T.U.), 516, 604. *See also* Temperance movement
Women's rights movement, 317–18, 343, 520, 930–32
Wood, Col. Leonard, 572–73, 576, 658, 697
Woodhull, Victoria, 514–15
Workday, campaign for eight-hour, 494–95
Workers: and Clayton Act, 639; federal legislation for, 641; and industrialization, 494; migrant, 935; post-war boom for, 928; unskilled, 764, 765; women, 930–31; work-

ingman's compensation laws, 604, 641; and World War I, 671. *See also* Labor
Workingman's compensation laws, 604, 641
Works Progress Administration (WPA), 757, 758, 798
World Court, 734
World War I: aftermath, 682–85; and American business, 640; American casualities of, 682; Armistice, 682; conscription, 677–78; costs of, 682–83; and Fourteen Points, 668–69, 681–82; German War acts, 663–64; Hooverizing, 671–73; origins of, 649–51; preparedness for, 658–59, 669–71; and progressivism, 685; propaganda during, 652–53, 665, 666, 674–75, 681; shipbuilding during, 673; submarine warfare of, 655–59, 662–63; troops in France, 677, 678–81; and U.S. exports, 653; U.S. involvement in, 664, 665–66; U.S. neutrality in, 650, 653; women in, 671
World War II: Allies in, 794–95, 814–15; American involvement in, 792–93; blacks in, 796; costs of, 799, 814; D-Day invasion, 807–809; declaration of war, 792; Hitler halted, 803–804, 810–11; invasion of Austria, 782; invasion of Czechoslovakia, 782; invasion of Italy, 806–807; invasion of Poland, 782, 783; Japan in, 800–802, 811–14; Japanese-Americans in, 795–96; North African front, 804, 805–806; Pacific strategy, 802–803; preparedness for, 784; rationing in, 797; war production, 795, 797–99; women in, 799, 930
Wounded Knee: Battle of, 527; Indian occupation of (1973), 934
Wright, Frank Lloyd, 719–20, 941
Wright, Orville and Wilbur, 713
Wright, Richard, 939
Wyoming, statehood for, 532
Wyoming Stock-Growers' Association, 530
Wyoming Territory, woman suffrage in, 515

XYZ Affair, 159, 179

Yalta Conference, 817–18
"Yankee Hessians," 395
Yazoo River, 212
"Yellow dog contracts," 493
Yellow fever, 573, 574, 576–77, 578
Yom Kippur War, 894
York, Alvin C., 681
Yorktown, Battle of, 114–15
Young, Andrew, 904, 905, 907
Young, Brigham, 304, 305
Youth, revolt of, 936–37

Zenger, John Peter, 75
Zero population growth (ZPG), 924
Zimmerman note, 663

1 2 3 4 5 6 7 8 9 0

The United States and Its Possessions